Framing the Early Middl

Framing the Early Middle Ages

Europe and the Mediterranean
400–800

CHRIS WICKHAM

OXFORD

UNIVERSITY PRESS

OXFORD
UNIVERSITY PRESS

Great Clarendon Street, Oxford OX2 6DP

Oxford University Press is a department of the University of Oxford.
It furthers the University's objective of excellence in research, scholarship,
and education by publishing worldwide in

Oxford New York

Auckland Cape Town Dar es Salaam Hong Kong Karachi
Kuala Lumpur Madrid Melbourne Mexico City Nairobi
New Delhi Shanghai Taipei Toronto

With offices in

Argentina Austria Brazil Chile Czech Republic France Greece
Guatemala Hungary Italy Japan Poland Portugal Singapore
South Korea Switzerland Thailand Turkey Ukraine Vietnam

Oxford is a registered trade mark of Oxford University Press
in the UK and in certain other countries

Published in the United States
by Oxford University Press Inc., New York

British Library Cataloging in Publication Data
Data available

Library of Congress Cataloging in Publication Data
Data available

Typeset by SPI Publisher Services, Pondicherry, India
Printed in Great Britain on acid-free paper by
Biddles Ltd., King's Lynn, Norfolk

ISBN 978-0-19-921296-5 (Pbk.)

3 5 7 9 10 8 6 4 2

For LESLIE

Acknowledgements

I HAVE BEEN working on this book for nearly seven years, and have discussed issues relating to it with nearly every late Romanist and early medievalist I have met during that time; I have gained insights from too many people to list. First of all, I should like to thank those who commented on sections of the book: Leslie Brubaker, who read almost the whole text; Paul Fouracre, John Haldon, Hugh Kennedy, and Eduardo Manzano, who read sections of Chapter 3; Mayke de Jong, Paul Fouracre, John Haldon, Guy Halsall, Peter Heather, Eduardo Manzano, and Peter Sarris, who read sections of Chapter 4; Jean-Pierre Devroey and Domenico Vera, who read sections of Chapter 5; Steven Bassett, Nicholas Brooks, Wendy Davies, Simon Esmonde-Cleary, and Patrick Wormald, who read Chapter 6; Steven Bassett, Matt Innes, and Peter Sarris, who read sections of Chapter 7; Sonia Gutiérrez, Helena Hamerow, Simon Loseby, and Mark Whittow, who read sections of Chapter 8; Domenico Vera and Chris Dyer, who read Chapter 9; Simon Loseby, who read all of, and Lisa Fentress and John Haldon, who read sections of, Chapter 10; Paul Arthur, Lisa Fentress, Jodi Magness, Olga Magoula, Eduardo Manzano, Paul Van Ossel, and Bryan Ward-Perkins, who read some or all of Chapter 11. They were often sharp critics, and I gained immensely from their insights, suggestions, and bibliographical references; I know they do not all agree with my conclusions.

Another group of people, partially overlapping, consists of friends with whom I started when I needed to get a sense of the bibliography of a given region: people I could not do without as guides to one area or another. These include Steven Bassett, Julio Escalona, Simon Esmonde-Cleary, Lisa Fentress, Riccardo Francovich, Hugh Kennedy, Eduardo Manzano, Ulf Näsman, Pierre Ouzoulias, Claude Raynaud, Peter Sarris, and Paul Van Ossel. I must also here express my great debt to Rosamond McKitterick, Ghislaine Noyé, and Pierre Toubert, who invited me to teach in, respectively, the University of Cambridge (to give the 2003 Trevelyan Lectures), the École des Chartes, and the Collège de France; the lectures I gave there are all, in more or less revised form, in this book and I gained enormously from the conversations and library access—and the time to research and write—that I had both in Cambridge and in Paris.

I benefited from ideas and bibliographical or other help from, apart from those mentioned above, Stuart Airlie, Donald Bailey, François Baratte, Bernard Bavant, Andrea Berlin, François Bougard, Monique Bourin, Alan Bowman, Luis Caballero, Federico Cantini, Gill Clark, Simon Corcoran, Bill Day, Paolo Delogu, Archie Dunn, Santiago Feijoo, Laurent Feller, Rebecca Foote, Sauro Gelichi, Sharon Gerstel, Mary Harlow, Jill Harries, Catherine Hills, Richard Hodges, Sonja Jilek, Jeremy Johns, Olga Karagiorgiou, Sean Kingsley, Luke Lavan, Stéphane Lebecq, Régine Le Jan, Wolf Liebeschuetz, Antonio Malpica, Cyril Mango, Alessandra Molinari, Jinty Nelson, Margaret O'Hea, Lauro Olmo, Helen Patterson, Walter Pohl, Andrew Poulter, Dominic Rathbone, Mark Redknap, Paul Reynolds, Charlotte Roueché, Riccardo Santangeli, Sven Schütte, Chris Scull, Trish Skinner, Jean-Pierre Sodini, Frédéric

Trement, Marco Valenti, Alan Walmsley, Mark Whyman, Ian Wood, and Enrico Zanini. A particular thanks is owed to Sue Bowen, who has spent what amounts to years typing this book, and to Harry Buglass, who drew the maps. The index was compiled by Alicia Corrêa. Here the list is certainly incomplete, but can be added to with some of the more specific acknowledgements in footnotes; I am also very grateful to the wide range of people who sent me their books and articles, many unpublished, including doctoral theses; I could not have written this book without you. I have tried to restrict this list to those who, knowingly or unknowingly, had a direct effect on the book; if I was to include the rest of the people with whom I have dealt fruitfully and intellectually since 1997, the list would be at least twice as long.

I must finally thank three institutions: the University of Birmingham Main Library, and the Ashmolean (now Sackler) Library in Oxford, where I did most of my research—I could not have written without the latter in particular; and the British Academy, whose granting of a Research Readership in 1997–9 enabled me to start this project in the first place. This book is the (delayed) result of that Readership.

Birmingham   C.J.W.
April 2004

For this paperback edition, only minor corrections have been made. There has of course been a steady stream of books and articles in the last two years which could be taken into account, and I have been greatly stimulated by the variety of critical reactions to the book, in public or private, some of which would result in modifications to the argument. But I stand by my main claims, and also by my empirical characterizations; I would not want to make any major changes to the text. Adding in new work would thus be not only an enormous operation, but also mostly cosmetic, so I have not attempted it. The book should be seen as remaining a work of 2004.

August 2006

Contents

List of maps   x

Abbreviations   xi

Notes on terminology   xiv

1. Introduction   1

Part I. States

2. Geography and politics   17
3. The form of the state   56

Part II. Aristocratic power-structures

4. Aristocracies   153
5. Managing the land   259
6. Political breakdown and state-building in the North   303

Part III. Peasantries

7. Peasants and local societies: case studies   383
8. Rural settlement and village societies   442
9. Peasant society and its problems   519

Part IV. Networks

10. Cities   591
11. Systems of exchange   693
12. General conclusions   825

Bibliography   832

1. Primary sources   832
2. Secondary sources   845

Index   945

List of maps

1. The regions discussed in this book and other placenames   xvi
2. The Roman empire in 400   xvii
3. Africa   xviii
4. Egypt   xix
5. Syria and Palestine   xx
6. The Byzantine heartland   xxi
7. Italy   xxii
8. Spain and Mauretania   xxiii
9. Central and southern Gaul   xxiv
10. Northern Gaul   xxv
11. Britain   xxvi
12. Ireland   xxvii
13. Denmark   xxviii

In Maps 3–10:

- ●   BENEVENTO   Roman city
- ○   MURCIA   New city in the post-Roman period
- +   Farfa   Monastery

Abbreviations

AA	*Auctores antiquissimi*
AEA	*Archivo español de arqueología*
Æthelberht	*The laws of the earliest English kings*, pp. 4–16
Aistulf	*Leges Aistulfi*
Alfred	*The laws of the earliest English kings*, pp. 62–92
AM	*Archeologia medievale*
APEL	*Arabic papyri in the Egyptian library*
ARS	African Red Slip ware
b.	ibn
BAR	British archaeological reports
BCS	*Cartularium saxonicum*
Cap.	*Capitularia*
CB	*Breviarium ecclesiae Ravennatis (Codice Bavaro)*
CDL	*Codice diplomatico longobardo*
ChLA	*Chartae latinae antiquiores*
CJ	*Codex Iustinianus*
CPR	*Corpus papyrorum Raineri*
CTh	*Theodosiani libri XVI*
Dip.	*Diplomata*
Dip. Kar.	*Diplomata Karolinorum*
Dip. Merov.	*Diplomata regum francorum e stirpe merovingica*
DSP	*derivées des sigillées paléochrétiennes*
Ep., Epp.	*Epistula* (or *Epistola*), *Epistulae* (or *Epistolae*)
ERS	Egyptian Red Slip ware
Form.	*Formulae*
Form. Wis.	*Formulae Wisigothicae*
GC	Gregory of Tours, *Liber in gloria confessorum*
GM	Gregory of Tours, *Liber in gloria martyrum*
GWW	Glazed White ware
HE	Bede, *Historia ecclesiastica gentis anglorum*
HGL	*Histoire générale de Languedoc*
HL	Paul the Deacon, *Historia Langobardorum*
Hlothhere	*The laws of the earliest English kings*, pp. 18–22
Ine	*The laws of the earliest English kings*, pp. 36–60
JRA	*Journal of Roman archaeology*
KRU	*Koptische Rechtsurkunden des achten Jahrhunderts aus Djême (Theben)*

LH	Gregory of Tours, *Decem libri historiarum*
Liutprand	*Leges Liutprandi*
LRA	Late Roman amphora (see Ch. 11, n. 24)
LRE	A. H. M. Jones, *The later Roman empire*
LV	*Leges Visigothorum*
MDL	*Memorie e documenti per servire all'istoria di Lucca*
MEFR	*Mélanges de l'École française de Rome*
MGH	*Monumenta Germaniae Historica*
NJ	*Novellae Iustiniani*
Nov. Maj.	*Novellae Maioriani*
Nov. Val.	*Novellae Valentiniani*
P. Ant.	*The Antinoopolis papyri*
P. Apoll.	*Papyrus grecs d'Apollônos Anô*
P. Bad.	*Veröffentlichungen aus den badischen Papyrus-Sammlungen*
P. Cair. Masp.	*Papyrus grecs d'époque byzantine*
P. Flor.	*Papiri greco-egizii*, III
P. Ital.	*Die nichtliterarischer lateinischen Papyri Italiens aus der Zeit 445–700*
P. Laur.	*Dai papiri della Biblioteca Medicea Laurenziana*
P. Lond.	*Greek papyri in the British museum*
P. Mich.	*The Aphrodite papyri in the University of Michigan papyrus collection*
P. Ness.	*Excavations at Nessana*, III
P. Oxy.	*The Oxyrhynchus papyri*
P. Petra	*The Petra papyri*
P. Ross.-Georg.	*Papyri russischer und georgischer Sammlungen*
P. Ryl. Ar.	*Catalogue of the Arabic papyri in the John Rylands library, Manchester*
P. Ryl. Copt.	*Catalogue of the Coptic manuscripts in the collection of the John Rylands library, Manchester*
P. Vatic. Aphrod.	*I papiri vaticani greci di Aphrodito*
PBE	J. R. Martindale (ed.), *Prosopography of the Byzantine empire*
PBSR	*Papers of the British School at Rome*
PERF	*Papyrus Erzherzog Rainer. Führer durch die Ausstellung*
PG	*Patrologiae cursus completus, series latina*
PL	*Patrologiae cursus completus, series graeca*
PLRE	J. R. Martindale, *et al.* (eds.), *Prosopography of the later Roman empire*
PO	*Patrologia orientalis*
Pol. St-Germain	*Polyptique de l'abbaye de Saint-Germain-des-Prés,* ed. A. Longnon

PSR	*Papyri Schott-Reinhardt*
Ratchis	*Leges Ratchis*
RF	*Regesto di Farfa*
Rothari	*Edictus Rothari*
RS	Red Slip ware
S	P. H. Sawyer, *Anglo-Saxon charters*
SRG	*Scriptores rerum germanicarum*
SRL	*Scriptores rerum langobardicarum et italicarum, saec. VI–IX*
SRM	*Scriptores rerum merovingicarum*
SS	*Scriptores*
Trad. Wiz.	*Traditiones Wizenburgenses*
TSHT	*terra sigillata hispánica tardía*
Ub.	*Urkundenbuch*
VM	Gregory of Tours, *De virtutibus sancti Martini*
VP	Gregory of Tours, *Liber vitae patrum*
Wihtred	*The laws of the earliest English kings*, pp. 24–30
ZPR	*Zeitschrift für Papyrologie und Epigraphik*

Notes on terminology

Placenames

I have done my best to refer to placenames in their modern, not ancient or medieval, spellings, so Mérida not Emerita, Bologna not Bononia, only using English spellings (generally in fact borrowed from French) for places like Milan, Athens, or Cologne, where Milano, Athēnai, Köln would seem precious. In the West this creates few problems, for most medieval historians do the same (ancient historians often use classical forms, however). For regions of the Roman empire now in Arab-speaking countries, and sometimes in Turkey and the Balkans, historians frequently use ancient or medieval names to the exclusion of modern ones, particularly when they are very different. Here I have used both, putting the modern one in brackets without an initial article, so Arsinoë (Madīnat al-Fayyūm); only where the ancient name (or an Anglicization of it) is so well known that to use the modern one genuinely contributes nothing, like Constantinople or Antioch, have I left it. So also I have left well-known ancient names where there is no modern settlement, as with Caesarea in modern Israel. Caesarea is also one of a handful of ancient Greek names that have been left in Latinized versions (others are Nicaea and Phocaea), on the grounds that they are so well known in this form that consistency would confuse. In Egypt, where Coptic texts often provide a third name, I have put in all three when using Coptic sources, so Sioout (Greek Lykopolis, modern Asyūṭ). Arabic transliterations are also very variable; when I have been able to pin down a classical Arabic form I have normally used it, except in the Maghreb, where I have used the Francicized transliterations current in the countries themselves, so Kairouan not Qayrawān.

Personal names

These create other difficulties. In general I have Anglicized the names of rulers, and names from the standard lexicon of saints: so Justinian not Justinianus/Ioustinianos, Clovis not Chlodovech(-us), John and George not Johannes, Geōrgios, etc. I have left nearly everybody else in the language of the texts, except that I have cut -us from Germanic names, so Gundulf not Gundulfus, and have sought to use modern standard transliterations of classical Arabic names, not the specific spelling forms of texts. In Greek, I have transliterated kappa as k, upsilon as y (except in diphthongs) and chi as ch. In Old Norse and Anglo-Saxon, I have transliterated thorn as th, and kept ð. I have used modern forms for well-known literary figures, such as Augustine or Bede. I have resisted the tendency of some Byzantinists to Latinize Greek names, which does violence to intellectuals as Hellenic as Prokopios, and I have also avoided their (even stranger) habit of Latinizing the titles of texts, though here I have generally used English, not the less familiar Greek, so Prokopios' *Buildings*, not *De aedificiis* or *Peri ktismatōn*.

Geographical terminology

The ten geographical units discussed in this book will normally be called 'regions', although, when they coincided with political units, I shall also use the names of these units for variation, as in the period, after the 620s, when the Visigothic kingdom roughly coincided with 'Spain'. How to name larger and smaller subdivisions of these regions caused me some difficulty, not least because the word 'region' is used for relatively small units in many countries, both in official usage and popular speech (the *regione* of Lazio, for example). I have had to choose, and stick by, one terminological system, to avoid confusion, even if it sometimes looks odd. Accordingly, formal subdivisions of my regions will be referred to by their then-used names, provinces, duchies, themes, and so on; but the major subdivisions will be referred to in general as 'sub-regions', a suitably imprecise and therefore neutral term that makes comparison between, say, the Lombard kingdom of northern Italy and Tuscany, the papal *patrimonium S. Petri* (i.e. Lazio), and the duchy of Benevento a linguistically more straightforward process. Smaller units will be called areas, zones, (city) territories—as well as, sometimes, counties or dioceses where this would be a technically exact usage. The smallest blocks, small river-valleys or groups of villages, will be called 'microregions'.

On villas

'Villa' in the text (pl. 'villas') means an isolated rural estate-complex from the Roman period, discoverable by archaeology or air photography. '*Villa*' (pl. '*villae*') is a Latin term, which may mean estate, or estate-centre (i.e. 'villa') or village, or even—later than our period—town; what it means in any given context will be discussed in the text, if it matters for the arguments, as in Chapter 8.

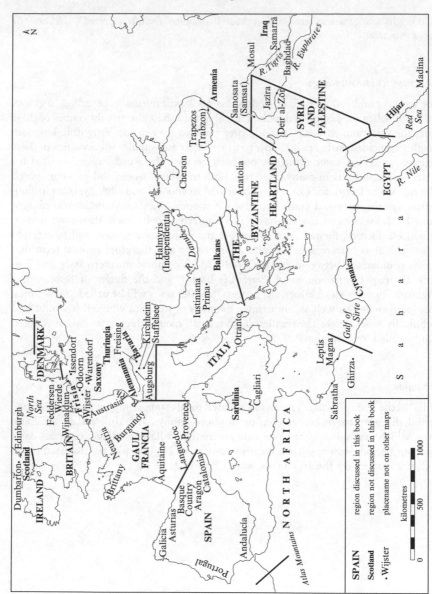

MAP 1. The regions discussed in this book and other placenames.

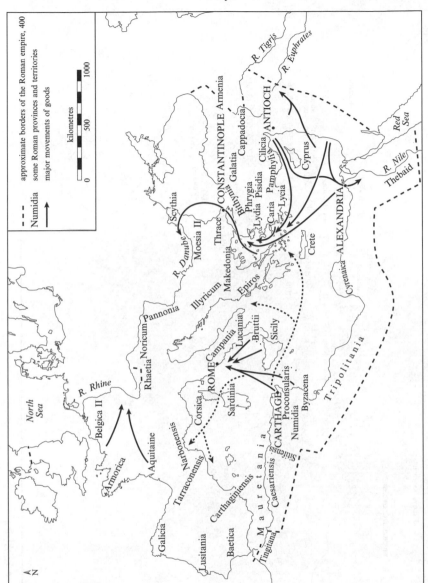

MAP 2. The Roman empire in 400.

Maps

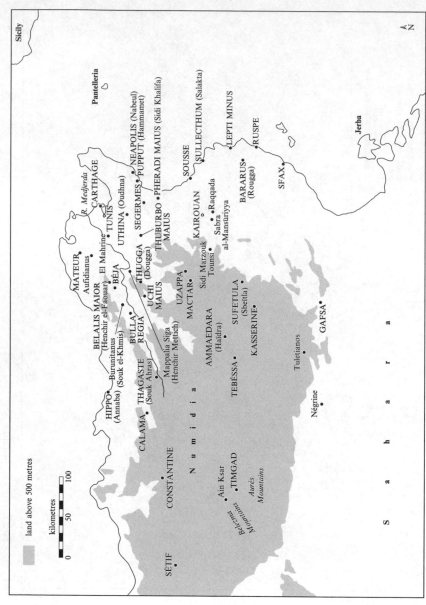

MAP 3. Africa.

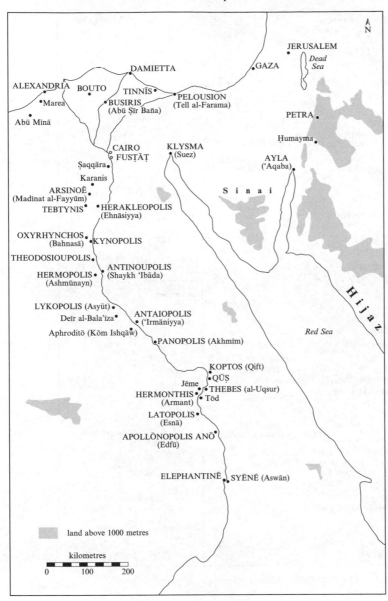

MAP 4. Egypt.

Maps

MAP 5. Syria and Palestine.

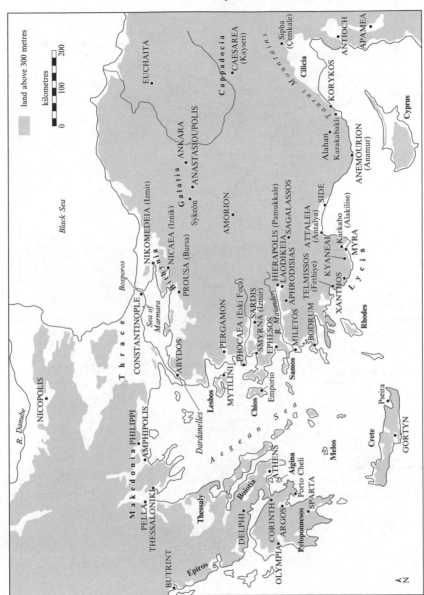

MAP 6. The Byzantine heartland.

MAP 7. Italy.

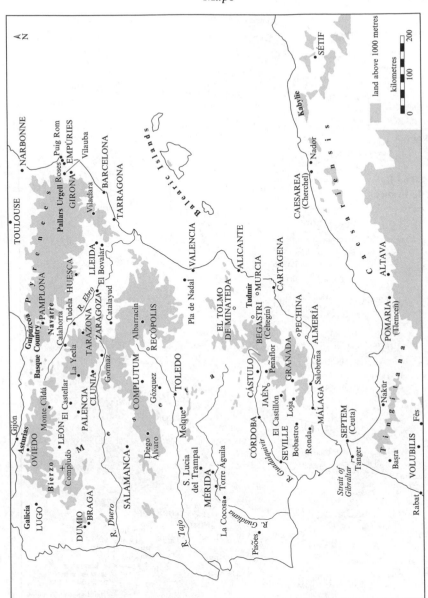

MAP 8. Spain and Mauretania.

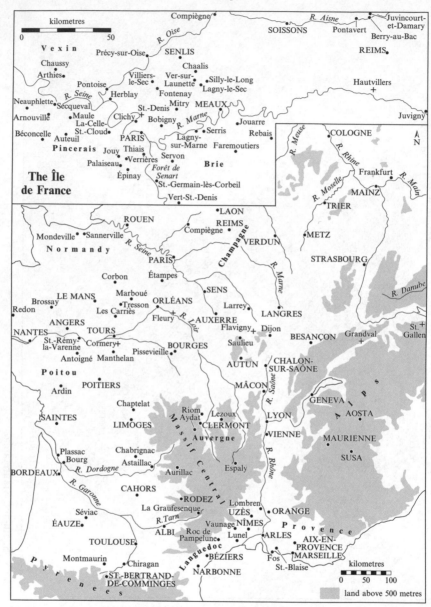

MAP 9. Central and southern Gaul.

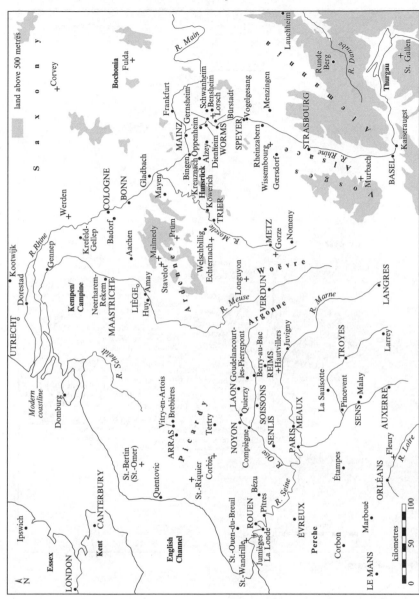

MAP 10. Northern Gaul.

Map 11. Britain.

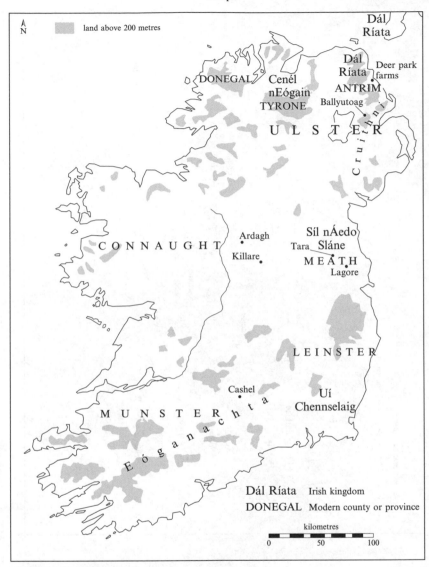

MAP 12. Ireland.

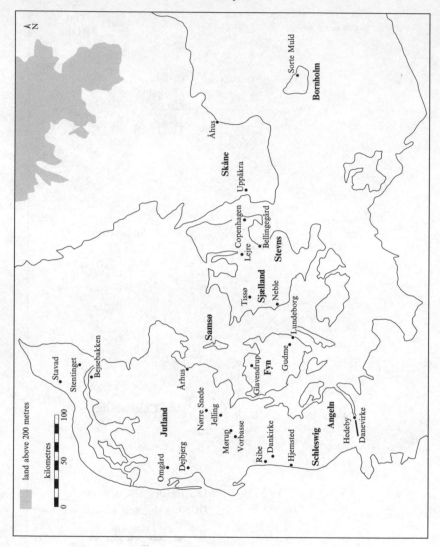

MAP 13. Denmark.

Introduction

IN THE LAST three decades the study of the early middle ages has been transformed. Far more people write about its documentary history; what we can say about its archaeology has multiplied tenfold—in some countries, a hundredfold. The sorts of questions asked about the material have changed radically too, with far more sophisticated analyses of political process and cultural change being now offered than ever existed before. This development is, of course, common to the historical profession as a whole; all the same, in some areas—the analysis of the construction of sanctity, for example—the period 400–800 is a trendsetter. The community of scholars is also more international than it was: this is an ongoing process, started for early medievalists above all by the Centro Italiano di Studi sull'Alto Medioevo and their Spoleto conferences from 1953 onwards, and in the last decade channelled, in highly stimulating ways, by the European Science Foundation's Transformation of the Roman World project of 1993–8.

These are all wholly positive developments. What has not developed, however, is a set of interpretative paradigms that fully reflect this flowering of scholarship. When I was a student around 1970, we looked for an overview of western European development in this period to Alfons Dopsch and Henri Pirenne, both born in the 1860s, who worked out their major rival contributions in the 1920s. Today, although Dopsch has (unjustly) faded a little into the background, he has not been replaced by any successor, and Pirenne is still a key point of reference, cited all the time. Historians of other periods argue over the theories of scholars who are often still living; the early middle ages, despite the fact that its scholarship (and even its evidence-base, thanks to archaeology) has been transformed more than those of most periods, has not seen a successful revision of its founding paradigms, and actually not even many unsuccessful ones. This is particularly the case for social and economic history, my principal interest in this book. There are some good economic surveys, but they are usually fairly summary accounts, as with Georges Duby's stimulating foray into the period, *Guerriers et paysans*, of 1975, or Richard Hodges's and David Whitehouse's archaeological rewriting of Pirenne, *Mohammed, Charlemagne and the origins of Europe*, of 1982, although our understanding of long-distance exchange has recently been transformed by Michael

McCormick's major survey, *The origins of the European economy*, of 2001. The very recent inclusion of early medieval western society in the topics for study for the French *agrégation* has also generated several excellent overviews.[1] But if one wants to go further, in social history in particular, one has to go back to Dopsch.

One reason for this is that the internationalism of scholarship is even now only skin deep. The early middle ages is a visceral period: it is the period when the polities first formed that are the genealogical ancestors of the nation states of today. The importance of these foundations continues to matter greatly to historians, whether consciously or unconsciously. All the sharpest debates about the period have always been about what are perceived as the major elements in national genealogies—the formation of unitary kingdoms in Denmark or England, their absence in Italy or Ireland, the reality and nature of the Arab break in Spanish or Palestinian history, the division on linguistic lines between France and Germany, and, all through every country of western Europe, the old issue of the exact role that 'Germanic' immigrants into the Roman empire had in the creation of those elements of national identity that are locally regarded as most significant. This latter issue remained important even in a decade like the 1990s, in which the pendulum moved resolutely in a Romanist direction, and against an overemphasis on the Germanic influence in any Roman province, a development which has some internationalist implications, as we shall see. The problem about all these debates is that, in their national forms, they make most sense only to scholars from one country, and sometimes no sense at all outside its borders—if indeed they are known about at all to other scholars, caged inside their own country-specific preoccupations. I called this situation 'cultural solipsism' when I lamented it a decade ago,[2] and, although the situation has eased slightly, as more people go to conferences abroad, it has by no means gone away: everybody who has done so has had the experience of finding in at least some international conferences that people from other countries were in reality talking about wholly different things, even when they were apparently using the same scientific language. Another development that could also potentially dissolve the national cultural traditions that dominate the field, the existence of a sizeable and

---

[1] Dopsch, *Economic and social foundations*; idem, *Die Wirtschaftsentwicklung*; Pirenne, *Mohammed and Charlemagne*; Duby, *Early growth* (the English translation of *Guerriers et paysans*); Hodges and Whitehouse, *Mohammed, Charlemagne*; McCormick, *Origins*; Depreux, *Les sociétés occidentales*; Le Jan, *La société*; Devroey, *Économie rurale*. See further the comparative social history of war in Halsall, *Warfare*. Pirenne, but not Dopsch, has been the focus of some historiographical interest recently, largely in Italian—perhaps paradoxically, given his relative lack of interest in Italy: Petralia, 'A proposito dell'immortalità'; Delogu, 'Reading Pirenne again'; Violante, *Uno storico europeo*. Note that throughout this book citations are given in short-title form, to save space.

[2] Wickham, *Land and power*, p. 203. But Marc Bloch made the point first, as usual, in 1928: *Mélanges historiques*, I, pp. 37–40. See further Geary, *Myth of nations*.

increasing contingent of scholars who study another country, has mostly up to now not had that effect either: by and large, such scholars have the choice between being absorbed into the national debates of the country they study, or else keeping a distance from them, but only because they have remained attached to the debates of their country of origin. In the latter situation they can add a critical element, and sometimes do, but in that case they have often been ignored by the historians in the country they study.

The other démarche chosen by recent scholars to get around these traps is continuity. A genuine arena for relatively neutral international scholarship is the Roman empire, given the size, the transnational scale, of its political system. Indeed, the Roman empire is too *often* seen as a whole, too *seldom* as a collection of provinces. This is a position that I shall argue against on occasion in the pages that follow; but at least the solipsism of the early middle ages is less often felt in its study, and people argue about issues covering wide geographical areas, often using a wide variety of foreign languages as they do so. The history of the Byzantine empire has carried on this international tradition, for the obvious reason that it can be regarded as the most direct heir of Rome. (I leave aside the issue of Orientalism here, the western European construction of the East as the history-less Other, which is these days less serious an issue for Byzantine than for Islamic studies.[3] There is, anyway, Greek scholarship on Byzantium—though less Turkish scholarship—which is integrated into the international network.) It cannot be said, unfortunately, that the study of Byzantium has had much impact on the West; only a handful of scholars, such as Dietrich Claude or Michael McCormick, have ever studied both with equal attention. All the same, it seems to me significant that one of the contexts in which internationally orientated scholarship of the post-Roman western world, too, has felt most at ease is the study of Roman continuity. In a sense, if the sixth-century West is refigured as still-Roman, and the seventh for that matter—indeed, even the Carolingians for some people—then national history-writing can be put off till later. This is fully legitimate in some areas—intellectual culture, most notably; religious history, perhaps; political practice, with more difficulty. But it comes at a price. Much of the most fruitful international debate has been achieved in the framework of the illusion that nothing of major importance had changed in the post-Roman world at all. This is further emphasized, I think, by the impact of two separate cultural traditions in 'late late Roman' studies. One is the by now considerable volume of British scholarship on continental European topics, for there is a strong strand of British (particularly English) national culture that seeks to stress historical continuities at all costs, and to play down any breaks, as can be seen in, for example, much recent English writing on the English/British Civil War, or the French Revolution. The second is a Catholic tradition,

---

[3] Said, *Orientalism*; the book does not discuss Byzantium.

largely French in recent years, which sees the real caesura as the Christian-ization of the Roman empire, and the religious continuity between the late empire and the early middle ages as more important than any political/institutional break (and even this latter has recently been denied by some). These two elements are very different, and have little influence on each other; nor do they by any means encompass all such scholarship on the period. But they contribute to continuitist readings in the same *sort* of ways, all the more because they are in general unconscious. This is why, perhaps, there are so few overviews, even in the framework of what one could call the 'Romanist paradigm': because it is so unconscious that it has not even reached paradigmatic status. It is not like this that we will substitute for Pirenne.

I am restricting myself to generalities here, because I wish to avoid critiquing individuals. Pretty well all early medievalists (including myself) are anyway implicated in this situation, all the more so because the param-eters outlined here are largely unperceived, and their importance in debates is largely instinctive. It could be argued, however, that the basic problems derive from a failure to confront difference, whether temporal or spatial, in a comparative way: before versus after a major change like the replacement of the western Roman empire by a dozen successor states, or the loss by the eastern empire of most of its provinces to the Arabs; or the geographical differences between parallel regional experiences, of both continuity and change. Major generalizations have been made either simply by taking one region as normal, and analysing divergent patterns, if at all, as exceptions (Dopsch and Pirenne already did this), or simply by concentrating on one country, one series of nationally focused questions, and attempting to solve these alone. The main national syntheses of the 1940s–1950s, which are still points of reference for debates in their respective countries, illustrate the latter point: it would be absurd even to imagine stitching, for example, Frank Stenton, Robert Latouche, Eugen Ewig, Gianpiero Bognetti, and Claudio Sánchez-Albornoz together in order to produce a history of early medieval western Europe. None of these people, although all excellent scholars in their own context, were interested in comparison; their separate concerns virtually created a Europe of islands, separated by treacherous channels. Their successors (mostly living) have sometimes made a better job of their syntheses, but they are often just as national-focused, to the exclusion of any outside reference-point—and in some countries they have not had successors at all. Hence the sense one sometimes feels of a lack of rootedness about early medieval scholarship, even when it avoids the wilder edges of unsupported or deluded theorizing that is only too common for the period (as is inevitable really: any period which has both very little evidence and a major importance for national identity is bound to generate it). Debates about continuity and discontinuity, in particular, continue to float without anchors in the sea of current research, with the continuitism of some (largely historical) scholarship, already referred to, fully matched by the catastrophe theories of other scholars, largely archaeologists, which are equally unclear in their articulation as real historical phenomena, in operation on the ground. It is that rooting, or anchoring, that we could usefully attempt in the immediate future, before we get near to shifting our paradigms; and this will only come, it seems to me, through more systematic regional comparison.

I have argued for more comparison in early medieval studies before, and I have attempted it in analyses of the central middle ages.[4] So it seemed to me appropriate to follow my own precepts and try the same for the earlier period. This book is focused on the period 400–800, long enough to include the Roman empire before its crisis period, and to explore the changes that derived from that crisis for some time thereafter. The cut-off date of 800 is arbitrary, but it means that I do not have to consider the effects of the Carolingian and 'Abbāsid takeovers, which introduce several new problems; the Carolingian period in Francia and Italy also coincides with a substantial increase in documentary evidence, which I have for the most part avoided using—in Francia this book in part stops in 751. The area covered by the book is western Europe and the Mediterranean, or, in other terms, the former Roman empire and some of its northern outliers. From North to South and West to East, the regions I have focused on, for comparative purposes, are: Denmark, Ireland, England and Wales, Gaul/Francia, Spain, Italy, North Africa, the Byzantine heartland of the Aegean and western Anatolia, Syria and Palestine, and Egypt.[5] Of these, only Denmark and Ireland were not once Roman. I chose Denmark as my major non-Roman parallel because, unlike the other Scandinavian countries, it was close enough to continental political and economic networks to accumulate quite a lot of diagnostic archaeological material; and because its state-building process, unlike those in the otherwise ecologically similar regions of Frisia and Saxony, was not interrupted by the Franks. Ireland, for its part, simply has so much early medieval documentation that it would have been wrong to exclude it, although its development was sufficiently *sui generis* that incorporating it has not been as easy as I hoped (see below, pp. 354–64). I excluded the Slav lands, both in the Roman empire (in the Balkans) and outside it, because of my own linguistic weaknesses. Armenia was excluded for the same reason, and also because its development ran along such

---

[4] Wickham, *Mountains*; idem, *Community and clientele*; idem, 'La signoria rurale'.
[5] These regional names deserve some comment. They are generally the easiest translations of Roman terms, so Spain means the whole Iberian peninsula, Roman *Hispania*, with due apologies to the Portuguese, Catalans, and Basques; Palestine means the region now constituted by the states of Israel, Palestine, and Jordan; North Africa (more usually, Africa) means the area from Tripolitania in modern western Libya to the Atlantic, north of the Sahara. Similarly, I shall use Britain as a synonym for England and Wales, stopping at Hadrian's Wall. I use Gaul and Francia more or less interchangeably to mean the whole area from the Pyrenees to the Rhine; after 550 or so, I use Francia more often than Gaul.

genuinely different lines; if it had been included, it would have been hard to exclude Iran, and then the book would really have got out of hand. There are other absences, but ten major regions are already hard to manipulate—adding each new one, I found, is quite like the qualitative leap in difficulty produced by adding each new ball while juggling.[6]

In the framework of that set of regions, I have concentrated on certain specific issues, each of which has a substantive chapter, or a group of chapters, to itself: the form of the state (in particular its financing), the aristocracy (in particular its wealth), the peasantry and the structures of local rural society, urban society and economy, and networks of exchange. In each case the regions have been treated as separate case studies, compared with each other in the course of presentation, and summed up in a comparative analysis at the end of each chapter. This method of exposition is imperfect, and I chose it with some misgivings; it seemed to me that it risked simply being a wearisome set of too many examples, strung together with relatively weak links between them. The reader will have to decide how far those fears are justified. One could argue, however, that the alternatives would be worse. The book could have simply consisted of a set of giant regional analyses, all of England then all of Francia, and so on. Actually, this is how I did the research, and it would have been easier to write. But drawing out the comparative elements in what would simply have been a set of separate histories, in effect national histories of a partially traditional type, seemed hard to envisage: particularly as one of the things that interests me most is what happened to aristocracies as a *whole* (in their different regional experiences), cities as a *whole* (in their different regional experiences), not just the regions themselves. An alternative procedure, to have looked at, for example, 'the city' and its development as a single unit, would conversely have involved a melting down of the comparative element that was, precisely, one of the main aims of this project.

Comparative analysis also requires a standard vocabulary. History, as is well known, uses an 'ordinary-language' vocabulary, with relatively little use of technical neologisms, unlike other social sciences or literary disciplines. This means that it uses words that have developed their meanings and overtones in daily use, which are not always consistent even inside single countries, and which are often substantially divergent across different languages. History also, not being a very self-reflexive discipline, has sometimes developed technical meanings for these words which vary greatly from one end of the discipline to the other, or else are fought over by practitioners, too often concerned as they are to lay claim to the 'right' meanings of words in technical historical language. ('Feudal' and 'feudalism'

---

[6] Three smaller absences which I regret are Scotland, Bavaria, and Cyrenaica; I left them out because in each case it seemed to me that the information available for them had parallels elsewhere.

are the most famously contested of such words, but there are plenty of others.) I do not believe that there are 'right' and 'wrong' examples of such usages—although some do seem to me unhelpful—and no policing is possible, anyway. All that one can do, when one uses words, is to have a clear and consistent idea of what they mean, and to explain them to the reader if necessary. I shall do this, in different chapters, for the words 'state', 'aristocracy', 'peasant', 'feudal', 'tribal', 'estate', 'village', and 'town/city', among others. Not everyone will agree with the meanings used here (and the level of agreement will vary from country to country: my use of the term 'feudal' is closest to that common in Spanish, for example, while that of 'town' is closest to uses in English); but I hope that it will not be found that the usages here are internally inconsistent. Most of these words evoke a sufficiently complex pattern of meanings that it is best to think of them as Weberian ideal types, and they will be presented as that when they are discussed, in the relevant chapters.[7]

The themes chosen for the book are those of a fairly classic social and economic history. This book does not offer a political narrative, except a minimum outline for each region in Chapter 2. Intellectual culture is certainly not part of its remit. It is more difficult to exclude the wider conception of culture that an anthropologist or cultural historian would mean by the word—values, attitudes, representations, discursive strategies, material culture, imagery—for these underpin all political and social action, and indeed give meaning to all our source material. Such cultural analysis will therefore appear in several chapters; but it is fair to warn the reader that a fully fledged cultural history of the period has simply been squeezed out by a feeling, as I wrote, that the book was already pretty long and should be tied down to its core themes. It will be treated more fully in a future work, volume 2 of the *Penguin History of Europe*.

My overall research procedure, as I went from region to region, was to treat each in the same way, and to ask the same questions of each, insofar as that was possible. This meant that I had to base my research on primary sources, whether written texts or archaeological reports, before engaging with the interpretations of modern historians/archaeologists, the premises of whom anyway often caused me difficulties, for reasons already outlined. In the end, of course, one learns whom to trust among modern scholars, and I hope I have properly recognized my great debts to them, in footnotes and acknowledgements—A. H. M. Jones's explanations of why he cited so few scholars, set out in his preface to his still marvellous late Roman synthesis, do not appeal to me, any more than does his mystifying neglect of archaeology.[8] Indeed, in this period secondary sources often overwhelm the scarce

---

[7] For a discussion of ideal types and of the diversities of the usages of the word 'feudalism', see Wickham, 'Le forme del feudalesimo'.

[8] Jones, *LRE*, pp. vi–vii.

primary material they are commenting on, even when substantially pruned, as here. But I have tried to read all the texts myself which were actually written in the period (or which report archaeological finds datable to the period), at least all those that seemed relevant. There are too many, and I am sure there must be serious omissions. If there are, they are the result of my error, not of any predetermined research strategy; that strategy was restricted to excluding later sources, even if they recounted events from the period, with certain clear exceptions that could not easily be done without, such as the *Vita Eligii* or al-Balādhurī. I have not looked at every cemetery report, or every sermon, but I should have done, and if the information contained in them undermines an argument then it is my fault. My Greek and Anglo-Saxon are pretty imperfect, and my Arabic, Coptic, and Irish almost non-existent (here I have relied on translations), but I have taken advice over interpretative cruxes in each, and I will stand by them.

The way I read sources needs a little comment. Sources used to be regarded as unproblematic; the statements they made were true or false, one could develop criteria for telling which, and then one believed their true information and reproduced it. In more recent years this has come to be regarded as a naive strategy. Indeed, every narrative text for the late Roman and early medieval period has recently been (or soon will be) analysed as a piece of free-standing rhetoric, often separated entirely from anything except the textual traditions its author was operating inside, and presented as useless for understanding anything except the mind and the education of the author. This is certainly more satisfactory than the positivism of a generation ago (except, at least, when scholars do both at the same time, which they often do), but neglects the fact that authors did also write in a contemporary environment, and for a contemporary audience. How we navigate this epistemological and practical minefield is of crucial importance, but complex: I could have spent ten pages discussing each reference to a source as a result. In practice, it was of course not possible to do this, so I had to get round the issue. I have usually taken legal documents more or less at face value, while recognizing of course the problems of typicality they represent, for, if genuine, they had at least some legal force in nearly all our societies, as court cases show. Normative sources I have treated as guides to the minds of legislators, rather than as reportage (see below, p. 383). As for narrative sources, I have, in general, tended to disbelieve them, but I have presumed that they reflect a rhetorical field, of acceptance of what was plausible to say to someone at any given moment. So it matters, for example, that Salvian (and his presumed audience) thought that in the 440s a corrupt tax system was something that one should emphasize in a denunciation of the age; that Gregory of Tours (and his presumed audience) in the 570s–590s paid attention to aristocratic and royal violence; that the author of the *Life* of Theodore of Sykeōn (and his presumed audience) in the 620s–630s thought that individual peasant greed could cause demons to take over villages. This does not mean that the exact details of fiscal corruption, or violence, or demonic possession actually ever happened at all, but it does mean that people thought they were possible: this is what *could* be said. This is a different procedure from 'there's no smoke without fire', or from the belief, shared by surprisingly many historians, that a historical source must be 'reliable' if even one member of the presumed audience was an eyewitness to events, because in that case the writer would not have been able to get away with inaccuracy. As has been said often before, it should be enough to read a day's newspapers to lose either of these illusions. But the image of the newspaper is a positive one, too: if you read the main stories, and even the editorials, of even the most irresponsible newspapers, across a decade, or else across different countries (say Belfast, Dublin, and London on Northern Irish issues, not to go farther afield), you will get a sense of the mindset and the reactions to daily events of significant sections of the population that you can (unfortunately) trust. So it is with Salvian, even if all his facts are wrong.

A final warning: I have not found it easy to keep a balance between general overview and the detailed *explication des textes* that early medievalists love. This book is long enough, but it also treats a large amount of material, often at much more restricted length than the experts in any given country are used to reading. Those experts—you, the reader—often also know far more than I about a given set of material, and may well find my treatment superficial. I have, of course, elided much detail, while also trying to respect difference. As a result, my image of Italy may ignore the special case of Tuscany, my image of Tuscany may ignore the special case of Pisa, and so on down, for every one of my regions. I have here done my best, however. Michael Mann, in his magnum opus on historical sociology, said: 'Having covered a large slice of recorded history, I have doubtless committed errors of fact, and probably a few howlers. I ask whether correcting them would invalidate the overall arguments.'[9] This book covers less ground than Mann's, but the question is still a fair one. If the errors do invalidate the arguments, however, that is another matter. I hope not; but I shall find out.

These warnings to the reader, partially apologetic in tone, are not insincere; but if I did not have confidence in the project I would not have embarked on it. Now does seem to be a good moment to write this book. The archaeological advances of the last generation offer a particularly good framework for comparison, of like with like, for the technology of cutting stone or throwing pots has fewer cultural barriers than textual strategies do (not *none*, but fewer). I shall be using pot-making technology and ceramic distribution as one of my main comparative elements, in fact. This procedure will be defended in Chapter 11 (pp. 700–6), but it underpins many of the earlier chapters in the book as well—indeed, the realization of how much

---

[9] Mann, *Sources*, I, p. 31.

one could now say about ceramic distributions (almost none of which could have been said in 1970) was one of the major impetuses behind the conception of the book in the first place. It is, equally, in the archaeological arena that the book's conclusions risk being outdated earliest; it needs to be stated explicitly that the period in which evidence was collected for this book was 1997–2000, with less systematic updating thereafter. (The last moment the bibliography was updated was April 2004.) I believe, all the same, that the materials already in existence are a secure enough basis for at least some of my generalizations.

I want to propose here two basic points about the early middle ages. The first concerns break-up. The Roman empire was a coherent political and economic system, operating on a scale that has seldom since been matched in Europe and the Mediterranean, and never for so long. (The early caliphate matched its scale, but the period of full *economic* centralization of the caliphate was a century at most, c.770–870; the Roman empire lasted four times that and more.) However much the successor states managed to imitate Roman political and economic patterns, which they did in very varying degrees, they did not match that scale. Anything in their local infrastructure that depended on a wider geographical framework, like the supply of grain from Africa to Rome, or the huge wealth of some late Roman senators, could not survive political localization. Areas like the Aegean, which were particularly closely linked into a wider exchange network, would similarly suffer when that network broke down. In general, there were parts of the empire that were more linked into a Mediterranean world-system, like southern Italy, the Aegean, and Africa, and other parts that were relatively separate from it, like inland Spain and northern Gaul. Other things being equal, one would expect more continuities in the latter than the former, and indeed, to an extent, this can be shown. It may be added that, although the 'fall of the Roman empire' is such a potent symbol that it has had the ill luck to be reinterpreted through every *idée fixe* of every decade and every national group in the last two centuries or longer, it has become at least easier, recently, to make this sort of analysis with the fall of the Soviet Union in mind; the unprepossessing successor states, with their regional economies in greater or lesser degrees of chaos, fare better or worse depending on how far from or how close to the former command economy they had been. The analogy cannot be pressed too far, for we actually at present have a clearer idea of the internal working of the post-Roman polities than of many of the post-Soviet ones, but it has been in my mind, so it is fair to make that fact explicit.

More generally, what happened when the empire broke up into its various pieces was that each piece took the surviving elements of Roman social, economic, and political structures and developed them in its own way. The parallel developments of the successor states are thus a very rough-and-ready research laboratory of alternatives: what happens to the way social change takes place if in any given region, each starting from an at least analogous starting-point, you have more urbanism (as in Egypt, in Palestine, and to an extent in Italy), more internal exchange (as in Egypt), richer aristocrats (as in Gaul), or a more centralized fiscal system (as in Byzantium)? Of course, many of these, and other, differences themselves go back to the Roman empire, and can also retrospectively illuminate regional identities there. More important for the arguments in this book is the recognition that some such differences also derive from the trauma of the break-up of the empire itself, which included in most cases the conquest of a given region by an external army and (partially) new ruling class. I would argue, however, that in each case the new elites essentially had to make the best of what they found; pre-existing differences were more important than the culture and economy of incoming groups in every case, even when we are dealing with situations of the most extreme change, as in Britain. This is to an extent a 'Romanist' reading, at least in the sense that it plays down the socio-economic effect of immigrant populations, who were always small minorities. It is not, however, a narrowly continuitist reading, for major social changes undoubtedly took place, nearly everywhere, across our period.

The second point leads on from this, for it concerns 'continuity' itself. This is a much misused concept, for it is often invoked for such specific things, in such isolation from wider problems of social change. People who invoke it often write as if the use of a Romano-British wall-building technique in an Anglo-Saxon house, the accessibility of manuscripts of Ovid in a Frankish monastery, the genealogical longevity of a local ruling family on the Christian–Muslim frontier in Spain, the squared street plan of a city in Carolingian Italy, the availability of Egyptian papyrus in the West, the existence of a Roman senatorial title in the Byzantium of 800, the match-up between provincial boundaries of the Roman and the Arab periods in Palestine, each, in themselves, simply represent 'continuity'. Well, on one level they certainly do; but the continuity they represent is in each case of a different order from the others. (If one had them all in any given region in 800, say, one could certainly invoke the concept of pretty slow social change; but one does not.) Historians or archaeologists who seize on these individual strands as signs of a wider development too often appear to have no conception of how the strands actually might fit into such wider developments. Nor, often, conversely, do the catastrophists who can in each case be found to deny the existence of these continuities, or others. One has to have a model for how social development takes place, which would allow one to say what elements were significant for what. And one has also to recognize that even the most extreme situations of social change are also full of elements of continuity, unless the entire population of a given region were to be killed or expelled and wholly replaced by another, an interpretation of the late Roman/early medieval change that was indeed once believed for some places, but is no longer accepted except on the fringes of scholarship. (Such radical replace-ments of populations are actually logistically very hard to achieve before the technological advances of the last century, and are in most cases so pointless that only unusually organized and ideologically driven invaders would conceive of them—the Athenians on Melos, the Mongols at Herāt, the Europeans in the Americas. The average Germanic tribe looking for its place in the sun hardly fits.) Where population continuities can be assumed, so will continuities of daily practice: agriculture, much ritual, most elements of social exchange. These in themselves do not disprove the existence of crisis in *other* elements of a social system, state structures, or exchange networks. One has to put them all together, and assess them as a whole, if one wants to get a sense of how social change as a whole takes place.

It must be added that this is, of course, the sort of debate that historians have all the time. How much of a break *was* the English Civil War? The French Revolution? The Russian Revolution? These debates are often not much more sophisticated than those around the fall of the Roman empire, for they too are full of people seizing isolated strands of continuity or change and claiming that they are widely representative, just as our debates are. Perhaps the only advantage they have over early medieval ones is that the theorists who dominate their debates are still alive, or only recently dead. These homologies are a product of the lack of interest historians have in social theory, in the understanding of how societies work as systems. Here, it is illusory to hope that the problem will go away soon; but a recognition that our debates are close in their own structure to those in other periods is something that could usefully be more widely felt.

I would argue, in general, for elements of both continuity and radical change. Broadly, the peasantry saw least change in the period 400–800, and they were around 90 per cent of the population in most regions (outside Egypt, and maybe Syria-Palestine, where cities were bigger). Not that noth-ing changed for them. Their landlords changed sometimes, and sometimes, indeed, faded away; they paid less tax in many places; the intensity of their exploitation in general decreased temporarily (this was often already chan-ging back by 800); their numbers probably decreased for a few centuries; and in many cases they had less access to artisanal products of decent quality. These shifts, taken together, are substantial. But they are not so radical that one needs to posit fundamental changes in peasant societies or household economies. I have argued this before (and been labelled a con-tinuitist for it), and I would stand by the picture: I shall seek to demonstrate it here most fully in Chapters 7–9. Conversely, the arena which saw most change was in the form of the state. In the Romano-Germanic kingdoms, the Roman state collapsed—not immediately in the fifth century (except in Britain), but steadily between 400 and 700; its entire fiscal basis dissolved, and all parameters of political power had to be constructed anew, even if many of their elements had older origins. I have argued this before as well (and been labelled a catastrophist for it), and I would only slightly modify the picture, as can be seen in Chapter 3, where the major Romano-Germanic kingdoms are set against the surviving—also changed, but to a far smaller extent—states of the eastern Mediterranean.[10]

In the other themes of this book, above all aristocracies, urbanism, and exchange (themselves all closely linked, as we shall see), the answer to questions of continuity and change lies much more in regional difference. Different provinces of the Roman empire had different experiences of each, and these experiences changed across time. I shall try to set these differences side by side and compare them, using them as guides to how similar and divergent developments took place, in all our regions, for such comparison is, as said above, one of the main aims of the book. It is worth noting, however, that I shall systematically in this book resist *deus ex machina* disaster theories for any major changes. Cities get burnt by enemies, or hit by earthquakes, throughout history, but if they are not rebuilt *afterwards* it is because of longer-term causes than one disaster encompasses on its own. This is so even when, conversely, the slow decline of such a city in previous centuries might have remained unnoticed, and maybe eventually have been reversed, had it not been for that crisis. The same sort of considerations can often be used for a polity defeated in war which then dissolves, or an aristocratic family that dies out (or is killed or expelled) whose local power is not replicated by another. These crises can best be seen as the flips in the 'catastrophe theory' of mathematicians, the modelling of when slow change finally reaches a situation where previous patterns cannot be sustained, and trends flip over into often precipitous crisis. Such patterns do not need external disasters to act as the catalyst, either; the sudden end of ceramic networks, for example, at different times between 500 and 700, often had nothing to do with immediate external crises—the catastrophe-flips happened on their own, as declining markets meant that, one day, transport and production costs made products just too expensive or too intermittent, and production plunged. The end of the Mediterranean Red Slip/*terra sigillata* networks, for example, seem often to have occurred like this: see below, pp. 712–13. Settlement change can take place in this way too.[11] I shall use the image of the catastrophe-flip in later pages, but it must be distinguished from the catastrophism of writers who seek an external cause for all major change in plague, volcanic eruption, or the old mantras of war and destruction. Rapid change did sometimes occur; you can indeed call it catastrophic if you like (as I will in this mathematical sense); but each time

---

[10] For earlier discussions of the issues referred to in this paragraph and the next, see Wickham, *Land and power*.

[11] For the mathematical image of catastrophe theory applied to settlement change, see Renfrew and Poston, 'Discontinuities'; applied to state breakdown, see Tainter, *The collapse of complex societies*, pp. 118–26, a more sociological version.

it had longer roots, which are more interesting and important to explore than the often contingent crisis.

This stress on regional difference is not intended to dissolve all general patterns into a mass of separate local experiences; far from it. The experiences of all the post-Roman regions—even their northern, un-Roman neighbours, like Denmark—can be *paralleled*. It is my aim to isolate the different trends in each region for each of my main themes, but then to put them together again, in generalizations that are rooted in the recognition of difference, rather than the pretence of uniformity, and in models of how societies work that are, whether right or wrong, at least more conscious than those often used by historians and archaeologists.[12] This will produce a series of generalizations that are too qualified for them simply to be able to replace the bolder paradigms of three generations ago, and in this respect the book is not, at all, aimed at a real paradigm shift; but it will, I hope, produce the raw material that will allow a better synthesist to do so in the future.

Researching this book has been pure pleasure. Never in my life have I been paid (thanks to the generosity of the British Academy) to tread on so many other people's territories. I discovered something excitingly new (to me) almost every day. I hope they do not become routinized and dull in my discussion of them here. I look forward to presenting here some of the things that surprised me most: the amazing documentation for some Egyptian villages, the startlingly well-preserved rural sites of Syria and Palestine, the real vigour of the late Visigothic state, the strangeness of Anglo-Saxon land tenure, the remarkable wealth of recent excavations in Denmark. These fit into wider patterns of parallelism and difference too, but they are interesting in themselves. Knowing that there is more like that to find in part makes up for the vertigo one feels in having taken on too much, with too much not accounted for.

---

[12] Two books which offer a standard to aim at when constructing coherent models for ancient and medieval societies are Runciman, *Treatise*, II, and Haldon, *The state and the tributary mode*.

PART I
States

2

Geography and politics

THIS CHAPTER, LIKE the last, is substantially introductory. In it, an overview of the geography and the political history (from 400 to 800) of each of the regions that this book will focus on will be set out as a point of reference. The regions are presented here in the form of a spiral, starting from North Africa, going anti-clockwise around the Mediterranean to Spain, then moving northwards to Denmark. The chapter is not intended to be particularly original, and will essentially be based on secondary literature; the footnotes cite fairly obvious guides. But it does need to be here, for not every reader has a very detailed knowledge of every part of western Europe and the Mediterranean, and an orientation point thus seems useful. I shall also include brief characterizations of some of the historiographical problems that are a feature of each region. But it must be stressed that my aim is to be introductory—an analysis of political history is not one of the purposes of this book (there are plenty of alternative guides); and a proper discussion of national historiographies would require a complex, book-length, characterization of national cultures, and of the role of historians, and national images of the past, in each. That task is much needed, but it will have to be carried out elsewhere.

1. Africa

Roman Africa consisted of a strip of the Mediterranean coast and its usually mountainous hinterland, running from Tanger to the Gulf of Syrtis (see Maps 1, 3, 8), essentially the western half of the part of the African continent north of the Sahara. Its economic powerhouse was beyond doubt the twin provinces of Proconsularis (or Zeugitania) and Byzacena, in modern terms northern and southern Tunisia and the eastern fringe of Algeria. Proconsularis was the grain-growing province par excellence, with a complex urban network focused on Africa's largest city by far, Carthage. Byzacena, notably drier and less urbanized except on the coast, was more an oil producer, though one should not be too schematic here—there were olives in the north and grain-fields in the south as well. Together, the two 'Tunisian' provinces produced one of the largest agrarian surpluses of the empire, second only to

Egypt, and remained rich thereafter, past the end of the time period discussed in this book.

The lands to the east and west of 'Tunisia' were more marginal. Tripolitania, modern western Libya, was a grain producer on its northern fringes, and indeed there was settled agriculture in the seasonal wadis to the south of that coastal strip, much further into the fringes of the Sahara than there is now, as the recent Libyan Valleys Survey has explored in some detail.[1] To the west, Numidia and Mauretania Sitifensis, together occupying the coast and the plateaux of modern eastern Algeria, were a slightly poorer and less market-orientated version of Proconsularis. From there to the Atlantic, however, in Mauretania Caesariensis and Tingitana, the percentage of highland becomes higher, as we move into the Atlas ranges, and the percentage of fertile land lower. The Romans tended to rule militarily in these provinces, and the Arabs never really controlled them at all. In the far west there is a substantial lowland area, the triangle between Tanger, Fès, and Rabat in modern Morocco, looking to the Atlantic rather than the Mediterranean. The Romans controlled this triangle from their city of Volubilis, but abandoned most of it as early as the late third century, for reasons that are unclear.[2]

The main feature that has dominated African history (and, indeed, African historiography) is the contrast between the settled agriculture of the coast and the nomadism of the Sahara. In historiographical terms, we owe the starkness of that opposition to Ibn Khaldūn in the fourteenth century, who regarded settled society as highly precarious, and only capable of being protected against nomadic conquerors by strong states.[3] But Ibn Khaldūn is more important here in the sophistication of his formulations than in their originality; in turn the Romans, the Arabs, and the French (in their guise as a colonial power) saw their role as the standard-bearers of civilization against the desert world. To an extent, they were right: the Sahara does offer more of a challenge to Mediterranean agriculture than does the other desert fringe that will appear in this book, the Syrian desert, for the former is so much bigger, and has been so much less influenced by settled societies. (The Arabian desert which connects with that of Syria is another matter, but it is outside our remit.) Not that there is in reality a sharp division between desert and sown; there is a wide grey area between them, as one moves south, into areas with steadily less rain. Dry-farming areas (which include most of Proconsularis) give way to areas that can only yield crops if they are irrigated, and to areas where agriculturalists and pastoralists coexist, often uneasily, and to areas where settled agriculture is at best a part-time

---

[1] Barker, *Farming the desert*; see in general Mattingly, *Tripolitania*, pp. 194–217.
[2] See e.g. Rebuffat, 'Recherches sur le bassin du Sebou'. Villaverde, *Tingitana*, surveys (and talks up) Roman finds from after 300 in central Morocco.
[3] Ibn Khaldūn, *Muqaddimah*, e.g. I, pp. 249–310; II, pp. 286–301.

occupation, by pastoralists who grow a few crops at the only rainy moment of the year, perhaps at one end of a semi-nomadic cycle, before one reaches the true desert. But the wide extent of the grey area was in itself the reason why the relationship between the settled and the nomadic world was so fraught: it was precisely that area whose economy, and culture, they fought over. When the settled world was dominant, grain was grown in the northern Libyan desert; when the unsettled world was dominant, the inland plain of Byzacena and the Numidian plateau (though never Proconsularis) were the home of shepherds, in a cycle of 'intensification' and 'abatement', as Øystein LaBianca has called it in the context of his studies of central Jordan.[4] These are simply cultural choices, although one need not be surprised that they have been moralized about so violently by two millennia of apologists for the settled ('civilized', literate) world, for the cultural/economic alternatives involved are very stark. The African provinces are the only ones in this book, apart from smaller sections of Syria and Palestine, where it was ever possible that settled agriculture could be abandoned. As a result of this reality, there is a certain edge to the modern historiography of Roman Africa, most of which is French, as the pioneer excavators of abandoned Roman cities (often apologists for the Roman—and French—*mission civilisatrice*) gave way to anti-colonial celebrators of *la résistance africaine*. Mutual accusations of neo-colonialism and Berber romanticism still appear in the literature.[5] The late and post-Roman period, although less sharply fought over, has been dominated, in an analogous way, by the metanarrative of the 'failure' of an urban/settled economy: when did that economy really begin to give way, to the relatively unagricultural world of the early modern period? In the late Roman period? with the Vandals? the Byzantines? the early Arabs? the Banū Hīlāl in the eleventh century? Every one of these has been canvassed by someone. It must be said at once that the answer almost certainly does not lie in simple invasion in any period, even by nomadic tribes like the Banū Hīlāl, whose devastations have been so written up in the past. (The force of invasion theories in part derives from a parallel belief, that tribal societies are inimical to settled economies, which is much more problematic, as will be seen in a moment.) But we do not have to solve the question in this book, at least. As we shall see in Chapters 10 and 11, the evidence points to the involution of an agricultural export economy in the sixth and seventh centuries, with a low point in the eighth, but not to a major retreat of settled agriculture, at least for subsistence, until well after our period ended.

---

[4] LaBianca, *Hesban 1*, pp. 12–19 (see below, Ch. 8, n. 47); for desert versus sown areas, see classically Braudel, *The Mediterranean*, pp. 171–88.
[5] The best introduction to African historiography is Mattingly and Hitchner, 'Roman Africa'; for the colonial edge, see pp. 169–70.

Africa was, as already said, one of the major sources of agricultural and artisanal products in the late Roman empire. Its grain and oil tax fed Rome, and extensive properties there made Roman senators rich; its pottery could in the fourth century be found on the tables of rich and poor alike throughout the western Mediterranean and into the East as well. It was lightly (and therefore cheaply) defended, for the tribal groups to its south were not considered much of a threat in the late empire. The world of the African Augustine of Hippo (354–430), by far the most prolific and original-minded intellectual in our period, was a violent, but essentially prosperous world.[6] Even when the Visigoths sacked Rome in 410, Augustine could be relatively uncatastrophist in his response to that unprecedented psychological blow: heretical Donatists were to him a more serious issue.[7]

The Vandals ended that. Not one of the major Germanic tribes, but by 417 located in southern Spain after a decade of movement from central Germany, they crossed over to Africa in 429 under their king Geiseric (d. 477), and by 430 were in control of the whole of its western half. In 439 they moved again, and occupied Proconsularis and Byzacena for a century, until 534. The Vandal century in Africa was decisive for the western Roman empire, for the Vandals were an independent kingdom, and the taxes from the region would not go to Rome henceforth; it is indeed after 439 that we first find clear signs of fiscal crisis in texts from the west Roman government, and the beginning of the spiral of ineffectiveness that would result in the end of imperial rule in the West itself (see below, pp. 87–92). The Vandals have a bad press as a consequence; and they had a worse press still from African authors, for they were fervent Arian Christians, fully prepared to persecute the Catholic Africans. Unfortunately, our main non-archaeological sources for the post-Augustine period are the Catholic apologists; there are no Vandal sources except a few praise-poems (by Roman poets), and no documents except the Tablettes Albertini, a set of estate documents of the 490s from an economically marginal zone of southern Byzacena. But it is reasonably clear from all of these that the Vandal state, notwithstanding its religious policies, was very Roman in style, and a certain prosperity is visible in the archaeology, at least until 500 or so. When the 'Vandal parenthesis' was ended, in the rapid conquest of the kingdom by the east Roman general Belisarios in 534, Africa was expected to return rapidly to its proper place as a major source of taxation for the empire, now focused on Constantinople.[8]

Africa under east Roman rule (it is universally called 'Byzantine Africa' to distinguish it from the pre-Vandal Roman period) is very badly documented, at least after the conquest period, which is described in detail by Prokopios

---

[6] So above all Lepelley, *Les cités*, I, pp. 29–36, 293–330.

[7] Brown, *Augustine*, pp. 288–95.

[8] Still basic is Courtois, *Les Vandales*; a good update is Cameron, 'Vandal and Byzantine Africa'.

and Corippus. It is clear that the hopes for its productivity were initially ill-founded, partly because the Vandals had apparently let taxation slip (below, p. 92), and partly because the east Romans had to keep a substantial army there, and to engage in extensive fortification, both of which were expensive. This military commitment was necessary in order to hold off native Berber tribes, which since the mid-fifth century dominated all the Mauretanias as independent political entities, and menaced the Vandal/ Byzantine-controlled territory from both the west and the south. By the second half of the sixth century Byzantine Africa had achieved a certain stability and showed moderate prosperity, which was sufficiently coherent that the exarch (governor) of Africa, Heraclius, could revolt and conquer Constantinople itself in 608–10, setting his son Heraclius in place as emperor for over thirty years.[9] But from then on there was more trouble. In 647 Arabs, raiding from Egypt, defeated and killed the exarch Gregorius, and from then on Tripolitania and Byzacena were lost to the empire. The Arabs were not yet acting as serious conquerors, but it was Berbers, not Romans, who filled the power vacuum in these southern lands—the empire by now only controlled Proconsularis. After 670 the Arabs returned, and in the next thirty years took over the core African provinces properly, resisted more by the Berbers than by the Romans. In the end they took Carthage too, in 698.[10]

The first century of Arab rule in what they called, following Roman usage, Ifrīqiya, is obscure. Its archaeology has been badly studied, and reliable historical sources are very few. It is at least clear that Kairouan, a new city founded in inland Byzacena, was their capital, with Tunis (another new city founded to replace neighbouring Carthage, now in ruins) reduced to second place. The *wālī* (governor) of Ifrīqiya had a similar position to the exarch before him, of some autonomy but also of some political marginality.[11] It was from here that Spain was conquered in 711 and onwards, with the enthusiastic involvement of the Berbers of the western Maghreb, the former Mauretanias, whom the Arabs had managed to co-opt into the *dar al-Islām*. But this co-operation did not last long, and the great Berber revolt of 739–40 severed Spain (temporarily) and Morocco (permanently) from the caliphate. Essentially, the core of Ifrīqiya was Tunisia, as it had been for the Vandals and Byzantines before. Eighth-century archaeology is, as noted, exiguous, but its simplicity implies that the confusion of the period 647–98 had done damage to African prosperity (see below, pp. 726–8). All the same, the intrinsic agrarian potential of the Tunisian provinces was still great. After 800 the autonomy of Africa turned into effective independence,

---

[9] See, in general, Cameron, 'Vandal and Byzantine Africa', with two basic monographic surveys, Diehl, *L'Afrique byzantine*, and Pringle, *The defence of Byzantine Africa*; and see below, pp. 641–2, 723–6.

[10] Brett, 'Arab conquest', is the best introduction to the seventh and eighth centuries.

[11] See above all Djaït, 'La wilaya d'Ifrīqiya'; idem, 'L'Afrique arabe', covering similar ground.

under the Aghlabid dynasty (800–909), and the economy of the region took an upward direction, to a new peak in the tenth century, after our period ends.[12]

As is clear from this brief account, the Berber tribes steadily increased their military strength and autonomy across our period. Already by 500 they were often organized in larger-scale alliances, like the Laguatan of what is now Libya, and some of them were ruled by kings with ambition.[13] (Exactly how large their polities were is in dispute, however; see below, pp. 335–7.) They left no written records, so can easily be constructed as the uncivilized Other, the main threat to the settled lands in our period. This, however, is misleading. There were settled Berber tribes, as much as there were nomadic ones; the development of tribal autonomies, which took more and more sections of Africa out of the power of the Carthage- (later, Kairouan-) based state, did not necessarily have any effect on agriculture at all, as is clear above all in the area covered by the best rural archaeology of Berber territories, the Libyan Valleys Survey. Indeed, some western Berber polities were even based on Roman cities, Altava and Volubilis. To Volubilis in 788 came the 'Alid exile Idrīs b. 'Abd Allāh, who founded the first Muslim dynasty of Morocco, the Idrīsids; their polity acted as the independent source of the Islamization of the Berber tribes of the Maghreb. Idrīs moved to Fès in 790, which is still the main centre of the settled plains of northern Morocco, in lineal succession to Volubilis.[14] The development of Berber autonomy will be discussed later in parallel with post-Roman Britain in Chapter 6, these two being the clearest instances we have of the breakdown of Roman-style political structures without invasion. In my view, however, the opposition between state and tribe is a more useful way of understanding Africa in our period than that between the desert and the sown. Not least because of the continuing wealth of the sown land in the region, which is an abiding feature of our whole period.

2. Egypt

Egypt was similarly located on the desert edge, but was much less exposed than Africa: partly because its desert is so inhospitable that very few people can live there; partly because the Nile made it so rich, and so populous, that its internal stability was enormously enhanced. The Nile and its annual flood essentially created Egypt (the region has almost no rainfall, and almost no other natural water apart from the river); Egypt as concept in human

---

[12] For the economy see in particular Vanacker, 'Géographie économique'.

[13] Mattingly, *Tripolitania*, pp. 173–6; and now Modéran, *Les Maures*, the basic historical survey of the Berbers in late Roman and post-Roman Africa.

[14] Brett, 'Arab conquest', pp. 525–6.

geography is in effect nothing other than the thin, winding strip of the valley, the 800 km stretch of Middle and Upper Egypt from Cairo to Aswān, plus the great triangle of the Delta, its base stretching between Alexandria and Pelousion on the Mediterranean and its apex at Cairo. (See Map 4.) The Nile had two other effects on the region, however. First, its flood, and the alluvium that came with it, captured in our period by thousands of local irrigation networks, made it more than twice as fertile as any other part of the Mediterranean or the rest of Europe (see below, pp. 65–6), which not only allowed it to produce a huge grain surplus for the eastern Roman empire and its Arab successors, but also fed an urban population which Roger Bagnall and Bruce Frier calculate as up to a third of the total population of Egypt, three times the standard estimate for most Mediterranean regions (see below, pp. 609–12).[15] Second, the Nile was a cheap and secure means of transport. This meant that Aswān was structurally linked to Alexandria, even though it was physically further from the Mediterranean coast than anywhere else in the empire except Britain—Aswān ceramics, indeed, dominate Egyptian sites in our period (below, pp. 761–3). It was possible for a complex economic network, both fiscal and commercial, to exist in Egypt even when interregional trade closed down, as it did at different times everywhere in our area of study. Egypt will thus always be the test case for what stability looks like in our period, when everything else changed—and when things changed even in Egypt, they certainly did so elsewhere.

Egypt, still more than Africa, was a core source of agricultural produce for the Roman state, and thus one of the mainstays of the east Roman fiscal network. The region was so straightforward to control, thanks to the Nile, that its political history is quiescent in the extreme in the late Roman period, which here extended to the 610s, with little to disturb it except the occasional bout of urban (sometimes religious) violence in Alexandria. What we know a large amount about, on the other hand, is its social and economic history. Egyptian archaeology for our period is as yet fairly restricted, despite its considerable potential; nor are narratives very numerous, outside the framework of a strictly ecclesiastical politics. But papyri are very well represented in our period (with the exception of a relative scarcity in the fifth century), surviving in their thousands. Egypt is by far the best-documented of our regions as a result, between 500 and the late eighth century. In the latest Roman period the two main documentary foci are Oxyrhynchos and Aphroditō, both in Middle Egypt, the former a centre of great landowning, the latter of small and medium properties; but there are scatters of papyrus for many other centres too, excepting only the Delta. The worlds these sets of papyrus illuminate are not 'typical' of the Roman world, but only because

---

[15] Bagnall and Frier, *Demography*, pp. 53–7.

nothing ever is; they are, nonetheless, comparable to many other Roman local realities, and they will be used as guides in that framework.[16]

The Persians took Egypt in 618–19, in a break as sharp as the Vandal conquest of Africa; they held it for a decade, until Heraclius defeated them in Armenia and won the last great Roman–Persian war. But the 630s, an ill-documented period in Egypt in fact, was the last Roman decade; in 639–42 the Arabs conquered the region, and it became (unlike Ifrīqiya) one of the central provinces of the caliphate. The Arabs did not settle in most of Egypt. They established themselves in a new capital, Fusṭāṭ, the ancestor of modern Cairo—Alexandria survived, unlike Carthage, but principally as a naval base—leaving Egypt as a whole under the control of its pre-existing local elites, which changed very little for a century. Egyptians in c.550 wrote documents in Greek, although they mostly spoke Coptic. Under Arab rule, Arabic slowly replaced Greek as the language of central government (though even this took a century); local documents were more and more written in Coptic. A second set of Aphroditō documents, from the 700s and the 710s, are in all three languages; the main later eighth-century collections, from Bala'īza in Middle Egypt and Jēme in western Thebes in Upper Egypt, are essentially in Coptic. Arabic only won out entirely after our period, in the ninth and tenth centuries, as Egypt began, very slowly, to go Muslim.[17]

Egypt's local politics was for a long time no more dramatic under the Arabs than it had been under the Romans, and is as quickly told. Its *amir* sat stably in Fusṭāṭ, and used the same mechanisms of rule, even the same tax mechanisms, as had his Roman predecessor at Alexandria. Being *amir* of Egypt was a high-ranking role: 'Abd al- 'Azīz, governor in 685–704, was the brother of 'Abd al-Malik, caliph in 685–705. In part, this is because being *amir* was arguably as profitable as being caliph. In the Umayyad period (661–750), the different provinces of the caliphate kept most of their taxation for themselves, to pay for local Arab armies. This was a practical, and politically necessary, solution in most cases, but it meant that the caliphate was for long much more fiscally decentralized than was the Roman empire.[18] In the case of Egypt, furthermore, this decentralization meant that early Arab Egypt was in a position that it had not been in since Cleopatra, one analogous to the Africa of the Vandals: it could consume the great part of its surplus inside the region. (The other great productive area of the caliphate, Iraq, had been the political focus of Sassanian Persia, and had thus always consumed its surplus locally—there was less change here. Indeed, when the 'Abbāsids recentralized the caliphal fiscal system in the late eighth century they were by now based in Iraq too, at Baghdad.) In Africa, this fiscal

[16] See as introductory guides Bagnall, *Egypt*; Keenan, 'Egypt'.
[17] McCoull, 'Strange death'.
[18] For the political structures of Arab Egypt, the best guide is Kennedy, 'Egypt as a province'; for fiscal decentralization in general, idem, *Armies*, pp. 59–79.

independence led in the end to economic simplification (below, pp. 722–8), but the Egyptian regional economy was so huge that a similar process did not occur. The Arabs in Fusṭāṭ must have become amazingly rich, nonetheless.

It may be in this context that, from the 720s onwards, tax revolts began in Egypt: they are constant, documented every decade or so, for a century, culminating in a general uprising in 831–2 (including by now Arabs, who had begun to settle in Egypt, as well as Christian Egyptians). These revolts largely correlated with periods of instability elsewhere in the caliphate, as with the 'Abbāsid revolution of 750 or the civil war of 811–19, but they had their own local roots in fiscal demands as well.[19] They will be discussed in more detail in the chapter on state structures (pp. 140–3). They show that, even in Egypt, taxation needed a justification that was more complex than simply the threat of force to legitimize it. Only when Egypt became effectively autonomous from the caliphate, from the Ṭūlūnids (868–905) onwards, did the Arabs, by then more numerous, more settled, and more closely linked to an increasingly Islamized native population, succeed in working out how to create a stable local state structure again.

Egypt is simpler to describe than Africa in an introductory framing, for it does not present the same sort of problems of interpretation—Egyptian geography is so uncompromising, and its papyrus evidence is so rich, that both overview and detailed socio-economic analysis are relatively straightforward. Its historiography is also less fraught, in the period of this book. Sixth-century surveys have not yet arrived at the remarkable level of Roger Bagnall's synthesis for the fourth century, but this may only be a matter of time, given the quality of what is being written at the moment. Its weakness is only that abiding Egyptological blind-spot, a lack of interest by most scholars in anywhere outside the Nile valley—a lack of interest, unfortunately, amply repaid by most scholars of the rest of the eastern Mediterranean in our period, who barely discuss Egypt at all, with a few notable exceptions such as Wolf Liebeschuetz and Jean-Michel Carrié.[20] In the Arab period, however, one has simply to register a falling-off in quality. Eighth-century Aphroditō has good work done on it, because its documentation is largely about the tax system, and Arab political/fiscal structures are well analysed; the later Coptic collections have had hardly any analysis at all, despite the richness of, especially, Jēme.[21] Here, as in Egyptian archaeology, there is work to be done.

---

[19] Morimoto, *Fiscal administration*, pp. 145–72.

[20] See above, n. 16; for Liebeschuetz, see e.g. *The decline*; for Jean-Michel Carrié, e.g. 'Observations sur la fiscalité'.

[21] See below, pp. 133–40, 419–28. An important exception to these observations is Wilfong, *Women of Jeme*.

3. Syria and Palestine

The region of the eastern, Levant, coast of the Mediterranean is in effect another long strip of land like Africa, set against the desert. A narrow coastal plain is backed by highlands running north from Jerusalem to the Taurus in modern Turkey, rising to serious mountains in Lebanon in the centre. Behind them, the top of the Rift Valley cuts a line up from the Red Sea parallel to the Mediterranean coast; it is desert in the Dead Sea area in the south, but highly fertile in the Jordan valley, Galilee, and the Beqa'a in the north. Then comes another line of uplands, marked by a string of historically important cities: from south to north, Petra, the Decapolis towns, Damascus, Emesa (Ḥimṣ), Epiphania (Ḥamā), Aleppo, that is to say the core of modern Jordan and Syria (see Map 5). Finally there is the full desert, with only oases to act as foci for habitation, most famously Palmyra (Tadmor). This linear pattern again recalls Africa, and many of the general observations made there apply here too, but there are differences. The coastal strip was in many places notably rich, especially between Gaza and Caesarea in the south in modern Israel, and around Antioch and in Cilicia in the north; but so were several inland areas, especially the valley and the uplands between 'Ammān and Damascus, and the Ḥimṣ–Aleppo region of northern Syria. Here, the desert margin was not a political fringe, as in Africa, but of central political importance. Indeed, there is a constant interpenetration between fertile land, mountain, and desert in the region. The desert is close to the coast in the south, in the Negev behind Gaza, but is itself backed by the grain country of the southern Jordan hills behind Petra; further north, if one travels the 60 km from Jerusalem eastwards to 'Ammān, one goes from a Mediterranean hill landscape to desert to an oasis (Jericho) and back into fertile hills. Even if one continues eastwards into the full desert, one can reach the great Mesopotamian rivers in a few weeks from the south or a few days from the north (days and hours by modern transport); the Euphrates in fact crosses the desert north-west to south-east, and in the north of Syria is only some 50 km from Aleppo, meaning that there is no significant break between the north Syrian cities and the middle Euphrates valley.

The desert between Syria and Mesopotamia is less threatening, as a result of these patterns, than is the Sahara. In the fifth and sixth centuries it was controlled by Arab tribes who were clients of the Romans and Persians, a far cry from the Berber tribal threat in Africa. Nor would Arab conquest in the seventh century bring any change to this; in the Umayyad period, indeed, the caliphs developed serious irrigation projects in the desert fringes of Syria and Jordan. (The late Romans, by contrast, with more of a Mediterranean orientation, had developed the Negev.)[22] In the end, however, there was an 'abatement' of agriculture on the desert fringe, south of Aleppo and in the

---

[22] Compare King, 'Settlement patterns', with Hirschfeld, 'Farms and villages', pp. 50–60.

drier south, in parts of the hill country of Jordan and Palestine.[23] As with Africa, there has long been a debate about who was 'responsible' for this, with a tendency in (among others) Israeli historiography to blame Arab conquest in the short or long term (the Israelis here taking the structural role of French colonial historiography in Africa). The 'Abbāsid revolution of 750, which removed political centrality from Syria, coinciding with at least one cataclysmic earthquake in the late 740s, which did much damage to cities in the southern Syrian/northern Jordanian sub-region, is another popular culprit. Recent archaeology, however, argues for very little economic weakening after 650, and not so much, perhaps, even after 750.[24] The main period of 'abatement' in the inland Levant probably did not begin until the ninth century, after our period ends. On the coast, Arab conquest may have been more of a blow, because of the heavy dependence in the Gaza and Antioch areas on interregional maritime links, for wine and oil respectively, but even then the marginal lands that became abandoned as a direct result, in parts of the northern Negev and the Limestone Massif of northern Syria, did not begin to lose their population until the eighth and tenth centuries respectively. In the latter case, the date is later because the area is not a desert environment.[25]

The late Roman period in Syria and Palestine in the fifth and sixth centuries was, as in the rest of the eastern Mediterranean, one of relative calm on the political level and great prosperity on the economic level, with a high point in the early sixth century, a period of large-scale urban rebuilding usually associated with the reign of Justinian (527–65). This is very clear in the archaeology, which is of particularly high quality for our period in this region (especially, but not only, in Jordan); the early sixth century was a period of great activity both on urban and rural sites. Nor is it contradicted by our written sources, although these are fairly scarce (hagiography is the most important element, including well-known texts like Theodoret of Cyrrhus' *Religious history*; documents are restricted to the Nessana and, now, the Petra papyri from the far south).[26] War with Persia, which led to considerable destruction in the 540s and 570s in the north, did not interrupt this prosperity; nor did the more localized conflict of the Samaritan revolts of the 480s–520s, except in Samaria itself (roughly the northern section of the modern Palestinian state), which suffered badly from the resultant repression.[27] There is less agreement about whether the period after 550 saw the start of a slow-down in the Syrian/Palestinian economy; if it did, the

[23] For 'abatement', see n. 4 above.
[24] See e.g. Walmsley, 'Production, exchange'; see below, Chapter 11.
[25] See below, Chapter 8.
[26] For the documents, see *P. Ness*; the first volume of the Petra papyri, *P. Petra*, is *The Petra papyri*, I. For urban archaeology see below, Chapter 10.
[27] Dauphin, *La Palestine byzantine*, pp. 285–95.

north is likely to have been more seriously affected than the centre-south
(below, pp. 620–5). But the Levant was still doing pretty well in 600.

Even more than in Egypt, the Persian occupation and then the Arab
conquest (614–28 and 636 onwards) caused structural reorientations.
Syria and Palestine had been heavily integrated into the Mediterranean
during the Roman empire, but the caliphate was only secondarily a Mediterranean power; conversely, the Arab conquest of the Sassanian empire as
well as half the eastern Roman empire united the Fertile Crescent for the first
time since Alexander. The coast faced economic difficulties, as already
noted; conversely, major inland route-centres like Aleppo began to develop.[28] All the same, the Umayyad period from the 660s onwards was, as
was seen in the Egyptian context, relatively fiscally decentralized, with little
revenue coming from the different provinces to central government. The
eighth century shows an economic localization in the Levant that would
only be reversed under the ʿAbbāsids (see below, pp. 774–80): not until the
ninth century did the Syria–Iraq link become more developed. But
the Umayyads had their power-base in Syria and Palestine, and their capital
in its centre, at Damascus; the region clearly prospered as a result, at least in
its internal economy.

We have extensive narratives of the Umayyad period, but they are mostly
late: the first major one is by al-Balādhurī (d. 892), and the most detailed
compilation is the work of al-Ṭabarī (d. 923). Recently there has been
considerable doubt cast on the utility of these and other texts as accurate
guides to the early Arab period, especially, but not only, the period of
Muḥammad's lifetime, a debate which exactly parallels those on all other
early medieval sources, but which has been sharpened, and driven to extremes, by the obvious importance of the period for Islam as a religion. The
implications of the most critical analyses of these texts are more serious for
political and religious historians, however, than they are for me. I have
used—with due caution—al-Balādhurī more than al-Ṭabarī, for the former
gives slightly more attention to socio-economic issues. (For the Jazīra, east of
Aleppo between the middle Euphrates and middle Tigris, there are some
more local histories in Syriac and Arabic, which will be used as appropriate,
but this area is on the margin of the Levant as a region.)[29] As a result of these
problems, and also as a result of the heavy military and prosopographical
slant of the narrative texts themselves, archaeology will stay at the centre of
our source material for the Umayyad period as well.

---

[28] See below, Chapters 8, 10, 11. A good introduction to the period is Canivet and
Rey-Cocquais, *La Syrie*.

[29] Critical accounts include Noth, *The early Arabic historical tradition*; Crone and Cook,
Hagarism; and the masterly microstudy by Conrad, 'The conquest of Arwād'. For the Jazīra, see
Segal, *Edessa*, and above all Robinson, *Empire and elites*. The classic account and the most
incisive analysis of the Umayyads are respectively Wellhausen, *The Arab kingdom*, and Crone,
Slaves on horses, pp. 29–57.

The Umayyad polity had its apogee from the late 680s to the early 740s; after the death of the caliph Hishām (724–43), it fell into crisis. In 750 the 'Abbāsid dynasty overthrew the Umayyads, and the capital moved to Iraq: Baghdad was founded in 762. Syria was treated virtually as a conquered territory by the early 'Abbāsids, and remained much more politically marginal thereafter, even though this process needs to be balanced against the development of the Fertile Crescent routes when estimating the degree of the economic recession of the 'Abbāsid Levant. The 'Abbāsids will not be discussed much here, for Iraq is out of the range of this book, and 800 is anyway a poor cut-off date for caliphal political processes; between 750 and 861, which are better ones, I have in practice gone for 750. But socio-economic patterns do not go by political dates, and we shall track the post-750 history of at least some cities when it is clear enough to discuss, at Pella for example (below, pp. 623–4). Syria and Palestine were a region in which many aspects of Roman society and the economy continued, almost as much as in Egypt, and the two regions complement each other, given Egypt's archaeological scarcities and documentary wealth, and the opposite situation in the Levant. I shall trace that complementarity in several chapters.

4. The Byzantine heartland

In 324 Constantine founded Constantinople as a new Roman capital, which by the fifth century was a city with a population of around half-a-million. The provinces around it were transformed into a political core area as a result, with Thrace and Bithynia at the forefront and the Aegean sub-region as a whole not far behind. The Aegean remained the political focus of the eastern Roman empire, and of the Byzantine empire that followed it. Exactly when one begins to use the word 'Byzantine' is a matter of debate (to modern historians, that is—by the Byzantines themselves, *romanus* and then *rhomaios* were the only terms ever used, and *byzantios* only meant an inhabitant of the capital); the two most common dates are 324 itself and c.640, the moment when the Arab conquests forced the Roman state to change its internal structures dramatically. I choose the latter; it seems to me by far the most important turning-point. In this book, the word 'Byzantine' will be used only for the period after 640, except in Africa and Italy, where, for reasons of convenience, it will describe the period after the Justinianic reconquests of the 530s.

The eastern Roman empire in 400 was a politically stable, fiscally integrated structure. As a fiscal system it will be described in Chapter 3 (pp. 62–80). As a political system it was not much under threat: the fifth century, which destroyed the western half of the empire, saw few ripples from that crisis come into the eastern Mediterranean, which indeed, as already noted, was reaching an economic high-point. The fifth-century emperors were not very striking figures, and others ruled through them until 474, but it was a period of not only calm, but a certain degree of political protagonism— the *Codex Theodosianus* of 439, the first great collection of imperial legislation, dates from this period. The only area that was dominated by the semi-autonomous 'barbarian' armies that were a standard feature of the late Roman West was the northern Balkans, modern Bulgaria and (former) Yugoslavia, from where most emperors also came; between the start of the fifth century and the end of the sixth these armies were only a serious political danger in the 470s–480s, under Theoderic Strabo and Theoderic the Amal, at a time when the emperor, the Isaurian general Zeno (474–91), was unpopular and the empire was short of money after a disastrous attempt to destroy the Vandals in 468. Anastasius (491–518), an administrator, restored imperial finance, and Justinian (527–65) used it to impose himself on all aspects of government—renewed legal systemization, administrative reorganization, extensive urban and military building, and the reconquest of Africa, Sicily, Italy, and south-east Spain. By 565 all the Mediterranean was in Roman hands again except the coast between Valencia and the Alps, and parts of Mauretania. Justinian's successors could not hold (most of) Italy, and the rest of the century may have seen economic stagnation, but as late as 600 the East (by now including Africa and Sicily) was still reasonably stable, integrated, and prosperous.[30]

The military balances which allowed Rome and Persia to spar without doing long-term damage throughout the sixth century ended abruptly when a mutiny against a winter campaign north of the Danube killed Maurice (582–602) and the Persians declared war. By 614 Syria and Palestine were lost, by 618–19 Egypt, as we have seen; in 615 the Persians invaded Anatolia. In 626 the Persians besieged Constantinople from one side, the Avars and Slavs—who had occupied most of the Balkans in the previous two decades—from the other. Remarkably, Heraclius, who was in the East at the time, managed to wrap up the Persians from behind and win the war in 628; but, when in 634 the Arabs, newly Muslim, began their conquests, neither the Romans nor the Persians had the strength to resist. By Heraclius' death in 641 the Romans/Byzantines were restricted to their heartland: the Aegean and parts of the coast of Greece, and the Anatolian interior as far east as the Taurus mountains, which was continually subject to Arab attack for another century—as well as to a few western Mediterranean outliers, of which by far the most important were Sicily and, for a few decades more, Africa.[31]

The great effects of this catastrophe on Byzantine state structures will be discussed later (pp. 124–9). Its effects on morale were equally great, and there was not much of a recovery until Leo III (717–41) saw off the second Arab siege of Constantinople in 718 and re-established the basic

[30] See in general Jones, *LRE*, pp. 204–37, 266–315.
[31] Haldon, *Byzantium in the seventh century*, pp. 41–53, gives a convenient survey.

underpinnings of peace. Leo and his son Constantine V (741–75), whom we call the Iconoclast emperors (although only Constantine was particularly hostile to religious images), were perhaps the most effective creators of the basic structures of the Byzantine polity which continued into the twelfth century. This was a highly centralized state, defended by a set of regional ('thematic') armies whose autonomous tendencies were kept in check by fiscal control from the capital, Constantinople, and by the trained troops (*tagmata*) which were based there.[32]

I have here given a political narrative before discussing geography, for it was the crises of the early seventh century that created the 'heartland region' of eastern Greece and Anatolia, a concept that would not have had much meaning as late as 600 (see Map 6). The Aegean and Marmara seas make up a naturally protected sub-region, with easy maritime communications thanks to the islands scattered across it, going up through the Dardanelles to Constantinople and through the Bosporos to the Black Sea. Greece is largely a network of limestone mountains, and even its coast is not particularly fertile (except for a few plains, notably that behind Thessaloniki); the Turkish coast is richer, however, in Thrace, Bithynia, and the great river valleys of western Anatolia. Even the latter areas went into crisis in the early seventh century, with deurbanization visible in the archaeology everywhere—only some of the island cities, like Gortyn on Crete, remained partially exempt from it (below, pp. 628–35). A systemic crisis even in the Aegean, which was so protected and inward-looking and also not so much under military threat, is a sign of how near the empire was to total breakdown. It was still more marked in the inland Balkans, by now no longer under Byzantine control (and outside the scope of this book), and on the militarily exposed Anatolian plateau. It is possible that the only zone which experienced a certain continuing prosperity was Thrace and Bithynia, the lowlands on each side of the capital, and its chief source of supply in the decades around 700.

The Byzantine empire is often analysed in terms of a long-term structural conflict between the (largely civilian) capital and the (militarized) provinces. It could be as easily looked at, however, through the discontinuities between the sea-coasts and the plateau. The Anatolian plateau is a large, poor, upland region, too cold in winter for olives, isolated from the sea by mountains to its north and south; it was for long separate from the Mediterranean economy and was certainly fairly marginal to the Roman empire except as a source of soldiers. For the Byzantines, however, it was a crucial military bulwark against the caliphate, and it became the major base of the increasingly powerful landed aristocracy after the late eighth century: hence, among other things, the elaboration and sophistication of the decoration of the

[32] Brubaker and Haldon, *Byzantium in the Iconoclast era*.

rock churches of one of the most remote and barren parts of the plateau,
Cappadocia, from the late ninth and tenth centuries onwards.[33]

Exactly how the plateau interrelated with the lowland river valleys to its
west and north-west (and also with the narrow coastal strips of Lycia and
Pamphylia to the south) is unfortunately obscure, for the archaeology of the
whole of Turkey is very underdeveloped for the Byzantine period, except for
some recent excavations of the latest levels of the great Roman cities, paralleled by some others in Greece. This is one area where future survey work and
rural excavation would be particularly fruitful, perhaps above all in Bithynia, the link between the plateau and the capital. Byzantine archaeology
is not as weak as that of Egypt, however, thanks to the urban sites, and it is set
against a notable sophistication in analyses of written texts, partly deriving
from the international scholarship of the late Roman world, which extends
to Byzantium as Rome's heir (above, p. 3). Late Roman and Byzantine
written source material for this region is limited, however, mostly to narratives (largely military in orientation), theology, and legislation from the
capital, and only a few hagiographies from the provinces. These limitations
are similar to those for Syria and Palestine, with the eighth century especially
poorly covered; the only advantage this region has is that most of its sources
are more or less contemporary. There is thus a particular need for future
archaeological work, to make sense of, in particular, the eighth century; it
must be hoped that current signs of renewed activity come to fruition.

The Byzantine heartland offers us a paradox: although it was the focus for
one of the two largest and most complex political systems in the whole of
Europe and the Mediterranean in the second half of our period, it consisted
of an uneasy coupling of two wildly different geographical zones, the Anatolian plateau and the Aegean, one of them ecologically poor and devastated
by political events, the other in parallel systemic crisis. This was a structure
with far more economic problems than many of the simpler polities of the
West. It will appear, as a result, in contexts where we look at both continuity
and sharp change. How the empire climbed out of the terminal crisis it
appeared to be in in 717–18, and established itself as a prosperous, coherent,
expansionist polity by the late ninth century, is not the subject of this book—
nor is it easy to explain, for that matter—but it must be remembered that this
revival did indeed occur: the crisis was superable, and was overcome. This
can act as a warning against the teleologies that are often applied to western
states in the same period; political structures did not have to break down
after major military defeat and territorial loss.[34]

---

[33] For the changing importance of the plateau, see Hendy, *Studies*, pp. 40–58, 90–108,
556–61. For the rock churches, e.g. Jolivet-Lévy, *La Cappadoce médiévale*.

[34] The ninth-century revival of the Byzantine state is not well studied as a whole. Haldon's
fiscal articles are important (collected to 1994 in his *State, army and society*); Treadgold, *The
Byzantine revival*, offers a synthesis, but a problematic one; Brubaker and Haldon's eighth-
century reinterpretation, *Byzantium in the Iconoclast era*, extends to 843.

5. Italy

Italy is created by the Appennines, as much as Egypt is created by the Nile: the long boot of the region is essentially the mountain ridge and its coastal appendages. But the peninsula is more fertile than Greece: less of its geology is limestone, and the sandy clays of Tuscany, plus the soft volcanic rock of Lazio and Campania, create substantial prosperous zones of plains and hills on the western side of the mountains (see Map 7). At the centre of these latter plains was Rome, artificially large throughout the empire (it had a million people in the first century, and roughly half-a-million in the early fifth); but even when Rome's population tumbled to the number of people that could be sustained by Lazio alone, somewhere between 20,000 and 40,000, which had happened by the seventh century at the latest, it was still the largest city in Europe after Constantinople, testimony not only to a surviving exchange infrastructure in Lazio, but also to the basic agricultural potential of that sub-region. Inland from the lowland territories of the west, the central mountains are poorer and more marginal, and so are most of the other coastlands except the wide plains of Puglia, which are close to Greece, and shared the eastern Mediterranean's fifth-century prosperity. But the closeness of even Italy's highest valleys to the sea on one side or the other, plus the centuries-old exchange networks that centred on Rome, enabled a commercial infrastructure to penetrate far into the ecologically poor mountains and valleys of central-southern Italy, as much as it did into, say, the Limestone Massif of northern Syria. Local specializations in, among others, pork (Lucania), sheep (the Adriatic side of the Appennines), or timber (Calabria), are visible in our evidence.[35] Much of this network ended with the fall of the empire and the decline of Rome as a market—and also with the breakdown of senatorial landowning, for senators owned so widely in the south and in Sicily—but some survived. The poverty of the modern Italian south was by no means a feature of our period; and Sicily, with its long-standing wealth in grain, was one of the richest provinces in the Mediterranean. (Sardinia was a grain-exporting island too, but it has very poor documentation, and it will not be discussed in this book.)

A little separate from peninsular Italy was the great alluvial plain of the Po in the north, overlooked by the Alps. Northern Italy is agriculturally rich, but much less Mediterranean: it is outside the olive-growing climatic area, for example (except for the protected south-facing lake areas of the Alpine fringe), and it was also only imperfectly part of the late Roman Mediterranean trading network, despite its coastline and easy river connections. From Rome, the Po plain for long seemed hardly Italian at all, and, although by the late empire this no longer held, the great cities of the north, chief of them

---

[35] See respectively Barnish, 'Pigs, plebeians'; Gabba and Pasquinucci, *Strutture agrarie*, pp. 152–82; Giardina, 'Allevamento', pp. 99–107. For Puglia see Volpe, *Contadini, pastori*.

Milan, were still seen as relatively provincial, even when Milan (briefly) and Ravenna (permanently, from 402) became the governmental centres of the western empire. Being close to the Alps also, however, made the north more exposed to invasion. In the end, this would reverse the political marginality of the Po sub-region, when the Lombards made it the focus of their kingdom, with Pavia, a long-standing military centre, their capital. As the peninsula fragmented into smaller polities (by 900 there were nine from Rome southwards), the *regnum Italiae* of the north became the new political centre of Italy, which it has usually remained. Although the economic shift to northern dominance was not a feature of our period, the political shift was.[36]

Italy was the last of the western provinces to face political crisis in the fifth century: it remained securely under the control of a succession of military leaders, who until 476 ruled through emperors (themselves mostly political ciphers, as in the East), and who after that ruled alone. The region barely even faced invasion except for occasional single campaigns, until Theoderic the Amal conquered the peninsula with an Ostrogothic army at the request of the emperor Zeno in 490–3, and ruled it as king until 526. The Ostrogothic period (490–552) has usually been seen as Italy's last period of Roman-style stability: it was a view current even at the time, and was encouraged by Theoderic himself. The Goths were more politically prominent (not least as landowners) than Roman armies had been, but the structures of government and civilian society remained substantially unchanged.[37] More important than 'barbarian' rule in itself was the simple fact that Italy was by now a separate kingdom, not any longer the centre of the whole of the western empire; the region lost a substantial amount of tax income as a result. Even this was mitigated by Theoderic's temporary control of Spain, Mediterranean Gaul, and the Danube provinces; but the loss of Africa hit Italy hard, and particularly Rome, which, as a result of the ending of the African taxation which fed the city, experienced its sharpest population fall in precisely this period. Demographic decline in the city of Rome was indeed probably the most important structural change in Italy between 400 and 535.

What ruined Italy was less conquest than war, above all in the seventy years after 535, when Belisarios moved from Africa to conquer Sicily at Justinian's command. The Romans retook Sicily with ease, but mainland Italy was more difficult, and it took nearly twenty years of war, 536–54, for Roman control to be properly established south of the Po—and in Verona and Brescia not until 561. Gothic and Roman counterattacks, together with Frankish invasions in the Po plain, devastated the peninsula, in particular its governmental infrastructure (local social patterns may have been

---

[36] See as a general overview Wickham, *Early medieval Italy*.
[37] See recently Moorhead, *Theoderic*; Amory, *People and identity*; Heather, 'Theoderic'; *Teoderico il Grande*.

less damaged, however, judging by the Ravenna papyri, even though Ravenna was a major war zone). And Italy had barely a decade of full peace: in 568–9 the Lombards invaded from Pannonia (modern Hungary). The Lombard conquest of the peninsula was never complete: at least initially, the Lombards were very disorganized, and by the early 580s they had divided into networks of competing groups led by dukes of different Italian cities, some fighting for the Romans, others against them. The Romans could not dominate this chaotic situation either, however, and Italy's coherence fragmented definitively—between 569 and 1870, unlike any other region described in this book, it was never under the control of a single ruler. The Lombards reunited under a king in 584 in the face of Frankish invasion, and a series of truces after 590 turned into longer-term peace in 605, but by then Italy's prosperity, as well as its political coherence, was in ruins.

In 605 the Lombard polity was divided into three pieces, the kingdom of the Po plain and Tuscany, ruled by Agilulf (590–616), and the geographically separate, autonomous, southern duchies of Spoleto and Benevento. The Roman parts of Italy (as with Africa, they are from now on most conveniently called Byzantine Italy to distinguish them from the pre-Ostrogothic period, and, in addition, to lessen confusion with the Romans of Rome) were divided into seven or eight unconnected or tenuously connected coastal areas, which, however, included the major centres of Rome, Naples and Ravenna, and also Sicily, relatively untouched by trouble and more integrated into the East.[38] The seventh and early eighth centuries were a quieter period, but this fragmented situation continued, and indeed partially increased, as the rulers of some of the Byzantine territories, particularly the bishops (popes) of Rome and the dukes of Naples and Venice, established ever greater autonomy from the exarch of Italy (based in Ravenna) and from Constantinople. The Lombard kingdom, however, became steadily more coherent, making increasing use of the city-based administration that had survived the wars; its first written law-code was set out by Rothari (636–52) in 643. The most powerful Lombard king, Liutprand (712–44), subdued the southern duchies, and Aistulf (749–56) took Ravenna and threatened Rome. The Lombards were by now in a position to reunite the peninsula. But after 751–2 the Carolingians owed their position as kings in Francia to papal recognition, and renewed Frankish invasions of Italy followed papal pleas for help. In 773–4 Charlemagne conquered all of Italy down to Rome; only Benevento, and the by-now small Byzantine enclaves in the south (plus Venice in the north), remained outside Frankish control.

Italy is relatively well served by evidence. Its narratives are weak, for historical accounts are exiguous except for the Gothic war and parts of the

---

[38] See for Byzantine Italy above all Brown, *Gentlemen and officers*; Zanini, *Le Italie bizantine*.

eighth century, and there are not even many hagiographies covering events in our period; but, conversely, there are governmental sources for the century-and-a-half up to 540 (above all, Cassidorus' *Variae*, his official letters for Theoderic and his successors), a long run of papal letters, especially from Gregory the Great (590–604), and several hundred private documents, from Ravenna in the sixth and early seventh centuries, and from Lucca and other cities in the eighth, making up the richest documentary set after Egypt and Francia. Italy's archaeology is also particularly good for this period: it is more extensive than that for any other Mediterranean region except Jordan.[39] The unusually promising possibilities for a proper dialogue between experts in documentary and archaeological evidence are by now beginning to be explored, too, even if historians and archaeologists are still capable of engaging in largely separate debates about the dating and extent of economic and political crisis. Some of these debates are pretty charged. The responsibility of the Lombards for the fragmentation of Italy, and the question of how Romanized they were, is as live an issue as it was in 1850; the more recent archaeological debate about the survival of urbanism has at times seemed even more intense. The issues of the unification of Italy and its urban character have, however, it must be recognized, always been charged, for they underpin the two central events of Italian pre-twentieth-century national memory, the Renaissance and the Risorgimento; this situation is not likely to change soon.

Italy's varied historical and archaeological evidence, its central geographical position, and the simple fact that I know its documentation much better than that for anywhere else, mean that Italian developments are inevitably in the back of my mind as I write as a 'typical' pattern, however hard I try to treat every region equally. It must be remembered, however, that they were atypical in one crucial respect. Nowhere else in Europe and the Mediterranean was brought down so fast by war (in this case in the mid- to late sixth century), from considerable regional-level prosperity and economic integration, to a series of isolated, sometimes very simple, microregional economies/societies. Only Anatolia in the seventh and eighth centuries offers any real parallel, as a region economically weakened by war, and political infrastructures maintained themselves there better than in Italy. Elsewhere, breakdown was either less severe (it was almost non-existent in Egypt) or a much more long-term process, or else, in other cases of free fall such as early fifth-century Britain, was the product of catastrophic internal involution, not simple destruction. Italy thus fits the old storyline of 'the barbarian invasions destroying the Roman world' better than most regions do, with the proviso that it was *Roman* invasion that caused the Gothic war, and it was Lombard weakness, not 'barbarism', that prevented the sort of quick

---

[39] See for a recent summary Wickham, 'Early medieval archaeology'.

and easy conquest that characterized the Vandal entry into Africa or that of the Ostrogoths into Italy itself, neither of which were systemic disasters. Even in Italy, it is possible to find internal factors—notably the negative impact of the political break-up of the Mediterranean—that made two generations of war so fatal. Outside Italy, however, as we shall see, internal developments were far more crucial for the types of change analysed in this book, at every stage.

6. Spain

Spain is the other great inland plateau of the Mediterranean, together with Anatolia (see Map 8). Most of its land-mass consists of the high Meseta plain, which is dry, cold in winter, and, at its highest points (as in the central mountain range), very barren—the most effective pre-industrial use of such areas has been for transhumant pastoralism. Mountains separate the northern Meseta (the Duero valley) from the wet Atlantic coastlands of Galicia, the Asturias, and the Basque Country, and also from the Ebro valley, the only major Mediterranean river of Spain (which is not as much of a route as it might be, for it passes through semi-desert in its lower reaches). The south-west Meseta, around Mérida, the capital of late Roman Spain, is good grain country, and has a significant river route, the Guadiana, down to the coast, but that coast is west of the straits of Gibraltar, slightly too far from the Mediterranean for easy bulk transport. The same is true for the only large area of rich lowland in the peninsula, the lower Guadalquivir valley between Córdoba and Seville (Roman Baetica, the heart of modern Andalucía): this was in the first century the main source of olive oil for Rome, but it lost out to Africa, which was geographically more convenient, and was never so important again for the Mediterranean. Still, inside Spain Baetica remained the richest sub-region by far, and was always central to any ambitious polity. Its archaeology is relatively poor for our period, and it would repay further study.

   This characterization leaves out most of the coasts. The north was marginal and poorly Romanized in parts (the Basques, of course, still do not speak a Romance language); the west, modern Portugal, contained more lowland, but is poorly documented and not much exploited archaeologically: we can say little about it, and I have used little Portuguese evidence except for in the Braga area. The Mediterranean coast was, not surprisingly, rather more integrated into the Roman world, and also has most of the best archaeological coverage for our period, with a string of local studies from the Pyrenees to Málaga. Most of it is not very fertile, however, except for the hilly Mediterranean landscape of Catalonia, and the irrigated *horta* of Valencia; elsewhere, the mountains come down too sharply to the sea, and the main specialized product of much of the coast seems to have been *garum*, salt fish sauce.[40] The mountain edge to most of eastern Spain of course matches the fact that most major Spanish rivers flow into the Atlantic; both features kept Spain from being a central element in any Mediterranean network, and indeed made its unity a difficult logistical task for any ruler.

Late Roman Spain is seldom referred to in our sources, although the archaeology for the period shows that it was prosperous enough, both in its cities and in the countryside. Germanic invasions began in 409, when the Vandals and Suevi came over the Pyrenees. The Vandals left in 429, leaving the Suevi dominant in western Spain; in 456 the Visigoths of Aquitaine began their own conquest, which seems to have been largely complete by the 480s (the Suevi survived for a century as a kingdom in Galicia). When the Franks conquered Aquitaine from the Visigoths in 507, the latter regrouped in Spain. Their kingdom was pretty incoherent for over sixty years, however. It was under Ostrogothic hegemony in the 510s–520s, and after that it was constantly troubled by revolt and regional separatism; even cities could establish their own independence, as did Córdoba between 550 and 572, and the east Roman empire also conquered the southern Mediterranean coast in 554, holding it until c.628. The fragmentary narrative evidence we have for Spain in this period makes it impossible to be sure where the boundaries of Visigothic power extended in any direction (it is likely, too, that the internal coherence of the kingdom was equally variable), but the list of conquests of the 570s (below, p. 94) shows that the Visigoths cannot have controlled more than two-thirds of the peninsula in 560, and maybe less.[41]

Leovigild (569–86) founded the united Visigothic kingdom of Spain. He conquered all of the peninsula except the areas controlled by the Basques in the north and the Byzantines in the south; he also established a measure of internal control that was lacking previously, and issued a substantial law-code. By the end of his reign Toledo (the main royal city since the 550s, situated in the middle of the Meseta, an upland but central location) was a real capital.[42] In 589 his son Reccared (586–601), at the Third Council of Toledo, formally abandoned Arian Christianity and established religious unity in his kingdom. Regular councils of bishops at Toledo remained a major feature of ceremonial aggregation in the Visigothic state, and their surviving proceedings are a major source for church policy, and indeed, in the absence of narratives, secular politics; by 694 they had got up to the Seventeenth Council (the proceedings of a later one do not survive).

[40] See below, pp. 488–90, 748–51 for the coastal surveys. For late Roman *garum* see Reynolds, *Trade*, pp. 60–7; he is very cautious about how widely it was exported, for the amphora distributions have not been fully tracked.

[41] See Arce, *El último siglo*, for the period to 409; overviews of the Visigothic period include Claude, *Adel, Kirche*; García Moreno, *Historia de España visigoda*; a brief and up-to-date survey with bibliography is Ripoll and Velázquez, *La Hispania visigoda*.

[42] Velázquez and Ripoll, '*Toletum*'.

Religious unity was more than usually ideologically important for the seventh-century Visigoths; hence, in particular, the fiercest anti-Jewish legislation that survives from anywhere in our period, which is a constant feature of our legal sources from 589 onwards, reaching its peak in 694. Roman ideology was important too; the Visigothic law-code is by far the most Roman-influenced of the 'barbarian' laws, and in its surviving versions, issued by Reccesuinth (649–72) in 654 and Ervig (680–7), it uses a heightened moral rhetoric that was inherited directly from the empire. This, plus the anti-Jewish polemic, makes reading Visigothic legal texts an unnerving experience. We must recognize the ambition and religious purpose of the seventh-century Visigothic state, nevertheless, however we estimate the degree of its real effectiveness (below, pp. 93–102), or however little we sympathize with its aims.

A run of coups produced nine kings in the forty years after Reccared's death; the tenth, Chindasuinth (642–53), controversially killed a large section of the aristocracy and ensured peaceful succession until 710.[43] The late Visigothic kings seem from our sources to have been mostly strong and ruthless, successfully presiding over an aristocratic and episcopal political world that was substantially focused on Toledo itself. How far this is an illusion of our sources—all legal except for a handful of saints' lives and short narratives (mostly written by or about political bishops), and a set of documents on slate from a corner of the northern Meseta—is not fully clear. The fact that when the Arabs and Berbers came in, defeating the last Visigothic king Roderic in 711, non-Muslim Spain at once broke up into several pieces, might indicate that royal control was in reality incomplete. But these pieces were all coastal, behind mountain barriers; the Visigoths certainly controlled the core lands of the Meseta and Andalucía. These were the core lands of Arab Spain, too, for that matter.

Arab Spain, al-Andalus, was in one respect different from the Visigothic kingdom, however, for it was ruled from the south, from Córdoba. The Meseta was largely seen as a set of frontier lands, controlled locally and semi-autonomously, as indeed also were the east and west coasts, and the Ebro valley, the farthest north the Arabs stably reached. Apart from Catalonia, which was occupied by the Franks, the northern mountain ranges were ruled by a string of small Christian rulers whom the Arabs never seriously tried to conquer, much as they had been in the early sixth century. Between them was a buffer area in the northern Meseta that was not obviously controlled by anyone until the most successful northern kings, of the Asturias, occupied it in the late ninth century under Alfonso III (866–910), moving their capital south from Oviedo to León after Alfonso's deposition in 910. Inside al-Andalus itself, governmental instability

---

[43] Claude, *Adel, Kirche*, pp. 115–22.

was great (and not helped by the 739 Berber revolt in Africa) until 'Abd al-Raḥmān I, a fugitive Umayyad, established himself as *amir* in 754. Even thereafter, however, emiral power and stable state structures did not always extend much beyond the Guadalquivir valley until 'Abd al-Raḥmān III (912–61), who established firm control over most of Arab Spain, and claimed the caliphal title itself in 929. Elsewhere, Arab and Berber—and, indeed, ethnically Visigothic—frontier lords maintained considerable autonomy up to the tenth century, and caliphal unity dissolved again into civil war after 1009. The tenth century nonetheless joins the seventh as the only long periods of peninsula-wide government between 409 and the end of the middle ages.[44]

Spain thus matches Italy as a region where disunity was greater than unity in our period. Unity was here actually possible, and sometimes achieved, but it was always difficult, and always temporary. Actually, regional difference in Spain was much greater than in Italy: the contrast between the wet Atlantic weather of Galicia and the desert of Almería is extreme, and every intermediate ecology is represented too. This was matched by huge differences in social organization, with Roman-style landowning dominant in the southern Meseta and Andalucía, but not necessarily in mountain lands, where social structures could sometimes be better called tribal, or kin-based (*gentilicio*). Given the poverty of Spanish documentation, at least until after the late ninth century in the Christian kingdoms, exactly what 'tribal' might mean in practice is hardly clear, and is often argued over—some mountain societies had clear leadership structures, some perhaps did not; some perhaps had collective landowning, some certainly did not; and so on (see below, pp. 226–32). The exact nature of ethnic Berber, and Basque, social influence is equally disputed. But the variety of Spanish society is clear all the same, at least after 711 and probably before.

The main historiographical divide between ancient and medieval in Spain is 711, even more firmly than is 568 in Italy: even the architectural dating of rural churches to before or after 711 is fraught.[45] The Arab period is a crucial focus of debate, for its legitimate position in the seamless narrative of (Christian) Spanish historical memory has always been contested; the fact that its sources are largely late, and inaccessible in the original to most Spanish historians, has made matters still more difficult. Cancelling the Arabs has been one solution, particularly among conservatives of different persuasions, as with Ignacio Olagüe's claim that there were never any at all, or with Claudio Sánchez-Albornoz's claim that large parts of the northern Meseta were never occupied by them, and were repopulated from scratch by

---

[44] See as overviews Chalmeta, *Invasión e islamización*; Manzano, *La frontera*; and the old classic, Lévi-Provençal, *Histoire de l'Espagne musulmane*.

[45] See e.g. Caballero, 'La arquitectura', with bibliography; cf. the debates over his datings in the volume in which that article appeared.

Christian conquerors.[46] The degree of Arab influence on Spanish history has indeed often been a specifically political debate, with the Left distinctly more Arabist (and, more recently, Berberist) than the Right; a stress on tribal/kin alternatives to landowning has often been a Left-wing tradition too, although here one can detect a contrary tendency even among the Left in recent years.[47] Spanish historiography has the merit of being more explicit in its political agendas than is that of most other western countries, which tend to hide them behind a rhetorical veneer of scientific neutrality. Where the mines are is more visible as a result, although, conversely, the violence of explosions is greater when one—inevitably—steps onto them. Here, Spain's reviving archaeology ought to help in the future, not least because settlement hierarchies and exchange systems do not have to be expressed in ethnic terms at all; but we have not yet reached that point, in particular because Spanish medieval archaeology is as yet in a constant state of flux, with new discoveries and reinterpretations very common—generalizing on the basis of it remains risky, although it will be attempted in several chapters of this book. Personally, however, I am more struck by the continuities between Arab/Berber political and social structures and those of their predecessors than by differences; I shall defend this position in later chapters.

7. Gaul and Francia

The region of Gaul/Francia has by far the best narrative sources for anywhere in Europe and the Mediterranean in our period, ranging from Gregory of Tours (who is, together with Prokopios, by far our most detailed single author), through a constant stream of letter-collections, to six thick volumes of saints' lives, nearly half of them contemporary or near-contemporary. When we add the richest set of documents after Egypt (more extensive than those of Italy, although rather less varied), it becomes clear that we can *say* more about the history of this region than about any other in the period up to 800. The continuities are not perfect: broadly, Aquitaine is best-documented in the fifth and sixth centuries, Neustria (north-west France in modern terms) in the seventh, the Rhineland in the eighth, and the Rhône valley least of all. The slow shift from 'Gaul' to 'Francia' is sharpened and made seemingly more radical by a steady move from 'Roman' areas to 'Frankish' areas in our evidence. The links with archaeology are imperfect,

---

[46] Olagüe, *Les Arabes*; Sánchez-Albornoz, *Despoblación*, the most substantial of his many analyses of the issue.

[47] On tribalism, see among others Barbero and Vigil, *La formación*, pp. 354–404 (for the north); Guichard, *Structures sociales*. Critical reactions from varying perspectives include Manzano, 'Arabes, bereberes'; Acién, 'Poblamiento y fortificación'; Larrea, *La Navarre*, pp. 111–29. For the history of the Christian north, a good recent survey is Isla Frez, *La alta edad media*.

too, for the latter is still more sporadic in its densities: the Rhineland has a long tradition of serious work, but its interpretative frameworks are often still dominated by post-war models, and badly need updating; the Mediterranean coast has been very active for two decades, but this is one area of Gaul that has little written documentation; Aquitaine has relatively little archaeological work at all. At present, the recent intense archaeological activity in Normandy and the Île de France, and northwards across the Neustrian heartland into Picardy, provides us with the best possibilities for a historical–archaeological dialogue.[48] These are cavils, however; the relative wealth of material for this region means that one often finds oneself establishing a Frankish-based model and then looking around vainly for anywhere with evidence as good to compare it with. In particular, when discussing the aristocracy I gave up pretending that I could give equivalent space to other regions, as Frankish examples regularly turned out to be the best ones available. This is why I start here with sources; they, even if nothing else, make this region distinct.

The historiography of the region is more problematic. It is now divided between three countries, France, Belgium, and Germany, with outliers in Switzerland and the Netherlands. The first three of these were the standard-bearers of systematic history writing by 1900, and all arguments about our period have a long history—one, furthermore, made more difficult by the divergencies between French and German scholarship. Wars between 1870 and 1945 hardly helped this, but the divergencies have continued since as well. Not surprisingly, the French have tended to Romanist positions and the Germans to Germanist ones; although this opposition has lessened sharply in recent years, the fiercest 'hyper-Romanists' still write in French.[49] There is also a traditional divide, still continuing, between a German preference for histories of political power, aristocratic identity, and socio-legal categories and a French one for regional socio-economic and socio-political studies—the Belgians have for their part dominated economic history, though this is an arena where all three national traditions meet. Here, I confess that my natural sympathies are with the French, but they have tended to decide that the evidence is not good enough for regional studies before around 900 (a mistaken assumption, above all in the Île de France and the middle Rhine). The year 900 is a date which has also been seen as the beginning of three centuries of *essor* or *croissance économique*, a point of reference popular in French medieval historiography.[50] For both of these reasons, there is less history written by French scholars about our period in this region than one

[48] See below, pp. 504–14. Significant examples of this dialogue include Halsall, *Settlement and social organisation*; Theuws, 'Landed property'; Bourgeois, *Térritoires, reseaux*.

[49] The most substantial 'hyper-Romanist' text is Durliat, *Les finances publiques*. Some German and Austrian scholars have developed more Romanist positions in recent years; see below, Ch. 3, n. 68.

[50] For the debate, see Ch. 5, n. 64.

might expect. There are exceptions here, of course (Michel Rouche's study of Aquitaine is the most notable regional analysis); there are also partial crossovers, like Régine Le Jan's book on aristocracies or Matthias Werner's local study of the Liège area.[51] It should be added that there has in the last twenty-five years been a strong British input to the study of this region, which has contributed above all to the establishment of a more pragmatic, 'social', approach to high politics and culture, a British historiographical speciality, which in this context could be said to represent a French-leaning approach to German themes, particularly as it has tended, at least implicitly, to stress continuities with the Roman past.[52] But it must be said that, despite a wealth of high-quality works on this region in our period, truly daunting in size in fact, the themes I have chosen in this book have often been less studied than one might expect.

Gaul is less fragmented a land-mass than is Spain (see Maps 9 and 10). For a start, it is mostly relatively low-lying, until one gets into the Alpine borderlands; the major internal barriers, and the only agriculturally poor areas, are the dissected pastoral uplands of the Massif Central in the centre-south and the German-style hilly forests of the north-east, from the Ardennes to the Vosges. These are not serious barriers to communication, however, and controlling the whole territory from the Rhine to the Pyrenees has never been logistically difficult, in sharp contrast to Spain, a block of similar size and shape. The western half of the region, right down to Bordeaux, is in effect an extension of the North European Plain; the hill country to its east is traversed by important Atlantic rivers, the Seine, Loire, and Garonne. On the eastern side of the region, the two greatest western European rivers, the Rhône and the Rhine, both prosperous valley zones, mark a south–north path from the Mediterranean to the Rhine frontier of the Roman empire, the main route into northern Europe in Roman times by far, and one of two or three ever after.

These are elements which aid unity; but Gaul is nonetheless ecologically divided, in important ways. The Mediterranean world does not extend very far into Gaul. Olives stop before Lyon; vines are hardly found north of Paris, Reims, and the sheltered Moselle and middle Rhine valleys. The silvo-pastoral economy is the main alternative to grain in the open country between the Seine and the Rhine; the relationship between human settlements and their territories changes considerably as a result. These divisions mirror the fact that northern Gaul has tended to be distinct from the Mediterranean in both its economy and its politics, and in our period, as later, looked north and east rather than south. In general, northern Gaul is

---

[51] Rouche, *L'Aquitaine*; Le Jan, *Famille et pouvoir*; Werner, *Der Lütticher Raum*. Other significant French local studies for this period include Fournier, *Le peuplement rural*; Gauthier, *L'évangélisation*; Pietri, *La ville de Tours*; Bourgeois, *Térritoires, reseaux*.
[52] See the bibliography for works by Fouracre, Innes, James, McKitterick, Nelson, Wood.

much more like England, northern Germany, and Denmark, whereas the
Rhône valley is much more like Catalonia, Italy, and Andalucía; and rulers
of the region have since 500 always lived in the north.[53] This division
between south and north will recur as an issue throughout the book, with
sub-regions on the boundary (Aquitaine, modern Burgundy) sometimes
treated with the north, sometimes the south.

Gaul in 400 was already experiencing divergent developments, in part
because of the ecological division just noted, in part because of an emerging
distinction between lands closer to the Rhine frontier of the empire and
lands further away and more protected from invasion. Aquitaine and the
Rhône valley were prosperous centres of provincial Roman aristocratic
society; in the north, by contrast, villas were already beginning to be abandoned, and the tone of social action was much more military, including
around the regional (for much of the fourth century, western imperial)
capital at Trier. This contrast had an urban aspect, too, for cities were in
general weaker in the north, with some important exceptions, like Trier
itself, Cologne, or Paris.

Border wars turned into full-scale invasion after 406, and the political
history of fifth-century Gaul is exceptionally complex. Broadly, however,
Gaul was settled by three main Germanic groups, the Visigoths, stably
located between Toulouse and Bordeaux after 418, the Burgundians, in the
Geneva area after 443, and the Franks, in the lands west of the Rhine below
Trier, from the second quarter of the century. These three were not the same:
the Visigoths could be seen as a rogue Roman army, who toured the whole
northern Mediterranean in the twenty-five years prior to their settlement;
the Burgundians were at least initially a defeated remnant, and little threat;
the Franks were a set of apparently unconnected war-bands and tribal
communities, who simply moved across the Rhine when the Roman defences weakened—of the three, they were by far the least Romanized. As late
as 460, the three groups may have seemed to be fairly contained. From then
on, however, they steadily expanded the areas they controlled. The 460s–
480s saw the remaining areas of Roman autonomy continually squeezed
from all three directions: the Visigoths under Euric (466–84) controlled the
whole of Aquitaine and Septimania (modern Languedoc) by 480, as well as
Spain, and the Burgundians came to control the Rhône–Saône valley. In the
north, the Frankish leader Clovis (481–511) removed the last traces of
independent Roman power north of the Loire in the 480s, leaving only the
far west, which had reorganized itself as an independent Celtic community,
the Bretons; Clovis also unified the Frankish people under a single ruling
family, the Merovingians.[54]

[53] The classic survey of difference is Bloch, *Les caractères originaux*.
[54] James, *The Franks*, pp. 51–108, and Wolfram, *History of the Goths*, pp. 173–93 provide
convenient surveys.

In the early sixth century it became clear that the most successful of these groups would be the newly united Franks. In 507 the Visigoths lost Aquitaine (though never Septimania), and between 523 and 534 the Burgundians were conquered and absorbed into the Merovingian political system; only the Bretons remained autonomous. The Franks were already a people who lived on both sides of the old Rhine border, and they expanded their hegemony east as well as south: to the Alemans in south-west Germany and the upper Rhine valley; to the communities which were only now crystallizing as the Bavarians, in the upper Danube valley (the Franks gave to the Bavarians their ruling dynasty, the Agilolfings); on occasion as far as Thuringia in east-central Germany; and, from 539, even into northern Italy, by then riven by the Gothic war.[55] Northern Gaul gained a political centrality as a result which it had never had in the Roman world, even when the capital was at Trier. That centrality was great: in 500 Theoderic's Ostrogoths looked like the hegemonic Germanic group, but by 550 that role was clearly in the hands of the Franks. A century later the steady strengthening of the Visigoths in Spain and the Lombards in Italy meant that the Franks were no longer as dominant a model for political development, but they remained the strongest military power in the West, even at moments of internal crisis.

The Franks, at least after Clovis's death in 511, did not see kingship as indivisible, and it was henceforth normal that Francia should be divided between eligible male Merovingians (or, later, Carolingians)—the tradition did not cease until the end of the ninth century. Not that heirs necessarily agreed about who was eligible, or even who was a Merovingian, and certainly not about where the boundaries were between the *Teilreiche*, as the Merovingian kingdoms are often called in modern historiography. Civil wars resulted, and were a recurrent, almost stable, feature of Merovingian history; the building-blocks of city territories were constantly transferred from one king to another, with predictably convulsive effects on local political power-balances, something that Merovingian evidence tells us more than usual about. Such conflicts did not, however, weaken the wealth and power of Merovingian kings, which in the sixth century was very great, thanks to landowning, tax-raising, and successful external war. They imposed themselves on their subjects with much vigour and little scruple, and so did several queens-regent, in particular Brunhild (d. 613).

In 613 Chlotar II (584–629) united the kingdom by force, and he and his son Dagobert I controlled it as, for the most part, a single unit. The courts of the three main *Teilreiche* continued, however, with a local palace official, called *maior domus* or *maior palatii*, as the head of each. The office of the 'mayor of the palace' soon became the focus for the competing rivalry of sub-regional aristocracies, as kingship itself was (unlike in Spain or Italy)

---

[55] See for this and what follows Wood, *The Merovingian kingdoms*; Lebecq, *Les origines franques*.

effectively inaccessible to them. Three political communities thus formed, with more stable boundaries than in the previous century because civil war was uncommon for two generations: Neustria in the north-west, focused on Paris, Austrasia in the north-east, focused on Metz and Cologne (and, more generally, the Rhineland), and Burgundy in the south-east, still essentially the Rhône–Saône valley. The fourth quarter, Aquitaine, occasionally had a sub-king too; but it, like Burgundy for that matter, remained a little marginal—there were never many Franks in the south, and the kings largely stayed in the palaces of the two *Königslandschaften*, 'royal landscapes', of the Île de France and the middle Rhine/Moselle.[56] In 639 Dagobert died, leaving children to succeed him, and the following fifty years saw a continuous period of political manoeuvring, sometimes including open war, between queens-regent, mayors of the palace, and kings when they achieved adulthood. The latter could still be powerful, but for the first time we can find mayors like Grimoald of Austrasia (d. c.657) and Ebroin of Neustria (d. 680) choosing their kings: the balance of power had shifted. The greatest moment of crisis was probably 675, when Childeric II was murdered, and stability only returned when Pippin II, mayor of Austrasia (d. 714), established his own hegemony in Neustria at the battle of Tertry in 687. In the meantime, however, wider Frankish hegemony was weakened. Thuringia, Bavaria, Alamannia, even the heartland province of Aquitaine, established autonomy under families of dukes.[57] Pippin II's era seems to be, despite a measure of political tranquillity, the low-point for both that hegemony and, briefly, for the activism of central government itself.

The last major civil war for over a century, in 715–19, was fought between Pippin's widow Plectrudis and his illegitimate son Charles (Martel). Charles won it, and he and his army carried on fighting; most summers in the eighth century saw a Frankish army crossing one border or another, and these borders got steadily further away, as the autonomous duchies were reconquered one by one.[58] Charles's post-victory settlement removed many rivals, and re-established governmental centrality, by now clearly focused on Austrasia. For the first time, the Merovingians became total ciphers, and in the last years of Charles's life (737–41) there was no king at all. Charles's son Pippin III (741–68) took the next step and claimed the throne in 751. His Carolingian dynasty owed their legitimacy to the ritual sanction of the church, and Carolingian political programmes were much more ecclesiastically influenced, indeed rather more systematic, than those of any other western post-Roman state except the Visigoths (and much more inclusive than the latter). Under Charlemagne (768–814) these programmes took off dramatically; Charlemagne also extended Frankish rule to territories

---

[56] For *palatia* see Barbier, 'Le système palatial franc'.
[57] Werner, 'Les principautés péripheriques'.
[58] Fouracre, *Charles Martel*; Jarnut et al., *Karl Martell*.

hitherto hardly touched by it, Saxony, northern Italy, and north-eastern Spain. These changes created a new political framework for continental western Europe, one that was by now in effect only Frankish (western Europeans were by the eleventh century simply called 'Franks' in the eastern Mediterranean). They take us well outside our period, however, and I shall tend in fact to regard the whole period after 751 in Francia as outside the strict remit of this book. In part, this is because the evidence changes in scale, but it is also in order to avoid teleology. Charlemagne's world has often been regarded as *the* end-point of the historical development of the early middle ages. The arguments of this book go in very different directions from that. Still, this is not to deny the power and lasting coherence of the Frankish political system; I shall try to explain some of the reasons for it in Chapters 4 and 11.

8. England and Wales

Britain is clearly divided into two halves, long called by historians and archaeologists the Lowland Zone and the Highland Zone, with a boundary between them running very roughly from Scarborough to Exeter (see Map 11). The Lowland Zone is another extension of the North European Plain, with few natural divisions—indeed, not even very much woodland in historic times. The Highland Zone is not actually very high by European standards, but Britain is far enough north for limestone and volcanic plateaux at 500 m above sea level to be fairly barren—in Scotland, the higher and more northerly equivalents are uninhabitable. The west and north consists of sets of narrow valleys and coastal strips between these plateaux, with only a fewer larger, richer belts, like the Severn valley and the central lowlands of Scotland; this terrain is as hard to control as is Spain, and arguably no one ever did control it on more than a local scale until the fourteenth century in the case of Wales and the eighteenth in northern Scotland. Even the Romans only conquered Britain up to Hadrian's Wall. I shall not discuss the kingdoms of what is now Scotland, however; the post-Roman history of *Britannia* is already complicated enough.

The Romans abandoned the province in c.410, and its archaeology shows a nearly immediate systemic collapse. We will look at possible reasons for this in Chapter 6, but one result is that post-Roman society was nearly completely de-Romanized in all respects.[59] The relatively small-scale Anglo-Saxon communities who crossed the sea into eastern Britain from c.450 onwards found communities whose social structure was more like that of the Anglo-Saxons themselves than that of their Roman ancestors. Among the communities whom the Anglo-Saxons never conquered, in modern

[59] See above all Esmonde-Cleary, *Ending*.

Wales, Latin did not survive except as a specialist ecclesiastical language—
Welsh is full of Latin loanwords, but it owes far less to Latin than, say,
modern English does to French. Latin was probably lost in the Lowland
Zone, too. The main visible Roman inheritance in lowland Britain was the
structure of the settled landscape; in highland Britain we could add Christianity (which did not return to the Lowland Zone until the seventh century),
but little more.

Around 550 we begin to have some sense of the political units of what is
now England and Wales. They were all very small; a single modern county
was a common size for kingdoms, and kings often ruled less; none of them as
yet controlled more than two or three. Among the Anglo-Saxon polities,
Kent, East Anglia, Wessex (then what is now Hampshire and Berkshire), and
Deira (Yorkshire) were probably the most coherent in 550; Mercia (the west
Midlands) and Bernicia (Northumberland) had crystallized by 600 as well;
in Wales, Gwynedd in the north-west, Dyfed in the south-west, and, from
the seventh century, Glywysing in the south-east, matched or surpassed them
in size, even if not in population. Early English and Welsh kingdoms all seem
to have had a very simple structure, focused on an itinerant king and his
armed retainers, whose main functions were to resolve disputes and to fight
small-scale campaigns against other kings; no Clovis emerged to establish a
larger-scale permanent political structure, and he would not have had the
means to do so if he had tried.[60] The above-named kingdoms did, nonetheless, slowly expand at the expense of their neighbours in the Lowland Zone
(though not in Wales, whose geography was rather harder to master). By 700
what is now England had four dominant kingdoms, in a pattern that continued until the Viking conquests of the ninth century: Northumbria (Bernicia plus Deira), Mercia (which had absorbed a host of neighbours, both
English and Welsh), Wessex (which would aim at a hegemony over the south
coast—it contested Kent with Mercia), and East Anglia, the smallest, but
based on the best land and economically the most developed. Even then, all
were still tiny by Frankish standards, and materially poor judging by the
archaeology; but the Franks sometimes pretended otherwise, and Offa of
Mercia (757–96), our period's strongest ruler in Britain, was treated as an
equal by Charlemagne.[61]

Offa had a more ambitious programme and a more sophisticated government than his predecessors. We can see it from many elements: his charters
and church councils; his preparedness to welcome papal legates into Mercia
in 786–7; his successful suppression of kingdoms; and, above all, the logistical feat of his dyke along the Mercian–Welsh border, the largest human
construction in Europe between the Roman road-network and the canal

---

[60] See Bassett, *Origins*, for a collective history of the early English kingdoms; Davies, *Wales in
the early middle ages*, pp. 85–140.
[61] See e.g. Wormald, 'Offa and Alcuin', p. 101.

systems of the seventeenth and eighteenth centuries.[62] Except the dyke, these are activities that have parallels in Francia, and we can detect Frankish cultural influence in most elements of royal protagonism in the English-speaking lands between 600 and 1200—the Lowland Zone was in many ways a cultural colony of Gaul/Francia centuries before it became a political colony of one of Neustria's successor states in 1066.[63] But England did not really resemble Francia; the origins of its political structures were too different, and, as we shall see in Chapter 6, its local social structures were quite distinct too—they continued for long to parallel, rather, those of Wales. As a result, paradoxically, in the tenth century England's political structure would be unusually coherent for the period by European standards, and one can begin to talk about the English 'nation state', which has survived ever since. That state, however, had its real origins in the crisis of the Viking invasions, and not in our period at all.

English historiography is traditionally Germanist, in that it begins with the Anglo-Saxons and ignores the social situation they found in Britain; this tradition is less dominant today, and some reactions to it have been quite sharp, but the question of how German the Anglo-Saxons were undoubtedly still matters to historians—more, say, than among Spanish scholars of the Visigoths. This historiography is also traditionally teleological, in that it sees the real historical process of our period, 'the general course of Anglo-Saxon history', as Frank Stenton put it in a letter, as being the steady move from fragmentation to national unification, that being the true destiny of English development; and this process, even now, is scarcely ever questioned at all. These preoccupations are not different in type from, say, Italian concern about the fate of urbanism; they have distorted English history-writing in the same sorts of ways. Exactly when England reached the point where unification was attempted, or became inevitable, has been a matter of fraught debate. Inside the realms of serious scholarship, the reigns of Offa (with Bede (d. 735) acting as the theorist of the concept of England) and of William I (1066–87) are the outer limits of the debate, with Alfred (871–99) recently gaining the most support, in my view rightly; but it is the fraughtness of the debate that is its most striking feature, not its conclusions.[64] Wales and Ireland, which did not move in the same direction, are often seen as failures; English kingdoms which were absorbed along the way are often seen as losers. The issue of state-formation in England is beyond doubt an interesting one, for that sub-region is the best-documented example of the process in northern Europe, thanks to both archaeology and (after c.670) documentary and narrative evidence. It compares equally interestingly with Wales, if one

---

[62] For which see, most recently, Squatriti, 'Digging ditches'.

[63] e.g. Campbell, *Essays*, pp. 159–71.

[64] Stenton's letter is reproduced on the back page of the 1996 edition of Keynes, *Anglo-Saxon history*. For Bede, see Brooks, 'English identity', which cites previous bibliography; for Alfred, see e.g. Wormald, *The making*, pp. 277–85.

strips the teleological issue away, as Wendy Davies has done.[65] But I am happy in this book to stop with Offa, who in my reading understood Mercia much better than he understood 'England'; the Lowland Zone of four kingdoms is a more meaningful end-point for the developments of the period than is the common English identity of Bede, which remained on the drawing-board for a long time.

Evidence for England and Wales is largely archaeological. A detailed political polemic by Gildas survives from c.550, and south-east Welsh documents begin in the late sixth or early seventh century; in England, documents and laws do not begin until the late seventh century except for Æthelbert's Kentish code of c.600, and only a handful of ecclesiastical texts pre-date Bede's history and his other works, written in the early eighth. It is the late seventh and eighth centuries above all that allow us to develop a dialogue between history and archaeology, a dialogue which is more active than in some other parts of western Europe. Some of this is in the arena of landscape studies, at least in the areas where both types of evidence exist, as in, say, Worcestershire. (Unfortunately, East Anglia, which is particularly interesting archaeologically, has left no documentation at all.) Much of it concerns the issue of state-formation, which can be seen in less regionally specific terms. Apart from these, I shall pursue English and Welsh concepts of land tenure, a more 'historical' issue, and regional exchange networks, a more 'archaeological' one, in Chapters 6 and 11.[66]

9. Ireland

Ireland is the first of the two regions discussed here that was never Roman: its early medieval polities could not deal even in the memory of the Roman world, unlike in Britain, and the organization of the church adapted itself to Irish society rather than the other way round after the conversion period of the fifth/sixth centuries, unlike in England. Christianity did bring writing, however, and the seventh century, in particular, resulted in the recording of the rules of a very distinct social system: we have hundreds of pages of law tracts in Old Irish, the teaching compilations of a caste of hereditary lawyers, which purport to describe social classifications in great detail. We also have heroic prose narratives, some of which date to the end of our period, which make up a much more substantial body of vernacular material than we have for either England or Wales; in Latin, some sixteen saints' lives also survive from before 800, and church legislation too. Secular narratives are unfortunately very sketchy (they largely consist of single-sentence annals); as in

---

[65] Davies, *Wales in the early middle ages*; eadem, *Patterns of power*.
[66] A model regional study using both history and archaeology is Blair, *Anglo-Saxon Oxfordshire*.

Spain, our evidence focuses on social theory rather than on real social relationships.[67] Nor does archaeology transform our knowledge: the sites that have been excavated—even royal ones—routinely show a very simple material culture, which certainly sets into critical perspective the amazing intricacies of the social gradations 'described' by the law tracts, but which does not favour a detailed archaeology-based examination of relationships (see below, pp. 354–7). Ireland often perplexes: its written evidence seems to point to social structures that could hardly work in practice at all.

Ireland is one of the smallest of our regions. It consists of a central plain, often marshy, with groups of 'Highland Zone-type' barren uplands to the north, south, and west, interspersed with smaller lowlands (see Map 12). This terrain is often fertile, with grain and cattle-raising the main agricultural activities, but there are quite strong contrasts in agricultural potential.[68] It is less logistically difficult to control Ireland than, say, Wales (still less Scotland), but Ireland emerges into the light of seventh-century documentation as the most politically fragmented region in Europe: up to 150 'kingdoms' coexisted on the island, and this number did not substantially change in our period. The word 'kingdom' represents Irish *túath*, which is most exactly translated 'people' (Latin texts of our period translate *túath* as *plebs*, not *regnum*)—or 'tribe', or even 'clan'; Irish scholars are uneasy about the latter two terms, but they do convey the scale of these polities rather better, and I shall use the word 'tribe' to describe them (the usage is defended in Chapter 6, pp. 305–6). They, and their 'kings' (the Irish *rí* corresponds to Latin *rex*, its standard translation in saints' lives), were subject to one or more levels of over-kings, the most powerful of which controlled groups of *túatha* covering about the size of medium-sized Welsh or Anglo-Saxon kingdoms in the period. This is still not huge, however, and there were crucial differences between the Irish and British situations: there was little expectation of permanence in these hierarchies of subjection (except among very weak *túatha*), few examples of absorption of one *túath* by another, and no development, until well past 800 (mostly in the context of the disruption brought by Viking invasion), of any systematic rights by over-kings to intervene in the affairs of their subject *túatha*.[69]

Political narrative, however summary, is impossible given a situation of this kind. Broadly, though, it is possible to present Ireland after 500 or so as having two particularly important families of kings, both of which consisted of several autonomous lineages, each controlling a separate *túath*, but united by a claimed common ancestry and a recognition that there was only one

[67] For a convenient survey of sources, see Hughes, *Early Christian Ireland*; for law, Kelly, *Early Irish law*, is basic; for saints' lives and their dating, see Sharpe, *Medieval Irish saints' lives*.

[68] For agriculture, see Kelly, *Early Irish farming*; for microregional difference, see Smyth, *Celtic Leinster*.

[69] The best guide is still Byrne, *Irish kings*, now supplemented by Ó Cróinín, *Early medieval Ireland*, and Charles-Edwards, *Early Christian Ireland*, pp. 1–144, 441–585.

supreme family head at any one time. The northern family was the Uí Néill, apparently descended from Níall Noígíallach, a mid-fifth-century semi-mythical conqueror; its position was strengthened by a more historical king, Díarmait mac Cerbaill (d. 565). Its *túatha* stretched from Donegal to Meath, with a ceremonial focus in the uninhabited Iron Age fort at Tara; its two most powerful lineages, the Cenél nEógain of modern Tyrone and the Síl nÁedo Sláne of modern Meath, tended to take turns at being family head. The southern family was the Eóganachta, based in Munster, with its ceremonial focus at Cashel. About half the *túatha* of the island were in loose hierarchical relations to one or other of the numerous lineages of these two families. The political activity of each family grouping was largely separate, however; no southern king claimed significant authority in the north, or vice versa, until the late tenth century. These broad groupings also left out the kings in Connaught, Leinster, and eastern Ulster. The former were pretty marginal to wider Irish affairs, but some of the Leinster and Ulster kings had links to Britain, and east Ulster seems to have had the most complex exchange system in the island.[70] One of the east Ulster *túatha*, Dál Ríata in modern Antrim, conquered part of western Scotland in the fifth century, and in the ninth century the Scottish section of Dál Ríata took over the whole of Scotland north of the central lowlands from the Picts. These developments had little effect on Dál Ríata's position in Ireland, however, unless it helped to keep Uí Néill hegemony out of the north-east. This lack of connection is typical. In Ireland, it is not easy to track consistent trends of development on the basis of the political geography just described between the period of its creation, at some point in the fifth century, and the Viking incursions of the ninth.

Irish historiography of this period has long been dominated by what one could call a 'nativist' tradition: these socio-political patterns are seen as very old, protected by elaborate rituals, with more parallels to ancient Indian material, at the opposite end of the Indo-European linguistic network, than to anything in Europe. Recent proponents of this view, such as Daniel Binchy or Francis John Byrne, establish high scientific standards, but they make the task of analysing change, and even comparing Ireland with elsewhere, very hard, before the need to resist the Vikings forced alterations to the rules. An alternative view, associated with Donnchadh Ó Corráin, Charles Doherty, and Liam Breatnach among others, stresses the Christianization of Ireland as an initial step that began to bring the island more into line with Europe, with considerable canon-law influence on the law tracts, and more state-building, even 'feudalism', than the 'nativist' tradition has assumed.[71] I am in sympathy with the comparativism inherent in the second

---

[70] For which see Mallory and McNeill, *The archaeology of Ulster*, pp. 217–25.

[71] e.g. Binchy, *Celtic and Anglo-Saxon kingship*; Byrne, *Irish kings*; contrasted with Ó Corráin, 'Nationality'; idem, Breatnach, and Breen, 'The laws of the Irish'; Doherty, 'Some

view, but I am not as yet convinced by its arguments: Irish society does appear to me more conservative and more different than the second view seems to suppose. We will look at how it may have worked in Chapter 6. The value of including Ireland in this survey, for me, is not to force it into continental European or British models, but simply to explore the fact that it provides the best written documentation by far of the assumptions of a society really unaffected by Roman political structures, which sets into relief how those structures (or those of their post-Roman successors, in particular Francia) conditioned political practice everywhere else, even in as de-Romanized a region as Britain. That it also provides us with difficult conundrums about how that political practice actually operated is not a reason to exclude it.

10. Denmark

Denmark, our other non-Roman region, is at the opposite extreme from Ireland, with no contemporary written evidence at all except a handful of runic inscriptions (the result of the fact that its conversion to Christianity did not occur until the tenth century), but, conversely, a very substantial amount of archaeology, including by far the richest site in northern Europe in our period, Gudme.[72] Denmark was a coherent culture-area which included the modern state of Denmark, plus Schleswig and Skåne, in what is now northern Germany and southern Sweden respectively (see Map 13). It consists of a series of low-lying peninsulas and islands, the largest of which is the Jutland peninsula in the west, with (from west to east) the islands of Fyn and Sjælland and the Skåne peninsula making up the other main components of the region, the total making up about two-thirds of the land area of Ireland. Sea communications are easy, and the land is mostly agriculturally prosperous enough, except where it is too sandy—Denmark is, like England and Ireland, rather less forested than most of continental northern Europe, and has always, like Ireland, specialized in grain and cattle. Denmark has, in particular, much better land than the rest of Scandinavia, which is ecologically and geographically quite different, heavily forested (Sweden) or mountainous (Norway), with much more difficult communications, and a much more fragmented social structure. Denmark has been a region of villages since the fifth century BC, unlike the rest of Scandinavia, which is a zone of highly dispersed settlement, but much more like the Netherlands and northern Germany, the Frisia and Saxony of our period, which it ecologically

aspects of hagiography'. Charles-Edwards's work (esp. *Early Irish and Welsh kinship*; *Early Christian Ireland*) tends towards the first group, but is notably more interested in parallelisms with other European societies.

[72] See Nielsen *et al.*, *Gudme*.

resembles (see below, pp. 496–500). It is linguistically associated with its northern neighbours, and, like them, many of its inhabitants devoted the ninth century to Viking raids, which have dominated the picture of early medieval Denmark ever since. In our period, however, its socio-economic affinities were with the South more than with the North, and I shall treat it as a model for what a 'free German' social system might develop into with minimal influence from Rome—or from their major successors in northern Europe, the Franks.

Denmark seems to have seen a slow process of state-formation. Of course, given the absence of written evidence, we cannot track its protagonists; leaving out later fictional accounts, we know the names of precisely three rulers in the region before 800,[73] compared with over a hundred in England and perhaps a thousand in Ireland. But we can trace a sequence of major political centres, with elaborate archaeological contexts, moving east to west from the Stevns area on Sjælland in the third and fourth centuries (the Late Roman Iron Age), to the Gudme area of Fyn in the fifth and sixth (the Early Germanic Iron Age), and then, after an apparent seventh-century break in which the richest centres were smaller and more scattered, the Ribe–Hedeby area in southern Jutland in the eighth century, at the end of the Late Germanic Iron Age. One must beware of seeing this as a single sequence, for there may well be, say, other Gudmes waiting to be discovered in Jutland, but it does look as if Denmark saw the establishment of clear hierarchies of wealth and perhaps power, which extended across substantial parts of the region, from quite early on: this contrasts not only with the rest of Scandinavia, but even with northern Germany, and certainly with Britain and Ireland. This wealth was presumably derived from Danish agriculture, but it is made visible to us by exchange networks which brought Roman and, later, Frankish metalwork and other luxuries northwards into the above-named centres, and, secondarily, into 'magnate farms' scattered across all the region. By the eighth century Ribe was an active commercial settlement which it would be cavilling not to call urban, and so, shortly, would Hedeby be.

Traditional Danish historiography saw the creation of a single Danish kingdom as a tenth-century phenomenon, with the central Jutland family of Gorm and Harald Bluetooth, who converted to Christianity, establishing power after the confusion of the Viking period. Recently, however, archaeologists, operating within a state-formation paradigm, have stressed the importance of the eighth century as one where there are real signs of political centralization: Ribe seems to have been deliberately founded in 705–10, and Denmark's own defensive dyke against southern invasion, the Danevirke, dates dendrochronologically to 737 or even before. This raises the strong

[73] Chlochilaich, Ongendus, and Sigifrid, referred to respectively in Gregory of Tours, *LH*, III.3; Alcuin, *Vita Willibrordi*, c. 9; *Annales Regni Francorum*, s.a. 771, 782, 798.

possibility that the family of King Godofrid (d. 810), who defended Jutland against the Carolingians, had a century and more of power in much of Denmark, perhaps even most of it. This issue is under considerable debate at present, with some people holding out for the tenth century, even 1000, as the date of Danish unification, and others going the other way, back as far as Gudme, as the moment of unity. We will look at the issue in more detail later (pp. 364–76); it is fascinating, however, that a group of archaeologists as uninfluenced by traditional nationalist debates as those of Denmark should end up as committed to debates about national unity as are the English.[74] The issue of state-formation looms large in Danish scholarship at present; we can avoid it in other contexts, however, for example when looking at settlement (below, pp. 496–8).

The foregoing is not intended to be a full introduction to the history of early medieval Europe and the Mediterranean. The resolutely regional focus of these brief characterizations precludes synthesis and comparison: even the Roman empire almost vanishes from sight as a single unit as a result, and so does the crucial issue of the impact on different regions of the breakdown in Mediterranean unity. Here, I have sought simply to introduce the dramatis personae of this book, and some of the historiographical issues that are hard to get around when setting the secondary literature on one region against that of another. In the next nine chapters we will pursue thematic comparative problems, with these ten regions as their building blocks; the aim of these chapters is to show how they can each, in practice, be paralleled and differentiated. Each region will be summed up in Chapter 11, with general comparative conclusions set out in Chapters 11 and 12.

[74] For the range of views, see Ch. 6, nn. 151–5. John Hines remarks in discussion in Ausenda, *After empire*, pp. 249–50, that Danish archaeologists feel free to discuss the origins of the state precisely because that had not been their original research agenda.

3

The form of the state

THE STATE FRAMED the activities of landowners and peasants, the focus of most of this book. The resources and the capacity for political aggregation of each political system, the public arena it offered, determined the choices of aristocrats, indeed their very identity, everywhere. The local protagonism of each polity—the degree to which rulers and their officials were capable of, and interested in, local intervention, whether through ad hoc trouble-shooting or formal legal action—likewise framed the conflictual relationship between lords and peasants (and, for that matter, lords and lords, peasants and peasants), everywhere. What must be recognized at the outset, however, are the ways states could be different from each other. Far too much political narrative of the early middle ages homogenizes political structures, making all kings pretty much the same, whether they ruled a single English county or the whole of Francia, or whether they ruled Francia in the sixth or in the tenth century, or else assigns difference only to the changing attitudes of clerics to lay politics. It is a fundamental proposition of this chapter that the crucial division is in resources.

This chapter will distinguish between three sorts of polities. First, strong states, the Roman empire and its Byzantine and Arab successors, based on taxation and a paid army as an independent resource for political power. Second, weak states, above all the major Romano-Germanic kingdoms such as Frankish Gaul, Lombard Italy, and Visigothic Spain, with a landed army but also a strong sense of public power acting as a focus for political legitimation, inherited from the Roman world. Third, the pre-state systems of the northern world—in this book, the kingdoms of England, Wales, Ireland, and Denmark, where royal centrality was for a long time much more ad hoc, much more personal, even if in England and Ireland kings and lawyers could at least issue legal guides to how society should regulate itself. By 800 in England, and conceivably also in Denmark, some kings were wealthy and powerful enough to claim more political space than that, but we can still rarely say much about their resources, or how they operated on the ground. For this reason, this chapter will not discuss the third category of political systems; their problems are best seen in the context of wider discussions about aristocratic wealth, power, and political action, and they will be looked at in more detail in Chapter 6. Here, we will concentrate on the differences between strong and weak states; the basic difference being in the role of taxation.

What is a state? The issue has not greatly bothered Roman historians, for the empire was one by any definition; but early medievalists worry at it, conscious as they are of the informality and the personal relationships that lay at the heart of the exercise of all kinds of power in their period—the essential lack of institutionalization of the political process, even under rulers as powerful as Charlemagne. To use the word 'state' at all seems to some scholars to imply a teleology towards a (re)establishment of 'modern'-style bureaucratic structures, or, at least, a scale of values, with the modern state at the top and simple political systems at the bottom.[1] My aim is different here; it is to establish criteria for comparing like with like. Accordingly, I offer a set of parameters for an ideal type of 'the state', adapted from those of Henri Claessen and W. G. Runciman: the centralization of legitimate enforceable authority (justice and the army); the specialization of governmental roles, with an official hierarchy which outlasted the people who held official position at any one time; the concept of a public power, that is, of a ruling system ideologically separable from the ruled population and from the individual rulers themselves; independent and stable resources for rulers; and a class-based system of surplus extraction and stratification.[2] These core elements characterized both the strong polities of the Roman period and the early medieval eastern Mediterranean and the weak polities of the Romano-Germanic West. So, for example, even though local power was in practice in the hands of local elites in the early medieval West, who had a measure of legitimate authority, these elites were in this period all (or nearly all) legitimized by their connections with the public sphere of power. Given that the main Romano-Germanic kingdoms can indeed be characterized in these ways, I shall call them 'states' with no further ado. This is an instance of the sort of discussion that these parameters support. Their general applicability in the first two sets of polities listed above means, however, that it is not necessary to discuss each in detail here. We shall return to how they interrelate in Chapter 6 (pp. 303–4), when we look at political systems in northern Europe, which did not in our period fit easily at all into the state model. But they lie at the core of the analyses made in this chapter.

I have discussed the importance of taxation in earlier articles of 1984–5, on the fall of the western Roman empire and on the relative stability of the

---

[1] One lucid argument along these lines is Innes, *State and society*, pp. 251–63; even Innes, though, uses the word 'state' to an extent.

[2] Claessen, 'The early state', pp. 586–9; Runciman, *Confessions*, p. 53. Claessen discusses this in much more detail, some of it more schematically than seems useful for the model. There are, of course, as many definitions of the state as there are social theorists; but, if the concept is seen as an ideal type, this does not really matter, for there is no 'right' characterization, only more—or less—useful ones.

empires of Asia.[3] I proposed then that the single major change that took place when the western empire broke up was the collapse of the tax system, because a political system that is based on tax-raising is fundamentally different in its basic structure to one that is not. In an ideal-type tax-based state, where wealth is taken from (nearly) everyone, the fiscal system provides an independent basis for political power, separate from the goodwill of the aristocracy, for the army is paid directly from public coffers, and complex bureaucracies, themselves usually salaried, handle the process of tax-collection (as well as other aspects of administration and law, which can also, as a result, in principle operate separately from aristocratic interest). This separation of the state from the aristocracy is seldom complete, for the aristocracy tend to dominate the fiscal and military administration too, if for no other reason than that anything to do with taxation is such a reliable source of enrichment, legal or illegal; public office may also be, in fact usually is, an important element of aristocratic status itself. But the complexity of the state is such that there are many levels of mediation between the interest of the ruler and the interests of aristocrats; and the wealth of the state is so great that it will keep aristocratic loyalty and commitment for a long time. Tax-raising rulers have one crucial advantage over their dependants, too: in the case of unreliability, whether through disloyalty, corruption, or simple ineptness, they can simply dismiss them, and stop paying their salaries. This process works, however badly the other checks and balances work, in any tax-based system. Subjects have only one practical recourse in return: the replacement of the ruler, by rebellion or coup. Regional autonomies, in particular, are hard to create, unless the state structures themselves can be regionalized, because any ambitious regional leader would regard separating himself from tax-raising powers as a pointless exercise. In practice, in fact, rulers were overthrown, and provinces did break off, in the history of any tax-raising system, from the Roman empire to the 'Abbāsid caliphate and beyond. But the state machinery continued to be central, even as its rulers were removed or defied.

Contrast an ideal-type land-based (or rent-based) state: here, the bulk of the wealth of a ruler is derived, not from a whole population, but only from the rent-paying inhabitants on the land he (very rarely she) directly controls, and that wealth is also the major support for all political aggregation. The administration is simpler, for the tax system is absent or rudimentary; the ruler's principal officials are his local representatives and his army leaders, and they too are based on the land, as indeed is the whole of the army. All political reward is dominated by the 'politics of land'—cessions of land and its rents, to officials or to other powerful aristocrats, in return for loyalty. Rulers have two basic problems here. The first is that land is finite, except in

---

[3] Respectively, 'The other transition: from the Ancient world to feudalism', and 'The uniqueness of the East', both now in *Land and power*, pp. 7–40, 43–74.

periods of political expansion: essentially, the more I have, the less you do. Rulers may achieve loyalty from one round of land-gifts, but they have less to give as a result, and may become less attractive over time; furthermore, land, once given, on whatever legal terms, is hard to get back, except by force. Rulers were often very good at force—societies of this type tend to be highly militarized, with a good deal of respect paid to ruthlessness; but still, in the long run, in the absence of wars of conquest, or the sort of civil war that is won so totally by one side that the victor can confiscate on a large scale and start again, polities risk becoming weaker. The second problem is regional fragmentation: in the absence of capillary administrative controls, and unless the centre is particularly powerful and effective, regional officials have little preventing them from increasing their autonomy, and maybe in the end breaking free altogether. This can again be countered by force, and often has been, across the centuries. Even more often, it has been countered by the generation of a political culture, a set of assumptions about legitimate political action and how to characterize and symbolize it, which favour central rather than regional power—whether this is the social position conveyed by being a king's guest, at his banquets or his Easter celebrations, or the ideological importance of unconditional political loyalty, or the greater status attached to being a dealer in central-government politics rather than being a regional leader—political systems have differed about which of these, and others, mattered more, but all polities have had to deal in one or more of them if they were to avoid total failure. Still, the standard risks in a land-based system are, other things being equal, structural weakness and centrifugal tendencies.[4]

These two systems have just been presented as ideal types: in historical reality, many polities have had elements of both. Even the Roman emperors were large-scale landowners as well, and the rent they received was significant, even if their tax returns always overshadowed it. More important, most land-based systems have managed to extract at least some tax, even if just from customs tolls and judicial fines, and have paid at least some of their dependants (mercenaries, for example), as well as being capable of dealing in the gift-exchange of treasure that was an important part of court ritual. (This exchange was important in pre-state polities, too.) But the basic distinction between the two systems, tax and land, seems to me to be fundamental, and it is inside that framework that I wish here to explore the detail of the different protocols and procedures that a variety of states adopted in the period 400 to 800, to see how they compare. The buying power, and the geographical scale, of tax-based states was, in particular, in most cases much greater than in land-based states, which in turn had a considerable impact on exchange, as we shall see later in this book.

---

[4] The major analytical account of this sort of system remains Bloch, *Feudal society*.

This chapter is empirical more than theoretical; for the theoretical implications of this distinction, the reader can be referred to the articles already
cited. But it needs to be added that now, twenty years later, I would nuance
the way I then developed the tax–land opposition, while still maintaining the
basic lines of my arguments, in three main ways. First, I then held that there
was a distinction in the whole economic base of the social system, seen in
Marxist terms, between tax-based systems and land-based systems, which
I defined respectively as the ancient (or tributary) and the feudal modes of
production. I would retreat from that position now, as a result of critiques by
Halil Berktay and John Haldon: it now seems to me that both are sub-types
of the same mode of production, in that both are based on agrarian surplus
extracted, by force if necessary, from the peasant majority. Second, I posited
that the moment of change in the West was above all in the fifth century:
that, in the crisis of the invasions and divisions of the western empire, local
aristocracies ceased to become interested in collecting—or paying—tax that
was not any longer funding successful military defence, and instead adapted
to new Germanic political structures that were no longer dependent on
taxation: 'it is because the tax-raising mechanisms of the empire were
already failing that the Germanic armies ended up on the land.'[5] This
I now believe, in empirical terms, to be at best half-true: Germanic armies
did indeed mostly end up on the land, but tax often carried on as well for a
time, as we shall see; the overall process was much the same, but it took
rather longer than I believed in 1984. Third, the opposition between salary
and land for the army, which underlies the sharpness of that change, is too
stark. There are many ways to fund an army, and in relatively few of them
are armies *only* landed, or *only* salaried. The 'feudal' armies of twelfth-
century England were full of mercenaries; conversely, the Roman empire
gave land to veterans, and indeed to several different types of serving troops.
Only the Umayyad and 'Abbāsid states, out of all the polities discussed in
this book, relied on an army that was entirely salaried.[6] What happened
in the fifth (and sixth) century in the West was that the balance between
money and land shifted: from an army that was *basically* paid (though given
land when necessary) to an army that was *basically* landed (though supplied
when necessary or useful: on campaign, in garrisons, or as one-off
royal largesse)—much less abrupt a shift, though a crucially significant one
nonetheless.

The foregoing paragraph has used the word 'feudal' in two distinct ways:
to characterize a whole economic system, as a mode of production, and
to characterize the armies of twelfth-century England. Actually, one can

---

[5] Berktay, 'The feudalism debate'; Haldon, 'The feudalism debate once more'; idem, *The
state and the tributary mode*, pp. 63–87 (where he proposes the term 'tributary' rather than
'feudal' for the mode). For the quote, Wickham, *Land and power*, p. 29.
[6] See Carrié, 'L'état à la recherche', compared to Kennedy, 'The financing of the military',
both in a volume focused on the funding of armies.

distinguish between three main meanings of the word in historical practice: feudalism as a mode of production; feudal society as the 'politics of land', characteristic of the land-based rather than the tax-based polities just discussed; and what is sometimes called 'military feudalism', or 'feudo-vassalic' relationships, characterized by a system of rewards based on conditional military tenures (fiefs) and complex rules of loyalty.[7] Each of these three uses is sanctioned by tradition, and it is pointless to make claims about which one is the 'real' meaning; in different works I have, indeed, used all three. In this book, however, the word will henceforth be used in the first sense. The third meaning certainly has no place here, for its concrete examples are all chronologically subsequent to our period. As for the second meaning: my own retraction of a modal difference between tax-based and land-based polities has not led me to conclude that the structural differences between them are minor, as the foregoing pages make clear, but I shall stick to 'tax' and 'land' as shorthands for them, since these words already make the opposition clear. In Chapters 6 and 9, however, the distinction between an economic and political system dominated by peasants, in a ranked society, and that dominated by aristocrats and aristocratic landowning, in a class society, will become relevant, and I will here use the terminology of feudalism and the feudal mode for the latter system.

This chapter, as already stated, is above all about resources: about how states are financed, about how taxation (if it existed) worked at a local level, and about how, and where, public resources were moved around. These issues are crucial if we are interested in analysing the geographical scale of economies, a concern which will underpin the whole book, and which, in particular, will be the subject-matter of Chapter 11. The aim in this chapter is not, however, to describe the whole public edifice in each political unit of the Roman and post-Roman world. There are already many monographs and manuals that aim to provide precisely that sort of overview, and to discuss institutional questions in any detail here would wildly overbalance the book.[8] Even then, just a discussion of how taxation worked (or what alternatives there were to it) entails quite a lot of exposition at times, in particular where we have a good deal of material, as, most notably, in Gaul and Egypt. More problematic is the issue of what was earlier termed political culture, the assumptions about the parameters of legitimate action held by political actors, which encompasses not only competing ideologies of legitimacy but also the discourses and representations which embody those ideologies. These are as crucial for any understanding of the way actors make the choices they do as are the resources of states; and, even if the huge

---

[7] See Wickham, 'Le forme del feudalesimo', for a bibliographical survey.

[8] There are too many analyses even to list; but see, as points of reference and guides, Jones, *LRE*; Delmaire, *Largesses sacrées*; Barnwell, *Emperor, prefects*; idem, *Kings, courtiers*; Brandes, *Finanzverwaltung*; Haldon, *Byzantium in the seventh century*; Kennedy, *Armies*.

public wealth of the Roman empire, say, can be assumed to have made
political action attractive to elites regardless of the details of their values,
the same cannot be said of weaker states in the post-Roman West, whose
centrality to the lives of local aristocracies was to a substantial degree
determined by the ideas the latter had about status, loyalty, obligation,
legitimate royal behaviour, and so on. But this chapter is more concerned
to explore state infrastructures; the transactional elements in the construction of political power will be discussed elsewhere. And, it must be stressed,
the aim here is not to provide an account of the successes and failures of any
political actors or political system. Rather, it is the establishment of a set of
parameters that will allow the development of comparisons between the
economic structures of political systems, at least inside the broad categories
of strong, tax-based states and weak, land-based states.

1. The later Roman empire

There is, of course, not much debate about whether the Roman empire was a
strong state. In recent years, it is true, quite a number of writers have talked
down the more totalizing elements of the traditional image of the *Zwang-
staat*, the 'coercive state' of the post-Diocletianic period: the bureaucracy of
the late empire was much smaller than is often believed, state fiscality did not
have a seriously negative effect, the efforts of the government to restrict
social mobility were failures, and so on. These revisionist arguments have
some force; they do not, however, alter the fact that the scale of the late
Roman political system was greater than that of any subsequent state in
Europe and the Mediterranean, and its internal coherence was not again
matched in Latin Europe until the late middle ages. The impact of the
Roman state needs to be briefly illustrated here as a starting-point for all
that follows; for the effect of its disintegration is a major turning-point in
every part of this book. I shall treat the empire in the period c.400–600 as a
whole; but in the West my illustrative material is mostly taken from the start
of the period, before disintegration began, whereas in the East the sixth
century is privileged, as the last prolonged period of stability before the
Persian and Arab conquests.

Roman taxation was perceived as heavy. Complaints about its weight
are endless;[9] whole rhetorical systems were developed to characterize its
oppressive nature. The most dramatic is that of Salvian, writing in Gaul in
the 440s, for whom the 'chains of taxation' were the main causes, along with
the barbarian invasions, of the 'death' of the Roman state. Salvian painted a
highly coloured picture of the way the tax system worked to ensure that
everybody oppressed everybody else, with the *curiales*, the city councillors

---

[9] For a list, see Demandt, *Die Spätantike*, p. 248.

with the main tax-collecting responsibilities, cast as *tyranni*, tyrants, or *latrones*, brigands; the *potentes*, powerful landowners, were Salvian's other serious culprits, as they invented new illegal exactions, forced the landowning poor into their patronage networks as their clients and then as their tenants, and—perhaps worst of all—reneged even on their promises to protect the poor from their tax obligations, with the latter, now stripped of their lands, even losing their freedom.[10] Add to this the harsh and often ferocious imperial laws about the *curiales* themselves, who are to be prevented in every possible way from leaving their duties, which they were apparently desperate to evade (for the *curiales* not only organized taxation, but underwrote it too), and we have a world in which pretty much everybody, from the top to the bottom, was oppressed by the tax system.[11]

As already implied, Salvian is far from the only source on the oppressiveness of late Roman taxation. An emperor himself, Valentinian III, issued a law in 450 which castigated the unjust and unbridled terrorism of his own central-government tax *discussores*, for example.[12] But most sources concentrate on the terror of the *moment* of taxation; where Salvian is unusual is in his careful tracing of the effects of tax oppression, from the top to the bottom. As a result, a literal reading of Salvian underpins a good percentage of the more negative analyses of the late Roman state.[13] But Salvian was above all a preacher, in the grand style: his attack on taxation is paralleled by exactly similar attacks on public entertainment and on sexual deviance, to neither of which historians pay much attention; still, it is not obvious why we should be any less cautious about Salvian's view that the poor lose all their property to the powerful than about his belief that a substantial part of the population of Carthage consisted of homosexuals and transvestites.[14] Salvian is almost certainly describing a real process in his account of the travails of the poor, just as doubtless there were indeed transvestites in Carthage; but it is naive to regard his account as any more a work of objective sociology than is any sermon, or political speech, today. Historians have, as a result, more recently reacted against these dark tones, arguing that taxation changed little in the fourth century with respect to the principate, and in the East not much more in the following two centuries; or else that it was never so out of control that it menaced the overall economy of the empire, as even the measured A. H. M. Jones thought.[15] Indeed, it could be said to be relatively light: 'Although late antiquity has acquired (along

---

[10] Salvian, *De gubernatione dei*, IV.30–1, V.17–45. See for *curiales* in this context Lepelley, 'Quot curiales, tot tyranni'.

[11] Core legislation can be found in *CTh*, XI–XIII.   [12] *Nov. Val.*, I.3.

[13] e.g. Stein, *Bas-empire*, I, pp. 344–7; Wickham, *Land and power*, p. 21. (See also below, pp. 527–9.) There are many others.

[14] Salvian on Carthage: *De gubernatione dei*, VII.76–83. The best critique is Krause, *Spätantike Patronatsformen*, pp. 233–331.

[15] Jones, *LRE*, pp. 450–69, gives a general survey of taxation; see also Cérati, *Caractère annonaire*. For its weight, Jones, *LRE*, pp. 468–9; idem, *Roman economy*, pp. 82–9. Against

with its undeserved reputation for bureaucracy) a high-tax profile, the reality is very different.'[16]

This seems to me to be going too far the other way. One does not have to believe Salvian as an accurate reporter to be struck by the fact that, for him, as for other writers, taxation defined and framed rural oppression.[17] Contrast medieval societies, where such oppression was overwhelmingly seen as the work of unjust lords, not state officials, until well into the fourteenth century. When peasants fled from the land, this, too, was seen as an evasion of fiscal obligations; contrast Visigothic Spain in the late seventh century, where such flight was from servile status, not taxation (see below, pp. 526–7). Under the empire, the tax system was generally seen as the major point of contact between the state and the citizen, along with the legal system, and the major point of difficulty.

It is also the case that tax was genuinely high. I will concentrate here on the land tax, overwhelmingly the dominant tax in this period. Jones, in his defining account of taxation, put his stress on two texts, both from the mid-sixth century, the Antaiopolis ('Irmāniyya) register from Middle Egypt (now dated by Jean Gascou to c.540) and a state grant to the church of Ravenna in Italy, newly reconquered by the east Roman empire, from c.555. The latter allows one to say that church taxes to the state made up 57 per cent of the combined tax plus rent that the church collected from its tenants. The former links a basket of taxes to land areas, and allowed Jones to argue, in a calculation that has not been successfully contested by other scholars, that taxation in the sixth century came to 3.2 *artabai* of wheat per *aroura* of land. (In Egypt, wheat was by far the most important agrarian product.) These are Egyptian measures, which are related, in that around 1 *artaba* is sufficient to sow an *aroura*. Figures from sixth-century leases tend to assume rents of 4 to 6 *artabai* per *aroura*; the best estimates of Egyptian yields are 10 to 12 *artabai* per *aroura*. Of those yields, then, a quarter to a third went in tax, perhaps 40 per cent in rent, 1 *artaba* in seed-corn, leaving between 2 and 4 *artabai* for peasant subsistence, if the peasants were tenants, and as much as 6–8 *artabai* if they were owners, in Antaiopolis around 540. Tax thus, unlike in Ravenna, did not quite match rent, but it was very substantial all the same.[18]

---

this, Whittaker, 'Inflation and the economy'; Duncan-Jones, *Money and government*, pp. 57–9; Carrié, 'L'economia e le finanze', pp. 767–8; idem, 'Observations sur la fiscalité'; Bagnall, 'Agricultural productivity'; idem, *Egypt*, pp. 153–60, among others.

[16] Bagnall, *Egypt*, p. 153.

[17] See in general Krause, *Spätantike Patronatsformen*, pp. 233–43. Another example is Agathias, *History*, IV.21.6–22.5.

[18] *P. Cair. Masp.* I 67057; *P. Ital.* 2. See Jones, *LRE*, pp. 484, 819–23; idem, review of Johnson and West, *Byzantine Egypt*, including for the detailed calculations. See along similar lines Wickham, *Land and power*, pp. 14–16 (which needs to be modified slightly in the light of the discussion here). For the date of the first document, see Gascou, 'La table budgétaire', pp. 281–6; for rents, Herrmann, *Studien*, pp. 274–88; for yields, Rathbone, *Economic rationalism*, pp. 243–4, Rowlandson, *Landowners*, p. 247, and Bowman, 'Landholding', p. 149.

It has been argued that this is only a single figure, and this is certainly true, although *P. Cair. Masp.* 67057, the papyrus that contains the Antaiopolis register, has more recently been substantially confirmed by the global figures contained in a slightly earlier text for the same city, *P. Freer* 08.45 c–d, published by Gascou (it lists part of the fiscal budget for Antaiopolis for two periods in the 520s–530s), and the orders of magnitude roughly fit other Egyptian tax figures from the same period. It is likely that tax had risen in Egypt since the fourth century, for Roger Bagnall has proposed global tax figures of 2.1 *artabai* per *aroura* (though often in practice 2.6 *artabai*), around a fifth of crop, for that period, but, even if tax had gone up by between a quarter and a half, it was never negligible.[19] Bagnall's image of the lightness of Egyptian taxation seems to derive more from the fact that urban society was barely taxed at all in the Roman fiscal system (urbanism was unusually dense in Egypt: below, pp. 609–12) than from the rural figures he himself presents.

More of a problem is that these figures are from Egypt. I do not subscribe to the view that Egypt is structurally different from the rest of the Mediterranean, and we will see the Egyptian model set out at several points in this book. But if there is one respect that Egypt does differ, radically, from almost all of the empire, it is in its yields. Irrigated land always provides higher yields than dry-farming, which was normal in the rest of the empire outside the desert margins of Africa and Palestine, and parts of Spain. Three- or fourfold wheat yields were common in dry-farming until the agricultural revolution; in Egypt three times as much could be calculated for, with no fallow period thanks to the mud that came with the annual Nile flood, the only uncertainty being the height of the flood itself (which was no more uncertain than was rainfall elsewhere).[20] Egypt was par excellence the source of wheat for the eastern empire, and would be as heavily taxed as was practicable. But we cannot extend Egyptian calculations to dry-farming regions without resorting to open guesswork. Jones himself argued that Egyptian taxation under Justinian was apparently at six or seven times the level per surface area that can be calculated for Numidia a century earlier, in c.450. The Numidian figures are not good, and tax rates fluctuated substantially, but this does seem to show that Egypt could support heavier rates of

---

[19] Against a single figure: e.g. Liebeschuetz, *Barbarians and bishops*, p. 247. The Freer papyrus is published in Gascou, 'La table budgétaire'. Ibid., pp. 307–8, and Rouillard, *L'Egypte byzantine*, pp. 124–6, argue that these citations are comparable to other figures for the period. For the fourth century, see Bagnall, *Egypt*, p. 157, with idem, 'Agricultural productivity', pp. 303–5. 20% is also proposed for the fourth century by Durliat, *Les finances*, pp. 19, 304–9, on the basis of *Panégyriques*, II, pp. 99–100, for Autun in 311–12, but it is not clear how he obtains the figure.

[20] Irrigation yields away from the Nile were less, although still higher than dry-farming: sevenfold yields are recorded at Nessana (*P. Ness.* 82, cf. 83). See Patlagean, *Pauvreté*, pp. 247–8; Kaplan, *Les hommes*, pp. 80–1.

tax than elsewhere.[21] The Ravenna figure for c.550 already cited, although it cannot be directly linked to production, is also from a dry-farming region, and may be a better guide; it might indicate, if half the yield was extracted in surplus, with a quarter going to peasant subsistence and a quarter to seed, a tax rate—as at Antaiopolis in fact—of between a quarter and a third, on land which was episcopal, and thus privileged as not being liable to extra taxes. Here we are already in guesstimates, and these are the best figures we have. For other provinces, and other centuries, we are even less certain.[22] One could at least argue, however, that sixth-century tax norms were often upwards of a quarter of total yields; and, even if these figures are atypical, they at least do not seem to be far out of the range that is implied by more generic figures, like those for imperial surpluses. If the Ravenna figure could stand for a wider area, which it cannot properly do, it might indicate that tax rates across the empire could be more stable than rents, which varied more according to agricultural fertility. But there is no sign from any of these figures that tax was other than a serious burden, which fully justified the huge amount of legislation (for example, most of books XI–XIII of the *Theodosian Code*) and political rhetoric that it generated.

It is not easy to collect tax in an agrarian society. It is not, actually, that easy to collect rent either, as subsistence peasants are understandably un-willing or resentful payers of their own surplus to outside powers in any society. But at least landowners tend to know who holds land from them, and their structural opponents are the peasants themselves, who rarely have much of the main force or the desire for risk that are necessary if they want to defy the aristocracy (see below, pp. 578–88). Tax-collectors, however, collect from rich and poor alike, 'the powerful and the poor', as they were called throughout our period,[23] and the rich/powerful are more dangerous opponents, whether they are supposed to pay tax themselves (having extracted it from their peasants already, something they have no problem doing) or whether they simply let the collectors in to tax their dependants directly, thus lessening the surplus they might claim themselves. Both of these two latter patterns were part of late Roman fiscal practice—broadly, tenants (*coloni*) who held all their land from one landlord paid tax through him; tenants with some land of their own paid tax directly.[24] Peasants were relatively straightforward to terrorize, as in the texts cited earlier; but their lords were less easy game. Small wonder that tax-collectors travelled with

[21] Jones, *LRE*, pp. 463–4, commenting on *Nov. Val.*, XXXIV.2 (cf. XIII). Jones saw Numidia as 'relatively poor', but this is an exaggeration. For Numidian prosperity see e.g. Fentress, 'Numidia'.

[22] Another well-known set of figures, in Ammianus' account of Julian reducing taxes in Gaul (*Res gestae*, XVI.5.14), seem to me too rhetorical to use.

[23] See e.g. Bosl, '*Potens* und *pauper*'; Morris, 'The powerful and the poor'. Of course, the rich were often themselves tax-collectors, as we shall see.

[24] This simplifies a complex structure; see further below, pp. 520–6.

armed support, in the Roman empire as in most other strong states. Unless one really needed to tax, it is hard to imagine that its rituals could have prevailed against so many structural opponents.[25]

All the same, the evidence that we have does point to a high level of regularity and ritual about the tax-raising process as well. The recently discovered tablet of Trinitapoli (in Puglia in southern Italy), dating from c.369, gives one starting-point.[26] This inscription is a decree of Valentinian I, apparently in response to the 'defraudations' perpetrated by provincial officials, in collusion with the local authorities responsible for collecting taxes, the *praepositi pagorum* (*pagi* are rural districts) and the city *tabularii* (notaries, acting for the city council, the *ordo* or *curia*). The taxation process is to be tightened up, with the *praepositi* made responsible for the writing of monthly accounts, and the *tabularii* henceforth are to co-ordinate these for the city territory and forward them to the provincial government. The governor, in turn, is to make spot checks on the ground by making a formal circuit of the province (called here an *adventus*, a term commonly used for the ceremonial entries of emperors),[27] asking landowners (*possesores*) about the process, then checking their declarations against the accounts. This system, had it really worked, would have been very tight: tighter even than other imperial laws envisage, for they tend to stress four-monthly written accounts, reflecting the fact that tax after 364 was paid three times a year, whereas the monthly accounts here could have allowed the tracking of delayed payments too, as the editors of the text remark. Of course, it could not really work, because—quite apart from the practical difficulties of actually making such tours on a regular basis—it entirely hung on the rectitude of the governors themselves, who were among the most famously corrupt of late Roman officials. But Valentinian's institution of the governor's inquest was not a temporary measure; it is still invoked in a law of 458.[28]

The tablet of Trinitapoli shows both the complexity of the tax-collection process and how easily it could be subverted. Let us run through some of the elements of both of these. Every year, the praetorian prefects (of which there were four in the empire) worked out the global tax sum to be required for the year, taking into account, above all, the costs of war, the main variable in the budget. These sums had a basic stability (often, contingent increases were regarded as extra taxes, *superindictiones*), but the

---

[25] Brown, *The rise of Western Christendom*, p. 14, stresses that delegation meant that taxation became a 'way of life' for all local elites; this overstates its acceptability as part of normal behaviour.

[26] Edited and commented on in Giardina and Grelle, 'La tavola di Trinitapoli'.

[27] MacCormack, *Art and ceremony*, pp. 17–89.

[28] See Giardina and Grelle, 'La tavola di Trinitapoli', esp. pp. 280–1 (monthly accounts), 294; cf. *CTh*, I.16.11 (the shorter law, from 369, that parallels the tablet); *Nov. Maj.*, II.4 (a. 458). See further Cecconi, 'Tradizione e novità', for the tendencies to fiscal centralization which underlay the latter law.

presupposition that tax levels could change regularly is assumed by a wide range of sources, and was a consistent feature of Roman and indeed post-Roman tax systems—the principle that tax rates were publicized yearly can still be found in 'Abbāsid Egypt.[29] The rates, set out in great detail, were communicated to provincial governors and thence, by formal proclamation, to cities, whose councillors had the task of ensuring collection, overseen by other councillors and/or by central government officials, in an ever-changing set of institutional protocols, as *curiales* or officials thought up new loopholes or abuses, which were corrected by later legislation. *Curiales* often had a specific geographical remit, which they regarded as their personal responsibility, and where they could often behave pretty much as they chose.[30] But they had to justify their local exactions with documentation: around 400, for example, Symmachus, major senatorial aristocrat and letter-writer, can be found asking an official about a case in which the tax-collectors sent by the city came to his estate without *publicae validitatis monumenta*, publicly valid documentation, which meant, he concluded, that they were taxing fraudulently.[31] One could assume that less exalted taxpayers had less chance to query such collections, but the principle of documentation did undoubtedly exist.

Curiales were for long the linchpins in this system. They constantly complained that they were being bankrupted by the burden of underwriting taxes, while all other taxpayers complained about their tyranny. Historians have stressed either side of this equation, or both at once, depending on their general view of the internal balances of late Roman political structures. In general, it seems true both that some councillors eagerly sought the opportunity to exact taxes and that others systematically evaded it: the major division could be seen, as Claude Lepelley has formulated it, as between rich and poor *curiales*. Libanios in Antioch in the later fourth century, in some fairly standard perorations about the decline in curial status and numbers (in Antioch's case, supposedly from 1,200 members to twelve, but in another oration from 600 to sixty: the figures are obviously rhetorical), stressed that the main cause of this was that the richer *bouleutai* (Greek for *curiales*) wanted to keep numbers small, so as not to have to share out profits.[32] The point was that tax-raising was always both profitable and risky. It was profitable, of course, because of the huge illegal (and often even legal)

---

[29] For changing tax levels, see Jones, *LRE*, pp. 449–53. For the 'Abbāsid period, see *P. Ryl. Copt.* 117 (dated to 764–70 by MacCoull, 'Strange death', p. 37—although it refers to the 9th and 10th indictions, which would be 755–7 or 770–2); *P. Ryl. Ar.* IX.6 (a. 798).

[30] A good description of the process of proclamation and of tax-collection in general is *NJ*, CXXVIII (a. 545). For *curiales*, see most recently Laniado, *Recherches*.

[31] Symmachus, *Ep.* IX.10; cf. *NJ*, CXXVIII, CXXX.5 for documentation.

[32] Lepelley, '*Quot curiales, tot tyranni*', p. 154; see in general, among many, Jones, *LRE*, pp. 737–66; Laniado, *Recherches*, pp. 3–26. For Libanos, see *Orations*, XLVIII.4, XLIX.8. Basil of Caesarea, *Letters*, n. 299, similarly comments that power and wealth both come from the control of the tax census.

perks that the system could bring in. But it was risky because the higher the tax rate, the harder it was to collect; because the at least intermittent central government controls on tax-collecting meant that state officials might correct abuses (and siphon profits off to themselves); and because it was considerably harder to collect taxes from the lands of the most powerful aristocrats, such as senators, who were much richer and more influential than most *curiales*. The last of these risks was highly variable, region by region, or even city by city, depending on the concentrations of senatorial land, and, indeed, on the level of law-abidingness of individual landowners. But certainly the ability of powerful owners and patrons to evade taxes, on their own estates or on those of clients, whether by fraud, outright defiance, or by feet-dragging that went on long enough that their tax was let off in one of the intermittent remittances of tax arrears, is well attested.[33] I shall return to the issue in Chapter 9 (pp. 527–9).

It is because of all these problems that *curiales* did, in the end, lose their responsibility for tax-raising. This will be discussed from the standpoint of the structures of urban society and politics in Chapter 10 (pp. 596–602); here, we can restrict ourselves to a brief narrative. In the East, the role of *curiales* as the principal collectors was partially undermined by Anastasius (491–518), who instituted new city-based central government tax officials known as *vindices* (in Egypt the apparently equivalent office was the pagarch, who remained the governor in Egyptian cities into the eighth century). *Curiales* certainly sometimes continued to collect taxes in Justinian's time, for the latter's *Novels* of the 530s–560s mention them (and legislate to safeguard their property). In Palestine, a Petra document of 538 shows a *politeuomenos* (city councillor) with a traditional tax-raising responsibility; a bishop from the Gaza area, seeking the religious advice of the ascetic John in the 530s, referring again to *politeuomenoi*, assumes the same. But after that they fade out of our tax evidence, and, importantly, do not appear in the extensive sixth-century Egyptian documentation for the practice of taxation, of which more shortly.[34] In the West the pattern is more regional: by the early sixth century *curiales* no longer collected taxes in Africa or Gaul as far as we know, and in Spain the only evidence for them is in the Breviary of Alaric, dating from 506, which may only repeat outdated legislation; but they were still active in Ostrogothic Italy, and in ex-Vandal Sardinia (by now Roman again, theoretically subject to Justinianic legislation) they are associated with taxation as late as 594.[35] But both East and West experienced the same process of centralization, with tax powers being taken away from local elites. The late sixth- and seventh-century taxation that is attested for Gaul

[33] Jones, *LRE*, pp. 466–7, lists remittances of arrears.

[34] *P. Petra* 3; Barsanouphios and John, *Correspondance*, n. 835; see in general Laniado, *Recherches*, pp. 27–62, and 98–9 for a commentary on the last-named text. For further bibliography, see Ch. 10, n. 6.

[35] Jones, *LRE*, p. 761; Gregory the Great, *Ep.* IV.26 for Sardinia.

and Spain (below, pp. 96–115) seems to have been collected directly by central government officials, and the same is emphatically true for the Byzantine and Arab eastern Mediterranean.

Any land tax system that is at all precise has to rely very heavily on documentation: of the amount to be exacted, the amount actually paid, and—above all—up-to-date materials on who actually owns land. Without these, the system will quickly become arbitrary, a system of legalized plunder, or ad hoc tribute at best. 'Tribute' can in fact be conceptually separated from 'tax', with the former consisting of lump sums due from communities or individuals, determined essentially by relations of armed force, and often arbitrary or irregular in their incidence; tax, by contrast, was based on assessments of relative wealth, in land or movables. This distinction, which I shall maintain in what follows, is an important one for state resources: for it is unlikely that any system of tribute will be as remunerative as an exactly assessed tax can be, simply because only the latter will effectively pinpoint who has the resources to pay.[36] Every tax-raising state has had to struggle with these constraints, with greater or lesser success. In the late empire, the idea was certainly that censuses of persons and property should be regularly revised, and also, at any rate from 444 (in the West, but with eastern analogues too), that land sales should be formally registered in each city. The censuses were not revised so very often, as far as we can tell, although the Trinitapoli text at least assumes that governors can know who is a *possessor* at any given moment, and there certainly were revisions, throughout the late empire, maybe in some detail; a military text from the Justinianic East assumes that even land quality was assessed in them.[37] We do, however, have clear evidence of the formal registration of land sales, in *gesta municipalia*, municipal registers. These are referred to in some of Gregory the Great's letters for Byzantine Italy in the 590s, and some actually survive in Italian papyri from the fifth to seventh centuries (see also below, pp. 110–11); in Egypt, too, although *gesta municipalia* do not appear to have existed, documents of sale or gift were accompanied by formal notifications to the public authorities, several of which survive, that tax liabilities were hereby transferred as well. The point is that procedures like these were essential, if taxation was to be accurately assessed. (So were adequate reference and retrieval systems in the archives where these records were kept, which are indeed harder still to imagine operating very well.)[38]

---

[36] These distinctions are discussed in Wickham, 'Lineages'.

[37] Infrequent censuses: Jones, *LRE*, pp. 454–5. For land quality, *Peri stratēgias*, c. 3. For sale registrations, *Nov. Val.*, XV.1.3; cf. for the East *NJ*, XVII.8.1 (but they seem not to be envisaged in *NJ*, CXXXV).

[38] Gregory the Great, *Epp.*, II.9, 15, VIII.5, IX.58, 71, 180, XIII.18; *P. Ital.* 4–5, 7, 8, 10–11, 12, 21, 29, 31–3. See in general Everett, 'Scribes and charters', pp. 73–8. For Egyptian sale and gift notifications, see e.g. *P. Oxy.* I 126, XVI 1887; *P. Laur.* II 26, III 77; *P. Cair. Masp.* I 67117–9. For retrieval problems, see Kelly, 'Later Roman bureaucracy'; cf. Clanchy, *From memory*, pp. 138–47, for the issue in medieval England.

The evidence is that they worked, after a fashion, throughout the Roman empire; they continued to work in Arab Egypt, too, for that matter. In the post-Roman West, however, their continuance was distinctly more intermittent, as we shall see.

Exactly how tax was exacted is clearest in the Egyptian papyri. Egyptian tax-collecting was always violent and coercive (Ammianus famously remarked that Egyptians were proud of the scars they received from floggings for tax-evasion); but it was remarkable in its systematization at the same time. For the sixth century, we have tax-rolls for the two best-documented localities of the region, the city of Oxyrhynchos (Bahnasā) and the fiscally autonomous village of Aphroditō (Kōm Ishqāw). It is clear, too, that such rolls were normal everywhere and regularly compiled—even if not so regularly updated.[39] On the basis of these rolls, local officials (in a complex hierarchy of dependence) went out and collected tax from each village, or else received the taxes from landowners who collected directly from their own tenants. It is a notable feature of the Egyptian evidence that the best-documented great estate of the sixth and early seventh centuries, the Apion estate at Oxyrhynchos (it is by far the best-documented estate for the whole period of this book, in fact, and will often appear in later chapters), regarded tax-collecting and taxpaying as an entirely routine matter; although late fourth- and early fifth-century laws on rural patronage, *patrocinium vicorum*, stress the tax-evasion in Egypt that resulted, this family of great owners and patrons saw no need to evade.[40] At the moment of the handover of tax, three times a year, every taxpayer received a receipt (*entagion*), often for each sort of tax, in wheat, in money, or any of the minor dues that were also owed. Hundreds of these receipts survive; we also have receipts from village leaders, to individual taxpayers or to government officials.[41] It is clear that Egyptian taxpaying was regulated and checked, down to the smallest detail (one letter from sixth-century Aphroditō asks for more money from village leaders, because the minor officials delivering the

---

[39] Ammianus, *Res gestae*, XXII.16.23; *P. Oxy.* I 127; *P. Cair. Masp.* I 67055, 67058–9; cf. Gascou, 'La table budgétaire', for Antaiopolis. (Aphroditō is the conventional spelling for the village, but strictly it is the eighth-century form; in the sixth it was usually Aphroditē.)

[40] For patronage laws, see below, Ch. 9, n. 19. Apion tax accounts survive in *P. Oxy.* XVI 1906–8, and elsewhere; agreements for the collection of taxes on the Apion estates are *P. Oxy.* LXII 4350–1. Gascou, 'Les grands domaines', argues that the Apions and other major Egyptian families were as much tax-farmers as landowners, with their 'estates' really quasi-public institutions, and their tenants paying 'rente-impôt', 'rent-tax'. This view has been both influential and controversial, with Bagnall, *Egypt*, pp. 159–60, accepting it, for example, but Liebeschuetz, 'Civic finance', pp. 395–8; Banaji, *Agrarian change*, pp. 93–100; and Sarris, *Economy and society*, ch. 8, contesting it. (It lies at the heart of Durliat's even more controversial view of the West, below, n. 68, while being far less schematic than Durliat.) For me, there are too many instances of an explicit separation between tax and rent in papyri for the theory to survive; for Oxyrhynchos, see below, Ch. 4, n. 238; for Aphroditō, for example, see *P. Cair. Masp.* II 67138–9, III 67300; *P. Lond.* V 1695; *P. Mich.* XIII 667; *P. Vatic. Aphrod.* 1.

[41] *Entagia*: e.g. *P. Cair. Masp.* I 67033–51 for Aphroditō.

money-tax refused to deliver it as it was seven carats too light). This of course did not prevent corruption, oppression, violence: the *megaloprepes-tatos* Theodosios, who kept Aphroditō's taxes for his own personal use (the village appealed to the emperor), the Antaiopolis officials who forced an inhabitant of the village of Poukhis to pay someone else's taxes (he appealed to the duke of the Thebaid), and so on. But it was oppression in a recognized institutional framework, and was, as far as can be seen, relatively stable: the system certainly long outlasted the Arab conquest, as we shall see (pp. 130–44). Egypt was probably not atypical in any of this except for the survival of its documentation (and, maybe, except for the easier availability of papyrus as a writing medium).[42] This is the sort of way that the Roman empire operated everywhere: as a corrupt, violent, but also stable system, and one whose social relations were largely structured by the taxpaying process.

The late Roman empire was territorially unified by its tax system, simply because so many goods were moved from place to place by the state, to supply the three main expenses of Roman government: the army, the capital cities of Rome and Constantinople (which were supplied by the state for symbolic purposes), and the civil administration. There has been much argument between historians about this, with some stressing the overwhelming dominance of fiscal mechanisms in the movement of all goods around the empire, others preferring to privilege commercial activity (particularly for city supply), and with a whole spectrum of intermediate theories.[43] The dramatic increase in archaeological knowledge in the last thirty years has led to a revival of views that there was a good deal of commerce in the late empire, although this does not in itself weaken the stress on fiscal movement of goods: it is indeed common to argue that commerce was given much of its impetus precisely by the fiscal movement of goods, and I have so argued myself.[44] The issue will be discussed in greater detail in Chapter 11. Here, however, what needs to be set out is some of the detailed regional relationships that were created by the fiscal system, which is an issue that has not been fully explored, despite the amount of work that has been devoted to certain aspects of it, most notably the food supplies (*annona*) to Rome and Constantinople.

[42] See, respectively, *P. Cair. Masp.* I 67070, 67029 (cf. *PLRE* III, Theodosius 9), III 67279. For the system as corrupt but stable, e.g. Bagnall, *Egypt*, p. 321. For papyrus, see Lewis, *Papyrus*, esp. pp. 88–94; it was certainly available all over the empire (see e.g. Sidonius, *Ep*. IV.3.1), but it is harder to tell if it had the capillary availability elsewhere that it had in Egypt.

[43] Fiscal mechanisms dominant: Jones, *LRE*, pp. 695–705; Durliat, *De la ville antique*. Commercial mechanisms dominant: Sirks, *Food for Rome*, pp. 19–23, with idem, 'The size of the grain distributions'. Different forms of intermediate position: Lo Cascio, '*Canon frumentarius*' (more fiscal), the argument that seems most plausible to me; Vera, 'Fra Egitto ed Africa' (less fiscal).

[44] Panella, 'Merci e scambi'; Wickham, *Land and power*, pp. 90–6.

I want in this book to avoid too much of a reliance on numbers games, for all statistics in our period—outside Egypt, at any rate—are pretty hypothetical. Even those which have some basis in contemporary calculations, such as some of the elements of the Rome and Constantinople *annona*, can be read in many different ways: as Andreas Müller has recently shown, for example, the 'eight million' of wheat, mostly for Constantinople, that Justinian expected from Egypt in 538 might represent 54,500 tonnes, or 163,000, or 245,000, and is the main basis for population estimates for Constantinople in the same period that vary from under 200,000 to 1 million (even if 400,000–600,000 is the most commonly cited range). Rome's population is as disputed between 300,000 and 700,000 on the basis of figures for the pork *annona* of 419.[45] So is the size of the army, between some 400,000 and some 650,000 at the end of the fourth century; and, if historians tend to agree that the civil administration of the empire numbered rather less, some 30,000 people on Jones's reckoning, they only do so because they only include government bureaucrats of aristocratic status[46]—the guards, messengers, ox-drivers of the public post, palace servants, and the like had to be fed or paid as well (as also did their municipal counterparts), but there is no evidence that would let us estimate them. What we can conclude from these modern calculations is partly that there is no way of really knowing the figures (especially when we add in a presumption that many of those we have were inflated—but by how much?—for corrupt purposes). It can be seen, however, that the figures for recipients do tend to settle around the same order of magnitude (those for the civil administration would do if their plebeian elements were counted in), even when one bears in mind that the urban figures are for total population, whereas the army and civil figures are only for adult males.[47] Historians, ancient and modern, concur almost unanimously that the army was the principal expense of the empire: 'most of the public revenues (*dēmosiōn eisodōn*) are devoted to it', as an anonymous military theorist of Justinian's reign stated. My guesstimate would be, however, that it at most made up half the budget, roughly matched by the expense of feeding cities and the civil administration, around 400. Michael Hendy puts the proportions still lower on the basis of sixth-century evidence, which might imply a third for the army, a third for Constantinople, and a third for the administration. As usual, the figures are heterogeneous,

[45] Müller, 'Getreide für Konstantinopel'; for Rome, Barnish, 'Pigs, plebeians', pp. 160–4; Lo Cascio, '*Canon frumentarius*'; Durliat, *De la ville antique*, pp. 250–7.

[46] For the army, Jones, *LRE*, pp. 679–84 (higher); Lee, 'The army', pp. 219–20 (lower). For the civil service as a whole, Jones, *LRE*, pp. 1057, 1411–12; Heather, 'New men', pp. 18–21, implies around 20,000.

[47] Durliat, *De la ville antique*, pp. 321–485, also argues that other cities were fed by *annona*. This is certain for Alexandria (Justinian, *Edictum*, XIII.4.2, ed. with *NJ*, pp. 780–95) and probable for Antioch (linked to Alexandria in *NJ*, VII.8); it is much less certain for smaller cities. Perhaps one might suppose that the Rome–Constantinople budget could be increased by roughly another 50% if we included other urban centres.

but a third to a half of the revenues of the empire seems a fair guess for the cost of the army around 550.[48]

Tax was not only in foodstuffs (or, more rarely, in manufactured goods, such as clothing for the army), but also in gold. From the fourth century onwards, the element that was collected in money increased substantially, largely because earlier inflations had stabilized, and indeed many provinces paid only in gold according to our sources, in the fifth and sixth centuries. These sources are mostly legal texts; our Egyptian tax documentation shows that actually much wheat (and wine) was taken directly in the sixth century. But peasants there did pay some money, around a third of the total, as well. Jones, who sets out the basic evidence for this, remarks blandly that 'commutation to gold greatly simplified the collection and the distribution of the revenue, and must have reduced the wastage of perishable goods collected in excess of needs, and the unnecessary transport of heavy goods'.[49] And, indeed, taxes in money do increase flexibility, and help to iron out regional differences in what products can be supplied. Army and civil-service pay involved a substantial money element in all periods (even at moments of collapse, as the *Vita Severini*, a nearly contemporary source, tells us for Noricum on the upper Danube—now northern Austria—in the 470s, whose army was still sometimes paid in coin from Italy), although the city *annona* and campaign supplies were certainly provided in kind.[50]

All the same, it has to be said that a model which invokes gold as a major, regular, medium for tax-collection in this period makes no sense. Keith Hopkins wrote an influential article over two decades ago which argued that early imperial money taxes were a powerful motor for empire-wide exchange, for only a large, long-distance, commercial network could possibly allow the coin paid, say, to the Rhine troops to get back to a relatively army-less province like Spain, whence it had been exacted, and whence it would be exacted again. His argument has been criticized, largely because it did not accurately predict the distribution of coinage on the ground, but it is hard to fault the logic behind it.[51] The higher levels of fifth- and sixth-century money taxation would indeed require even higher levels of commercial activity. For how else could the peasants of the inland areas of the provinces, the Thebaid, or the plateaux of central Numidia, or Spain again, get all that metal, year after year, to pay their taxes? The problem about this is twofold. First, even the most optimistic proponents of late

[48] *Peri stratēgias*, c. 2; Hendy, *Studies*, p. 171.

[49] In general, Jones, *LRE*, pp. 460–1 (p. 461 for the quote); Barnish, 'Government and administration', pp. 194–8; Banaji, *Agrarian change*, pp. 39–88. Detailed reservations in Cérati, *Caractère annonaire*, pp. 153–83; Carrié, 'L'economia e le finanze', pp. 760–6; idem, 'Observations sur la fiscalité', pp. 131–8.

[50] *Vita Severini*, c. 20; but the presuppositions of this story are not backed up by coin-finds in fifth-century Noricum, which are few: Ladstätter, *Die materielle Kultur*, pp. 82–3.

[51] Hopkins, 'Taxes and trade'; criticized by Duncan-Jones, *Structure and scale*, pp. 30–48; Howgego, 'Coin circulation'.

Roman commerce (which certainly did not include Jones, despite the remarks just cited) do not offer a picture of the empire as commercialized as that, with merchants swarming around buying primary products for money and taking them out of the region. Indeed, most commerce would, as we shall see, have been local, uniting city and country, and this would not have helped the tax cycle, for cities could no more pluck gold out of the air than the country could. Second, gold was not, in most cases, what the state needed either. Africa and Egypt's wealth was in grain, not gold; cities and soldiers needed to eat, as well as to have money in their pockets.

The only way these processes can be explained is by invoking *coemptio* (Greek *synōnē*), the systematic buying of goods by the state, at state-determined prices, for the state's needs. There is certainly plenty of evidence for this. It is true that *coemptio* was often reckoned as an unsatisfactory procedure except in emergencies (by the emperor Anastasius, for example), but in the sixth century it was certainly frequent, as many narratives tell— such as an account in Agathias (writing in Constantinople in the 560s–570s) of a military scam, that involved soldiers demanding plough-animals, which peasants could not spare, and accepting bribes to go away, or the story that appears in two mid-sixth-century Constantinopolitan sources of the peasants of the remote central Anatolian plateau, whose only market was the public post, the state transport system, and who supposedly could not sell their produce, and thus pay their taxes, when the post was abolished in their area in 541.[52] One can go further, indeed: outside main commercial highways, that is to say the main sea-roads and a handful of major rivers, even though (as will be argued in Chapter 11) a far wider pattern of commerce can be postulated on the basis of archaeology than Jones ever assumed, sales of primary produce at a level necessary to pay money-taxes would have to have been almost always to the state. As a result, the state's adoption of money-taxation must above all have been an accounting device, which ensured that the state got its food relatively cheap (state prices were often low), as well as allowing for a certain flexibility in determining what products to buy, and also the accumulation of reserves, which certainly did have to be in money. Money-tax was only feasible as part of an autonomous commercial system in areas where the state's personnel were close enough to the producers whose food they consumed to buy it directly: in the Rhineland, say, major army centre as it was, and westward as far as Trier, maybe Metz, but probably not Reims or Paris; the 'free market' would not easily have reached as far as the latter two towns, and the state's forced sales would already have to have

---

[52] Hendy, *Studies*, pp. 295–6, 602–7; Haldon, 'Synônê', pp. 118–22; Banaji, *Agrarian change*, pp. 57–60, all give good accounts. For Anastasius, *CJ*, X.27.2 (but Justinian regulated the practice in *NJ*, CXXX). For Agathias, *Histories*, IV.22; cf. Prokopios, *Secret history*, XXIII.11–15, and a more neutral account in *Wars*, VII.1.9. For Anatolia, *Secret history*, XXX.5–11, and John Lydos, *On powers*, III.61. For *coemptio* in Ostrogothic Italy, see Ruggini, *Economia e società*, pp. 211–21, 232–8.

stepped in. On one level of analysis, forced sales were still sales; Jairus Banaji has stressed that state prices were at least related to market prices, and contributed to a generalized commercialization of the economy—as well as to the capillary presence and use of coinage in most regions, his major concern. But the macroeconomic point made in the previous paragraph still holds. Overall, whatever the detail of the mechanism of payment on the ground, the state's tax-collectors must have expected to leave any given region with food, far more often than with gold. This is shown, for example, by the highly complex fiscal accounts for olive oil from different places in Africa, dating to (perhaps) 373, which have been found on ostraka (potsherds with writing) in the Carthage harbour area.[53] The state had mouths to feed.

A more important question for us, however, is where these mouths to feed actually lived, and where they were fed from. This is not at all straightforward, and involves hypotheses that are of a different order from the issue of, say, whether *curiales* were more oppressors or oppressed. It is relatively easy to provide a list of major suppliers of agrarian surplus: Africa and Sicily in the West, and Egypt in the East, all great wheat-producing regions, and in the case of Africa olive oil as well. Smaller exporter sub-regions included Sardinia for grain, the Palestinian coast and parts of the Aegean for wine, and the Antioch area (north-western Syria, Cyprus, and Cilicia) for olive oil. There is ample evidence for the importance of these areas, both in our written documentation and in archaeology. There is further evidence for the grain regions, and for African olive oil, that much of their surplus was exported as a result of fiscal exactions: mostly because we have evidence for the state *annona* to Rome and Constantinople. Rome got its grain from Africa, secondarily from Sicily; Sicilian grain presumably became dominant after the Vandals took the main grain-producing province of Africa, Proconsularis (together with Byzacena, which produced more olives), in 439, and Sardinia and also Puglia in southern Italy were other sources. (Rome's pork came from southern Italy throughout; where its wine came from is less clear, and it was probably not part of the *annona*, but Calabria and the Aegean supplied much of it: below, p. 708.) Constantinople's wheat came from Egypt, without any doubt; and, given the evidence we have for coastal Palestinian wine specialization and coastal Syrian/Cilician oil specialization, we probably know some of the prime sources of these elements in the feeding of the capital, though the Aegean supplied it substantially too, and African oil came to Constantinople as well, both before 439 and after the Vandal century ended in 534—by 600, in fact, even some grain also came to Constantinople from Africa.[54]

[53] Banaji, *Agrarian change*, pp. 58–9; for Carthage, Peña, 'The mobilisation'.
[54] Durliat, *De la ville antique*, collects all the literary references. (Rome got Egyptian grain only very rarely; a late example is *Liber Pontificalis*, LXIV.1 for the 570s.) In these lists, wine was not necessarily part of the *annona*; Palestinian wine, for example, may have reached Constantinople commercially.

So far so good; and the second item in state expense, the civil service, is not a logistical problem whatever its size, for it was evenly distributed across the empire, including areas remote from water transport, such as the Spanish Meseta and the Anatolian plateau, and could always be supplied locally—in this case, indeed, even largely salaried in money. The difficulty comes with the army, for the sources of its supply are much less systematically presented in our documentation. Essentially, we are forced to rely on anecdote, and on rural ceramic patterns, which are often less clear than they are for cities. The bulk of the army was still in the late empire located on or near frontiers, above all the northern and eastern frontiers of the empire; in any given area it would have been mostly too large for local supplies to be sufficient, except on the southern frontier, where the agrarian surpluses of Africa and Egypt could easily cope.[55]

The Rhine army seems most plausibly to have been supplied from Gaul, and perhaps also Britain. There is anecdotal evidence that Arles was an important entrepôt for goods travelling up the Rhône and destined for the Rhine, which would hint at some Mediterranean support for the army there; all the same, the most systematic publication of a Rhine fort, for Kaiseraugst near Basel, shows that the scale of Mediterranean amphora imports there, although substantial in the early empire, dropped off greatly in the late empire, and Mediterranean supplies here would have to be considered relatively marginal after 300 or so (they were restricted to olive oil, not wine; olive oil, of course, unlike wine, cannot be produced on the Rhine). The oil here came from southern Spain more than North Africa, a pattern also found at Trier, and it could thus be proposed, fairly tentatively, that Spanish oil was still directed to the Rhine army after African oil became dominant in Rome, in the third century; but quantities by now seem to have been small. For grain Ammianus indicates for the fourth century that it was normal to take grain even from Aquitaine—and for that matter Britain—for army needs. Northern and central/eastern Gaul seem to have been the privileged army suppliers, all the same, with south-western Gaul and Britain added in times of war (though war was, admittedly, fairly common).[56] The fiscal circuit in Gaul and Britain, although itself complex, was the only major Roman network that was essentially separate from the Mediterranean world.

The Danube army was more of a problem, for the lands the river runs through are, even though fertile enough in the immediate river valleys,

---

[55] See in general Whittaker, *Frontiers*, pp. 98–131, which pays due attention to supply.

[56] For Arles, *Expositio*, c. 58; Ausonius, *Ordo urbium nobilium*, X (in *Works*, I, p. 276). For Kaiseraugst and Trier, Martin-Kilcher, *Die römischen Amphoren*, pp. 186–93, 469–71, 554–77, with wider generalizations in Baudoux, *Les amphores*, pp. 157–9, who shows that Spanish oil stopped altogether by 350 around Metz and in Alsace (here, though, African oil is documented on a small scale for longer). For Ammianus, *Res gestae*, XVII.8.1, XVIII.2.3. I am grateful to Simon Esmonde-Cleary for advice on this section.

mostly backed by mountain and forest. The upper Danube, down to Pannonia (roughly modern Hungary), was largely supplied from the Po plain in northern Italy.[57] The lower Danube quite plausibly got much of its supplies from the Aegean, as the distribution of Aegean amphorae (LRA 2 in particular) is beginning to show; this is also the best explanation for the fact that Justinian created an institutional link, the *quaestura exercitus*, between the provinces of Moesia II and Scythia (the Bulgarian Danube region) and the Aegean islands, Cyprus, and Caria (in south-west Turkey), skipping over Constantinople supply routes. These patterns clearly indicate extra-regional support for the Danube army, above all from north-eastern Mediterranean provinces.[58]

The eastern frontier was the hardest of all, for the army here had to face the Persian military machine, which was, apart from a long fifth-century parenthesis, a permanent danger; but much of the frontier lay across high mountain and desert, with only the middle Euphrates sector of any real fertility—although the high mountain area to the north had far fewer troops than the Euphrates valley did. At least one must assume that very little of the grain-tax from Syria and Palestine had to leave that region; it is also likely that Egypt partly fed the southern sections of the eastern frontier. This latter statement is remarkably hard to prove, for Egyptian evidence stresses Constantinople above all; but at least the *Expositio totius mundi*, a mid-fourth-century Latin collection of clichés about the economic activities of different provinces, states that Egypt provided food for the 'Persian war'. It is, unfortunately, hard to see how future archaeology will help to fill out this picture, for our best evidence for food distribution, amphorae, are not a direct guide to grain export, especially not into wine- and oil-producing regions like Palestine and Syria.[59]

These characterizations are fairly tentative, for, surprisingly, not much work has been done on the supply aspect of late Roman military logistics. But they do allow us to fill out our picture of the geography of the city *annona*. An extremely rough picture of the global patterns of where the foodstuffs taken in tax in say, 400, went can be found in Map 2. Overall, the major exporter regions and sub-regions were Africa and Sicily (above all to Rome) and Egypt (to Constantinople, and to an extent to the eastern frontier), with lesser export from northern Italy (to the Danube), the Aegean

---

[57] For the supply of Mediterranean goods from Italy to Noricum (roughly modern Austria), see Ladstätter, *Die materielle Kultur*, pp. 110–17, 164–9; this doubtless began as a state-backed exchange, but it reached private buyers (including churches), and lasted into the late sixth century, well after the end of political unity between Noricum and Italy. See Ruggini, *Economia e società*, pp. 112–15 for Italy–Pannonia commercial links (she is perhaps overoptimistic when she says on pp. 114–15 that Pannonia regularly exported grain in this period).

[58] Jones, *LRE*, pp. 482–3 for the *quaestura exercitus*; Karagiorgou, 'LR2', for the amphorae; see below, p. 781.

[59] *Expositio*, c. 36; cf. Isaac, *The limits of empire*, pp. 290–1, although he barely discusses the issue. I am grateful to Michael Whitby for advice on this matter.

(to Constantinople and the Danube), and perhaps Britain (to the Rhine—though Britain had a frontier army too). Importer sub-regions were southern Italy (because of Rome), the Marmara sub-region, and of course the frontiers. There were also several regions that were relatively self-sufficient: Gaul, Syria, and Palestine, which essentially provided for the frontiers in their areas; here, all the same, one would postulate an internal fiscal drag of goods towards the frontiers themselves, running south-west to north-east in Gaul, west to east in Syria and Palestine, routes of several hundred kilometres in some cases, with the Rhineland certainly counting as an importer sub-region. The only two regions that do not clearly have a role in this network of relationships are Spain and Anatolia, both dominated by inland plateaux of difficult access. The Anatolian economy was recognized as a problem at the time, because it was both poor and had few outlets—hence the stress on the public post as a local source for cash, as already mentioned. Spain, which gets relatively few references in the late empire, is the most mysterious; the ceramic evidence for the Meseta indicates an exchange system that, though active, scarcely had any links with the Mediterranean at all by the fourth century; Andalucía, the richest sub-region, is unfortunately ill-studied in our period, and where its oil and other goods went by now (apart from small quantities to the Rhine) is far from clear. Only the Mediterranean coast, a thin line of agricultural land backed by mountains, was clearly linked into the standard fiscal and commercial networks of the late empire (below, pp. 748–9). But the Spanish interior may have been the most isolated, detached, part of the whole Roman world-system in 400 or so, when our period starts.[60]

These patterns are very schematic, it must be stressed. The movement of goods was always more complicated than that, as the startlingly complex distributions of both amphorae and fine wares attest for the late Roman Mediterranean.[61] This is partly a sign that there was commercial activity alongside fiscal movement of goods; partly a sign that the state itself was capable of greater subtleties, making up shortfalls from one region with extra surpluses from another; partly a sign that grain, wine, and oil (not to speak of other goods) did not have identical trajectories. But, as a global picture, this seems the most plausible one currently available. And it is important as a picture, for two reasons. First, because I would indeed argue that the fiscal process was a major motor for the commercial movement of goods, and these global distribution patterns were the routes that commerce had to build on. Second, because, in the West in the fifth century and in the East in the seventh century, all the interregional elements in this fiscal system would abruptly end, as the Roman empire was divided up into successor states. *Ex hypothesi*, this division ought to have had very serious effects on regions that were more linked into the fiscal exchange system, like Africa, and less on those that were more self-sufficient, like Gaul. We will see that this is true in some cases, but, interestingly, not in others. Both of these points will be developed in Chapter 11.

2. The Romano-Germanic kingdoms

It should be clear from the foregoing that I would not argue that there were any inherent instabilities in the Roman state that would explain its collapse in the West in the fifth century. This is by now not a controversial position: the majority of scholars would argue that the period around 400 was one of institutional stability and also economic prosperity; the late empire was a period of violence, injustice, and brutal exploitation, but these were standard features of ancient (indeed, most) societies, and can, as noted earlier, easily coexist with stability. Such a position would thus put considerable stress on the 'barbarian' invasions as the major catalyst that resulted in the end of the western empire;[62] but recent work on the Germanic peoples, too, has stressed the degree to which they sought to fit, as far as possible, into Roman social and political patterns, as indeed aristocratic Romans themselves ardently desired—if one had to have a Germanic ruler, it was best if he were as Roman in style as possible, and fifth- and sixth-century literature contains several attempts by Roman authors to depict their Germanic kings in a highly Roman manner: Sidonius on Theoderic II of the Visigoths, Ennodius and Cassiodorus (and indeed Prokopios) on Theoderic of the Ostrogoths, Florentinus on Thrasamund of the Vandals, Venantius on Charibert and Chilperic of the Franks, and so on. This ability by the Romans to absorb Germanic leaders into their own conceptual framework is not lessened by the fact that other authors (or, often, as with Sidonius in other contexts, the same authors) depict invaders whom they are hostile to with all the standard rhetoric about savagery and barbarism that figures in every century of ancient discussions of the uncivilized Other.[63] Essentially, even if Germanic kings did not always completely imitate the Virgil-reading, *otium*-loving, senatorial aristocracy (a highly atypical stratum of Roman society,

---

[62] The word 'barbarian' is loose, and has negative connotations, but *barbarus* was the standard Latin term for non-Roman peoples in the fifth century. It is arguably anyway better than 'Germanic', which implicitly imposes a cultural homogeneity on peoples who felt no common identity at all (see e.g. Pohl, *Die Germanen*, pp. 1–7; Goffart, *Barbarians and Romans*, pp. 12–28).

[63] Respectively, Sidonius, *Ep.* I.2; Ennodius, *Panegyricus* (*Opera*, n. 263); Cassidorus, *Variae*, I.1, XI.1; Prokopios, *Wars*, V.1.26–30; *Anthologia latina*, n. 376, ed. Riese (cf. Chalon, 'Memorabile factum', pp. 214–24); Venantius, *Carmina*, VI.1–2, IX.1–3.

but the source of most of our literature), they greatly resembled most emperors, who since the third century had tended to have had military careers, to have little cultural capital (senators were snobbish about them too), and to have originated from the same frontier regions (notably the Balkans) as many Germanic leaders were from.[64]

This 'Romanist' view of the new Germanic leaders who partitioned the West in the fifth century can be taken in several directions. For historians principally interested in political and intellectual culture, it has allowed the development of continuitist readings of the early medieval polities that go up to the Carolingian period at least—and quite legitimately so on one level, for there are many elements of a cultural genealogy going back without a break to Roman times in (say) the Carolingian royal courts of the first half of the ninth century, not least their concept of the importance and responsibility of 'public' power.[65] Institutional continuities are more problematic. They are of course much easier to propose once one has made the first step, as in the preceding paragraph, and admitted the ability of the new Germanic leaders to fit into pre-existing Roman models of political culture, and of the Romans, not always but increasingly often, to accept them in those terms—especially as Roman aristocracies had less and less alternative, as the fifth century wore on, to doing so, as has been traced in some detail for our best-documented region, central and southern Gaul.[66] In principle, there might have been no problem in having a large number of sub-imperial states coexisting inside the boundaries of the former western empire, each with the same internal structure as its predecessor, thus maintaining the Roman world on a smaller scale, in just the same way as the ten or so post-'Abbāsid successor states did in the tenth century in the land-area of the caliphate. In 500 these would be the Franks, Burgundians, Ostrogoths, Visigoths, and Vandals (with rather greater doubt about the situation in more marginal areas, the upper Danube, Britain, Armorica, Galicia, the Basque Country, and Mauretania—though Romanist readings have been tried for some of these too);[67] in 600 they were the Franks, Lombards, Visigoths, and the reconquered Roman territories of Italy, Africa, and the Spanish coast. The problem comes in determining how institutional change actually did take place, if it was not during the tornado of fifth-century events: for, most certainly, by 800 (say), none of the political structures of the West any longer resembled those of the Roman world, with the exception of those of Sicily, still fully integrated into the eastern empire. Only one attempt has been made to argue that political structures had not changed at all by then, by the 'hyper-Romanist' school (as their opponents call them) in France, led by Jean

[64] So also Amory, *People and identity*, pp. 282–91, with different emphases.
[65] For the 'public' in the ninth century, which had different nuances to classical or modern usage, see Schlesinger, *Die Entstehung*, pp. 109–14 for some ideas.
[66] See most recently Mathisen, *Roman aristocrats*, pp. 119–31.
[67] For the Basques, Larrea, *La Navarre*, pp. 111–34.

Durliat and Elisabeth Magnou-Nortier. As I have argued elsewhere, their views can be challenged in every detail; nor have any of their basic arguments won acceptance, except for some partial use of them by historians in Germany and Austria.[68] If this position is excluded, however, the problem of institutional change remains to be explained, even if now in terms of 'transformation' (as in the international European Science Foundation project of 1993–8, the Transformation of the Roman World) rather than 'crisis' or 'decline': but sometimes, for sure, in terms of 'crisis' too.

It is not part of the remit of this book to explain the fall of the Roman empire in the West.[69] But the issue of the transformation/crisis in political structures, political institutions, and—above all—in the economic basis of the state in the Romano-Germanic kingdoms is a central problem here, for the Roman fiscal system was arguably the most effective way of extracting surplus from a large population yet known, and it did not survive in the long or even medium term. Several elements in the successor kingdoms could, however, be said to have acted to undermine the maintenance of a Roman political structure and fiscal system inside the geographical compass of each polity.

As already implied, one of these elements was not the cultural difference between the new ruling class in any given kingdom and the older Roman aristocracy. It could in principle be argued that, however easily Germanic royal families fitted into their new Roman-provincial environment, Germanic aristocracies might not necessarily do so with the same enthusiasm. But the degree to which the latter remained committed to ancestral values is considerably in doubt. How 'Germanic' each ethnic group was at all in its successor state has in fact been the object of considerable debate in recent years, as historians move from an essentialist view of ethnicity (once a Frank, always a Frank), through a recognition that people could often adopt new ethnic identities (as, again in Francia, the fact that by 750 everyone north of the Loire was a Frank, regardless of their ethnic origin: *Romani* were by then the inhabitants of Aquitaine), to the broader 'ethnogenesis' model of Reinhard Wenskus and above all Herwig Wolfram, in which ethnic identity is a 'situational construct', and can be easily changed as circumstances dictate.[70] Although, in the case of the Germanic tribes,

---

[68] Durliat, *Les finances publiques*, is the most substantial contribution to this position; Magnou-Nortier, 'La gestion publique', is perhaps the briskest synthesis. For criticisms, see e.g. Wickham, 'La chute de Rome'; Delmaire, 'Cités et fiscalité', pp. 66–70. For a more sympathetic reception with respect to the settlement period, see e.g. Wolfram and Schwarcz, *Anerkennung*; Wolfram, *History of the Goths*, pp. 222–5, 295–7; Werner, *La naissance*, pp. 462–4.

[69] Neat characterizations are Heather, 'The Huns', with idem, 'The western empire'.

[70] The bibliography here is very large. Significant monographs are Wenskus, *Stammesbildung*, and Wolfram, *History of the Goths* (and, for a non-Germanic people, Pohl, *Die Awaren*). For articles, see e.g. Wolfram and Pohl, *Typen der Ethnogenese*, I; Geary, 'Ethnic identity as a situational construct'; Pohl, *Le origini etniche*; Wolfram, 'Typen der Ethnogenese'.

identity became notably more stable once an army had taken control of a Roman province, its content could continue to shift: so, for example, 'being' a Visigoth by 650 or so had come to involve, not only being a free inhabitant of the territory ruled by the Visigothic kings, thus probably having some Roman ancestors in almost every case, but also following a legal system which was far closer to Roman law than it was to the law of other Germanic kingdoms. The ethnogenesis model is now widely accepted. There have been further versions of it, however, which refine it in different directions: Peter Heather would argue that each Germanic people had at its core a group with a stronger longer-term ethnic identity, for example (a position not actually so far from Wolfram's), whereas Patrick Amory has argued that Germanic identity hardly existed at all except as a variant of Roman identity—the Goths in Italy, for example, were nothing other than the Italian army, redefined in ethnic terms, with 'Goth' just being a new word for 'soldier'.[71]

I record all these views as historiographical developments, rather than going straight to the sources. This is partly because there is a bit of truth in most of them,[72] given the extremely wide range of local experiences in the post-Roman West. Amory's position, however stimulating and original, might be referred to as extremist, in that on one reading of it the 'barbarian' invasions could be said to have taken place without any population movements at all on more than a small scale, a position that is not difficult to reject (although it has been argued explicitly for, of all places, Anglo-Saxon England, as well as in Ignacio Olagüe's crazy but systematic work, *Les Arabes n'ont jamais envahi l'Espagne*, which is relevant here in as much as it at least confronts the problem of how to explain dramatic cultural and linguistic change without any population movement).[73] Even if one does not go this far, however, one must recognize that the success of ethnogenesis as a model has contributed to weakening any argument that held that the incoming Germanic ruling classes would ever have felt so alien to the Roman system that they could not enthusiastically take on, manage, or copy all the aspects of it that had survived in any given area. This I am sure is true; and it goes for aristocratic landowning as well, as we will see in the next chapter. Where the variability came was not in Germanic willingness to appropriate *romanitas*, but in how much *romanitas* there was to appropriate.

[71] Heather, e.g. in *Goths and Romans*, pp. 317–30 (his core group is larger than Wolfram's, who stressed royal families above all: *History of the Goths*, e.g. pp. 5–16); Amory, *People and identity*.

[72] Except the essentialist position. Oddly, although historians have abandoned this, archaeologists often remain attached to it, particularly in the German tradition of ethnic readings of grave-goods. A recent defence is Bierbrauer, 'Frühe langobardische Siedlung'. Critiques, largely in English, are many; recent detailed ones include Halsall, 'The origins of the *Reihengräberzivilisation*'; Curta, *The making of the Slavs*, pp. 6–35; Effros, *Merovingian mortuary archaeology*, pp. 100–10; Jentgens, *Die Alamannen* (a focused critique of the German tradition); Brather, 'Ethnische Identitäten', esp. pp. 158–72.

[73] For England, esp. Hodges, *Anglo-Saxon achievement*, pp. 25–32; Olagüe, *Les Arabes*, esp. pp. 191–284.

Three other elements in the successor kingdoms seem to me to be more important in understanding the way the west Roman political/fiscal system broke down. The first is indeed crisis: the degree of confusion and of war-induced disturbance that there was in any given region of the western empire, such that it would be hard for institutions to continue to function properly. The second is what the successor-states needed to spend money on: for if the army was landed, the civil administration (based, except for Ostrogothic Italy, on provincial not central Roman government) much reduced, and the food supply for Rome not in the picture outside Italy either, then the need to collect taxes would have been hugely lessened. The third, closely related, is that the social status of the army changed in the post-Roman period, for the ethnically defined armies of the Romano-Germanic kingdoms were not just replacements for their Roman predecessors; they were a new aristocracy, with a more extensive socio-political role and much wider ambitions. These parameters will be borne in mind as we look at, in turn, four of these kingdoms: Vandal Africa, Visigothic Spain, Frankish Gaul, and Lombard Italy.

Before we look at those examples, however, we need to consider one more general issue: the debate about Walter Goffart's theories of 'barbarian' settlement. Goffart in 1981 proposed, essentially, that the armies that were settled in the different regions of the West (at least, south of the Loire) were not given shares in land, the one-third or two-thirds of Roman estates that was the traditional picture of the *hospitalitas* settlements of the Germanic peoples, but rather shares in the tax system, which still continued to operate. That is to say, the 'barbarian' armies remained salaried, though with tax shares associated with specific areas of land, of which each army-man was a *hospes*, a guest, and from where he collected the tax directly. Such direct collection could soon turn into de facto landowning, and indeed did—for Goffart also holds that many of the key elements in the ninth- and tenth-century power of landowners over their tenants had origins in the detail of late Roman taxation; in the end, that is to say, armies became landed. But the process was much slower and more complex than previous historians had ever thought, and the fifth century did not have in itself to be a period of institutional crisis, only of decentralization—both at the level of the division of the empire into kingdoms and at the level of the tax-gathering mechanism itself, which was taken out of the hands of *curiales* and transferred directly to its individual recipients. This Goffart justified on the basis of rereadings of texts for Ostrogothic Italy and the Visigothic and Burgundian kingdoms in Gaul.[74]

Goffart's theory is not impossible. States can indeed hand out individual tax shares to soldiers. The post-'Abbāsid states did it with the generalization

---

[74] Goffart, *Barbarians and Romans*; for the ninth–tenth century, idem, *Rome's fall*, pp. 190–211.

of *iqṭāʿ* cessions, which were just such tax shares, and the practice continued into the modern period in the Islamic world (the best-known example is the *timar* system of the Ottomans); it was also adopted, possibly in imitation, by the middle Byzantine state, where it was called *pronoia*. Goffart, as already noted, supposed that such localized tax-collection would eventually turn in practice into ownership, and this would indeed have happened if the state could not police the tax process, as presumably would have occurred in the early medieval West, for all references to taxation stop there after 700 or so at the latest—although such a development was not inevitable: tax shares turned into landowning in eighteenth- and nineteenth-century Iran, for example, but never fully in the Ottoman world.[75] The problem is that no single text clearly supports Goffart's theory. His critics have been able to show that even his best instances are at the least ambiguous. One such is *Variae* II.17 on the granting of a *sors* (a tax share according to Goffart, a portion of an estate according to the older theory) to the Gothic priest Butila in Italy in c.510, which resulted directly in the lessening of the tax burden on the relevant city, Trento. Goffart interprets it as a demonstration that Trento's tax went down because Butila would now collect some of it directly. Wolf Liebeschuetz, however, notes that it could equally mean that Butila's estate-portion was tax-exempt; global taxation would still go down.[76] And it is very striking how often the terminology of the cession of land to the 'barbarians' actually does appear in contemporary sources, whereas the use of traditional terminologies for taxes do not; there are laws of the late fifth-century Visigothic king Euric envisaging boundary disputes between Goths and Romans, which are hard to explain unless a land division is postulated.[77] A land settlement of some kind still seems the one that, on empirical grounds, is best supported by the *sources* in every region.

Goffart's view has nonetheless attracted not insignificant support.[78] Essentially, this is because he offers a big picture: Germanic groups could settle inside a still-functioning Roman fiscal system, as with the Visigoths in 418, the Burgundians in 443, the Ostrogoths in 493, without recorded difficulty, because all that had to change were taxation details; the fiddly aspects of one-third and two-third cessions of estates can be avoided at the

[75] For *iqṭāʿ*, see Cahen, 'L'évolution de l'iqtaʿ'; cf. Wickham, *Land and power*, pp. 57–66. The parallel between Goffart's tax shares and the *iqṭāʿ* was recognized by Hendy, 'From public to private', p. 43 n. Tax to landowning in the West: Goffart, *Barbarians and Romans*, pp. 206–30.

[76] Goffart, *Barbarians and Romans*, pp. 77–9; *contra*, Liebeschuetz, 'Cities, taxes', pp. 142–3. Other critics include Cesa, 'Hospitalitas'; Barnish, 'Taxation, land'; Wood, 'Ethnicity', pp. 65–9.

[77] Notably *Chronica gallica ad annum 452*, s.a. 442; Cassiodorus, *Variae*, II.16; Ennodius, *Ep.* IX.23 (*Opera*, n. 447); *Passio S. Vincentii*, c. 6; *Vita Lupicini*, c. 94; *Leges Burgundionum*, cc. 31, 54, 55, 84; *Codex Euricianus*, cc. 276–7. These sources are discussed by Goffart. I would accept the unreliability of Prokopios, *Wars*, V.1.8, 28, with Goffart (*Barbarians and Romans*, pp. 60–70), against several scholars.

[78] Hendy, 'From public to private', pp. 42–3, is an important instance.

same time. Conversely, however, it can be said that the big picture is not altogether with him in other respects: too many Germanic settlements were distinctly less ordered than this (the Vandals, the Franks, the Lombards); there is no particular reason why the same protocols should be used for each settlement anyway, given the ad hoc remedies of most fifth-century political problem-solving; and, perhaps above all, if this problem-solving was aimed at changing as little as possible, then why abolish centuries of rules of army-supply and entrust tax-raising to individual soldiers—but, if sharp change was indeed necessary, then why not give those soldiers land, as so many sources imply? Actually, I would suppose rather more ad hoc procedures than traditional theories of *hospitalitas* assumed. We know that Visigothic soldiers were billeted, along Roman lines, as *hospites*, in the initial period of their invasion of southern Gaul in the early 410s; it is not unlikely that such billeting became routinized and more firmly associated with land after 418, when the Goths made peace with Rome, but not necessarily in any consistent way. The percentage calculations could come later, when tax rates were refigured to take account of that land-settlement. It is quite possible that Goths, both in Gaul and in Italy, got payments out of the land tax as well, in hybrid patterns that had Roman analogues already, and some of Goffart's Italian material might well indicate it (the evidence is not good enough to be sure for Gaul).[79] But any model that supposes a smooth, merely administrative, changeover does violence to the evidence we have for the confusion of the fifth century.

On the other hand, it does, finally, have to be stressed that fifth-century evidence by no means supports the view that the tax system was so soon in ruins. In the 440s Salvian's anti-fiscal rhetoric is so sharp-edged (above, p. 62) that it can scarcely be supposed that it was as yet visibly in decay. More important still, perhaps, are the letters of Sidonius, dating from the 460s–470s, the final moment of the ending of Roman authority in Gaul, which do not at any stage imply a breakdown of the fiscal system: tax terminology, even if not all-pervasive, and never stressed rhetorically, is at least regular in his writings.[80] The collapse of taxation was not yet an issue; we shall see that some tax still survived in Gaul a century later and more (pp. 105–15). And in Ostrogothic Italy it is systematically documented: the Ostrogothic state, which still included Rome and the western imperial central government at Ravenna, was for sure the successor state that most fully continued the complete array of Roman tax procedures.[81] The break-

---

[79] Goffart, *Barbarians and Romans*, pp. 162–75, for billeting; for early Visigothic billeting, the clearest is Paulinus of Pella, *Eucharisticos*, ll. 285–90. Wood, 'Ethnicity', pp. 65–9, on the Burgundians, also sees billeting as the core of the land settlement. For Italy, see n. 81.

[80] Sidonius, *Epp.*, II.1.2–3, V.7.3, V.19.2, VII.12.3, VIII.8.3.

[81] For commentary, Cassiodorus, *Variae*, e.g. I.14, II.17, IV.14, V.26–7, VI.24, VII.45, VIII.26; Goffart, *Barbarians and Romans*, pp. 60–102; Barnish, 'Taxation, land', the best account; Thibault, 'L'impôt direct', pp. 699–728.

down of the fiscal system of the Roman empire clearly postdated the foundation of the 'barbarian' kingdoms. But what, by now, was it actually used for? This cannot be easily answered with fifth-century material. To get any sense of it at all, we will have to take a longer-term perspective, and look at the issue regionally.

The Vandals invaded North Africa from Spain in 429; they were already in Numidia in 430, besieging Hippo (Annaba) and its dying bishop, Augustine; in 435 they were granted two provinces in roughly modern eastern Algeria by treaty, in return for acting as soldiers for the Romans. In 439 they broke the treaty and took Carthage, and the core of African agrarian prosperity, the provinces of Proconsularis and Byzacena, respectively modern northern and southern Tunisia. The Vandal attack is often seen as an almost chance disaster: no one took them seriously as a danger, but they sneaked into Africa by the back way. This might be true for 429, but it is certainly untrue for 435–9, when the Vandals were a very visible threat but no one did anything about them. They did after 439; there were constant Roman plans to retake Africa for the whole of the next century, though all came to nothing until Belisarios' conquest in 534. These plans were anyway too late. Geiseric's conquest of Carthage in 439 is arguably the turning-point in the 'fall' of the western empire.[82]

This was chiefly for infrastructural reasons. Africa lay at the heart of the grain and oil *annona* for Rome, and, without that permanent supply of food, the western capital (as Rome remained at least in symbolic terms) could scarcely function. Geiseric turned the screw further when he took Sardinia in the 460s and, from as early as 440 right up to 476, systematically attacked the Sicilian coast, for these islands were the major alternative grain suppliers in the western Mediterranean. 'L'empire du blé', as Christian Courtois called it, was Geiseric's evident aim, as the basis for his desire to determine Roman politics in the West: the maritime element to the Vandal kingdom was, indeed, itself made possible by the grain fleet that had presumably lain in Carthage harbour in 439.[83] The Vandals had their control of the African grain lands confirmed by treaty in 442, which according to Prokopios involved Geiseric giving annual tribute (*dasmos*) to the western empire, a treaty which held until 455. Boudewijn Sirks has interpreted this as the temporary continuance of the *annona*; even if Prokopios' claim was an accurate one, this reading of it can be regarded as highly unlikely, given the weight of that taxation and the weakness of Roman bargaining power in

---

[82] For a narrative, Courtois, *Les Vandales*, is still basic, updated by Gil Egea, *África*. Aetius' obsession with Gaul and lack of interest in Africa must be the main reason why the Romans paid no attention to the Vandal threat in 435–9: so e.g. Moss, 'Aetius'.

[83] Courtois, *Les Vandales*, pp. 187–90, 205–14 (p. 213 for quote). Courtois, ibid., pp. 192–3, thinks the Vandals conquered Sicily in 468, but this control is minimized by historians of Sicily; see e.g. Ruggini, 'La Sicilia', pp. 497, 521–2.

442. And it is in the period from 440 onwards that we first begin to get signs that the western empire was seriously short of resources, in the legislation of Valentinian III, much of which is about tax shortfalls.[84] Rome, in particular, must have faced a swift crisis; and if, as is far from impossible, Geiseric did indeed continue to supply the city, but as a commercial, not a fiscal, transaction (for Vandal commerce, see pp. 711–12), that is, in return for money, then the effect on the tax resources of the West would have been similar.

Thanks to the breaking of the Carthage–Rome fiscal axis, Italy was the chief sufferer from Geiseric's conquests: all the more so because one element in them was a substantial expropriation of aristocratic land, and the great absentee landowners who were such a substantial feature of the African economy were also based for the most part in Rome. Africa itself, however, was conquered sufficiently quickly that, notwithstanding highly coloured reports of Vandal atrocity ('Les Vandales n'étaient pas, à coup sûr, de petits saints', Courtois dryly conceded), it is hard to see there being much institutional discontinuity there when Geiseric took over. The Vandals, after 439 (or 442), stably controlled the richest region in the West, including the standard mechanisms of provincial-level tax-raising. For the first time since the Roman conquest, that taxation stayed in Carthage, and could enrich a local ruling class; this localization of African wealth was further emphasized by the end of absentee landowning.[85]

The internal structure of the Vandal state is, it must be said at once, exceptionally ill-documented. Africa is nonetheless useful to discuss, as a good example of how a successor state *could* be organized if it was established in a period when Roman institutions were still fully functioning, with a minimum of disruption. The state was, for a start, highly Romanized, and the Vandal kings behaved like Roman rulers in many ways. This is most notable in their religious policies, even though it is precisely these that have gained them a poor press in the eyes of later generations, for, as did any emperor, they regarded their own variant of Christianity, Arianism, as the only legitimate one, and, at least intermittently (notably in 484, and in the 510s), persecuted those whom they saw as heretics, who were, however, the entire Roman population of Africa, whether Catholic, Donatist, or Manichee. Their persecution was exactly analogous to that of any Catholic emperor, nonetheless. Indeed, it was copied from Roman models: Huneric's Edict of 484 against Catholicism is a direct, explicit, copy of a law of Honorius of 412 against Donatism in Africa, down to the table of fines,

---

[84] Prokopios, *Wars*, III.4.13; Sirks, *Food for Rome*, pp. 162–4. For tax shortfalls, *Nov. Val.*, I.3, IV, VI.3, X, XV; *Nov. Maj.*, II.

[85] Courtois, *Les Vandales*, p. 168 for quote. Accounts of Vandal expropriations (and atrocities) are numerous: Possidius, *Vita Augustini*, c. 28; *Nov. Val.*, XXXIV.3; Victor of Vita, *Historia persecutionis*, I. 8–47; Ferrandus, *Vita Fulgentii*, c. 1; Prokopios, *Wars*, III.5.8–17.

different for each member of the Roman social hierarchy.[86] Imperial models are indeed the only visible sources for nearly every aspect of the Vandal state. The administration was certainly hardly different, and was run by a complex network of (mostly ethnic Roman) officials, who are prominent in our poor evidence. These officials may have adopted a Vandal dress code, but in other respects were unchanged except in detail (the *proconsul*, for example, cannot have had the same role as governor of Africa as he had had before 439—that role was now taken by the king—and may have been, as Paul Barnwell has proposed, more similar to the *praefectus urbis* of Rome). They were paid in money and in kind, as before 439. They included provincial officials, such as the overseer of the public post whom Belisarios met in Sullecthum (Salakta) in 533, and such as the city-based tax official, *procurator*, that Fulgentius, a future saint, briefly was around 490.[87] In imperial legislation, *procuratores* would have been *curiales*, but this is the only argument for the latter keeping tax responsibilities under the Vandals, and they are nowhere referred to in this role after the Byzantine conquest, indicating that their role had ceased by then. The Vandal century is the most likely period for the end of city-based taxation, and indeed city political autonomy, as the decline of forum areas in African cities in the same period (below, pp. 636–8) further indicates. It is at least possible that taxation was simply centralized by the Vandals, in the same sort of way as it was for the east Romans (above, p. 69), and in the same period, the years around 500.[88]

Taxation evidently continued in the Vandal period, anyway; there are several references to it, as well as, as usual, to its weight and oppression. It paid for the civil administration; it also made the Vandal kings immensely rich, as is shown by praise poems about their buildings in the Carthage area,

---

[86] The best account of these persecutions remains Courtois, *Les Vandales*, pp. 289–310. For Huneric's Edict, see Victor of Vita, *Historia persecutionis*, III.3–14, citing *CTh*, XVI.5.52 (cf. also 54). The whole of the 484 persecution was in fact posed as an almost playful copy of the 411–12 Donatist persecution, as Victor knew well (*Historia persecutionis*, II.40, III.2). Huneric's table of fines in ibid., III.10, graduated by social category, since it is taken directly from Honorius' law of 411, cannot be used as a guide to the social groups of the 480s, *contra* Overbeck, *Untersuchungen*, pp. 67–8; Gil, *África*, pp. 296–7; and others.

[87] For the administration, see Courtois, *Les Vandales*, pp. 248–60; Gil, *África*, pp. 276–330; Barnwell, *Emperor, prefects*, pp. 114–24. Victor of Vita, *Historia persecutionis*, I.48–50, II.8 (dress code), 10 (pay), III.27, 62, gives several important anecdotal examples of Roman administrators (all the more important because he greatly opposed such collaboration). The dress code is doubted by von Rummer, 'Habitus Vandalorum?' Public post: Victor of Vita, *Historia persecutionis*, II.38; Prokopios, *Wars*, III.16.12. *Procurator*: Ferrandus, *Vita Fulgentii*, c. 1 (see Modéran, 'La chronologie', pp. 176ff.). Clover, 'Emperor worship', even argues that the Vandals recognized the sovereignty of the emperor; this seems improbable.

[88] *Procuratores* as *curiales*: *CTh*, VII.4.32. For the curial title of *flamen perpetuus* under the Vandals, see e.g. Duval and Prévot, *Haïdra*, I, nn. 401, 413, for inscriptions, and *Tablettes Albertini*, nn. 3–24, for the 490s; see further Chastagnol and Duval, 'Les survivances'; Modéran, 'La chronologie', pp. 174–81; Gil, *África*, pp. 291–7. The survival of these titles does not, however, prove the survival of the *curia* as a tax-raising body. *Curiae* are not documented in Africa after 534, either; Durliat, 'Les finances municipales', pp. 378–9, wants to prove the opposite, but his only clear examples are from Sardinia.

Prokopios' admiring comments on a royal palace on the coast south of Carthage, and, not least, the latter's dramatic account of the huge size of the treasury of King Gelimer, captured to the west of the capital by the Roman conquerors in 534, which as Prokopios notes, could be so huge because African revenue had not had to leave the country for ninety-five years.[89] It is much less clear, however, that this taxation was spent on the army. African taxation never had been, to any great extent, for the army was historically small (the Berbers on and beyond the frontier had not been considered a major danger by the Romans, although in fact they were becoming so in the Vandal period, and continued to be a serious threat under both the Byzantines and the Arabs). The Vandal army, although not one of the major Germanic armies, was bigger than that; but the evidence is that it was settled on the land, on *sortes* (the standard fifth-century term for land-shares), in particular in Proconsularis—the royal family kept control of Byzacena. The Vandals probably settled on imperial land, which was very extensive in Africa, as well as (as Prokopios claims) on land confiscated from the Roman aristocracy; after the reconquest, Justinian reconfiscated their land back to the fisc. This land was, as was normal in Germanic land-settlements, exempt from taxation, for the Vandals were performing military duties in exchange for it.[90]

It is in one sense more surprising than I am making it seem that Geiseric settled the Vandals on the land. In Africa, the Roman fiscal system was intact; and Roman armies had always been principally salaried. If ever there was a case for proposing that a Germanic king divided up tax-assessments, it might be here. Furthermore, the evidence for the Vandal land-settlement is not that good; it amounts to only three pieces of evidence, and the most explicit, Prokopios' description of Geiseric's expropriations, was written down a century later. Prokopios, furthermore, tends to move into romantic and sometimes fanciful storytelling whenever he is not dealing with contemporary events, and, although he uses the word *klēros*, the correct Greek translation of *sors*, for the settlement, *klēros* meant 'estate' more often in Greek than *sors* did in Latin: Prokopios could simply have misunderstood a technical term in tax-assessment, and, since the Vandals

---

[89] Victor of Vita, *Historia persecutionis*, I.22, II.2; Ferrandus, *Vita Fulgentii*, cc. 1–2; Prokopios, *Wars*, III.5.15, 10.25–8, 17.8–10, IV.3.25–7 (for Gelimer's treasure, which was not all the Vandal treasury—see IV.4.33–41). Chalon, '*Memorabile factum*', collects the building poems in the *Anthologia latina*.

[90] Prokopios, *Wars*, III.5.11–15 for the *klēroi Bandilōn* after 439; Victor of Vita, *Historia persecutionis*, I.12–13 (less explicit, although he is clear about the geographical division of Vandal occuption); ibid., II.39, III.4, for the third source, Huneric's Edicts of 483–4, the only ones to use the word *sors*. Prokopios, *Wars*, IV.14.8–10, on Justinian's confiscations, shows that the Vandals had land by 534; ibid., III.5.14, for tax immunities. See Courtois, *Les Vandales*, pp. 275–89, for general discussion, and pp. 218–20n. for other evidence for the Vandals in Proconsularis; Modéran, 'L'établissement territorial', updates and develops the argument. For imperial land before 439 (leased out for the most part), see Vera, 'Enfiteusi, colonato'.

were landowners in 534, assumed that they always had been.[91] But the Vandals did not come from nowhere in 429. They had had two decades-worth of experience of occupying a Roman province, north-west and then southern Spain, where they presumably gained a taste for landed wealth, the major source of status in the Roman empire, as in any agrarian civilization; nor had they ever been a Roman army, even nominally (unlike the Visigoths in 418). All Germanic soldiers whose careers we can track wanted land, or more land, as soon as they could get it: the *Variae* in Ostrogothic Italy are full of examples of illegal land-claims by them, and there are parallel Gallic narratives.[92] It is far from clear that a newly conquering army, with no need to negotiate, would have wanted simply to receive salaries. The Vandals are referred to as landed in 484, and again in 534, so, even if they were only handed out tax-assessments in 439, they at least became landowners soon. They wanted to be aristocrats, not simply soldiers, and as many of them as possible became so. They were not simply an army, that is to say, but a militarized ruling class.[93] This is the essential difference between Roman armies and the Germanic armies that replaced them: Roman armies did not constitute an elite, except in the case of their leaders, but Germanic armies for the most part did. And land came logically with this. Geiseric had a free hand in 439, but it is highly unlikely that he would have tried to resist such a logic. Compare the caliph 'Umar I, who did resist it in the aftermath of the early Arab conquests, and enacted in 640/2 that his armies must remain in barracks, or barrack towns, receiving pay ('*aṭā*'), and not acquiring land: the decision was hard, had huge implications, and is endlessly cited in our sources.[94] The absence of similar choices in descriptions of Germanic conquest is to me significant, even in the case of sources as sketchy as those for Africa in the 440s.

But in this case Africa becomes paradoxical: it contained a highly effective tax system, but the principal expenses of the state, the *annona* for Rome and the army, were no longer paid out of it. Even if we move into the realms of hypothesis, and propose supplementary payments to Vandal soldiers (when they were on campaign they must have got them, and also when they were garrisoning *castra*, which they certainly did—Fulgentius, in one of his anti-Arian perorations, refers to them), we still are dealing with a notably unbalanced budget. Not only must the royal family have become amazingly

---

[91] Durliat, 'Le salaire', pp. 40–5, develops an argument analogous (not identical) to this, opposed sharply by Modéran, 'L'établissement territorial', pp. 102–22.

[92] *Variae*, e.g. IV.39, V.12, VIII.28 (the first two for Theodahad; cf. Prokopios, *Wars*, V.3.2). In Gaul, Paulinus of Pella, *Eucharisticos*, ll. 309–27, a fifth-century text; *Vita Bibiani*, c. 4, ascribed to c.800 by its editor Bruno Krusch.

[93] So e.g. Prokopios, *Wars*, IV.6.6–9 on Vandal luxury. It was a rhetorical trope, a formal counterpoint to Berber asceticism, ibid., 6.10–13. All the same, no text refers to the Vandals after 439 as including peasants. Victor of Vita, who hated Vandals and despised peasants (see below, p. 566), might have made something of the link if it had been empirically available.

[94] Puin, *Der Dīwān*, esp. pp. 80–116, is the fullest discussion.

rich, but many others too, as Prokopios says. Prokopios in fact goes further, claiming that Geiseric had actually destroyed the Roman documentation for taxation. We can doubt this: it would be a strange thing to do, it does not fit the fact that the Vandals still taxed, but it does fit the extravagant way Prokopios wrote about Geiseric. But Prokopios was an eyewitness to what did happen in 534: Justinian needed to reassess African taxes as a result of the inadequacies of Vandal record-keeping, sent two men to do so, and the latter were hated by the Africans for their lack of moderation.[95] It looks as if, at the least, the Vandals had let record-keeping slip, and probably, given the African reaction in 534, exactions as well. Why go through the considerable effort of updating registers if you already have almost too much already? This sort of budgetary imbalance led, steadily, to a breakdown in the basic infrastructure of taxation. If Justinian, who had other needs, had not come in, it would doubtless have slipped further. The fiscal infrastructure was certainly revived in the region; by 600 at the latest, Africa was feeding Constantinople again (see below, p. 124). But, under the Vandals, the lack of need for tax allowed for an involution in tax-raising. This, in the long run, would have changed the whole basis of the state.

I have spent some time on relatively scarce material in the case of the Vandals, because they represent the best example in the fifth century of the quick conquest of a rich province. The only parallel to the efficacy and ease of their conquest is the Arab conquest of Syria, Palestine, and Egypt (as well as Iraq) under 'Umar, already cited as having made different choices from those of Geiseric. But, precisely because of that firm, institutionally strong, starting-point, they represent a model: this is how a tax system could break down even in favourable circumstances, if it was not structurally necessary to a polity. The closest parallel to the Vandals in the West are the Ostrogoths; they are far better documented, too. If I skip over them here as a case study it is largely because their rule in Italy was less than half as long as the Vandal hegemony, and long-term change is less visible as a result. They were not identical to the Vandals, however, in some key respects. First, Italy had gone through considerable trauma in the half-century before Theoderic entered the peninsula in 490: not invasion, perhaps, but at least the disturbance of its fiscal equilibria, precisely because of the Vandals in Africa; it was not as strong in its institutional structure, and indeed Theoderic is credited, not implausibly, with considerable reconstruction. Secondly, Italy did not have the same budgetary imbalance as Africa had, for it still had to feed Rome from its own territory, even if the Ostrogothic army, like the Vandal one, settled on the land, and even though Rome was steadily decreasing in size. As a result, one thing the *Variae* do not at all attest is fiscal breakdown. Prokopios refers to back-taxes being exacted by the Roman conquerors in

<hr>

[95] Prokopios, *Wars*, IV.8.25 (cf. *Secret history*, XVIII.10); for garrisons, Fulgentius, *Ad Trasamundum*, I.1.3.

541, but not, here, to any need for new assessments.[96] Italy might have continued for a long time as a successor-state run almost entirely along Roman lines. But we cannot test this hypothesis, for not only did the Romans destroy the Ostrogoths, but their wars, in 535–54, destroyed most of Italy too. The Lombards, as we shall see, inherited a different Italy in 568–9 and onwards.

My second example is the Visigoths. They at least allow for the long view, for Visigothic kings ruled in the land-area of the Roman empire for three centuries; even if one restricts one's analysis to the Visigoths in Spain, as will be done here, one can use a time-span of over two. Visigothic written evidence is also better than that of the Vandals, for we have a very large amount of legislation from them, both secular and ecclesiastical; this is not very well balanced by other types of evidence, unfortunately—we know a lot about Visigothic theory, far less about practice—although we do have an interesting handful of saints' lives and other narratives, and a document collection, on slate, that is still underused by historians (see Chapter 4, pp. 223–5).

The Visigoths in Spain stand out in one respect in the post-Roman West: their state did not get weaker over time, but stronger. As usual in early medieval historiography, this statement has been contested: the period around 700, in particular, has been seen by several scholars as one of breakdown, in law and order and in the power of kings over the aristocracy, leading to the incapacity of the Visigoths to resist the Arabs in 711. An alternative view, which seems much more convincing, is to point out that the major evidence for breakdown comes from the law-code, whose late laws are full of highly coloured characterizations of illegalities, expressed in shrill rhetoric, and countered, furthermore, by violent measures. As usual with legislation, one can read lists of illegalities either as evidence for crisis, or as evidence for royal commitment to impose control on civil society. There is, in fact, reasonable evidence for increases both in royal ambition and royal control. But this strengthening state was nonetheless set against an increasingly fragmented set of local societies.[97] This can best be seen in a brief narrative, which partly amplifies the political survey in Chapter 2 (pp. 38–40).

Spain, as we saw in Chapter 2, is hard to govern: its richer areas are all peripheral, and separated by mountains both from each other and from the high central plateau. How the Visigoths controlled it in the first years of their occupation, which began in the third quarter of the fifth century, is totally unclear, but the early fifth century had been a period of confusion and

---

[96] Prokopios, *Wars*, VII.1.32. For Ostrogothic taxation, see above, n. 81.

[97] For crisis, García Moreno, *Historia de España visigoda*, pp. 176–90, out of many. For no crisis, Claude, *Adel, Kirche*, pp. 202–10; Collins, *Arab conquest*, pp. 6–22.

continual conquest by a number of invading peoples, which seems to have enveloped the whole peninsula except Tarraconensis (roughly modern Catalonia and Aragón) in the north-east, and it is unclear exactly how much there was left of Roman political structures by the time the Visigoths established stable control over most of the peninsula in the 480s. After the Visigothic defeat by Clovis at Vouillé in 507, and their loss of all their lands in Gaul except Septimania (Languedoc), the kingdom went into a two-generation political crisis. When Leovigild re-established royal authority in the 570s–580s he had to do it by conquest, for many more parts of the peninsula were wholly independent: the Basques in the north, the Suevic kingdom in the north-east, the territory of Cantabria (probably based in the upper Ebro valley, and apparently ruled in Romanizing style by a *senatus*), the lands of the *senior* Aspidius (just south of Suevic Galicia), the city of Córdoba in the south, the unlocated Orospeda and Sabaria territories, and the Byzantine-controlled south-eastern coast, around Cartagena.[98] He conquered all of these apart from the first and last, but the ability of the peninsula to break up like this at least indicates how little its different sections depended on each other. Spain was, as we have seen, relatively disconnected from the Roman fiscal network (above, p. 79); its internal integration was probably never strong. But one must conclude that by the mid-sixth century economic and political fragmentation had gone quite far.

Leovigild and his son Reccared (d. 601) maintained stable control in Spain, issuing a systematic law-code and beginning the sequence of large-scale church councils of Toledo that dominate the seventh century. Toledo emerges clearly as the Visigothic capital in this period, and as a major ceremonial centre: secular and ecclesiastical ritual both focused on the city from now on, in increasingly elaborate forms.[99] The kings clearly intended to rule the whole peninsula, for Toledo is in the high plateau at its centre, and not in the richer lands of the edge, where the major Roman provincial capitals, Mérida, Seville, Cartagena, and Tarragona, were. Toledo remained the focus of the kingdom in the next half-century, which is one of weaker kingship and continual coups: provincial rulers aimed at central power, not independence, in this period, demonstrating how effective the political unification of Leovigild and Reccared had been. In 642 Chindasuinth took power, and, as noted earlier (p. 39), killed a substantial group of the

---

[98] See John of Biclar, *Chronica*, s.aa. 569–85; Braulio, *Vita S. Emiliani*, c. 33, for the Cantabrian *senatus*. Aspidius (John of Biclar, *Chronica*, s.a. 575) seems to have been an informal rural boss; the others were autonomous local communities of different types. Other communities claimed more temporary autonomy, such as Seville, which revolted under Leovigild's son Hermenegild (ibid., s.a. 579); Mérida, too, a major city relatively close to Toledo, was socially fairly separate in the period (*Vitas patrum Emeretensium*, V.4–8). See in general Stroheker, 'Leowigild'; Collins, 'Merida and Toledo'; and, for Cantabria, Castellanos, *Hagiografía y sociedad*, pp. 52–60.

[99] Velázquez and Ripoll, '*Toletum*'; McCormick, *Eternal victory*, pp. 297–327; for the church councils, Stocking, *Bishops, councils*.

aristocracy, depriving others of their civil rights, so as to ensure that the coups would end, which they did: succession was thenceforth often highly tense and dubious, but not violent for the rest of the century. The late seventh-century kings legislated, including two reissues of the law-code, and called numerous church councils; a highly articulated ceremonial practice is well attested in Toledo, and dubious successions, in particular, were legitimated by it. The political structure was strong enough to cope with frequent changes in political orientation, as each king sought to differentiate himself from his predecessor, Wamba (672–80) with respect to Chindasuinth's son Reccesuinth, Ervig (680–7) with respect to Wamba, Egica (687–702) with respect to Ervig, and onwards; the laws and the councils preserve each change of direction, with an increasing heightening of political rhetoric each time, which reached its peak under Egica.[100]

It is this constant changing of political position in the late seventh century which creates the impression that things were going wrong for the Visigoths. Each king legislated to 'correct' the illegalities or the inadequacies of his predecessor's rule, which he listed, often in detail. The list of enemies became ever greater: Jews, heretics, *servi* (probably the bulk of the dependent peasantry: below, pp. 526–7), army deserters, rapacious bishops and aristocrats... small wonder that the kingdom seems to some historians to have been in ruins. But the rhetoric is borrowed from late Roman legislation, which influenced the Visigothic state far more than it did any other successor kingdom after 550, as did all aspects of Roman culture in fact: the literary world of Isidore of Seville (d. 636) or Braulio of Zaragoza (d. 651) would hardly have been out of place in the Gaul of Sidonius.[101] The Visigothic state of the late seventh century, in its zeal for moralizing centralization and reconstruction, is more like that of the eighth-century Byzantines than that of any other Romano-Germanic kingdom. It is in this context that the increasing aggregation of the kingdom's elite around the court was a sign of stability, and the shrillness of the legislation a sign of ambition. 'Enemies' were effectively overcome: there is more anecdotal evidence of royal destruction of local aristocrats in the period from Chindasuinth onward than there ever had been before,[102] and no example of successful provincial separatism, very unlike the cases of the Franks and Lombards in the same period. We do not even have clear evidence of articulated factions in this period, although they abound in Frankish sources, except the failed

---

[100] Claude, *Adel, Kirche*, pp. 115–210, is the best account.

[101] Isidore's *Etymologiae*, classic repository of 'knowledge' as they are, are in something of a time-warp, with their 250-plus citations of Virgil, but one each of Augustine and Ambrose, and four of Jerome (and only one reference to the contemporary Goths, V.39.41). Braulio's *Epistulae* similarly show a world of late Roman *amicitia* (on whose survival see Wood, 'Family and friendship'). Collins, *Early medieval Spain*, pp. 59–87, gives a sensible survey.

[102] e.g. VIII Toledo, *Decretum* (ed. Vives, *Concilios*, p. 292); Julian of Toledo, *Historia Wambae*, passim; Valerius of Bierzo, *Ordo querimoniae*, c. 7.

conspiracy of Paul in Tarraconensis and Septimania in 672–3. Our primarily legal evidence must surely have deliberately covered them up; the way the laws—and even our rare political narratives, such as the *Historia Wambae*—pose politics is in terms of more muted power-struggles, among a political community by now determined to be cohesive in a way reminiscent of Leninist democratic centralism.[103] The very sharpness of the criticism of royal predecessors in the late seventh-century legislation (as well as occasional reference to failed coups) itself implies the existence of conflicts inside the elite, which must have had some form of factional articulation. But, at the least, there was no rhetorical space for disagreement, whether ideological or political, even as the kingdom continually changed line.

On one level, this was phony. Spain was becoming, in economic terms, even more localized in the seventh century, as archaeology is making increasingly clear; aristocrats may have clustered in Toledo, but at home their environments were becoming ever more isolated from each other (below, Chapter 4, pp. 221–6, Chapter 11, pp. 741–58). When the Arabs killed the last king of Toledo on the battlefield in 711, the peninsula abruptly broke up again, into almost as many pieces as had been in existence in 570.[104] The kingdom of Toledo, left to itself, might have established a renewed integration of the peninsula at the economic level, as the Byzantines after all did in the ninth century and onwards, and as indeed as the Arabs eventually would in Spain too; but it had not begun to do so by 711. Still, given this economic fragmentation, the Visigothic kings were remarkably effective, and their confidence is consistently visible.

This brief political analysis can serve as a framing for what we know about the economic basis of the state, which makes it a little easier to see why political practice in the Visigothic kingdom worked as it did. For a start, the Visigoths kept the land tax right up to the end of the kingdom, as laws regularly make clear; by 700 they were the only Germanic state to do so on a national level. In the sixth century one of Cassiodorus' *Variae*, from 523–6, in the period of Ostrogothic control over Spain, makes it clear that tax-collecting there was seen by Italians to be out of control, with collectors very much exceeding their rights; but this is the rhetoric of abuse, not of collapse. In 594 a text entitled *De fisco Barcinonensi* shows how tax-collecting

[103] Julian of Toledo, *Historia Wambae*, is in fact curiously short of references to factions, in strong contrast to Frankish sources such as the *Passio prima Leudegarii* (e.g. cc. 8–11, 16–20). It must be reasonable, all the same, to assume that Paul's Tarraconensis–Septimania group of aristocratic allies (*Historia Wambae*, esp. cc. 6–8) were a regional faction prior to Paul's usurpation. See in general García Lopes, 'La cronología'; de Jong, 'Adding insult to injury'.

[104] Akhila held out in the north-east for several years; the Asturias established its own autonomy shortly afterwards. See most recently Manzano, 'La conquista del 711', for the variety of local, ad hoc, agreements elsewhere with the Arab/Berber forces—the much-debated role of the sons of King Witiza, Theudemir's pact in the eponymous Tudmīr area, the mixed lineages of the north-east. Each of these different solutions to the end of the Visigothic kingdom represented different local socio-political structures.

worked by then in the Barcelona region: it was run by local *comites patri-monii* and bishops, who appointed *numerarii* to make annual collections in money of 14 *siliquae* (just over half a gold *solidus*) per *modius* of barley—the text is in fact a letter to the *numerarii* from local bishops, telling them how to do it. The rate they quote cannot easily be pinned to percentages, for how big a *modius*, probably a land-area in this instance, was here is impossible to say, but it would have to have been unusually large for this tax to have been significantly lower than Roman imperial levels (above, p. 64). In this corner of Spain—which was, it is important to add, the corner least affected by the troubles of the fifth century—tax-gathering seems to have been alive and well in 594.[105]

De fisco is a highly unusual text for the early middle ages in its clarity; it is not surprising that seventh-century evidence is less explicit. But we do have evidence in the law-code for tax records, the *poliptica publica*, in the 610s, and even a handful of references to *gesta municipalia* (although city councils were by now not involved in taxation, and indeed were probably defunct); in the 640s sellers of land were instructed to ensure that tax would still be paid; counts and *numerarii* (still chosen by bishops, though in other texts by the king) were instructed not to oppress people or be corrupt. In 683 Ervig, whose political position was arguably shakier than most kings, remitted unpaid tax up to 681, stating, with rhetoric typical of the period, that fiscal debts were by now so great that they undermined peoples and would lead to the destruction of the world. This material would not have been out of place in the legislation of any late Roman ruler. Only one change is visible, but it is a significant one: in one of Ervig's enactments about his tax remission, he says that officials sometimes took land from taxpayers, so as to use its fruits for taxpaying. In other words, a tendency was developing for landowners to hand over a section of property to the fisc, as a permanent alternative to paying tax.[106] This, if at all generalized, will have marked a fundamental shift, from a state funded by taxation to a state based on land (even if, for sure, a lot of land).

Taken on its own, this is pretty clear. Like the Vandals, the Visigoths took tax, on a systematic basis, in the 680s as much as in the fifth century. Were *De fisco* to be typical, which we cannot say, above all not for a century later,

---

[105] *Variae*, V.39; Vives, *Concilios*, p. 54 for *De fisco* (cf. III Toledo, c. 18, in ibid., p. 131). For commentaries, see Hendy, 'From public to private', pp. 53–7 (particularly important for its analyses of the monetary situation); King, *Law and society*, pp. 69–71 (p. 70 n. for the figures).
[106] *Poliptica*: LV, XII.2.13. *Gesta municipalia*, now called the *gesta publica* of the *curia*: *Form. Wis.*, nn. 21, 25; for the defunct state of the *curia*, Sánchez-Albornoz, 'Ruina y extinción', in *Estudios visigodos*, pp. 50–110. For tax references, LV, V.4.19, XII.1.2, 3; XIII Toledo, *Tomus* (ed. Vives, *Concilios*, p. 413) for the destruction of the world; and, for the land, a law appended to XIV Toledo (ed. ibid., p. 437). Egica remitted taxes too, in 693: XVI Toledo, c. 8 (ed. ibid., p. 506). See in general King, *Law and society*, pp. 64–71; García Moreno, 'Imposición y política fiscal'; Barbero and Vigil, *Sobre los orígenes sociales*, pp. 107–37; Castellanos, 'The political nature of taxation'.

rates were high as well. There were not, however, very many tax laws in the extensive array of Visigothic legislation: I have cited more than half of them in the previous paragraph. In the generous array of royal rhetorical materials, taxation did not figure very largely: this was certainly unlike the late empire. Nor does the government administration compare in its elaboration to late Roman practice; although there was a complex palace organization (the *palatinum officium*) in Toledo, there seems to have been usually only one *numerarius* per city, and the rest of the provincial administrative (and indeed judicial) system was restricted to counts, dukes, and other military figures.[107] And the army was here clearly quite different from late Rome. Sixth-century laws are relatively sketchy; they refer casually to the *expeditio publica* (i.e. campaigning), and list penalties for avoidance of army service; one law protects the supplies (*annona*) of garrisons from loss due to peculation. Wamba and Ervig in 673 and 681–3 discussed the problem of avoiding military service in rather greater detail and enacted different provisions to deal with it: Wamba deprived deserters of all civil rights, including the right to testify; Ervig declared that this was excessive, for it had affected, so he claimed, 'nearly half the population', and reversed it—though his alternative measures, loss of property, fines, flogging, and *decalvatio* (scalping or head-shaving), were hardly less severe. But Wamba and (especially) Ervig's laws also make it much clearer who was liable to army service, and how: all free adult and able-bodied males, and also 10 per cent of all the unfree; the free were to follow their duke, count, or private patron (*patronus*), and the unfree their free masters (*domini*).[108] The salaried Roman army had gone, and an army based on public obligation had taken its place.

The amount of scholarly attention that has been paid to these laws is huge. In part, this is because they are supposed to show military crisis—a crisis not visible to me, unless it is that a *levée en masse* on this scale would have produced an unfeedable army of hundreds of thousands, on any count of the total population (and the total free population) of Spain, in a period, furthermore, when wars were fairly rare (although Wamba in 673 had just, rather efficiently in fact, defeated Paul's uprising). In part, it is because of the role of the *patroni* in them. This is not the only evidence we have for private military clientèles in Spain. Euric legislated about *buccellarii*, a standard late Roman term for private men-at-arms, who were commended to *patroni*; Leovigild renewed and extended this—armed robbers, for

---

[107] For administration in general, see King, *Law and society*, pp. 52–121. But the *palatinum officium* had its own legal status (ibid., p. 56), and the judicial system was apparently largely standardized—see above all Velázquez, *Las pizarras*, n. 39 (dating to the 560s–580s), which fits *Form. Wis.*, n. 39; cf. Diaz y Diaz, 'Un document privé', pp. 60–6. For palace officials see further Isla Frez, 'El "officium palatinum" visigodo'.

[108] *LV*, IX.2.1–7 (sixth century), 8 (Wamba), 9 (Ervig: see also XII Toledo, *Tomus* and c. 7, ed. Vives, *Concilios*, pp. 383, 394–5). See in general Pérez, *El ejército*, which cites earlier bibliography.

example, who were *in patrocinio vel obsequio*, 'in a clientèle or following', were not to be seen as personally guilty, for they were only following their *patronus*. Prokopios claimed that King Theudis (531–48) had a private army of two thousand men, recruited from his (Roman) wife's estates. The epitaph of a certain Oppila, from near Córdoba, refers to his death in 642 while fighting the Basques with his *clintes*, clients. These details show that powerful men had military dependants from the beginning of Visigothic rule onwards, even if not, except perhaps in the last example, that these dependants were integral parts of regular armies. By Ervig's time, though, they clearly were.[109] His law closely parallels ninth-century Frankish legislation, where, again, soldiers can choose to follow either their local count or their personal lord. Military service could indeed be associated with gifts of land: Fructuosus of Braga, a monastic founder and bishop of the mid-seventh century from the highest Visigothic aristocracy, gave all his property to the monastery of Compludo; his brother-in-law went to the king and asked to be given that land, *quasi pro exercenda publica expeditione*, 'as if for carrying out a public military campaign'.[110] It is not surprising that these texts have become a crux of discussions of the 'pre-' or 'proto-feudalism' (as Claudio Sánchez-Albornoz and Luís A. García Moreno call it—'proto' because there were no fiefs or vassals) or the 'feudalism' (as Abilio Barbero and Marcelo Vigil call it) of the Visigothic state. In Ervig's law in particular, the army is becoming a set of personal clientèles, whose members, as Leovigild assumed already, owe their primary loyalty to their lord, not to the king. Nor would I disagree, especially not with Barbero and Vigil, who are particularly effective in the way they track the terminology of private dependence through every section of society, whether in the king's personal relationship to the aristocracy, structured by oaths of fidelity on the one side and gifts of land of various kinds on the other (this is common ground in all discussions of Visigothic feudalism/proto-feudalism), or in the personal relationship between bishops and clerics, which increasingly came to have the same structure. Visigothic society was following the standard track of all Romano-Germanic societies, in the translation of public obligations into relationships of personal dependence, and the association of these with landholding. In this respect, the army was simply part of the same set of developments. The Visigoths had entered the 'feudal society' of Marc Bloch, with the politics of land foremost in the construction of political relationships.[111]

[109] Respectively, *Codex Euricianus*, c. 310 = *LV*, V.3.1; *LV*, V.3.3–4 (in the latter, a *patronus* gives land: cf. *LV*, IV.5.5); and *LV*, VI.4.2 for armed robbers; Prokopios, *Wars*, V.12.50–1 (a text it would be naive to trust without caution); Vives, *Inscripciones cristianas*, n. 287. Pérez argues from those texts that the sixth-century army was largely composed of private clientèles (*El ejército*, p. 113–18); Barbero and Vigil, *La formación*, pp. 44–52, argue similarly for the sixth and seventh centuries. It seems to me that the evidence is clearer for the seventh than the sixth.

[110] For Francia, see e.g. *MGH, Cap.*, I, n. 50, c. 1 (a. 808); *Vita S. Fructuosi*, c. 3.

[111] Sánchez-Albornoz, 'El "stipendium" hispano-godo', in his *Estudios visigodos*, pp. 355–63; García Moreno, *Historia de España visigoda*, pp. 224, 250–4, 332–7; idem, 'El estado proto-

This, of course, as with the Vandals but even more sharply, forces us to ask what purpose taxation still served. Military service was universal for the free, but, as all kings knew, war needed more specialized expertise. In the above-cited text, it is likely enough that Fructuosus' brother-in-law was asking for land in return for expert service; the alternative is that it was for the funding of a specific campaign. Either way, it was land that was requested by an aristocrat as a personal concession, in return for military activity. Even specialist army service, that is to say, was not associated with salaries, in other words with tax. Tax probably funded the *palatinum officium* (though its members could well have been given land as well), and all that Toledan ceremonial; going to Toledo would anyway have been all the more necessary for the elite if the capital was awash with tax wealth— although our sources tell us little about the detail of royal munificence, unlike those for the Franks.[112] But it is very difficult to tell what else it could have been for. The imagery of royal negotiations with the aristocracy was always in terms of land, not salaries. In this context, the reference in Ervig's laws to the transformation of tax obligations into cessions of land is highly significant: land was the currency of politics, and even tax was turning into it by now. Tax was still being exacted in the 680s, but I propose that it was becoming, and perhaps had become, politically marginal: perhaps light, perhaps intermittent, and capable of being dispensed with. This would doubtless have resulted, in the end, in a more fragmented political system, as the logic of the 'politics of land' indicates (above, p. 58), but the enormous size of the royal patrimony, further enlarged by these tax com- mutations, would have made for wealthy, and thus politically relevant, kingship for a long time to come. This must be why, although Spain could break up very quickly when the Arabs won in 711, it did not do so while the king was in Toledo.

The internal construction of al-Andalus, the Arab polity that succeeded the Visigoths, is not at all clear, at least until the tenth century, when the Umayyad emirs of al-Andalus claimed the title of caliph, and the state achieved for three generations a centralization and stability that eluded both its predecessors and successors. Our sources are late, tenth-century at the earliest (Ibn al-Qūṭiya, al-Rāzī, the latter in part preserved in sources of the eleventh century and later), apart from a few details preserved in the eighth-century Latin *Chronicle of 754*; they disagree substantially over major issues as well, such as whether the different parts of Spain were conquered by force or not, which had different implications for who had

feudal'; cf. Diesner's use of *Frühfeudalismus* in 'König Wamba'. Alternatively, Barbero and Vigil, *Sobre los orígines sociales*, pp. 107–37; iidem, *La formación*, pp. 21–200, rather less legalistic. Arguments about whether land was held conditionally or not are particularly irrele- vant in Visigothic Spain, where kings could take anything back from the unfaithful: ibid., pp. 122–5. For the politics of land, see Bloch, *Feudal society*.

[112] For royal gifts, one example is *Vitas patrum Emeretensium*, V.4.6.

legal rights over the land. It seems fairly clear, however, that the initial settlement of the Berber and Arab armies was on the land, in return for military service; these *baladīyūn* might have been salaried at the start, but they were settled, and no longer paid, by the middle of the century. A second group of incomers, the Syrian armies who came in in 742–3, were certainly paid '*aṭā*'; but they seem to have been distributed across different localities, in each of which they were assigned, as al-Rāzī puts it, 'a third of the goods (*amwāl*) of the Christians'. This could allow us to propose a Goffartian model of localized tax-collection by single soldiers or detachments, or, again, a developing land-settlement. From 'Abd al-Raḥmān I's time onwards, in the second half of the eighth century, a permanent army and a *dīwān*, a register for army pay, was established, the army being recruited from North Africa and from slave groups; this army is associated with Córdoba, and continues without a break thereafter.[113] The Arabs taxed from the start, as these citations make clear; indeed, the eighth-century *Chronicle of 754* is full of taxation imagery, for the first time in early medieval Spanish history, in its characterizations (and condemnations) of the Arabs.[114] But Spain is unique among the provinces the Arabs conquered (apart from Syria, where there were so many Arabs already: below, p. 130) in the absence of a clear separation between the conquering armies and the local population. Elsewhere, Arab conquest brought a set of paid garrisoned troops and no land-settlement. It was quite different in Spain: Arabs and especially Berbers settled fast, and we find in ninth-century sources a landed aristocracy of mixed origin, Visigothic as well as Arab/Berber, which the Umayyad emirs had to subdue in the first *fitna*, the civil wars of the decades around 900, and which continued thereafter as well (see below, pp. 226–7). This mixing is what one would expect if a conquering military elite settled on the land, among the strata of indigenous society. It looks as if the first attempts to establish a paid army in al-Andalus failed, with, by 800 at the latest, a two-level system emerging, a paid army in and around the capital, and a military settlement elsewhere, which would fight it out in the *fitna*.

The best way of reading these observations is through the realization that Spain was the only major province of the Umayyad caliphate which had not been ruled by a tax-based state at the time of the conquest. The Arabs could not here simply inherit a tax system which could continue unchanged, as can be seen most clearly in Egypt (pp. 133–44), until its personnel and, eventually, its principles were Arabized; in Spain, they had to re-establish one,

---

[113] For the sources, see Manzano, 'Las fuentes árabes'; idem, 'La conquista del 711'. Vallvé, 'España en el siglo VIII', offers in effect a Goffartian model of the Arab settlement, in that it was patterned on that supposedly practised by the Visigoths, but his arguments do not convince. For the different armies, see Chalmeta, *Invasión*, pp. 316, 331, 333 (quote from al-Rāzī), 334, 362, 382–4; Guichard, *Structures sociales*, pp. 213–23; Manzano, 'El asentamiento'. I am grateful to Eduardo Manzano for advice about this section.

[114] *Chronicle of 754*, cc. 51, 62, 69, 76, 82, 91. See Barceló, *El sol que salió*, pp. 23–54.

almost—even if not quite—from scratch. So early armies had, in practice, to be landed; there was no other permanent way of paying them. (Since the *baladīyūn* were mostly Berbers, who had been associated with the Arabs for two or three decades at the most, it should be added that this was also doubtless what they expected, and desired, most.) And the lack of continuity in the capacity of the eighth- and ninth-century emirs, based in Córdoba, to assert their control over large sections of their state fits best with a political system based principally on landowning rather than one based on taxation. In the tenth century, under ʿAbd al-Raḥmān III, al-Ḥakam II, and al-Manṣūr, things changed; but subjecting the aristocracy was a difficult process, and never fully complete. Spain remained different, and in the eleventh century the power of the caliphate collapsed.[115] This development is outside the period of this book, and had complex roots, but it is not unreasonable to see it as a distant consequence of the steady decline of taxation in the Visigothic kingdom.

The Franks are much better documented than either the Vandals or the Visigoths, and far more can be said about the development of their state structures. Essentially, they tell the same story as the Visigothic evidence does, but the Frankish evidence includes a decent quantity of public and private documents, which allow not only an impression of how the fiscal system worked—and changed—in practice, but also an analysis of sub-regional differences.

Late Roman Gaul, as noted earlier, was probably fiscally self-sufficient, in that the Rhine army was mostly supplied from the resources of the Gaulish hinterland: the northern lowlands and eastern valleys first, Aquitaine second. Northern Gaul is by far the obscurest part of the region in the late fifth century; it was fought over by Franks, Alemans, and Bretons, with local political structures still owing nominal allegiance to Rome persisting in the Trier area until the 470s and the Soissons and maybe Paris area until the 480s. One of the late fifth-century Frankish groups established itself at Cologne by c.440, possibly initially as a federate group, given Cologne's long-standing importance for the Roman military machine.[116] But the political subdivision of the north, plus the disappearance of the Rhine army (the latest date for the occupation of the best-excavated Rhine forts, such as

---

[115] For recent general guides to these developments, see Manzano, *La frontera*, pp. 261–389; Kennedy, *Muslim Spain*, pp. 44–129; Barceló, *El sol que salió*, pp. 103–36; Acién, *'Umar ibn Hafsūn*, pp. 105–24.

[116] James, *The Franks*, contains a good overview of the fifth century in the north: pp. 56–7 for the possible federate origins of the Franks of Cologne; pp. 67–74 for Romans in the north. There are (amazingly) five recent collections of articles on fifth-century Gaul, none of which, however, amount to a new synthesis: Drinkwater and Elton, *Fifth-century Gaul*; *Die Franken, Wegbereiter Europas*; Rouche, *Clovis, histoire et mémoire* (the strangest of the five); Geuenich, *Die Franken*; and Mathisen and Schanzer, *Society and culture*. For Trier, Sidonius, *Ep.* IV.17; for Soissons, Gregory of Tours, *LH*, II.27.

Alzey, is c.450), meant that one certain casualty of the century was the fiscal infrastructure which channelled money and produce taken in taxation to the Rhine.[117] The only information about food supply that we have for the second half of the century consists of ad hoc local initiatives. In southern Gaul, surviving infrastructures could allow Bishop Patiens of Lyon to send substantial supplies down the Rhône to the cities of Provence in c.471 when their resources were upset by war, and a generation later, in c.510, the Burgundian kings did the same. In the north, by contrast, the *Vita Genove-fae*, probably written in the 520s, relates Genovefa's travels up the Seine into Champagne to get *annona* for besieged Paris in (perhaps) the 470s, which is depicted as a considerable expedition, complete with river monsters and storms, although Troyes, the furthest point she reached, is only 160 km from Paris.[118] In these areas, in much the same way perhaps as in western Spain in the same period, political and fiscal reconstruction would have to start virtually from scratch. But these were also the heartlands of the Merovingian Frankish kingdom, after the reunification of nearly the whole of Gaul under Clovis and his sons. The ex-Visigothic and ex-Burgundian provinces of the south, which had a less complex experience of conquest, show far more evidence of Roman traditions, in culture, aristocratic landowning, and political/ecclesiastical institutions; indeed, after the Visigoths left Aquitaine in the early sixth century, in that sector of Gaul there were few non-Romans at all. The Franks saw the south, except the northern parts of the Burgundian kingdom (roughly modern Burgundy), as 'Roman' territory, as can be seen for example in the *Vita Eligii*, a seventh-century life rewritten in the Carolingian period, which shows Eligius (d. 660) coming from Limoges north to 'the soil of the Franks', and, when bishop of Noyon, being reviled by (supposedly) paganizing Franks as a *romanus*.[119] The Merovingians were based above all in the Paris–Oise basin and eastwards to the Cologne–Trier–Metz area of the Rhine, Moselle, and Meuse valleys. These areas may have been less disrupted than some parts of the north, as we shall see (pp. 178–81), but they were certainly not areas of large-scale institutional continuity.

The Merovingians kept kingship strictly inside the family; internal wars were wars between kin. The family treated Gaul and its outliers, Francia as we can now call it, in effect as personal property, to be divided between heirs if necessary, in a never-ending sequence of redivisions: half-a-dozen major ones for the sixth century alone. After Clovis's death, only very rarely was there only one king, in particular in 558–61, 613–23, and after 679; and, apart from in the first of these periods, there were always at least two, often

---

[117] See for Alzey, Oldenstein, 'Die letzten Jahrzehnte'.

[118] Sidonius, *Ep.* VI.12; *Vita Caesarii*, II.9; *Vita Genovefae*, cc. 35–40 (see Heinzelmann and Poulin, *Les vies anciennes*, pp. 8, 51–7, 115–45, for the early date of the last of these).

[119] *Vita Eligii*, I.4, II.20. The clearest statement of the 'Romanness' of the south is Rouche, *L'Aquitaine*; see below, p. 111.

three, separate courts, each with its own palace, official staff, treasury, and aristocratic aggregation. The courts were the most stable feature of the system. They moved around from *palatium* to *palatium*, but inside quite small areas—between Paris and Compiègne, a distance of 65 km, in the western, Neustrian, 'royal landscape'; the palaces did not have the architectural solidity of Toledo, but each 'royal landscape' had a parallel centrality.[120]

It is generally reckoned that the Merovingian kings were strong rulers until at least the death of Dagobert I, in 639. They were immensely rich, suffered few checks on their activities, and were happy to kill any of their entourage of ambitious aristocrats with only sporadic criticism in contemporary narrative sources, Gregory of Tours, 'Fredegar', and an array of saints' lives. Royal minorities did sometimes lead to the weakening of one of the Merovingian courts, but these periods were reversed when the kings concerned reached adulthood. A traditional picture (characterized briefly above, pp. 45–6) has the family losing power, however, when Dagobert was succeeded by two children, for this was the first time there actually was no adult Merovingian, except for a brief period in the years around 600. Each court increasingly came to focus on its main aristocratic administrator or *maior domus* ('mayor of the palace'), notably Ebroin and then the Warattonids in Neustria, and the Pippinids in the eastern kingdom, Austrasia. There was a confused period in the mid- to late seventh century in which the outlying provinces of the Frankish kingdom gained ever greater autonomy, and when local powers even in the northern heartland—notably bishops—began to act as de facto autonomous units. This process of disintegration began to be reversed after Pippin II established the supremacy of his mayoral family in 687, and was fully reversed as a result of the effective reconquest of the Frankish heartland by Pippin's son Charles Martel in the civil war of 715–19. The following 120 years were the first years of full unity for Francia since Clovis, almost unbroken under four generations of rule by Charles and his descendants, the Carolingians, who claimed the kingship in 751 and the imperial title itself in 800; the Carolingians re-established the uncontested centrality of pre-639 Frankish kingship, and greatly extended its geographical area of control.[121]

Recent scholarship has revised this picture to an extent, at least as it describes the period 639–714. One by one, the late Merovingian kings have been rehabilitated as effective rulers; even if this rehabilitation will never be entirely complete, the state is now often seen as relatively little changed until the mid-670s; some Merovingians are seen as maintaining

---

[120] For royal centres, see Dierkens and Périn, 'Les *sedes regiae* mérovingiennes', and Barbier, 'Le système palatial franc'; for 'royal landscapes', see above, p. 46; below, pp. 393–406; and Cardot, *L'espace et le pouvoir*, pp. 134–7, for Austrasia.

[121] The classic picture is well described by Ewig, 'Die fränkischen Teilreiche'. For the outlying provinces, see Werner, 'Les principautés péripheriques'.

political relevance if ever they reached adulthood even after that date, most notably Childebert III in the period 694–711; and the courts as remaining significant centres of political aggregation throughout, until Charles Martel swept them away and started again.[122] I would argue that this puts the shifts too late: mayors chose their own Merovingians in c.656 in Austrasia and 675 in Neustria; the unpopularity and eventual murder of Childeric II in Neustria in 673–5 seem to show that a king could now be regarded as tyrannical for doing what would have been totally normal half a century earlier (see below, p. 198); Merovingian family authority was, that is to say, already weakened by these dates, and it is not easy to be sure that it ever recovered.[123] Nor does the new scholarship argue away the strong tendencies towards autonomy outside the Frankish heartland in the late seventh century, which were only reversed, slowly, under Charles Martel and his sons. But the continuing importance of the Neustrian and Austrasian courts throughout the period is much clearer than it was twenty years ago. They were the places where magnates needed to go if they wanted to settle their disputes peacefully, for example, in every decade of the seventh century; indeed, the courts were full of aristocrats and bishops seeking honours and preferment, even at low points for strictly royal authority. They did not replicate Toledo in the elaboration of royal ceremonial; nor did the late Merovingians legislate, in sharp contrast to their Visigothic contemporaries.[124] The Frankish normative sources we have are almost devoid of that Romanizing ambition, verbal aggression, and zeal for social exclusion that one finds in Spain. But the state did not collapse, for all that; its elements could be reconstructed, with willpower, a lack of scruple, and military good fortune, as Charles Martel shows us.

These political changes, as sketched out here, are underpinned by the history of taxation and other royal resources. Here, there is more lasting agreement by most historians: sixth-century Merovingians taxed their Roman population (Franks remained immune), but taxation was increasingly unpopular, and in the seventh century any taxation at all was generally seen as an abuse of power. Indeed, land-tax imagery had largely vanished from privileges to churches of immunity from royal exactions, which begin to survive from the second half of the seventh century, indicating that

---

[122] Wood, *Merovingian kingdoms*, pp. 262–6; Fouracre, 'The outgrowth of Pippinid influence'; idem, *Charles Martel*, pp. 38–54.

[123] See e.g. *Vita Boniti*, c. 5, a contemporary text, for Pippin II appointing a bishop of Clermont in 690, when the then king, Theuderic III, was in his thirties. Childebert III, talked up by Wood and Fouracre (see n. 122), is above all visible in court-cases, but most of these are formulaic (see Bergmann, 'Untersuchungen', pp. 93–102), and do not in themselves show royal protagonism. The exceptions, *ChLA*, XIV, nn. 581, 586, 587, show Pippinids losing cases, it is true, but n. 587, at least, is structured by Pippinid, not royal, decision-making.

[124] For disputes, see above all Bergmann, 'Untersuchungen'; Fouracre, ' "Placita" '. Not all dispute-settlement was peaceful by any means: see Fouracre, 'Attitudes towards violence'; Busch, 'Vom Attentat zur Haft'.

taxation was by now not normally exacted. Henceforth, it was royal lands, not tax rights, which were the main currency of political ambitions— although kings kept control of commercial tolls and judicial fines.[125] Here, as with the Visigoths and probably the Vandals, the underlying reason for this was the lack of need for a complex tax infrastructure, for the army was landed and the civil administration relatively sketchy. The amazing wealth of sixth-century Merovingians was derived from the fact that they had no structural outgoings; they used their tax to give gifts to their aristocrats, which could be enormous when aristocrats were in favour (hence the continuing attraction of the dangerous places that royal courts were).[126] But of course, under these circumstances tax itself could be one of those concessions. As early as the 550s, the city territory of Tours had a tax immunity; so did Bourges in the 630s. This sequence of concessions was focused in particular on church lands, which were themselves steadily increasing. It was matched, as Walter Goffart in particular has stressed, by the increasing landed wealth of the effectively tax-immune Frankish aristocracy, and indeed by the extension of Frankish ethnic identity, which may have carried further assumptions about immunity, to the whole free population of the lands north of the Loire.[127] But given the immense lands that the Merovingians still had access to, which, even if generously given away, were constantly also being added to by confiscation from factional losers, as well as smaller-scale fiscal rights like tolls and the profits of justice, the weakening of taxation did not in this case necessarily lead to the weakening of public authority. Its trajectory does not fit the trajectory of Merovingian political power, and even less does it fit the continuing political importance of the royal courts. Throughout the seventh century, and indeed the eighth, narrative sources continually stress that any successful ruler needed to have a *thesaurus*, a treasury, at his disposition, in order to attract the core of an army by gifts.[128] Clearly, political rivals were not ever poor; and Carolingian expansion would make them richer still. One might see Chlotar II (who renounced any *census novus* in 614) and Dagobert I, the early seventh-century kings who seem to have presided over the catastrophe-flip in

---

[125] The main discussions of Merovingian taxation are Lot, *L'impôt foncier*, pp. 83–107; Goffart, *Rome's fall*, pp. 213–31 (the article 'Old and new'); Kaiser, 'Steuer und Zoll'; Durliat, *Les finances publiques*, pp. 95–187, the latter of which stresses continuities very greatly (cf. above, n. 68). For tolls, see also Ganshof, 'À propos du tonlieu'.

[126] Cf. Lot, *L'impôt foncier*, p. 99, in moralistic mode. For the army as landed, see in general Bachrach, *Merovingian military organisation*, e.g. pp. 65–73.

[127] Goffart, *Rome's fall*, pp. 213–31.

[128] For *thesaurus* imagery, see Gregory of Tours, *LH*, II.40–2, IV.20, V.34, VII.4, Fredegar, *Chronica*, IV.38, 42, 60, 67, 75, 85; Fredegar, *Continuationes*, cc. 2, 5, 10; *Liber historiae Francorum*, cc. 45, 48, 52–3; *Passio prima Leudegarii*, cc. 6, 18. This imagery is much less strong in narratives for Lombard Italy, although this may be because kings were more based in a single palace at Pavia (Paul, *HL*, II.29 and VI.35, nevertheless mentions treasure being removed from it, and Aistulf had a *thesaurus* in Fredegar, *Continuationes*, c. 38). See in general Doehaerd, 'La richesse des Mérovingiens'; Gasparri, 'Il tesoro del re'.

which taxation became finally only one out of many resources, and not the most essential one, as the Frankish versions of Henry II of England, the king who felt himself strong enough and rich enough to abandon the Anglo-Saxon land tax in 1161.[129] But the basis of the state changed very substantially as a result. And, even if the Merovingians were not destroyed by the centrifugal tendencies of the politics of land, the Carolingians would be, in the century after the end of the political unity and military success of the years 720–830.

This picture seems to me still to stand. Where it needs to be nuanced is in recognizing the substantial regional differences characteristic of the Merovingian period from start to finish. We do not know much about taxation in Frankish Gaul before Gregory of Tours's writings in the 570s–590s, but it is extremely unlikely that there was substantive survival of any sort of planned, Gaul-wide taxation structure: first, because the Merovingian heartland had seen such confusion and political division in the fifth century; second, because the frequent partitions of the kingdom would have made any renewed integration impossible as well. Tax was at best collected locally, at the level of the city territory (the basic building block of the sixth-century kingdom), and then sent to whichever king happened to control that city at any given time.[130] There would have been little reason why each city territory could not have developed its taxpaying practices completely separately. It is also the case that Gregory only tells us much about one part of Francia: the Loire basin, northern Aquitaine, and northern Burgundy. This happens, as we shall see, to be the area where survivals in taxation are best attested in the seventh century as well, so we must remain very cautious about how widely Gregory's evidence can be generalized. Let us trace the documentation we have for this region first, and then look at other areas.

Gregory disapproved of the land tax, but had no doubt that it existed. It was mostly called *tributum* or *census*, it was in kind, and it was apparently exacted regularly by public officials, either local counts or central officials like the *referendarius* Marcus—who was active in 579–83, and hugely rich from peculation according to Gregory. It was based on written assessments of the population, which apparently excluded widows, orphans, the poor, and the infirm, and which could also include an assessment of land areas: these seem to have had Roman roots, though the protocols were somewhat simplified. Gregory's evidence is most explicit for Tours, Poitiers, Limoges, and Clermont, all ex-Visigothic territories. The citizens of Limoges rose up against the new taxation of King Chilperic in 579 and burnt the *libri discriptionum*; by comparison, in 589 Bishop Maroveus of Poitiers asked

---

[129] *Census novus*: MGH, *Cap.*, I, n. 9, c. 8. The end of Dagobert's reign saw a sharp drop in the fineness of Merovingian gold coins, which may be a consequence of this: Hendy, 'From public to private', pp. 62–8; Lafaurie, 'Eligius monetarius', pp. 134–9. For Henry II, see Green, 'The last century of Danegeld'.

[130] So Gregory of Tours, *LH*, VI.22.

Childebert II to send *discriptores* (they were major court officials) to reassess his town, to update the registers, which had not been done since before 575, and make them more just; in Clermont in 590, too, the same king had tax registers revised, because the 'succession of generations and the division of properties in many parts' made the levy of *tributum* almost impossible. In Tours in 589 Gregory forcefully defended the tax privileges of the city, which had been, he said, established by Chlotar I (d. 561) and confirmed by all his successors—more than once the local bishop had had to appeal to the king against collectors who tried to do so anyway, using old registers. The picture we gain from Gregory is that taxation is always unjust (though Maroveus may have thought differently); that good kings remit it, especially from church land (as happened twice in Clermont, in the 530s and in 590)— even wicked kings remit it if they have attacks of guilt, as did Chilperic and his wife Fredegund in 580, who threw the registers in the fire, an image Gregory uses on several occasions.[131] These are generic political points, but the frequency of the image of pious remission is still significant. More important is that assessments were by now not often revised, and the Poitiers reassessment was a sufficiently momentous process for the *discriptores* to be close associates of the king: this was certainly a major change from the Roman period. Finally, and again importantly, the sixth-century Merovingians, so unwilling to accept any other restrictions on their powers, did back down over taxes: on the only two occasions that kings tried to increase taxes, they were met with sharp opposition and eventually conceded. But Chilperic's new punitive tax of 579, the only one Gregory describes in any detail, was 1 *anfora* of wine per *aripennis* of land (Gregory does not give the grain figures), which Ferdinand Lot worked out as being 10 per cent of the crop: far below Roman levels.[132] This is the only figure for a tax rate we have for Merovingian Gaul, but it is a strikingly low one, especially for a newly increased tax, even if Gregory was not exaggerating its incidence for effect. Tax had probably become a relatively marginal imposition by the 570s; hence, too, the possibility of leaving decades between ad hoc reassessments.

But this does not mean that it necessarily was about to end, at least in this part of Gaul. Bourges was still paying *census* in the 640s, as already noted; Bishop Sulpicius supposedly got it lifted in one account, the *Vita Sulpicii*, which closely parallels the narratives recounted by Gregory. In the Limousin, *census* was also still exacted in the same period; Eligius again had it

---

[131] See *LH*, V.28, 34, VI.28 (Marcus); V.28, IX.30, X.7 (Limoges, Poitiers, Clermont); IX.30 (Tours); III.25, X.7 (Clermont remissions); V.28, 34, IX.30 (registers thrown in the fire). For commentary, see above, n. 125, with Weidemann, *Kulturgeschichte*, I, pp. 327–31, a very literal account. Gregory also says that the dependants of St-Martin and the cathedral at Tours were exempt from military service (*LH*, V.26, VII.42).

[132] Gregory of Tours, *LH*, IV.2, V.34 for kings backing down. See Goffart, *Rome's fall*, p. 221; and, for the 10% figure, *LH*, V.28; Lot, *L'impôt foncier*, pp 85–6. Note that wine yields are higher than grain yields, and that there is no equivalent to seed-corn; this 10% is thus even lower by the standards of Roman figures for grain taxes (above, pp. 64–5).

lifted for his own estates in 632. (In the *Vita Eligii*, tax was apparently taken in gold, unlike in the previous century.)[133] And from the 660s we also begin to have documentary references to taxation, generally called *inferenda* here, though also *annona*, *tributum*, and *agrarium*. The evidence for this focuses on Le Mans, north of the Loire this time but only 80 km from Tours; we have a good set of late seventh- and eighth-century documents for Le Mans, which also include texts from the outlying estate of Ardin in Poitou. This is not the chance of document survival, for it is significant that the only reference to taxation in the St-Denis originals from the same period, which generally concern the Paris basin, is also associated with the *inferenda* of Le Mans. This tax was sometimes in cows, sometimes in money. At Ardin in 721 it was exacted by the bishop of Le Mans as the local landowner, through his *agentes* and *iuniores*, who had to return documentary proof of the exactions to him, and then it was apparently sent on to the king: the bishop had an immunity for some of his land, but not all.[134] These partial immunities are documented elsewhere in the Loire valley, too: Childebert III (694–711) granted one to a monastery in Angers (here, the *inferenda* would evidently still be collected from monastic estates, but only some of it would henceforth go to the king); even in Tours there are hints that the *fiscus* still expected at least some taxation, for the monastery of St-Martin reportedly got an immunity from tax on its own properties from Dagobert I in the 630s, which in Gregory's time it would not have needed, and in the 700s and 710s it got two others from the bishops, from taxation which was apparently still exacted both by the bishop and the *fiscus*, despite explicit reference in one of the texts to Dagobert's *emunitas*, this time to the whole city.[135] It is in the light of this that the lists of payments of *agrarium* to St-Martin, surviving in accounts dating from the end of the seventh century, peasant by peasant from properties (*villae*, *colonicae*) across the Touraine and Poitou, can probably best be seen as tax, in this case mostly in grain, more rarely in wood—although it is unclear in the accounts whether the monastery kept it or passed it on to the king. The former is the most likely, judging by the texts just cited; in which case it would effectively be turning into a rent.[136]

[133] *Vita Sulpicii*, c. 6; *Vita Eligii*, I.15. Gregory, *LH*, V.28, 34, is directly copied in the analogous account for Limoges in *Vita Aridii*, cc. 38, 41. (*Miracula Austrigisili*, cc. 2–3, used by Rouche, *L'Aquitaine*, p. 347, which would back-date the Bourges immunity to the previous bishop, is an eleventh-century text.)

[134] For Le Mans, *ChLA*, XIV, n. 591 (a. 716; cf. the Carolingian compilation, the *Gesta Dagoberti*, c. 37). For Ardin, Busson and Ledru, *Actus*, pp. 219–20, 220–2, 228–30, 237–8, 238–40, 242–4, for confirmations, 240–2 for the 721 text. Compare the *census* 'to be brought', *inferendus*, to the royal treasury in *Vita Eligii*, I.15, and the Saxon tribute of *vaccas inferendalis* (the same phrase as in *ChLA*, n. 591) in Fredegar, *Chronica*, IV.74. See in general Lot, 'Ardin'; Goffart, *Rome's fall*, pp. 204 n., 243–6.

[135] *MGH, Dip. Merov.*, n. 145, for Angers; *Vita Eligii*, I.32, for Dagobert and Tours; Debus, 'Studien', II, nn. 21–2, for Tours in 703–11 and 711–22.

[136] *ChLA*, XVIII, n. 659 (also published with commentary by Gasnault in *Documents comptables*), with the new leaves ed. in XLVII, nn. 1404–5. See Goffart, *Rome's fall*, pp. 241–52; Durliat, 'Qu'est-ce qu'un polyptyche?', a useful analysis; and Sato, 'The Merovin-

These late taxes seem to be more standardized, customary, than those of the sixth century, still more those of the Roman empire. The *inferenda* or *annona* of Ardin is worth exactly 400 *solidi* in 721, a figure that seems to have been stable, for it is apparently already referred to in 713. Similarly, St-Denis's Le Mans tax-concession amounts to a fixed annual due of 100 *vaccas inferendalis*. Reassessments, that is to say, had stopped, making tax potentially more arbitrary: in effect, turning into tribute (above, p. 70). The taxes all seem to be due from estates which the churches figuring in our documentation actually own—this is not always certain, but it is for Ardin, and for the Angers and St-Martin tax-concessions, and it is likely for the others. Landowners were assessing the tax on their own estates, that is to say, and sometimes getting to keep it as well. Fiscal exactions in the latter case—not just taxation but *servitutis operas, mansiones, pastus, munera, freta* (labour-services, hospitality, donatives, and judicial dues), as the 710s Tours immunity put it—would here in effect turn into rent. All the same, whether tax, tribute, or rent, some public exactions were alive and well in the early decades of the eighth century, in the Loire valley at least. How widely they were exacted even in this area—from lay aristocratic land? from peasant owners? and who by, in those cases?—cannot be said; nor can their real weight be estimated. But they had certainly not died out at the moment assumed by much secondary literature, the early seventh century.[137]

The Loire valley is also special for another reason: it is the sub-region where *gesta municipalia* survived best. We encountered these in Ravenna in the late fifth to early seventh centuries (above, p. 70), as the municipal land registers that *curiales* used to keep track on landowning for tax purposes, and there are signs of them in seventh-century Spain as well (p. 97). But there is no sign anywhere in Italy (or indeed Spain) that such practices were still in existence after 650. In the Loire valley, however, they appear with an elaborate ritual of registration, involving a good deal of formal dialogue and numerous participants, in Poitiers in 677–8 and Angers as late as 804. Private documents that refer to future registration in the *gesta* also come from Le Mans in 616 and 643, Orléans in 667, Flavigny in 721 (the latter two in northern Burgundy), and, further afield, Murbach in Alsace in 728; the practice also appears in formularies, collections of charter formulae, from Angers (very early, probably dating to 514–15), Clermont, Tours,

gian accounting documents'. All commentators stress that they are annually constructed working documents. Sato, '*L'agrarium*', pp. 122–3, implies that the *agrarium*, notwithstanding its fiscal origins, could now be regarded as a rent; but in 'The Merovingian accounting documents', p. 144 n., he is uncertain whether to plump for rent or for tax. On this occasion, I agree with Durliat that it is most likely to be a tax. But we are here on the cusp of a structural shift.

[137] *Annona* remained associated with Aquitaine for another century, in *Vita Pardulfi*, c. 17; Astronomer, *Vita Hludovici*, c. 7—cf. *MGH, Cap.*, II, n. 192, c. 15 (a. 829) for the *inferenda*. But these references are vaguer, and are not certainly more than ad hoc military exactions (or, indeed, sometimes usurpations). See Lot, *L'impôt foncier*, p. 110; Fouracre, *Charles Martel*, p. 86; Rouche, *L'Aquitaine*, pp. 348–9.

Bourges (very late, dating to 805), and in the Paris region, in the formularies of Sens and Marculf, mostly in the sixth and seventh centuries.[138] As can be seen, these examples do also extend outside the Loire region, quite far in the Murbach document. They must sometimes be purely formulaic survivals, as indeed can be presumed from their preservation in formulary books. In fact, given the complete absence of *curiales* in any of our materials for taxation,[139] and, for that matter, given the increasing standardization of surviving taxation practice, they could perhaps best be seen as evidence of meaningless civic ritual. But it is at least interesting that Poitiers and Angers, the locations of our clearest evidence for the *gesta*, are also centres of late taxpaying. Civic ritual and the collection of the *inferenda* may have diverged substantially by now, but they both belonged to a public practice that had roots going back to the late empire.

The Loire valley, seen broadly, was thus particularly traditional in its fiscal practices. This does not seem to indicate *Romanitas*, at least not in any simple sense, for these patterns have few clear parallels in the other major area of Roman 'continuity', the Rhône–Sâone valley; nor does it mark a common political history, for Le Mans was never Visigothic, and the Loire valley was continually redivided between Merovingian kings. Most strikingly, the Loire was not an area of particular centrality for the kings: it was divided up more often than it was fought over, and kings were happy to hand out fiscal immunities to churches here.[140] Its maintenance of tax did not, that is to say, make it obviously more valuable, which probably further confirms the point made earlier about Chilperic's rates—tax was by now not so high that it had any effect on a politics by now dominated by land. But it does operate as a warning against teleology: tax did not *have* to disappear once it ceased to be essential, and nor did it have to disappear at an even rate everywhere.

Implicit in this account of this seventh- and eighth-century evidence is that it is not paralleled elsewhere in Francia, and this is indeed the case. Actually, this is even true of the sixth century to a considerable extent, given that Gregory tells us most of all about the Loire valley and its environs. Outside his main area, he only mentions taxation a handful of times: a fantastic

---

[138] Respectively, Tardif, 'Les chartes mérovingiennes', nn. 1–3; *Ub. Coblenz und Trier*, I, n. 42; Busson and Ledru, *Actus*, pp. 141, 162; Pardessus, *Diplomata*, nn. 358, 544; *Cartulary of Flavigny*, n. 1; *Form. Andecavenses*, n. 1; *Form. Arvernenses*, nn. 1–2; *Form. Turonenses*, n. 3; *Form. Bituricenses*, n. 15; *Marculfi Formulae*, II.37–8; *Cartae Senonicae*, nn. 39–40 (in *MGH*, *Formulae*, pp. 4–5, 28–9, 136–7, 174–6, 97–8, 202–3). The best discussion is in Classen, 'Fortleben und Wandel', pp. 42–9.

[139] The only possibility (cited by Rouche, *L'Aquitaine*, p. 345) is Gregory of Tours, *LH*, X.7, referring to *exactores* in Clermont: these would have been of curial status under the empire (see *CTh*, XII.6.22), but it is not clear how far a fairly generic technical term had changed meaning by 590.

[140] As Régine Le Jan pointed out to me in discussion. Rouche, *L'Aquitaine*, pp. 338–50, argues that this continuity is specifically Aquitainian, but he elides the Le Mans material to do so.

account of a tax-exemption for Lyon in the 470s, which is anyway well before Frankish rule in the area, and two narratives about the Franks refusing to be taxed in northern Gaul in the mid-sixth century; other sixth-century sources add nothing that is sub-regionally specific.[141] We could not assume that there was no tax in the sixth-century Frankish heartland— Gregory would surely have complained about the unfairness of taxing his own areas if so, given his attitudes to fiscal exactions; but there were certainly more Franks, and thus more potentially immune landowners, in the north, and Francisization was developing apace. Taxation may well have been in rapid decay around Paris or Metz just as it was being revised in Poitiers. At the Council of Clichy outside Paris in 626–7, under Chlotar II, payers of the *publicus census* were excluded from the clergy without special permission; lawmakers in the Frankish heartland were beginning to regard taxpayers as a special, inferior, category. By Marculf's time in the late seventh-century Paris area, free status itself was beginning to be associated with tax-exemption.[142] St-Denis documents from the period never (apart from the one Le Mans reference) refer to any public due except transport tolls; contemporary royal privileges from northern Neustria and Austrasia similarly only refer to tolls, hospitality, and judicial fines; so, it can be argued, do the more fragmentary episcopal records from Reims.[143] The only clear reference to a tax-collector known to me for the whole area north or east of the Loire valley in the seventh century comes from Lyon in c.660, and the context is a rhetorical insult against a bishop, not an account of tax actually being collected. There are references to rulers wickedly exacting taxes, but they are very generic.[144] Words that had formerly had a fiscal edge to them, like *census*, or *describere/descriptio* (assess, assessment), are coming to be used only for rent-paying: whether this means that the rents themselves had ex-fiscal elements, as Goffart argues, or whether the words have simply shifted meaning, the tax process had ended.[145] The sharpness of

[141] Gregory of Tours, *GC*, c. 62, for Lyon; *LH*, III.36, VII.15, for Franks. The Lyon story all the same seems to show that the city had an exemption (for 3 miles around the city) in Gregory's time.

[142] Clichy, c. 8 (in *Les canons des conciles*, p. 532); *Marculfi formulae*, I.19 (in *MGH, Formulae*, pp. 55–6).

[143] *ChLA*, XIII, n. 568, XIV, n. 574, for St-Denis tolls; for elsewhere, *ChLA*, XIX, n. 674; *MGH, Dip. Merov.*, e.g. nn. 96, 99 (perhaps interpolated), 171; *Dip. Maiorum domus*, nn. 17, 19; *Marculfi formulae*, I.2–4, 14–17, II.1, Suppl., n. 1 (in *MGH, Formulae*, pp. 41–5, 52–5, 70–4, 107). For Reims, see the texts excerpted in Flodoard, *Historia Remensis ecclesiae*, II.5, 7, 11; see Devroey, 'Les premiers polyptyques rémois' (for Flodoard's methods, see Sot, *Un historien*, e.g. pp. 418–59).

[144] *Acta Aunemundi*, c. 8, for Lyon; cf. Stephanus, *Vita Wilfridi*, c. 33, for Dagobert II's biblical-style exaction of *tributum*; *Vita Balthildis*, c. 6, has the virtuous queen halting *exactiones publicae* (*actiones* in the earlier A text). Taxation might, of course, have survived in Lyon, with the Rhône valley here matching Aquitaine; see also the ref. in n. 141; but the evidence for the area is too sketchy to allow us to go further.

[145] For *descriptio* and its analogues, see e.g. Desiderius of Cahors, *Ep.* II.7; *Passio Praejecti*, c. 37; Flodoard, *Historia Remensis ecclesiae*, II.7. For a more fiscalist commentary, see Goffart, *Rome's fall*, pp. 208–9, 249–51; Durliat, 'Les attributions civiles', p. 247.

the shift from normal taxpaying in the late sixth century to a post-tax politics in the immunities of the mid- to late seventh century could thus be seen simply as a shift in our documentation (and in the attention of historians) from Gregory's Loire valley narratives to the northern Frankish charter collections. In the Merovingian heartland, fiscal involution had probably begun earlier, and all that kings like Chlotar II perhaps did was register what had, in the heartland, already occurred. This might be too radical a revision of the narrative of tax decline; really, we cannot say what happened in the north and when, and the decisive shifts still tend to concentrate in the Chlotar–Dagobert period. But the distinction between the Paris–Rhine heartland and the Loire basin of southern Neustria and northern Aquitaine must be recognized, as also must the point that the kings were strongest in the areas where taxation was weakest—the opposite to what one would expect, given the demonstrable advantages of taxation for kings, and an indication in itself of how marginal that tax really was, perhaps across the whole Merovingian period.

The greater quantity of documentation that survives for the early medieval Franks does not make their political economy more transparent, unfortunately; indeed, quite the opposite, as the previous sentences imply. But it would be very wrong to conclude that the weakness of taxation in northern Francia meant that it was in economic terms a wasteland, along the lines that could be argued for Britain (pp. 306–10). The wealth of the Frankish kings, particularly in the late sixth century but also in the seventh, gives the lie to that; the seventh-century north is increasingly seen as a forerunner of Carolingian economic revival, and the continuities of royal wealth—by now based on landowning, but also to an extent on other public rights such as tolls—argue against a low point that lasted very long at all. Actually, as we shall see (pp. 178–86), one can equally argue for considerable continuities in the structures of large-scale landowning in much of the north, both public and private, in strong contrast to the British situation, and for that matter on a larger scale than in either Italy or Spain. It may be that the weakness of the tax structure in the same areas simply derives from the end of the Rhine army and the cessation of tax-collection (or its rapid privatization by landowners) in the Rhine-supply catchment area, which did not involve western Gaul/Aquitaine as much as it did the north, and not from any wider disruption there. This is wholly speculative, of course. But the disjuncture between the patterns of tax-raising and the patterns of rent-taking is particularly clear in this latter area all the same.

A final point about Gaul/Francia is this. This part of the Roman empire gives us the best evidence we have—despite its evident deficiencies—for how taxation in practice declined. The decline was local in its incidence, because the fiscal system was seen as a set of local resources, no longer as an integrated framework. In each city territory, at different speeds, tax assessment became more occasional and more standardized; rates lessened;

responsibility shifted from city councillors to central officials and then to landowners; the tax burden became slowly privatized and assimilated to rents, with or without the help of a formal immunity; taxpayers became regarded as not fully free. These are all steps from a political system funded by taxation to one based on land, and they are steps that have been recognized as such for a century, except perhaps the local differences: what historians have mostly argued about is the pacing. It seems to me significant, however, that one development that does not seem often to have taken place is the takeover by private individuals (or by non-royal institutions, such as bishoprics) of *territorial* tax-raising. One might have expected tax-immunities to have resulted in *potentes* with fiscal control over a city territory, or a *pagus*, or a smaller area: fiscal control over people who were not, in a strictly landed sense, their tenants, as in the Arab *iqṭāʿ* system (above, p. 85). Such control would have had its microregional analogues in the *seigneurie banale* of the late tenth century and onwards, in which surviving public rights such as justice and hospitality were territorialized in precisely such a way.[146] There might be some instances of this pattern, it is true: the tax-cession by the bishop of Tours to St-Martin in the 710s may be one example, in that the bishop apparently had territorial rights to cede; others of the 'episcopal republics' of Eugen Ewig and Reinhold Kaiser could perhaps have had similar resources.[147] But the main element of the privatization of tax rights, which anyway only took place after tax levels declined seriously, seems to be the devolution to landowners of dues owed to the fisc from their *own* lands, not those of others. I guess that one development that was relatively unlikely was the power of any immunist to tax effectively the lands of any major landowner in his district—senators had been hard to tax even under the empire, let alone their successors or descendants in a seventh-century city territory, and Frankish aristocrats would hardly have been easier. But it is interesting that we also have no record of peasants who own their own land but owe *census* to an immunist. The peasant owners who emerge in our documentation in the late seventh and eighth centuries, above all in the eastern parts of the Frankish kingdom, do not seem to owe anything to private powers. Instead, they were—or became regarded as— Franks: liable (in theory) to military service.[148] It cannot be excluded, of

---

[146] Still classic is Duby, *La société*, pp. 174–90; for subsequent bibliography, see Carocci, 'Signoria rurale'.

[147] Ewig, 'Milo', pp. 211–19; Kaiser, *Bischofsherrschaft*, pp. 55–74. Kaiser, 'Royauté et pouvoir épiscopal', pp. 147–50, develops the fiscal point with reference to Tours. The last 'episcopal republic', Chur, lasted until after 800: Kaiser, *Churrätien*, pp. 45–53.

[148] For peasant owners, see below, pp. 394–8; for military obligations, e.g. Ganshof, *Frankish institutions*, pp. 59–68. But not all peasants, of course, served in the army in any period. In the ninth century there are occasional signs of the development of more standardized dues paid in lieu of army service, particularly east of the Rhine: the *haribannus*, as well as the *osterstopha*, perhaps a form of tribute. See Gockel, *Karolingische Königshöfe*, pp. 96–100; Lot, *L'impôt foncier*, pp. 107–18; and particularly Innes, *State and society*, pp. 153–9. These may be

course, that in other areas it was different; we simply do not have the evidence to be sure of it. But on the face of it, one aspect of the decline of Frankish taxation was that peasant owners, not only aristocrats and churches, were for the first time free of obligations. Only tenants sometimes found their fiscal burdens continued, now compounded with their rents.

The fourth and final Romano-Germanic example is the Lombards. It will take less space, for the Lombard kingdom did not, as far as we can see, tax after 600 or so at the latest: but it offers examples of different sorts of public resources and of political integration, which can be compared to those of the Franks of the late seventh century and onwards, after the developments just discussed had mostly taken place.

The situation in Italy had changed as a result of the Gothic war. Italy's former geo-political fiscal networks, the Carthage–Rome axis in the south and the (less important) Po–Danube connection in the north, ended in the mid- to late fifth century, as we have seen (pp. 76–9, 87). In the Ostrogothic period a fiscal focus on Ravenna is the most clearly evidenced pattern in the *Variae*, although Rome was still supplied from public sources inside mainland Italy and Sicily. The war, however, would have seriously damaged the remaining internal structures of the region, and it is from now on that archaeologists and historians begin to stress the breakdown of the economic coherence of the peninsula. Rome (and the army and civil administration) did still need to be fed, and when peace returned after 552–4 (561 in the northern Po plain), there is clear evidence of the intent of Justinian and his officials to re-establish the fiscal system of the pre-war period.[149] But it must have been at least temporarily weaker; it may not have offered in all areas a secure basis for the Lombard polity even in the years of the establishment of the kingdom, 569–74, after which the latter anyway dissolved for another decade into a network of autonomous duchies. This would be the best context for positioning the Lombard kingdom as for the most part a post-tax state from the start.

Actually, the proposal that the Lombards did not ever tax is now contested. It might be said to be contradicted by two famous short passages from Paul the Deacon's *Historia Longobardorum*, written in the 790s, about the Lombard settlement in the 570s–580s, which clearly refer to some or all of the Romans being made *tributarii*, among other atrocities. Were these

---

paralleled by the *hostilitium*, an army due, in the polyptych of St-Germain-des-Prés (see esp. Devroey, 'Problèmes de critique', pp. 456–60). Such a fiscalization of public service obligations would indeed be one of the ways that taxation revived, in the twelfth century and later. But it does not seem to have been particularly systematic in the Carolingian period, and did not outlast the ninth century. The fact that armies remained landed was a limit to any renewal of fiscal burdens of this type.

[149] *Constitutio pragmatica*, cc. 9–12, 18 (ed. with *NJ*, pp. 799–802) for Justinian; see Zanini, *Le Italie*, pp. 291–334; Marazzi, 'The destinies', pp. 132–59, for economic fragmentation.

passages to have been taken from an earlier account by Secundus of Non (d. 612), whom Paul cites elsewhere, who was in the Lombard court by around 600—an assertion that cannot be proved—then they would at least be closer to the years of the invasion.[150] The two texts have been subject to innumerable contrasting interpretations over the last two centuries, as they contain almost the only usable evidence for the Lombard settlement, but can be very variously construed; new interpretations, indeed, continue to be produced. Recent examples of these, however, first by Goffart, and then, following him, by Paolo Delogu, Jean Durliat, Walter Pohl, and Nick Everett, stress the tax element in the Lombard settlement far more than had been normal hitherto. Previous analysts of Paul had been more concerned with quantifying the violence of the Lombards, which seemed entirely to exclude anything as Romanized as a fiscal system (for *tributarius* does not strictly have to mean 'taxpayer'; it might just mean 'tributary' in a very generic sense); but Goffart was more interested in the double appearance of the word *hospes* in these passages, which fitted into his tax-allotment model of 'barbarian' settlement, and it is true that one of the readings of Paul's passages would indeed fit that model. The most interesting developments of this reading are in recent articles by Pohl, who points out that the terminology Paul uses (*tributarius*, but also *adgravatus*) matches very well that of Gregory of Tours when he defended Tours's tax-exemption in 589. Following this argument, Paul (borrowing from Secundus) could be seen as simply using a standard fiscal terminology of the late sixth century, which was as operative in Italy as it was in Gaul.[151]

I have elsewhere declared my distrust of any argument that is based too closely on texts as late, fragmentary, and ambiguous as these, and these recent discussions do not convince me to change position. But it does at least have to be recognized that it is striking that a writer at the end of the eighth century should use (or copy) tax-related terms for the sixth-century settlement, given how outdated such a terminology was by then. Furthermore, since the Byzantines had reorganized the tax system in Italy (it was operational at least in Ravenna, as the papyri make clear), the Lombards would have to have been unusually hostile to taxation—or unusually disorganized—not to have employed it at all, at least in the first years of the settlement. These arguments, taken from Pohl, are the best ones we have to support, at least prima facie, the proposition that the Lombards did use a version of the Roman tax system when they first came into Italy. This is the

---

[150] Paul, *HL*, II.32, III.16. Secundus is cited at III.29, IV.27, 40.
[151] Goffart, *Barbarians and Romans*, pp. 176–89; Delogu, 'Longobardi e Romani', pp. 111–20; Durliat, 'Le salaire', pp. 48–9; Pohl, 'The empire and the Lombards'; idem, '*Per hospites divisi*' (of the last two, respectively pp. 118–21 and 197–200 for Paul and Gregory); Everett, *Literacy*, pp. 75–9. These also cite the extensive earlier bibliography. For Gregory, see esp. *LH*, IX.30.

conclusion which the balance of argument seems best to favour at the present time.[152]

More important than these possible proofs of the institutions of the early Lombard settlement, however, is the fact that the Lombard kings can never be seen exacting, or even referring to, land tax in any subsequent documentation, whether laws (surviving from the Edict of Rothari in 643 onwards), documents (surviving, with a few early outliers, from 710 onwards), or indeed Paul himself. Stefano Gasparri has analysed all possible citations of taxation in the seventh and eighth centuries, and come to an essentially negative conclusion: no systematic, or even unsystematic, pattern of land-based fiscal exactions can be derived from them. If the Lombards had ever taxed the land, all sign of the process had vanished by the mid-seventh century, in a way that has no parallel in Francia or Spain. All that the kings could take from inside the kingdom was occasional ad hoc tribute, like the 30 pounds of soap owed by the city of Piacenza as a *pensio*, which King Liutprand (712–44) ceded to the local church, and, more systematically, public works, judicial fines, and tolls, of types that, as we have seen, were maintained by the Franks as well (indeed, they were to remain royal rights, and became the bases of territorial seigneuries in the eleventh century, in Italy as in Francia).[153] Almost all the wealth of the Lombard state in the last century of its existence before the Frankish conquest of 773–4, the period of the great bulk of its documentation, was derived from the exploitation of public land. This we do have documentation for, in laws and charters; it is also the politics of land that dominates the narratives of Paul the Deacon. The seventh- and eighth-century Lombards are thus the first clear example of a fully post-tax state in the West—an example which would shortly be matched by the Carolingian Franks. If, then, they did tax at their arrival, the system swiftly collapsed, presumably in the upheaval of the period after 574, when the Lombards managed for a decade without a king, and their kings after 584 had to face semi-autonomous dukes in the north for a generation. Tax must indeed not have ever been more than a marginal resource for the Lombards, or this process would not have been so fast, judging by parallels elsewhere.

One point that does need to be made, however, is that the Lombard kingdom, in the late seventh century and onwards, was not notably frail as a result. The central administration does not seem to have been as complex as that of the Visigoths, in particular (in the main because, in the absence of any tax system, there was less to run); but the capacity of its administrators

---

[152] Pohl, '*Per hospites divisi*', pp. 189, 201, with 202–17 for the Ravenna papyri (esp. *P. Ital.* 2). Wickham, *Early medieval Italy*, p. 66, is critical of tight textual analysis of Paul's passages.

[153] Gasparri, 'Il regno longobardo', pp. 262–8, with the addition of *MGH, Dip. Kar.*, I, n. 174 (a. 792). Piacenza: *CDL*, III, n. 18 (note that the pounds of soap are *inferebantur* to Pavia, the same terminology as in Francia). Leicht, *Studi sulla proprietà*, II, pp. 47–54 and Brühl, 'Zentral- und Finanzverwaltung', pp. 90–3, were more upbeat about Lombard taxation.

to react swiftly to local situations seems to have been considerable. As has been argued elsewhere, it was normal for people to appeal to the king, in order to resolve disputes big and small, or even to ratify documents; in one case, the diocesan boundary dispute between Siena and Arezzo of 714–15, appeals went to King Liutprand four times, and the king twice sent *missi* to hear the case on the ground, a practice we can trace on other occasions too.[154] Liutprand heard cases of all kinds, in fact, which we can sometimes reconstruct, for he turned many of his judgments into legislation: in 732–4 he pronounced on, among other things, bigamy, an attack on a woman while defecating, a husband prostituting his wife, group agrarian violence, a man stealing a woman's clothes while she was bathing, who should be responsible in the case of a man killed by the counterweight of a well, who should be responsible in the case of a foal who killed a child, adultery which took place with a slave between a marriage agreement and the marriage itself, group agrarian violence by women, and so on. Royal judicial authority was respected; we have a document from 771 in which King Desiderius directed the bishop of Lucca to reverse his decision over a case of incest among the holders of a private church, and the bishop did so.[155] Going to the royal capital at Pavia was probably less ritualized than it was in the case of Toledo, and apparently also less momentous and high-aristocratic than going to a Frankish *palatium*. It was, simply, normal; and so was the reception of instructions from the capital. One should not see this capillary power as straightforward or uncontested; at the same time kings could complain in their laws, often at great length, about the abuses and corruption of local judges and administrators (*iudices*), or about the tendency of royal *actores* illegally to appropriate royal land.[156] But these complaints were standard in all pre-industrial political systems; by contrast, detailed royal interventions were rather less common, particularly in the early middle ages.

The cohesion of the Lombard kingdom had three main bases. First, a simple geographical one: it was not so very large, and it was based on a single river-valley, the Po plain and its outliers, with the addition of Tuscany over the Appennines, making up roughly the size of a single Frankish *Teilreich*. The southern duchies of Spoleto and Benevento were separate: they were always as independent as Bavaria, or indeed more so. Pavia was accessible; Liutprand reckoned that crucial judicial business between the Po plain and Tuscany could be done in twenty-four days, though he usually

---

[154] For local administration, see Gasparri, 'Il regno longobardo', and Wickham, 'Aristocratic power', pp. 153–8. For Siena and Arezzo, *CDL*, I, nn. 17, 19, 20, III, nn. 12, 13—the area was as far from Pavia as any part of the kingdom in 714. Other examples of royal intervention include parallel boundary disputes in Tuscany and Emilia, *CDL*, III, nn. 4, 6, and I, n. 21.

[155] Liutprand 122, 125, 130, 134–7, 139, 141; *CDL*, II, n. 255 for Lucca; cf. for other royal interventions, nn. 137, 163, 170.

[156] e.g. Liutprand, *Notitia de actoribus regis*, c. 5; Ratchis 1, 10.

allowed sixty.[157] Secondly, it was a territory of cities, as the Frankish heart-land was not (though Aquitaine and the Rhône valley still largely were), and as much of Visigothic Spain may have decreasingly been (see below, Chapter 10). The Roman city network, tight and fairly regular across the Lombard kingdom, was still in operation, and it structured everything: the church, of course, but also royal government, and the socio-political activity of local aristocracies, who, crucially, remained urban-based as well. One must not overstress continuity here: by Roman standards, as we shall see (pp. 647–50), Italian cities were by now materially unimpressive foci. But the political network persisted. Everything essentially took place in the same location. In Lucca, by far the best-documented city in this period, the *curtis regia* in the centre of the city near the old forum, focus of royal justice and the admin-istration of royal land, balanced the *curtis ducalis* of the duke of Lucca in the west of the city and the episcopal palace in the south-east. Between all of them and around the Roman walls were the private churches of the urban aristocracy. Considerable local aggregation was possible here, and also considerable royal control, in part because the leaders of political society were all here, in part because their inevitable disagreements could be bal-anced from above, just as in the Roman world. It looks as though the confusion of the Lombard invasions, which was greater than that of the Visigoths or Franks (the Lombards never managed to conquer the whole of Italy, after all), did not disrupt the internal cohesion of the city units of northern Italy, or the expectation that political power was city-based—indeed, the Lombards themselves settled in cities as soon as they could.[158] Reconstruction in the early seventh century was easier as a result, and so was institutional stability, by Rothari's time.

The third basis of the cohesion of the kingdom was the balance of landed power. The king was a landowner on a grand scale, as were his counterparts in Francia and Spain. But, unlike at least in Francia, most of his aristocrats were not. As we shall see (pp. 209–19), very few indeed of the Lombard magnates were major owners: perhaps some of the ducal families, but not all even of them. Most of the *viri magnifici* of our private documents owned only a handful of estates: enough to make them prosperous, but not enough for them to build up clientèles of lesser aristocrats and armed retainers—each of whom would have needed their own lands—and thus create the basis for sub-regional power. What is lacking in our (admittedly scanty) narrative sources, especially when viewed from Francia, is any sign of the swirl of aristocratic faction, the sorts of ambitious aristocratic leaders whose loyal-ties it was so essential for mid-seventh-century Merovingians (and, for that

---

[157] Liutprand 61, cf. 44, 88, 108–9.
[158] Basic for the urban focus of Lombard administration is Harrison, *The early state*. For Lucca, see Belli Barsali, 'La topografia di Lucca', esp. pp. 506–15; de Conno, 'L'insediamento longobardo'. For early city occupation, Paul, *HL*, III.17 (a. 584).

matter, mid-ninth-century Carolingians) to court. When Paul describes the construction of armed support by rival kings (which he does at least once, in his account of the Cunipert–Alahis civil war of c.688), he characterizes it as being done city by city—first Brescia, then Pavia, then Vicenza, then Treviso, with (aristocratic) *cives* operating together. He does not refer to any large-scale dealers like Flaochad and Willebad in Burgundy (d. 643) or Leodegar bishop of Autun (d. 678) or Eucherius, bishop of Orléans (d. 738) or so many others in the Frankish world, lay or episcopal alike.[159] This may reflect Paul's late eighth-century assumptions about how politics worked, not reportage about the 680s, but it is significant all the same. Nor does it seem to result from elision, unlike, perhaps, the *Historia Wambae* in Spain (above, p. 96), for Paul is certainly happy enough to pose political choices in terms of feuds, fears, and jealousies. These, all the same, take place on the level of the city faction, or sometimes the noble entourage, rather than on the level of grand aristocratic politics. As a result of this small scale for the aristocracy, however, not only was the king an inescapable magnet for ambition, but the king did not even have to give very much land away to satisfy it. Central or local office-holding was sought after by the aristocracy, and, while corruption was to be expected from officials, disloyalty usually was not. The kingdom remained cohesive, only fraying slightly at the edges when the Franks showed interest in hegemony over it, as in the 590s, perhaps in the 660s, and above all in the twenty years between the Frankish invasion of 754 and the final fall of Pavia to Charlemagne in 774.[160] It may be added that these observations seem to be largely valid for Spoleto and Benevento too, although documentation for these two independent duchies is much more patchy.[161]

These final observations allow us to look at the issue of political aggregation in the Romano-Germanic kingdoms, after the period of the breakdown in taxation, in comparative perspective. A ruler who is in charge of a fully effective tax-raising system can finance his own army and salaried officials, and has a secure independent basis of authority. Challenges to it will of course exist: all rulers need the consent at least of their armed men, either by creating an ideology of obedience, by training, indoctrination, or

---

[159] Paul, *HL*, V.36–9; cf. Fredegar, *Chronica*, IV.89–90; *Passio prima Leudegarii*; *Vita Eucherii*, cc. 7–9.

[160] For the aristocracy and office-holding, Tabacco, 'La connessione'. For the last years of the Lombard kingdom, Schmid, 'Zur Ablösung' (more downbeat); Delogu, 'Lombard and Carolingian Italy', pp. 301–3, and Wickham, *Early medieval Italy*, pp. 45–7 (more upbeat).

[161] See most recently Gasparri, 'Il ducato di Spoleto', esp. pp. 104–12; idem, 'Il ducato e principato di Benevento', esp. pp. 122–3; and Collavini, 'Duchi e società locali'. The best-documented aristocratic groups in each, the Rieti families in the former and those of Benevento itself, seem to have been closely linked to ducal power (see also below, p. 217). By the 830s, however, Benevento certainly had factions, and broke up because of their infighting: see above all Cilento, *Le origini della signoria capuana*, pp. 81–104.

ceremonial, or, more simply, just by giving them what they want—indeed, preferably all of these; coups are the ever-present alternative, as Roman emperors knew from the start to the finish. Sub-regional or local breakdown, by contrast, can only occur if separatist leaders seek to reconstruct the state machinery on a sub-regional or local basis, which is not always easy. None of these patterns existed, however, once armies were landed, as they were in all of the Romano-Germanic kingdoms. Land-based military power in itself created a land-based, and potentially localized, politics. We do not know enough about Vandal Africa to develop the point there, but there is no doubt about it in Spain, Francia, and Italy. In Spain, political fragmentation was kept under careful control between c.580 and 711, but its potential is obvious as soon as one looks at before and after; in Italy it was certainly a feature of the early Lombard kingdom, and, even if it is less visible in the period after 620 or so, this must be set against the fact that the kings hardly ever even attempted to control the Lombard duchies of the central and southern Appennines, Spoleto and Benevento. In Francia, political separatism was a constant possibility, by subject peoples, or even at the level of single counties. Before the late Carolingian break-up, royal courts remained extremely powerful, but aristocrats could be as well—the stakes were certainly high in Francia, arguably higher than anywhere else.

The basic problem that rulers faced in all three regions was thus the same: the potential localization of the politics of land. Some of the ways they could deal with it were similar, too. In all three regions, kings were at least far richer than anyone else. In Visigothic Spain they still taxed, into the late seventh century (with an Arab-period revival after 711); Visigothic taxation was by now too low to act as an independent basis for the state, but, given that the army was no longer paid from it, it could serve to keep kings very rich indeed, particularly when added to the revenues from their extensive lands. In Lombard Italy, tax soon ceased, but the relatively small scale of the aristocracy at least meant that kings were proportionately as dominant, even if everyone, kings and landowners alike, were less generously resourced than in Francia. This wealth was of course in part ceded away in permanent gifts of land, to the church and the laity, or else was tied up in local office-holding, in that local dukes and counts controlled it as part of their office (and did not always give it back): this was the standard gift-exchange of the politics of land discussed by Marc Bloch. But there was still a lot; and much of this wealth was accumulated in movables, whether food, manufactured goods, or treasure. It made coming to court to receive some of it, and maybe to stay there as a central government official, worthwhile for any aristocrat, large or small. Courts thus maintained their positions as foci for political aggrega-tion, throughout our period; and with this aggregation (and wealth) belonged the ideology of public power, inherited from the Roman world, which supported all royal ambition and responsibility, and which did not begin to break down in these regions until the foundering of Carolingian government in the late ninth and tenth centuries, after the end of our period.

Beyond this, however, the protocols that attached the centre to the regions differed quite substantially. In seventh-century Spain, the ceremonial of Toledo and the Romanizing imagery of royal legislation govern our evidence. We cannot be entirely sure how much this is simply the rhetoric of central government, with no reality in the localities. All the same, occasional non-royal sources indicate that aristocrats did fear and respect royal arbitrary authority; and bishops were often genuinely committed to conciliar decision-making. At the institutional level, too, we can find standardized formats used locally for court-cases.[162] What we can be sure of, however, as already observed, is that Spanish ceremonial had no parallels elsewhere. The Franks and the Lombards (and also smaller political groupings) legislated, but never like this—their forum was the annual army meeting, and it was much more pragmatic, much less rhetorical.[163] The Franks, too, made relatively little political use of their church councils before the Carolingian period, and the Lombards had almost no councils at all—indeed, they made very little use of bishops as political figures, far less than in the other two regions.[164]

For the Lombards, on the other hand, we can lay stress on capillary government. The king's *missi*, representatives, may have been ad hoc, but they came by often; justice was local, but regular, and was regularly appealed to Pavia. The city network helped greatly here, as we have seen. Royal legislation is at least sometimes referred to in documents (something we cannot say for the Franks, though we have more documents for them); people knew what it contained.[165] Lombard government was pragmatic, but it seems to have continued to work; after 774 the Franks borrowed from it. Above all, the aristocracy of Italy seems to have operated inside its ground-rules.

[162] See above, n. 107, for court-cases; the Count Bulgar letters in *Epistolae Wisigothicae*, nn. 11–16, indicate a very cautious aristocratic respect for royal power already in the 610s. Stocking, *Bishops, councils*, stresses the collective nature of decision-making, with bishops as involved as kings.

[163] Childebert II and Liutprand both favoured 1 March, the day of army muster, for legislation: *MGH, Cap.*, I, n. 7; Liutprand, prologues to 7, 15, 19, 30, 54, 65, 70, 84, 96, 104, 117, 139, 143—and also Ratchis 1, prologue to 5; Aistulf, prologue to 1, 10.

[164] For Frankish church councils, see *Les canons des conciles*; they focus on ecclesiastical affairs almost exclusively, unlike Spanish councils (in Vives, *Concilios*). Kings did call them, however—and even cancelled them on occasion (Desiderius of Cahors, *Ep*. II.17). Their acts do not survive between 675 and 742, and they probably hardly met (though see the cautionary remarks of Wood, *Merovingian kingdoms*, pp. 250–1). For Lombard councils, our only source is the verse account of the 698 Council of Pavia, *Carmen de synodo Ticinensi*; for bishops, Bertolini, 'I vescovi del "regnum langobardorum" '.

[165] e.g. *CDL*, I, nn. 81, 96, II, nn. 226, 230, 293; for the Franks, contrast Nehlsen, 'Zur Aktualität und Effektivität', pp 461–83 (though Brown, 'The use of norms in disputes', establishes a nuanced argument for recognized procedural norms being often followed in court-cases, at least in Bavaria). For the density of royal government, see Everett, *Literacy*, pp. 163–96.

The Merovingian Franks are in some ways the hardest to characterize, because their aristocracies were so unruly and powerful, and their political expedients were so ad hoc. One must at least stress that they were far from devoid of the sort of local intervention we have seen for Italy. What survived of taxation in the Loire valley is one instance, although its devolution and standardization at least made it easier to administer by now. The range of seventh-century royal interventions that we can see in diplomata and in Marculf's formulary are perhaps better guides. Kings were asked to oversee marriage arrangements, to confirm wills, and to help divide property between heirs; their *agentes* travelled to the localities, much as Lombard (and, later, Carolingian) *missi* did; they regularly patronized even privately owned monasteries, characteristically ceding the land on which the church was built, even if not the rest; and they were much sought after for their justice and their judicial ratification of property-owning, in the grand public *placita* which began in the early seventh century and continued as a major aspect of royal ritual for 300 years and more.[166] Kings, and their courts, were relevant to private life, and their ratification of private activity was important, throughout the areas that charters illuminate. It seems to me that one can trace a lessening in this activity between the 670s and the 720s, which marks a genuine weakening in central authority (cf. above, p. 105), but it was only relative, and it was later reversed.[167] Two more important limitations, however, are these. First, this administrative centrality seems to be reactive more than proactive; people went to the king more often than the king sent out to them. The Merovingians appear to have seen it as their main task to ratify and to legitimate, not to change, the behaviour of others: a self-restriction of royal responsibility that was unlike even the Lombards, let alone the Visigoths, or for that matter their Carolingian successors. Second, it seems restricted to the highest level of aristocratic society. This may be a problem of our documents, which are very aristocratic; but when we begin to get collections that reflect more local, even sometimes peasant society, like the Wissembourg cartulary, beginning in the late seventh century, kings abruptly disappear.[168] It may indeed be that Frankish politics was seen as much more the affair of elites than Lombard politics was. But, conversely, since elites were so powerful in Francia, it at least mattered that they considered government relevant. In this context, the ideological pull of the courts

---

[166] Marriages: *Marculfi formulae*, I.12 (in *MGH, Formulae*, pp. 50–1). Wills, *ChLA*, XIII, nn. 550, 559 (probably); Flodoard, *Historia Remensis ecclesiae*, II.4. Divisions: *ChLA*, XIII, n. 554; Havet, 'Questions mérovingiennes', V, n. 3; *Marculfi formulae*, I.20 (in *MGH, Formulae*, p. 56). *Agentes*: ibid., I.11, 23 (pp. 49, 57). Monastic patronage: Pardessus, *Diplomata*, nn. 273, 275, 350, 358, 423. For *placita*, see refs. in n. 124 above. For Merovingian governmental literacy, see Wood, 'Administration, law', and Linger, 'L'écrit'.

[167] The interventions referred to in the previous note all pre-date 677, except the *placita*, which carry on without a break.

[168] There are no royal charters among the 76 Wissembourg documents pre-dating 750 (ed. in *Trad. Wiz.*).

continued to be strong, even at its low point around 700. Frankish kings needed to be successful warriors to gain, and above all to regain, political support from their aristocrats, in a way that in Spain and Italy was apparently less essential; but this was at least possible, even after 700, as Charles Martel so clearly showed.[169] At their height, the Frankish kings were of absolutely central interest to their aristocrats—as we can see, for example, in letters of the 630s to Desiderius, bishop of Cahors, from other bishops, which are devoted to telling him where King Dagobert is at any given time, as he moved from Verdun to Reims then Laon then the Rhineland, all of them 700 km and more from Cahors.[170] They achieved this partly through ceremony (but less than the Visigoths), partly through administrative action (but less than the Lombards), and largely through the enormous opportunities for wealth and power that they offered, at all times—very matter-of-fact successors of the Roman emperors, but effective ones for all that.

3. The east Mediterranean empires

The east Roman empire around 600 maintained the fiscal structures, and the regional interrelationships, described earlier for Rome (pp. 72–9). Constantinople was still principally fed from Egypt, by far the richest province, and any pressure on that source was by now alleviated by the fact that the stable result of Justinian's reconquests was the acquisition to the East of the other two great grain provinces, Sicily and Africa. Exactly how these two were balanced against Egypt is not clear—sources for the years around 600 are not very helpful for these sorts of issues, and nor would they be again for centuries. But the Justinianic reconstruction of the African fiscal system (cf. p. 92) must have eventually borne fruit: the clearest proof is the fact that its exarch Heraclius could use the same blackmailing tactics against Phocas in 608, that is to say, withholding the grain supply to Constantinople, as pre-Vandal governors like Gildo had done against Rome; Africa was in fact organized enough for the exarch's son Heraclius (emperor 610–41) actually to conquer Constantinople from Carthage in 608–10. All the same, it is probable that the region never had the same importance in the eastern Mediterranean that it had once had in the West (cf. below, pp. 724–6).[171]

---

[169] See in general Reuter, 'Plunder and tribute'. For the relatively unmilitary style of the Lombard aristocracy, the best texts are the wills made by men going to war: see Gasparri, 'Strutture militari', esp. pp. 681–4.

[170] Desiderius of Cahors, *Epp.*, II.12, 15.

[171] For the exarch Heraclius in 608, Theophanes, *Chronographia*, p. 296. For the organization of Africa in the period, see Diehl, *L'Afrique byzantine*, pp. 501–2 (seals which show the organization of taxation—cf. Dunn, 'The *kommerkiarios*', pp. 4–15), 517–32. For archaeological signs of involution, see below, pp. 723–4.

The supply of the eastern frontier army was still, presumably, principally from Syria and Palestine, with some Egyptian help: the logistics here had not changed from earlier centuries.

It is in this context that the military disasters of the seventh century must be understood, in order to understand the fiscal problems the state faced. As we saw in Chapter 2, in 613–14 the Persians occupied Syria and Palestine, and Egypt in 618–19. The Roman counter-offensive restored these provinces to imperial rule in 628–9, but the Arabs began their own conquests shortly after, taking Syria and Palestine in 636–8 and Egypt in 640–2: this time the losses were permanent, and Anatolia, already a war zone in the 620s, was attacked systematically for a century. The east Roman state at two blows lost, as Michael Hendy has argued, two-thirds of its land area and three-quarters of its wealth;[172] its central core for a time was not much more substantial than the Aegean and Marmara sea-coasts, yet it had to defend itself still, and also feed Constantinople. At least the western empire had had two or three generations in which to adjust to conquest; the east Roman state had to do it in a handful of years, if it was to survive. Nothing could stay the same, and, in the necessary reorganizations that followed, the basis of the state—which we can now call Byzantine—profoundly shifted.

The impact on Constantinople in 618–19 of the loss of Egypt was immediate, just as that of Africa had been on Rome in 439; but not necessarily catastrophic. Two chronicles that cover the period state that the *sitēresion*, the grain *annona*, was suspended in 618/19, and one adds that grain ceased to be free; by the end of the eighth century it was forgotten that it ever had been.[173] Abolishing free grain did not, of course, solve the problem of supplying the city, but Egypt was, as we have seen, by now not the only source of urban grain. In the three decades after 618 Africa and Sicily must have been particularly important. After 647 the Arabs were in Africa as well, however; although they initially concentrated on its southern province, oil-rich Byzacena, rather than on the grain-lands of Proconsularis which they only conquered in the 690s, all the same African supplies would have been severely disrupted in the second half of the century. This left Sicily, which was firmly in Byzantine hands until it was conquered from Arab Africa in the decades after 827, as the pre-eminent grain province of the empire for a century-and-a-half. This major role for Sicily is barely documented, it is true, and has not been much considered by Byzantine historians. It does explain, however, the otherwise quixotic decision of Constans II to move the capital there in 662–8, and it is further underlined by the evidence of numismatics, which shows a more active circulation of coinage, copper as

---

[172] Hendy, *Studies*, p. 620.
[173] *Easter chronicle*, p. 711; Nikephoros, *Short history*, c. 8. It is forgotten in the *Parastaseis*, c. 12. See in general Durliat, *De la ville antique*, pp. 271–5.

much as gold, in eighth-century Sicily than in any part of the empire outside Constantinople. (Archaeology for Sicily in this period is, however, sketchy, so its material prosperity cannot be effectively tested as yet.)[174]

The western provinces could thus cushion Constantinople from the full effects of the loss of Egypt. So, conceivably, did grain sales from Persian and Arab Egypt itself, though these are not documented, and it would have been unwise to count on them given the risks involved in dependence on an enemy. Essentially, though, Constantinople's population must have slowly dropped, to levels that could be supported from more immediate suppliers like Thrace and northern Bithynia, both of them reasonably fertile territories, situated very close to the city around the Sea of Marmara, which is the situation we find by the tenth and eleventh centuries, after the loss of Sicily.[175] The drop in the population doubtless began as soon as the distribution of free grain ceased; it is generally reckoned to have been especially fast after the aqueduct of Valens was broken in the siege of 626, and supposedly not rebuilt till 766—hence also the city's ability to withstand siege again in 674–8 (in the summers only) and, above all, in 717–18. (Where the city got its reserves to survive these sieges is unclear, except the last: in 713 Anastasios II ordered that only people with their own three-year food reserve could stay in the city.) Although it may be doubted that the aqueduct was really fully out of action as long as 140 years—for Heraclius, in particular, was perfectly capable of serious building projects—all the same the population-drop fits all the available evidence: historians only argue about how low it got, with Cyril Mango proposing 40,000 and Paul Magdalino 70,000.[176] It is significant that the lower of these two figures is the highest that has been proposed for Rome in the eighth century: indeed, Constantinople was by now, and remained, substantially the bigger of the two, indeed the largest city in Europe until perhaps tenth-century Córdoba and, more certainly, late thirteenth-century Paris, Milan, and Florence. But its supply, whether from Sicily or from the Marmara area, did not again pose infrastructural problems to the state, at least in our period.

The army is more of a problem. Unlike the capital, it could not safely become dramatically smaller, and after the retreat from the eastern provinces (and from the Balkans), it was going to have to be located above all in

---

[174] Haldon, *Byzantium in the seventh century*, pp. 59–61 for Constans II; Morrisson, 'La Sicile byzantine', for coins. *Liber pontificalis*, LXXVIII.4, refers to a reassessment by Constans of Calabrian, Sicilian, Sardinian, and African taxation, linked to the move of the capital. For Sicilian archaeology, see below, p. 737.

[175] See, for the middle Byzantine period, Teall, 'The grain supply', pp. 117–32; Magdalino, 'The grain supply'.

[176] Mango, *Le développement urbain*, p. 54; Magdalino, *Constantinople médiévale*, p. 18. For the aqueduct and Anastasios II, Theophanes, *Chronographia*, pp. 440, 384. For the archaeology of the aqueduct, see Bono *et al.*, 'Water supply'; I am grateful to Jim Crow for discussion on this point, and for his scepticism about the completeness of the breakdown of water supply to the city.

Anatolia, which, except around the edges, is poor land with poor communications. The army was, as far as can be seen, spread out across the plateau, in five sections, with the defensive role of each linked to a zone of relative agrarian prosperity, in areas which are first referred to as *themata*, 'themes', in narratives for the period 669–87; the themes gained clear geographical identity in the early eighth century, and fiscal autonomy in the late eighth century. The issue of the origin of the themes is another much-contested question; here I follow John Haldon's dating.[177] But, however it is dated, what is clear is that the army, like the capital, came to be supplied locally, and indeed recruited locally. In the late eighth century a new centralized force of troops, called the *tagmata*, was developed, which was salaried, more highly trained, and directly reliant on the emperor;[178] but the bulk of the army had become regionalized, almost as much as in the West. Once this happened, which must have been a quick process in the mid-seventh century, the whole interregional exchange network, which the Roman state had supported for its infrastructural needs, came to an end, with the single exception of the Sicilian grain supply.

The catastrophic nature of the mid-seventh-century crisis has of course always been known, but it was not until Michael Hendy's work on it that its full dimensions became clear: the fiscal crisis was as great as the political-military crisis. Anatolia, whose fiscal marginality in the sixth century has already been noted (p. 79), and which was being constantly attacked by the Arabs, suddenly had to support an army large enough to hold off invaders without any support from elsewhere, in a situation of acute political confusion. Hendy could also point to the cessation of large-scale minting after 658, in that coin-finds almost dry up after that date, outside Constantinople (and Sicily). He concluded that the monetized tax system had collapsed, and that the thematic armies must have been settled on the land, much as they were in the West; only with Nikephoros I (802–11) did taxation revive, as the chronicler Theophanes' complaints about that emperor imply, a revival which is further indicated by an increase in coin-finds from the 820s.[179] But there are other references to the continuance of taxation in Theophanes: to registers of pay in 706 (which seem to parallel Arabic *dīwān* registers), to the supposedly oppressive tax policies of Constantine V in 767, to tax-remissions by Irene in 801, as well as those to army pay in the *Ekloga*, a law-code of 741. Furthermore, there are hundreds of surviving lead seals which attest

---

[177] Haldon, *Byzantium in the seventh century*, pp. 208–32; idem, 'Military service' (pp. 4–7 for previous bibliography).

[178] Haldon, *Byzantine praetorians*, pp. 228–337.

[179] Hendy, *Studies*, esp. pp. 619–67 (and pp. 424–5 for the coins: see further n. 228 below); Theophanes, *Chronographia*, pp. 486–8. For the size of the army, see Haldon, *Warfare*, pp. 99–103; Whittow, *The making*, pp. 181–93 (with lower figures). Treadgold, *Byzantine state finances*, pp. 13, 62–5, reaches parallel conclusions to those of Hendy, though he also stresses continuities in taxation; idem, *Byzantine revival*, pp. 149–52, discusses Nikephoros.

to the operation of a complex central and local bureaucracy throughout the seventh and eighth centuries, much of which was devoted to the organization of taxation.[180] Tax, as we have seen, does not have to be in money; and, as Haldon has argued, it is significant that the word *synōnē*, which had meant forced sales to the state in the sixth century, by the early ninth century simply meant land tax. He argues that the thematic armies continued to be paid, but paid in kind: what had changed was the end of a large-scale use of coin by the state outside the capital. Soldiers not unnaturally settled on the land too, but the principle of army pay (and also weapon supply), and the resultant maintenance of a relatively complex fiscal system, was never broken.[181]

This seems to me the most convincing formulation. Had the army become basically landed, then the revival of the fiscal system, including of developed patterns of army pay, would have been far more difficult than it was. Even Justinian found it difficult in Africa (above, p. 92), and the Umayyads in Spain harder (pp. 100–2); it would have been harder still for the economically and politically insecure emperors of the late eighth and the early ninth centuries, but the *tagmata* were established then, and a mid-ninth-century Arab chronicler, Ibn Khurdādhbih, is explicit about differential rates of pay for the Byzantine army.[182] The bureaucracy of the capital continued to exist, too, on a scale unmatched by the largely landed polities of the West, even Visigothic Spain; and we can trace not only tax officials and the supply of military equipment through the seals, but even the *cursus publicus* (*dromos* in Greek). Hendy is fully aware of these continuities, many of which he tracked himself in his analyses of the surviving fiscal system.[183] But in my view they go better with a basically paid than with a basically landed army; here, the shift to land did not have to be made.

The late seventh- and eighth-century Byzantine empire thus presents us with a double face. On one level, it was fiscally as localized as any Romano-Germanic kingdom, with armies supplied entirely from the local theme, and indeed with the emergence of thematic loyalties which bear some formal parallels to the provincial autonomies of the contemporary Frankish world. As we shall see, this fiscal localization is also matched by a dramatic fall in

---

[180] Theophanes, *Chronographia*, pp. 375, 443, 475; *Ekloga*, c. 162. Theophanes' account—especially his praise and blame—cannot be taken literally, but, as in the West, the continuity of the rhetoric of taxation as an element in his assignment of praise and blame is significant. For seals, see the references in Brubaker and Haldon, *Iconoclasm. The sources*, pp. 129–40, esp. Zacos and Veglery, *Byzantine lead seals*, and Nesbitt and Oikonomides, *Catalogue*. The central bureaucracy that can be deduced from the seals is analysed definitively in Brandes, *Finanzverwaltung*, esp. pp. 180–426.

[181] Haldon, esp. 'Synônê'; and, in general, 'Military service', pp. 11–20.

[182] Hendy, *Studies*, p. 182; Haldon, *Warfare*, p. 127; Treadgold, *Byzantine revival*, p. 318; all are based on Ibn Khurdādhbih, *Kitāb al-masālik wa'l mamālik*, pp. 83–5 of de Goeje's translation.

[183] Hendy, *Studies*, eg. pp. 607–13; for the *dromos*, Avramea, 'Land and sea communications', pp. 58–61.

the evidence for the landed aristocracy, in the evidence for urban society, and in the complexities of the networks of material culture in Anatolia and the Aegean (Chapters 4, 10, 11). On another level, however, Byzantium maintained a strong tax system, which, even if it was above all in kind, had a money element too, at least in the Constantinople area. Constantinople as a city was still dependent on it, in that, even if supplying the capital as a whole had become largely commercial, it was at least partly administered by the state; and the civil administration, which dominated the city and its buying-power, was certainly salaried. The wealth of the capital, and the complexity of its culture, were unequalled in the Christian world.[184] The armies, too, however localized, were at least circumscribed territorially by their own administrative systems, and the idea that private power-centres could exist was unthinkable in this period—the political danger to emperors remained coups, from regional armies (in the eighth century) or the capital (in the ninth), never political fragmentation.[185] Indeed, given the central control of all tax-raising by now, and the weakness of the aristocracy, eighth-century Byzantium was actually more centralized than was the eastern empire in 500. The small amount we know about local administration, largely from the late seventh-century sections of the *Miracles* of S. Demetrios from Thessaloniki, also indicates central control, with frequent imperial intervention, in particular to safeguard food supplies. Thessaloniki was a large and strategically crucial city, isolated from its natural hinterland by Slav settlement, but the involvement of the emperor is striking nonetheless.[186] The Byzantine empire was at its historic low point in the late seventh and eighth centuries, but its coherence is still significant. One is tempted to compare it to Lombard Italy, as a polity with relatively few concentrations of wealth but a relatively great capacity for internal organization, but the comparison certainly favours Byzantium—even the isolated exarchate of Ravenna was more structured than the Lombard kingdom, let alone Constantinople and its hinterland.[187] Even the weakest tax-raising state, that is to say, was more coherent than the most organized post-tax system.

[184] For the supply of the city, see above, n. 175. The unusual complexity of the society of the capital is clear in two rather different texts, the *Miracles* of S. Artemios of the mid-seventh century, and the *Parastaseis* of the late eighth: neither of them have contemporary parallels elsewhere, even in the Arab world.

[185] See in particular Haldon, 'Ideology and social change', pp. 178–89.

[186] *Miracles de St Démétrius*, II.4 (§§ 244–54, 281); Thessaloniki also had an official called an *abydikos* (e.g. Nesbitt and Oikonomides, *Catalogue*, I.18.8), whose name was taken from Abydos on the Dardanelles, one of the key points on the supply routes to Constantinople, and whose role must have included the overseeing of food availability. See Oikonomidès, 'Le kommerkion d'Abydos', pp. 244–8, with caution, and Brandes, *Finanzverwaltung*, p. 416 n.

[187] Brown, *Gentlemen*, pp. 109–43. Manaresi, *I placiti*, n. 17, is a dispute of 804 over the dues owed by the inhabitants of Istria to the Carolingians and their representatives, which makes extensive reference to the public dues of the previous Byzantine regime, which had lasted until the 780s; these, too, although much lighter than they had been, were more complex than anything in Lombard Italy.

What the Byzantine empire could not match, on the other hand, was the wealth of the early caliphate, which in many ways was the clearest lineal descendent of the Roman empire. Still, the fiscal localization that we have seen in both the West and in Byzantium can be tracked even in the Arab world, at least up to a point. Here, the political choices of the early caliphs were crucial, and these need to be surveyed first. We will then look at Egypt, for the best concrete example at our disposal of how those choices worked in practice.

The Muslim Arab armies conquered half of one empire, that of east Rome, and all of another, Sassanian Persia, and most of this process was completed in six years, 636–42. The caliphs could have stabilized this rule in a variety of ways. The most obvious might have been to settle the Arab armies as a new ruling class, scattered across this huge territory, but this was risky, both in military and cultural terms. A scattered army of occupancy, hugely outnumbered (Arabia is of course largely desert, and cannot sustain a substantial population except in the Yemen), was at risk from revolt, particularly from the highly militarized Persian aristocracy; it also might not have maintained either Arab culture or the new Muslim religion, which were the legitimating forces behind Arab conquest. 'Umar I accordingly, as already noted (p. 91), established a system by which the Arab armies should remain as permanent, hereditary garrisons, separate from the conquered populations, receiving pay ('*aṭā*'), with each individual's rights and pay registered on a provincial register known as the *dīwān*. This system was first established in 640/2, after the conquest of Iraq, when the Arabs were settled in the new cities of Kūfa and Baṣra (not necessarily willingly—some of them had got land immediately after the first Arab victories in 637–8); this was closely matched in the case of the settlement of Egypt, where the garrison city of Fusṭāṭ was similarly established in 642, in the area of modern Cairo, 150 km inland from the Roman capital at Alexandria. In Syria and Palestine, where there were already Arabs before the conquest, settlement was also permitted in the old urban centres and elsewhere, presumably privileging the political centres of the provinces, Caesarea, Tiberias, Damascus, Emesa (Ḥimṣ), as well as in smaller army camps; it may in fact be that the Syrian settlement was more ad hoc than elsewhere, at least until the 690s.[188] The pay that the Arab armies received could theoretically be spent on buying land, but this was not encouraged. In Egypt, in particular, where our evidence is better, there is almost no known Arab landowning before a small land-settlement in

---

[188] Puin, *Der Dīwān*; Morony, *Iraq*, pp. 236–53; Kennedy, *Armies*, pp. 59–65. For Syria, see esp. Donner, *Early Islamic conquests*, pp. 245–50. The period before the 690s is one in which Arab coins were not minted in Syria, except localized imitations of Byzantine copper coins, hinting at an unambitious fiscal system (cf. Kennedy, *Armies*, pp. 69, 72), probably based on a land tax in kind. Taxation and army pay certainly continued throughout, however. See Bates, 'Arab-Byzantine coinage', for the most likely of several accounts of the coinage of the period. See also below, n. 193.

the eastern Delta in 727, and large-scale landowning is relatively ill-attested before as late as 850.[189] The Arabs were of course paid out of taxation, which was never interrupted in the provinces they conquered, in large part precisely because of the maintenance of a paid army, unlike in the West. In fact, judging by Egyptian materials, the basic structures of the fiscal system only changed very slowly—in particular, the 'classic' Muslim tax dyad of *kharāj*, land tax, and *jizya*, the poll tax on non-Muslims, is hardly detectable until the mid-eighth century; initially, as far as we can see, a poll tax was simply added to previous patterns.[190] Initial continuities were further emphasized by the fact that the Arabs left the Roman and Persian administrative élites in place. In Syria, the focus of government under the Damascus-based Umayyad caliphate (661–750), even the language of administration was not changed until c.700; in Egypt, tax documents survive in Greek and Coptic as well as Arabic well into the eighth century. The Arab settlement was entirely new, and in no sense replicated the organization of the Roman army; but it entailed very substantial fiscal continuities.

There were changes, nonetheless. The first is an obvious geopolitical one: Syria, Palestine, and Egypt now belonged to an inland polity which stretched eastwards into Iran, not westwards across the Mediterranean. Egyptian grain would never go to Constantinople again until the Ottoman period. The ships of the Alexandria–Constantinople tax spine no longer structured Mediterranean exchange—just the opposite, in fact, for Alexandria housed a publicly funded war fleet, as many tax documents make clear, especially for the well-documented period around 710: as with the Vandals under Geiseric, the fleet would henceforth raid more than it would transport goods. The border with the Byzantine empire was rather differently constructed, too, for Arab armies could be supported from Syria, the middle Euphrates valley (now part of the province called the Jazīra, the 'island' between the middle Euphrates and middle Tigris), and Iraq—that is to say, with much greater logistical ease then either the east Romans or the Sassanians had managed, a situation of course mirrored by the organizational crisis the Byzantines faced.

The major difference in the fiscal structure of the early caliphate is, however, a much greater regionalization than the Romans had ever envisaged. The crucial linking role of sea traffic in the Roman world was out of

---

[189] Morimoto, 'Land tenure', pp. 114–15, 130ff. (pp. 124–30 probably overstate Arab landowning in Egypt after 730).

[190] See Simonsen, *Studies in the genesis*; Rémondon, 'P. Hamb. 56' (pp. 411–13, 426, 428, for the poll tax, *diagraphon* in Greek—even that tax had some institutional links with the pre-Arab period); Morimoto, *Fiscal administration* (with Gascou's review, 'De Byzance à l'Islam'); and the still classic survey by H. I. Bell in *P. Lond.* IV, pp. xi–xli. *Jizya* first appears with something like its later meaning in *APEL* III 174, 175 (aa. 722, 731): see Simonsen, *Studies in the genesis*, pp. 85–6; *kharāj* appears at some time in the eighth century too (e.g. *Arabische Briefe*, n. 26); the first dated reference to *kharāj* in this sense is in 773 (see Frantz-Murphy in *CPR* XXI, p. 141).

the question in an empire based on land routes, whose capitals were always inland too; communications were simply harder. More important still: the *dīwān* system was organized province by province, and the Arabs on each register expected to keep all the tax exacted in each province. The whole Umayyad period witnessed constant battles between the caliph and the provinces, to get any tax to Damascus at all; only a few provincial governors were keen to help the caliph in this respect, and the hostility of local armies could be guaranteed. Daniel Dennett's much-cited estimate that in the Umayyad period Egypt sent only 5 per cent of its revenue to Damascus is only a factoid, for there is no evidence supporting it at all, but the sums must have been pretty low; al-Balādhurī thought the figure was 6.5 per cent for Iraq in Muʿāwiya's time. Actually, in all the extensive Egyptian tax papyri there is no evidence for *anything* being sent to the Umayyad caliphs except construction materials, builders, and sawyers for the building of the al-Aqsa mosque at Jerusalem and the Great Mosque at Damascus.[191] The Arabs repaired Trajan's canal to Egypt's main Red Sea port at Klysma (Suez), which indicates an interest in sending goods eastwards; this is confirmed by an early eighth-century text which refers to ships 'laden with grain' leaving Klysma. The presence of Egyptian LRA 7 amphorae in Umayyad Ayla ('Aqaba) is a further demonstration of that eastern link. But this link was probably focused above all on the supply of Madīna in the Hijaz, which did depend on Egypt; Egyptian products are only occasionally found on sites in inland Syria and Palestine in this period. Archaeology does not help us, then, any more than documents do, to establish a link between Egypt and the caliphs.[192] If we were to assume that the Umayyad caliphate's central administration was funded almost exclusively from Syria and Palestine, we would not go far wrong. This region was divided into several relatively small provinces, which might not have been able to maintain full fiscal autonomy from nearby Damascus. The fragments of a *dīwān* register of c.685 that survive among the Nessana papyri from the Negev seem to indicate that Arabs from three separate provinces were collecting their pay there, apparently directly, that is to say that the boundaries between provinces were here more permeable than elsewhere. But the region was essentially dependent on its own resources. Only with the 'Abbāsid period, from 750 onwards, were the caliphs able to force taxation out of

[191] Kennedy, *Armies*, pp. 63–5, 71–6, is a key survey of tax conflicts; p. 71 for the al-Balādhurī reference (but Iraq doubtless paid more under al-Ḥajjāj at the end of the century); p. 75 for the changing amounts probably coming to Syria from Egypt. For Dennett, see e.g. Kennedy, 'The financing of the military', p. 371. For the al-Aqsa mosque, *P. Lond.* IV 1403, 1435, *P. Ross.-Georg.* IV 4, *CPR* XXII 43; for the Damascus mosque, *P. Lond.* IV 1341, 1368, 1411, *P. Ross.-Georg.* IV 3, *CPR* XXII 53. *P. Lond.* IV 1434 l. 26 may refer to the building of 'Anjar.

[192] For grain ships, see *CPR* XXII 44. For LRA 7, see Whitcomb, 'The "commercial crescent" '; it can be found down the Hijaz coast of the Red Sea too. For inland Syria and Palestine, see below, p. 774.

their local officials on any scale: the first century of 'Abbāsid rule marks the only period of full financial centralization of the caliphate.[193]

Hugh Kennedy is the historian who has stressed this fiscal regionalization more than any other, in a number of influential books and articles. He argues that the pattern seriously undermined the coherence of the Umayyad state, for the caliph had no real control over the provinces at all, except the right (not an insignificant one, though) to dismiss governors at will. Indeed, he has proposed that the well-attested interest of the eighth-century Umayyads in systematic desert irrigation projects in eastern Syria and Palestine was in part in order to supplement this fiscal weakness—with landowning here coming to equal the tax system in its remuneration.[194] This seems to me to go too far. The most substantial surviving building projects of the whole world dating to the early eighth century (at least outside China, Japan, and Yucatán) are in Syria and Palestine, and most of them are the work of the caliphs. These would have been hardly possible unless caliphal wealth was on an altogether larger scale than the irrigation projects would indicate; Damascus must have done pretty well out of Syrian-Palestinian taxation, in fact, supplemented by occasional windfalls from elsewhere. All armies and provincial administrators, it must be remembered, were paid for locally— that was what a *dīwān* was for, after all—and this was the great bulk of state expenses, in this period as in others. Syria and Palestine made up a still highly prosperous (although economically fragmented) region in itself, as we shall see (pp. 774–80), and its tax would have been substantial. The regionalization of the state is clear, but the accumulation of wealth possible *inside* each region was not less for that, whether in case of a province like Egypt or Iraq, or the 'central-government region' of Syria–Palestine, as long as the fiscal system held up.[195]

Egypt is even more predominantly the source of our material for seventh- and eighth-century taxation than it was for the sixth. Indeed, one interesting feature of the main Umayyad-period archives for Egypt is that most of them privilege tax records even above those for landowning—an observation that

---

[193] *P. Ness.* 92–3 (cf. Kennedy, 'The financing of the military', pp. 376–8), mentioning the provinces of Urdunn, Filasṭīn, and even Egypt (which is not so far from Nessana). This may also fit the patterns of post-690s coin finds in Jerash and Jericho, both of which include substantial proportions of coin from several different provinces of Syria and Palestine: Walmsley, 'Production, exchange', pp. 334–9. 'Abbāsid fiscal centralization essentially began with the Barmakids in the last quarter of the eighth century: Kennedy, 'The Barmakid revolution'.

[194] Kennedy, 'The impact of Muslim rule'; cf. above, nn. 191, 193.

[195] Conversely, if the fiscal system did not hold up inside a region, there would be trouble, as the Arabs found in Spain (above, pp. 100–2). It may be that the material simplicity of eighth-century North Africa shows something similar, after the confusion of a fifty-year Arab conquest period: below, pp. 726–8. Another example might be the Jazīra before the 690s, if we accepted Chase Robinson's view (*Empire and élites*, pp. 44–53) that the 'tribute' in Syriac sources for the period was not a standard land tax; but it seems more likely that it was indeed the latter.

is valid for the Arab-period Nessana papyri in Palestine too.[196] It was evidently very important to keep taxation materials in that period, to our considerable benefit: for we can track tax structures, the complexities of payment mechanisms, the patterns of central control, and attitudes to fiscal morality. Thanks in part to the survival of tax receipts (still called *entagia*) in large numbers, both on papyrus and on ostraka, local collections of documents are, as in previous periods of Egyptian history, almost unfairly rich by the standards of other regions: over 400 texts for Aphroditō, 300 for Bala'īza, both just south of Asyūt in Middle Egypt, and well over 1000 for Jēme, a village in the ruins of Western Thebes. Jēme in particular will recur in later chapters (esp. pp. 419–28): its local society is better documented than any other village anywhere in the eighth century. But Aphroditō is the best source for fiscal evidence, and we shall start here.

Aphroditō was the Greek name for the village (*kōmē*); in Coptic it was Jkōw, hence in contemporary Arabic Ashqaw; today it is Kōm Ishqāw. We know this variety of names because of our surviving Umayyad-period texts: some 45 per cent Greek, 35 per cent Coptic, 20 per cent Arabic, all dating from the period 698–722. The village had by now established fiscal independence from Antaiopolis ('Irmāniyya: see above, pp. 71–2; below, pp. 412–13), and had its own pagarch and administrative district. Arabic and Greek were the languages of communication between the governor of Egypt at Fustāt and the pagarch (sometimes *dioikētēs*; *sāhib* in Arabic) of Aphroditō; Greek was the language of administration of the pagarchy; Coptic was the language of administration of its subordinate localities (*chōria* or *epoikia*), and probably of its inhabitants as a whole—private letters and documents, in Aphroditō as elsewhere in Egypt, are overwhelmingly in Coptic by the eighth century.[197] The narrow time-range of the texts for this period indicate that they were the archive of a single person, almost certainly the pagarch Basilios, who figures in large numbers of them; indeed, the main time-range is even narrower, for most of our texts come from a single three-year period, 709–11, the beginning of the governorate of Qurra ibn Sharīk (709–15), from whom nearly 200 letters survive. The Qurra–Basilios letters are, to use yet another superlative, easily the best guide to day-to-day administrative processes anywhere in our period. Qurra and Basilios, as an agonistic duo, with Qurra constantly making demands and never fully being satisfied, can become emblematic of an entire system as a

---

[196] This is true of Aphroditō (see n. 197), of Bala'īza (see *Bala'izah*, II), of Nessana (*P. Ness.* 60–93)—though not of Jēme in Upper Egypt. *Bala'izah*, nn. 290–301, shows a monastery keeping systematic accounts of tax paid in the eighth century.

[197] The basic collections are *P. Lond.* IV and *P. Ross.-Georg.* IV for the Greek and Coptic material, and, for the Arabic material, *PSR*; *APEL* III 146–66; *The Kurrah papyri*; Becker, 'Arabische Papyri'. See also Cadell, 'Nouveaux fragments'; Rāġib, 'Lettres nouvelles'; Pintaudi and Sijpesteijn, 'Testi dell'VIII sec.'; *CPR* XXII 52–9. The analyses of Egyptian taxation in n. 190 are principally based on the Aphroditō material. Note that *epoikion* just means 'village' now, not 'dependent settlement' (see below, Ch. 5, n. 29).

result—especially as more fragmentary survivals from other pagarchies attest that Qurra did this to everybody.[198] What the governor of Egypt wanted, and expected, from Aphroditō around 710 can stand for what he wanted from Egypt as a whole.

What Qurra was principally concerned with, of course, was taxes: each of the separate taxes due from Aphroditō, the poll tax (*andrismos* or *diagraphon*), the land tax, in money (*chrysikon dēmosion*) and grain (*embolē*), and expenses for men on public service (*dapanē*). The latter were ad hoc exactions, but the three main taxes were regular, and due three times a year as far as we can see, just as in the Roman period. But they were often late. In a dozen letters and more, Qurra chides Basilios for delays, and demands that the back taxes be sent at once; sometimes the taxes risk arriving so late that the fleet may have already left Alexandria for its annual raiding (*kourson*), or else the water in Trajan's canal will have fallen so low that boats cannot get through to Klysma; once Basilios had not sent sailors in time for the *kourson*, so Qurra had to hire substitutes, billing Basilios for the money, which the latter sent. Sometimes, however, the taxes were just slightly delayed, with Qurra's complaints simply showing unusually high expectations, as when he upbraided Basilios for being 1300 *artabai* in arrears on the grain tax only four months after the harvest.[199] Qurra could get very cross about this: in 709 Basilios was commanded to come to Fusṭāṭ with all his tax registers and his arrears to do a full account—a letter repeated a month later, for he still had not arrived. In another letter of the same year, Basilios had not responded to a requisition of acacia-wood for the fleet after twenty days; send the wood now, Qurra said, or I'll send you 'a recompense intended to destroy your life'.[200] Qurra could be pretty shrill in his letters, but Basilios survived. One gains the clear impression of a pagarch devoted to dragging his feet, but with a good knowledge of how far he could do so without provoking reprisals. But he could not get out of paying the taxes in the end, and indeed sometimes had to pay penalties too—though if he did any fining for tax arrears on his own behalf, Qurra was capable of second-guessing it.[201]

[198] Qurra to Herakleopolis (Ehnāsiyya): *PERF* 593; to Ashmūnayn: *PSR* 10, 11; to Antinoupolis (Shaykh 'Ibāda): *Bala'izah*, nn. 180–2.

[199] Respectively, *P. Lond.* IV 1349; Cadell, 'Nouveaux fragments', n. 7; *P. Lond.* IV 1337 (cf. 1450), 1370.

[200] *P. Lond.* IV 1338, 1339, *P. Laur.* IV 192. *The Kurrah papyri*, n. 4, also threatens Basilios' life, as well as chiding him for being a disappointment to Qurra. *APEL* III 146, another letter about arrears, says: 'when I sent you to your post, it was with the expectation that you would show trustworthiness', implying that Basilios was Qurra's man. He was indeed appointed close to the date of Qurra's own appointment; but he was also the brother of his predecessor Epimachos (*P. Lond.* IV 1512, 1592), and a local landowner, judging by the few leases that survive in the archive (*P. Lond.* IV 1592–4): see below, p. 251.

[201] Penalties (it is not clear for what) are cited in *P. Lond.* IV 1345, 1359; *P. Ross.-Georg.* IV 15. In *APEL* III 153, Basilios' own fines are cancelled by Qurra.

It is already clear from the above that Qurra did not only want taxes from Aphroditō, but men as well (with their wages and travel expenses), and we must add a wide array of ad hoc dues—butter, milk, bread (only good bread would do), wood, post-horses, shirts for the army, and building-supplies, such as palm roof-beams for the palace of Fusṭāṭ, and iron chains for the Great Mosque of Damascus.[202] The men were shipbuilders and construction-workers, both skilled and unskilled, for these and other major public building projects, and also sailors for the fleet. Qurra even put out ship-building locally: he sent iron to Aphroditō to get turned into nails for the shipyard at Fusṭāṭ.[203] It must here be recalled that the habitable areas of Egypt are all connected by waterways, the Nile and its tributary canals, or else the scale of these requisitions would have simply been impossible, given that Aphroditō is over 350 km up the Nile from Fusṭāṭ, and over 500 km from Alexandria; but they are notably dense requirements nonetheless, which were expected to be satisfied very fast, as we have seen. If the taxes were regular, these ad hoc demands were not, and they were, as far as we can see, in principle limitless—the only local flexibility was that Aphroditō could generally, if it preferred, send money rather than the men or goods.[204] We must recognize the hardship that these unpredictable demands would cause locally; it is also worth noting how much work they would have caused for the governor's office in Fusṭāṭ, involving the apportionment of such dues across fifty-plus pagarchies, the sending of messengers to demand them, more messengers to demand them again, and the signing off of each part of each requisition when it was sent and when it arrived. These procedures really did (at least usually) take place, as we see from a couple of particularly unexpected texts, in which Qurra or his officials actually sent back items the state did not eventually need: grain for the *kourson* in 710 (but not the vinegar and beans, which were still needed), and the wages due for a workman in Fusṭāṭ, who had in the end been requisitioned locally.[205] This fiscal responsibility (such a phrase seems a fair way of describing it) was grudging and probably rare, but, almost more important, it entailed a careful accounting system for it to be possible at all.

Qurra did not only requisition; we can see him in other roles too. In a handful of texts he orders Basilios to get private debts repaid, presumably in response to the appeals of creditors. In a dozen more he gives instructions about the apprehension of fugitives from taxpaying and their return to their correct tax districts—or their registration as taxpayers in Aphroditō

---

[202] Butter and milk: *P. Lond.* IV 1392, 1397, 1414. Bread: Rāġib, 'Lettres nouvelles', n. 1. Wood: *P. Laur.* IV 192. Post-horses: *P. Lond.* IV 1347; shirts: 1352; roof-beams: 1362, 1378; chains: 1368. Cf., in general, the lists of requisitions in 1375, 1414 (especially), 1433.

[203] See in general *P Lond.* IV 1433. Men: 1336, 1337, 1342, and many others. Iron: 1369, 1399, 1408; *P. Ross.-Georg.* IV 9; Becker, 'Arabische Papyri', n. 9; Cadell, 'Nouveaux fragments', n. 6. Less common are dyke-building, ibid., n. 6; and tree-planting, *P. Ross.-Georg.* IV 6.

[204] e.g. *P. Lond.* IV 1408.   [205] *P. Lond.* IV 1354, 1508-9.

itself.[206] In one letter, of 710, he commands Basilios not to use any torture that makes the victim sick and incapable of work—especially not the forced drinking of quicklime!—and tells him to instruct village headmen in the same way, with the threat of punishment. (Evidently such activities were standard on the ground.) Qurra is concerned for fair local tax-assessments, and insists not only that Basilios avoid (or stop) unfair behaviour, but also that village-level assessors formally swear to be just. He lectures Basilios on his duties: 'the first and chief of the duties of an offical is tax-collecting' (the second is watching for fugitives), and criticizes Basilios because he is inaccessible to the people and does not hear their petitions.[207] The style of Qurra's letters is of an autocratic and haughty ruler, who makes his own rules, demands immediate obedience, but obeys them himself; and, above all, of an obsessive micro-manager, concerned that every detail of public life be accountable at a distance of 350 km, month by month, even day by day: in Aphroditō, but also in every other pagarchy of Egypt.

One should not over-personalize the Qurra letters. He did not, of course, write or even compose most of them himself—we have one about every five days for Aphroditō as it is, and it was one of the smallest of Egypt's pagarchies. We do, furthermore, have a few parallel texts from some other governors, as well as some forty similar letters from the officials of the dukes of the Thebaid in (probably) the 670s to the pagarch Papas of Apollonopolis Anō (Edfū) in Upper Egypt: this form of hands-on government was standard. Qurra does seem to stand out in his exactness, nevertheless—it is interesting that his is the commonest governor's name on letters of this kind even for other places than Basilios' Aphroditō. He had a reputation as an efficient, not to say oppressive, administrator in later narrative sources.[208] But, as already noted, however atypical he was as a person, he could not have acted as he (and his administrators) did if the system had not been awesomely regular in its procedures. This, at least, seems to be a general feature of Umayyad government in Egypt. Papas, certainly, responded in a similar way in the 670s to Basilios in 710; he too had to

---

[206] Debts: *APEL* III 154; *The Kurrah papyri*, n. 3; Becker, 'Arabische Papyri', n. 1 (cf. *PSR*, 10, 11, for Ashmūnayn). Fugitives: *P. Lond.* IV 1332–3, 1339, 1343–4, 1349, 1382–4, 1438, 1460–1 (for registers), 1484, 1494, 1518–23, 1545; *P. Ross.-Georg.* IV 1, 2; *PSR*, n. 12; Becker, 'Arabische Papyri', n. 14; Rāġib, 'Lettres nouvelles', n. 2; Cadell, 'Nouveaux fragments', n. 5.

[207] Torture: *P. Ross.-Georg.* IV 16; cf. *P. Jernstedt*, ed. in the same volume, pp. 99–105, from the time of the Persian occupation, in which a man complains of the Persians forcing him to drink marble-dust and vinegar. Fair tax assessments are discussed in *P. Lond.* IV 1345, 1356, and perhaps 1367; cf. the formal statement by local tax-collectors from Aphroditō that they are not fraudulent in *Bala'izah*, n. 240. Qurra lectures Basilios in *P. Lond.* IV 1349 (quote), 1356, and also in *The Kurrah papyri*, n. 2, where he opines that cultivation by the people 'is their chief duty, after their duty to God'.

[208] Other governors: *Bala'izah*, n. 130 (with the 724 Jēme document edited there); *P. Apoll.* 1–36 (cf. 37–51). For the dating of the Apollōnopolis texts, see Gascou and Worp, 'Problèmes de documentation'. For Qurra, see the attack in Sāwīrus, *History*, in *PO*, V.1, pp. 57–64; and the balanced assessment by Nabia Abbott in *The Kurrah papyri*, pp. 57–69.

send taxes and dues regularly, including having boats made, with wood sent upstream, perhaps all the way from Fusṭāṭ, and also ironwork, silver ankle-rings for the duke (or *amīr*) of the Thebaid, and apparently embroidery as well; he also sent shipbuilders to the arsenal at Fusṭāṭ (some of them fled) and canal-diggers to Latopolis (Esnā), 50 km away, who had to be back by the next tax deadline. He sometimes lent workers, too, to his friend Platōn, the pagarch of Latopolis, who certainly resented the duke's requisitions ('may he taste water!'—i.e. drown—as he wrote to Papas once).[209] And, if we do not get so many letters of this kind from other places, we can at least see the generalization of the administrative context: detailed tax-assessments; hundreds of receipts for different taxes and requisitions; punishments for tax delays; in a rare document for the Delta, from Pousire (Greek Busiris, modern Abū Ṣīr Banā), a tax on cloth, which may show some concern for local productive specializations; and instructions to make registers—in one case, a text for Shmoun (Greek Hermopolis, modern Ashmūnayn), including lists of adult and child artisans, and individual date-palms and acacias.[210]

Upper Egypt in the 670s, where there were few Arabs as yet, as we see in the Papas archive, bridges the gap back to the conquest in 640–2, and we must ask how much this documentation simply reflects continuity from Roman, indeed pre-Roman times (see above, pp. 64–72). The main taxes certainly seem to have been Roman in their essentials, although, as already stated, the poll tax was new in this form, and probably imposed on non-Muslims only (not that there was anyone else in Egypt, outside Fusṭāṭ and Alexandria, till well into the eighth century). The tightness of organization was old, as well; so was forced labour, as sailors or canal-diggers, although this does now seem more frequent and more arbitrary. Indeed, as Roger Rémondon has shown, even the form of tax registers, and their basic assessment structures, had changed relatively little.[211] What we do not have from the late Roman period, however, is the density of instructions from the office of a major central official to local officials that we have from (especially, but not only) Qurra. This is partly because government was more decentralized under the Roman empire, with cities more—even if decreasingly—autonomous; it is partly because there were more powerful land-owners in the Roman period, which allowed, enforced, another level of mediation, as for example on the Apion estates (above, p. 71, below, p. 247). In the Umayyad period there were fewer levels, and the Egyptian

[209] *P. Apoll.* 11, 12 (boats), 25 (iron), 20 (silver), 38 (embroidery), 9, 28 (shipbuilders), 26 (canal-diggers), 37–40 (Platōn letters: 37 for the quote).

[210] The Delta text is *Bala'izah*, n. 132 (it is rare because papyrus does not survive in the wet lands of the Delta). Shmoun: *CPR* XIV 1 (cf. *P. Ryl. Copt.* 346, c. 770); cf. W. E. Crum in *P. Lond.* IV, p. xlviii.

[211] Rémondon, '*P. Hamb.* 56'; for general continuities, see Simonsen, *Studies in the genesis*, pp. 81–112, 127–31; Gascou, 'De Byzance à l'Islam'. For fourth-century labour services, see Bagnall, *Egypt*, pp. 133–6, 153–60.

governor could expect to speak to pagarchs—indeed, sometimes villages and their headmen—directly, and indeed did so.[212] It is this process of communication which gives the evidence for tax-raising in Umayyad Egypt its special flavour.

For how it worked as a structure, let us go back to Aphroditō. It seems that taxes were established yearly by the governor and apportioned by pagarchy; the pagarch's office then apportioned by village, and village leaders did the same inside the village—although there were also short-cuts, for Qurra could send assessments to village leaders directly; and the village tax registers which we have for the early eighth century, listing the extents of private land plots and the tax due on each, seem to have been drawn up by the pagarch's office. These registers show, for example, that irrigated and unirrigated land were taxed at different rates, at least as regards the money-tax, although not very different—1 *nomisma* per 4 *arourai* is fairly common. Village officials then collected them and passed them to the pagarch for onward delivery; village officials were also responsible for the requisitions of sailors and workmen. The central role of formal village leaders, especially the headman or *lashane* (Greek *meizōn*, Arabic *mazūt*), is very clear in the Aphroditō texts, and fits what we know of the considerable power a *lashane* could have in his village elsewhere (see below, pp. 422–4). How the system knew that land had changed hands is unclear—the formal registrations of land-sales that we know from the sixth century in Aphroditō do not have parallels in the eighth. We do have separate tax registers for one locality from 706 and 714, however: it may simply be that reassessments were frequent.[213]

From Aphroditō, tax essentially went north: above all to the army and government in Fusṭāṭ and, secondarily, to the fleet in Alexandria. The money-tax for Fusṭāṭ is sometimes referred to as *roga* in Greek documents, the Roman/Byzantine word; the grain is sometimes *rouzikon* (< Arabic *rizq*, sustenance). It has recently been argued, fairly convincingly, that these are in effect synonyms, and that the structural distinction between the two taxes should not be overstressed; but the dual etymology is interesting all the same. The recipients of the taxes are referred to by Qurra as the *mōagaritai*

---

[212] Qurra to villages: *APEL* III 160–3; Becker, 'Arabische Papyri', nn. 5, 9. For the lack of autonomy of pagarchs, see Banaji, *Agrarian change*, pp. 154–5. One sixth-century parallel to Qurra's interventions is *P. Cair. Masp.* I 67060, in which the pagarch Menas of Antaiopolis demands that Dioskoros of Aphroditō come personally to account for the late taxes of the latter village; but this was part of the long-running battle over Aphroditō's fiscal autonomy (see below, pp. 412–13), so is not necessarily typical.

[213] For registers, see above all *P. Lond.* IV 1412–32 (cf. 1433–61; and, for elsewhere, *Bala'izah*, nn. 286–301; *P. Apoll.* 73–92; *CPR* XXII 17–33; *PERF* 597, 616). *P. Lond.* IV 1433 is a division of taxation between and inside villages (cf. *PSR*, Appendix); 1356, 1367, relate to divisions inside villages. For headmen, see n. 212; their responsibilities are clear in *P. Lond.* IV 1494–511. The two tax registers for one village, Pente Pediades, are ibid. 1420, 1424. In *CPR* XXII 28, a probably slightly later text, perhaps from Arsinoë or Herakleopolis, vineyards, grain-fields, orchards, and other land types are all taxed at different rates.

(Arabic *muhājirūn*), that is, the Arabs on the *dīwān*, although once he refers to his own household, whose expenses Basilios must cover, as *araboi kai christianoi*, 'Arabs and Christians'—the administration in Egypt had only switched to Arabic in 706, three years before Qurra was appointed. Most of the beneficiaries of this taxation were, nonetheless, the Arabs of the capital.[214] This will have made more feasible the money-taxes that Egyptians all paid; as we shall see in Chapter 11 (pp. 759–69), there was enough exchange inside Egypt for private spending in Fusṭāṭ to get back up the Nile to small towns like Aphroditō. But exactly what all this money was spent on, as yet, is not at all clear. Fusṭāṭ was certainly growing, and the governors spent money building and rebuilding the palace and the Great Mosque, but the dramatic surviving buildings of medieval Cairo, which make it the true heir of Ptolemaic Alexandria and Pharaonic Memphis or Thebes, only really began to be put up after 820.[215] One simply gains the impression that the Arabs on the Egyptian *dīwān* were absurdly rich. But tax pressures never slackened in Egypt. Structurally unnecessary taxation came to be abandoned, or at least eased up on, in the Romano-Germanic West, as we have seen. But we can now conclude that, if tax remains the sole resource of an army, that army is very unlikely ever to think any of it is unnecessary, and, in this case, certainly did not—indeed, tax went up more often than down, not least, according to our sources, in 725 under the *ṣāḥib al-kharāj*, 'head of taxation', 'Ubayd Allāh. This provoked a tax revolt, almost the first in Umayyad Egypt, but not the last—indeed, in the next century there were a dozen more, culminating in a full-scale civil war in the 820s.[216]

We know about the Egyptian tax revolts almost entirely from narrative sources, the Christian Sāwīrus ibn al-Muqaffaʿ and the Muslim al-Kindī, both from the tenth century, but apparently writing independently of each other; they agree on major details, nonetheless. Kosei Morimoto has analysed them most fully, and I largely follow his account. The first revolt was 'Coptic', that is, by the Christian inhabitants of the eastern Delta, and dates to 726, just after the tax rises of 725. The second, in 739, was in Upper Egypt, and is again linked by Sāwīrus to tax problems. In 750 there were

---

[214] *Roga*: e.g. *P. Lond.* IV 1349, 1357; *rouzikon*: e.g. 1335, 1404; Becker, 'Arabische Papyri', n. 10. Mayerson, 'Rouzikón', argues that they are synonyms, and gives more references. (*Rizq* was itself an Arab loan-word from Persian: Kennedy, *Armies*, p. 73.) For *araboi kai christianoi*, see *P. Lond.* IV 1375. For the change to Arabic, see Kennedy, 'Egypt', p. 72.

[215] For the palace and the mosque, see *P. Lond.* IV 1334, 1362, 1378; *P. Ross.-Georg.* IV 7. ʿAbd al-ʿAzīz b. Marwān, governor in 685–705, i.e. shortly before Qurra, was famous as a builder, both in Fusṭāṭ and more widely in Egypt; 'he used men like Pharaoh did', as Sāwīrus remarks (*History*, *PO*, V.1, pp. 42–3). Fusṭāṭ had 40,000 Arabs on the *dīwān* already in the 660s–670s according to Ibn ʿAbd al-Ḥakam (Kennedy, *Armies*, p. 72), a figure which seems to me implausibly high, but which was one which Egyptian taxation could certainly have funded. For the first standing buildings, see Creswell, *Early Muslim architecture*, II, pp. 171–96, 327–60.

[216] Sāwīrus, *History*, *PO*, V.1, p. 76 for ʿUbayd Allāh; but see below, n. 219. For an earlier tax revolt from the 690s, see below, Ch. 7, n. 127.

generalized revolts, of both Arabs and Christians, in the context of the 'Abbāsid overthrow of the Umayyads—as noted above, Arab settlement had by now begun in the eastern Delta. Small-scale Coptic tax revolts, from single localities, are ascribed to 753, 767, and 773, and a larger-scale mixed Arab and Coptic revolt in Upper Egypt took place in 783–6. In 784–5 and 794, 801–2, and 807–9 the Arabs of the Delta began to revolt over rising taxes too. Finally, the period 812–32 was one of nearly continuous war, set off by the contemporary civil war in Iraq, but, as in 750, soon taking on local concerns; by 819 an anti-tax element in Coptic rebellion is clear, and by 830 in Arab rebellion too. In 831–2, above all, the Copts and the Arabs of the Delta joined forces to oppose the government and to expel its tax-collectors, in response to fiscal harshness, and only an army led by Caliph al-Ma'mūn himself was sufficient to quell them.[217] After this, the country became quieter. This was, perhaps, more as a result of reforming measures than because of the violent repression of the rebellion itself: a lot of people were killed or enslaved in 831–2, it is true, but so had they been after previous rebellions, and tax resistance had never previously died down. It is anyway clear that Copts, and after a while Arab settlers too, were committed to opposition to the fiscal regime, and were prepared, across a whole century, to take the extreme risk of doing it by force. Given the habitual caution of most peasantries, that regime must have been genuinely seen as unacceptably oppressive.

These tax revolts are a particular feature of Umayyad and 'Abbāsid Egypt. They have few parallels elsewhere in the caliphate (the major one was the peasant's revolt against a particularly tyrannical governor of Mosul in the eastern Jazīra in the 770s; the famous Zanj revolt of the 870s in southern Iraq was of slaves, a very different matter),[218] and they are also unparalleled in late Roman Egypt. It is hard to avoid the conclusion that the Arabs in Egypt did mishandle their governing and their tax-raising role, as our narratives claim, even if our documentary evidence does not make it easy to see how. It is not clear, first of all, that Arab taxation was in global terms dramatically heavier than that of the sixth century, although Aphroditō certainly paid more, and the more frequent requisitions of the Umayyad period may also have been particularly unpopular because they were arbitrary.[219] A peasant from Ashmūnayn who refused to sow his land because his

[217] Morimoto, *Fiscal administration*, pp. 145–72, supplemented by Kennedy, 'Egypt', pp. 74–84.

[218] For recent translations of the basic Mosul text, the *Zuqnīn Chronicle*, see *Chronicon anonymum pseudo-Dionysianum*, pp. 198–309, and *Chronicle of Zuqnīn*, pp. 223–320; see in general Cahen, 'Fiscalité, propriété'. For the Zanj, the basic account is Popovic, *La révolte des esclaves*, esp. pp. 79–168; for the social status of the Zanj, see ibid., pp. 64–6, and al-Ṭabarī, *Ta'rīkh*, III, pp. 1742, 1747–51 (trans. *The history*, XXXVI, pp. 29–30, 34–8).

[219] The relative weight of Arab taxation has not yet been fully established. Globally, the figures we have from al-Balādhurī, *Futūḥ al buldān*, trans. Hitti, p. 340, for the early period compare with Justinianic levels (Banaji, *Agrarian change*, p. 65; el-Abbadi, 'Historians and the

taxes were too high, referred to in a letter between two village officials (the text is unfortunately undated, but dated texts in the same collection are eighth-century), may be one straw in the wind, though that at least has late Roman parallels. Another undated, but at least eighth-century, text from Shmin (Greek Panopolis, Arabic Akhmīm) in Middle Egypt, almost unique in that it is trilingual, may be another indicator: it records the formal oaths of the inhabitants of several villages in the city territory to the pagarch Yazīd that his tax-collector 'Amr had never oppressed them, contrary to previous assertions, which had apparently included a formal appeal.[220] More import-ant than these essentially anecdotal indicators is, however, the evidence for peasant flight. Peasants had always used this recourse in Egypt, despite the difficulties involved—unlike in most places, there are few marginal areas in Egypt where fugitives can easily hide out, for irrigated land gives way to full uninhabitable desert in a few kilometres at most. We find no shortage of references to fugitives in the fourth century, or the sixth.[221] But in the Umayyad period they spiral. Qurra, as already noted, was obsessive on the issue, almost as shrill as Egica in the Spain of the same period (below, p. 526); he set up special fugitive-hunters, even if they admittedly only amounted to three commissioners for the whole of Middle and Upper Egypt, with three clerks per official. But here Qurra was not unusual at all. Nearly every other collection of eighth-century documents has references to the hunting down of fugitives, including formal registers of the missing.[222] Sāwīrus says that after Qurra's death in 715 the government went so far as to bring in internal passports for all travellers, so as to allow checks on fugitives, a process which, he says, was administered in such an inefficient way that trade was brought to a standstill; and it is certainly from around this time that the

papyri', presents more figures). But in Aphroditō the figures for money-tax paid in the early eighth century are seven times those of the early Justinianic period: Rémondon, '*P. Hamb.* 56', pp. 428–9; Banaji, *Agrarian change*, pp. 83, 230. This may be partly explained by territorial boundary changes (and fluctuations in the percentage of tax paid in money), but the difference is still striking. Christian narratives complain endlessly about tax rises, but one would expect them to; the papyri are a better source. Contrast Sāwīrus on 'Ubayd Allāh's exactions in 725 (above, n. 216) with the apparent drop in taxation paid in Aphroditō in the late 720s (*P. Lond.* IV 1412–13 set against 1416: the figures are presented in Rémondon, '*P. Hamb.* 56', p. 430 and Banaji, *Agrarian change*, p. 230).

[220] Respectively, *P. Ryl. Copt.* 323 (cf. 324, a village headman who has 'eaten', i.e. embezzled, local taxes); *APEL* III 167. The latter is undated, but cannot be too early, as pagarchs were not Arabs, with few exceptions, before the 730s (below, Ch. 4, n. 274).

[221] For the fourth century, Bagnall, *Egypt*, p. 144; Krause, *Spätantike Patronatsformen*, pp. 157–8; for the sixth, *P. Lond.* III 1032; *P. Laur.* II 46; *P. Oxy.* XVI 2055, XXVII 2479; *P. Ant.* III 189.

[222] See n. 206 for Qurra. *CPR* XXII 1, 3–4, 33–42, mostly for the Fayyūm, are an important set (4 for a fugitive hunter; 1 for the association of flight with the first Arab fiscal innovation, the capitation tax, at the start of Arab rule). Elsewhere, e.g. *Bala'izah*, n. 289; *APEL* III 151; *P. Ryl. Copt.* 277; *P. Apoll.* 9, 13, 18; *P. Apoll. Copt.* 5 (discussed in MacCoull, 'Apollonos Anô', pp. 142–3); Norsa, 'Un circolare'; *KRU*, n. 115 (see below, Ch. 7, nn. 90, 101). See in general Morimoto, *Fiscal administration*, pp. 119–25.

passports that actually survive do begin to date—as far as we can see, they all had to be issued by pagarchies, and only for a few months at a time, which must have caused endless difficulties, thus supporting Sāwīrus's claims. (They contain physical descriptions, as is logical over a millennium before photographs: Constantine Papostolos was, in 731, 'a young man, flat-nosed, with a scar on his cheek and two moles on his neck, having lank hair'.)[223] These remedies for tax-evasion were so heavy-handed that it is less surprising that open revolt was one of their results.

All the same, as already noted, it is not clear that taxation was much heavier. Rather, it was more stringently enforced, and more aggressively policed. There may well not even have been more fugitives; but the Umayyad government was more concerned with controlling them, again in unusually aggressive ways. And here it is worthwhile returning to the issue of patronage. Patricia Crone, in a typically perceptive phrase, remarks that in the Umayyad period, as a result of the weakening of local aristocracies, 'because the countryside was thus denuded of its protective network, flight from the land replaced the traditional search for a rural patron as the primary mode of tax-evasion'.[224] This certainly seems to fit Egypt, where patronage and evasion had gone together since the fourth century (above, p. 71). It is not that aristocracies had actually gone, as we shall see in the next chapter (pp. 251–5), but patronage and all the other complex mediations of the Roman world were much less available in Umayyad and 'Abbāsid society. The Arabs did, actually, have an extremely elaborate conception of political patronage, but one usually had to become a convert to be a client (*mawlā*); clientage meant Arabization, in effect, which was a ninth-century, not an eighth-century, development in Egypt.[225] For everyone else, there was only Qurra. Unlike their predecessors, the Arabs set themselves up as a separated 'state class' of recipients of taxation, with no structural social links to taxpayers, whether rich or poor; and they were unremitting in the way they exacted tax and controlled the population for the purposes of exaction. It would be much easier for them to lose consent as a result; and the trouble that ensued caused problems for a century.

Egypt may have been at an extreme here. Certainly Arabs were much better integrated into Syria and Palestine, where they had lived, both as ordinary Roman citizens and as frontier allies, for centuries. In Nessana, for example, the village headman (*dioikētēs*) was liable to the governor of Palestine for taxation and requisitions, just as in Egypt (though here

---

[223] Sāwīrus, *History*, PO, V.1, pp. 69–70. For surviving passports, see the editions in Rāġib, 'Sauf-conduits', and his lists on pp. 143–6; the quote is from *APEL* III 175. Add to Rāġib's lists *CPR* IV 19, 22c, 102; *CLT*, n. 3 (see Ch. 7, n. 90). Not all of these are dated, but none clearly predate 715, and there are, significantly, none in the Qurra collections. *P. Lond.* IV 1633, from the Qurra period, may however be a more informal precursor.

[224] Crone, *Slaves on horses*, p. 51.

[225] See in general Crone, *Roman, provincial and Islamic law.*

bypassing the city), but it cannot have hurt that so many people in Nessana were ethnic Arabs, even if Christian ones. We have a remarkable late seventh-century text from Nessana in which *kyrios* (Lord) Samuel invites village representatives, through a sort of chain letter, to go with him the following day to the governor in Gaza to protest against the tax burden (*phortion*).[226] This may parallel the 'popular petitions' Qurra thought Basilios should hear, but this time it is directed to the governor, not the pagarch, and led by a local notable, a local patron that is to say. Samuel evidently expected this sort of popular protest to work, and it fell considerably short of armed revolt. It is unique, but it is closer in feel to Roman than to Umayyad Egyptian procedures. Even the 770s Mosul revolt involved, in part, peasants seeking protection against taxation from local chiefs, not simply violent uprising against the state—there, as in Palestine, Arabs were by now landowners as well as a tax-based military elite, and could mediate.[227] But in Egypt even Arabs, once they settled on the land, felt themselves subject to an uncontrollable system, for the Fusṭāṭ Arabs, who had come into the province much earlier, were socially separate from them as well. The Arab elites were better able than any other post-Roman ruling class to maintain the basic political structures of the Roman empire; they modified them slowly, of course, but the continuities of control were unbroken, as, probably, was not true even in Byzantium, at least in the crisis period of the 650s. But when they tried to do without patronage networks as part of their political practice, they came unstuck. The implications of this will be developed in a moment.

I have discussed Egyptian taxation in some detail. This is partly because there is a lot of evidence, it is intrinsically interesting, and it should be better known outside the circles of the experts. It is also because Egypt is, out of all the Roman provinces, the model for continuity across the early middle ages. It is not that nothing changed at all, as the crisis in consent to tax-raising shows. But *less* changed in Egypt, in particular in its state structures and, as we shall see in Chapter 11, its exchange networks, than it did in any other region. As a result, as we shall also see in future chapters, it is the comparator against which the more inconsistent experiences of the other regions need to be set.

4. Conclusion

This chapter has focused on the resources of states, and, in that arena, above all on tax-raising; for tax, if it was collected with commitment, dwarfed

---

[226] *P. Ness.* 68, 70, 74, for village headmen, 75, for Samuel. Cf. the headman (?) as dealer in *Arabic papyri from Ḥirbet al-Mird*, n. 18, from the late seventh-century Dead Sea.

[227] Cahen, 'Fiscalité, propriété', pp. 149–50.

other types of resource that rulers had access to. In general, tax-based states were therefore richer and more powerful than rent-based, land-based, states. This is not entirely the case; in 800 the Byzantine empire, although securely based on a tax system, was almost certainly less militarily powerful than Charlemagne's Francia, and it is possible, too, that the Frankish ruler at that moment controlled more resources than did the empress Irene in Byzantium, even though Frankish wealth was largely derived from the rents due from land. But Merovingian and Carolingian Francia was unusual in the medieval West, in the scale of the landed resources available to its rulers (and to its aristocrats: below, pp. 168–95); it is also worth noting that, although this scale had existed since the sixth century, it would not for much longer. By 900 the balance of power had in fact reversed itself, with Byzantium on a roll of increasing internal organization and, soon, military success, and Francia swiftly dividing itself into several pieces, many of them themselves internally incoherent. This difference in the future history of Francia and Byzantium is not chance. Even at the weakest point of the eastern empire, roughly 650–750, Byzantine political structures were more coherent than those even of the best-organized land-based states, such as Lombard Italy in the same period; tax-based structures had more staying-power, and the risk of decentralization, a feature of all land-based states, was less great. If taxation disappeared as the basis of any given state, then, no matter how much cultural, ideological, or legislative continuity there was (which could be a large amount in some cases, such as Visigothic Spain), it would not prevent fundamental changes in political resources, infrastructures, and practice.

We will see in the rest of this book why this issue was so important to society as a whole. Aristocracies were largely defined and legitimized by their relationships to states, particularly strong states (see Chapter 4); peasants were more distanced from the state, but a tax-raising polity had a considerable capacity to constrain peasant autonomy, and to intervene in the basic patterns of local society (see Chapter 9). A rich state (usually rich through taxation, except in the case of Francia) was also an independent source of demand, which directly affected the complexity of regional structures of agrarian and artisanal production (see Chapters 5 and 11). And a large-scale public distribution network, such as that of the Roman empire, had a direct effect on the scale of all forms of exchange (see Chapter 11). These were not direct causal relationships, with the form of the state somehow determining every other aspect of society and the economy, in a statist version of a very traditional Marxist analysis; but public demand, and the capillary influence of public power, were nonetheless important elements in local social and economic structures in nearly every post-Roman region, and their nature and extent have constantly to be borne in mind.

Taxation is also useful as a guide to comparison: for the structures of the tax-raising process, although they are regionally diverse, and change across time, have enough in common for their differences themselves to be usable as a window onto the different structures of early medieval societies. This process has been the underpinning of most of this chapter; to conclude, let us look at some of its more general features. Six of them seem worth setting out in this context, although they are not entirely analytically distinct.

First, taxation is difficult; it is never popular, and it has powerful enemies. For states to continue with the considerable effort required to maintain an effective fiscal system, it has to be obviously necessary: that is, there has to be something essential to spend it on. In the Roman empire that essential expense was the army, and secondarily the great cities. The continuity of a salaried army was also a crucial element in the Byzantine inheritance from Rome; it meant that, however extreme the political and economic crisis the Byzantines faced around 700, they maintained an infrastructure that they could build on later. The Romano-Germanic kingdoms, by contrast, had conquering ethnic groups who wished to become aristocracies, and thus became landowners; the main expense of the Roman state moved out of the public sector, for people henceforth did army service because they were free landowners, as an obligation, and without pay. As we saw at length earlier on in this chapter, this shift did not mean the end of taxation. Taxes became one element in royal wealth among many, and could be—and were—given away or otherwise dispensed with; or else they came to seem too complex to collect, and withered away, as we shall see in a moment. The Arabs, the other great conquering group in the post-Roman Mediterranean, by contrast took the decision to persist as a salaried army. This decision has tended to be studied as a cause of the continuing social separation of the Arabs as a people, at least until the fall of the Umayyads in 750, and thus the survival (and eventual cultural takeover) of the Arabic language and religion; but it was equally important as the direct cause of the continuing strength of the state structures of the Umayyad and 'Abbāsid caliphate. If the Arab armies had settled on the land, the fiscal systems of the different regions of the caliphate would have eventually withered, as surely as did those of the West, and the history of the eastern Mediterranean would have been very different. Some of this can be seen in Umayyad Spain, for long the weakest of the Arab regions in its political structures, and also that whose full fiscal centralization, later than our period, was most short-lived (above, pp. 100–2).

Conversely, tax is seldom opposed outright by its enemies. The wealthy and locally powerful, those who might pay most, have a stake in most tax-based political systems; they tend to want to profit from being among the beneficiaries of the state, as office-holders in its hierarchies, and they understand that this means that tax must continue. Their aim is not to destroy it, but to pay less themselves. A fiscal system whose major potential contributors avoid paying tax is often seen by historians as one which is doomed to failure, but this is naive; patently unjust fiscal systems can continue for centuries, and often have done. Powerful tax-evaders, whether aristocrats or ecclesiastical leaders, can also increase their local power by offering protection to their neighbours, who thus become their clients. This was common in the later Roman empire (above, p. 63; below, pp. 527–9), and has again been seen as an element of structural weakness in the late Roman political system, as wider and wider social groups managed to evade fiscal obligations. Here, too, I would resist this interpretation; the late empire was corrupt and unjust, but also essentially stable, and indeed Syria and Egypt, two of the regions of the empire with the best-documented patronage systems, were places where taxation survived best in the long run. One can go further: patronage was one of the elements which actually promoted the stability of the Roman state. The Arabs in Egypt, who apparently dispensed with it, faced foot-dragging and an opposition which eventually turned into outright revolt, in a way that had few parallels in the late Roman period, except in moments of crisis (below, pp. 529–33). But the Arabs also dispensed with the services of the indigenous elites, except for those few who made it to the office of pagarch; they cut an entire section of the locally powerful out from their traditional role as patrons and mediators, at least in the two centuries before the conversion/Arabization of the bulk of the Egyptian population. It would not be surprising if local leaders took up the position of standard-bearers for the opposition of the poor to taxation, rather than their traditional (and more remunerative) role of local representatives and mediators for the state, if the state itself excluded them from the latter. If the Umayyads had maintained the more complex, more informal, and probably less equitable procedures of late Roman political and fiscal practice, they would arguably have avoided revolt in Egypt. Patronage hierarchies have been remarkably effective across history in promoting the illusion among the poor and the excluded that they are in some way benefiting from the social system; this explains some of the more counter-intuitive choices of voting publics, in Italy, say, or Russia, or the United States, even today.

A third point, and a more important one if we want to find explanations for when and why taxation did decay, is that a successful taxation system depends on information, and on a substantial amount of hard work. In part, this hard work is coercion, for it is false to imagine that taxpaying was ever a cosy and accepted ritual. Mostly, however, it is the compilation of registers of those liable to pay, of how much they should pay, and of whether they have paid it; and the continual updating of those registers, as taxpayers die, or sell land, or expand their taxable activities. Here, the very wealth of our documentary material for Egypt, a region with unusual fiscal stability, makes the point clearly enough; Egyptians of all periods spent a lot of time and papyrus dealing with the fiscal system at all its levels, and that system had to be notably complex and—to an extent—ordered to be able to cope at all. This complexity, above all the constant need for updating, is the main reason why states have abandoned taxation when it was not structurally

necessary. The way this happened is clearest in Francia, where the updating
of taxation was intermittent already in the later sixth century and had ceased
altogether by the later seventh; in effect, the capillary procedures of tax-
assessment had turned into the blunter processes of the extraction of tribute
(above, p. 70)—blunter, and also much less remunerative—before they
finally ended. It needs to be clearly understood that effective taxation cannot
work without detailed information. And, although we might not find out
much at all about the detail of taxpaying itself from early medieval sources
(or ancient ones for that matter), outside Egypt at any rate, we tend to find at
least the shadow of the information-gathering process appearing somewhere
in our evidence, every time we have an effective tax system. We also find
fiscal imagery in our narrative sources, as taxation, owing to its weight and
all-pervasiveness, finds its way onto the rhetorical palette of every writer
who wishes to express moralizing images of the world. If we find neither tax-
recording nor tax rhetoric in any given society (in Charlemagne's Francia,
for example, where public records and moralization are both pretty well
documented), then that was a society where taxation was marginal or
entirely absent. This is not a controversial view of Charlemagne's Francia,
but it is not universally held, so it is still worth repeating. Francia around
800 is better-documented than Gaul around 450, but taxation is clearly
visible in the sources for the earlier date, as it is not for the later. Neither
compare with Egypt in any period, but it is not necessary to have Egyptian
evidence to find the shadow of taxation.

Taxation requires work; but it also brings control. Tax-collectors go
everywhere in a strong state; no public official is as pervasive in a land-
based political system. And those collectors are themselves always salaried,
or otherwise remunerated from the tax system itself, and can be dispensed
with if necessary. It was stressed at the start of this chapter that land-based
states had constantly to confront the dangers of insufficient control, notably
the decentralization of relevant political practice and the resultant potential
disintegration of the state itself. By and large, these processes did not occur
in our period, except temporarily in moments of political crisis, in the main
Romano-Germanic states (though they certainly did in Britain: below,
pp. 306–10); but they were potential dangers all the same, and all such
states had procedures to guard against them. One procedure was the elaboration of public ceremonial in royal courts and capitals, which legitimated
people who participated in it, delegitimated political practices which were
seen as in opposition to it, and helped to underpin consensus about the
power of the king and his political system. A second was the concentration
of what public wealth there was in royal courts and capitals, such that any
political player needed to maintain access to royal largesse in order to be
successful (and to be perceived as successful). A third was the construction of
other forms of capillary intervention in local society by kings and their
representatives; these, if they did not involve tax, generally tended to involve

justice and the law. The Visigoths, Merovingian Franks, and Lombards practised all three of these; the Visigoths seem to have stressed the first most, the Merovingian Franks the second, the Lombards the third. (The Carolingians stressed all three.) Rulers needed to do this, in order to maintain their relevance in a potentially decentralizing political system. Roman and Byzantine emperors and Arab caliphs did all three as well, of course, and it was important for the success of their affairs (sometimes, for their very survival as rulers) that they did so; but their state structures did not need it in the same way, for they were based on taxation, and had an existence independent of the interests of aristocrats and other locally influential elites.

A fifth observation concerns scale. One thing that made the Roman empire stand out was the geographical range of its fiscal structures, with Rome fed from Africa, Constantinople from Egypt, and the frontier army from nearly everywhere. The Roman tax system was not centrally controlled for a long time—until the sixth century it was run by local urban elites—but it linked together wide areas. Almost none of its successors did the same. Interestingly, all of its successors were more centralized in organizational terms, with central-government officials by 550 or so replacing the semi-autonomous elites of the past; but the movement of taxation, and of all other supplies controlled by the state, became much more localized. Of course, the simple division of the empire into independent kingdoms accomplished this in the West; when taxation foundered there as well, in the sixth and seventh centuries, economic localization was all the greater. In the East, too, however, at least after 650, we see a similar process. Both the Byzantines and the Umayyads adopted regional or sub-regional tax regimes, where tax mostly paid for armies and officials inside a single theme or province, and relatively little moved more widely. The 'Abbāsids reversed this process in the late eighth century, ensuring that much more taxation flowed to Baghdad and its hinterland, but that centralization only lasted a century, until the break-up of the caliphate itself, with the establishment of politically, not just fiscally, autonomous regimes in its various regions in the late ninth century and onwards. The considerable, and often dramatic, reduction in the economic scale of political systems everywhere in the post-Roman world had a considerable impact on exchange. Only a few regions (notably Egypt, and perhaps Syria and Palestine) maintained fiscal unity even at the regional level; elsewhere, even medium-distance exchange came to be linked to the geographical scale of aristocratic demand inside regions, which as far as we can see was only substantial in Francia. These issues will be explored further in Chapters 4 and 11, in some detail, for they are crucial for the arguments of this book.

The final point is that taxation, once abandoned, can of course be re-established, as has happened often enough in history; it is just that it is much harder to do so. In our period, as already noted, we can see this in Spain: the Arabs did begin to tax again after 711, but re-establishing a fully working tax system took two centuries and a civil war. Contrast the re-organization of the Byzantine state in the mid- to late eighth century: it was not a smooth task, but it was that much easier because the basic fiscal structures of the past had never fully broken down, and from the 820s a more monetized economic system begins to be visible. In Francia, which was richer than either, such procedures were never successful. Francia did not have to pay an army, of course, so it lacked the incentive to try; it is significant, though, that even when the Franks did institute a new tax, in order to pay Danegeld to the Vikings in the 860s, they did not maintain it. It is in fact much easier to extract tax as a one-off than to establish a taxation *system*, with all the record-keeping that this involves. No state in the Latin West managed that again until the late tenth century in England, a tax which also began as a Danegeld, but which was regularized with time into a more permanent obligation.[228] This takes us into a very different world, however; how it relates to the reconstruction of western states in the central middle ages, and why it took place in England nearly two centuries before it did anywhere else, are problems for a different study. I wish to try to avoid teleologies in this book, in fact; it is enough to say that, in 800, the future developments of taxation and the form of the state in the West could have been predicted by no one.

---

[228] For Byzantine remonetization in the 820s, see e.g. Haldon, 'Production, distribution', pp. 241–3. For Charles the Bald's Danegeld, see *Annales Bertiniani*, s.aa. 866, 877, with Nelson, *Charles the Bald*, pp. 28–9, 250–1. For other ninth-century Frankish developments that might have resulted in the re-establishment of a stable tax system (but did not), see above, n. 148. For English Danegeld in a comparative European perspective, see Wickham, 'Lineages'.

PART II
Aristocratic power-structures

4

Aristocracies

WHAT MAKES WHAT we call an aristocrat in most societies is a complex, often negotiable, process. In modern societies, legal determinations bring certainty: one is either in the *Almanach de Gotha*, or in the (pre-1999) House of Lords, or one is not; in Great Britain, all hereditary peers with the same sort of title are the same sort of aristocrats, whether their ancestors were the protégés (or bastards) of Henry I, Charles II, or David Lloyd George, and no one else is one. This sort of certainty hangs on a process by which royal (now, ministerial) favour, backed up by law, is all-powerful, and other determinations do not exist at all—Winston Churchill, aristocratic in lifestyle, politically powerful, nephew and descendant of dukes, remained a 'commoner' because he stayed out of the House of Lords. This can rarely be said for any society before the late middle ages. In late Antiquity and the early middle ages, the situation was certainly far more fluid. In our period, indeed, there was no single word for 'aristocrat' in most of our societies, and we must recognize that the concept is ours, not theirs. What I mean by an aristocrat is a member of a (normally landed) political elite, someone who could wield some form of power simply because of who he (or, rather more rarely, she) was. There were many levels of political elites in the more complex societies of our period, above all the Roman empire and the Arab caliphate, but Merovingian Francia too, and there were therefore different levels of aristocrats there. It must also be recognized, right from the start, that the aristocrats of different societies often had very little in common, the *gesithcundmenn* of early Anglo-Saxon England (below, p. 343) set against the Anicii in Rome, or the wide-owning *proceres* of Merovingian Francia set against the *milites* of eleventh-century France, with their highly localized lordships. The last-named might well not have been recognized as political players at all by their Merovingian forebears, and in the early medieval world, where status was seldom precisely defined, whether we see a given local leader as 'aristocratic' or not depends largely on our own decisions about where to draw the line in any given period or region. All of these points make the apparently simple characterization described here rather more complicated in reality. Indeed, what made an 'aristocrat' has always been made up of several different elements; even in the England of the late middle ages, where 'nobility' was already defined by membership of the House of Lords, more informal criteria defined local elites, the 'gentry', who can certainly be regarded as aristocratic by the definition used here. Of these different criteria, six seem to me particularly important as guides to the membership of a broad aristocratic stratum in our period. These are, put briefly: distinction of ancestry; landed wealth; position in an official hierarchy; imperial or royal favour (what the Germans call *Königsnähe*); recognition by other political leaders; and lifestyle.[1]

These six are doubtless not exhaustive; more important, they were not autonomous. Recognition or reputation, in particular, tends to depend on satisfactory performance in whichever of the other five are currently regarded as most important, and it will be referred to less here (it was more important as an independent criterion in the eleventh-century West, when central powers were weaker). But all the criteria are at least identifiably different, and they tended to have different histories in our period. The six together can be seen as making up an 'ideal-type aristocrat'. All the same, real societies privileged different combinations and hierarchies of criteria at different times. In particular, there were periods—periods of crisis in all cases—in which ancestry was relatively unimportant (a good example is the Byzantine empire in the period after 650).[2] The importance of office also tended to wax and wane depending on the fortunes of public power, with a maximum in late Antiquity and a minimum in the eleventh-century West, although large-scale and complex official hierarchies like those of the 'Abbāsid caliphate could also allow less official, gentry-like, aristocracies to exist in the provinces as well.[3] These complexities made all forms of political position transactional. At the margins, where an ambitious man[4] was trying to make it without ancestry or family land, his success would depend on his negotiating skills with kings and other aristocrats: perhaps his charm, often his military success, and certainly his luck. Very often, 'low'

---

[1] Cf. for example the multifaceted characterization of the Carolingian aristocracy in Goetz, ' "Nobilis" ', or Depreux, *Les sociétés occidentales*, pp. 116–18 (extending beyond the Carolingian period), or the ninefold elements of senatorial identity in Näf, *Senatorisches Standesbewusstsein*, pp. 8–11.

[2] For the Byzantines, see below, pp. 233–9.

[3] For the 'Abbāsids, Kennedy, 'Central government'; cf. Bulliet, 'Local politics', for a slightly later period. Note that periods where ancestry is genuinely unimportant tend to last only for a single generation after a major political upheaval; in the second generation family loyalties will already impose themselves. For this, see Runciman, *Treatise*, II, esp. pp. 138–45.

[4] This discussion is necessarily gendered; men could sometimes establish themselves without land and family backing, but women could not. Politically powerful women were universally so either because of their ancestry (as with, for example, Pulcheria and Galla Placidia in the early fifth century) or else, if they had no high-status ancestry, because of their husbands or consorts (as with Fredegund and other queens-regent for the lineage-obsessed Merovingian kings, or Verina and Theodora in the Roman East); more strictly aristocratic versions of these would be respectively Anicia Juliana and Antonina in early sixth-century Constantinople. For the general issues, see among many Nelson, 'Queens as jezebels'; Holum, *Theodosian empresses*; Brubaker, 'Memories of Helena'. My focus on the control of land will lead me largely to concentrate on male actors.

birth was forgotten (particularly by his friends) when a man was successful, but remembered again (especially, though not only, by his opponents) when he was not.[5] The constant ambiguities and changes of meaning of the word *nobilis* across space and time are themselves markers of how the negotiation of aristocratic status changed; although *nobilis* never simply meant 'aristocrat' according to the criteria set out here, one could pretty much write the history of the ideal type just from the history of the word.[6] ('Noble', though, has its own baggage as a word in English, and its use will be here restricted to the criterion of distinguished ancestry, 'blood nobility', or 'nobility of birth'.) These complexities do, however, also mean that one cannot, whatever one's interests, write any account of aristocracies without taking into consideration all the criteria that mattered at any given moment. The focus of this book will lead me to say most here about landed wealth, but the other criteria will remain essential as a framing, for aristocratic identity itself depended on it.

In this chapter, like the last, I shall begin with the later Roman empire, and then track the post-Roman world. This is inevitable, given the considerations already set out, for the heavy involvement of all the Roman aristocratic hierarchies in the structures of the state was similar everywhere, and would lead to huge repetition if it was described regionally; we need to get a sense of a *status quo ante* before we can see how, and how far, aristocracies changed. But in this chapter the imperial starting-point will only be that; my main interest is in the regions, and in the other sections of the chapter these will be considered in turn, setting aside the regions of the northern world (including Britain, where Roman continuity was particularly weak), which will be discussed in Chapter 6. In each case, the scale and organization of landowning will be the structuring element, but always located in relation to the other five criteria as well. In the next chapter we shall look at some aspects of estate management: these are not really separable from the general issue of the scale of landowning, but have a separate historiography (indeed, several separate historiographies), which deserves separate treatment.

1. Roman imperial hierarchies

The aristocracy of late Rome can be divided into three parts: the senates of Rome and Constantinople; the imperial office-holders, whether in the civil

---

[5] Sidonius on his fallen friend Arvandus in 469 is an instance, *Ep.* I.7; would Sidonius have made much of his 'plebeian' origins (I.7.3, 11) had he still been praetorian prefect?

[6] See Goetz, ' "Nobilis" ' (for whom *nobilis* does mean 'aristocratic' in the Carolingian period), or, more generally, Niermeyer, *Lexicon minus*, s.v., for the complexity of the word. In the late empire, *nobilis* generally denotes the senatorial strata rather than any wider group (see e.g. Schlinkert, *Ordo senatorius*, pp. 171–88, 210–19); but the word could be used to denote more fluid categories, as Barnish, 'Transformation and survival', pp. 122–3, shows.

service or the army; and the provincial aristocracies of the city *curiae*.
These three substantially overlapped, for ambitious *curiales* were the main
sources of 'new men' for the senate and the administration, and entry to
the senate was largely through holding an administrative position. The
differences between them remained important, however; local senatorial
families, for example, were at the centre of provincial aristocratic society
precisely because they were not members of the *curia*, as we shall see. All of
them, particularly the senate, have been the focus of so much secondary
work, not least in recent decades, that it would be both impossible and
superfluous to characterize them in detail here: what follows is only a sketch,
with particular attention paid to senators, as the exceptional feature of the
period.

The senate was the oldest marker of political position in the empire, older
indeed than the empire. It brought privilege in the law courts and exemption
from taxation (not from the basic land tax, but from *superindictiones* and a
variety of services); it brought exemption from curial duties, for the most
part; above all, it brought status. It mattered to the state; as a result, the
criteria for membership of the senate were constantly being changed,
throughout the late empire. By 400 the highest senatorial grade, that of
illustris, itself only introduced in 372, could only be gained by holding public
office or through direct imperial nomination (*adlectio*); this was partially
true also of the second grade, *spectabilis*; only the third grade, *clarissimus*,
was wholly hereditary, in that the male children of all three grades were
clarissimi of right.[7] At some point in the fifth century (A. H. M. Jones
thought after 450, Ernst Stein c.440, Stefano Giglio the 420s), the title of
senator became restricted to *illustres*, thus making the senate an aristocracy
of office only, dependent on having been a civil servant or on other signs of
imperial favour.[8] Certainly, this allowed 'new men' into the senate; it also
meant that pre-existing senatorial families were ever more determined to
hold imperial offices, which in the fifth century they anyway largely dominated, at least in the West. The fact is that the western senatorial elite was in
reality no less hereditary than any other great aristocracy, which means that
its core membership could boast both ancestry (back to the third century,
anyway, a period of a certain turnover of senatorial families) and gigantic
wealth, possibly, in the case of its leaders, greater in relative terms than any
other aristocracy ever; but its identity was perforce more tied up with
governmental service than other aristocracies have mostly been, for not
only the wealth that accrued to any official, but also senatorial status itself,

---

[7] Among recent general accounts (but there are many) are Jones, *LRE*, pp. 523–62; Arnheim,
The senatorial aristocracy; Matthews, *Western aristocracies*; Roda, *La parte migliore*; Näf,
Senatorische Standesbewusstsein; Heather, 'Senators and senates'. See also n. 9.

[8] Jones, *LRE*, p. 529; Stein, *Bas-Empire*, I, p. 220; Giglio, *Il tardo impero*, pp. 27–46 for
dates.

was associated with it.[9] This was still truer of the eastern senate, which was far newer (Constantinople had only been founded in 324, and its senate not until 340), and whose members, ex-*curiales*, or, indeed, occasionally ex-artisans, had no equivalents to the hyper-rich western elite;[10] when one refers to the great wealth of senators, one is always thinking of a dozen families in the senate of Rome.

We have a quantity of evidence about what being a (western) senator was like, thanks to the aristocratic provenance of so many late Roman literary texts. Office certainly counted, but it was not necessarily the main focus of the ambition of every senator. For a start, many of the entry offices were only ceremonial, notably the quaestorship and praetorship: these offices brought with them the obligation to provide games in Rome, often in the case of the praetorship at gigantic cost (extravagance was not legally necessary, but it was a sure way to social status), but no political duties, and indeed their members were nominated by the senate itself. Secondly, the palatine offices of central government had a high turnover rate; a senator did not need to spend more than a few years in one of them, and most did not do so—career politicians, like, most famously, Petronius Probus in the 360s–380s, or Petronius Maximus in the 410s–440s, were relative rarities, and in general the most long-lasting political careers were those of military, not civilian, leaders.[11] Senators did not exactly shun government; to some extent they saw its powers and its perks—less often its responsibilities—as theirs by right. But as important was their right to leisure, *otium*, to living the role of the senatorial elite, moving from luxurious town house (in the winter) to luxurious country house (in the summer), in a permanent round of feasts, games, and literary activities. Western senators indeed had to know classical Latin literature well to keep their moral and cultural status, and deeply despised those who did not. They did not really make a distinction between Virgil and the dice-board, but people who could *only* cope with the dice-board were defined as déclassé: a true senator dealt with both. Ammianus in the 380s could attack senators because they only *really* read Juvenal and Marius Maximus, as it were the easy or spicy bits of the literature, but he did not doubt that they at least read that, and many of them were serious poets and philosophers in their own right, up to Boethius in the early sixth century. Senatorial identity was thus, in large part, the identity of a complex shared culture—hence, indeed, the literary productions that make senators so well

---

[9] On practical hereditary, see e.g. Jones, *LRE*, pp. 529–30. For turnover in the third century and its limits, Jacques, 'L'ordine senatorio'; for a slower process of replacement subsequently, Barnish, 'Transformation and survival'.

[10] The key text here is Libanios, *Oration* XLII.22–6, but this certainly overstates the déclassé elements of the eastern senate. See above all Skinner, ' "Byzantine" senatorial perspective'; cf. Jones, *LRE*, pp. 527, 546, 551, 555; Näf, *Senatorische Standesbewusstsein*, pp. 251–3.

[11] For the two Petronii, see *PLRE*, I, s.v. Probus 5, and II, s.v. Maximus 22. For games and their expense, see most recently Lim, 'People as power'.

documented, as also the grand town houses and rural villas that help to make late Roman archaeology so impressive. It was a culture of leisure, to the extent that Symmachus could write to Petronius Probus (among others) formally to console him for the burden of having to take office once more. Still, that leisure has to be balanced against the fact that office defined the senate itself.[12]

This emphasis on a literary lifestyle is unusual among aristocracies. Essentially, it derives from the one overriding feature of this elite: it was a civilian one. Most aristocracies are above all military; they derive their power and elite status from their control of the army, and they are educated to arms. The dominant elite of the Roman empire is indeed unique in the pre-industrial world, with the sole exception of China, in that it was civilian. The Roman army held power, for sure; its generals dominated politics, and provided most of the emperors. To that extent it had plenty of parallels in world history, including, in our period, the caliphate, controlled as the latter was by a military elite, who excluded the older civilian (and, as yet, non-Muslim) landed elites of the provinces from most political power. But the cultural status of the Roman senate was not in any sense a consolation prize for political marginality. Senators with a civilian background could, if they wanted, rule provinces (Africa's *proconsul* was always a senator), or a quarter of the whole empire, as praetorian prefects; they could indeed, if they really wanted, run armies. Conversely, the major military leaders, like Aspar in the East and Aetius in the West in the mid-fifth century, were respected senators (Aspar at his death in 471 was the senior senator in Constantinople). But to be a respected senator one had to have cultural capital too. Aspar, from a military family of Alan extraction, is not, it is true, recorded as being a major literary figure, but he was at least not attacked for his cultural inadequacy; he was anyway an active patron of public building in Constantinople, another sign of civilian seriousness.[13] This would change. After 500 in the West, 650 in the East, the aristocracy became sharply more military, both in the centre and in the provinces; all these cultural markers disappeared, and aristocratic identity itself shifted dramatically, as we shall see.

By 400 the senatorial aristocracy was also predominantly Christian, and by 450 exclusively so. This did not make much cultural difference;

---

[12] Ammianus, *Res gestae*, XXVIII.4.14 (cf. in general XIV.6, XXVIII.4); Symmachus, *Ep.* I.58 to Petronius Probus. Sidonius, *Ep.* V.17.6, says 'I have [the ball] no less than the book as my companion'—he is proud that, in his forties, he is a ball-player as much as a dice-player. For *otium*, see Matthews, *Western aristocracies*, pp. 1–12; Forlin Patrucco and Roda, 'Crisi di potere', pp. 267–72; Roda, 'Fuga nel privato'.

[13] For Aspar, *PLRE*, II, s.v. (p. 168 for his seniority); for the building of the Cistern of Aspar, *Easter chronicle*, s.a. 459. For cultural capital, Bourdieu, *Distinction*, esp. pp. 1–96. For military–civilian interpenetration, see also Whitby, 'Armies and society', p. 473. Sidonius, *Ep.* IV.17, to Arbogast, is rather patronizing about the culture of his friend, who is a military governor.

knowledge of the Bible and of Augustine (or Basil of Caesarea) were simply set alongside Virgil and Sallust (or Homer and Thucydides) as (subsidiary) elements of one's credibility as an educated and virtuous person. But it did open up a different route for advancement, the church. The church was a totally separate hierarchy; the episcopate did not, for example, have senatorial status. It had the advantage of being partially tax-exempt, as senators were, and of bringing similar exemptions from curial duties, but it was formally distinct from the basic structures of the Roman state. Nevertheless, bishops, in particular, were gaining considerable informal influence in the late fourth and fifth centuries as leaders of their cities, and increasingly this influence was sanctioned by law too. Furthermore, as Christian gift-giving to the church increased, episcopal office could mean the control of substantial estates. By 450 the status of being a bishop had become considerable, and was sought even by senators, initially as a retirement position, later as a career path. This development is first seen fully in Gaul, in the crisis of imperial power there; by the mid-sixth century we can find parallels in Italy and Spain as well. In the East, too, although senatorial bishops are harder to track, the episcopate certainly had local status.[14] After 500, as western aristocracies became more military, civilian aristocratic culture became largely restricted to clerics. It was then that that culture itself began to change, dropping most of its secular literary elements and becoming much more ecclesiastical in orientation. But by then, too, it was seen as a marker, not of aristocratic, but of clerical identity. This process was not yet complete in the time of Venantius Fortunatus and Gregory the Great at the end of the sixth century, but it would be soon after. Aristocratic identity by then was in most places expressed in military terms.

Rome's senate was dominated by half-a-dozen great family clans, all interrelated: the Anicii above all, linked to the Petronii, the Symmachi, and probably the Acilii; the Caeionii and their fifth-century heirs the Decii and probably the Rufii Festi; and so on. How to distinguish them is very difficult. This is particularly so with the Anicii, whose status was sufficiently high that all kinds of lesser senators (like Cassiodorus) and parvenus could claim kinship with them on the most tenuous of grounds, the marriage of a cousin to a minor Anician or whatever.[15] The criteria which different people

---

[14] See for Gaul, Van Dam, *Leadership and community*, pp. 153–78; Mathisen, *Roman aristocrats*, pp. 89–104. Contrast for Italy Barnish, 'Transformation and survival', p. 138 (senators tended to choose bishops rather than became bishops themselves); Brown, *Gentlemen and officers*, pp. 34, 181. For the East, see most recently Rapp, 'Bishops in late Antiquity'.

[15] This is an ill-studied subject. Arnheim, *The senatorial aristocracy*, pp. 103–42, is not an adequate account of family structures. Some impression can be gained from the genealogical tables in *PLRE* (esp. vol. I). For the Anicii, see most recently Ruggini, 'Gli Anicii', with previous bibliography, which is more extensive on this family than on others. For the Rufii Festii, see Matthews, 'Continuity'. For the claims of Cassiodorus and also Ennodius to Anician kinship, see respectively *Institutiones*, I.23.1 and *Ep.* I.18 (*Opera*, n. 23, much vaguer)—see in general Ruggini, 'Nobiltà romana'. The peculiarly loose identity of the Anicii might in principle be

used for family membership in the late empire have never been systematically analysed, but it is at least clear that there were no strict rules: male- and female-line inheritance both worked for family identity (as indeed they did for the transmission of property), and individuals could probably, at times, identify with more than one family at once, as did Petronius Probus, one of the Petronii obviously, but also *Anicianae domus culmen*, the summit of the Anician house, in an inscription. We can now only trace links by marriage between him and the Anicii, through his wife and his daughter-in-law, but Petronius presumably knew, or claimed, different.[16] The Anicii maintained their centrality in Rome right up to the Gothic war, though they vanished thereafter—it is interesting that Gregory the Great (pope 590–604), who was proud that his great-grandfather was Felix III (pope 483–92), makes nothing of his great-grandmother Petronia, known from a tomb inscription, who could well have been an Anician. By the 590s family identity, too, was constructed on other grounds.[17]

These core senatorial families were all based in Rome. Around them there was a large penumbra of western provincial families, notably in northern Italy and Gaul, who were descended from senators (and thus remained *clarissimi*), but whose continuing senatorial status was less assured, either because they could not afford the expense of senatorial entry offices, or because, being provincial, they had less access to any ceremonial or governmental position. We can see this very clearly in the upper aristocracy of Gaul, whose links to Rome were never more than occasional, and whose links to government were only strong in the fourth century, when Trier and Arles were imperial residences.[18] Sidonius Apollinaris (c.430–85) is a good example (as well as unusually well-documented, thanks to his poems and extensive letter collection). Grandson of Apollinaris, a praetorian prefect of the Gauls (though for a usurper) in 408–9 and son-in-law of the emperor Eparchius Avitus (455–6), himself of a family of praetorian prefects, Sidonius was from one of the premier families of Gaul, and under Avitus, and his successor Majorian (456–61), he had a position at court, dining with the latter in what might be called Majorian's *Kaisersnähe*. But we do not know of any office Sidonius held that would have technically attached him to the

explained by Demandt's proposition ('The osmosis', p. 82) that the family died out in the male line in the fourth century, but he offers no support for this, and one can track a male line through *PLRE* with some plausibility into the mid-fifth century, after which most detailed family relationships are obscure for two generations.

[16] *Inscriptiones latinae selectae*, I, n. 1267; cf. *PLRE*, I, stemma 24.

[17] Anician centrality in the 520s is well illustrated by Cassiodorus, *Variae*, X.11 (referring to one of the Petronii—clearly the two families had fused conceptually by now). See Gregory the Great, *Dialogi*, IV.17, for Felix, and *Inscriptiones latinae Christianae veteres*, I, n. 167, for Petronia (cf. Pietri and Pietri, *Prosopographie*, II. pp. 777, 1721—note that even her marriage to Felix is not fully certain, let alone her family background). Historians often refer to Gregory as 'an Anician', but this is the only grounds.

[18] Matthews, *Western aristocracies*, pp. 329–51.

senate as a *vir illustris* until he was nominated *praefectus urbis* in 468, the first Gaul known to have been prefect of the city of Rome for over fifty years. Sidonius was obsessed by exact titles and the status that derived from them, but it is significant that we cannot be totally sure when he entered the senate: in part this may be because it preceded the letters we have (he might have been directly promoted by Avitus in the 450s), but largely it seems to be because, as a Gaul, family *nobilitas*—senatorial identity—was not so strictly attached to the ever-changing legal rules for senatorial eligibility. In 461 in Arles Sidonius could look down on the former praetorian prefect Paeonius as *municipaliter natus*, of curial origin, when he himself was only a *comes*, a very vague title indeed; his family status was enough to allow him to do so. Had they both been in Rome, where the rules were sharper, this would have been harder. Even in something as empire-wide as senatorial status, that is to say, there were already regional differences. And indeed in the following century, in Gaul, the leading families continued to regard themselves as 'senatorial' even though they seldom left the region at all, and the senate in Rome was, after the 540s, in ruins.[19]

One implication of the foregoing is worth bringing out: the senatorial elites were profoundly dependent on the survival of the empire. Their members were certainly greedy, selfish, hypocritical, and short-sighted, as aristocratic communities generally are. It is sometimes claimed that the fall of the western empire itself owed much to the renewed importance in the fifth century of senatorial occupation of palatine offices. But this is to go too far the other way—after all, anyone who reads John Lydos, writing about Justinian's Constantinople, can hardly come out feeling that career civil servants were much more altruistic. Senators, above all, could not go it alone. Without an empire, traditional senatorial position was inconceivable. Even the most 'disloyal' aristocrats, Attalus and Jovinus and Paulinus of Pella in the Visigothic entourage of the 410s, Arvandus in that of the late 460s, re-erected the empire locally, or tried to convince themselves they were doing so. All those titles that a Sidonius cared so much about could not exist otherwise. In the end, the unintended result of much local aristocratic action was that the empire did indeed break up. It is significant that Anician identity did not survive thereafter—for, even though southern Italy was by 550 Roman again, the senate and its offices were failing, and the Anicii

[19] See *PLRE*, II, s.v. Apollinaris 1, 6 (Sidonius' unnamed father was also praetorian prefect in 449: *Ep*. VIII.6.5, cf. V.9.2), and above all Harries, *Sidonius Apollinaris*, e.g. pp. 25–30. Sidonius claimed that his was a family of officials: *Ep*. I.3; for office mattering to him, e.g. VIII.2, VIII.6; against Paeonius, I.11.5–7. Jill Harries suggested to me that Eparchius Avitus could well have appointed him to the senate when he delivered a panegyric to the emperor in Rome in 456 (*Carmen* VII). The other focus for senatorial identity in fifth-century Gaul was the Council of the Seven Provinces: see Matthews, *Western aristocracies*, pp. 334–6. For the sixth century, see Stroheker, *Der senatorische Adel*, pp. 112–36; Näf, *Senatorisches Standesbewusstsein*, pp. 178–92, largely commenting on Venantius Fortunatus and Gregory of Tours, for whom see below, pp. 171–84.

depended on these to exist. In Gaul, the local value attached to senatorial birth permitted the families who carried it to continue longer; but this was second best to the apparatus of titular status which was still so valued in the fifth century. Senators would have never voluntarily done anything to weaken this, and they greatly lamented its loss when they did recognize it.[20]

For the wealth of senators we are reliant on only a few, much-cited, texts. Olympiodoros, in particular, writing in Greek in c.425, tells us that annual income in rents for many aristocratic families (*oikoi*, 'houses') in Rome amounted to 5,000-plus pounds of gold (c.375,000 *solidi*), three-quarters of it from rents in money. He also gives figures for three praetorian games, that of Probus son of Olympius, implicitly a lesser senator, of 1,200 pounds of gold in c.424, of Symmachus 'the *logographos*', that is, the writer, a 'middling' (*metrios*) senator, of 2,000 pounds for his son in 401, and of Maximus, of the 'wealthy' (*euporoi*), of 4,000 pounds (300,000 *solidi*), for his son, probably in 411 if his son was the future senatorial politician Petronius Maximus.[21] How do we rate these figures? Olympiodoros only survives in fragments, so we cannot assess their full rhetorical context, except that they are certainly part of an extended laudatory account of senatorial wealth, which makes the unlikely claim, along other things, that Roman aristocratic town houses had a hippodrome inside each one. Olympiodoros did like figures, and used them elsewhere, but this does not make them any more authentic than the hippodromes. Still, they do fit, in terms of orders of magnitude, the account in the *Vita Melaniae* that Melania the younger (d. 439), from the Valerii, or alternatively her husband Pinianus, got 120,000 *solidi* in annual rents (when they sold off their land it wrecked the land market), and one may also note a sixth-century account in John Lydos of the emperor Anastasius' gift of 1,000 pounds of gold to a bankrupt Constantinopolitan senator, Paul, a former consul (in 498), to re-establish him financially (though this represented his total resources, not his annual rents).[22] It would be wrong to try to locate Melania and Paul too tightly inside Olympiodoros' hierarchies of wealth, but the scales are analogous. They also compare strikingly with our figures for the taxation of Numidia in 445, which survive in a law remitting seven-eighths of the burden owing to

---

[20] For self-deception about a senator's role in imperial break-up, see Paulinus of Pella, *Eucharisticos*, ll. 291–310. For a lament, see Sidonius, *Ep.* VIII.2: education is all that is left, if the political power-structure goes. For the limits of John Lydos' altruism, see *On powers*, III.27, on the profits he made.

[21] Olympiodoros, *Frag.* 41.2 (ed. Blockley). Probus' father's name is often emended 'Olybrius', putting him firmly into the Anicii-Petronii, along with Maximus, but this makes his lesser wealth hard to understand.

[22] Olympiodorus, *Frag.* 41.1, 23, 25; *Life* of Melania/*Vita Melaniae latina*, c. 15 (the Latin version says it is Melania's property, the Greek version Pinianus')—see Giardina, 'Carità eversiva', for the stupidity of selling off land on that scale; John Lydos, *On powers*, III. 48 (cf. Jones, *LRE*, pp. 554–5). For Roman town houses in the period, see Guidobaldi, 'Le *domus* tardoantiche'.

twelve years of Vandal occupation; the full total, if reckoned in money, comes to just over 78,000 *solidi* (some 1,050 pounds of gold).[23] It was possible, that is, for senators to get rent income that was on the scale of the taxation from entire provinces, and, if we were to be sufficiently trusting to take these figures all literally, up to four or five times more. Numidia was a smallish province, but not a poor one. Small wonder then that an estate of Melania and Pinianus near Thagaste (Souk Ahras), on the Numidian border, could be described as 'larger than the city [territory] itself'. Small wonder too that the richest senators could afford only to dip their toes into the potential wealth of government—though when they went for the latter, as in the case of Petronius Probus, they took peculation seriously as well.[24]

The wealthiest senators, the level of the hyper-rich, were all Rome-based. No account of any wealth attached to either Constantinopolitan senators or western provincial senatorial families ever matches figures like these. Where did they own land? Ammianus says that Petronius Probus 'possessed estates (*patrimonia*) scattered across almost the whole Roman world'. The *Life* of Melania says that Melania and Pinianus, when they decided on an ascetic life in c.405, owned in Rome, Campania, Sicily, Africa (Proconsularis, Numidia, and Mauretania), Spain, and Britain. Symmachus' letters mention, more casually but less rhetorically, lands in Rome, several places in Italy, Sicily, and Mauretania. The Caeionii were also rich in African land, and often took on African provincial offices. So must the Anicii have been, because they actually came originally from Uzappa, near Mactar in Proconsularis, at the start of the third century.[25] In general, we can conclude two things: first, that it was normal for these aristocrats to own very widely indeed, and not to concentrate their estates in single areas; second, that the 'senatorial region' par excellence was southern Italy, Sicily, and Africa. Other regions were decidedly secondary as far as senatorial landowning was concerned, although Gaul, Spain, and northern Italy of course had their own regional elites, who were at least of analogous status, as we have seen. The tax spine of the grain *annona* tied Africa and Sicily to Rome (above, pp. 76, 87); we can now see that senatorial land, often held on a giant scale, reinforced exactly the same axis. But its extent did depend on the unity of the Mediterranean. The Vandal occupation of Proconsularis in 439 would have broken the senatorial axis, as it broke the fiscal one; the Vandals were not shy of expelling local aristocrats, and can hardly have been

---

[23] *Nov. Val.*, XIII (see Jones, *LRE*, pp. 462–3). Useful on orders of magnitude are the lists in Banaji, *Agrarian change*, pp. 227–9.

[24] *Vita Melaniae latina*, c. 21; for Petronius Probus, Ammianus, *Res gestae*, XXVII.11, XXX.5.4–11. For Numidian prosperity, above, Ch. 3, n. 23.

[25] Ammianus, *Res gestae*, XXVII.11.1; *Life* of Melania, cc. 11, 19, 20. For Symmachus, see *PLRE*, I, s.v. Symmachus 4. For the Caeonii in Africa, Matthews, *Western aristocracies*, pp. 27–8; for the Anicii in Africa, Jacques, 'L'ordine senatorio', pp. 158–9; Novak, 'The early history'; Corbier, 'Les familles clarissimes', pp. 740–1.

expected to be more generous to absentee senators. The subsequent division of the rest of the western empire between the other Romano-Germanic kingdoms, although in general the latter were less hostile to Roman aristocratic landowning, would have made absentee property less easy to manage as well. The senators were pushed back to Italy and Sicily by the time of the Ostrogothic kingdom, and the wars of the 540s would have damaged many of their mainland estates. In Gregory the Great's time, nonetheless, Campania and Sicily were still the main centres of senatorial activity. The Roman senate was by then failing as an institution for a variety of reasons, few of which have to do with any senatorial poverty (which should anyway not be exaggerated); but the gigantic wealth of the leading early fifth-century senators, and its ability to link together whole geographical regions, had gone.[26]

Outside the elite of Rome, interregional landowning is less easy to document, but it certainly did exist. Paulinus of Nola (d. 431), a Bordeaux senator, the richest Gallic landowner we have documentation for, owned in Campania (whither he went as a priest, later to become bishop of Nola) and in Spain. Even his elder contemporary, the poet Ausonius of Bordeaux (d. c.395), whose estates were far smaller and also restricted to Aquitaine, could marry his daughter to a *praeses* in Illyricum, hence bringing property in Epiros and Makedonia into the family, as we know because that daughter's son (by her second marriage) Paulinus of Pella, a notably unsuccessful Gallic politician of the 410s, refers to it.[27] In the East, too, we can see some evidence of similar patterns. The Constantinople senate was new, as already noted, and its members were not rich on an Anician scale, but they were, of course, taken from the elites of the whole of the East (particularly Antioch), and by 400 or so the eastern senators were at the top of the landowning hierarchy there. Olympias, a major landowner from a senatorial family, gave to the patriarch John Chrysostom in c.400 large sections of her property, which lay in Constantinople, in Thrace and Bithynia in the urban hinterland, and in Galatia and Cappadocia on the Anatolian plateau. Hierios, a leading senator of the late fifth century (he may have been the praetorian prefect of the East in 494–6), left a will involving subsequent legal problems only resolved in a *Novel* of Justinian in 555, which includes the will itself: he owned in Constantinople and in Antioch. Only a handful of other senators can be seen to have owned land outside the Constantinople area, however, in Phrygia or again in Antioch.[28] Essentially, what we find in the East is what

---

[26] Brown, *Gentlemen and officers*, pp. 21–37; Barnish, 'Transformation and survival', pp. 150–4.

[27] *PLRE*, I, s.vv. Paulinus 21, Therasia; for Ausonius, Étienne, 'Ausone'; Paulinus of Pella, *Eucharisticos*, ll. 24–6, 412–15, 481–8 (cf. *PLRE*, I, s.v. Paulinus 10).

[28] *Life* of Olympias, c. 5; *NJ*, CLIX. See in general Čekulova, who overstates the significance of the absence of evidence for eastern senatorial land, but lists it; Skinner, ' "Byzantine" senatorial perspective'; and Haldon, 'The fate of the late Roman senatorial élite'.

we find in Gaul: that most people owned inside single regions, plus, for the wealthy, one or two outliers. This is even so for the most remunerative location for landowning, Egypt. The Apions, the best-documented landowners we have, hugely wealthy in the territories of Oxyrhynchos and Arsinoë in Egypt, are not certainly known to have owned anywhere else at all except Constantinople, where in the sixth century they were senators and often palatine officials.[29] These examples, when put together, essentially show that long-distance political links, those which the empire developed and depended on, also allowed substantial regional owners to pick up property elsewhere, most notably in the areas nearest to Rome and Constantinople. But I have listed the best examples of this process that I know, and none of them compare with the Rome-based senatorial hyper-rich. Only the latter really *contributed* to the Mediterranean-wide networks that the empire made possible. Only the latter, too, would be seriously affected by its end.

This discussion has focused on the empire-wide aristocratic elite from the standpoint of its senatorial element. If it was viewed from the imperial court and army, through the wealth and identity of civil and military officials, it would look only slightly different. By and large, career officials who were not from the Roman senatorial elite already discussed were landowners on a lesser scale, at the Paulinus or the Ausonius level: still rich, but part of regional, not interregional, aristocracies. The senators of northern Italy, such as the Ennodii of Provence and Pavia, who looked to the administrative capitals of Ravenna and Milan more than to Rome, were at this sort of level of wealth; so were the Cassiodori of Squillace in Bruttii (modern Calabria).[30] These were people who needed the perks of government more than did the Anicii, and who would not, unlike the Anicii, have been powerful without it. As far as we can see, this is also true of the military leaders of the late empire as well, who were usually from frontier provinces (most often in the Balkans), and who are rarely associated with enormous landed wealth; even the rich exceptions, such as Gildo (d. 398) or Belisarios (d. 565), are only associated as owners with single provinces, in these cases Mauretania Caesariensis and Bithynia respectively.[31] The only major difference between the civilian and military governing elites was cultural: a Cassiodorus was—indeed, had to be—fully part of the senatorial literary establishment, while a Belisarios was (as Prokopios' patron) only at second hand. But as noted already for Aspar, military leaders without exception

[29] For the Constantinople land of the Apions, Malalas, *Chronographia*, p. 490; Gregory the Great, *Epp.*, II.27, IV.44. Apion III's Anician mother-in-law Rusticiana, Gregory's correspondent, also owned in Sicily—see below, n. 137.
[30] *PLRE*, II, s.v. Ennodius 3, Cassiodorus 1–4.
[31] *PLRE*, I, s.v. Gildo, III, s.v. Belisarius 1. Gildo was from a major Berber ruling family in the Kabylie; see below, p. 334; Belisarios' reputedly huge wealth (cf. *PLRE*, III, pp. 221–2) was not necessarily put into land.

played the senatorial game, at least in part. Essentially, they occupied the same cultural space as emperors, who mostly came from military families, and who were often indeed derided as uncultured by our literary arbiters, but who were large-scale patrons of culture as the holders of power and the disbursers of wealth. The new independent Germanic leaders like Theoderic II of the Visigoths (d. 466), Theoderic the Amal of the Ostrogoths (d. 526), and Thrasamund of the Vandals (d. 523), were identical. In the period up to 500 in the West, civilian culture maintained a certain hegemony even over these figures; only later would this change.

The other major landowners in the empire, the emperor himself and the church, only need a brief note, for they did not affect the patterns outlined above. The emperor was far and away the largest owner, owning, for example, perhaps a sixth of Africa (though, by contrast with earlier centuries, rather less of Egypt), and in general, estates in every province. These were generally, however, as far as we can see, let out for relatively low rents, by now on long-term *emphyteusis* leases, to local figures, who in effect added imperial leases to their own local and regional landowning. Some imperial lessees could be relatively small-scale people, indeed, such as Crispinus, Donatist bishop of the small town of Calama in Numidia, who dared to baptize his imperial *coloni* as Donatists, as Augustine complained in c.402.[32] Imperial land thus can effectively be seen as part of provincial-level patterns, not as part of the Mediterranean network itself. This was still more true of church land, for this was in nearly every case restricted to the diocese of the bishop that controlled it, or close by: the age of wide-ranging church landowning, whether focused on cathedrals or monasteries, had not yet begun. Only the churches of Rome and Constantinople as yet owned outside their immediate regions on a large scale, on a senatorial level. Already in the fourth century, thanks to imperial gifts, the papacy owned extensively in southern Italy, Sicily, and in Africa, and also in the East; by the sixth century it had Gaulish and Sardinian estates too (the eastern lands, however, seem to have gone). The patriarchs of Constantinople owned almost as widely in the eastern provinces.[33] Unlike the emperors, the popes controlled their estates relatively closely, and Gregory the Great's correspondence about it rivals the Apion papyri as a guide to landowners' assumptions about estate management (see below, pp. 270–1). But the papacy, at least, did not change the patterns already described, for the main focus of its lands was in the 'senatorial region', the Italy–Africa axis. What one can say about the papal estates, and perhaps those of the patriarch as well, is that

---

[32] Jones, *LRE*, pp. 412–27 for imperial land; pp. 415–16 for Africa. *Emphyteusis*: see e.g. Vera, 'Enfiteusi, colonato'; Kaplan, 'Novelle de Tibère', pp. 239, 241. Crispinus: Augustine, *Ep.* 66, with *Contra litteras Petiliani*, II.184 (he had 80 dependants, not a large estate given that this apparently included whole families).

[33] Jones, *LRE*, pp. 781–2, with, for the papacy, Recchia, *Gregorio magno*, and Kaplan, *Les hommes*, p. 143, for the patriarch.

they were better able to survive the political localization which destroyed the greatest senatorial families: by 600 or so they must have been the largest private estates left anywhere in the Mediterranean. But, though they had a staying-power that lay owners did not have, it was not infinite. Patriarchal land was cut back seriously after the Arab conquests; the popes for their part lost their Sicilian and south Italian estates as a result of fiscal measures taken by the emperors against them in around 730, and were forced back into Lazio, the immediate hinterland of Rome—they returned then to being just a provincial power, even if, to be sure, still a rich one.[34]

Finally, let us look quickly at city-level aristocracies. They will recur in more detail, both in the next section and in Chapter 10; here, it is enough to say that they existed, in every city of the empire, and indeed made up the great bulk of aristocratic landowning in the empire as a whole. They were the *curiales* or *decuriones* (Greek *bouleutai* or *politeuomenoi*) of the early and late empire, the city hierarchy who built the municipal buildings of the second century and the cathedrals of the fourth, and who underwrote the tax system at the level of the city territory (above, p. 68). In the fifth and sixth centuries *curiae* weakened: their richest members got senatorial or ecclesiastical privileges and rose above the curial level; their poorer members went under. As we shall see later (p. 597), around the end of the fifth century *curiales* largely lost their tax-raising responsibilities to imperial or royal officials; they also lost their roles as city patrons to more informally constructed groups, to the local senatorial-level families, to a handful of local (but not curial) officials, and to bishops.[35] But the major urban families in most cases continued to exist, surviving every one of these institutional shifts, and they did so later on as well.

The Aviti of Clermont can serve as an example of what changed and what stayed the same at the city level. By the start of the fifth century they were a locally based senatorial family, probably with curial roots, producing an emperor, Eparchius Avitus, in 455–6 and a local warlord, his son Ecdicius, in the 470s; collaterals were bishops in Vienne and elsewhere around 500. In the 540s they provided a senior administrator, Parthenius, to the Frankish king Theudebert; later on in the century an Avitus was bishop in Clermont, and two brothers, Avitus II and Bonitus, were bishops there at the end of the seventh century and into the early eighth. Here lay the real continuities of the Roman world: at the city level, despite any number of changes of regime, the continuous patterns of landowning structured local politics. What did change was, however, identity. Curial politics was a clearly circumscribed city-focused politics, with a formal structure and a recognized cursus. When this broke down, the informal patronage networks that replaced it were

---

[34] Marazzi, 'Il conflitto' is the basic survey; see further below, n. 143.
[35] See Liebeschuetz, *The decline*, pp. 110 ff. In general for municipal-level wealth, see Laniado, *Recherches*, pp. 154–60.

different: less literary, and soon less civilian—as already with Ecdicius, and indeed Eparchius Avitus, himself a general with Aetius, as well as praetorian prefect, before becoming emperor. In the case of major families, they might also be less tied to a single city—the Aviti had close marriage links to Narbonne and Lyon by the mid-fifth century and collaterals, as already noted, in Vienne; Parthenius was based in Arles and then Trier. Had Parthenius not been lynched at his king's death, his descendants might have shifted again, and become Franks, as so many others did. But the episcopate, necessarily more local, did keep the Aviti in Clermont. The civic identity had become an ecclesiastical one; the aristocratic identity a military one. The Clermont lands of the Aviti may, conceivably, have stayed roughly the same, keeping a city attachment with it, but everything else changed.[36] After 700 or so the names changed even in the episcopal context, and who the family then became is lost. This mixture, of structural (landowning) continuity and discontinuity in identity, marks the early middle ages, as it emerged from the ruins of the Roman empire, in both East and West. The aristocracies of the empire, both central and local, were too imbricated with the state, from which they derived all their essential distinguishing marks, not to be altered totally when the state changed. By 800 there is not a single person, anywhere in the former empire, with the sole exceptions of the Mamikonean and Bagratuni families in Armenia, whose male-line ancestors in 400 are securely known.[37] And yet, in 800 a high proportion of the city-level aristocratic families of the late empire were assuredly still around, speaking Latin, Greek, Coptic, Arabic, Berber, German, Welsh. Let us look at how this change occurred in more detail.

2. Gaul to Francia

The best-documented aristocracies of the post-Roman world are in Gaul and Italy, and the contrasting fates of these two areas in the pre-Carolingian period, taking southern Gaul, northern Gaul, and Italy in turn, are the best beginning to a discussion of what happened to late Roman aristocratic patterns. Spain will follow, and then the three main eastern regions, the Byzantine heartland, Syria-Palestine, and Egypt. In each case, the way aristocratic wealth and identity adapted to the world after the end of imperial unity was partially, and interestingly, different. But Gaul/Francia

---

[36] See in general Wood, 'Ecclesiastical politics'; *PLRE*, II, s.vv. Avitus 4 (bishop of Vienne), 5 (emperor), Ecdicius 3, Parthenius 3. The Apollinares were closely linked; see above, n. 19.

[37] For the Mamikonean and Bagratuni see Toumanoff, *Studies*, pp. 201–3, 209–11; see in general pp. 192–222 for all the Armenian families, mostly in areas never stably part of the late empire. A possible parallel are the descendants of Cunedda in north Wales (Bartrum, *Early Welsh genealogical tracts*, pp. 9–13, etc.; see Davies, *Early medieval Wales*, pp. 89, 92), but the authenticity of the early parts of this genealogy is problematic.

is the most clearly documented of all; it will be considered at length and in some detail.

In late Roman Gaul, as already noted, there was not much systematic linkage between regional landowners and land elsewhere: even Paulinus of Nola was basically an owner in the Bordeaux area, with only outlying estates in other provinces. This undoubtedly contributed to the Gaulish political identity that has been attributed to the fifth century in the region. John Matthews has commented that Gaul was substantially separate, both in political and social terms, from the rest of the empire already in the third century (it indeed formed an independent empire in 260–74); it was the fourth century, when emperors were based in Trier and Gaul was closely integrated with Italy, that was the exception, not the more regionalist fifth.[38] By the mid-fifth century Gaulish senators seldom even went to Italy except on political business.[39] This separation (not yet consciously separatist) was further reinforced by the economic separation between Gaul and the Mediterranean, discussed in Chapter 3 (p. 77). As already observed, the Gaulish senatorial-level elites had a conception of a birth nobility that could allow families to keep their sense of privilege even if their links to senatorial office were cut. In the 470s their feeling of distance from Italy and the empire steadily increased, first when the 'Greek' Anthemius was western emperor in 467–72, and then, still more, when the only emperors were eastern, after 476–80; but they could survive on their own. Both in landowning and in independent identity, the leading Gaulish families were equipped to cope with political break-up.[40]

Political break-up did not, however, just mean a separation between Gaul and Italy. Gaul in the late fifth century was made up of several fully independent polities, the Visigoths in the south-west and Provence, the Burgundians in the Rhône valley, the Franks in the north, the latter expanding at the expense of a set of surviving Roman generals. These included Arbogast in Trier, Syagrius in Soissons, and, obscurest of all, Riothamus in the Loire valley, with his British army; they no longer necessarily looked to Rome, and Syagrius and Riothamus are called *rex* in our sources.[41] The Gallo-Roman aristocracy had to adjust to life in different *regna*, and to the problems of travelling, or potentially even owning land, outside them.[42] But here, too,

---

[38] Matthews, *Western aristocracies*, pp. 338–51; for the third century, Drinkwater, *The Gallic empire* (who argues convincingly against an innate Gaulish separatism, pp. 251–6); Witschel, *Krise-Rezession*, pp. 307–37.

[39] Mathisen, 'Fifth-century visitors to Italy'. For the political focus in fifth-century Gaul, see above, n. 19.

[40] Sidonius, *Ep.* I.7.5 says that Arvandus preferred the Goths to the Greeks; in V.6, 7, he himself prefers the Burgundians to Julius Nepos. In general on aristocratic adaptation to the post-Roman world, see Mathisen, *Roman aristocrats*.

[41] See *PLRE*, II, s.vv. Arbogastes, Syagrius 2, Riothamus for the few references; for Syagrius, see James, *The Franks*, pp. 70–1 and Fanning, 'Emperors and empires'.

[42] See e.g. Sidonius, *Ep.* IX.5.

this increasing political localization may not necessarily have had a negative impact on them. For a start, both in the late fifth century and the sixth we can see both ecclesiastical and secular figures making career moves between kingdoms with relatively little difficulty. Caesarius, bishop of Arles (d. 542), came to Visigothic Provence from Chalon-sur-Saône in the Burgundian lands in the 490s. Parthenius (d. 548), from Clermont in the Visigothic kingdom as we have seen, later moved in the opposite direction, from Ostrogothic military service in Arles (the Ostrogoths occupied Provence in 508) to Frankish service in Trier.[43] Secondly, and more important, the networks of Gallo-Roman *amicitia* and landowning were by now themselves on a more restricted scale. The addressees of Sidonius Apollinaris' (d. c.480) letter collection do still cover the whole of Gaul south of the Loire (Sidonius' base was Clermont, which was roughly in the middle of the geographical area), even though by now very few of them lived in the north.[44] But a generation later Ruricius, bishop of Limoges (d. 510), further to the west in Aquitaine, restricted his correspondence to the Visigothic kingdom, including its outlier in Provence. Avitus, bishop of Vienne (d. c.518) in the Rhône valley, for his part mostly restricted his letters to the Burgundian kingdom, plus the borderlands of Clermont to the west and Provence to the south, and a handful of more formal letters to Ostrogothic Italy. Here, too, there was only a small overlap with the third main letter collection of the post-Sidonius generation, that of Ennodius, bishop of Pavia (d. 521), which is focused on northern Italy and (by now Ostrogothic) Provence. The curious thing is that all these aristocrats were actually related to each other, through a network of marriage-alliances focused on the Aviti, who were probably, thanks to their ex-imperial status, the central family of southern Gaul in the period. But they had evidently adapted themselves to the new regionalization, without much difficulty.[45] Provence appears from these collections as a crucial point of contact, which must have given some centrality to its capital, Arles, and its then bishop, Caesarius (Caesarius in fact capitalized on this with some enthusiasm—Ruricius, among others, clearly resented him).[46] All the kings, indeed, wanted to control Provence, including the still rich commercial traffic of the lower Rhône, and Arles was besieged twice in Caesarius' time; later, after the Franks occupied the whole of Gaul except Septimania (Languedoc), their kings often partitioned it. But Provence was more a hinge between separate social networks than a political centre in its own right;

---

[43] See Klingshirn, *Caesarius*, esp. pp. 20–3, 72–5, and *PLRE*, II, s.v. Parthenius 3.

[44] Sidonius, *Epp.*, III.9, IV.17, are his only ones to recipients clearly living north of the Loire. For *amicitia* in the fifth and sixth centuries, see Wood, 'Family and friendship', pp. 434–6.

[45] The three letter collections are edited in *MGH, AA*, VI–VIII; see Mathisen, *Ruricius of Limoges*, pp. 31–3, and cf. Schanzer and Wood, *Avitus of Vienne*, p. 6, recent translations and commentaries, for the lack of overlap. Barnish, 'Transformation and survival', pp. 134–8, argues for a northern Italy–southern Gaul senatorial continuum, but this continuum did not really extend past Provence.

[46] Ruricius, *Ep.* II.33.

these networks were already moving apart.[47] The Frankish conquest of the south, in the years 507–33, did not reunify southern society, which tended to remain divided between a Loire–Garonne network—Aquitaine—and a Saône–Rhône network—Burgundy and Provence. Indeed the Frankish north would in the seventh century slowly split into two as well, Neustria focused on the Seine valley, and Austrasia focused on the Meuse and Rhine.

The ability of Gaul to divide itself, so to speak, into four parts without disturbing the families of each sub-region probably shows that family land-owning was itself relatively concentrated inside each, or, at least, could split easily into sub-regional groupings. In this period, before our document collections begin in the early seventh century, we do not have many detailed accounts of landowning, but what we can deduce certainly fits this. If Paulinus of Nola owned widely around 400, his heirs, the Leontii of Bordeaux, seem rather more locally restricted. They were rich; in the 460s Sidonius immortalized the walled villa (*burgus*) of his friend Pontius Leontius at Bourg, near Bordeaux, in verse. They were politically influential into the next century, for in the period 541–65 there are two bishops called Leontius in Bordeaux, each of high *nobilitas* of birth, according to epitaphs by Venantius Fortunatus; the second Bishop Leontius tried to defy the Frankish king Charibert. Ruricius of Limoges (and his descendant there, another Bishop Ruricius) may well have been members of the same family; Ruricius' relatives also seem to have largely dominated the bishopric of Tours in the late fifth century. When we add to this the more certain knowledge that Leontius II of Bordeaux married Sidonius Apollinaris' great-granddaughter Placidina, thus linking himself to the Aviti-Apollinares in Clermont, who had their own links with the Ruricii, we build up a picture of a considerable pan-Aquitainian family grouping, focused on episcopal office. Still, the family is not seen outside Aquitaine. It had remained strong on a sub-regional level, but remained, as far as we can tell, inside the borders of the pre-507 Visigothic kingdom.[48]

The family of Gregory of Tours (d. 594) is another instance of this. His father's family was firmly from Clermont, rivals to the Aviti-Apollinares for the local bishopric, and his lands were probably mostly there. He had

---

[47] On Provençal centrality see e.g. Klingshirn, *Caesarius*, pp. 33–71; Delaplace, 'La Provence'.

[48] See above all Sidonius, *Carmina*, XXII (Bourg); Venantius, *Carmina*, IV.9, 10 (the epitaphs for the Leontii), I.6, 15, 17 (Placidina); Gregory of Tours, *LH*, IV.26 (Charibert). On the Leontii see in general Heinzelmann, *Bischofsherrschaft*, pp. 217–20; and the entries in Stroheker, *Der senatorische Adel*, p. 188 (cf. genealogy I); *PLRE*, III, s.vv. Leontius 3, 4. Heinzelmann proposes the Ruricius link on plausible prosopographical grounds; see further Pietri, *La ville de Tours*, pp. 131–7, for Ruricius' probable kin in Tours. Venantius, *Carmen* IV.5, also proposes an Anician link for the Ruricii, perhaps the latest reference to that family, but not obviously an authentic one, for reasons outlined earlier (p. 159); Heinzelmann, *Bischofsherrschaft*, pp. 215–20, and Näf, *Senatorisches Standesbewusstsein*, p. 188, are respectively more optimistic and more pessimistic about the link.

relatives in Tours too, including his predecessor there as bishop, Euphronius (d. 573); he claimed once that all his predecessors but five were 'related to the family of our kin' (*parentum nostrorum prosapiae coniuncti*). This must, at best, have been on a generous interpretation of family, on the level of the claims of Cassiodorus to Anician kinship; as we have just seen, the Tours bishops were more often linked to Limoges, and Gregory had opponents in Tours who saw him as an outsider. Gregory's best-documented family links outside Clermont instead go eastward, to Lyon and Langres in the Burgundian kingdom, whence his mother came: his mother's family produced two bishops of each, plus one of Geneva, and Euphronius of Tours. But his links to the Saône valley were less organic than those in his Aquitaine–Loire stamping ground. It is the latter that are the focus of his histories and saints' lives, rather more seldom the former.[49] Gregory relates the chance visit to Tours in 581 of his mother's uncle, Gundulf, a recently appointed *dux* in (what would soon be called) Austrasia. Gundulf is a much-cited figure in modern historiography, as one of the first Gallo-Romans *de genere senatorio*, as Gregory puts it, to bear a Frankish (or Burgundian) name—his parents (or he himself, in adulthood) must have regarded an expected political/military career as involving at least one element of 'Germanic' identity. We cannot, however, be as certain as was Gregory (and as are modern scholars) of his exact family location; the best-known moments of his strictly military career date to 581–3, when Gundulf would have been in his sixties at least if he were really Gregory's great-uncle, which is implausible for a military leader, newly promoted, in the sixth century. Gundulf's Roman origin and military choice are not at issue; I would see it as significant, nonetheless, that Gregory was sufficiently distanced from his Saône-valley kin to get the exact details of their kinship wrong.[50] Gregory's orientation was decisively towards Aquitaine.

Two examples (three with the Aviti) must suffice here of these patterns, especially as in each case, as with the letter collections of two generations earlier, it is matrimonial and episcopal connections that are most clearly documented, with landowning and transfers of revenues only indirectly attested at best. The patterns they demonstrate match up, however, and

---

[49] For Gregory's family see above all Heinzelmann, *Gregory of Tours*, pp. 7–35, who stresses Gregory's Clermont base (on which see esp. Wood, 'Ecclesiastical politics', pp. 39–41). His links to the Saône became weaker after his brother Peter, a priest in Langres, died in 574, the year after he became bishop (*LH*, V.5). For his 'kin' in Tours, *LH*, V.49; see Pietri, *La ville de Tours*, p. 135, Heinzelmann, *Gregory of Tours*, pp. 23–8 (both less sceptical than I would be). For Lyon, see Heinzelmann, *Bischofsherrschaft*, pp. 98–179.

[50] Gregory of Tours, *LH*, VI.11, 26 for Gundulf; for commentary, see Stroheker, *Der senatorische Adel*, p. 180; Werner, 'Important noble families', pp. 154–5; *PLRE*, III, s.v. Gundulfus; Heinzelmann, *Gregory of Tours*, pp. 20–1. Of these, only Werner sees Gundulf's career and genealogy as a problem. Overall, historians are much happier to accuse Gregory of half-truths and evasions than to suppose that he could be factually inaccurate. For Gregory on the senatorial *ordo* and *nobilitas*, see e.g. *LH*, II.2, *GM*, c. 86, and *VP*, VI, VII.1; cf. Näf, *Senatorisches Standesbewusstsein*, pp. 178–87.

are not contradicted by others we know about.[51] We are dealing here with sub-regional aristocracies, not networks that cover the whole of Gaul, still less interregional powers. But they are, in southern Gaul, 'senatorial' family groupings, with continuous roots in the Roman past; and links across the whole of Aquitaine are not to be underestimated. It must furthermore be stressed that these are, by early medieval standards, not narrow but wide; even in the late empire this had probably been true outside the Rome-based senatorial elite, and a tiny handful of major provincial families. We shall see that normal aristocratic landholding in the post-Roman Mediterranean was restricted to single city territories, and political networks did not go much further, except when they were extended by kings and other rulers. In Gaul however, at least in the more Roman south, kings in this period had little to do with the sub-regional networks just discussed. Kings did intervene in episcopal appointments, indeed as regularly as they could, but most of their appointees were from local families—the scale of the clientèles they were intervening in did not change as a result. (Gregory's appointment at Tours in 573, certainly the work of King Sigibert I, may have been an exception: it depends on how well rooted his family really was there. But Luce Pietri has pointed out that most sixth-century Tourangeau bishops were not local, and the city itself may have been more exceptional than was Gregory.[52]) We can legitimately see Aquitaine, at least—doubtless the Rhône basin was similar—as the focus for a large-scale aristocratic network, partially autonomous of Frankish patronage, that linked the Loire, the Garonne, and the western valleys of the Massif Central, lasting at least to the end of the sixth century, and probably, as the Aviti indicate, to the end of the seventh. We are missing any direct documentation for their landed property networks, unfortunately. The will of Aredius of Limoges, together with a donation by him, both dating to 572, are the only surviving Aquitainian charters for the period up to 600, and the estates listed in them, when identifiable, are all restricted to the southern Limousin, a single city territory (though Aredius' fifteen or so estates, some carefully characterized in the will, undoubtedly made him wealthy, on the Ausonius level of two centuries earlier). It is probable that Aredius' city-level scale of landowning was a norm for most aristocrats even in southern Gaul, with the sub-regional families a clear elite inside the elite: this would have parallels in the north, as we shall see.[53] We also do not yet have for Aquitaine the full dimensions of local networks of

[51] Provence is another sub-region with aristocratic links that spread across several cities in the later sixth century (notably Marseille, Arles, and Uzès): see Gregory of Tours, *LH*, IV.43, VI.7, 11, and *PLRE*, III, s.v. Dynamius 1, for the most powerful and best-documented Provençal figure in the 560s–590s.

[52] For Gregory's appointment, see Venantius, *Carmen* V.3. For Tours bishops in general, see Pietri, *Tours*, p. 186.

[53] For Aredius see *Testamentum S. Aredii* and Debus, 'Studien', n. 19; see below, pp. 284–5 for estate structures. Cf. above, n. 27, for Ausonius. Rouche, *L'Aquitaine*, pp. 327–8, argues that the city level of landowning was commoner than the sub-regional level, which is probable

material culture, which would give us a sense of the geographical scale of local economies.[54] We do have a good number of rich late villas, nonetheless, some with identifiable sixth- (occasionally even seventh-) century finds surviving from excavations that were often fairly sketchy: Plassac near Bordeaux (and near Leontius' Bourg), Séviac near Éauze (the best-excavated by far), Espaly in the Velay south-east of Clermont, St-Rémy-la-Varenne in Poitou on the Loire downstream from Tours. The aristocrats who continued to live in these were committed to a life that could be lived—and funded—in a way that resembled the centres of late Roman *otium* so often praised by Sidonius. It is not unreasonable to suppose that they were people on the social level of the sub-regional elite just discussed, and in the case of Plassac, which belonged to the mother of the enormously wealthy Bertram, bishop of Le Mans (d. after 616), we can show it.[55]

Apart from the scale of this aristocracy, or at least of its richest members, one other aspect of their social praxis, the separation between military and episcopal careers, needs further development, for this had considerable cultural implications. The civilian career structure of the fifth century became very restricted in the Romano-Germanic kingdoms, whose state structures were simpler than the empire (above, pp. 87–124) and needed fewer personnel. The stress in both central and local administration moved towards men who were prepared to run armies, as well as other governmental responsibilities such as law courts: the *duces* (central or sub-regional figures) and *comites* (for each city) who dominate the narratives of Gregory of Tours and our other Merovingian-period sources. This led to cultural shifts among military leaders of Roman extraction, of which there were many, some even operating in northern Gaul (Lupus, duke of Champagne, is the best-known in the sixth century). In effect, the dominant tone of ambition had changed between the fifth century and the sixth: successful military leaders took on a senatorial lifestyle in the fifth century, but all successful secular politicians had a military aspect to them in the sixth. In particular, the classical secular culture and the *otium* imagery of a Sidonius became less relevant, as secular figures moved towards hunting, and civilian figures, by now above all ecclesiastics, concentrated on the church fathers, as noted earlier (p. 159). One must not overstate this: Eparchius Avitus and his son Ecdicius, Sidonius' brother-in-law, had been pretty martial already.

everywhere, but does not invalidate the points made here. The sixth-century *Formulae Andecavenses* and *Arvernenses* (in *MGH, Formulae*, pp. 4–31) seem to deal above all with the city level, but do not mention locations. For the seventh century, see below, p. 188 and n. 96.

[54] See below, pp. 746–8, for what can so far be said about the geography of Aquitainian exchange in our period.

[55] For references, see Balmelle, *Les demeures aristocratiques*, pp. 393–5 (Plassac) and pp. 121–2, 386–90 (Séviac); O'Hea, *The conceptual and material transformation*, site n. 51 (Espaly); Blanchard-Lemée, *Recueil general des mosaïques*, II.4, pp. 90–2 (St-Rémy). Plassac was certainly the *villa Blacciago* near the *castro Blaivit* on the Garonne in Bertram's will of 616: Weidemann, *Das Testament*, n. 34 (Busson and Ledru, *Actus*, p. 121).

Conversely, Venantius Fortunatus could arrive from Italy at the northern Frankish courts in the 560s and gain instant success as a Latin praise-poet of the most traditional of types, full of classical allusions; he was patronized by kings, queens, aristocrats, and bishops alike.[56] But there was a shift, nonetheless; by the later seventh century most traces of that secular literary culture had gone. And other aspects of it were changing already. Clothes were one. What the third-century Romans would have seen as military costume—long tunic and cloak, a heavy belt, trousers—became the standard clothing of a secular aristocrat.[57] The Romans used the imagery of the *cingulum militiae*, the belt of (military) service, as a characterization of public service as a whole, even in the civil administration; in the post-Roman world, the belt itself, *cingulum* or *balteum*, recurs over and over in texts as a physical representation of status and service. By the seventh century, if not earlier, aristocrats were also putting a lot of gold and jewels on their persons as well. This shift, also paralleled in Byzantium, marks a clear move towards a military bearing for the aristocracy at large.[58] A second shift is the end of the heavily decorated *villa rustica*, which will be discussed in more detail later (pp. 473–81), but which arguably also marks a more militarized cultural context. The secular career structure became focused on the royal entourage (being a *conviva regis*), and on the royal patronage of local political position; the great public assembly on 1 March at (or near) the start of the campaigning season became the essential meeting point for the political society of each kingdom.[59] This linked together with the politics of land discussed in the previous chapter (pp. 58–9), to produce a world which already by 600 in many respects resembled the courts of the central middle ages rather more than those of the fifth century.

The military world was, very much, a king-centred world, for kings were the direct sources of all political patronage, as well as of the lavish gifts that characterized Merovingian political practice. At the local level, counts (*comites*) were also royal appointees, although most of them were from already-established local families whose ambitions did not need to extend to the dangers of the court, and who remained city or city territory leaders. We cannot easily track comital families in our period, for our documentation is above all ecclesiastical, but there is no doubt that they operated at the heart of city-level landowning and political practice, both in the Merovingian

---

[56] See in general George, *Venantius*. Duke Lupus, one of Venantius' patrons (Venantius, *Carmina*, VII.7–10—the first of these mentions his Roman origins), also patronized Andarchius, a literary scholar of servile origins (Gregory of Tours, *LH*, IV.46).

[57] See in general Harlow, 'Clothes maketh the man'.

[58] For the Roman *cingulum militiae*, see Delmaire, *Largesses sacrées*, pp. 54, 138; Werner, *Naissance*, pp. 189–225. For the Merovingian period, see the very concrete references in e.g. Gregory of Tours, *GM*, c. 60; Venantius, *Carmen* VII.6; *Vita S. Germani*, cc. 62, 91, 162; *Vita Balthildis*, c. 8; *Vita Eligii*, I.10–12 (including for jewels on clothing).

[59] For the assembly, see Ch. 3, n. 163 (and the critical observations of Bachrach, 'Was the Marchfield'); for *conviva regis*, see below, n. 110.

period and later, until the breakdown of Carolingian political practices in the decades around 1000.[60] But bishops were the main leaders of their localities: they represented and defended their cities, whereas counts (if they had to choose) represented their king. Bishops often had close links with kings as well, of course. Kings approved their appointments, sometimes overruling local communities; many well-known bishops were parachuted in from a long way away, as with Eligius of Limoges, made bishop of Noyon, north of Paris, by Clovis II in 641. Some bishops wielded power at the level of the kingdom, come to that, like Leudegar of Autun (d. 678), or headed armies. But all bishops had a local stage as well. Eligius' friend Desiderius of Cahors, another of the school of officials and future bishops of the court of Chlotar II and Dagobert I, made bishop of Cahors in 630, was a local man and actually succeeded his brother; and, overall, Desiderius was more typical than Eligius.[61] It is thus not at all surprising to find the autonomous 'senatorial' families of the south structuring their local power through episcopal office, both in the sixth century and the seventh; and we can find the same patterns in the north too.[62]

Two aspects of these cultural changes, however, should not be over-stressed. The first is the 'Germanization' of military Romans. Gundulf bore a 'Germanic' name; if Lupus apparently did not, his brother Magulf and son Romulf did (even though Romulf was assigned to an ecclesiastical career, becoming bishop of Reims in 590).[63] But we should not see military identity as necessarily involving ethnic Frankish (or Burgundian) identity *instead* of Roman identity, as has been argued for Ostrogothic Italy. The military tradition in the southern half of the Frankish lands, where there were, for sure, very few Germanic incomers ever, is associated very largely with people who keep Roman names, until past 700: from Duke Victorius of Clermont and Vincentius *dux Hispaniarum* in Euric's Visigothic army, through Mummolus of Auxerre and Desiderius of Albi in the 570s–580s, to Bonitus of Clermont in the 680s and Maurontus of Provence in the 730s. It was not necessary to do otherwise; the Roman tradition of military activity was perfectly adequate. The north of Gaul became militarized earlier (towards 400 rather than towards 500), and also more Germanized; unlike the south, it went over to Frankish names (one of the last people to be called *romanus* in the north was Chramnelen, a *dux* from the Besançon area,

---

[60] For Merovingian counts, see esp. Claude, 'Untersuchungen'.

[61] *Vita Eligii*, II.1; *Passio prima Leudegarii*, cc. 8–10; *Vita Desiderii*, cc. 7–15. For bishops and war, see Prinz, *Klerus und Krieg*, pp. 47–72. For Leudegar see Fouracre, 'Merovingian history', pp. 13–35; and idem and Gerberding, *Late Merovingian France*, pp. 196–205.

[62] Note that reputation mattered alongside descent in episcopal politics: see e.g. Brown, 'Relics and social status', pp. 243–50.

[63] For Magulf see Venantius, *Carmen* VII.10; for Romulf see Gregory of Tours, *LH*, X.19; Flodoard, *Historia Remensis ecclesiae*, II.4. But note that Lupus, 'wolf', is represented in the -ulf ending of these two names; Lupus himself may have been differently addressed in Frankish-speaking circles.

in 636), and then to generalized Frankish ethnicity. But the difference is essentially sub-regional.[64] Gregory of Tours is famous for not distinguishing Franks and Romans in his histories; he saw ethnicity as, if anything, conveyed by political loyalties, not birth, and senatorial status, not Roman origin, was what mattered to him. By 700 the *Romani* are simply the inhabitants of Aquitaine, who did not at that moment always recognize Frankish suzerainty; in effect, everyone else was a Frank. On the other hand, this does not imply an unchanging social world in the south. Michel Rouche has argued that Aquitaine remained sharply distinct from the Frankish north, as Roman in culture and tradition.[65] Gregory's ethnic blindness is already a counter-argument to such a claim; but more generally the differences Rouche sees (in attitudes to oaths, for example) are less visible in my readings of the texts. The few eighth-century Aquitainian texts show an atmosphere identical to that in the north; the *Vita Pardulfi* has the same sorts of stories of aristocratic bad behaviour as in any contemporary northern life.[66] The crucial shift was the militarization of secular hierarchies; that Frankish identity had not yet developed in the south is irrelevant.

The second point is, however, in some respects the converse of this. It is often argued that the militarization of society also made aristocrats behave worse than they had done in the Roman world: more violently, more unjustly, as chronicled with relish by Gregory of Tours, and as in the supernatural-vengeance anecdotes of many saints' lives.[67] This seems to me a misreading of the material. Gregory, in particular, wrote up the violent behaviour of his contemporaries for rhetorical reasons and, actually, hagiographical anecdotes of what the *Vita Pardulfi* calls 'usurpation', private appropriation by elites, although they certainly exist, are not as numerous as they would be in later centuries, especially after 950.[68] Such a view also misreads the late Roman world. Querolus, in the early fifth-century Gallic comedy of the same name, seeks *potentia* from his household god, who asks him what he means; he replies: 'that I should be allowed to despoil nondebtors, kill strangers, and despoil and kill neighbours'. The god laughs and says that is *latrocinium*, brigandage, not *potentia*, but Querolus had got one basic element of the idea right. Faustus of Riez (d. c.490) remarked in a

---

[64] See respectively *PLRE*, II, s.vv. Victorius 4, Vincentius 3, III, s.vv. Desiderius 2, Mummolus 2; Ebling, *Prosopographie*, pp. 89–90, 192, 110–11. Chramnelen is *ex genere romano* in Fredegar, *Chronica*, IV.78; cf. Werner, 'Important noble families', pp. 155–7. Contrast for Ostrogothic Italy Amory, *People and identity*. For ethnic identity as a sub-regional development, a good guide is Ewig, *Spätantikes und Fränkisches Gallien*, pp. 246–73.

[65] Rouche, *L'Aquitaine*, pp. 362–85. For Gregory's ethnic blindness see e.g. James, 'Gregory of Tours and the Franks'; for the flexibility of ethnicity, Geary, *Aristocracy in Provence*, pp. 101–14.

[66] *Vita Pardulfi*, cc. 9, 17. Cf. *Vita Eligii*, I.6, overinterpreted in Rouche, *L'Aquitaine*, pp. 367–8.

[67] Mathisen, *Roman aristocrats*, pp. 139–43, is an example of this.

[68] Goffart, *Narrators*, pp. 168–83, for rhetoric; *Vita Pardulfi*, c. 9, for *usurpare*; for pre- and post-950, see most recently Fisher, *Miracle stories*, pp. 107–57.

sermon that we are silent if any *potens persona* does us injury or curses us, but we would certainly take revenge (*vindicamus*) if any equal or inferior did so. Aristocratic bad behaviour was normal.[69] In the case of kings, as with emperors before, it was even expected. The basic eye-for-an-eye ethic of violent revenge existed throughout the Roman period; so did all forms of abuse of power. It is arguable that the Romano-Germanic period brought a space for the structured private vengeance etiquette that we generally call feud, and this is possible; there are certainly some episodes of revenge in the Frankish world, such as Sichar versus Chramnesind in Tours in 585–7 and Dodo versus Landibert in Maastricht in the 680s, which fit standard feuding models.[70] Gregory's rhetorical field indeed seems to treat this as legitimate; and, of course, the fact that Gregory's rhetorical field gives so much space to violence is in itself a sign that at least the imagery of violence was normal in his time. But this is as much as can be said. We need to avoid romanticizing either the *civilitas* of the Roman world or the ultra-violence of that of Gregory of Tours.

This account has so far looked at the Frankish world as a whole from south of the Loire, up to 600 or so; let us look at it again from the north, because here the parameters are at least initially somewhat different, before looking at north and south together in the seventh century. The north was much more 'Frankish', in the sense that the kings and their courts were all situated there, that any Frankish settlement took place there, and that Roman aristocratic continuities are harder to find. It is indeed possible, in fact common, to argue that aristocracies were absent altogether from the north, at least in the sixth century; versions of this argument go back to the nineteenth century; and have a substantial historiographical import-ance.[71] This is a tenable position, though I do not myself agree with it. Given how much has traditionally ridden on it, it is worth setting out the main lines of the discontinuitist position first, before attempting to counter it.

[69] *Querolus*, c. 30; Faustus of Riez, *Sermo in natali S. Stephani*, p. 236, both cited in Mathisen, *Roman aristocrats*, pp. 50–1.

[70] Gregory, *LH*, VII.47, IX.19 (in the latter he is much more sympathetic than in the former); *Vita Landiberti*, cc. 11–17. These well-known examples, and others, are discussed in Wallace-Hadrill, *Long-haired kings*, pp. 121–47; White, 'Clotild's revenge'; Fouracre, 'Attitudes to-wards violence'; Halsall, 'Violence and society'. The last two, particularly Halsall, minimize the role of feud, and they seem to be right that much Frankish violence was part of a public political practice, not 'feud' as classically characterized (e.g. in Black-Michaud, *Cohesive force*, pp. 1–32). But the two cited examples still look like classic feuds to me; so do some others in Gregory, e.g. *LH*, X.27.

[71] Staab, 'A reconstruction', gives a useful historiographical account. For the aristocracy debate, key post-war texts are Bergengruen, *Adel und Grundherrschaft*; Irsigler, *Untersuchun-gen*; Grahn-Hoek, *Die fränkische Oberschicht*; Zotz, 'Adel, Oberschicht, Freie'. Halsall, *Settle-ment and society*, pp. 33–9, has recently revived a version of the no-aristocracy model, which he links to burial patterns (see below, n. 74).

The north of Gaul had seen crisis from much earlier on than any other part of the western Roman empire, even Britain. Its villas became steadily less numerous after 350 or so, and few exist at all in stone and brick after 450. It was under constant military threat, and the major structuring element in its economy, the Rhine *limes*, was in ruins by 450 as well.[72] Its society was militarized early, already by 400, so was probably better able to respond to crisis than many parts of the empire (see below, pp. 331–2); all the same, the mid- to late fifth century was a period of particular confusion. Furthermore, the Franks, who had taken over the area by c.490, were initially politically fragmented; Clovis had to conquer rival Frankish kings, much as he conquered rival Roman and Germanic territories. Before him, political power was highly localized throughout the north, and even after him fiscal structures remained substantially weaker in the north than in the Loire valley or Aquitaine, as we have seen in Chapter 3 (pp. 102–15). The *Pactus legis salicae* of c.510, the earliest Frankish law-code, focuses on the sorts of disputes that are most important in a peasant, not an aristocratic-dominated, society, giving a lot of space to agricultural delicts, and it gives little or no sign of any firm status-differences at all apart from that between free and unfree.[73] The archaeology of the north between 450 and 550 so far discovered is unimpressive in the extreme, privileging small wooden houses and *Grubenhäuser* rather than more developed/expensive architectural patterns (below, pp. 476–7). Even the cemeteries of the north from the same period, which sometimes include expensive metalwork, show that a competition for status through public burial in the ground (in effect, the public destruction of goods) extended widely through society—there was thus, arguably, not a secure social hierarchy that would have rendered such competition pointless.[74] The Frankish aristocrats who appear in Gregory of Tours's histories are almost never called *nobilis*, unlike his Roman 'senatorial' families. They are all, again unlike the Romans, royal appointees, products of specifically royal entourages, and are in fact a newly created aristocracy of royal dependants, whether officials or dining companions (*convivae regis*) or both. They are rich, because the kings are rich; they have land by 600, and are by then a proper landed aristocracy, but the lands are themselves relatively recent gifts (indeed, some authors have argued that all this landholding was for a long time dependent on the king's pleasure). The seventh-century aristocratic factions are thus a new start for north Frankish society;

---

[72] Van Ossel, *Établissements*, pp. 72–84, and below, pp. 795–6. For militarization, Whittaker, *Frontiers*, pp. 222–40, 260–78.

[73] *Pactus*, e.g. cc. 2–9, 34; cf. Wickham, *Land and power*, pp. 212–14. The *Pactus* does recognize the social status of (Roman) royal *convivae*—see below, p. 196.

[74] Halsall, *Settlement and society*, pp. 252–61, makes this basic point. See further below, pp. 340, 575, for comments on the force of the assumption that grave-goods imply status anxiety and on some of its problems. Note also that these assumptions also presume that metalwork in graves is not an ethnic indicator; for this view, which I fully share, see above, Ch. 3, n. 72.

it is only then that the area comes back into the norms of the rest of the former empire, after a period of dissolution more similar to Anglo-Saxon England.

This is a powerful argument, all the more powerful in that most of the statements that it is based on are in themselves fully convincing—it is only in the last three sentences of the previous paragraph that I am repeating assertions that I would not myself accept. But they need framing in a counter-argument, that stresses some other elements of the early Frankish period in Gaul.

Political logic is one problem. The Franks had several petty kings in 450; by 511, at Clovis's death, they had all gone. So far so good; but it would stretch the imagination if we were to suppose that Clovis actually managed to destroy all of them, and their families, creating a political *terra rasa* in the whole of the north, which was then replaced by a totally different system. The most ruthless Anglo-Saxon kings—Offa, Alfred—reduced rival kings to the aristocratic level; they did not wipe them out. So did the Huns. The Normans in England removed a whole aristocracy, but they simply replaced it with another one just the same. We would have to look as far as the Mongols to find an analogous commitment to such root-and-branch change. But the Mongols are famous for their violence; Clovis by contrast got a reasonable press, even from people relatively indifferent to his world-histor-ical-turning-point conversion to Christianity.[75] It is also hard to see how Clovis could have maintained the sort of infrastructure that allowed him to conquer and rule all the north and then Aquitaine without a strong aristoc-racy to do his bidding locally; even if that aristocracy was newly created, from, say, the entourage he inherited from his father, which is at least a plausible hypothesis, then it would have stepped into the shoes of its prede-cessors, the kings of the *regna* of the north, and would have been hard to shift. The notion of any aristocracy in this environment remaining a *Dien-stadel*, an aristocracy of service subject to the absolute control of a ruler, is highly implausible; Clovis did not have the sort of political system that would have enabled such control, as we saw in Chapter 3.

The second problem is the continuity of Roman landowning we do see in the Reims area. The leader of the episcopate of the north, Remigius (d. c.532), who is said to have died in his nineties, and who certainly lived through the whole period of crisis in the region, left us his will. It is a strikingly ordinary document: it consists of gifts of slaves, movables, money, and family land to his own church of Reims, to the church of Lyon and a few others, and to his kin. Remigius' family land (he once explicitly says he inherited it from his parents) was not huge, and was all situated in a

---

[75] Cassiodorus, *Variae*, II.40–1, III.1–4, is not impolite; nor are Avitus, *Ep.* 46, and, more vaguely, Jordanes, *Getica*, cc. 295–6. (The mythic Clovis is above all visible in Gregory of Tours, *LH*, II.27–43.)

fairly restricted area south of the road from Laon to Reims, but it resembles all other late Roman estates we have documentation for.[76] His successors as bishops were also often local landowners, as we know from Flodoard's history of the see—written in the tenth century, but largely based on archival records still then existing in Reims. We can be less sure than with Remigius that this landowning is old, especially as the wills Flodoard cites only begin in the 590s, but the first, that of Romulf, is of the son of Duke Lupus, who was, as already noted, of Roman origin. The lands Romulf lists (they include land in Poitou) could have been given to either Lupus or Romulf by any king or queen, but Lupus was almost certainly a local man—his links are all with Champagne—and his family land is most likely to have had a pre-Frankish core. The existence of this sort of localized property-owning does not in itself show a survival of a large-scale, sub-regional, aristocratic network of an Aquitainian type, but it is difficult to fit it into the north Frankish meltdown theory. Lupus is just the sort of military aristocrat who already existed in northern Gaul in 400, and whose family could have carried on there without much change across the two following centuries. Reims has no claim to be a model for the whole of northern Gaul, which must have experienced the shift from Roman to Merovingian very differently in different microregions, but why it should be unique is difficult to see.[77]

The third problem is archaeological. It is true that the end of villas and the sudden appearance of furnished graves shows a major shift of some sort; but these are not the only features of the period. As will be discussed in more detail in Chapter 11, the ceramic history of the sub-region shows the survival of rather more elaborate exchange systems than one might expect if crisis was extreme. Argonne ware, the main Roman fine ware from northern Gaul, survived into the late sixth century, and Mayen ware, together with its local versions in the Seine valley and elsewhere, the main mass-produced coarse wares of the late Roman period, survived into the Carolingian period and beyond—in both cases with distribution networks reduced from those of c.400, but still involving kiln productions being sold across many city territories at once (in the case of Mayen, down the Rhine from near Trier to the sea). The late fifth century also saw the development, again on Roman lines, of a new fine carinated or 'biconic' pottery, usually black or grey and decorated with rouletting, that can soon be found across the whole of the north, though its kilns seem here to be more localized, perhaps one or two city territories each (see below, pp. 796–8). Ceramics are not necessarily

[76] *Testamentum Remigii*; its authenticity is defended in Jones, Grierson, and Crook, 'The authenticity'. See further Castellanos, 'Propiedad de la tierra'.

[77] See above, nn. 56, 63. Kings and queens patronized Reims already in the 530s–540s: see Flodoard, *Historia Remensis ecclesiae*, II.1, for Queen Suavegotha. Ewig, *Trier*, pp. 69–71, makes a similar argument for the Trier area; continuities were probably as great there as in Champagne, or greater, but the documentation is sketchier. See further Ch. 8, n. 88.

made for elites, but their geographical scale shows the size of exchange systems, which in the case of these wares is actually larger than that of any known sixth-century Mediterranean wares north of Rome, and after 700 has its closest comparators as far away as Egypt. It is again unfortunate that we cannot yet compare this in detail with Aquitaine, or, indeed, the Rhône basin, north of the coast at any rate. But the patterns are anyway strikingly different from those in Britain, where a major political and economic crisis did occur, which was by 500 either close to aceramic (in the west) or characterized by hand-made pottery of very simple types and microregional distributions (see below, pp. 806–8). These patterns do not argue for any radical economic fragmentation in northern Gaul of the type that a meltdown model would predict.

The fourth point is the evidence we have for the earliest Frankish aristocracy. We would not expect this to be very extensive; Venantius only came to Francia in the 560s, and Gregory does not begin to be detailed until the 570s; before that, we have little contemporary material for the sixth-century north apart from the *Pactus* and a handful of church councils. Some points can be made, all the same. It is true that Gregory does not usually use *nobilis* for Franks (though he does once, at least), but he means 'senatorial' by *nobilis* in most cases, which is not a word that would be applicable to Franks—and anyway Venantius does call Frankish aristocrats *nobilis* several times, invoking ancient ancestry when he does so, a significant rhetorical device under the circumstances, whether or not it was true in any given case. There are also accounts of the 520s–540s in Gregory which feature aristocrats acting independently of kings—in one case, that of Munderic, claiming kinship to kings, whether Merovingian or not it is hard to tell.[78] These will doubtless have been the same social group as the *potentes* of ecclesiastical and secular legislation of the same period, who apparently could own widely, and influence episcopal appointments.[79] All this fits the early 'princely' male graves at the core of *Reihengräberfelder*, the 'row-grave' furnished cemeteries of the early Frankish period—most famously Krefeld-Gellep no. 1782, the first obviously post-Roman grave in one of the Rhine's largest early medieval cemeteries, which dates to the 520s at the latest: such a burial maybe showed status anxiety, but it also showed wealth on a large scale, with sword, spear, axe, a gilded helmet, gold jewellery, and glass, all associated with the body. Renate Pirling proposes that the dead man was Clovis's local lieutenant, which is far from implausible, but he was rich, and

---

[78] Gregory of Tours, *LH*, VIII.16, uses *nobilissimus* for a Frank; for Venantius, see *Carmina*, II.8, IV.26. For Munderic, Gregory, *LH*, III.14.

[79] *Potentes* own widely (*per diversa*) in MGH, *Cap.*, I, n. 3, c. 12 (= *Pactus*, c. 88), from the period before 561, and influence episcopal elections in the Council of Clermont (a. 535), c. 2 (ed. *Les canons des conciles*, p. 212), though this is a southern text. See in general Irsigler, *Untersuchungen*, pp. 142–86.

died 500 km from Clovis's own base in Paris; it would be difficult to suppose a priori that his aristocratic status only depended on the king.[80]

Gregory's accounts of Frankish aristocratic landholding date later, to the 570s–580s, but they are nevertheless interesting. For a start, they clearly distinguish between royal gifts and family property. Kings killed a lot of their major aristocrats, who were all dukes or other central-government officials; if they have no known title they were at least, as with Ursio of the Woëvre (d. 589), *Königsnähe*. When kings did this, they confiscated their property; very often it is property the kings gave them out of the *fiscus*, but sometimes it is explicitly land they inherited, as in the case of the land left to Eberulf the *cubicularius* (d. 585) by his ancestors (*priores*). On one occasion, in 589, King Childebert II exiled two plotters against his mother, confiscating all the land which they held from the *fiscus*, but allowing them to keep their *proprium*.[81] These texts are well known, and have been used for a variety of arguments, mostly unhelpfully because based on the untenable position that one can construct out of them a series of consistent legal principles, which kings would have respected. We know full well that Merovingian kings routinely took land *iniuste*; it was, to an extent, a royal prerogative.[82] Although the very existence of the word implies a sense of a set of norms that they were not respecting, we could not usefully in these instances, or in any others, distinguish between legal and illegal royal acts, and attitudes to justice doubtless depended on the observer. What we can say, however, is that the difference between family land and royal gifts was understood, and that kings, if they wanted to make a distinction, confiscated royal gifts first. This does not mean that either type of property was precarious (any more than it is now, when people can nonetheless be bankrupted by judicial fines). But the existence of family land is certainly clear, by the 580s. If this, too, was a royal gift in a previous generation, it was sufficiently far in the past for kings to have forgotten it.[83]

What we see in Gregory of Tours, therefore, is a powerful landed aristocracy, in northern Gaul as in the south, behaving in much the same ways—'Frankish' dukes like Guntram Boso, 'Roman' dukes like Mummolus. It would be, as Karl Ferdinand Werner has observed, highly unlikely that, of these two, the 'Frankish' section was *more* precarious than the 'Roman' section, and there anyway is no sign of it at all by the 570s–580s.[84] It is quite

---

[80] Pirling, *Römer und Franken*, pp. 162–4. Heidinga, 'Gennep', reports on a Rhineland site which may have been the home of one of the pre-Clovis aristocracy, abandoned c.500.

[81] For Ursio, Gregory of Tours, *LH*, VI.4, IX.9, 12; he has no mentioned office, one of the only major figures in Gregory not to have one, but he was active at court. For Eberulf, *LH*, VII.22, 29; for the two plotters, IX.38. Other confiscations, either of land given by the king or of all property, are in III.14, 24, IV.13, V.3, 17, VI.28, VII.40, VIII.21, IX.9.

[82] e.g. Gregory of Tours, *LH*, VI.46, VII.7, 19, all concerning Chilperic.

[83] *LH*, VIII.22, IX.35, do not seem to me to show that aristocratic property was in itself precarious, *contra* Halsall, *Settlement and society*, p. 36. *Pactus*, c. 59, defends the inheritance of *aloda*, with no qualifications. [84] Werner, 'Important noble families', p. 145.

possible that the 'Frankish' section was as a whole newer than the 'Roman' section, but the evidence we have supports the argument that the northern aristocrats were, at the very latest, in place by the second quarter of the sixth century. What seems most likely is, first, that there was *some* aristocratic continuity in the Frankish north, of both Roman and Frankish families, which Clovis could not eliminate. (Of course we will never know exactly who; if I had to guess, however, I would propose, along with other scholars, the Agilolfings, powerful in Bavaria already in the 550s, presumably by royal patronage in the previous generation, active all over the north, and with their own family name by the early seventh century, uniquely among Frankish aristocrats before 900.)[85] Second, that Clovis's dramatic political success transformed the social position of both these families and those of Clovis's own newer protégés, creating an aristocracy much more focused on royal courts and patronage—and less on birth and ancestry, as yet—than it would otherwise have been, much as the Byzantine aristocracy did in the period of the transformation of the state, 650–750 (below, pp. 233–9). But, third, that these families, old and new, rooted themselves quickly in their lands, old and new, and assumed local powers that had in many cases themselves survived the confusion of the Frankish conquests, as with the Champagne of Remigius and Lupus, or the Trierer Land, or for that matter the Paris urban society of the *Vita Genovefae*.[86] The survival of the economic networks represented by northern ceramic production would in principle have allowed some of this new aristocratic landowning to be widely scattered across the north, too. We shall see that when, in the seventh century, we have actual evidence for the extent of aristocratic landholding, we find exactly that.

Before we move into the seventh century, there are two caveats to be added. The first is that this aristocracy did not have a clearly marked legal identity. This is shown by the lack of interest in aristocratic status markers in the *Pactus*, and also by the notable vagueness of aristocratic terminology in all our sources—*maiores, seniores, optimates, proceres, potentes, meliores* being the preferred words, whether in Gregory or in the sixth-century post-*Pactus* royal capitularies. This is common ground in the two best contributions to the sixth-century aristocracy debate, those of Franz Irsigler and Heike Grahn-Hoek (the former tending to stress aristocratic power and identity, the latter to underplay it).[87] If ancestry was an important element

---

[85] Agilolfing historiography is extensive; examples, with bibliography, are Werner, 'Important noble families', pp. 161–8; Jarnut, *Agilolfingerstudien* (detailed, although unconvincing on the family's supposed Suevic/Visigothic origins); Le Jan, *Famille et pouvoir*, pp. 387–96, the best brief survey. The surname is cited in Fredegar, *Chronica*, IV.52.

[86] *Vita Genovefae, passim.*

[87] Irsigler, *Untersuchungen*, pp. 107–85 (with Claude, 'Untersuchungen', pp. 59–65); Grahn-Hoek, *Die fränkische Oberschicht*, pp. 55–123. See also the lists in Weidemann, 'Adel im Merowingerreich'.

in any part of early 'Frankish' aristocratic identity (which it may not have been, at least not on the level of the *genus senatorius* in the south), it did not have a legal dimension, in this respect unlike the Anglo-Saxons, the Bavarians, or the early Lombards, even though the average Frankish aristocrat was far more powerful than the equivalent aristocracies of any of these peoples. By the seventh century this was irrelevant, for (as Irsigler stresses) by then the imagery of *nobilitas* is strong in all our texts, giving the clear sense of a de facto stable elite. In the sixth century, however (as Grahn-Hoek stresses), the elite may have been more open, more dependent on royal patronage, and also less culturally separate from the *populus*, ordinary Franks, who as yet maintained some political protagonism.[88]

The second point is linked to that *populus* imagery: we must not overstress the aristocratic nature of early Frankish society. Twentieth-century historians reacted against romantic nineteenth-century ideas of early Frankish freedom and equality, which were reinforced by the legalist presupposition that, since the *Pactus* did not mention aristocrats, there could not have been any at the time, only the king and his 'common free' (*Gemeinfrei*) warriors; but the alternative proposed in the middle decades of the century by Heinrich Dannenbauer or Theodor Mayer or Walter Schlesinger, that all the so-called 'free' of the *Pactus* and other texts were really specialized warrior elites of royal dependants, *Königsfreie*, was even more unacceptable as a general theory, and has now been mostly abandoned in its turn.[89] All these theories have tended to be too legalist, too generalizing, too inflexible. Reality was local in the early middle ages, based on local practices, not on law. In particular, local differences were, or could be, acute. When our documents begin, for example, we find some areas (such as the Seine valley) where land was owned in huge blocks, estate-sized; others (such as the middle Rhine) where it was highly fragmented. (See further below, pp. 393–406.) It is only common sense to presume that these differences, and others, had their analogues in local social activity as well. And it is in particular plausible that there were some *areas* where the sort of peasant society described in the *Pactus* predominated, and others (again, such as the Seine valley) where an aristocratic practice was already so dominant that the peasantry was reduced to marginality. These points will be looked at again in Chapters 7, 9, and 11, but it is necessary already to stress them here. The great aristocrats of our seventh-century texts did not necessarily dominate

[88] Ine 51, 54, 70; *Lex Baiwariorum*, III.1; Rothari, *Prologus*. For the Franks, Irsigler, *Untersuchungen*, pp. 233–42; Grahn-Hoek, *Die fränkische Oberschicht*, pp. 263–75. The word *nobilis* remained a key reference-point into the Carolingian period: see Goetz, ' "Nobilis" '; Le Jan, *Famille et pouvoir*, pp. 32–4, among many.

[89] See n. 71, with, as critics of *Königsfreie* theory, Tabacco, *Liberi del re*, pp. 3–12; Schulze, 'Rodungsfreiheit'; Schmitt, *Untersuchungen*. Dopsch, *Economic foundations*, pp. 202–9, coming out of the *Gemeinfreie* tradition, never denied the existence of aristocrats, and I still find myself close to him.

all the different microregions of the north; they coexisted with relatively independent peasantries as well, for a long time.

After 600 documents begin, and they deserve a careful analysis, above all to bring out their geographical dimension, something that has not always been studied. Our early documents privilege the Seine basin and the lands west and south of Paris, as far as Le Mans and Orléans, the heartland of what was becoming Neustria, thanks above all to the St-Denis originals and the genuine texts in the Le Mans cartulary-chronicle. Later in the century we can move north, for the cartularies of the recently founded western Austrasian and northern Neustrian monasteries, such as Stavelot-Malmedy and St-Bertin (modern St-Omer) allow these areas to come into the light as well; only at the end of the seventh century and into the eighth, however, do the Rhineland collections, Wissembourg, Echternach, St Gallen, and then, in the Carolingian period, Murbach, Fulda, Lorsch allow our attention to move eastwards into the Austrasian heartland in a systematic way. The south, both Aquitaine and (still more) the Rhône valley, is much less well documented, and here will be used only as a subsidiary source of information.[90]

Let us begin with the largest, most famous, and in many respects least typical of these charters, the will of Bertram, bishop of Le Mans, dating to 616, for it can be seen as a bridge from the sixth-century focus in the preceding pages. Bertram's will is immense, forty pages in the standard edition; it includes well over a hundred properties, mostly estates, in at least seventeen city territories, from Le Mans (the largest collection) southwards as far as Bordeaux and Cahors, and eastwards to a line from Provence to Soissons. It defies easy synthesis, not least because Bertram was an unusually chatty will-maker, happy to tell us the histories of individual estates; but some aspects of it are clear. Bertram, a former archdeacon of Paris, was from a Le Mans–Paris basin landowning family on his father's side, and a Saintes–Bordeaux family on his mother's. Margarete Weidemann has argued that on his father's side Bertram was related to two Merovingian queens and Bertram, bishop of Bordeaux, and on his mother's side to Roman senatorial families. This is fairly speculative, although that he was paternally Frankish and maternally Roman is pretty certain; still, more important than Bertram's dual ethnicity is the fact that this sort of marriage alliance allowed

---

[90] Editions are very numerous, but the most important collections are *ChLA*, XIII, XIV; Busson and Ledru, *Actus*; *Recueil des chartes de l'Abbaye de Stavelot-Malmedy*; *Trad. Wiz.*; Wampach, *Geschichte*, I.2; *Codex Laureshamensis*; *Ub. St Gallen*, I; *Ub. Fulda*. Royal documents are in Theo Kölzer's *MGH, Dip. Merov.* (replacing Karl Pertz's previous edition, except for Arnulfing/Pippinid mayoral texts). Pardessus, *Diplomata*, the classic nineteenth-century edition, picks up most of the rest. There is no complete guide to Merovingian charters, though see Debus, 'Studien'; Kölzer, *Merowingerstudien*, although focused on royal charters, surveys some of the main manuscript collections.

for the development of landowning linking (above all) Neustria and Aquitaine, presumably in the mid-sixth century, in a way that we have not seen
hitherto. And Bertram's *Königsnähe* did still more. He was a loyal follower
of Chlotar II, as were his kin, and he had lost much of his property in the
long period of Chlotar's weakness, c.585–610. Chlotar, however, reversed
his fortunes dramatically in 613, becoming the first sole king of the Franks
for over fifty years, and Bertram got dozens of estates in royal gift to him
personally, not only former family lands but much more. It was Chlotar who
extended his lands throughout two-thirds of Francia, and who facilitated his
acquisitions of others—most of Bertram's property, that is to say, had been
gained or regained in the last three years. The resultant spread, well beyond
the sub-regional level, was in this case stabilized, in that some two-thirds of
it went to two churches in Le Mans (including the cathedral); it was the
starting-point for a long-standing interest by the church of Le Mans in
Aquitaine. If this sort of political fortune in any sense matched that of
Clovis's entourage, it would help to explain the 'royal-ness' of the sixth-
century aristocracy, no matter what their roots. And by now such patronage
extended to Aquitaine as well.[91]

The other charters for large-scale seventh-century aristocrats (mostly
wills, but not all) are different, in that they put much less stress on royal
intervention. All the same, they sometimes show wide geographical spreads,
even if not on as large a scale as Bertram. In the St-Denis charters, Wademir
and Ercamberta's will, from 690–1, is the only one that comes close in size,
with thirty-three estates (and another four in an earlier text), scattered across
the south and west of the middle Seine valley and into what is now Normandy, with substantial outliers south from there to Le Mans and Angers in
southern Neustria and Cahors in southern Aquitaine. This was undeniably a
Paris-focused property, for the couple gave all this land to sixteen churches
in the Paris basin, up to half of them in the city itself, but it extended well
beyond the local area: above all inside a single sub-region, but extending into
Aquitaine as well.[92] The Aquitaine link is present in quite a number of
Neustrian aristocratic documents, in fact: in 626–7, and again in the 630s,
we have royal ratifications of the division of family land between heirs,
which show owners in the Beauvaisis north of Paris with lands in central-
southern Aquitaine (in one case as a result of a marriage alliance; the other
probably through royal patronage, for it is the family of a Merovingian
queen, Chlotar II's last wife Sichild). Several Reims owners owned beyond

---

[91] Busson and Ledru, *Actus*, pp. 102–41, re-edited in Weidemann, *Das Testament*, pp. 7–49.
Ibid., pp. 124–38, discusses Bertram's kin; pp. 156–67 discusses Chlotar. Nonn, 'Eine fränkische
Adelssippe', accepts that Bertram's kinsman was the bishop of Bordeaux, which is the
most likely of these genealogical hypotheses. For the Le Mans background, see Sprandel,
'Grundbesitz'.
[92] *ChLA*, XIII, n. 571, with XIV, n. 594 (a. 682). There is no indication as to where Wademir
and Ercamberta's land came from.

the Loire as well, from Romulf in the 590s (in Poitou) to Nivard in the 660s—both of them bishops, but also local aristocrats with considerable private land. When these texts—largely consisting of donations to Neustrian churches—are put together with the other texts we have for northern church-owning in Aquitaine, we have a substantial documentation for Neustrians owning south of the Loire, with not much sign of Aquitainians owning in the north. It would be hard to disagree with Rouche when he stresses the exploitation which this involved; the Aquitainian aristocracy were beginning to face rivals from the north.[93] But, more important, it shows how widely dispersed both secular and ecclesiastical landowning could be in seventh-century Francia, at least its western half.

To give a better idea of what these estate collections are like, let us look at two, one more focused, one more scattered. The will of the 'son of Idda' (we do not know his name or the exact date, for the top of the text is missing, but it is late seventh-century, one of the last Frankish papyri) distributes nine *villae* and three *villares* (smaller estates), mostly in the Vexin west of Paris, and the rest in the Seine valley between Paris and Évreux, stretching south only to Étampes, 30 km south of Paris. Idda's son probably lived at Arthies in the Vexin, close to the centre of this group: the charter was written there, and he willed the *villa* to his wife, the only permanent gift he made to his family (they must have been a childless couple)—the others went to Paris churches or, once, the king. The other focus for the estate set was Chaussy, just to the west of Arthies, where the family church and grave-site was; here, apparently, Idda's son's freed *servientes* had their land. This was a relatively concentrated property, although even here the estates did stretch across 80 km, and across four of the small counties (*pagi*) of the seventh century. The Vexin was evidently its core, and it was not city-focused. Arthies is, however, only 20 km from the River Oise, where so many Neustrian royal palaces were concentrated, and his gift of a *villa* to the *sacratissimus fiscus* shows that he was at least linked to the Neustrian central political network.[94]

The second property set is that of Adalgisel-Grimo, a deacon of the church of Verdun, who made his will in 634. It is not substantially larger than that of Idda's son, with thirteen *villae* and some more scattered land, largely vineyards, but is much more widely spread. His land went to his own monastery at Longuyon, 40 km north of Verdun, to Verdun cathedral, and

---

[93] Respectively, Havet, 'Questions mérovingiennes', V, nn. 3, 4; *ChLA*, XIII, n. 554; Flodoard, *Historia Remensis ecclesiae*, II.4, 10. Others are Pardessus, *Diplomata*, nn. 369, 406, and cf. 442. Reims is in Champagne, which was more often in Austrasia, but it is geographically part of the Seine valley, and its landowning best fits Neustrian patterns. See in general Rouche, *L'Aquitaine*, pp. 239–48, with map at pp. 232–3. But some major Aquitainian landowners were part of Chlotar and Dagobert's court politics, notably Desiderius of Cahors: see Heinzelmann, *Bischofsherrschaft*, pp. 112–13, and Stroheker, *Der senatorische Adel*, nn. 57, 103, 187, 335, 346, 350, 378, for his family.
[94] *ChLA*, XIII, n. 569.

to numerous other churches in Trier, Metz, Tours, Maastricht, Huy, Amay, covering much of Austrasia and indeed further afield; only two estates, both in the Longuyon area, went to his nephews. The land itself was similarly spread. Much of it was around Longuyon, but it also extended outwards; as much was on the Moselle between Trier and Metz (including several vine-yards), two estates were in the Vosges 150 km to the south-east, and three were in the middle Meuse between Huy and Maastricht, 150 km to the north, down the river from Verdun. Most of this land was family property, for Adalgisel-Grimo only held portions of it, indicating that they were inherited shares; Longuyon was certainly the organizational centre of it, but the rest was not recently acquired. The king is not mentioned here, although Metz was one of the centres of the Austrasian kingdom. Adalgi-sel-Grimo must have been all the same part of a king-connected aristocracy, for his nephew Bobo was a *dux*, although he cannot be securely linked to any of the other major families of the period. But the spread of his lands did cover the whole of the west of Austrasia; if a minor member of an elite family had land on this sort of sub-regional geographical scale, then one can imagine that bigger political players were often at least as widely endowed. This geographical scale is the opposite of that of the son of Idda.[95] These two forms of landowning, the relatively concentrated and the more widely dispersed, can be found both among the lesser and the greater aristocracy of the Frankish world; and there were always some aristocrats with widely dispersed lands in every sub-region.

There are several observations to be made here. First, that we are dealing with what are often really large properties. It helps that we have numerous wills from Merovingian Francia as a whole, at least sixteen between Aredius in 572 and Abbo of Maurienne, another major owner, in 739: we can be reasonably sure of the near-complete extent of a person's landowning in most of these cases. Of those wills, only three list fewer than ten separate estates, and four list over seventy-five. As a group, these are, in absolute, the largest secular non-royal properties attested in our period from anywhere in the post-Roman world; and nor do the wills exhaust the charters that list lands on this scale.[96] Where did aristocrats get such large collections of

---

[95] Levison, 'Das Testament'.

[96] The four with over 75 estates are Bertram of Le Mans (above, n. 91); *Vita Desiderii*, c. 30, for Desiderius of Cahors; *Cartulary of Flavigny*, nn. 1–2, 57–8, for Widerad of Flavigny; Geary, *Aristocracy in Provence*, pp. 38–78, for Abbo: the second and fourth of these are for the south. The three with less than 10 are *ChLA*, XIV, n. 592; Guérout, 'Le testament', pp. 817–20; Flodoard, *Historia Remensis ecclesiae*, II.5: the first two of these, for Erminethrudis and Burgundofara, are for the only women acting on their own in these wills, which is an indicator of the restricted wealth most aristocratic women had independent access to in Francia. Other wills are those of Aredius, the son of Idda, Wademir and Ercamberta, Adalgisel-Grimo (above, nn. 53, 94, 92, 95); also Busson and Ledru, *Actus*, pp. 157–62; Pardessus, *Diplomata*, nn. 358, 437; Flodoard, *Historia Remensis ecclesiae*, II.4, 6. Large groups of land mentioned in other texts include Pardessus, *Diplomata*, nn. 363 (*Cartulaire général*, n. 8), 475; Devic and Vaissete,

estates? Often from kings, presumably, but often several generations earlier than the wills we have, for only a few mention royal gifts even casually; anyway, royal gifts were often of estates confiscated off some other aristocrat of a similar level. Perhaps one should simply say that the scale of Frankish political power, the size of the kingdom, the wealth of the kings, and the potential size of the perks of office, were such that any aristocrat who had any royal connection could end up exceptionally rich, and, by extension, locally powerful, even though at whose expense—royal lands, rival aristocrats, peasantries—is less easy to see. The monasteries they founded and the churches they patronized perpetuated this wealth in the ecclesiastical sphere too.

The second point is about spread, building on the comments made about Adalgisel-Grimo. Few of these big estate sets were quite as widely scattered as Bertram's; dispersed estates tended to be inside sub-regions, with only outliers outside, as with Wademir and Ercamberta's lands. So, the other really big collections of land, over seventy-five estates that is to say, were very largely focused on more restricted zones: the territories of Cahors and Albi for Desiderius of Cahors in 649–50, eleven small counties around Dijon for Widerad of Flavigny in 717–19, the western Alps and eastern Provence for Abbo of Maurienne in 739. These are by no means tight concentrations, but they are relatively localized given their scale, and they emphasize the sub-regional political practice that marked Francia in this period. Conversely, they allowed for expansion to wider areas. A marriage alliance might immediately link two areas, as it did for Bertram's parents. The Pippinids of the seventh century, unquestionably one of the leading families of Austrasia but (before c.690) located too far east to appear much in charters, seem to have been based in the Liège area, which they presumably dominated as firmly as Desiderius, say, would have dominated Cahors; but they extended their influence systematically southwards by marriage, notably to the Trier area. One of the major roles for aristocratic women was to facilitate these wider geographical links; Plectrudis, Pippin II's powerful wife, was all the more influential because it was she who provided the Pippinids with their Trier connection.[97] And we can trace groups of aristocrats in narrative sources for the seventh century with power-bases apparently even more widely spaced than this, above all the Agilolfings and the related Faronids, who between 590 and 640 can be found with major centres in the Brie south of Meaux, in the Verdun area, and probably in the Main

HGL, II, preuves, pp. 42–4 (for the south); Wampach, *Geschichte*, I.2, nn. 3, 4, 6, 9, 10 (all for Ermina abbess of Ören in Trier, probably Plectrudis' mother—see the next n.). The only parallels in the Roman and ex-Roman world after 550 would be the Apions, and after the 620s they had gone too: see below, p. 249.

[97] See Werner, *Der Lütticher Raum*, pp. 216–27, 341–475, for the fullest analysis; he extends his analyses to the Trier families in *Adelsfamilien*, although he is more unwilling than I would be to accept Ermina as Plectrudis' mother (pp. 121–48, 174–5).

valley east of the Rhine, as well as controlling the autonomous duchy of Bavaria, which they did until 788, a century after their eclipse elsewhere, and supplying kings to Lombard Italy for sixty years, 653–712. Régine Le Jan has argued that a grouping as big as this was probably too loose to act as a permanent faction, and was certainly polycentric in the sense that single family-members did not necessarily ever own land both on the Seine and on the Danube; but slightly smaller powers like the Pippinids could own across the whole of a Frankish sub-region, and sometimes further.[98] Even aristocratic families with local bases, in two or three counties perhaps, were not only interested in local affairs; royal politics and marriages could extend their range notably, and often did so. Doubtless it was the richer local families who were most often likely to have the opportunity to extend their land and political activity to a sub-regional level, thus creating two levels inside the aristocracy, of much the same type as in sixth-century Aquitaine (above, p. 173). Both in Aquitaine and in the north, however, we are entitled to conclude that the geographical scale of the economy as a whole could sustain—and would have been supported by—landowning that could often span two or three hundred kilometres, and sometimes more. The monasteries they founded inherited these large spans of property too, and indeed organized them in economic terms increasingly systematically between the seventh century and the ninth.[99] This brings us back to the issue of archaeologically attested exchange networks, which will be discussed further in Chapter 11, but which, as already noted, were unusually wide-ranging in Merovingian Francia.

A third point is about the direction of political interest. The long-distance landowning that is documented in our Merovingian charter-collections is almost always north–south, almost never east–west: it connects Neustria with Aquitaine (or northern Austrasia with southern Austrasia, as with the Pippinids, or with Adalgisel-Grimo), but it does not connect Neustria with Austrasia. This may be because our charters only really begin in the 610s, when Neustria and Austrasia had started to crystallize out as separate (and opposed) polities.[100] Here, it would be helpful to have more early Austrasian

---

[98] Le Jan, *Famille et pouvoir*, pp. 387–96, contrasting the Agilolfings to the more focused Pippinids (pp. 398–401), who were more like the Carolingian *Reichsaristokratie* (pp. 401–13). Le Jan stresses the importance of the sub-regional scale of landowning too, ibid., pp. 122–6. For the Faronids around Meaux, the basic account is Bergengruen, *Adel und Grundherrschaft*, pp. 65–80. See above, n. 85.

[99] Lebecq, 'The role of the monasteries', pp. 129–39; see below, pp. 280–93.

[100] There was also Austrasian land in Aquitaine: Rouche, *L'Aquitaine*, pp. 232–3. Neustria went politically with Burgundy for most of the seventh century, but there is little sign of this in these patterns of landowning (although Burgundy is very poorly documented). Bertram's will shows some Austrasian links (Weidemann, *Das Testament*, nn. 50, 59; Busson and Ledru, *Actus*, pp. 129, 132), but that is a text from the 610s. Champagne, the border (cf. n. 93), is the area with the clearest links both east and west. Austrasians, finally, could give or sell to St-Martin in Tours; ecclesiastical charisma on its own seems to have underpinned that link. See Levison, 'Das Testament', p. 132; Debus, 'Studien', n. 24.

charters, but at least one can say that Neustrian aristocrats rarely refer to land in Austrasia in our documentation. It may be significant that the Agilolfings, whose landed interests can be traced back to the 580s, did have an east–west orientation: this may represent a set of possibilities which was more sixth-century than seventh-century, which also may help to explain why the Agilolfing 'connection' eventually failed.[101] Only with the reunification of all of the sixth-century Frankish regions under the Carolingians (the former Pippinids, that is to say) did wider east–west links become normal again, as—to name only the most important families—with the Rupertiner/Robertines of Neustria (below, pp. 393–4) and the Guidonids of the Breton march (not to speak of Spoleto in central Italy), both of whom had Rhineland roots. But that aristocracy, the Carolingian *Reichsaristokratie*, were by now responding to a substantially different political situation, in which Austrasia was the core region par excellence.[102] In a sense, Neustria in the Carolingian period was a 'colonial' territory, almost in the same way as Aquitaine had been in the seventh century, and continued to be for that matter.

A fourth point is about what this wealth was used for. Over and above living well, it was used to promote political power, principally at the level of royal politics, at least in the case of the sub-regional elites. Major aristocrats linked themselves to kings, as we shall see in a moment; but they were political players because they had networks of patronage extending downwards to city-level aristocrats, who were their political clients, whose interests they could favour in return for local support. They were also, of course, powerful because they had a wider network of sworn military dependants, *satellites*, *leudes*—in the future, *vassi*—whose upkeep they paid for, often in the end by ceding them land. The politics of land thus reappeared in the relationship between aristocrats and their armed entourages, whether based on unconditional gifts or on temporary ones (called *precariae* in this period). This did not present problems of control before 800; the 'fragmentation of powers', as Marc Bloch put it, was not a problem of this period. But it must be recognized that it was enormously expensive. Roman senators could spend so much on games or housing because they mostly did not need private armies on this scale, and their outgoings may in general have been less than those of Merovingian *proceres*, outside the city of Rome at least. This would remain a feature of aristocratic politics for centuries to come.[103]

---

[101] See above, n. 85. The Agilolfings were also the only major family before 750 known to have significant links to the lands east of the Rhine valley.

[102] Werner, 'Important noble families'; Le Jan, *Famille et pouvoir*, esp. pp. 403–5 for Austrasian dominance; Airlie, 'The aristocracy'; Le Jan, *La royauté et les élites*, among many.

[103] For an aristocrat's responsibility to his clients, see e.g. *Marculfi formulae*, I.23–4 (ed. *MGH, Formulae*, pp. 57–8). For how patronage worked in practice, see e.g. *Passio Praejecti*, cc. 23–5 (a bishop of Clermont entrusting a case to a queen mother, Himnechild, when up against

A fifth point is the simple density of aristocratic land in some regions. I have already noted that the Paris basin is unlikely ever to have been the sort of territory where peasants had a great deal of independence. This is in a way an understatement: it was a territory overwhelmingly dominated by kings and aristocrats, not just a *Königslandschaft* (cf. above, p. 46), but an *Adelslandschaft* too. Dozens of aristocrats owned large numbers of estates in the area, as the St-Denis documents make clear, and so did kings and churches/monasteries. If the Brie was slightly more aristocratic (thanks to the Faronids and their monasteries, Faremoutiers, Jouarre, and Rebais), and the Val d'Oise slightly more royal (thanks to a string of royal *palatia* from Clichy to Compiègne), overall the area was one of extensive large-scale landowning, a chequerboard of estates, representing a striking balance of power, for no one could dominate an area with so many rivals in it. The Île de France will be discussed again as a local study in Chapter 7 (pp. 398–406), but it represents an extreme: nowhere which is documented to the same extent, in all the lands of the former Roman empire (let alone outside it), has such a density of major political figures. It may be that if we had the equivalent of the St-Denis charters for other core areas, Reims or Metz or even Liège, we would find similar patterns. We would not find them, on the other hand, in the Rhineland, where peasant landowning is altogether better documented (below, pp. 393–8). It is in part as a result of this concentration of extensive aristocratic landowning, all around the kings of the Neustrian *Teilreich* (and, as we have seen, spreading elsewhere as well), that we have such clear evidence of aristocratic faction in the seventh century. The seventh-century Frankish kings faced a swirl of faction, increasingly coherent rival aristocratic groups, who have no real parallel in Spain and Italy. Our best evidence for it is Neustrian, in the period c.640–715 (Austrasia has less hagiography as well as fewer charters, so we can be less sure about exactly what happened there before Pippinid supremacy was assured in the 680s); and most of the major actors in it, Erchinoald (d. 657), Ebroin (d. 680), the Warattonids, had land in the Paris basin.[104] This was a focus for an intense politics, both at the level of the kingdom and at that of the locality, a combination which had few equivalents elsewhere in our period, outside perhaps the Marmara region around Constantinople.

This is as far as I shall take the Franks chronologically. Once we get past 751 the Carolingian world provides a sufficiently different set of parameters that we would have to discuss it in as much detail as the preceding two

two much more powerful aristocrats). For *leudes*, etc., see Kienast, *Die fränkische Vasallität*, pp. 3–51, for the sources; Le Jan, *Famille et pouvoir*, pp. 112–13. For Bloch, *Feudal society*, p. 446. Cf., for the later empire, Sidonius on Ecdicius (*Ep.* III.3.7), who implies how unusual it was that he paid for his own army.

[104] See, *ChLA*, XIII, nn. 557, 570, XIV, n. 587. The Pippinid versus Gundoin factional dispute may be a product of a parallel density of landowning in parts of Austrasia: Werner, *Der Lütticher Raum*, pp. 110–12, 220–6.

centuries, which is simply impractical.[105] To conclude this section, however, let us look at how aristocratic culture and practice changed in Gaul/Francia, across the period c.450–750, according to the criteria that were sketched out at the beginning of the chapter.

The first criterion is ancestry. For late Roman aristocrats in Gaul, this mattered a lot, as Sidonius shows; by Gregory's time in Aquitaine it may have mattered even more, for it conveyed to Gregory status entirely independently of ever holding office (Gregory remarks of Paulinus of Nola that, when he sold all his property, he possessed 'nothing except his own rank (*status*)'—for Gregory, he could never lose that). This may contrast with sixth-century north Frankish aristocrats, about whose ancestry we know very little. Venantius refers to noble birth, however, and, if one could feel that this may be because his classical rhetoric required it, it is at least true that once he praised a high official, Conda, whose ancestry (*genus*) was sufficiently humble that it was Conda's career which 'ennobled' it—Conda was born in 515 at the latest, judging by the steps of his career, in a period when we might suppose that the Frankish aristocracy was pretty fluid, but Venantius treated him as exceptional all the same.[106] The extreme speed of the success of Clovis and his entourage nonetheless probably created an environment in which ancestry mattered unusually little in northern Gaul. This would change; in the seventh century hagiographies routinely stressed the noble birth of as many saints as they could plausibly make claims for. *Nobilitas* of ancestry was by now a standard feature of aristocrats in both the north and the south; Paul Fouracre has indeed argued that non-noble origin was virtually impossible for a major secular player after 600 or so, and rare enough for bishops too.[107] This indicates a certain stabilization in the political system, which would not be disturbed for several centuries. The Carolingian takeover did not bring a substantial renewal of aristocratic families beyond the standard turnover expected in any elite, even though that elite did increase in size, thanks to the recruitment of families east of the Rhine. The next shift, the rise of the castellan stratum to aristocratic status, would not be until the fall of public power in France in the tenth century, which was arguably the most momentous change in the parameters of high politics in the region since Clovis.[108]

The second criterion, landed wealth, was the most stable feature of all. In every century between the fourth and the eighth we can find a very wealthy

[105] See n. 102. There is no good guide to Carolingian aristocratic landowning as a whole, but see Devroey, *Économie rurale*, I, pp. 260–96, for a significant introduction.

[106] Respectively, Gregory of Tours, *GC*, c. 108 (cf. the 'senatorial' priest of Riom in *GM*, c. 86); Venantius, *Carmen* VII.16. For a negative view of social ascent, see Gregory on Leudast, *LH*, V.48.

[107] Fouracre, 'Merovingians, mayors of the palace'.

[108] This seems to me to remain a valid statement despite the criticisms that the concept of 'feudal revolution' has had, e.g. in Barthélemy, *La mutation*, pp. 13–28.

social stratum in most parts of Gaul/Francia, with two levels, aristocrats owning across a whole sub-region like Aquitaine or Neustria, and those by and large restricted to a single city territory. There was not really a structural separation between the two; every sub-regional aristocrat had a local core of landed power, and some less ambitious country cousins, who were happy with the exercise of power at the city level, as bishops, counts, or local bosses. All the same, the two levels remained distinct, much as they had in the Roman world, and indeed patron–client relationships linked sub-regional and city-level aristocrats, and underpinned the factions of the Merovingian period and later. Another striking fact about aristocratic landowning in this region is that, although seventh-century northern aristocrats inhabited areas with a substantially different history from the more Roman south, the structures of their landed properties, including their size and their geographical dispersal, were so similar. This may be chance, due to the fact that Clovis and his sons were able to recreate a polity that matched the shape of Roman Gaul quite closely. But it may also be that there were continuities in even northern Gaul from the Roman period that facilitated the maintenance of large-scale landowning, even if usually by different families in 550 from those around in 450. The continuities in ceramic networks in the north at least show that long-distance economic relationships, which had be present if an aristocrat living in (say) Le Mans wanted to call in rents from land in (say) Reims, did indeed exist, throughout that invasion period. In this sense, the scale of seventh-century northern landowning did have Roman roots. Unfortunately, our evidence for Aquitaine becomes much less generous after the seventh century, so we cannot track north–south parallelisms side by side; still less can we tell if the military reconquest of Aquitaine in the 760s brought structural discontinuities in that sub-region. The example of Provence, however, which was violently brought under the hegemony of Charles Martel a generation earlier, might argue for continuity, for Abbo of Maurienne, one of Charles's main Provençal lieutenants, was certainly of long-rooted local origin, and the social patterns visible in Provence in the early ninth century are those of sub-regional and local aristocrats, just as they had been in Gaul as a whole in the seventh.[109] In general, the Carolingian period saw considerable continuity from the Merovingians in landowning patterns.

The ways in which personal links to rulers worked did not change much, either, in their basic parameters, as fifth-century emperors were replaced by sixth-/seventh-century kings. They hung substantially on collective dining in all periods. The etiquette probably changed (dining with rulers was much less formal in the seventh century than in the fifth), and probably also the

---

[109] For Provence, see e.g. *Gallia christiana novissima*, III, nn. 195, 196, for Leibulf in Provence in 824–5; just over the Rhône, cf. Devic and Vaissete, *HGL*, II, preuves, pp. 75–9, for Braiding of Nîmes in 813. Provence was never cut off from the north, though; see Geary, *Aristocracy in Provence*, pp. 103–5, 130–48, for the interconnections of its aristocracies already in the seventh century. Carolingian conquest only accentuated that.

food (the roast meat dominance in medieval aristocratic diet developed across this period). But being a *conviva regis* was the quintessence of *Königsnähe* in all periods; it is even privileged in the 'egalitarian' *Pactus legis Salicae*.[110] It brought rich gifts from emperors and kings, and the ear of the powerful, thus potential for the patronage of others. It also brought office, a separate criterion for aristocratic identity; but here the differences were much more marked. The official career structure that defined the landed aristocracy was largely civilian in the fifth century, and it was also very complex, as the ambitious moved between curial, military, senatorial, and palatine office. As we saw earlier, this changed as soon as the successor-states established themselves, and by the sixth century the military hierarchy had become dominant even in royal courts, focused on *maiores domus*, *duces*, and *domestici*; locally, royal officials were all military leaders before anything else; and even the separate ecclesiastical hierarchy often had military roles by the seventh century.[111] This shift in the public parameters of social hierarchies was sufficiently great that it would have itself often created discontinuities in identity—particularly in the north, where the imagery of senatorial ancestry was less strong, but even sometimes in the south, where some sixth-century military leaders perhaps came from fairly obscure backgrounds.[112]

The seventh century has been traditionally distinguished from the sixth as an age of aristocratic power, both in the localities and increasingly at court as well, with symbolic dates in 614, when Chlotar II supposedly conceded autonomous local power to his aristocracy at the Edict of Paris,[113] and 639, when an age of royal minorities and over-mighty courtiers began; by the end of the century Francia was breaking up into semi-independent territories, ruled by dukes or bishops, who had to be reconquered by Charles Martel in the decades after 715. As we saw earlier (above, pp. 104–5), the image of the slow weakening of the Merovingians as a family still has some credibility, but the rest does not. One important element in this is that the sub-regional

[110] For Roman formality, see e.g. Sidonius, *Ep.* I.11. For the start of medieval meat-eating, see Anthimus, *De observatione ciborum*, cc. 3–33, for the Franks in the period 511–34 (the *domni Francorum* were particularly fond of speck, *crudum laredum*: ibid., c. 14); commentary in Effros, *Creating community*, pp. 61–7. For *convivae regis*, see *Pactus*, c. 41.8; for comments and other refs., Claude, 'Untersuchungen', pp. 74–6; Irsigler, *Untersuchungen*, pp. 239–42. For changes in etiquette, see Hen, *Culture and religion*, pp. 209–10, 234–49, the latter section emphasizing Merovingian-period drunkenness; see further the eighth-century parody of Salic law ed. in Beckmann, 'Aus den letzten Jahrzehnten', p. 307, concerning the drinking games of a *senior* and his *vassalli*.

[111] A convenient guide to the hierarchy is Barnwell, *Kings, courtiers*, pp. 23–51.

[112] See Gregory of Tours, *LH*, V.13, VIII.27, 45, for the *dux* Desiderius of Albi, none of whose kin are ever mentioned. (But if Desiderius of Cahors two generations later, who was probably born in Albi (see below, p. 606), was from the same family, it fast became extremely rich.)

[113] For the Edict, Dopsch, *Economic and social foundations*, pp. 200–1, is a classic formulation of the position; Murray, 'The *Edict of Paris*', is a recent critique.

spans of landowning of the major aristocratic families themselves made such fragmentation very difficult, except at the level of the largest territories, Aquitaine or (outside our region) Bavaria. The standard pattern of scattered landowning enforced co-operation and competition, and itself contributed to the continuing centrality of the royal courts of the *Teilreiche*. Political clientèles stretched across whole kingdoms and indeed beyond, and them- selves, through marriage alliances, contributed to the maintenance of geo- graphically extended landowning and thus once again kingdom-wide politics. The only figures who might have thought of focusing on local autonomy—in fact probably did, at Trier, Mainz, Orléans—were bishops; church land, at least, tended to be based in single dioceses (even if this was no longer to be taken for granted, as the extensive lands of the church of Le Mans in Aquitaine show). Nonetheless, any time that episcopal office was held by a member of a sub-regional family, which was often, the episcopate was tied into kingdom-level politics again. As Fouracre has stressed, the politics of a bishop like Leudegar of Autun (d. 678) make no sense at all either at an exclusively royal or at an exclusively local level—both were crucial for Leudegar's success and survival, or (as in the end occurred) his failure and death.[114] The courts stayed central, as the venues for political rivalry, even when the kings did not; they could not be done without. The imagery of the court as a place of power and danger, a sort of moral labyrinth, pervades even the most locally orientated of our texts, such as the *Passio Praejecti* from Clermont in c.680 or the *Vita Eucherii* from Orléans in the 750s.[115] At least some political activity at the level of the *regnum* could simply not be avoided, if one wanted to stay afloat, even if only at the level of city politics.

The Merovingian kings were very rich, but, as we have seen in Chapter 3 (pp. 102–15), dealt above all in the politics of land, not in a tax-based political system, even before Chlotar II, and certainly afterwards. The ar- ticulation of the official hierarchy was not only more military, but also less complex as a result. In this respect, it is very likely that the stability of *Königsnähe* masked a real expansion of its role: unlike the Roman empire, where the hierarchy of titles was fought over by aristocrats who mostly seldom if ever met the emperor, Frankish aristocrats were often educated at court, and sought to be close to kings—and queens—on a regular basis; kings and queens could know them well (and love or hate them too, a phraseology that narratives constantly employ). Major aristocrats are rou- tinely called *vir inluster* in seventh-century documents, a usage obviously

[114] For Fouracre, see n. 61; note that Leudegar did not by any means come from an exclusively local family, for his uncle was Dido, bishop of Poitiers, himself an active episcopal dealer (*Passio prima Leudegarii*, c. 1). For more localized episcopal families and politics, see above, Ch. 3, n. 166.

[115] *Passio Praejecti*, cc. 23–7 (the bishop as an innocent and not very able dealer); *Vita Eucherii*, c. 8 (the bishop fails to get Charles Martel to eat with him).

inherited from the *illustres* of the late Roman senate, but it is hard to say that this meant anything other than *Königsnähe*—many *inlustri* do not obviously have any office at all, and the hierarchy of titles (though not, of course, the power that office could convey) had lost its lustre by the seventh century, in apparent contrast with the sixth.[116] We might conclude that this meant that attachment to kings was potentially weaker in the seventh century, simply as a result of the centrifugal tendencies of the politics of land, above all if kings became poorer because of their previous generosity, as in the traditional model of tenth-century royal decline. It might thereafter be the case that loyalty became associated only with such intangibles as royal charisma (less effective after Dagobert I's death in 639?) or military success (which began to falter after the Austrasian army failed to subdue Thuringia in the same year); indeed it is after this date that royal tyranny is more often condemned in our sources, in a way that had seldom been the case when kings before 639 had behaved badly, which was very often indeed.[117]

These arguments have often been made, and they have partial force: in particular, the arena of legitimate royal behaviour seems genuinely to have shrunk. Childeric II was condemned in 675 for having an aristocrat, one Bodilo, tied up and flogged, which was held to be more demeaning and thus tyrannous than simple killing.[118] It is hard to reconcile this with the inventive slow execution methods that many sixth-century kings and queens specialized in—Gregory of Tours reports them very grimly, but he does not regard them as going beyond practical royal prerogatives.[119] This does seem to be a change. But the attachment to court politics remained a constant throughout the Merovingian period. This was so no matter how young a king was or how unpopular his *maior domus*, or how much and how violently the aristocracy was divided by factional dispute: it did not depend on the charisma of its central figures. Indeed, the only way to successfully oppose Merovingian or, later, Pippinid rule was to set up a new court, in the outlying principalities: first Bavaria and Thuringia, then Aquitaine and Alemannia.[120] The main courts did, of course, stay rich; it may be that their continued wealth helped them to avoid the catastrophe-flip over to royal marginality that occurred in tenth-century France. This wealth aided the continuity of court-level faction-fighting just discussed, which in turn reinforced the centrality of court politics. But I think myself that the scale and spread of the landowning of Merovingian Francia's principal aristocrats was the major

---

[116] For *viri inlustri*, see e.g. Le Jan, *Famille et pouvoir*, pp. 122–3, who stresses office more than I would.

[117] For this general argument, see e.g. Ewig, 'Die fränkischen Teilreiche', pp. 201–21.

[118] Fredegar, *Continuationes*, c. 2; *Liber historiae Francorum*, c. 45.

[119] See e.g. Gregory, *LH*, VI.32, X.10; cf. also Fredegar, *Chronica*, IV.54 on the choreographing of the death of Godin by Chlotar II.

[120] Werner, 'Les principautés péripheriques'; Fouracre, *Charles Martel*, pp. 79 ff., who stresses that such principalities tended to be Merovingian legitimist in the generations of Pippinid mayoralty.

structural support for that centrality. The extreme fragmentation that late tenth-century France experienced occurred in an age of a much more localized aristocracy, focused on single counties, and, inside counties, on single castle-based *seigneuries*. Such a process would have, in the seventh century, menaced the widely spread powers of the aristocratic leadership itself, and was not on the agenda in most places.[121] Here, the politics of land actually aided the survival of political centralization, at least on the sub-regional level. How seventh-century parameters gradually changed into tenth-century ones—across the Carolingian period, the period of the greatest political-geographical expansion of all, for kings and aristocrats alike—is, however, outside the remit of this book.

One can turn these observations around, and make another point: as yet, the commitment of Frankish aristocrats to local political dominance seems to have been incomplete. If we look back at our period from the castellanies, the territorial *seigneuries*, of the eleventh century, then the way aristocrats in the fifth to eighth centuries organized local power was usually different from that. Late Roman urban aristocrats like Libanios, or, in Gaul, Sidonius, practised patronage over peasantries as a matter of course, which could certainly be coercive (as Salvian stressed), but which involved a systematic *mediation* between public powers that were already in place and individual peasants, rather than of any form of direct domination over an area, large or small—apart, of course, from the properties, usually fairly fragmented, which such aristocrats actually owned.[122] This sort of patronage, rather than domination, seems to have been the most likely pattern in Merovingian Gaul as well, if only because landowning remained so scattered and intercut. It is far from clear, indeed, that rural landowners even had structured, permanent, political centres, which are the best places from which to establish local domination. Perhaps the family of the son of Idda had had one at Arthies (above, p. 188), but Bertram, based in a city it is true, was happy to see his entire proprietorial focus move across Gaul in the wake of royal gifts (above, p. 187). The absence of reference to any monumentality in the proprietorial centres of these aristocrats (in contrast with the fortifications of the tenth century, the first private castles, that is to say)[123] may fit this too: aristocratic power was great, but it was fluid, and its quantity was more important than its local coherence or impact, for any magnate who wanted to make a political impression at court. Private coercion was a simple

---

[121] See for a general survey Fouracre, 'Space, culture and kingdoms'.

[122] See above, pp. 63, 71. Formal immunities from royal intervention were in this period restricted to the lands owned by immunists, and are anyway now seen as an emanation of royal power, quite as much as a sign of ecclesiastical or lay aristocratic autonomy: e.g. Rosenwein, *Negotiating space*, pp. 3–9, 75–96. Nubel's family in Mauretania in the fourth century may have aimed at a more direct local domination, but in a local context in which, atypically, political practice was beginning to change radically: see below, pp. 334–5.

[123] Samson, 'The Merovingian nobleman's house'; see further below, pp. 506–7.

spin-off of aristocratic status, rather than a systematic policy, and one indeed has the sense that a lord who committed himself to local dominance rather than the king-centred political hierarchy would have been something of a failure—indeed, even in the tenth and eleventh centuries the driving force behind the *seigneurie banale* was an aristocracy so small-scale that, as was noted at the start of this chapter, a Merovingian *vir inluster* might not have recognized them as aristocratic at all.[124] The first landowners to make the shift to a politics of local control may have been monasteries, if they were sufficiently isolated, concentrated in their landowning, and independent of lay control: one example of this is Redon in eastern Brittany in the late ninth century.[125] Only after 900, when aristocratic clientèles began to break down, did these have secular counterparts. This links to the one criterion for aristocratic status and identity, listed at the start (p. 154), that has here had least attention, peer-group respect: title and *Königsnähe* meant far more to other aristocrats, under the Merovingians, than simple de facto control over a county, or half a county, or less still. De jure control, as a local duke or count or, increasingly, bishop was not a problem, for this had always been part of the Merovingian political structure; but even here, de facto autonomy was not necessarily in itself the best direction for a local official to pursue. It is of course possible that there were already geographically marginal areas where this was not the case. Chur in the east-central Alps was one, under the continuous control of a single family, the Victorids, from the sixth century until c. 800, and sufficiently culturally distinct that it may have been semi-autonomous. In more hypothetical vein, we may note that Gerald of Aurillac (d. 909) had an effectively autonomous lordship in the mountains of the southern Auvergne in the decades just after Carolingian kingship began to fail in the area; we do not have any sources for this area in the Merovingian period, so we could not deny with certainty an analogous pattern in 700.[126] But such areas would, as yet, have been marginal; the main areas of documented aristocratic power worked differently. This discussion is relevant here, as a guide to how aristocrats might have seen local power; it will also be important later, when we come on to peasantries. The survival of autonomous landowning peasantries in the interstices of aristocratic power, in at least some areas (notably the Rhineland), was made much easier by the relative lack of concern such aristocrats had, as yet, to control them directly. We shall look at how such peasant societies worked in Chapters 7 and 9.

The militarization of the official hierarchy also had a profound effect on aristocratic lifestyles. There were shifts in styles of clothing, which were

---

[124] e.g. Duby, *Hommes et structures*, pp. 395–422.
[125] Davies, *Small worlds*, pp. 192–9.
[126] See Kaiser, *Churrätien*, pp. 45–53; for Gerald, Lauranson-Rosaz, *L'Auvergne*, pp. 345–51, commenting on Odo of Cluny, *Vita Geraldi*, who does his best to establish the public roots of Gerald's authority.

certainly the product of a more military tone to social action (p. 175). Shifts in the etiquette of feasting might be linked to this too, though it is harder to be sure about that. Another element is architectural display. The rural estates and town houses of Sidonius' time were the basic stage-sets for *otium* and *negotium*, and the flashier the better: we have half-a-dozen detailed description of rural *villae* in Sidonius alone, and some of them were very elaborate constructions indeed. Those of them that have been found by archaeologists, the richest late Roman villas, show in their mosaics and architectural complexities that Sidonius was not exaggerating. But villas drop out of the architectural record everywhere: in the period 350–450 in northern Gaul, in the sixth and early seventh century in the south—as also in Spain and Italy—with only a handful of later examples in each region.[127] This is sometimes simply treated as a marker for wider economic, political, demographic crisis, but this sort of interpretation marks a lack of awareness of external parallels. The end of the architectural style *everywhere* must mark a substantial cultural shift. It has been hard for scholars of the issue to avoid the terminology of decline; nothing so grand again can be associated with private landowners until the castles of the twelfth century; why would anyone have voluntarily abandoned underfloor heating and a bath-house except in an acute crisis? We do not have any secure archaeological evidence for aristocratic residences in the immediately succeeding centuries; what they actually looked like cannot, unfortunately, be easily worked out from literary sources either. Were aristocratic *villae* more like the wooden halls which are the most elaborate houses Merovingian archaeologists have discovered? (There is certainly some literary evidence for aristocratic housing in wood, as Dietrich Claude has shown.) Did they sometimes involve some form of continuing use of masonry and brick, something that was far from technologically unfeasible, for that was how they built their prestige churches?[128] We shall look at the problem in more detail from an archaeological perspective in Chapter 8. But the signs are that architectural display had become rather less important for the aristocracies of post-Roman Gaul.

And yet, notwithstanding the end of *villa* culture, it should be clear from the preceding pages that in Gaul/Francia, at any rate, aristocratic wealth remained enormous. They must have been spending their money on something: on churches, certainly (which generally maintained Roman architectural styles, more or less); on movable decorations in their houses perhaps, gold ornaments and hangings; on bejewelled clothing, for sure; and on private armies, the most expensive item of all. These came to be the markers of status and display, and they were much more military in style. It may be added that the military aspect of even late Roman archaeology is not always

---

[127] See below, pp 473-81.
[128] For villas with a wooden phase, see e.g. Van Ossel, 'Structure, évolution'; see below, pp. 506–7. For references to wood, see Claude, 'Haus und Hof', p. 333.

easy to pin down, apart of course from defensive walls; *castra* are fairly simple in their internal structures, for example.[129] The army had, one can deduce, always stressed display in its housing less than had the senatorial elite. I would argue that the end of the villa system is best seen as a marker, with a different date in each region, of the militarization of aristocratic lifestyles, rather than of crisis. What it was *like* living in the halls (or whatever) of the new militarized elites is not as yet clear; this change so far can only be described in terms of a negative, not a positive, shift. But this at least will be partially clarified in the future, maybe fairly soon, given the considerable advances of Merovingian archaeology already in the last fifteen years or so.

This militarization was not, finally, the only cultural shift in the aristocracy of sixth- and seventh-century Gaul/Francia. The self-identity of aristocratic elites as morally superior had always been important to them, and in our period this was not only expressed through the literary snobbery of senatorial *otium* or the bravery in battle of medieval *proceres*, *nobiles*, knights; it had a religious element to it as well. The local political role of bishops from the fifth century onwards was sufficiently important that aristocratic families settled into episcopal office from the start, and some of their members were soon content to aim at a purely ecclesiastical career structures.[130] But the seventh century, in particular, saw a change: as well as aristocrats using the ecclesiastical structures that existed, they began to create their own, founding and patronizing monasteries across all the Frankish kingdoms. Kings, indeed, did much the same; so did many bishops. The major reason why we can say so much more about the seventh century than the sixth (outside Gregory of Tours's fields of interest, at least) is because these monasteries kept their documents. Monasteries indeed contributed to the stability of the sub-regional scale of wealth that has been emphasized in this section, for they inherited it from aristocratic gift-giving, and then kept hold of it—more effectively than many secular aristocrats, who were more exposed to the dangers of royal disfavour. But family monasteries were also crucial for aristocratic identity: they were one of the underpinnings of the religious legitimation of the great landed elites. As was noted earlier, saints' lives in this period stress *nobilitas* of birth where possible. Sanctity and aristocracy went together; this is the great period of *Adelsheiligen*, 'noble' saints.[131] That numinosity rubbed off on Merovingian lay aristocrats too; and it may not be chance that their churches seem to have been built with more architectural ostentation than their houses. There is a religious protagonism here which is new, and which marked identity as surely as did

[129] e.g. Oldenstein, 'Die letzte Jahrzehnte', pp. 73–81, for Alzey.

[130] Heinzelmann, *Bischofsherrschaft*, pp. 211–46.

[131] See e.g. Bosl, 'Der "Adelsheilige" ', based on Bavarian sources, with the cautious notes of, among others, Berschin, *Biographie und Epochenstil*, II, pp. 79–80.

jewelled belts (perhaps more surely, for it was more under aristocratic control). It would continue in later centuries as well.

The fate of the aristocracy is better documented in Gaul/Francia than anywhere else in the former empire, in part precisely because it continued to be so rich and influential, in part because of the wealth of our local narratives. It has also been, for nearly two centuries, the focus for an unusually large amount of attention by historians, far more than its analogues in other regions—proof of the long-standing dominance of Germany, the Low Countries, and France in the historical profession, and of the symbolic importance of the issue for national identity, attentive as the latter always has been in western Europe to the early medieval emergence of national difference. For both of these reasons, it seems to me fair to have discussed its problems at relative length here. Francia can indeed in part serve as a model, in particular for the militarization of aristocratic identity, which will largely be taken for granted when we look at Italy and Spain—where anyway a dearth of evidence means that any characterization of the issue would have to be much less dense and more hypothetical. Where Francia cannot, however, serve as a model is in the wealth of its aristocracy. It is in this respect that Italy and Spain's differences can most clearly be characterized, and it is here that the following discussions will be concentrated.

3. Italy and Spain

Italy's aristocracies, much more than those of Gaul, saw major discontinuities in the period 400–800. These were the result of several different factors: first, the breakdown in Mediterranean unity, which seriously weakened the richest levels of the senatorial elite; second, the Gothic war of 535–54, which marked one of the most continuous and serious periods of violence anywhere in the late and post-Roman West; third, the Lombard invasion of 568–9. The Lombard occupation was portrayed in later centuries as itself unusually violent; although this violence was clearly exaggerated by its chroniclers, one aspect of it was particularly disruptive: the fact that the Lombards never managed to conquer the whole of Italy. Seventh-century Italy in fact resembled a chequerboard, with three separate Lombard polities (with centres at Pavia, Spoleto, and Benevento) bounded by eight geographically separate Roman/Byzantine territories (with centres at Grado and the Venice area, Ravenna, Pescara (up to c.620), Otranto, Reggio, Naples, Rome, and Genoa (up to 643)), not counting the islands. This fragmentation continued throughout our period, and for centuries to come; it could be expected to have seriously negative effects on aristocracies with more than local interests, and indeed did. So: if the richest landowners of Italy in 400 had unusually widely spread lands, far more than those in Gaul, by 750–800 the divisions in the peninsula ensured that landowning outside relatively small regions was very rare, far rarer than in Gaul. Although sub-regional landowning was theoretically possible in the largest polity in Italy, the Lombard kingdom of the Po plain and Tuscany, we shall see that even that was virtually unknown; most property was owned inside single city territories.

I shall here spend most time on the sixth century and the eighth, for the seventh century in Italy is a near blank in terms of evidence. Here, the Carolingian break is 774; although the Carolingian conquest of the north and centre changed aristocratic structures relatively little in Italy, the date is once again a convenient stopping-point. Sixth-century evidence tells us most about Rome (including its southern interests) and Ravenna; only the latter city has a surviving document collection for the period. In the eighth century we have many more documents, but they are also localized, and illuminate different parts of the peninsula, above all the Lombard kingdom of northern Italy and Tuscany and small parts of the duchies of Spoleto and Benevento; conversely, evidence for landowning in the Byzantine lands dries up after the end of Gregory the Great's letter collection in 604, and, apart from a little continuing evidence for Ravenna, hardly restarts until the late ninth century or later.[132] Broadly put, the south, and the future Byzantine lands, are better documented in the sixth century; the Lombard lands are better documented in the eighth. The region will be discussed here in two tranches as a result, moving from south to north.

The south of Italy was by far the richest section of the peninsula in the late Roman period. Under the empire the lowlands between Rome and Naples, and the Sicilian plains and plateaux, the two major centres of aristocratic property, structured a network of landowning between them in the coastal strips and valleys of Lucania and Bruttii (modern Calabria), with Puglia a more distant spinoff. This is where the senators were focused; the Rome–Naples axis, in particular, must have surpassed even the seventh-century Paris basin as a location for intermingled large-scale properties. Of course, as we have seen, the scale of wealth of the richest senators was fully established above all by their pan-Mediterranean landowning, especially in Africa; the fall of Carthage in 439 and the expropriation of aristocratic land by the Vandals must have been a major blow. From c.450 we see unmistakable archaeological signs of retreat: the end of villa phases in the rich sites of Piazza Armerina and Patti Marina in Sicily (though they survived as settlements), or the substantial weakening of ceramic imports in the still-surviving villa of S. Giovanni di Ruoti, 100 km inland from the coast in

---

[132] *CDL*, the basic collection of documents for Lombard Italy to 774 (787 in the south), illuminates above all Lombardy, Emilia, north-west Tuscany, and the Sabina; *Chronicon S. Sophiae* supplements it for the Benevento area. For Ravenna, *P. Ital.* and *CB* publish most documents.

Lucania.[133] But the senators remained a sub-regional elite. Even our casual information about late Roman senatorial land continually records major property-owning in Campania or Sicily, or both. And, if imported ceramics from now on less often got past the coast, the south still had an articulated set of local good-quality painted wares, produced industrially at several centres and widely available.[134]

The Anicii, Rufii Festi, and others of the major senatorial families remained active and influential in the Ostrogothic kingdom. Boethius worried about the expense of the praetorian games (while congratulating himself for being able to pay for consular games in 522 in the old style), which may indicate that senatorial public waste was pitched at a level the families could no longer afford so easily, but his father-in-law Symmachus could still in c.508 rebuild the Theatre of Pompey (this was, nonetheless, held an unusual act of evergetism by Theoderic, who reimbursed him).[135] Theoderic was very respectful of the senate; he treated it very seriously, notwithstanding his execution of Boethius and Symmachus in 525. One would not guess from the political narratives of Theoderic's reign that senators were getting poorer. It is important, nonetheless, to note that the archaeology of the south hints at a further involution in the wealth and complexity of the aristocratic network whose lands were there. In the early to mid-sixth century, villas like S. Giovanni di Ruoti, or Mola di Monte Gelato just north of Rome, were abandoned or lost their monumentality. The large-scale painted-ware productions of the south similarly began to face trouble, with kilns going out first in the Caserta area, then at Calle di Tricarico in central Lucania, the largest kiln-site so far found. This process was often the specific result of the Gothic war, but the failure of ceramic systems indicates that the private economic networks of the 'senatorial region' were increasingly in disarray. This one can see as the long-term effect of the breaking of the Africa–Italy link in senatorial landowning: the south as a whole was weakened as a result.[136] The Gothic war certainly damaged those networks further, however, and after 550 they were ever more clearly in retreat.

It is not that the senatorial aristocracy was even then in free fall. It is true that a number of *illustres, clarissimi,* or the new title of *magnifici,* were on Gregory the Great's poor-relief books; but others were evidently still pretty rich. Cethegus, an Anician who was important enough to be consul in his youth, in 504, stayed in Rome until 545 at least, and returned from

---

[133] Wilson, *Roman Sicily,* pp. 335–6; Small and Buck, *S. Giovanni di Ruoti,* I, pp. 82–5, 89–90, 119–21. For Sicilian landowning, Ruggini, 'La Sicilia', is basic.

[134] Tortorella, 'La sigillata africana' (who also shows that some imports did continue); di Giuseppe, 'La fornace di Calle'.

[135] Boethius, *Consolatio,* II.3, III.4 (a topos, as Barnish, 'Transformation and survival', p. 141, comments); Cassiodorius, *Variae,* IV.51 for the Theatre of Pompey.

[136] Small and Buck, *S. Giovanni di Ruoti,* I, p. 121; Potter and King, *Mola,* pp. 76–7; Arthur, 'Local pottery', p. 507; di Giuseppe, 'La fornace di Calle'.

Constantinople to his Sicilian estates by 558; his presumed heir, another
Cethegus, lived in Rome and owned in Sicily in 598. Boethius' descendant
(granddaughter?) Rusticiana, a close friend of Gregory the Great, lived in
Constantinople in the 590s, where she had married her daughter into the
Apion family of Egypt, a classic example of the Mediterranean-wide links
that might be thought to have by now been impossible; she still owned
extensively in Sicily and probably elsewhere.[137] Tullianus, a Lucanian aristocrat, was capable of gathering a private army of (his own?) peasants
against the Goths in 546, which was countered only by Totila's promise of
land to pro-Gothic tenants—Tullianus fled, but either he or a homonym had
a daughter in a Roman nunnery still in 597. Cassiodorus himself, probably
always a provincial figure in Roman eyes, kept his Squillace estates in
Bruttii, and retired there after the wars, living until c.580.[138] Gregory's
letters are full of citations of people with 'senatorial' names, Decius or
Basilius or Faustus: we cannot usually be sure how they fit into the old
families, but they were certainly still important political figures. Tom Brown
has counted thirty-five people with senatorial titles in these letters, twenty-
nine of whom still lived in Rome, Campania or Sicily. Still, Gregory never
mentions the Anicii as a family (cf. above, p. 160); the senate as an institution cannot be traced for sure past 580; the *curia* building itself was transformed into a church shortly after 625.[139] The old parameters of aristocratic
identity were going, undermined by war, and by the end of Italy as an
independent source of traditional title and position. Justinian's Italy was
uncompromisingly ruled from Constantinople, and if the exarchate of Ravenna, in place by 584 as a bulwark against the Lombards, brought government back to Italy, this government was above all military. There was only
room for one senate in the empire by now, that of Constantinople. The old
families of Rome had to choose, between a (relatively) traditional politics in
the eastern capital, a traditional *otium* in Sicily, or new forms of political
protagonism in the Italian peninsula.

Senators changed identity, then, rather than necessarily declining to ex-
tinction. Forty political figures, excluding clerics, were called John in Italy in
the period 550–625, judging from the lists in PLRE III, nearly four times as
many as in the equivalent period a century earlier; names were changing in
the latest Roman empire as surely as they were in northern Francia, and

---

[137] The basic secondary source for this paragraph and the next two is Brown, *Gentlemen and
officers*; p. 31 for poor relief, p. 191 for Rusticiana, with *PLRE*, III, s.v. Rusticiana 2, and
Gregory the Great, *Epp.*, IX.83, XIII.26 for landowning. For Cethegus, *PLRE*, II, s.v., III, s.v.;
for the elder, see esp. Prokopios, *Wars*, VII.13.12; Pelagius I, *Ep.* 33; for the younger, Gregory
the Great, *Ep.* IX.72.

[138] For Tullianus, Prokopios, *Wars*, VII.18.20–3, 22.1–5, 20–2; cf. *PLRE*, III, s.v. Tullianus,
Venantius 1.

[139] Brown, *Gentlemen and officers*, p. 23, for numbers; pp. 21–4, for the last references to the
senate, with Stein, *Bas-Empire*, II, pp. 617–19. (Gregory only mentions the *xenodochium
Aniciorum*—*Ep.* IX.8—an earlier family foundation.)

faster than they were in Aquitaine. There was still less of a military tradition among the senatorial elites in Italy than there was in Aquitaine; armies had been for the most part made up of frontier communities, whether Roman, mixed Roman and Germanic, or, after 493, Ostrogothic. After 550, however, and especially after the Lombard settlement began in 568–9, the Italians were increasingly expected to defend themselves. The military career structure, focused on the exarch, and expressed through military offices such as *dux/magister militum*, *tribunus*, and *primicerius*, steadily increased in importance. So did episcopal office, at least in the case of the richest sees, Rome, Ravenna, and Naples. Aristocratic identity changed with this, and John, followed by Gregory, Stephen, Theodore, Sergius, saints' names above all, became the standard name set for seventh- and eighth-century elites in what we now call Byzantine Italy, not the senatorial family markers of the past. This development, infuriating for prosopographers, marks a fundamental break in the boundaries of elite status. No senatorial families can be traced past the early seventh century, unlike in southern Gaul. With the demise of the civilian title system, elite membership became much more fluid, and vaguer words like *optimates* and *proceres* surface in our few seventh-century sources; *nobilis* is rare between the sixth and the eighth.[140] Seventh-century Byzantine Italy thus replicated sixth-century northern Gaul in the melting away of previous status criteria, and the temporary lack of stress on descent, and all this without the confusing element of a newly dominant group of incomers: changes in the form of the state had that effect on their own. After 650 the Byzantine heartland would experience the same shifts.[141]

It is normal for new elite criteria to make rapid social ascent easier, whether in the military or the ecclesiastical hierarchy, before the return of the importance of descent pulls up the ladder again, which it was doing in Byzantine Italy by the eighth century.[142] So it doubtless did in this case. It is

---

[140] Brown, *Gentlemen and officers*, pp. 61–81, discusses these processes; pp. 62, 165–9, for *nobilis* and equivalents, pp. 93–101 for the army. For Johns, see *PLRE*, III, pp. 624–712; Brown, *Gentlemen and officers*, pp. 263–5, counts 65 among the aristocratic laity in Byzantine Italy between 554 and 800. The name was as common among the clergy; in the latter period four popes and five archbishops of Ravenna were called John.

[141] A probable parallel here is Africa; the region has too little information after 439 to be discussed in detail, but a process of militarization is visible in our scarce sources for Byzantine Africa in the late sixth century, as it had not been for ethnic Romans in the Vandal period; Ostrogothic and then Byzantine Italy are the best analogues to this. See in general Diehl, *L'Afrique byzantine*, pp. 492–502; Pringle, *The defence*, pp. 39–50, 89–94. For the very small amount one can say about Byzantine and Arab aristocracies from documents (which does not include anything about their wealth), see respectively Durliat, 'Les grands propriétaires', and Brett, 'The Arab conquest', pp. 520–4, 534–5. How African aristocratic wealth changed is irrecoverable, then; all we can say is that it is likely that it changed less than in Italy, for there was never a hyper-rich senatorial stratum actually living in the region. For what we can see of urban wealth, see below, pp. 635–44. There observations only relate to the core lands of modern Tunisia; for the Berber parts of Africa, see pp. 333–7.

[142] Brown, *Gentlemen and officers*, pp. 169–74.

hardly possible, however, that the Campania-plus-Sicily landowning families should have failed to make an impact on this new hierarchy as well, as
their ancestors had always done. We cannot do more than assume this, as
after the end of Gregory the Great's letters our evidence decreases rapidly,
but it remains the most likely scenario. What did happen, on the other hand,
between 600 and 750, after which our evidence becomes slightly fuller
again, is that the scale of aristocratic activity contracted further. The politics
of Rome by the late eighth century had almost no links with Sicily at all, and
few enough with anywhere outside Lazio, the sub-region immediately
around the city. The popes, as we have seen (p. 167), had lost their extensive
Calabrian and Sicilian estates in or soon after the 730s, but it is striking that
Sicily was not by now a location for any landowning sufficiently important
for Roman sources to mention. On the mainland, steady Lombard expansion cut back the Byzantine-controlled parts of Italy to small enclaves, but
Sicily remained untouched until Arab attacks began in 827. It was probably
being absorbed into the Constantinople orbit, rather than the Italian one.[143]
But the impact on aristocratic scale in Italy was great all the same. With or
without the military change, Byzantine Italian aristocracies were becoming
steadily more localized. The 'senatorial region' ceased to exist.

A traditional focus on the senatorial elites leaves the city aristocracies of
Italy rather neglected. We might expect them to survive better, for the
localization of landowning would hardly have affected them; even the end
of *curiae* (cf. pp. 68–70) could easily have left city elites focused on local
military and ecclesiastical offices, as occurred in Gaul. Here too, however,
we are left to rely on supposition. Rome, the heart of traditional senatorial
power, could well have seen a greater than average family turnover; only five
out of twenty popes in the period 618–715 came from the city at all. Naples,
whose local elite had been thriving and troublesome in Gregory the Great's
time, and which was now in effect an isolated city state surrounded by
Lombards, probably experienced greater continuities; the family that controlled it in the late eighth century was certainly well rooted.[144] Ravenna, the
best-documented of the Byzantine cities, shows another break in names: the

[143] Sicily provided three late seventh-century popes, in a period in which the eastern empire
was influential in Rome, but only one in the eighth, Stephen III (768–72): see *Liber pontificalis*,
LXXXI.1, LXXXIII.1, LXXXV.1, XCVI.1. Late eighth-century papal interest in Sicily is visible
in letters: *Codex carolinus*, nn. 61, 64; but it was by then clearly foreign (i.e. Byzantine)
territory. An eighth-century seal from Syracuse refers to a *patēr tēs poleōs*, a civic title very
much in an eastern Mediterranean tradition (cf. below, p. 597); see further pp. 125–6, for Sicily's
role in the Byzantine empire; but documentary evidence for the island is by now fragmentary.
See Ruggini, 'La Sicilia', pp. 505–6, n. 23, for a handful of citations, including the seal, and
Nichanian and Prigent, 'Les stratèges de Sicile', for a prosopography of Sicilian *strategoi*
(governors), whose succession can be more or less reconstructed. The popes themselves were
by the eighth century overwhelmingly focused on Lazio, with only a few outliers elsewhere: see
Marazzi, *I 'patrimonia'*.
[144] For Naples, Gregory the Great, *Epp.*, I.11, III.1, IX.53, 76, 85, X.6, 7, etc.; *Gesta
episcoporum neapolitanorum*, cc. 42, 46, 53; Cassandro, 'Il ducato', pp. 24–52.

curial families of the sixth century (notably the Melminii, five of whose members are known in the period 550–75), abruptly cease to be documented thereafter, and our seventh-century texts privilege military officials, and, as usual, names like John and Theodore and Martin. If there were genealogical continuities here, they are as hard to see as at the senatorial level.[145] Although it is in city elite families that survivals were doubtless greatest in practice, we can only speculate about them. What is clear, nonetheless, in the seventh- and eighth-century Ravenna documents we do have, mostly leases by the archbishop to aristocrats, is that lay elite landowning operated above all at the city level, and no further. The archbishop's land in Rimini was leased to men of Rimini, that in Senigallia to men of Senigallia. Only the archbishop himself owned more widely.[146] This was typical of Byzantine Italy, with the partial exception of Lazio, whose cities were closely linked to the still-dominant sub-regional focus of Rome.[147] It was dramatically unlike the situation in Gaul; it was matched by Lombard Italy, however, as we shall now see.

In the north of Italy the scale of landowning had always been smaller. There certainly were senators there in the fifth and early sixth centuries, focused on the court at Ravenna, but their land was above all restricted to the Po plain (and perhaps Provence), rather than stretching across the Mediterranean. The Po plain was traditionally somewhat separate from the Mediterranean networks—even African pottery was less common there than elsewhere; only the great port cities, Ravenna and Aquileia, were really part of that wider world. The Gothic war broke down wider links even more, for Ravenna was throughout the 540s in Roman hands, whereas the rest of the north was under Gothic and Frankish control. It has been strongly argued in recent years that the political fragmentation of the Lombard period onwards had its origins, not just in Lombard offensive (and Roman defensive) incapacity, but also in an economic regionalization that had already begun to be acute: Federico Marazzi in particular has argued that the Lombards simply took over the territories that were already losing their links with the Mediterranean.[148] This would certainly fit the territory of Modena, 100 km inland from Ravenna. Here, a dozen so-called 'pozzi-deposito' have been found dating to c.600: these are Roman wells filled with ceramics and other goods, apparently for safe-keeping (the groups of objects are sometimes protected by wooden lids, which still survive in the

---

[145] For Ravenna, *P. Ital.* 4–5, 6, 14–15, for the Melminii; for the later seventh century, Brown, *Gentlemen and officers*, p. 216.

[146] For Ravenna, *CB*, nn. 27, 29, 36, 64, 80; add 33, 63, 71, for a lessee of land in Rimini in 748–69, Mauricius *gloriosus magister militum*, who is a duke of Rimini in 770 in *Liber pontificalis*, XCVI.25.

[147] For Rome, *Liber pontificalis*, XCVI.3 for Toto, a *dux* from the city of Nepi but owning a *domus* in Rome; see for Toto's politics Noble, *The republic of St Peter*, pp. 112–17; the pattern was still there until the tenth century: Toubert, *Structures*, pp. 1026–30.

[148] Marazzi, 'The destinies', pp. 152–9.

wet environment of the well). It is quite plausible that these deposits were left by local communities fleeing war (the Lombards occupied Modena in this period, and the area became a political boundary) and not returning. They thus represent a snapshot of what was possessed, and seen as worth keeping, at the time. There were bronze objects, jugs and bowls, but they were almost all old, from the early empire, and abraded or mended. There was African Red Slip, too, but almost all from before 500. Both of these products were evidently no longer available on the market, but families were still using what they had been able to buy before. There was no north Italian glazed pottery, but there was local Red-Painted pottery, still produced industrially, as well as some very simple, sometimes hand-made, coarse ware. There was still in 600, that is to say, a local market for good pottery (and presumably other commodities); but the wider exchange system had ceased to reach Modena at some time in the sixth century.[149]

It was into this already regionalizing world that the Lombards came in 568–9. What effect they had on it has long been debated, with positions ranging from the view that they dispossessed all Roman landowners (maybe reducing them to slavery) to the view, popular in recent years, that they simply replicated the regional Roman state, and changed very little at all (cf. above, pp. 115–20). But the main impression of the first decades of Lombard occupation is of chaos, with dukes of individual cities acting autonomously, many of them indeed fighting for the exarch rather than for the Lombard kings, though certainly prone to abrupt shifts of allegiance. This would hardly have helped continuities of sub-regional-level landowning, even if the latter had existed on a substantial scale before 568. Conversely, however, there is little secure evidence of widespread expropriation of Roman landed property; although there must have been some, or else the new elites would not have had land of their own, there were certainly Roman aristocratic families continuing, for Roman officials can be found in the early seventh-century royal court, together with the *nobilissima romana* Theodota in the Pavia of the 680s. One family, that of Senator and Liceria, children of Albinus, documented in a Pavese charter of 714, preserved senatorial names: they were probably a family of pre-Lombard origin, but they had royal gifts of land in their possession, and were clearly *Königsnähe*. As with Remigius and Lupus in Champagne, there is no reason to think that they were unique. Continuities in Roman attitudes to property law, and to city-dwelling by elites, are other signs of Roman influence on the Lombards, and thus of the survival of elite families and their lands.[150] Again, we are reduced to speculation, for the seventh century has left us so little evidence for the

---

[149] See in general Gelichi and Giordani, *Il tesoro nel pozzo*. These sentences are adapted from Wickham, 'Early medieval archaeology', p. 10.

[150] See *CDL*, I, n. 18 for Senator and Liceria (cf. Barnish, 'Transformation and survival', pp. 154–5); Paul, *HL*, V.37 for Theodota. For property law, cf. Wickham, *Early medieval Italy*, pp. 69–70.

Lombard kingdom, but these propositions receive support from the patterns we can see in the eighth century, when our documents begin.

The first feature of our eighth-century texts that needs stressing is the fact that we cannot say much about the origins of almost any of the aristocracy in them. Senator and Liceria are perhaps an exception, in that classical names are sufficiently rare by now that they may be a marker of family origins. Other Romans must have 'Lombardized' themselves, adapting to the presumption that military activity and even political participation went with Lombard ethnicity, along lines we have seen for Francia. But even kings cannot after 712 be traced back genealogically more than a generation. The Lombard blood-aristocratic *genera* referred to by Rothari in his Edict of 643 (he himself was of the *genus* Harodos, and could list eleven male-line ancestors) are by now invisible. It is true that Paul the Deacon, writing his *Historia Langobardorum* in the 780s or 790s, could trace four generations of ancestors. He believed, wrongly, that this took him back to the Lombard invasion, but at least this shows that a family-focused memory could exist; if we had more narratives than just Paul, we might have records of others.[151] But even Paul does not bother with anyone else's families: the political actors in his narrative are not defined by them. Paolo Cammarosano has argued from this that elite status in Lombard Italy was derived from office-holding, not from ancestry. This is plausible, for eighth-century Italian documents stress the titles of offices of aristocrats to a considerable degree, with *vir magnificus*, the Lombard equivalent of the Frankish *vir inluster*, and royal offices like *strator* or gastald—or *Königsnähe*, represented by the term *gasindius regis*—regularly appearing in texts.[152] One would have to modify the argument to accommodate Giovanni Tabacco's earlier demonstration that office itself was in effect the prerogative of major landowners: in other words, landed wealth, office/*Königsnähe*, and aristocratic status were all closely linked, and land, at least, was heritable. But Cammarosano is right to play down ancestry; as in Byzantine Italy, the word *nobilis* is relatively rare in our sources, and does not seem to denote high birth exclusively, for Paul in a poem refers to *nobilitas* as being an antonym to *aegestas*, poverty—if you were without land, you were not 'noble'. The Lombards may have kept a lack of stress on ancestry that the Franks had lost already by 600 or so.[153]

A second feature of eighth-century elites was attachment to a city. The Lombard aristocracy seem above all to have been city-based and city-orientated. They are called *cives*, or they state in documents that their *casa habitationis* is in a city or its immediate suburbs, or they privilege urban churches in their pious gifts. Of the thirteen richest families documented in

---

[151] Rothari, *prologus*; Paul, *HL*, IV.37.   [152] Cammarosano, *Nobili e re*, pp. 81–4.
[153] Paul's poem is edited in *MGH*, *Poetae*, I, p. 48; he refers to *nobiles* in Brescia in *HL*, V.36. See Tabacco, 'La connessione fra potere e possesso'; cf. in general Gasparri, 'Grandi proprietari'; idem, 'Strutture militari'.

Lucca and its territory in the late Lombard period (Lucca being far and away the best documented city in Italy, then and later), only two or three seem to have lived in the countryside, and this pattern repeats itself across most of the kingdom.[154] The origins of this urban identity seem to go back to the very start of the Lombard period, for the Lombards had already fortified themselves in cities against Frankish attack in 583–4, according to Paul at least, and the boundaries of the city territories of Parma and Piacenza mattered enormously to the inhabitants of each, as two seventh-century court cases make clear. In the eighth century urban society had a clear political form. As at the national level, power at the level of the city was closely linked to landowning. The five bishops of Lucca between 713 and 818 were all from the local landowning elite just mentioned, and again there are many parallels to this elsewhere; on the secular side, to take just one example, Walpert, the father of Bishop Walprand of Lucca (737–54), had earlier been the city's duke (fl. 713–36). Each city, with its local government and local tribunals, and its episcopal structures as well, was the focus of the immediate political activity of most of the landed elite of its territory. It was also the focus of local military identity (as with the *exercitus Senensium civitatis* in a document of 730 from Siena); and there were indeed possibilities for collective urban political activity in the national arena, as with the shifting allegiances of the *nobiles* of Brescia in the 680s, narrated by Paul the Deacon.[155]

Why does this focus on the city matter? One reason, as we saw in the last chapter (pp. 118–19), is simply that the infrastructure of the Lombard kingdom was much more concentrated on the city than that of many parts of the early medieval West: institutions and officials were all essentially in the same place, and were as a result much easier to reach. Cities were also major points of reference even for country-dwellers. Another dispute, that between Siena and Arezzo in 714–15, over the diocesan boundaries of the two (which did not match those of the secular city territories), makes it clear that the small and medium owners of the contested territories, some of them living deep in the countryside of southern Tuscany, cared where the boundaries of the diocese of Arezzo lay; and they looked politically to the gastald of Siena, in an apparently systematic manner, even while disagreeing with his

---

154 In turn, *CDL*, I, n. 28, II, nn. 154, 161 (with *ChLA*, XXXVI, nn. 1065–6 = *MDL*, V, n. 170); I, nn. 30, 70; I, nn. 48, 73; I, nn. 80, 88, 102, 106, II, n. 179; I, nn. 89, 111 (with *MDL*, V, n. 231); I, nn. 105, 114, 118; II, n. 178; II, n. 214; II, n. 250; II, n. 287, for urban figures; for rural figures, II, n. 148, and the documents for Gunduald of Campori (see Wickham, *Mountains*, pp. 40–51). The landowners of Brescia in II, nn. 228, 257, are less well documented but seem similar. This paragraph and those in the next few pages are revised versions of Wickham, 'Aristocratic power', pp. 158–62.

155 For 583–4, see Paul, *HL*, III.17; for Parma and Piacenza, *CDL*, III, nn. 4, 6. For Walpert and Walprand, see esp. *CDL*, I, nn. 16, 21, 30, 40, 56, 114; see further Schwarzmaier, *Lucca*, pp. 74–8; Andreolli, *Uomini nel medioevo*, pp. 19–32. For Siena, *CDL*, I, n. 50; for Brescia in the 680s, Paul, *HL*, V.36, 38–9. Paul uses city-based political imagery elsewhere, too: e.g. *HL*, IV. 3, 51, V.2, VI.20.

attempt to make them subject to the bishop of Siena (see below, p. 393).[156] And the city focus of local politics also made the maintenance of checks and balances far easier; cities were dominated, not by one family, but many, and one local official could relatively easily be balanced by another, potentially from a rival family. We do not have precise documentation of city rivalries and factions in our period, but they must have existed; there were certainly fewer major civic offices in a place like Lucca than there were families to fill them, and the resultant struggles probably made Italian cities look very much like the highly factious Clermont of the Merovingian period, analysed by Ian Wood.[157]

Italian cities were, then, strong social and political foci for the eighth-century upper classes. We shall see in Chapter 10, however, that the period around 700 marks more or less the low point in the material prosperity of cities in the peninsula (pp. 644–56). It is true that some elements of ambitious building survived, as can be argued from an early eighth-century list of building prices, the *Memoratorium de mercedibus comacinorum*, which lists the costs of different kinds of roofing and walling, internal decoration in wood, gypsum, and marble, and even, perhaps, a hypocaust.[158] In the exarchate, some fairly impressive town houses in Rimini are described in eighth-century leases, with two storeys, a dining-room (*triclineum*) and bedrooms above, kitchen, storeroom, and furnace below, the whole tiled; in one case there were columns and a tower, in another a portico, privy, and private bath. These probably show that urban display was more developed in Byzantine parts of northern Italy, and excavations of similar buildings in Italian cities tend to confirm that, as we shall see (pp. 648–9).[159] But the material framing of these buildings even in the exarchate, and still more in the Lombard kingdom, was relatively simple; the display which is clear in these texts has not been found archaeologically, except in churches. The same goes for the exchange networks of the north, which by the eighth century had become very localized indeed, far more than those of northern Francia (below, pp. 730–41). Thanks to the archaeology of the last two decades, we have a double image of Lombard aristocrats: as relatively city-focused (above all with respect to the Franks, very few of whose elite were obviously city-dwelling), but also as living in a materially simple environment, with smaller-scale exchange networks than those of Francia. Put simply, the Lombard aristocracy was both more urbanized and poorer than that of the Franks.

[156] For the gastald of Siena in the countryside, see above all *CDL*, I, n. 19 (pp. 63, 67, 71, 74); cf. above, Ch. 3, n. 174.

[157] Wood, 'Ecclesiastical politics'.

[158] The *Memoratorium* is edited in *Leges langobardorum*, pp. 177–9. A rare reference to stone in an aristocratic house description for Lombard Italy is *CDL*, II, n. 127.

[159] *CB*, nn. 64–5, 69, 71–3; cf. Cagiano de Azevedo, 'Le case descritte'; Ortalli, 'L'edilizia abitativa'. For private baths, see Ward-Perkins, *From classical antiquity*, pp. 146–8.

This material weakness is not restricted to the ceramic record and to urban archaeology; it can be inferred from our private charters, too, for Lombard aristocratic landowning does not seem to have been particularly extensive. King Aistulf in 750 used the phrase *maiores et potentes* for soldiers with the equivalent of seven tenant-houses: this is not a large number. Did seven tenant-houses really make one an 'aristocrat'? It is hard to tell, for phrases like *maior et potens* are pretty vague, but if we were to restrict our definition of aristocracy further, say to people in our documents with more than five *curtes* (estates, the Italian equivalent of *villae*) each, which is not an ambitious criterion for wealth even in the early middle ages, then only about ten 'aristocrats' would be documented in the nearly 300 charters for the Lombard period. None of this last group have much more land than that, either, even though they are *viri magnifici*, *gasindi*, royal officials, or bishops. Even the greatest Lombard aristocrats could not compete with men like Bertram or Abbo in Francia, and they would often indeed have been outclassed even by middling Frankish *proceres*.[160] It seems clear, in fact, that the effective Lombard aristocracy regularly operated on a pretty small scale: five *curtes* would be closer to a maximum than to a minimum. Rotpert *vir magnificus* of Agrate, north-east of Milan, left four estates, two or more tenant houses and two fields to his female heirs and his favourite churches in 745; the bequest is atypical only in that Rotpert made an apparently complete list of half his property—the scale of the document is widely parallelled elsewhere.[161] Four or eight estates is of course enough to live very comfortably from; but it is not much if one wants to buy enough to maintain a complex interregional exchange system, to maintain a powerful armed entourage, or to fund a rich urban church, at the same time as endowing one's heirs properly. Nor could kings (who certainly were hugely rich) underwrite an entire exchange economy on their own. On the economic level, Lombard Italy, however urban, looks decidedly modest.

The stratum of society that does seem to be more prosperous than in Francia—and is certainly better documented—is that of small and medium landowners, owner-cultivators and small-scale rentiers, most of them with less than the seven tenants stressed by Aistulf. In Francia the evidence for

---

[160] Aistulf, 2, 3. Cf. *MGH, Concilia*, I, n. 18, for Francia in 792–3, in which royal *vassi* are envisaged as holding 30 tenant-houses (*casatae*) for the smallest, 200 *casatae* for the biggest—an order of magnitude higher than in Italy. An approximate list of the seven absolutely richest documented landowners before 774 might be Walfred of Pisa (*CDL*, I, n. 116), Gisulf of Lodi (II, nn. 137, 155, 226), Erfo of Friuli (II, n. 162), Gaidoald of Pistoia (II, n. 203), John of Persiceta (II, n. 271), Taido of Bergamo (II, n. 293), Peredeus of Lucca (II, nn. 154, 161; *ChLA*, XXXVI, nn. 1065–6 = *MDL*, V, n. 170). The most powerful ducal families, like those of Ratchis and Aistulf in Friuli and Desiderius in Brescia (before they became kings), would have to be added as well. Friuli may well have been the focus of a relatively rich aristocratic grouping; Gasparri, 'Istituzioni e poteri', reconstructs the family and monastic networks of Erfo and John in particular.

[161] *CDL*, I, n. 82 (Wickham, 'Aristocratic power', p. 161, incorrectly states that four estates made up the whole of Rotpert's land); on this will see La Rocca, 'Segni di distinzione'.

them is so fleeting in some areas that scholars have doubted their existence. Such a doubt is misplaced, but no one who works on Italy has ever had it. Modest landholders dominate our documentation; some of them are even city-dwelling, though of course most lived in the countryside. Their lands were scattered across the territories of every city, intercutting with lands of the rich that were themselves highly scattered. They formed the Lombard army as its *exercitales*, and often used military titles, such as *vir devotus*, though they were probably mostly seldom called up and of doubtful use when they were.[162] Their existence in such large numbers is an essential explanation for the relatively small scale of aristocratic landowning: it is likely that a rather larger percentage of the land-area of the Lombard kingdom was in the hands of modest landholders than would have been the case in much of Francia, particularly its Seine valley heartland. Their impact on social action will be discussed, above all using Lucchese material, in Chapter 7 (pp. 387–93).

As with Francia, it may be useful to give a couple of more detailed examples of how aristocratic properties were structured. Gaidoald *medicus regum* (he had been a royal doctor since at least 726) in 767 gave to his own monastery, S. Bartolomeo just outside Pistoia, what may have been half his properties: they amounted to six *curtes*, in the territories of Pistoia, Lucca, probably Florence, and Cornino down the Tuscan coast; the only property he had outside northern Tuscany was a religious foundation in the royal capital at Pavia. Gaidoald's properties are among the largest we have documented. He was clearly a civic aristocrat from Pistoia, with a royal link that had brought him land 250 km away, but the rest of his land was in three contiguous dioceses, plus Lucca's outlying dependency in Cornino. Another of the major magnates we have, Taido, *civis* of Bergamo and *gasindio domni regis*, made his will in 774, while Charlemagne was actually besieging Pavia: his eight *curtes* were all in the territories of Bergamo, Sirmione, and Verona, a span of 100 km, and so were ten unattached *casae massariciae*, tenant houses, apart from one on the Po, probably close to Pavia, for it was given to a Pavese church. Taido was explicitly city-based, and half his land was in his native city territory; one might guess that his family had a marriage connection in Verona. Although he was a royal retainer, *gasindio*, he cites no gifts from the king and, as in the case of Gaidoald, if they existed, they did not transform his position, that is to say of a very spatially circumscribed landowner.[163]

These examples are entirely typical of Lombard Italy. The largest owners whose properties survive in our documents—and they are not very large by

---

[162] Lombard landowners made wills before campaigns in *CDL*, I, nn. 114 (Bishop Walprand of Lucca), 117, II, n. 230, V, n. 52; see Gasparri, 'Strutture militari', pp. 681–4.

[163] *CDL*, II, nn. 203 (cf. I, n. 38 for Gaidoald in 726), 293; cf. Wickham, *Early medieval Italy*, pp. 132–5.

Frankish standards—were focused on two or three contiguous city territories at the most, with a couple of outlying properties maybe, in Pavia perhaps, or (in the case of Tuscan owners) Corsica, which had been recently conquered by the Lombards.[164] Smaller landowners, which make up the huge bulk of our documents, owned inside one city territory only. Tassilo *vir devotus* of Lucca, one of the thirteen richest Lucchese owners mentioned earlier, made his will in 768, giving lands to ten Lucchese churches, urban and rural (unless they were sold off for alms). They included between one and five estates (depending on how generous we are in translating the word *res*), eight unattached *casae massariciae*, and six isolated fields, all in the territory of Lucca (including one house in Cornino).[165] The high degree of fragmentation of estate structures that this text shows is entirely normal in Italy (see below, pp. 295–6). If this was an eleventh-century text, one might also, paradoxically, use it to argue how widely spread elite landowning could be, for it extended to 20 km north of the city, 30 km west of the city, and 30 km to the south-east, as well as the Cornino land 100 km down the coast, stretching across nearly the whole of the Lucchesia, and helping to maintain it as an economic unit focused on the city.[166] Such an argument assumes that aristocrats were mostly restricted to single cities, which by the eleventh century one can treat as established. The argument indeed, taken on its own terms, works equally well for the eighth century; Lucca and its territory must have been a very effective unit, given the fact that scattered estates like this one are fairly frequent in our documentation. Nevertheless, the geographical presuppositions it involves show that we are a long way from Adalgisel-Grimo, let alone the really big Frankish aristocrats. The subregional range of landowning that is dimly visible for the north in the Ostrogothic period (p. 209) had entirely gone by the eighth century.

One element in the construction of aristocratic properties is much better documented in Italy than in Gaul/Francia: the 'land market'. In Francia, land sales were certainly normal, both of whole *villae* (as in Bertram's will) and smaller plots, but they tend to be referred to casually in other documents, and relatively few charters of sale survive.[167] In Italy, however, such documents are common, making up 24 per cent of our eighth-century private charters for the north up to 774. In one case, the so called 'Alahis list', we have an atypical but illuminating sidelight on the process: a document listing the forty-four charters of a certain Alahis, a protégé of King Liutprand

[164] For Corsica, see *CDL*, I, nn. 114, 116, II, n. 295, for important Lucchese and Pisan landowners.

[165] *CDL*, I, n. 214.

[166] e.g. Wickham, 'Economia e società rurale'.

[167] Among the few sale documents for Merovingian Francia west of the Rhine are Debus, 'Studien', n. 24; Pardessus, *Diplomata*, nn. 460, 470, 528, 546; *ChLA*, XLVII, n. 1465. For the 'land market' in the early middle ages, see Davies, 'Sale, price'; Feller, Gramain, Weber, 'La marché de la terre'.

(712–44), made for the nun Ghittia, probably of Pisa, probably around 770. Three-quarters of the group are sales to Alahis by laymen and women. Of the others, three are *cartulae de mundio accepto*, probably meaning documents in which the other party transferred the *mundium*, the legal guardianship, of a daughter or sister whom Alahis had married; one text, the *cartula da Iohanni de morte germani sui in Alahis*, seems to refer to a homicide composition; six are royal diplomas from Liutprand to Alahis, mostly confirming property—one, however, confirms all of Alahis's acquisitions, which, as we can see, were many. Exactly who Alahis was we cannot be sure, except that he obviously had royal links and was probably also based in Pisa, and how much family land he had is irrecoverable.[168] But land dealing was normal for him, much more normal than any other activity that might involve the writing of documents. It is entirely possible that, already (or still) in the eighth century in Italy, substantial sets of properties could be bought and sold as easily as they could be inherited. But if so it is no less striking that they were almost all localized in single city-territories: the economic circuits most people operated inside, although dense and complex, remained relatively small scale.

The foregoing observations all relate to the Lombard kingdom of the north; the two southern duchies are less well documented, but do show parallels. The Farfa documents, for the southern fringe of the duchy of Spoleto, show a set of prosperous urban owners in Rieti who are similar to those in Lucca: they own above all in the Rietino, though sometimes including a house in Spoleto, and seldom mention land elsewhere.[169] Beneventan texts, above all for S. Sofia in Benevento itself and, at the very end of the eighth century, for S. Vincenzo al Volturno, show an aristocracy closely linked with ducal (after 787, princely) politics, and one could say that in the case of Benevento we have a documentation for the capital that is missing for Pavia and Spoleto. The Beneventan texts show a geographical range for landowning that is hard to identify further north; aristocrats based in the capital not infrequently have land on the Adriatic coast, up to 200 km to the east, and also to the north-west, up to the frontier with Lazio. Even then, however, the largest spreads of lay land in our texts do not actually constitute more than eight or ten estates, and usually less. Eighth-century Benevento may well have shown a more integrated aristocratic community

---

[168] *CDL*, II, n. 295. Alahis's charters were listed in this text together with those of other owners, as a list 'of charters which Teuspert returned to the nun Ghittia and her daughters Aliperga and Willerada'. How the participants fit together is obscure, although several of the charter-makers have names beginning in Al-, as does Ghittia's daughter, and they may have been her former husband's family.

[169] See for Pando and his family esp. *CDL*, IV.1, n. 35, V, nn. 3, 26, 58, 99; for Hilderic, gastald of Rieti, esp. V, nn. 60, 100; the widest spread of land is owned by Acerisius in 770 (V, n. 55), who lived in Rieti, had an estate in Spoleto, and owned unspecified quantities of land in four other territories. See for commentary Gasparri, 'Il ducato di Spoleto'; Costambeys, *Piety, property*, pp. 273–6; and above all Collavini, 'Duchi e società locali', pp. 132–9.

than in the north, unifying a whole sub-region, but not necessarily a richer one. This fits some features of its archaeology, as we shall see (pp. 736–7). But S. Sofia and S. Vincenzo (and also Montecassino, the most important of the three, though with fewer surviving documents) were emerging in the years around 800 as really serious landowners in their own right, taking the scale of private ownership to levels not known for the peninsula for two centuries and more.[170]

I have been arguing that Lombard aristocrats, indeed Italian aristocrats as a whole, were by the eighth century primarily locally focused, with single city territories the norm, and more than two or three very rare, except sometimes in the duchy of Benevento; that that focus included a clearly identifiable urban orientation, usually indeed a town house at the centre; and that the global extent of aristocratic landowning was by the eighth century fairly restricted, in sharp contrast to the huge properties of the highest-ranking aristocrats of the late empire, and also to the major figures of contemporary Francia. One could rephrase this by saying that Italy by now simply lacked the top levels of landowning that the other two societies had; the only owners in Italy who could match Bertram or Abbo would have been the pope, the Lombard king, and the two southern ruling dukes; and no one would have come anywhere near the landowning of the Frankish kings themselves. It is hardly surprising that the Franks could sweep into the Po plain three times in the twenty years 754–74. In the ninth century this would change, as some aristocratic landowning on a larger scale began to be visible under the aegis of Carolingian patronage, of families of both Lombard and Frankish origin, and as ecclesiastical institutions became steadily richer through gifts and sales, both in the north and in the south.[171] In the eighth century, however, this pattern sharply reduced the ability of the Lombard aristocracy to operate politically outside the orbit of the kings and dukes, who were so much richer than they. As we have seen, the urban focus of royal government allowed the Lombard kings to have a capillary political presence; the relative poverty of their aristocracy made royal patronage that much more attractive, too. In terms of the six criteria for aristocratic identity set out at the start of the chapter, ancestry was, as already argued, relatively marginal; lifestyle is barely documented (it seems to have paralleled that in

---

[170] See *Chronicon S. Sophiae*, II.1, 3, 4, 8–9, III.30, for Wadulf in the early years of the century; *Chronicon Vulturnense*, nn. 34, 36–9, 41, 43, 47, for owners in the years 800–17. See further Gasparri, 'Il ducato e il principato', pp. 122–3. Poto, a hugely rich owner with fifty estates, notes for whose will survive from the middle decades of the ninth century (ed. Pohl, *Werkstätte*, pp. 197–9; commentaries in ibid., pp. 53–5 and Martin, *La Pouille*, p. 177; Martin *et al.*, *Regesti*, n. 734, dates it to the 830s–840s), was probably from one of the princely families, and so would show the scale of princely, rather than private, land. See in general Martin, *La Pouille*, pp. 176–81, and for the monasteries Wickham, 'Monastic lands'.

[171] For the ninth century see in general Hlawitschka, *Franken, Alemannen*; Feller, *Les Abruzzes*, pp. 180–90; Collavini, *Honorabilis domus*, pp. 38–70; Cammarosano, *Nobili e re*, pp. 117–22, 174–85.

Francia);[172] land was an indispensable starting-point, but not sufficient for independent action; office and *Königsnähe* were of major importance. The Lombard political system was very coherent as a result. By contrast, however, it was economically and socially fragmented between its city territories, and of course was even more so if we take the Italian peninsula as a whole, as we shall see more clearly in Chapter 11.

We know much less about Spain. What documentary evidence we have for the Visigothic period indicates that the scale of its aristocratic property-owning was more similar to Italy than to Francia. But Spain also presents a problem. In northern Francia and Italy, as we have seen, what we know about the exchange networks of the early middle ages, mostly from archaeology, tends to support and fill out what the documents tell us about aristocratic property-owning. These networks will be analysed in Chapter 11 on their own terms, because ceramic studies (their main element) are tailor-made for comparative analysis, and indeed can only be understood comparatively, but they do essentially fit the contrast between the worlds on each side of the Alps that we have been exploring. In Spain we do not have a fit of this kind; to an extent, our written evidence and our archaeology point in opposite directions, for the Visigothic period at least. Given that our written evidence is largely normative and narrative, mostly laws and hagiographies, with only two land-transfer documents surviving in full for the whole of the fifth to seventh centuries (although they are supported by a formulary and by the slate archive, of which more in a moment)—and only half-a-dozen others for the eighth century for that matter[173]—one might legitimately conclude that the archaeology had greater weight; but the written evidence is at least homogeneous. Essentially, one has to work out how to reconcile two somewhat different sets of data, or else how to choose between them. And here a second problem appears, one of presentation. The ceramic evidence for Spain is only going to make full sense in the context of other regions, and therefore the full implications of an alternative model to the Visigothic documentary material will only be explicable in that context. I have therefore chosen to split the argument into two, presenting one perspective in detail here, and the other in Chapter 11. Spain's aristocracy, and its changing resources across our period, will be summed up in the later

---

[172] Lifestyle markers are much scarcer than in Francia, but see the stories in Paul, *HL*, IV.37, 51, V.34, 40, VI.24, 26, 51, 55, for aristocratic courage, prickly honour, and revenge. Drunkenness was more frowned on than in Francia: ibid., V.2–3, 39.

[173] For the two documents, both for Vicentius of Huesca, see n. 180. There are also some fragments of parchment originals, ed. in *ChLA*, XLVI, nn. 1398–402. The formulary is *Form. Wis.* Eighth-century Latin documents are edited in Floriano, *Diplomática española*, nn. 7, 9, 12, 14, 15 (9, a charter of King Silo of the Asturias, the only original, is in *ChLA*, XLVI, n. 1397). The only Arab document is the Pact of Theudemir of 713, of which there is a convenient text in Melville and Ubaydli, *Christians and Moors*, pp. 10–13 (it is attacked as a forgery in Barceló, 'Els *fulūs* de Ṭanǧa', pp. 8–9).

chapter. Here, nonetheless, the written sources will be analysed, so that the parallels they offer to Francia and Italy can be explored.

Spain was, as we saw in Chapter 3 (pp. 78–9), relatively isolated from the Mediterranean network of the Roman empire, especially its internal regions. But it certainly had elements of a rich aristocracy. Not that late Roman Spain is well served by written sources of any kind, but one clear evidence for it is the imperial house of Theodosius, for Theodosius came from Spain, and many family members remained there. Two of them, Didymus and Verenianus, in 408–9 organized a private army of peasants and slaves in Lusitania (the south-west of the peninsula) against the usurpers Constantine III and Constans, very much along the lines of Ecdicius in Gaul and Tullianus in Italy in the next century or so. Late Roman Spain does not yet show the dissonance between documentary and archaeological evidence just mentioned: another sign of aristocratic prosperity is a substantial set of rich fourth-century villas, as can be seen in Jean-Gérard Gorges's detailed survey, evenly spread across most of the peninsula, though concentrating in Catalonia, the Ebro valley and the northern Meseta in the north, and the rich lands of Baetica (the Guadalquivir valley) in the south, stretching up to Mérida and southern Portugal. The first two of these groups are also linked by the basic network of late Roman fine wares in inland Spain, *terra sigillata hispánica tardía* (TSHT), whose kilns were concentrated in the upper Duero and Ebro valleys; there are parallel TSHT networks on the Tajo and going down to the Guadalquivir (see below, p. 742). Gorges supposed that his rich villas marked urban decline and increasing self-sufficiency; one could anyway doubt that specialized mosaicists were exactly a sign of self-sufficiency, but TSHT distributions point to a network of markets selling industrial fine wares across most of the inland of the peninsula. Here, we seem to have a prosperous local aristocracy sustaining a local exchange system which was unusually independent of the structures of the Roman state, and which ought, in principle, to have been able to maintain itself thereafter.[174]

The late fifth and early sixth centuries, the first two generations of Visigothic rule, are a near blank in the written documentation for Spain. Later regional evidence allows us to make some proposals about the survival of aristocracies in some parts of the peninsula, as we shall see in a moment; but apart from that we can say little until after Leovigild's unification in the 570s. From then on, Visigothic secular and ecclesiastical legislation certainly indicates that major landowners, whether laymen or churches, were important. The wealth and status of *nobiles* is taken for granted in the royal lawcode. Ecclesiastical legislation refigured church hierarchies in terms of the sorts of private dependence characteristic of landowning (see above, p. 99). That legislation is also harsh in its protection of church lands, to the extent

---

[174] *PLRE*, II, s.v. Didymus 1; for the villas, Gorges, *Les villas hispano-romaines*, pp. 51–7 (p. 51 for self-sufficiency).

that in 656 the Tenth Council of Toledo voided the will of Bishop Riccimir of Dumio (near Braga in northern Portugal) because he had freed fifty unfree dependants (*mancipia*) of the church—this was illegal because it defrauded church property, which had to be maintained 'for the needs of the poor'. The fact that the unfree tenants of Spain were also systematically pursued (according to the laws) if they fled their estates, with the shrillest legislation on this subject dating to as late as 702 (see below, p. 526), confirms one in the view that the Visigothic rulers valued aristocratic wealth as a principle, and were keen to protect it.[175] How rich these landowners were is much harder to tell from the laws. Chindasuinth in 645 promulgated a dower law prohibiting husbands from giving more than 10 per cent of their property to brides, although allowing *primates vel seniores* to add to this 1,000 *solidi*, twenty (unfree) boys and girls, and twenty horses: these additions seem essentially to be decorative, so we might conclude that Chindasuinth envisaged that aristocratic wealth could come to well over 10,000 *solidi*—not a huge sum by Roman standards, but far from negligible.[176] Beyond this, we can say that aristocratic collective identity was sufficiently great that in 683 a council of Toledo restored the noble status (*nobilitas*, or *titulus honestioris*) and the property of all those who had lost civil rights through the acts of kings for nearly fifty years, since 639: although they had been politically and economically marginalized, they still mattered to the rest of the elite.[177] This elite was by the seventh century a mix of ethnic Romans and Visigoths, living by Visigothic law, but operating in what one could characterize as a relatively militarized late Roman world, and even maintaining Roman-style legal distinctions between aristocrats and the ordinary free. It was one which had parallels to Aquitaine; even though, unlike in Aquitaine, Roman law had gone, a number of Roman presuppositions about elite cultural traditions had survived in Spain. Isidore of Seville's classicizing tendencies (above, p. 95) had a substantial resonance in the peninsula.

Regional evidence supports this picture of Roman traditions for aristocratic identity and wealth, but adds one important element: a visible tendency to geographical localization. Mérida is one case, as seen in the *Vitas patrum Emeritensium*, a text of the 630s which discusses, above all, three sixth-century bishops of the city. In the first half of the century a gift by two local aristocrats, unnamed but certainly Roman, a 'very noble man of senatorial origin, of first rank in the city' (*primarius civitatis ex genere*

---

[175] For *nobiles* (and other equivalent words) in *LV*, see King, *Law and society*, pp. 183–6; Claude, *Adel, Kirche*, pp. 80–91, is a basic guide. For the church and landed dependence, Barbero and Vigil, *La formación*, pp. 53–104. Riccimir: X Toledo, *Aliud decretum* (ed. Vives, *Concilios*, pp. 322–4). 702 law: *LV*, IX.1.21.

[176] *LV*, III.1.5. Note Prokopios, *Wars*, V.12.51–4, on the 2,000 armed men that King Theudis's Roman wife could fund from her estates (*oikia*): a lot, if the story is reliable (see also above, p. 99).

[177] XIII Toledo, c. 1 (ed. Vives, *Concilios*, pp. 415–16); see Claude, *Adel, Kirche*, pp. 88–9.

senatorum nobilissimus vir) and his wife of a *nobilis prosapies*, of their whole property to Bishop Paul made him 'more powerful than all the powerful', and when this property came to the church it became the richest in Spain. This account is highly unusual in hagiographies, as is the unorthodox use that was made of the wealth: Paul's heir Fidelis was imposed by Paul on his church as his successor in return for a commitment to leave that land to the church at Fidelis' death if he was accepted as bishop, a clearly simoniac move—Fidelis later indeed reportedly saw off opponents by threatening to leave and take his estates with him. Mérida was the capital of late Roman Spain, so urban landowning on a large scale makes more sense than in some other places. Masona, the next bishop (c. 570–610), was so rich that at Easter boys dressed in silk paraded before him 'as if before a king'. The bishops of Mérida were, furthermore, in Masona's time also matched by a network of city-based civil officials focused on the *dux civitatis*. In the late 580s the latter was Claudius, a Roman *nobili genere* (contrasting with Masona, who, although a Catholic bishop, was ethnically a Goth); his subordinates were rich Gothic *nobiles*, who plotted against Masona on religious grounds and lost their lands, their *patrimonia vel honores*, as a result.[178] So an urban aristocracy of Goths and Romans and ecclesiastics, who were landowners, sometimes on a large scale, is visible in this text. But this was also a very localized hierarchy. Mérida had links with the king in Toledo, 200 km away, at least from Leovigild's time, it is true. The Gothic aristocracy of the city included some who were counts of other cities, although their locations are unspecified. No other Spanish city is even named in the text; the rest of Spain is only represented as a place of exile for Masona, in the period, probably in the 580s, when Leovigild expelled him from the city. Méridan politics, however rich its participants, was exclusively focused on one place, with even Toledo only appearing as an external threat. And yet the city was, and remained, one of the main centres of Spain, dominating its major north–south road as late as the seventh century, in no sense a marginal location.[179]

A second area is the middle Ebro valley. This is the location for another hagiography, Braulio of Zaragoza's *Vita S. Aemiliani*, written around 636 about the saint now known as S. Millán, who died in 576 (supposedly at the age of 100), as well as for our only two fully surviving Visigothic-period documents, from 551 and c. 576, listing the lands of Bishop Vicentius of Huesca. In the documents we find evidence of a property scattered across around thirty *loci* in the Zaragoza–Lleida–Huesca triangle, about 100 km in

---

[178] *Vitas patrum emeritensium*, IV.2–5, for Paul and Fidelis, V.3 for Masona's boys, V.10, 11, for lay aristocrats.

[179] For Toledo and the kings, ibid., III, V.4–11. Counts of cities: V.10. Exile: V.6–7. Outside Spain, Narbonne appears in V.12; African and east Mediterranean links appear in III, IV.1, 3, V.11. For the road in the seventh century, see *Vita Fructuosi*, cc. 11–12. The best analysis of the situation of Mérida remains Collins, 'Merida and Toledo'.

length on each side, and into the Pyrenees. How large the fragments were is entirely unclear—some were probably estates, some houses, some only collections of single fields; but the scale of property-owning is closer to Remigius or Aredius in Gaul, or to any of the Italian owners we have looked at, than to the major Frankish landowners. The life of Aemilianus depicts a set of landowners in the Ebro valley above Zaragoza, all with late Roman names and titles—the *senatores* Sicorius, Nepotianus, Honorius, the *curialis* Maximus, whose relatives and servile dependants Aemilianus cured of blindness and demonic possession. *Senator* and *curialis* do not seem to be Roman technical terms; rather, they are markers of local status. This group was a local ruling class, operating independently of the Visigothic kingdom, until the latter conquered them in c.574. Their autonomy presupposes that they too did not possess widely, if at all, outside the middle Ebro; they can plausibly be seen as similar to Vicentius in the scale of their properties.[180] The whole zone seems to be one of locally owning aristocrats in a late Roman tradition, at least throughout the sixth century. By the mid-seventh century Zaragoza was certainly integrally absorbed into the kingdom of Toledo, as Braulio's own career shows: bishop of the city, he was a friend of Isidore of Seville, and close to King Chindasuinth; he may have been the dominant cleric in Spain from Isidore's death in 636 to his own in 651, and was the focus of a network of *amicitia* that included every other contemporary literary figure. But Braulio was himself part of a local episcopal dynasty, for he succeeded his brother, the *nobilis* John, in office; his letters include several to what appear to be other Zaragozan notables. The local aristocracy of the Ebro was absorbed into the kingdom, but was not necessarily much changed.[181]

A third area, the northern Meseta, is larger and less homogeneous. We know of Visigothic royal estates here: King Reccesuinth in 672 died in one, the *villula* Gerticos, unlocated but in the territory of Salamanca; private estates can be added if we include the *opulentissimus domus* of the *illustris vir* Riccimir in the Bierzo, a mountain river basin just to the north-east of the Meseta, referred to in the late seventh-century writings of the crazed ascetic Valerius.[182] What gives the Meseta its particular interest in the Visigothic period, however, is the collection of slate texts, around a half of them from Diego Álvaro on the edge of the central mountains, around 50 km south of

---

[180] The Vicentius texts are edited in Fita, 'Patrologia visigótica', pp. 151–7; the more recent edition in Fortacín, 'La donación', is almost inaccessible, but is reproduced in Corcoran, 'The donation'. For a commentary, see Díaz, 'El testamento de Vicente', with Ariño and Díaz, 'Poblamiento y organización del espacio'. For Braulio, *Vita S. Emiliani*, cc. 18, 22–4; see above all Castellanos, *Poder social*, pp. 37–78.

[181] For John, Ildefonsus of Toledo, *De viris illustribus*, c. 11; Eugenius of Toledo, *Carmen* XXI, ll.17–18; for Braulio's letters to probable Zaragozan notables see his *Epp.*, nn. 19, 20, 28–30, 34. Cf. Castellanos, *Poder social*, pp. 29–33.

[182] Julian of Toledo, *Historia Wambae*, c. 3; Valerius of Bierzo, *Ordo querimoniae*, cc. 5, 7. See for the terminology, Isla, '*Villa, villula*'.

Salamanca, and secondarily from a group of villages just nearby, which had
equal access to the slate of the zone. They survive because slate was locally
convenient as an alternative to the wax tablets that most late Roman
landowners used as scratch pads, an alternative that was far less destructible
(even if fragile: few of these texts survive intact). The Diego Álvaro texts
were found in a small group of neighbouring sites, excavated in the
1940s–1950s and never published; they are the only known dating evidence
for them, and are from the period c.560–700. They vary substantially in
type, from sale agreements to registrations of witnessing (all fragmentary);
in particular, there are numerous texts simply consisting of lists, often called
notitiae. These are essentially estate-management documents, mostly for
Diego Álvaro though with exact parallels in the other Salmantine find-
sites. (I shall treat them as if they were from one estate, as they are so
homogeneous; the argument would not change substantially if they were
from more than one.) They are the best evidence for the northern Mediterranean in our period of the daily level of land management, for many of
them are ad hoc registrations of renders or expenses, a *notitia de casios*
(cheeses) from Galinduste, consisting of a list of names and one *froma*
(*forma*, cheese-round) each, apparently owed in rent; a *notitia de vervices*
listing sheep which were given out on specific occasions; several lists of
names with quantities of grain ascribed to each, which are certainly rents;
a *notitia* in which 'it is set down that we gave to Simplicius' grain, a lamb, a
pig, a cow, and so on. These texts show the level of practical literacy that one
could evidently consider normal even in the far corners of the landscape.[183]

What concerns do the Diego Álvaro slates show? The estate economy was
clearly built up out of rents, which were catalogued separately by type.
Grain is the most common item in our lists, followed by animals and animal
products—one list is of fifty-plus cows and horses, and may be a register of
animals the estate actually held. One text lists just people and their children:
dependants of the estate of some kind. Others list outgoings, like the goods
given to Simplicius, which could go through the *erarium* (the villa's strong-
room), as another text said. There is no money mentioned in the rentals: this
was a kind-based economic system, although carefully controlled. But coins
were used as well: sales, and even debt agreements, in money survive in the
slate set. Two court-case fragments concern animals, which were undoubtedly important in the area (it is above all a pastoral zone today); another
mentions a vineyard. Four texts list artisanal products, in two cases perhaps

---

[183] Isabel Velázquez's *Las pizarras* is the basic edition, updated with more slates and better
photographs in *Documentos de época visigoda*. (The new slates do not change the interpretations offered here; my citations are mostly from the previous edn., the numbering of which is
the same.) See *Las pizarras*, pp. 42–51, on the find-sites of the slates, pp. 58–9 on the source of
the rock, and pp. 72–4 on the dating (only one slate, not from this area, may date later, to c.750).
Texts cited here are nn. 11 (cheese), not from Diego Álvaro, 97 (sheep), 45–8 (grain rents), 54
(Simplicius). See also *Documentos de época visigoda*, nn. 124, 141.

movables that had been stolen: they include clothes and tools, mostly of a fairly basic type, which could have been made locally.[184]

On one level, these texts show that Diego Álvaro was in the seventh century fully part of a political and cultural system stretching across the whole of Spain. Their attestation of capillary literacy—shared among many people, for the hands are different—is itself one aspect of this; so is the formal witnessing, in one case in front of six public officials; so is the fact that the sales and witnessing on occasion reflect the formularies surviving in the *Formulae Wisigothicae*, a Visigothic text which was widely used from the eighth century to the eleventh in northern Spanish documents. On another, however, they are even more localized than the Ebro material. No cities are mentioned in any of these texts except, once, Toledo, which was only 120 km away (over the mountains, however). The estate documents themselves barely mention place-names at all; it is likely that all the rent-payers in them were highly local, though whether the estate was itself large or small is unknown. Economic links to the outside world are almost entirely absent, in fact. Diego Álvaro shows a Roman tradition reduced to the level of the microregion.[185]

The written sources for Visigothic landowning, taken as a whole, show a remarkably Roman Spain, a set of social patterns that had changed relatively little since the fifth century, with the important caveat that they had become very localized, restricted to single city territories or little more, often indeed (as with Diego Álvaro) less, with only political, not economic, links to the capital. They resemble Italy more than Gaul in their restricted geographical scale; as already noted, they resemble Aquitaine rather than Italy (both Byzantine and Lombard) or northern Gaul in their political and cultural continuities, for the aristocracy as a whole seems to have been less culturally or ideologically reshaped than elsewhere. It is not that there is nothing Visigothic about the areas I have described: names slowly became more Gothic, particularly in the seventh century (though never as fully as in Lombard Italy or the Frankish heartland); law was certainly fully Gothic, by 650 at the latest and probably from the start; furnished burials in the Meseta in the sixth century begin to show Germanic influence in the metal-work found in female graves, which is at least an indicator of the cultural influence of a partially new ruling class on the local population (the ceramics

---

[184] *Las pizarras*, nn. 53 (animals), 55 (people), 97 (the '*erararium*', recte *erarium*). Velázquez, ibid., p. 665, sees the latter word as meaning the public treasury, but the text does not make much sense to me as a tax account. For money, nn. 8, 40A (sales), 75 (debt). Court-case fragments: nn. 39, 40B, 92. Artisanal products: nn. 49, 50, 102, with *Documentos de época visigoda*, n. 115. (*Las pizarras*, nn. 8, 92, 102 are not from Diego Álvaro.) The slates as a whole show tight management; nn. 5 (not from Diego Álvaro) and 97 show incomings and outgoings together, and n. 103 (for a little south of the Salamanca area) deals with the problem of *fraudem* when *mancipii* pick olives for a lord.

[185] For sales, cf. *Las Pizarras*, n. 8 with *Form. Wis.*, n. 32; for witnessing, see Ch. 3, n. 120. For Toledo, *Las pizarras*, n. 75 (cf. p. 667).

in the same graves are in a Roman tradition, however).[186] But Spain seems to have become the Visigothic kingdom without experiencing the breaks from the Roman world that were common elsewhere, something that was made possible, perhaps, by the relative marginality of most of Spain (except the coast, and Baetica) to that Roman world. Hence also the ambition, and the unadulterated Roman legal rhetoric, of the kings of the seventh century, as outlined in Chapter 3 (pp. 95–6). The local aristocracies of each area often had Roman roots (most clearly in the case of the middle Ebro), or mixed roots that were expressed in largely Roman terms (as at Mérida); the 'senatorial' elite of the Ebro and the clearly marked *honestiores* or *nobiles* of the laws were aristocracies who were, doubtless, focused on office and land rather than ancestry, but who were often old families for all that. At most, they had become militarized or ecclesiastical, but even their militarization was perhaps incomplete. They were probably not hugely wealthy; the history of the Mérida bishops is the only hint of that, and the other signs we have of their activity are rather more modest, on Italian rather than Frankish (or late Roman) levels. But they were at least a stable elite, and they appear so throughout our written documentation.

It must, finally, be added that these patterns extended into the post-Visigothic period too, at least in some areas. Mérida's archaeological continuities, which go on into the ninth century, are one instance of this (below, pp. 661–2), and the Guadalquivir valley from Seville to Córdoba, the core of the emirate, is probably another. The Visigothic ancestry claimed by several ninth- and tenth-century Arab figures, most notably the chronicler Ibn al-Qūṭiya ('Son of the Gothic woman') and the southern aristocrat and famous rebel 'Umar ibn Ḥafṣūn (d. 917), is another. Most of all, perhaps, the Banū Qasī, the lineage of lords who ruled the frontier lands of the middle Ebro between the late eighth century and the early tenth (they were based between Tudela and Calahorra, upstream from Zaragoza), can be seen as heirs of the world of Aemilianus and Braulio, for Ibn Ḥazm says in the eleventh century that the original Qasī was a 'frontier count' (*qūmis al-thagr*) in the Gothic period. Such a Gothic 'Count Casius' presents serious problems, not least that Cas(s)ius is not attested elsewhere in the period as a name, and the 'frontier' did not exist here before the Arab conquest (the 'Basque *limes*' of recent historiography does not have contemporary support as a formal territory); but that the family claimed (or were ascribed) local Visigothic roots is not undermined by doubts about which Visigoth they were actually descended from. Nor is the fact that they operated as an effectively independent political unit throughout the ninth century, one of

---

[186] For furnished burials, see the exhaustive survey of Ebel-Zepezauer, *Studien*, with a traditional ethnic approach, slightly nuanced (e.g. pp. 155, 165–7); beyond this, the works of Gisela Ripoll are the basic starting-point, e.g. 'Materiales funerarios' and 'La necrópolis de El Carpio de Tajo'; she too takes a more ethnic line than I would, but she has softened it in recent years. For Roman ceramics, Izquierdo, 'Ensayo'.

the many, whether Muslim or Christian, in northern Spain; in this respect too they acted as the structural heirs of the Ebro senators of the sixth century.[187]

This Roman (perhaps better, Aquitainian) reading of the history of early medieval Spain is, as noted earlier, based on relatively few texts, but they are consistent with one another. The problems come from the other evidence we have, or rather the other evidences, for they are twofold. One aspect of this evidence is actually more documentary than archaeological: it is that other parts of the Spain of the ninth century were quite different. By then, the Arabs ruled to the Duero and Ebro, with Christian principalities to the north; but the Asturias, the main northern kingdom, was a very different polity, with a very simple political structure indeed, and a population characterized as much by independent peasants as by aristocrats—the entire social structure of the north, from Galicia to Catalonia, is often said by historians to be *gentilicio*, kin-based or tribal, rather than *feudal*, based on landowning. This is even more true of the Duero valley, the northern Meseta, which when it was reoccupied by the Christian polities after 900 showed very flat landowning hierarchies indeed, dominated by village communities and only slowly brought under aristocratic/ecclesiastical control— by means of royal concession from above and the growth of social differentiation (and thus a small-scale military elite) inside the communities themselves. This was certainly a change from the organized estates, some of them royal, that are documented there before 700. And, inside the Arab emirate (later, caliphate) of al-Andalus, Berber communities are seen as dominating large sections of the eastern mountains, once again characterized by village-based collectivities and kin-based/tribal social relationships, owing military service and/or tax to Córdoba but nothing else.

Of these areas, the Asturias is the best documented by far before 900, thanks to a group of early charters, a set of (admittedly sketchy) chronicles, and a remarkable set of ninth-century royal churches in and around the capital at Oviedo. Its symbolism as the lineal ancestor of the united Christian Spain of 1492 has led to a charged historiography, even by Spanish standards (cf. above, p. 41). It does have to be said that there is very little sign in Asturian documentation of anything other than Roman traditions of landowning; at most, there is reference to the standard forms of collective silvo-pastoral exploitation that can be found in any mountain area (for the

---

[187] For Ibn al-Qūṭiya, see idem, *Historia*, pp. 1–4, for the chronicler's descent from King Witiza, a fantastic account, but one which lays considerable stress on inherited land. For commentary, see Christys, *Christians*, pp. 158–83. For Ibn Ḥafṣūn, see Acién, '*Umar ibn Ḥafṣūn*, pp. xxv–xxx, 88–91, 111–13, for his ancestry. Fierro, 'Cuatro cuestiones', pp. 222–4, although in general critical of Acién's argument, accepts this point. For the Banū Qasī, see most recently Manzano, *La frontera*, pp. 110–24 (p. 112 for Ibn Ḥazm). The Basque *limes*, proposed in Barbero and Vigil, *Sobre los orígines*, esp. pp. 67–89, has been strongly doubted by Arce, 'Un "limes" innecesario', and Larrea, *La Navarre*, pp. 117–18 (but see below, n. 190).

Asturias largely consists of mountain valleys). I remain unconvinced that this area, at least, was a society fully dominated by *gentilicio*, tribal, models of social organization (for the word 'tribal' see below, pp. 305–6), and indeed the evidence for some Roman socio-economic patterns in the period before 500, such as villas and exchange links with elsewhere, is growing. But its documented landowners operated on a very small scale for a long time, in terms of both global wealth and geographical range—ownership inside a single valley was the norm.[188] Diego Álvaro's localization is the most we could expect in this area, except for kings, who could certainly afford prestige buildings by the ninth century. And the Asturias was also, in other areas, characterized by a survival of pre-Roman traditions of concentrated settlement, called *castros* both in documents and by archaeologists; these by no means necessarily represent a 'non-Roman' world (the western Asturias was an active centre of Roman mining), and they indeed must have been the focus of socio-political as well as settlement hierarchies, but at least they would have aided collective social action of some form.[189] Under these circumstances, although the core lands of the Asturias maintained Roman landowning patterns, it remains plausible to postulate other, more collective or communitarian, traditions in the north as well, including tribal ones: in the present-day Basque lands, in particular, never fully subjected by the Visigoths, and never linguistically Romanized.[190] Such traditions could

[188] For modern politics, see some of the discussion in *La época de la monarquía asturiana* for a sharp-edged recent example. For Roman landowning, see the documents edited in Floriano, *Diplomática española*; these seem entirely normal in Italian or Frankish terms. Ibid., n. 30 (a. 822) is a good text for land-clearance. For its restricted geographical scale, see e.g. nn. 17, 26, 44, 70 (aa. 803–60), for a single family, probably of aristocrats. The *gentilicio* interpretation of some of the later northern documents for peasant landowning in Barbero and Vigil, *La formación*, pp. 354–80, for the most part does not convince; but it is fair to note that land documents tend by their nature to privilege Roman landowning patterns. For the Oviedo monuments, see most recently Noack-Haley and Arbeiter, *Asturische Königsbauten*. For the Romanization of material culture in the central Asturias, see Calleja and Beltrán, 'El espacio centro-oriental', pp. 66–78, with the discussion at pp. 127–59.

[189] Floriano, *Diplomática española*, nn. 9, 28, for early documentary references to *castros* in Asturias; for a regional analysis, Fernández Mier, *Génesis del territorio*, is basic (see pp. 41–60 for a general survey); see further Gutiérrez, 'Sobre los orígines de la sociedad asturleonesa'; cf. for other parts of northern Spain below, n. 196 and pp. 338–9. See further p. 584 for the Asturian peasants' revolt of 770, which may possibly represent the political response of an autonomous peasantry to increased aristocratic encroachment. For strong peasant communities and collective action, although also Roman-style landowning, in the eastern Pyrenees (in Pallars and Urgell) in the ninth century, see Wickham, 'Rural society', pp. 512–16. But one must insist on microregional difference here; each small area had its own local patterns of development, and has to be analysed on its own terms.

[190] Larrea, *La Navarre*, pp. 111–60, doubts this view of the Basques, and provides a Romanist reading of the Pamplona area, in particular. This latter reading is broadly acceptable; but it cannot be extended without question to the present-day Basque Country, a generally more isolated and ill-documented territory in our period. Larrea does not present a convincing reason for continued Basque resistance to everyone, if they were all exactly the same as the inhabitants of the rest of Spain. For some continuing Basque autonomy into the eleventh century, at least in Guipúzcoa, see e.g. Besga Marroquín, 'El reino de Asturias', pp. 412–13. The differences of position in the historiography on this issue are, however, endless.

well have had parallels even in the Asturias in more marginal zones, and were probably expanding rather than contracting, at least in the eighth century. Even though attempts to track specific evidence for tribal structures in northern documents are mostly inconclusive, it would strain one's imagination to propose an entirely Romanized north, and the tiny scale of political practice in the Christian polities of the Cantabrian mountains and the Pyrenees into the tenth century and even, sometimes, later does not fit with that either. I would see areas of small-scale Roman-style landowning, with small aristocrats and independent peasants (as in the core of the Asturias, Navarre, or Pallars and Urgell), separated by more autonomous areas, some of them more tribal in structure; and one substantial area, the northern Meseta, under no obvious external control at all, in which communities of different types (whether tribal or Roman-style) existed autonomously between the early eighth century and the early tenth.[191] The process of development that this presumes (particularly in the Meseta, where larger-scale properties certainly existed earlier) will be returned to later (pp. 338, 755–7); but any currently available picture of the post-Visigothic north is very different from that of the Visigothic period as a whole.

It is this set of local realities, relatively unhierarchical in social terms, that much of the post-Roman archaeology fits, rather better than the 'late late Roman' model presented hitherto. But the archaeology introduces a series of data that are much more opposed to that model than is the simple recognition that things were different later. That change was, before the archaeology began to be clear—which is only in the last decade or so—ascribable to the Arab conquest itself. The archaeology, however, pushes many of the shifts rather earlier. The villa system weakened substantially from the fifth century onwards, and already in the sixth it can only be clearly identified in a few areas. These actually map quite well onto our zones of regional Visigothic aristocracies, for they include the middle Ebro valley around Lleida and Huesca, the northern Meseta, and central Baetica and western Lusitania between Córdoba and the Atlantic (a fourth area, the Catalan–Valencian coast, is not well represented in written documentation).[192] They could be

---

[191] Local case studies of the northern Meseta which attempt to reconstruct social structures in this period include Martín, *Poblamiento*, pp. 107–211; Escalona, *Sociedad y territorio*, pp. 62–77; Pastor, *Castilla*, pp. 83–143. Martín and Escalona stress tribal and small-scale communities; Pastor a continuity from Visigothic political structures. This latter seems overgeneralized, in such a microregionally diverse area; all the same, if Luis Caballero's redating of the Meseta's 'Visigothic' churches to the eighth century and later gains acceptance (see e.g. 'La arquitectura denominada de época visigoda'), then their patrons, at least, maintained sources of landed wealth that would have had Roman/Visigothic antecedents. For settlement archaeology in this area, see further below, p. 491. For overviews of the history of the Meseta in the period, see Martín, 'La articulación del poder'; Castellanos and Martín, 'The local articulation of central power'; García de Cortázar, 'La formación de la sociedad feudal'.

[192] For these areas, Gorges, *Les villas hispanoromaines*, p. 56 n., gives lists. For Catalonia and Valencia, see further Ch. 8, nn. 99, 101; for central Baetica, Carr, *Vandals to Visigoths*, pp. 92, 183–8, shows sixth-century villa survival on the basis of ceramic imports, even though she herself argues for sharp crisis after 400.

said to fit the surviving Roman cultural traditions already proposed, and once again their best parallels are in Aquitaine. But these are fairly restricted areas of Spain; in other areas such survivals cannot clearly be traced at all. The TSHT market network, too, can scarcely be found by 500. And, above all, in most of the areas that have had decent regional archaeological analyses, such as the Alicante–Murcia region, the coastlands of the province of Granada, or the upper Guadalquivir around Jaén, we see evidence of some quite sharp regional involution, with not only the local market networks of late Rome vanishing, but even in some cases settlement hierarchies; indeed, not only does industrial ceramic production break down, but hand-made wares begin to dominate on much of the east coast, indicating a complete deprofessionalization of artisan production, in a development hardly paralleled in any part of the early medieval Mediterranean except for sectors of Greece.[193] These patterns will, as said earlier, be developed more in Chapter 11 (see also pp. 488–93, for settlement archaeology); but they certainly cause problems for the 'late late Roman' model, for it is important to recognize that these involutions are in many cases fully under way by the seventh century (if not before), only to be reversed after 850 or so.

Two broad models have dominated the interpretation of these issues in Spain. One is an interpretation focused on ethnic discontinuities, adopted by Claudio Sánchez-Albornoz and Ramon d'Abadal for the Christian polities and (rather uneasy bedfellows with the former) Pierre Guichard and Miquel Barceló for al-Andalus. For these theorists, the Arab invasions brought dramatic population changes. The whole of the lands north of the Duero and Ebro were depopulated in the eighth century in Sánchez-Albornoz's and Abadal's theory, thus allowing social development to begin once more with peasant settlement from the northern mountains at the end of the ninth.[194] For Guichard and Barceló, similarly, Berber settlement brought profound social change, as well as a new kin-based segmentary model of social development that could spread outside strictly Berber areas: 'el medi tribal produeix tribus', the tribal milieu generates tribes, in Barceló's much-cited phrase. The Visigoths could be as late Roman as they liked; history would start again.[195] An alternative model is that the Arab conquest (and/or the Berber revolts of the 740s) sharply weakened the power of the aristocracy, in particular in the Meseta, and that the survival of Christian polities only in the much less feudalized mountains of the far north meant that slow political

---

[193] See Ch. 8, nn. 132–4.

[194] The classic for Sánchez-Albornoz (out of many) is *Despoblación*; for Abadal, *Els primers comtes*, pp. 75–120.

[195] Guichard, *Structures sociales*, is the classic here (trans. into Spanish as *Al-Andalus*); Barceló has set out his views above all in articles, e.g. 'Assentaments berbers'; 'Vespres de feudals'. For the quote, see ibid., p. 245. Glick, *From Muslim fortress*, pp. 29–37, gives a good brisk survey.

expansion southwards did not immediately bring aristocratic hierarchies with it—they developed later, often in situations of violent conflict. This position is common to the current leaders of the historiography of the northern half of the peninsula, despite their other differences: over how far the breakdown of Visigothic hierarchies was associated with the breakdown of the slave mode of production, as Pierre Bonnassie and José Maria Mínguez argue in different ways; over how far the kin-based communities of the far north were not only relatively socially undifferentiated, but also economic collectivities, without much private property, as in Abilio Barbero and Marcelo Vigil's work.[196] I would myself regard the slavery issue as irrelevant, for the *servi* of seventh-century society were tenants, not slaves in a modal sense (below, pp. 526–7); nor, as already argued, is there much evidence for collective property, at least in agricultural areas. But this general picture is certainly more satisfactory than that of Sánchez-Albornoz, and indeed his depopulationist model has by now effectively been abandoned.[197] It is also a model that can fit the Arab south, and versions of it have been argued there too, as with Eduardo Manzano's stress on the weakness and division of the pre-tenth-century Arab state, at least outside its Guadalquivir heartland, which emphasized the localization of political power—although the aristocracy certainly remained stronger there.[198]

There is more common ground in these different interpretations than one would sometimes realize from the violent debates that they have often—indeed, usually—engendered (post-Visigothic Spanish scholarship is stimulating, but not exactly eirenic), for 711 and its impact is seen as the major element of change, in almost every case. But the archaeology forces us to ask to what extent the changes were already beginning under the Visigoths; and, if so, whether the Arab conquest represented as total a change as is often said. This will be the key issue to be explored in Chapter 11 (see below, pp. 741–58). I shall argue there for the importance of regional differences in Spanish socio-economic development, which, broadly, could be said to be more important than the changes brought in by the Arabs. A regional approach above all helps to get over some of the disjuncture between documentary and archaeological sources. But it is worth leaving a discussion of Spain which privileges written texts with an explicit recognition that the written evidence is incomplete. The domain of Roman cultural and economic structures stretched to an unprepossessing place like Diego Álvaro, but not necessarily up into the mountains; and it was, at least slowly, in

---

[196] Barbero and Vigil, *La formación*, pp. 279–404; Bonnassie, *From slavery*, pp. 71–4, 93–6; Pastor, *Resistencias*, pp. 20–73; Mínguez, (among many) 'Ruptura social'; García de Cortázar, (among many) 'La formación de la sociedad feudal', a full recent bibliographical survey and presentation of his own views.

[197] The works cited in nn. 191, 196, all presuppose the abandonment of the theory.

[198] Manzano, *La frontera*; see Acién, as above, n. 187, and Manzano, 'Señores y emires', for pre-caliphal al-Andalus as being one of a relatively strong local aristocracy.

retreat. In general, unfortunately, the parts of the world illuminated by written sources are most likely in our period to show relative Roman continuity; it is dangerous to assume too blithely that they were typical, and Spain is, of all our regions, the most likely counter-instance to such an assumption. Spain was highly differentiated ecologically, which is one important context for this; it may be that it is a model for other highly differentiated regions too.

4. The eastern Mediterranean

When we move into the eastern Mediterranean, we move into the territories of consistently strong political systems. Some of the parameters governing aristocratic continuities were therefore different. The wealth and power of states meant that they were even more important for the career choices of any aristocrat with ambition, and access to government, than they were in the West. In particular, that continued strength means that if state structures changed, aristocracies would transform their identities as well, at least as much as one might expect in the Romano-Germanic kingdoms, and indeed even more so. We have already seen this in Byzantine Italy after 570; two generations later, the Byzantine heartland and the Syro-Palestinian core of the caliphate saw the same sort of intensity of aristocratic change. Egypt saw the greatest continuities, but there were shifts there, too, notably in the direction of ever more localized property structures. We will look at each in turn, in much the same way as the West has been presented, although in less detail, for problems with the evidence are either fewer, or else insuperably great.

We have already seen (pp. 164–5) that late Roman aristocrats in the eastern Mediterranean were rarely hugely rich, and even more rarely were widely spread landowners. Aristocratic landowning was normally focused on single city territories, and little more. Even inside these territories, we get the impression that it was substantially dispersed; the evidence for this is largely for Syria-Palestine and Egypt, as we shall see, but the patterns can probably be extended to the other areas of the eastern empire as well. In the future Byzantine heartland two areas tend to appear as locations for aristocratic property, the Constantinople–Marmara sub-region from Thrace to Bithynia, and the central Anatolian plateau, notably Cappadocia, where there were substantial imperial estates too. The former must have been a standard rural base for landowners living in the capital. For the plateau our evidence is fairly heterogeneous, but it seems as if substantial landowners and independent peasantries lived in neighbouring provinces. The *Novels* of Justinian from the 530s which stress aristocratic landowning in Cappadocia (and its menace to the peasantry) equally stress the peasantry (and their unwillingness to pay taxes) in Pisidia, just to its west, whereas in Galatia to their north we find in the *Life* of Theodore of Sykeōn, written not long after 613, villages of peasant proprietors together with the leading landowners of Ankara and Anastasioupolis, called *protiktores*, an apparently informal title, in the text. The local city focus of landowning politics is clear in the *Life* of Theodore. It postdated the end of the formal tax-raising responsibilities of city councillors, but Ankara was no less important a centre because its civic aristocracy had lost their formal identification markers.[199]

In the fourth and fifth centuries the social system was structured by official titles, at the levels both of the senate and central government and of city aristocracies, in the East as in the West (above, pp. 155–68). In the sixth century this remained true at the centre, as we can see in the office-obsessed descriptions of the governmental system in John Lydos, writing in the 550s; at the city level, however, the gradual suppression of city councils led to a more informal de facto local aristocratic network, as we have just seen. It is not clear that an Ankaran *protiktor*, or his equally informal equivalents elsewhere, the *illoustrioi* of Amorion or the *scholarioi* of Nikomedeia (Izmit), strictly needed an imperial position in order to have 'real' aristocratic status, by the start of the seventh century.[200] Local imperial offices did nonetheless exist, which brought both power and wealth: the *archontes* (magistrates) and *anytai* (tax-collectors) of Anastasioupolis, who could be tyrannical to the local peasantry. We will look at Sykeōn and Ankara in more detail in Chapter 7 (pp. 406–11) and at the issue of the parameters of city society in Chapter 10 (pp. 626–35). In general, however, the patterns we have here, at the start of the seventh century, are similar to those in earlier centuries of the later Roman empire, which was always made up of a set of aristocratic societies with strong local loyalties but, equally, many-levelled links to the state.

It can already be seen that the late Roman evidence for the aristocracy in the future Byzantine lands is not generous. In the absence of any documents, and in a world where our narrative materials concentrate on the army and the politics of the capital, we are reduced to dealing with not much more than anecdotes. But at least the continuities of the Roman empire were such that we can assume that the public hierarchies that are better documented elsewhere existed here too. After c.650 it becomes far more difficult: in part because even the slight evidence we have for the previous two centuries is much better than that for 650–800; in part because we cannot use parallels

---

[199] For the Marmara, see above, p. 164. For the plateau, *NJ*, XXX.5.1 (Cappadocia), XXIV.1 (Pisidia). For *protiktores*, *Vie de Théodore*, cc. 25, 45, 76 (the word had formerly been a military title—see e.g. Jones, *LRE*, pp. 636–8—but clearly is not in this text). For city councils, see below, pp. 597–602. See in general, especially for aristocratic power, Patlagean, *Pauvreté*, pp. 287–96; Kaplan, *Les hommes*, pp. 169–74; Köpstein, 'Zu den Agrarverhältnissen', pp. 14–18, 28–34.

[200] John Lydos, *On powers, passim*; see Maas, *John Lydus*, esp. pp. 39–43. *Illoustrioi* and *scholarioi*: *Vie de Théodore*, cc. 107, 156, 158 (it is possible that *scholarios* is more of a formal title than are the other words).

from anywhere else to flesh out the fragmentary information we have for the Byzantine heartland—not even that from Byzantine Italy, for developments there, although certainly parallel, were not identical. After the great crisis of the mid-seventh century there is actually no direct evidence for aristocratic landowning at all before 800. As a result, it was not uncommon in the first half of the twentieth century to argue that it had all vanished; that the aristocracy dissolved in the face of the Persian–Arab crisis, leaving nothing but the state and the peasantry.[201]

This argument has some analogies to arguments made for the West, whether in the northern Gaul of the sixth century or the Spain of the eighth, as we have seen; it is unlikely to work for Byzantium, however, given what we know of later periods—Byzantine aristocracies are certainly much more visible in the tenth century than they are in the northern Meseta, for example—and such a radical view has few followers at present. All the same, in order to obtain any picture of the early Byzantine aristocracy one has to do it by extrapolating back from a small number of later sources, not all of them easy to wield. The considerable use made of the early ninth-century *Life* of Philaretos (d. 792) is a measure of the desperation of scholars, for this text is a skilled reworking of classic folk-tale motifs into the plotline of the Book of Job, and all its apparently circumstantial material about the scale of landowning derives from that rhetorical framing—as a source for the aristocracy it is virtually useless.[202] If we abandon this text, however, we have little indeed. Methodios' *Life* of the chronicler Theophanes (d. 818), a text of c.830, says he was son of a provincial governor, and had lands in Bithynia. A nearly contemporary text, Ignatios the Deacon's *Life* of the patriarch Tarasios (d. 806), who was from a family of high officials, shows him with land on the Bosporos. The family of Theodore of Stoudios (d. 826) had Bithynia estates as well, and so did several other monastic founders from the capital's official elites in the eighth and ninth centuries. This geographical focus fits with the Marmara landowning of late Roman Constantinopolitan figures. It is significant that a third of all the surviving Byzantine churches from the eighth and early ninth centuries, at least some of them the result of private patronage, are found in the Marmara area; this seems to have remained the sub-region with the most notable concentrations of wealth in the empire. Outside that area, about all we can say about landowning is that imperial and church estates continued to

---

[201] Ostrogorsky, *History*, pp. 87–8, 120, is a crisp survey along these lines; he stresses above all Slav settlement and the granting of land to soldiers.

[202] See Fourmy and Leroy, 'La vie de S. Philarète', esp. pp. 113–39. This text is accepted by, among others, Lemerle, *Agrarian history*, pp. 52 ff.; Ševčenko, 'Hagiography', p. 126; Každan and Ševčenko, 'Philaretos the merciful'; Kaplan, *Les hommes*, pp. 332–3. Speck, *Kaiser Konstantin VI.*, pp. 204–6, 626 n., is more cautious. Major criticisms are Polyakova, 'Fol'klornyi syuzhet', for folkloric elements, and Ludwig, *Sonderformen*, pp. 74–166, for the Book of Job. These, particularly the latter, are to me devastating; little remains except anecdote—perhaps the story of a poor soldier (Fourmy and Leroy, 'La vie de S. Philarète', p. 127), or the layout of a dining-room (ibid., pp. 137–9), or assumptions about gender roles.

exist, for seals of their administrators (*kouratores* and *oikonomoi*) survive; that tenancy as a concept turns up in eighth-century legislation; and that local *archontes* are referred to as controlling private churches in the acts of the Council of Nicaea in 787.[203] No one really doubts that major civil and military officials were always landowners, as were emperors and patriarchs. But whether large-scale landownership retreated in this period or roughly stayed the same is hard to say on the basis of material like this.[204]

What is fully clear, on the other hand, is that the official hierarchies that aristocrats aspired to were transformed after 650. The senate survived the seventh-century crisis, but it became more and more the ceremonial version of the civil and military official hierarchy. The civil administration in Constantinople survived too; it had its own collective identity and even group memory, as is seen in the *Parastaseis*, an eighth-century text which recounts the antiquarian interests of a group of officials, who supposedly went around the statues of the capital in the 710s and onwards, trying to make sense of their inscriptions. But the whole administrative structure of the empire changed radically in this period, as Byzantium adjusted to its reduced border and its fiscal weakness (above, pp. 124–9). John Lydos could recount the administrative history of each arm of government, going back centuries; the new arms of government, however, the *genikon*, *eidikon*, and *stratiotikon*, as they were called by the ninth century at the latest, had a less obvious institutional genealogy. The *Parastaseis* antiquarians found even making sense of the history of the city as a whole a perplexing process, and as much as anything they saw Constantinople as a city of signs, which were as important as a guide to the future as to the past.[205] The

---

[203] Methodios, *Life* of Theophanes, cc. 5, 21; Ignatios, *Life* of Tarasios, cc. 4, 24 (cf. Efthymiadis' editorial comments on pp. 6–13); *Life* of Theodore, B, c. 5 (cf. c. 15). For landowning in general, and other monastic foundations, see Cheynet, 'L'époque byzantine', pp. 319–20, and Auzépy, 'Les monastères', pp. 432–50. For the churches, see Robert Ousterhout's architectural contribution to Brubaker and Haldon, *Iconoclasm. The sources*, pp. 8–15. Sample seals are Zacos and Veglery, *Byzantine lead seals*, I, nn. 3014, 3218, 3230; Nesbitt and Oikonomides, *Catalogue*, III, 14.10, 35.5; see Kaplan, 'Maisons impériales', pp. 350–1, for a list of *kouratores*, and idem, *Les hommes*, pp. 312–23, for imperial land. For tenancy, see Ashburner, 'Farmer's law', cc. 9–17; *Ekloga*, cc. 12–13. For II Nicaea, canon 10, see *Sacrorum conciliorum collectio*, XIII, col. 430. The empress Irene is often said to be from an Athenian landowning family, but there is no basis for this; even the statement that she was Athenian is not recorded before the twelfth century (*PBE*, I, s.v. Eirene 1)—Theophanes only says that she arrived from Athens for her wedding in Constantinople in 769 (*Chronographia*, p. 444).

[204] See e.g. Köpstein, 'Zu den Agrarverhältnissen', pp. 60–72; Haldon, *Byzantium in the seventh century*, pp. 128–31. Köpstein provides a standard argument for aristocratic weakening; Haldon would see the answer to the question as substantially different in different parts of the empire.

[205] The *Parastaseis* is edited and commented on in Cameron and Herrin, *Constantinople*; see e.g. cc. 20, 64–5, for the city of signs. See also Dagron, *Constantinople imaginaire*, pp. 115–23, 143–56. For the senate, Haldon, 'The fate of the late Roman senatorial élite'. For the main subdivisions of government, see above all Brandes, *Finanzverwaltung*. He stresses (pp. 165–79) that the *eidikon* is not called that until the ninth century, in a classicizing renaming that covers institutional discontinuities; he may be going too far here, as Haldon argues in his review of the book (review of Brandes, pp. 719–20), but the discontinuities are nonetheless clear.

predominance of a totally new set of administrative hierarchies is even more marked in local government and the army, for this was the period of the development of the themes, as military commands and then as provincial administrations as well. In the West, the dukes and counts of cities and provinces largely survived the fall of the empire as the basic building-blocks of local political organization; the army might become landed rather than salaried, but its local administrative responsibilities remained structured by Roman territorial patterns. In Byzantium, thematic reorganization was substantially greater than that. This was probably helped by the fact that the army was still paid, for the state as a result kept more control over its internal structures. Indeed, the continued, for that matter increasing, dominance of central government over all official hierarchies is one clear feature of the late seventh and eighth centuries. Constantinople thus determined the new structure of public provincial position, as much as it did the new structures of central governmental hierarchy.

The result of all this was that the parameters of aristocratic identity all shifted. City hierarchies had already gone; military hierarchies became the dominant public positions in the provinces by 700; by 800 the surviving civilian provincial hierarchies were folded into the military career structure, leaving only Constantinople with a free-standing civilian hierarchy—although a largely new one. Senatorial titles cease to be recorded on Byzantine seals after c.750, and only palatine and military offices are attested from then on. Friedhelm Winkelmann is tempted to argue that this emphasis on imperial title reflects a temporary lack of stress on landowning among the parameters that created aristocratic identity.[206] This is indeed possible, although the state was so dominant in Byzantium, and it had changed so radically, that any private identities might have been transformed in its wake. One thing that is very clear is that any focus on high birth was temporarily of relatively minor importance. All names changed, here as in the West; even in Constantinople, no families can be traced past the early seventh century. Theophanes twice (in annals for 677 and 713) refers to people of 'ancient lineage' (*archaiogenēs*), and the state treasurer (*logothetēs tou genikou*) Theodotos in 694, a man of humble origin (he had been a hermit), was criticized for confiscating property from *periphanesteroi*, prominent people. These show that the concept of privileged birth did at least exist, whether around 700 or around 800, when Theophanes was writing.[207] Only from the eighth century onward, however, did the great families of the middle Byzantine period begin to emerge. The relatively obscure Rendakioi are the first surnamed family to appear in Theophanes,

---

[206] Basic are Haldon, *Byzantium in the seventh century*, pp. 387–402, and idem, 'The fate of the late Roman senatorial élite', Winkelmann, *Quellenstudien*, pp. 28–31 (for the lack of stress on land), 221–8.

[207] Theophanes, *Chronographia*, pp. 355, 383, 367; another version of the third example is in Nikephoros, *Short history*, c. 39, with the word *periphanesteros*.

in 719; the Melissēnoi are the first major family who are documented, with Michael Melissēnos, *strategos* of the Anatolikon theme in the mid-eighth century; after 800 we find the Sklēroi, after 850 the Phokades and Doukai. By the tenth century Byzantine sources include many aristocratic family names; a nobility of birth certainly existed by then.[208] This makes the hiatus of the seventh century still clearer; the structures of aristocratic identity had changed for a second time.

The great Byzantine families take us out of our period, but it is worth considering what their crystallization means, because this, at least, was beginning before 800. The development of a consciousness of family identity that is sufficiently strong that it is attached to a surname is a clear sign of an identity independent of state office, one which has its own rules and values. In the tenth and eleventh centuries these were above all military values; the greatest families were above all a military aristocracy. In those centuries we begin finally to know something of their landowning: the Anatolia-based families mostly owned on the plateau, relatively close to the frontier, which further stresses their military identity.[209] These patterns are of course paralleled in the West, though surnames for non-royal families rarely appear before the eleventh century there, except in Venice, which, significantly, was itself Byzantine. It is interesting that it was in Byzantium that family surnames appeared first, and not in the West, where public power was so much weaker, and local family power so much more secure a point of reference. This probably tells us that Byzantine family identity was more patrilineal (male-line) than it was in the Carolingian and immediately post-Carolingian West, so could more easily be carried by patrilineal family names.[210] This was certainly a feature of societies where family names were older, like the Irish, the Arabs, or the Armenians. It is, for that matter, possible that surnames were sometimes a sign of Armenian cultural influence: a frontier location for a Byzantine family meant a location closer to Armenia, after all. But, either way, it is clear that by the ninth century Byzantine elites were stable enough to lay claim to lineage identity again, after a century or more of uncertainty. By 900 the balance of ancestry, land, office, and lifestyle is clear in our steadily increasing source material. It was not all military—the eleventh-century rivalry between civilian and military

---

[208] Before 800, see Winkelmann, *Quellenstudien*, pp. 143–219; Patlagean, 'Les débuts'; Kaplan, *Les hommes*, pp. 326–31. After 800, see ibid., pp. 281–373; Cheynet, *Pouvoir et contestations*, pp. 207–86. Family names are not actually very common in sources before the late tenth century, though: Stephenson, 'A development'; Kazhdan, 'The formation'.

[209] Hendy, *Studies*, pp. 100–8; Cheynet, *Pouvoir et contestations*, pp. 207–48.

[210] For family structures, Cheynet, *Pouvoir et contestations*, pp. 261–7; Patlagean, 'Les débuts', pp. 29 ff. Cf., for the West, Schmid, 'Zur Problematik'; Le Jan, *Famille et pouvoir*, pp. 159–77, 387–427. For Venice, see John the Deacon, *Istoria Veneticorum*, II.35, 44, 48, III.1, 32, 35, 40 (in this early eleventh-century text, surnames begin in the ninth); cf. Castagnetti, 'Famiglie e affermazione politica', pp. 614–20.

elites is famous, and the capital was always the focus of alternative identities to the army. But it was by now more separate from the state.

What the implications of this are for the period 650–800 is more hypothetical. The rapid rerooting of aristocratic families in the ninth century is of course a major reason why scholars generally argue for a period of relative weakness in large landowning in the previous period, and it is not implausible that Winkelmann and others are right to propose that aristocratic landowning could often have been a casualty of the confusion of the mid-seventh century, just as it often was in the most generalized periods of crisis in western regions. The reorganization of the army in that crisis period, added to a temporary lack of stress on family ancestry, also undoubtedly helped the rise of new families, sometimes from Armenia, sometimes from the Byzantine provinces themselves.[211] But it must also be emphasized that the dissolution of aristocratic identity hides not only change, but any potential continuity. It is worth asking how a *protiktor* from Ankara, and still more a local notable from one of the less ravaged regions of Anatolia, the lower Maiander valley or the southern coast, would have reacted to the new political situation of the late seventh century. He might well have fled from exposed areas, leaving his peasantry as de facto landowners (if they themselves survived). If he stayed, however, he would probably have maintained his wealth, for his landowning was predominantly local, and could thus survive periods of uncertainty more easily. But local position was by now more difficult to legitimate. Cities themselves were weakening, and the urban political stage was thus a less attractive option, except in the remaining provincial centres, Smyrna (Izmir), Antalya, Trabzon, Thessaloniki, and a few others. Even there, however, an autonomous urban politics was not what it was. The *Miracles* of S. Demetrios, a text from seventh-century Thessaloniki, shows a level of city notables with clear political roles, to be sure, but it is striking how vaguely they are described, as *kratountes*, 'powerful' (cf. *potentes* in the West), *archontes*, 'magistrates' (but already also perhaps just meaning local leaders), *exochoi tōn prōtōn*, 'outstanding among the leaders', or *ta prōta pherontes*, 'the bearers of rule'; this is public position in dissolution, something we shall also see for Egypt (below, pp. 600–1). Under these circumstances, the continuing strength of the formal hierarchies of the state in Byzantium (substantially more structured than in the West, by now) must have been compelling; to remain a local informal elite could even have seemed déclassé.[212] Those who stayed in the surviving cities—above all Constantinople, to where ambitious provincials continued to come—would have been absorbed into local state hierarchies

---

[211] See e.g. Haldon, 'The fate of the late Roman senatorial élite'.

[212] *Miracles de St Démétrius*, I.13–14, II.1, 3–5 (§§ 121, 136, 193, 224, 231, 252, 254, 281, 293). For the interplay in Thessaloniki between informal city elites and formal imperial and ecclesiastical hierarchies, and the public presence of the latter, see Brubaker, 'Élites and patronage'.

fairly fast. Elsewhere, the essential structure was the army, which was local as a result of the theme system and thus accessible, or the (increasingly military) provincial administration, for that was all there was. In most of the empire, then, any surviving city-level landowner of even medium ambition would have found himself in the thematic hierarchies by the eighth century. His identity would change as a result, becoming military, with new family naming in most cases too; everything would change so that everything could stay the same. To move further still into guesswork, I would suppose that some regions were likely to show relatively high cultural continuity, notably the Marmara sub-region around the capital, where civil administrators had most of their land; some only slightly less (as in protected coastal areas such as Caria or Pamphylia). The greatest dissolution of identities would come on the militarized plateau, although not necessarily the greatest dissolution of landowning, for it was here that the great families were later based, after all. We cannot test this, however, until the rural archaeology of this period is more firmly rooted in Turkey (cf. below, pp. 628–34).

It is impossible to be sure what happened to the aristocracy of the Aegean and Anatolia in the seventh century, but the implication of the above arguments is that they survived. One could suppose that they probably became rather more locally restricted, until the ninth and especially the tenth centuries allowed an expansion of their property and power; they may as a result have become poorer. This supposition is given further support by the archaeology of the Byzantine heartland, which shows a sharp drop in the sophistication of production, and a substantial decrease in interregional exchange, between 650 and 800, at least outside the capital (below, pp. 784–93). For this reason above all, I am inclined to think that large-scale landowning weakened in the period. But one should resist reasoning from this weakening, or from the breaks in the parameters of aristocratic identity, to any genealogical discontinuity in aristocratic power. The discontinuities were on the level of the state, not of the localities; it is much more likely that the same families held land locally, for the most part, across all the traumas of the post-crisis period.

This analysis matches that for Byzantine Italy very closely, and indeed repeats many of the arguments made in that context (above, pp. 205–9). There are two main differences, however. The first is that in Italy the shifts discussed here had already begun two generations earlier, in the 580s rather than the 650s. The reshaping of the Italian aristocracy can hardly be seen as a model for the Byzantine heartland; what it shows is that a militarization of hierarchies reshaped aristocratic identity twice in Byzantium, in roughly the same ways and at the same speed—something of a tribute to the consistency of state power, in fact. The second point is that aristocracies in Italy stayed more urban. It is not that urban economies all survived there, particularly in the numerous tiny cities of the Italian south: even the major centres were materially simpler, as we shall see (pp. 644–56). But in the cities which we have documents for, even small centres like Senigallia (above, p. 209), the newly militarized aristocracy stayed rooted. The transformations of Byzantine political structures did not, as has sometimes been argued, necessarily bring cities down with them. This argues for a difference in the way military and provincial hierarchies worked between the Byzantine East and the Byzantine West.

The evidence for Syrian and Palestinian aristocracies is too fragmentary to merit more than a brief reference. As elsewhere in the East, city-level aristocracies were dominant in the fifth and sixth centuries, as with the Gaza aristocrats praised in Chorikios' orations in the early sixth century, or the rich notables of Emesa (Ḥimṣ), Askalon (Ashqelon), and Caesarea in Prokopios, or those of Apamea mentioned by a pilgrim in the 560s.[213] The recently discovered Petra papyri show a prosperous sixth-century urban family with lands scattered across the plateau east of that city, up to 50 km away to the south-east and south. The aristocracy of Edessa (Urfa), a major entrepôt for trade with Persia, appears in a number of texts as being immensely rich, but its base was again one city.[214] The only exception to this single-city focus was Antioch, whose elites had much more widely extended landowning, from the fourth to the sixth centuries: partly in Antioch's immediate hinterland, small cities such as Cyrrhus as we see in Theodoret's *Religious History*, but also further east to the Euphrates, south down the Orontes to Epiphania (Ḥamā), and down the coast to Palestine proper—a former city leader of Antioch, Kaisarios, patronized a monastery outside Jerusalem around 500, for example.[215] Many of the city aristocrats of the region were all the same visibly rich, notwithstanding their local focus, which fits the wealth of urban archaeology, in particular in the late fifth and sixth centuries (below, pp. 613–26).[216]

This set of patterns did not have to change when the Arabs conquered Syria and Palestine in 634–8. The Arabs left the cities alone, and they stayed prosperous, with few exceptions (one being Antioch itself, now a frontier

---

[213] Chorikios, *Orations*, III–VI; Prokopios, *Secret history*, XXVIII.1–15, XXIX.17–25 (the latter is an Askalon–Caesarea marriage alliance, linking cities); for the Piacenza pilgrim in c.570, *Itinerarium Antonini*, c. 46.8 (cf., also for Apamea, John Moschos, *Spiritual meadow*, c. 196).

[214] For Petra, see *P. Petra* I (the only volume published as yet) 2, 3, with pp. 9–10, and Gagos and Frösén, 'Petra papyri', one out of several interim reports. Only one of the Petra papyri (n. 2) mentions property outside the city's own territory or very close; it is for land near Gaza. For Edessa, Joshua the Stylite, *Chronicle*, c. 93; Prokopios, *Secret history*, XII.6–10; *Chronicle of AD 1234*, pp. 122–4, 140.

[215] For Antioch, see Libanios, *Orations*, XLII.37, XLVII.13–4; Theodoret, *Histoire des moines*, XIV.4; Cyril of Scythopolis, *Life* of Euthymios, cc. 47–8; *PLRE*, III, s.v. Evagrius. NJ, CLIX, for a rich Antioch owner, develops the Constantinople link too (cf. above, p. 164).

[216] Specific material signs of aristocratic wealth include Megas at Kaper Koraon and the Madaba mosaics: see Ch. 8, n. 16, Ch. 10, n. 52.

town, and no longer the centre of a whole region). It is sometimes supposed that the Arab conquest would have resulted in an aristocratic emigration, but it is hard to see why—such émigrés would have abandoned the sources of wealth they had in favour of a new life in the world of crisis that was mid-seventh-century Byzantium. Such emigration is occasionally mentioned in Arab sources, notably al-Balādhurī, who refers to it for Tripoli (Tarābulus), Damascus, and Ḥimṣ, as well as Bālis in the middle Euphrates valley, but it was probably not a widespread phenomenon.[217] The Edessa elites certainly stayed; Athanasios bar Gūmōyē was a sufficiently rich and important player around 700 that the Umayyads used him as an administrator in Egypt, where he made even more money (below, p. 621), and the great Edessan families are documented into the ninth century. *Kyrios* Samuel stayed in the Gaza hinterland in the 680s, too (above, p. 144); so did the patrons of the strikingly rich churches of Madaba and its region, which were still being given high-quality mosaic floors into the 770s. The city-focused provincial aristocracy remained an important feature of Syro-Palestinian society, and indeed eastwards too: the Edessene city elite is matched in the late eighth century by that in and around Mosul, 300 km to the east, just the other side of the old Persian frontier.[218]

The Arabs added certain things to these continuing patterns. One was immigration: al-Balādhurī mentions Arabs moving into abandoned houses in Tarābulus and Damascus, and in general the Muslim Arabs, the new military elite, settled among the Christians—many of whom, in the south and east, were Arabs themselves—in this region, unlike in others (above, pp. 130–1). A second was a certain revival of long-distance landowning, in that one family, the Umayyads themselves, owned across the whole region: most extensively in the Jazīra, but westwards to Iskenderun and southwards into the Balqā' south of 'Ammān, and probably in Askalon too.[219] A third was the introduction of a central administration to Damascus, which attracted Christian administrators, at least until the administrative language changed from Greek to Arabic in c.700, notably the Christian Arab family of Manṣūr b. Sarjūn (Sergios), who a tenth-century history says was a local administrator under Heraclius who went over to the Muslims in 636. His existence is not assured, but that of his probable son is, Sergios/Sarjūn b. Manṣūr, active around 700, for he is mentioned as head of the tax office for 'Abd al-Malik by both Theophanes and al-Balādhurī. His son was probably

---

[217] See al-Balādhurī, *Futūḥ al-buldān*, trans. Hitti, pp. 189, 194, 201, 232; cf. below, p. 621.

[218] *Chronicle of AD 1234*, pp. 202–4 for Athanasios; see in general Segal, *Edessa*, pp. 202–3; Liebeschuetz, *The decline*, pp. 306–7. P. *Ness.* 75, for Samuel; Ch. 10, n. 52, for Madaba. For Mosul, see Robinson, *Empire and elites*, pp. 90–108.

[219] For Umayyad landowning, see al-Balādhurī, *Futūḥ al-buldān*, trans. Hitti, pp. 197, 228, 232–3, 280–2; cf. Kennedy, 'The impact of Muslim rule', pp. 293–4; for the private estate of the 'Abbāsids at Ḥumayma, see the excavation interim in Foote, 'Frescoes'.

the theologian John of Damascus (d. 749/54), whom Iconoclast opponents called Mansour.[220] Apart from these three shifts, however, there was little structural change in Syro-Palestinian aristocratic life until at least the end of the Umayyad period, and perhaps even later. Families who stayed Christian were for the most part marginal to caliphal politics and official position, but they could regard themselves as secure in their local political frameworks. The density of exchange networks in Syria-Palestine, as well as their relative localization, especially after the Arab conquest, fits this picture of local-level continuity too (below, pp. 774–80).

These patterns are clear enough, and show an evident stability. The curious thing about Syria and Palestine, however, is that they end there. One thing that we do not find in this region is the sort of continuity with the pre-Islamic past that can be seen in al-Andalus or Iran in the tenth century, with genealogical links to former aristocracies written up, and stories of earlier civilizations recorded (as in al-Mas'ūdī's *Meadows of gold*, and most emblematically, in Firdawsī's *Shāhnāma*).[221] Later Syrian and Palestinian elites looked to their Arab, not their pre-Arab, past. The Syriac chronicles, mostly Edessene in origin, are an exception to this, but those chronicles were from the Jazīra, always slightly marginal to caliphal power.[222] Syria and Palestine, by contrast, were at the core of the Umayyad state, and much more exposed to the transformative power of a strong new political system, just as Byzantine elites were. Essentially, what happened in Syria and Palestine was that local aristocratic identities largely Islamized/Arabized themselves, and transformed themselves into something new, without a traceable Roman past: a development that one could roughly locate in the eighth century, for it was complete by the time our sources become more numerous after 800. In this respect, this region can best be located in the framework of shifting regional aristocratic identities that we have seen elsewhere: as in northern Francia, local elites took on the ethnic identity of their new rulers; as in Italy, their urban focus remained unchanged. Here, unusually, militarization was perhaps less important in the new Arab identity of local elites than was Islamization, and this may be a reason why Syria and Palestine show greater material cultural continuities than are visible almost anywhere else. But apart from that the region fits in with elsewhere, as another example, analogous to others but, once again, slightly different, of what happened to aristocracies when the Roman empire stopped.

There were probably never many really big owners in Roman Egypt. Roger Bagnall reckons for the fourth century, largely on the basis of a land register

[220] See in general Auzépy, 'De la Palestine à Constantinople', pp. 194–203, with refs. to sources.

[221] al-Mas'ūdī, *Murūj al-dhahab*, ed. and trans. Barbier de Meynard and Pavet de Courteille; Firdawsī, *Shāhnāma*, ed. and trans. Mohl.

[222] *Chronicle of AD 1234* is the main source here.

from Hermopolis (Ashmūnayn), that the 'average village' had between two-thirds and three-quarters of its land owned by villagers, whether cultivators or village-level notables. There were always some great private landlords, however: the Appianos family in the third century was one, the archive of one of whose estate managers in Arsinoë (Madīnat al-Fayyūm) survives, studied by Dominic Rathbone. In the sixth century and early seventh the role of emblematic landlords is taken by the (unrelated) Apion family of Oxyrhynchos (Bahnasā), some of whose estate archive survives too, some 300 papyri in all.[223] After a generation in which the rise of great estates in the late Roman period was accepted by many, as a result of E. R. Hardy's work on the Apions in 1931, one strand of Egyptian scholarship has gone sharply the other way, and is tending to deny their importance at all. Both positions seem to me to be exaggerations.[224] What Egypt shows, better than anywhere else in this period, is the way large landowning *interpenetrated* with small landowning, sometimes indeed field by field, with great landlords constructing estates out of thousands of often tiny building-blocks. If one concentrates on the estate archives, one only sees the estates; if one concentrates on the fields, one may not see the estates at all. But both were there, throughout.

The intermingling of larger and smaller owners in Egypt created very complex local social structures, with many links between different levels of society, expressed through political patronage, dependent tenure, the ad hoc leasing of small land-parcels, wage labour—all of which are visible in the papyri (see below, pp. 411–19). The resultant picture has some parallels in other parts of the former Roman empire, although only in later periods. The Rhineland in c.800 gives us a dimly seen version of the picture (see pp. 393–8); a clearer analogy, including in the density of documentation, can be found in the northern Italy and Tuscany of the twelfth century, which, since I have studied it myself, is inevitably in the back of my mind when I interpret Egyptian material.[225] The ready availability of these parallels makes the Egyptian evidence important as a model for other parts of Europe and the Mediterranean in our period, for it is highly unlikely that the West only developed similar structures at the very end of our period, to take them on into the central middle ages. Indeed, the interpenetration of village-level and aristocratic landowning, and the existence of complex interrelationships between the two, seem to me features of any rural society where aristocratic landowning is not in single, village-sized, blocks: before 800 there are signs

---

[223] Bagnall, *Egypt*, p. 148; cf. idem, 'Landholding', and Bowman, 'Landholding'; Rathbone, *Economic rationalism*. The published Oxyrhynchos documents are almost all in *P. Oxy.*, esp. in I, XVI, LVIII; they are not all for the Apions, but most are (see in general Mazza, *L'archivio degli Apioni*, esp. pp. 20–45).

[224] Hardy, *Large estates*; critical are Bagnall, *Egypt*, pp. 159–60, Gascou, 'Les grands domaines' (see Ch. 3, n. 44). Banaji, *Agrarian change*, pp. 119–70, and Sarris, *Economy and society*, ch. 9, convincingly reassert the view that great estates were developing in this period; but they were certainly not dominant everywhere.

[225] Wickham, *Community and clientele*.

of this interpenetration in Syria, Italy, much of Africa, parts of Spain and the south of Gaul, and the Rhineland, and it probably was a standard feature in other areas too, since it is the consistent result of partible inheritance, a normal characteristic of the Roman and post-Roman world.[226] This has often been missed by scholars whose mental model of aristocratic land-owning is the huge dependent villages of St-Germain-des-Prés, and who deny aristocratic power altogether if those blocks of land are invisible. Actually, although big single blocks of landholding certainly could exist everywhere as well, and once again can be tracked in nearly every province of the empire and the successor states, they can only be shown to have been dominant over wide areas in relatively few places, notably parts of north-western Gaul/Francia, and post-Roman Britain.[227] (Their origins in Britain will be analysed in Chapter 6, pp. 318–33, for they are highly particular; see pp. 398–406 for Francia.) Again, the list might well be longer if we had more evidence, but known areas of fragmented landowning are far more numerous. For them, Egypt is an important model.

This manifesto is aimed once again at the presupposition that Egypt is too different to be included in a set of analogous regions such as the ones chosen for this book. The points in it will be developed further in later chapters, for they are above all relevant for understanding how local societies worked. In the particular context of aristocratic landowning, however, they are relevant in that they remind us that aristocrats were located in a peasant environ-ment, with which they reacted in a wide range of ways. In other parts of the empire we only really hear about the equivalents to the Apions; in Egypt we can get a sight of their social context. But this does not, conversely, mean that Egypt was exactly the same as everywhere else, so as to allow the sleight of hand so characteristic of much of the historiography of the Roman period, in which details from every province of the empire are set beside each other to create a picture of a single 'Roman' society. In what respects *was* aristo-cratic landowning in Egypt atypical? It was probably better organized, with more wage labour, as we shall see (below, pp. 274–6). Nonetheless, it was probably, as already indicated, less dominant than aristocracies often were: Bagnall's figure, given at the start of this section, was certainly not matched in, say, the parts of Africa and Sicily dominated by the Anicii and their colleagues (though we should not underestimate independent peasants even there).

In the late sixth century we have figures for the *embolē* in wheat for the nomes (the Egyptian term for city territories) of Oxyrhynchos and

---

[226] See below, Chapter 7, and pp. 552–4.

[227] Examples of large blocks of land outside the latter two regions include Devic and Vaissete, *HGL*, II, preuves, pp. 42–4, and Debus, 'Studien', n. 5, for Aquitaine; for the Adriatic coast of Abruzzo, Feller, *Les Abruzzes*, pp. 143–7 (here the land is fiscal, but, unusually, it is located in fertile lowland areas—large tracts of fiscal land were usually in the mountains); *Life* of Melania, c. 18, for Italy or Sicily; and above, n. 24, for Africa.

Kynopolis, the latter being a small city cut out of the Oxyrhynchite nome, and also those for the Apion estates in the two cities. If these figures were for years of analogous taxation (both texts are unfortunately undated), the Apions paid 40 per cent of the total. Other more partial lists, of leading contributors only, to a barley tax, and to the expenses of the public baths of Oxyrhynchos, have the Apions making up 23–32 per cent of the total tax paid. None of these figures are flawless; indeed, they are contradictory, for the Apion family could not have paid a larger percentage of the taxes of the whole nome than it paid of the contributions of major taxpayers; but they at least converge, giving the major family of the nome a notable dominance.[228] Indeed, Oxyrhynchos as a whole was a territory dominated by substantial landowners, with the Apions only the largest of them. It was, of course, this sort of scale that impressed Hardy, and there can be no doubt that in Oxyrhynchos itself large landowning had grown substantially since the third century.[229] Jairus Banaji has shown how a new provincial aristocracy developed throughout Egypt after the mid-fifth century, out of families of state officials, who were much wealthier than before; their power was a specific feature of the sixth and early seventh centuries. It must, however, equally be stressed that Oxyrhynchos was atypical. There are some parallels to large-scale aristocratic landowning in the Fayyūm (some of it, indeed, by Apions), but not to the local dominance attested at Oxyrhynchos.[230] In the next best-documented sixth-century centre, Antaiopolis ('Irmāniyya) with its semi-autonomous dependency of Aphroditō, although there were certainly large owners there, no such dominance can be seen at all, and our evidence is above all of prosperous medium owners and owner-cultivators (see below pp. 411–19); this is also true of other centres which have left us documents, such as Herakleopolis (Ehnāsiyya) or Hermopolis. So Oxyrhynchos is our best guide to how estates worked, not our best guide to Egypt. We will look briefly at the Apions and their landowning here, and then look at what can be said about aristocrats elsewhere in Egypt, in the sixth century and later.

The Apion estates were highly organized. We have a number of detailed accounts for them from the last half of the sixth century; they list income in rents, and wages, capital costs, and other outgoings.[231] Supervision at every

---

[228] *P. Oxy.* I 127 set against XVI 1909 give the 40% figure; XVI 2020, 2040, for leading contributors. See Jones, *LRE*, pp. 780, 783–4; Gascou, 'Les grands domaines', pp. 45–8; Sarris, *Economy and society*, ch. 5; Mazza, *L'archivio degli Apioni*, pp. 80–3; Banaji, *Agrarian change*, pp. 148–52, more critical; Wipszycka, *Les ressources*, pp. 48–50.

[229] Rowlandson, *Landowners*, the best study of a local Egyptian society in the early empire, makes the absence of major owners clear for Oxyrhynchos (see esp. pp. 102–38).

[230] Banaji, *Agrarian change*, pp. 119–41; for the Fayyūm, pp. 141–9, 176–80, 241–50.

[231] Basic account collections are in *P. Oxy.* XVI 1905–21, 2016–53; particularly useful texts are 1911, 1913, 1919, 1921, XVIII 2195, 2197, XIX 2243A, XXVII 2480, LV 3804, LVIII 3960. See Sarris, *Economy and society*, ch. 2, based above all on the first, fifth, seventh, and ninth of these; Johnson and West, *Byzantine Egypt*, pp. 50–65; Mazza, *L'archivio degli Apioni*, pp. 75–156, for an overview of the estate.

level was normal, of the estate workforce and of the supervisors themselves. We have, among many, a striking set of letters from a senior estate official, Victor *antigeouchos* (*geouchos* means 'great owner'; Victor was the Apions' chief administrator) to a slightly less senior official, George *komēs* or *dioikētēs*, dating probably to the 610s, requiring a wide range of things: requests for people to be sent, for money to be deposited or paid, for some lesser officials to be released (the Apions had an estate prison), for a dispute about a cistern between some Apion tenants to be arbitrated, for an inter-village quarrel to be sorted out, for a damaged boat to be repaired, since it was needed for a journey to Alexandria. To other officials Victor asked similar things: he requested from Theodore *meizoteros* some Rhodian wine, and also asparagus, 'for the vegetables here are rotten'; he told Kosmas *komēs* to make sure that two brickmakers did not flee without finishing their contract satisfactorily.[232] These sorts of instruction recall Qurra in their specificity (above, pp. 133–40); but this time they are for a private estate, not the tax system, and their range was wider. We should, really, think of them as memos rather than letters: the Apion estate was a vast organization, whose middle management spent a good deal of time communicating with each other. The control over local agriculture, and indeed rural artisans, that they show is also notable at every stage, as with the receipts we have for the new axles of waterwheels for the irrigation network (and the return of the old ones), which the Apions made available to their tenants on a regular basis, apparently every seven years (we have axle accounts, too).[233] We have contracts for estate managers, tax-collectors, and artisans (as for example a millstone-cutter in 544), credit notes for wages, and sureties (*enguai*), in which someone acts as guarantor that an Apion dependant, usually a peasant, will serve the family satisfactorily, and not flee.[234] We do not have many Apion leases, curiously, unlike the more fragmented Aphroditō properties, which have left us several; there are three or four, all the same, and it may be that the Apion leases were in general simply located in a separate part of the archive, and have not survived.[235] It is clear, however, that the Apions relied quite substantially on wage labour in addition to leasing, which required a

[232] *P. Oxy.* VI 943, XVI 1844–8, 1853–5, 1936–7, 1940, 2011, for Victor and George (the last of these dates to 618), 1851, 1849 (quote), I 158, for Theodore and Kosmas. XVI has other linked letters. Maybe the same George to Theodore in LVI 3871 refers to their common 'lord' (*despotēs*) the *antigeouchos*, unfortunately unnamed; there is a clear hierarchy here. See Sarris, *Economy and society*, ch. 4. For the estate prison, see Gascou, 'Les grands domaines', p. 24 n.
[233] See *P. Oxy.* I 137, 195, XVI 1899, 1900, 1988–91, XXXVI 2779, for receipts, etc., XIX 2244 for an account.
[234] Estate managers (not all for the Apions): *P. Oxy.* I 136, XVI 1894, XIX 2239, LVIII 3952, 3958. Tax-collectors: LXII 4350–1. Millstone-cutter: LI 3641. Credit notes: see below, Ch. 5, n. 30. *Enguai*: see Gascou, 'Les grands domaines', pp. 24–6; Sarris, *Economy and society*, ch. 3 (from which I draw much of this); Mazza, *L'archivio degli Apioni*, pp. 122–4.
[235] *P. Flor.* III 325; *P. Oxy.* LXIII 4390, LXVII 4615 (still in press); XVI 1968 is another probable example. These are taken from the full account in Mazza, *L'archivio degli Apioni*, pp. 106–20 (cf. 189–91).

further level of control, over payment and the quality of work (below, pp. 274–5).

The level of organization of the Apion estate is very striking. Of course, we would not expect as much documentation to survive outside papyrus areas, but the estate-management collections that do exist elsewhere, from places like Nessana and Diego Álvaro, are very much less complex than this; nor do Gregory the Great's letters or, later, the polyptychs of the ninth century suggest much more by way of documentation than rent rolls (see below, pp. 265–8). Why was there so much in Oxyrhynchos? One reason is that there was a tradition of such accounting in Egypt: we find it in the Appianos estate already, for example (though third-century estate-management was not entirely the same as it was three centuries later).[236] A second is that the tax system had an equally complex accounting structure, which the Apions, who had an 'autopract' estate (that is, they collected the taxation from their estates themselves and passed it on), had partially borrowed from.[237] The Apions did distinguish between tax and rent—hence the special contracts they made with their own dependants to collect the taxes of specific sections of their property—but they extracted them both, and had an evident interest in ensuring accurate and detailed payment of both.[238] A third reason is that Egypt was an irrigated economy, and that irrigation systems require rather more detailed attention than do dry-farming systems, including a continuous attention to maintenance; this, too, would have underpinned the Apion interest in micromanagement. A fourth reason is that the Apion estate was at least in part orientated towards profit. A frequent theme of the Oxyrhynchos papyri is the shipment of goods along the Nile, which made access to nearly the whole of Egypt so easy that it reduced transport costs in the region virtually to zero. The range of those goods is once again striking; one early sixth-century papyrus lists on one ship: wallets, a cupboard door, a bag, bread, wine, salt fish and meat, preserves, anise, cumin, garlic, oil, cheese, saucepans, locks and keys, geese and chickens, a wineskin, and a silver chest; another lists papyrus, a rug, and numerous amphorae, some empty, some containing wine, soap, cedar-oil, garum, and olive oil. These must be mostly imports rather than exports, but we know that the Apion estate produced wine, grain, and sheep, as well as artisanal goods made out of brick, pottery, and stone. Peter Sarris has observed that its subsidiary villages (*epoikia*) seem, in an account of 566,

---

[236] Rathbone, *Economic rationalism*, pp. 331–87; cf. above, pp. 71–2; compare for Palestine *P. Ness.* 82–8.

[237] See in general Gascou, 'Les grands domaines', pp. 38–52.

[238] So *P. Oxy.* LXII 4350–1, agreements with tax-collectors, explicitly refer only to taxes, *dēmosion* and *embolē*, not to rents. See above, Ch. 3, n. 44, for Gascou's alternative view and for criticisms of it; idem, 'Les grands domaines', pp. 13–15 cites documents confusing tax and rent. But not many of these are for Oxyrhynchos—very few if one considers how easy it would have been for the Apions to amalgamate the two.

even to have had crop specializations, even though the land between Oxy-rhynchos and the Nile is relatively homogeneous.[239] Egypt's cities were the main destination of such exchange, for most artisans lived in them, and bought their food from the countryside. If cities in Egypt housed as much as a third of the population of the region (p. 611), this fact alone would have ensured that exchange, both inside city territories and along the Nile, must have been unusually active. This certainly fits the evidence of ceramic distributions, which extend the whole length of Egypt, from Aswān to the sea, in the whole period 400–800, without a break (pp. 759–69). This density of commercial activity was further underpinned by the tax system, for the tax boats plied the Nile as well, taking goods up to Alexandria and beyond. All this would have encouraged any owner to keep a close check on the goods coming from his or her land, and on the peasants working it—for withheld and pilfered rents could be sold too, after all.

It must be obvious that the Apions were not detached from daily land management; even though they largely lived in Constantinople, they had a complex hierarchy of direct managers, and indeed even the most basic contracts and surety agreements were often, at least nominally, made with the Apion family head, not any subordinate. This is linked with the fact that the Apions were also not at all detached from Oxyrhynchos society. They were regularly pagarchs there (they also appear as pagarchs of Arsinoë and neighbouring Theodosioupolis, and dukes of the Thebaid, further south in Middle Egypt), which meant both local power and local responsibility for tax-raising and justice/order. They apparently rose to local position and imperial attention already by 440 or so, and they were soon a senatorial family, with no need for curial office. All the same, Strategios II appears as *politeuomenos* (city councillor) for Oxyrhynchos in 489, and probably *riparios* (a city councillor with responsibility for security) of Herakleopolis, another area of Apion interest, in 505/6; his heirs were sometimes called *patēr tēs poleōs*, city leader, in Oxyrhynchos later in the sixth century, and the family had their own racing stable for the city's hippodrome into the 610s. The Apions are the richest aristocrats known for the whole of the sixth-century eastern empire, but they remained very attached indeed to the society of their city.[240] Nor were they very widely spread. It is true, as already noted, that they had Arsinoë and Herakleopolis interests, and we know of

---

[239] *P. Oxy.* XVI 1922–4. For crop specializations, LV 3804, commented on in Sarris, *Economy and society*, ch. 2.

[240] See in general Mazza, *L'archivio degli Apioni*, pp. 47–74 for the fullest recent account; earlier, *PLRE*, II, s.v. Apion 1, 2, Strategius 8, 9; III, s.v. Apion 3, 4, Strategius 3, 5, 10, where the refs. are not entirely complete. The Strategios II citations are *P. Flor.* III 325, *CPR* XIV 48; see ibid., pp. 41–8, for pagarchs of Arsinoë and Theodosioupolis, and, in general on that office, Mazza, 'Ricerche sul pagarca'. For the early period of the Apions, around 440, see also Banaji, *Agrarian change*, pp. 129–30. For Apion II as *pater tēs poleōs* in 571, Mazza, *L'archivio degli Apioni*, p. 61 n.; for the racing stables, *P. Oxy.* I 138, 140, 145, 152—cf. XXXIV 2707 for a racing programme, and LXI 4132 for a vet.

properties owned by them in both nomes, but the distance between these cities and Oxyrhynchos is only 90 km, and anyway their lands there were probably on a smaller scale than those in Oxyrhynchos.[241] They were local aristocrats who, when they made good, kept all their local links, and did so right up to their end, which seems to have been the 620s: they are not documented after 621, in the middle of the Persian occupation, and their archive stops abruptly almost at once, with only two documents surviving from the 630s, and none thereafter.[242]

The Apions are highly atypical in their wealth, and in the extent of their documentation, but they are typical in other respects. The other leading families in Oxyrhynchos paid alongside them for the city's public baths, for example (so did the cathedral, coming in in fifth place by tax obligation).[243] In other cities we find the same kind of people, too. The best-documented is Ammonios of Antaiopolis in the second quarter of the sixth century, for whom we have a set of accounts for land in Antaiopolis and Aphroditō— they survive because one of his estate administrators was Apollōs, son of Dioskoros and father of Dioskoros the poet (fl. c.520–85), from the main family in the papyri of Aphroditō (below, pp. 411–19). Ammonios was clearly a substantial local landowner, and several references to his properties can be found among the lands of smaller owners in Aphroditō, in the cadaster of c.525; he probably owned in Hermopolis too, 150 km downstream, and also had imperial office. His accounts are quite as complex as those of the Apions, and probably for the same reasons, although he was far from as locally dominant as the Apions were.[244] It is likely enough that the sixth-century pagarchs of Antaiopolis were aristocrats of a similar level, for, even though we cannot track their estates, they had senatorial-level titles, *endoxotatos (gloriosissimus)* or *megaloprepestatos*, and one, the *endoxotatē* Patrikia, pagarch in 553, was actually a woman: it is hardly imaginable that a woman, however able, would get to exercise this office, against all Roman assumptions about gender roles, unless she was of a rich and/or prominent family already. Even in the Aphroditō area, then, a major focus of small and medium landowning, we can find an aristocratic stratum, who were both

---

[241] For Arsinoë, see also Mazza, *L'archivio degli Apioni*, pp. 68–72; Banaji, *Agrarian change*, pp. 141–6. Outside Egypt, see above, n. 29.

[242] The last secure references to the Apions are *P. Oxy.* XVI 1921, LVIII 3960, both for 621, and, probably for the Apion estate, LI 3637 for 623. Two Oxyrhynchos charters for the 630s are LVIII 3961 and Sijpesteijn, 'A late deed of surety'.

[243] *P. Oxy.* XVI 2040; Wipszycka, *Les ressources*, pp. 48–9, discusses the cathedral; Fikhman, *Oksirinkh*, pp. 80–7, with Banaji, *Agrarian change*, pp. 149–52, discuss other families.

[244] *PLRE*, III, s.v. Ammonius 1. The main texts are *P. Cair. Masp.* I 67138–41, III 67327, 67347; *P. Ross.-Georg.* III 37; with *P. Flor.* III 304 for Hermopolis. For Ammonios in Aphroditō, see further Gascou and MacCoull, 'Le cadastre d'Aphroditô', p. 152, s.v.; Sarris, *Economy and society*, ch. 6. Cf. the seventh-century accounts in *P. Bad.* IV 95 for Hermopolis: Hardy, *Large estates*, pp. 58–9; Johnson and West, *Byzantine Egypt*, pp. 56–8; Banaji, *Agrarian change*, pp. 166–7.

large owners (*geouchoi*) and important imperial or city-level officials. This is likely to have been true of the whole of Egypt.[245]

That said, it has to be repeated that most of our documents are not from the large landowning stratum, outside Oxyrhynchos at least. In Aphroditō there was a complex mixture, and links of clientage between the village leadership and the powerful are in fact better documented than the latter's landowning, thanks to Dioskoros of Aphroditō's poems to the dukes of the Thebaid and other notables (indeed, once, to Patrikia). Dioskoros' own lands were in fact substantial, even though not on the *geouchos* level, and extended out of his village 60 km upstream to Panopolis (Akhmīm); we even have some accounts for them, from the 580s.[246] This level of prosperous medium owners can indeed be found all over Egypt; others are the family of Patermouthis of Syene (Aswān) in the 570s–580s, the family of Thekla of Apollōnopolis (Edfū) in the 620s–640s, and the monastery of Phoibammon at Jēme (in Western Thebes), which begins to be documented around 600.[247] How the church as a whole fitted into this network of landowning is not actually very clear; unlike the situation elsewhere, most Egyptian archives are not ecclesiastical. The level of ownership of major churches probably extended from that of the lower rungs of the aristocracy, as with the cathedral of Oxyrhynchos, down to the fairly restricted level represented by the monastery of Jēme; probably only the patriarch of Alexandria was a really major owner, as is implied by the large resources referred to in Leontios' contemporary *Life* of the patriarch John the Almsgiver (d. 619). But how far Alexandrian landowning, ecclesiastical or lay, really extended we cannot tell, for we have no documents from the Delta, the city's most obvious hinterland.[248]

---

[245] For this stratum, see Banaji, *Agrarian change*, pp. 159–63; Sarris, *Economy and society*, ch. 6; for pagarchs, Mazza, 'Ricerche sul pagarca', pp. 227–32. For Patrikia as pagarch, *P. Lond.* V 1660; see the suspicious discussion in Beaucamp, *Le statut de la femme*, II, pp. 11–13. For other major female landowners, see Banaji, *Agrarian change*, pp. 134–5, 137–8, 141–2, for Kyria of Oxyrhynchos, Christodotē of Oxyrhynchos (perhaps), Sophia of Arsinoë and elsewhere in the Fayyūm.

[246] See in general MacCoull, *Dioscorus*, and Fournet, *Hellenisme*, for the poems; McCoull, *Dioscorus*, pp. 81–4 for the poem to Patrikia and her husband. Accounts: *P. Cair. Masp.* III 67325; land in Panopolis: I 67095. See further Ch. 7, n. 81.

[247] For Patermouthios see esp. *P. Lond.* V 1719–37, which has several recent commentaries, esp. Farber and Portens, 'The Patermouthis archive'; Farber, 'Family financial disputes'; Clackson, 'Four Coptic papyri'. For Thekla, *P. Budge* (ed. and commented on in Schiller, 'The Budge papyrus'), with Zilliacus, 'Griechische Papyrusurkunden', nn. 2017–18. For the monastery of Phoibammon, see Godlewski, *Le monastère*, pp. 79–88.

[248] See in general Wipszycka, *Les ressources*, pp. 34–56, an excellent analysis of ecclesiastical landowning. The Alexandrian church did own as far as the Arsinoite: ibid., p. 53 n. A third of Aphroditō's lands belonged to seven churches in c.525: Gascou and MacCoull, 'Le cadastre d'Aphroditô', p. 118. For John the Almsgiver, see Leontios of Neapolis, *Life*, cc. 1, 6, 10, 18, 57, etc.; cf. for the late seventh century Sāwīrus, *History of the patriarchs*, PO, V.1, p. 18, for land in Fusṭāṭ. See in general for patriarchal wealth Haas, *Alexandria*, pp. 249–51. In the third century Alexandrian land had extended well beyond the Delta: Rathbone, *Economic rationalism*, pp. 44–58; Banaji, *Agrarian change*, pp. 102–11.

How a society of many levels of landowning worked we will see in Chapter 7, using the example of Aphroditō itself. In terms of the geographical range of landowning, however, each of the nomes of Egypt can be regarded as fairly locally focused. The evidence for Egypt in fact substantially fits what we have seen for the rest of the late Roman east Mediterranean: that, however rich aristocracies were, they tended to be centred on single cities, with rather less landowning outside them. Even really large lay owners like the Apions cannot be seen owning more widely than two or three city territories, apart from links to the capital. Nor were ecclesiastical owners different, except perhaps the patriarch of Alexandria. This may be the chance of our papyrus evidence, which is only for parts of Middle and Upper Egypt, and not the Delta; but it is worth adding that the Apions are also by far the best-known Egyptian family even in non-Egyptian documentation, so there are unlikely to have been many others like them or ahead of them. It is curious, in a sense, that people did not own over long distances more often, given the ease of communications in Egypt. They did, very occasionally: Thekla of Apollōnopolis, though not obviously a major owner, had land in Oxyrhynchos and Herakleopolis, to which she moved in the 620s, during the Persian occupation, a distance of some 600 km.[249] But this was not common. All our document collections are relatively localized, and make little reference to worlds outside their city-level compass. The true integration of the Nile valley was created, not by landowning, but by exchange, and of course by the tax system.

The Arab conquest did not change so very much in these patterns, but their scale became substantially smaller. The Apions had already gone, and we find no one else to take their place who was a *geouchos* on that scale. The Arabs certainly did not; they stayed in Fusṭāṭ, and, if they acquired land, did so in areas we do not have documents for. Egyptian local elites stayed in place, however, for a century. We have several examples of families of pagarchs in this period, all of them from Greco-Coptic families, presumably local ones. Kyros of Herakleopolis (638–42) was pagarch during the Arab conquest itself—the first surviving Arabic documents mention him—and was succeeded by his sons Christopher (643–7) and Theodorakios. Liberios of Apollōnopolis (649) was succeeded, even if not immediately, by his son Papas (675–6?). Petterios of Arsinoë (668–99) was not visibly succeeded by his sons, but at least controlled his territory, probably off and on, for a generation, if we accept Peter Sijpesteijn's dating of his texts. Epimachos of Aphroditō was succeeded by his brother Basilios (see above, pp. 133–7) in 709. All of these families can be found owning land as well, for we have a few leases for most of them.[250] We cannot say how much land in any case, for

---

[249] Banaji, *Agrarian change*, p. 137, lists some wide owners, but the distances are not enormous. For Thekla, see n. 247.

[250] Kyros, Christopher, and Theodorakios: *PERF* 550 (a. 638); Grohmann, 'Greek papyri', nn. 2–4, 7–8; *CPR* VIII 71, XXII 4–6. Liberios and Papas: Crum, 'Koptische Zünfte', p. 106;

papyrus archives from the two centuries after the Arab conquest usually stress tax records rather than estate documents, but one could well guess that they were important local owners, important enough to try to control the pagarchy and thus the determination of tax liability—it is probably significant that, although we have a wealth of documentation for Aphroditō's tax obligations in the 710s, Basilios does not appear in any of it.

All in all, our documentation for large property in the early Arab period is fragmentary: only about a dozen papyri in our period seem to refer to it at all, and then only casually.[251] Probably the best-documented estate for Arab Egypt up to 800 is the monastery of Apa Apollō, now called Deīr al-Bala'īza, 20 km south of Sioout (Greek Lykopolis, modern Asyūṭ), whose eighth-century archive survives. It contains several private accounts of different types. There are lists of taxes paid and the peasants who paid them, and a list of fugitives (cf. above, pp. 136–43). There are also accounts of expenses: lists of foodstuffs, lists of to whom wine was to be distributed among the monks and the estate workers. One list of expenses mixes taxation and miscellaneous outgoings in an instructive way: listing from the top, 1 *nomisma* for the money-tax of [the village of] Pektēs, 1 *nom.* for rope for Pateron, $\frac{1}{24}$ *nom.* for freight costs by boat to Antinoupolis, $\frac{2}{3}$ *nom.* in receipt from Sioout, $\frac{1}{2}$ *nom.* for the poll-tax of Pğōl the deacon, $\frac{1}{6}$ *nom.* for the horse-doctor from Sioout, and so on. Apart from these lists, there are contracts (for debt, and once for marriage), there are standard tax receipts, and there are several letters about the management of monastic property, of the Victor-George type: you must return the goat you extorted; I don't think it is a good idea to expel the palm-leaf picker, as we need him—also, bring me lentils and salt fish when you come; do not pay him, but here is the money for the tax, and give two camels to [name lost]. Bala'īza was a much simpler and smaller estate than anything on the Apion level, and its attachment to lists recalls Diego Álvaro; its management seems to have focused on moving goods around and checking on its transport-workers rather than on organizing agrarian production.[252] It is likely, however, that it represents well enough the way a medium-level landowner saw management in the eighth century, and its concern with accounting had certainly carried over from the sixth century and earlier.

P. Apoll. 3–50 (all these texts are redated in Gascou and Worp, 'Problèmes de documentation', pp. 83–9). Petterios: Sijpesteijn, 'Der Pagarch Petterios'; Gascou and Worp, ibid., p. 88, doubt the 690s dating of some of the texts. Epimachos: *P. Lond.* IV 1512, 1521, 1530, 1592, 1613, *APEL* III 164. Leases, etc.: Grohmann, 'Greek papyri', n. 3 (Christopher lending money); *P. Apoll.* 57, 63–4; *P. Vindob.* G. 20796 (ed. in Sijpesteijn, 'Der Pagarch Petterios'); *P. Lond.* IV 1592.

251 References to large property in the period 640–800 are very heterogeneous, but see *CPR* VIII 71, 82, X 135, XIV 52; *PERF* 616; *P. Lond.* IV 1631; *APEL* IV 223, 231–2, VI 378. Hardy, *Large estates*, pp. 146–7 and Banaji, *Agrarian change*, pp. 153–4, 156–7 both argue that the great sixth-century estates had gone by now; I entirely agree, as the following will make clear.

252 *Bala'izah*, nn. 286–346 for accounts; cited is n. 291; a good parallel is n. 303B. Debt contracts: nn. 102–18; marriage: n. 152. Letters are nn. 186–273; nn. 256, 259, 214 are cited. For a simpler parallel, see *CPR* XXII 60.

Any conclusion one draws from this fairly heterogeneous material for the early Arab period will have to be impressionistic, but the clear impression given by it is that the scale of aristocratic landowning had decreased. Not only had the Apions gone, but Dioskoros of Aphroditō would be accounted a major figure by the eighth century had his documents been for two centuries later. Certainly the pagarch level would fill out our sense of the scale of landowning more if it had left us more than fragmentary documentation, but, on the other hand, our densest local collections do not give us the sort of frequent, even if chance, reference to substantial owners that those of the sixth century had. Bala'īza's scale was, as has just been noted, medium-level at best. The Jēme documents, although they include several eighth-century wills, show nothing beyond the same level, and the largest owner there was probably the already-cited monastery of Phoibammon, which may have been smaller than Bala'īza (below, pp. 419–26). Aphroditō's tax records miss out Basilios, but also do not include any other major owners— *Apa* Kyros son of Samuel, *lashane* (headman) of the village of Treis Pediades ('Three Fields'), was the largest owner and taxpayer there, owing in 705 around six times the local average in taxes, with land scattered across seven separate sections of the village, but here we are at the level of the rich peasantry. Even though Aphroditō was among the most insignificant pagarchies of Egypt, its tax assessments in 550 would have listed many people richer than *Apa* Kyros, including major outside owners. Either they were by now all more skilled in tax-evasion than in 550 (and that would have to have been very skilled, given the intensity of Arab tax controls), or the top level of the Egyptian aristocracy had lost much of its wealth.[253] If it did, it was probably slowly; the Arab impact on Egyptian society was as yet relatively external, and seldom violent until the tax revolts began. It is likely that the restriction of official position for Christian Egyptians to the level of the pagarchy meant that opportunities to profit from the state hierarchy were cut back substantially. The weakness of patronage relationships in early Arab Egypt (above, p. 143) was both cause and consequence of this relative weakness of local elites. After c.730 all our pagarchs have Arab names, too, either because they were now chosen from among the Fusṭāṭ Arabs or because they had converted. (Before the early eighth century the only probable Arab pagarch in our documents is Atias of Arsinoë, pagarch 694–8 and then duke of the Thebaid in 698–700.)[254] This marked the beginning of the

[253] For *Apa* Kyros, see esp. *P. Lond.* IV 1421, with 1494; cf. Morimoto, 'Land tenure', pp. 117–18. MacCoull, 'Notes on the social structure', pp. 74–5, shows that church landowning survived into the eighth century at Aphroditō (e.g. the monastery of *Abba* Souros in *P. Lond.* IV 1419), and suggests that Psibanōbet in the same text (ll. 527, 539, 550, 906) is an heir of Dioskoros. This is quite likely; but the tenurial scale of both is only that of *Apa* Kyros by now.

[254] For Atias, see *CPR* VIII 72–84, and the documents listed on pp. 190–7. His ethnicity is not entirely certain, but likely. The editors worry (p. 197) that he is called Flavios, but unnecessarily: as they concede, the certainly Arab pagarch Sahal of Armant in 739 (*KRU*, n. 50) was called

Arabization/Islamization of local political structures in Egypt, although this was still a slow process, very incomplete by 800; but it further cut out Christian families from official position, and thus access to state wealth. The state remained powerful and rich, as we saw in Chapter 3; it was rich enough to integrate the whole of the economy of Egypt on its own, as the ceramic continuities of the region imply (below, pp. 759–69). The period 640–800 may have been the clearest instance in Egyptian history in which this wealth was relatively unconnected to a localized aristocracy. In Arab Egypt there is a disjuncture between the archaeological and the documentary evidence for wealth, as there is in Spain, but it goes in the opposite direction, with the archaeology indicating a larger scale than does the documentation for landowning, not a smaller one. But here, at least, the principal missing link is evident: it is the state.

The non-Arab elites of Egypt, whether Greek- or (mostly) Coptic-speaking, were more separated from public power than were their equals in Syria-Palestine; they also changed more slowly. We do not have the sort of contemporary narratives that would tell us what the local Christian aristocracy thought of ancestry, but the visibly semi-hereditary pagarchies of the late seventh century imply that it was more important in Egypt around 700 than in most of the rest of the eastern Mediterranean at that moment. Access to official position was still possible for non-Muslims, although only at the level of the pagarchy, for a century; access to central government patronage was almost absent. Landed wealth was less extensive, but probably more essential for status than ever. We cannot say anything about aristocratic lifestyles, although we can be sure that Christian Egyptians stayed civilian, even at the aristocratic level, longer than they did elsewhere. The Arab elites stayed isolated in Fusṭāṭ, and did not fill the gap between state and society; even Arab landowning seems to have been relatively small scale, outside the area of Arab settlement in the eastern Delta, before 850.[255] This situation could not, however, last. In the end, the rich Arabs of Fusṭāṭ would buy land, and the Christian elites would convert in order to get access to the wealth of the capital. After 850, indeed, we begin to find evidence of substantial grants of land by the state to Muslim aristocrats, and also the beginning of large-scale

Flavios too. The Arab pagarchs of Armant seem to begin around 730: see *KRU*, nn. 12, 13, 42, 45, 50, 52, 106, for the 730s. I follow Till's datings in *Datierung*, except for *KRU*, n. 50, which is dated to 739 rather than 724, surely more correctly, in Till, *Erbrechtliche Untersuchungen*, p. 147. In Herakleopolis and Arsinoë, too, Arab pagarchs are regularly documented from the 720s onwards (with some uncertain earlier examples): see *CPR* XXII 7–13 and the comments on the texts. No non-Arab pagarch is known from later. Note that this trend was independent of legislation; the Caliph 'Umar II (717–20) had enacted that even village headmen should be Muslims (Morimoto, 'Land tenure', p. 126), and this certainly did not occur (below, pp. 422–4).

[255] Morimoto, 'Land tenure', pp. 124–30 (cf. Ch. 3, n. 214): most of his early evidence is for small-scale landowning.

tax-farming grants, that could turn into de facto landowning.[256] Landed wealth comes back into our documentation from then on, and society began to change. But it had taken two centuries from 640.

5. Conclusions: regional aristocracies in the post-Roman world

If we want to generalize about the trends in the aristocracies of the whole of the former empire in the post-Roman period, we can identify certain common features, which unify nearly every region of the Roman world, and which put the exceptions into high relief. First of all, post-Roman aristocracies tended to be poorer. This is a clear tendency, which is common to every region except two, Francia and Syria. Historians who suppose that the break-up of the Roman world was to the benefit of aristocracies are wrong; in no case did they increase their prosperity. Indeed, in some places they lost wealth dramatically: most notably in the 'senatorial region' of southern Italy and the Rome–Carthage axis of the great families of late imperial Rome, which was destroyed by the regionalization of the Mediterranean. The level of the hyper-rich did not survive the end of the empire, that is to say. But perhaps still more important is that even regional and sub-regional elites disappeared, with the important exception of Francia, the only region in which aristocrats stayed both wealthy and geographically wide-ranging in their land tenure. This continued scale of aristocratic power made Francia unique: it created considerable problems for kings when the latter faltered in their authority, but it was a secure support for the remarkable scale of Carolingian ambition at the end of our period.

The second common feature is implied already in the preceding paragraph: except again in Francia, aristocracies became more localized, and those who were based on non-local power-bases went to the wall. The real continuities between the Roman world and the early middle ages are all at the level of the city and its territory: this is indeed true of Francia as well, where our securest examples of family survival are all at the city level. In Syria aristocratic continuities were helped by the small geographical scale of wealthy landowning even under late Rome. In Egypt, too, private ownership remained restricted to the city level, more indeed after 640 than before. In Italy the collapse of the senatorial level left urban society and local land-owning largely unchanged; by contrast, in the Byzantine heartland cities

---

[256] Ibid., pp. 130–6, for land grants. For tax-farming, see Frantz-Murphy, 'Land tenure', who traces its origins in Fayyūm documents back to the 770s; she edits most of them in *CPR* XXI. Frantz-Murphy calls tax-farming contracts 'leases', and argues that there was already a genuine blurring between land-leasing and tax-farming, in ibid., pp. 17, 27–31; this seems rather early to me, but, either way, her use of the word 'lease' in this context seems to me unfortunate, and it leads to confusion.

went as well, but it is likely that that level of landowning did at least survive. The result of this generalized localization was that any economic relation- ships beyond the level of the city territory would have to be carried by the state. The eastern empires could do this (most successfully in Egypt); the Romano-Germanic kingdoms could not. Only, once again, in (northern) Francia do we find extra-local exchange networks surviving throughout our period, in the context, however, of an extra-local aristocracy. This too made the Seine–Rhine region different from elsewhere around 800 (see below, pp. 797–805).

The reasons why aristocracies became poorer and more localized in most of the Roman world can partly be associated with political decentralization, as has been implied; it was simply too difficult to maintain widely scattered lands in several independent states for more than short periods of time. But the end of sub-regional elites as well in most of the post-Roman world indicates that aristocrats faced more problems that that, for the post- Roman polities were mostly large enough to have accommodated at least some sub-regional landowning. Here, one has to recognize that political crisis was in itself not good for aristocracies. As states changed, new families appeared to rival the old, either from lower down the social scale or from different regions altogether; they did not necessarily replicate the wealth of older elites, at least not immediately. And crisis could undermine aristocratic local control more directly, as older families were destroyed (which they were at least sometimes) without newer ones being created, or as owners lost control of their peasants in situations of political disturbance. A rare empir- ical example of the latter process is represented by a plea of the monastery of Murbach in Alsace to Charlemagne, from the period 774–800, in which, according to the abbot, 'many' of the monastery's *mancipia* supposedly, in a time of *turbatio* between the Alsatians and the Alemans (i.e. probably in the 740s, a full generation before), 'escaped from its service, and now claim to be free (*ingenui*)'; the abbot asked Charlemagne to return them to servitude. It is clear that these unfree dependants had not moved; if the abbot was telling the truth, they had profited from a moment of instability to improve their tenurial position, and maintained it for a generation—in the full Carolingian period, too, and not so far from the political heartlands of the dynasty.[257] Even if the abbot was lying, such a process was possible to set out as a rhetorical image; either way, the abbot evidently could not subject these dependants by force. Practical aristocratic control depended on local rela- tions of force between lords and peasants, which could vary even from village to village; this was so in the sixth and seventh centuries, periods of greater aristocratic difficulty in different parts of the post-Roman world, just as it was in the eighth in Alsace. Under these circumstances, although

---

[257] *Formulae Morbacenses*, n. 5 (in *MGH, Formulae*, p. 331).

aristocrats doubtless sometimes found themselves able to profit from crisis, as the rule of law slipped, thanks to their armed men, they did not always: hence, then, the fact that we find them tending to be less wealthy in global terms. The consequences for peasantries were potentially considerable, as we shall see in Chapter 9.

The way aristocratic identities changed had different parameters. Here, the exceptions are southern Gaul/Francia and Spain, which are the two post-Roman regions in which aristocrats seem to have continued longest to operate inside a broadly defined Roman socio-political habitus; to these we must add the Christian aristocracy of Egypt, as long as it resisted the temptations of Arabization/Islamization, which was until our period ended, though not much longer. Elsewhere, names changed, the importance of ancestry temporarily dissolved, and a 'new' aristocracy appeared. Even though its genealogical relationship to an older one was not necessarily negated by these changes, its relationship to the state was in each case—northern Francia, Lombard and Byzantine Italy, the Byzantine heartland, Syria-Palestine—quite different from before. In fact, it was the changing culture of the state that was itself responsible for these transformations: the state was so important for the way aristocrats imagined themselves every-where that, when it changed, so, inevitably, did they (even if, as in Egypt, they held out for two centuries). This was so whether a part of the ruling class was clearly new, immigrants from outside, as in Francia, Lombard Italy, or Syria, or whether it was not, as in Byzantium. It follows that the culture of the state in Visigothic Spain was relatively unchanged from the Roman period, which I think is a legitimate conclusion to draw: less changed even than in the surviving Roman empire that we call Byzantium. The form of the state was not obviously so unchanged in Aquitaine, but Frankish power was much more distant and perhaps less influential locally as an identification marker; furthermore, the local state was never well defined there, and went under in the eighth century. The capacity of the state to dominate over aristocratic identity is further underlined by the fact that states were far richer than the by-now-localized aristocrats in most of our regions; this may have been least true in Francia, but the Merovingian kings were never poor, and the Carolingians were for long rich as well.

A final near-consistent pattern is a tendency to the militarization of aristocratic identity and values. This militarization was indeed a key element of the changes in the form of the state just discussed. The church was the only civilian alternative in the West, with the added feature (an advantage or a disadvantage according to the local situation) that it brought a relative autonomy from state hierarchies. This autonomy was never more than relative in our period, however, apart from a few short-lasting Frankish 'episcopal republics' around 700, and with the major exception of the papacy. In the East the church was more politically marginal (except for the patriarch of Constantinople, and probably also that of Alexandria, a leader of Christian Egyptians until well after our period ends),[258] and there was more scope for surviving civilian administrative groups; but military leadership dominated there too, in Byzantium and the caliphate alike. It was argued earlier that this military shift may well underpin some of the major changes in the material culture of the West, particularly the fate of rural villas. In the East this is harder to ascertain, for archaeology is less good for the post-Roman period—except in Palestinian cities, which in fact show little change. But, uniformly across the former Roman empire, the major marker of an aristocratic lifestyle in the imperial period, an educated civilian literary culture, vanished (it had even gone in still-civilian Egypt by 800, for so few people there by now spoke Greek). This change was regarded by generations of historians as the most momentous one of all. Not by me; but it is nonetheless significant, as a marker of the military identity that would characterize aristocrats in the rest of the middle ages in most of Europe and the Mediterranean.

These are the major shifts in the post-Roman aristocracies of Europe and the Mediterranean that I can identify. To an extent they mark continuities rather than change; in particular, at the level of cities and city-territories, the parameters of aristocratic power very largely remained as they were. Only in a few regions was change more radical than that, regions where one of the essential presuppositions of that continuity, a Roman-style concept of property-owning, was swept away. This was in particular a feature of marginal areas, the African desert and mountain fringe, perhaps parts of the northern and eastern Spanish mountains, and above all Britain. There, the post-Roman world was so different that it needs separate treatment; we shall look at it in Chapter 6.

---

[258] Sāwīrus, *History of the patriarchs, passim.*

5

Managing the land

1. Metanarratives

THIS CHAPTER FOCUSES on the organization of agricultural production, as seen from the standpoint of landowners. (Some peasant reactions will be discussed in Chapters 7 and 9.) We will only look at agriculture here, not artisan production. The late Roman and post-Roman world was, of course, overwhelmingly an agrarian society; artisanal work was only a small proportion of the total productive activity of any of our regions, even in Egypt, where it was probably most extensive. Furthermore, we know even less about the social organization of artisan production than we know about agriculture—the little that can be said (again, mostly about Egypt) will be set out in Chapter 11. Agriculture is thus our essential concern for the moment.

The organization of agriculture has not been neglected by late Roman and early medieval historians. Far from it; it lies at the heart of almost all economic analyses of our period, and one of the major images of the way Antiquity changed into the middle ages was, traditionally, the account of how a society based on slavery was replaced by a society based on serfdom. This was an image already strong at the start of the nineteenth century, and was developed, among others, by Karl Marx and Friedrich Engels; it still exercises a strong hold in the field as an underlying metanarrative. There certainly were slave plantations in, say, the Italy of the first century AD, just as there were unfree tenants (serfs), and also free tenants who were dominated by the legal coercion of their lords, in much of Europe in the twelfth century; that contrast can still, if one chooses, be elevated into an ideal-type opposition between 'ancient' and 'medieval' economies. But the path between them was by no means a straight one, and in the period 400–800, the actual period of the shift between ancient and medieval, the contrast is considerably less useful. Given the hold of the traditional narrative, we need to see why it is problematic before we move on.

First, slavery. Both ancient and medieval societies were full of people who had few or no legal rights, called *servi* and *ancillae* in Latin (with *mancipia* as an alternative neuter noun that covered both sexes, though see below, pp. 562–4, for complications)—every other language had its own terminology too, of course. They were substantially commoner in the West than in the East, but they existed everywhere. Their practical rights varied: usually their de facto possession of goods, their *peculium* in Latin, was recognized (slaves could buy freedom with them on occasion); sometimes their nuclear families were legally recognized—though very rarely their wider kin; sometimes the punishment that their masters/owners could give them was restricted by law. But they were defined in law as unfree, in that they had no access to public legal recourses (except sometimes to claim that they were illegally enslaved), and still less to political rights; they were the property of masters/owners. Much of the literature on slavery in our period stresses this legal and proprietorial aspect, and the 'social death' it implies, in Orlando Patterson's words. It is an aspect that did not significantly change as the ancient world became the medieval one, and this fact has been used to underscore some of the essential continuities between the one and the other.[1]

Up to a point, this is fully legitimate. The problem comes, however, when moving from legal subjection to economic activity. In human history, most cultivators have been peasants, who work the land autonomously, in family groups (see below, p. 386, for definitions). There are differences in the organization of their labour (sometimes wide kin-groups are involved, sometimes nuclear families, sometimes only the men in the family, sometimes wider non-kin collectivities organized on the level of the village or the estate); there are, furthermore, great differences in their legal and tenurial independence; but these are not such as to remove the basic resemblance between all peasant economies. Peasant families control a given set of lands at any one time, cultivate it, rely on its produce to survive, and also give a part of the produce to a landlord if they have one, and/or to the state if it exists. The structural economic shift, away from a peasantry, comes when agricultural workers are not given that control. This may be because they are slaves, who are, like animals, wholly the property of the lord, wholly maintained by him/her, and—this being the crucial point here—wholly under the lord's direction in their economic activity. This directed slave production is often called plantation slavery, for it was the basic pattern of the antebellum United States, the Caribbean, and Brazil. The other main alternative to peasant production is that of wage labour, in which workers are paid a salary for working at an employer's orders rather than having land from which they draw their subsistence; this is the basic feature of the agrarian capitalism of recent centuries.

Slave plantations, peasant farming, and wage labour are in empirical terms the only major ways in which settled agriculture has ever been

---

[1] Patterson, *Slavery and social death*. (On pp. 182–6, he gives a good cross-cultural survey of *peculium*.) For the early middle ages, good examples are Bonnassie, *From slavery*, pp. 1–59; Hammer, *A large-scale slave society*; and Bois, *La mutation*, pp. 31–61, a less convincing account. From a different standpoint, Whittaker, 'Circe's pigs', plays down the slave mode of production in the early Roman empire and emphasizes economic continuities with the early middle ages.

practised, and they are fundamentally different in the way labour power is organized. Marx distinguished between them as 'modes of production', stressing above all that the relations of dominance and expropriation, which themselves underpinned the whole of society, were structured differently if a master fed and directed his slaves, or if a lord took surplus from a subsistence peasant, or if an employer paid and directed a worker who then used the money to pay for food and shelter independently—in the slave mode, the feudal mode, and the (agrarian) capitalist mode respectively. In each case, a dominant class lived off the labour of others, but the relations of production were entirely different, and, crucially, had a different economic logic. These categories do not need to be developed further here; they anyway have an endless bibliography, dating largely to the 1970s. It needs only to be said that they have always seemed fundamental distinctions to me, and I shall use them throughout this book. They are fundamental distinctions even though they could in real societies be combined, with peasants, say, owning their own slaves and using them as farmhands, or hiring themselves or their children out as labourers to supplement their incomes, patterns to which we shall return in this and later chapters.[2] I shall add to these three modes a fourth: the patterns of the peasant economy that can be found when landlords or the state do *not* take surplus in a systematic way, which I call here the 'peasant mode of production'. This mode will be characterized in more detail in Chapter 9 (pp. 535–47), where it is contrasted above all with the feudal mode. This chapter, however, concerns the landlord's perspective on production and estate management, and thus presupposes the existence of landlords.

If one wants to understand how slavery works economically, then it should be clear that how rural labour was actually organized is more important than the issue of legal disability discussed by other historians. The slave mode of production of course needs slaves, as defined in legal terms, for such a totalizing economic control presupposes a denial of rights to the workers involved; but *servi, ancillae, mancipia* do not have to be organized according to the slave mode. Plenty of tenants throughout the ancient and medieval periods were referred to in these words (and their analogues in other languages), and were unfree in legal terms, but their *economic* relationship to their lords was effectively identical to that of their free tenant neighbours. I would argue that the de facto economic autonomy that such tenants had as peasants was more important than

---

[2] Marx discussed these issues in most detail in *Grundrisse*, pp. 459–514. For some bibliography, see Wickham, *Land and power*, pp. 9–12, 45–50, 84–9 (I have abandoned, however the tax–rent modal distinction argued for there: see above, p. 60); and Carandini, *Anatomia*, one of the 1970s analyses that has held up best. Banaji, 'The fictions of free labour', has recently and effectively argued that the coercive environment of much wage labour lessens the distinctions between it and other modes, but this does not change the fact that each presupposes a different economic logic.

their legal unfreedom, and that slaves in the slave mode were on the other side of a divide from them. For this reason, I shall avoid calling unfree tenants 'slaves', restricting this terminology to the slave mode (as well as to servile domestic labour in the households of both aristocrats and peasants, which was quite common everywhere in our period). Of course, it mattered enormously to individual tenants whether they were free or not; their capacity to negotiate their rents and to deal with their wider social environment was crucially affected by their legal condition (see below, pp. 558–66). Peasant collectivities, too, found their bargaining capacity considerably lessened if too many of their number were unfree. But there is still a gulf between this level of differentiation and the radical separation from any control over one's own labour that is the experience of the plantation slave, which justifies the modal difference between them, the feudal mode for the former, the slave mode for the latter.

These characterizations are hardly controversial; I have also set out my own views on the slave mode in earlier work.[3] Here, they serve to underline one essential empirical point: plantation slaves were very rare anywhere in our period, even though *servi* were so common. Actually, plantations had never been frequent outside central Italy, Sicily, and parts of Greece, and even there the basic economic shift from the slave to the feudal mode had already taken place well before 400, in particular in the second and third centuries.[4] Throughout our period the slave mode was only a minor survival, everywhere marginal to the basic economic structure, the landlord–peasant relationship (where there were landlords at all). This was not less so because the legal systems of the period all ascribed so much importance to the slave–free boundary, and because so many peasants were legally unfree.[5] This contrast between economic and legal distinctions has sometimes caught ancient and medieval economic historians in a game of mirrors: medievalists, less aware that ancient historians do not see the slave mode as continuing much past 200, look too hard for this 'ancient' survival in their evidence for *servi*, and think they can find it; ancient historians, unaware of this misunderstanding, then conclude that the slave mode must have revived again in the early middle ages, perhaps in the context of the fifth-century wars,

---

[3] For the slave mode, see the bibliographical survey in Wickham, *Land and power*, pp. 84–9, referring to work up to 1986. (The historiography on the Roman slave mode is largely in Italian, for in the imperial period its geographical focus was Italy. Carandini, *Schiavi* is a later article collection.)

[4] For late Rome, see Jones, *LRE*, pp. 793–5, as a basic starting-point, although now outdated; more recently, important surveys include Vera, 'Forme e funzoni', 'Schiavitù rurale', 'Dalla "villa perfecta" ', and 'Le forme del lavoro rurale'; Giardina, *L'Italia romana*, pp. 233–64. I rely substantially on Vera's numerous articles in what follows.

[5] See the basic survey in Bloch, *Mélanges historiques*, I, pp. 261–85, together with the collections of data, mostly from law-codes, in Verlinden, *L'esclavage*, I, pp. 61–122, 637–728; II, pp. 30–96—although Verlinden gratuitously assumes that *servi* and *mancipia* in our period were plantation slaves unless there is explicit contrary evidence.

and so on.[6] One of my intentions in this chapter will therefore be to try to show quite how unimportant slave-mode production actually was, empirically, in all the regions studied in this book.

The other end of the story, the 'serfdom' of the central middle ages, is equally problematic. The sort of legal subjection to lordly control that one can find in (say) twelfth-century France or England had many separate elements, each with its own separate history. One, certainly, was legal unfreedom, which descended genealogically from that of the Roman world (and also from that of all the non-Roman societies of northern Europe), but which had changed considerably in its practical content. Among other things, of course, the content of unfreedom depends on the changing content of the legal rights of the free, which the unfree do not have access to, and free tenants were finding their legal autonomy diminished by that time. Not least by the second element, what the French call the *seigneurie banale*, the subjection of tenants to the private justice of lords, which was in its main essentials a new development of the late tenth century onwards (although the de facto local political dominance of lords is as old as the lord–tenant relation itself).[7] This latter development considerably lessened the old free–unfree divide, and free and unfree tenure were moving together, becoming equally subject and 'serf-like', in many parts of twelfth-century Europe. But this means that the twelfth century was not at all like the sixth to ninth centuries, when that divide was still very sharp.

A third element in central medieval productive relations was the manorial system (in French, the *régime domanial classique*; in Italian, the *sistema curtense*; in German, a common term is *Villikationswirtschaft*), the 'bipartite' division of an estate into a demesne and tenant holdings. Before 1200, the demesne on a manor was worked by the labour service (corvée) of tenants, as part of their rent, and/or (although, as we shall see, less often than some have thought) by household slaves. This directed labour resembles the slave mode, and in the latter variant could indeed be characterized as the slave mode. It is thus tempting to trace the genealogy of demesne labour back to the slave plantations of Columella, as well as to the corvées of free peasants, to the state or to private landlords, which are documented on a small scale in the early empire, particularly in Africa. Nor would this be unreasonable, if a link could be shown; all the same, both labour service and demesnes were relatively rare in the immediately post-Roman period. Whether or not the link is there (see below, p. 299), there was a systemic break between all the patterns of direct labour in the Roman world and medieval demesne

---

[6] Vera, 'Le forme del lavoro rurale', unveils many of the misunderstandings, although even he falls into the mirror game once, on p. 327.

[7] A basic survey of *seigneurie banale* and its origins is Poly and Bournazel, *La mutation*, pp. 71–95, 193–219; for Italy, Carocci, 'Signoria rurale'; most recently, *Señores, siervos*, and Bourin and Martínez, *Pour une anthropologie*. For the origins of 'serfdom', a good survey is Panero, *Schiavi servi*.

agriculture, which begins to be extensively documented in northern Francia and northern Italy only in the late eighth century. This, too, is an empirical assertion, which this chapter will need to explore. But we can take for granted from the start that the generalized rural subjection represented by the mutual dialectic of personal unfreedom, directed corvée labour, and the private justice of the *seigneurie banale* is simply absent from our period, and from before the late tenth century.[8] It needs no more description in this book than do the idealized slave plantations of Columella, and I shall avoid calling my unfree tenants 'serfs', as a result, as well. Late Roman and early medieval productive relations in the countryside must be seen in their own terms, not in those of the periods before and after, and that will be the task of this chapter.

The marginality of the slave mode in our period is matched by the relative unimportance of wage labour, at least outside Egypt (below, pp. 274–6); essentially, throughout our period, agriculture on estates was above all performed by peasant, tenant, cultivators. (Hence, among other things, the importance in late Roman legislation of laws about the tax liability of the 'colonate', the representation in fiscal terms of the basic landlord–tenant relationship: below, pp. 519–26.) But an agrarian system based on tenancy is also one whose basic productive processes are under peasant, not landlord, control, for it is the peasant family on its tenant plot which is actually making most of the strategic choices about production and, of course, doing the work. Direct intervention by the landlord is certainly possible, but it is an intrusion from above, against the grain of the labour process; it requires much attention and constant (often coercive) reinforcement, and will only be partially successful. Landlords generally have to have good reasons for such attentiveness, and, if the reasons go away and the attentiveness is relaxed, tenants will return to cultivating in the ways that best suit them, not their lords. This is indeed, as I shall argue, what happened in the early middle ages in most regions. The economy will be looked at from the peasant point of view in Chapter 9, but the fact that peasants, on their plots, control their own labour power in all default situations must not be forgotten in what follows.

I want to set out two basic arguments in this chapter, and a section will be devoted to each. First, that the slave mode and the demesne have in common something different to their hypothetical genealogical link: they are both signs of the intensification of landlordly control over agrarian production. Nor are they the only such signs: tight accounting procedures, systematic attempts to direct the labour of peasants even on their own holdings, moves to cash-cropping specializations, and wage labour are others. In the case of

---

[8] For genealogical continuities, out of many, Percival, 'Seigneurial aspects', is perhaps the most sustained argument. Davies, 'On servile status', is an analysis close to mine, with some differences in uses of terminology; there are also parallels in Goetz, 'Serfdom'.

plantations and full-time wage labour, landlordly intervention pushes the agricultural labour-force out of the peasantry altogether, as outlined above; but both these cases and the others, all of them to be found in the late Roman world at least somewhere, are united by a common concern for intensified control on the part of landowners. Lords sometimes want to dominate the economic activity of their dependants simply in order to assert and underline their local power; but the infrastructure needed to do so often takes a lot of work to set up (this is particularly true for the plantation, for that degree of systematic coercion, unless it is on a very small scale, is complex and expensive to maintain), and generally needs to have a stronger rationale than just a desire for local dominance, which can be achieved in simpler ways. It is argued here that all these patterns of direct management are responses to the needs and opportunities of exchange: lords react to the possibilities of the sale of surplus (and also the requirement to pay taxes) by intervening in ways that might increase the surpluses that could be sold. It follows—and this is my second argument—that the less exchange there was in any given region, the less need there would be for such intense control, and one would expect to find much less complex methods of taking surplus from peasants. In the next section we shall look at late Rome, and at the examples it gives us of the control over surplus extraction by landowners. In the third section we shall look at the period after 550/600 in the two western regions with most evidence, Francia and Italy, where the patterns of rent-taking became simpler, until a renewed intensification of production begins to be visible at the very end of our period. This latter shift is to an extent a sign of an upturn in exchange, at least in northern Francia, a point further developed in Chapter 11.

2. Types of late Roman intensification

It is hard to direct agriculture without some form of accounting. What is the rent, from this field or this holding? Has it been paid this year? Has it been paid in full? In twelfth-century Italy, where at least written leases existed but where written accounts were uncommon, interminable disputes could arise when tenants and lords were at odds over rent-paying, for there were no yearly records. There, no intensification from above could easily be contemplated, except by lords demanding specific crops in rent, which, if they wanted to, they could then sell. Annual accounts seem only to have come in in the thirteenth century, in England most precociously, on the back of state record-keeping, in Italy slightly later, also on the back of the state, and perhaps also on that of mercantile records.[9] In the late Roman empire, by

---

[9] Wickham, *Courts*, pp. 79–81, 292–6, for the twelfth century; for accounts, Clanchy, *From memory*, pp. 71–4; Cammarosano, *Italia medievale*, e.g. pp. 175–6, 230–1, 272–86.

contrast, accounting was normal, and we have several surviving examples of it.

The most elaborate are certainly Egyptian. Those of the Apions are the fullest for our period, and they have already been discussed in Chapter 4 (pp. 245–9). They derive, as was noted in that context, from older Egyptian traditions of accounting; from the elaborate papyruswork associated with the tax system; from the organization of irrigation agriculture, which, if it was landlord-run, as often in Egypt, could require very specific planned interventions; and also from a need to know exactly what surpluses existed so that they could be sold. Egypt may represent an extreme, but many of these patterns were paralleled elsewhere in the empire. Gregory the Great certainly regarded accounting as normal on his Sicilian estates. Simpler accounts can be found elsewhere, too, where casual discoveries have been made, usually in an archaeological context. The Nessana papyri preserve some for sixth- and seventh-century Palestine, in an irrigated area in the desert behind the export centre of Gaza, relatively close to Egypt. The most substantial account is from the late seventh century, a *gnōsis* of grain sown and reaped on several tracts of land, which allows a calculation of yields there (above, p. 65); there are also a threshing account and some commercial accounts. North Africa ought to have been another region where accounting was important, given its grain and oil export, and indeed we can find traces of it, in chance finds of ostraka (potsherds with writing) with receipts on them, in what was in our period southern Numidia (modern eastern Algeria). Four from the 480s–490s, which list the measures of barley a certain Massiesa got out of his *pars dominica* (see below, p. 273), survive from the edge of the Aurès mountains, and several that list quantities of olive oil survive from the Négrine oasis to the south-east of those mountains, and from the hill country which stretches from Négrine north to Tebéssa, dating mostly to the early sixth century (the Négrine ostrakon, dated to 542–3, refers again to the *portio dominica*). These are again marginal irrigated areas, but that is not surprising, for the survival of writing on ostraka (or indeed papyrus) usually depends on dry conditions. They at least show that receipts were systematically recorded, some way from the most important African production areas in what is now Tunisia, and they are presumably a guide to accounting practices in the latter too.[10]

---

[10] For Gregory, see Recchia, *Gregorio Magno*, pp. 103–4. For Nessana accounts, see *P. Ness.* 36–8, 40 (all sixth-century, probably military), and above all 81–91 (seventh-century; 82 is the *gnōsis*, literally 'knowledge'). The ostraka are in Bonnal and Février, 'Ostraka de la région de Bir Trouch' (for the Aurès), Albertini, 'Ostrakon byzantin de Négrine', which also, on pp. 60–2, gives a list of the other African ostraka known in 1932. The most important of these, from Henchir el Maïz, are edited, badly, in *Inscriptions latines*, n. 3719, and in *Corpus inscriptionum latinarum*, VIII, n. 22646.20: here, oil receipts are referred to as *PD*, perhaps *pars dominica* again, and this latter phrase recurs on another ostrakon from near Négrine (Albertini, 'Ostrakon

Our knowledge of this sort of registration of incomings and outgoings is reliant on fragments like these. So far, they all come from export-orientated regions, and could not be presumed to be guides to regions with less exchange. The source which makes the best case for our assuming that Romans in general usually kept updated records of receipts and outgoings is the collection of seventh-century slates from Diego Álvaro and nearby in central Spain (above, pp. 223–5), whose *notitiae* list cheese and grain rents, gifts of sheep and other goods, and so on. They are less articulated than our southern Mediterranean examples (they are undated, for a start, which must have limited their use); all the same, if in one of the poorest areas of the northern Meseta in the seventh century this sort of estate recording was going on, then it is likely that it was common elsewhere as well, up to that period at any rate. It was part of the normal behaviour of the Roman and immediately post-Roman world.

From 700 onwards, however, references to estate accounts are few. The Frankish *Capitulare de villis* of the early ninth century, it is true, demands that each estate manager (*iudex*) should make an annual statement of a wide range of incomings for the king, divided up by category (*distincta et ordinata*), as well as recording other incomings and outgoings in *brevia* or *rationes*.[11] As is well known, a concern for recording estate structures was promoted by the Carolingian court, and we would expect such recording to be most systematically practised on royal estates. But the *Capitulare de villis* is normative, not descriptive; and the estate surveys we have for the ninth century are lists of tenants, holdings, and standard rents, not registers of whether and when such rents were actually paid. By the eighth and ninth centuries, in fact, written accounts only survive from Egypt. It is likely that by now in practice, in most places in the West, registration of payment was largely oral, or organized by means of tallies and other non-written recording methods, as would be common into the thirteenth century, when accounts began again. These observations are based on absences; it is far from impossible that annual accounting persisted or was reinvented here and there in the Carolingian and post-Carolingian period.[12] But there is little to

byzantin de Négrine', p. 62, n. 10). The contemporary Tablettes Albertini, which were found not far east of these ostraka, do not include any agrarian accounts. Cf. also the long list of receipts for the years 499–510 in *P. Ital.* 47–8, for an Italian usurer and agricultural dealer.

[11] *MGH, Cap.* I, n. 32, cc. 44, 55, 62 (in particular), 66.

[12] Eighth-century Egyptian accounts include Kahle, *Bala'izah*, nn. 291, 303B, 309–12; *CPR* XIV 42; *APEL* VI 378; *CO* (see Ch. 7, n. 90), n. 452—cf. also rent receipts such as Crum, *Short texts*, n. 70. For tallies, see Clanchy, *From memory*, pp. 72, 95–6. The Marseille polyptych of 813–14 (ed. in *Cartulaire de l'abbaye de Saint-Victor*, II, pp. 633–56) may have been a temporary register, with some updating as Jean-Pierre Devroey argues ('Elaboration et usage des polyptyques'), but there is no sign of a regular accounting system here. The exactness of a polyptych like that of S. Tommaso di Reggio, from tenth-century northern Italy, which lists yields, points towards accounting, but here, too, the text does not seem to have been intended to have followed up on an annual basis: *Inventari*, IX, pp. 195–8 (ed. A. Castagnetti).

allow us to assume that it was common in the West between 700 and 1200, and, without such record-keeping, an important element of potential landlordly control over agriculture was lost. It seems to me likely that the main stimulus, and model, for private accounting was always the record-keeping that taxation depended upon, and these are the centuries when taxation was more or less absent in the West. There was at least some tax in seventh-century Spain (above, p. 97), and the last annual records of payments known to me from Gaul in our period, the Tours documents of c.700 (above, p. 109), are probably tax records; the thirteenth-century revival of accounting had fiscal records as a model, too. It follows that we might expect accounts to have persisted in the Byzantine and Arab worlds throughout; we can show this for Egypt, where written receipts and the like were continuous, but for Byzantium we simply do not have enough evidence for the period after 600, not until the eleventh century, although accounts do appear by then.[13]

On the basis of the information provided by accounting, one way of exercising landlordly control over peasant agricultural practices is to keep one's tenants under surveillance. There are signs that some late Roman landowners kept a regular eye on how tenants practised their cultivation, with an interest in improvement. Palladius' *Opus agriculturae*, a fifth-century estate manual from Italy written by, as the text claims, a senator (*vir illustris*), is a sign of this concern. Palladius relied heavily on previous manualistic literature, but he did aim for practicality, setting out agricultural needs month by month. He was concerned for the quality of rural labour at every stage, and for the effective organization of the agricultural infrastructure. Palladius clearly expected his dependants to be constantly watched, to ensure that they cultivated correctly. He was, as one of his editors has remarked, just the sort of agriculturally minded aristocrat that his contemporary Sidonius condemned (pp. 467–8). His manual was popular in the Carolingian and post-Carolingian period, too, with eight manuscripts surviving from the ninth and tenth centuries; the author of the *Capitulare de villis* would certainly have sympathized with his concerns. It is significant, however, that his control did not extend to any interest in labour relations. Palladius says that he cannot usefully discuss them, in view of the 'very great diversity of lands', *tanta diversitate terrarum*; he was dealing with late Roman aristocratic estates, which were often dispersed over many provinces (above, pp. 163–4). But there is no sign that he had any agricultural workers who were not tenants (whether free or unfree); the sections of Columella dealing with slave management were not reprised in his text, except for a warning against using slave favourites as estate managers, for

---

[13] For the first references to Byzantine estate accounts, see Lefort, 'The rural economy', pp. 295–6.

they will take advantage of their position. I would myself agree with Andrea Giardina and Domenico Vera that, had the slave mode still been an import- ant part of Palladius' experience, he could not have avoided discussing it. But anyway the *diversitas* must have included tenants, given their promin- ence in other sources, and this is important: Palladius would have been a rather relaxed manager of plantation slaves, but, as a manager of tenants, he was highly attentive.[14]

We gain the same impression of a concern for micromanaging tenants from a number of late Roman texts. The Victor–George letters from the Apion estates are one clear instance (above, p. 246), and, in general, the Apions and other landowners in Egypt kept tight controls over all their agricultural concerns, as can be seen in several contracts with overseers, which could specify the crops to be planted.[15] It can be added that most Egyptian leases to cultivators (which survive from several parts of the Nile valley, although only very rarely from the Apion estates) are for short periods of time, seldom over six years and very often only for one. This fast turnover for lease negotiations—which after all, a year later, would frequently be between the same people—is itself a sign of a desire for land- lordly control, which could indeed extend further in Egypt, as we shall see in a moment. Leases as short-term as this were an old Egyptian tradition, however, and were probably less typical in other regions.[16] The laws on *coloni* (below, pp. 519–26) certainly regard long-term tenurial relationships as normal; and the Mancian tenures of Africa were sufficiently stable that

[14] For Palladius as a whole see the edition by Rodgers, *Opus agriculturae*; that by Martin, *Traité d'agriculture*, edits the first two books with a substantial introduction. Martin's argument (pp. vii–xx) that he was an Italian landowner with a Gaulish background is plausible, and his date of the 460s–470s is quite possible (the outer limits of dating for the text are 372–550). See ibid., p. xvii for the Sidonius parallel; pp. lv–lviii for manuscripts. See Palladius, *Opus agricul- turae*, I.6.3, for *tanta diversitate terrarum*; I.6.18 for *servuli dilecti* as managers (cf. Columella, *Res rustica*, I.8.1). For commentary, Giardina, 'Le due Italie', pp. 31–6; Vera, 'Dalla "villa perfecta" ', pp. 342–52, with previous references. An alternative view, that Palladius was partly describing slave plantations, is put very tentatively by de Martino, 'Il colonato', pp. 805–6, and by Whittaker and Garnsey, 'Rural life', pp. 295–6, 306.

[15] *P. Oxy.* I 136, XVI 1894, XIX 2239, LVIII 3952, 3958, all aa. 573–614.

[16] For lists of leases, see Johnson and West, *Byzantine Egypt*, pp. 80–93 (not all to cultiv- ators); Herrmann, *Studien*, pp. 274–88 (the completest lists; see pp. 91–4 for comments); Mazza, *L'archivio degli Apioni*, pp. 189–91 (for Oxyrhynchos; pp. 106–20 for commentary). The percentage of single-year leases slowly dropped; on Herrmann's figures the main moment of decline was the fifth century, after which they stabilized at around a third. They still existed in the seventh century, as shown by, for example, *P. Oxy.* LVIII 3955 (a. 611). See in general Banaji, *Agrarian change*, pp. 199, 205–6, 237–8. For earlier periods, see among others Rowlandson, *Landowners*, pp. 209, 252–9. For Egypt's short-term leases as exceptional, see Jones, *LRE*, pp. 802–3. Note that some leases, in each case certainly to cultivators, are sharecropping contracts, with the landowner (usually) supplying seed and taking half of the rent or more: e.g. *P. Lond.* I 113.3, V 1694; *P. Mich.* XIII 666 (all from the sixth century); and some of the leases for Jēme, cit. in Ch. 7, n. 106. As with the late medieval Italian *mezzadria* contract, an exact parallel, such landowners were taking on more risk, and were highly likely to exercise close control over the tenant. Banaji, *Agrarian change*, pp. 126, 167–8, 200–1, links the growth of sharecropping with the growth in wine production.

the owner of the *fundus Tuletianos* in southern Byzacena actually had to buy them back from his tenants in the 490s, in the documents on wood published as the Tablettes Albertini.[17] But even where tenure was stable, and mediated through many levels of *conductores* (tenants of whole estates), *actores* and *villici* (estate managers), owners could be very concerned with the detail of local practices. One example is Gregory the Great's provisions for the investigation of bad management, notably the defrauding of tenants by rent-collectors; Gregory was concerned even to specify the weights and measures the latter could use, and to have unjust weights, *iniusta pondera*, broken.[18] Gregory may, as a saint, have been atypical in his concern for a just treatment for his tenants, but the detail of his interventions fits some found elsewhere.

The involvement of late Roman landlords in estate management was in some respects paradoxical. On one level, it was beneath them; *otium* was not for mundane things like that, as Sidonius often said, and political involvement left little time for it, especially as the greatest landowners had so many estates, far too many to deal with properly or even to visit. Palladius states, in an agronomist's cliché, that 'the presence of the *dominus* brings prosperity to the *ager*';[19] if that was really so, there would have been no prosperity on the estates of the Anicii, or the Apions, or Pope Gregory. They had to delegate. If an owner chose to manage his or her estates directly, through hierarchies of paid officials, as the Apions did, delegation was a complicated matter—the Victor–George letters show this clearly—and was as potentially corrupt as the tax system. If the owner instead leased estates to *conductores*, then any form of detailed control from above was more difficult. A good example of the latter comes from a Ravenna papyrus of 445/6 concerning the estates in Sicily of a court official, Lauricius, which were evidently all let to *conductores*; the text includes copies of three of Lauricius' letters, which focused on the need to check that rents in individual years had been paid by each *conductor*. Lauricius had all the documentation, but he still experienced serious managerial problems, with one lessee, the *tribunus* Pyrrus, seriously neglectful, another in debt, and, overall, a constant danger of delay and fraud.[20] So it was hard for owners to engage in the day-to-day management of estates, and many doubtless did not bother. *Conductores* indeed frequently behaved as de facto owners (especially on imperial estates, which

[17] *Tablettes Albertini*, nn. 3–32. The prices were very low, however (ibid., pp. 203–5), perhaps indicating a tenurial weakness on the part of the peasants—though Tuletianos was also very remote, and the landowner may simply have been able to coerce low prices out of his dependants.

[18] Gregory, *Epp.*, esp. I. 42 (quote), XIII.37. See, among many, Vera, 'Forme e funzioni', pp. 430–47, and the full survey in Recchia, *Gregorio Magno*, pp. 85–105.

[19] Palladius, *Opus agriculturae*, I.6.1.

[20] *P. Ital.* 1; see Vera, 'Forme e funzioni', pp. 418–22. Lauricius may himself have been an emphyteutic tenant for the church of Ravenna, which is mentioned in the last line of the text; his *conductores* evidently had short-term leases, for they could be replaced.

were so enormous, and by now regularly leased in long-term emphyteutic tenure).[21] *Domini* at the top of the layer-cake of leasing and delegation did not have to be interested in anything other than the total quantities of rents.

But, in this context, it is striking how many of them *were* interested and involved, from Palladius to Gregory. Here, the issue of commercialization comes to the fore. Large Roman landowners were not simply rentiers; they sold produce. If they did not, their *conductores* did. Olympiodoros says in the 420s that the major Roman senators got three-quarters of their huge rents in money, a quarter in kind; this probably roughly reflects the proportion between money rents paid by *conductores* and estates that were directly managed. Lauricius, too, whose documented *conductores* mostly paid in money, owned a *horreum* for produce in Rome.[22] The peasants for the most part paid rents in kind, for much the same reasons that, as I have argued (pp. 74–6), they paid taxes in kind: most peasants did not have sufficiently easy access to long-distance markets that they could obtain the metal for money-rents on a regular basis. These rents might be assessed in money, and then converted to kind in a process which Gregory the Great refers to as *comparatio*, performed at the moment of rent-paying on his Sicilian estates, a practice surely modelled on the *coemptio* of the tax system (above, p. 75), and one which gave assessors yet more opportunity to defraud peasants by unfair pricing and false weights.[23] Either way, it was produce that was mostly extracted from cultivators; this was, however, then sold, either by *conductores* or by landowners, presumably to cities, including to Rome itself as a supplement to the *annona*. Although it would be anachronistic to swing the pendulum from an image of late Roman large owners as idle rentiers to one of agrarian entrepreneurs, the fact remains that there was *space* for at least some agrarian entrepreneurship in the complex economy of the late empire for anyone who wanted to practise it, and most of the well-documented super-rich can be seen engaging in it at one moment or another. This possibility of sale created an incentive for any landlord who wanted to direct agrarian production.[24]

The obvious next step, to be taken by any owner or *conductor* who wished to sell produce, was to cash-crop. We must not imagine that this ever meant the monocultures of the twentieth century, so totalizing that no other crops are grown at all, and peasants have to sell even to get their own food; the peasantry of the late Roman period will all have produced for their own

[21] See for a survey Vera, 'Enfiteusi, colonato'.

[22] Olympiodoros, *Frag.* 41.2 (ed. Blockley); *P.Ital.* 1; cf. Symmachus, *Ep.* VI 12.

[23] Gregory, *Ep.* I.42; see in general Recchia, *Gregorio Magno*, pp. 87–92. For the complexities of rent paid in kind but assessed in money, see Vera, 'Forme e funzioni', pp. 435–7. Egypt was an exception here; its capillary exchange more easily allowed for rents in money, at least to local owners (see below, pp. 759–69).

[24] Vera, 'Strutture agrarie', pp. 516–21; 'Fra Egitto e Africa' (Vera makes analogous points in several other articles); see also, classically, Ruggini, *Economia e società*, p. 131, and *passim* for agricultural exchange.

subsistence as well as specializing in the specific types of crop that their lords wanted in rent: wine from Calabria and Palestine, oil from Africa and Syria, and so on (we shall look at these geographical patterns in more detail in Chapter 11). All the same, it must be recognized that such specialisms did exist; and, furthermore, they were chosen by owners and *conductores*, and were developed in the context of known markets, rather than simply being the 'natural' products of given areas. Some African epitaphs from the third and fourth centuries make this development explicit, notably that for the *conductor* of the *fundus Aufidianus* west of Carthage in the late third century, whose widow was proud of his agrarian improvements: he planted numerous olive trees, as well as fruit trees and vines, at the end (perhaps at the steepest point) of Africa's century-long rise to dominance over the oil production of two-thirds of the Mediterranean.[25] These were serious, committed, interventions in agricultural practice, and they happened in different measure across nearly the whole of the late Roman empire, although most of all in regions most orientated towards export, Egypt, Africa, southern Italy and Sicily, Syria and Palestine.

The export-orientated regions are also those in which the next step up in agricultural management is best documented, the development of tracts of land where owners directly controlled labour and the detail of agrarian exploitation. I shall call these tracts by the medievalists' word 'demesne', despite the dangers of anachronism, for reasons which will appear in a moment. Not that demesnes were common in either the Roman or (as has already been noted) the immediately post-Roman world, but they did exist: as little islands of direct management in the sea of the 'colonate', places where landlordly control became sufficiently tight that owners could break through the mediating veil of subsistence peasant agriculture, and, in part, create an environment in which they could begin to organize their own agricultural processes.

One problem is that to talk about Roman demesnes at all has become difficult. In so doing, one seems to have taken a step backwards, and to be returning to the metanarrative of how plantation slavery turned into

---

[25] Peyras, 'Le *fundus Aufidianus*', esp. pp. 198–203, for the inscription; idem, *Le Tell*, pp. 438–41, shows further that the Aufidianus area was not one of full monoculture. See Mattingly, 'Oil for export?', pp. 47–8, for the third-century oil boom in the archaeology; idem, 'First fruit?', for a wider context. A similar pattern, of export specialization inside a subsistence economy (one, however, where landlords were weak), can be seen very clearly in Syria: see below, pp. 443–9. One common way subsistence and specialization were balanced was through 'promiscuous' cultivation, with grain or legumes planted between olives or vines (grain takes water from a different level of the soil from tree crops). See Desplanques, *Campagnes ombriennes*, pp. 345–82, for a good modern description. Vera in 'Enfiteusi, colonato', pp. 290–1, and '*Conductores domus nostrae*', esp. pp. 474–8, argues that permanent emphyteutic leasing by *conductores*, characteristic of the late empire, as at Aufidianus, itself helped agrarian investment.

serfdom and the manorial system, criticized above. Hence, above all, the edginess with which many recent historians have dealt with the single late Roman document that attests to tenant labour service on a demesne, *P. Ital.* 3 for Padua in the mid-sixth century; for them, it has seemed necessary to reject that text altogether as a guide to agricultural realities. It will be proposed shortly that such a rejection is mistaken (pp. 278–9); all the same, the metanarrative, having been thrown out the door, should not be brought back in through the window. The problem is that the demesne has been seen as so particular a way of organizing agriculture that all examples of it must have been genealogically related. I would argue the opposite: demesnes are most likely to have been invented more than once, not just in history, but even in the Roman empire. The clearest examples of them are actually in Egypt, which had never had slave agriculture and never would develop manors. Demesnes can be seen simply as lands which have become, thanks to the possibilities for the sale of agricultural produce, more advantageous to run directly than through tenancies. Such lands may be cultivated by household slaves in plantation format, or by the labour service of tenants, or by wage labour; the choice is one between modes of production, which is not at all a small difference, but it will be made in practice according to which of these labour relations is most easily available already. To use a Darwinian image, I see the demesne as a little like the development of the wing: separately, pterodactyls, birds, and bats evolved wings from different sets of body parts to meet the same sort of environmental needs and opportunities. We see their wings as analogous, and all three can/could certainly fly, but the three developments are actually entirely unrelated, and could in principle recur in different ways again.

Let us begin with Africa: not because it tells us much that we can use about how demesnes were organized there, but because it at least establishes the existence in the late Roman period of the terminology of the *pars dominica*, the standard terminology for demesnes after 800 or so, and indeed the etymological origin of the modern word. This is shown by the ostraka from fifth- and sixth-century Numidia, discussed earlier (p. 266). Not that one should assume that every use of the word *dominica* necessarily means 'demesne'; it is simply an adjective deriving from *dominus*, and it is not uncommon. Any of the Numidian ostraka, taken on its own, might simply be referring to 'the lord's portion', perhaps of rent. But the phrase appears sufficiently often to allow one to conclude that it probably has a more precise meaning here; and it is anyway not the only evidence for direct management in Africa. One is a law of 319 for the region, referring to *coloni* who are occupying the irrigated land of imperial emphyteutic tenants, which by implication should be being cultivated by people who are not *coloni*. Another is perhaps the buying-up of the Mancian tenures of the *fundus Tuletianos* in 493–6, for it is not clear why a landlord should want to buy out tenants only to replace them with others.[26] All these data, labile though they are, imply that late Roman estate management in Africa did envisage areas of greater landlordly control, which could be called a *pars dominica*, and which in principle were run directly rather than through peasant tenures. They do not, however, give us any idea of what labour process was used on them. Africa is also, of course, the location of the well-known second-century inscriptions which refer to labour service (*operae*) by tenants (*coloni*). Their scale is trivially small, however: six days labour per year on the *saltus Burunitanus* (Souk el-Khmis), six again on the *fundus* of Mappalia Siga (Henchir Mettich)—either the demesnes there were at most a thirtieth part of the tenures around them, or else other workers, slaves or wage labourers, were used as well.[27] It would be unwise to assume automatically that the demesnes of the later empire in Africa were cultivated by labour service. But the region did at least have demesnes, however small, as early as the second century.

To see how direct labour actually was organized, three other regions need discussion, each of which gives us clear evidence of each of the three different kinds of demesne labour. The first, and by far the best-documented, is Egypt, where wage labour was widely used, in particular but not only on the Apion estates. It was common back into the third century, at least in the most intensely exploited estates, like the Appianos lands in the nome of Arsinoë (Madīnat al-Fayyūm), where, as Dominic Rathbone has shown, there were at least two different levels of wage labourers, differentiated by the permanence of their employment: on such estates, a high percentage of the land could be directly managed. Outside such estates, however, in the third and (still more) the fourth century, leasing to tenants was much more normal, and wage labour above all appears in the context of casual labour for the harvest, or else in that of specialist labour—irrigation-machinery operators, or field guards, or herdsmen, or vine-dressers.[28]

In our period the Apions certainly exploited their Oxyrhynchos land intensively, and a more substantial use of wage labour returned, as shown by Jairus Banaji and Peter Sarris, to the parts of estates that were cultivated directly (called in this period *autourgiai*), by workers living in *epoikia*, estate

---

[26] *CJ*, XI.63.1, cf. Vera, 'Terra e lavoro'; *Tablettes Albertini*, pp. 210–11. Augustine, *Sermo* CCCLVI.15, sometimes cited in this context, seems to me only to refer to a *fundus* whose *possessor* could not find a *conductor* to lease the entire estate.

[27] *Corpus inscriptionum latinarum*, VIII, nn. 10570, 25902, and also 14428. The most recent commentary on these texts is Kehoe, *Economics of agriculture*, which includes a re-edition at pp. 28–70. The word *dominica* appears in the second of them, for Henchir Mettich, but in a syntactically very obscure context.

[28] Rathbone, *Economic rationalism*, esp. pp. 88–174. For the general third-century context, see Kehoe, *Management and investment*, pp. 119–72, and Rowlandson, *Landowners*, pp. 202–79 (pp. 205–8 for wage labour; see also eadem, 'Agricultural tenancy'), who argue that leases were normal outside the Arsinoite. For the fourth century, Bagnall, *Egypt*, pp. 121–3, 126, 150–3, takes a similar position, although he stresses the normality of casual wage labour; for the best wage labour text for that period, dating to 338, see Bagnall, *Egypt*, p. 126.

villages.[29] It has already been noted that we do not have many Apion leases; we do not have many hire contracts either, a handful at the most, but there is other documentation concerning the payment of estate workers. Some of the overseer contracts, already cited, imply the handling of such payments, and even on occasion the issuing of credit notes (*pittakia*) in lieu of wages, which could be cashed on request.[30] Exactly how much of the Apion lands in Oxyrhynchos was organized in *autourgiai* in the sixth century is not fully clear in the material we have, so the exact importance of this wage labour cannot be assessed. It is less well documented than its third-century equivalent on the Appianos estate, in fact. But there is no doubt about its significance, which is anyway buttressed by the regularity of more casual references to agricultural wage labour throughout our period in Egypt, both in the sixth century and later, going into and beyond the eighth century, with some wage contracts surviving from nearly every major collection of documents. This was a recourse that was available to any Egyptian land-owner who wanted to get involved in direct management.[31]

Peasant agriculture and a salaried labour-force are structurally, modally, distinct, but, as noted earlier, this does not mean that they cannot coexist. Empirically, peasant families have often themselves hired labour at particular moments in the life-cycle; adult sons have often hired themselves out before inheriting the family farm; poorer owners and tenants have often taken on paid work for others to make ends meet. In Greek, such intercuttings of the two systems were, in a sense, made easier by a striking overlap in the terminologies available for each, with the word *misthōsis* meaning a lease and *misthōtēs* a tenant, but *misthos* meaning a wage and *misthios* a hired labourer: this range was fully used by the Egyptians, who did not draw sharp distinctions between the two.[32] The predominant system in Egypt was

---

[29] Banaji, 'Agrarian history'; idem, *Agrarian change*, pp. 180–206, 217–18, 231–2; Mazza, *L'archivio degli Apioni*, pp. 129–34; Sarris, *Economy and society*, chs. 2, 3. For *epoikia*, in effect barracks in some cases, see, in chronological order, Rathbone, *Economic rationalism*, pp. 177–83; Bagnall, *Egypt*, p. 151; Sarris, *Economy and society*, ch. 2. By the eighth century, however, the word just meant 'small village' in Aphroditō in Middle Egypt; *P. Lond.* IV 1412–19, 1432, etc., show *epoikia* full of small owners. But, as was argued earlier (pp. 251–5), large estates were fewer by the eighth century.

[30] *P. Oxy.* XVI 1992, 2032 (probably), LV 3804, LVII 3914, refer to wages; see above, n. 15 for overseers, esp. *P. Oxy.* LVIII 3958 for *pittakia* (cf. LV 3804); for *pittakia*, see also XVI 1845 (cashing one), LV 3804. Sarris, as n. 29, discusses these texts in detail; see also the classic account in Hardy, *Large estates*, pp. 113–32.

[31] Other agricultural hire contracts include *P. Cair. Masp.* I 67095 for the sixth century; Gerstinger, 'Neue gräko-ägyptische Vertragsurkunden', n. 1, for the seventh. For the Arab period: *CPR* IV 165, 175; *P. Ryl. Copt.* 159; *APEL* VI 378 (for the eighth/ninth century, with several workers with Arab names); Hall, *Coptic and Greek texts*, n. 72/1.

[32] Cf. *P. Vatic. Aphrod.* 1 (*misthōtēs* as a tenant) with *P. Cair. Masp.* I 67095 (*misthios* as a hired labourer), both from sixth-century Aphroditō. *P. Lond.* V 1796 from sixth-century Hermopolis, an atypical text because the lessor probably both takes rent and hires himself out as a worker on the same land, uses both terminologies simultaneously. Thanks to John Haldon for guidance concerning this document.

tenancy, but the interest in direct control for sale that landowners had in the region, plus the reliability of local market relationships (we have hire contracts for artisans, too), allowed owners to move to wage labour whenever they wished. There was even some space for the slave mode, for there are occasional references to *paidaria*, who were at least sometimes agricultural slaves, although they were economically and socially marginal.[33]

Egypt was not unparalleled in other parts of the empire. Wage labour does appear elsewhere, and is not remarkable when it does. A certain Rōmanos hired labourers (*ergatai*) to work his *agros* near Gaza in the early sixth century, for example, according to Cyril of Scythopolis; and the ambiguities—indeed, confusions—in *misthos* terminology can be found in imperial legislation in our period and later, as much as in Egypt.[34] But the scale of Egyptian wage labour is not visible outside that region. There is perhaps a reference to peasants working as wage labourers in Sardinia in 599, although the text is not fully conclusive; the only clear examples of partly salaried agricultural workers in Gregory the Great are shepherds, that is, specialists. In Gregory of Tours there is a clear reference to casual workers (*operarii*), perhaps from the local city, working at the harvest in the territory of Clermont around 570; but this latter, harvest work, was everywhere the commonest form of wage labour.[35] We could not conclude from these citations, and others like them, that the *substantial* use of wage labour that is visible for Egypt was fully matched elsewhere; there is not enough evidence to allow us to assume it, and in other regions the tendency for our sources to stress tenants as the archetypal rural workers is overwhelming. Essentially, Egypt was just more economically developed. If the same patterns did exist elsewhere, we might presume that the Levant and Africa, other regions with relatively high levels of exchange, would be the most plausible candidates. At present, however, how far wage labour extended is guesswork.

The slave mode was, by contrast, certainly restricted, indeed hardly used at all. There is no certain example of a slave plantation in Italy after 300 or so, even though such estates had reached the height of their ancient development in the peninsula a couple of centuries earlier. Two slave estates are

[33] *Paidaria*: Bagnall, *Egypt*, pp. 123–7; Sarris, *Economy and society*, ch. 2. It was very subsidiary to wage labour; as Bagnall shows, most rural slaves were farmhands for peasants, not organized in groups at all (cf. the slaves of northern European peasantries, below, pp. 543–4). For artisan hire contracts, see below, p. 764.

[34] Cyril of Scythopolis, *Life* of Euthymios, c. 57; cf. John Moschos, *Spiritual meadow*, c. 154, and probably John Chrysostom, *Homilies on Matthew*, LXI.3. For agricultural hire, see Diocletian, *Edict on prices*, VII.1, 18. For later imperial legislation and other examples, Kaplan, *Les hommes*, pp. 150–63, 262, 273–4, although his example from the *Life* of Theodore of Sykeōn does not seem to me to involve agricultural work.

[35] Gregory, *Epp.*, IX.203 (for Sardinia), II.38 (but even these shepherds have housing); see also V.5 (for Sicily, more ambiguous still). Vera, 'Forme and funzioni', pp. 431–2, sees these as wage labour, however. For Gaul, Gregory of Tours, *GC*, c. 1 (a Syrian example is Joshua the Stylite, *Chronicle*, c. 52, for 502 in Edessa). For harvest labour see Jones, *LRE*, p. 792.

documented in the late empire in the Aegean, both in a census register from Lesbos surviving on a fourth-century inscription, each with twenty-plus slaves; but other similar inscriptions from the Aegean, and even other Lesbos estates, show slave workers as marginal.[36] Indeed, it could not be securely argued from the Lesbos text that the slave mode was here significantly more important than it was in Egypt. It did exist, but its marginality seems clear. And, although there were many other estates with no cultivators except the unfree (some of Melania and Pinianus' lands, for example), there is no sign that they were anything other than tenants.[37]

On one level, it is actually strange how little evidence there is for the slave mode in the late empire (and the post-Roman world: below, p. 282). In the world of tenants, unfreedom was very common. Among more directly subjected workers, there were unfree domestic servants, in aristocratic and even peasant households; in fact, as an extension of this, there were unfree farmhands on peasant holdings, from Egypt to Scandinavia. There was, that is to say, the raw material for the productive relations of the slave mode, readily available in every period; plantations could in principle have been invented anew at every stage. But slaves are a risk. The more numerous they are, the more dangerous and expensive they are to police. Furthermore, they have to be maintained, in high seasons and low, in good years and bad, when hired labour can be laid off, and tenants left to their own holdings. They presuppose high levels of profitability, of the sale of products, for these risks to be covered; but if there is that much exchange, then wage labour is equally feasible. As has been argued in recent decades, the context in which plantations are most likely to become attractive is when there is a secure market for produce at the same time as an easily available slave market.[38] By and large, in the late empire and later, if there was one of these there was not the other: the wars in fifth-century Gaul or sixth-century Italy produced many slaves but were also linked to economic crisis, whereas the stable prosperity of the fifth- and sixth-century East was in a time of relative peace and less large-scale access to new slave groups. As a result, slaves turned into unfree tenants in the former, as Marc Bloch proposed,[39] and land management for profit looked to free wage labour in the latter. The expanding Roman empire, which had brought in all the slaves of the last centuries BC, or the predatory slave trade with Africa which created the gang slavery of ninth-century Iraq[40] or the plantations of the eighteenth-century

---

[36] *Inscriptiones graecae*, XII, 2, nn. 76, 78, cited and analysed by Jones, *Roman economy*, pp. 243–4 (cf. 242–4 for the other inscriptions).

[37] *Vita Melaniae latina*, c. 18, for 400 *servi agricultores* in 60 *villae* (cf. below, Ch. 8, n. 74), an over-commented text. For cautious arguments in favour of some continuing slave-mode cultivation, see Whittaker, 'Circe's pigs', pp. 93–4, and above, n. 14; for strong doubts see Vera, 'Le forme del lavoro', which sums up his own work.

[38] e.g. Hopkins, *Conquerors and slaves*, pp. 12, 99–111.

[39] Bloch, *Mélanges historiques*, I, pp. 261–85.

[40] For Iraq and the Zanj slaves, whose economic role was to dig fertilizer on river terraces rather than to work agriculturally on plantations, see above, Ch. 3, n. 218.

Americas, were phenomena on a scale which did not have parallels in our period.

The final alternative was labour service, by tenants on a demesne. This, like the slave mode, is only clearly attested in one document—in this case, the already cited *P. Ital.* 3 for Padua in north-eastern Italy. This has attracted rather more discussion from historians than has the Lesbos census, or even Egyptian wage labour, for reasons which have already been mentioned: that is, the key position of the document in the slavery-to-serfdom metanarrative, and also in the linked manorial genealogy that some historians have seen as stretching from the Henchir Mettich inscription to the *Capitulare de villis* and the polyptych of St-Germain. *P. Ital.* 3 is a fragment of an estate description, presumably for the church of Ravenna, plausibly from the period between the Gothic and the Lombard wars, that is, c.560. Its surviving two columns contain, on the left, the dues owed by a set of tenants but not their names or their holdings; on the right, in a second set, which relates to the territory of Padua, we have both the names and (probably all) the attached dues. Totals at the bottom of the text indicate that there might have been ten columns in all on the full document. The dues are in money, *xenia* (the standard medieval Italian term for symbolic gifts like chickens and eggs—here, these two and also ducks, lard, honey, and milk), and *operae*, labour, measured *per ebdomada*, and varying between no days and three days per week; *operae* are only listed for the left-hand column. The first holding on the left has no labour, but the largest money rent; it is conceivable that it parallels the first holding on the right, which is held by a *vilicus*, an estate manager.[41]

I characterize the text in more detail than usual so as to make one point clear: this text does indeed list labour service, and, unlike the second-century African texts, at quite high levels. Against it, it has been argued that it is a one-off, unique in Italy until the 730s, which is true, although not very surprising since no rents paid by cultivators are characterized in any detail in mainland Italy from now until the 730s; and that it does not fit the total absence of such service in Gregory the Great's letters, which is also true, although this only shows that Sicily was different from the Po plain (in the ninth century, when labour service was certainly common in northern Italy, it is almost unknown south of Rome). The point is that, however isolated

---

[41] For the date of *P. Ital.* 3, see the comments of its editor, Tjäder, *Die nichtliterarischen lateinischen Papyri*, I, pp. 185–6; my observations do not depend on the exact date, however, which could at a pinch oscillate half a century either way. It is also edited, again by Tjäder, in *ChLA*, XX, n. 709. The fullest commentaries on the text are Percival, 'P.Ital. 3'; Vera, 'Forme e funzioni', pp. 425–30; the former stresses its importance, the latter minimizes it. Other positive analyses: Jones, 'L'Italia agraria', pp. 83–4; Percival, 'Seigneurial aspects', pp. 454–5, 460. Other negative analyses: Toubert, *Les structures*, pp. 466–7; Verhulst, 'Quelques remarques', pp. 92–3; Andreolli, 'La corvée precarolingia', p. 29. See also the neutral accounts in Jones, *LRE*, pp. 805–6; Pasquali, 'L'azienda curtense', pp. 10–14. Note that the text says that one rent is due *in domnico*, although it is not clear whether this means the rent is special in some way.

P. Ital. 3 is, there is not any body of different evidence about rents in sixth-century northern Italy, or for the next two centuries, which would make it legitimate to set the text aside. The only strong argument for its intrinsic atypicality is one made by Domenico Vera: that it is surprising to find so much emphasis on money rent in an estate survey, and no reference at all to what land generally produced in north-eastern Italy, that is, grain and wine.[42] It seems to me, all the same, that the text cannot be argued away as a guide to *one* local reality; and that local reality expected, from some tenants, large amounts of labour service, making up in some cases half the working week.

As a guide to 'the origin of the manor', this text is too isolated to be probative. I shall argue below that it may, in fact, show that the demesnes worked by labour in the Italy of the eighth century did have roots in the late Roman world, but that this proposition about genealogical origins is less important than the fact that there was a *systemic* break between the demesnes of late Rome and those of the period after the 730s (pp. 293–9). The real significance of *P. Ital.* 3 is, rather, a different one: it is a guide to another way of exploiting a demesne in the specific circumstances of the late Roman period, filling out the array of possibilities in the clearest fashion. Rather than calling on non-peasants, who were always in a small minority in the late Roman countryside, at least one Italian estate used tenants (*coloni*), who anyway cultivated the *coloniae* of the area, as direct labourers. If an owner wanted to manage part of an estate directly for profit, but wanted to play safe economically, then tenant labour was arguably the safest solution of all. The practicability of profit from these estates in the period when the Padua text was written is further underlined by the heavy stress on money rent alongside the labour: atypical or not, even peasants could be expected to sell their produce here. This was the context of the Padua demesne, then: the possibility of the sale of agricultural goods; the intensification of agriculture to match it; but the desire (perhaps the necessity) to do this without transforming peasant-based productive relations.

It simply cannot be said how common demesnes were in the late Roman empire, and still less how they were cultivated in regions such as Africa, where their existence seems clear but their mode of exploitation is not. Of the three types of exploitation discussed here, the only one I doubt was widely used in our period is the slave mode; it must also be recognized that wage labour is, overall, the best evidenced of the three. What the existence of

---

[42] Vera, 'Forme e funzioni', p. 427. Of course, this money rent may only be an accounting device, with peasants paying rent in produce, priced in money, as in Sicily (above, p. 271), but the detail of the other types of produce mentioned in the document argues against that. The main other reference to *operae* in the late empire is *CJ*, XI.51.3 (a. 371) for Illyricum, a vague citation. The only other references to rents in the period 550–730 in northern Italy are contained in *P. Ital.* 44, 45, and in the *Codice Bavaro*; none of these seem to be, however, leases to cultivators (*CB*, n. 129 is the only possible instance in my view, and not a very likely one.)

even these few clearly documented demesnes does show, however, is that the economy was sufficiently complex that there was sometimes some point in landowners taking the trouble to manage part of their land directly without the mediation of the peasant cultivators who were otherwise the great majority of the population of the empire. Their choice was far from inevitable: for every owner who went into demesnes we could find another, equally attentive to exchange, who did not—Gregory the Great, for example. But the strength, at least by post-Roman standards, of the commercial network of the late empire does seem to me the best explanation of the emergence of demesnes, the final step in the moves towards the intensification of control over peasant production that have been surveyed in the previous pages. As noted earlier, owners who went into demesne agriculture would presumably use the organizational techniques that were most readily to hand locally: whether these were a controllable servile work-force, tenants capable of being subjected in new ways, or simply an exchange economy strong enough to reward the rural underemployed with wages.

Conversely, it must be repeated that this model means that such intensification depended on the commercial network. Without it, such control was pointless, and it would break down. Demesnes would for the most part get leased out, to their pre-existing work-force most likely, as landlords returned to the simplest and easiest method of getting surplus, that is to say, the taking of rent. To test this part of the model, however, we must look at the period after the end of the exchange activity of the late empire, to see what happened to surpluses; this will be the focus of the next section. Here, we have looked at estate management right up to 600, and beyond it, going up to 800 in the East, where states and exchange survived throughout our period. In the next section, we shall focus on the best documented Romano-Germanic kingdoms, Francia and Lombard Italy, in the period after 550–600, so as to get an idea of what happened in regions where the complexity of exchange had partially, or substantially, lessened.

3. Estates in Francia and Italy, 600–800

Up to the 1960s, most historians assumed without difficulty that early medieval estates in the West were generally bipartite, run through the *régime domanial classique*, the *sistema curtense*, the manorial system, with demesnes cultivated by tenant labour. Adriaan Verhulst, in a classic article of 1966, overturned this paradigm, and made it clearer than it had ever been that only in the estates of the Carolingian heartland, from the Seine to the Rhine, was this pattern at all common, and hardly before the eighth century. Verhulst attributed the change to land-clearance, particularly in the Paris basin, and also to royal initiative, since the first explicit references to agricultural labour service in the Frankish world are actually in (Aleman and

Bavarian) legislation. Merovingian demesnes, where they existed, he argued, were by contrast cultivated by slaves, not by labour service, and there was no true link between the two halves of such estates at all.[43] This late origin for the manor has been generally accepted since, and its regional restriction to the Seine–Rhine area (and eastwards into parts of what is now central and southern Germany) has been confirmed by studies of other parts of Francia. We must add northern Italy and Tuscany, which Verhulst did not then consider, but in southern Francia, or indeed southern Italy, manors did not exist in the early middle ages. They spread into, or developed in, Anglo-Saxon England as well, but not certainly before 900.[44]

If we want to investigate the West between the end of the Roman empire and the development of manorial patterns after c.750, we must start with Francia, the only region to give us any significant evidence for the seventh and early eighth centuries. For the Merovingian period, the major refinement to Verhulst's model has been an important article by Marie-Jeanne Tits-Dieuaide, published in 1985, which analysed in detail the documentary evidence for all forms of estate structure up to 750. She argued that most estates were simply run by tenants, with no demesnes; that there was a scatter of entirely slave-run estates, *villae cum mancipiis*, throughout the region, although they were a minority; and that there was also a handful of early manors, although this was the smallest group of all.[45] This picture can broadly be accepted, but I would go further: there is, it can be argued, even less evidence than Tits-Dieuaide thought for anything other than tenants, whether free or unfree, in our Merovingian Frankish material. I shall go through what evidence there is, and then offer some hypotheses as to how direct exploitation developed anew in the eighth century, before turning to analogous problems in Italy.

Let us begin with the will of Bishop Bertram of Le Mans from 616, the largest Merovingian document that survives. It is, as noted earlier (p. 186), far from the most typical text of the period, but its chattiness enables us to get a sense of how Bertram thought about his estates, which is a useful way into how estates worked in the period. Bertram was proud of his management, and, for example, listed the vineyards which he had planted at Cariliacum (perhaps Les Carriès near La Chartre, south-east of Le Mans), 'for previously this *ager* only had a couple of vineyards, nor did my predecessors as bishops want to add any there'. He 'built houses (*domos*) and established

---

[43] Verhulst, 'La genèse'; pp. 145–7 for Merovingian demesnes. He was preceded by Latouche, *Les origines*, pp. 74–85, and Fournier, *Le peuplement*, pp. 201–16, 326–7, who argued respectively for their weakness in Maine and in the Auvergne in the Merovingian period; and in general Ganshof, 'Quelques aspects principaux', pp. 75–91, who accepted the existence of Merovingian manors, without much discussion, but downplayed their significance.

[44] Southern Francia: see below, n. 67. England: see Ch. 6, n. 111; they could be regarded as an independent development there too.

[45] Tits-Dieuaide, 'Grands domaines'.

mancipiae' at Brossay, west of Le Mans; and, at Fontenay in the Seine valley below Paris, where the late Eugenius had planted vineyards, he placed *mancipia* as well. These *mancipia* seem consistently to have been unfree tenant families, living in their separate houses; indeed, on every estate he gave to the church where he would be buried, Sts-Pierre-et-Paul du Mans, he freed the *nitidior condoma*, the 'healthiest dependent family', to serve his tomb in perpetuity, which presupposes a family structure for his unfree dependants, and probably a separate tenant plot, judging by the normal meanings of the word *condoma*. Bertram's estates were, it appears, generally divided into tenant plots, which he elsewhere calls *colonicae*, although his general assumption was that his tenants were unfree, or to be freed on his death.[46]

This is the general pattern of most Merovingian estates. It is assumed by many charter-makers that dependants are largely unfree; but there are no indications of any pattern of exploitation of *mancipia* other than putting them into tenures. Because of this, I see no reason to read the *villa cum mancipiis* formula, which Tits-Dieuaide used as a prima facie case of a slave-mode estate, as anything other than a set of unfree tenures. In 572 Domnolus, one of Bertram's predecessors at Le Mans, gave to St-Vincent du Mans the often-cited Tresson estate, a large tract of woodland with eight named *mancipia*, in two or three families, and a horse-herd: perhaps a small slave estate? But in other properties which Domnolus gave to St-Vincent his *mancipia* were demonstrably unfree tenants (in one case he gave a *villa* plus the *accolae*, tenants, living there; in another, nine family groups of freedmen, evidently still cultivating; in a third, a *colonita* with its family of *mancipia*), so there is no particular reason to think that Tresson was different. Tits-Dieuaide was already concerned to minimize the existence of slave estates in Francia, so why did she read estates like these as directly managed? Her explicit assumption is that this is because they could be seen as a survival, after the invasion period, of Roman patterns of exploitation: she had fallen into the trap of the mirror game described earlier (p. 262), for slave plantations are not documented before the invasions either, and had never been, as far as we know, a feature of Gaulish agricultural management. If one takes away the presupposition, then this evidence for the slave mode in Francia vanishes at once.[47]

[46] Weidemann, *Das Testament*, respectively nn. 32 (cf. 25), 1, 17, 69; for *colonicae*, e.g. nn. 6, 9, 20, 25, 32, 35 (Busson and Ledru, *Actus*, pp. 118–19 (cf. 114), 104, 112, 138, 108, 109, 113, 114, 118, 122); for analysis, most recently Weidemann, *Das Testament*, pp. 102–12. For the word *condoma*, Goffart, *Rome's fall*, pp. 177–89; Martin, *La Pouille*, pp. 206–8; Billy, *La 'condamine'*, pp. 106–16 (the latter two show that Goffart's fiscal reading is unnecessary); and below, n. 81.

[47] Tits-Dieuaide, 'Grands domaines', pp. 32, 35–6. For Domnolus, Busson and Ledru, *Actus*, pp. 84–7 (a. 572), 87–9 (a. 581, for the *colonita*). See below, pp. 526–7, for the seventh-century *servi* of Spain, about whom one can make similar points.

This might not be true if Merovingian estates could at all often be bipartite, of course. Verhulst and Tits-Dieuaide correctly stress that labour service is in general documented only later (we shall look at it in a moment), so, if estates were divided into demesnes and tenures earlier, then the time-difference would entail that demesnes were initially exploited in a different way, by wage labour, or, far more likely by now, by direct slave management. Actually, however, the evidence for Merovingian demesnes is as scanty as that for estates entirely run by slaves. As Tits-Dieuaide notes, there are a handful of references to 'demesne-type' words, *dominicus, dominicatus, indominicatus*, in seventh-century and early eighth-century texts; I have counted nine before 740.[48] We find references to *curtes indominicatae, mansi indominicati/dominici*, and so on, and historians have understandably related these to the *dominicum* on which unfree tenants did labour service in the Aleman and Bavarian laws of the 710s and 740s (below, p. 288), or the *pars dominica* of ninth-century northern Francia (and we can add fifth-century Africa: above, p. 266), that is to say, demesnes in the technical sense. We do not need, however, to assume this equivalence for most of our Merovingian references. We saw earlier that *dominicus/-atus* does not have to mean anything more than 'belonging to a *dominus*', and this remained so in Francia; *dominicus* means 'royal' in the *Pactus legis Salicae*, for example. In the Mâcon survey of the 750s–760s, the word *dominicatus* simply described estates (monasteries in this case) that remained under the immediate control of a church rather than being ceded in benefice.[49] This sort of meaning, that is to say, immediate lordly possession rather than any specific type of agrarian management, seems to be commonest in our Merovingian references: hence the fact that most of them explicitly refer to whole estates, not just to one *pars* of them. The first in time, a charter for the territory of Laon in 671, refers to the *mansi dominici* in the *villa* of Macerias, which either had been lived in by Audeliana, grandmother of the donor Huntbert, or else had been built by Huntbert later: this seems simply to be a collection of tenant houses, with, presumably, an estate centre as well. When Nizezius and Irmitrudis in 680 sold their *curtes indominicatae*, with attached churches, buildings, orchards, fisheries, mills, and four subordinate settlements (here called *apendicia*), in a single large block of land north of Toulouse, with its *servi, coloni*, and *liberti*, we have no grounds for concluding that they meant anything other than their estates in the area. And when Abbo of Maurienne in 739 referred to *colonicas, terras et vineas dominicales* that had been leased out to Iocos the harpist (*lerator*), and

---

[48] Tits-Dieuaide, 'Grands domaines', pp. 33–8. References: Pardessus, *Diplomata*, nn. 365 (a. 671), 369 (a. 673), 432 (a. 694—*Cartulaire général*, n. 10, not really a better edition, dates it to 719), 544 (a. 728); Devic and Vaissete, *HGL*, II, preuves, pp. 42–5 (a. 680); *Dip. maiorum domus*, n. 2 (a. 691); *Leges Alamannorum*, c. 21 (a. 717–19); *Trad. Wiz.*, n. 3 (a. 739); Geary, *Aristocracy*, pp. 56, 68, cc. 26, 48 (a. 739).

[49] *Pactus*, cc. 1.1, 1.4, 41.5, 42.1–2, 50.4, 63.2. For Mâcon, Heidrich, 'Das Breve', pp. 21–2.

were also ceded to Opilonicus *in benefitium*, one of whom (it is not clear which) was now to be freed, then we are dealing with the opposite of any demesne. These loose meanings continue to be normal well past the first unambiguous references to *dominicum* as demesne, in the Aleman and Bavarian laws.[50]

The most detailed description of a set of Merovingian estates can be found in one of the earliest texts we have, the will of Aredius (modern French St Yrieix) and his mother Pelagia, dating to 572. At Sioussac, situated like the other estates in the will in the southern Limousin, Aredius and Pelagia ceded all the *mancipiola* of the estate, including three named ploughmen, and Ursacius and his family, whose task it was to cultivate four *aripenni* (around half a hectare) of vineyard. At Louhac, the families of *mancipia* similarly cultivated vineyards, and paid money to their landowners; these families also had their own *campelli* and *vineolae* as their *peculiaria*. At Chabrignac and the unlocated Scauriniacum, other *vinitores* had particular plots of vineyard they were responsible for; at Astaillac twenty-five freed families and eleven unfree had, again, their own *campelli* and *vineolae* apart from the lands they cultivated for their lord; some of them had to do cart service, pay money-rent, and give *eulogiae* (symbolic gifts), although these were separate from the six families of *mancipia quae colonaria appellantur*, who just paid money.[51] How this is to be read is a matter of some debate. It is possible to see the references to vine-cultivation as labour service by unfree tenants who are based on their own plots of land; the cart service is of course an explicit corvée, though not an agrarian one. Conversely, the ploughmen, at least, were probably slave specialists, and some of the vineyards might have been cultivated by the slave mode, on a micro-scale.[52] But the great bulk of these unfree dependants were tenants, and the agricultural labour service, if that is what it is, is specific to vineyards. This text is the closest we get to the *régime domanial classique* for another hundred years, but it is notably circumscribed. One could most easily conclude from it that Aredius and his mother were concerned for the tight control of their wine production, but in the framework of a standard set of unfree tenures.

It is important not to be schematic about these texts. It is hard to prove negatives, and tempting to talk away ambiguous evidence. But our evidence for any form of bipartite pattern in our Merovingian documentary evidence is never anything other than ambiguous, before the eighth-century

[50] Pardessus, *Diplomata*, n. 365; Devic and Vaissete, *HGL*, II, preuves, pp. 42–5; Geary, *Aristocracy*, p. 68, c. 48. Loose meanings continued in the Auvergne: Fournier, *Le peuplement*, pp. 285–91.
[51] *Testamentum S. Aredii*; see Tits-Dieuaide, 'Grands domaines', pp. 36–8, for commentary; Rouche, *L'Aquitaine*, p. 209, for identifications of placenames; and Debus, 'Studien', II, pp. 11–13 and n. 19 for another Aredius text and the textual tradition.
[52] Cart service: also *Marculfi formulae* I.11, II.36 (*MGH, Formulae*, pp. 49, 97). Specialist slaves, all herdsmen: also Levison, 'Adalgisel-Grimo', p. 129; Wampach, *Geschichte*, I.2, n. 3; Heidrich, 'Das Breve', p. 22. But such specialists were common in early medieval Europe.

codes. It does not seem to me that it would be easy for anyone to read a manorial pattern into the will of Aredius and Pelagia (unlike the case of the near-contemporary *P. Ital.* 3) who did not have the metanarrative of the origins of the bipartite estates of the ninth century ringing in their ear. On the other hand, what this text does show, explicitly, is a specialization in wine production; this, at least, does have clear parallels in other texts, right across the Merovingian period. Remigius of Reims in the 530s owned vineyards and an unfree *vinitor*, whom he freed. Erminethrudis of Paris around 600 owned quite a number of vineyards, at least thirteen, around the city, separate from her main estates and from each other; each of them had one or more attached vine-dressers, often clearly unfree. We find the same pattern near Laon in 664, at Echternach in 697, at Trier in 704, at Bingen on the Rhine and Köwerich on the Moselle in 710, near Saulieu in northern Burgundy in 717, in Alsace in 737, near Gorze in 745.[53] Vineyards were the only type of land that was regularly cultivated by slave specialists, in effect as mini-demesnes. Even on Aredius' *vineae*, more explicitly characterized than these, it was not possible to be entirely sure whether we were dealing with labour service or the slave mode, but it would be better, probably, to recognize that the distinction is pointless at the level of the single plot. More important is that vineyards lent themselves, rather more often than did any other kind of cultivation in Francia, to specialist treatment. Even when they were not cultivated in any obviously unusual way, *vineae* were also the most common land to be alienated separately from estates, in north-western Francia at least, where estates described as single blocks of land were more frequent than they were elsewhere (below, pp. 398–406).[54] It is vineyards that were special, I would argue, not the estate structures of Aredius and Pelagia in the southern Limousin.

Aredius' estate was unusual among this group in one respect only: it lay in the south. All the others lay on the extreme northern border of large-scale wine production in Europe. Wine was a standard part of the diet in the Mediterranean, but north of the Le Mans–Paris–Reims–Cologne line it immediately became a luxury, and was bought as such by political leaders in northern Europe even in the early middle ages, as with, for example, the wine served at the court of Mynyddog of Gododdin, situated at Edinburgh,

---

[53] Respectively, *Testamentum Remigii*; *ChLA*, XIV, n. 592 (dated in Laporte, 'Pour une nouvelle datation'); Pardessus, *Diplomata*, n. 350; Wampach, *Geschichte*, I.2, nn. 3, 10, 19; *Cartulary of Flavigny*, nn. 1, 57; *Trad. Wiz.*, n. 8; *Cartulaire de l'abbaye de Gorze*, n. 1 (four *vinitores*). In the first of these, one *vinitor* is free, and co-owns with Remigius. In *ChLA*, XIV, n. 592, we sometimes find a free dependent tenant and a slave *vinitor* each associated with the same *vinea*.

[54] e.g. Weidemann, *Das Testament*, cc. 22, 25, 32, 33, 44 (Busson and Ledru, *Actus*, pp. 113–14, 118–19, 127, largely for Maine); Levison, 'Adalgisel-Grimo', p. 130 (the Moselle); *Cartulary of Flavigny*, n. 1 (Flavigny in Burgundy).

around 600.[55] Throughout the post-Roman period, that is to say, there was a commercial reason why one might want to specialize in wine production at the access points for northern trade, which certainly included Paris, on the Seine, and probably Echternach and Gorze, both close to the Moselle, and Le Mans, where Bertram mentioned *negotiantes* as an outlet for his new vineyards at Cariliacum, linked by river to the Loire mouth. Later, in the eighth century, Paris became a major wine entrepôt, as Jean Durliat and Jean-Pierre Devroey have argued on the basis of the polyptych of St-Germain; the great St-Denis market was itself in part a wine market, as a diploma of 753 makes explicit.[56] Aredius' estates, although further south, may fit with this, in that they were close to the Dordogne, which may mean that their wine was meant for export too.

I argued in the previous section that direct management of demesnes made most sense in the framework of the sale of produce. Francia in the early middle ages was never a region where exchange collapsed, as we shall see in Chapter 11 (pp. 794–805), but that exchange hardly matched the late Roman Mediterranean in its overall intensity. Wine may have been the one agrarian product whose trade maintained its vitality, thanks to the ecological margin that ran across the north Frankish heartland.[57] It is, accordingly, less surprising that wine production is consistently associated with forms of special land management in northern Francia, however obscurely characterized these are. I would argue that there was a systemic break in the intensity of land management in the region after the end of imperial rule, which was complete by the time of the first Merovingian land documents, such as the will of Aredius and Pelagia. The general dominance of tenant production in our evidence is the clearest sign of it, and it correlates with a relative weakening of exchange. Wine production was the major exception to that break, and it was more of an exception the closer it was to the margin

---

[55] Aneirin, *Y Gododdin*, IV, XXXIXA, B, LXXXI. The dating of this text is almost as contested as is *Beowulf*, and there are currently proponents of a variety of dates from as early as 550 right up to the tenth century. A dating to c.800 remains a fairly safe assumption, however, and the poem could well be earlier. See for a convenient bibliographical survey Evans, *Heroic poetry*, pp. 65–87. For Frankish wine in Ireland, see Lebecq, 'Les échanges', p. 187; Wooding, *Communication*, pp. 32–4, 68–70, minimizing it.

[56] Weidemann, *Das Testament*, c. 32 (Busson and Ledru, *Actus*, p. 119); *MGH, Dip. Kar.*, I, n. 6 (a. 753)—cf. Durliat, 'Le vigne et le vin'; Devroey, 'Un monastère', pp. 577–81; and below, Ch. 11, n. 187. By the eighth century the Rhineland was showing a particularly active wine specialization: see below, pp. 393–6. The Champagne was slower to develop as a wine region: Devroey, 'Vin, vignes et vignerons'. Bruand, *Voyageurs et marchandises*, pp. 216–34, discusses the circulation of wine in the period after 750 in detail; by then it used roads as well as rivers.

[57] One might argue the same for olive oil; we certainly have enough evidence of the concern by northern Frankish kings and monasteries to get oil from the South, especially, via Marseille, from Africa: see Claude, 'Aspekte des Binnenhandels', pp. 17, 79–80; Fouracre, 'Eternal light', pp. 68–72; Loseby, 'Marseille, II', pp. 176–80. But how this affected oil production in Gaul/Francia itself cannot be seen at present, for the ecological boundary ran across parts of the far south of the region for which there is no significant documentation, for this period or for some time after.

beyond which wine cannot be reliably produced. The specialist *vineae* were the main examples, in seventh-century Francia, of demesnes, the local equivalents to the *autourgiai* of sixth-century Oxyrhynchos. But they were pretty small and pretty marginal. Nor were they, as far as we can see, directed with the same intensity that even tenants could be in the late Roman world. The vine-dressers of Aredius' or Erminethrudis' estates do not seem to be working under the immediate surveillance of a landlord or his/her agents; it seems fairly clear that they organized the cultivation of their handful of fields themselves, as long as they grew wine there. This sort of specialist management was the weakest we have so far seen, the one in which landlords were most distant from the labour process, even though it was the most intensive we have documented for the Merovingian period.

It is, conversely, quite possible that these vineyards were one of the models for the renewed direct management of the end of the eighth century. We have two further probable references to demesne from before 700, four *cingas* of land at Flivenasa near Auxerre in 670, and a citation of the *riga* as a form of tenure in Marculf's Paris-based formulary of around the same time. Both terms mean the same in later texts (the first in the form *andecinga* or similar): tracts of land which tenants are required to cultivate, from which the whole surplus goes to the lord.[58] The provision of the Bavarian law-code of the 740s which describes labour service also relates it largely to *andecingae* or *andecenae*, which here are fields 400 by 40 feet in size, as well as to vineyards. This sort of labour service leaves the actual organization of work to the peasant; the lord simply provides the seed and takes the harvest.[59] It is thus similar to the specialist *vineae* in its structure. Although it is clear that (*ande*)*cingae* and *rigae* were predominantly grain-fields, the geographical location of the first two references fits that of the *vineae*, and I would propose that the idea of demanding this sort of labour spread from the vineyards of the north.

---

[58] Pardessus, *Diplomata*, n. 363 (*Cartulaire général*, n. 8, dates it to c.680); *Marculfi Formulae* II.36 (*MGH*, *Formulae*, p. 97); see Tits-Dieuaide, 'Grands domaines', p. 38; and, for *andecingae*, Perrin, 'De la condition des terres'.

[59] *Leges Baiuwariorum*, I.13. See Rivers, 'Seigneurial obligations'; Hägermann, 'Einige Aspekte', pp. 72–7, among many. This law and *Leges Alamannorum*, c. 21, from twenty years earlier, which are the first explicit texts for labour service in Francia, come from codes known to have been influenced by seventh-century Frankish royal models, but it would be illegitimate to use this as an argument for dating any specific law to the seventh century, still less as evidence of royal interest in labour service. Nor can we lightly assume that corvées were already generalized in Alemannia and Bavaria, just because they are referred to in a law. Hammer, *A large-scale slave society*, pp. 19–20, stresses that bipartite estates are rare in Bavaria before 800, in fact. They were commoner in Alemannia, as is seen in some of the early charters for St Gallen, *Ub. St Gallen*, nn. 18, 24, 29, 33, 39, 56 (aa. 754–70), which list the rents that donors to St Gallen must pay for the usufruct of the land they gave, usually in the Thurgau; these include some *operae* or *angaria*. But the scale is small, and *operae* are by no means universal in these usufructs; this is not as yet a developed demesne system.

Such an argument is speculative, of course; and, indeed, the concept of large-scale labour service had several other possible origins. One was transport service, which is occasionally documented in the Merovingian period, as we have seen; it is the form of labour which is most likely to have had fiscal roots, and indeed road-building and the like were still in this period standard public burdens for the free in most of the post-Roman world.[60] Another was perhaps the direction of large-scale land-clearance, as Verhulst argued, although his major example, the Paris basin, is increasingly regarded as having had rather less woodland in the early Merovingian period than was believed a generation ago (below, pp. 402–3). Another again, perhaps more important, was forced labour as a sign of legal subjection, as in the *opera* or *servicium* (measured in days per week) that several formulary collections (from sixth-century Angers, from seventh-century Paris, from late eighth-century Sens) require in return for a loan of money, for the period of the loan—in the Angers formulary associated with a diminution of the debtor's *status*. This association of *operae* (of unspecified type in the formulae) with subjection recurs in the Aleman and Bavarian laws, where it explicitly denotes agricultural labour service on demesnes, and is only due from the unfree; we shall find this imagery again in Italy (pp. 296–7). The difference is that, between the late sixth century in Angers and the 710s in Alemannia, such *operae* had become part of normal agrarian relations of production.[61] All these strands came together in the *régime domanial classique* of the Carolingian period. But it needs also to be stressed that to search for the genealogical origins of ninth-century demesnes in isolated elements of this kind is a misrepresentation of the problem. We have amply seen in the late Roman context that demesnes can develop more than once, if other conditions are right. The key issue here is that the first well-documented examples of demesnes, such as Rihbald's upper Rhineland estates in 774, or the *rigae* in the Pithou formulary from the Paris area in the late eighth century, or the Staffelsee estate of the bishop of Augsburg not long after 800, or of course the *villae* of St-Germain-des-Prés in the 820s, as well as their later successors, existed on a scale that is simply unparalleled before 750.[62] These demesnes were cultivated by labour service in increasingly

[60] See n. 52 for refs. Goffart, *Rome's fall*, pp. 207–8, 217, suggests that early medieval labour services had a Roman, fiscal, origin; but cultivation was never a fiscal obligation, and agrarian corvées are absent from southern Francia and Byzantine Italy, where structural continuities with Rome were, overall, greater.

[61] *Form. Andecavenses*, n. 38, *Marculfi Formulae* II.27, *Cartae Senonicae*, n. 3 (MGH, *Formulae*, pp. 17, 93, 186); see for comment Hägermann, 'Einige Aspekte', pp. 57, 60–1; for the laws, see n. 52.

[62] *Trad. Wiz.*, n. 63; Poupardin, ' "Formulae Pithoei" ', cc. 34–8, 72, 102/4; MGH, *Cap.*, I, n. 128, cc. 2–9 (see for comment Elmshäuser, 'Untersuchungen'); *Pol. St-Germain*. For later Frankish polyptychs, see Fossier, *Polyptyques*, pp. 25–33, written before the wave of recent editions however. In the later eighth century casual references to demesnes in our document collections increase: see Halsall, *Settlement*, pp. 192–4, for the Metz region. The Wissembourg

elaborate ways, and the pre-existing patterns of unpaid labour, especially in vineyards, that have just been listed help to show why this Frankish agrarian intensification took the form of labour service rather than any other (such as wage labour or slave plantations)—Frankish landlords, like their counterparts elsewhere, used what was already locally available. But the demesnes of the Carolingian period represent a new phenomenon, simply because of their scale, and the need for organization that they posed. This needs to be explained not in terms of earlier roots, but in terms of contemporary function and purpose.

Until fairly recently, it used often to be argued that the bipartite manors of the Carolingian period were examples of a 'closed', self-sufficient economy, in which everything was made on the spot, and nothing needed to be exchanged. This is increasingly being discarded as a model: it derived too much from a rhetoric of self-sufficiency which is used by some of the leading texts for the period, such as the *Capitulare de villis* of c.800, and which is no more authentic than is the parallel rhetoric in Cato's *De agricultura*.[63] Recent work by a wide array of scholars, such as Waltraut Bleiber, Olivier Bruand, Jean-Pierre Devroey, Richard Hodges, Stéphane Lebecq, Werner Rösener, Pierre Toubert, and Adriaan Verhulst, stresses instead the productive advances of the *régime domanial classique*, and the evidence in the polyptychs for a concern for the sale of produce.[64] The economic upturn of the late eighth and ninth centuries (below, pp. 801–5) seems to me the most plausible context for the development of more intensive, in this case manorial, exploitation. It was doubtless a result of a specifically landlord pressure on dependent peasants, an increase in their level of exploitation, and, above all, an increase in control over them, in the substantial portions of the week in which many of them came to work on demesnes for lords.[65] But

documents, which begin as early as the 690s, perhaps show this most clearly: here, after two references to *indominicata* in 739–42, neither of them clearly demesne, the Rihbald document for 774 is the next; more or less clear demesne terminology only begins in the 770s. See *Trad. Wiz.*, nn. 3, 1, 54, 57, 19, 127, etc.

[63] *MGH, Cap.*, I, n. 32, cc. 17–23 and *passim*; Cato, *De agricultura*, II.7.

[64] Bleiber, *Naturwirtschaft*, pp. 127–58; eadem, 'Grundherrschaft und Markt'; Bruand, *Voyageurs et marchandises*; Devroey, *Études*; Hodges, *Towns and trade*; Lebecq, 'The role of the monasteries'; Morimoto, 'État et perspectives'; Rösener, 'Strukturformen'; Toubert, *Dalla terra*; Verhulst, 'La diversité'; idem, 'Marchés'. This is only a small proportion of the work of each author, and of recent work in general, on the subject; Toubert, *Dalla terra*, pp. 246–50, and Verhulst's two pieces contain extensive bibliographies. Two syntheses now frame the subject: Verhulst, *The Carolingian economy*; Devroey, *Économie rurale*. As early as 1951 Cipolla, 'Questioni aperte', although more or less adhering to the then dominant closed-economy model, recognized how complex Carolingian manors were. For recent contrary views see Duby, *Early growth*, pp. 83–107 (with some important nuances); Fossier, 'Les tendances'; and the debate at the end of *Flaran*, X, pp. 183–203: these represent a current of opinion that survived latest in France.

[65] Verhulst, 'La diversité', pp. 138–41; Kuchenbuch, 'Die Klostergrundherrschaft', pp. 325–30. It must be added that this landlordly pressure also involved increased rents in some cases, as around 800 on the Antoigné estate in Poitou of the monastery of Cormery: see Nelson, 'Dispute settlement', pp. 48–51.

there was only any point in doing such things if the outlets for the sale of produce were clear.

The Carolingian manor lies outside our period, and cannot be looked at in detail here. Its documentation in empirical terms almost all postdates 800. In the first decades of the ninth century demesnes and large-scale labour service suddenly appear all over the northern half of the Carolingian empire, from the Seine to the Danube. It is a transformation that has too often been associated with kings, above all Charlemagne, in particular because the *Capitulare de villis* is a normative account of an ideal estate deriving from the royal court, and because the polyptych surveys seem to have begun with royal encouragement, as the *Brevium exempla* of the years after 800 makes explicit. I have always found it hard to imagine kings specializing in this level of micro-managerial interest. The Le Mans capitulary of c.800, which shows Charlemagne regulating labour services in the area, is explicitly a response to the complaints of the tenants of ecclesiastical and royal land about the more variegated services demanded by *seniores* of all kinds there. It seems to me most likely that these trends were common to all landowners, but that these included royal managers (such as the *iudices* of the *Capitulare de villis*), who were close enough to the king's court for their actions to be translated into the highly moralistic terms characteristic of Carolingian governance.[66] What seems to have happened is that the increasing possibility of the sale of produce encouraged the crystallization of demesnes, in the context of a more generalized intensification of surveillance and control (very clear in the *Capitulare de villis*, which, probably over-optimistically, even envisages accounting, as we have seen—p. 267). This concentrated on the direction of the labour of tenants, both because this was less complex to develop, and because, on a small scale, it already existed as a concept, especially in vineyard cultivation. The possibilities of exchange encouraged a pattern of emulation that moved from estate to estate, in a few decades at most. Hence or otherwise, it could even be found in England a century later (below, p. 349).

Before we leave Francia, two aspects of this development need to be looked at briefly. The first is its geography. The *régime domanial classique* in Francia was overwhelmingly a northern phenomenon, at least in the Carolingian period. It is almost invisible in the estate records we have for the Auvergne, the Saône valley, and for anywhere south of that.[67] The Seine–Rhine region, the Frankish royal heartland, was its core, extending eastwards into the Danube valley of Alemannia and Bavaria. Following Carolingian armies and the extension of aristocratic power, it soon spread into Saxony. East of the Rhine, however, demesnes remained small and

---

[66] *MGH, Cap.*, I, nn. 31, 32, 128 (e.g. cc. 16, 23: *et sic cetera breviare debes*).
[67] Fournier, *Le peuplement*, pp. 284–307, 326–7; Rouche, *L'Aquitaine*, p. 211; Poly, 'Régime domanial', pp. 57–67.

manorial organization less tight.[68] The absence of manors from southern Gaul may have been because, where estates were fragmented and tenants by now generally free, new forms of exploitation may have been harder to achieve; from the Rhineland eastwards tenurial fragmentation was as great, but tenants were generally *mancipia*, so their conditions of labour may have been easier to change (see below, pp. 560–6).

These unevennesses of development led to what Ludolf Kuchenbuch has called *Rentenlandschaften*: different areas, all across ninth-century Francia, which had different patterns of rents and services, largely irrespective of which great lords owned in each, as the geographical contrasts inside polyptychs show. These showed lasting differences in local assumptions about the rents that ought to be paid, which survived landlordly pressure in the eighth and ninth centuries, whether or not in the direction of manorial structures. There must, in fact, everywhere have been a dialectic between aristocratic pressure and local norms, the latter underpinned by peasant resistance, which produced different organizational results in different microregions.[69] The variables would thus not only be the size of estates and the level of landlordly coercive power, plus the density of exchange in different areas, but also the nature of pre-existing local practices with regard to rents and services, and the capacity of local peasantries to resist, all of which would be different from place to place. How these variables actually converged to produce different *Rentenlandschaften* cannot easily be seen for Francia, for the evidence is lacking; we shall see some examples in Italy in a moment. The key point that comes out of a recognition of these differences is, however, that the same *sort* of pressure from above could produce locally distinct socio-economic realities, depending on what was there before. Carolingian manorialization, even when it occurred, was not a fully homogenizing process. And that pressure did not have even to result in manorialization, as it did not in southern Francia; as the Romans knew, one could derive sufficient profit from simple tenure, if rents were high enough.

The second point is a problem. Recent historiography lays considerable stress on exchange as an underpinning of the manor, I am sure rightly. What is less clear is whom the produce of the newly coherent great estates of the ninth century was actually sold to. Wine is easy, as we have seen; so are artisanal products (below, pp. 796–805); but by the time of the polyptychs most demesnes specialized in the production of cereals. If every royal and monastic estate sold its grain surplus, who was there around who had the resources to buy it, but not the land to produce it? Certainly not aristocrats, who may have been doing the same; there was anyway a limit to the amount

[68] Verhulst, 'Étude comparative'; Rösener, *Strukturen*, for monographic analyses.
[69] Kuchenbuch, *Bäuerliche Gesellschaft*, pp. 236–44; idem, 'Probleme der Rententwicklung'; see also n. 65. For the force of peasant norms, see also Vollrath, 'Herrschaft und Genossenschaft', and, for the lord–peasant dialectic, Goetz, 'Herrschaft und Recht'. See below, pp. 580–1, for peasant resistance.

of bread that even the most voracious mead-hall could consume. Overseas export, to the undeveloped economies of the North, offers even greater difficulties of explanation. One answer is certainly towns, the expanding cathedral cities of the great river-valleys and the coastal *emporia* (below, pp. 676–88), although even the most optimistic analyst of the Carolingian economy would probably not argue that this was the only motor of the exchange system. Another, however, may have been the army. Carolingian armies were not fed by the state, unlike in the Roman world, but the campaigning season (pre-harvest, one must remember, therefore in the most difficult months for supplies) involved larger numbers of men than any equivalent gathering in the West, for up to three months of the year. They were supposed to provide their own supplies, and indeed presumably did, for there is no public military commissariat recorded in our period. These supplies, logically, either came from their own lands, or from the marketed surplus of others. Either way, the intensification of grain production in the decades around 800 may have had a purpose.[70] This would link the great years of the Carolingian *régime domanial classique* to the great years of the state's mobilization of armed men on a large scale, which had ended by 900 at the latest in most of the Carolingian lands. This would certainly fit the era of the polyptychs, which ended in Francia at the same time (in Italy, a few decades later), although manorial structures, now in place, would continue for centuries to come, feeding, by now, the enlarged military entourages of the post-Carolingian period.

The problem of agrarian demand nonetheless seems to me to mark the limit of the economic expansion of the ninth century. There is much less evidence for agricultural exchange (or for other elements of absolute agrarian expansion, such as land-clearance) in this period than there is for the eleventh and twelfth centuries; the major evidence for it is actually the development of manorial organization itself, including its market outlets, plus the clear documentation of *artisanal* exchange that archaeology now provides us with. The underlying problem of northern agricultural exchange is the homogeneity of the terrain in the North European Plain, which extends from Paris and London eastwards into Poland, as much the same crops can be grown in every part of it. For agricultural products, apart from wine, to be exchanged on any scale across long or medium distances, the moorland and woodland areas of the North needed to be developed as well, so as to allow for the growth of specialist silvo-pastoral productions, such as sheep (for wool) and timber, a development which itself depended on the import of grain. This development was, broadly, later than our period, for the marginal lands of the North were for the most part those which

---

[70] *MGH, Cap.*, I, nn. 32, c. 64; 74, c. 8; 75; 77, c. 10; 171. Cf. Ganshof, *Frankish institutions*, p. 67, who gives a different interpretation. This paragraph is a revised version of Wickham, 'Overview II', pp. 354–5.

aristocratic power had not yet come to dominate. In this respect, the eleventh century was indeed more of a period of agrarian growth than was the ninth; one does not have to dismiss Carolingian prosperity, as Georges Duby and Robert Fossier did, to recognize it. These specialist, mutually dependent, productions (further underpinned by substantially increased urban demand) were in fact, in my view, more important to the increasing economic complexity of the eleventh to thirteenth centuries than was the land-clearance that has often been seen as its core.[71] Although this point cannot be developed here, it puts further into relief the question of who bought the grain from the demesnes of the Carolingian monasteries. All the same, as we shall see further in Chapter 11, there was *enough* exchange in the late eighth and ninth centuries to encourage the first medieval evidence of systematic aristocratic interest in, and at least partial control of, agrarian production, which is what the growth of the *régime domanial classique* comes down to.

The development of the manor, in Italian the *sistema curtense*, in Lombard Italy is clearly analogous to that in Francia, but demesnes here had a different structure, and, I would argue, different roots. In order to understand how the two were related, we must begin here in the eighth century, for we have no evidence for the seventh. How the situation in sixth-century Italy characterized earlier (pp. 278–80) related to that of the best-documented sub-regions of the eighth century, Tuscany, the Sabina, and Lombardy-Emilia, can only be guessed at, but we shall look at some hypotheses later.

The first point to make is that, unlike any other of our regions except Egypt, the bulk of our evidence for the management of estates in Italy in the eighth century—and still more in centuries following—consists of leases to cultivators. This allows us a much more exact assessment of what obligations peasants actually owed than does any other source except the most detailed polyptych; we even have some leases from lay landowners, paralleling Egypt (where they are normal) but unmatched in most of western Europe for centuries, so we can extend our observations beyond the restricted arena of church property. Conversely, we must be careful about overgeneralization, for not all tenants had leases. Unfree tenants could not make legal contracts, by definition; ninth-century Italian sources also sometimes draw distinctions, even among free tenants, between tenants with a charter (*livellarii*) and those without, who owed rents established by local custom. Leases, even when to cultivators (which by no means all leases were, and it is sometimes hard to be sure whether they were or not), would in this case only tell us about one stratum of tenancy, the highest. In northern Italy, in particular, ninth-century leases (in the Po plain only three leases precede 800) show considerable divergences from the great monastic polyptychs of the same period, those for Bobbio (862, 883) and that for S. Giulia di Brescia

[71] Cf. Wickham, *Land and power*, pp. 193–8. For Duby and Fossier, above, n. 64.

(c.900): for example, a third of the tenants of S. Giulia owed three days a week labour service, but not one of the leases requires more than two days, and in fact 75 per cent of the latter require only two weeks or less per year, not much more than a recognitive obligation. Here, leases are no guide to the obligations of tenants as a whole.[72] In Tuscany, on the other hand, where leases to cultivators are most frequent (there are over thirty for the eighth century, nearly 300 for the ninth), the pattern of their terms fits pretty well what we know about the dues and services of other tenants, referred to more casually in charters of gift, or, in the case of Lucca, listed in the inventories of the cathedral from the late ninth century, so here one can trust the evidence of the leases. The Tuscan documentation is by far the richest in Italy for the eighth century, so it must be our first point of reference. From the start, labour services on demesnes are more prominent than in contemporary Francia.

Tuscan documents in our period come mostly from two ecclesiastical archives, of the bishop of Lucca in the north and of the monastery of Monte Amiata in the south. The Amiata documents, although less numerous, include our first reference to a peasant rent in Italy since the sixth century, in a lease of 735/6 for Gello, east of the monastery, from a lay landlord, Taso *centinarius*. It already assumes a manorial pattern for Taso's estate, for it requires one week's labour service (*angaria*) in three, a typical figure (along with one week in four) in the Amiata collection up to the 880s.[73] The Lucchese evidence also shows us that bipartite estates, and labour service, were common by the 740s, and indeed earlier: here, our first lease, for Guamo just south of Lucca in 746, for an unspecified customary rent and *angaria*, is a renewal of a lease previously held by the tenant's father. By the middle of the century Lucchese documents routinely distinguish between demesne (*sundrium, domus cultilis*) and tenures (*casae massariciae*), and 60 per cent of Lucchese leases for the century require labour service. It was usually as yet referred to in fairly vague terms, as 'according to the custom of the house', *secundum consuetudinem de ipsa casa*, or 'as much as is needed', *quantas utilitas fuerit*, both of which probably refer to standardized local customs. After the Carolingian conquest in 774, however, labour became more frequently specified: thereafter, between one and three days per week (or their equivalents in weeks) were common obligations for another century. As the number of leases climbed in the ninth century, the percentage that required labour dropped, to 29 per cent, almost all before

---

[72] For the polyptychs, see *Inventari*, nn. V (ed. G. F. Pasquali), VIII.1, 2 (ed. A. Castagnetti). For leases set against the polyptychs, see Montanari, 'La corvée' (esp. p. 46), Galetti, 'Un caso particolare', pp. 82–6, set against Pasquali, 'La corvée', pp. 115–18. For *livellarii*, see classically Leicht, 'Livellario nomine', the best contribution in a historiographical tradition dominated in Italy by an excessive legalism until the 1960s.

[73] First Amiata lease: *CDL*, I, n. 57 (*Codex diplomaticus Amiatinus*, n. 2). For statistics, see Andreolli, 'Contratti agrari', pp. 72, 148–54, the basic article on Tuscan estate management.

875.[74] Not all tenants were involved in manorial organization, that is to say, and indeed there were estates with no demesne at all. But, although the manorialization of the Lucchesia was incomplete, it was entirely normal, at least up to 875, and on some estates later. It could involve a heavy commitment for many tenants, as the first inventory of episcopal estates, probably dating from before 880, makes clear.[75]

On the other hand, the economic organization presupposed by this bipartite pattern cannot easily be compared to that of major Frankish polyptychs such as St-Germain-des-Prés. We possess a brief description of the *sundrium* of one of the main family estates of one of Lucca's major landowners, Bishop Peredeus (d. 779), at Rosignano on the coast south of Pisa, dating to 762: it seems to have been remarkably small, consisting of two or four grain-fields, two vineyards, a wood, an orchard, and a *sala antiqua*, an estate-centre, apparently abandoned. The Rosignano demesne was not only small, but also highly fragmented, and this was indeed a feature of Italian property-owning as a whole.[76] As we shall see (pp. 387–92), villages owned by a single proprietor were rare, and most estates were divided up into dozens, sometimes hundreds, of separate fields or groups of fields. As a result, the *sistema curtense* in Italy was itself fragmented, with, often, tenants from one village required to do labour service in another, not even necessarily neighbouring, and with landowners entirely happy to separate out demesnes and tenures and to give either piecemeal to the church. This fragmentation did not in itself make manors less common, but it at least imposed a limit on their internal organization, for scattered tenants could not be as secure a work-force as tenants living on the spot—journey times had to be taken into consideration, even if nothing else. Bruno Andreolli has argued, on the basis of the fact that Carolingian-period corvées are more tightly characterized than their predecessors, for a systemization of labour service from the late 770s onwards, probably under Frankish influence. This is in my view unlikely, especially given the late date of manorial development in Francia itself; but, anyway, Lucchese manorial organization remained very heterogeneous by north Frankish standards. Andreolli has also shown that the rates of labour in Carolingian Tuscany were actually rather high for Lucca's small demesnes, and he has therefore proposed, convincingly, that corvées represented control and subjection in symbolic terms, as well as, or more than, tighter economic organization. This certainly has Frankish parallels, and would locate Tuscan manors in a framework of the exercise of

---

[74] First Lucchese lease: *CDL*, I, n. 85; for demesne, e.g. *CDL*, II, nn. 139, 165, 175; for custom quotes, *CDL*, II, nn. 166, 167. For statistics, see Andreolli, 'Contratti agrari', *passim*.

[75] Varieties of estates: e.g. Wickham, *Mountains*, pp. 68–81; see Andreolli, 'Contratti agrari', pp. 119–20; idem, 'L'evoluzione', pp. 39–44, for manorial discontinuities and continuities after 875. For the first inventory, *Inventari*, XI.1 (ed. M. Luzzati); Andreolli, 'Contratti agrari', pp. 129–31, for the figures; Wickham, *Mountains*, p. 86, for the date.

[76] *CDL*, II, n. 161.III; cf. n. 178 for another good example of fragmentation.

landed power quite as much as that of productive intensification, to the extent that the two can be distinguished.[77]

Some of these patterns recur in the Rietino and the Sabina, the hill country on the boundary between the duchy of Spoleto and that of Rome, which is known to us because of the cartularies of the monastery of Farfa. Here, gifts to the monastery often specify that the dues owned by tenants should not be increased, and from the first references to these, in 748–9, such dues include *angaria*. One, in 773, protects the tenants from doing future *angaria* outside their estate (*casale*), implying that Farfa might have considered the rationalization of its management. From the later eighth century this labour begins to be specified more exactly, and turns out to be three weeks per year in most cases: not a high figure, much smaller than the averages in Lucca, and not present on all estates. Only in the mid-ninth century are there a few citations of genuinely heavy labour service, up to one week in two, all of them concentrated in the higher mountain valleys north-east of the monastery.[78] This may have developed in the context of the imposition of monastic power by force on isolated free populations, as the corvées of the 850s in the Valle Trita, a mountain estate of the monastery of S. Vincenzo at Volturno, certainly were.[79]

Pierre Toubert, who studied the Farfa evidence in most detail, stressed how unlike the *régime domanial classique* of northern Francia these patterns were. He reckoned that there were three types of estate management here, and that only a small minority were manors of a 'classic' type. He also argued that there were bipartite estates in the Sabina which were largely, or wholly, cultivated by slaves, the *servi manuales* who in some texts are counterposed to *servi in casis* or *in portionibus*, unfree tenants. But *servi manuales* are not actually associated in our texts with demesne labour in any explicit way. I am not convinced, in fact, that we can be sure that there were slave-run demesnes in the Sabina; as in the Frankish case (p. 282), if one was not persuaded by the historiography that such estates still existed, the texts would not require them. But it is anyway clear, as Toubert stressed, that estates in and around the Sabina had highly fluid structures, as indeed they did in Tuscany; here, any development and systematization of manorial

---

[77] Andreolli on Carolingian influence: 'Contratti agrari', p. 88; idem, 'La corvée precarolingia'; idem and Montanari, *L'azienda curtense*, pp. 52–64. Andreolli on labour rates too high for demesnes: 'L'evoluzione', pp. 36–40.

[78] *RF*, nn. 20, 21, 23, 36, 88, 102, 142 (*CDL*, V, nn. 11, 12, 14, 21, 63, 73, 100), *RF*, n. 152 for the eighth century; cf. *RF*, n. 25 (*CDL*, IV.1, n. 12), for an estate in 750 consisting only of *casae colonicae* except for one *casa* of *domusculta*. For heavy labour service, *Liber largitorius*, nn. 7, 15, 17, 24, 31–3, 51, from the 820s–870s. For all this see Toubert, *Les structures*, pp. 462–73.

[79] *Chronicon Vulturnense*, I, pp. 333–7 (twelve weeks per year, i.e. roughly one week in four); cf. Wickham, *Studi*, pp. 18–28, 44–8; and Feller, *Les Abruzzes*, pp. 321–2, 339, for a handful of ninth-century examples around Casauria. See below, pp. 582–4, for resistance in the Valle Trita.

relationships was only occasional, spatially restricted, and temporary.[80] It can be added that this is even more the case for what we know of all the rest of central and southern Italy, whether Lombard or not. Here, in material from both before and after 800, any reference to anything more complex than tenants simply paying rent to estate-centres is exceptionally rare, much as it had been in Gregory the Great's Sicily. In Beneventan documents, indeed, estates themselves often dissolve into collections of unfree tenants, *condomae*, who were often simply alienated as single family units, together with their land.[81] When Popes Zacharias and Hadrian I (741–52, 773–96) established a set of *domuscultae* around Rome, they may well have been creating a manorial system, given the meaning of the word *domusculta* in all the Lombard territories. Still, if they were, it was regarded as unusual enough for specific sections of the *Liber pontificalis* to be devoted to it; they were locally controversial, and did not necessarily last much beyond 815, when, while Pope Leo III was dying, several were burnt.[82] The southern boundary of the *sistema curtense* did not significantly extend beyond Farfa and the Amiata.

In northern Italy, finally, we have less eighth-century evidence, as already noted. The first leases we have, for the territories of Piacenza and Imola, only date to 783–4, although they already contain reference to labour service: in the first Piacenza contract, on average one-and-a-half days per week. Earlier, too, at least the existence of corvées is made explicit by a court-case from the period 721–44 for Campione in the Alpine foothills of Lombardy, in which a freedman does *operas a prados et a vitis* for his lord, as well as transport service.[83] Put this evidence beside the frequent use from the 740s onwards of standard bipartite terminology to describe estates, *curte domoculta cum casas massaricias* and the like, and we could conclude, here too, that manors and demesne labour already existed in the Po plain. How *important* demesnes were in the eighth century is, however, no clearer than anywhere else. Two exchanges, from 761 and 771, detail land more carefully than usual; in

---

[80] Toubert, *Dalla terra*, pp. 156–82, for estate-management types; idem, *Les structures*, pp. 469, 476, for *servi manuales* (for texts, see esp. *RF*, nn. 85, 142 (*CDL*, V, nn. 56, 100), 175), and pp. 462–5 for fluidity.

[81] *Condomae* before 800: *Chronicon S. Sophiae*, I.5, 8, 9, 12, 15, 19, 24, II.10, 11, 15, III.1, 6, 26; *Chronicon Vulturnense*, nn. 22, 32, 38, 69. Isolated houses of *servi* would further increase the list. See above, n. 46, for bibliography, with Wickham, *Il problema*, pp. 19–22. For possible bipartite estates in Benevento see *CDL*, V, n. IX (764/70); *Chronicon S. Sophiae*, II.1, 10, III.11 (724–57); all of these show *domoculta* in possession clauses, without further characterization. Note also that the ex-Byzantine Romagna was another area of weak manorialization: Fumagalli, *Coloni e signori*, pp. 93–110; Andreolli and Montanari, *L'azienda curtense*, pp. 161–75; Montanari, 'La corvée'.

[82] *Liber pontificalis*, XCIII.25–6, XCVII.54–5, 63, 69, 77; see for comment and context Wickham, 'Historical and topographical notes', I, pp. 173–7; Marazzi, *I 'patrimonia'*, pp. 235–66 (259–60 for the events of 815), the basic current account.

[83] *Le carte private*, I, n. 1 (cf. n. 2; *ChLA*, XXVII, nn. 828–9, are another edition); Mazzotti and Curradi, 'La più antica pergamena imolese' (also ed. *ChLA*, XXIX, n. 888); *CDL*, I, n. 81. For commentary, see Montanari, 'La corvée'; Galetti, 'Un caso particolare'.

each, the areas of *domuscultilis* are both fragmented and fairly restricted in size.[84] Interestingly, these were exchanges involving S. Salvatore di Brescia, the monastery which would be called S. Giulia in the ninth century, and whose polyptych would show the most complex version of the *sistema curtense* hitherto recorded in Italy. There is no sign of that at all in our material before 800.

Lombard northern and central Italy presents, before the ninth century, a fairly consistent picture. It had bipartite estates, intermingled with estates with only tenant plots. On the former, demesnes were not necessarily large, and certainly not always—even often—territorially coherent; it can be added that, in parts of northern Italy and the Sabina, demesne land could often have a silvo-pastoral focus. But the bulk of the evidence we have supports the view that these demesnes were cultivated by tenant labour. Such labour could vary greatly, from very heavy (three days a week) to simply recognitive (a few days a year), although many tenants (most, in some areas) owed none at all. These were markers of status differences among tenants—between *angariales* and *redditales*, as one of the ninth-century Lucchese inventories put it. It is significant that, in our Lucchese leases (i.e. among free tenants), those who did not owe labour service generally paid money rents instead, another sign of status difference.[85] These patterns were already well established before the Frankish conquest; manors are in fact better documented in Italy than in Francia itself in the middle third of the century. I would argue that the most that early Carolingian influence might have brought was the encouragement of a greater rationalization of, and a greater explicitness in, the requirement of tenant labour.

This early documentation of manorial patterns, which appear at the start of our evidence in the 730s–740s in three separate sub-regions of Italy, reproposes the issue of origins. It seems to me unnecessarily restrictive to postulate that they were new in that period; labour in the Lucchesia was, indeed, a standard part of local *consuetudo* by then. Conversely, however, bipartite patterns and labour service in eighth-century Italy do not seem to be part of any intensification of the labour process, in the context of exchange opportunities, unlike in contemporary Francia, or indeed the later Roman empire. Indeed, the complicated patterns of service on distant and/or fragmented demesnes, evidenced in numerous Italian documents, do not make obvious economic sense at all; nor is there much evidence of exchange activity in eighth-century Italy, again unlike in Francia (below, Chapter 11).

---

[84] *Domuscultae* in formulae: *CDL*, I, n. 82, II, nn. 137, 188, 228, 231, 293 (quote); 155 and 257 for the exchanges.

[85] *Inventari*, XI.1 (ed. M. Luzzati), e.g. p. 219; cf. the figures in Andreolli, 'Contratti agrari', pp. 128–34. For money versus labour, see the lease tables in ibid., pp. 92–113. For rent-types as signs of status in northern Italy, see most recently Montanari, 'La corvée', pp. 49–52; Pasquali, 'La corvée', pp. 117–19, both carefully nuanced.

Corvées in the peninsula seem, rather, to be part of a set of patterns of rural subjection, markers of lower status, and of the local political dominance of landlords. So how did they come to exist in the first place? Here, it does seem to me relevant that northern Italy is also the only clearly evidenced location for late Roman labour service, the Paduan estate described in *P. Ital.* 3 in the mid-sixth century (above, pp. 278–9). That property existed in an economic context in which cultivation for profit was conceivable, which does not seem to have been the case in the economic world of two centuries later. There had been a break in the patterns of agricultural management, that is to say. But it does not seem unreasonable to postulate that the practice of demanding labour had survived here, across the economic divide, as a constituent element in the patterns of rural subjection, in a simpler and more unstructured form. We could, here, recognize a genealogical link between the two, as long as we also recognize the systemic break, as what had begun as an instrument of economic intensification turned into one of social dominance.

I have argued, throughout this chapter, against the metanarrative that sees bipartite estates, linked by labour service, as a sufficiently peculiar form of land management that all instances of it have to be related to each other—at its extreme, from second-century Africa right into the central middle ages in northern Europe. Instead, demesnes, as markers of the intensification of exploitation, have been invented more than once, and cover a variety of distinct developments. In Italy, the existence of demesnes in the eighth century, in a relatively unintensified economy, could be seen as the simplification of an older economic model, in the context of continuing rural power structures. In Francia, by contrast, it can be argued that demesnes had different origins. We have no evidence of late Roman labour service there, so we do not have to worry about postulating Roman survivals when we encounter corvées in the eighth century; they are anyway rare by Italian standards before the last decades of that century. In northern Francia, we can see the gradual extension of demesne structures (perhaps on the model of vineyard exploitation) as signs of renewed intensification for profit, in a way that is impossible to postulate for the rather more muted economy of Italy in the decades around 800. This difference in origin has that much greater a level of defensibility when one considers how rare the highly structured village-size estates of the Paris lands of St-Germain-des-Prés were in Italy. The contrast between St-Germain's Palaiseau and Peredeus' Rosignano is very considerable, and it seems entirely justified to be cautious about the assumption that the developments leading to each need be comparable.

As in Francia, studies of the *sistema curtense* in Italy have usually been dominated by polyptychs, particularly those of Bobbio and S. Giulia di Brescia. In Francia this is justifiable, because there are fewer alternative sources, and anyway the *Brevium exempla* and the polyptych of St-Germain stand close to the beginning of (a long) manorial history. In Italy, however, they stand near the end; indeed, S. Giulia's polyptych, dating to c.900, the text that best shows the degree of internal organization that Italian manors were capable of, may postdate the start of their decline.[86] I think it can be argued that Bobbio and S. Giulia, far from being typical, are best seen as a subsequent stage in manorial development, this time indeed on a Frankish model—not by chance, both were imperial monasteries—and for profit: the demand, here, coming from the expansion of exchange (however fitful it was: below, pp. 732–4) in the later ninth century in northern Italy. S. Giulia had its own merchants, after all, such as the often-cited Ianuarius, for whom it obtained an exemption from tolls from Louis II in 861.[87] This would align the most organized manors of late ninth-century northern Italy with those of Francia, while also stressing their atypicality with respect to most Italian bipartite estates. The profit-orientated demesne would not have a future in Italy, probably because most land was just too fragmented for such large-scale organization to be generalized. Italian exchange anyway soon became sufficiently capillary, at least at the level of the local city–countryside relationship, that in the early tenth century money-rents for cultivators could expand rapidly: peasants were here selling produce themselves.[88] But how these developments worked is beyond the remit of this book.

Some of the S. Giulia demesnes were not only cultivated by tenant labour, but by slaves, called *prebendarii*, who could make up substantial groups: the monastery had 740 of them (meaning around 200 adult males?)—scattered across some 60 *curtes*, it is true, and set against nearly 600 peasant tenures, but reaching concentrations of thirty or more on four estates.[89] These demesne slaves have a few parallels: in Italy on the early tenth-century estates of S. Tommaso di Reggio; in Bavaria on the Staffelsee estate of the bishop of Augsburg shortly after 800; maybe in northern Francia on the Corbie estates described by Adalhard of Corbie in 822, among others. Such

---

[86] *Inventari*, V (ed. G. F. Pasquali). There is some debate about when corvées actually did decline in northern Italy (as against Tuscany, where the date is c.875: above, n. 75). Fumagalli argued for a 'crisis' of demesne at Bobbio between 862 and 883: *Coloni e signori*, pp. 37–49; this has been doubted by Toubert (*Dalla terra*, pp. 207–9), and, implicitly, by Montanari, 'La corvée', pp. 39–41, and Pasquali, 'La corvée', whose evidence would date the decline of demesne labour to, perhaps, the 920s. The major recent analyses of the Italian polyptychs are contained in these works, together with Fumagalli, *Terra e società*, Andreolli and Montanari, *L'azienda curtense*, Pasquali, 'L'azienda curtense', and the early classic, Luzzatto, *Dai servi*, pp. 3–177, dating originally to 1909.

[87] *MGH, Ludovici II Dipl.*, n. 32. For the *sistema curtense* and agrarian exchange, see Violante, *La società milanese*, pp. 12–21, 62–3; Jones, 'La storia economica', pp. 1619–21, 1643–6; Toubert, *Dalla terra*, pp. 150–1, 198–9, 214–24; and, for the case of S. Giulia, Pasquali, 'I problemi dell'approvigionamento', who shows that not estates turned a surplus.

[88] Andreolli, 'L'evoluzione', pp. 42–4, for the Lucchesia.

[89] *Inventari*, V (ed. G. F. Pasquali); for the figures, Luzzatto, *Dai servi*, pp. 172–7; cf. Pasquali, 'I problemi dell'approvigionamento', and commentary in Toubert, *Dalla terra*, pp. 199–201. Luzzatto, *Dai servi*, pp. 92–3, and Montanari, *L'alimentazione*, pp. 168–9, 184–6, 217–18, show that *prebendarii* ate more grain than did tenants, which probably indicates some de facto privilege. See further Pasquali, 'La condizione', pp. 84–90.

slaves have been seen often enough as survivals of Roman slave plantations, mostly because of the mirror game discussed earlier (p. 262). This is hardly possible in the case of Staffelsee, of course, on the very edge of the former empire and in an area of poor continuity; but even in Italy, where such a genealogy might at least be conceivable, they do not appear early in the development of demesnes. Most important, in none of these instances do *prebendarii* constitute more than a minority of demesne labour; they are a core work-force, often a substantial one, but tenants are always integrated with them. They may to an extent have been privileged slave specialists, which would at least have made it easier to control them, in the absence of the complex coercive institutions of the slave mode of Columella's time, which are nowhere attested in the early middle ages. Such slave specialists existed in all periods; but the relatively large numbers of *prebendarii* seem to me to be a further step towards the intensification of labour in the period after 800, not any sort of survival from an earlier period. Significantly, even wage labour reappears in Adalhard of Corbie's statutes for his monastery, at least at the high points of the agricultural year.[90] Unlike labour service, however, this sort of slave-mode exploitation did not anywhere survive as a productive form: large slave groups, even privileged ones, were far too difficult to manage and expensive to maintain in early medieval conditions. Here, the limits of economic expansion in the period soon imposed themselves.

At the very end of our period, in the eighth century, a few of our regions show some signs of the revival of agrarian intensification. We have seen this in Francia—although not yet in Italy; in the eastern Mediterranean, too, there are a few indicators of the same process. In Syria and Palestine, the Umayyad caliphs were committed to developing at least sections of the desert borders, through the intensive irrigation projects associated with the palaces of the 720s–740s. This interest in irrigation, al-Balādhurī tells us, extended even to peasants, for the owner-cultivators of Bālis on the middle Euphrates were prepared in the 710s to become the tenants of the Umayyad prince Maslāma b. ʿAbd al-Malik in return for his building an irrigation canal to their former properties. Arab (and Berber) commitment to irrigation would indeed in the next centuries allow for substantial agrarian development in some of the barren uplands of south-eastern Spain; even if we cannot date

---

[90] *Inventari*, IX (ed. A. Castagnetti); *MGH, Cap.*, I, n. 128, c. 7 (but are these really slaves? they are not fed all year); Levillain, 'Les statuts', esp. pp. 369–70 (and p. 361 for wage labourers; wage labour in vineyards reappears in the Edict of Pîtres in 864, too: *MGH, Cap.*, II, n. 273, c. 31). For the privileged position of *prebendarii*, see n. 89. Note that nearly every estate in what is now Germany was full of *mancipia* in the eighth and ninth centuries, who were given along with estates, and were often named—see, for one example out of many, *Ub. Fulda*, nn. 22, 40, 51, 57–60, 64, 85, 87, etc. These must have simply been unfree dependants, doubtless with their own tenures; demesnes in these areas were never large, as the refs. cit. in n. 68 show. See Renard, 'Les *mancipia* carolingiens', for the vagueness of the term in the ninth century.

these with any precision, they were fully in place by the twelfth century, and probably began rather earlier, although it would be over-optimistic to locate such intensification as early as 800.[91] Even in Egypt, where no let-up in agricultural exploitation can be detected, the eighth century (perhaps) and the ninth century (certainly) show the development of sugar production for the first time, one of the first of a range of Asian crops that reached the Mediterranean only after the Arab conquest.[92] Essentially, however, these patterns of development are, up to 800, restricted to the two extremities of our research area, northern Francia and Egypt/the Levant. These were the regions with the most substantial concentrations of wealth—a rich aristocracy in the Carolingian world, a powerful state in that of the Umayyads and 'Abbāsids. They were, therefore, the regions with most potential for exchange, and thus with the most stimulus for agrarian intensification. How exchange worked in them will be looked at in more detail in Chapter 11; but that exchange is the major underpinning for the sort of developments in estate management discussed here. In the West, northern Francia was the first region to generate these patterns, by 800. Italy, Spain, even England would follow in the next centuries, allowing for western interregional exchange patterns to become more firmly rooted by 1100 than they could yet be in the Carolingian period, because there were more regions to exchange with. In the West, this specifically means that northern Francia was the first region where demesne agriculture became a focus for intensification since the exchange crises of the fifth and sixth centuries. Its crystallization can be put squarely into the half-century of Charlemagne's reign, as many historians have indeed argued, but it was the economic wealth of Charlemagne's elites and the needs of his armies, rather than any specific royal economic interventions, that fuelled this first step in agrarian intensification. Planned economic development, organized from above, would have to wait awhile; few European rulers have had it on their conscious agenda before Stalin.

[91] For the 'desert palaces', see Sauvaget, 'Châteaux umayyades'; Grabar, *City in the desert*; Kennedy, 'The impact of Muslim rule'. For Bālis, al-Balādhurī, *Futuḥ al-buldān*, trans. Hitti, pp. 232–3. For Spain, among many, Barceló, *Les aïgues cercades*, and the wide synthesis, with bibliography, in Glick, *From Muslim fortress*, pp. 64–91.

[92] *PERF* 642, 705; *APEL* IV 216, 234–5, VI 367; see Watson, *Agricultural innovation*, pp. 26–9, and *passim* for other crops: a problematic but important survey.

6

Political breakdown
and state-building in the North

1. From aristocratic to tribal societies

THIS CHAPTER FOCUSES on the lands north of the Roman empire and of
the Frankish world, or, at least, on selected regions among them: Ireland and
Denmark, which were never under Roman rule, and Britain, which lost most
of its specifically Roman characteristics in the fifth century. Britain is indeed
the most striking example anywhere of a province of the empire whose
Roman socio-economic structures and identity broke down, quickly and
almost totally, apparently for internal reasons; it will for that reason be the
focus of the first half of this chapter, with parallel instances (in particular
Berber North Africa) brought in for comparative purposes at the end. Of our
three regions, two, Britain and Denmark, were moving (or returning) to
increasingly elaborate and hierarchical political and socio-economic structures by the end of our period, which can be referred to as a process of state-
building. Why these two moved in this direction, and the third region,
Ireland, did not, and also why, inside Britain, the Anglo-Saxon kingdoms
did so more consistently than the Welsh ones, will be the subject-matter of
the second half of the chapter. This process of 'state'-building was, however,
at least as much one of the creation of a stable aristocracy, in particular of
power and wealth based on the exclusive control of land; hence the location
of this chapter among those on the aristocracy, rather than alongside
Chapter 3.

At the start of Chapter 3 I characterized the ideal type of 'the state'
according to five main criteria: (i) the centralization of legitimate enforceable authority (justice and the army); (ii) specialization of governmental
roles, with an official hierarchy which outlasted the people who held official
position at any one time; (iii) the concept of a public power; (iv) independent
and stable resources for rulers; and (v) a class-based system of surplus-
extraction and stratification. These criteria were not developed further
there, for all the polities discussed in that chapter fell easily into the framework of such an ideal type. In this chapter, however, one could argue that
only the Mercia of Offa and Cenwulf, at the very end of our period, could

adequately be characterized by most of this list of features, and, even there, element (v) would still be in dispute. The issue of how these elements were articulated internally thus poses itself. I would argue that the full development of the institutional and ideological elements in the ideal-type state as characterized here, elements (i) to (iii), depended on an economic underpinning to ruling-class power, elements (iv) and/or (v), for only stable resources made the stable exercise of power possible. It is worth distinguishing between the resources of rulers and those of the ruling class, because one can often, even though not always, draw a sharp distinction between the two (e.g. tax or tribute versus rent). In theory, one might argue that (v) could be subsumed into (iv), as with a state whose taxation dominated over all other surplus-extraction, and whose ruling class were simply public employees, with no autonomous sources of wealth available, as for example the Ottoman empire has often been claimed to be.[1] In practice, however, dominant classes have almost always been distinguishable from state institutions; they are independently wealthy, although they also characteristically seek wealth as well as power from official positions in public hierarchies. Indeed, in the land-based, weak, states of the post-Roman West, such as Francia and Lombard Italy after 600 or so (above, pp. 102–24), the relationship was reversed, with (iv) being subsumed into (v): the resources of kings became nearly identical to that of the ruling class as a whole, the aristocracy, as royal wealth came to be based almost entirely on landowning. This was the model that any ambitious northern king had to follow, in fact—as long, at least, as land was available to be owned, and its surplus was available to be extracted.

This was, however, not as universal as it sometimes seems to us. I draw in this book an analytical distinction between societies in which landlords dominate over peasants and live off the surpluses of dependent tenant cultivators, 'feudal-mode' societies (above, p. 261), and societies in which peasants are mostly independent producers, and the local rich and powerful are dominant only over a minority of the peasantry, or are partly direct producers themselves. The latter I shall call 'peasant-mode' societies, when analysing their economic structure, or 'ranked' societies when analysing their social patterns—the latter in order to represent the fact that there are clear status differences in such societies, but they are not necessarily stable or heavily marked, except for the distinction, always present, between free and unfree.[2] (Among the societies of the regions studied in this chapter, the articulation of the social divisions among the free was probably greatest in Ireland, although in the Irish case largely for ideological and ritual, not economic, reasons.) How the peasant mode worked economically will be looked at most fully in Chapter 9; here its social and political implications

---

[1] e.g. Inalcık, *Economic and social history*, I, pp. 103–17.
[2] A sensible survey of ranking can be found in Fried, *Evolution*, pp. 109–54, 182–4.

are our main concern. I shall argue that all the societies of the North were in large part, or entirely, peasant-mode societies in c.600, although by 800 most of them were moving in a feudal direction (particularly England; Ireland least of all). This shift, or at least its beginnings, was a key element in state-building, for, without an effective, coercive, predominance by land-owning aristocrats—including kings—over the peasantry, and the subjection of the latter to economic dependence, the resources of the political systems of our regions would remain very limited, and fully fledged state structures could not be funded. It is because of this that, as proposed at the start of the chapter, state-building was closely related to the development of a land-owning aristocracy.

One version of a ranked, peasant-mode, society that has been common in history, including in our period, is one in which a ruler, or local lord, is less the owner of land than the leader of a free people, who are often at least in theory his distant relatives, but who are above all tied to him by tight bonds of mutual obligation and loyalty, of common identity. The dependants of such a ruler are, in settled societies, mostly free peasants; they owe military obliga-tions, and/or (often intermittent) tribute, but on an economic level they are largely autonomous, and indeed rulers also have to give to them in return, for example by means of elaborate hospitality and feasting. The land both ruler and people live on may be the same, but, if so, rights to it are frequently overlapping, without the exclusivity of feudal-mode land tenure, in which one person is an owner and the others tenants. Indeed, the absence of exclusive ownership rights is a good sign of the presence of a society of this kind, although the reverse is not the case, as we shall see. I shall here call such societies 'tribal'. Historians are often cautious of this word, which can be seen as demeaning, or else as characteristic only of non-settled societies (even though the original 'tribes' came from an entirely settled environment, early republican Rome). Social theorists are, these days, equally cautious.[3] But I have not found a better one, and I hope that it is used here sufficiently neutrally and consistently for its more ideological baggage to be lost. Some of the small-scale polities of the North clearly had kinship-based ideological associations, for they were named after families, such as the Uí Chennselaig or the Cenél nEógain and dozens of other 'kingdoms' of Ireland, or the Hroth-ingas and many other small early political units in England; these have further parallels in Arab and Berber Africa and Spain, in the Banū Hilāl or the Aït Kaci. Such polities do not, nonetheless, seem structurally distin-guished from those which were simply the names of peoples, the Cruithni or the Gewissae or the Laguatan, or those which had taken the names of pre-existing geographical territories, such as Kent or Dyfed: I shall use the word

---

[3] Typical of this caution is Fried, *The notion of tribe*, a demolition of earlier, fuzzy, uses of the term by sociologists and anthropologists.

'tribal' for all of them, as a result. Tribal societies could easily turn into aristocratic, feudal, societies, as we shall see in the next section; the purpose of this one is to explore the superficially more difficult process by which aristocratic societies could turn into tribal ones.

The experience of Britain in our period was different from that of the Continent (above all from northern Gaul, its nearest neighbour, and ecologically very similar to lowland Britain) in three main ways. First, the fifth century saw a dramatic collapse in the sophistication of material culture on the island. Second, when we have written sources again, from roughly 600, we find a highly fragmented political structure, with dozens of small autonomous units in both 'England' and 'Wales' (i.e. the Anglo-Saxon- and Welsh-speaking parts of the island of Britain—the two words are anachronistic but convenient). These were ruled by men who are called *reges* in our Latin sources, so we call them 'kingdoms', but they had little or nothing in common with the Romano-Germanic kingdoms of the Continent, ten or even a hundred times the size of insular ones. Third, when we find out more about British land tenure, after 670 in England thanks to the beginning of the Anglo-Saxon charter tradition, up to a century earlier in south-eastern Wales, it has such a peculiar set of characteristics by Continental standards that it seems to many, including me, to represent a set of social relations without parallel in the Roman land law that had been inherited by the Romano-Germanic kingdoms. That these three differences are related is not in itself controversial, but exactly how, and what the implications are, is more contested. We must characterize each in more detail, before looking at their implications.

Late Roman lowland Britain was, as far as can be seen, a fairly ordinary part of the Roman empire: more provincial than most, for sure, but not structurally different. Highland Britain was more obviously a military zone, its cultural Romanization incomplete, as in what would become Wales, which had few cities or rural villas (they were restricted to the south coast) but a network of forts; Hadrian's Wall, in particular, was an area of highly structured defensive settlements, with a hinterland stretching southwards as far as York. But the Lowland Zone was made up of standard Roman settlement hierarchies: around twenty *civitates*, some smaller towns, several hundred villas, a few villages, and many small-scale hamlets and isolated farmsteads, very much as northern Gaul was. Indeed, when around 350 north Gaulish villas began to become fewer, British villas arguably stayed prosperous for another generation. Culturally, too, Britain was not unlike other parts of the empire, with Christianization developing across the century, and the epigraphy on tombstones paralleling that elsewhere; the only substantive difference was probably that Latin remained the language of a minority, with Brittonic widely spoken still, but this has plenty of Roman provincial parallels, such as Africa.[4] Lowland Britain was also, probably, rather less militarized than was most of northern Gaul, up to 400 at least. By 400, however, villas and towns alike were in recession. After that date economic crisis was precipitous. By 450 it is close to impossible to track any villa as surviving in a recognizably Roman form, even in a wooden version of the Roman tradition (for wood would be henceforth the over-whelmingly dominant building material in Britain for centuries).[5] Nor can urban economies be traced far into the fifth century; the latest known, Verulamium, cannot be traced securely past 450, although continued occu-pation of a non-urban type in *civitates* is likely in Wroxeter and York among others, and could be defended for Canterbury.[6] In the early fifth century industrial ceramic production, which had been elaborate into the late fourth, also ended, with even the potter's wheel vanishing for several centuries, and no other large-scale artisanal production can be traced either: all forms of market exchange beyond the simplest, that is to say, must have ceased.[7]

Britain may have been like northern Gaul in 350, then, at least on the surface; but by 450 it was completely different. The end of villas in each is in many respects similar, and it may be, as we shall see in Chapter 8 (pp. 473–81), that it represents a cultural shift rather than necessarily an economic or political crisis. In other respects, though, we can see greater contrasts. In Gaul, the Roman network of cities survived as political foci, and in some of them, such as Paris and Cologne, surviving urban economies can clearly be identified (below, pp. 677–81); Gaulish ceramic production, too, survived the fifth century rather well (below, pp. 795–8). There was, certainly, a recession in northern Gaul in that century, but it had stabilized by 500 or so, and would soon begin to be reversed; in Britain, by contrast, recession, or crisis, turned into catastrophe. By the third quarter of the fifth century our insular archaeological evidence consists of a set of disconnected fragments, resembling the opaque clues of a Richard Hannay novel: the packed-rubble foundations of a putative timber-frame building at Wroxeter; a handful of *Grubenhäuser* (sunken-floored huts) inside the Roman walls of Canterbury; a post-hole building and some ditches, which apparently re-spect the alignments of Roman villa buildings, at Orton Hall Farm near

---

[4] Esmonde-Cleary, *Ending*, pp. 41–130. Millett, *Romanization*, pp. 181–211, is another useful survey. For Wales, Arnold and Davies, *Roman and early medieval Wales*, pp. 28–32, 44–6, 65–87. For epigraphy, Handley, 'Christian commemoration'.

[5] Branigan, *Latimer*, pp. 89–99, 173–5, publishes a Buckinghamshire villa with final wooden phases going into the mid- or late fifth century, but his dating seems too late; wheel-thrown ceramics (cf. ibid., pp. 130–1) have not elsewhere been found as late as that. Rivenhall in Essex, a parallel example, has less secure dating still: Rodwell and Rodwell, *Rivenhall*, pp. 62–75; Millett, 'The question of continuity'.

[6] For an overview, see Loseby, 'Power and towns'; see further below, p. 686.

[7] For the end of Roman ceramics, see Tyers, *Roman pottery*, pp. 77–80; see further below, pp. 805–7. For the early Anglo-Saxon period, Arnold, *An archaeology*, pp. 67–100, 126–48, in its revised form, is easily the best overview at present.

Peterborough; some box-framed buildings with almost no finds on top of a Roman cemetery at Poundbury in Dorset, dated only by radiocarbon.[8]

This dramatic material collapse might seem too total to be credible, but it derives from what is by now a very wide evidence-base by the standards of our regions, and its existence is hard to dispute (although its significance is certainly contested). Simon Esmonde-Cleary describes it best, in a book over a decade old but scarcely outdated in any of its main elements.[9] That is to say, more examples of a sort of grudging continuity turn up, but they are all of the same type: Roman sites with later occupation so simple that writers often tend to describe the period as if it was the early pre-Roman Iron Age. One important result follows from this material collapse: Anglo-Saxon settlements, when they appear after the mid-fifth century, show almost no indigenous British cultural influence. There has been a sharp argument over whether Anglo-Saxon house types were influenced by Romano-British ones, which is at present won by those who argue that they were not: there are Continental parallels for nearly every one of their features, and anyway excavations of early medieval non-Anglo-Saxon sites in Britain generally show house structures that are so evanescent that it is hard even to hypothesize what they looked like.[10] Similarly, early Anglo-Saxon ceramics were hand-made, showing very simple market structures and a marked lack of specialization; their styles and techniques closely resemble those of northern Germany, and have no relation to Roman patterns anywhere (see below, Chapter 11); non-Anglo-Saxon areas of Britain were anyway by now almost aceramic, except for small quantities of imports in some political centres in the far west (below, p. 327).

Taken on its own, a material break of this kind might well encourage people to look for a substantial population break; if this was Germany, an important section of scholarship would probably still be advocating it, given the way the argument has run for the Rhineland (below, p. 509). As the strongly Germanist element in the English scholarship of a century ago has waned, English cultural tendencies to argue for continuities rather than discontinuities have become dominant here too, so the population-break model has not had many supporters recently (it was never strong among the Welsh, who take their Roman as well as their Celtic ancestry for granted).[11] On a more scientific level, however, the strength of landscape analysis in Britain has helped to bury the discontinuity argument, for field systems have

---

[8] Barker *et al.*, *Baths basilica*, pp. 138–68, generalized to Wroxeter as a whole (and beyond) in White, 'Wroxeter'; Blockley, *Marlowe Car Park*, pp. 279–350; Mackreth, *Orton Hall Farm*, pp. 27–42, 87–91, 237–9; Green, *Poundbury*, I, pp. 71–92, 151–3.

[9] Esmonde-Cleary, *Ending*. The difficulty of dispute is shown by the extravagant hypotheses necessary for Dark's alternative reading, *Civitas to kingdom*, pp. 50–70.

[10] See most recently Hamerow, 'Migration theory', pp. 169–73; eadem, 'Anglo-Saxon timber buildings'; for contrary views, e.g. Dixon, 'Saxon house'; James *et al.*, 'An early medieval building tradition'.

[11] For the English–German contrast, see e.g. Härke, 'Archaeologists and migrations'.

often been shown to pre-date even the Romans, never mind the Anglo-Saxons, thus providing prima facie grounds for continuous cultivation of at least the better soils.[12] The evidence for broad agricultural continuities in recent pollen analyses (with the exception of the Hadrian's Wall area) backs this up further.[13] There must have been a population decline, as we shall see in a moment, but Anglo-Saxon tribal communities evidently came into a landscape that was still occupied. On the other hand, such demographic continuities make material cultural discontinuities even more evident. Something dramatic happened to the basic fabric of all socio-economic activity in Britain, above all in the early fifth century, in the generation after the withdrawal of Roman imperial power from the province in c.410. Nor was this involution reversed, except on a small scale, until the eighth century and later.

It seems inescapable to link this collapse with the withdrawal of the Roman state. One point, for sure, is that arguments for Roman governmental continuity into a later period in the fifth century, made on scholarly grounds by Horst Wolfgang Böhme and on more fantastic grounds by others, are made very difficult by the generalized nature of this collapse, including in political centres (Böhme argues strongly for military continuities, but coins ceased to be imported after c.410 as well). Conversely, too, the fact that Britain rarely gets mentioned in any of our numerous fifth-century Gallic sources is a reasonably sure sign that their writers no longer considered Britain to be part of their world.[14] Nor, it should be added, can we give much credence to Gildas's account from the Britain of a century later, which is governed by a series of patterned cycles, for polemic effect. Here, the most important thing to take from that account is that Gildas had no idea how Roman rule worked: its structures of government had become by now irrecoverable.[15] Esmonde-Cleary argues that the economy of Britain had been tied too closely to the Roman fiscal system, that the withdrawal of Rome led to the abrupt end of taxation, and that a systemic crisis of the elite ensued, bringing everything down with it, before the Anglo-Saxons arrived.[16]

[12] See for eastern England e.g. Bassett, 'Beyond the edge of excavation', pp. 34–8; Rodwell, 'Relict landscapes in Essex'; Williamson, 'Early co-axial field systems'.

[13] Dark, 'Palaeoecological evidence'; eadem, *Environment*, pp. 140–56.

[14] Böhme, 'Das Ende der Römerherrschaft', pp. 522–3, 538–42, 558–9. For other theories, Dark, *Civitas to kingdom*; earlier, Morris, *Age of Arthur*, pp. 44–141 (on the sources for which see Dumville, 'Sub-Roman Britain'); there are several others. Snyder, *An age of tyrants*, esp. pp. 217–50, much more continuitist than I would be, is a good recent overview. For what can be got out of Gallic sources, Wood, 'The end of Roman Britain'.

[15] Gildas, *De excidio*, esp. I.10–27: his cyclical pattern has the Romans, and then committed British minorities, repeatedly saving the Britons from themselves, with the saved British thereafter causing disaster again through their wickedness, in ways intended to prefigure his critique of the present (cf. e.g. I.21 with I.26–7). I would also agree with Sims-Williams's critical assessment of the paucity of Gildas's sources: 'Gildas and the Anglo-Saxons'; see further James, *Britain*, pp. 94–9.

[16] Esmonde-Cleary, *Ending*, pp. 138–61.

This is the most effective argument that I have seen, but it needs to be taken further, for it does not in itself explain the contrast with Gaul. The Roman state must have lost a good deal of its coherence in fifth-century northern Gaul too (above, pp. 111–13), but, as just noted, its economy did not collapse. It is true that at least some aspects of a political-military infrastructure must have persisted there, which Clovis could use as a basis for territorial control, already wide before his southern conquests; Remigius of Reims could regard him simply as the new ruler of the Roman province of Belgica Secunda.[17] But it is also the case that one thing that clearly survived in at least parts of northern Gaul was a landowning aristocracy, capable of operating on a substantial scale: Remigius is a type-example here, too, thanks to the lands listed in his will (above, pp. 180–1). We cannot see any parallels to this aristocracy in post-Roman Britain. In my view, in fact, the traditional form of aristocratic landed power was one of the major casualties of the withdrawal of the state in Britain, and it is this, aristocratic, crisis which meant that the breakdown of the fiscal system, which would anyway have brought economic recession as in Gaul, led to economic meltdown in Britain.[18] It also would explain why Britain could not maintain the *local* structures of the Roman state, in at least a vestigial, land-based, form, as other post-Roman polities managed to do throughout the West. Such an argument relocates the problem of the Gaulish parallel to the contrasting fates of the aristocracy of each region. I shall return to the issue, after having looked at two more questions, the nature of the Anglo-Saxon settlement and of early Anglo-Saxon political structures, and the nature of post-Roman land tenure in eastern Britain, for both of these have to be understood before we can look clearly at what happened to the British aristocracy of c.400. These arguments here will be based initially on the evidence from the 'English' parts of Britain; Wales will be discussed separately, so that it can be used as a control (pp. 326–30).

Around 500 the archaeology of eastern Britain is more variegated, for now we have Anglo-Saxon sites as well, but it remains materially very simple. In 'English' areas, the earliest early medieval settlements we have tend to consist of relatively simple post-hole buildings associated with *Grubenhäuser*, probably making up the same sorts of modular building units that one finds in sixth-century northern Gaul (see pp. 502–7), although as yet without fenced compounds. They tend to have few finds; only in East Anglia and Essex are finds slightly commoner. It is not that their inhabitants had no artisanal products at all, for they put metalwork and

---

[17] *Epp. Austrasicae*, n. 2.
[18] Millett, *Romanisation*, pp. 227–30, and Jones, *End*, pp. 244–57, are the most recent writers to argue for an alternative view, an aristocratic revolt as the cause of the end of Roman rule in the region. This is not impossible, although the evidence is circumstantial; but it does not seem to me the point. Such a revolt does not explain, at all, the fifth-century material collapse, which is surely more significant than British recognition (or not) of Honorius.

decorated pots in their graves, but they were careful not to lose them in life—although such products do not show great specialization for the most part, they were valuable. These sites were very often on or close to Roman sites, as with Spong Hill in Norfolk, West Stow in Suffolk, Mucking in Essex, Bishopstone in Sussex, Barrow Hills and Barton Court Farm, close to each other in Oxfordshire. In each case, the excavators argued for a settlement discontinuity (unlike for the already-cited Orton Hall Farm, otherwise a parallel example, where the excavator proposed a—rather circumstantial—continuity), but the consistent pattern of associations is important. Overall, these settlements were located in a Roman landscape, which is in fact particularly visible in eastern England (where later open fields have not wiped out Roman field systems), and it is thus significant that they are so often linked spatially to the centres of that landscape.[19]

I have called these sites 'Anglo-Saxon', simply because all their material parallels are Continental; but we cannot simply assume that they were inhabited by people with any version of an Anglo-Saxon ethnic identity, and/or who spoke Germanic languages. The material weakness of the post-Roman British was so great that, once Anglo-Saxon immigrants brought a new material cultural tradition in, one that was technologically simple to imitate, then it could have spread widely among non-Anglo-Saxons too. This argument has been often used in recent years to justify a further step: that there were very few Anglo-Saxons indeed, perhaps only a narrow elite of aristocratic conquerors.[20] This attempt to extend continuity theories even to the Anglo-Saxon invasions is unconvincing, on two grounds. First, the fact that early Anglo-Saxon settlements are so materially simple: either they were ethnically marked, in which case that 'aristocracy' was absurdly poor, or they were not, in which case a tiny minority had managed to impose a totally new material culture on the indigenous majority inside a generation at most. Second, the fact that lowland England ended up speaking a Germanic, not a Celtic (still less a Romance), language is so out of keeping with the situation on the Continent, except very close to the Roman frontier, that it is hard indeed to imagine that only a conquering elite brought the language. This second point is further sharpened by the absence of Brittonic/Welsh influence on the Anglo-Saxon language (or languages—John Hines has convincingly argued that the relatively homogeneous language of early sources is a sixth-century development). This absence is perplexing, and

---

[19] Respectively Ricketts, *Spong Hill, part VII*, pp. 41–58, 126–30, 152–8; West, *West Stow*, I, pp. 167–8; Hamerow, *Mucking*, II, pp. 93–8; Bell, 'Bishopstone', pp. 238–41; Dodd and McAdam, 'L'habitat rural', pp. 228–9; Miles, *Barton Court Farm*, p. 52. Rivenhall (see above, n. 5) must be added to this list, for early Anglo-Saxon occupation of a villa site, whether or not with a break, is here certain. For a wider spatial context, Williamson, *Norfolk*, pp. 57–62; Baker, *Chilterns and Essex*, pp. 86–122.

[20] e.g. Higham, *Rome, Britain and the Anglo-Saxons*, pp. 165–208; Hodges, *Anglo-Saxon achievement*, pp. 22–42.

extremely atypical in situations of cultural contact. It may be, as has often been argued, that it was partly a result of the weakness of Latin in Britain, a language with higher cultural status. But it must at least show that there was a popular stratum to the Anglo-Saxon immigration, a peasant element to the incoming culture, which could preserve the new language sufficiently completely that the slowly acculturating indigenous British found they had to learn Anglo-Saxon, rather than vice versa.[21] The existence of this peasant element further contributed to the flat social hierarchies visible in the sixth century, as we shall see.

All the same, this non-aristocratic immigration does not mean that the Anglo-Saxons were ever more than a minority, in any part of England. Recent calculations of the population of fourth-century Britain focus on the 3–4 million range (Martin Millett, in a well-argued contribution, proposes 3.7 million), most of which must have been in the Lowland Zone, where the Anglo-Saxons settled. From here, the numbers game moves further into guesswork, but if the population fell by as much as half in the fifth century (a figure which has been proposed for northern Gaul, and which might fit the sort of settlement retreat which has been proposed for eastern England, out of poorer open soils, which were often left to pasture, and into river valleys), then we might be seeing a million or more indigenous inhabitants in the lands under Anglo-Saxon control by 500.[22] On the other hand, the notable settlement continuities now recognized for Denmark, and the weakness of settlement in early fifth-century Frisia, only leaves the northern German coast as a plausible source for a large-scale migration to England. (Angeln may have been substantially depopulated by such a migration, but it is a pretty small area.)[23] I see no reason at all to imagine that there were more Anglo-Saxons migrating than there were in the average Germanic migration, which tends to be put around the 100,000 mark, and there may very well have been fewer. Overall, one would end up with the rough calculation that the Anglo-Saxons were outnumbered at least 10 : 1 by the indigenous British—the difference would be rather lower in East Anglia, but rather higher in

---

[21] As critics of the books cited in the previous note have also argued: Hines, 'The Anglo-Saxons reviewed', pp. 317–18; Brooks, review of Hodges. See Ward-Perkins, 'Why did the Anglo-Saxons', for a useful problematization. (All the same, an Anglo-Saxon peasant settlement does have to be argued, not taken for granted, as others do: Welch, *Anglo-Saxon England*, pp. 11–12; Gelling, 'Why aren't we speaking Welsh?', p. 51.) For a sixth-century homogenization of 'Old English', see Hines, 'Philology, archaeology', pp. 29–33; this would of course not explain the lack of Brittonic loan-words, for by the sixth century it would not have been clear which these were.

[22] See for the figures Jones, *End*, pp. 13–17 for a useful conspectus, with Millett, *Romanisation*, pp. 181–6. For settlement retreat, Williamson, *Norfolk*, pp. 57–8, is the best characterization; for other bibliography, Williamson, 'Settlement chronology'; Newman, 'The Sandlings'; see below, pp. 507–10, for northern Gaul.

[23] See as quick surveys Hvass, 'Jernalderens bebyggelse', for Denmark; Gerrets, 'Evidence of political centralisation', for Frisia. For Angeln, the focus of major scholarship for two generations, see most recently Gebühr, 'Angulus desertus?' with previous bibliography.

Oxfordshire, at the limit of the early settlement. These are bald guesses, but they work as ballpark figures, to give a measure of the problem. The Anglo-Saxon immigration included a peasant element, as we have seen; but this peasantry was surrounded by an indigenous majority—initially almost invisible, but whose existence as a sort of 'dark matter', to use an astronomical image, must be posited. The major changes in the material culture of sixth-century eastern England can therefore simply be seen in terms of the acculturation of that majority into 'Anglo-Saxon' material norms: the steady increase in identifiable settlements, and, particularly, in Anglo-Saxon-style cemetery ritual.[24] If there was any accommodation of the practices of the majority into that of the minority, it was in the use of the landscape itself, which, as we have seen, remained Roman in structure, even if settlement density thinned somewhat. In most other respects, as far as we can see, early acculturation was one-way. By 600 or so, when our first literary evidence begins, it would already have been close to complete, and one has to go a long way north or west to find any British or Welsh named in our sources at all.[25]

Early Anglo-Saxon settlement patterns will be discussed in Chapter 8 (pp. 502–4). It is sufficient here to say that there is no archaeological evidence of any form of hierarchy in the settlements of the fifth and sixth centuries, either in spatial structure or in small finds; there is more in cemetery sites, but even there rich burials are relatively rare, outside Kent at any rate.[26] When we get written evidence for the kingdoms of England, in the seventh century (with reasonably coherent narratives going back to around 550), we find more hierarchy than before, but also a substantial degree of political fragmentation. The larger kingdoms of around 600, East Anglia, Wessex, Deira, maybe already Mercia and the Hwicce, had a size of around two modern counties each or a little more, and they were surrounded by many polities that were a single county in size, Kent or Sussex or Essex, or indeed much smaller, as in the lists of tiny East Midland tribes in the *Tribal Hidage*, a text of probably seventh-century date. Steven Bassett in particular has argued convincingly, following the implications of work by Wendy Davies and Hayo Vierck, that these tiny tribes were typical of the original scale of most Anglo-Saxon polities, and derived either from the local development of stable hierarchies out of even simpler tribal structures, usually kinship-based, or from the takeover of small indigenous British territories by

---

[24] See e.g. for the British tradition, Esmonde-Cleary, *Ending*, pp. 173–87, 201–5; Crawford, 'Wasperton', pp. 25–6; Wise, 'Wasperton'; Rahtz, 'Late Roman cemeteries', pp. 56–9; Chambers, 'Queenford Farm'. For acculturation, see e.g. Dickinson, 'The present state', p. 23; Scull, 'Approaches', pp. 77–9; Hamerow, 'The earliest Anglo-Saxon kingdoms'; Baker, *Chilterns and Essex*, pp. 167–72.

[25] See e.g. Bede, *HE*, II.2; Ine 23.3, 24.2, etc.

[26] For cemeteries and status, see as useful surveys Arnold, *An archaeology*, pp. 103–25; idem, 'Wealth and social structure'; Huggett, 'Imported grave-goods'. For furnished burials and competition over ranking see below, n. 88.

external invaders who already had a tribal composition.[27] County-size king-doms like Essex would be the next step along, or perhaps two steps, in political amalgamation; two-county kingdoms the one after. One thing of course follows from this: that the indigenous British polities which lost ground to Anglo-Saxon-led ones were no larger or more developed than these small tribal groups, or they would never have lost to them militarily: it is once again clear that the dramatic change in scale with respect to the late Roman world of c.400 was accomplished before the Anglo-Saxons arrived, rather than as a result of their invasion. Even the one-county and two-county kingdoms remained relatively simple political structures. There are clearly characterized social hierarchies in our early sources—seventh-century saints' lives and law-codes, and Bede half-a-century later—with kings and aristo-crats separated out from free peasants; but government and dispute-settle-ment seem very ad hoc, and there are few references to permanent political roles.[28] These kingdoms did not at all, that is to say, fit into the ideal type of the state, as discussed at the start of this chapter. We shall return to what this means in the next section (p. 342), for the county-size kingdoms are already signs of political recomposition, not of dissolution; all the same, they show that, even after a period of recomposition, we are still dealing with very small-scale and simple parameters of political power.

The final major difference between Britain and the Continent lies in land tenure. This deserves some exposition, more than Roman and post-Roman tenure as a concept was discussed in Chapter 4, for it is crucial to our understanding of what happened to aristocracies in Britain. It is also a complex and contested issue: among the twenty-odd writers who have discussed some detail of Anglo-Saxon land tenure (not to speak of Welsh tenure, which will be dealt with separately), one can detect a dozen or more separate positions. Most of our early charters are from three areas, Kent (with a few south-eastern outliers), central Wessex, and the diocese of Worcester (under Hwiccean, and then Mercian, rule), to which we must add some circumstantial Northumbrian evidence in Bede. All the evidence is for the period after 670, in an age when kingdoms were expanding quickly—by the 720s most of England was dominated by four kingdoms only, East Anglia, Northumbria, Mercia, and Wessex. They thus come firmly from the period of political recomposition in England. But they are also the only guide we have to how tenure had worked in the preceding period; once we have established how it worked in 700, we can use our knowledge to move back,

---

[27] Bassett, 'In search of the origins'; Davies and Vierck, 'The contexts of Tribal Hidage'. For the kingdoms, the best introductions are Bassett, *Origins*; Yorke, *Kings and kingdoms*; Scull, 'Archaeology, early Anglo-Saxon society'; Hamerow, 'The earliest Anglo-Saxon kingdoms'. Woolf, 'Community, identity', offers an alternative view of greater (though incomplete) English unity—sophisticated, but not empirically grounded where it gets controversial.

[28] Loyn, *Governance*, pp. 41–50, is a decent quick survey.

retrospectively, into the sixth and fifth centuries, to meet up with the archaeology.

Charters came in with the conversion of England, and not, it seems, at once; the fact that the basic sequences of authentic charters all begin in the 670s points to the period of Theodore of Tarsus (archbishop of Canterbury 668–90) as the one in which the charter form was imported.[29] They are not complicated documents in this period; they essentially consist of rulers giving properties to churches as permanent gifts. At a later stage, such gifts come with exemptions from secular obligations; exactly when is not wholly clear, for early examples of it tend to be forged or interpolated, but by early in the eighth century such cessions are common. By the mid-eighth century there has come to be a clear distinction between obligations that are exempted in the text and those that are not; in a charter of 767 for Stoke Prior in Worcestershire from a Hwiccean sub-king, the text grants freedom from *omni tributo parvo vel maiore publicalium rerum et a cunctis operibus vel regis vel principis*, 'all tribute of public goods, small or great, and all work due to the king or the prince', though not from *instructionibus pontium, necessariis defensionibus*, and *arcium contra hostes*. The latter exclusions soon tended to be threefold, bridge- and fortification-building, and, above all, army service; Nicholas Brooks has convincingly argued that they are increasingly often listed from the mid-eighth century only because charters became more precise, not because the exclusions were new—at least in the case of army service, the oldest of the three.[30] The Stoke Prior text is actually to a lay aristocrat, but it is explicitly stated to be held *iure ecclesiastico possedendam*, 'to be possessed by ecclesiastical right'. Charters created a special form of ecclesiastical possession, which only rulers could grant; it was sufficiently privileged that in the eighth century the laity wanted it as well, in ever increasing numbers. This form of landholding is in the ninth century sometimes called *bocland*, 'bookland' or 'charter-land', in vernacular texts. It is very occasionally counterposed to *folcland*, 'folkland' or 'people-land', which was not held with the same rights; even without that explicit counterposition, however, it is already clear that this was privileged land, atypical at the outset (though perhaps not by, say, 1000, when nearly

---

[29] For the debate about the date of introduction of charters see Wormald, *Bede and the conversion*, pp. 13–17, which cautiously defends the traditional Theodoran dating. Idem, *The making*, II, ch. 11 (5), gives renewed reasons for a possible earlier date, so the debate may not be closed yet. I am grateful to the late Patrick Wormald for letting me see this text in advance of publication. Charters are cited here for convenience from *Cartularium saxonicum* [*BCS*], except for the vernacular texts ed. in *Anglo-Saxon charters*; later editions are all listed in the hand-lists in Sawyer, *Anglo-Saxon Charters* [S], whose numeration I shall also include.

[30] *BCS* 202 (S 58); see Brooks, 'Development'. Justice was also reserved to kings; even in the late Saxon period, there was little private justice in England, and the judicial aspects of Continental-style immunities were also absent: see Wormald, 'Lordship and justice', and cf. below, n. 48.

all non-royal land could have had charters), which was different from unchartered land.

This situation immediately makes England different from any documented region of the Continent; it also creates a problem. Since unchartered land is by definition undocumented, it is far from straightforward to tell what these privileges really consisted of, and therefore what constituted 'normal' non-church landholding at the end of the seventh century—and, by extension, earlier. It is equally hard to tell, furthermore, what rights over land and people were actually possessed, even by those who did have charters. The texts seem clear enough on the surface: they convey full property rights over estates. But there are enough inconsistencies in our evidence to allow us to doubt whether this is really what they mean: it may simply be that the imported formulae of the charter form, which derived from the Roman land-law worlds of Italy and Francia, convey a false impression of what rights really were in an Anglo-Saxon environment. Hence the considerable divergencies between historians, already referred to. We need to start, briefly, with what made bookland special, before we can move onto what land rights actually were in the period, whether in charters or outside them.

Put at its simplest, bookland and *ius ecclesiasticum* seem to have conveyed a particularly solid form of possessory right, of a sort that churchmen from Italy and Francia would feel comfortable with. Churches wanted as full a control as possible of whatever the land brought, permanently and without the possibility of legal reversion; the imported charter was solemn enough to convey this. Alienation rights were also an intrinsic part of the transfer of property in Italy and Francia, as in Roman law, and very soon (the first text is as early as 688) this began to be explicit in England too. Churches would have found alienation rights less useful, for they seldom let land go, and church councils soon prevented them from doing so anyway. Laymen, however, when they began to be granted charters, found this right particularly valuable.[31] Initially, such alienation rights above all allowed laymen to give land to the church; early lay charters are generally associated with such gifts in explicit ways, and some of them may well have concerned land that the laity held already, re-ceded by a king with extra rights attached.[32] By the end of the eighth century charters to the laity had snowballed, and such rights were held to be valuable in themselves. They were becoming a standard element in land tenure, whether for churches or for laymen. Æthelric son

[31] This largely follows Wormald, *Bede and the conversion*, pp. 19–23, who cites the previous bibliography, and Reynolds, *Fiefs and vassals*, pp. 324–30. Wormald further argues that alienation rights in bookland derived from its status as acquired land, which seems to me an unnecessary refinement. The 688 text, from Wessex, is *BCS* 72 (S 235); it is discussed in Wormald, *The Making*, II, ch. 11 (5). For church councils, see Brooks, *Early history*, p. 159.

[32] Unfortunately, the only early example of a royal charter to laity who already possessed the land, *BCS* 248 (S 125, a. 786), is a reworking from c.1000 of the authentic *BCS* 247 (S 123, a. 785), as Nicholas Brooks points out to me.

of Æthelmund in 804 went to two Mercian church councils, which looked at his *scripturae* and confirmed that he could give his land and *libellae* (charters) where he liked. He then gave some of them to his family burial church, Deerhurst in Gloucestershire, and others to two kinswomen for life, with reversion to the bishopric of Worcester, in return for episcopal protection against the Berclingas, the monastic community (and ruling family?) of Berkeley. The latter were determined opponents, as a text of 824 further shows, which partially explains why Æthelric took the trouble to get ratification twice for perfectly legal acts, but we could also perhaps conclude that his alienation rights were not so secure that they would have been safe from contestation without that ratification. From now on they would be; but the array of rights attached to land tenure on the Continent had taken over a century to become standard in England.[33]

This is a minimalist reading of the special rights conveyed by bookland, but I do not think that more is required. The discussion of these rights, although extensive, has often been vitiated by too legalistic a reading of the implications of our sources. Bede's letter to Bishop Ecgbert of York, dating to 734, is the most important text we have for the consequences of land grants, and has often been both used and misused. Bede complained that laymen paid Northumbrian kings to grant them *territoria* on which to build false monasteries, which they held in *ius haereditarium*, hereditary right, by royal *edicta* (presumably charters), free from both divine and human *servitium*. This was not only wrong in itself, but meant that there was not enough land to give to the sons of *nobiles* or *emeriti milites*, who therefore either remained unmarried or left the country. Bede's characterizations, it is generally agreed, can be associated with the growing practice of granting bookland to the laity (although the monasteries they endowed were not necessarily as false as Bede thought).[34] Beyond this, however, the implications of the text are unclear. It does not, for example, demonstrate that charters were essential to establish hereditary rights in land, as Eric John argued.[35] For a start, Bede in other writings clearly envisaged hereditary succession in land to be normal; what he was decrying in his letter was particularly the hereditary control of monasteries by the laity. Surviving charters themselves from the 740s sometimes use the phrase

---

[33] BCS 313, cf. 379 (S 1187, 1433). For commentary, extensive in part because of the survival of the Deerhurst church up to the present, see Wormald, 'Charters, law', pp. 152–7; Bassett, *Deerhurst*; Sims-Williams, *Religion and literature*, pp. 174–6. Æthelric and his father, it should be noted, were major aristocrats, and not pushovers.

[34] Bede, *Epistola*, esp. cc. 10–13. Sims-Williams, *Religion and literature*, pp. 126–9, is a crisp critique of Bede's views on false monasteries.

[35] John, *Land tenure*, esp. pp. 39–63, a position he maintains 35 years later in *Reassessing Anglo-Saxon England*, pp. 11–14; Abels, *Lordship*, pp. 28–33, follows him. John, *Land tenure*, pp. 53–6, also finds support in poetry, especially *Widsith*, ll. 93–6, for kings granting family lands to heirs, but all such citations can be regarded as the rhetorical talking-up of royal munificence.

ius hereditarium, which may mean that Bede was quoting their terms (though the reverse is also possible); even then, this phrase seems only to be a gloss on the strong, solid, tenure that bookland was intended to convey, just as the various formulations for the irrevocability of grants did, and indeed as the phrase *ius ecclesiasticum* and its variants did.[36] It must be added that John's argument also implied that early Anglo-Saxon kings had total legal control over land tenure, such that it was theoretically possible for it to be revoked at the holder's death for the whole lay population; this would have given the small-scale English kings of 700, with no developed governmental infrastructure, more legal power than the Merovingian kings, or for that matter Roman emperors. But arguments of this kind are also based on presuppositions about the legal force of charter terminology that are inappropriate for our period (particularly in England, given the simplicity of early Anglo-Saxon political structures). After all, notwithstanding the supposed irrevocability of charters, kings clearly had the power to confiscate bookland from disloyal laymen, and even clerics. All that the solemn form of the document could achieve was, perhaps, a greater caution on the part of kings, a use of legal recourses to justify their actions rather than arbitrary power.[37]

Charters were in material terms the concessions of economic rights over land, rights that had previously gone to kings or (more seldom) to aristocrats. Let us look more closely at what these rights could have consisted of. Unfortunately, charters themselves are strikingly vague; the *omne tributum* ceded in the Stoke Prior charter is never spelled out in any single text. We have to approach the problem of what it meant through more indirect methods. A starting-point is the scale of gifts. In 672/4 Frithuwold *subregulus* of Surrey endowed the monastery of Chertsey with 205 *manentes* of land (this and several other Latin terms seem to translate Old English *hida*, 'hides' in the standard modernization), making 300 hides when it was added to land the monastery presumably already had; these 300 hides, following the reconstruction of John Blair, enclosed some 100 km² of land. When the West Saxon king Caedwalla took the Isle of Wight, a territory of 1,200 hides (*familiae*), in c.686, he gave 300 of them to Bishop Wilfrid according to Bede (the charter itself does not survive), which, given the size of the island, would amount to just under 100 km² of land again.[38]

---

[36] Bede, *HE*, V.12, *Historia abbatum*, c. 11; see also Felix, *Vita Guthlaci*, c. 26. For sensible comment, Wormald, *Bede and the conversion*, pp. 21–2; Charles-Edwards, 'The distinction', esp. 99–101.

[37] For the confiscation of bookland from a cleric, see Stephanus, *Vita Wilfridi*, c. 47; a lay example is BCS 595 (S 362), a. 901, which however shows that two kings, Alfred and Edward the Elder, before confiscating bookland for disloyalty, were careful to go through at least two judicial assemblies. Loss of charters, even by theft, could mean the loss of title to the land in some cases, as BCS 291 (S 1258) shows, although not always, as in BCS 186 (S 1256); both are from the later eighth century.

[38] See, respectively, BCS 34 (S 1165; cf. Blair, 'Frithuwold's kingdom'); Bede, *HE*, IV.14. Another 300 hide territory was *Iogneshomme*, perhaps Eynsham in Oxfordshire, confiscated from the archbishop of Canterbury in c.821 by Cenwulf of Mercia, but in this case, as also with

The Anglo-Saxon obsession with the quantification of land, unparalleled in Continental sources, helps us to see exactly how large such units could sometimes be. Not that the hide was ever a standard size (and it probably included more than one 'family'), but that other insular particularity, an interest in tracking the detailed bounds of land in charters, allows us to accept that the value of the hide indicated by these texts was fairly typical, with 5 hides representing up to roughly 2 km². Three hundred hides was at the upper limit of the land-units ceded in charters, to be sure, but 100 hides is found in several eighth-century charters, 10 or 20 is normal, and less than 5 is rare. Five hides was still a substantial land-area, as we have just seen; it 'made a *thegn*', a small aristocrat, in the words of a law tract of 1008–14.[39] The blocks given in all these gifts were characteristically whole village territories, or groups of villages, in fact (see below, pp. 516–17, for the word 'village'). Charter boundaries allow us to create jigsaw puzzles of adjoining blocks to make large areas of continuous tenure in the areas of our densest charters, such as Worcestershire, where the cathedral eventually controlled a quarter of the county, by the tenth century.[40]

If these large units were 'estates', in the Roman or modern understanding of the word, absolutely held properties, cultivated by rent-paying tenants— as indeed the texts of charters imply—then they would have been very big ones, their owners would have been very rich (indeed, on the Frankish level of aristocratic/ecclesiastical wealth), and their inhabitants would have been highly subjected, across wide and homogeneous areas, already by the late seventh century. Some historians, such as H. M. Chadwick, Trevor Aston, and H. P. R. Finberg, have in fact argued this.[41] But there are problems about such an interpretation: three, above all. The first is that the kings who handed out these blocks would have been, in effect, owners of all or most of the land in their kingdoms before they started to cede property to the church: absolutely dominant figures with only tenants (whether peasants or aristocrats) as their subjects. This would re-create the absolute royal power that was implicit in John's idea of non-heritable lay landowning, and is subject to the same criticisms. The second is that the first Anglo-Saxon law-codes, which are all seventh-century (there is then a hiatus until the late ninth), give much space to free peasants (*ceorlas*) and their agricultural problems; the laws admittedly do not include an unambiguous textual

---

other substantial early territories, we cannot be sure how the land was acquired. See *BCS* 384 (S 1436), and Brooks, *Early history*, pp. 104, 181–2.

[39] *Gethyncðu*, c. 2. For hidages, see esp. Maitland, *Domesday Book*, pp. 416–21.

[40] e.g. Hooke, *The Anglo-Saxon landscape*, p. 89. A quarter of the county: Maitland, *Domesday Book*, p. 272. In the ninth century, Canterbury and the Kentish monasteries controlled as much of Kent: Brooks, *Early history*, p. 206.

[41] Chadwick, *Studies*, pp. 367–77; Aston, 'Origins'; Finberg, 'Anglo-Saxon England', pp. 446–8, etc. Patrick Wormald also accepts this position in *The making*, II, ch. 11 (5), though see n. 54.

statement that such peasants 'owned' their land, but we certainly get a clear sense that many were autonomous in their local activities. Some are described as tenants, but of aristocrats, not kings (it must be repeated that if kings did own their entire kingdom, they would exclude not just independent peasants, but also independent aristocrats). I have argued elsewhere that the sort of attention to the agricultural problems of the free peasantry shown by the West Saxon laws of Ine from around 700—as also by the *Pactus legis Salicae*—only make any sense as the focus of royal legislation if at least some of such peasants had a certain public position, with a certain respect accredited to them by legislators; such a position seems to me inconsistent with the proposition that they were all or mostly heavily subjected tenants.[42]

The third problem is archaeological. The simplicity of early Anglo-Saxon material culture around 500 has already been stressed; around 700 it was not much more elaborate. Villages were more articulated by now, but most show a notable paucity of finds, except in eastern England (see below, pp. 810–11). We even have a seventh-century royal site, Yeavering in Northumberland, with a complex and ambitious set of wooden constructions (showing possible indigenous influence, too, for once), but with, again, almost no finds at all.[43] As in the earlier period, we must recognize that there was rich metalwork around, which survives in graves (it is enough to mention Sutton Hoo in Suffolk, Mound 1 of which can still be dated to c.625), and cloth production could probably be equally high-quality.[44] But, apart from these specialist artisanal productions, we have no support for the proposal that there were even modest concentrations of wealth in England, never mind the extreme hierarchy that the estate model would entail. This would begin to change in the eighth century (see below, pp. 809–14), but that was part of the next phase of English development, which was scarcely visible in 700—and even the richest Middle Saxon sites, Hamwic or Ipswich or Flixborough, do not match their Frankish counterparts as yet.

For all these reasons, I conclude that the estate model for early Anglo-Saxon land units does not work. There has always been an alternative view, however, espoused by Frederic Maitland and Frank Stenton at the start of the twentieth century and Steven Bassett, John Blair, Rosamond Faith, and Dawn Hadley now, which sees early landholding in more fluid terms.[45] According to this model, kings had 'superiority', as Maitland put it, over

[42] Ine, e.g. 40–4. Cf. Wickham, *Land and power*, pp. 214–15, 221–2.

[43] Hope-Taylor, *Yeavering* (pp. 170–203 for the very few finds, pp. 205–9 for the 'native' Great Enclosure, pp. 119–22, 241–4 for the Roman-style theatre). Tinniswood and Harding, 'Anglo-Saxon occupation', gives evidence for ironworking there as well, but finds remain sparse.

[44] For Sutton Hoo, see Carver, 'Sutton Hoo'. For cloth, see e.g. Budny, 'Maaseik', with Ch. 11, n. 197.

[45] Maitland, *Domesday Book*, pp. 272–90 (still the classic account); Stenton, *Anglo-Saxon England*, pp. 302–5; Bassett, 'In search of the origins'; Blair, *Anglo-Saxon Oxfordshire*, pp. 77–9; Faith, *English peasantry*, pp. 7–14; Hadley, *The northern Danelaw*, pp. 60–93, who offers a rare comparative perspective.

these large tracts of land; they did not so much take rent from tenants as take tribute from free followers, who themselves had rights in the land. It was this tribute that kings were ceding to churches in charters, and it was not necessarily huge. Ine once indicates the scale of at least one kind of tribute, which he calls *foster* (it probably represents the *pastum*, 'feeding', of some Latin charters): from 10 hides, he expected ten vats of honey, 300 loaves, 42 'ambers' of ale, two cows or ten wethers, thirty geese and chickens, ten cheeses, an amber of butter, five salmon, twenty measures of fodder, 100 eels. This is clearly an idealized list, but, even though it looks a lot, 300 loaves is actually the annual produce of only around a hectare of land, a tiny proportion of 10 hides—on the Isle of Wight calculation, around a three-hundredth.[46] There are half-a-dozen similar lists in charters dating to between 780 and 900. Their status is usually uncertain; above all, it is generally unclear what cultivators paid out, rather than what was owed by ecclesiastical and aristocratic middlemen—they cannot, that is to say, ever be shown to constitute *omne tributum*, and indeed they normally character-ized what was still paid to the king, not what he ceded away. All the same, the variety of products in them is as wide as in Ine, and the scale is even smaller. In c.810 the Kentish estate of Stanhamstead, whose vernacular charter contains the most likely candidate for a list of peasant dues, in this case paid to Christ Church Canterbury, only owed, for 20 sulungs (probably 40 hides), 150 loaves, a bullock, four sheep, two sides of bacon, fifteen poultry, ten pounds of cheese, thirty ambers of ale, and two ambers of honey. This is around an eighth of the weight of the Ine *foster*, and is significantly low even if it was not all that was paid out.[47]

Curiously, the development of these obligations, and their internal articu-lation, have not had systematic study since Maitland and Chadwick around 1900. Not that this is the place for the intricate reassemblage of sources that would be a necessary part of such an analysis; how they developed anyway belongs to the analysis of the recomposition of aristocratic power in the eighth and ninth centuries, and will be discussed, although still sketchily, later (pp. 344–9). It is at least clear, however, that land could owe a variety of regular obligations, some of which kings ceded to churches, and others of which they kept for themselves, and that the division between them could often be negotiated ad hoc.[48] But we need to recognize two points about these obligations. The first is that there is no early sign that any of them were

---

[46] Ine 70.1. *Pastum* and similar: e.g. BCS 241, 309, 324, 350 (S 1257, 1431, 1263, 172); *feorm* was a common later term, e.g. BCS 454 (S 197), Alfred 2. For the calculation of loaves to hectares, using late medieval yield figures, see Dyer, *Lords and peasants*, pp. 28–9.

[47] BCS 330 (S 1188, *Select documents*, n. 1); cf. Crick, 'Church, land', for an 830s date for the text. Other such lists are BCS 273, 324, 364 (S 146, 1263, 1861), and Finberg, *West Midlands*, p. 103.

[48] Maitland, *Domesday Book*, pp. 280–6, 319–45; Chadwick, *Studies*, pp. 100–2, rather more sketchily. It can be added that the uncertain nature of the boundary between these dues argues against the utility of using the word 'immunity' to describe such grants. That is a concept

heavy; the references we have to different kinds of dues are very variegated, but all low. This fits the absence of major foci of wealth in the archaeology. The second is that they were not clearly separated conceptually. Ine's *foster* seems to have denoted supplies to an itinerant royal household, not rent (whether to kings or others), which the text calls *gafol*. Conversely, however, a charter of King Offa lists in Old English the renders he still expected from 60 hides at Westbury on Trym in Gloucestershire in 793/6, even after the land had been given to the church of Worcester, and uses the word *gafoles* for these renders (*vectigalia* in the Latin), although they were similar in type to Ine's *foster*.[49] It is true that similar semantic shifts can be found in many societies, including those with clearly distinguished legal categories; overall, however, there is no sign that the difference between 'rent' and 'tribute' was systematically marked in seventh- to ninth-century texts in England, and it may not have been fully understood yet. Land-units had many people living on them; they all owed dues to at least one lord, perhaps more than one at all times, whether or not the land was granted out by charter. But it does not seem to be the case that these dues yet marked the exclusive ownership of Roman land tenure; they just marked obligation, and hierarchy, among people who could all have seen themselves as in some sense landholders, as in the Maitland model of 'superiority', at least if they were legally free.

This framework fits Ine's assumptions about *ceorlas*: they lived on land that, presumably, could be granted away by charter, but they were autonomous. Even the one law of Ine which does unequivocally refer to rent-paying (*rædegafol*) to a lord (*hlaford*), Ine 67, envisages the possibility that that tenant might possess his own home, although he could well have still paid a different sort of *gafol* to another lord for it, for all we know, in a political rather than a tenurial context, however.[50] There could indeed have been quite complex and variable socio-economic hierarchies inside a 300-hide territory such as around Chertsey, including aristocrats and small-scale estate relationships, as well as autonomous *ceorlas*. But the structuring of free society did not depend on exclusive rights to land, and it therefore fits my definitions of tribal society (above, p. 305); this pattern, not a land-owning-based feudal society, still characterized the England of the late seventh and early eighth centuries.

Maitland and, in particular, Stenton saw early Anglo-Saxon society as dominated by free peasants, along the lines of the *Gemeinfreie* theory

which has a precise, quasi-judicial, meaning on the Continent, and which exists in the context of clear separations between different sorts of rights; early Anglo-Saxon grants are altogether different. See most recently Rosenwein, *Negotiating space*.

[49] BCS 272–3 (S 146). This text is now often seen as a Worcester rewriting, dating to soon after Offa's grant (see the bibliography in the second edition of S), but the point in the text still stands.

[50] Ine 67 has had much commentary, especially from estate theorists, as above, n. 41. Helpful remarks in Charles-Edwards, 'The distinction', pp. 101–3.

prominent in German historiography up to the 1930s.[51] This must be wrong; we have plenty of evidence of aristocrats from our first texts, as with the contrast between *eorl* and *ceorl* in Æthelberht's early seventh-century code—indeed, early Anglo-Saxon law pays more attention to status differences than early Frankish law does. Bede's writings are full of *nobiles*; early English literature is full of aristocratic heroism.[52] The relative wealth of such high-status people may have been established through ad hoc tributes from the free; it will also, however, have been based on the rather greater dependence of the unfree. The unfree were not landholders; they did, certainly, cultivate for other people and pay what we would call rent to them. Wilfrid was given a royal residence (*villa*) at Selsey in the 680s by the king of Sussex as the basis for his new bishopric, with 87 hides (*mansiones*) attached, according to his biographer Stephanus, writing in the 710s. Bede, who used Stephanus two decades later, added that Wilfrid baptized and freed 250 *servi* and *ancillae* there. Even if we do not treat these figures as gospel, it was clearly conceivable to Bede that such a land-unit could have a lot of unfree workers.[53] Elsewhere, it is likely that land-units could have both free and unfree peasants living on them, and it could well be that the unfree paid most of the *foster/feorm/gafol/tributum* due from that land, and the free relatively little. Faith has developed a model as a result which distinguishes sharply between the 'inland' on such land-units, where more dependent inhabitants paid something akin to rent, and wider areas of 'outland' or 'warland', of extensive lordship, where more autonomous inhabitants paid more political, and lower, tributes. This is a helpful and convincing way to see how we can set the evidence for the vagueness of 'superiority' attached to land-units alongside the evidence we also have for some estate structures, even for free peasants, as early as Ine 67. 'Inland' must have been a minority of tenure in 700, but it was destined to grow at the expense of 'outland' across the next centuries (below, pp. 347–51).[54]

The underlying reason why these issues have perplexed scholars for so long, and caused so much disagreement, is that the Anglo-Saxons were entirely happy to be vague about the whole issue. Their own Old English mental terminology is ill-documented, for we cannot assume one-to-one translations into Latin, the language of most of our sources, as the multifarious words which translate 'hide' show. All the same, we have seen that *gafol* had a wide semantic range, running from our 'tax' to our 'rent'; *lond* or

---

51 Maitland, *Domesday Book*, pp. 374 ff.; Stenton, *Anglo-Saxon England*, pp. 274–310.
52 See e.g. Wormald, 'Bede, "Beowulf" '; Campbell, *Essays*, pp. 131–8.
53 Stephanus, *Vita Wilfridi*, c. 41; Bede, *HE*, IV.13.
54 Faith, *English peasantry*, *passim*. Patrick Wormald suggested to me that the *cassati*, *manentes*, etc., of the Latin charters may have only meant the (usually unfree) 'inland' workers on the land-units ceded by kings, over which kings indeed had effective proprietorial rights, and not the 'outland' inhabitants of the same territories. This hypothesis needs development. It would restore some authority to the terminology charters use, but would not otherwise affect the arguments made above, for such dependants would have been a minority for some time.

land, too, which is found in the laws and also in vernacular charters, which begin in the early ninth century, seems to mean 'an extent of land' without any conceptual distinctions.[55] This is matched by the use of *terra* in Latin charters, in fact—and it may be added that even that word is absent in many eighth-century charters, which often only refer to 'X hides at Y'. Nor is Bede, who was certainly bilingual in Old English and Latin, any more helpful: his topographical precision, so considerable at the level of kingdoms, is much vaguer at the land-unit level, with *terra*, *locus*, *possessio*, *territorium*, arguably all just translating *lond* as well. The mental hierarchy that allows one in Italy or the Rhineland or Egypt to distinguish between separate terminologies for villages, estates, peasant holdings, and isolated fields in our sources (below, Chapter 7) is simply absent here. Bede is indeed strikingly uninterested in the detail of how local landed relationships might work; he deals exclusively in royal/aristocratic/ecclesiastical levels of tenure. Interestingly, Bede was himself, unlike almost any other major writer in our period, perhaps not aristocratic (the only immediate parallel that comes to mind is George, author of the seventh-century *Life* of Theodore of Sykeōn); he has no known kin (and no saint's life), and was in many respects unsympathetic to aristocratic values. He was born, in 672/3, on the *territorium* which would shortly be given by King Ecgfrith to found the monastery of Monk-wearmouth, which he himself joined at the age of 7.[56] What this meant for his own family's tenurial dependence we do not know; but Bede would certainly have known if the imprecision of Anglo-Saxon tenurial arrangements was threatening, or even problematic, and he gives no sign of it.

These opacities are unhelpful to historians, but, taken as a whole, they have their own significance. Ine's laws on tenure assume fairly complex social arrangements. Bede also makes it clear that inheritance was partible, and this would inevitably, as universally on the Continent, have created equally complex, not to say messy, tenurial patterns.[57] None of these are apparent in the bland cessions of land in our early charters and other sources. We must conclude that they simply happened at a different social level from that recorded in charters and the like. Tenure was not an issue simply *because* it did not, in this period, imply exclusive rights in the way that Roman or modern—or Frankish or Lombard—legal concepts assume. How many aristocrats, *ceorlas*, or unfree lived in any given *territorium*— and who was paying a lot and who was not—was not relevant at the royal/ ecclesiastical level, so we have no record of it. We can, in fact, hardly deduce anything secure about how landholding actually worked on the ground from

[55] See for *lond* e.g. *Anglo-Saxon charters*, n. 3 (S 1500), BCS 330 (S 1188, *Selected documents*, n. 1).

[56] Bede, *HE*, V.24 for his geographical origins, cf. pp. ix–xi of Plummer's edition, and de Jong, *In Samuel's image*, pp. 48–9, 212–13. On Bede's unaristocratic sensibilities, Wormald, 'Bede, "Beowulf" ', pp. 62–3.

[57] Bede, *HE*, V.12, *Historia abbatum*, c. 11.

seventh- and eighth-century charters. How it *might* have worked is an issue to which we shall return in Chapter 7 (pp. 428–34).

Seventh-century England was a sub-region in which political power was often, by European standards, tiny in scale; it was, however, constructed out of land-units which could, by European standards, be huge. I have been arguing that these units were therefore political divisions, not yet estates. There must have been a large number of them, in every part of the country, fitting inside each other like Russian dolls, the territory of Chertsey inside the sub-kingdom of Surrey and so on. How old were they? Bassett and others have proposed that they were in many cases early, their boundaries delineating the territories of fifth- and sixth-century kings or tribal leaders which, as noted earlier, had often become swallowed up into larger polities by the seventh.[58] This is necessarily guesswork, and it would be too schematic to presume that they all were, a priori; but the proposal, taken as a generalization, seems convincing. Three hundred hides, the size of the Chertsey territory in 674, itself cut out of a larger unit in all likelihood, was also the size of the smallest polities in the roughly contemporary *Tribal Hidage*, after all. At the least, one could propose that the Anglo-Saxons originally organized themselves *like* this: in tenurially informal units, tribal units, of the Chertsey scale or smaller still, some of which could well still have been visible in the local territories of the seventh century. It is in this way that we can move back retrospectively from the documented world around 700 to the undocumented (and archaeologically very simple) world of 500 and earlier. And, as also noted earlier, this sort of scale for Anglo-Saxon political action would not have been a winning strategy had the indigenous British operated on a larger scale in the Lowland Zone. We can conclude that this form of micro-regional politics preceded the Anglo-Saxon immigration and that it was simply taken over by the new people and made their own.

It might in principle be argued that these large, tribal, land-units were much older, a Romano-British provincial specificity that could have had pre-Roman roots. To test that view fully, one would have to track the spatial networks assumed by Romano-British archaeological patterns across the first four centuries AD, which is not part of my project. But such a view is at least locally falsified by the only two land documents as yet found for Roman Britain, both of which use standard Roman law; the clearer one, part of a court-case from Kent dating to 118, involves the full Roman-law ownership of 15 *arepennia*, roughly 2 hectares, of woodland—the sort of

---

[58] Bassett, 'In search of the origins'. Analyses of early territories were given an important push thirty years ago by Glanville Jones's theory of 'multiple estates' (see e.g. 'Post-Roman Wales', pp. 358 ff.), which persuaded people to go and look for territories everywhere—see Sawyer, *English Medieval settlement*, for examples. But Jones's image of the multiple estate, apart from the late date of his evidence, is far too static and legalist; it also presupposes the identity of these units as estates, a position denied here. Barrow's parallel image of 'extensive lordship' (*The kingdom of the Scots*, pp. 7–28) could be seen as a more satisfactory formulation.

small-scale property that is normal elsewhere in the empire, and barely visible again in documents from the island until the tenth century.[59] In my view, this backs up the impression one derives from the 'ordinariness' of fourth-century Romano-British archaeology, and gives further support to the proposal that it was in the early fifth century that Roman traditions in property-holding broke down, in the same context as the well-documented breakdown of material culture. The Anglo-Saxons would, on this model, have found small-scale tribal territories when they arrived, but these would only have been a generation or two old.

If this were so, however, then we cannot simply restrict ourselves to Anglo-Saxon evidence; we ought to find these territories in the Welsh areas of the island as well. I would argue that we do, but the point needs to be established by setting out the Welsh evidence, using the same sort of arguments that we have just seen for England. Only when we have done that can we come back to some hypotheses about what actually might have happened in the early fifth century to cause changes of this type.

Wales was one of the very few parts of the western Roman empire not to have been conquered at any time by Germanic invaders, and half of the sub-region stayed independent until the thirteenth century. But there is not much evidence of Roman cultural traditions (except for writing, and Christianity) by the seventh and eighth centuries, a plausible date for our earliest vernacular texts: here, and in later poetry, we have the same sort of small-scale military aristocratic societies that we find in Anglo-Saxon literature and narratives.[60] The *Vita Samsonis*, too, a probably seventh-century saint's life from the sister sub-region of Brittany, much of which is at least nominally set in Britain, describes small-scale political structures which are similar to those depicted in contemporary Anglo-Saxon lives, and which contrast notably with the court of the Frankish kings in the same text.[61] It is in fact not much in dispute that by the seventh century Wales was divided among four major kingdoms (Gwynedd, Powys, Dyfed, and Glywysing) and maybe half-a-dozen minor ones. Without any invasion, Wales had developed a political structure quite unlike that of the Roman empire.

As with England, we must ask when these kingdoms originated. Gwynedd was the core of the least Romanized part of Wales, in the north-west, and its political structure may well show some continuities with the tribal patterns of Roman and pre-Roman times, although its name was new, and its rulers may have been immigrants from northern Britain. Dyfed, the Demetae in

[59] Tomlin, 'A five-acre wood'; cf. Turner, 'A Roman writing tablet'.

[60] There is always dispute about the dating of early Welsh poetry (cf. Ch. 5, n. 55), but see Rowland, *Early Welsh saga poetry*, pp. 121–41, 174–8, for a seventh-century dating for, and an edition of, *Marwnad Cynddylan*.

[61] *Vita Samsonis*, I.1, 6, 53–9; for the date, see Davies, *Wales in the early middle ages*, p. 215; Wood, 'Forgery', pp. 380–4.

Gildas's mid-sixth-century Latin, preserved the name of the Romano-British tribe of the south-west, but here, too, its intervening history was not entirely linear. It was an area of Irish settlement in the fifth century, and its Gildas-period ruler, Vortipor, has left a bilingual Latin and Irish stone memorial at Castelldwyran in modern Pembrokeshire which calls him *protictor*, a Roman military title (with illuminating Mafia overtones), which was used to mean local aristocrat in Anatolia as well (p. 233); Vortipor may have been constructing local legitimacy out of a bricolage of different elements, local non-Roman, military Roman, and Irish, in ways paralleled elsewhere. These two kingdoms were the most likely ones in Wales to have had some core of pre-existing tribal identity, surviving beneath the Roman imperial structure, but even they had elements of discontinuity with the past.[62] In the sixth century they may have been the largest polities in post-Roman Britain, although, if so, their coherence would have been based on local situations, not easily exported beyond the incompletely Romanized mountains (a king of Gwynedd might and did conquer elsewhere, but did not have the infrastructure to keep his conquests); also, that relative physical size did not translate into substantially greater populations, given that half of Gwynedd and much of Dyfed is non-agricultural upland.

The lowland sections of non-Anglo-Saxon Britain—Lancashire, Gwent in south-east Wales, and, until past 550, the Severn valley and Somerset—had by contrast been entirely Romanized, and ought to have undergone the same sort of material and political collapse that we have seen in eastern Britain. In archaeological terms, they certainly did; ceramics, villas, and towns vanished as they did elsewhere. In the lowland west, however, we see material signs of the reconstruction of an elite in the late fifth century. After c.475 a series of hill-forts on or near the sea on both sides of the Bristol Channel was reoccupied, with evidence of high-status occupation, in that we find small quantities of Mediterranean (mostly Aegean) *terra sigillata*, amphorae and glass, and evidence of metalworking, sometimes in silver—although, by contrast, the quality of building construction was very low. It does not seem to have taken much to make an elite here, but these are at least signs of conspicuous consumption that contemporary (Anglo-Saxon) settlements in eastern Britain, or indeed inland indigenous centres such as Wroxeter, did not yet match. Were each hill-fort to be the centre for a 'king', then the scale of each polity might have been very roughly a third of a modern county.

---

[62] Davies, *Wales in the early middle ages*, pp. 85–93. For Vortipor, Gildas, *De Excidio*, II.31 and *Early Christian monuments*, n. 138: cf. Dumville, 'The idea of government', pp. 182–3. Vortipor's use of the title *protictor* (not present, interestingly, in the Irish ogham—the Irish perhaps did not recognize its cultural connotations) recalls the word *tyrannus* in Gildas, a very informal title. Of course, Gildas used it polemically; one can wonder, all the same, whether 'Vortigern', Gildas' *superbus tyrannus* (*De Excidio*, I.23), was the first of these bricoleurs, using *tyrannus* to Latinize *tigernos* (*teyrn*, 'ruler', in modern Welsh) and thus to bring it, too, into a Roman tradition, as Snyder, *An age of tyrants*, pp. 97–108, proposes. Cf. Davies, *Small worlds*, p. 138, for Brittany.

This was also the apparent scale of the earliest known kings in Gwent and Ergyng, around 600. It is larger than that of the 300-hide units found in parts of eastern Britain, but is in the same order of magnitude in terms of landed resources. These kings could plausibly be seen as the survivors of fifth-century lowland tribalization who had not become Anglo-Saxonized, and who by the late fifth century were beginning to develop their own characteristic material culture, and, presumably, value-system. By the mid-sixth century the Mediterranean link had gone, but a ceramic link with western Gaul (again unparalleled in eastern Britain) replaced it in the areas which still resisted Anglo-Saxon expansion.[63]

There is only one area of the west which has any charter documentation, Gwent in south-east Wales, with outliers in Ergyng, Glamorgan, and Brycheiniog to the east, west, and north. The charters we have survive in the *Book of Llandaff* and the *Vita S. Cadoci* (of Llancarfan), both twelfth-century compilations, with many forgeries in the former. Wendy Davies in the 1970s finally established criteria for identifying their authenticity and dating, making them usable by historians. By her dating, the texts begin after 550, and some ninety charters pre-date 800; Patrick Sims-Williams prefers a date for most of these of about half-a-century later, but this is the only modification that the last thirty years has produced.[64] These texts are from an area whose cultural traditions descended directly from the Roman world, without the ethnic and religious breaks of Anglo-Saxon England; it is interesting, however, how many similarities to contemporary English material they show.

The first similarity is that, initially, only kings gave to the church. This hardly changed throughout the seventh century; lay donations only began to be numerous in the eighth (see below, pp. 352–4). Before then, restrictions on alienation seem, as in England, but unlike anywhere on the Continent, only to have been breakable at the royal level.[65] The second similarity is that early gifts were of substantial properties, usually whole estates (often called *villae* or *agri*) measuring one or more *unciae* (Davies gives the figure of approximately 500 acres, some 2 km², for an *uncia*) in most cases, and never in this period less than $\frac{1}{2}$ km². We are here on the five-hide level, not the 300-hide level, using Anglo-Saxon terminology, but we are also in a more localized stage of political development than that of late

---

[63] For all this, see Thomas, *Tintagel*, pp. 85–99; Alcock, *Dinas Powys*, pp. 26–34, 47–61; Alcock, *Cadbury castle*; Rahtz, *Cadbury Congresbury*, pp. 230–46; Campbell and Lane, 'Longbury bank'. For a gazetteer, see Snyder, *Sub-Roman Britain*. For exchange, see above all Campbell, 'The archaeological evidence', and Wooding, *Communication and commerce*. Three centres per county: this is a guesstimate based on the two Cadbury's in Somerset, given that it is very unlikely that we have found all of them. For Wroxeter (and also the non-high-status structures at Poundbury in Dorset) see above, n. 8.

[64] Davies, *Microcosm*; eadem, *The Llandaff charters*; eadem, 'Land and power'; Sims-Williams, 'The Llandaff charters', in idem, *Britain*, n. VI.

[65] Davies, 'Land and power', p. 16; *Microcosm*, pp. 165 ff., for a calendar of texts.

seventh-century England, with kingdoms themselves not so much larger than 300 hides.[66] A third similarity is that the dues from these gifts were expressed in terms of food: as a (probably) eighth-century text for the monastery of Llancarfan puts it, 9 *modii* of beer, plus bread, meat, and honey, 'wherever the clerics of Cadog want to eat and drink'. Exactly how heavy these dues were is not clear in this period, but 9 *modii* (78 litres by Roman measures), itself quite high by Llancarfan standards, is not much for a whole estate, and as late as 1086 documented rents on the Welsh border were very low by comparison with England.[67]

These charters do not at all resemble those of the Anglo-Saxon tradition in format, but they seem to be describing the same sorts of things: large, formerly royal-dominated lands with fairly small 'rents'. Even if one proposes that the more aristocratic eighth-century gifts were of land that had always been outside royal control, which is uncertain, we find the same situation as in England: small kingdoms and large land-units. Autonomous peasant owners would be squeezed out in the areas dominated by these land-units, even though such people are assumed to exist in later Welsh legislation—if the units were estates.[68] But if the picture of the breakdown of Roman-style landowning before the Anglo-Saxons came is valid, then we would not expect them to be estates; they would be the building-blocks of the small tribal kingdoms. This, in my view, is what the Welsh land-units have to be. It would explain, as in England, the absence of fragmented landowning and peasant proprietors, and also the low 'rents' in the Llancarfan texts, which would once again be best seen as tribal tributes. It is true that there is a genealogical link between Ergyng and Gwent, named from Roman Ariconium and Venta, and the late empire, which we cannot assume a priori for the territories of the English lowlands. But it can be argued that the socio-economic break was as great in western as in eastern lowland Britain: each saw the dissolution of Roman land tenure into small tribal units, and the maintenance (or reintroduction) of Roman land terminology only at the political/tribal level. The situation in Gwent can in fact be proposed to be a rough model for what the eastern lowlands looked like before the Anglo-Saxons came in, with tribal leaders of the community of each *ager* operating as the direct successors of the local landowners of c.400, and themselves owing allegiance and tribute to kings on the Ergyng scale. Inside *agri*, we could once again expect a more complex mix of free social strata, and also servile cultivators, maybe living on what Faith would call an 'inland' in the Anglo-Saxon context; the latter could well have produced

---

[66] Davies, *Microcosm*, pp. 32–42; eadem, '*Unciae*', for land size.

[67] Llancarfan: *Vita S. Cadoci*, c. 59, cf. cc. 55–66. 1086: Darby and Terrett, *Domesday geography*, pp. 53–5, 110–11, 155–8. Cf. Davies, *Wales in the early middle ages*, p. 46.

[68] *Llyfr Iorwerth*, e.g. cc. 84–5 (trans. Jenkins, *The law*, pp. 101–5), a thirteenth-century text in its present form. Cf. below, n. 119. For charter format, see Davies, 'Latin charter tradition'.

most of the dues that lords received.[69] This structure could be seen as being as tribal as Gwynedd, but newer in that form, and much smaller in size.

I argued earlier (pp. 306–10) that the collapse in the material culture of Britain in the first half of the fifth century could best be explained in the context of the breakdown, not only of state structures, but of Roman traditions of private landowning. Seventh-century evidence both from England and from Wales fills this latter point out a little: by then, and probably already by 450, hierarchies had ceased to be based on exclusive tenurial rights, and had become associated with dues representing political, tribal, relationships of dependence. How local elites moved from one to the other is entirely a matter of guesswork; what follows is what makes most sense to me, rather than what can in any way be documented.

What would a (male) aristocrat do in lowland Britain when the state infrastructure collapsed around him in the early fifth century? He could flee Britain (if he was by any chance already militarized, he could by the 470s have joined Riothamus' *Britanni* on the Loire[70]); he could have lost control of his land to a hostile peasantry. If he stayed put, however, he would have to have defended his land, somehow, by himself; he would have to arm himself and his most reliable servants. The most straightforward solution would be to seek a territory, for the scattered estates implied by the Kentish document of 118 would be hard to defend, and outlying lands would be soon lost; conversely, lands of weaker neighbours or absentee owners could be seized. One would probably find that the people in such a territory would be of three types: one's most trustworthy retainers, military specialists; a wider penumbra of tributary clients of different types and statuses, who could defend the territory if it was particularly menaced, but who were otherwise not militarily orientated; and the most dependent of all, maybe the descendants of the unfree tenants of the Roman period, who simply worked some of the land and transferred surpluses upwards.

This sort of pattern already recalls the world of Ine, in fact; but it is important to note that it tends to be found whenever civil society breaks down. It is not actually that dissimilar to the Palermo of the Mafia, which has a core of 'military' experts in each zone and a wider penumbra of the loyal and protected, as well as the exploited (in Palermo, where the concept of unfreedom is not available, these latter two groups interpenetrate, without at least a minimum form of loyalty being undermined). What would happen, though, if all public social hierarchies dissolved: if not only the Italian state and the Carabinieri left Palermo, but the city council as well?

---

[69] Tidenham in Gloucestershire, source of one of the first (tenth-century) references to labour service in England (*Anglo-Saxon charters*, n. 109, S 1555; see most recently Faith, 'Tidenham'), was formerly a Llandaff property in Wales: *Liber Landavensis*, pp. 174b, 229b.

[70] Sidonius, *Ep.* III.9. Where Riothamus came from in Britain cannot be said, although, as usual, that has not prevented historians from speculating about it.

The Mafia would have to run it on their own. They would have to draw on the loyalties they already have in a much more organized, explicit, way, including a visible leadership with recognizable responsibilities. They would have to create local communities, with links that stretched from top to bottom. So would a fifth-century British landowner. He could use the imagery of kinship, or of common geographical identity, or of religion, or—probably—all three; he would, however, want 'his people' to identify with him, for if they did not he would go under. He would need to create a collectivity, tight enough to be called a tribe. He would become a leader or chieftain, a 'protector', a ruler on a small scale, but he would not necessarily need to stay a land*owner*, for his control of his community would no longer be based on property rights. All the same, he would need to make material concessions to his people to gain their support, for they could always join a rival instead; he would probably be much less rich as a result, hence, in Britain, the rapid decline of the market infrastructure as well. He could do this while still maintaining an attachment to Roman imagery, as did St Patrick's family (Patrick's father was a *decorio*, at least nominally a city councillor, which brought him *nobilitas*; Patrick uses the imagery of *cives* to describe his community), but the real content of that ideology would soon change out of recognition, and *Romanitas* had been abandoned as an image by Gildas's time, in the mid-sixth century.[71]

In Gaul, this process in most places worked very differently. There, political crisis did not result in tribalization, but, rather, in the hegemony of an unusually powerful landowning military aristocracy, whose lands interpenetrated with those of other aristocrats. In most of Gaul, the lack of wealth and restriction in geographical scale characteristic of Britain cannot be seen, and Roman traditions of landowning were by no means given up (above, pp. 178–99). Why Gaulish and British aristocrats had quite such contrasting fates cannot as yet fully be explained, but one reason probably lies in the different role of the army. As C. R. Whittaker has shown, the aristocracy of fourth-century northern Gaul had already become substantially militarized, under the influence of the Rhine frontier zone; they could go it alone more easily without changing their local practices in a radical way, indeed maintaining (military) Roman traditions as they did so. In lowland Britain, where external threats had been fewer, aristocratic society was much more civilian, much less prepared for the dangers and

[71] Patrick, *Epistola*, c. 10; Coroticus, his addressee, is clearly a British warlord, although probably in the Highland Zone, so in an incompletely Romanized area (or, indeed, an entirely un-Romanized area, if he was ruler in Dumbarton, as many think). See also Handley, 'Christian commemoration', for Roman identity. The extensive historiography on Patrick does not need citation here; most people agree that he wrote in the fifth century, although they disagree about when in the fifth century. See Charles-Edwards, *Early Christian Ireland*, pp. 214–39, for a sensible survey. For Gildas, see above, n. 15. The imagery of *cives* (and a *magistratus*) did survive in sixth-century Gwynedd: see *Early Christian monuments*, nn. 33, 103. See Snyder, *An age of tyrants*, pp. 76–81, for discussion.

opportunities of local autonomy.[72] Britain also, however, had a less Romanized fringe in the Highland Zone, where tribal practices had never gone away entirely, which offered a potential model for local social activity if it became necessary to go it alone. Lowland British aristocrats in c.400 were thus simultaneously 'more Roman' (more civilian) than their Gaulish counterparts, and 'less Roman' (physically closer to tribal alternatives—with which, one can add, they also shared a Celtic language); they chose the tribal option as a result. That this option would quickly lead to a drastic lessening of their living standards and political horizons could not easily have been foreseen. And by then it was too late to backtrack.

Such newly invented lowland tribes, crystallizing on the basis of whatever infrastructure and ideology they could generate or preserve locally, were much more small-scale than the Catuvellauni of the past, or the highland Demetae/Dyfed of the sixth century, precisely because they had to start from scratch. Exactly what size they could sustain would certainly vary, depending on that local socio-political or economic infrastructure; it might be bigger around relatively large population centres, for example, or where two communities structurally depended on each other (as, perhaps, with the elongated agricultural-cum-pastoral units that have been identified in and around the Weald in Kent, Surrey, and Sussex).[73] But there have as yet been no successful demonstrations that any *civitas* managed to keep control of its imperial-period territory, and the scale of such units, by the standards of the rest of the empire, seems throughout the Lowland Zone to have remained very small. It can also be repeated that the control of the new tribal leaders over their clients and dependants must have been fairly incomplete. As we saw in Chapter 4, throughout the post-Roman world the weakening of the state tended to lead to a lessening, not an increase, in aristocratic power and wealth, and the material weakness of late fifth-century Britain certainly fits with this. We could indeed suppose that, at least by the early Anglo-Saxon period, tribal society could have permitted the existence of polycentric hierarchies, focused on a range of relatively rich people in any single territory, which might further relate to problems of control for individual leaders. At an earlier stage, even leadership might have been contested, with several local leaders in competition for followers, using short-term success, personality, and generosity as a means to persuade clients to switch loyalties; such a 'big man' model can be found later in Iceland (below, p. 374). If this were so, then wealth could have been dispersed downwards from leaders to clients in ways that would be hard to detect archaeologically (such as

[72] Whittaker, *Frontiers*, pp. 222–78; ibid., pp. 238–9, and Esmonde-Cleary, *Ending*, p. 174, make points similar to the one made here. Hadrian's Wall was in the Highland Zone, and its infrastructure had less effect on lowland Britain than did the Rhine frontier in Gaul. Whyman, *Late Roman Britain*, pp. 359–90, sets out an interesting model for how the process may have worked in the East Riding of Yorkshire, on the edge of the northern military zone.

[73] Witney, *Jutish forest*, pp. 49–55; Blair, 'Frithuwold's kingdom', pp. 98–101.

feasting), which would further help to explain the material weakness of the period.[74]

One could continue with this form of hypothesizing as long as one wanted; there is no direct evidence for any of it. I have discussed it over three pages simply to put some flesh on the bones of our knowledge of the extreme weakening of economic, political, and tenurial structures in fifth-century Britain. This is how it *could* have happened; these are the most plausible parameters for abrupt (catastrophic in a mathematical sense) social change that currently present themselves. If we want to go further, but not simply build hypothesis on hypothesis, then we must leave Britain, and look for parallels. Actually, none of them are quite as clearly marked out as Britain, for archaeology on that island is unusually well developed, and no society that 'went tribal' has left us good written sources; but they can help us to understand certain aspects of the tribalization process a little better. The most interesting parallel is Berber North Africa, which has some useful similarities, as well as some important differences. Let us conclude this section with a brief look at Africa, and at a handful of other potential examples.

Historians and archaeologists of Africa are less shy than many of using the word 'tribe', for it is commonly associated with desert/nomadic communities. However, as was noted in Chapter 2 (p. 22), there were also settled Berber communities, better-evidenced than the nomads, who increasingly show a tribal social structure in our period; it is these who offer the parallel case to Britain. That said, it is important to keep in mind that the nomadic tribes were always there in the African semi-desert, as an organizational alternative. They were not dominated by Rome, and they grew steadily more powerful across the imperial centuries, probably as a spin-off of stable exchange and political relationships with Rome (including military employment as federate troops), much as Germanic settled tribal communities did north of the Rhine–Danube frontier. Sometimes these expanding tribes attacked Roman power directly, as in the bloody raids described by Synesios in early fifth-century Cyrenaica, which were probably the work of the Laguatan alliance.[75] Further west, however, they seem to have moved more gently into settled/Roman territory. The Tripolitanian semi-desert was settled in Roman style, with dispersed farms along the irrigated seasonal wadis, in the first century AD; by the third, the population had concentrated into small, partially fortified, settlements, now called *gsur* (Classical Arabic *quṣūr*). The largest of these was Ghirza, some 180 km south of the coast, whose high point was the fourth to sixth centuries, and which has several surviving monumental buildings, temples, and mausolea. Increasingly, the

---

[74] Cf. Wickham, *Land and power*, pp. 216–25.
[75] Synesios, *Correspondance*, nn. 107–8, 125, 132 (aa. 405–12).

style of decoration on them is more 'Libyan' than Roman, sometimes depicting what seem to be local leaders receiving gifts. These leaders, elsewhere in inscriptions called *tribuni* ('tribal leaders'?), look less and less like landowners and more and more like tribal chieftains. The area slowly moved, in effect, from the Romans to the Laguatan, both in social structure and in political allegiance (we cannot tell which came first). The fall-off in finds of African and Tripolitanian Red Slip pottery in most of the semi-desert (Ghirza itself is in the fifth and sixth centuries one of the few sites with any) indicates that economic exchange with the coast lessened considerably with this tribal shift; but settled agriculture itself was not undermined by it, and perhaps still survived in the eleventh century. When Ghirza was burnt down around 550, it was probably the work of the Byzantine general John Troglita, whose campaigns are documented in the 540s, not any external Berber attack.[76]

This Tripolitanian example is one of tribalization directly affected by outside influence; but the process could be an internal one, too. Flavius Nubel was a *regulus*, 'very powerful among the Moorish/Berber (*Mauricae*) nations' in the mid-fourth century, as Ammianus puts it. He built a church in the Kabylie mountains of Mauretania Caesariensis, to the west of the African grain heartland, and he appears on an inscription found there as a *praepositus* in the Roman army. His sons had mixed Berber and Roman names, and operated in a similar way between tribal and Roman values: Sammac built a fortified estate in the same area *in modum urbis*, 'in the manner of a town', whose Latin inscription survives, claiming for him military success for the Romans against the *gentes*, who have now sought treaties (*foedera*). Firmus, his brother, who killed him, by contrast rose up against Rome in 373 in a revolt which Ammianus paints as tribal, although Firmus claimed the imperial title. Gildo, another brother, who stayed with Rome, ended up as *magister utriusque militiae* of Africa, its military governor, with huge estates and imperial marriage links; when he revolted in 397 he did so as one of a long line of insubordinate Roman rulers of Africa. Were these people 'really' tribal chiefs or 'really' a local Roman military family? Evidently, the question is badly posed: they were both.[77] On their

[76] Barker *et al.*, *Farming the desert*, I, pp. 118–33, 326–42, II, pp. 321–3; Mattingly, *Tripolitania*, pp. 194–217 (pp. 216 f., with Sjöström, *Tripolitania*, pp. 101, 112–14, for notes on the eleventh century); Brogan and Smith, *Ghirza*, pp. 80–8, 230–9 (p. 229 for *tribuni*). The title *tribunus* may, however, be a piece of local bricolage, like Vortipor's use of *protictor*; it is also found in the fifth-century St Albans of Constantius, *Vita Germani*, c. 15. For Ghirza's role in the wars, see Modéran, *Les Maures*, pp. 291–2, 633, 647; for terminological bricolage, ibid., pp. 435–41; this whole book is now the basic account of Berber society and politics in Tripolitania and Numidia in our period. On pp. 421–8 Modéran defends the terminology of the 'tribe', along lines similar to mine. See also Whittaker, *Frontiers*, pp. 246–50, 259–60, in comparative perspective.

[77] Ammianus, *Res gestae*, XXIX.5.2 for Nubel (with *Inscriptiones christianae latinae veteres*, I, n. 1822), XXIX.5.13 for Sammac (with *Inscriptiones latinae selectae*, III.2, n. 9351); XXIX.5

'estates', indeed, we could easily suppose that what the Romans (and Sammac) saw as landed properties, some or all of the local inhabitants saw as tribal communities. The Romanization process could certainly turn tribesmen into tenants in Africa, slowly subject them, that is to say, create situations in which they could no longer consider themselves in any way as tenurially autonomous. But a family with sufficient traditional identity that as late as the fourth century its head could be called a *regulus*—and in the Kabylie too, admittedly always (including today) hard to subdue, but close to the coast and far from the desert—had presumably kept many elements of the tribal infrastructure of the pre-Roman period, legitimized by Roman military office. Here we are looking at a rather richer version of Roman Wales, one much more integrated into the state, into city culture, even into imperial politics, but with the same capacity to reclaim tribal autonomy if the state faltered.

The state did falter, and the Mauretanias, Caesariensis and Tingitana (modern central/western Algeria and Morocco), did go tribal. There is no sign that most of this part of Africa was ever ruled from outside after the Vandal conquests of 429–39, either by Vandals or by Romans/Byzantines (or indeed, except intermittently, by the caliphs). From then on, our written evidence is fragmentary, and the archaeology for this sub-region has hardly been begun. Caesarea (Cherchel) itself and its hinterland, further west than the Kabylie, have been studied; it had a period of late fifth-century prosperity, and did not close down in archaeological terms until well into the sixth. But this area almost certainly remained an isolated Vandal (and then Byzantine) outpost, as also did Septem (Ceuta) opposite Gibraltar.[78] Elsewhere, what we find in our literary evidence is *Mauri*, Berbers, and their kings. These kings maintained close ideological connections with Rome, however. Masuna, in an inscription of 508 from Altava in western Algeria, referred to himself as *rex gentium Maurorum et Romanorum*. Prokopios, who was keen to write up the barbarism of the Berbers, nonetheless recounted that they would not recognize any ruler who did not receive formal tokens of office, a staff, cap, and cloak, from the Romans (then the Vandals, then the Byzantines). Not least, Berber polities continued to be based in cities. Altava has not been properly excavated, but it seems to have been a real political centre; Masuna's *Romani* may be in part represented by the remarkable run of over

---

in general for Firmus; cf. *PLRE*, I, s.v. Firmus 3, Gildo. Good analyses: Modéran, 'Gildon'; Brett and Fentress, *Berbers*, pp. 71–5. For detribalization and retribalization in Numidia and Byzacena, see Modéran, *Les Maures*, pp. 504–10.

[78] Leveau, *Caesarea*, pp. 209–15, 455–64; Benseddik and Potter, *Forum de Cherchel*, I, pp. 55–66, II, pp. 377–82; Anselmino *et al.*, *Nador*, pp. 76–88, 96–101; Bernal Casasola and Pérez Rivera, '*Septem*' (occupation up to 650 at least). For *Septem* and cities further south in modern Morocco, see also Villaverde, *Tingitana*, pp. 141–3, 166–74, 214–20, 309–10; Villaverde argues that Roman power continued to extend into central Morocco into the seventh century, but here he does not convince.

a hundred fifth- and sixth-century dated tombstones surviving from there, recording people with Roman or part-Roman names (Iulius Leontius in 542 but also Aurelius Tifzalis in 450) in a duonominal system; the numbers only begin to fall off after 560, and continue to 599.[79] These inscriptions are paralleled by a smaller number in nearby Pomaria (Tlemcen), which go up to 589; Pomaria was still a political centre, with a mint, as late as 813.[80] Volubilis in modern central Morocco is a third example, and the best studied. It was in the part of Tingitana abandoned by the Romans in the third century, but it continued to be occupied in some form for another half-millennium and more. African Red Slip is found there at least into the late fifth century (unlike in Volubilis's rural hinterland, where, as in the Tripolitanian semi-desert, it stopped as soon as Roman rule did). At the end of the sixth it too picked up the memorial habit, probably from Altava; four tombstones survive from the period 599–655 for people with Roman names (all had Iulius as a *gens* name, as often at Altava too; one woman explicitly came from Altava), two with titles, a *princeps* and a *viceprepositus*. These were found in a necropolis which continued to the eighth century, when we know that Volubilis was the centre of a Berber kingdom; a late eighth-century bath-house has been found as well, with other eighth-century buildings, and, near the city, a seventh-century monumental tomb. Both urban continuity in an economic sense (at least on a small scale) and a continuous political centrality is likely at Volubilis, up to the very end of the eighth century, when its rulers moved to Fès, and the site remained occupied thereafter as well.[81] All three of these former Roman cities kept their roles as the foci for Berber political power, for centuries after the end of imperial government in the sub-region, as the African equivalents of Wroxeter and Canterbury (and, at least as it seems at present, rather more impressive ones). Tribalization did not necessarily mean the rejection of Roman imagery, whatever else it meant.

Mauretanian social development resembles Britain more than it does Tripolitania, in that it was internally driven, and on one level it is easier to understand than the British case. Non-Roman traditions were closer to the centre of political life in Mauretania than in Britain in the fourth century, and were thus more easily available when the state failed. It is very likely that the pre-existence of powerful families such as that of Nubel made the

---

[79] *Les inscriptions d'Altava*, n. 194, for Masuna (cf. Camps, '*Rex gentium*'), nn. 111–224 for the full sequence (cited are nn. 209, 166); Prokopios, *Wars*, III.25.3–9, IV.6.10–14.

[80] *Corpus inscriptionum latinarum*, VIII, nn. 21782–92 for Pomaria, with García-Arenal and Manzano Moreno, 'Idrīssisme', pp. 27–8, for the mint; cf. Courtois, *Les Vandales*, pp. 329–30, for other cities.

[81] See esp. *Inscriptions antiques du Maroc*, II, nn. 506, 603, 608, 619; Euzennat, 'Les édifices de culte'; Camps, 'Le Gour'; Lenoir, 'Les fossiles directeurs', pp. 240–1 (no rural ARS); Villaverde, *Tingitana*, pp. 433–7 (urban ceramic imports); El Khayeri, 'Les thermes'; Akerraz, 'Les rapports'; Akerraz, 'Recherches'. See www.sitedevolubilis.org, and Elizabeth Fentress (pers. comm.), for the excavations of 2001 onwards.

re-establishment of tribal structures on Roman-style estates rather easier in the fifth century, as the different areas of Mauretania dropped out of the state system: 'the tribal milieu generates tribes', as Miquel Barceló put it for Spain (above, p. 230). Conversely, the acceptability of Roman aspects to political power that is clear for the Nubel family seems to have continued, with some recognition of Roman ceremonial hegemony, with city bases for political power, and with a long-term respect for elements of local Roman cultural identity, presumably alongside the tribal solidarity (what Ibn Khaldūn called *'aṣabiyya*) which is well attested in later centuries.[82] What we cannot yet tell is what effect this relative de-Romanization had on local political and economic structures in our period. We could at least doubt that Mauretania experienced the extreme political fragmentation that we have seen in lowland Britain; its closest British analogues would be with more traditional highland Wales, Gwynedd and Dyfed, rather than with Chertsey—lowland Britain's crisis was so great because it had committed itself so *fully* to the Roman world-system, not because it was not Roman enough. The Berber kingdoms did, nonetheless, see some economic involution. It is significant that imported pottery dries up both in Tripolitania and in Tingitana in the post-Roman period, except in political centres, where it may have become a prestige item (as it did in the late fifth century on the Welsh and Cornish coast); it is thus likely that market exchange was rather weaker by now, and this has implications for the wealth of Berber leaders. How large any autonomous polity could be if economic infrastructures were simplifying in this way is an issue for future research; all the same, I am inclined to think that Gabriel Camps's arguments that Berber kingdoms could cover whole Roman provinces is considerably over-optimistic (even if not as over-optimistic as the parallel arguments in Britain for figures like Vortigern). Without developed political and economic infrastructures, the maintenance of power at a sub-regional level would have been hard. The smaller tribal groupings hypothesized by Christian Courtois make more sense; some of them may have been, in effect, city states, some more rural, but Mauretania could easily have seen a substantial number of them.[83] The smallest might have been something like the size of Gwynedd, perhaps; but there is space in Mauretania for a dozen of them even if they were all as large as Wales.

These two examples, the British and the Berber North African, show different sorts of reaction to the break-up of Roman political power, which relate closely to the differences in local late Roman social structures. Roman-style political structures collapsed in both, even if (different) elements of Roman

---

[82] Ibn Khaldūn, *Muqaddimah*, e.g. I, pp. 261–78. Cf. Guichard, *Structures sociales*, pp. 66–70, 185–9.

[83] Camps, '*Rex gentium*'; Courtois, *Les Vandales*, pp. 333–9. Modéran, *Les Maures*, pp. 315–415, is with Courtois here, although he is also very critical of the latter.

culture remained in both; in Britain, however, exchange structures collapsed everywhere too, perhaps (although we cannot be sure here) to a greater extent than in the Berber lands; so did the scale of political action, probably much more than in Africa. In Britain, Roman concepts of property-owning disappeared as well; this we cannot say for Africa, though it is entirely conceivable. Overall, however, the similarities between the two are greater than their differences, and they distinguish both regions from (most of) Gaul, (most of) Spain, Italy, or indeed the African heartland of Proconsularis and Byzacena, modern Tunisia, where Roman traditions remained much more substantial at all these levels. They point up the fact that the survival of aristocracies and of sub-regional exchange networks was not inevitable in the post-Roman centuries; the radical de-Romanization of Britain was extreme, but not unparalleled. It must be added that something similar occurred in the post-Roman Balkans, although that region is not analysed in this book.[84]

Other, smaller, areas may well have undergone the same experience as well. One is eastern Brittany, in the early ninth century an area of strong local communities (*plebes*), with hegemonic leaders (*machtierns*) who did not control their communities tenurially: these chieftains could be seen as having a tribal relationship to their *plebes*, although, here, Roman concepts of property-ownership survived at the level of the peasantry, as another protection against the power of local leaders.[85] In Spain, too, there seems to have been more than one area which moved towards tribal relationships, whether in the fifth century or the eighth: the northern mountains, including parts of the Asturias, next door to the partially autonomous Basque lands; the south-eastern mountains and coasts, even before Berber immigration; and finally parts of the high plains of the northern Meseta. The evidence for this was briefly discussed earlier (pp. 227–32; see also below, pp. 755–7), but this is the context in which it makes most sense. Some of the Spanish areas may have been more similar to the African pattern, in that tribal relationships may always have been a local alternative to, or have coexisted with, state and estate structures: the northern mountains are arguably an example. The northern Meseta in the eighth century may have been closer to the lowland British case, in that a highland model spread to a formerly urbanized region in a situation of political collapse. In all these Spanish cases, however, landowning aristocracies had to reassert themselves, with difficulty, and not before the tenth century.

[84] See in general Curta, *The making of the Slavs*, pp. 311–34. For the Croatian lands, recent and linguistically accessible (to me) surveys are Ančić, 'I territori sud-orientali'; Milošević, 'Influenze carolingie'.

[85] Davies, *Small worlds*. Eastern Brittany had been part of the urban-focused network of late Roman Gaul: Pietri and Biarne, *Topographie chrétienne*, V. pp. 57–66, 95–100. In the sixth or seventh century, Roman-style property law is assumed in the *Canones Wallici*, cc. 25, 43, 49; the text is ascribed to Brittany by Bieler, 'Towards an interpretation'.

The experience of de-Romanization and tribalization was different in each of these examples.[86] But they do have one basic feature in common: that of an acute political and/or economic crisis, in a sub-region which had a geographical and thus perhaps a cultural connection to areas of relatively traditional social structures—Gwynedd with respect to lowland Britain, the Kabylie for Mauretania Caesariensis, the Basque lands for the Asturias and the Meseta. I would tentatively argue that the crisis in itself would not have been, in any of these cases, sufficient to generate a tribal society; in each case the nearby tribal or quasi-tribal model was necessary as well. This would be hard to prove beyond doubt.[87] But two aspects of the process are relatively clear across these examples, and deserve stress: that the development of tribal structures could occur in parts of the Roman empire which look quite 'normal' in the fourth century; and that this process could occur without any invasion from outside. This was certainly so in pre-Anglo-Saxon lowland Britain, and even (at least the second aspect) in Berber Africa. So, in Spain, it is not necessary to postulate that the whole of the northern mountains had *always* been tribal in order to explain its particular development in the eighth century, or that south-eastern Spain had been *settled* by tribal groups as an explanation for its particular development in the ninth. Internal crisis could newly generate tribal society, if the circumstances were right. If other tribal groups subsequently settled in such areas, as in Anglo-Saxonized lowland Britain, or Berberized south-eastern Spain, local culture would change, of course; but the main structural shift had already taken place.

2. From tribal to aristocratic societies

This section has as its theme the linked processes of state-formation and the creation of aristocratic landed power. In it, we shall look at four culture areas separately, the English kingdoms, the Welsh kingdoms, Ireland, and Denmark, before moving to generalization. England will again be discussed in most detail, simply because it is the best-documented of the four, with a

---

[86] A less likely example is Bavaria: an area of considerable dislocation in the late Roman period, it is true, as Eugippius, *Vita Severini* makes depressingly clear, but one in which—as the same text shows—Roman cities, landowning, and even armies survived into the late fifth century at least; in the eighth century, too, documents show sharp property-based hierarchies of a Frankish or Italian type (as in *Die Traditionen des Hochstifts Freising*). See among many Störmer, *Früher Adel*, pp. 44–50, 118–56; Pearson, *Conflicting loyalties*, pp. 20–1, 75–110.

[87] Not least because small-scale traditional communities could be found all over the Roman world, in marginal areas, as with the *gualdi* of Appennine Italy, whose tenurial patterns had arguably never been governed by Roman law (Wickham, *Società degli Appennini*, pp. 18–44; idem, *Land and power*, pp. 156–68). How much impact such areas had on their neighbours would depend on how large they were, how solid and how ecologically constrained their social structures were, and how much crisis their neighbours experienced.

relatively wide range of types of evidence: archaeology, land documents, and normative texts (narratives, poetic texts, and laws)—Wales has all three, but less of them; Ireland has above all the third; Denmark exclusively the first. To an extent, indeed, England provides the basic model for the social changes described here. But it is not a guide for understanding the other three, for in crucial respects English developments were quite unlike those elsewhere. Indeed, in Ireland and to an extent in Wales state-formation and aristocratic tenurial control did not develop; my task here is to explain not only change but also its absence. As elsewhere in this book, the differences between regions are as illuminating as their similarities.

The lowland British political crisis was a fifth-century development; after 550 or so, in the Anglo-Saxon lands, it began to be reversed. This reversal, a reconstruction of political power, was much slower than the crisis (it took at least three centuries), but is at least better documented. At the royal level, this recomposition was quite far advanced by the eighth century; at the level of land tenure it was rather slower, and indeed I could defend using eighth-century evidence for Anglo-Saxon landholding in the previous section of the chapter, although by 800 patterns of power were beginning to change here too. Changes in material culture, in royal power and political culture, and in land tenure will be discussed separately; they are linked, of course, but they had different rhythms of development. These discussions will be brisker than in the previous section, however, for the evidence is clearer, and less in dispute.

In the archaeological record, a first turning-point in England is the late sixth century. Before then signs of wealth are few, and, as noted above (p. 311), restricted to burials. Archaeologists in recent years have written interestingly about the meaning of the differences in wealth implied by the furnishings of individual burials inside cemeteries. A significant strand of interpretation links the practice of furnished burial itself to the competition for status inside communities. This theory, influenced by Marcel Mauss's analysis of the *potlatch*, the public destruction of objects to gain social status in nineteenth-century Pacific Canada, argues that the moment of furnished burial was a similar public display of the disposal (into the ground) of valuable possessions. The corollary would be that the communities practising it had unstable hierarchies, negotiable through (among other things) local displays of wealth, based therefore on temporary distinctions of rank rather than permanent social status. This is an attractive model, even though it may be too schematic as an automatic a priori interpretation; in particular, burial communities were almost always spatially restricted face-to-face groups, and uncertainties of ranking in such local contexts do not tell us anything directly about whether larger-scale status differences existed. In the Anglo-Saxon lands, all the same, the hypothesis that the differences in wealth visible in burial communities did not necessarily represent stable differences in wealth and power at least fits the absence of social differentiation in sixth-century settlements (below, pp. 502–4).[88] We can see changes in burial practice, too. In the early sixth century the differences in wealth in cemeteries were not very great as yet; in the later sixth there was a clear tendency towards greater funerary display for a minority, with some burials marked out by, for example, being put in barrows. After 600 really rich burials begin to appear, Sutton Hoo and now Prittlewell in Essex above all, and these were often separated from more ordinary cemeteries, which by contrast, across the seventh century, the so-called 'final phase' of furnished burial, show steadily fewer objects associated with burials. It is arguable that by now some serious and permanent status differences were being represented by rich burials; conversely, local communities, which had given up competitive burial furnishing, may have recognized that status was less negotiable at the local level too.[89]

This argument thus allows us to propose that by 600 status difference was stabilizing at all social levels in England. Settlement archaeology fits this as well; seventh-century settlements were beginning to be more structured than those of the sixth, and a few, notably Cowdery's Down in Hampshire, show greater differentiation in their building types after 600, with large wooden halls and internal enclosures—at Cowdery's Down there seems to have been a local elite group living on site, spatially marked.[90] The elaborate network of halls and the unique theatre-like structure at the royal centre of Yeavering (above, p. 320) come from the same period. These sites are at least architecturally ambitious. In the later seventh century this ambition could increase, with the newly introduced Christian church importing construction in brick and stone from the Continent; some churches were genuinely wealthy, on a level otherwise only linked with kings, judging by the extent of Benedict Biscop's buying for Monkwearmouth of books, silks, and wall-decorations in the 670s, as described by Bede. Archaeologists are beginning to find rich sites in eastern England which partially match this wealth, such as Flixborough near the Humber, beginning in the late seventh century and flourishing in the eighth, which is associated with imported ceramics, good-quality ironwork, lead, glass, craft tools, and varied food residues—we can easily accept Chris Loveluck's assessment of this site as an estate-centre, probably for a monastery, as long as we are cautious about the word 'estate', and Flixborough is only the best example of an increasing range of such sites.[91]

[88] Mauss, *The gift*, pp. 33–46. See, for the theory, Halsall, *Early medieval cemeteries*, pp. 66–8 (and his Frankish monograph, *Settlement*, pp. 251–61); Arnold, 'Wealth and social structure', among others.

[89] For basic surveys, see Arnold, 'Territories'; idem, *An archaeology*, pp. 176–218; Scull, 'Before Sutton Hoo'; idem, 'Archaeology, early Anglo-Saxon society'; Hamerow, 'The earliest Anglo-Saxon kingdoms'. For the final phase, Boddington, 'Models of burial'; Geake, 'Burial practice'.

[90] Millett and James, 'Cowdery's Down', pp. 215–17, 247–50.

[91] Bede, *Historia abbatum*, cc. 5–9; Loveluck, 'Flixborough' (pp. 158–60 for the nature of the site). See for a context Richards, 'What's so special about "productive sites"?'.

After 700 or so we find several coastal *emporia* for channelling imports, York or Ipswich or London or Hamwic (below, pp. 681–8). The Anglo-Saxon economy was by now much more articulated, at all levels.

These are considerable material changes (nor are they unique in the North, as we shall see later for Denmark: pp. 367–71). If 550/600 might be seen as a rough date for the stabilization of status, it is not until after 700 that substantial accumulations of wealth are visible. Thereafter, we also find sub-regional distinctions, with a much greater exchange complexity in eastern England (especially in East Anglia), a more politically controlled structure of imports in the south, Kent or Wessex, and, although there is much less evidence of exchange in the Midlands, the Mercian heartland, the latter area does provide material signs of political dominance, such as the defences of some proto-urban centres and, of course, Offa's Dyke.[92] These developments and differences will be explored in greater detail in Chapter 11 (pp. 805–14); they must, though, all be seen, in their different ways, as signs of an increasing ability of elites to control resources.

We thus do not need written sources to allow us to argue that both political power and elite wealth were increasing in England between 550/600 and 800. Written sources both put these changes into a wider context and are contextualized by them in their turn. Bede's *Historia ecclesiastica*, our major narrative source, does not discuss in detail the period before the 590s, the decade when missionaries first came to England from the Continent, and it is fullest for the seventh century. Before Bede, we have to use the royal genealogies and chronicle entries of the eighth and ninth centuries, which indeed record events assigned to the fifth; but three decades of critical study have radically undermined the plausibility of their early elements, and the most commonly accepted starting-date for relatively credible material in them is some time in the mid- to late sixth century as well. This date was argued on criteria internal to the texts themselves by writers such as Nicholas Brooks, David Dumville, and Barbara Yorke, but it clearly fits the archaeological date for the stabilization of social status around 550/600, even if the archaeology tells us more about village elites, whereas the written sources are referring to kings.[93] We can reasonably suppose that what we find in the late sixth-century sections of written sources is the immediate ancestry of the kings of the one- or two-county kingdoms of the Bedan narrative. If we accept, however, that the earliest Anglo-Saxon polities were generally very small, much smaller than even single counties, indeed around the 100–300 hide mark (30–120 km²), as was argued earlier (p. 325), then we can conclude two things. First, the movement between that level and the

---

[92] Biddle, 'Towns', pp. 120–2; Hill, 'Offa's Dyke', for the most recent overview; see Squatriti, 'Digging ditches', for international parallels.
[93] Brooks, 'Kingdom of Kent'; idem, 'Mercian kingdom'; Dumville, 'Kingship', pp. 91–3; Yorke, *Kings and kingdoms*, pp. 4, 46, 61, 102, etc.

one- or two-county level was in many parts of England a relatively quick process, taking only a couple of generations in the late sixth century and very early seventh. Indeed, the fathers of the first Bedan kings of East Anglia and Wessex in the 610s may only have been kings of tiny political units, who were only then beginning to conquer and absorb their neighbours; and their fathers in turn were hardly remembered at all, with political action earlier than that having to be reinvented in later centuries. Secondly, that the bounce forwards to county- and two-county-size kingdoms coincided with the crystallization of social status at the local level, with, probably, the two processes reinforcing each other.[94]

The seventh century itself is dominated by Bede's history. The faith of many historians in the reliability and importance of every line of Bede's account (whole political narratives have hung on where the full-stop is put in a Bedan sentence) often seems excessive, given the degree to which he manipulated known sources such as the *Vita Wilfridi*; all the same, his image of how kingship and aristocratic power worked seems plausible, at least for the 720s–730s, when he wrote.[95] This is the well-known image of an England of five to ten principal kings, each always aiming at ever wider but always temporary military hegemonies—Bede was unenthusiastic about unwarlike kings, in fact, even if their policies had Christian motivations. Bede's picture is also highly aristocratic: it is kings and their *duces*, *fideles*, *milites*, or *viri nobilissimi* who fight the wars that are the main secular political activities in his narrative. In the famous story of Imma, a Northumbrian *miles* who tried to escape from the battle of Trent in 678 by claiming to be a *rusticus*, Imma was recognized as a *nobilis*, not a *pauper*, 'by his face and dress and speech', and was enslaved as a result: whether these are the criteria of the 670s, or Bede's assumptions fifty years later, the story shows that real social and cultural differences existed by then between aristocrats and peasants.[96] This aristocratic society is also the world of *Beowulf* and other, more fragmentary, poetic texts, whatever date one puts on them, and is further assumed by seventh-century laws, as with the *eorl* of Æthelbert's Kentish laws of c.600 or soon after, already cited (p. 323), the *gesithcundman* or *gesith* (Wihtred of Kent in 695, Ine of Wessex in c.690), or, in Ine again and Alfred later, the 'twelve-hundred [shillings of wergild] man' and 'six-hundred man', as opposed to the 'two-hundred man' who is in Alfred a *ceorl*, a free peasant. Kings still ruled administratively simple polities, with relatively few official subordinates (above, p. 314), but they were the centres of networks of aristocratic dependence, linked outwards

---

[94] The best document-based overviews of this are Bassett, 'In search of the origins'; Blair, *Anglo-Saxon Oxfordshire*, pp. 29–52.

[95] For the full-stop, Prestwich, 'King Æthelhere'; for the *Vita Wilfridi*, e.g. Wallace-Hadrill, *Bede's Ecclesiastical history*, pp. 191–4 (a book which in itself testifies to the continuing authority of every detail of Bede's prose).

[96] Bede, *HE*, IV.22. See above, n. 52.

and downwards, through more than one level of lordship sometimes, to the peasantry.[97]

This Bedan pattern is at least internally consistent; but it can now, and must, be viewed through the archaeology-based awareness that it was not very old. On the tenurially inchoate land units of the fifth and sixth centuries there were doubtless always some status differentiations; the ancestors of Bede's aristocrats would often already have been the privileged retainers of small-scale kings, with inherited status, and some would have been those kings themselves. But these differentiations had had to be established against a background of a relative lack of economic distinction between aristocrats and peasants, and before 600 still had to be negotiated and fought for; only after that date could they be taken for granted, and, indeed, as we have seen, the seventh century is still a period of relatively flat economic hierarchies in the archaeological record.

In the eighth century the most important kings claimed more powers. We can see this most clearly in Mercian charters, at least after Bede's death in 735. These show that Mercian kings for a century (c.725–825) controlled, in one way or another, most of southern England. Sometimes this was through a vague military hegemony of a seventh-century type (as with Wessex), sometimes through conquest and violent dispossession (as with Kent), sometimes through the simple absorption of kingdoms which had hitherto been dependent directly into the Mercian kingdom (as with Sussex and the Hwicce, whose *reges* became *reguli* or *subreguli*, and then *duces*). These processes were not unilinear. Kent often revolted; and, although Æthelbald of Mercia (716–57) could in 737/40 call Osred of the Hwicce 'my very faithful retainer (*minister*) who is from the not ignoble lineage, the royal stock of the people of the Hwicce', he was a little premature, for Osred's family were at least *subreguli* for another generation. All the same, the general direction is clear. Æthelbald, Offa (757–96), and Cenwulf (796–821) furthermore controlled many rights that had not been given much stress in previous generations: tolls at major ports, especially London; and an increasingly articulated set of rights of hospitality, which churches often had to buy exemption from—by the early ninth century they included feeding not only kings and *principes*, but, even in the absence of rulers, their falconers, hunters, ostlers, heralds, and other *iuniores* or *fæstincmenn*. They also controlled, at least de facto, a complex sequence of church councils, which heard court-cases, and made legislation on occasion; and, of course, they developed the logistical infrastructure that could send workmen to barren hill-country to build over 100 km of dyke along the Welsh border.[98]

---

[97] Æthelberht 13; Wihtred 5; Ine 6, 30, 34.1, 45, 50, 51, 63, 68, 70; Alfred 10, 26–8, 39, 40; cf. Loyn, 'Gesiths', pp. 529–40. For *Beowulf* see Wormald, 'Bede, "Beowulf" '. It is not clear, however, who would have had the authority to collect Ine's food-rents on any regular basis.

[98] The basic surveys are still Stenton, 'Supremacy'; idem, *Anglo-Saxon England*, pp. 201–36; Wormald, 'Offa and Alcuin'. For Osred, *BCS* 165 (S 99). For London, Kelly, 'Trading privil-

These powers represent most of the elements of the ideal type of the state, as characterized at the start of this chapter; the only element that was not yet fully present was exclusive land tenure, which we shall return to in a moment. By 800 the nature of political power had fundamentally changed, and the initial state-building process in England can be regarded as largely completed.

From the late sixth century to the late eighth in England, we are looking at a consistent sequence of political accumulation. Generation after generation, it was possible for rulers to absorb their neighbours, and then, if they were successful, to build on that and absorb new neighbours at a later date. The slow tendency for numbers of kingdoms to get smaller, and kingdoms to get larger, with former rulers (if they survived) turning into aristocrats and royal retainers, has been known as the 'FA Cup model' since Steven Bassett's seminal account of it fifteen years ago.[99] Sub-kingdoms did move about: the upper Thames was West Saxon before it was Mercian, Kent was Mercian before it was West Saxon. And there were certainly glitches; Offa had to rebuild some of Æthelbald's hegemony after a brief civil war; Cenwulf had similar difficulties; after Cenwulf's death, his successors had notably narrower hegemonies. But the edifice constructed in one generation did not for the most part break down in the next. It was another large kingdom, Wessex, not the building-blocks of Mercia, which benefited from the ninth-century weakening of Mercian power. Even civil wars, common in the eighth century, can be seen as significant. The three or four major families who fought over Northumbria in the period, the four in Mercia, the two or more in Wessex, are signs of the *success* of each kingdom, for such families (often probably the descendants of the rulers of former independent polities) could, one might have thought, have gone for independence as easily as for wider rule. (Only the Kentish royal family did that, doggedly, for over a generation after Offa's conquest in c.764.)[100]

To English eyes, this process has often seemed inevitable, desirable, and therefore logical and not needing explanation. As we shall see when looking at Wales and Ireland, however, such a steady process of the expansion of the scale of political power is not a necessary consequence of royal ambition at all, so it needs more analysis. State-building in northern Europe seems to me to be linked to four main variables: one external, the influence of outside

---

eges'. For hospitality, see e.g. *BCS* 848, 443, 450, 454 (S 134, 1271, 198, 197); cf. Chadwick, *Studies*, pp. 100–2. Nobles had always, of course, owed hospitality to kings and their entourages (e.g. Stephanus, *Vita Wilfridi*, c. 2; cf. above, pp. 320–1); but these sorts of text remit a substantially extended range of obligations. For church councils, see Cubitt, *Anglo-Saxon church councils*; on pp. 49–59 she points out that royal control was less overt in England than in Spain or Francia. See n. 92 for the dyke.

[99] Bassett, 'In search of the origins', pp. 26–7.

[100] Civil wars: Wormald, 'Offa and Alcuin', pp. 114–16. Kent: Brooks, *Early history*, pp. 111–25; Keynes, 'Kent'.

political structures that is to say; and three internal, the tightness of the links between kings and aristocrats, the growth of economic differentiation, and the establishment of aristocratic landed power. Economic differentiation has already been sketched out (and will be discussed in more detail in Chapter 11); here, let us look at the other three in turn.

Too much has often been made of the impact of the conversion to Christianity on the Anglo-Saxons—or, later, of Bede's commitment to what seems to be a common language-based English identity; but conversion was the instrument for the introduction of important external influences into England. One was the creation of an England-wide organizational template for the church, the hierarchy of bishops and archbishops, which was imposed from outside, and already by the 670s was associated with common ecclesiastical decision-making, well outside the boundaries of individual kingdoms: this could be, and was, a useful support for any ambitious king. Each bishop also soon picked up a sizeable portion of local power, in the form of the large-scale cessions of land by kings, as already discussed. But bishops in Anglo-Saxon England rarely had the political space as independent protagonists that bishops in Francia had; unlike on the Continent, where bishops pre-existed Romano-Germanic kings, their local power was a royal creation. Bishops cannot be seen going for local autonomy (if, at any rate, we except some of the archbishops of Canterbury in the years of Mercian rule in Kent, whose actions fitted in with a wider Kentish resistance), and indeed could have been seen as standing in the way of any lay attempts at autonomy.[101] Overall, again unlike in Francia, the episcopal network in England tended to be an instrument of royal authority rather than of independent power. It was, indeed, kings rather than bishops who imitated Frankish political practice, in the wake of the conversion process. Legislation, trade tolls, even royal legitimation when Offa had his son Ecgfrith anointed in 787, were all borrowed from the Franks. Nor is this surprising: Charlemagne's realm was ten times the size of Offa's; Chlotar II's had been fifty times that of Æthelberht of Kent. What ambitious king would not do his best to copy the building-blocks of Frankish royal power? In the tenth century they copied Carolingian models so well that they could keep England united when Francia itself was collapsing.[102]

The bond between king and aristocrats is attested in a wide range of sources. We can see it in the *Anglo-Saxon Chronicle* entry for 755 (*recte* 757), in which two rival groups of loyal retainers separately fought to the death around their royal lords. It is equally clear in *Beowulf*, where good aristocrats are absolutely loyal, and failures in the tight link between a king

---

[101] For Canterbury, Brooks, *Early history*, pp. 111–42. Wilfrid was the other exception as a 'political' bishop, presumably following his experience in Gaul, and he was arguably a failure because of it.

[102] Campbell, *Essays*, pp. 53–67, 155–70, for Frankish influence; for Ecgfrith, *Anglo-Saxon Chronicle*, s.a. 785.

and his entourage (as in the Heremod episode, and in the dragon-fighting sequence) are depicted in the most chilling terms.[103] Not that aristocrats were really always loyal; in the seventh century they changed sides with ease if a rival king was more successful; Bede could imagine in his letter to Ecgbert that *milites* whose king had run out of land would logically leave the kingdom.[104] But unconditional loyalty was normative, however common it was to change sides; and disloyalty was generally associated with seeking alternative lordship, not with going it alone as a local lord, unlike the situation in Wales and Ireland, as we shall see. In England, but not in its western neighbours, the force of the old tribal relationship that must have kept small-scale kingdoms together everywhere in the early sixth century did not work against kings as kingdoms increased in size and face-to-face familiarities became less intense. It seems to me that this is most likely to be because, as kingdoms expanded, aristocratic power itself became more locally stable and politically secure. Aristocratic land tenure was beginning slowly to crystallize: this was only incipient in the eighth century, as we shall see in a moment, but its possibilities were doubtless already visible, and in the ninth century were beginning to be realized. This might not have been taken for granted if Mercia, say, had fallen back into its tribal constituent parts after its kings lost hegemony in the 820s. The slow growth of state power was a joint project in England, with kings and aristocrats linked in the search for mutual advantage. Nor did this change: the West Saxon conquest of eastern England in the tenth century was a similar joint project, an experiment almost in oligarchic rule as it sometimes seemed.[105]

Closely linked to this, then, is the question of changes in land tenure in England. The haziness of English (and also Welsh) land tenure around 700 has already been discussed at length (pp. 314–30); it was argued there that the concept of exclusive property rights, the ownership of estates, was not yet available in Britain, despite the Roman-law terminology of charters, and that the land-units of our documents could contain within them complex social hierarchies, from aristocrats to the unfree. Rosamond Faith has argued that the latter, on 'inland', owed rather higher dues, and already in Ine's laws some free men could pay rent for tenures as well, but as yet only a minority of land in any unit was organized in this way (above, p. 323); other inhabitants on the land owed dues to superiors without necessarily

---

[103] *Anglo-Saxon Chronicle*, s.a. 755 (but really datable to 786; the best analysis is White, 'Kinship and lordship'). *Beowulf*, ll. 1709–24, 2596–601, 2845–91. *Beowulf*'s date is highly controversial; recently, Lapidge, 'The archetype of *Beowulf*', argues for a version of the text in existence by the early eighth century, which I am happy to accept.

[104] Bede, *Epistola*, c. 11. Narratives of every kind contain references to *exules*, exiles, in fact, although many of these were loyal, to losing sides: see e.g. Bede, *HE*, IV.15, 23; Stephanus, *Vita Wilfridi*, c. 33; *Vita Guthlaci*, cc. 40, 42; *The Wanderer*; cf. perhaps Ine 63–6. Cf. the exile imagery in Ireland: Charles-Edwards, 'The social background'.

[105] See e.g. Williams, '*Princeps Merciorum gentis*'.

recognizing that the latter had ownership rights there, and these dues were still generally low.

The content of tenure steadily changed across time; England did, of course, eventually develop exclusively owned estates. We cannot easily tell when or how, unfortunately, precisely because property formulae in our documents assume that development from the start; all we can do is look for inconsistencies, or track the implications of new patterns. One of the latter is the grant of special types of land, the tenure of which is likely always to have been less complex, and the control of whose productive processes rather more complete: for example, salt-making areas (documented at Droitwich in Worcestershire from 716, and on the Kentish coast from 732), and urban property (documented in Canterbury from 762).[106] Another is the development of leasing: the new ecclesiastical holders of land-units began to cede them to the laity, for between one and four lifetimes. This process seems to have initially been part of aristocratic-level political relationships, and rents were generally not required until around 900; when rents did appear in such cessions, however, one of the basic principles of exclusive land tenure had begun to be accepted. (A rare early exception is the life grant in c.814 by the church of Worcester of 2 hides of land at Harvington to Eanswith, in return for her washing and mending the church's clothing—*ut semper illius aecclesiae indumentum innovet et mundet et augeat*—though 2 hides seems a lot for laundry service, and there may have been some other relationship involved.)[107] A third development is the beginning of land accumulation by acquisition, first visible in the land transactions of Archbishop Wulfred of Canterbury (805–32), a few of which were the sort of small-scale acquisitions that Continental land tenure normally assumed, but which were a novelty in England.[108] They are only visible in Kent as yet, and are probably a marker of the relative economic complexity of eastern England. A fourth is the sharpening in some royal grants of the difference between which dues were ceded and which were retained by the king, which begins under Offa, and which implies both that the grantee was getting rather more from the inhabitants of the unit than he was still giving to the king, and that these differences mattered more—both of which argue for an increase in the renders that local inhabitants were paying.[109]

The ninth century is the main period for these shifts. This is a period of growing archaeological evidence for concentrations of lay aristocratic wealth, in sites like Raunds in Northamptonshire and Goltho in Lincolnshire;

---

[106] *BCS* 137, 138, 148 (S 102, 97, 23), for salt; 192–3, 196, 242, for Canterbury and Rochester (S 1182, 32, 34, 266).

[107] *BCS* 307 (S 1261); the first rents for leases I have seen are in 492 (S 208, a. 857, a London charter, so perhaps atypical), and 617 (*Anglo-Saxon charters*, n. 15; S 1287), for 879/908.

[108] *BCS* 335, 344, and cf. the fluidity of transaction in 332 (S 168, 176, 1264); see Brooks, *Early history*, pp. 137–41.

[109] See above, n. 47.

surplus extraction was becoming more complex, heavier, and indeed more marketable.[110] As we shall see in Chapter 11 (pp. 808–13), it is arguable that market relations themselves are a guide to the intensity of aristocratic control; if so, it began in East Anglia and elsewhere on the east coast in the eighth century, and became generalized across England in the late ninth. This probably links to the tendency for land-units to become smaller in the ninth century and after, as cessions of land to aristocrats were for single village territories, not the big blocks of the past, and control over these may well have been tighter. 'Inland' exploitation itself could have become more intense, as well as more widespread; by 900 the chance survival of an estate description from Hurstborne Priors in Hampshire shows us a notable level of organization, with *ceorlas* owing substantial rents, and also labour service: the first unequivocal evidence we have from England of a 'manorial' demesne paralleling those in Francia and Italy discussed in Chapter 5. Such manorial patterns are steadily better documented thereafter, and are prominent in 1086 in *Domesday Book*.[111]

These changes, it must be stressed, were of two types. On the one hand, the dues and obligations owed by some or all dependent landholders, free as well as unfree, became heavier and more systematic; on the other, it seems that the concept of exclusive ownership slowly began to be accepted more widely. These are not identical; it would be perfectly possible for a lord to impose the idea of ownership on a land-unit without increasing the dues extracted from it, or indeed vice versa. The development of the one would all the same have helped the development of the other, and the two processes probably went in parallel. Faith thinks that the steady expansion of 'inland' areas of tighter control was very slow indeed, far from complete at the time of *Domesday Book*; Hurstborne would on that reading be a guide only to restricted percentages of the country in 900. Her minimalist reading of the *Domesday* figures can be questioned, and, overall, I am inclined to regard the tenth century as the other side of the line from the eighth and early ninth in terms of the weight of rents from most of the estates in most of the country; by the tenth century, indeed, it seems to me legitimate to use the word 'estate', and to think in terms of exclusive ownership, in most of

---

110 Cadman and Foard, 'Raunds'; Cadman, 'Raunds'; Beresford, *Goltho*, pp. 29–60.

111 For Hurstborne Priors, see *Anglo-Saxon charters*, n. 110 (S 359); for commentary, see Finberg, *Lucerna*, pp. 131–43, and in general Faith, *English peasantry*, pp. 56–88; other major later texts are treated in Faith, 'Tidenham', and Harvey, '*Rectitudines*'. Ine 67 must refer to some kind of service when it counterposes *weorc* to *gafol*; if that service was demesne work (a big if), then the earliest sign of the manorial system in England would date to two centuries earlier than the Hurstborne text, and, actually, to earlier than most references in Francia (above, pp. 284–90). But, as I argued there, demesnes could develop separately anywhere if local economic stimuli were sufficient, and this could in principle have occurred even on the tiny 'inlands' of c.700. What these stimuli in the Wessex of that period actually might have been is a more difficult problem. I owe much here to discussion with Steven Bassett and Nicholas Brooks.

England.[112] The tenth century is well outside our period, so the point need not be argued further here. But even if we regard this shift, from land-units to estates, and from 'extensive' lordship to much more oppressive forms of surplus extraction, as being already relatively complete by 900 or so, it still took a century, and perhaps two. 'Manorial' structures such as high rent and labour service crystallized only slowly inside land-units, extending first to the unfree, then to the weaker sections of the free; there were always people who remained outside them, up to *Domesday Book* and indeed beyond.

This slow internal crystallization process must be the major reason why one thing we do not have evidence for in England is peasant resistance. We shall see at least some signs of opposition to aristocratic power in most parts of western Europe, in the eighth and (particularly) the ninth century (below, pp. 576–88). In England, despite the magnitude of this change in peasant autonomy, we do not. But Continental resistance was generally to landlords subjecting or expropriating whole groups of peasants, in relatively swift acts of power. In England the shift was longer-term, and more insidious in that it seems to have concentrated on the weakest, leaving richer peasants (i.e. potential leaders) untouched for a long time. In the end, all the same, the result was striking. In 700, out of all the regions of the former Roman empire studied in this book, England, together with Wales, was the one in which aristocrats (and churches, and kings) had the least control over peasantries. But the land-units in which they exercised their powers were so large that, when in England they managed to turn their 'superiority' into real propri-etorial power, they arguably came to exercise a greater control over peasan-tries than anywhere else. (It needs to be repeated here that an estate consisting of a whole village territory, as was common in England at the time of *Domesday Book*—even though not universal, particularly in the east—is very large by the standards of our other regions, if we set aside exceptions such as the Paris basin.) This was a shift not just in generalized aristocratic hegemony, but in the mode of production itself, as a ranked, peasant-dominated, mode was replaced by the feudal mode, more com-pletely than elsewhere (cf. below, Chapter 9), with a cusp in the ninth century. But the completeness of this shift was masked by its slowness. This does not only explain the lack of resistance; it also explains one notable feature of the late Anglo-Saxon state, its unusually lasting relationship with the military service, and eventually the organized taxation, of the free peasantry—a relationship which in its turn partly explains the durability of state power in England. The strength of the English state thus went hand

[112] For Faith on *Domesday*, see *English peasantry*, pp. 85–8; her decision to exclude *Domes-day's villani* from her 'inland' figures because they were 'a miscellaneous group' effectively means that she treats them as 'outland' dependants, which is equally unsustainable. I am grateful here to discussions with Chris Dyer. See below, p. 813, for one regional difference, the independent peasantry of eastern England. The classic account of this process remains Maitland, *Domesday Book*, pp. 374–97.

in hand with an unusually extensive aristocratic proprietorial dominance, throughout the rest of the middle ages: a paradoxical relationship, but one between two consequences of the same slow development.

The main political power of the end of our period in England, the Mercian hegemony of Offa and Cenwulf, managed to create developed state structures, and a clear concentration of power, without land tenure yet becoming fully exclusive and detribalized. One need not doubt that the power of the Mercian kings, and the West Saxon kings from the 830s onwards, materially helped churches and aristocracies to crystallize their local landowning structures. But it must be recognized that Offa's power was already considerable without that crystallization process yet having fully developed—indeed, the evidence of its early development is least great in his Mercian heartland (below, pp. 813–14). Offa clearly expected at least some dues and services from everybody, some of which were newly exacted. In order to achieve this, however, he must have been able to count on an aristocracy that was both loyal and effective. We could suppose that his success was sufficiently long-term and consistent that aristocrats had an incentive to be loyal to him anyway. It is also probable that, as implied earlier, Offa's aristocracy could already see the tenurial advantages of a stable political system, as 'inlands' began to expand and peasants began to be more subjected, even though the process had only just begun. All the same, we discover from Offa's Mercia that coherent state power can develop in a society when peasant subjection was by no means fully complete. It must have begun, or else Offa and his aristocracy would both have been starved of resources, but it did not have to have got very far.

Wales experienced the beginning of these English developments, but not the end. We have seen that around 600, say, its kingdoms in the mountainous north and west were two-county-size and probably always had been, whereas in the south-east they were much smaller (pp. 326–30). The signs are that the seventh century showed the same sort of process of accumulation that can be seen in England, although a little more slowly. This is particularly evident in the south-east, where a single dynasty, that of Meurig ap Tewdrig, emerged to control the whole of Glywysing, modern Glamorgan and Gwent, by the mid-eighth century; Gwynedd, too, may have expanded into the minor kingdoms at its edges. But political accumulation stopped there. It is true that ninth-century kings of Gwynedd began to claim hegemonies over quite wide areas of Wales, and that tenth- and eleventh-century ones occasionally dominated all or nearly all the sub-region, for brief periods at least; but we see nothing of the internal developments of English kingship. The capillary governmental intervention of an Offa was not established by any Welsh king except over very small areas; nor were his official hierarchies; nor was the stability of his power. The hegemonic rulers of the period after 850 were more like contemporary Irish over-kings, or seventh-century over-kings in England, in that they claimed very little local control in subjected areas, and only lasted until the next successful revolt.[113]

Explanations for this have never been more than inconclusive, for Welsh evidence is not good enough to allow more than speculation. A popular explanation, the common 'Celtic' culture of disunited Wales and Ireland working against the establishment of wide-ranging political power, can be abandoned from the start: common 'Germanic' cultures had widely differing historical experiences, and Wales and Ireland were only superficially similar.[114] A better reason is simple geography: Wales consists of a series of relatively fertile coastal strips of varying depth, and a barren central plateau with few good communications. It is, as is Spain on a rather larger scale, physically difficult to move around in except by sea, and to control in detail; kings could easily find outlying microregions slipping out of their control, and it would be harder to subdue them if they did. One may add to this a difference from England in the way external influences operated in the sub-region. Wales was certainly influenced by the success of the English state by the tenth century, as were the English by the Franks in the eighth, and several royal initiatives by then bear an English stamp. Conversely, however, the English wished to intervene in Wales, unlike the Franks in England (outside Kent, perhaps), and their interventions were as disruptive to Welsh political centralization as their example was helpful.[115] And in Wales the ecclesiastical structure was not an Italian/Frankish import, but an autonomous inheritance from the Roman empire; as a result, it had itself undergone the same sort of radical decentralization that secular power did, with autonomous bishops and monasteries matching, or modelled on, the autonomous kingdoms. Unlike in England, church organization thus added no coherence or scale to secular politics.[116]

Another important reason for the Welsh–English difference in political development is the history of the aristocracy (called *meliores, seniores, principes,* among other terms, in Welsh texts). As noted earlier (p. 328), our Welsh seventh-century documentary material, like that for England, is dominated by kings, with aristocratic gift-giving to the church only appearing in the eighth. It is most likely that aristocratic land (the charters tend to call it *hereditas*) had always existed, but only became alienable after 700 or so; this has parallels to the English situation. But what appears to be the case

---

[113] Davies, *Wales in the early middle ages*, pp. 90–112, 125–40; eadem, *Microcosm*, pp. 65–107 for Gwent; eadem, *Patterns*, esp. pp. 80–91 for the ninth century and after.

[114] Binchy, *Celtic and Anglo-Saxon kingship*, proposed close Welsh and Irish parallels, at least by implication. Davies, *Patterns*, pp. 89–90, and Charles-Edwards, *Kinship*, pp. 1–3, 477, minimize them.

[115] Davies, *Wales in the early middle ages*, pp. 112–20; eadem, *Patterns*, pp. 48–79; after 850 the Vikings were another disruptive element.

[116] Davies, *Wales in the early middle ages*, pp. 141–69.

is that, once such alienation became possible, aristocrats became more autonomous from kings. They dealt directly with the church rather earlier than in England; they seldom asked kings to approve or confirm their grants. Wendy Davies has cautiously detected a breakdown in authority and in traditional peacemaking processes in the ninth to eleventh centuries, which could be linked to that greater aristocratic autonomy.[117] Kings went on claiming hegemonic rights, over steadily wider land-areas in fact, but local aristocracies were less clearly co-opted into that project. As a result, those wider hegemonies had less content than the smaller-scale political centralizations of the seventh century in Wales had had. This is where the divergence from England can be located: in the breakdown of a common project, of both kings and aristocrats, to increase the scale and density of their power together. In eighth-century Wales (as, later, in tenth-century Francia on a rather larger scale), unlike in eighth- or tenth-century England, royal power and aristocratic power began to rival each other rather than being complementary. The further structural development of royal power, full 'state-building', was checked as a result, until as late as the thirteenth century.[118]

This explanation is partly speculative: it fits the evidence as far as it goes, but the evidence is so sparse that it could be interpreted in other ways too. We cannot explore it in detail here, for most of it postdates 800. But some other structural implications are worth pointing out. I argued that the aristocracies of the English kingdoms saw the advantages of royal power increasing, as a framework in which they could increase their own local control, turning autonomous peasants into tenurial dependants, who were more subject to aristocratic political authority, and paid larger proportions of their surplus to lords. Otherwise put, these aristocracies came to prefer the wealth and political hierarchy of a strong kingdom to the tight, small-scale, local bonds, and also the relative economic equalities, of autonomous tribal leadership. If this is right, it would follow that in Wales aristocracies preferred to stay tribal; and that this also means that the aristocratic victory over peasant economic autonomies probably did not occur, or was restricted to the unfree (and perhaps—given the large percentage of legally unfree Welsh—to only a minority even of them). We have little secure evidence about the levels of exploitation in Wales until the thirteenth century (for *Domesday Book*, which covers only frontier areas, see above, p. 329), but it can at least be noted that in archaeological terms Welsh material culture remained fairly simple: there are only a few rich sites before the Norman period, and no traces of artisanal development apart from the high-quality metalwork that had been a sign of aristocratic patronage since the late fifth

---

[117] Davies, *Microcosm*, pp. 105–16; eadem, 'Land and power', pp. 15, 21–3.
[118] 'There were always people with power in early Wales, but no one ever had enough': Davies *Patterns*, p. 91. Wendy Davies in this work, esp. pp. 9–31, 80–91, develops the problem of how power worked in Wales in the eighth to eleventh centuries more densely than anyone else. I attribute less local power to landowners in Wales than she does.

century. Wealth accumulation did not visibly take place. We could conclude that the Welsh remained in a tribal political and economic environment until long after our period ends. Aristocratic autonomy from kings meant that the aristocratic dominance over the peasantry remained incomplete.[119]

I briefly characterized some of the paradoxes of early medieval Ireland in Chapter 2, but they now need to be confronted from closer to. Let us begin with the archaeological evidence, and then compare it with the written sources for the period 650–800, laws and saints' lives above all (though the vernacular prose 'sagas' most likely begin in the eighth century too, and several can at least be ascribed to the ninth).[120]

Irish archaeology for our period is not extensive, but is at least homogeneous. It shows an unusually even and dispersed settlement, based on ringforts (raths), smallish round fortified enclosures, with a few island sites (crannógs) on lakes too. Of the very large numbers of ringforts known for Ireland, up to 60,000, only 200 or so have any excavation, but recent radiocarbon datings from over 100 of them (mostly from Ulster) put the great bulk of these into the early medieval period, after the year 400 in every known case, and it is plausible to suppose that they were the dominant settlement form after that date, into the ninth century without doubt. They seem to have housed kings and peasants alike. The law tracts imply that royal housing was bigger, but this is not so far confirmed archaeologically. Indeed, the internal structure of Irish settlements seems to have been fairly standard: ringforts and crannógs had one or more round-houses in them, mostly made of wattle and planks without roof supports, which were not significantly more elaborate in the highest-status settlements.[121] Archaeologists argue about the percentage of the population that lived in ringforts: these arguments hang on how long the average ringfort was actually occupied, which is difficult to ascertain at present on the basis of the very small number of scientific excavations there have been, but it does seem clear that

---

[119] See, for a survey of the post-eleventh-century period, (R. R.) Davies, *Wales 1063–1415*, pp. 115–38 (with idem, *The first English empire*, pp. 104–6, a succinct set of generalizations covering Ireland and western Scotland too); note that 'freedom' and 'nobility' were synonyms in thirteenth-century Welsh law, without all the 'nobility' being non-peasants or all the unfree being sharply economically subject, which complicates the aristocrat versus peasant pattern that I am discussing here. For a survey of the as yet sparse archaeology of the period 800–1000, see Arnold and (J. L.) Davies, *Roman and early medieval Wales*, pp. 163–97; for richer sites, (W.) Davies, 'Thinking about the Welsh environment', pp. 10–14.

[120] For law, the basic starting-point is Kelly, *Early Irish law*; for saints' lives in this period, Sharpe, *Medieval Irish saints' lives*, who establishes dating criteria.

[121] See in general Stout, *The Irish ringfort* (pp. 21–31 for chronology); Edwards, *The archaeology*, pp. 6–48; for Ulster, the best-studied area, Mallory and McNeill, *The archaeology of Ulster*, pp. 185–204. The most useful single excavations are Hencken, 'Lagore crannog', with Warner, 'The date', for a foundation date in the seventh or eighth centuries; Lynn, 'Deer Park Farms', unfortunately only an interim report. For the size of houses varying by ranking, see *Críth Gablach*, ed. Binchy, cc. 10–45 (tr. MacNeill, cc. 79–133: see below, n. 135). In the west, many ringforts had stone houses; this is the main regional difference.

they were not exclusively aristocratic. It may be that low-status settlement was sometimes extramural, perhaps close by, but it is not possible to be sure of this as yet.[122] Settlements seem, at any rate, to have been small-scale. When monasteries developed in the seventh century and onwards, the largest of them could well have been the largest settlements in Ireland.[123] There was thus no developed settlement hierarchy in our period, although the scale of the earthworks of even the simplest ringfort shows that we are not looking at a society devoid of social organization. Some had several rings, and the *Vita* of Áed mac Bricc of Killare, dating to around 800, refers to an itinerant ringfort-maker who was asked by a rich man (*dives*) to make a *triplex murus* around his *arx*, clearly a significant status-symbol.[124]

As striking as this relative settlement homogeneity is the simplicity of the material culture attached to such sites, some of which are waterlogged, allowing the survival of an unusually wide range of objects. Ireland was a country of wood and iron. Its woodworking was often highly skilled, and iron is found on every site. Leather and cloth were made at a good level of technical skill, too. What is lacking is archaeological evidence of more organized artisanal activity. Ceramics seem only to have been made and distributed in the north-east, the Souterrain ware of the seventh century and later, and were hand-made even there. Nor was there much pottery imported: only the 'E ware' of seventh-century western Gaul is relatively widely found, and not in large quantities. There is some imported glass, some of it reworked on prestige sites like Lagore. Apart from this, the largest-scale high-status artisanal activity was copper-working, some of which was of very high quality. Silver was much rarer before the Viking period, and only half-a-dozen items of gold, mostly tiny, have been found in our period at all. In archaeological terms, it is hard to doubt that copper alloy and glass/enamel were the main markers of wealth. Ireland either could not, or chose not to, import the more expensive status goods that were normal everywhere else (including in Denmark: see pp. 364–71), and hardly

---

[122] Mytum, *The origins*, pp. 131–2, argues that ringforts were only aristocratic, but his arguments are not fully convincing; see Charles-Edwards, *Early Christian Ireland*, p. 151, for a brief critical comment. For open settlements, for which some fairly fragmentary evidence exists, see Edwards, *The archaeology*, pp. 44–7; and above all Williams, 'Ballyutoag'. If this site, of 23 unenclosed houses from the seventh and eighth centuries, had parallels elsewhere, our image of Irish settlement would substantially change; could it have been like the Scottish *vicus* in Adomnán, *Vita S. Columbae*, I.34? But the excavator sees it as an upland pastoral settlement, i.e. atypical ecologically. A tentative trend towards a greater nucleation has been identified as beginning in the ninth century: for a survey, see Fleming, 'Lords and labour', pp. 118–20.

[123] See e.g. Doherty, 'The monastic town'; Graham, 'Early medieval Ireland', pp. 26–38. Their arguments for monastic urbanism seem far too optimistic for this period. Monasteries were sometimes called *civitates* (e.g. Cogitosus, *Vita Brigitae*, c. 32), but so were ringforts (*Vita S. Aidi Killariensis*, c. 13).

[124] *Vita S. Aidi Killariensis*, c. 13, cf. Charles-Edwards, *Early Christian Ireland*, p. 150.

sought even to imitate them.[125] An increasingly wealthy church, with more international links, could by the eighth century commission the Ardagh Chalice and the Tara Brooch (both in silver with some gilding and glass), and sometimes elaborate manuscripts too.[126] But whatever was happening in Ireland, it did not involve much of a concentration of wealth in our period outside ecclesiastical circles, or any complex pattern of exchange; not even many elite imports. One might postulate internal exchange between more agricultural and more pastoral areas, for Ireland is not ecologically homogeneous, but it cannot as yet be shown empirically;[127] craftsmen were sometimes itinerant, moving from patron to patron, but above all working in a dependent, not a market, context. Ireland was by far the archaeologically simplest of our regions (together with Wales), throughout the early medieval period. It is therefore with fascination that one also discovers that it is one of the only two regions in this book (the other is Denmark) whose economy was more *developed* than it had been in the Roman period: before the fifth century there is almost no evidence of settlement, and little enough for artisanal activity, at all.[128]

This simplicity partly fits our written sources, and partly not. In one respect it contrasts markedly with them, in that the apparent absence of gold and silver did not prevent the Irish from expressing the image of wealth in terms of precious metal and jewelled objects throughout our narrative and even legal texts: the Irish clearly valued them, which may imply that their absence was not entirely the result of choice.[129] It is important, however, to recognize that, if there was one universal marker of wealth and status in Ireland, it was cattle, not any artisanal object. Cows (together with slave women) were the standard medium of gift-giving, rent, and tribute, in effect the Irish equivalent of currency, and sufficiently symbolically important that a cattle-raid is the main focus of our principal vernacular narrative, the *Táin Bó Cúailnge*. More generally, nearly all relations of dependence in free society were expressed in cattle, to the exclusion even of land. This focus

---

[125] Good surveys are Edwards, *The archaeology*, pp. 68–98; Mytum, *The origins*, pp. 210–51; Hencken, 'Lagore crannog'. On imports, Wooding, *Communication and commerce*, p. 64–92. Of course, the closest sub-region for imports was Britain, whose own material development was in crisis after 400, as we have seen; all the same, Britain was seen as the natural source of gold in the admittedly fantastic story in *Vita S. Cainnechi*, c. 53. Roman influence on Ireland was never great, either; Laing, 'Romanization', overstates the case.

[126] Edwards, *The archaeology*, pp. 92, 132–71, for church commissions.

[127] For Irish agriculture, see most recently Kelly, *Early Irish farming*; Edwards, *The archaeology*, pp. 49–67; they stress a mixed economy, against earlier emphases on pastoralism (cf. also Wickham, *Land and power*, pp. 137–9). Smyth, *Celtic Leinster*, stresses microregional difference, esp. pp. 21–40, and plates XI–XVI. Mills are first documented archaeologically in the seventh century: see Rynne, 'The introduction', for the most recent overview. Kelly, *Early Irish farming*, p. 319, doubts there was much exchange of foodstuffs.

[128] Raftery, *Pagan Celtic Ireland*.

[129] See e.g. *Táin Bó Cúailnge*, ed. O'Rahilly, ll. 33, 819, 1089–90, 1303, etc.; *Críth Gablach*, ed. Binchy, cc. 17, 27 (tr. MacNeill, cc. 90, 112).

on an essentially perishable item may help to explain the weakness of artisanally created markers of wealth in the archaeological record; whatever he wore, and however he lived, a man with a lot of cattle already had high status in early medieval Ireland.[130] But the way the cattle were actually exchanged may also help to explain the weakness of the archaeological markers of wealth that are standard elsewhere, as we shall see in a moment.

Irish evidence about the detail of social relationships is, as noted in Chapter 2, almost all legal. It must be added that the law tracts are all lawyers' handbooks, constructed through the establishment of elaborate legal distinctions (nine types of marriage, and so on), which presumably had more meaning in teaching and disputation than in the daily lives of most Irish, thus accentuating the standard difficulties of deducing social practice from law. But at least lawyers were genuinely important in Ireland; law-making was the work of a specialist legal caste, the *brithemoin* or 'brehons', in a way unparalleled in other regions studied in this book (though brehon law does have analogues in the jurists' law of third-century Rome, and in the Qu'rānic law-schools of the late eighth century onwards). The brehons ran law-courts, too; it is significant that it has been possible to argue about whether kings had any role in justice in Ireland at all (although they clearly did). The law tracts thus represent the thinking of a social group which had real power. Furthermore, at least in principle, the brehons underpinned a homogeneous legal system across a highly disunited island; nor can we often pin down local differences in our legal sources (only Munster law is sometimes identifiably distinct).[131] But this lack of geographical specificity, added to the elaboration of the social theory expressed in the tracts, has meant that early Irish social history has been very abstract; one tends to have to proceed by logic rather than by example, and local realities are very hard to get at.

But these local realities must, actually, have been quite distinct. As observed in Chapter 2, Ireland was made up of up to 150 *túatha*, 'peoples' or 'tribes' as much as 'kingdoms', although each had its own king (*rí*). These were very various in wealth and power, and it is hard to imagine that a powerful lowland kingdom in Meath and an upland one in Kerry had a lot in common. Politically, they were organized into hierarchies, expressed by the exchange of cattle, by aid in warfare, and by the presence of lesser kings at the court and assemblies of superior kings. The two major dominant dynasties after c.500, the Uí Néill in the centre and north-west and the Eóganachta in the south-west (i.e. Munster), were made up of sets of related kings, each with a separate *túath*, who fought for superiority inside their

---

[130] For cattle, see *Críth Gablach, passim.* Cattle and other animals were also consumed in competitive feasting, commemorated in numerous prose narratives, such as *Scéla Mucce meic Dathó*, ed. Thurneysen, or *Fled Bricrend*, ed. Windisch. This feasting has plenty of parallels in all the regions discussed in this book, however (cf. pp. 196, 695).

[131] See in general Kelly, *Early Irish law*; p. 246 for Munster; pp. 18, 238–40, for justice, set against the neat survey in Sharpe, 'Dispute settlement', pp. 183–7.

loose alliance, at least in part through the competitive accumulation of patron–client relationships with lesser kings. Some of these relationships of king-to-king subjection were long-term and stable, involving little *túatha* which would have no realistic chance—or reason—to achieve full autonomy, or even sometimes to change their overlord: these *aithechthúatha* (base-client peoples) or *dóerthúatha* (unfree peoples) perhaps made up a majority of kingdoms. But in principle they could still shift their loyalties; clientship was not legally permanent.[132] As in Wales, the geographical scale of over-kingship increased in our period, particularly in the eighth century, but not its density. We cannot as yet trace any overall trend for these subject peoples to be fully absorbed into larger polities in any systematic way, as, for example, in Offa's Mercia (above, p. 344). Nor are there many signs even of superior kings intervening in the affairs of client *túatha*—although there are a handful, for example a story in Cogitosus' *Vita Brigitae* of the seventh century in which an over-king instructs all his *plebes* (i.e. *túatha*) to construct a road for him. Kings made war, but did not do much 'governing'; law was partially in the hands of the brehons, as we have seen, decision-making was by assembly (*óenach*), and only a skeleton set of official positions is visible in our period. Conversely, kings had an elaborate ritual relationship with their *túatha*, which is stressed in all our sources, full of ceremonials and taboos. These rituals were overemphasized in the past as signs of Ireland's archaic Indo-European roots, but they cannot be argued away.[133] They underpinned local tribal solidarities, as firmly as did the *'aṣabiyya* of Ibn Khaldūn (above, p. 337); they were a strong safeguard against the full abolition of the local political identity of even an *aithechthúath*.

It would be misleading to attribute the continued structural fragmentation of Ireland's politics to tribal ritual and archaism; the ceremonial force of local kingship, or the legal right of kings to change overlords, would be convincing to any subordinate *túath*, no doubt, but would not soften the heart of an incipient Irish Clovis or Offa. We can see some parallels to the latter in Ireland after the confusion of the Viking period, but barely before, and we need to ask why.[134] One reason is that the political infrastructure that would allow state-building in England, in particular, was hardly developed yet in Ireland; not one of the elements of a 'state' listed on pp. 303–4 can be seen there, except for the royal concern for war, and it is hard to see how even an ambitious and successful king could really have enforced his local

---

[132] See in general Byrne, *Irish kings* (p. 7 for 150 *túatha*); Charles-Edwards, *Early Christian Ireland*, pp. 8–67, 469–585.

[133] For the *óenach*, Charles-Edwards, *Early Christian Ireland*, pp. 556–9; for the rituals, Byrne, *Irish kings*, pp. 15–33. For some early absorption of smaller *túatha* into larger ones, see Ó Corráin, 'Nationality', pp. 9–10. Cogitosus: *Vita Brigitae*, c. 30.

[134] Charles-Edwards, *Early Christian Ireland*, pp. 594–8 stresses the unusual ambition and violence of Donnchad mac Domnaill in the 760s–790s, and Byrne, *Irish kings*, pp. 211–29, stresses that of Feidlimid mac Crimthainn in the 820s–840s; all the same, these kings expressed a new scale of warmaking, not, as far as can be seen, of political infrastructure.

control, even if he had wanted to. Linked to this is the fact that the four elements that were identified earlier (pp. 345–6) as underpinning political change, external influence, tight links between kings and aristocrats, economic differentiation, and aristocratic landed power, were all largely absent in Ireland—although some changes can be associated with the church, as we shall see. In order to understand this, let us look at aristocratic hierarchies first, to see how they worked, and come back to political developments afterwards.

The main legal texts (out of over fifty that survive) that tell us significant amounts about social relationships, *Críth Gablach* (the most detailed), *Cáin Aicillne, Cáin Sóerraith*, and the Munster tract *Uraicecht Becc*, all probably from the early eighth century, list for us a remarkable range of status categories. In *Críth Gablach* there are five separate ranks for the non-royal aristocracy (plus two for kings), seven for the non-aristocratic free; in *Uraicecht Becc* it is five and six respectively. Each grade of aristocrat (*flaith*) in the tracts is characterized in considerable detail, with a specified, different, number of non-aristocratic clients (*céli*)—ten even for the lowest grade—a specified size of house with its accoutrements listed, a specified set of dues from clients, and so on.[135] It is generally accepted that such detailed characterizations are formulaic, even arbitrary, for no society works like that, although there have been many attempts to disentangle legal theory from supposed social description in them. It seems to me that it is necessary also to say that the overall articulation of this ranking is impossible, as a general statement about Ireland. If we return for a moment to guesswork numbers games, and propose, with other historians, that the ballpark population of Ireland was half-a-million people in our period (which at least fits with the one-and-a-half million guessed earlier for post-Roman Britain),[136] then, even supposing there were only 100 *túatha*, this would average 5,000 people for each *túath*: maybe 1,000 nuclear families, and a rather smaller number of effective kin-groups (which were unusually socially and economically coherent in Ireland),[137] a good percentage of

---

[135] *Críth Gablach*, ed. Binchy, tr. MacNeill, 'The law of status and franchise', pp. 281–306 (Binchy, c. 24, MacNeill, c. 107, for the lowest rank of aristocrat); *Cáin Aicillne*, ed. and tr. Thurneysen, 'Aus dem irischen Recht', I, pp. 338–94; *Cáin Sóerraith*, ed. and tr. ibid., II, pp. 239–53; *Uraicecht Becc*, tr. MacNeill, 'The law of status and franchise', pp. 272–81. Convenient status tables are in Charles-Edwards, *Early Christian Ireland*, pp. 130–2; Charles-Edwards, '*Críth Gablach*', is now the basic analysis of that text, and stresses its quality as a piece of legal sociology. I translate *flaith* as 'aristocrat'; Irish experts use 'lord' (or 'lordship', for the word denotes his powers too). Lords in Ireland were clearly quite unlike their colleagues in other parts of Europe, but their status and social roles fit into the ideal type of the aristocracy outlined here on pp. 153–4.

[136] For half-a-million, see e.g. Kelly, *Early Irish law*, p. 4 (he quotes it through two authorities, however, and it is itself derived by analogy from *Domesday Book* figures).

[137] The extensive evidence for kin-groups is most recently discussed in Charles-Edwards, *Kinship*, pp. 21–88, and, differently, in Patterson, 'Patrilineal kinship'. Common ground is the socio-political importance, often the co-ownership of property, of three- or four-generation

which would have been unfree and therefore outside the ranking. There is already no space in such a *túath* for all these ranks, even if each aristocrat had only ten non-aristocratic clients. On the other hand, it is unreasonable to assume that *túatha* were of uniform size; let us imagine that the smaller *aithechthúatha* had as little as 1,000 people, 200 nuclear families, and big tribes like the Cenél nEógain (of Co. Tyrone) or the Eóganacht Chaisil (of Co. Tipperary) ten or more times that number. Of course, the small tribes could not conceivably have sustained an articulated aristocracy, and may well have had no ranks between the immediate royal kindred and the non-aristocratic free; but the big tribes could have managed to include several distinct aristocratic levels, even if with some difficulty.

These speculations, typical in their abstraction, are at least starting-points. They seem to me at least to introduce an element of local differen-tiation into the tracts on status, for these tracts only make sense at all as rationalizations of the social systems of the *larger* polities of Ireland. It is possible also that the difference in detail in the law tracts, which are numer-ous, are products of different local rationalizations, although, out of those cited here, only *Uraicecht Becc* has been pinned to a specific part of the island. They are still schematic in the extreme, however, and one could not easily justify any argument about what the tracts 'allow' in any *túath*, even in Cenél nEógain and its peers. It may be better to restrict oneself to one simple but amply documented point about Irish social ideology: it was obsessed with pointillistic status and ranking differences, even when these could not have been sustained. This makes even more significant the archae-ology-based observation that there was very little material difference at all between how each rank lived.

How did aristocratic power work locally? This is not difficult, for the law tracts are consistent about it: it was based on *célsine*, 'clientage'. There were two main forms of clientage relationships, 'free clientage' (*sóer-rath*) and 'base clientage' (*gíallnae* or *aicillne*), both of which essentially linked non-aristocratic freemen to aristocrats. Their complex rules varied rather more from tract to tract, but they essentially hung on gifts of cattle from lord to client. Free clientage involved the cession of a (probably restricted) number of cattle to the client, who in *Cáin Sóerraith* paid one cow back per year for every three granted, as well as largely political services; the relationship could be broken by either side at any time with the return of the cattle, and ended after seven years. Base clientage was much more important to aristocratic prosperity, judging by the law tracts, and was probably much commoner: it was a real economic relationship, in which the cession to the client of cattle was made in return for fewer cattle per year, but also

kin-groups. But the signs are that the nuclear family was the core day-to-day unit of kinship even in Ireland; it would be hard to fit more than one into a round-house, as Lisa Bitel has observed (*Land of women*, pp. 4–7).

hospitality renders, services, and military obligations. The base client was more obviously a legal dependant of a lord, and most such clientage relationships, although in theory terminable, were in practice probably permanent; all the same, the agreement had to be renewed at the lord's death, with the lord's heir giving more cattle to do so, for the base client had the right to keep them if the relationship had lasted over seven years (except, apparently, in Munster).[138]

Aristocrats could construct followings of dependants out of relationships like this; indeed, successful non-aristocrats could in principle rise to aristocratic status eventually if they had enough clients as well. We could easily see base clients as economically subject, furnishing some of the basic elements of aristocratic wealth; free clients as retainers and supporters more than dependants. Aristocratic wealth also had at its core a half-free and unfree stratum of uncertain size, who were tenants and domestic workers (non-aristocrats could have such dependants too). All this has analogies to the sort of tribal social structure that was earlier postulated for fifth- and sixth-century Britain (above, p. 305). But there are two crucial specificities to this legal material. The first is that the client relationship was expressed in cattle, not in land, in nearly every instance. Clients were, even at the bottom of the scale, themselves autonomous landholders, whose lands were indeed specified in the tracts. That is to say: the tracts construct for us a system of hierarchy and dependence based on an economically independent peasantry, not a world of tenants.[139] Even the unfree seem to have been fairly restricted in their duties, and may have resembled the servile labourers of central medieval Iceland rather than the tenants of great estates; the basic economic units of both aristocrats and free peasants seem to have constituted single family farms, presumably the territories around single ringforts. It should be added that tenure in Ireland, unlike in early Britain (though like that of ninth-century Brittany: above, p. 338), seems to have been exclusive. There is nothing in Ireland that resembles English and Welsh land-units, unless the *túatha* themselves were this; but no king of a *túath* claimed any generalized

---

[138] The most detailed texts are *Cáin Aicillne*, cc. 2–3, 14–19, 22–5 ; *Cáin Sóerraith*, cc. 3, 6; see in general Kelly, *Early Irish law*, pp. 29–33; Charles-Edwards, *Kinship*, pp. 337–63; idem, *Early Christian Ireland*, pp. 68–80 (pp. 74–9 for Munster); Patterson, *Cattle-lords*, pp. 150–78.

[139] For the specification of land, see *Críth Gablach*, ed. Binchy, cc. 10–14 (tr. MacNeill, cc. 77–89); for a rising freeman, Binchy, c. 19 (MacNeill, c. 94). Once, in the same text (Binchy, c. 10; MacNeill, c. 80), the cession to a client is in land; Charles-Edwards, 'Críth Gablach', pp. 69–70, minimizes this, convincingly. Charles-Edwards, *Early Christian Ireland*, pp. 71–3 (and also in earlier writings) argues for a structural analogy between these cattle cessions and the lord–*colonus* relationship in Francia; the analogy, though useful, seems to me flawed, for he supposes that the cattle were necessary in order to work the land, yet no normal agrarian holding requires more than a couple of plough-oxen. Even allowing for the pastoral stress to the Irish economy, the cattle of standard clientship agreements seem to go well beyond subsistence. For half-free and unfree workers, see Charles-Edwards, *Kinship*, pp. 307–36; Patterson, *Cattle-lords*, pp. 152–5, who argues that their agricultural importance was limited.

control over its land, unlike in England.[140] Relationships of dependence here presumed a stable free peasantry.

The second crucial point is that these relationships were not permanent; even base clientage, the more lasting of the two, required renewed cessions of cattle every generation. Aristocrats did not only receive in client relations; they had to give, to every level of client, on a regular basis. Overall, they gained economically from base clientage, and at least politically from the more autonomous free clients. But what we do not find here is the presumption of unlimited dominance over *free* economic dependants that one can find even in Ine, and very extensively on the Continent. Political links, too, had to be renewed formally and often; there was nothing remotely similar to the notionally unconditional loyalty of England. Even kings, although their links to their *túath* were not temporary, had to fulfil certain criteria for their rule to last, such as justice, physical perfection, and the maintenance of taboos, and it is clear that peasant loyalty to aristocrats was more conditional than that. There are further implications to this. One is that the existence of a substantial autonomous free peasantry in itself limited the wealth that the aristocracy could accumulate: base clientage was not insignificant in its economic benefit to lords, but it hardly matched a real dependent tenure for rent—and anyway not all free peasants were necessarily base clients. Another is that the breakability of these relationships considerably conditioned the ability of lords to impose their own terms on their non-aristocratic neighbours: an oppressive lord could lose clients to a rival. They must have had to negotiate, at least by offering feasts and the like: a further expense for lords, which further inhibited the growth of economic hierarchies and more developed forms of private lordship. The cattle emphasis of our sources shows how surplus was not only based on perishable (and eatable) materials, but was also constantly distributed and redistributed among the ranks of the free. The tendency by some historians to call these relationships 'feudal' (or else to call cattle 'fiefs' and clients 'vassals') therefore seems to me fundamentally unhelpful, whatever definition of 'feudal' one uses. Indeed, even in the law tracts it is clear that some aristocrats were hardly more prosperous than rich peasants, something which in this context does indeed fit the archaeology. In economic terms, early medieval Ireland seems to have been a peasant-mode, ranked, society (above, p. 304; below, pp. 536–41), even if its rankings were largely fixed and so obsessively articulated, and even if, as a result, peasant political autonomy was virtually impossible. Only kings, at least of the major *túatha*, and by the eighth century some churches, may have been able to amass wealth on a largish scale.

It is in this context that the absence in Ireland of the accumulation of political power that one sees in England, and for a time even in Wales, seems

---

[140] For tenure, see Kelly, *Early Irish farming*, pp. 399–408. For the Breton analogy and its problems see Davies, 'La comunidad local'; for the Icelandic analogy, Karras, *Slavery*, pp. 80–3.

to me significant. These characterizations of local power structures show that economic differentiation and aristocratic landed power were not great, and there was as yet no tendency for them to increase. When we recall that the political hierarchies among kings were also structured by the rules of free and base clientship, at least in theory, then it can be seen that the ideology of impermanent and negotiable bonds operated at the royal level too. This was not a socio-political system that had as yet either the conceptual or the economic building blocks in place for state-building of an Anglo-Saxon type.[141]

I do not want to picture Ireland as an unchanging archaic world, as it has been too often in the past. Its focus on cattle rather than land does at least make it structurally different in its relations of dependence from every other region discussed in this book. But we need not think that Ireland *could* not generate larger political structures and stronger economic hierarchies (supposing indeed that these are always desirable); only that it *did* not, at least in our period. Actually, there were several quite sharp moments of change that we need to signal. One was the appearance of the society of the ringforts, by around 500, which certainly marked a considerable development in social articulation over whatever had gone before, quite possibly (as has been proposed) in the framework of population growth, even if that set of developments stopped there. Another, after our period, was the move towards at least some elements of larger-scale political power in the wake of Viking disruptions, particularly in the two centuries after 950: this was an indigenous development (it was certainly not the result of the small-scale town-based polities that the Vikings themselves introduced into Ireland), so it shows that such changes were possible in the end; it is just that there was no real sign of them before 800.[142]

Inside our period, it is also necessary to signal the role of the church. The church in Ireland was obviously the product of external influence, the Christianization process of the fifth and sixth centuries. The major churches developed their own patterns of ecclesiastical politics, with some quite ambitious synodal assemblies and claims to supremacy as in England, indeed at times with military aggression against clerical or lay rivals. Church hierarchies, however, both of bishops and abbots, mapped closely onto the secular hierarchies of the *túatha*. This is in part because the church was not associated with any external secular political models, unlike the Frankish example for England; in part because the Christian priesthood could, and did, fit easily into the pre-existing social niche of the learned orders, lawyers

---

[141] Wormald, 'Celtic and Anglo-Saxon kingship', develops the Irish–English comparison, but his conclusion, that the Irish lacked movable wealth, itself requires further explanation.

[142] Ó Corráin, 'Nationality', an important analysis, seems to me to put the start of the process of political accumulation too early; so does Patterson, *Cattle-lords*, pp. 343–60, coming from a rather different position.

and poets.[143] The church did, nonetheless, offer some pathways for social change. Church leaders wanted to obtain land in perpetuity, as in England, and did so, thus providing a model for clientage-free property-holding, from the late seventh century at least. By the eighth, even if ecclesiastical dependants (*manaig*) were socially very similar to lay clients, with cessions of cattle and the rest, they perhaps functioned in an economic context more similar to dependent tenants than did free people in lay society, which would have allowed for more economic accumulation by churches.[144] This could well have been a model for social development elsewhere; as we have seen, the best evidence for material wealth in the eighth century is church-related, and churches are indeed likely to have been richer than many kings. They were ever more obviously a resource for ambitious rulers. But the Irish church had as yet a limited impact on the protocols of land tenure, and its economic templates would be disrupted by Viking attack. These changes were potential, not actual, ones, even if they too help to undermine the assumption that Ireland was unchangeable.

It is crucial that Ireland had never been Roman. Not because this prevented its development, as indeed I have just argued, but because it meant that Irish developments were inevitably going to be along indigenous lines. Even the greatest external influence on the region in our period, the church, adopted predominantly indigenous social practices, at most providing a legitimation for (and occasional critique of, and occasional tinkering with) secular practices. Ireland was also a long way from the dominant power in the North, Francia, and much less exposed to its influence and example than was England. The social structures that inhibited the accumulation of wealth and power in the island were thus not countered by any outside force. It was social breakdown, not external influence, that changed that in the end, but even then political construction was a slow process (far from complete by the time of the Anglo-Norman invasion of 1170), and outside our period.

Denmark's documentation is almost all archaeological, until 800 at any rate, but in that context the contrast with Ireland could not be more acute: Denmark is full of gold-rich sites of the third to sixth centuries, and silver-rich ones from the Viking period, the ninth and tenth. Denmark was almost as distant from Francia as was Ireland, at least before the Carolingian period, and more distant still from the Roman empire and its wealth in the

---

[143] See in general Hughes, *The church*; Davies, 'Clerics as rulers'; Herbert, *Iona*, pp. 47–67; Charles-Edwards, *Early Christian Ireland*, pp. 241–81. For the argument that canon law also affected the content of the secular law tracts, see Ó Corráin, Breatnach, and Breen, 'The laws of the Irish'.

[144] For evidence of ecclesiastical landholding, deriving from quite small-scale lay gifts and a sale, see Tírechán, *Additamenta*, ed. Bieler, 5.2, 5.4, 8, 10, 11.2. For *manaig*, see for a good survey Bitel, *Isle of the saints*, pp. 115–28; also Kelly, *Early Irish farming*, pp. 452–5; I am grateful to Wendy Davies for helpful ideas.

fourth century, but it was considerably more effective in gaining the most expensive signs of prestige available than Ireland was. These imports serve as markers for articulated settlement hierarchies, whose meaning has been the focus of considerable debate in Denmark (and elsewhere in Scandinavia) in the last fifteen years or so. Not only does Denmark give us the material basis for a potentially complex socio-economic analysis, then, but this analysis is that much easier because of a commitment to systemic interpretation by Danish archaeologists that is relatively unusual among national archaeological communities. Uncertainties remain, nonetheless, particularly over how to interpret the first half of our period. For this reason, it seems to me most useful to start around 800 and work backwards, from the more agreed to the more controversial. We will then be in a better position to consider the implications of Danish evidence for the sorts of issues that have been discussed for Britain and Ireland.

There is good evidence for a relatively cohesive political system in Denmark, based in south-central Jutland (Danish Jylland), between c.700 and c.870. The Frankish annals refer to a *rex Danorum* from 777, first Sigfrid (fl. 777–98), then Godofrid (fl. 804–10), then to a contested and/or collective kingship for a couple of decades until Godofrid's son Horic I (fl. 827–54) established himself as sole king around 830. Members of the two families who contested that kingship had similar names, so were probably related; so did an earlier king, Ongendus, referred to in Alcuin's *Vita Willibrordi* as active around 700. This large family grouping supplied nearly twenty known Danish kings up to the death of Horic II some time after 864. They crop up quite often in Frankish sources, for they successfully resisted Charlemagne and his successors (surviving a serious invasion in 815); then, from the 830s onwards, they played a more ambiguous role, with the two Horics acting as both patrons and (unsuccessful) opponents of Viking raids on Francia, with royal losers acting both as Viking raiders themselves and as representatives of the Frankish kings in Frisia, combating such raids.[145] It is not certain how widely the direct rule of Godofrid's family actually extended, from their base in south-central Jutland: to Fyn, the nearest large island, almost certainly; to Skåne on the Swedish mainland, probably but less securely; maybe not to the far north of Jutland itself. Conversely, the family also had a wider hegemony as a naval power: Godofrid took tribute from the Obodrites, a Slav tribe on (what is now) the north-east German coast; he claimed some form of allegiance from Vestfold, the Oslo region of Norway; and he was bold enough to attack Frisia under Charlemagne's very eyes in 810, the year of Godofrid's death. A late ninth-century source,

---

[145] *Annales Regni Francorum*, s.aa. 777–828; *Annales Bertiniani*, s.aa. 831–73; Alcuin, *Vita Willibrordi*, c. 9. Sawyer, 'Kings and royal power', gives a good brief political survey; Randsborg, *The Viking age*, gives basic background; see also Lund, 'Scandinavia', pp. 205–13; for royal family members in Frisia, Coupland, 'From poachers to gamekeepers'.

Rimbert's *Vita Anskarii*, depicts the Denmark of the 840s–860s as a strong kingdom, which seems to have extended as far east as the kingdom of the *Sueones*, the Swedes, with no intervening polities referred to at all—and Rimbert was a Dane, so should have known. The Franks made peace with the Danes in 811 and 813 as equals, not as superiors, even if they subsequently interfered in Danish politics whenever they could.[146] These are all signs of an organized political system. Organized, but not necessarily fully stable: the kingdom fell apart after the 860s, probably in the context of the instabilities inherent in Viking politics, and had to be re-established from the mid-tenth century by a new family based at Jelling in central Jutland, that of Gorm and Harald Blåtand (Bluetooth), the ancestors of the central medieval Danish monarchy.[147]

The resources of the Jutland kingdom of Godofrid's family have recently become rather clearer, thanks to two decades of archaeological discoveries. The Frankish annals say that Godofrid built the Danevirke, a dyke across the peninsula at the level of Hedeby, in 808 against Charlemagne; dendrochronology can now show that this was at least the third period of building there, with a second in 737 and some prior activity too. A political power also took the trouble to build the Kanhave ship canal across the small island of Samsø opposite Århus in eastern Jutland in 726, a pointless act unless one controlled the Jutland coast. Earlier still, in 705–10 (once again the dates are dendrochronological), the town of Ribe on the west coast of the peninsula was laid out, quite systematically, as a commercial *emporium* (see below, pp. 681–8), inhabited at least seasonally; this was also presumably the work of a political power. This sort of protagonism fits with the later development of Hedeby at the Baltic end of the Danevirke before 800; and a trading centre in Skåne, too, Åhus, had close economic connection to Ribe in the eighth century. Hedeby and Ribe were certainly ruled by the Danish kings in the ninth century. It makes sense to associate all these acts with a single political system, which thus can be seen to have been coherent enough to organize substantial public works throughout the eighth century and the early ninth.[148] Not that we should overstress their scale; the Danevirke is under 10 km long, less than a tenth the length of Offa's Dyke. Still, this was a

---

[146] For arguments about Fyn and Skåne, see the works cited in the previous note. For tribute, *Annales Regni Francorum*, s.aa. 808, 810, 813; for peace as equals, s.aa. 811, 813 (less so 825), *Annales Bertiniani*, s.a. 839; for Frankish destabilization, *Annales Regni Francorum*, s.a. 817, *Annales Fuldenses*, s.a. 857. Rimbert, *Vita Anskarii*, cc. 24–6, 30 discusses the Danes as against the Swedes (c. 33 for Rimbert as a Dane). Note also that the late ninth-century travel accounts of Wulfstan and Ohthere imply that the Danes controlled Skåne: a convenient analysis is Lebecq, 'Ohthere et Wulfstan'.

[147] For the Jelling kingdom, see Skovgaard-Petersen, 'The making', with bibliography.

[148] Texts: *Annales Regni Francorum*, s.a. 808; Rimbert, *Vita Anskarii*, cc. 24, 31. Archaeology: Olsen, 'Royal power'; Axboe, 'Danish kings and dendrochronology'; Näsman, 'Exchange and politics' (pp. 58–60 for Åhus); Bencard *et al.*, *Ribe*, IV, pp. 137–48. For the Danevirke in the context of other earthworks, Squatriti, 'Digging ditches'.

polity that resisted Charlemagne, never an easy task, and (uniquely in the latter's reign) actually attacked back.

Rimbert's image of the political infrastructure of the Danish kingdom is helpful here, for it seems to have been quite articulated. There were different levels of *principes* and *primores* around the king; Hedeby was ruled in the 860s by a *comes*, who was also a royal kinsman. In Sweden, royal decisions had to be ratified by assemblies (*placita*), which the king could manipulate, but not control. Such assemblies certainly existed in Denmark, as in the whole of the medieval Scandinavian world (they were called *thingar* in Old Norse), but Rimbert's picture is that a Danish ruler could make decisions without them, whereas a Swedish ruler could not. The Danish king ruled through his aristocratic retinue, and through officials in his towns (*vici*) of Hedeby and Ribe, which as the archaeology shows were consistent sources of wealth. In addition, as we have seen, he could control the labour service of his dependants so as to build large earthworks, and the military service of enough people to equip naval expeditions.[149] So, we have a kingdom that probably covered most of the medieval Danish region (significantly, losers in royal power-struggles in the first half of the ninth century went to the Frankish court or turned Viking—there was nowhere in Denmark to go[150]), with a substantial level of internal integration. This polity did not last, and, when it broke up, it took more than two generations before any king aimed at control over Denmark again—we do not find here the un-broken political accumulation that we found in England. But Godofrid's kingdom was unusually large and unusually durable by the standards of the North, with only Offa's Mercia operating on a larger scale.

The eighth- and ninth-century Danish kingdom is already striking, but other recent discoveries have encouraged archaeologists to wonder whether it was really so new around 700. Lotte Hedeager, for example, proposed in a book first published in Danish in 1990 that something significant happened in Denmark in the two centuries spanning the end of the Late Roman Iron Age (c.300–500). Starting in the third century, villages were reorganized and became more highly structured, indicating a sharpening of local social organization; in the fourth, one part of the island of Sjælland, the Stevns area to the south of modern Copenhagen, was the focus for a set of very rich burials full of Roman imported goods, representing some form of political centre, at least for Sjælland. In the fourth and fifth centuries we find large sets of bog deposits of weapons, especially in eastern Jutland, the so-called 'weapon sacrifices', which, whatever they meant symbolically, at least indicate the existence of substantial communities involved with (among other things) military activity; these stop in the late fifth century, indicating, perhaps, peace. In the same period furnished burials cease as

---

149 Rimbert, *Vita Anskarii*, cc. 19, 24, 26–7, 31–2.
150 As Wormald, 'Viking studies', pp. 147–8, notes.

well, indicating, perhaps, the end of *potlatch* competition and the establishment of stable local hierarchies (see above, pp. 340–1, for analogous arguments for seventh-century England). Hedeager concluded from all this that a
single Danish kingdom could be postulated from, very approximately, the
early sixth century onwards.[151]

This argument might seem rather bold, but it was given further support by
the discovery in the late 1980s of an amazingly rich site at Gudme on the
island of Fyn, a little inland from the associated port of Lundeborg. It is now
clear that at its height, in c.400–550, this site consisted of at least fifty houses
in several clusters, a very large number for the period, with a substantial hall
in the middle, associated with uniquely large numbers of gold finds, in
graves, in hoards, and in the houses themselves. Many of these were clearly
made on the spot; so were silver and bronze objects. There were also
imported Roman precious-metal objects, glass and pottery, and many
other finds.[152] Even outside Gudme's peak, it was an active craft centre
from the third century to the tenth and onwards. But at its peak it must
have been a major political focus: of a single Danish kingdom? It no longer
seemed improbable, and this theory, or versions of it, today has quite strong
support, as can be seen in the numerous conferences on the issue that have
been published since *Fra stamme til stat i Danmark* in 1988.[153] Perhaps, as
Jytte Ringtved has argued, the Gudme-focused polity was only one out of
perhaps four in Denmark; perhaps, as Charlotte Fabech and Klavs Randsborg have argued, Gudme was a ritual centre for other independent polities,
a sort of Danish Delphi (though it seems to me too rich by regional standards
for that); perhaps, as Ulf Näsman sometimes argues, the process of state-
building was only begun in the Gudme period, and was not complete until
700.[154] But Gudme and Lundeborg around 500 document an accumulation
of wealth on a scale so far unmatched anywhere in the North for half-a-
millennium. It is not unreasonable to propose that this could be structurally
linked to the political organization, also unmatched in at least the Scandinavian parts of the North, that can be documented from both archaeological
and written sources only two centuries later.

[151] Hedeager, *Iron-Age societies*, esp. pp. 246–53.
[152] The fullest presentation of material is in Nielsen *et al.*, *Gudme*, especially Jørgensen, 'The
find material'; see further Østergård Sørensen, 'Gudmehallerne', for the hall. Sacral interpretations of the site are numerous; for a recent example, with bibliography, see Hedeager, '*Asgard*
reconstructed?' A more secular analysis is Jørgensen, 'The warrior aristocracy of Gudme'.
[153] Mortensen and Rasmussen, *Fra stamme til stat*; Fabech and Ringtved, *Samfundsorganisation*; Nielsen *et al.*, *Gudme*; Resi, *Produksjon og samfunn*; *Anglo-Saxon studies in society and
history*, X (1999) are the main ones.
[154] Ringtved, 'Regionalitet'; eadem, 'The geography of power'; Fabech, 'Reading society';
Randsborg, 'Gudme-Lundeborg'; Näsman, 'Analogislutning'; idem, 'Exchange and politics'—
though Näsman is more positive about a sixth-century kingdom in 'The Justinianic era of south
Scandinavia' and 'The ethnogenesis of the Danes'.

Not unreasonable, but still, I think, problematic; there are at least three reasons why one should be cautious here. The first is that Gudme is not actually in Jutland, where the eighth-century kingdom was focused, and indeed the period 550–700, between the two, marks something of an archaeological caesura. Only a decade ago it was hard to pin anything to the seventh century at all. By now, at the level of elite settlements, we can find several equivalents to Gudme in that period (called 'central places', Danish *centrale pladser*, in current Scandinavian technical vocabulary, to avoid prejudging their status): at Neble on Sjælland, Stentinget and Bejsebakken in north Jutland, Uppåkra in Skåne, Sorte Muld on the always rather separate island of Bornholm—the last two being the only ones to have been more than fragmentarily excavated. None seems to have been as rich as was Gudme before 550, but nor was Gudme by now.[155] It looks as if any political aggregation marked by Gudme had by now broken down, just as Godefrid's Jutland-based kingdom did two generations after his death. Again, there is no equivalent to the steady political accumulation that one finds in England. The second reason derives from a separate question: why, exactly, was Gudme quite so rich, just then, in the period 400–550? Here, one must remember that this is the period of the fall of the Roman empire in the West. The steady movement of Roman goods northwards to, for example, the Stevns area in the fourth century was presumably largely controlled by the Roman state: it was the result of political largesse, army pay for federates, maybe occasionally commerce.[156] When the western empire fell, however, and Germanic armies helped themselves, it would hardly be surprising if large quantities of precious metal ended up in the political centres of the North. After 550, on the other hand, the Franks had re-established a stable hegemony, and could control exports more effectively—and Francia, although rich and powerful, could not match the empire for wealth, hence the fact that there is less from that period in Denmark. These observations do not make Gudme less of a political centre, but they relativize its fifth- and sixth-century wealth a bit: this was a sign of Roman crisis, not Danish strength, and it may be better to see Gudme as a sub-regional centre (i.e. for Fyn) at most, in which guise it in fact continued as a central place from before our period starts until after it ends. If this were so, then we ought to find more Gudmes in the fifth-century levels of central places elsewhere: this will be tested in the future, as more of them are properly excavated. Uppåkra, at least, has high-quality fifth- and early sixth-century finds in its latest excavations.

---

[155] See as surveys Näsman, 'Det syvende århundrede'; Axboe, 'Towards the kingdom'. For the cited central places, see Nissen-Joubert, *Peuplement*, p. 192, for a good synthesis of Neble; Nilsson, 'Stentinget'; Nielsen, 'Bejsebakken'; Larsson and Hårdh, 'Uppåkra'; Hårdh and Larsson, *Central places* (esp. pp. 19–54 for articles on the recent Uppåkra excavations); Watt, 'Sorte Muld'.

[156] Lund Hansen, 'Himlingøje-undersøgelserne'; Hedeager, *Iron-Age societies*, pp. 46–51.

The third reason for my caution is a priori: not a strong basis for argument on its own, but rendered more forceful by the empirical points just made. It is very unclear indeed how a late fifth-century Danish 'kingdom' would actually work. What infrastructure would it have? What land tenure? How would wealth be channelled upwards? How would kings control outlying areas? These are not easy questions for archaeological evidence to answer, so it is often unreasonable to ask them, but it has to be said that none of the documentary evidence we have for nearby regions in the North—the Anglo-Saxon polities, Frisia, the Franks before Clovis—indicates that any-one else in that period had any form of large-scale permanent infrastructure, or indeed in the Anglo-Saxon case even a small-scale one. Denmark was so much richer than England until the seventh century that one could certainly postulate more accumulation of wealth in the former (needless to say, the contrast with Ireland is in all respects even more extreme), but the step between that and a stable regional state (cf. the definitions set out above, pp. 303–4) is a large one.

I should like to reframe the debate somewhat, therefore, arguing from a position closer to that of Ringtved than those of others. One thing that Denmark clearly shows, from the fourth century at the latest, is a settlement hierarchy. A set of well-organized small villages (five to ten farmsteads is a common size) can be found across the region, and seems to represent the basic settlement pattern throughout our period (though there are isolated peasant farms too, perhaps more often on the islands). Like Cowdery's Down in England, they are well built but not notably rich in finds; they sometimes have one larger farmstead in them, plausibly of a village headman.[157] (See below, pp. 496–8, for a more detailed discussion.) On a second level, we find what are called by archaeologists *stormandsgårder* (normally translated 'magnate farms'): isolated halls with associated buildings, as at Lejre in Sjælland, the largest, or Dankirke near Ribe, the best-studied. These have rather more finds, including in the case of Dankirke much imported late Roman glass, and bronze-working. *Stormandsgårder* often date from the late Roman period onwards, and frequently show settlement continuities into the eighth century and later: the social level they represent—that of the *stormænd*/'magnates', sometimes called *høvdinger*/'chieftains'—was thus relatively stable. It was clearly somehow privileged, but not necessarily hugely rich; 'magnate farms' parallel in their wealth the small-scale political centres of sixth-century western Britain, but not rich eighth-century eastern English sites such as Flixborough (cf. above, pp. 327, 341).[158] The third level

157 Basic village introductions are Hvass, 'Jernalderens bebyggelse'; Nissen-Joubert, *Peuple-ment*, pp. 219–73. For isolated farms, ibid., pp. 221–2; Kaldal Mikkelsen, 'Single farm', minimizes them.

158 For *stormandsgårder* (a term also, confusingly, used for the largest farmsteads in villages) see Hansen, 'Dankirke' (with Jensen, 'Dankirke-Ribe'); Christensen, 'Lejre beyond legend' (unfortunately, the late seventh-century levels of the hall were not fully excavated); Hansen,

is that of the 'central places': groups of small settlement clusters, some with artisanal specializations, associated at Gudme with a hall and with a port, as we have seen. Up to twelve of these have been hypothesized in the Danish region, although barely half of these have any form of archaeological study and thus dating. They seem sometimes to have been less lasting than 'magnate farms', but some (particularly Gudme) had a long history. Even in the seventh century, perhaps their low point, they were richer than normal in northern Europe, with gold finds not uncommon.[159] A fourth level, urban centres, did not develop until the eighth century, with Ribe and Hedeby.

This picture has only become clear in the last decade, but it is based by now on a substantial number of sites. If it holds, then it points in my view to a relatively decentralized political system, at least before 700. Ringtved, as already noted, argued for four separate polities in the sixth century, and stresses long-standing cultural differences in the one she has studied most closely, northern Jutland.[160] If 'central places' really were the centres of such polities, four would be a minimum, given the number of them which seem to have coexisted at any particular moment. These sites can perhaps most usefully be seen as foci for the political aggregation of greater and lesser elites, whether 'chieftains' or village leaders. But aggregation does not necessarily point to control. 'Central places' and their rulers did not have an exclusive monopoly over imports, which certainly reached the 'magnate farm' level as well; if such rulers had anything that could be understood as a political territory, their hold over it was probably fairly loose. At the next level down, villages were reasonably prosperous, and were probably inhabited by a relatively independent free peasantry (with their own slaves); here, too, there is no sign that their production was under 'chieftain' direction. Elites were stable, then, but at every level there are more signs of autonomy than control, just as in the tribal societies of early England, Wales, and Ireland. These are very hypothetical propositions, as is inevitable when one invents social history out of purely archaeological patterns. It could reasonably be argued, though, that these patterns resemble more those of England in the seventh century than afterwards, even if at every level Danish material culture was rather richer—particularly at the highest level, where the difference between Gudme and Yeavering (above, p. 320) is acute. If that was so, then one might postulate a Denmark made up of equivalents to the one-county and two-county tribal kingdoms[161] of seventh-century England

'Et jernalderhus med drikkeglas i Dejbjerg'; perhaps Tissø (Jørgensen and Pedersen, 'Vikinger ved Tissø'), although recent work may show Tissø was a central place, as Catherine Hills has pointed out to me.

[159] See nn. 152, 155 for the best-studied sites; for an overview, Fabech, 'Organising the landscape', cf. eadem, 'Centrality in sites'; Brink, 'Political and social structures'.

[160] Ringtved, arts. cit. n. 154.

[161] Of course, since we have no early documents for Denmark, we would have no way of knowing which level to ascribe the word 'kingdom' to; perhaps only the rulers of 'central places'

(which would roughly match, respectively, Fyn and Sjælland for size), although, if so, that pattern lasted longer than it did in England, from the fifth century to the beginning of the eighth, or perhaps indeed into the tenth.

On the basis of this pattern, one could at least postulate some political developments. It may well be, for example, that Gudme established itself as hegemonic for a period; there are parallels to this in the over-kings of seventh-century England, and in the hegemonies of later Wales and Ireland. If so, however, we should not be surprised that such a hegemony broke down, for it was precisely at the highest level that political power was most unstable in tribal societies like these. The seventh century was clearly such a period of breakdown, with a possible lessening in the concentration of wealth itself (although the relative obscurity of the seventh century may also be, as already noted, because less was coming north out of Francia). In the eighth century another two-county-level polity, south-central Jutland, managed to develop sufficient internal coherence for it to dominate the others in the ninth. Though that hegemony failed as well, the internal coherence of Jutland probably survived, for it was from the same sub-region that Denmark was finally united in the mid-tenth century. It cannot be chance, I think, that this was the Danish polity closest to Francia; the model of large-scale power that the latter offered would have been an encouragement to the *reges Danorum* of our Frankish sources, even before Charlemagne took Saxony and established a border with Denmark—after all, Ribe was in close commercial contact with Frankish *emporia* from the start (below, p. 685).[162]

Denmark has some parallels to England in this. Not that Offa's heartland was the closest sub-region to the Franks; still, as we have seen (p. 346), Frankish political models, made more accessible in England thanks to the church, were often visibly copied there. But Denmark was both faster and slower than England in its state-building. There is no English equivalent to the degree of the concentration of wealth—still less to the gross level of wealth—that can be found in Gudme in 500, for centuries; conversely, Offa's state system in the later eighth century was not matched in Denmark until the eleventh. Denmark's constantly rising and falling hegemonies were, however, arguably more typical of these crystallizing tribal societies than was England's linear political accumulation. The reasons for this must above all have been internal to Danish society.

I laid considerable stress in my discussions of England, Wales, and Ireland on the control aristocrats had over their peasant neighbours, arguing that, unless aristocrats began to develop (feudal) proprietorial rights over

in the seventh century would have been called *reges* by a Latin speaker (or *konungar* by an Old Norse speaker); perhaps the 'chieftains' would have had this title too. But the issue is not really important.

[162] See Näsman, 'Exchange and politics', for the most recent survey.

peasants, state-formation was impractical as a stable development, because effective, that is, adequately coercive, political infrastructures depended on a territorially dominant aristocracy. If we assume that 'chieftains' in 'magnate farms' were the equivalent of aristocrats elsewhere in the North, then we could say that they were both more and less than landed proprietors. The concentration of imports, such as the Dankirke glass, on 'magnate farms' rather than villages could be said to identify the holders of the former as political leaders, not merely landlords. But the relative homogeneity of villages points, as already noted, to a peasantry not yet entirely subjected by anyone. This points to a pattern in which a free peasantry recognizes an aristocrat as a leader, but not as a landlord; it may give him tribute, but only on a restricted scale. This is precisely the tribal social structure that was discussed earlier in the context of England, Ireland, Wales, and indeed Mauretania, on the basis of more evidence than we have for Denmark, at least for the first two. And there are no archaeological signs in the Denmark of our period of this structure beginning to shift towards landed proprietorship, unlike in Offa's England.[163] This, as in Wales and Ireland, must have been a considerable constraint on any permanent political aggregation. Nor, indeed, were peasants entirely subjected in Denmark for a long time. Central medieval Denmark does not have the peasant protagonism that one can still find in Sweden in the same period, but its local assemblies persisted throughout the middle ages; when documents begin in the late eleventh century, showing by then the existence of substantial aristocratic and ecclesiastical ownership, peasant landowners were still there too. The ancestors of central medieval aristocrats could well have been the 'chieftains', the elites that had been continuously locally prominent since the fifth-century levels at Dankirke, with successful village leaders joining them by the eleventh century, perhaps; but it may not have been until that period that peasantries were generally subjected, and some peasant autonomies survived later as well.[164]

The small-scale tribal leadership of local 'chieftains' that has just been proposed for early medieval Denmark has one well-known documentary parallel in Scandinavia: the relationship between *goðar* and *thingmenn* in tenth- to twelfth-century Iceland. *Goðar* were local ritual leaders and legal representatives (in the *thing*) of their lesser neighbours, but not owners of the

---

[163] There is some support for a change in local power-structures, perhaps indicating a new aristocratic dominance, in, roughly, the tenth century. Fabech, 'Organising the landscape', pp. 38–40, discusses how it might have taken place, using the example of Dejbjerg (cf. above, n. 158). The example of Vorbasse, however (below, p. 497), might point to the eleventh.

[164] For large-scale landowning in the twelfth century and for its fragmentation, leaving space for peasant ownership in its interstices, see *Diplomatarium danicum*, I.2, esp. nn. 21, 56, 63–5, 88; for case studies, see McGuire, 'Property and politics'; idem, 'Patrons, privileges' (e.g. pp. 11–13). For Danish assemblies, *Kulturhistorisk leksikon*, XVIII, cc. 359–66, s.v. *ting*. For a comparative survey, Sawyer and Sawyer, *Medieval Scandinavia*, pp. 129–42. For continuities back to the early middle ages, Jørgensen, 'The warrior aristocracy of Gudme', and above, n. 163.

latter's land. They could dominate their neighbours, but not too much, or else their *thingmenn* would simply transfer to another *goði*. This has Irish parallels (p. 362), and so has the complex network of gift-giving to *goðar* and hospitality of different types that our Icelandic narratives refer to, although in Iceland this was very ad hoc, and not subject to the complex rules of Irish clientship. A *goðorð*, the position of *goði*, was heritable, and the home farms of individual *goðar* (also, obviously, heritable) were invariably on the best land; there was a considerable level of long-term stability in Icelandic social ranking as a result. But the structures of power of any individual *goði* were much less stable, and dependent on the personal political skills of each one, on analogy with the 'big men' of early twentieth-century Melanesia. It was not until the twelfth century at the earliest that *goði* authority began to turn into lasting tenurial power, and before that *goðar* were hardly more than rich peasants themselves.[165] The Icelandic social structure was a variant of the Norwegian, not the Danish, one, and was built on a pastoral economy, on an ecological margin, which has no relation to the Danish situation. But the combination of the stability of ranking and the instability of practical political authority at the local level in my view fits the relationship between 'magnate farms' and villages that has just been discussed for Denmark. Given this, the Icelandic narratives may give us an indication of concrete elements of the political constraints for 'chieftains' in Denmark as well.

The Icelandic parallel has been badly applied in the past; indeed, the enthusiasm with which thirteenth-century saga narratives have been pitchforked into early medieval Scandinavian socio-economic history has sometimes run close to fantasy (only *Beowulf* is as misused). But at least it can be recognized that the idea of a local ritual and political leadership which did not necessarily involve real economic control may be what is being represented in our earliest Danish rune-stones, inscribed standing-stones, often memorials or grave markers, which begin in Denmark in small numbers in the ninth century. These commemorate people who are sometimes given titles: Rhuulfr, who appears four times in ninth-century Fyn, was *Nura-kuthi* (cf. *goði*), religious leader of (the) Nura; Ruhalt in ninth-century Sjælland is *thular* (cf. the *thulr*, sage or singer, in the *Hávamál*, a tenth-century Norwegian poem). Titles like these represent the sort of local ritual level I am proposing here, and perhaps Rhuulfr and Ruhalt could be imagined to have lived in 'magnate farms'. A generation or so later, around 900, we have the Glavendrup stone ship-setting on Fyn, whose rune-stone celebrates Ala, both *kutha* and *thiakn* (cf. Old English *thegn*) of a *lith* (war-band or

---

[165] See in general Byock, *Viking age Iceland*, esp. pp. 118–37; cf. Wickham, *Land and power*, pp. 217–20 (including for the Melanesian parallel); for the twelfth-century shift, Gunnar Karlsson, *Iceland's 1100 years*, pp. 24–7, 72–8, which briefly sums up recent literature; Callow, *Landscape, tradition and power*, pp. 177–96, 223–4.

group of retainers); it was put up by his wife and children, and carved by Suti 'for his lord' (*trutin*, cf. Old English *dryhten*). *Kutha* may point to Iceland, but *thiakn* and *trutin* point to a more solid, permanent dependence, of a type much celebrated in Anglo-Saxon literary texts, and the *lith* may have been the war-band of a king. Maybe this is how 'chieftains' always organized themselves, in the halls of their 'magnate farms'; but maybe we are also gaining a glimpse of the beginning of larger-scale political organization.[166] Still, c.900 is late for this book. It took until then for us to find signs in Denmark of the world even of Beowulf; Offa's world, and a world of landowners and tenants, would come later still.

I conclude that even in the eighth and ninth centuries, and still more in the fifth and sixth, aristocratic economic dominance over peasant neighbours was not established in Denmark; indeed, unlike in England, it had not even begun at the end of our period or for some time thereafter. Ritual/political, tribal, leadership by local-level 'chieftains' over autonomous peasants is a more plausible reading of our sources, however uncertain they are, and the control of wider rulers over both 'chieftains' and peasants was probably no more firmly established. This political hierarchy has more analogies with the ritualized but unstable multi-level hierarchies of Ireland than with any state structure, however distant Denmark was from Ireland economically. It did not prohibit the growth of larger political structures, which are clearly attested in the eighth and ninth centuries, and less clearly in the fifth and early sixth, but it made the permanence of such larger-scale polities much more difficult, and indeed, before 950 or so, they all failed in Denmark. Godofrid's and Horic's kingdom may well have resembled most closely that of Ine in Wessex a century earlier, with the beginnings of a set of officials and a control over developing *emporia* (above, p. 685). In England this political structure would in two or three generations develop towards a state; in Denmark not yet. I would argue that this was above all because the aristocracy in the latter were much slower to establish direct power over the peasantry than they were in the former. There were doubtless more contingent reasons as well, of course. The Vikings are outside the remit of this book, but it is worth reiterating that the instability caused by those roving, autonomous war-bands in England and Francia was fully matched in Denmark; and Alfred's political system, in part heir to that of Offa, survived the Viking onslaught, whereas that of the two Horics did not survive the internal confusion which Viking activity produced at home. In England

---

[166] *Danmarks runeinskrifter*, nn. 189–93 (Rhuulfr; note that the editor sees Nura in n. 192 as a people), 248 (Ruhalt), 209 (Glavendrup; cf. 202, 230). For an overview, Randsborg, *The Viking age*, pp. 25–33; Roesdahl, *Viking age Denmark*, pp. 25–7. For *thulr*, see *Hávamál*, stanza 111. For *trutin/dryhten*, see Green, *Language and history*, pp. 127–30, who shows a slow semantic move towards the meaning 'king'. For *lith*, see e.g. *Kulturhistorisk leksikon*, X, cc. 534–7, s.v. *lide*. For halls, recent interesting (but rather speculative) works are Brink, 'Political and social structures'; Herschend, *The idea of the good*, pp. 14–46, 181–5.

the state had developed just far enough to survive this instability, but not in Denmark. When the Danish state did form, in the two or three generations after 950, through conquest, organized external warfare, public works, the regularization of hospitality obligations into tribute, and (probably) the crystallization of aristocratic landed property, the processes involved were interestingly similar to those visible in the England of Offa and his successors.[167] But there was no inevitable trend towards it in our period.

It is, as with Ireland, crucial that Denmark had never been Roman—or, later, even Frankish; its development was indigenous, and its internal continuities were as great as in Ireland, with not even a church structure to influence its political ideology and tenurial geography before the late tenth century at the earliest. But Denmark was always, from well before the fifth century, more hierarchical in archaeological—that is, economic—terms than was Ireland; it had already developed one element that could allow the eventual accumulation of power. It was the others, in particular the tenurial power of aristocrats over peasants, that were slow to develop. As a result, the state was not yet incipient in Denmark in 800. All the same, some of the elements that would in the end contribute to state-building were beginning to be visible. By the ninth century the parallels for Danish political culture tend to be closer to England than to Ireland, and it may be that by then the cultural barriers to political accumulation were less than in Ireland; by 1000, in Denmark but not in Ireland, a unitary state did indeed come to exist, as a result of indigenous development. So we can reverse the points made at the end of the previous paragraph as well. Denmark's state formation was autonomous and intermittent, but it is important to recognize that, when it is compared to English political developments of two centuries earlier, we can see that the two processes ran along roughly the same lines.

As noted earlier (p. 54), I chose to discuss Denmark as a case study, rather than Frisia or Saxony, because its development was not cut short by the Franks. Recent work on Frisia is beginning to argue that its pre-Frankish developments may have their closest parallels in Denmark (or England), with concentrations of power beginning on a small scale in the sixth century, and best visible in the late seventh century and early eighth, just before the end of its independence.[168] Pre-Carolingian Saxony, by contrast, may be Wales to Frisia's England, with an avoidance of centralization, often seen as an ideological choice by local elites.[169] These instances further fill out the

---

[167] One instructive example is the concept of *veizla*, which initially (at least in Norwegian texts) meant 'hospitality', but came to mean 'benefice': *Kulturhistorisk leksikon*, XIX, cc. 631–2, s.v. *veitsle*.

[168] For recent surveys, see Heidinga, *Frisia*, pp. 17–22; Gerrets, 'Evidence of political centralisation'; earlier, Lebecq, *Marchands et navigateurs*, I, pp. 101–11.

[169] For surveys, see Lintzel, *Ausgewählte Schriften*, I, pp. 115–27; Hässler, 'Völkerwanderungs- und Merowingerzeit', pp. 310–14. See further below, pp. 585–8.

range of developments towards political aggregation, which, as we have seen, span both the Germanic and the Celtic lands of the North, and indeed potentially cover the Slav lands as well. Ireland would be at one end (maybe together with the Iceland of a later period), with few moves towards an increase in political scale for a long time. Wales would be next (maybe together with Saxony, and probably also Norway[170] and Sweden, at least during our period), as culture areas which began to move towards at least small-scale political dominance, but which stopped that movement at a given point. Denmark would come next, as a region which developed wider hegemonies (maybe paralleled by those of Frisia), but more intermittently. In England, finally, the process of aggregation, at least up to sub-regional level (Northumbria, Mercia, East Anglia, Wessex), was hardly broken at all, and a political structure that could be called a state had become visible by 800, in Mercia at least, and, as will be proposed later (p. 813), perhaps East Anglia too. This is, to repeat, not a league-table for failure and success; rather, it is a set of independent responses to an initial situation in, say, 500 of political fragmentation into small political units which have been called here tribal, which had not as yet begun even to be organized into archaeologically visible hierarchies except in Denmark. I shall conclude this chapter with an overview of the variables that arguably produced such an array of different solutions.

Four main factors affecting the development of states have been discussed across this section. One was the impact of political models from abroad, especially Francia: this had a substantial effect on England, less on Denmark (except perhaps in the south), none at all in Wales and Ireland, unless the relative prosperity of Irish churches in the eighth century can be used as a sign of potential (but unrealized) aggregation there. A second is the tightness of links between aristocrats and kings (and, in Ireland, lesser and greater kings). These remained relatively tight in England, and remained impermanent in Ireland; in Wales they perhaps started tight and then broke down. For Denmark we can only guess, though what we know of the ninth century perhaps shows that any links that did exist could be broken if kings went too far, or failed. Third is economic differentiation, which developed early in Denmark, later but steadily in England, relatively early but much less steadily in Wales, most hesitantly in Ireland. The fourth is the development of an aristocracy of estate-owners, dominating dependent peasantries through feudal landowning, out of an aristocracy of tribal leaders with economically autonomous followers, clients, political dependants. I have argued that this occurred first in England, uncertainly, on 'inlands', in the eighth century, and more comprehensively in the ninth; in Denmark it did not begin until after 900 at the earliest, and in Wales and Ireland it hardly occurred for many centuries. This latter is not essential for early signs of

---

[170] See e.g. Myhre, 'Chieftains' graves'.

wide-ranging and structured political power, as with Ine or Godofrid, but it has to have at least begun to develop for any stable and coercive state system to be created—as with Offa's and Cenwulf's Mercia, the only polity discussed in this chapter that could be called a state according to my definitions. From Gaul southwards, a Roman-style aristocracy survived almost everywhere; from the English Channel and the Rhine northwards, it had to be created or re-created, and the long-term stability of state-formation depended on it.

One parameter that I have not much discussed here is market relations. Twenty years ago Richard Hodges put them at the centre of his innovative analyses of state-formation in Francia and the northern lands, going so far as to argue that Charlemagne consciously developed the market to buttress the state in Francia.[171] Neither the market nor the state really needed much buttressing in Francia in 800, however, even setting aside the issue of whether this form of economic consciousness existed in our period. Nor do I think that markets are essential for state power in themselves, although they are certainly valuable resources if they are there. One could instead argue that they are relevant to the issues discussed in this chapter, but in a more indirect way: the presence of an integrated market system is a sure sign of local concentrations of private landed wealth; indeed, the more market exchange there is the richer landowners are. Markets are thus a guide to my fourth factor, aristocratic dominance, rather than a factor in their own right. They will be discussed in that light, and the overall argument will be defended, in Chapter 11. But it must be said immediately that, as we shall see in that chapter, an integrated market system is not at all easy to track in northern regions. Absent in Wales and Ireland, it is only visible in a politically controlled framework in most of England and Denmark before 800; autonomous markets, as late as the eighth century, can at present only be postulated on the North Sea coast of England (including the whole of East Anglia) and soon, perhaps, in the hinterland of Hedeby in Denmark. Market exchange is an important issue to pursue, but its association with state-formation (such as it is) takes us well past the closing date of this book.

Let us finish by returning to resources. I argued at the beginning of the chapter that states cannot exist without independent and stable resources; what sorts of resources did the various types of ruler discussed in this chapter actually command, from Offa, through Ine and Godofrid, to Vortipor and Feidlimid mac Crimthainn? They all had various forms of ad hoc tribute, for one. Offa's was heavier, more systematically characterized, and more frequently collected than was Ine's, and probably Ine's was more than that of any Welsh or Irish king, although we can be less sure about that. Stronger kings—Godofrid and Ine as well as Offa—controlled trade-outlets and the tolls they generated (below, pp. 681–8). They also could direct peasant

---

[171] Hodges, *Dark age economics*, pp. 151–98, is the classic text.

labour, as with the vast earthworks that Godofrid and especially Offa could promote—although even Irish kings could do that on a small scale, with the defences of their ringforts, and perhaps with roads too. Judicial fines and confiscations probably as yet produced less; they were more of a political than an economic resource. Successful warfare was certainly profitable, though its economic advantages were both risky and finite, as even the Carolingians found in the end.[172] But the major resource for all strong kings must have been what it was for aristocrats: the land they directly controlled. Kings controlled much more of it than aristocrats did, and indeed had enough to give it away to aristocrats for political support. Even before 700, English (and Welsh) kings can be seen doing this sort of thing; they were already participating in the land-based political processes that were discussed at some length for Spain, Francia, and Italy in Chapter 3. But this made it all the more essential for stable state-building, that the peasantry should become subordinated to aristocratic economic control, for that latter control was the main economic basis for successful kings as well—tribute was never enough on its own. That feudal power, of lords over peasants, was essential for lasting royal wealth and dominance. Offa was probably beginning to claim it, over the expanding 'inlands' of his estates; Ine had rather less of it; Godofrid probably did not have it yet. And what Offa and his successors were doing was to aim at the sort of land-based public power that Frankish and Italian kings already possessed, even if on a rather smaller geographical scale. When in the ninth century they managed that, the state-formation process could be seen to be completed.

---

[172] Reuter, 'The end of Carolingian military expansion', pp. 401–5.

PART III
Peasantries

7

Peasants and local societies: case studies

THIS CHAPTER AND the next two look at early medieval society from a different perspective, that of the peasantry. This is not at all easy in our period, or indeed in most periods before the nineteenth century at the earliest, for peasants were seldom literate until very recently, and the huge majority of narrative accounts which discuss them at all were the work of outsiders—clerics, notaries, more recently academics; even modern accounts of peasant experience by peasants themselves are typically the work of members of village elites, or of ex-peasants, distanced from their former traditions by education and urbanization. At best, these accounts are external reconstructions, and they are usually full-blown constructions, inventing peasant experience on ideological grounds, through the lens of moral exemplification, class-based hostility and contempt, or (in the case of ex-peasants) nostalgia.[1] This is certainly true for the late Roman and early medieval periods, where hostile constructions dominate accounts of peasantries, where indeed these exist at all.

There are some exceptions to this in our sources. One is some saints' lives, usually external to peasant experience of course, and always highly moralized and exemplified, but also occasionally using as a basis for their narratives assumptions about peasant perceptions and social relationships that are not exclusively negative. A second, on the surface, is law, which, in particular in the Romano-Germanic West, often appears to give us direct evidence about peasant social practices. This type of evidence was traditionally given by far the greatest weight by early medieval historians who were interested in peasants, not only because it gives us more information than most other sources do, but also because medieval social history came out of legal history, thus making it easier for historians to write as if law-codes were accurate accounts of peasant social action. Such assumptions were common into the 1960s. This reading of legislation is, however, naive.[2] It cannot be the case that schematic legal texts exactly encapsulated the range of social

---

[1] For hostile and distanced views in the later middle ages, Freedman, *Images*, is now classic.
[2] Cf. Wickham, *Land and power*, pp. 205–7.

practice anywhere, or that they could even begin to reflect the huge micro-regional differences in that practice that will have existed everywhere (no one village is quite like its neighbour in a peasant society even today, never mind in 600). More important, this is not the purpose of law, which is normative, not descriptive. In today's society it is more detailed, and also has strong coercive back-up, so legal norms are in theory more often imposed on the population at large, but no social analyst would dream of using modern statutes as sources in preference to the evidence of what people do in practice in their daily lives, and the latter, furthermore, remains hugely diverse from place to place. Ordinary people do not, essentially, spend much time dealing with legal niceties, even though these will surely affect their lives when they do. These observations are valid for the Roman empire as well, with its articulated legal and coercive system. In early medieval societies, where a coercive apparatus was far simpler, and (in many places) surviving court cases make no reference to written law at all, law could be nothing except social theory, a theory which doubtless derived from the local society the legislator knew best, but which would not have been a direct description of practice even there.[3] What laws focus on is certainly of relevance to us; as with narratives, their rhetorical fields are significant (see, for example, below, p. 513). But social history written exclusively from law-codes is a depressing experience to read, made worse by the fact that many historians, even when they do not have laws to rely on, often try to invent institutions and norms out of the anecdotes they encounter in the narrative sources. History of this kind both perpetuates the illusion of the descriptive nature of law and strips such anecdotes of the local contexts in which they gain meaning as events.

A third type of source is charters, legal documents. These have their own aridities: they are formulaic and repetitive; they need to exist in large numbers to be analytically useful, which is rare in our period. But as guides to peasant society, they can be important, for they often mention peasant activities, and are sometimes the work of peasants themselves (mediated through the scribes of the texts, at least); they are also locally specific by definition, dealing as they do with named people, in a named place, in (usually) a named year. They thus allow the sorts of comparisons, between patterns of social relationships and practices rather than abstract rules, that I have been aiming at throughout this book. This in my view justifies the

---

[3] Court-cases are themselves one way of getting over this gap; they have been an important evidence-base for much sophisticated social history in recent decades, as they show conflict and local social practices, often in some detail. I shall use them when I can. For all our period, however, and from all our regions, only some 300 cases survive, by my own very rough estimates. For lists, see Hübner, 'Gerichtsurkunden', I and II, for Francia and Italy respectively; Wormald, 'A hand-list', for England; Gagos and van Minnen, *Settling a dispute*, pp. 123–7, for Egypt—only a small handful survive for other regions; in general, see Davies and Fouracre, *The settlement of disputes*.

privileged use made of them here. All the same, two specific problems exist in any use of charters to characterize peasant society. First, they above all concern land, and thus only give a picture of those types of social relationship that relate to land, as it is given, sold, or leased to others. It is true that land is of crucial importance in any settled agrarian society, for it is the most direct marker of wealth and status (except in Ireland: above, p. 356), so that social relations linked to land are likely to be representative of others as well; but dealings which involve it are always among the most formal and solemn acts that peasants engage in, and analyses based on land transactions risk conveying too hieratic, too insufficiently nuanced, a picture of the range of social behaviour. Second, in a study of peasant society, one always has to read any given set of charters through an awareness that most 'authors' (the people who had them drawn up) were not peasants, and which of them actually were is not at all easy to tell—a peasant will not give five estates to a church, but an aristocrat can easily give a single field. The local reconstructions which follow in this chapter will as a result have to deal with peasants and their richer neighbours alike, at least initially, and a specifically peasant society will have to be located in the framework of evidence that often enough tells us more about aristocrats and churches. These two problems will have to be faced, systematically, in our case studies. But, notwithstanding them, charters, sometimes backed up by other sources such as saints' lives, seem to me the best starting-point for the peasantry that we have.

This chapter focuses on case studies. I want here to characterize a set of individual social realities, located specifically in time and place. The set consists of: the territory of Lucca in the eighth century; the middle Rhine in the eighth century; the Île de France in the seventh and eighth centuries; central Anatolia around 600; two large Egyptian villages, Aphroditō in the sixth century and Jēme in the seventh and eighth; and a village in England in the seventh century. These are not the only possible case studies for the period, but they are a high percentage, a good half perhaps (cf. below, p. 434), of the best ones. The purpose of beginning with these examples is simple: if we do not start a discussion of the peasantry with some clearly localized specificities, then we risk falling straight into the legalist abstractions already criticized—talking about, for example, the legal constraints of 'the unfree', rather than how unfree men and women actually fitted into different societies (cf. below, pp. 394–5, 405). In this chapter there will be relatively little generalization; that will be left to Chapter 9, which discusses the wider parameters of peasant society and socio-economic change. Chapter 8 will focus on the only homogeneous set of evidence for peasant activities that can be compared across all our regions in the way that was done for aristocracies in Chapter 4: the archaeology of rural settlement.

I have published detailed local analyses based on early medieval document collections before, including studies of Lucca (in particular) and the Rhineland. In order to avoid excessive repetition, the first two case studies here will be presented with a broader brush, less detailed and more synthetic. The Île de France has not been fully studied in this way before, however, and the two Egyptian villages are little known outside Egyptological circles; these examples will present more empirical material. The Anatolian case study is largely based on a single saint's life, that of Theodore of Sykeōn, for there are no documents for the zone; the argument there will have to be slightly different in type, and somewhat more interpretative. The English case is frankly speculative, indeed partially invented; but it is useful to include in this chapter, for comparative purposes, an account of the somewhat different peasant experience that was the counterpart to the weak aristocratic hegemonies discussed in Chapter 6, even though there is not the direct evidence that would be necessary for a properly empirical local study. All seven cases are, as far as is possible, looked at from the same standpoint: with attention paid to specific microregional realities, and with a systematic concern to look at social relations from the perspective of the peasantry, as far as our documentation permits.

What is a peasant? I had some trouble defining an aristocrat in Chapter 4, for one has to use a number of different criteria to do so, given that few of the aristocracies of our period were separated off on any consistent grounds from the rest of free society. For the peasantry it is a little easier, however, as one can regard the concept as a strictly economic one. Out of the competing characterizations of a peasant that exist, mine will be simply: a settled cultivator (or, more rarely, pastoralist), cultivating largely for subsistence, who does at least some agricultural work personally, and who controls his or her labour on the land. The issue of the control by peasants of their labour was discussed at the start of Chapter 5 (pp. 259–61), where dependent peasants were distinguished on this basis from slaves and wage labourers. Peasants could further either be landowners ('small owners') or tenants; they could be part-time—though not full-time—artisans; they could also have tenants or labourers working part of their land, as many cultivators do, especially richer ones.[4] If a rich peasant, however, accumulated so much land that s/he did not have to farm any of it directly, by my definition s/he would stop being a peasant and become a 'medium landowner'. Such medium owners characteristically, where they existed, stayed in villages, and made up village elites along with their richer peasant neighbours. They generally behaved like other villagers, and intermarried with them, but medium owners in particular were in a structurally dominant position that could often last across generations; furthermore, given that there was seldom in our period a policed boundary between peasants and aristocrats, medium owners were at the bottom of a social ladder that could, for the ambitious and the lucky, lead up into the aristocracy. These features mark medium owners off from the peasantry as a whole, which is particularly

---

[4] A valuable discussion is Hilton, *English peasantry*, pp. 3–19.

important when we remember that our documentation, even when it tells us about village society, tends to tell us about its richer rather than its poorer members. Even when we get through the veil of the aristocratic and ecclesiastical nature of our documentation, that is to say, it is often medium owners rather than peasants who become visible—another veil. But sometimes, as long as we are aware of it, we can break through even this, and discuss peasants as well. Such is the aim of this chapter.

1. Lucca and the Lucchesia

Lucca (Map 7, inset) was the main political centre in Tuscany in the eighth century, home of a duke, a rich cathedral church, over fifty other churches, and large numbers of urban landowners (above, pp. 211–12; below, p. 646). From the point of view of the rural inhabitants of the Lucchesia, the secular territory and diocese of Lucca, the city was a real focus. Even in the eighth century its market must have been important, for we can track agrarian specializations in the small plain around it and the hill slopes that bordered the plain, in grain and wine respectively, that must have been exchanged in the city.[5] And its landowners, whether secular or ecclesiastical, owned land in nearly every village of the Lucchesia, including right up in the Appennine valleys, 50 km and more from the city. Even though the overall scale of this landowning was not great by Frankish standards, it was all-pervasive, as the 300 or so Lucchese documents for the century show us.[6]

The other feature of Lucchese landowning, both large- and small-scale, including that of peasants, is that it was highly fragmented. We have a charter from 762 in which Bishop Peredeus (bishop 755–79), from one of the major landowning families in the diocese, divided some lands with his nephew Sunderad. They split a small demesne, itself consisting of several pieces, as discussed earlier (p. 295); they then divided twenty individual fields and two apple orchards (the latter tree by tree, *per numerum*). Lucchese documents often describe estates in terms of demesne, tenant houses and isolated plots of land scattered across several villages. We have no record at all of large-scale blocks of land owned by a single person, and it is likely, taking into account later evidence, that they were rare.[7] If one looks at this

---

[5] For Lucca's political structure Schwarzmaier, *Lucca und das Reich*, pp. 36–51, 74–90, 156–69 remains basic. For agrarian specializations, Wickham, 'Economic and social institutions', p. 13; there was greater subsistence in the mountains, however—see Wickham, *Mountains*, pp. 22–6.

[6] For Appennine landowning, ibid., pp. 56–8. For eighth-century Lucchese documents, the best edition is *ChLA*, vols. XXX–XL, but this only covers original charters and eighth-century copies; although these are the great majority, I have usually found it more convenient here to cite the older editions, *CDL*, I–II (to 774) and *MDL*, V.2 (which also registers some documents edited in *MDL*, IV, the only really poor edition of this set).

[7] *CDL*, II, n. 161 (n. 154 also divides servile dependants). For tenurial fragmentation see e.g. Mailloux, 'Pour une étude des paysages'.

situation from the perspective of a village and its peasant inhabitants, it meant to them that few if any single landowners were likely to own enough land locally to dominate a village society from the outside. Indeed, although few villages had no land of urban owners in them, it was also the case that few villages had lands of only *one* external owner in them. Rather, in most villages there was a complex mixture of property-ownership, with external owners, prosperous medium owners, and owner-cultivators, intermingled in a stable pattern of fractioned tenure which had probably changed little since the Roman empire.

Put another way, this fragmentation also meant that peasants who owned their own land lived next door to peasants who cultivated the lands of others. Indeed, it is likely (it would certainly be true in later centuries) that there was a large grey area of minor status differences, from peasants who owned all their land, to those who owned most of it and leased single fields, to those who were basically tenants but owned a couple of land plots,[8] to totally dependent free tenants. There was then a sharper status break between free and unfree tenants, which was hard to cross even by manumission (below, p. 564), although it has to be added that even here, when out in the fields, it was hard to be sure which was which. In a court-case of 796 from neighbouring Pisa, for example, which concerned the claim to freedom of a family of tenants, it was impossible to tell from the work they did whether they were free or not; they only lost because hostile witnesses said that they had been beaten by episcopal bailiffs 'as unfree', *pro servo*. Even such punishment may have been a matter of interpretation, for free tenants, too, were routinely subjected from the late eighth century onwards to the justice of their landlords for infractions specifically linked to their tenurial relationship.[9] A second grey area, as already implied, extended upwards, from owner-cultivators to medium owners, and then up, slowly, towards the lower strata of the aristocracy; for, in terms of the ideology of the eighth-century kingdom, these were all free Lombards, with public obligations at all levels, and no legal separation between peasants and *nobiles*.[10] The society of the village was doubtless structured around an acute awareness of the status gradations just described; but these gradations remained minor, at least in free society, and any free family could in principle claw its way up the ladder, until bad weather, debt, or the wrong number of children pushed it back down again.

This flexibility was helped further by alienations of land outside the family, of which there were many in the Lucchesia. Aristocrats bought and sold land, as we saw earlier (pp. 216–17), but peasants did so too, both

---

[8] Leases could sometimes be sold between tenants, indicating a certain tenurial autonomy, as with *MDL*, V.2, n. 159 (a. 776).

[9] Manaresi, *I placiti*, n. 9. For the *iustitia* of landlords over tenants, see Endres, 'Das Kirchengut', pp. 264–5; cf., for other parts of Italy, Panero, 'Servi, coltivatori dipendenti'.

[10] Tabacco, 'Dai possessori'.

single fields and whole properties. Our documentation stresses alienations (whether gifts or sales) to the church, for our Lucchese documents are all from the archive of the bishop of Lucca (including his subordinate churches, urban and rural). Indeed, our charters hardly begin before the start of the first great period of the foundation and endowment of churches (c.720–860) in Italy.[11] But when land came to the church, so did the most recent documentation for it (for one thing, this protected the church against the legal claims of others, most typically that a donor to the church was not the rightful owner); when this survives, it allows us to see a more secular network of land exchange. So, for example, Natalis, a master builder from northern Italy (*homo transpadanus magister casarius*), founded a church in Lucca in 805; at his death and those of his priests, the church and its properties, including a house in Vicopelago just south of the city, would go to the bishop. When that happened, the bishop also got a charter in which Nozo son of Raduald of Vicopelago sold the house there to Natalis and his brother in 787, which he had earlier bought from Gausprand son of Peredeus. Natalis was by no means a peasant, but Nozo probably was. He was a rich peasant, for he could own a tenant house; he also had some public standing, with the title of *vir devotus*, and witnessed charters around Vicopelago for others. But he was a local figure above all, and his documented identity does not show him as linked with the slow haemor-rhage of land to the church—this was the work of others. Instead, he carried on owning land, as a charter of 788 makes clear; his local position, including his interest in land sales, need not have changed at all. Despite the accumu-lation of church land, this must have been true for most people in the countryside, for the same complex array of gradations of landowners and tenants is as visible in the eleventh and twelfth centuries as it is in the eighth.[12]

One can thus argue for a considerable stability in Lucchese village society, which was not undermined either by outside powers or by the generosity of the faithful. Outside powers in effect cancelled each other out: city owner X could hardly aim to dominate a village by force if city owner Y and church Z owned land there too, without a great deal of trouble. It is also probably the case that the long-standing urban focus of political action in Lucca, as elsewhere in Italy, made local domination in villages less interesting for lords to establish: nowhere in Italy can we see a trend to this before 900, and often not until after 1000 (actually, in the specific case of Lucca, it barely occurred

---

[11] The cycle of gift-giving began with Liutprand's law of 714 on the endowment of churches (Liutprand 6); for its end, see Wickham, *Mountains*, pp. 54–5 (documents from then on are predominantly church leases in most of Italy for a century and more); for an overview, see Mailloux, 'Modalités'.

[12] *MDL*, V.2, nn. 216, 221, 322 (= IV.2, n. 6); cf. *CDL*, II, n. 269 for Nozo, *MDL*, V.2, n. 428 for Natalis (cf., for the latter, Violante, 'I traspadani', pp. 408–13). For the patterns in the eleventh and twelfth centuries, Wickham, *Community*, pp. 21–8.

even then).[13] As was argued in Chapter 4, what usually mattered to the powerful in our period was the net amount of land, thus rents, thus wealth they had, not where the land was. Villages, and villagers, could be allowed to get on with their own lives with relatively little interference. But this did not mean that they avoided the powerful; broadly, the opposite was true, as we shall see in a moment.

Villages may have been left alone, but they were not very strong as communities in the eighth-century Lucchesia. Settlement was generally dispersed in the diocese, except in the mountains, and in the plain around the city this reached an extreme. Here, individual houses were often scattered across village territories (*vici* or *loci*), in no apparent order, as they had probably been since the Romans centuriated the landscape (a division into squares that is still visible today), and as they have been without a break since. There are some cases in which village boundaries were themselves uncertain, with the same rural church ascribed to different territories in different documents: people were by no means sure what village they were actually in. The lowland Lucchesia was a typical zone of Mediterranean dry farming, which involves little structured co-operation (unlike stock-raising, which is often on common land, or the more collective co-operation assumed by irrigation, or by north European open fields); under these circumstances, villages do not have to have a strong economic role (see below, pp. 481–95). But even in this context, Lucca's villages seem to mark something of an extreme. This may be because they were not only scattered, but small; in parts of the Lucca plain they were only half a kilometre or a kilometre apart, and landowning by individuals across several of them was common, further weakening the presumption that village cohesion was the most important social bond. One example is Aunefrid *clericus* of Guamo, 5 km south of the city, who gave all his possessions to a church in Vaccoli, a neighbouring village, in 720, consisting of third shares (at most) of two houses, his own and that of a tenant in Mugnano, on the Arno some 20 km away. Aunefrid can hardly have been more than a prosperous peasant, and we can only guess at how his family got a house on the Arno (by marriage? did they move?), but the instance shows, all the same, that even peasants could own over widish geographical areas. The importance of Guamo itself to Aunefrid need not have been great at all. Villages with more of a social or political role are in a minority in the Lucchesia. One is apparently visible in a document of 746, in which two *centinarii* and the whole *plebs* of Musciano in the Arno valley consented to the ordination of a local priest; but this has no analogues elsewhere.[14] The collective solidarity that all peasants need to

---

[13] For Lucca and Tuscany, Wickham, 'La signoria rurale', and refs. cited.

[14] For village incoherence, Wickham, *Community*, pp. 54–62. Aunefrid: *CDL*, I, n. 27; Musciano: n. 86. *Centinarii* were probably local leaders; they may have had some official status (cf. the *centinus* in Ratchis 1), but their powers are notably obscure, and were perhaps ad hoc. (The office is above all in our period documented in Francia: see the survey by Murray, 'From Roman to Frankish Gaul'.)

survive is far more likely to have been based on links of extended family, that is, kinship, and more or less formalized relations of friendship, like the *consortes* that some documents refer to,[15] than village communities, in this part of the world. These may not have been elaborate either, however; groups of brothers are quite common in Lucchese documents, but groups of cousins are distinctly rare.

If these horizontal relationships were not enough, then peasants could seek the support of the more powerful: by patronage links to other villagers or to external landowners, both lay and ecclesiastical. Indeed, gifts of land to churches could themselves fit into vertical relationships of this kind. Such gifts of course had spiritual motives; they helped to save one's soul, as the proems to many charters make clear. But there were also other reasons than simple piety to give land to any given church. Such a church could be a useful support in times of economic need or legal difficulty: the church (or its owner, whether a founding family or the bishop) was here acting as a patron.[16] Peasants indeed had choices here. In the village of Asulari, just north of Lucca, we find three separate church foundations, two in one year, 759, and one not long before 765; the founders seem to be local, and it would be hardly unreasonable to see them as competitive, probably between families of medium owners, the village elite. After such foundations were established, the decisions of local donors to give to one or another would not have been neutral. At a different political level, the church of S. Colombano in Lucca was refounded by Bishop Peredeus in the early 760s. Between that date and 774, when Peredeus was exiled to Francia after the Carolingian conquest of Italy (he returned in 777 and died in 779), we have a coherent group of six gifts to the church, all from parts of the countryside where Peredeus' family is known to have held land; after 774 these gifts abruptly stop. One could thus conclude that these were the gifts of Peredeus' family clients, in the period when the family head had particular prominence and power; and at least one of the gifts was from a peasant owner. Patronage links in Lucca could extend from the highest stratum in landowning society to the lowest.[17]

Patronage can take many forms. One is the tight link between land gifts and military dependence that has become encapsulated for historians as the 'feudo-vassalic' relationship. This, at least, was not a major feature of our period in Italy. Lombard kings had *gasindi*, personal followers, very like

---

[15] e.g. *MDL*, V.2, nn. 208, 227.

[16] See Costambeys, *Piety, property*, ch. 2, for proems; for patronage, Rosenwein, *To be the neighbor*, pp. 132–43; Wickham, *Mountains*, pp. 190–215; Innes, *State and society*, pp. 16–34. Note that most people gave only restricted percentages of their land, except for the childless. But churches did massively increase their global landholding across the whole of Carolingian Europe: see below, Ch. 9, n. 110.

[17] Asulari: *CDL*, II, nn. 138 (cf. *MDL*, V.2, n. 215 = IV, n. 103), 140, 186 (cf. 255). For S. Colombano, Wickham, 'Aristocratic power', pp. 164–6.

later vassals, but their patronage of them did not necessarily involve land (above, p. 215). Conversely, we have a handful of lifetime or permanent cessions of land in Lucca to retainers or servants in return for past service, but they are fairly heterogeneous, and the service seems not to have been military.[18] Gifts to churches by personal clients, however, are signs that a far wider range for possible patronage relations existed than just the military service of traditional aristocratic patronage networks: exchanges of favours, political and legal support, preferment, protection. The fact that they extended to the peasant majority shows that peasant owners, at least, had access to the political-social framework of urban aristocratic dominance and competition, rather than being excluded from it. I would argue indeed that these patronage relationships created a network in which Italian aristocrats, although poorer than their Frankish neighbours, and incapable of aiming at local domination because of the fragmentation of their lands, could at least achieve local hegemonies for their values and their practices.[19]

A male free peasant in the Lucchese countryside thus operated in an interestingly fluid situation. (Women did not: for their situation, see below, pp. 554–7.) He was linked to his kin but tightly linked only to his nearest kin. He was not closely identified with his village, at least in our best-documented villages; at most, different village social structures gave to peasants different sets of possible internal and external relationships—different stages, that is to say, to act on. As for vertical networks: tenants were doubtless tied fairly closely to their landlords, as they are in most societies. Small owners, however, seem to have been able to choose which patronage networks they participated in, with high- or low-ranking, local or urban, lay or ecclesiastical patrons all available, at least in principle, to most land-owning peasants. It is probable, nevertheless, that very few Lucchese peasants could avoid patronage links altogether; village collectivities were too weak for horizontal relationships to be able to replace vertical ones. Peasants in the Lucchesia, however independent, were thus part of an aristocratic-dominated social and economic world.

The peasant voice is rarely heard directly in this period, but here is one Lucchese peasant testifying in Siena in 715. 'Gaudiosus, an old free man, said: "It is fifty years since I moved here [to the Senese] from the city of Lucca, and I dwell on the land of the late Zotto; I know that the churches of S. Pietro and S. Vincenzo, where Bishop Deodatus [of Siena] has just built a font, are under the church of S. Maria Alteserra, and that church was, from the day of its foundation, in the diocese of S. Donato [of Arezzo] and still is." ' Alteserra, now Monte Benichi in the Val d'Ambra, a remote outlier of the Chianti hills, was part of a network of churches subject ecclesiastically to Arezzo and for secular matters to Siena, which the bishop of Siena tried

---

[18] *CDL*, I, n. 61, 124 (for Pisa), II, n. 143 (a female servant).
[19] Wickham, 'Aristocratic power', pp. 162–70. See further below, pp. 438–41.

to claim for his diocese consistently from the early eighth century to the early thirteenth. In 715 seventy-seven men, mostly inhabitants of the zone, all testified in favour of the bishop of Arezzo (as their heirs in later centuries usually would too), despite the threats of Warnefrit, gastald of Siena, their secular ruler.[20] Gaudiosus is here particularly significant: he was an incomer from 120 km away, one of the lowest-status people who testified in the inquisition, and was a tenant of Zotto, son of a former gastald of Siena; but he was still capable of being sufficient of a political agent to testify four-square with his neighbours in favour of Arezzo. Firm institutions of horizontal solidarity may have been lacking, but the complex networks of power in the countryside of Tuscany gave even peasants the possibility of choice, and occasionally we can see them taking it.

2. The middle Rhineland

On many levels, the middle Rhineland (Map 10) was not so dissimilar to the Lucchesia. Historians mean by the term 'Mittelrhein' a fairly restricted part of the river valley: the northern third of the long, agriculturally rich plain, surrounded by forests, some 30 km wide and 300 km long, running between Basel and Mainz, from the river's northward turn out of Switzerland to the Rhine 'gorge' going down to Bonn and Cologne. This northern third, north of Speyer, included three bishoprics, Speyer, Worms, and Mainz. Mainz, at least, was a significant urban centre in the period after 750, and perhaps also before; it was a real economic and political focus, probably not matching Lucca, but at least paralleling it, and must have been the main commercial centre for the wine export down the Rhine that was a major source of wealth for the area.[21] But the middle Rhine valley was also dotted with other political foci, which were entirely lacking in the Lucchesia. There were important estate-centres of the kings, such as Trebur, Gernsheim, and Frankfurt, which were densely enough clustered to make the area a real *Königslandschaft* in the Carolingian period; there were also power-bases of some of the major Austrasian aristocrats, above all the 'Rupertiner', the ancestors of the Capetian kings of France; and there was one of the principal east Frankish monasteries of the Carolingians, Lorsch, actually founded by the Rupertiner in 764, but already by 772 under royal control.[22] Lorsch's huge cartulary, by far the largest single document collection in eighth- and

---

[20] *CDL*, I, n. 19 (p. 76 for Gaudiosus, p. 74 for threats by the gastald). See in general Gasparri, 'Il regno longobardo', pp. 241–9; Delumeau, *Arezzo*, pp. 475–85. The Val d'Ambra was probably an area of weak aristocratic power in general: below, p. 546.

[21] For Mainz, see Wamers, *Die frühmittelalterlichen Lesefunde*, esp. pp. 19–49, 195–7, for archaeology; Staab, *Untersuchungen*, pp. 122–32, and Falck, *Mainz*, pp. 8–34, for documents.

[22] The basic accounts of the middle Rhine are Gockel, *Karolingische Königshöfe*; Staab, *Untersuchungen*; Innes, *State and society*.

ninth-century Europe, is the major source for the area (which is thus documented above all from the very end of our period), together with the cartularies of Fulda, another major monastery, founded in 743–4 in the hill country some 80 km north-east of Frankfurt, which are an important subsidiary source.[23] Almost all of the several hundred documents for the eighth-century middle Rhine (around a hundred of them for one village, Dienheim) are donations, and those in the Lorsch cartulary are very abbreviated, which restricts their value, but the scale of the material we have once again parallels Lucca, and indeed it is more concentrated, since it is almost all from the last third of the century (and the first third of the next—gifts fell off from the 840s, as in Lucca).

One major difference from Lucca was, then, that there were more political centres than just one city, or even three: as elsewhere in Francia, power foci were above all rural, and thus more scattered across the landscape. But the landowning structure based on these centres was just as fragmented as at Lucca. There were a few single-block estates, but mostly land was owned in scattered parcels, even by aristocrats—and certainly by Lorsch and Fulda, who accumulated their huge properties in many cases field by field. In our best-documented villages, above all Dienheim, but also Bensheim, Bürstadt, Oppenheim, or Menzingen, we find complex networks of substantial land-owners, all intermingled: really large owners, like the king and the Rupertiner and, eventually, Lorsch; substantial local aristocrats, like Walaram (d. 802), father of Hraban Maur, abbot of Fulda and then archbishop of Mainz (d. 856); and a set of lesser owners, who can be found controlling one or more estates, stretching across several villages, but whose participation in an 'aristocracy' would have been more variable.[24] These three broadly defined groups are particularly well documented, for they made up the main donors to the monasteries. Beneath them were village-based medium owners and small peasant owners, just as in Italy; these turn up in the documents as donors, as witnesses, and as owners listed on land boundaries. Free tenants were probably less common, however, in that all the dependants referred to in our charters are unfree, *servi* and *mancipia*; this seems to be fairly typical of east Frankish estates, as ninth-century documents make plain.[25] We could assume, however, even though we have no leases, that a

[23] The major eighth-century collections are thus *Codex Laureshamensis*, and *Ub. Fulda*. The next great collection, moving southwards up the Rhine, is that of Wissembourg for Alsace (*Trad. Wiz.*).

[24] For Dienheim, see Gockel, *Karolingische Königshöfe*, pp. 184–203, 222–7; Staab, *Untersuchungen*, pp. 262–78; Freise, 'Studien zum Einzugsbereich', pp. 1187–98; Wickham, 'Rural society', pp. 519–23; Innes, *State and society*, esp. pp. 22–3, 108–9, 126–8. For Bürstadt, see Gockel, *Karolingische Königshöfe*, pp. 228–312. For Menzingen, on the far south-east edge of the middle Rhine, see Schwind, 'Beobachtungen', pp. 457–64; this whole article is the best overview of Carolingian villages in the German lands, and it emphasizes the fragmented nature of landholding. For aristocrats, see most recently Innes, *State and society*, pp. 51–77.

[25] See below, Ch. 9, n. 81.

good percentage of the isolated grain-fields and vineyards given to Lorsch must have been let out for rent, either to the families of their donors or to the free peasants whose lands often adjoined them—presumably in *precariae*, the most normal forms of leases on the Wissembourg estates south of Speyer and in other east Frankish document collections (Lorsch's compilers explicitly kept no *precariae*).[26] We could further expect the wholly undocumented relationship *between* medium and small owners to have a tenurial element, as was certainly the case in Lucca. But most tenure remained unfree, and it is unlikely that there were many free families in the middle Rhine who owned no land.

Two other differences from the Lucchesia need signalling. One is the wealth of the richest Rhine aristocrats. Peredeus of Lucca, one of that city's major owners, could not have even tried to match the Rupertiner; his economic level would have been more that of Walaram and Hraban, whose activity in the Rhineland was circumscribed by richer and more powerful figures.[27] This fully fits the wider contrast between the aristocratic wealth of Francia and Italy discussed in Chapter 4. The scatter of aristocratic property made claims to village-level political dominance as complicated a task as in Lucca, but the greater power of any given aristocrat made even their unplanned acts potentially more dangerous to their peasant and village-level neighbours, who must have watched carefully for the casual flicks of the tails of the dinosaurs marching across their landscape. If an aristocrat happened to live or own a major estate-centre in one's own village, then his local influence would have been greater, even if peasants would perhaps have been still more on their guard. Dienheim's privileged documentation is at least in part because there were probably two such centres there, a royal estate, which Charlemagne gave (most of) to Fulda in 782, and most likely a Rupertiner centre, rather more closely linked to Lorsch: hence the fact that other people in Dienheim gave to both monasteries as well.[28]

A third difference from Lucca is that village social structures seem to have been significantly more coherent. Settlement archaeology from neighbouring parts of modern Germany shows grouped settlements in existence by 600 at the latest, consisting of sets of farmsteads, rectangular post-hole houses with associated outbuildings (below, pp. 500–2). This would roughly fit the Rhenish documents, which divide the landscape into clearly characterized *villae*, here evidently meaning villages, and their territories, including fields

---

[26] Examples of Wissembourg *precariae* are *Trad. Wiz.*, nn. 208, 226, 229, 256–7, 264; cf. Morelle, 'Les "actes de précaire" ', pp. 618–22, for Gorze, and Depreux, 'L'apparition de la précaire', for St Gallen. For the Lorsch compilers, see *Codex Laureshamensis*, II, p. 3; cf. Innes, *State and Society*, p. 14.

[27] For Walaram, see Staab, *Untersuchungen*, pp. 387–91; Innes, *State and society*, pp. 64–8; Staab, 'La circulation des biens', pp. 924–30. For documents, see esp. *Ub. Fulda*, nn. 38, 177–8, 283.

[28] See *Ub. Fulda*, nn. 149 (= *MGH, Dip. Kar.*, I, n. 145), 246 (cf. 236, 277).

and woodland or pasture land, often called *marcae*. It is rare for houses to be situated in *marcae*; settlement seems to have generally been concentrated in the centre of the *villa*, with grain-fields and vineyards around it. Some of these *villae* must have been fairly large: excavated settlements seem to average only around ten farmsteads, but Dienheim could have had four times that in 800 or more, judging by the documents.[29] The spatial coherence of such villages is clear from both sorts of evidence. Village territories structured the landscape. They seem to have been socially coherent, too. They did not have any visible administrative structures, however informal, but we do have examples of villages acting collectively, with all their free men turning out to formal acts; public tribunals were also centred in them. More occasionally, villages, or groups of villages, seem to be ascribed collective obligations such as labour service. These patterns are much easier to find in the Rhineland (and, more generally, in the German lands) than in Italy.[30]

Dienheim is well enough documented to allow us to go further than that. It had a village-based witness-group which appeared particularly regularly in documents, especially (but not only) if the charters were redacted in the *vicus publicus* or *villa publica* of Dienheim itself; Eckhard Freise identified thirty-six of its members. These men must have acted as a de facto leadership for the public activity of the village. They were doubtless linked to the aristocrats whose power-structures surrounded them, and we can sometimes find groups of village witnesses transported wholesale to another village to witness for a local aristocrat, presumably acting in some way as part of his entourage.[31] In this way, we can posit at least one form of social linkage extending from the aristocracy into the villages of the whole of the middle Rhine. But it is also noteworthy that the further down the social strata we go, the less we find villagers giving to the monasteries. There is a particularly explicit short text for Dienheim from 796, referring to a dispute about tolls payable at the *nautis*, the Rhine port that the village also had; the twenty-two witnesses listed in it are described thus: *isti habent hereditatem*, 'these men have inherited land', *in Dienenheim*. These witnesses were headed by Count Rupert of the Rupertiner, and included Hraban Maur's father and several other substantial aristocrats. Less than half this group seem to have been villagers, in that they were part of the standard set of regular Dienheimer witnesses, and those that were in that set were probably its

---

[29] For the size of excavated settlements, see Damminger, 'Dwellings, settlements', p. 60. For *villa* and *marca*, see e.g. Schwind, 'Beobachtungen', pp. 453–4. *Ub. Fulda*, n. 279 (a. 801), for Dienheim, is a rare reference to a building in a *marca*.

[30] Innes, *State and society*, pp. 108–9, 111, 126–7, 159–64, with reference to the more institutional readings of previous historiography.

[31] Freise, 'Studien zum Einzugsbereich', pp. 1187–98. For the witness group moving, see e.g. their witnessing around Kreuznach, 20 km from Dienheim, in each case with the same aristocrat, Ediram: *Ub. Fulda*, n. 278; *Codex diplomaticus Fuldensis*, n. 335 (cf. Staab, *Untersuchungen*, pp. 386–7 for Ediram).

leaders, for they often witness first in other texts; they also included some of the more systematic donors from the village. By contrast, the rest of Freise's witness group gave little or (usually) nothing to the monasteries, maybe only two or three fields at the end of their public lives, mostly to Lorsch. It looks as though there were two sets of Dienheimers who had a certain public role: a richer group, more closely linked to aristocrats, who gave more land and often witnessed less; and a more modest group, who witnessed more and gave distinctly less.[32] This can best be seen as a distinction between local medium owners and the landowning peasantry.

Dienheim may have been quite politically divided, even though it could operate as a collectivity. As Matthew Innes has stressed, there was very little overlap there between donors to Lorsch and donors to Fulda; this may well represent a factional difference, with donors choosing to link themselves to more Rupertiner Lorsch or more royal Fulda, maybe depending on longer-standing patronage links to the royal and Rupertiner centres in the village itself.[33] But an equally sharp divide was that between the donor group, relatively rich people, and those who hardly gave anything at all. Unlike in the Lucchesia, the peasant leaders of Dienheim, and the middle Rhine in general, were not sufficiently involved with external clientèles to follow the aristocratic practice of linking themselves to the great monastic houses. This must have been deliberate: the structures of aristocratic power were probably more threatening than inviting, and only a minority of village leaders committed themselves fully to them. Peasants who were not owners were, as already noted, as a rule unfree in the middle Rhine, and the free–unfree divide needs to be added to the divisions already mentioned; it must have seemed to be a further threat to the stratum of peasant owners, whose freedom would be at risk if they lost their land.

It is not that no peasants participated in aristocratic clientèles at all. One, as Innes has made particularly clear, was Ripwin of Bensheim, fl. 768–806. He went to Italy in the Carolingian army in, probably, 792, making his will in favour of Lorsch (which is close to Bensheim) as he did so. He seems to have been a military client of the monastery (he and his brother sold land to Lorsch in return for a horse in 768–9); he was also, along with his father and brother, a charter witness for Bensheim and for Lorsch. He was doubtless a beneficiary of monastic patronage, but he did not rise very far, all the same; his gift to the monastery at the end of his life, in 806, was of probably no more than a handful of tenant houses—he had become a medium owner at

---

[32] *Ub. Fulda*, n. 246. For commentary, Staab, *Untersuchungen*, pp. 262–78; Freise, 'Studien zum Einzugsbereich', pp. 1190–5, 1259–60.

[33] For the lack of overlap in gifts, see Innes, *State and society*, p. 22. The clearest exception is Siggo, who gave to Fulda in *Codex diplomaticus Fuldensis*, n. 198, and to Lorsch in *Codex Laureshamensis*, n. 1670 (see Staab, *Untersuchungen*, p. 274; Friese, 'Studien zum Einzugsbereich', p. 1189)—Siggo is also one of the only people both to be a (fairly) substantial donor and a frequent witness.

best. Ripwin is an interesting figure, unusually well documented for a peasant, thanks to his military role.[34] But he puts into relief the others, who kept away from such power structures, and from gifts to churches. We seem to have a class opposition in the middle Rhine villages which we did not see in the Lucchesia, with peasant leaders for the most part following different practices from the aristocracy.

From the standpoint of free peasant cultivators in Dienheim or Bensheim around 800, the world was probably more sharply characterized than around Lucca. The economic environment was fairly open in both, with markets for produce clearly available: the urban market in Lucca, the river trade route for wine in the Rhineland. Landowning was equally fragmented in each. But the aristocracy was much stronger in the middle Rhine, and village collectivities were also considerably more visible. In the Lucchesia, peasants could and did choose between a variety of patronage networks, which were not necessarily threatening, and which are likely to have re-inforced the ideological hegemony, the legitimation, of the aristocratic world. (Patronage networks work like that in parts of rural Italy even today.) In the middle Rhine, however, patronage networks were more po-tentially dangerous, for aristocrats were more powerful; they also did not encompass the whole of the village elite. Peasants, even those with a public standing, tended to keep out of them. It is most likely that village structures, although informal, were sufficiently coherent to provide horizontal support groups for the peasantry that would get the free sector of the village (al-though probably not the unfree) through bad times without needing the support of lords. The larger the village, the stronger that collectivity. The village as a social group thus acted as a buffer between aristocratic demands and peasant needs, in a way that it did not do in Italy, well before the more developed, but also more subject, village communities of the twelfth century and onwards.[35]

3. The Île de France

The territory around Paris, the Paris basin of the rivers Seine and Oise, a circle of some 50 km radius around the city (Map 9, inset), was much more aristocratic than either of the two previous areas discussed: there aristocrats were hegemonic over peasant owners from a distance, but here they exer-cised direct control, and peasant owners are distinctly difficult to find. This case study thus illuminates peasant dependence, not autonomy, and great landowning will have to be discussed in more detail. The Île de France is

---

[34] Innes, *State and society*, pp. 147–52 (better than Gockel, *Karolingische Königshöfe*, pp. 260–2); the key texts are *Codex Laureshamensis*, nn. 247, 257, 259.
[35] See for these communities Bader, *Studien*, II, a classic legalist account.

documented from early in the seventh century, thanks largely to the extensive endowment of St-Denis by King Dagobert in the 630s and its subsequent accumulation of royal and aristocratic estates, in donations often surviving in the original. Just after the end of the eighth century, around 820, the run of St-Denis charters can be set against a very different text, the estate survey (polyptych) of another royal monastery, St-Germain-des-Prés. We will thus be able to look at this area across two centuries of history. Very broadly, the St-Denis material focuses on the lands north of the Seine, the St-Germain survey on the lands to its south. But here, unlike in the middle Rhine, these two monasteries, although rivals, do not represent geographically separate power centres, for both are Parisian: St-Germain immediately extramural to the Roman and Merovingian city, St-Denis some 10 km to the north. Paris was a significant urban centre (below, p. 677), and its other churches accumulated lay donations too, but the two great monasteries, together probably with the cathedral, were by far the dominant ecclesiastical centres of the area.[36]

The Île de France was another *Königslandschaft*, even more than was the middle Rhine. Away from Paris, the Oise valley, in particular, was studded with royal *palatia*, from Clichy just outside the city up to Compiègne and Quierzy, which were the main residences of the seventh-century Merovingians in Neustria, and of the Carolingians when they were in the western Frankish lands too. The Frankish kings may have lived in rural centres, but Paris was their focus; the Paris basin was dominated by them. In the seventh century one can almost construct a ceremonial landscape out of royal movements to the north of the city. One of its tracks became visible when Audoin, bishop of Rouen, died in 680 at Clichy and his body was carried in procession back to Rouen: the king and queen accompanied the bier the 30 km to Pontoise, but then returned, leaving bishops and aristocrats to take it across the Oise into the Vexin and on into what would become Normandy.[37] This royal dominance did not mean that the Île de France was not an aristocratic centre as well, however. As we saw in Chapter 4 (pp. 187–93), most of the major Neustrian aristocrats owned land around Paris in the seventh century, providing a strong tenurial focus for

[36] *ChLA*, XIII–XVI collects the seventh- and eighth-century originals for St-Denis (and a handful for St-Germain and other churches); *Recueil des chartes de Saint-Germain-des-Prés*, I, adds other documents for that monastery; *MGH, Dip. Merov.* adds other royal cessions to St-Denis. The polyptych of St-Germain has had three major editions, by Guérard, Longnon, and Hägemann and his associates. I have mostly used Longnon's edition, *Pol. St-Germain*, referring to Hägemann, *Das Polyptychon*, where necessary; the numeration of the text is the same. For the cathedral there is no surviving charter collection, but Marculf's seventh-century formulary (in *MGH, Formulae*, pp. 36–106) was most plausibly compiled for a bishop of Paris, and its second book, containing private formulae, could be seen as a guide to episcopal transactions. Lay donations to sets of Paris churches include *ChLA*, XIII, nn. 569, 571.

[37] For the *palatia*, see esp. Barbier, 'Le système palatial franc'. For the procession, *Vita Audoini*, cc. 15–17.

the power-struggles of the half-century after 640. This density of large landholders meant, as in the Lucchesia and the middle Rhine, that territorial control by single figures was barely possible; here, however, the density of large estates was such that, seen as a whole, aristocratic (including royal) dominance over the peasantry could be taken for granted.

This picture is reinforced by the overall structures of landowning themselves. In the Rhineland landowners owned scattered estates inside *villae*, 'villages'; in the Île de France they owned the *villae* themselves, a word which here, before 800 or so, is better translated 'estates'. Such *villae* were much more often single blocks of land than they were in either of my previous examples, or, indeed, than almost anywhere in the former Roman empire outside Britain (above, p. 319). The abiding image of the Paris basin is the huge *villae*, with highly subject tenants, of the polyptych of St-Germain, the 117 *mansi* at Palaiseau, the 110 at Jouy, the eighty-nine at Verrières, the forty-three at Épinay, and the seventy-nine at Thiais, all neighbouring estates just south of the city, around what is now Orly airport.[38] Overall, the lands around Paris were structured by estate boundaries, which could include large land areas. In the end, these estates would become villages (the process was arguably well under way by the time of the polyptych: below, pp. 510–14), but this in itself seems to show that the landscape was simply divided up between village/estate blocks. Inside this chequerboard, there was at first sight little space for the smaller-scale levels of landowning that we saw in our first two case studies.

Before we get to the peasantry, it is worth facing two linked questions about this pattern: whether it was quite as regular as initially appears, and how it came to exist in the first place. Overall, the image that we get in documents is that single-block *villae* were a feature of a fairly wide region, stretching north to St-Bertin (modern St-Omer) and west to Le Mans— essentially, the heartland of Neustria; eastwards, the sort of fragmented landholding that we have seen for the middle Rhine seems to begin around Verdun.[39] But it would be wrong to take this image too literally; if one looks closely enough, there are signs that it is exaggerated. Let us look at one *villa*, Lagny-le-Sec, some 40 km north-east of Paris, to develop the point. One of its subordinate properties was certainly situated elsewhere, the *res* in the *locus* of Silly-le-Long in 688, about 5 km away, which had formerly been added to Lagny, but when the king gave Lagny to St-Denis in that year was separated off again and given to the bishop of Lyon. A second document, a court-case between Lagny's new owner St-Denis and the mayor of the palace Grimoald

---

[38] *Pol. St-Germain*, I, II, V, VI, XIV, for the Palaiseau group.

[39] For Le Mans, see in general Weidemann, *Das Testament*, and Busson and Ledru, *Actus*, pp. 157–62. For fragmented land beyond Verdun, see e.g. Pardessus, *Diplomata*, nn. 375, 475, and above all *Trad. Wiz.*, for the Metz area. South-east towards Burgundy, scattered land already begins around Auxerre and Fleury (modern St-Benoit-sur-Loire): Pardessus, *Diplomata*, nn. 273, 358, 363 (*Cartulaire général*, n. 8); 437, 554; *Cartulary of Flavigny*, n. 1.

in 709–10, concerns the question of whether a mill at Chaalis, 8 km from Lagny, *infra termeno Verninse*, inside the territory of Ver-sur-Launette (Grimoald's own *villa*, between Lagny and Chaalis), belonged to Lagny or Ver. Witnesses from both *villae* testified in favour of St-Denis, and Grimoald (who was, interestingly, running the court) ceded. Here we can see two opposing geographical principles in operation: that an estate had bounds, and what was inside it belonged to the estate; and that an estate could own outliers in other territories. The second won in this case, and the idea that Lagny could have outliers is supported by the history of Silly as well. Lagny was not, then, a single landowning block, but rather an estate centre with a certain scatter of dependencies. We cannot tell how substantial that scatter was—or, conversely, whether others owned in Lagny—but the estate was nonetheless, as one might say, fuzzy at the edges.[40] This might give us some space for a wider range of landowning than the purely aristocratic.

If we go looking for anomalies of this kind, properties that were separable from the *villa* chequerboard, we can find some others. Vineyards were one, as we have already seen (p. 285); Erminethrudis had some around 600, for example, organizationally separate from her two *villae* east of Paris at Lagny-sur-Marne and Bobigny, although located in the same rough area. A couple of documents from the 690s concern the exchange of single fields (with an array of different landowners on their boundaries) situated in the Pincerais just west of Paris, and a sale of another field in the same territory dates to 769: these transactions would not look out of place in the middle Rhine.[41] The area west of the city seems in fact to have been one where the *villa* structure was rather more complex and scattered than elsewhere, as has recently been stressed by Luc Bourgeois. We have one text of 720–2, surviving in a late summary, in which a certain Chulberta sells to St-Germain her *res* in two *villae*, including Maule, near the Seine some 30 km west of Paris, 'in a time of hunger' (*tempore famis*), receiving the land back in lease (*precarium*). Chulberta was most plausibly a peasant, forced to give up landowning in adverse economic circumstances (a rather rare occurrence in our documents, actually, although prominent in an older historiography). If one looks at the patterns of landowning in the polyptych of St-Germain,

---

[40] *ChLA*, XIII, n. 570, XIV, n. 587. Lagny's tenurial history was quite complicated; it seems to have gone from the king to Ebroin and other mayors of the palace, then back to the fisc, then to St-Denis, in the course of the seventh century, with Ebroin as well as the king being associated with the gift to the monastery. This may show contested claims, or overlapping rights, or, just conceivably, more than one estate-centre in Lagny. (The *Gesta Dagoberti*, c. 49, says Lagny went straight from the king to St-Denis before 639; we should probably disregard this late text.)

[41] *ChLA*, XIV, n. 592 for Erminethrudis (her vineyards were run by largely unfree vine-dressers, and were very dependent); for the Pincerais, XIII, n. 563, XIV, n. 582, XV, n. 609. Cf. also the apparently smallish owners in XIV, nn. 572, 590, in Bézu (Dept. Eure), further west (although Bézu would have an imperial *palatium* in the ninth century: Barbier, 'Le système palatial franc', p. 250). Other separate portions of estates are XIII, nn. 564 (especially), 566, 570, perhaps XIV, n. 578; Pardessus, *Diplomata*, nn. 358, 432, 480; *Dip. Maiorum domus*, n. 18.

too, it is not actually the case that all the estates described in it are solid geographical blocks; this is only a feature of around half of them, in particular the Palaiseau group already mentioned, and a group around the Forêt de Sénart just across the Seine. The others are rather more fragmented, with, for example, the Maule estate spread across ten localities, and the Béconcelle estate to its south across as many as twenty-seven (including Auteuil and Beule, where the Maule estate had land too). It is, furthermore, in the context of the western estates around Maule that the polyptych actually makes reference a few times to landowning peasants, who once held, or still held, *proprietas* or *hereditas* inside the boundary of the estates—or, as one might say here, of the villages—at their centre. As soon as we can pin down some fragmentation in the *villa* pattern of the Île de France, that is to say, we can find evidence of other owners too, including peasants. Bourgeois concludes that the St-Germain estates west of Paris are 'artificial reassemblages' of sets of separable land. We might further conclude that it is the estate blocks south of the city that are atypical, not the more scattered properties to the west.[42] Palaiseau (Latin *Palatiolum*, from *palatium*), at least, was originally a Merovingian royal centre, probably given to St-Germain by Pippin III in 755, and its neighbouring *villae* may have been fiscal too.[43]

This brings up the issue of the origins of such estate blocks. It was easier to accept that the whole of the Paris basin was a network of huge estates when the theories of Maurice Roblin were influential, for he argued that almost the whole area was forest, until much later land-clearances, and that human occupation was isolated along river valleys. This argument cannot now be sustained; two decades of Roman and early medieval archaeology, which has been particularly active in the Île de France, shows substantial continuities of settlement, often fairly dense, with the exception of parts of the chalk plateaux between the various Seine tributaries (pp. 507–8)—and not all of them, given that Lagny-le-Sec, for example, is on a plateau.[44] An alternative view might be that estates consisting of large blocks of land were originally fiscal; nearly 40 per cent of the land in the seventh-century St-Denis documents is visibly ex-royal, and many of the St-Germain estates were too. Such an argument is easier to sustain if the territory characterized by contiguous

---

[42] For all this see Bourgeois, *Térritoires, reseaux*, I, pp. 404–14 (p. 409 for quote); this thesis, the best regional study for the Île de France, is focused on the west of Paris as a whole. For Chulberta, see ibid., III, p. 63, from *Annales ordinis S. Benedicti*, II, pp. 60–1. The fragmented St-Germain estates are *Pol. St-Germain*, IX, XXI–XXV, and also XII, XIII for the Perche, further west (XII, for Corbon, is just a set of gifts, not yet formed into an estate). Peasant owning: IX.247, XXI.78, XXII.95–6, XXV. 8 (mostly cited in Bourgeois, *Térritoires, reseaux*, I, p. 411); cf. also Déleage, *Bourgogne*, pp. 221–2, 239–51.

[43] Böhmer, *Regesta imperii*, I, p. 41, n. 77a; for the Merovingian palace, Barbier, 'Le système palatial franc', p. 251 n. An array of spurious royal cessions of estates around the city may preserve the memory of fiscal land in the Paris suburbs: e.g. *MGH, Dip. Merov.*, nn. 13, 41, 51.

[44] Roblin, *Le terroir de Paris*, passim; for recent archaeology see e.g. Ouzoulias and Van Ossel, 'Dynamiques de peuplement'; for a recent overview, Bourgeois, *Térritoires, reseaux*, pp. 209–16, 240–9, 389–401.

chequerboard estates is seen as relatively restricted, for there is certainly no sign that Clovis, or any of his successors, expropriated the whole of the Parisis from the landowners of the city, who must have existed (Paris, to repeat, was a significant urban centre throughout our period, one of the best-attested in northern Gaul), and there are plenty of lay landowners with no obvious royal connections at all in the Merovingian period, including the earliest in our surviving documents, Erminethrudis around 600.[45] It may, however, be that there were substantial zones dominated by royal land, such as the Palaiseau group, and more generally some of the other city suburbs, linked to the royal *palatia* we know were there, and also, certainly, up the River Oise; these could well have contained large land areas, lumps of which were cut off and given to churches and monasteries. Such zones might even sometimes have been imperial or public land in the Roman period; we cannot show such a thing for the Île de France, but a possible parallel is the huge, probably imperial, estate around Welschbillig, not far from the major urban centre of Trier.[46] They would, all the same, have been interspersed with zones of private landowning, such as the tenurially more fragmented lands west of Paris, where in fact Merovingian and Carolingian fiscal land seems to have been relatively sparse. It may indeed be that some others of the aristocratic *villae* that lay owners gave to St-Denis—in the wills of Wademir and the son of Idda, for example (above, pp. 187–8)—were relatively fragmented estates, as Lagny-le-Sec turns out to be when looked at closely enough.[47] The Île de France would thus turn out to be an area *structured* by royal and ex-royal property, which is inevitable considering the number of palaces and estates we know the kings had, but not *defined* by it—a sociologically more plausible proposition.

This long excursus is necessary in order to characterize the peasant experience in the Paris basin a little more clearly. Even with all the loose ends of our evidence for *villae* unravelled as proposed here, we are still left with a very coherent set of estates by the standards of the post-Roman provinces. *Villae* may well have often been more scattered than they seem, but they were not so scattered that it is at all common for documents to refer to *adiacentia* or other dependent lands in named places elsewhere. Nor are

[45] For the active society of late fifth-century Paris, see the *Vita Genovefae* (the date of the text is shown to be early sixth-century by Heinzelmann and Poulin, *Les vies anciennes*, pp. 8, 51–7, 115–45). For Erminethrudis, *ChLA*, XIV, n. 592; for a date of around 600, see Laporte, 'Pour une nouvelle datation'.

[46] For the *palatia*, see Barbier, 'Le système palatial franc'; they ring the city. Roblin, *Le terroir de Paris*, p. 253, speculates about a Roman origin for Merovingian fiscal land; Bergengruen, *Adel und Grundherrschaft*, pp. 86–101, is much more negative, with good reason (although his underlying discontinuism is hard now to accept). But there was certainly private landowning in the suburbs too, as, once again, with Erminethrudis's Bobigny estate, *ChLA*, XIV, n. 592; there were aristocrats on the Oise as well. For Welschbillig, see below, p. 469n.

[47] Lagny was fiscal, but its known history was so complex (above, n. 40) that it would be impossible to say that it was necessarily so 'originally'. For relatively little fiscal land to the west, see Bourgeois, *Térritoires, reseaux*, vol. III, map 185b.

villae often obviously divided among kin, the first step towards a more flexible and fractioned tenurial system;[48] perhaps Parisian aristocrats were so rich that they could simply apportion whole estates among heirs rather than split them up. But we do at least have space now, especially west of Paris but elsewhere as well, to envisage a wider range of owners than simply the aristocracy, the church, and the kings. Below the *viri inlustri* of most of our secular material, we find occasional lesser owners, without titles, negotiating smaller numbers of estates.[49] And the handful of known peasant owners west of the city almost certainly represent a larger number, above all (but not only) in the numerous villages we have no early documentation for, as at Neauphlette, again west of the city, where fourteen peasant owners ceded their *alodi* to St-Germain in the tenth century because they could not do military service (*quia militiam regis non valebant exercere*).[50] There was a spectrum of ownership everywhere; it would be a misreading of the evidence to conclude that all the peasantry of the Île de France were subject tenants on great estates of the Palaiseau type.

But more of them were than elsewhere. From the standpoint of the peasantry, there were too many great powers about for effective autonomies to be plausible. The most one could hope to achieve in most cases was village-level status among dependent tenants. In Arnouville, a dependency of the St-Germain estate of Secqueval on the Seine near Maule, we find thirty-five separate tenant holdings in the polyptych, eighteen free tenants and seventeen *servi*, mostly doing analogous labour service on the monastery's fields and vineyards. Four holdings at the end of the list are assigned horse service (*paraveredum*), generally a sign of privilege; two of these holdings are double *mansi*, and the families that control them also divide a mill between them. Tenants in three of the four, Adric and his family, Ermenold, and Randuic and his associates, also own some of their own property, for which they do no service. So: the privileged tenants of Arnouville, including the millers, were also the only known landowners in the village. We can safely assume that they were the village leaders. But we could not conclude that they could do much outside the remit given them by the monastery, or by Laifin, the monastic *maior* at Secqueval.[51] Conversely, St-Germain did not treat every estate in the same way; there

---

[48] A rare example is *ChLA*, XIII, n. 564.

[49] e.g. *ChLA*, XIV, nn. 572, 590 (cf. 575–6).

[50] The text is an addition to the polyptych: see *Pol. St-Germain*, III.61. Longnon's dating, based on the handwriting, is accepted in Hägemann, *Das Polyptychon*, p. 23, and in Devroey, 'Problèmes de critique', p. 460, who suggests c.900. Tenants in Corbon, further west, are also occasionally visible as buying land allodially (*de libera potestate*): *Pol. St-Germain*, XII.22—see Devroey, *Économie rurale*, I, pp. 292–4.

[51] *Pol. St-Germain*, XXII.70–96 for Arnouville (.92–5 for *paraveredum*, .95–6 for property; .2 for the *maior*). Were there any inhabitants there who were not St-Germain's tenants? Maybe Peter and Eodimia, co-owning with Randuic in .95 but not listed as tenants. Gunthar in .76 ter also has a very small tenure indeed, and could have owned land too.

were microregional differences in the sorts of rents and labour it exacted, for example, as Hans-Werner Goetz has shown (the Palaiseau group of estates were the most standardized).[52] Social structures were just as differentiated from place to place. St-Germain could not control them entirely; such differences related to local realities that developed independently of land-lordly intervention, in an essentially peasant context. But they developed in an overall framework of aristocratic power, not real peasant autonomy.

Peasant society in most of the Île de France was thus a society of tenants, with social divisions largely determined by outside forces. Where there were peasant owners, they will have made up village elites, and will have con-trolled village-level decision-making (at least unless an aristocrat or other major owner happened to live in the village, as with the son of Idda at Arthies in the Vexin: above, p. 188). Where there were no local owners, social division will have turned on tenurial status: how much land each tenant had (very variable, at least on St-Germain's estates), how much rent and labour each paid, and of which type; and, above all, whether tenants were free (*ingenui, coloni*), half-free (*lidi*), or unfree (*servi*). There are clear signs that the free–unfree line was not unbridgeable on Parisian estates: most of the *servi* in the polyptych had free wives, and thus (probably) free children. This also indicates a level of solidarity between the two status-groups, rather greater than in many places (below, p. 561), or else the free would not have married their daughters off to the unfree.[53] A further sign of the weakening of this boundary was the fact that *coloni* are often found holding *mansi serviles*, and *servi* holding *mansi ingenuiles*, with different quantities of attached land and services. Unfreedom was not due to end soon on estates like these, but around 800 its particular stigma may have been felt less around Paris than around Lucca or Mainz: on a St-Germain estate, unfreedom, although important, was only one element out of several in the village-level pecking order. Further than this into peasant society it is diffi-cult to go without engaging in considerable imaginative reconstruction; but this has already been done admirably by Eileen Power, in her famous account of the lives of Bodo and Ermentrudis on the La-Celle-St-Cloud estate, and I refer the reader to it.[54]

The Île de France is a type example for early medieval peasant subjection. Peasants could choose their patrons in the Lucchesia, and their leaders could have public roles in the middle Rhine; all they could do here was maybe negotiate a locally specific set of rules for labour service, or else (as at Neauphlette) keep their heads down and stay very quiet. This is the closest

---

[52] Goetz, 'Bäuerliche Arbeit'.

[53] Goetz, *Frauen*, pp. 263–7 for mixed marriages.

[54] Power, *Medieval people*, ch. 1, pp. 18–38. This analysis stands the test of time, although Power perhaps understates status differentiations inside the village (p. 21). Bodo was the first tenant listed at La-Celle (*Pol. St-Germain*, VII.4), and actually had half a mill, which will have substantially reinforced his local position.

that we will get to the eleventh- or twelfth-century world of outright aristocratic dominance over peasantries that is part of the 'classic' image of the middle ages. And, of course, the polyptych of St-Germain has long been seen in that light, as a model not only for later developments but also for most of Carolingian Europe. But we have already seen that its estate structures do not constitute such a model (pp. 280–93); even less was it typical in the light it sheds on peasant social relationships. The post-Roman world was, in general, far more like Lucca and Mainz than it was like Paris. And that goes for the eastern Mediterranean as well, as in my next examples.

4. Around Ankara

For the centre of the Anatolian plateau (Map 6), we have no documents for our period, and relatively few before the sixteenth century. But in our period we have one of the saints' lives that best conveys a feeling for rural life, the *Life* of Theodore of Sykeōn (d. 613), whose author, the monk George, was his younger contemporary.[55] This *Life* will be the basic source for this section.

Ankara was the capital of Galatia, and also probably the main city of the whole plateau. The plateau as a whole was one of the sub-regions least integrated into the Roman economy (above, p. 79), but Ankara was an important route centre, and the *Life* depicts a constant movement along the main post road from Constantinople, which was one of the two major land routes from the capital to Syria and the eastern frontier. According to the text, Theodore's mother Maria, with his grandmother and aunt, were prostitutes in a roadside inn at Sykeōn; they could make enough money from the road to leave the trade and become innkeepers and restauranteurs. Maria could afford to equip Theodore for a military career as a result (until a vision told her of God's alternative plans), and she eventually married an Ankaran aristocrat (*protiktor*). The road also brought all manner of imperial officials in Theodore's lifetime, including the future emperor Maurice and, later, Heraclius.[56] But most of the *Life* depicts a rather more localized society, prosperous and independent of much outside influence, probably in the last generation of its prosperity (George was writing after the Persian invasions,

[55] *Vie de Théodore*, cc. 165–6 for George; in c. 166, George refers to Heraclius' death, which probably dates its completion to the 640s. For Theodore, see Patlagean, *Pauvrété*, pp. 252–71; Kaplan, *Les hommes*, pp. 98–9, 127–8, 197–202, 224–8. There are useful comments in Cormack, *Writing in gold*, pp. 17–49; Whittow, 'Ruling the city', pp. 25–8; Trombley, 'Monastic foundations', pp. 46–51. The topography of the zone is reconstructed as far as possible in Belke and Restle, *Galatien*, esp. pp. 125–6, 228–9, and the maps; most of the documented villages cannot be traced.

[56] Theodore's family: *Vie de Théodore*, cc. 3–6, 25. Maurice, Heraclius: cc. 54, 166. In c. 147, Theodore protects villagers from the billeting of travellers.

but before the start of long-term Arab raiding in the plateau). This society was focused on a hierarchy of settlement: Sykeōn was in the city territory of Anastasioupolis, which in turn looked to Ankara, some 100 km to the east. Theodore became bishop of Anastasioupolis for a time; as the *Life* puts it, the city became great through his merits, not through men of wealth and power, or its walls or imperial patronage, which were presumably relatively unimpressive there (though the city did have landowners and tax-collectors). He was also in demand in Ankara, whose *protiktores* asked him to curb a plague; conversely, Ankara's provincial governor (*archōn*) intervened in village society in the Anastasioupolis area.[57] Ankara was a major centre, with fifth- and sixth-century building and rebuilding, extramural residences, and urban patronage extending some way out of town, as shown by an inscription recording Bishop Paul's building of a bridge roughly 50 km to the west in the late sixth century. It was sacked by the Persians in c.622, and a fire in the gymnasion certainly dates to then; later, either around 630 under Heraclius or around 660 under Constans II, a large citadel was built, with spolia reused to monumental effect, as the military focus of a surviving political centre (see below, p. 629).[58] In the period 570–610, the focus of the *Life*, Ankara dominated the cities around, and the villages (*chōria*) subject to them.

The villages of western Galatia are the main focus of the action of the *Life*. They were apparently concentrated settlements (as are almost all the contemporary villages studied by archaeologists elsewhere in Turkey and Syria: below, pp. 443–65); each was an identifiable community (*koinon*), with its own feasts and local rituals. Processions were a popular means of expressing, or (as often in the *Life*) re-establishing, village solidarity. These village collectivities were stronger than anything that can be found in the West in our period, although their solidity seems fairly typical in the East.[59] Villages had leaders, who are variously named in the *Life*: *prooikoi*, *presbyteroi*, *prōtopresbyteroi* (the most recent editor, André-Jean Festugière, argued convincingly that they could not be village priests). The implication of the text is that these leaders had formal roles, which presumably included directing the collective action that the *Life* describes: building a bridge to join two halves of a village, fighting a neighbouring village over woodland, rising up against an unjust episcopal

---

[57] Anastasioupolis: ibid., cc. 58 (Theodore's merits), 76, 78, 148. Ankara: cc. 45 (*protiktores*), 114, 116 (the *archōn* acting).

[58] See in general Foss, 'Late antique and Byzantine Ankara'. For suburban residences, ibid., p. 43 (cf. *Vie de Théodore*, c. 107 for Amorion). For the building of the citadel and its dating, see Ch. 10, n. 88. For Paul's bridge, Ramsay, *Historical geography*, p. 238; it was not on the road to Anastasioupolis and Sykeōn.

[59] *Vie de Théodore*, cc. 72, 114 (concentrated settlement—cf. cc. 52, 116, for boundaries of village territories), 143 (a community feast—cf. *Life of St Nicholas of Sion*, c. 57), and 43, 67, 114, 127 (processions—cf. cc. 45, 101, 107, 127, for city processions, and below, p. 634).

administrator, and, over and over, going to Theodore of Sykeōn to beg his help.[60]

Theodore was essentially a holy man, in Peter Brown's sense. Not that he was opposed to the church hierarchy, unlike some such men: he was an abbot of a monastery, and a priest, and a bishop for eleven years until he resigned, with, throughout, strong institutional support from the bishop of Ankara and from Constantinople. But he was an ascetic, and as a result a healer, a caster-out of demons, a patron, and a mediator: village communities valued him for this, not for his institutional status.[61] As a patron, he protected peasants from oppression by tax-collectors, although the most detailed record of this, concerning his dealings with a certain Megethios, do not show him as so very effective (it was secular powers who did for Megethios, nothing miraculous). He also, as bishop, protected his tenants from the depredations of his own aristocratic administrator, whom he dismissed, although only after a revolt by the peasants of Eukraoi; he protected fugitives too. As a miracle-worker, perhaps more successfully, he protected village communities from hail, rain at the wrong moment, locusts, and food-poisoning. As a mediator, he tried to stop the woodland dispute already mentioned, and ensured that the bad losers were punished by hail.[62] Theodore was typically called in, rather than stepping into problems himself, and in this context it is significant that it was often whole communities, or their leaders, who asked for his help. The solidarity of the village is made clear by these patterns. But in rural societies it is often the most coherent villages that are at the same time the most riven; the stronger the community, the more there is to fight over. In Galatia around 600 this is clearest in Theodore's dealings with demons. Here again Peter Brown has given us important keys to interpretation, indeed using the *Life* of Theodore as an example; Michel Kaplan has developed them further; but some of the key narratives deserve discussion here.[63]

Eutolmios the *oikodespotēs* (house-owner) in the village of Sandos had a large grain crop and wanted to enlarge his threshing-floor, so he levelled the ground around, lifted a stone, and demons flew out. They infected many animals and villagers; others thought—wrongly—that Eutolmios was digging for treasure, which would make the *archōn* punish the village, so they

[60] *Vie de Théodore*, cc. 72, 111, 124, 143, for *prooikoi*, etc.; for Festugière on priests, ibid., II, pp. 217–18; Kaplan, *Les hommes*, pp. 227–8, agrees. For local clergy (*klēros*) see *Vie de Théodore*, c. 116. For collective activities, cc. 43 (the bridge), 150 (the woodland), 76 (the uprising).

[61] Brown, 'Rise and function'. Theodore as bishop: *Vie de Théodore*, c. 58; he resigns in cc. 78–9. A general summing-up of his role in village is in cc. 145–7.

[62] *Vie de Théodore*, cc. 148 (Megethios), 147 (other extortions by tax-collectors—cf. *NJ*, XXIV.3 for Pisidia, XXX.3 for Cappadocia, etc.), 76 (peasant rising), 52, 144 (hail), 56 (rain), 36, 101, 115 (locusts), 143 (food-poisoning), 150 (woodland mediation). In cc. 37 and 143 he has magic-working rivals.

[63] Brown, 'Rise and function', p. 89; Kaplan, *Les hommes*, pp. 199–202, 224–7.

tried to burn down his house. Village leaders (here described more vaguely than usual, *hoi ta prōta telountoi presbeutai*) and peacemakers (*eirēnopoioi androi*) calmed them down and sent for Theodore. Theodore took them all in a procession around the village, and put the demons back in the ground. The next day he did the same with the escaped demons of the nearby village of Permetaia. He wrapped up his task by writing to the *archōn* to dispel the charge of treasure-hunting. Similarly, in Eukraoi, Timothy, a peasant (*geōrgios*), also dug into a hill—maybe to take treasure, maybe not, but the villagers certainly thought so. It brought both demons and the punishment of Timothy by the *archōn* for tomb-robbing. This time the demons really let fly: they possessed most of the villagers, who burned down Timothy's grain stores, then those of others, then broke up their own homes and killed animals. The *oikodespotai* and local clergy who were still demon-free begged for Theodore's help; he prayed all night in the village church and eventually got them back into the hill.[64]

Here we have a number of different causes of tension operating at once. Demons for one, of course: obviously Theodore's job. It is interesting, however, that they lived in the ground, and could so easily be let out. Of course, peasants turned over the soil (and stones) all the time in their standard agricultural work, without suffering much demonic attack, but targeted excavation always seems to have created trouble. Two other examples of this were the stone-cutting for a bridge, at Bouzaiai, and the opening of a pagan sarcophagus to make a water-trough, at Sandos again.[65] Demons duly emerged on both occasions; and at Bouzaiai most people again thought that the stone-cutting (done at diabolic instigation, an image also used for Eutolmios) was a cover for treasure-hunting. Treasure-hunting was evidently a very negative activity in sixth-century Galatia. This is presumably in part because this activity targeted tombs, and the dead were dangerous; but so also was excessive profit by individuals. Too much profit undermined community cohesion, and that was not only as bad as demons but difficult to distinguish from them. Hence also the physical violence against perpetrators, which was not only the work of demoniacs.

The villages inside Theodore's remit do not seem tenurially dependent on outsiders for the most part. At Eukraoi there was a church estate, hence the revolt against its administrator; but, as we have just seen, there were *oikodespotai*, house-owners, there as well. Hence, doubtless, the possibility of effective revolt, for this tends to need fairly confident leaders; but the balance of local power must have been, to say the least, very different from that at Arnouville west of Paris two centuries later, even though village leaders were property-owners there too—no revolting peasants would have stayed alive,

---

[64] *Vie de Théodore*, cc. 114–15, 116–17 (in c. 117 the *oikodespotai* are called *prōtoi*, the leading men). *Oikodespotai* also ask for Theodore's help in a flood situation in c. 141.
[65] Ibid., cc. 43, 118.

much less won their case, in the Paris hinterland, as the peasant militias of 859 indeed found (below, p. 581). Overall, the protagonism and autonomous action of all these villages implies that their inhabitants were very commonly property-owners. It seems also that *oikodespotai* were the richest of these; they were evidently, judging by references in the *Life*, normally the group from which village leaders were drawn, and sometimes they were virtually synonymous with that leadership. This identity between the richest villagers and the local political elite is normal in rural societies. All the same, as Kaplan has stressed, it is also not chance that Eutolmios of Sandos, an *oikodespotēs* with an unusual amount of grain, or Timothy of Eukraoi, who had two grain stores, were the targets of village anger.[66] One would indeed expect local wealth to generate not only leadership but also opposition; and unusually increased wealth, even if from something as legitimate as a good harvest, was on the same spectrum as finds of treasure: it risked the disruption of collective relationships, and this was threatening. When Eutolmios enlarged his threshing-floor, he may also have been making his wealth too obvious, and the resultant tension was the right context for demons. Perhaps only pious or collectively orientated acts, like rural church-building (not documented in the *Life*, but a feature of villages elsewhere in the East), or indeed the extreme personal piety of the most obvious social upstarts in the text, Theodore himself and his mother Maria, were safe ways of rising socially and showing it.[67] It is also likely that Theodore and Maria, who grew prosperous in the marginal environment of an inn and went into the ranks of the sub-regional aristocracy, would have been seen as a different matter from Eutolmios, who was still a peasant organizing his own threshing-floor. The rich villagers of Galatia do not seem to have reached the status of medium landowners, who did not have to do any cultivation, and often had a certain local legitimacy as leaders; they remained peasants, and not so much richer than their neighbours. In principle, even if not very frequently, good and bad fortune could have changed their relative status fairly quickly. This potential instability produces trouble in all sorts of rural societies, which can take many forms—brigandage, long-term family feuds, the wrapping of faction-struggles in heresy; demons might be seen as a safer option.[68] It should be added, too, that demons, and Theodore, only intervened in extreme situations; normally, local *eirēnopoioi androi* could presumably handle discord.

---

[66] Kaplan, *Les hommes*, pp. 224–5.

[67] Cf. ibid., pp. 279–80, for Theodore and Maria. For village church-building elsewhere, see *Inscriptions de Cilicie*, n. 113 (a local builder in Sipha (Çemkale) in 590, acting with the help of his village, *komē*), and below, pp. 443–8, for Syria.

[68] For brigandage and its use as a political image, see Patlagean, *Pauvreté*, pp. 297–301; Shaw, 'Bandit highlands', pp. 237–70. For heresy, compare its relation to faction in Le Roy Ladurie, *Montaillou*. For feud, see as a type-example Wilson, *Corsica*.

The *Life* of Theodore of Sykeōn is an unusually good text for peasant society. This must in part be due to the fact that its author was himself from a peasant family,[69] and perhaps also that Theodore's own origins were unprepossessing. It is also probably the case that in this part of Galatia it was not necessary to abandon peasant values when one gained an education (one of the bigger villages even had a schoolteacher[70]), or a clerical career—a further sign of the generalized autonomy and prosperity of village society. One must not exaggerate; the *protiktores* of the cities, and of course the churches, must have had land and tenants somewhere. As we saw earlier (p. 232), Justinian in his *Novels*, indeed, envisages the possibility of serious aristocratic oppression in parts of the Anatolian plateau, especially Cappadocia to the east of Galatia, even though Pisidia to the south-west was equally excoriated for its excessively independent villages, who evaded taxes.[71] Western Galatia was perhaps more like Pisidia, but doubtless not all of it. Even where outside landowning did exist, however, it was probably fragmented, intermingled with that of peasant owners, as we have seen for Lucca and the middle Rhine. Put that beside the coherent centralized village communities of the eastern Mediterranean, and one finds a very self-confident peasant class. This coherence and self-confidence would outlast the seventh-century crisis in Anatolia (see below, pp. 462–4). It is also likely to have been a feature of other parts of the East, notably parts of Syria and Palestine, whose archaeology implies village societies of relative equals. We shall look at these patterns more generally in Chapter 8.

5. Aphroditō in the sixth century

Our next two examples, single settlements, are both Egyptian (Map 4). Together they span the Arab conquest, for our Aphroditō texts are all sixth-century and our Jēme texts are largely from the late seventh and the eighth. We have encountered eighth-century Aphroditō texts already, but they essentially focus on tax-paying, and hardly illuminate village society from the inside at all (pp. 133–40); it is not easy to gain a sense of the effect of the Arab takeover there. Nor is it by comparing Aphroditō and Jēme, for there are indications that these two villages were always structurally different, as we shall see. But we can at least get at some of the parameters of an earlier and a later peasant society. Both villages are illuminated by documents, not narratives of any standard kind, but we have over 500 published texts for sixth-century Aphroditō and 1,000 and more for Jēme, ranging from the most banal receipts, through leases and sales, to

---

[69] *Vie de Théodore*, c. 170. [70] Ibid., c. 26.
[71] *NJ*, XXX.5.1 for Cappadocia, XXIV.1 for Pisidia (its non-tax-paying *kōmai*, and its brigands); for bibliography, see Ch. 4, n. 199.

letters and court-case transcripts—and, in Aphroditō, also some lengthy and circumstantial petitions, and even poems. We can thus say more about social relations than is often possible.

The sixth-century Aphroditō archive is essentially the archive of one man, Dioskoros son of Apollōs, living c.520 to c.585 (see also above, p. 249).[72] We also have some documents for his father, Apollōs son of Dioskoros son of Psimanobet (d. 546/7), but few for his sons, even though the family continued, which implies a personal, not a family, archive. Conversely, since the 'Psimanobet family' was among the leading families of Aphroditō, we also have documents that were in effect those of the village as a whole.

Aphroditō (Coptic Jkōw, modern Arabic Kōm Ishkāw) is and was a large concentrated settlement on a low mound above the plain in the middle Nile valley—concentrated settlement being the only type practicable in an annually flooded landscape.[73] It is not on the river, but is and was linked to it by canals. In our period it was an 'autopract' village (*komē*), that is, it had a grant of fiscal autonomy from the local pagarchy, of Antaiopolis ('Irmāniyya), apparently made by the emperor Leo I (457–74). Successive pagarchs were very hostile to its autonomy, and the villagers had to defend it, often against violent attack. In 541 Apollōs and his nephew Victor went as far as Constantinople to argue their case (they overstayed and overspent, and had to borrow money to get home). It may have been then that the village placed itself under the direct patronage of the empress Theodora, to whom it also in c.547 appealed against the pagarch; the village sent a further deputation to Justinian in c.551, and we have the emperor's reply, supporting their claims. Even an imperial letter was not enough, however; the villagers had to hire in Constantinople two high-ranking officials, one of them Palladios, count of the sacred consistory, to come to Aphroditō to enforce Justinian's judgment. Apollōs probably went to the capital as a village headman (*prōtokōmētēs*), a title he certainly held earlier; Dioskoros, too, is known to have held the position in 547 and 553. In the latter year, Justinian and Palladios notwithstanding, the pagarch Mēnas was still demanding the village's taxes from its *prōtokōmētai*. Mēnas was again pagarch in 566–7, and pushed the village still harder that time, imprisoning several villagers, raping nuns, burning part of the village, blocking the main canal from the Nile at flood time (a particularly serious act), confiscating 700 *nomismata*, sequestering animals, and appropriating some

---

[72] Sixth-century Aphroditō texts are to be found above all in P. *Lond.* V and P. *Cair. Masp.* Others include P. *Mich.* XIII, P. *Ross.-Georg.* III, P. *Vatic. Aphrod.* No more than a small handful postdate 585: see MacCoull, 'Notes', p. 72.

[73] Bell, 'An Egyptian village', p. 21, describes it in the early twentieth century. For concentrated settlement as normal, see Bagnall, *Late Roman Egypt*, pp. 110–14. In sixth-century Aphroditō, charters show courtyard houses on named streets, bounded by other houses, in a pattern characteristic both of other villages and of cities (below, pp. 609–12): e.g. P. *Mich.* XIII 662, 665.

of Dioskoros' own property (something which Dioskoros, who wrote the petition to Duke Athanasios of the Thebaid which lists all this, put first). A later pagarch, Julian, was again trying to undermine Aphroditō's autonomy in 570, raising taxes and attacking the village with soldiers in reprisal for non-payment.[74] It might not look as if Aphroditō could easily have withstood such a concerted, long-term opposition, but it must be remembered that when we next know about it, in the early eighth century, it was independent enough to have become a pagarchy in its own right. The anger of Mēnas and his colleagues was perhaps largely because the village really was out of their control.

Aphroditō's success in establishing fiscal autonomy may have been in part due to the fact that it was not only an agricultural centre. It had been a small *polis* in the Ptolemaic period, and, although later annexed to Antaiopolis, it maintained some urban-style economic characteristics.[75] It was a market centre, and a number of its artisans are named in documents: a potter who made wine amphorae, lessee of a workshop in 565, for example. In the 547 petition to Theodora, we have the signatures of the heads of six local guilds, the coppersmiths, fullers, carpenters, cloak-weavers, shipwrights, and wine-sellers; seven more guilds (including sculptors) and many other artisans appear on tax lists.[76] If this was the West, it would be impressive evidence of urban activity; in Egypt, however, it is relatively modest. Most of the rest of what we know of Aphroditō is its agricultural activity, through the land-sales, leases, loans, accounts, tax records of its landowners (*ktētores*), twenty-two of whom signed near the head of the 547 petition. The Psima-nobet family was probably the richest of these *ktētores* by the mid-sixth century, but even they seem to have been little more than prosperous medium owners (above, p. 386). Dioskoros' father Apollōs was active as an estate manager (*hypodektēs*) for Count Ammonios, a great owner who owned land locally (above, p. 249), and was a lessee of at least seven other landowners, mostly city councillors and officials from Antaiopolis and other cities. James Keenan has argued that it was on the basis of the local management of the lands of others that Apollōs established the family's social

---

[74] Accounts of the dispute are in Bell, 'An Egyptian village', and Sarris, *Economy and society*, ch. 6. The main texts are *P. Cair. Masp.* II 67126 (a. 541—cf. Keenan, 'A Constantinople loan'), III 67283 (c.547), I 67024 (c.551), 67032 (a. 551, the contract with Palladios), 67060–1 (undated, but probably a. 553, as Dioskoros is here *prōtokōmētēs*, as he is also in 67094, a. 553, and Mēnas was pagarch then—see *PLRE*, III, s.v. Menas 5), 67002 (c.567—cf. Bell, 'An Egyptian village', pp. 33–4), *P. Lond.* V 1677 (c.567, in which Mēnas also arrests Dioskoros' son, the *boēthos* Apollōs, a lesser village official), 1674 (c.570). For the elder Apollōs, see n. 77.

[75] MacCoull, *Dioscorus*, p. 7 proposes that it had 15,000 inhabitants; this figure seems far too high, as we shall see.

[76] Lease: *P. Cair. Masp.* I 67110. 547 guilds: III 67283 (the word 'guild' is not used, but each craft has a formal leader); tax lists: II 67147, III 67288 (cf. Jones, *LRE*, p. 847). Many other trades are referred to casually, e.g. the butcher (*mageiros*), the coppersmith (*galkitēs*), and the vetch-seller (*orbiopōlēs*), in *P. Mich.* XIII 665. For the social mix, see in general MacCoull, 'Notes', who lists all known occupations.

position in the village, which was eventually crystallized in their use of the prestigious personal title of Flavios from c.540, and the foundation of a family monastery, to which Apollōs retired.[77] But if this sort of middle-level agrarian entrepreneurship was the cause of the prosperity of one of Aphroditō's leading families in 550, then we can scarcely equate it with the urban centres we know for the rest of the empire, dominated as they were by landowning aristocrats. Aphroditō's society, by contrast, was run by medium owners and rich peasants; it belongs in a chapter on villages, that is to say, even though it had non-agricultural characteristics too.

The network of owners in Aphroditō is first documented in detail in a land cadaster of the mid-520s, for 5,906 *arourai* of land (16.3 km²), 88 per cent of which was grain-fields. (This would argue for a population of 2,000 people or a little more on Roger Bagnall's figures, only a medium-sized village by Egyptian standards—if, at least, the cadaster included all its land.) We have the totals at the end of the text, but we do not have most of its content, so we cannot be sure of the total landowning structure of the village (Apollōs, for example, admittedly fairly early in his career, only appears once, as a co-owner of a single land-plot), but nearly 200 plots are mentioned, each with their owners and tenants, many of them less than an *aroura* (just over a quarter of a hectare) and none more than 27 *arourai* (7.4 hectares). The fragmented landowning pattern that can be deduced elsewhere is here immediately evident, and almost total; landowners built their estates out of single fields. The largest owners were monasteries, the largest of which, Apa Sourous, controlled a fifth of the land in the surviving section of the text; Ammonios figures several times too; but most owners only appear once or twice.[78] It is these latter owners who were the backbone of the village in later texts across the century: so much so that in two papyri from 567–70 the whole village was referred to as being made up of small owners (*leptoktē-tores*).[79] This was in petitions against pagarchal excesses, and was thus part of a rhetorical frame which stressed the political weakness and poverty of the village's inhabitants; it certainly did not reflect the prosperity of a Dioskoros. It is not insignificant, all the same, that the village could be summed up in this way. There was a complex of levels of ownership

[77] For Apollōs, see Keenan, 'Aurelius Apollos'; idem, 'Absentee landlordism'; ibid., pp. 147–51 for *P. Cair. Masp.* III 67327, which lists some of Apollōs' landlords; Banaji, *Agrarian change*, pp. 194–7. For Ammonios, see the estate accounts, *P. Cair. Masp.* II 67138–40, III 67347. Apollōs rose from being Aurelios, the standard title of the free peasantry and artisans, to Flavios, the prestige title of professionals, officials, and aristocrats, in 537–41: Bell, 'An Egyptian village', p. 26; Dioskoros was always Flavios, and possibly even became *lamprotatos*, i.e. *vir clarissimus*—see *PLRE*, III, s.v. Dioscorus 5, commenting on *P. Cair. Masp.* I 67066.

[78] *P. Freer*, 08.45 a + b, edited and translated in Gascou and MacCoull, 'Le cadastre'. Ibid., p. 118 for overall figures and a brief socio-economic commentary. Line 105 of the text refers to Apollōs. For Apa Sourous, Banaji, *Agrarian change*, pp. 11, 147. For population figures, Bagnall, *Late Roman Egypt*, p. 110.

[79] *P. Lond.* V 1574, *P. Cair. Masp.* I 67002. The latter also refers to the 'old big owners' (*archaioi ktētores megaloi*) whose houses stood out in the village: the local elite.

in it, from medium owners downwards to dependent tenants with only a few fields of their own, but most people living there were probably peasants who were proprietors of at least some land.

The Psimanobet family are easily the best-documented family of medium landowners in the whole of late Antiquity and the early middle ages, and have often been discussed.[80] Summarizing, we can see the family as active as local owners and tenants, as monastic patrons and administrators, and as village officials. Dioskoros himself was trained in law, presumably in Alexandria, and was active both as a lawyer and a notary; he also had a collection of literary texts in his archive, and was the author of nearly forty Greek poems, largely praise-poems to dukes and other magnates of the Thebaid. These have often been criticized for their appalling quality (H. I. Bell called them 'probably the worst Greek poems which a whimsical Fortune has preserved for us from the wreckage of ancient literature'). Leslie MacCoull has put up a spirited defence of their merits, reasoning that they are best seen in the context of a Coptic, not a Greek, literary aesthetic; all the same, they are notable for their bathos, ending as they do, after the standard tropes of classical panegyric, with commonplace requests for employment and protection against opponents. This banality makes them unusually personal, all the same; we find that Dioskoros, although a leading figure in his village, felt himself to have his back to the wall, oppressed by pagarchs, mercenary troops, creditors, personal enemies, neighbours, tenants, and nomadic attackers of the Nile villages. In other documents, more pragmatic texts, Dioskoros can be seen as a local dealer: he loans money, buys and sells land, leases to tenants, disputes with his neighbours and tenants, and arbitrates the disputes of others (including his relatives), who were evidently behaving in the same ways as he was.[81] This was, on one level, an even more fluid society than the Lucchesia, full of transactions of all kinds; it was also more threatening than the Lucchesia, with both the powerful and the weak capable of using violence. Dioskoros' poems show that he felt exposed to this, and none of the documents show that he had it under control.

This is the best way into understanding Aphroditō from the standpoint of the peasantry. One of the main conclusions one can draw from the documents is how difficult it would have been for any single person to dominate the village. Not only medium owners but small owners could be dealers, and rise in village society. Keenan has analysed the way a peasant

---

[80] Bell, 'An Egyptian village'; MacCoull, *Dioscorus*; eadem, 'The Coptic archive'; eadem, *Coptic perspectives, passim*; Keenan, 'Absentee landlordism'; idem, 'Egypt', pp. 633–6; *PLRE*, III, s.v. Dioscorus 5; Fournet, *Hellénisme*; Sarris, *Economy and society*, ch. 6.

[81] Bell, 'An Egyptian village', p. 27; MacCoull, *Dioscorus*, esp. pp. 57–146, which collects the poems; but the definitive edition is now Fournet, *Hellénisme* (pp. 1–3 for a critique of MacCoull; pp. 326–36 for the dukes; 684–90 for Dioskoros' culture). For Dioskoros as a Coptic writer, MacCoull, *Dioscorus*, pp. 37–47, 59–63; eadem, 'The Coptic archive'. For Dioskoros as a dealer, see e.g. *P. Cair. Masp.* I 67028, 67087, 67095, 67116, II 67127, 67128, *P. Lond.* V 1686, for a sample range.

called Phoibammōn loaned grain to Samuel, a medium-landowning soldier, in 526–7 in return for leases on favourable terms and then a mortgage on his estate; across the next fifty years Phoibammōn took leases on ever more land, and bought systematically as well, turning himself into another medium owner and village leader on the Dioskoros level. Samuel was not protected by his wealth and military status from economic hard times and poorer neighbours with an eye to the main chance.[82] Nor were others: Dioskoros could not easily command his tenants, as can be seen from an arbitration of the 560s in which he accused a certain Joseph of working his land so badly that not only did Dioskoros not get the rent, but he had to underwrite its taxes; and, in addition, of allowing animal trespass on the land and covering up that trespass. Dioskoros won the case, but, no matter who was in the right, it is clear that he had no power to coerce Joseph without wider community support. Shepherds might have been used to coerce such tenants; they were certainly used as field guards by the village community (*koinotēs*). But shepherds were hard to control too; Dioskoros complains about their violence in other texts.[83] Underpinning the fluidity of Aphroditan society was the fact that we seldom see simple bilateral relationships, with a tenant holding from a single landlord. Tenants held from many owners, and indeed could take leases, cultivate land in full property, hire wage labourers to cultivate more of it, and let out land to others. Often there was more than one level of lease, and these multiple levels were further complicated by the frequency of pledging land for debts, and mortgage agreements.[84] In this kaleidoscope of economic relationships, even if reinforced by violence or menace, stable dominance was almost impossible.

This economic openness was matched by a political one. Aphroditō's collectivity of richer owners had a certain local hegemony, but this hegemony could be contested on the inside by new rising figures, and also from the outside by anyone who sought an external patron. Dioskoros did this with the dukes of the Thebaid; but so did some of his own neighbours and tenants against him, using the support of the pagarchs of Antaiopolis, always keen to cause trouble locally. That is to say, peasants could use the patronage system in the same way that village leaders could, using influential outsiders (many of whom were themselves local landowners) to balance out the power of the local elite.[85] It must be added that this did not mean that these

---

[82] Keenan, 'Aurelius Phoibammon', with *P. Vatic. Aphrod.* 10, a court-case, as an extra text: see Gagos and van Minnen, *Settling a dispute*.

[83] *P. Berol.* 11349, summarized in MacCoull, *Dioscorus*, pp. 22–3; for shepherds, Keenan, 'Village shepherds', re-editing *P. Cair. Masp.* I 67087, a complaint by Dioskoros, and 67001 for the *koinotēs* employing them.

[84] For leases, see Ch. 4, n. 235. An aristocrat is a tenant in *P. Cair. Masp.* III 67298. *P. Vatic. Aphrod.* 1 is a particularly detailed lease to a rich tenant. For loans, see e.g. *P. Cair. Masp.* II 67127–9, 67166–7; *P. Lond.* V 1701.

[85] *P. Cair. Masp.* I 67002, *P. Lond.* V 1677. (Other tenants of Dioskoros were troubled by the pagarch's clients too—cf. Keenan, 'Village shepherds', pp. 258–9.) Cf. Libanios, *Oration* XLVII,

outsiders gained power in the long run either. We have seen that Aphroditō as a community resisted the pagarchs of Antaiopolis, with success. Nor is there any sign that great estates there became larger; and after the Arab conquest they must indeed have got smaller, for they are absent from early eighth-century tax records (above, p. 253). Landowning power, land-based dominance, was all too mediated. Ammonios' local lands were administered by, and therefore his local patronage was channelled through, the Psimano-bet family, but the latter family's own lands were leased to others, and so on down. This, plus the external patronage opportunities just mentioned, allowed for an unusual freedom of action for peasants, and even for entre-preneurship if they wanted to take it on; violence and oppression were systemic, but they were relatively ad hoc, relatively individual.

Another element in the equation was the state as a public body. We have some of the witnesses for a mid-sixth-century court-case concerning an accusation of murder made against a senatorial-level aristocrat, the *mega-loprepestatos* Sarapammōn, and a soldier named Mēnas. They were accused of beating to death a certain Victor and ordering Aphroditō village officials (*kephalaiōtai*) to arrest and kill another victim, Hērakleios, and burn his body. Mēnas denied that Victor died unnaturally, and said he was not in the village for Hērakleios' death; Sarapammōn put the blame for the death of Hērakleios, whom he said was an informer, on the villagers themselves, and had actually fined them a pound of gold or more for it; this or other money he had then paid to a blackmailer. This murky business, made murkier by the fragmentary nature of the text, at least shows violent oppression of Aphro-ditō inhabitants, both by outsiders and locals. But it is significant that the text is a trial transcript, and the witnesses—including the high-ranking perpetrators in person—were being interrogated by a *vir illustris comes militum*, the title (unusually, in Latin) of the senatorial head of a military detachment, in effect a senior police chief. Even though the result of this trial does not survive, the tone of the *comes militum*'s questions is markedly hostile to Sarapammōn and Mēnas, and anyway we might guess that Dios-koros kept the text because it went against them in the end. We see the state in Aphroditō in negative guise usually, with tax-collection a highly system-atic and coercive process (above, pp. 71–2), and pagarchs a constant danger, but it could intervene to oppose coercion too. Pleas to the duke of the Thebaid, or to his official subordinates, apparently for once paid off.[86]

lamenting that his tenants used military patrons against him in fourth-century Syria. Note that Aphroditō's village elite was not formally constituted; the common argument that *syntelestai* were structured groups of elite landowning taxpayers has been convincingly opposed, partly on the basis of Aphroditō evidence, in Laniado, 'Syntelestēs' (esp. pp. 37–48), who shows that the word means any taxpayer, although in Aphroditō village notables used it as a title more often than others did.

[86] *P. Mich.* XIII 660–1, with a commentary by the editor. The later commentaries of Mac-Coull, 'The Aphrodito murder mystery', and Keenan, 'The Aphrodito murder mystery', add insights but just about cancel each other out.

Aphroditō's sixth-century society was, like that of the villages around Ankara in the next generation, subject to the Roman empire. In this respect they were different from the western examples I began with, which are all from two centuries later, and fully part of an early medieval world. I would, however, argue that, from the peasant standpoint, participation in the local framework of the Roman state only served to make social relations more complex, not to make them structurally different. The state regularly cost peasants produce and money, in taxation; tax-collectors and other officials appear equally often as individual oppressors, rivalling aristocratic or ecclesiastical landowners. Patronage networks were necessary to protect from taxation, as much as from private landlords; when taxation ended in the West, local social relationships greatly simplified as a result, as we shall see in Chapter 9 (pp. 527–35). Conversely, however, public officials could, as we have just seen, intervene to alleviate the oppression of others; and the pagarchs who were invoked by Dioskoros' neighbours may have said they were doing—or actually had been doing—the same. In a sense, what the capillary presence of the state offered was simply an alternative power network to private landowning-based clientèles. These two networks might simply back each other up (as in Oxyrhynchos, modern Bahnasā, where the same people controlled both: above, pp. 244–7); but where they did not, they could in principle be manipulated, set against each other, even by peasants and village leaders, if these groups were canny enough in taking advantage of the two-way obligations of patron–client relationships. The double patronage network of state and land tenure added further to the fluidity of Egyptian society, and peasants could use this too.

Of the two, all the same, land tenure remained the more important. The many levels of Aphroditō society, or the less hierarchical village society of Galatia, allowed some peasants to manipulate their environments because of fragmented ownership patterns that were not the result of the Roman state. The possibility was less likely at Oxyrhynchos because of Apion landowning, and, in the (few) other parts of the empire where a single owner dominated an entire village, there was very little effective recourse against him or her; the rules established by the landowner were usually in those cases the inescapable ground-rules for village-level social action, state or no state.[87] This counterposition simply matches that, already discussed for the early medieval West, between Lucca and Mainz on one side and Paris on the other. At the village level, that is to say, the history of land tenure was in the last resort more central for the articulation and autonomy of peasant social action than was the history of the state, and of the fiscal system which supported it. These points will be developed later.

---

[87] As with the isolated tenants in the Tablettes Albertini, who sold their land to their landlord for very low prices (above, Ch. 5, n. 17).

To return to Aphroditō, we can end with a paradox. The fluidity of possibilities discussed for the village, the instability of the fate of individuals (even elite members), and the violent edge to village interactions, did not mean that the social structure itself was in flux. Quite the opposite: individuals might rise and fall, but the same networks continued. Indeed, there were continuities at the level of the village elite: MacCoull has shown that both the largest local monastery of the sixth century and the Psimanobet family were still landowners in the tax lists of the eighth.[88] It is likely that the variety of possible patronage networks there, economic and political, private and public, internal and external, cancelled each other out, and prevented, not only the local dominance of individual people in Aphroditō, but also the local dominance of individual systems of power. But it is also the case that the fluidity we have seen existed against the background of a strong and lasting village community, which ran its own taxes and irrigation, and was thus economically influential as well. In this respect Aphroditō was quite unlike the Lucchesia; the village was an inescapable part of all social interaction, and structured it from top to bottom.

6. Jēme in the eighth century

Jēme (its name in Coptic; Memnonia and variants in Greek) was a settlement in the territory of Ermont (Greek Hermōnthis; Arabic Armant), situated in what is often called Western Thebes, over the Nile from the core of the ancient city of Thebes (al-Uqsur/Luxor). It lay between the desert hills, where the Valleys of the Kings and Queens are, and the Nile, on the edge of the cultivable area, in and around Madīnat Habū, the mortuary temple of Ramesses III. It was excavated by the University of Chicago in the years around 1930 as part of the clearance of that temple, but, predictably, the early medieval housing of Jēme was not published, except for interims and a (very valuable) plan, and some of the documents found there. This could in principle provide us with the best chance anywhere for a real linkage between a rich document collection and a settlement site in our period, and some beginnings have been made (Terry Wilfong's association between the ostraka of a female moneylender, Kolōje, and House 34 of the Chicago excavations is the best example). But without further publication, of texts and site notebooks, or further excavation of the surviving remnants of Jēme outside the temple, this linkage will not be realized.[89] Even the published documents for the settlement, over a thousand, are in a state of confusion,

---

[88] MacCoull, 'Notes', pp. 74–5.

[89] For the excavations, see Nelson and Hölscher, *Medinet Habu reports*, pp. 50–6, and Hölscher, *Medinet Habu*, I, esp. plates 10, 32, 34; see Wilfong, 'Western Thebes', pp. 96–103, for a critical survey. Wilfong, 'The archive', reconstructs Kolōje's family archive.

appearing as they do in well over twenty separate publications, and substantially more remain unpublished. Wilfong and, before him, Walter Till have provided invaluable guides to them, without which one could scarcely start; Till also translated almost all the known documents (but not the letters) from Coptic into German, and I have heavily relied on his translations, and also those of Walter Crum, Arthur Schiller, and others into English.[90] The confusion of Jēme's documentation, together with the language of most of the texts and the fragmentary nature of many of them, are the main reasons why there has been so little work on the area; this has furthermore, mostly been restricted to legal history, given the prevailing interests of the Coptic scholars of the 1930s to 1950s. Wilfong's recent innovative work on gender begins to redress the balance here, but Jēme remains an open field for study.[91]

Jēme was, as was Aphroditō, a sizable concentrated settlement, with a considerable density of courtyard houses with two or more storeys each, crowded along its narrow streets and around its four churches; they are visible on the Chicago plan, and several are described in great detail in our eighth-century documents. Jēme was also roughly as large as Aphroditō, judging by the excavations, and it was a significant exchange centre (and moneylending centre) for its immediate hinterland, but, like Aphroditō, it was above all dependent on agriculture, and it can best be seen as a large and prosperous village.[92] Unlike Aphroditō, it had no fiscal autonomy or special administrative status, although it was always called a *kastron*, perhaps because of the solidity of the Ramessean temple. It was surrounded by monasteries, which were both on the hills above the monastery (the 'holy mountain' as some texts call them) and on the plain; these furnished substantial parts of our written documentation, notably the monastery of

---

[90] Wilfong, 'Western Thebes', and Till, *Die koptischen Rechtsurkunden*, are the essential starting-points. The latter, and Till, *Erbrechtliche Untersuchungen*, are the core translations; others include *Coptic Ostraca* [CO]; *Short texts*; Winlock and Crum, *The monastery of Epiphanius*, II [Ep.]; *Ten Coptic legal texts* [CLT]; Schiller, 'A family archive'; Stefanski and Lichtheim, *Coptic ostraca from Medinet Habu* [OMH]. Coptic documents have acquired an arcane set of abbreviations (see Schiller, 'A checklist'); I shall only use the ones marked here, with the addition of *Koptische Rechtsurkunden* [KRU], the main edition of papyri and parchments, which is translated by Till. All the texts I cite are translated by Till, or else are letters of Epiphanios and others, which are translated by Crum. A handful of post-1960s publications of documents include Hintze, 'Koptische Steuerquittungsostraka'; MacCoull, 'O. Wilck. 1224'; Gascou, 'Documents grecs de Qurnat Mar'y'; more are urgently awaited.

[91] For legal history, see esp. Steinwenter, *Studien*; idem, *Das Recht*; Schiller, 'A family archive'. For gender history, and the best general introduction, Wilfong, *Women of Jeme*.

[92] Wilfong, *Women of Jeme*, pp. 12–18, gives the best description of the village, and plausibly suggests a population of 1,000–2,000. He sees the settlement as primarily agricultural, and indeed we do not see the range of artisans for Jēme that we did for Aphroditō. The monasteries made shoes, clothing, and ropes (Winlock and Crum, *The monastery of Epiphanius*, I, pp. 67–78; Godlewski, *Le monastère*, pp. 87–8); there was cloth-making and wine-selling by women in the village (below, n. 106, with Wilfong, *Women of Jeme*, p. 143); there was ceramic production nearby too (below, n. 96). But this is all fairly standard for Egyptian villages. For house details, see Schiller, 'A family archive', pp. 364–8, and the excavation reports in n. 89.

Epiphanios and that of Apa Phoibammōn (now called Deir al-Bahri, in the temple of Hatshepsut), probably the richest landowner in the area. Both of these have published excavations.[93] Jēme's high point seems to have been the later seventh and eighth centuries—this is, at any rate, the date of our documents, which by no means come from one single archive, unlike at Aphroditō. There are very few from the late sixth century, and none after the end of the eighth, the probable date of the abandonment of Jēme. The settlement may have been a casualty of the tax revolts and their repression (above, p. 141); at any rate, it can be seen as a one-period site, and this makes (or, rather, will in the future make) the reconstruction of its society easier.[94]

Jēme's most formal legal documents were on papyrus and (more rarely) on parchment. The ostraka, by contrast (both potsherds and limestone flakes) contain more ephemeral documentation: tax receipts, loan receipts, accounts, lists, and letters. The ostraka are by far the most numerous documents from the area. Letters often began with a semi-formal apology for not using papyrus—we are in Upper Egypt, over 600 km from the reedbeds of the Delta, and papyrus was evidently not cheap (or, perhaps, always available) in a minor centre like Jēme. As already implied, nearly all our texts are in Coptic, although a Coptic larded with Greek technical terms. Even the Greek texts betray a non-Greek-speaking environment, as in the case of one of our earliest, the will of Bishop Abraham of Ermont, founder and owner of the monastery of Apa Phoibammōn, dating to around 610. This text states that it was read to the testator in Coptic (*dia tēs Aigyptiakēs dialaleias*) so that he could understand it; if a bishop, only a generation younger than Dioskoros of Aphroditō, could not cope with Greek, it is unlikely that more than a handful of the laity, mostly notaries, ever dealt with it at all. As for Arabic later, it is close to entirely absent.[95] But the ubiquity of documentation in the village and its territory points to a capillary literacy there, even if not in the successive administrative languages of Egypt.

This essentially monoglot culture was therefore already different to Aphroditō, some 200 km downstream. Indeed, the village seems to have been more isolated than Aphroditō. In Egypt such statements are always relative; the Nile flowed past its doors, and Aswān pottery is very common on the site—although there was also substantial ceramic production in Western Thebes, in the kiln complex inside the temple of Seti I at Gurna,

---

[93] For the 'holy mountain', see *P. Lond.* I 77, among many. Excavations: Winlock and Crum, *The monastery of Epiphanius*; Godlewski, *Le monastère*.

[94] Godlewski, *Le monastère*, pp. 76–8, followed by Wilfong, *Women of Jeme*, pp. 152–3, suggests that the settlement was abandoned in the context of disturbances of the 780s in Upper Egypt, which is quite possible.

[95] Apologies for not using papyrus are discussed by W. E. Crum in CO, p. x, and in Biedenkopf-Ziehner, *Untersuchungen*, pp. 29–31. Abraham's will is *P. Lond.* I 77; for his career, Godlewski, *Le monastère*, pp. 62–6.

into the seventh and probably eighth centuries.[96] Jēme paid its taxes as did everywhere else, and participated in the complex network of fiscal movement of goods that characterized the whole Nile valley. But we have almost no reference to the detailed local interventions of dukes of the Thebaid or Arab governors of Egypt that are documented around 700, both north and south of Jēme, at Aphroditō and Apollōnopolis Anō (Edfū); the only Arabs mentioned in these texts are the mid- to late eighth-century pagarchs of Ermont. Jēme was part of an economic network that stretched 40 km up and down the river, into the neighbouring city territories of Koptos (Qift) and Latopolis (Esnā). Beyond that, however, connections are rare in our texts—two references to journeys to Antinoupolis (Shaykh 'Ibāda), a gift of two children from Shmin (Greek Panopolis, Arabic Akhmīm) to a Jēme monastery, both of these cities being in Middle Egypt; a reference to a journey to the capital at Fusṭāṭ; an application for a three-month passport to go to Arsinoë (Madīnat al-Fayyūm) just south of the capital in 728/9 or 743/4; several references to Aswān in the far south. This is not a lot for Egypt. Jēme and its territory were relatively inward-looking in the seventh and eighth centuries. In particular, outside landowners are not recorded at all.[97]

The major figure in Jēme was the village headman or *lashane*—the Coptic word, though Greek *dioikētēs* was often used as an alternative even in Coptic documents, and *prōtokōmētēs* in the seventh century too.[98] The *lashane* (pl. *lashaniou* or *lashnou*—there were often two or three) was so important in Jēme that documents were routinely dated by the *lashane* of the year, together, sometimes, with the pagarch—a degree of documentary prominence that is quite unparalleled for a headman. He was often called *lamprotatos* too (the Greek equivalent of Latin *clarissimus*), doubtless no longer a technical term, but indicative of his local standing. *Lashaniou* changed yearly, so that all of the male members of the village elite could expect to become headmen at one time or another; we know the names of over thirty from the eighth century. Of these, the most active seem to be related: Chael son of Psmo in 733–5, Komes son of Chael in 748–59 (possibly continuously), Psmo son of Komes in 766 and 770–2.[99] We could

---

[96] Myśliwiec, *Keramik und Kleinfunde*, pp. 98–179, 192, for Gurna; Hayes, *Late Roman pottery*, p. 387 for Aswān wares.

[97] For Jēme's overall economic network, see Wilfong, *Women of Jeme*, p. 8; idem, 'The archive', p. 174. For Ermont (Armant) pagarchs, see above, Ch. 4, n. 254. The citations in the text are respectively *KRU*, n. 10 (a judicial appeal to the duke of the Thebaid); *OMH*, n. 82; *KRU*, nn. 99, 93; *CLT*, n. 3; and, for Aswān, *KRU*, nn. 38, 68; *CO*, n. 452; *Short texts*, n. 91.

[98] *Prōtokōmētēs* in, e.g. *KRU*, nn. 77, 105, *CO*, n. 131, and MacCoull, 'O. Wilck. 1224'; *meizoteros* is also occasionally used (*KRU*, nn. 10, 12, and perhaps 37). *Lashane* and *dioikētēs* are too frequent to list. Steinwenter, *Studien*, pp. 19–60, and Schiller, 'A family archive', pp. 370–2, regarded the latter two as separate offices; *KRU*, nn. 7 and 13, for the same man, are only one demonstration of the contrary out of many.

[99] For the basic *lashane* lists, see Till, *Datierung*, pp. 234–5. He does not link the *lashane* Psmo of c.770, attested in *KRU*, nn. 84, 86, 97, 104, to the contemporary witness Psmo son of Komes attested in *KRU*, nn. 82, 83, 112.

see them as a leading family, but probably only as a *primus inter pares*, given the number of other headmen we know of; they are in this respect analogous to the Psimanobet family in Aphroditō. We cannot compare their wealth, however, for we have no documents for them as private persons; nor indeed do we have for most other headmen. One exception is Peter son of Komes, *lashane* in 724–5, who accuses a husband and wife of theft from him in the 730s, and who makes a financial agreement with a co-villager in 735; the scale of the theft, 10 $\frac{2}{3}$ *nomismata*, roughly the value of a house, indicates that Peter was a reasonably prosperous dealer, but we cannot be more precise about it.[100] At a guess, Jēme's headmen were sometimes rich peasants, sometimes medium owners; but it is only a guess.

A *lashane* also had considerable powers. He was responsible for taxation, and routinely signed off tax receipts. *Lashaniou* heard the numerous legal disputes from the village, which were either put to them directly or delegated from the pagarch, and also presided over less formal arbitrations. The *lashane* controlled the village prison (*phylakē*, the standard Greek term), into which he put fugitives in a mid-eighth-century text; this was in no sense a novelty of the eighth century, for already in the late sixth Bishop Abraham (probably acting as abbot of Apa Phoibammōn) had threatened the *lashane* Pesynthios with an interdict for imprisoning a man unjustly, and in the early seventh the *lashane* Shenoute and thirteen other representatives of the community (*koinon*) of Jēme asked Abbot Epiphanios if he would intercede with the *lashane* of Taut to get men out of the prison there. Indeed, in seventh-century texts, which include more letters and informal transactions, *lashaniou* are quite commanding: they punish (including putting a man in the stocks), give safe-conducts, order the presentation of legal documents, and so on.[101] They both represented and policed their community, that is to say they essentially controlled it. The only immediate checks on their power were the superior authority of the pagarch (though this is seldom documented), and the interventions of local abbots, who could be prestigious and at least locally powerful. But, of course, a *lashane* was only in office for a year in the first instance, which was probably the most effective check of all, for a headman who oppressed too many of his community was in for trouble later. Perhaps it is better to say that the *lashane* was a temporary representative of a much more permanent group of village elite. This group was at least

[100] *KRU*, nn. 52, 55; cf. also *Varia Coptica*, n. 26. A house is worth 12 *nomismata* in *KRU*, n. 25. Two other *lashaniou*, John and Pekysios, leased out land, in the late seventh century and 695 respectively, in rare Greek documents: Gascou, 'Documents grecs de Qurnat Mar'y', n. 3; MacCoull, 'O.Wilck. 1224'. But these may have been leasing out land of the village community.

[101] For tax receipts, see e.g. *OMH*, nn. 218–400. For disputes, *Ep.*, nn. 116, 278 (seventh-century); *KRU*, nn. 10, 25–6, 36–45, 47, 50–2, 56, with *CLT*, n. 5 (eighth-century). Other powers: *KRU*, n. 115, *CO*, n. 61, *Ep.*, n. 163 for the prison citations (cf. *Ep.*, nn. 176–7, accounts of torture in prison in the early seventh century, but whose prison is unclear); *CO*, nn. 115, Ad. 60 for other punishment; *Ep.* 181 for the stocks; *CO*, nn. 108–12 for safe-conducts; *Ep.*, n. 257 for legal documents.

informally defined, for its members are referred to in several eighth-century disputes as the *noc nrōme*, the 'elders' or 'big men' of the village, who heard cases with the *lashane/-iou* at their head.[102] The practical domination of the *noc nrōme* over their lesser neighbours was probably fairly firm, with the legally supported coercive back-up of the *lashane*. We cannot develop this, though, for we do not see it contested.

The documents themselves show a lively land market in houses and portions of houses inside the village. Aaron son of Shenoute, for example, certainly a medium owner, bought them nine times in 730s–750s, before willing some of them to the monastery of Apa Phoibammōn. Families could also dispute over the apportionment of houses in inheritance, as with the disagreement between the sons of Germanos, resolved in 749–50 by the *noc nrōme* and the headman Komes son of Chael, who drew lots; or the long-running trouble over the division of a house between the daughters of Epiphanios, Tshenoute and Elizabeth, and their mostly female heirs, which ran across numerous documents between 719 and 763, a dispute analysed by both Schiller and Wilfong. Elizabeth is a type-example of the sort of tough women that the Jēme documentation tells us about fairly often, excluded from public office, but economically active as dealers and tenacious as disputants; she may well be the Elizabeth who commissioned a donor portrait in one of the village churches, which survived into the 1930s. Her family, and those of Aaron and Germanos, are the most prominent in the documents, and they were probably all three of a similar socio-economic standing. None of their members are documented as *lashaniou*, but they must have been among the *noc nrōme*, and Shenoute son of Germanos went fugitive-hunting for the *lashane* Kollouthos son of Konstantinos in one text, indicating some position of responsibility.[103]

It is interesting, and unusual, that this network of sales and disputes focuses so heavily on houses, not agricultural land. Although land could be used as a pledge on a loan, and it was certainly given to monasteries, indicating a certain movement in property-owning, land-sales are rare in even our most formal documents, and land disputes do not survive at all.[104]

---

[102] For the *noc nrōme*, see e.g. *CLT*, n. 5 (cf. 6, where the term is not used); *KRU*, nn. 36, 39–40, 42, 45, 52. In 42 and 45, an *ekot*, a housing expert, participated in the hearing. For parallels to this group elsewhere, see below, pp. 600–1.

[103] For Aaron, *KRU*, nn. 1–2, 4–6, 12–15, 72 (the will, but most of it is lost; the monastery is not named, but it was probably a beneficiary). For Germanos' family, nn. 10, 20–1, 39–40, 66, 76, 115 (for the fugitives). For Epiphanios' descendants, nn. 24–6, 28, 35–8, 45–8, 50, 56, 68. It is worth noting that these elite families are above all documented in papyrus texts, not in ostraka: Wilfong, *Women of Jeme*, p. 23. For the Tshenoute–Elizabeth dispute, ibid., pp. 47–68, and above all Schiller, 'A family archive'. For Elizabeth's portrait, fragmentary except for the inscription, see Wilber, 'The Coptic frescoes', p. 98; Wilfong, *Women of Jeme*, pp. 95–8, who is tempted, as am I, to see her as the same Elizabeth.

[104] A rare agricultural land sale is *CLT*, n. 9. For land gifts to the church, *KRU*, nn. 107–11; Godlewski, *Le monastère*, pp. 81–2. Pledges in land are discussed in Wilfong, *Women of Jeme*, pp. 130–1. Note that Aphroditō documents do not include a huge number of straight sales

It may be that houses were more difficult to divide, so occasioned more disputes; they were described in detail in wills, as fields were not. So, when Germanos' mother Sousanna made her will in the early eighth century, she simply specified portions of her fields, crops, and tax obligations (*dēmosion*), but she carefully divided out a house between her grandchildren, Germanos being already dead.[105] But the relative absence of land from the exchange economy is striking, for there is every sign that exchange was capillary. Loans, usually for money, were frequent (they were often to pay the tax in advance of the harvest), and there were semi-professional moneylenders in Jēme, both male and female; we have one quite detailed fragment of a journal, perhaps of a pawnbroker, which lists ingoings and outgoings of wheat and dates (the standard local crops, along with flax) and wine. We have contracts with artisans; and we have documents that show agricultural wage labour (mostly for payment in kind), as well as leases, for Apa Phoibammōn and other landowners.[106] These texts show a wide variety of lessors and employers, not at all restricted to the privileged house-owners already discussed, some rich, like the monasteries, but some of no obvious status at all. The fragmentary nature of many of the documents makes it hard to track individuals, but it looks as if we have a similar network of complex ownership to that of Aphroditō, with medium and small owners leasing out fields to others, and hiring for wages as well; Jēme thus fitted into the standard patterns of Egyptian villages elsewhere. If land itself was kept out of the active exchange economy that involved its products (as well as money, which circulated freely, and houses), then this would show an unusual degree of family control over the basic source of wealth—for land circulated more easily than this in less active village economies elsewhere in the former empire.

Jēme seems to have been a less flexible society than Aphroditō. Aphroditō had more administrative autonomy, of course, and by the eighth century, when it had a pagarch, it also had subordinate villages with their own

---

either: *P. Cair. Masp.* I 67097–9, *P. Lond.* V 1686, are among the few that survive, although they can be supplemented by documents transferring tax liability to new owners: see Keenan, 'Absentee landlordism', pp. 154–6. For the fourth century, see Bagnall, *Late Roman Egypt*, p. 72.

[105] Sousanna: *KRU*, nn. 66, 76 (doublets); cf. 67, 68, for fields tacked on to house descriptions. Family disputes over inheritance were normal in Egypt, even though sibling bonds were tight; for Aphroditō see *P. Cair. Masp.* I 67026, 67028; *P. Lond.* V 1707–9; for the fourth century see Bagnall, *Late Roman Egypt*, pp. 167, 204–7.

[106] For loans, see among many, *OMH*, nn. 51–81; *Short texts*, nn. 85–95; and Wilfong, 'The archive', idem, *Women of Jeme*, pp. 117–49, the basic discussions. The journal is *Ep.*, n. 531. For artisan contracts, e.g. *CO*, n. Ad. 44; *Short texts*, n. 46; Crum, 'Coptic ostraca in Milan', n. 11; *Coptic and Greek texts*, plate 83, n. 2, for woodwork and weaving. For wage labour, e.g. ibid., plates 72, n. 1, 74, n. 1; *Ägyptische Urkunden*, I, n. 45. For leases, e.g. ibid., nn. 48, 65, 75, 79, 82; *Coptic and Greek texts*, plate 66, n. 3; *OMH*, n. 81; *CO*, n. 138; *Short texts*, nn. 38, 39, 70; *Varia Coptica*, nn. 28, 33; and the lists and discussion for Apa Phoibammōn in Godlewski, *Le monastère*, pp. 82–5.

lashaniou, who had similar powers over taxation to those of Jēme (and who misused them, too: above, p. 137). Jēme, for its part, seems in the eighth century to have been under the stable control of a group of families, medium landowners at most, the *noc nrōme*. The active exchange economy just described did not visibly undermine that; although it is quite conceivable that this would have allowed individuals to rise into it and fall out of it, it is my sense that status was relatively stable. The smaller owners of Jēme may have had to recognize that they were excluded from political dominance in the village, that is, that they had to accept a local hegemony controlled by their richer neighbours. Although the exchange network, and probably the landowning network, of Jēme extended to other villages in the territory of Ermont, and presumably vice versa, we see no external patronage networks, even from Ermont. The only alternative patrons to the hierarchy of village officials were the abbots of the local monasteries; they, at least, were very active in that role, and they did include a bishop of Ermont, Abraham. But we do not see the range of possible political support that we saw in Aphroditō.

From the standpoint of peasant cultivators, Egyptian society was arguably riskier than it was elsewhere in the Roman and post-Roman world. Egypt was agriculturally rich, with unusual crop yields thanks to the Nile (above, p. 65), but irrigation required a lot of work, and both landowners and the state expected much from the peasantry, including in years of low flood and reduced fertility. The opportunities of small-scale accumulation were probably greater than elsewhere, but so were the dangers of ruin. Both were increased by the level of capillary, often highly localized, commercial exchange and rural credit. As we have seen (pp. 274–6), there was rather more wage labour in Egypt than elsewhere, which probably shows a social stratum of cultivators who did not control enough landed resources to live on. Wage labour is less clearly evidenced in Aphroditō and Jēme than on the Apion estates of Oxyrhynchos, but it was present in both as well. The level of risk, both positive and negative, in Egypt may also have underpinned greater social tension, and the greater possibility of violence. This may just be the product of a denser and more varied documentation in Egypt; violent acts were, after all, legislated for in great detail in law-codes in the early medieval West. All the same, it is my impression that Egyptian villagers were more conscious than those elsewhere that their neighbours might do them harm. Village organization was tighter than it was elsewhere, at least in the West, but this very tightness can increase tension, as has already been noted for Galatia.

What could peasants do to survive and prosper in this sort of society? They could aim to rise socially, either by economic entrepreneurship, as with Phoibammōn of Aphroditō, or by working their way up the hierarchy of village offices. They could also look for patrons: medium owners in the villages most obviously, the village leadership that is to say, but there were alternatives—external landowners and powerful officials in Aphroditō, leading churchmen in Jēme. This patronage was useful in all aspects of village life. How taxation was apportioned locally, for example, depended largely on village notables, and one thus needed either their favour or a patron to get around them. Patronage was also crucial in dealing with the law, which was immediate and much feared at the village level, thanks to the judicial powers of headmen; it was necessary for those facing economic trouble as well. It did not necessarily come free—peasant land was at risk from rapacious patrons here as elsewhere, especially in moments of economic crisis. Conversely, however, there is no sign in our letters from seventh-century monastic patrons to *lashaniou* of Jēme that the former were getting anything but status out of it;[107] and Mēnas of Antaiopolis did not need to be paid to undermine Dioskoros' control over his tenants. All village-level patrons, everywhere, benefit simply from being seen to be successful patrons: they gain supporters, who may work for them, decide for them in village-level disputes, sell them goods cheap, or be good men in a fight. I have argued that Aphroditō had a more open society, with more possibilities for peasants to choose patrons, than had Jēme, but their basic structures were otherwise similar.

The assumption that village communities were strong in Egypt has not been uncontested. Danielle Bonneau and Roger Bagnall have argued that village communities in late Roman/'Byzantine' Egypt were very weak, and only constructed from above, as taxpaying collectivities. For Bagnall, who is writing about the fourth century, only the church would eventually bring village leadership, perhaps in the fifth.[108] Aphroditō and Jēme are documented for later periods than that, but I have to say that I find this picture unrecognizable. Village councils were not formally constituted in either case, and nor did the church have any structured political role, but the communities of each were active protagonists, with clearly constituted and powerful leaders in the *prōtōkomētai* and *lashaniou* of each (who do not seem that dissimilar, for that matter, to the *kōmarchoi* of the fourth century).[109] The Aphroditō *ktētores* who fought off the local pagarch, the Jēme *noc nrōme* who handled local disputes, were actively engaged in the control and administration of their villages. The violent disputes

---

[107] As with the considerable standing of Abbot Epiphanios, witnessed to by *Ep.*, n. 216 (almost certainly to Epiphanios), a fawning letter in which Shenoute, *lashane* of Jēme, invites him to the village church, saying the whole village is 'filled with perfume' as a result of his sermon.

[108] Bonneau, 'Communauté rurale'; Bagnall, *Late Roman Egypt*, pp. 137–8. Bonneau, who discusses the fourth to sixth centuries, has a definition of 'rural community' that seems to me far too restrictive.

[109] Aphroditō community: *P. Cair. Masp.* I 67001; *P. Lond.* V 1687. Jēme community: *Ep.*, n. 163; *KRU*, n. 105; perhaps Jernstedt, *Koptskie teksty*, n. 43; and *CLT*, n. 6, which is a mutual aid agreement for fiscal duties, probably by village elite members. See also above, n. 100. For fourth-century *kōmarchoi*, Bagnall, *Late Roman Egypt*, pp. 133–6.

between sixth-century villages in the Oxyrhynchos papyri, and the evidence from the same archive of village leaders acting for the economic benefit of the village, borrowing seed-corn from the Apions or building a village storehouse, further supports this picture.[110] In the eighth century, too, village communities or their representatives around Arsinoë (Madīnat al-Fayyūm) and Hermopolis (Ashmūnayn) leased out land, hired dependants, and took out loans, as well as fulfilling more standard tax duties, and in Panopolis/ Shmin (Akhmīm) village headmen formally protested against tax oppression to their pagarch.[111] These patterns do not seem to have been new in 500. Indeed, I would go further: these densely inhabited Egyptian villages seem to me to furnish the best-documented example of active village communities in the late Roman and post-Roman world. There were others in the eastern Mediterranean that may have been as strong, as we shall see in the next chapter (pp. 443–65), but those of Egypt are the most clearly characterized, and can be regarded as models for what one might look for elsewhere. This was so even though the social structures inside villages were much more variable, as the contrast between Aphroditō and Jēme shows.

7. Peasant societies in the northern world: Malling

We do not have any equivalent in the North to the sort of village-level documentation that we have seen in these six examples. But, as noted at the start of this chapter, it seems to me worthwhile to write an account of a northern village that can be set in parallel to those already discussed, even if the evidence has to be invented. Society and the economy in the North was much less dominated by aristocratic landholding for a long time, and even exclusive land tenure hardly existed before the eighth century and later, as we saw in Chapter 6; these meant that the parameters in which peasants operated were in several significant respects different to those we have looked at so far in this chapter—although there were, certainly, parallels too. What follows is a hypothetical reconstruction of a village society, which I shall call Malling;[112] it could be said to be located somewhere in lowland England in the late seventh century, the date of many of the sketchy sources that lie at the heart of this characterization, although I shall use some of the insights that can be gained from later Scandinavian evidence as well.

---

[110] *P. Oxy.* I 133 (seed-corn, borrowed in 550 by seven *kōmarchoi* from the *koinon tōn prōtokōmētōn tēs komēs*, led by a *meizōn*, a very structured group), XVI 1853, 1866–7, 1897 (quarrels), 2005 (storehouse).

[111] *CPR* IV 127, 170; *P. Ross.-Georg.* III 57; *P. Ryl. Copt.* 127; *APEL* III 167 (the protest). (Note also *P. Ryl. Copt.* 324, in which a village headman, *ape*, who has 'eaten' the village's tax, is declared liable for it.)

[112] I chose the name Malling simply because it is a placename found not only in England (in Sussex and Kent) but also in Denmark (south of Århus). For Anglo-Saxon settlements of this period as 'villages', see below, pp. 516–17.

Malling was a village of relative equals, at least as far as its free peasants were concerned (the unfree were a different matter, as we shall see). It had some 150 people in about twelve household compounds, each fairly similar: they consisted of a rectangular wooden building, with an anteroom, a main hall, and a bedchamber for the householder at the back surrounded by smaller square buildings, some of them sunken-floored. Each was the main living and working area for the members of a nuclear peasant family, their unmarried relatives and elderly parents (if living), and their unfree servants and farm labourers, who made up one or two families of dependants. Only two of the houses in Malling were slightly larger and better made (though not significantly better furnished), with a fenced enclosure around each.[113] The families which lived in the latter were also cultivators, but controlled more land, and each had an extra unfree family to help cultivate it; one of them also let out a couple of fields to a poorer neighbour for rent. This was, then, a society of agriculturalists (and stock-raisers, for they all had some animals too); clothmaking was done by the women of each household, and one of the male householders was a smith in the winter—pottery they bought from the next village, where there was a part-time potter, but no smith. Skilled unfree men did some of the specialist agricultural labour, such as beekeeping, and their children looked after animals, to keep them off crops and from straying.

Most exchange was internal to Malling, and was regulated more by the tightness of social relations than by more abstract calculations of value. There was not much of a market link to the world beyond the next-door village, although travelling metalworkers and pedlars did sometimes come by, prepared to exchange beads, brooches, and buckles for agricultural products. Only these transactions could be called commercial; they were marked by mistrust, and had to be done in public, to avoid accusations of theft.[114] Internal village gift-exchange was nonetheless often marked by power plays, as neighbours sought to take advantage of each other, at times of economic or political need (below, pp. 538–9). It was by exploiting neighbours in this way that Ælfwine, one of the larger householders in Malling, had built up his position, and he now cultivated some lands that his neighbours had previously controlled as a result. He was therefore less popular than Ealhmund, the other larger householder, whose social position was older (it was based on lucky marriage alliances a century earlier); the other villagers hoped that all the children Ælfwine had at present would live to adulthood and split the family holding down to a reasonable size again,

[113] This picture roughly fits that of Cowdery's Down in Hampshire, and also Vorbasse in Jutland, though Danish houses were more elaborate. See Ch. 8, nn. 145, 160.

[114] Arnold, *An archaeology*, pp. 126–48 is a good guide to small-scale artisanal exchange in England. For mistrust, see Ine 25 (cf. Liutprand 79 for Italy), and for general suspicion see also Hlothhere 15, Wihtred 28, Ine 20.

before one of the family made it to being a king's retainer or *gesith*, as Ealhmund was already.

This was a village without huge inequalities of wealth, but it must be stressed that inequality was also structural to it, for free families and unfree ones were profoundly distinct. The free–unfree boundary was sharper even than around Lucca, and far sharper than on the St-Germain estates, for it marked not only real status difference, but also direct economic power inside the household. The unfree did the same sort of agricultural labour as their masters, working alongside them in fact, but the subordinate relationship remained structural.[115] There was little chance of free–unfree marriage here, for that would undermine that subordination too much— although the status distinction was not impermeable, for some unfree in the kingdom had lost their free status because of crime, some free had bought their freedom, and many of the unfree children of the village had masters who were also their fathers.

Malling as a community had until recently paid tribute in agricultural products to the king, though on a fairly small scale. The king only needed from his entire kingdom as much food as he, his family and servants, and his (numerous) guests could eat, together with the surplus necessary to feed and supply more specialist artisans, weapon-smiths and workers of precious metals. Ealhmund, being a *gesith*, often went to eat at the king's court, and had a few treasured objects from the king to show for it; he fought for the king, too, in the campaigning season, sometimes with a couple of his neighbours who could afford swords. The king had taken little else from the village, except that two of the smaller households were wholly unfree and had owed a much heavier set of agricultural dues directly to the royal court. The kingdom had recently gone Christian, and the king had transferred Malling to the new bishop; the villagers had already noticed that tribute was now collected yearly, whereas neighbouring villages still paid only when the king asked for it. The public labour service the villagers had been occasionally asked to do—road maintenance was the most important in their area—was now due to the church as well, and they had been called to help build the cathedral. The church used the Roman terminology of ownership when describing Malling, but only in Latin documents, which no one outside the cathedral could read or understand.

Malling was not a legal entity, but it had a certain identity as a village. Villagers did not yet co-operate so much in economic terms, for open fields were in the future, but they did run livestock collectively, and also together took wood from the part of the woodland 10 km away that Malling had

---

[115] For domestic unfreedom see in general Karras, *Slavery and society*, esp. pp. 78–83, focused on western Scandinavia; for early Anglo-Saxon England, Finberg, 'Anglo-Saxon England', pp. 430–2, 435–8, rather a legalistic survey. Pelteret's comprehensive analysis, *Slavery*, only begins around 900. See above, p. 323; below, p. 435.

rights to. Many of the villagers were related by kinship or marriage, of course, but these horizontal links did not cover the whole village, and extended beyond it too. The free men of Malling (women were not allowed) did however go together to the local legal assembly, the *gemot*—in Scandinavia it was called a *thing*—which was the meeting-point of a dozen villages. It had once been the main collective focus for the small kingdom (*regio*) which had been swallowed up in the larger kingdom Malling was now in; in the future it would be an organized hundred court. In the seventh century, however, it was just an assembly for the surrounding area, presided over by the heir of the old local king. The latter was still a close associate of the new, more powerful, king, and in his own village, two or three away from Malling, he still received an elaborate set of dues from his neighbours, particularly the unfree ones.[116]

The men of Malling went to the *gemot* with Ealhmund, their *gesith*. The title of *gesith* did not mean much inside Malling except status, but Ealhmund was their leader in other ways as well. His family ran the local religious rituals for the village, and had done so since before Christianization; he was in close contact with the new bishop, as were all the king's immediate entourage. Ealhmund's family graves were publicly furnished with the richest grave-goods, to underpin their status, though Ælfwine's by now often matched them too.[117] In the *gemot*, Ealhmund was the patron of his neighbours, for, if any of them were accused of anything, they needed to obtain supporters who would swear formally on their behalf, a solemn and serious act, and the more serious the accusation the more supporters they needed; someone was needed to round up support, including from outside the village, for one's kin might well not be enough on their own. Recently, however, Ealhmund had not been as assiduous in the collecting of such oath-swearers as he should have been, and one of the villagers had lost a case unfairly as a result. His neighbours were now wondering whether they ought to ask Ælfwine, the newer large householder, to sponsor their court-cases instead, much as they distrusted him, for at least he did what he said he would, at a price. In England there is no sign that the right to sponsor cases was restricted to a legally defined elite, so the villagers could change patron; all the same, only relatively prosperous people could deal effectively in the *gemot*, for only they had the right level and range of links of obligation to do so. One had to balance the degree of practical effectiveness of one's

---

[116] For the *gemot*, see Stenton, *Anglo-Saxon England*, pp. 294–5; Wormald, ' "Inter cetera bona" ', for early law. The only early reference to Anglo-Saxon legal assemblies is *BCS* 201 (S 106), a reference to *popularia concilia* in c.800, but we cannot be sure of their geographical scale, or their relation to villages. A useful model for the relationship between a *gemot* and a *regio* is Brooks's reconstruction of the territory of Micheldever in Hampshire in 'Alfredian government', pp. 165–73. The local position of the ex-royal family is based on speculation.

[117] For local religious rituals, see above, p. 374 for Denmark. For the local rights of *gesithas* see e.g. Ine 23.1, 50. For burials and claims to status, above, p. 340; below, p. 575.

patrons against what they would demand in return, whether now or in the future.[118]

In this society there were several elements of instability. Families could rise and fall, for sure, as they became too large or too small, as their crops throve or failed, as their heads gained or lost local status through the effectiveness of their dealing. We could easily imagine that Ealhmund, more popular than his rival Ælfwine but also lazier as a dealer, slowly lost his support, had too many sons, and split his lands; his sons then found that they did not have the time or the weapons (which they had had to sell) to make any showing at the king's court. Ælfwine, by contrast, a less scrupulous but also a more effective operator, accumulated more surplus and land parcels from his neighbours, and replaced Ealhmund at the latter's death at the king's court as a *gesith*. His son negotiated with the bishop to build a small church in the village, thus replacing the ritual dominance of Ealhmund's family; his local status was more permanent as a result. A generation later Ælfwine's family, by now rich enough to be letting out many of its fields in Malling for rent, obtained a *læn*, a lease, of all the village tributes from the bishop.[119] The family by now directly controlled the surplus of the two unfree households of the village, which had gone from the king to the church, and was now part of the *læn*; as already noted, it rented out land to several free neighbours, who by now had less of their own; and it was getting tribute from everyone else. These rights had different origins, but they became part of the family's lordship as a single block. By 900 Ælfwine's heirs were regarded, by themselves and their neighbours, as *owners* of Malling; some of their higher-status neighbours only owed them relatively little, but others, both free and unfree, owed them a lot, both in rent and labour.[120] As small aristocrats, now called *thegnas*, they were well placed to serve in the newly crystallizing English state.

This was Malling's trajectory, but it should be added that it was not the only possible one. In a second village nearby, also given to the church, no peasant family had risen to dominance, and the church controlled the whole village as its tenants in 900. In a third, the king had given his local rights directly to a *gesith*, who had established the same sort of external lordship as the church had elsewhere. In a fourth, the village of the heirs of the former king of the *regio*, the village remained stably in their hands throughout, without local tribute relationships changing much. In a fifth, the king had kept control of local tribute, but the free householders had remained

---

[118] For the need to support oaths in Anglo-Saxon courts, see e.g. Ine 46, 52, 54; cf. 50, 62. For the de facto control by Icelandic *goðar* of sponsorship in the *thing*, and their political problems if they did not do it properly, see Byock, *Viking age Iceland*, pp. 99–137; Miller, *Bloodtaking*, pp. 234–47.

[119] For *læn*, see Maitland, *Domesday Book*, pp. 354 ff.

[120] For this model of how landowning developed, see Faith, *English peasantry*, and above, pp. 347–51.

prosperous; they now regarded themselves as small proprietors who simply owed military and corvée service to the state. Overall, however, there were more Mallings, and many more externally dominated villages, by 900 in lowland England than there were villages whose societies had remained stable since the seventh century.

This account is invented, but it does represent a picture, plausible to me at least, of how village societies worked and changed in England—and, later, in Scandinavia too. It is a picture of a society that for a long time did not deal in the exclusive land tenure of the Roman world; but there were some parallels between it and the better-documented societies we have been looking at, all the same. Even if we set aside the unfree, there were richer and poorer peasants in Malling and its real-life counterparts in the North, and the opportunities and necessities for patron–client relationships at every level must have been as great as in any Italian, Frankish, or Egyptian village—for peasants regularly need help, and the help that their kin give them is often not enough. We have little direct documentation of such relationships in England in our period, but we do not lack parallels in the rest of the North—the *goði–thingmaðr* relationship in Iceland, or the clientage networks of Ireland (above, pp. 373, 360). Such associations were not necessarily permanent (and certainly not necessarily military, unlike the more aristocratic links of dependence that are well documented everywhere, including England), but they were between unequals, for mutual support, just like the manifold forms of *patrocinium* in the Roman and post-Roman Mediterranean.

There were two major differences between *patrocinium* and these northern relationships. One was in its relation to land tenure. Frankish and Mediterranean patronage was structured in apposition to clear hierarchies of ownership. Sometimes patrons were the landowners themselves; sometimes they were their rivals (if peasants sought patronage against their landlords); sometimes they simply operated in different spheres, in particular if patrons were other villagers, offering help and support in village-level crises, when landowners were rather further away. In England, and the rest of the North, this dialectic with landowning was for long largely absent: either there were few or no external landowners, or the patronage relationship itself constituted the main relationship of exploitation there was—as in Ireland and Iceland, and arguably in England before 700 as well, when small levels of tribute-paying to patrons/rulers were the principal external, and tenurial, link that villagers had. The other major difference was that contrasts in wealth were so much less strong in most of the North (except perhaps Denmark) until well after 800, as is clear in our archaeological evidence: even the most important non-royal patrons were less rich, and therefore presumably in some respects less powerful, than they were in the Mediterranean. One might propose that this lack of power corresponded to an impermanence in most vertical relationships in the North. This can certainly be argued for Ireland, where indeed even political structures were generally impermanent (unlike probably in England: above, pp. 344–51). Elsewhere, one can only speculate. But it seems to me most likely that a relative impermanence characterized northern patronage relationships at the village level; this would be another potential contrast with the Frankish and Mediterranean worlds.

8. Parameters of analysis

Given that we are dealing here with the earliest middle ages, we can say a surprising amount about most of the local case studies set out here, and, to an extent, we can get through the veils in our sources and say something about the concrete social activities of the peasantry. This is important; it shows that at least in these examples we are not restricted to tiny elites of kings, leading clerics, and aristocrats, if we want to study human behaviour in the past in detail. (There are not many other areas that could be studied for our period in similar detail, but there are some: Numidia in the early fifth century, Oxyrhynchos in the sixth, the upper Rhine, central Bavaria, and the Sabina in the eighth, and Arsinoë and Hermopolis probably all through, are others.) We need now, however, to draw some comparisons, so that we can explore some of the criteria by which peasant social practices can be set against each other. These comparisons will in turn feed into wider general-izations about peasant societies in Chapter 9.

I shall focus in this section on two main issues, the coherence of the village, and the nature of patronage. Before we reach them, however, four briefer points need to be made about the case studies as a group. First, our snapshots of local societies have tended to show relatively stable social structures. Some elements of potential future change have been visible, but these were not societies obviously facing social breakdown or transform-ation. In part, a static image is privileged by the sort of analysis presented here, for one needs to treat a body of material as a single unit, given the fact that one is dealing with such small amounts of evidence in this period, in order to be able to say anything at all. But I would anyway wish to argue that social change at the peasant level was often pretty slow. The Lucchesia, whose long-term history I know best out of these examples, had villages in 1150 whose local societies had not altered much since 750. The scansion of historical change is often much faster at the level of elites and political systems than it is for peasantries, and is certainly differently paced. Not even the 'fall' of the western Roman empire had all that dramatic an immediate effect on peasants, outside (usually restricted) war zones at least, even though some spin-offs of that political breakdown—the end of tax, the weakening of aristocracies—would in the end be important for them (see below, pp. 519–35).

Second, it emerges from these case studies that a crucial parameter for how peasant society works is the fragmentation of large landowning, more even than the latter's simple extent: the more fragmented that landowning is, the more space there is for peasant social action. In these seven examples, aristocratic power was all-pervasive in only one, the Île de France, largely because large blocks of land owned by single owners are well documented only there. External landowning was considerable in three others (Lucca, the middle Rhine, Aphroditō), and more marginal in the other three (Galatia, Jēme, and Malling), but all these cases were characterized by a similar social mix between peasant owners and tenants. Aristocrats were more powerful in the first group than the second, obviously, but there were visible signs of peasant protagonism, of autonomous peasant initiatives, in both groups. Even where it was present, aristocratic landowning was too dispersed, and local domination was as a result too difficult, unless a good deal of effort was put into it, which was by and large not a feature of our period.

Third, it should be clear that, although in all these societies there was a division between free and unfree,[121] the importance of that division was highly variable, and was greatly influenced by the patterns of landowning. Where all peasants in a village were subject to one lord, as often in the Île de France, the free–unfree division, although a relevant status marker, was no more than that, and could be bridged. Where there were peasant owners, free tenants, and unfree tenants in a village, as often around Lucca, the division was more important, for it marked the limit of participation in autonomous social action, which was a genuine possibility at village level and even beyond, and mattered for the free; when most tenants were in practice unfree, as around Mainz, such a distinction will have had an extra edge. Above all, though, where peasant owners dominated the economy, as in England, any free–unfree division that existed was a structural part of the relations of intra-household exploitation, and could not easily be diminished. It must be stressed that these contrasts, although very great, are invisible in our legal sources, which restrict themselves to establishing a line beyond which people were excluded from free, political, society, and to policing it with great vigour. 'Slaves' thus seem to be much the same in the Roman world, Italy, Francia, and Anglo-Saxon England, and have often been analysed as if they were. Such analyses are basically flawed. Even after the end of slavery as a mode of production (above, pp. 259–63, 276–7), which radically changed the economic position of the unfree, the latter's socio-economic standing was substantially different from place to place. This variation was so closely tied up with the differences in landowning that

---

[121] This was so even in the East, although the unfree were much less numerous there. They were largely domestic servants and household labourers: Bagnall, *Late Roman Egypt*, pp. 123–7; Kaplan, *Les hommes*, pp. 275–7; *Vie de Théodore*, cc. 7, 116; Ashburner, 'Farmers' law', cc. 45–7. The latter will have had some formal parallels to Anglo-Saxon unfree workers.

the unfree could have had a different practical position not only from region to region but from village to village. This point will be further explored later (pp. 559–66).

Fourth, inside free society, legal or formal status markers seem to have had little independent importance at the peasant level. There were some, like village official position in the East, or the quasi-military titles sometimes attested around Lucca; there were informal versions, too, like the *noc nrōme* of Coptic-speaking Egypt. But the most important criteria for status seem to have been economic: how much land each family held, and on what terms. This meant that good or bad management, good or bad luck, could allow any given peasant family to rise or fall socially; there was more opportunity, and also more risk. One should not exaggerate this; land and thus status was inherited, and the local pecking order did not necessarily change all that much across the generations. But it could in principle, and this would have affected peasant strategies. Relevant here to add is that this de facto social gradation also extended upwards into the aristocracy: there were no legal barriers to peasant ambition in any of our societies. The chances of success-ful upward mobility into the aristocracy were trivially small, of course, but they did affect the choices available to the richest members of village elites, and this had an impact on peasant strategies too, as with Ripwin of Ben-sheim (p. 397). This impact, too, will be developed further later (pp. 566–70).

With these points clearer in our minds, let us look at the coherence of villages as economic, political, social units, as seen in our case studies. In institu-tional terms, the most organized villages were those of the eastern Mediter-ranean, where we find regular references to community action and to village leaders, indeed sometimes several village officials. In the West village activity was much more informal, and also varied considerably between the public presence of village leaders in the middle Rhine and the near-invisibility of the village level except as a geographical reference point around Lucca. In only two of our examples, Malling and the Île de France, was there no direct evidence on this issue. About England we can only guess; on the St-Germain estates, however, we could postulate that common subjection to a single landlord would in practice have created a certain coherence for the commu-nity, giving the *maior* of each village, himself a peasant, the sort of de facto authority that an eastern village headman had. We shall see in Chapter 8 that these contrasts extend well beyond these seven case studies, and do indeed mark genuine differences between regions.

The main variables that created stronger or weaker villages were, as far as can be seen, the degree of organization of political power and collective life in the village; the pattern of settlement; the economic role of the village collectivity; and the degree to which village leaders were committed to their communities. In order to get closer to them, let us summarize their main features in the five examples for which we have evidence, in sequence. Around Lucca, villages were spatially fragmented, to the extent that people could be uncertain where they began or ended; they seldom had any clear economic role. They also had close to no social function, and peasants could construct their own support networks as they liked, almost as one might do nowadays, although this doubtless meant uncertainty as much as freedom. Around Mainz, villages were more concentrated settlements, and their inhabitants perhaps co-operated more over silvo-pastoral activities, but we can also see more coherent groups of village leaders acting in public contexts, who could operate both as a bulwark and as a barrier between free peasant society and the middle Rhine aristocracy. Around Ankara, villages were much more organized: potentially riven by jealousies and conflicts, but also capable of generating the unheard-of, a successful peasants' revolt against a landlord. This coherence partly derived from pastoral co-operation, partly from long-standing local institutions, but above all, perhaps, from the fact that village leaders, themselves peasant cultivators, had social and political horizons that did not go far beyond the boundaries of their settlements. Local peasant culture was unusually cohesive and self-confident; and even internal divisions in the villages at least show that there was a local community worth fighting over. Aphroditō was a strong community of a different kind: it had a wide variety of social levels in it, and a good deal of structural discord, but a sufficiently complex organizational structure, and a sufficiently wide range of economic and political functions, that it could operate as a focus for local loyalty, including solidarity against the next-door city. Jēme, finally, had the most developed village-level political structure, with headmen endowed with notable coercive power, backed up by a village elite who decided local disputes. Its solidity blocked independent communication between local peasants and outside patrons, much as in the middle Rhine. The economic functions of Jēme as a village were similar to those of Aphroditō, but the local social structure was rather less fluid, and the village elite rather more inward-looking.

Our case studies thus show how the basic variables that underpin village coherence worked in practice. One could plot them on a graph, according to whether a given society had more or less institutional solidity, or economic co-operation, or concentrated settlement. The way they worked in detail would doubtless have been sufficiently specific that two neighbouring villages could quite easily have had distinct types of village community: not all of Egypt's villages were like Aphroditō and Jēme (which were themselves different), Rhenish villages were not all like Dienheim, and so on. But in each case these local differences could be put back together, so as to characterize village society on a regional level as well.

The solidity of the society of any given village was in itself crucial for the framing of peasant choices. Protagonism, an autonomy from the decisions of outsiders, was easier for peasants if some of them owned their own land, and if outside powers did not have their own local proprietorial power-bases; but such autonomy was still firmer if the village operated as an effective body, for it could be more of a support group in cases of individual difficulty. If villages were very weak, as around Lucca, peasants would have to link themselves to external patrons in order to have firm back-up in a crisis. Conversely, if such patronage links were easy to establish (and, in particular, if village elites chose to use them, in order to dominate their neighbours, or to rise into the lower rungs of the aristocracy), then villages would in turn have less of a social role. In both cases, the local autonomy of the peasantry would be reduced again. Peasant autonomy was not always more benign than dependence on outside powers, landowners, and/or patrons, for peasants can be unpleasant to each other too (as the people rotting in the *lashane*'s prison at Jēme knew); but it was at least not defined by inequality and subjection, and is worth signalling when we can find it. All this takes us on to the parameters of patronage, however; we shall return to villages in the next chapter.

Patronage is the most elusive element of all, for it is so diverse. Indeed, it is common to all human societies in one form or another, for even the most public, meritocratic societies give some space, however informal, to powerful people helping weaker ones and getting support back in various forms, both political and economic.[122] There were many different types of it even inside single communities in our period, let alone across the whole of Europe and the Mediterranean. Patron–client relations coexisted with other vertical relationships, either in competition with them or mutually reinforcing them: the public hierarchies of power (as with counts or tax-collectors or *prōto-kōmētai*), and the landlord–tenant relationship. They also coexisted with horizontal relations of solidarity, with kin, neighbours, and, as we have just seen, the village community. The village community was, however, both a horizontal and a vertical power network: it was a relationship of mutual support between relative equals, but it was also a terrain for the power-broking, the village-level patronage, of local officials and medium landowners. The more effective such communities were as an alternative to external patronage networks, the more they were a support for the internal patronage of members of village elites.

Once again, it is worth reprising briefly the specific forms of patronage that we have seen in each of our case studies. Around Lucca, we could not see the content and the purpose of patron–client relationships, but it was at least possible to see that they were eclectic, with peasants looking to both local and city figures, who did not have to be their landlords as well. In the middle Rhine, peasant relationships to the various strata of the aristocracy

---

[122] For patronage seen cross-culturally see e.g. Runciman, *Treatise*, II, pp. 52, 105–6, 257–8, 406–9.

seem to have been rather more distant, probably because the latter were perceived as threatening; the village was a more likely focus of support. Around Paris, peasants and aristocrats seem to have lived in different worlds; aristocrats were simply the landlords of peasants, and any peasant social relationships would be in practice, as far as we can see, on the village level. This was mostly true around Ankara as well, but for the opposite reason: outside landlords were not powerful enough, rather than too powerful. Galatian peasants looked to St Theodore as a neutral, not too elevated, not too external, mediator if their village rivalries got out of hand, rather than any secular power.[123] In Aphroditō, we see the greatest variability, with village-level patronage, village landlordship, formal village leadership, external landlords, and competing external political powers being called upon by peasants and medium owners at different times, against both other villagers and external dangers. In Jēme, by contrast, patronage stopped with the village leadership, and the only alternatives to it were heads of monasteries, themselves significant landowners but also religious leaders. In Malling, finally, I would suppose that patronage operated at the village level for the most part, between people who did not differ very greatly in wealth and status. Only rather later in England would churches and aristocrats be strong enough to offer themselves as alternative patrons—as in the tenth century, when we can see aristocratic patrons being very useful in court-cases.[124]

We cannot easily tell what peasants wanted patronage for. To sidestep economic difficulties, certainly: we can see Egyptian patrons doing that. To evade taxation and other public dues and duties: our case studies do not give us evidence for this, but other sources do (below, pp. 527–9). To mediate in situations of local tension: we can see a Galatian patron doing that. To construct support networks in situations of formal conflict, for sure: we can see this later in Scandinavia, and, as just noted, in England, and overall one could expect it virtually everywhere. Aristocrats were *supposed* to be patrons of parties to court-cases; one classic instance is from Marculf's seventh-century formulary from, probably, the Paris region, which envisages that, if an aristocrat was sent away by the king on public business, then 'all his court-cases, and those for his friends, for his sworn dependants, and for those in his legitimate sphere of influence (*legitimo mitio*)', would be suspended until he returned.[125] Perhaps the Parisis was the least likely context of all for this *mitium* extending to peasants, but these sentiments will have been normal at every social level. Patronage could also be used against

---

[123] Our evidence for Galatia obviously stresses Theodore at the expense of alternative patrons, but the *Life* is sufficiently detailed that one might expect at least a hint of secular patronage, and it is absent. Internal village peacemakers do appear, however (above, p. 409).

[124] See Wormald, 'Charters, law', pp. 159–67; Keynes, 'The Fonthill letter'.

[125] *Marculfi formulae*, I. 23 (MGH, *Formulae*, p. 57). Patronage in lawsuits was of course usually seen much more negatively in our sources: Ratchis 1, 10, are a locus classicus.

landlords, as Dioskoros found—as did, earlier, Libanios of Antioch (p. 527). But how each of these weighed for individual peasants we cannot tell; even in the societies in which we get closest to the thought-world of the peasantry—which among these case studies are probably Galatia and Aphroditō—we cannot get more than a few fragments of insight. A detailed knowledge of peasant states of mind is largely closed to us before the fourteenth century.

All the same, we can see clear regularities in our case studies, which have their own significance. The most important contrast is between communities where peasants principally looked to other villagers for support, and those where they tended to look outside. The peasants of the Lucchesia and of Aphroditō most often looked outside the village; the others notably less. This valuing of outside patrons has considerable implications for the ideological hegemony of those outsiders. 'Hegemony' in this context is a term coined by Antonio Gramsci, to denote, not simply the dominance of a social class, but the acceptance of that dominance by the dominated, the internalization of the value-system of the ruling class, including those parts of the system which allow rulers to punish the dominated for not obeying the rules. Peasants have accepted aristocratic hegemony often enough in history, at least in part. This has not prevented them from engaging in the small-scale signs of disobedience and disaffection that James Scott analysed in his classic account of Malaysia in the 1970s, *Weapons of the weak*; but it has made it harder for them to organize their own societies autonomously, or to move towards the clearest sign of protagonism of all, that is to say revolt.[126] Out of our case studies, the Lucchesia in the eighth century and Aphroditō in the sixth are the best bets for societies in which the aristocratic strata had a hegemony over peasant society.

This is significant, for these were not, actually, the societies where aristocrats were strongest. Paris and the Rhineland in the eighth century fit that picture better: here, aristocrats could simply dominate, with overwhelming physical force, without worrying about whether peasants had internalized their values, which they probably had not. A third group was made up of Galatia in sixth-century Anatolia and Jēme in eighth-century Egypt, where, by contrast, aristocrats were rather less dominant, but probably not ideologically hegemonic either. This is where we might expect revolt: in a society which did not necessarily accept aristocratic ground-rules, and was not exposed to overwhelming aristocratic power. And we find it, too: at the village level in Galatia, against landlords; in Egypt, at the level of the whole region, in the great eighth- and ninth-century tax revolts against the state. It is not, one must stress, that we can see direct signs of these revolts at Jēme,

---

[126] Gramsci, *Quaderni del carcere*; Scott, *Weapons*. Scott sees his resistances as a proof that Gramsci was wrong, and that peasants do not collude in their subjection: see ibid., pp. 314–50, and idem, *Domination*, pp. 70–107. The two seem to me to be able to coexist.

even if, as noted already (p. 421), they are the most plausible cause of the village's abandonment.[127] Nor can we say for sure that the absence of links between Jēme peasants and Arab patrons in Ermont were either the cause or the consequence of fiscal tensions. But I noted already when discussing the Arab state in Egypt that the weakness of patronage at the level of the state was a major cause of the weakness of its hegemony over the issue of whether taxation was legitimate (pp. 140–4); we now find the same point suggested independently at the level of at least one village, and this seems to me significant. The absence of hegemony is only one reason why peasants revolt, of course; they must have something concrete to oppose as well. We shall look at this in more detail when we come to the general issue of revolts in Chapter 9 (pp. 578–88). But it is, at least, a necessary element in all peasant uprisings. Conversely, the lasting interest of peasants in the Lucchesia in links of external patronage can be seen as a sign of quiescence, and indeed the Lucchesia—and Tuscany as a whole—is one of the most stable sub-regions in the whole of Europe in the rest of the early middle ages and beyond. There was unusually little social conflict there even at the next major moment of political instability, the replacement of the march of Tuscany by urban communes and private rural lordships around 1100. The Tuscan aristocracy could not dominate the peasantry directly in 800, but they could control the basic ground-rules of society, thanks to the hegemony they did possess. This latter would be crucial when they aimed for domination too.[128]

---

[127] But see Bell, 'Two official letters', pp. 272–4, a little-known letter from Atias, duke of the Thebaid, to one of the Jēme-area monasteries, dating to, almost certainly, 697; it refers to the monks defaulting on their poll-tax in the time of *antarsia*, 'insurrection'. This revolt pre-dates the better-known sequence of revolts that began in the 720s, but at least shows that Jēme was not isolated from resistances of this kind.

[128] See, for Tuscany, Wickham, 'Property ownership', pp. 226–44.

8

Rural settlement
and village societies

THIS CHAPTER AIMS to present an overview of the state of archaeological knowledge on rural settlement, and to link it with the textual evidence on village identity. (For a definition of the word 'village', see below, p. 470, and for a discussion of alternative definitions see pp. 516–17.) Like other chapters with a largely archaeological evidence base, notably Chapters 10 and 11, the syntheses presented here are provisional, for new discoveries are being made all the time. Overall, the areas of this survey that are most hypothetical, most subject to reinterpretation in the light of future research, lie in the post-Roman western Mediterranean: in those regions, research methodologies capable of identifying rural settlement in the early middle ages at all have only been generated relatively recently, in the last two decades in Italy, the last decade or little more in southern France and eastern Spain, not yet in most of North Africa; and what has been found is so sub-regionally or microregionally variable that generalization proves unusually difficult. Elsewhere, however, most of the basic patterns set out here seem fairly sound, reinforced by numerous research projects all finding similar things—even if unstudied sub-regions might well, of course, spring surprises on us, that is to say, local realities whose existence we had not hitherto suspected. Two caesurae run through the subject-matter of this chapter, one geographical, the other chronological. First, there is a real difference between the eastern Roman empire and the western in the importance of villages in the rural landscape, which has stood up to all attempts at critique that I have seen; as a result, I shall look at the villages of the East first, as a separate topic from the more dispersed rural settlement of the Roman West. Second, around the period of the end of the Roman empire in the West, one particularly characteristic settlement form, the rural villa, went out of use, and was replaced by a wider range of patterns; my treatment of the West will as a result be divided into three parts, a discussion of the villa-focused rural settlement hierarchies of the Roman world, and two surveys of the post-Roman forms that replaced them, in the western Mediterranean and finally in northern Gaul and its northern neighbours.

1. Villages in the eastern Mediterranean

The best evidence for rural settlement in the eastern Mediterranean, indeed for anywhere in our period, comes from Syria and Palestine. What makes this region special are the astonishing standing ruins of villages that still survive in, especially, the Limestone Massif of north-east Syria, the Hawran in what is now southern Syria and northern Jordan, and the north-west Negev in what is now Israel: arguably the most significant monuments to the late Roman world surviving anywhere, for they are monuments to the peasant majority, not to rich but atypical elites. Topographical study of these zones has been backed up by excavation and field-survey across the region: this has been more intermittent, particularly in Syria, but it is still denser than elsewhere in the East. We shall see that the evidence for Anatolia and Egypt differs from it only in detail, so the Levant will be the type-region for the East, in this chapter at least.

There are some 700 deserted late Roman villages on the Limestone Massif, which is today a barren belt of low karstic hills between Aleppo and the Orontes plain above Antioch (see the inset in Map 5), of which at least fifty are well enough preserved to be capable of study without excavation. They consist of groups of houses, built without much sign of planning, with only rudimentary streets and public spaces. Villages vary between eight and 200 houses, and seem simply to have accumulated in size, through infill and steady expansion outwards; this is true even of the largest villages, which have relatively few urban characteristics.[1] The houses are made out of well-cut squared limestone, and are generally two-storeyed, usually with two or three rooms on the ground floor, with an ample courtyard in front that fits into neighbouring courtyards in jigsaw form. These houses were built with considerable care, 'comme des temples romains', as Georges Tate has written, and are often elaborately decorated with mouldings, relief sculpture, and colonnading; they are solid enough to have survived a millennium-and-a-half of earthquake and abandonment, sometimes almost intact—there are houses surviving to the roof pediment, 10 metres above the ground, and others with their doors (always made of basalt, imported from the plains some 40 km to the east) still in place. They were built across the first six centuries of the Christian era, but their main period is c. 350–550, with a peak in the fifth century and early sixth. Villages were in general overwhelmingly made up of these houses, which were differentiated from each other only by the number of rooms they had on each floor (this varied

---

[1] The basic surveys are Butler, *Publications*, II; idem, *Syria*, II B; Tchalenko, *Villages antiques*; Tate, *Les campagnes*. A useful brief overview is Foss, 'Syria', pp. 197–204, 226–9. The largest centres, notably Brād and Bāra, had more artisans, a market in the latter, and some richer houses, but were not in other respects distinct from other villages: Tchalenko, *Villages antiques*, I, pp. 387–90. Cf. above, pp. 411–28 for Aphroditō and Jēme in Egypt.

between one and thirteen, though 86 per cent had four or less; the larger ones were built up by continuous extensions).[2] The number of public buildings was very small—a small number of open-arcaded buildings, generally called 'androns', perhaps centres of village political institutions, and some structures that can best be seen as inns, make up most of them; half-a-dozen villages had bath complexes.[3] Every village had at least one church, however, and often several, as befits a zone so active in the Christian Roman period. It was in the centre of this area, overlooking the edge of the plain of Antioch, that Simeon the Stylite had his column in the early fifth century; the great church of Qaʿlat Simʿān was built there in the 470s, probably with imperial patronage, and a network of inns for pilgrims soon developed just beneath, at Deir Simʿan. The architectural and decorative styles of the main church spread across the limestone country thereafter, and can be found on many of the churches built in the next century.[4]

The solidity and decoration of these villages spells wealth. The main questions have to be: from what? for whom—peasants, peasant communities, or landowners? and when and why did it stop? Georges Tchalenko argued in 1953 that the wealth of the zone derived from an olive monoculture, particularly from the fifth century onwards, and that the period was marked by the steady fragmentation of earlier larger properties: the beneficiaries of the oil boom were independent peasants, who exported right up to the breaking of eastern Mediterranean unity by the Persian and Arab conquests, after which the zone was abandoned.[5] Tchalenko's book was an influential analysis; it was not the first study of the area (H. C. Butler had surveyed it in 1899–1905), but it was the first attempt to integrate topography with economic explanation, and it caught attention with its upbeat portrayal of the late Roman economy, something that was distinctly rare in 1953. Not everyone wanted to accept the argument, but its solidity was difficult to disregard; even A. H. M. Jones, whose view of late Roman exchange was decidedly different and who generally avoided using archaeology, grudgingly accepted Syria's limestone country as an exception, and cited Tchalenko in a footnote.[6] Recent work has undermined some of Tchalenko's propositions, however. One of the only excavations in the area (and the only one of houses), the 1970s French study of three house groupings at Dēḥes (with two houses added later), showed that, although the

---

[2] Basic for housing is now Tate, *Les campagnes*, pp. 15–188, 257–65 (p. 340 for the quote, p. 260 for statistics of house sizes). For mouldings and relief, see e.g. Naccache, 'Le décor des maisons', for Serjilla.

[3] Tate, *Les campagnes*, pp. 72–81, for androns and inns; Charpentier, 'Les bains de Sergilla', for baths.

[4] Naccache, *Le décor des églises*, pp. 270–9; for Qaʿlat Simʿān see Tchalenko, *Villages antiques*, pp. 223–76; for Deir Simʿān, ibid., pp. 205–22; Claude, *Die byzantinische Stadt*, pp. 208–10.

[5] Tchalenko, *Villages antiques*, I, pp. 394–438.

[6] Jones, *LRE*, pp. 823, 1340 n. 119.

buildings dated to the fourth and sixth centuries, occupation continued in them until after 900. Georges Tate, one of the Dēḥes excavators, published a study of the house-types of the Limestone Massif in 1992 which refines Tchalenko's datings for them, stresses even more than Tchalenko that they were always the habitations of peasant proprietors, but also denies the oil argument, arguing instead that they were prosperous, largely subsistence cultivators, with at most a market in neighbouring towns, whose prosperity grew as the population increased, until overpopulation and reduced urban demand caused a steady lessening in wealth and thus new building— although the local population stayed on for centuries.[7] We need to look at some of the elements in this debate, for they have wider implications.

The first point to be made is that Tate is correct to doubt Tchalenko's arguments about oil monoculture. The Limestone Massif, despite its barren appearance today, is actually well enough watered to allow dry farming, and a detailed analysis of the evidence for agriculture shows all the standard features of Mediterranean polyculture in our period: in particular, stock-raising was important, and indeed the ground levels and courtyards of houses were mostly given over to cows and sheep, with humans living on the first floor. All the same, there was a lot of oil being produced there: Tate counted 245 oil-presses in the forty-five villages he focused on, some of them quite elaborate.[8] What seems to be likely is that oil was the main *exchange* specialization of the Massif. Villagers did not exclusively rely on it as a cash-crop, because for peasants to depend on the market for their own food was not something that the Roman economy, even at its most elaborate, could normally sustain; hence the evidence for a mixed economy in the area. All the same, oil was what they exported, and the source of their wealth, the sort of wealth that allowed them to employ specialized itinerant builders, such as Kosmas *technitēs*, who left his name on five buildings between 489 and 505. In 'Amudiye, a village on the Antioch–Apamea road, rock-cut oil containers have been found, capable of holding over a thousand litres each, which are signs of the first stage of the export process.[9] At this point it is worth recalling that the north-eastern corner of the Mediterranean, Antioch and its hinterland, Cilicia, and parts of Cyprus, are the main region that produced LRA 1 amphorae, largely for oil, which are the most widely spread late Roman amphorae in the eastern Mediterranean between the fourth and seventh centuries.[10] The Limestone Massif is part of this specialist oil region,

[7] Sodini, 'Déhès'; Bavant and Orssaud, 'Stratigraphie et typologie' (on later seasons at Dēḥes); Tate, *Les campagnes*, pp. 243–350.

[8] Tate, *Les campagnes*, pp. 243–56; cf. Callot, *Huileries*. Decker, 'Food for an empire', wonders if the area produced wine for export too, although Callot, *Huileries*, p. 5 excludes it for the northern half of the Massif.

[9] For Kosmas, Tchalenko, *Villages antiques*, I, p. 51 n. For 'Amudiye, Peña, *Christian art*, p. 57. See further Callot, *Huileries*, p. 106, for storage at Kāfr Nabo.

[10] Overviews: Panella, 'Merci e scambi', pp. 665–6; Sodini and Villeneuve, 'Le passage', p. 197; Van Alfen, 'New light', pp. 208–10. LRA 1 amphorae were often resinated, and were in

and is better suited to oil production than is the plain behind Antioch itself; there is no reason why its surplus should not have been an integral part of the Mediterranean oil export of the period, as indeed Tchalenko argued.

Even if Tate is right about the household economy in these villages, then, it all the same seems probable that Tchalenko better characterizes the macro-economy of the area. As will be argued in a moment, this model also better fits the pacing of its later history. Why does Tate, whose study is now the starting-point for research in the area (he is much more scientific, less impressionistic, than his predecessor), not accept the idea of an interregional export economy? He does have some significant support, it is true: LRA 1 amphorae are not actually very common at Dēḥes, for example, or indeed elsewhere in the Limestone Massif. On the other hand, sixth- and seventh-century Phocaean Red Slip fine ware, imported from the Aegean, is common there, and a hundred copper coins were found too, a substantial number for a rural site, peaking in the seventh and eighth centuries, and including Byzantine coins into the 670s, even though northern Syria was Arab from 638.[11] These do indicate exchange; it may be that the amphorae were mostly used for sea-voyages, and that oil came to the coast in skins, as appears to be the case in fourth-century Africa. It is indeed true that the great Syrian cities would have been a significant source of demand, regardless of the scale of Mediterranean exchange, as Tate proposed; another outlet was the army on the Euphrates frontier.[12] But it does also seem that Tate is relying on a macroeconomic model of a relatively unmoving and economically localized late Roman Mediterranean, derived from A. H. M. Jones and Évelyne Patlagean, which is essentially pre-archaeological—a model that is still quite powerful in France, as shown, for example, in the works of Michel Kaplan and Jean Durliat, whatever their other differences, although it is rarer to find archaeologists using it.[13] I shall discuss further the density of late Roman exchange in Chapter 11; but even at a local level, the remarkable flourishing of the late Roman period in the Massif, followed by its eventual

that case for wine, not oil, but they also did not all come from the Antioch area (see below, p. 714).

[11] Tate, *Les campagnes*, esp. p. 331; For Dēḥes ceramics, see Sodini, 'Déhès', pp. 234–66, updated by Orssaud, 'Le passage', and Bavant and Orssaud, 'Stratigraphie et typologie' (a full publication is planned). LRA 3 amphorae, from the Aegean, were found there too: Sodini and Villeneuve, 'Le passage', p. 199. For coins, Sodini, 'Déhès', pp. 267–87; they begin around 600 because the levels begin then, and few are residual. For comments on other sites, see Reynolds, 'Levantine amphorae'.

[12] African skins: Peña, 'Mobilisation', e.g. pp. 118, 135, 212. Skins were used in the vine-yards of the upper Euphrates, too, although we do not know if they were used for export: Ammianus, *Res gestae*, XXX.1.9; but there were amphorae there too, for a 'North Syrian' carinated amphora type, probably for wine, links inland sites (including Dēḥes and other nearby sites) with the Euphrates—see below, p. 772.

[13] Patlagean, *Pauvreté*, pp. 156–235; Durliat, *De la ville*, pp. 513–40 (who does confront archaeology), Kaplan, *Les hommes*, pp. 562–73 (the latter now distances himself from the model—pers. comm.).

near-abandonment, seems to me to require a more dynamic explanation, and the link between this area and oil export is the most plausible one we have.

The beneficiaries of this prosperity seem mostly to have been the peasantry. Literary sources, our best sources for ownership, are ambiguous on this issue, it is true: Libanios and Theodoret refer to both villages with peasant owners (*despotai*) and villages with a single external owner in the lands behind Antioch—including in the latter category a village in the territory of Cyrrhus, part of which covered the northern section of the Limestone Massif, which was wholly owned by an Antioch city councillor. As a result, there has been some questioning of the peasant-focused assumptions of Tchalenko and Tate, which seem to go against standard views of late Roman proprietorial power—Peregrine Horden and Nicholas Purcell, for example, have recently proposed that these villages were generally owned by Antiochenes.[14] I find this alternative view mostly unconvincing. The quality of village houses by itself disproves it: it would be hard to argue that peasants would have enough surplus left to pay for them after not only tax but rent as well, and even less credible that landlords should put up the money. The general homogeneity of housing also argues against large-scale landowning: would not one expect central buildings acting as collection-centres, or indeed clearly marked-out residences if landowners were local? (There are one or two of the latter, showing they could be recognizable, but they are few.) Obviously, there must have been some larger owners. Continuously enlarged houses, or the bath-building at Serjilla put up by Julian and Domna in 473, must be signs of the village elite, the most successful and the richest, that is to say medium owners, whose lesser neighbours acted as part-time tenants and seasonal labourers.[15] Some still larger properties must surely have existed too; one would certainly have been that of Megas *komēs*, curator of an imperial estate, a major political figure at Constantinople in the 580s, who paid for some of the silver objects in the Kaper Koraon treasure, found in the southern hills of the Massif in 1908. But it is significant that large estates can rarely be identified, and they were probably fairly fragmented.[16] One could propose that, given that the

[14] Libanios, *Oration* XLVII.4, 11; Theodoret, *Histoire des moines*, XIV.4, XVII.3; other references to large owners in the Antioch hinterland are John Chrysostom, *Homilies on Matthew*, LXI.3 (without a reference to location, but probably dating from Chrysostom's time in the city), and Severus of Antioch, *Homily* XIX, pp. 38–43; cf. Horden and Purcell, *Corrupting Sea*, pp. 274–5.

[15] Serjilla: Charpentier, 'Les bains de Sergilla' (but that village, unusually well preserved, has a very homogeneous housing stock, and thus few structural social divisions: Butler, *Syria*, II B, pp. 113–33). For larger houses, see e.g. Tchalenko, *Villages antiques*, I, pp. 352–60, for Behyo (redated by Tate, *Les campagnes*, p. 294).

[16] Epigraphy also gives us a *komis* in Bāra (Tchalenko, *Villages antiques*, III, p. 33). For Megas, see Mango, *Silver*, pp. 6–13; Feissel, 'Magnus, Megas', pp. 469–72. Cf. the cautious remarks in Gatier, 'Villages du Proche-Orient protobyzantin', pp. 28–30.

density of large-scale landowning is not usually even, this upland area could well have been largely left to peasants until the oil boom, with Antiochenes focusing on the plains below, and that, once the boom occurred, peasant prosperity itself could have helped to protect the area from external land-lords. Instead, peasants engaged in competitive house-building, and, soon, church-building—though we cannot for the most part be sure whether churches were only built by individuals or by communities as well.[17]

Village communities are hard, in fact, to pin down in archaeology, unless they commemorate themselves with inscriptions, which they seldom do in the Limestone Massif; there are only two clear examples of it, a village *kankellarios* at Brād and a council (*boulē*) at Ṭurīn.[18] We must recognize that communities probably had little directive role in the olive economy, which tends to be an individualist one, especially in dry-farming areas; it is possible that they were not as dominant a feature of limestone village society as they were in Egypt (above, pp. 426–8). But Libanios assumes that villages act collectively, at least when confronting outsiders, and that they have a headman (*meizōn*). These concentrated settlements, however internally stratified and fractious, must have had a fairly clear identity on the political level, particularly when they were big, as many were (including Brād and Ṭurīn)—the *kōmai megalai* of Libanios, the *metrocomiae* of Latin-language eastern legislation.[19]

If these villages depended on oil export for their prosperity, then one would expect a seventh-century economic recession, following the Persian and Arab conquests and the end of the eastern Mediterranean exchange network. Tate puts such a recession back to 550, his date for when house-building stops; this does actually fit one date of the eastern Mediterranean downturn, although it seems to me too early—one can argue for exchange continuities for another two generations without much difficulty (below, pp. 716–17). But, actually, dated houses go on to the 570s, and churches up to 610, as well as later epigraphy on into the eighth century (though there are no mosques in the area); the silver in the Kaper Koraon treasure, probably presented to a church across the century 540–640 by both rich and middling donors, also shows the continued existence of local wealth up to the Arab conquest. In Dēḥes, too, even though building there may have stopped around 550 and the build-up of ground-floor occupation levels (that is to say the end of the systematic use and therefore cleaning of ground floors) began around 600, both perhaps indicating some economic difficulty, none-theless coin availability continued without a break to 800 (including, as

---

[17] Naccache, *Le décor des églises*, does not discuss the issue, in the absence of clear inscriptional evidence; but see pp. 261–3 for local master builders.

[18] *Inscriptions grecques et latines*, II, nn. 530, 652; note also the village boundary stones put up under Diocletian (Tchalenko, *Villages antiques*, I, pp. 130–1; III, pp. 6–11).

[19] Libanios, *Orations*, XI.230, XLVII.4, 7; *CTh*, XI.24.6; *CJ*, X.19.8, XI.56.1. For large villages see in general Dagron, 'Entre village et cité'.

already noted, Byzantine coins), with only a slight lessening in the eighth century; even its cessation only reflects the general absence of coinage on ninth-century sites in Syria and Iraq. Imported pottery, too, continued as long as it did elsewhere, up to 650 or so. But the latter date does at least mark the end of large-scale eastern Mediterranean demand for olive oil (below, Chapter 11), and this fits the fact that new building ended in the seventh century too. The end of the Roman *limes* on the Euphrates in the face of Persian and Arab conquest, and the early seventh-century difficulties of Antioch and Apamea, two of the major urban markets for goods around the Massif, will have further reduced the number of immediately accessible buyers of oil. By the eighth century the Limestone Massif was probably only producing oil for the still-prosperous inland cities of Aleppo and Qinnasrīn (former Beroia and Chalkis): a much more localized economic role. It did not yet, however, face serious economic or demographic crisis; only in later centuries did it empty out altogether, perhaps in the context of tenth- and eleventh-century frontier wars, leaving just a handful of centres, such as Bāra, to continue up to the present day.[20]

The limestone villages are at an extreme in their density and in their architectural and decorative ambition, but they are not unique, as indeed Tate stressed. Nearly all the sectors of Syria and Palestine that have been studied show a high point in the fifth or sixth centuries, which often extends into the seventh and eighth. We can go through them in rather less detail. The coastal hill country of western Cilicia is an area of villages and occasional isolated houses, again focused on oil—it was on the western edge of the Antioch export network, and thus parallels the Limestone Massif for the east, although it is rather less well studied.[21] The basalt plain on the desert margin east of Chalkis, an irrigation area for the most part, had a couple of major villages dating particularly to the sixth and seventh centuries, one of which, Andarin, is currently being excavated: here, the major crop might

[20] Mango, *Silver*, for Kaper Koraon; Sodini, 'Déhès'. Dated buildings: Tate, *Les campagnes*, p. 179; Naccache, *Le décor des églises*, p. 25. For late epigraphy, see Trombley, 'War and society', pp. 197–8: eight inscriptions from 653 to 772, and four from 843 to 954. For the tenth century as a break, see Sodini and Eddé, 'Les villages'. For 'Abbāsid copper coins as rare in the ninth century, see Whittow, 'Decline and fall?', p. 412; Alastair Northedge (pers. comm.) confirms this for Samarrā'. Magness, *The archaeology*, pp. 196–206, indeed argues that the Dēḥes houses were not built till the late sixth century, and that they were prosperous into the ninth. But Bernard Bavant (pers. comm.) sees the ninth century as a period of economic weakening for Dēḥes in particular, given that no glaze was found there; 800 was probably the end-point for the village's stability.

[21] Eyice, 'Ricerche'; Hild and Hellenkemper, *Kilikien* (esp. pp. 109 for olive presses, and 260–1, 285–7, 290, 299–300, 412, for important sites, two of them isolated estate-centres); these focus on the hills behind Silifke, and in particular the village of Karakabaklı. See also *Inscriptions de Cilicie*, esp. nn. 113, 118, for village churches, one sponsored by a village community, in northern Cilicia in the 590s. Further west along the Cilician coast, settlements were not linked to the oil network: see Blanton, *Rough Cilicia*, p. 71, by implication.

perhaps have been wine, and the market perhaps the Euphrates army.[22] To the north-east, surveys around Samosata (Samsat) and Zeugma on the upper Euphrates showed a sixth-century settlement peak and a probable eighth-century population decline, but this stands in interesting contrast to the Balīkh valley survey a little further south, where the settlement peak is in the late eighth and ninth centuries. The latter lay in the hinterland of Raqqa, an 'Abbāsid capital between 796 and 808, which in part explains its history, but we must nonetheless recognize that this contrast shows how micro-regionally differentiated the pacing of settlement in Syria could be. 'Abbāsid-period expansion was atypical in the Levant as a whole (it was a period where economic hegemony passed to Iraq; Raqqa was in effect on the boundary), but the Balīkh valley is not unique in Syria and Palestine; the hinterland of Ayla ('Aqaba) on the Red Sea has recently been recognized as a parallel.[23]

Further south, the Hawran is another basalt area on the edge of the desert, between Damascus and 'Ammān; it can be cultivated (mostly with cereals) without irrigation, although with difficulty. It is again a zone of large villages, with dispersed settlement hardly documented except immediately around its major city, Bostra (Buṣrā). Here, the sixth century was again the height, though the seventh and eighth centuries were hardly less active; only in the ninth did occupation contract quickly. The villages that have been studied here, notably Umm al-Jimal in Jordan, have houses and courtyards paralleling those of the Limestone Massif, although (apart from churches, at least) with less decoration; they are equally unplanned as communities. Excavation at Umm al-Jimal has shown a general refurbishing around 700, including a house where floors were relaid, and debris was not accumulating in ground-floor rooms before the mid-eighth century: here, then, new building continued a century or so later than at Dēhes.[24] If local prosperity was based on exchange here, it was between the settled lands and the desert, which doubtless explains why it continued well after the start of the seventh century, for the desert became more important with the Arab conquest, not (as with the Mediterranean) less. South of 'Ammān, the Balqā' around Madaba, dry-farming cereal land, had villages which were prosperous into the eighth century, as is shown by a number of rural churches with

[22] Mango, 'Oxford excavations at Andarin', with previous references; wider surveys are in train; the older survey of the area is Poidebard and Mouterde, *Le limes de Chalcis*. For the army, see below, p. 772.

[23] Wilkinson, *Town and country*, pp. 117–29, with Algaze, 'The Tigris–Euphrates project', pp. 21–3 (though a sharp drop in the 'early Islamic' period, really the ninth century, depends again on the assumption that glazed pottery was already common on rural sites); Bartl, *Frühislamische Besiedlung*, pp. 186–7, 244–5, for the Balīkh valley; Avner and Magness, 'Early Islamic settlement', for the Negev.

[24] Villeneuve, 'L'économie rurale'; de Vries, *Umm el-Jimal*, I, pp. 24–6, 109–11, 175–84, 195–204 (the house), 229–41, with idem, 'Continuity and change'; Kennedy and Freeman, 'Southern Hauran survey'; see Foss, 'Syria', pp. 245–58 for an overview.

high-quality mosaic floors dating to after 700, and as late as 756 at Umm al-Rasas. Settlement in this area seems overall to have showed continuities into the eleventh and twelfth centuries, and, even if there were progressive abandonments in the Balqā' after 800, individual settlements carried on into the late middle ages, as at Khirbet Faris, a village with occupation into the thirteenth century in the south of the area. Muslim Arabs settled in the Balqā' (as in the Hawran, but unlike in the other zones so far cited), but they brought little new by way of settlement forms; even the fortified *quṣūr* they built had antecedents in Roman military *kastra*, and most of these were simply villages with walls. In this area, too, concentrated villages predominated; only around Pella to the north-west of 'Ammān, on the edge of the River Jordan, has some dispersed settlement been found, perhaps again reflecting its closeness to a substantial urban centre; there were also some isolated monastic communities near Madaba, presumably with their own estates, for they too could afford mosaicists.[25]

Palestine west of the Jordan has been fairly intensively surveyed, mostly by Israeli archaeologists, with more rural excavation as well, even if it is not always adequately published. Unfortunately, the ceramic identifications the field surveys have used are mostly by now outdated; the dramatic fall in seventh-century occupation that they purportedly show is based on the assumption that the late ceramics on rural sites all pre-date 650, although stratigraphic excavations in the modern state of Jordan (and increasingly in Israel as well) show continuities in ceramic production and human occupation through the Umayyad and indeed, sometimes, 'Abbāsid periods.[26] Apart from their dating, the overall patterns they show are similar to the foregoing, with the same network of unplanned concentrated villages, and little dispersed settlement except in the environs of Caesarea, that is to say

[25] For mosaics, see Piccirillo, *Mosaics*, pp. 22–37; idem and Alliata, *Umm al-Rasas*, I, pp. 106–10. The Hesban survey claims a settlement retreat in the seventh to twelfth centuries (LaBianca, *Hesban* 1, pp. 178–81, 203–18), but this is subject to the same criticisms as the Israeli datings discussed in the next note; for Khirbet Faris, see McQuitty and Falkner, 'The Faris project', and for overall continuities across the central middle ages see Johns, 'The longue durée'. Miller, *Archaeological survey*, pp. 221–32, recognizes that the Kerak survey could not identify most early Islamic wares. For *quṣūr* see e.g. Haldimann, 'Les implantations omeyyades'. For Pella settlement, Watson, 'Pella hinterland survey', and Margaret O'Hea (pers. comm.). For monasteries, see Piccirillo and Alliata, *Mount Nebo*. Note also the prosperous Arab and Muslim community from the seventh to ninth centuries just west of the Dead Sea, whose fragmentary papyri were ed. in *Arabic papyri from Ḥirbet el-Mird*.

[26] See in general Hirschfeld, 'Farms and villages'; Mayerson, 'Some observations', is one critic of Israeli ceramic dating; but Magness, *The archaeology*, is the most comprehensive critique. This dating is seen as unproblematic in the most detailed survey, Dauphin, *La Palestine byzantine*, who thus spends a lot of pages trying to explain a sixth- and seventh-century demographic decline which probably did not occur (pp. 351–2, 368–72, 512–25, etc.). The Southern Samaria survey, presented (but not analysed) in Finkelstein, *Highlands*, recognizes the late (eighth-century) dating of some of its 'Byzantine' ceramics, but its maps do not reflect that (pp. 36, 955–7). For Umayyad prosperity see e.g. Haiman, 'Agriculture'; Avner and Magness, 'Early Islamic settlement'; Walmsley, 'Production, exchange', pp. 309–12; Magness, *The archaeology*. See also Eshel, 'Khirbet Yattir', for continuities in a settlement in southern Judea.

once again in a suburban area, and in particular in the desert areas of the northern Negev, where there is a scatter of isolated farmsteads, each dependent on small-scale irrigation. Galilee was, and remained, a strong Jewish area, by 600 the largest non-Christian area anywhere in the Roman empire, but in settlement terms it too was much the same as elsewhere. (So was Samaria, although the failure of the Samaritan revolts of the late fifth and early sixth centuries resulted in the abandonment of some Samaritan villages.)[27] In Galilee, prosperity into the eighth century is visible in several places, such as Tel Jezreel, Chorazin, and Ḥorvat Dinʿila, and new settlements were founded, as at near Capernaum around 700; village autonomy seems to have been as great as in the Limestone Massif, with synagogues operating as community foci.[28]

The north-west Negev is the last area which needs to be mentioned here, and it deserves slightly more discussion, for three reasons: because it is the (desert) hinterland of the prosperous Gaza–Askalon (Ashqelon) coast; because it has several very well-preserved villages; and because one of these, Nessana (Niẓẓana), furnishes us with the largest collection of papyri to survive outside Egypt. The Gaza–Ashqelon coast is not well synthesized (and Gaza itself not well studied), but what is clear is that in the fourth to sixth/seventh centuries, at least, it was very densely populated indeed. This is the core area from which LRA 4 (Gaza) amphorae were exported, and its major export crop was wine: its wealth was above all wine-based, and its agrarian commercialization must have been as great as in the hinterland of Antioch. A recent excavation has uncovered an industrial-level wine installation near Ashqelon (with an olive-press too), and five kilns for LRA 4 amphorae; we may expect more of this in the future.[29] The desert behind Gaza, the city territory of Elousa (Ḥaluẓa), was also known for wine, and wine-presses are common in the surviving villages, although it is clear from the Nessana papyri that grain was important there, and oil and dates as well.[30] The desert villages are each associated with walled irrigated fields in neighbouring seasonal stream valleys; we are close to the ecological edge here, even for irrigated land, but the papyri show how high yields could be locally (sevenfold for wheat, eightfold for barley), so we must conclude that water management was pretty effective.[31] Villages here began in the first

[27] Dispersed settlement near Caesarea: Hirschfeld, *Ramat Hanadiv*, pp. 722–7; in the Negev, idem, 'Farms and villages', pp. 52–60; Haiman, 'Naḥal Mitnan'; Magness, *The archaeology*, pp. 72–4, 130–76. Galilee: Hirschfeld, 'Farms and villages', pp. 42–4. Samaritan revolts: Dauphin, *La Palestine byzantine*, pp. 285–95.

[28] See respectively Grey, 'The pottery from Tel Jezreel'; Yeivin, 'Chorazin'; Hirschfeld, 'Farms and villages', p. 43; Tzaferis, *Excavations at Capernaum*, I, pp. 1–29, 213–21, with Magness, 'The chronology of Capernaum'.

[29] Israel, 'Ashqelon'; Dauphin, *La Palestine byzantine*, maps 15, 23, for site densities on the coast. For LRA 4, see below, p. 771.

[30] Crops in the Nessana area: *P. Ness.*, e.g. 32, 60–7, 69, 90. Wine-presses in the desert villages: Mazor, 'The wine-presses'.

[31] Yields: see above, Ch. 3, n. 20. Shereshevski, *Byzantine urban settlements*, pp. 189–200, discusses water.

century or so, with a high point in the sixth, as usual—by then they varied in size from c.500 to c.4,500 people; one, Mampsis (Mamshit), the smallest, may have been abandoned in the seventh century, but the others went on into the eighth, and Nessana survived into the tenth. As elsewhere, they are comprised of courtyard houses without significant planning—although Sobata (Shivta), the best-preserved village, was structured around two great rock-cut pools at its centre, with streets leading off from there—and two to four churches per village, added in the fifth/sixth centuries (in Sobata there was also a mosque, a clear sign of active building in the eighth century).[32] Exactly what economic relationship these villages had with Gaza is not clear from either the archaeology or the papyri, but one of the better excavations there, in the northern church at Rehovot, showed all the Mediterranean Red Slip fine wares, indicating external exchange up to the seventh century; this pattern is matched in recent excavations at Nessana.[33] It is also arguable that for relatively large villages to be built so far into the desert there must have been a demand for agricultural products and extra land that was greater than usual. I would hypothesize that it may be that a heavy concentration on wine-production nearer the coast created a local demand for other agrarian products, which stimulated both vineyards and a more broad-based agricultural production further inland. This is only hypothesis at the present stage, but it does produce a model that links the fate of the villages to the fate of Gaza. As will be argued later (p. 774), the Gaza area is one of the few parts of the Levant whose exchange networks weakened under the Umayyads (Antioch is the other clear example), and this may explain why most of the Negev villages were in trouble during the eighth century too.

The Negev villages that still stand seem to show a relatively socially homogeneous population, each family with its own house, much as in the Limestone Massif at the other end of the Levant. This picture is backed up by the Nessana papyri, which document a population of local owners between the 510s and the 680s. In the first third of the period, the papyri focus on soldier-farmers based in Nessana's *kastron*, which was part of the village (*kome*); the soldiers were doubtless of local origin, since they owned land locally and several had Arab names. Some of the inhabitants of Nessana were medium owners, as one substantial property-division shows, others were owner-cultivators, but there is no reference to external landowning.[34]

[32] Ibid., *passim*, is the most detailed overview; for the Shivta mosque, ibid., p. 74. Magness, *The archaeology*, pp. 177–94, gives the most authoritative dates; cf. p. 148 for the twelve mosques known from the Negev.

[33] Tsafrir, *Excavations at Rehovot*, I, pp. 78–96; Magness, *The archaeology*, pp. 183–5. In *P. Ness.*, esp. 70, and 75, a tax protest (cf. above, p. 144), the Umayyad-period political centre is clearly Gaza; there is not much evidence of external exchange in those texts, but see 89–90 (cf. 91, 95), for mixed cargoes for pedlars, and dates probably sold to Egypt.

[34] *P. Ness.* 14–29, for soldiers; 31 for larger local property-owning (and 22 for a courtyard-house in 566).

Later documents, from around 600 and from the 670s–680s, are for a church, S. Sergios, and for the family that controlled it; by the 680s George, headman (*dioikētēs*) of the village (*khōrion*) of Nessana, was from this family, and his son Sergios was the priest. By then this family was locally rich, from its inherited land, the land and goods offered to its church, from moneylending, and also from a cession by the Arab governor of local tribal lands. George got a few of the same sort of detailed orders from the governor that Basilios of Aphroditō did in Egypt (above, pp. 134–9), above all about taxation. One tax document, unfortunately fragmentary, shows a range of tax payments from $1\frac{1}{2}$ to 23 *nomismata*: quite a wide variation, which, if it is related to landed wealth, fits with the substantial property-owning of the church patrons, and probably of one or two other families as well.[35] We could postulate that the richest inhabitants of Nessana had got richer across these two centuries. But wealth stayed at the village level, and owner-cultivators continued; Nessana operated as a community, with village representatives and local judges as well as its headman, and was not simply dominated by one family.[36]

Before we move away from Syria and Palestine, we need to look at what generalizations can be drawn from this array of material, and at its problems and implications. Syrian and Palestinian peasant society was clearly for the most part a village society. Study after study shows that agglomerations of well-built stone houses were normal almost everywhere, across dry-farming and irrigated areas alike. The main exceptions in settled areas were closest to cities, where residential villas (as at Daphnē just outside Antioch) and scattered farms can sometimes be found. Isolated estate-centres are not unknown elsewhere, but are rare.[37] The northern Negev desert showed a partially dispersed settlement pattern too, which might turn out to be a model for other desert areas.[38] Another group of isolated complexes are the well-known Umayyad palaces, situated both in fertile land and in the desert; in the latter case they are associated with quite elaborate irrigation systems.[39] These palaces are the closest Syro-Palestinian equivalents to the most ambitious rural villas of the West. But they, too, are only a marginal phenomenon with respect to rural settlement as a whole in the Levant, where, overwhelmingly, villages predominated. The patterns of these

[35] *P. Ness.* 44–80 for S. Sergios; 68, 70, 74, for George as *dioikētēs*, 55–8, 76–7, for Sergios, 55, 59(?), for moneylending, 58 for the governor's gift, 68, 70–4, for the governor's orders, 77 for the tax document (and 75 for another local notable, *Kyrios* Samuel).

[36] *P. Ness.* 57–8, for representatives and a judge.

[37] For isolated estate-centres, apart from those already cited, see Balty, *Le mosaïque de Sarrîn*. LaBianca, *Hesban* I, p. 185, seems to show fifth- and sixth-century dispersal in that area.

[38] See above, n. 27; in the desert behind 'Aqaba, most settlement was in villages, but not all (Avner and Magness, 'Early Islamic settlement').

[39] A useful overview is King, 'Settlement patterns'; the best monographic study is Grabar, *City in the desert*.

villages are indeed strikingly homogeneous, privileging two-storeyed court-yard houses, each somewhat closed off to the outside world (windows tended to be mostly onto the courtyard), arranged in compact groups with little planning. They often look so impressive that they have been called 'cities' by some recent writers (and, perhaps particularly, by tourist bro-chures), a terminology that has in turn encouraged people to see, in their absence of planning and of public spaces, the germs of future urban devel-opment in the Muslim period. This is a mistake; they were unplanned *because* they were not cities, and it is enough to go from Shivta to neighbour-ing Elousa, or from Serjilla to Apamea, to see that city status and planned public spaces went together routinely, into the seventh century and indeed beyond (below, p. 619).[40] Spatially incoherent or not, villages expanded in the fifth and sixth centuries nearly everywhere; they contracted again with less of a regularity of dating, but rarely before the eighth century, and often well after the end of our period. I shall discuss that process in a moment; here, however, it may be noted that the other feature of Levantine villages was their stability, including the absence of any major changes in settlement structure (except the addition of churches), right up to the periods of their contraction or abandonment.

Our evidence for these villages is almost all archaeological, with the addition of epigraphy and iconography in the case of the more ambitious building and decorative programmes. Narrative sources focused on the countryside are rare for our period outside the saints' lives of Theodoret and the Symeon biographers in the far north; documents are unknown outside the papyri of Nessana and Petra in the far south. What can we say about rural social structures? In general, the archaeologists who have stud-ied Syrian and Palestinian villages have stressed that they show few signs of large landowning. Sometimes one has a suspicion that this is only because the mental model the archaeologist has for such landowning is an isolated villa, a settlement form that is, as we have seen, unusual in this region. But Georges Tate's careful analysis of house types in the Limestone Massif is a better guide: his arguments for a predominance of village-level landowning, of (in my terminology) medium and small ownership, are more convincing. There was, certainly, a level of prosperous local owning that appears in several different contexts: in the already-cited patronage of the baths of Serjilla in the 470s by Julian and Domna, or of those of Andarin in the 550s by Thomas, or of the synagogue of Duyūk in Galilee by Pinḥas in the late sixth century, or in the church documents of Nessana in the late seventh, or with the rich village headman of Beth Laha in the Limestone Massif in the fifth-century Syriac life of Simeon the Stylite. But, as noted

[40] See e.g. Kennedy, 'From *polis* to *madina*', pp. 13–15; Shereshevski, *Byzantine urban settlements*, pp. 147–9. For Elousa as different, see ibid., pp. 82–90, 141; for Apamea, below, p. 620.

earlier, there is no house in Serjilla that is clearly marked out as different from the others, and the bath patrons of that village need not have been more than medium owners—after all, even small owners there could afford quality housing.[41]

The problem is, however, that this reading of village society eliminates one economic category that must have been widespread in the Levant: city-based landowners. Syrian and Palestinian cities remained, for the most part, unusually prosperous by Mediterranean standards into the seventh and eighth centuries (pp. 613–25), just as did the villages of the region; indeed, urban continuities and rural continuities were presumably related, at least at the level of exchange, the basic exchange of (mostly urban) artisanal products for (mostly rural) agricultural ones that lay at the core of all urban growth in our period. But these cities were also the residences of substantial landowners, indeed, as we have seen, their only residences; some of the countryside must have been owned by them. Such landowning was doubtless, as elsewhere, mostly fragmented, scattered across wide territories rather than organized in village-sized blocks (such fragmentation is clear in the Petra papyri), although we do have reference to single-owner villages in Libanios, Theodoret, John Moschos, and Prokopios.[42] Where was this land? Here, it must be admitted that our knowledge of the Syrian and Palestinian countryside is incomplete. It is probable that most urban property was closest to cities, where indeed dispersed settlement has sometimes been found, as we have seen. It would be too schematic, however, to propose that dispersed settlement went with urban property, concentrated villages with local ownership; nor would this give urban landowning much space. I have argued against much external landowning for the Limestone Massif, but I would be more cautious about the argument elsewhere. In some of our areas, most notably the Hawran, which constituted the whole hinterland of an important city, Bostra, we would have to presume that urban owners did indeed have tenants in many of the villages that archaeologists have investigated. The Balqā', with its richly decorated rural churches resembling those in Madaba at its centre, may be another. Perhaps not all villages had such owners, however; as we saw in Chapter 4 (p. 240), our evidence for really large-scale landowning is restricted in this region, with the exception of the Antiochene elite. A plausible hypothesis is that the unusually high level of exchange in the Levant allowed both rich citizens and independent peasantries to coexist, with urban wealth partly deriving from the intensity of exchange itself, not just from taking rents from tenants (see below, p. 777).

---

[41] Tate, *Les campagnes*, pp. 257–67. For Serjilla and Andarin, see above, nn. 15, 22; for Duyūk and several parallel examples, Dauphin, *La Palestine byzantine*, pp. 333–4; for Beth Laha, *The Syriac life of Simeon*, c. 33.

[42] *P. Petra* 2; Libanios, *Oration* XLVII.11; Theodoret, *Histoire des moines*, XIV.4; John Moschos, *Spiritual meadow*, c. 196; Prokopios, *Secret history*, XXX.18–19. See above, n. 14.

Village communities have been referred to on occasion in the foregoing: they were not very clearly documented in the Limestone Massif, but, by contrast, the Nessana papyri show that they could be quite articulated. But it has to be said that any substantial, closely intermingled settlement, as all these were, must have had a clearly characterized identity, simply because people had to deal with each other on a daily basis. They had mutual interests, in defending common grazing lands[43] against rival villages and nomads, in keeping up irrigation systems in some areas (notably the Negev, and probably the Hawran), in organizing the local church(es) or synagogue, in keeping the peace,[44] and, of course, throughout our period, in distributing tax liability. These features link Syria and Palestine northwards, to the communities of the Byzantine *Farmer's law* (below, p. 463), and southwards, to the Egyptian villages discussed in Chapter 7. The nature of community action is better known in these neighbouring regions than in the Levant, although, conversely, what villages themselves actually looked like, and how they developed, is better known in the Levant. With care, however, we can put them together; rural society, in its prosperous autonomy and inward-lookingness, had certain features in common from Ankara to Aswān, throughout our period.[45]

Before we move into these neighbouring regions, however, we must look at the issue of abandonment; for, of course, one major reason why late Roman/early Islamic villages survive so well in many areas of Syria and Palestine is that at a given moment they ceased to be occupied. This abandonment has often been expressed in apocalyptic terms, with a variety of different human or non-human causes to blame: the plague of 541–2,[46] the Arab conquerors of the 630s, the 'Abbāsid removal of political centrality from Syria to Iraq in 750, or the nomadic threat at dates of choice (this is often linked to the Arab conquest, for, even among scholars who are aware that the new Muslim elites were by no means nomads, indeed committed to extending irrigation, the belief that they were less good at confronting Arab-speaking nomads than the Romans had been is surprisingly common). In recent years this rhetorical style has eased off somewhat, for two reasons. One is the growing realization that in many places the dates for depopulation and agricultural recession have been set too early: in the Limestone Massif the date is the ninth or tenth century now, not the early seventh; in the Hawran it may be the ninth; in the Balīkh valley it is the eleventh or twelfth; in the Balqā' it may be as late as the twelfth or thirteenth. The second is that, in the wake of Øystein LaBianca's work on the Hesban survey, the more neutral terminology of intensification and 'abatement' has begun to be used

---

[43] Patlagean, *Pauvrété*, p. 262.

[44] *P. Ness.* 15, 19 (cf. 21–2, 31), 57, mostly intra-family disputes: cf. for Egypt, above, pp. 423–8.

[45] See in general Patlagean, *Pauvrété*, pp. 236–71, covering the Levant and Anatolia.

[46] Stressed by Dauphin, *La Palestine byzantine*, pp. 512–18; but see below, pp. 548–9.

more: the tendency for some periods to show an increase in cultivation, and for others to show an increase of pastoralism, which are both fully legitimate ways to use a landscape on the edge of the desert, as are most of those in the Levant. Pastoralism permits less population in any given area, and always implies the continuance of settled agriculturalists elsewhere to sell grain to the stock-raisers, but it is also less labour-intensive—that is, it requires less work—than agriculture; the principal losers when a land-scape goes pastoral are external landowners and tax-collectors.[47] One must add that the shift to 'abatement' would have to be linked to demographic decline, which might after a while have gone down sufficiently far that the catastrophe-flip to pastoralism became possible, as well as desirable; we would then still have to explain the population decline (see below, p. 549). But the terminology is a useful one all the same; it takes some of the moral urgency out of these changes in land-use, an urgency which is still felt by some.

All the same, agricultural recession and demographic decline, as just noted, cannot be explained away by this terminology. I would propose that it is easiest to explain in the far north and south, the limestone lands behind Antioch and the Negev nearest Gaza, for these two areas were most clearly linked to an international exchange network that was in crisis in the seventh century. This crisis had a different effect in each: in the limestone lands, it forced an exporting economy back into local exchange, lessening the rural wealth that (judging by the density of local occupation, and the greater quality of house-building than anywhere else that has been studied) was unusually great even by Syro-Palestinian standards, but not resulting in demographic recession for some centuries; by contrast, in the Negev, a highly marginal area, it resulted in agrarian abandonment by the end of the eighth century. In both cases, however, we can propose a systemic cause for agrarian change. Out of well-studied areas that do 'abate' in or near our period, perhaps the hardest to explain is the Hawran: not notably focused on long-distance exchange, and in a long-standing equilibrium with the neigh-bouring desert, including with pastoral and semi-pastoral patrons on the desert fringe (made easier because it had always been ethnically Arab), it is not clear what motors for change existed here at all. It may be that in this case a political explanation does work: the Hawran looked to the Ghassa-nids for protection against at least occasional nomadic incursion in the sixth century, and was an important locus for Umayyad building in the early eighth, but the 'Abbāsids may have considered it too much associated with Umayyad political structures, and may have withdrawn that protection, thus

---

[47] LaBianca, *Hesban* 1, pp. 9–21, 41, a reference I owe originally to Mark Whittow; see also Horden and Purcell, *Corrupting sea*, pp. 263–70. Even LaBianca uses unhelpfully negative images when characterizing 'abatement', but they are not necessary to the model. For pastor-alism dependent on agricultural exchange, see Wickham, *Land and power*, pp. 125 ff.

inviting a local 'abatement'.[48] But, if this explanation works here, it is important to stress that it does not work elsewhere. The neighbouring Balqā', for example, survived with much less difficulty for longer; so, even more clearly, did lands closer to the coast; and even areas that did 'abate' did so, as has just been argued, for different reasons than the Hawran. The Syro-Palestinian landscape can be seen as a single block in many respects, but the crises it faced were all local.

Egyptian village society has already been discussed in some detail in Chapter 7 (pp. 411–28), and needs little development here, above all because Egyptian rural archaeology for our period is so poor. The villages of the Nile valley had varying social structures, depending on how much external landowning they had, and how rich local owners were—microregional distinctions that are probably widely applicable, although we do not have enough evidence to comment on them outside Egypt. But Egyptian villages were all linked: by the concentration of their settlement patterns—here not determining, but rather determined by, the irrigation networks around them; by the tightness of village society; and by the tension of local social practice, a tension and competitiveness which was arguably greater than elsewhere (above, p. 426), but which only the naive would imagine was absent in other regions.

Egyptian village archaeology is particularly difficult, of course, because of the extreme continuities in the region. Leaving aside the unusual example of Jēme (pp. 419–21), most village sites from our period are still occupied. One exception is the Fayyūm, an outlying basin not far south-west of Cairo, part of whose Nile access slowly dried up, leaving substantial areas of Roman and post-Roman agricultural landscape as desert. Even here, survey and excavation are still at relatively early stages; the main excavation that has taken place, at Karanis, has focused on the period up to the third century, and only very recently has it been recognized that the village remained occupied into the sixth. In both Jēme and the latest levels of Karanis, courtyard-house blocks, although maintaining a rough common alignment, were inserted into each other in a jigsaw pattern, that recalls contemporary and later Syro-Palestinian villages; the orthogonal plan of the Ptolemaic period at Karanis had been lost.[49] Egyptian villages were generally made of mud brick, not of stone, which doubtless increased their flexibility; houses could be rebuilt as family structures changed. Literary sources indicate that two- and three-storey houses were common, even in villages; as in the Levant, courtyards were largely for animals or storage.[50] All of this means

---

[48] For protection, see e.g. Foss, 'Syria', pp. 250–7; this is an area where settlements were walled, as they were not in areas further from deserts.
[49] For Karanis, see Bagnall, *Late Roman Egypt*, pp. 111–12 and plate 4, with Pollard, 'The chronology'. For Jēme, Ch. 7, n. 89.   [50] Husson, *Oikia*, pp. 45–54, 257–67.

that we can probably carry most of our Syro-Palestinian images of what villages looked like to the Nile, just as we can carry some of those about how villagers behaved to the Levant. But for more articulated information we will have to wait until more excavation has been carried out.

The clearest secular exceptions yet known to this village world are on the coast. Behind Alexandria, to the west of the Delta, and around Pelousion, to the east, we find isolated villas, at Huwariya and Tell al-Fadda respectively, the former occupied to the seventh century, the latter to the eighth. These are among the few areas of Egypt that are neither flooded, nor (in our period) desert; they also conform to the model of more dispersed settlement closer to cities that we have seen in the Levant. The Apions, too, had rural estate-centres, called *proasteia*, in the territory of Oxyrhynchos, as we can see from some of the documents for that zone; probably other great landlords had similar structures.[51] But these are exceptions that prove rules: the rest of Egypt was villages, and still is.

The sector of Anatolia that has had the most systematic rural archaeological study for our period (if one excepts Cilicia, which has here been put with Syria) is Lycia: a sub-region that lies on the Mediterranean, not on the plateau, and is cut off from any easy land access by 3,000-metre-high mountains that come close to the coast. Lycia, like Egypt and the Levant, was a land of villages, in this case limestone-built, some of them substantial in size, like Lebissos, on an island south of the city of Telmissos (Fethiye), and Karkabo (Alakilise), a village with thirty houses in the mountains some 10 km from the coast. Only in the immediate surroundings of the city of Kyaneai, studied by a German team in 1989, has any dispersed settlement been found, and there were villages near that city too.[52]

These Lycian villages seem above all, on the basis of architectural analysis and some inscriptions, to be sixth-century. Unfortunately, no excavation has been undertaken there, so how late they extend after 600 is not at all clear. We are by now in the Byzantine sector of the eastern Mediterranean, after it was divided into two by the Arab conquests, and we could thus expect a rather earlier period of generalized crisis than needs to be assumed further east, in the wars of the seventh century. Lycia was protected by mountains from any land-raiding, but Arab coastal attacks are documented. Furthermore, although the Byzantines generally controlled the sea-roads along the Anatolian coast, the network of easy sea transport that is assumed by the late

[51] Rodziewicz, 'Alexandria and district of Mareotis', pp. 204–7; Vogt, 'La céramique de Tell el-Fadda'; Husson, 'Recherches sur les sens du mot "proastion" ', pp. 182–6, commenting on *P. Oxy.* XVI 1913, 1925.

[52] The best overview is Foss, 'Lycian coast'; see idem, 'Cities and villages', pp. 310–12 for the identification of Karkabo. For the Kyaneai survey, focused on the area immediately around the city, see Kolb, 'Spätantike und byzantinische Besiedlung', pp. 579–82. Other Lycian surveys are reported in Tsuji, 'Ölüdeniz', and (briefly) in Coulton, 'Highland cities', pp. 234–6.

sixth-century *Life* of Nicholas of Sion (a monastery near Karkabo) was substantially weaker after 650; any export-led economy would have become very difficult as a result. Clive Foss argues for a seventh-century crisis in both cities and countryside, against a characterization by Frank Kolb and his team of some degree of later continuity in the Kyaneai area. Karkabo did survive, all the same: its sixth-century church was rebuilt on the same scale in 812.[53] How typical this village is of others by 800 will have to await excavation, but it shows that local economic structures which permitted architectural spending on some scale could continue in at least some places, past the end of our period and into one in which economic revival was possible.

The *Life* of Nicholas of Sion describes a local monastic founder who was used as a demon-buster by neighbouring villages; he patronized their village feasts, too. The villagers of Lycia the text describes were not obviously tenurially dependent; in the time of the 542 plague the peasantry kept out of the city of Myra to avoid infection, and the city suffered famine as a result—they must have been selling their surplus, rather than being required to pay it in rent.[54] This image of a largely autonomous village-based peasantry matches that of several sections of Theodoret of Cyrrhus' *Religious history*, and thus connects us with another area of standing limestone ruins. The other main parallel to the interrelationship between such a peasantry and a local holy man is, of course, with Theodore of Sykeōn on the plateau, in Galatia (above, pp. 406–11): there are few significant divergences in our saints' lives between the Lycia of the one and the Galatia of the other, despite the considerable ecological differences between the coast and the high interior. The archaeological surveys that have begun on the plateau, such as that around Konya, and the province-by-province publications of standing buildings by the Austrian Academy of Sciences, show the same sort of villages as in Lycia as well.[55] With caution, we can talk of a single peasant society that spans both highland and lowland in Anatolia. In Chapter 4 I discussed the areas of Anatolia where large landowners seem to have been concentrated before 650; the Marmara coast and Cappadocia are the best-documented areas for such landowning (pp. 164, 232). Outside such areas, the only substantial owners will have been the aristocracies of the network of Anatolian cities, which, apart from the major urban centres of the Aegean

---

[53] For transport, *Life* of St Nicholas, cc. 8, 27, 32, 36; cf. for a later period *Nomos rodiōn nautikos*, III.10–11, 20–35, 38–40. Tsuji, 'Ölüdeniz', focused on two islands, found ceramics with Constantinopolitan parallels up to 800 or so, later than usual (ibid., pp. 142–3); cf. Kolb, 'Spätantike und byzantinische Besiedlung', pp. 584–5. For seventh-century crisis, Foss, 'Lycian coast', pp. 22, 48–51; for Karkabo's church, ibid., p. 32.

[54] *Life* of St Nicholas, cc. 18, 52, 57.

[55] For surveys, see as interims, Baird, 'Konya plain survey'; Belke, 'Das byzantinische Dorf'; Matthews, 'Project Paphlagonia' (here, north of Ankara, some dispersed settlement was found: ibid., pp. 203–4); Vanhaverbeke, 'Sagalassos'. For Austrian work, see the various volumes of the *Tabula Imperii Byzantini*, though these largely depend on the quality of previous studies.

coast and the river valleys leading into it, and of Pamphylia along the south coast, were mostly fairly small: the autonomous villages near Anastasiou-polis in Galatia and Myra in Lycia may therefore have been typical of substantial sections of the plateau and even the coast in the whole period before 650. It should be added that rural villas are almost as little documen-ted in Anatolia as in Syria or Egypt. John Rossiter has collected all the literary evidence for them; they are mostly close to towns, as elsewhere in the East (counting the Marmara coast of Bithynia, a popular senatorial hangout, as being close to Constantinople, for access to it was by an easy sea crossing). The exceptions are accounts by Basil of Caesarea and Gregory of Nyssa of apparently more isolated estate-centres in Pontos and Cappa-docia, as luxuriously appointed as a western villa in one case.[56] It may thus be that one area of villas of a western type was the eastern Anatolian plateau. All the same, the only excavations of such estate-centres are for suburban sites, easy of access for an essentially urban ruling class.[57] Once again, this meant that rural life was largely confined to peasants, whether landowning or dependent; they had more of a chance to run their lives by their own rules as a result. The social cohesion of villages, which we have seen expressed both in Galatia and, now, Lycia, will have further favoured peasant cultural autonomy from urban/aristocratic values, which in Galatia could even include violence against oppressive external landlords. Powerful landowners and the *kouratores* of imperial estates could be both oppressors and patrons, at least in the sixth century, in Cappadocia and doubtless elsewhere as well;[58] but autonomous peasant action was a standard possibility in the village society of Anatolia.

One of the most interesting texts for rural society that survives in our period is the *Nomos geōrgikos* or *Farmer's law*; as a piece of peasant-focused legislation it is only matched by the *Pactus legis Salicae* for north-western Francia around 510 (see below, pp. 512–14).[59] The *Farmer's law*, however, is even less easy to pin down than is the *Pactus*; it appears to be a private legal compilation, and claims to be derived from Justinianic law, but, apart from the question of which Justinian this might be (the emblematic lawgiver, ruler 527–65, or Justinian II, 685–95, 705–11), such an ascription is very generic, and could be a later addition. Its tax terminology seems to date it to the period before the late ninth century; the necessity for a private legal hand-book probably puts it into the period after the late sixth century when

---

[56] Rossiter, 'Roman villas'. The major Pontos and Cappadocia texts are Basil of Caesarea, *Letters*, n. 14 (cf. n. 88 for city leaders of Caesarea (Kayseri) in the countryside, presumably in summer); Gregory of Nyssa, *Letters*, n. 20. Cf. John Chrysostom, *Lettres à Olympias*, IX.2–3, for a village and an estate-centre (*proasteion*) near Caesarea; and *Vie de Théodore*, c. 107, for Amorion.

[57] Rossiter, 'Roman villas', p. 102, for Ephesus; Foss, 'Ankara', p. 67, for Ankara.

[58] *NJ*, XXX.5.1; Kaplan, 'Novelle de Tibère II'.

[59] Ashburner, 'Farmer's law'.

legislation virtually ceased for two centuries, apart from the *Ekloga* of 741, an imperially sponsored handbook which indeed appears with the *Farmer's law* (and the *Rhodian sea law*) in many manuscripts. In common with most historians, I see this as a text which postdates 650, although when it dates to in the next two centuries is impossible to say.[60] Where it derives from is hardly easier to be sure of; one hesitates to offer any precise location, given the fanciful attempts to do so in the past (particularly to Slav areas of the Balkans, even though there is nothing Slavonic about the text at all—all its points of reference are totally Roman).[61] All the same, the absence of any reference to olives in it is perhaps the best sign that it can be linked to the Anatolian plateau, the only part of the Byzantine-controlled world after 650 that was out of the olive zone. Irrespective of this, however, the *Nomos geōrgikos* can be seen as the emblematic text for Byzantine rural society after the crisis of the conquest period, and it is, in fact, as such that it has generally been used.

The text of the *Farmer's law* focuses on peasant agricultural disputes in villages (*chōria*). The *geōrgoi*, peasants, of the text are generally landowners, though hired herdsmen and field guards are referred to; there is some leaseholding too, from landowners (*khōrodotoi*) and from peasant neighbours, and some household unfree labour.[62] How powerful the *khōrodotoi* are is unclear, but the rent they are paid is only 10 per cent, which is pretty low. Paradoxically, however, leases from peasant owners produce a far higher rent, 50 per cent: perhaps the owner supplied the seed, as with Italian *mezzadria* leases, and almost certainly s/he paid the taxes too—for this was evidently a society that paid taxes routinely, given that there are laws to cover what happens to vineyards if their owner flees without paying. Another sign of the presence of the state is several references to judges (*akroatai*), external to the village.[63] The most interesting laws are those which cover the dividing-up of common land (*topos koinos*), which is clearly controlled by the village as a community (*koinotēs*): the lots (*merides*) are apparently permanent divisions, although they are reversible if they are unjust; undivided land may already be cultivated, at least with tree crops, but is not necessarily. These show an economic role for the village community that we have not seen so much of elsewhere in the East; it is backed up by a political role as well, in boundary disputes with neighbouring villages.[64]

---

[60] See for manuscripts *Nomos rodiōn nautikos*, pp. cxiii–cxiv; for dating Haldon, *Byzantium in the seventh century*, pp. 132–3, which summarizes previous arguments. John Haldon (pers. comm.) adds that it has to pre-date c.880 because its terminology pre-dates the *Basilika* compilation, which also changes the tax law that the *Farmer's law* presumes. Burgmann redates the *Ekloga* to 741 in *Ecloga*, pp. 10–12.

[61] For the Slavs, see e.g. Margetić, 'La legge agraria', pp. 124–35. For the Roman origins of its substantive law, see Köpstein, 'Zu den Agrarverhältnissen', pp. 59–60.

[62] Ashburner, 'Farmer's law', cc. 4, 5 (owners), 16, 33–4 (hiring), 9–17 (leases).

[63] Ibid., cc. 18–19 (taxation), 7, 37, 67 (judges).

[64] Ibid., cc. 1, 7, 8, 32, 78–9, 81–2.

The debates about these laws have often in the past been trapped inside the old legalist belief that laws were accurate descriptions of the whole of society, and they do not need to be reprised here. The best recent work on them, however, goes some way to reduce their special status as witnesses to the ill-documented centuries after 650.[65] The fact is that the sort of village society described in the *Nomos geōrgikos* is not very dissimilar to that in the *Life* of Theodore of Sykeōn, which describes Anatolia before the seventh-century crisis. It involves a coherent community which is a point of reference for individual peasant proprietors both rich and poor, and is strong enough to take on the outside world, although disputes inside that community are frequent too. Even the most atypical task of the community, land division, had ancient parallels in Anatolia, as with a Lydian inscription from the first or second centuries which describes a village assembly (*ekklēsia*) dividing up a common field, and is a practice that fits very well with the open spaces of the plateau. Anatolian peasantries behaved like this well before 650, that is to say; the *Farmer's law* is a guide to plateau society in any period (if the reader accepts such a location for the text), more than to Byzantine society after 650 as a whole. Even the parts of the plateau that had more large landowning, either before or after 650, could perfectly well have had village-level practices resembling these. What this text presupposes, however, as does the *Life* of Theodore, is a functioning village collectivity. The *Farmer's law* says nothing about settlement patterns, and community identity is possible without nucleation, but the spatially closed-in villages that we have seen throughout the East are the most plausible background to these laws as well. Although it has usually proved difficult for archaeologists in this region to track the villages of the Roman period past the seventh century, similar spatial structures probably carried on, whether on the same sites as in earlier periods or on different ones.[66]

Eastern Mediterranean rural societies were very diverse. On one level, there is a world of difference between the rich, fractious village of Aphroditō, divided between its internal and external patronage networks, though united by its irrigation network and its common hostility to Antaiopolis; the more homogeneous village of Serjilla, with its internal competitive building, but no strong economic role for the community; and the mixed farming villages of the Anatolian plateau, where relatively tight communities had weaker exchange and patronage links to the outside world, and often gained further coherence through the exploitation and division of common land. Some of the parameters for how to analyse differences of this sort were set out at the

[65] Good analyses are Köpstein, 'Zu den Agrarverhältnissen', pp. 40–60; Haldon, *Byzantium in the seventh century*, pp. 132–41; Kaplan, *Les hommes*, e.g. pp. 203–5, 258–63, 383–7; Lemerle, *Agrarian history*, pp. 27–65; Maslev, 'Die soziale Struktur'.

[66] Loos, 'Quelques remarques', p. 5, for the inscription; see above, n. 55, for the archaeology, together with Barnes and Whittow, 'The survey of medieval castles'.

end of Chapter 7 (pp. 436–41). But when we look at Eastern villages through their material forms, the constantly recurring patterns of unplanned but nonetheless tightly packed houses and courtyards that can be tracked across all our regions, we can see that those varying social structures were at least played out on the same stage. Nor, in each of these three regions, is there any reason to think that settlement patterns, and the way settlements articulated internally, changed at all in the four centuries 400–800; the stage remained the same across time as well as across space. What we see, then, is the way that different ecological constraints, different economic roles for communities, different relationships to markets, different landowning patterns, created different local societies in that consistent village environment. Peasants in the East may have hated and feared each other, as well as, at other times, being deeply supportive of each other; but they could not get away from each other. Village identity was a given, as important, often, as family identity or tenurial status. It must always have helped social cohesiveness, even if it could not always create it out of wholecloth. The *koinotēs* of the village, although weaker or stronger in different places, was in place throughout the East, right at the start of our period as at its end, as a social actor in its own right. This is crucial to bear in mind as we go westwards. For western rural societies could not necessarily take that village identity for granted, and indeed in many cases centuries were needed for it to become fully rooted—not until the twelfth century were communities, as articulated as in the East, a standard feature of the majority of the western regions. Many misapprehensions will be avoided if, when we look at western rural societies across our period, we remember the solidity of eastern villages as an alternative model for social organization—matched, perhaps, in parts of northern Europe, Denmark or Saxony or Frisia, but in few other places.

2. The rural villa in the West and its problems

The western boundary of Roman village society was, very roughly, somewhere in Illyricum to the north of the Mediterranean, and the desert bordering the Gulf of Syrtis, between Cyrenaica and Tripolitania, to the south. West of this, we tend to find much more dispersed settlement patterns. Such a clear statement immediately invites modification, of course; we have seen some dispersal in the East, and we shall see a few village areas in the West. But broadly the statement appears tenable, and it marks a real East–West distinction. What are now Bulgaria, Macedonia, and northern Greece appear to belong with the eastern world of villages in the fifth and sixth centuries (although they perhaps saw more settlement change: a partially dispersed landscape existed on the lower Danube up to the late fourth century but then ended, and northern Greece saw an apparent shift of villages into the hills by the fifth century—both were areas under military threat).[67] Southern Greece, by contrast, seems to have had more of a 'western' pattern, with villas and isolated farms, even though its language and socio-political framework were otherwise entirely 'eastern'. These are the patterns at present visible in the Balkans up to the seventh century, after which rural settlement there is very hard indeed to track.[68] The rest of this section will focus on the Latin lands of the West, up to the end of imperial unity and a little beyond, where a surprisingly uniform picture could for a long time be found.

There are two general features of western Roman settlement patterns that need to be stressed here. The first is that there was a network of many thousands of rural aristocratic residences and other estate-centres, 'villas', extending from around York to around Lepcis Magna; the second is that this network coexisted with, and indeed structured, a rural settlement hierarchy which tended to be dispersed in most of the western Roman empire. These two features are obviously linked, but are not identical, and need to be treated separately, before we look at how territorial identity worked in the countryside.

Rural villas were by no means all the same. They varied from enormous, elaborate residential structures, with anterooms, colonnaded peristyles, mosaic halls, and bath-houses, to more utilitarian complexes, devoted to the running of an estate, though still solidly built in brick and stone. There is much argument about the definition of a 'villa' as a result, with some stressing size, some a rather ill-defined 'Romanness', some the combination of the residential elaboration just referred to (what Columella in the first century called the *pars urbana*) and the *pars rustica*, the working estate-centre, which even the flashiest villa had as well. All the same, the similarities between modest oil-producing centres like Nador in Mauretania and palatial residences like Welschbillig near Trier, Chiragan south of Toulouse, Desenzano on Lake Garda, La Cocosa near Mérida, seem more important than their differences, and the homogeneity of the entire group is indeed a marker of the homogeneity of Roman culture

[67] I am particularly grateful to the advice of Archie Dunn, Vince Gaffney, and Andrew Poulter concerning the Balkans and northern Greece. See in particular Poulter, 'Roman to Byzantine transition', pp. 353–8; idem, 'Cataclysm'; Dunn, 'The problem of early Byzantine rural settlement'; and, for the clearest overview, Henning, *Südosteuropa*, pp. 22–41. For the southern coast of the Mediterranean, cf. Goodchild, *Libyan studies*, pp. 145–54, for a Cyrenaica consisting both of villages and single farms, with Mattingly, *Tripolitania*, pp. 140–7. In inland Tripolitania, the villa hierarchy was replaced by networks of fortified farms (*gsur*) by the third or fourth centuries (ibid., pp. 202–9), but this was in the context of a local tribalization of society, and is a rather different phenomenon—cf. above, pp. 333–4.

[68] See Bintliff, 'Frankish countryside', pp. 2–4, for Boiotia; Jameson, *A Greek countryside*, pp. 400–4, 554; Mee and Forbes, *A rough and rocky place*, pp. 84–94. The last two deal with the same area, the Argolid; the latter is notably more scientific. Perhaps as a result, it is also more cautious about the more traditional population-collapse explanation for the period after 700 (ibid., pp. 93–4); but clear evidence was lacking there, too. See in general Avraméa, *Le Peloponnèse*, pp. 116–17, 127–8.

itself.[69] Roman landowners in the West structured their estate-management through estate-centres which were as elaborate as they could afford, and located them as single complexes in the country, independent of any village structure. The larger the landowner, the more estate-centres he owned; only some of them, presumably, needed to be palatial. But the imagery of rural display was important; hence, among other things, the frequency of depictions of elaborate villas inside the standard iconography of mosaic and fresco decoration of private houses, both rural and urban.[70]

Western aristocrats regarded the possession of expensively equipped estate-centres as normal. They were where one went to spend a summer of *otium*, of playing games, or reading and writing, or eating and drinking. The sources for this are copious, but in our period Sidonius Apollinaris has left several particularly good accounts of such villas (he sometimes indeed called them *villae*, although also *domus*, *agri*, *praedia*) in the 460s–470s, such as his own at Avitacum (perhaps modern Aydat) outside Clermont, or those where he stayed with friends. Sidonius wrote up the baths, marble, colonnades, and libraries of these complexes for rhetorical effect, but this in itself shows that display was a significant aspect of them (for Avitacum he does not even mention the *pars rustica*, which will certainly have existed however). Sidonius is an important witness, not only because he was writing late in western imperial history, but also because his literary works are sufficiently detailed to get beyond these panegyrics.[71] He felt in general that rural living was appropriate to the summer, whereas in the autumn one should be back in town, where real action, civilization, *negotium*, was located. We have several admonitory letters to friends in which he criticizes them for not returning to town and for caring more about agriculture than politics: living 'not only among them [agricultural activities], but, what is more shameful, because of them'; as he says in another text, 'if you cultivate an estate in moderation, you possess it; if too much, it possesses you'. Historians have argued about whether this means that less traditionalist aristocrats by now were less convinced of the superiority of urban living than was Sidonius. It is likely, however, that Sidonius was most concerned that local notables should participate in politics; as long as they did that, he could be much more tolerant about them staying in the countryside in the winter—in one letter, indeed, he writes to a friend, Maurusius, saying that if he is still on his estate after the wine-harvest, into January and February, in 'sooty *otium*', Sidonius

---

[69] Percival, *Roman villa*, is still a good survey. See also Anselmino *et al.*, *Nador*; Columella, *Res rustica*, I.6.1. I have published versions of parts of what follows in the next two sections before, in 'Asentamientos rurales'; 'Development of villages'; 'Un pas vers le moyen âge'; and 'Early medieval archaeology'. Bowden *et al.*, *Recent research on the late Antique countryside*, and Christie, *Landscapes of change*, were published when this book was going to press, and could not be taken into consideration.

[70] e.g. Sarnowski, *Les répresentations des villas*.

[71] Sidonius, *Carmina*, XVIII, XXII; *Epp.*, II.2, 9, 12, 14, VIII.4, 17.6. For *otium*, see above, Ch. 4, n. 12.

might well join him, more for friendship than for the wealth of the estate however.[72] Sidonius had no obligation to be consistent in his letters, of course, any more than we are. It is certainly not true that he considered that paying any attention at all to agriculture was déclassé—the letter to Maurusius also expresses pleasure that the wine-harvest was better than expected; still, he would have been, on the basis of his other letters, distinctly less enthusiastic about the agrarian commitment of a senator like Palladius (above, p. 268). But the crucial point which his writings show here is that rural estates mattered, both for display and for wealth creation, sufficiently that some major landowners lived on them semi-permanently, and that even the most urbanized and conservative observers could be enthusiastic about their virtues. This certainly fits with the huge expense lavished on them that is attested by archaeology. It would be mistaken to see this expense (or Sidonius' words) as a proof that western aristocracies really were deserting cities, still less that the exchange economy was weakened by rural living (the mosaics and so on are themselves, of course, proof of its vitality; cf. above, p. 220). Rather, the reverse is true: villas exported an urban lifestyle into the countryside, as long as such a style continued to exist in cities (see below, Chapter 10). But the interest shown by aristocrats in rural living, comfort, and display—unmatched in most of the East, outside suburban areas at least—was firmly part of western Roman aristocratic identity.

Villas were in general the foci of rural settlement hierarchies in the Roman West, which were mostly highly dispersed. A really big villa, of course, could have hundreds of inhabitants, more than many villages; but it was a network of medium-sized villas, smaller ones, and isolated farmsteads that predominated in most places in the Roman period, with other forms of concentrated settlement generally rarer. This pattern can be deduced in most of the West from field surveys and from excavations (almost always, unfortunately, only of the villas). Villages (generally called *vici*) could coexist with this pattern, all the same. There were several types. Some were large, nodal settlements with commercial roles, on major road and river crossings, for example—the French call them *agglomérations secondaires*, to show that they fit into the urban settlement hierarchy. Smaller *vici*, by contrast, are often seen by scholars as rural alternatives to the villa pattern, populated by small peasant owners. This has tended to follow from the assumption that rural land-owning was organized in big blocks, which would then entail the existence of separate territories owned independently by small owners, living in separate settlements, if such owners were to exist at all. Blocks of this kind have even been reconstructed by more optimistic archaeologists, such as the well-known, but wholly hypothetical, 'estates' of the villas of Montmaurin

---

[72] Sidonius, *Epp.*, I.6 (quote), VII.15, VIII.8 (quote) for agriculture; II.14 (quote) and *Carmen* XXII, ll. 180–91, for winter. In I.6 and VIII.8 he is criticizing young people who were avoiding the civic *cursus*; it may be that Maurusius, being older, had done his turn.

and Chiragan in the Haute-Garonne south of Toulouse.[73] Actually, however, most of the evidence we have suggests much more fragmented landowning patterns, with very few exceptions (above, pp. 243–4). Under these circumstances, a peasant who owed rents to a villa-owning landlord could perfectly well live in a neighbouring village, if there was one, or a small owner live on an isolated farm not too far from a villa; apart from the fact that villas were estate-centres, settlement patterns and ownership structures did not have to be linked at all.[74]

How villas really articulated with concentrated villages in the West is better dealt with empirically. There were places where villages were commoner than villas, mountain areas in some cases, such as parts of the Italian Appennines; these were, however, relatively rare.[75] There were others, by contrast, in which villas and villages could be found in the same territory; when that was the case, it is important to ask which one dominated the settlement hierarchy. This is not easy to establish, but there have been some attempts. Around Kasserine in southern Tunisia in the late Roman period, for example (an unpublished field survey with good interim reports), villages seem to have been part of a hierarchy focused on villas, with tenants living, perhaps, both in the villages and in isolated farms.[76] By contrast, St-Blaise near Marseille, a fifth- and sixth-century hilltop settlement, seems to have been the focus of a landscape that contained small villas and small farms alike: here, medium landowners, if not city-dwelling, probably lived both in the central settlement and in some of the dispersed villas. This latter pattern, of newly developing agglomerated (often fortified) sites in a still-dispersed landscape, seems to have been particularly common in Mediterranean Gaul around 500, for it is found again on the other side of the Rhône mouth, around Lunel and in the Vaunage west and south-west of Nîmes, from the late fifth century at the latest, and extending into the ninth century, without the villages yet absorbing the dispersed settlements around them.[77] This

---

[73] For nodal settlements, see Petit *et al.*, *Les agglomérations sécondaires*; Negro Ponzi, *S. Michele di Trino*, pp. 473–6. For blocks of land, see for Montmaurin (the block itself is called Nébouzan) Fouet, *Montmaurin*, pp. 289–92, extended to Chiragan by Percival, *Roman villa*, pp. 123–4, 129–30. A more plausible case by far is the Langmauerbezirk around (among other things) the villa of Welschbillig near Trier; this was a real late Roman boundary, but almost certainly for an imperial, not a private estate: see Steinhausen, 'Die Langmauer', esp. pp. 65–79.

[74] Tenant villages (*villae*) are referred to in *Vita Melaniae latina*, c. 18—although this, probably a translation from Greek (the Greek version of the *Life* uses the standard eastern term for small tenant hamlets, *epoikia*), may simply be an east Mediterranean image of peasant society; but for African dependent villages (*vici*) see Banaji, *Agrarian change*, p. 12.

[75] For the Appennines, Ciampoltrini, 'Materiali tardoantichi', pp. 699–706; Giannichedda, *Filattiera*; La Regina, 'Ricerche'. Note also the *castros* of the Asturias and related areas of northern Spain: see Fernandez Mier, *Génesis del territorio*, pp. 41–60, for a recent synthesis, which also discusses villas, and also above, p. 228.

[76] Hitchner, 'Kasserine 1982–1985', pp. 162–3; idem, 'Kasserine 1987', pp. 245–6.

[77] Demians d'Archimbaud, *Saint-Blaise*, with Trément, *Archéologie du paysage*, pp. 205–17, 242–3; Raynaud, *Lunel Viel*; Parodi, 'La Vaunage', pp. 8–9, 14–15, 22–5. Durand, *Les paysages médiévaux*, pp. 85–95, 102–3, reaches similar conclusions for ninth-century Languedoc on the

apparent centrality of villages in a continuing landscape of villas and farms is new in the late Roman period in the south of France, but it is relatively stable; it precedes the decline of villas, which was a separate phenomenon, and does not seem to lead inexorably to generalized settlement-concentration either, even though from 1000 this would be a very marked feature of south French *incastellamento*.[78] We will probably find parallels to it elsewhere as more areas are studied in depth; a similar pattern has, for example, recently been proposed for fifth- and sixth-century Puglia. But areas where the villa network remained central are more normal in the late empire: the whole of lowland Britain and northern Gaul; almost the whole of Spain (these three have particularly good overviews); the major plains of Italy and Sicily; all the half-dozen surveyed areas of Tunisia and Algeria; and probably Aquitaine too, given our literary texts and the wealth of its biggest villas, although systematic survey-work there is virtually absent.[79]

The other aspect of the centrality of villas is the terminology of territorial identity in the Roman West. Country-dwellers live today in village territories, named from and focused on settlements. These settlements can be concentrated or dispersed, but the sense of being part of a single village does not entirely depend on living close together, and can be present even if everyone lives in scattered farms. This geographical territorialization, with a common identity being shared by everyone living in that territory no matter what their tenurial status, is at the core of what the word 'village' means in this book (see further below, p. 516). Such village territories are distinct from each other, and are normally unitary blocks. This pattern was normal in the eastern Mediterranean from the start of our period, as we have seen; the boundaries of village territories mattered, and could be fought over. In the West, however, at least while the Roman empire lasted, we cannot see such village territories in the majority of our texts. Instead, geographical locations were for the most part named *fundi*: units of ownership, sometimes linked together in *massae*. These dominate the land transactions of the sixth-century Ravenna papyri, for example, both whole and subdivided (into one or more twelfth-portions). In general, *fundi* could be large or small, and they could themselves be fragmented. Examples of small *fundi* can be found in

basis of the documentary record. For general archaeological surveys, see Mercier and Raynaud, 'L'habitat rural'; Schneider, '*Oppida* et *castra*'; idem, 'Nouvelles recherches'. For villa survival, see Carru, 'Les *villae*'; Pellecuer and Pomarèdes, 'Crise, survie', for Provence and Languedoc respectively.

[78] Bourin-Derruau, *Villages médiévaux*, I, pp. 45–77.

[79] For Puglia, Volpe, 'Paesaggi' is basic; see also the parallel discussions of Piemonte in Negro Ponzi, *S, Michele di Trino*, pp. 479–92, of Sicily in Molinari, 'Le campagne siciliane', p. 224, and of Calabria (see below, n. 123). Regional overviews of villas: Scott, *A gazetteer*; Van Ossel, *Établissements ruraux*; Gorges, *Les villas hispano-romaines* (updated in Ariño and Díaz, 'El campo' and in Chavarría, 'Interpreting the transformation', which was published too recently for me to use). For Aquitaine, see O'Hea, *Conceptual and material transformation*; Balmelle, *Les demeures aristocratiques*.

the Veleia tablet from the second-century Emilian Appennines, a list of the liabilities for local poor-relief of the small city of Veleia, estate by estate, with almost no reference to villages (*vici*) at all—only nine are cited among hundreds of *fundi*.[80] A larger one was the *fundus Tuletianos* of the Tablettes Albertini, documents of the 490s on wood from the Tunisian desert margin. This estate was divided into *loci* or *agri* which were not settlement-units but, rather, groups of olive groves and orchards in irrigated wadis—where the peasants who worked them actually lived was not necessary to say.[81] A *fundus* was thought by Roman lawyers normally to have a house on it,[82] which implies some degree of dispersed settlement, although in practice things were more complex; if Tuletianos was anything like the territory of Kasserine, a little further north, its peasants could have lived in villages as well as in isolated houses. But the crucial point is that a world of *fundi* was a world in which property structures had overwhelmed settlement structures as points of reference for rural identification. In most societies one looks to both, even if the dominance of one's lord or the cohesion of one's village may favour one or the other. In the Roman East, village community identity seems to have been pretty dominant, whatever the landowning structures of each village. In the West, at the opposite extreme, community identity may sometimes barely have existed at all. A settlement as substantial as St-Blaise must have had some collective identity, even though the Rhône delta, where it is situated, was characterized by an estate-based terminology for the localization of land, as we see in the will of Caesarius of Arles, dating to 542 (he calls estates *agella*, little *agri*).[83] Where dispersed settlement dominated, however, estate identification must have given support at a conceptual level to villa-focused rural hierarchies, for villas were the centres of estate territories, almost by definition, whether these territories were fragmented or not. Estates were still called *fundi* in the fifth and sixth centuries in Africa and Italy, following classical Latin usage; in Gaul by 600 they were called *villae*. As we shall see (pp. 510–13), the changes in meaning of the latter word are of some interest.

The contrast between the villa focus of the West and the village focus of the East is worth some further observations. The first is to stress again the weakness of most western peasant communities, for it has implications, as we shall see. The second is to stress that the flashy residential end of the villa spectrum represents a cultural difference from the East: in the West, rural

---

[80] For Ravenna, see *P. Ital.*, e.g. 8, 22–3, 35–7. For *fundi* and *massae*, recent discussions include de Neeve, 'Fundus as economic unit'; Castagnetti, *L'organizzazione*, pp. 171–9; Vera, 'Massa fundorum'. The most recent edition and commentary for the Veleia tablet is Criniti, *La tabula alimentaria*; pp. 242–4 for *vici*. The Veleiate *fundi* were located in fifteen *pagi* (pp. 232–42), which were local administrative territories, but not linked to settlement.

[81] *Tablettes Albertini*, passim. For a comparison with Kasserine, see Hitchner, 'Historical text and archaeological context'.

[82] *Digesta*, L.16.211: *ager cum aedificio fundus dicitur.*

[83] *Testamentum sancti Caesarii.*

otium, and thus rural aristocratic display, was impressive, whereas in the East, where aristocrats remained essentially urban-focused, it was mostly unnecessary. Villas were a marker of the range of civilian cultural values of western elites, from taking baths to reading Virgil. If they vanished, this might be a sign of the ruin of such elites; but it might also simply be a sign of changes in these values. If the comfortable otium celebrated by people like Sidonius became outdated, villas would have to change fairly fast; we shall return to this. A third and final point is an argument against economic determinism. The East and the West were both prosperous in the later empire, even if their settlement patterns were so different. Both concentrated and dispersed settlement patterns are sometimes hailed by different scholars as more economically 'rational', the former because it allows greater specialization of artisanal activity and greater access to markets, the latter because it allows cultivators to be closer to their fields. Both of these points are to an extent valid, but they are only partial characterizations (the highly dispersed population of fourth-century Italy had unrestricted market access to African ceramics, for example), and they have no explanatory value—it could be argued that a result of the heavy concentration of population found in fifth-century north-western Syria was the development of artisanal specialization, but it certainly was not a cause. Much the same is true of another possible economic explanation of these differences in settlement patterns, that they reflect the density of aristocratic control over the countryside. According to such a model, the dispersed, villa/estate-centred, patterns of the West would show a relative dominance of great landlords and great estates, whereas the eastern villages would show a tendency to independent peasant landowning. This latter difference is a real one, for landowning genuinely was more large-scale in the West (above, pp. 162–5), but the correlation is nonetheless once again misleading. For a start, there were great landowners in the East too, some of whom owned whole (concentrated) villages. Furthermore, the eventual victory of agglomerated settlement in most of the West, in the tenth and eleventh centuries, is itself often seen as a sign of aristocratic control, not weakness, the exact opposite of the late Roman argument. Actually, aristocrats can, if they are strong enough, dominate either a concentrated or a dispersed landscape with ease; conversely, peasant autonomy can be expressed through both settlement types too. In specific periods, particular aspects of control or autonomy may perhaps favour one or the other (the sharply territorialized local seigneurial control of the eleventh century often genuinely favoured agglomerations, for example—I have argued the point elsewhere myself), but that is as much as can safely be said.[84] Settlement patterns do not in themselves stably define or reflect particular economic relationships.

---

[84] Wickham, 'A che serve l'incastellamento?', pp. 33–9. For the prosperity of the fourth-century West, see in general Lewit, Agricultural production.

To sum up: a villa-focused settlement-pattern was not necessarily one where a great estate controlled a landscape; but it was certainly one where the estate run from that villa, whether a single block or (more often) a scatter of properties, was the major point of reference. Similarly, a conceptual geography based on *fundi* had space for smaller properties, but it privileged landowning over all other forms of geographical or collective identity. This did not mean that peasant co-operation was impossible; the *circumcelliones* in fourth- and fifth-century Africa, the Bagaudae in fifth-century Gaul and Spain, however contested their status as peasant rebels (below, pp. 529–33), at least represent (partially) peasant groups acting autonomously, and often against the interests of landowners. On the anecdotal level, Augustine's letter of 422–3 about Antoninus, the tyrannical bishop of Fussala, is one of the most illuminating single texts about late Roman rural behaviour (largely because Augustine had behaved so unwisely, and was so embarrassed about it). It describes how Antoninus terrorized the *castellum* of Fussala, by implication a relatively independent village, but when the church tried to transfer him to the *fundus* of Thogonoetum, the *coloni* there told its owner that they would leave if he came—here, the solidarity of the estate was at least as effective as that of the village.[85] All the same, a combination of dispersed peasant settlement and estate-based identity hardly could be said to *help* peasant collective coherence. A world of villages would be a significant social change, when it came, however great any continuities of settlement were.

The villa pattern was a Roman phenomenon, and it did not long outlast the end of the empire. As soon as we move from its hegemony to its crisis, however, the empire-wide focus we have been using dissolves. This fits the microregionality of the whole of the post-Roman world; every region and microregion would henceforth not only have its own settlement history, but also its own frame of reference within which settlement changes had meanings. We will see more homogeneities at the sub-regional level in northern Gaul, but, along the arc of the Mediterranean coast from Naples to Málaga, microregional differences are acute, and we will have to proceed case by case in the next two sections of this chapter. The dating of the end of villas, on the other hand, is something that can be generalized about, at least at the regional level, so this section will conclude with some of the conclusions that can be drawn from it.

Villas dominated in the West in 300, but by 700 they had almost entirely vanished. The patterns of their disappearance were very various.[86] Some

---

[85] Augustine, *Ep*. XX*, ed. Divjak. See Lancel, 'L'affaire d'Antoninus'.
[86] For general comments, see Percival, *Roman villa*, pp. 166–99; idem, 'The fifth-century villa'; above all now Ripoll and Arce, 'Transformation and end'; and most recently Lewit, '"Vanishing villas"'.

were simply abandoned, in some cases after fires, sometimes indeed as a result of wars: the revolt of Magnentius in 351–3, any number of barbarian invasions, or the Gothic war in Italy. Others—it is a feature that has been tracked, for example, in Catalonia—steadily lost their monumental features and became simpler estate-centres;[87] this I would read simply as a shift in estate-management, not necessarily as 'decline', but it often preceded more substantial changes. In other cases villas were replaced by churches or monasteries; this might be because the whole rural estate-complex was given to a church, which remodelled it as an ecclesiastical institution, or else because the villa-owner had built a church in the complex, which was the only building to survive a subsequent abandonment, or else because an abandoned villa was (as frequently happened) given over to a cemetery thereafter, with which a church was subsequently associated. These three patterns, covering the range from substantial settlement continuity to total discontinuity, can of course easily be distinguished in excavation, but much less easily when (as is more often the case) all we have is a standing church, maybe of the twelfth century, and the unexcavated vestiges of a villa visible under or around it. Other villas had late settlement on the site that reused decaying buildings in a much more ad hoc fashion, often labelled squatter occupation by archaeologists; recent excavations of post-hole wooden build-ings on such sites have sometimes shown a use of the structures of the villa so systematic that it could well be that the site was occupied without a break, maybe even by the same people, but their material culture nonetheless changed dramatically. In other cases, villa occupation seems to have been replaced by occupation on a nearby site, normally in new building styles; the same observations apply. Finally, villas in some cases continued to be occu-pied, but slowly changed their identity, turning into geographically, not tenurially, defined settlements—villages, that is to say. It is often the case that we can only deduce this from placenames (modern villages, unexca-vated, whose names end in *-ano* or *-aco* or *-ate* in Italy, *-an* and *-ac* in southern France, *-y* in northern France, representing old tenurial names such as the *fundus Cornelianus* or *Corneliacus*). These are, however, uncer-tain guides, for the old estate names might have persisted as territorial markers for abandoned or never-occupied sites before new villages devel-oped there—historians and archaeologists are sometimes too optimistic when they presume villa-to-village continuities without excavation. Still, there is no doubt that this development did occur, and in some areas might even have been normal.

Of all these developments, only that of the villa directly remodelled as a less monumental building or as a church estate-centre reflects any real organizational continuity. Several others reflect continuous settlement on

---

[87] For Catalonia, see below, n. 101. This development had already taken place in Africa: Ellis, 'North African villages', pp. 74–5.

the site, at least potentially, but also considerable economic and cultural change. Others (the cemetery option, the new site) at least reflect the continued occupation of the agrarian landscape, but not necessarily by the same people. Others might represent more radical breaks still. In general, recent villa studies mostly at least stress the continuity of human settlement, I am sure rightly.[88] But these must be set against cultural breaks that are often dramatic. The question is what these mean, and also whether they mean the same things from region to region.

Let us begin with a quick overview of the dating of the end of the villa, for this varies considerably across the regions of the West. In Britain, villas started to be abandoned in the late fourth century, and in the fifth this tendency became very swift: by 450 or so they had all gone, and in no case yet is there an unambiguous continuity of site usage into the Anglo-Saxon period (though in several cases later occupation, in 'Anglo-Saxon' style, was very close, and used the same agricultural terrain: see above, pp. 310–11). In northern Gaul, their disappearance began around 350, and was nearly complete by 450. In Mediterranean Gaul, the sixth century is the main period of villa abandonment, and there are few known after 600. In Aquitaine, too, we can at least identify a few villas which continued into the seventh century without abandoning their basic organizational structures, though not, probably, beyond that. In Italy villas disappear in the late fifth and sixth centuries, perhaps above all the early to mid-sixth; only in Sicily are a few seventh-century villas known for sure. In Spain, the process of abandonment began in the fifth century, and there were few villas by the end of the sixth, but it was a slower process than elsewhere, and some of them survived right up to 700, maybe into the early eighth.[89] In Africa, finally, post-Roman rural settlement is so ill-studied that what replaced it is usually unknown, and even the date of the change is unclear; all the same, discontinuities are invisible before 550.[90] These variabilities are substantial, but it can be recognized that they resolve themselves into two broad groups: in the North, the end of the villa is concentrated on the period around 400, whereas in the Mediterranean the equivalent date centres on the sixth century. It may be added that one standard cause for it is immediately excluded, for 400 is generally too early for an association with barbarian invasion and the military overthrow of aristocracies, whereas the sixth century is generally too late. Let us look a little more closely at the shifts in Gaul, Italy, and Spain, to see if we can pin down more detailed explanations.

[88] See e.g. Ouzoulias, 'La déprise agricole du Bas-Empire' (his specific target is an earlier depopulationist historiography, for which see e.g. below, n. 176); Lewit, '"Vanishing villas"'.

[89] For northern Gaul, see below, n. 91; for southern Gaul, see above, nn. 77, 79; for Italy, Brogiolo, *La fine delle ville*; idem, 'Continuità fra tardo antico e alto medioevo'; for Spain, above, n. 79.

[90] For 550 in Africa see e.g. Dietz, *Africa Proconsularis*, II, pp. 781–5; but see below, pp. 723–4.

In northern Gaul, between the Seine and the Rhine, it is clear, above all thanks to recent empirical overviews and syntheses by Paul Van Ossel and Pierre Ouzoulias, that villas began most consistently to lose their old identities in the late fourth century, probably slightly earlier even than Britain. Fifth-century villas are densest around Trier, in the Île de France, and around Maastricht and Aachen, but they too are gone by the late fifth century.[91] This dating is a significant one, for the fourth century was for the most part a period of peace and stability in Gaul, with the capital of the western empire for a time located at Trier. And, indeed, the end of villas does not seem to reflect economic or political weakness; ceramic patterns continued without much change until well past 400, indeed never ending entirely (below, p. 796), and perhaps half the villas recently excavated have continuing occupation on the site with little or no break. This occupation was in much simpler materials, however, spolia or, above all, wood, and on a rather smaller scale; it could involve artisanal activity, but heating and baths were abandoned. Areas of complete absence of later occupation do exist (see below, p. 509); but this sort of simplification can be found in most places.[92] In a small number of cases, so far—notably Servon (Seine-et-Marne)—wooden constructions were quite ambitious, with several aisles and rooms, which may have been aiming at a 'villa-like' architectural form,[93] but mostly such buildings were smaller, and associated with *Grubenhäuser*, the sunken-floored buildings that would be common in the early middle ages. Such complexes were already, in fact, quite similar to 'Germanic' settlement types, although it must be said that the villages in Gaul that can be most clearly associated typologically with those beyond the Rhine (they are largely found in the lower Rhine and Meuse in the fifth century, although right across to the Seine and beyond in the sixth: below, p. 505) are actually more elaborate, with larger post-hole buildings, and associated smaller buildings and *Grubenhäuser* in structured groups. In this sense, all the same, one could say that north Gaulish villas were already evolving towards early medieval villages in the last century of Roman rule. The Franks settled, from the middle decades of the fifth century onwards, in a landscape that was already mostly 'de-Romanized' in its material culture.

C. R. Whittaker has argued strongly that the fourth century is a period in which the frontiers of the Roman empire functioned more as zones of interaction than as boundaries, and that the militarization of social and political action was a general feature of northern Gaul, well before the

---

[91] Van Ossel, *Établissements ruraux*, pp. 81–2, 428; idem, 'Structure, évolution'; Van Ossel and Ouzoulias, 'Rural settlement'; Lenz, 'Late Roman rural settlement'. Cf. above, p. 179.

[92] Ouzoulias and Van Ossel, 'Dynamiques de peuplement', pp. 162–71; more widely, Van Ossel and Ouzoulias, 'Rural settlement', pp. 145–9.

[93] Gentili and Hourlier, 'L'habitat', for Servon; cf. Petit and Parthuisot, 'L'évolution de la villa', for the similar construction at St-Germain-lès-Corbeil (Essonne). A parallel further south is Pissevieille (Cher) in the Berry: O'Hara, *Conceptual and material transformations*, site n. 32.

invasion period. This is a convincing and important argument; it helps to explain many of the continuities between the Roman and the post-Roman world. It also, as Whittaker himself notes, helps to explain the transformation in villa culture, and I set out a version of this argument earlier (pp. 201–2, 331): military elites in the Roman empire had always stressed comfort and architectural display less than had civilian aristocracies, although in the late empire at least they often paid considerable attention to lavish personal adornment; the end of villas as an architectural form simply represents the militarization of the values and social behaviour of their owners, which substantially preceded the failure of the state in the North.[94] It must be added, however, in a chapter that focuses on peasants, that the other side of this cultural shift is that, in architectural terms, the difference had diminished substantially between buildings that might be aristocratic—those on villa sites—and those that there is no reason to consider aristocratic at all—including those on new sites of the fifth century, some of which have been recently found in the Île de France.[95] The first thing that militarization did was not to make post-villa constructions more 'Germanic', but to make them more like those of the surrounding peasantry. We must be careful about this, for, as we shall see later (p. 506), we have not yet found the residences of the kings and aristocrats of the early Merovingian period in northern Gaul, and some of these may well have remained architecturally elaborate. Even if they were not, they will have been distinguished in other ways, by rich wall-hangings and the like. But the relative homogeneity of surviving material culture in the fifth century is still striking; and it was a development that had already taken place before the Franks arrived.

In contrast to this pattern is the Mediterranean tradition of rather later villa survival: away from the frontier, there is no reason to suppose that aristocratic militarization occurred so early, and indeed, as we have seen (pp. 165–8, 174–6), it was generally uncommon until the very late fifth century. A sixth-century date for such militarization in the Mediterranean area would roughly fit both the end of villas and the literary evidence for southern Gaul and Italy. Slight differences in the scansion of villa abandonment could perhaps even be used as a guide to the speed of that social change; the fact that some Italian archaeologists are beginning to argue that the process already began before the Gothic war (though accelerating fast during it) might perhaps tell us something about local aristocratic reactions to Ostrogothic military hegemony, the beginning of a Roman mimetic response to that hegemony that our heavily classicizing texts from the Gothic period, Cassiodorus or Ennodius, largely hide.[96] But this is an

---

[94] Whittaker, *Frontiers*, pp. 222–40, 257–78; cf. Halsall, 'The origins of the *Reihengräberzivilisation*', for possible reflections of these processes in burials.

[95] See e.g. Valais, 'Herblay'; Bertin *et al.*, 'Une occupation mérovingienne précoce'.

[96] See e.g. Ortalli, 'La fine delle ville', pp. 15–16, for Casteldebole in Emilia; Roffia and Ghiroldi, 'Sirmione, la villa di via Antiche Mura'. Small and Buck, *S. Giovanni di Ruoti*, I,

argument that must be used with caution, for only in a few areas do we know what post-villa settlement actually looked like, and without some wider archaeological context, of a type that we are now beginning to find in northern Gaul, we risk circular arguments. I want to conclude this section by offering three possible models for the context in which villas ended in the Mediterranean, each of which is valid for at least some areas of each post-Roman polity. This is hardly an exhaustive overview, but the current state of knowledge does not allow us to go further.

The first model is very late villa survival. Aquitaine is not well studied archaeologically, but work on some of the largest villas shows that a few were still occupied, and sometimes refurbished, into the seventh century (above, p. 174). This area of cultural and economic survival may have extended quite far north, for a villa with late fifth-century mosaics and seventh-century architectural ornament has been found at Marboué (Eure-et-Loir), only some 100 km south of Paris.[97] It was proposed in Chapter 4 that in Aquitaine this late use of villas fits with a surviving Roman aristocracy, which maintained many of its traditional practices rather longer than elsewhere. There are parallels to this in Sicily, where at least one villa, at Contrada Saraceno near Agrigento, has been identified as surviving into the seventh century (and even into the eighth), although without luxury elements;[98] and in particular in Spain, where a group of large seventh-century, possibly eighth-century, villas are known, including at least one new foundation, at Pla de Nadal near Valencia.[99] In both Aquitaine and Spain, secular civilian traditions were steadily replaced, as elsewhere in the West, with aristocrats having to choose between a militarized secular hierarchy or the church; but both maintained an urban focus, and on the ecclesiastical side, at least, they continued some of the literary cultural practices of the Roman senatorial elite (above, p. 95). It must be said, however, on the basis of the

p. 121, shows a classic case of a villa that seems to have failed during the Gothic war, although settlement apparently continued on the site. See in general for military identity in the Ostrogothic period Amory, *People and identity*, pp. 149–65.

[97] O'Hara, *Conceptual and material transformation*, ch. 5; Balmelle, *Demeures aristocratiques*, pp. 118–23. For Marboué, Blanchard-Lemée, 'La villa à mosaïques'. (A fifth-century mosaic there names Steleco as its patron: he cannot easily have been a Frank, from the name and date, but may have been from a Romano-Germanic military family.) For fifth-century parallels south of Paris to this villa, see Van Ossel and Ouzoulias, 'Rural settlement', p. 145.

[98] Castellana and McConnell, 'A rural settlement'; see also Bernardini *et al.*, 'Il territorio di Segesta', pp. 118–22 for an inland parallel; and, in general, Wilson, *Sicily*, pp. 335–6; Molinari, 'Il popolamento rurale', pp. 366–70; eadem, 'Insediamento rurale'. For population continuities throughout the early middle ages, see further Rizzo, 'Le dinamiche'; Maurici, *Medioevo trapanese*, pp. 40–4.

[99] For Pla de Nadal see Juan and Pastor, 'Los visigodos'. Luis Caballero would redate the site to the eighth century, as part of his general redating of 'Visigothic' monuments (see 'La arquitectura'); Sonia Gutiérrez cautiously prefers the late seventh century, as proposed by the excavators (see eadem, 'Algunas consideraciones', pp. 102–5). The other very late villas are between Mérida and the Atlantic; they include La Cocosa, Torre Águila, and Pisões. See Gorges, *Les villas hispano-romaines*, pp. 189–90, 474–5; Rodríguez, 'La villa romana de Torre Águila'.

Spanish material, that the percentage of villas still occupied in traditional ways in the seventh century was probably low, and presumably restricted only to a portion of the elite; what slower social change achieved was a more gradual pacing of the abandonment of the villa lifestyle, rather than its general persistence to a late date.

A second model (which may indeed sometimes coexist with the first) is one where villas were only one part of a settlement hierarchy, which continued without any other changes when they ceased to be occupied. The village focus of settlement patterns on the Mediterranean coast of Gaul in the late fifth century is a particularly good example of this; villas began to disappear in the next century, but the rest of the network seems to have stayed more or less the same.[100] These patterns probably show that cultural change was rather more moderate there than in northern Gaul; richer villa owners, maybe still city-dwelling, could well have simply given up rural *otium* patterns and transferred their estate-management to smaller complexes, perhaps in villages, with lesser villa owners moving to the villages as well. The end of the world of *otium* was probably already prefigured by the transformation of many residential villas into more utilitarian estate-centres in the fifth century, as has been analysed in particular for neighbouring Catalonia, and as has also been identified in parts of northern Italy.[101] This sort of pattern may be one that could be found elsewhere, perhaps in the vicinity of the fifth- and sixth-century fortified *castra* that can be found across much of the northern Mediterranean countryside: Monte Cildá, La Yecla, and Puig Rom in northern Spain, Monte Barro, Belmonte, and Invillino in northern Italy join those south French villages that were fortified, like Lombren, Roc de Pampelune, and St-Blaise, as examples of this.[102] One should not overemphasize the significance of such *castra* in settlement terms, though; again, in the absence of detailed survey work around them, which has only been carried out in France, we would risk circular argument. Two points should be made about *castra*, however: first, although one can

---

[100] See n. 77 above.

[101] For Catalonia see Chavarría, 'Transformaciones arquitectónicas'; eadem, 'Els establiments rurals'; eadem, 'El món rural'; Gurt and Palet, 'Structuration du territoire'. For a case study, Vilauba, see Jones *et al.*, 'Vilauba'; Castanyer and Tremoleda, *La vil.la romana de Vilauba*, pp. 149–61, 345. For Italy, Ortalli, 'La fine delle ville'; see in general Ripoll and Arce, 'Transformation and end', pp. 71–4.

[102] See García Guinea, *Excavationes de Monte Cildá*; González Salas, *El castro de Yecla*; Palol, 'Castro hispanovisigodo de "Puig Rom" '; Brogiolo and Castelletti, *Archeologia a Monte Barro*, I; Micheletto, 'Forme di insediamento', pp. 56–8 (for Belmonte, a potentially significant site); Bierbrauer, *Invillino-Ibligo in Friaul*, I; Charmasson, *L'oppidum bas-rhodanien de Lombren*'; Schneider, 'Nouvelles recherches'; Demians d'Archambaud, *Saint-Blaise*. For overviews and parallels, see Brogiolo and Gelichi, *Nuove ricerche sui castelli altomedievali*; Murialdo, 'Prima dell'incastellamento'; Schneider, '*Oppida* et *castra* tardo-antiques'. In northern Spain, we would need to distinguish these late Roman military *castra* from the *castros* of indigenous origin, which may represent quite different social structures (see Ch. 4, nn. 189, 191); but at present there is no way of doing this archaeologically or topographically.

make quite a long list of these fortifications, and it would get longer if one added the fortifications that marked every one of the borders of the disunited Italy of the Lombard–Byzantine period, they do not ever seem to have been so common that they could in themselves match villas as the focus of a settlement hierarchy.[103] Second, these *castra* seem to have been public, marking state strategic networks, rather than being private fortifications: they do not mark a new period in which the security of walls was in general preferable to open settlements, and in fact fortified houses of any kind were not common before the castles of the tenth and eleventh centuries. *Castra* do show much greater levels of continuity between the late Roman empire and the early middle ages than villas do, all the same, and must have been a stabilizing element for local settlement hierarchies when villas disappeared.[104]

The third model is that of a more substantial breakdown in settlement hierarchies as villas disappeared. One example seems to be parts of eastern Emilia in northern Italy, where villas already ceased for the most part to be residential in the fourth and fifth centuries, and in the fifth and sixth lost most of their old roles altogether. Casteldebole near Bologna, a very large complex in 300, by the early sixth century was reduced to a sixth of its former size, with a cemetery on part of the rest of the site, and no later occupation; in other villas, simple and sometimes temporary structures succeeded the last villa-phases. But the early medieval period does not show more in the countryside than this, anywhere in that microregion. In one part of Emilia, the Modenese of the '*pozzi-deposito*' (above, pp. 209–10), there seems to have been a partial rural abandonment, although this is probably atypical, for it was a frontier area by 600.[105] Elsewhere in this area there was still occupation at least, but rural settlement hierarchies seem to have largely broken down; the difference between elite and peasant rural housing had become invisible, although one must not forget that most aristocrats, as elsewhere in the Mediterranean, remained city-dwelling. And exchange seems to have become considerably less complex at the same time: very little sixth-century African Red Slip has been found in the area, for example.[106] I would argue that a combination of the weakening of rural settlement hierarchies and the weakening of exchange is a good

---

[103] For Italian border fortifications, see Christie, 'The limes bizantino reviewed'; Zanini, *Le Italie bizantine*, pp. 209–90. The type-site for a Byzantine *castrum* in Italy is Mannoni and Murialdo, *S. Antonino*. The regular presence of *castra* and *castella* in the lists of terms for rural settlement in Spanish civil and ecclesiastical legislation at least shows that they were an important mental category: see Isla, '*Villa, villula*'.

[104] Samson, 'The Merovingian nobleman's home', is the best overview of unfortified housing in Gaul. Schneider, 'Entre antiquité et haut moyen âge', implies that around half the *castra* of southern Gaul survive past 600 or so.

[105] Ortalli, 'La fine delle ville', pp. 15–17; Gelichi and Giordani, *Il tesoro nel pozzo*, pp. 135–67. The equivalent area to the north of the Po, the lower Verona plain, certainly maintained occupation, and more of a settlement hierarchy: Saggioro, *Paesaggi rurali medievali*, II, pp. 35–53.

[106] Gelichi and Giordani, *Il tesoro nel pozzo*, p. 81.

guide to the weakening of elites (see below, pp. 545–6); it is anyway hard to doubt that the replacement of a villa pattern by nothing except scattered settlement is a rather sharper break than that of my second model, where the other elements in total spatial patterns continued unchanged. Mid- to late sixth-century Italy was a period of protracted military crisis, and breakdown of all kinds has been attributed to the Gothic and Lombard wars. This does not mean that a weakening in settlement hierarchies was universal in Italy—as we shall see, it was not—but it could happen; nor was it unique to Italy. We have seen it very clearly in lowland Britain (above, pp. 306–14), and analogous developments have also been found on the south-east Spanish coast, around Alicante and around Salobreña south of Granada, and perhaps elsewhere as well.[107] The implications of these developments take us further into the early middle ages, however, and I will discuss them in the next section.

What these models of villa breakdown already show is the microregionality of local settlement change once the homogeneity of Roman culture and economy could no longer be assured; even though villas in a given region generally went out of use in the same period, what replaced them was very much more diverse, depending on local socio-economic structures and agricultural practices. But the end of the villa as a settlement type is a more general phenomenon; it marked the end of one of the major elements of western Roman elite identity and display. I have been arguing here, as in Chapter 4, that this was a cultural shift, as aristocracies adapted to a more militarized post-Roman world, not a marker of economic and political crisis. But it was a very substantial shift, all the same, and power relations in the countryside could not have avoided being affected by it. This needs to be kept firmly in mind as we move into the early middle ages.

3. Early medieval settlement in the western Mediterranean

As already noted (p. 442), post-Roman settlement in this group of regions has been studied for a relatively short period of time; not everywhere has a critical mass of sub-regional surveys built up, that would allow us to generalize usefully over wider areas. Furthermore, the degree of microregional variability that has been discovered is extreme, which also discourages generalization: it could even be that an entirely new interpretative overview for how settlement change works here is just over the horizon, and will only become clear in the next generation of research. This section is, therefore, both partial and speculative. I shall try to restrict myself to characterizing only zones of the western Mediterranean that one can really say something about, without trying to guess about others; furthermore, I shall restrict

---

[107] See below, pp. 489–90.

myself to the Mediterranean coast between Rome and Málaga, where much of the best work on rural settlement as a system has been done, referring to other well-studied areas only in passing. On the basis of this, I shall offer some suggestions as to what different settlement systems might imply: these will be for future work in the field to test.

Let us start with Lazio in central Italy. (For Lazio and Tuscany, see the inset in Map 7.) This is the hinterland of Rome, by far the largest city in the Roman empire in 400, and, although only some 5 per cent of its fourth-century size by 800, still the largest city in the former western empire. Notwithstanding this, late Roman rural Lazio does not seem to have prospered as much as it had in the early empire. The extensive survey work done in the northern quadrant of the Roman hinterland since the 1950s, mostly under the aegis of the South Etruria Survey of the British School at Rome, has shown a steady decrease in the number of rural sites after the second century.[108] Exactly what this means is less easy to tell, however. In general, nowhere in the West shows the fifth- and sixth-century peak so visible throughout the eastern Mediterranean, except Puglia, whose economy paralleled that of Greece as much as that of Italy;[109] but recent work in the western Mediterranean (more recent than most of the British School survey work) suggests relative continuities in settlement and exchange at least to the fifth century. A continuitist reading of Lazial evidence could lead one to postulate a period of partial settlement concentration in the later empire, focused on large villa complexes; the excavations of the last two decades give some support to this, for several of them show surviving earlier villas rebuilt on a larger scale, though with less architectural elaboration, notably at Mola di Monte Gelato, 30 km north of Rome, in (roughly) the fifth century. This sort of continuitist reading becomes harder after around 550, when villas stopped; for what replaced them, survey becomes much less sure a guide after the end of African Red Slip imports in the countryside around the same date.[110] John Moreland's work around the monastery of Farfa, carried out with a specific eye to early medieval problems, does however indicate a surviving hierarchy of dispersed settlement, with medium-sized and small-scale complexes, similar to Roman patterns, but by now with the villa level partially stripped off. Even then, several villa sites in that area had Forum ware, Rome's new late eighth-century glazed fine ware, which could well imply continuity of occupation on them in some form; at the centre of

---

[108] See for a general overview Potter, *Changing landscape*, pp. 139–43; for an account of more recent surveys, including outside the south Etruria context, see Nardi Combescure, *Paesaggi*, pp. 11–45.

[109] Volpe, *Contadini, pastori*, pp. 372–4; idem, 'Paesaggi', pp. 314–21. The fourth century is the peak in most of the western Mediterranean: see above, n. 84.

[110] Potter and King, *Mola di Monte Gelato*, pp. 46–77, 423–5, for Mola: the late villa is c.350–550. For more continuitist readings see Wickham, 'Historical and topographical notes', II, pp. 85–7 and, particularly, Fiocchi Niccolai, 'Considerazioni', who synthesizes neglected cemetery and church archaeology; see also the next note.

one local settlement network, at Casale S. Donato, a substantial wooden building was excavated, on a new site in this case but near an abandoned villa, datable to the late seventh century.[111] This could well have been an estate-centre, and may show what villas with surviving habitation looked like by now too—if it does, they had some parallels with north French sites like Servon. We have, here, around 700, a simpler version of the late Roman rural site hierarchy, with a significant shift to wood.

A concept of elaborate stone architecture had not left the countryside around Rome. In the late eighth century the popes systematized many of their rural landholdings into manorial estates (*domuscultae*), and two centres of the *domusculta Capracorum* have been excavated, both in the context of British School work in the northern quadrant, S. Cornelia and Mola di Monte Gelato.[112] Both had a similar structure: a stone-built estate complex focused on a church. Their closest rural architectural forerunners are villas, although no direct continuities can be traced in these cases, for S. Cornelia is on a new site, and Mola's villa seems to have been abandoned after 550. It is possible that church-based estates, specifically around Rome, borrowed architectural forms from the city, which was still large and architecturally imposing, or else that there was a continuing, more generic, assumption that stone building was appropriate to churches. This latter view would be supported by the fact that far and away the most elaborate rural buildings known in early medieval Italy are the great late eighth- and ninth-century monastic complexes: Farfa in this area, Novalesa, S. Vincenzo al Volturno, Montecassino elsewhere.[113] Either way, however, *domuscultae* firmly restated the sort of rural estate-based site hierarchy which had been a feature of the Roman empire, and which had probably continued in Lazio without a break. The weakening of hierarchies that we have seen in Emilia was probably never likely to occur in the hinterland of a city whose elites remained as rich (on a sub-regional level) as those of Rome (above, pp. 205–8). In the areas of Lazio where they dominated, the first major settlement shift would only be with the sharp concentration of settlement into fortified villages that marked *incastellamento* in the tenth and eleventh centuries.[114] Estate-centres and dispersal were, all the same, not the only eighth-century settlement forms in this sub-region. A few kilometres to the

[111] Moreland, 'Casale San Donato, 1992'; at pp. 197–8 he shows this was called Cicilianus in the eighth century (cf. below, p. 555). For the survey, idem, 'The Farfa survey'; idem and Pluciennik, 'Casale San Donato', pp. 478–80. For a tighter dating of the site, see Patterson and Roberts, 'New light', p. 423.

[112] Christie, *Three South Etrurian churches*, pp. 13–68, 175–88; Potter and King, *Mola di Monte Gelato*, pp. 78–98. For *domuscultae*, see above, p. 297.

[113] See respectively Clark, *Farfa*; Cantino Wataghin, 'Monasteri in Piemonte', pp. 172–9; Hodges, *San Vincenzo*, I, II, with idem and Mitchell, *The basilica*; Pantoni, *Le vicende*.

[114] Toubert, *Les structures*, pp. 303–48; Hubert, 'L'*incastellamento*', is a survey of recent excavations in Lazio, which doubts that there was much concentrated settlement before 900; cf. Wickham, *Il problema dell'incastellamento*, pp. 53–66, for microregional difference.

north of Mola, we begin also to find hilltop sites from the late eighth century onwards, for example, at Ponte Nepesino and Mazzano Romano: these are both future fortified villages. Whether they were either fortified or agglomerated before 900 is not wholly clear, but at Ponte Nepesino there is evidence of at least a small concentrated settlement, with wooden buildings.[115] This shift in the focus of settlement hierarchies (which probably still included scattered houses as well) was new, but it coexisted with the nearby survival of older patterns.

Tuscany shows similar variabilities, which are visible both in its archaeology and in its documents. Marco Valenti's work on two areas of the southern Chianti is remarkable in that the two areas seem so different. North of Castelnuovo di Berardenga, a relatively remote area north-east of Siena, villas seem to stop around 500; what replaces them is a 'chaotic' network of very simple isolated houses on hill slopes, usually built of wood or even pressed earth, with no settlement hierarchy at all until villages began to crystallize, perhaps in the eighth century, but perhaps not until the *incastellamento* period around 1000—and it was far from complete even then.[116] At Poggibonsi and Montarrenti, by contrast, 30 km to the west, in the fertile Valdelsa, on or near what would soon be the major inland road of Italy, relatively articulated hilltop villages with wooden buildings have been dated to, respectively, the late sixth century and the late seventh century onwards. These may well represent the basic local settlement model by 700, and have parallels in several parts of inland southern Tuscany.[117] Further north, a village pattern can be postulated for the Appennine mountains of northern Tuscany on the basis of documentary evidence for the Garfagnana and the late Roman/early medieval excavation of Filattiera in the Lunigiana (which was, unlike other villages, a valley site).[118] Around Monte Amiata in the south of Tuscany, a mixture of hilltop villages and, closer to the monastery of the Amiata, scattered estate-centres and peasant houses can be identified in eighth- and ninth-century documents. The estate-centres in that zone seem sometimes, though not always, to be on hills too, although the real period for the flowering of hilltop settlement would once again be in

---

[115] Cameron, 'Il castello di Ponte Nepesino'; Potter, 'Excavations in Mazzano Romano'. For Byzantine *castra* in this area, see most recently Zanini, *Le Italie bizantine*, pp. 260–8. Abruzzo is another zone with a similarly complex mix of late dispersed settlement and occasional early concentration, both largely replaced by the settlement concentration of the *incastellamento* period: see Staffa, 'Le campagne abruzzesi'; Feller, *Les Abruzzes*, pp. 128–34.

[116] Valenti, *Carta archeologica*, I, pp. 360–3, 401–5; idem, 'La Toscana', pp. 95–9. For the late survival of fragmented settlement in part of the area, see Wickham, 'Documenti scritti', pp. 84–91.

[117] Valenti, *Poggio Imperiale*; idem, 'La collina di Poggio Imperiale', pp. 18–30; idem and Salvadori, 'Il periodo altomedievale'; for Montarrenti see Cantini, *Il castello di Montarrenti*. These two sites are set into the context of an array of similar sites in central and southern Tuscany, generally less fully published as yet, in Valenti, *L'insediamento altomedievale*, who argues that they are typical of Tuscany as a whole.

[118] Giannichedda, *Filattiera*, pp. 31–7; Wickham, *Mountains*, pp. 33–7.

the *incastellamento* period.[119] Hilltop locations for estate-centres can also be proposed for parts of the coast, and for the Chianti, and also elsewhere. Some of these were, again, large enough to be villages, like Scarlino on the coast, but others seem as yet to have been isolated complexes of the S. Donato or Mola type, and would thus fit into a more general dispersed settlement hierarchy like that we have seen for much of Lazio.[120] This latter model can also be identified from the eighth-century documents for the Lucca plain, in which a network of estate-centres, churches, and scattered houses is clearly visible, with no concentrations of settlement at all.[121]

This array of microregional differences—doubtless incomplete, for only the Lucchesia and the Senese have been studied in detail—is only alarming if one forgets that just the same level of variability is visible in the Tuscan countryside today. It may well be that we shall discover that such differentiation had always existed, even if subordinated before 500 to the regular spatial articulation of the villa network; after *incastellamento*, castles would articulate equally divergent settlement hierarchies.[122] But the Tuscan situation can be separated out into three major types of settlement pattern after 500. The first is the continuance of a dispersed hierarchy of estate-centres and scattered peasant houses, analogous to that of the empire. The second is the beginnings of an articulation of the landscape by relatively concentrated villages, which sometimes still coexisted with dispersed patterns. The third is the complete breakdown of all settlement hierarchies, as in the south-eastern Chianti. These have different sorts of implications for the way local social structures worked, as we shall see later.

Two other points need to be made about this network. The first is that there is in some places, in the earliest middle ages, the beginning of a move to hilltop settlement, normally as a dominant element in a hierarchy, although the patterns of such hierarchies are of very varying types. But this trend is not universal; nor is it part of a steady move from a lowland-focused (villa) pattern in, say, 400 to an upland-focused (castle or village) pattern in, say, 1000, for it can coexist with dispersed settlement for centuries. This inconsistent *perchement*, to use the French term, is a common feature in the western Mediterranean in the early middle ages. We have already seen it for early medieval Provence and Languedoc, where it started a little earlier than in Italy, in the fifth century (p. 469)—though it should be noted that not every village in the settlement patterns of Mediterranean Gaul was actually

---

[119] Wickham, 'Paesaggi sepolti', pp. 106–22; Augenti, 'Dai *castra* tardoantichi', p. 36, for an eighth-century hilltop site (pp. 34–7 for previous settlement found on later castle sites).

[120] Ceccarelli Lemut, 'Scarlino', pp. 33 ff., for coastal estate-centres; Francovich, 'Changing structures', p. 165, for Scarlino. For coastal hilltop and hill-slope settlement in the sixth and seventh centuries, see further Guideri, 'Il popolamento medievale', pp. 15–21; Dallai, 'Prospezioni archeologiche'; Dallai and Farinelli, 'Castel di Pietra', pp. 55–8, for field surveys.

[121] See above, p. 390.

[122] As argued in Wickham, 'Documenti scritti'; see now for more detailed analyses Francovich and Ginatempo, *Castelli*, I.

on a hilltop site (one well-studied counter-example is Lunel). Exactly what it means in Italy is as yet unclear. It has no direct relationship to defence, for so much other settlement was not in the hills, and few hilltop settlements were fortified as yet, except the public *castra*, which are documented here and there, in Lazio and Tuscany as elsewhere.[123] One might hesitate to attribute to it a clear overarching economic cause, either, for its incidence is too variable, and I have anyway already expressed caution about standard systemic economic explanations for settlement change (p. 472). But, in a framework of settlement patterns that were still mostly dominated by dispersal, *perchement* is certainly a new development; it marks at least a cultural change.

The second point is to stress that, in Italy, early medieval settlement was overwhelmingly in wood. As in northern Gaul in the fourth century, this marks a clear cultural change: the generalized adoption of a form of building technique that had previously been restricted to the simplest peasant housing (and not all of that). Elite groups adopted it, too, for estate-centres are also in wood (except the *domuscultae*, at least), and so are, often, even castles in their earliest phases.[124] Elite difference no longer depended on architectural elaboration; it must have been expressed in different ways, for elites certainly continued to exist in most places. (Hilltop locations themselves may indeed have been one example of the alternative forms of elite expression.) One reason for this shift is that wood is a medium that is easy to deal with: peasants could easily build their own houses without expert help, and also the houses of their lords if they had them; it therefore fits a world with fewer expert artisans. But one should not overstress this; stone is hardly impossible for peasants to cut, and anyway artisans in, for example, ceramics continued to exist, in Tuscany as elsewhere (pp. 731–41). Economic exigencies do not explain the whole process; again, a cultural shift had taken place as well. Recent work shows that a similar development took place in northern Spain too (below, p. 491)

---

[123] For Lunel, see above, n. 77. Lowland villas also eventually turned into villages at Villandro in the Alto Adige (Dal Ri and Rizzi, 'L'edilizia residenziale'), and probably in Sicily (see above, n. 98). For public *castra* in Lazio, see above, n. 115; for Tuscany see Augenti, 'Dai *castra* tardoantichi'; for northern Italy, see above, n. 102. One sub-region where a mixture of villas and villages was replaced by a hilltop village network by 700 or so was Calabria: Noyé, 'Économie et société', pp. 254–6, 261–3; eadem, 'Economia e società', pp. 598–600, 623–9. A parallel pattern has been argued more hypothetically for the Garda area: Mancassola and Saggioro, 'Ricerche sul territorio'. Saggioro, *Paesaggi rurali medievali*, II, pp. 38–53, for the lower Veronese plain, argues for dispersed huts being replaced by small grouped settlements by the eighth century, interrelated with estate-centres, although he avoids arguing for an early settlement concentration. But Francovich, 'Changing structures', pp. 158–67, and Francovich and Hodges, *Villa to village*, pp. 61–105, see *perchement* as normal in Italy by the eighth century. Debate in this area is still in flux.

[124] See in general Brogiolo, *Edilizia residenziale*; Valenti, *Poggio Imperiale*, pp. 159–218; and the documentary survey in Galetti, *Abitare nel medioevo*, pp. 78–93.

A final, but important, point about Italy is that although Lazio and Tuscany are similar in the arrays of settlement pattern they show, they were very different in the articulation of local territorial identity. In the Byzantine parts of Italy (which include Lazio), the *fundus* pattern, already described (p. 470), continued, right up to the *incastellamento* period; that was the first time that settlement territories became important in our Lazial documentation.[125] Contrast the areas under Lombard rule (which include Tuscany): here, as soon as documents begin around 700, geographical/ settlement-based units, rather than property-based units, dominate. People sell and donate, not portions of named estates, *fundi*, but lands in *vicus* X or *locus* Y (to use the Lucchese terminology of the period—around the Amiata it is *casale* or *vicus* or *locus*; around Varsi in the territory of Parma it is *casale* or *vicus*).[126] These were the territories of what can be called villages. Villages like this did not have to be concentrated settlements; in the Lucchesia they certainly were not, for example. Nor were they necessarily socially active or strong; in the Lucchesia, as we have seen (p. 390), people were sometimes uncertain even where village boundaries lay. But they now regularly defined identity, and, where necessary, could structure collective action, in a way that was rather harder in areas patterned by *fundi*. People identified with villages, and often stated which village they were from in documents. Rothari, legislating in 643, does not refer to villages (*vici* in his text) so very often, but, when they appear, they are clearly characterized. Serious rural violence consists of people going into villages to attack others, and to burn down houses; villagers (*vicini*) swear oaths to each other under some circumstances; villages have territories, called *viciniae*, and horse-theft is more serious if one takes the horse out of them.[127] Rothari was probably thinking of relatively concentrated settlements, which were maybe more common around his capital at Pavia (not an area of archaeological survey), but such conceptualizations were taken up in parts of the Lombard kingdom where settlement was dispersed, and applied there too.

One can hardly imagine that the concept of the village was invented by Rothari; this is not the sort of task that kings undertake. Nor is there any reason to suppose that the Lombards as an incoming group were particularly committed to it. But in early medieval Italy the concept does stop at the edge of the Lombard kingdom, with *fundi* still dominant beyond it, and it seems to be largely new—Varsi, for example, with its eighth-century *vici* and

---

[125] On *fundi* in Lazio, see Migliario, *Strutture*, pp. 58–71; Marazzi, *I 'patrimonia'*, e.g. p. 216. For the Romagna, Castagnetti, *L'organizzazione*, pp. 171–9.

[126] See *CDL*, I, II, *passim*. For the Lombard–Byzantine contrast, see Castagnetti, *L'organizzazione*, pp. 205–12. For Varsi as formerly in the Veleiate, see Criniti, *La tabula alimentaria*, p. 237. For the complex situation in the Sabina, in the Lombard duchy of Spoleto but on the edge of the Byzantine territory of Rome, see Costambeys, *Piety, property*, ch. 3.1.ii–v; a geographical basis for territorial units predominated here too.

[127] Rothari 19, 279, 340, 346; cf. also Liutprand 134, 141.

casalia, had been part of the territory of Veleia, with its second-century *fundi*. Its existence does not simply derive from the development of concentrated settlement, either, for, although overall there were probably more of such settlements by 700 than there had been in 500 in Italy, there was still dispersal in Tuscany, and, conversely, there may have been some concentrated settlement in the *fundus* areas of Lazio. Andrea Castagnetti has argued that the survival of *fundi* in Byzantine areas can be linked to their continuing use as a structure in tax cadasters, which is possible; their continuity into and after the eighth century, when tax ceased, may have been because by then the period of crisis was over.[128] We might suppose, conversely, that the confusion of the Lombard invasions encouraged a general sense among peasants in the Lombard zones that their local relationships mattered more than who owned their land. Whether the territorial solidarities that emerged were strong or weak (which would have depended on the power of landowners and on local agrarian practices, as well as settlement pattern), this conquest of an identity was an important step towards peasant co-operative action, a significant moment for peasant collectivity in Italy. It did not create a community in itself; it is enough to compare an eighth-century Italian *vicus* with a *chōrion* in the East to see how far the former had to go (see above, pp. 462–4). Large collective settlements were in the future, the tenth and eleventh centuries; politically organized communities would have to wait until the twelfth.[129] But the first step was taken here.

Let us move on from Italy, passing Mediterranean Gaul, which has already been discussed, and into the Iberian peninsula. Here, too, settlement structures after the end of villas were highly diverse. In Catalonia, first, the pattern that seems to predominate by the eighth century is a network of small villages. We cannot be fully sure of this in the absence of field surveys, but some quite concentrated settlements have been found in excavation. At El Bovalar, an inland site near Lleida, there was a set of square stone houses, clustered closely around a church, with a communal oil-press; its ceramics are all local and largely hand-made, but its later phases can be dated by a group of coins of 690–715. At Vilaclara, in hill country slightly nearer to the coast, a similar site was excavated, although without a church this time and also much smaller, with local ceramics of slightly better quality, dating from the seventh and eighth centuries. Puig Rom, on the coast, although a *castrum*, is sufficiently similar in its structures to make a third example.[130] We have no documents for Catalonia until the ninth century, but in the late ninth and tenth centuries village territories, here called *villae*, were so numerous in

---

[128] Castagnetti, *L'organizzazione*, pp. 172–5.
[129] Wickham, *Community and clientele*, pp, 185–241.
[130] See, respectively, Palol, *El Bovalar*; Enrich i Hoja, *Vilaclara*; Palol, 'Castro hispanovisigodo de "Puig Rom" '. See below, Ch. 11, n. 109, for the ceramics of these sites. Other parallels are referred to in Gurt and Palet, 'Structuration du territoire', p. 323.

lowland areas that they must have been very small, and maybe less concentrated than El Bovalar. In the Pyrenees, by contrast, ninth-century documents are unequivocal in their picture of coherent *villae* and *castra*, concentrated settlements of up to a hundred people and more, with structured identities, including collective church-building by peasant proprietors.[131] We must be cautious about generalizing out from as ecologically specific a zone as the Pyrenees; the local dominance of peasant landowners is unlikely to have been quite so normal closer to the coast. But the Pyrenean picture does at least roughly fit the measure of El Bovalar, and it is possible that such villages could be found across much of inland Catalonia. We thus gain an impression of mountain and inland areas dominated by concentrated settlement, and of lowland villages with, possibly, a more fluid settlement pattern. This would parallel the coexistence of both concentrated and dispersed settlement in neighbouring Languedoc and Provence.

The area of Spain with the most systematic local study up to now is the coast of Alicante–Murcia and the mountains behind, thanks to parallel field researches by Paul Reynolds and Sonia Gutiérrez. They focus on ceramic networks (see below, pp. 748–51), but, in Gutiérrez's work at least, settlement change is also analysed in some detail. This is an area where most villas ended in the fifth and sixth centuries; instead of a villa hierarchy, a network of small settlements can be found from the fifth century onwards. Lowland settlements seem to show a break in the eighth century, with new ones appearing in the early Arab period; highland settlements tend to show greater continuities from the fifth century to the tenth, even if not every century has necessarily been identified in the ceramics found in each in survey. These settlements could best be regarded as very small villages, but they do not seem to be located in an articulated pattern: less than are the villages of Catalonia. This point is reinforced in the eighth century by two other developments: the breakdown of most of the Roman/Visigothic urban network (here, unusually for the Mediterranean, and certainly unlike Catalonia, urban revival in the ninth and tenth centuries was focused on new centres, with Murcia replacing the old regional centre of Cartagena: see below, pp. 659–60), and the collapse of ceramic specialization along the coast, for most pottery in the eighth and early ninth centuries there was hand-made. Only in the tenth century, with urban revival and the establishment of a network of fortifications (*ḥuṣūn*), some of them substantial

---

[131] For the small *villae* of the lowlands around Girona, see To, 'El marc de les comunitats pageses', pp. 212–26; and Abad, *Pautes de poblament*, pp. 135–42, with tables and map. For church-building, Bonnassie, *From slavery*, pp. 243–6 (with P. Guichard); the texts are in Baraut, 'Les actes de consacracions', nn. 1, 4–26. For substantial settlements, see e.g. Baraut, 'Els documents', nn. 39–40; *El archivo condal*, n. 38 with appendix II-A; Abadal, *Catalunya carolíngia*, III, n. 132. These Pyrenean *castra* probably resembled the *castros* of the Asturias; see above, n. 102, and Ch. 4, n. 189.

population-centres, did a settlement hierarchy and a specialized artisanal tradition return.[132]

Two other surveys, that of Antonio Gómez for the Granada coast around Salobreña, and that of Juan Carlos Castillo for the upper Guadalquivir valley around Jaén, fill out this picture; the former is similar, the latter less so. The Granada coast, a rather more barren area than that of Alicante, shows steady fifth- and sixth-century recession, with some site abandonment, in the context of the steady breakdown of Mediterranean exchange, which perhaps affected this part of the coast earlier than those further north (p. 748), and then the development of small upland sites with more of a subsistence orientation. As around Alicante, this seems to represent a period of relatively weak settlement hierarchies, and is only reversed with the development of *ḥuṣūn* around 900, which also coincides with the revival of relatively sophisticated ceramics, both unglazed and glazed (glazed pottery along the coast seems to begin with the Pechina kilns of the late ninth century, situated between the coastlands of Alicante-Murcia and of Granada).[133] The Jaén area, by contrast, is close to the major economic and political focus of southern Spain, the Guadalquivir valley between Córdoba and Seville, although it is higher and more marginal than that zone. Here, survey shows the continued occupation of a substantial number of late Roman/Visigothic sites into the early Arab period, with a tendency for upland settlements to show more continuity (though there are some along the river as well); this emphasis on the uplands has parallels with patterns found on the coast. But the major upland settlement from our period that has been excavated in this area, Peñaflor, an eighth- to early tenth-century site, is quite a substantial village, and has relatively well-made pottery, better than that found in the same time-range on the coast; we cannot here deduce the same breakdown of settlement hierarchies and artisanal specialization that we could there.[134] This is likely to be because Córdoba, the Arab capital, is only 100 km from Peñaflor; this was probably a zone of continuing landowning and exchange structures. Unfortunately, there has been no systematic work further down the Guadalquivir for the Arab period, so we cannot check this hypothesis as yet; but overlooking another city-orientated area, the irrigated land (*vega*) around Granada, a similar village settlement has been excavated, El Castillón de Montefrío, this time with possible seventh-century origins, which also has quite good-quality ceramics across the three centuries of its occupation. The Loja survey, slightly further west, supports this picture, and presents us with a settlement hierarchy, focused on

---

[132] Reynolds, *Settlement and pottery*, esp. pp. 13–14, 25, and figs. 108–12; Gutiérrez Lloret, *La cora de Tudmīr*, esp. pp. 275–89, 327–36 (and *passim* for ceramics; see below, Ch. 11, n. 110).

[133] Gómez Becerra, *El poblamento altomedieval*, esp. pp. 430, 447–87.

[134] Castillo, *La Campiña de Jaén*, esp. pp. 147–209; for Peñaflor, see ibid., pp. 241–7, with Salvatierra and Castillo, 'Peñaflor'; idem, *La Campiña de Jaén*, pp. 40–124, for ceramics.

hilltop sites, which lasted throughout our period; the surveyer, Miguel Jiménez, links this to the survival of aristocratic landowning.[135] We could thus postulate a continuation of settlement hierarchies and relatively developed ceramic production on and above the major plains of this part of Spain, contrasting with a greater breakdown of settlement pattern and exchange, and a drift into the mountains, in more marginal areas, especially in the coastal provinces. Both, however, would become more clearly restructured in the tenth century, the century of the Umayyad caliphate, the period of the most coherent political system in Spain in the whole early middle ages.

These patterns are even less a guide to Spain as a whole than Lazio and Tuscany are for Italy. The Mediterranean coast of Spain became increasingly marginalized from c.550 onwards, when politics focused on inland centres (Toledo, then Córdoba), and seaborne commerce steadily weakened (below, pp. 748–55). We cannot, however, easily fill out these brief observations for areas further inland than Jaén. Significant excavations in the countryside around Madrid and elsewhere are beginning to show small Visigothic-period settlements, prevalently in wood, some of which continue into later centuries. How these fitted into sub-regional settlement structures is not yet clear, although a recent small field survey near Salamanca suggests the maintenance of a dispersed pattern in that area throughout the Visigothic period. On a larger geographical scale, however, although good area studies are beginning, notably in the northern Meseta and the Cordillera Cantábrica, they are as yet only registering absences for the period after the fifth or sixth century, with only isolated sites filling the gap before the tenth century—enough to disprove Claudio Sánchez-Albornoz's depopulation theory (above, pp. 230–1), but not yet enough to allow us to be sure what detailed settlement patterns were there instead.[136] It is the coast, as yet, which gives us our best material for Spain. Let us return to the coast, then, for a few final observations.

The first point is that the summaries made for each of the coastal areas have been based above all on the archaeological register. Neither Visigothic nor Arab documents are sufficiently locally specific to allow us to use them to back up such very variable microregional patterns. All that one can say about them is that texts of both periods attest geographical, village-based, identifications, the *loci* of many Visigothic texts,[137] the *qurā* (cf. modern

---

[135] Motos, *El poblado medieval de 'El Castillón'*; Jiménez, *El poblamiento*, pp. 67–122.

[136] For the Madrid area, see esp. Vigil-Escalera, 'Cabaños de época visigoda'. Azkarate and Quirós, 'Arquitectura doméstica altomedieval', pp. 43–56, generalize this to northern Spain and discuss the wood. For Salamanca, see Ariño and Rodríguez, 'El poblamiento romano'. For area studies, see Escalona, *Sociedad y territorio*, esp. pp. 58–72; Fernández Mier, *Génesis del territorio*; Martín, *Poblamiento*, esp. pp. 107–17; Gutiérrez, 'Sobre los orígines'.

[137] Visigothic law is somewhat vague about settlement, but certainly assumes the existence of villages (*vici* or *loci*): e.g. *LV*, III.4.17, IX.1.21, 2.8, and the more precise *Form. Wis.*, nn. 5, 8. Historiography on this issue is often generic: see e.g. García Moreno, *Historia de la España*

Spanish *alquerías*) of many Arab texts, with fortified settlements (*ḥuṣūn*) becoming more common after the end of our period;[138] the more detailed northern charters from Catalonia and Asturias (–León), beginning after 900, similarly stress villages (here *vilae* or *villae*), as we have seen for Catalonia.[139] But village-focused territorial identifications are not in themselves signs of concentrated settlement, as we have already seen in the Italian context.

Another point is that I have implicitly stressed internal developments when discussing these Spanish case studies. This is a controverted position with respect to the Muslim areas of Spain, which after 710 included all the coastal areas except Catalonia, with some people arguing for a considerable weight to be put on Berber (or Arab) settlement, especially in eastern al-Andalus, the location of these case studies, and others preferring to stress 'indigenous' occupation, which became 'Islamicized' in the tenth century. As implied in the context of earlier discussions of the aristocracy (above, p. 339), it seems to me that it is not necessary, when characterizing these shifts in settlement hierarchies, to assume that any of them were necessarily the result of immigration. It is, of course, quite *possible* that some new upland settlements, say, had Berbers in them; but many others had not, as far as can yet be seen, greatly changed since 700, and even new settlements could perfectly easily be the result of population shifts by peasants who were there already, as was the case in southern Gaul or Italy.[140] Finally, there is no reason to see in these shifts any sign of global agrarian 'decline'. This image is often used by historians and archaeologists, following chronicle references to wars, plagues, locusts, and so on, to underpin the idea of a sharp break at the end of the Visigothic period—sharp enough, for example, to destroy the Roman irrigation system of the *horta* of Valencia, or to harm even the more mundane and marginal dry agriculture that was practised in most of the pre-Islamic eastern mountains.[141] Such chronicle references are, of course, a standard feature of the rhetoric of medieval narratives, and it is anyway hard to see why Spain should have been so much worse hit by disasters than anywhere else was, not least the North Africa the Berbers came from. Settlement shifts of the kinds just described can certainly coexist with a largely unchanged agrarian landscape. The Spanish coast is not, in fact,

visigoda, pp. 204–11; Isla, '*Villa, villula*', gives a much more precise and detailed analysis, although he does not confront the issue of settlement patterns.

[138] See in general Acién, 'Poblamiento y fortificación', and Glick, *From Muslim fortress*, pp. 13–29, a good survey of the state of research in the mid-1990s; the most significant monograph on *ḥuṣūn* is Bazzana *et al.*, *Les châteaux ruraux*.

[139] For Catalonia, see n. 131; for Asturias and León, see n. 136, with the surveys of Mínguez, *El dominio*, pp. 55–63; Martínez Sopena, *La Tierra de Campos*, pp. 106–25.

[140] See Ch. 4, n. 195, and above, n. 132, for general bibliography. Some of the more detailed discussion of this issue has recently been very fraught.

[141] For irrigation continuity, Glick, *From Muslim fortress*, pp. 64–7, is sensible; the Arabs enormously expanded it, of course.

dramatically out of line in its *types* of settlement change with respect to other parts of the western Mediterranean, and one can conclude that the sorts of explanations that can be found elsewhere would work here, too.

I suggested in the context of Italy that three settlement models dominated the early middle ages, between the end of villas and the appearance of castles: first, a dispersed hierarchy focused on estate-centres of a rather simpler kind than villas had been; second, a pattern focused on concentrated settlements, though often containing a substantial percentage of scattered houses between these concentrations; third, a breakdown of hierarchies altogether. Spain seems to fit this array of possibilities without difficulty; broadly, the case studies just discussed tend to fit into either model 2 (Catalonia, Jaén, Loja) or model 3 (Alicante, the Granada coast), with only the small Salamanca survey suggesting model 1, at least up to the generalization of fortified settlements in the tenth century. A warning to the reader must be added: in survey work, it is not easy to tell an isolated and unmonumental estate-centre from a peasant house, and model 1 may thus be under-represented in these case studies; also, if the apparently small and unstructured settlements of the eighth and ninth centuries on the Alicante coast turned out to resemble Peñaflor, then the contrast that has been cautiously drawn here between Jaén and the coast would have to be nuanced somewhat. But on the basis of what has been published, the major opposition in well-studied areas of Spain in this period is between areas looking to villages and areas without much differentiation in a largely scattered habitat, although even villages were rarely yet as structured a feature of the rural landscape as they would be in the 'land of *ḥuṣūn*', to use Manuel Acién's phrase, of the tenth century and onwards.[142] Finally, in the Italian (and French) context, we have seen what can be called an inconsistent *perchement*, an occasional trend to hilltop sites; in Spain, too, this can be found, and it was perhaps more generalized than in Italy, for a majority of known early medieval sites in Spanish survey areas are in hill or mountain country. This is a significant homogeneity, although it partly depends on the fact that plains areas in Spain have had little significant field survey. Here, too, future work may well significantly change our current impressions of the period.

If one wants to identify social differentiation on the basis of archaeological research, then, as has already been proposed, two good guides are the complexity of exchange, and the articulation of settlement hierarchies. Broadly, the elaboration of artisanal goods (as seen, for example, in ceramic production and distribution) implies people rich enough to provide demand sufficient to sustain production; and, if one finds that production decreased rapidly in complexity, one can conclude that demand for products beyond the level of the local peasantry—whose needs could be supplied by part-time

[142] The phrase appears in the subtitle of Acién, 'Poblamiento y fortificación'.

(peasant) artisans—must have decreased too. This argument will be discussed in detail in Chapter 11; see also pp. 535–47. As for settlement: a hierarchy focused on estate-centres is obviously one that privileges landowners. One that consists only of concentrated settlements is more ambiguous, for such villages could have one or more external landlords, grouping and controlling dependants from outside, or a major landowner living inside the settlement, or no large owners at all (as in the ninth-century Pyrenees, demonstrably a zone of autonomous peasant owners); but even the latter situation is at least one of some social complexity, involving articulated sets of local relationships, as we saw in Chapter 7. But where, instead of villas and villages, one only finds homogeneous arrays of houses, isolated or in small groups, then it is harder to argue for major status differences. And where, in addition to this breakdown in rural settlement differentiation, which we have seen for example in eastern Chianti, we also have a radical deurbanization and a breakdown in ceramic complexity, as on the Alicante to Granada coast, then a major social simplification must have taken place, in this case beginning in the seventh century and reaching an extreme, probably, in the late eighth, before a recuperation in hierarchies of all kinds at the end of the ninth. This coastal strip must have been an area of particularly poor aristocratic survival in that period. Manuel Acién has argued on documentary grounds for a survival of a Roman/Visigothic aristocracy in the south until the civil wars in the decades around 900, the 'first *fitna*', which were won definitively by Córdoba in the 920s. The best-known of these aristocrats, 'Umar ibn Ḥafṣūn (d. 917), was based in Bobastro, in the mountains west of Málaga. The surveys of areas of al-Andalus that have been discussed here at least imply one thing: that aristocratic equivalents to Ibn Ḥafṣūn, whether of Roman-Visigothic or Arab-Berber origin, are unlikely to have existed further up the coast to the east of Malaga. They may, on the other hand, have existed in the uplands of Jaén, if the relative articulation in settlement and artisanal production proposed for the latter area are any guide; and indeed it can be shown that those uplands contained leaders who participated actively in the first *fitna*.[143] Predictions of this kind may be further testable in the future, when survey work comes closer to areas that are (by the standards of Arab-period narrative sources) relatively well documented.

The settlements discussed in this section fall into the relatively unstructured period between the villa network and the castle network. They are difficult to seize as a whole, for no easily visible framing device can be used to characterize them; they are hard to find, in the absence of well-studied ceramics and impressive ruins; the area studies that we can use to identify

---

[143] For the first *fitna*, see Acién, 'Poblamiento y fortificación', and idem, '*Umar ibn Ḥafṣūn*; the second edition of the latter contains reference to recent debates on the issue. For Jaén, see Castillo, *La Campiña de Jaén*, pp. 207–9, and now above all Salvatierra, *La crisis del emirato omeya*.

them are still relatively few, and often ambiguous. There need to be more of the latter. But the absence of regularity in the settlement patterns discussed here is an indicator in itself: it is a normal feature of the western Mediterranean. *Incastellamento* itself, the next major change in settlement patterns, had highly diverse sub-regional and microregional forms, for that reason (even leaving out of consideration the fact that the appearance of private *castra/castella* in Latin Christian lands and of the *ḥuṣūn* of the highly centralized Umayyad caliphate were two very separate socio-political processes). Outside irrigated areas, Mediterranean agriculture is a highly individualistic practice, and peasants who carry it out can exercise considerable choice as to how to combine spatially, with kin or neighbours, in order to do so. Although I have correlated the simple existence of settlement hierarchies to aristocratic power, the way those hierarchies work out in detail—how much dispersed settlement there is, how large villages are—is to a substantial extent a peasant choice. The early middle ages in the western Mediterranean was a period in which the concept of village identity became available to peasants, mostly as a new development. This did not mean that peasants quickly developed strong communities, all the same; their settlement did not always crystallize into substantial villages, often not for a long while, and their collective action does not seem to have been very highly articulated (cf. above, pp. 389–93, for Lucca), in strong contrast to their east Mediterranean contemporaries. Without other indicators, we cannot tell what the parameters of peasant choices actually were, especially as they could vary very greatly in both time and space. But settlement patterns are peasant artefacts (they built the buildings, after all), and they need to be treated as such: they are, however hard to explain, the clearest imprint of the peasantry on the landscape.

4. Early medieval northern Europe

The last two sentences of the previous section apply equally to northern Europe. But villages are much more visible there too, and have also been more fully studied, thanks to a series of major excavations across the whole post-war period (and, more, sporadically, even before). Fieldwork, in fact, is a more recent development (the South Etruria survey was pathbreaking not only in southern Europe), and only in a small number of places—East Anglia, parts of the Netherlands, the Île de France—has it produced results that really help our analyses. On the other hand, northern Europe seems to show greater homogeneities than does the western Mediterranean, and it is easier to generalize there. Broadly, one can distinguish between two large regional groupings in the North in the early middle ages: one of relatively articulated villages, with larger houses inside them, and one of looser concentrations and smaller house-types, the boundary between them being very roughly a line running east from the Rhine mouth. We will look at the northern group first, focusing on Denmark, northern Germany, and the Netherlands; then at the southern group, focusing on southern Germany, northern France, and England. This survey will also be less detailed than was that for the Mediterranean, for in this field, unlike in the Mediterranean, there are several good syntheses already.[144]

A type-site for the northern group, the best village site for Denmark in our period and one of the most significant early medieval village excavations yet conducted, is Vorbasse in central Jutland. This is a village which has existed since the first century BC, although it has moved regularly, with nine different sites up to and including the present site, which has been stable since the twelfth century. These shifts have all been inside the same agricultural territory, however, the settlement never moving more than 400 metres at a time and usually less, until a leap of 800 metres to the present site. These shifts have not yet been satisfactorily explained, but they affirm the stability of the village as a social whole, for the same pattern recurs over and over on each site, a chessboard of rectangular farm complexes, each of them fenced since the third century, each with one or more long-houses at its centre, divided into a habitation area and a byre area, and one or two smaller rectangular houses and further subsidiary buildings. Buildings were all made of wood, generally solidly built with a post-hole construction. From the third century until the eighth, one of the farm complexes was in each village site rather larger, with a longer long-house and more subsidiary buildings, showing a village leader of some kind (cf. above, pp. 370–1). The settlement slowly changed in size, doubling from ten farms to twenty in around 300, returning to ten around 500, remaining steady thereafter until around 700, then decreasing to around seven farm enclosures, which were conversely rather larger in size, until 1100. The most substantial shifts in terms of village structures were made around 200, with the beginning of farm enclosures and the larger farmstead, and around 700, when enclosures were enlarged, and the village's layout became much more regularized, with, for example, sunken-floored buildings (*Grubenhäuser*) situated in the areas of farmsteads closest to the central road. (It is particularly interesting that neither of these structural changes coincides with the *Völkerwänderung* period of the fifth century, or the Viking period of the ninth.) Only from the eighth century are imported goods other than rare at Vorbasse, and in earlier periods the only impressive feature of peasant material culture there was the quality of house-building, but this was indeed impressive. Overall, it points to a network of prosperous peasant cultivators, each family with its

---

[144] The best overview is now Hamerow, *Early medieval settlements*; before that, Donat, *Haus, Hof und Dorf*, and Chapelot and Fossier, *The village and house*, pp. 27–128. More localized syntheses include Chapelot, 'L'habitat rural'; Lorren and Périn, 'Images de la Gaule rurale'; Theuws, 'Haus, Hof und Siedlung'; and Damminger, 'Dwellings, settlements'; and see n. 145 for Denmark and n. 166 for northern Francia.

own (perhaps unfree) dependants living in the same compound. The main farmstead, although larger and associated with more imported goods, was not typologically distinct from the others. It disappeared in the Viking period, but reappeared in the eleventh century; it is conceivable that by then it was the house of a village landlord, but there is no reason to believe this of earlier centuries. All the same, in our period village leadership was evidently stable, and probably hereditary; when, for example, the village shifted site around 300 to slightly further north, the main farm kept its original position. I discussed earlier (pp. 370–5) some hypotheses about the nature of village-level and other local leadership in Denmark; the society of Vorbasse probably worked in ways that were analogous to that of Malling, too (even if that example is essentially based on English material: pp. 428–34), although with a much slower and less consistent move towards dominance by a single landowner.[145]

Vorbasse is at present unique—not just in Denmark, but, I believe, among the rural excavations of the whole of Europe—in its continuous occupation for over two millennia; but it does have parallels, both inside Denmark and outside. Several other early medieval Danish sites match its shifting but stable community: Nørre Snede, not far away in central Jutland (the best-studied), Stavad and Hjemsted elsewhere in the Jutland peninsula, Bellinge-gård in eastern Sjælland. These have shorter time-frames for the most part, presumably because some of the village shifts have not been found; one village which did not shift, Omgård in western Jutland, was occupied for rather longer, from the fourth (at the latest) to the tenth centuries. At Nørre Snede, the number of farms stayed at ten with each shift, between c.200 and c.700; a larger farm has not been found there.[146] As already noted, precisely why villages shifted is unclear, although one can at least propose some reasons why they did not have to remain in the same place before the twelfth century: the absence of three-field collective agriculture (in Denmark, agriculture seems to have focused on permanent manured infields, around which settlement could move, with two-field systems only developing later) and the absence of a church to fix the settlement being two important elements. One might simply say, that is, that village geography had not quite crystallized, in the way that churches, castles, and the carapace of the three-field system would impose, and that Vorbasse was simply moving around in the way that most dispersed peasant farms do everywhere. This does not explain the shifts, but it at least makes them less strange, less *necessary* to

---

[145] Vorbasse has no full publication, but its interims are good, and so are the overviews of its excavator, Steen Hvass. See Hvass, 'Die völkerwänderungszeitliche Siedlung'; 'The Viking age settlement'; 'Wikingerzeitliche Siedlungen'; and, for overviews, 'Jernalderens bebyggelse'; 'Rural settlements'. See further the comprehensive survey in Nissen-Joubert, *Peuplement*. On the status of the village leader, ibid., pp. 232–3, is sensible.

[146] See respectively Hansen, 'Nørre Snede'; Nissen-Joubert, *Peuplement*, pp. 222–3; Ethelberg, 'Hjemsted Banke'; Tornbjerg, 'Bellingegård'; Nielsen, 'Omgård'.

explain.[147] Richer sites, the isolated *stormandsgårder* and central places, remained in the same place, however, indicating that shifting settlement related to peasant, not elite, practices.

Villages began in Denmark around the fifth century BC; they coexisted with more dispersed settlement throughout. Concentrated villages are arguably commonest in Jutland in our period, with more dispersal on the islands.[148] It is also notable that villages were not, as in the early medieval western Mediterranean, near the top of a settlement hierarchy, but, rather, at its base. The political elites of Denmark lived in central places and isolated farms, leaving villages to the peasantry. As we saw in Chapter 6, that settlement hierarchy is unusually clear in this region, and acts as the core empirical underpinning of arguments about state-formation. In this chapter, the pattern is most important as a reminder that the autonomy of the prosperous peasant owners of villages like Vorbasse was not unlimited: they lived inside a network of political structures which, though weaker than those of more southern regions, were nonetheless always present. But that consistent pattern of wider power only reinforces the striking impression of stability that Danish peasant evidence gives us. There is no evidence that Danish villages like Vorbasse were under anyone's direct domination, either external or internal. Denmark's socio-economic framework was not unchanging, it is true. There were steady small-scale developments in village morphologies and building construction, and probably in agriculture; state-formation had faster ups and downs, with a low-point in 550–700 and then a revival; after 700 urbanization brought more exchange into the region, as we shall see (pp. 684–5), and another level of settlement hierarchy. But it did not undergo *dramatic* changes in its material culture or what we can deduce of its social structures, at any point in our period—less so than any of our regions outside the south-east Mediterranean. It is itself a type-example, of what a stable northern society looks like, which we can compare others to.

Frisia and Saxony were not at all unlike Denmark in some of their basic village structures. We can see sharper breaks here in the *Völkerwänderung* period, but excavated villages have some close parallels to Vorbasse. Feddersen Wierde, on the north German coast, on an artifical mound in a wetlands area, inhabited between the first century BC and the fifth AD, did not show the farmstead pattern of Vorbasse, probably because space did not permit; but its long-houses, arranged radially on the mound, are closely analogous to Danish ones. Elsewhere, where space was less at a premium, at Wijster in central Frisia, occupied from the mid-second century to the early

---

[147] For shifting settlement, see Hamerow, *Early medieval settlements*, pp. 100–2, 116–19.

[148] Hvass, 'Jernalderens bebyggelse'; for the island point, Nissen-Joubert, *Peuplement*, pp. 221–2, although see also Ch. 6, n. 157. For excavated isolated houses, apart from 'magnate farms' (for which see above, p. 370), see esp. Kaldal Mikkelson, 'Single farm', pp. 183–5, for Mørup in Jutland.

fifth, at nearby Odoorn, occupied from the seventh to the ninth, at Wijnaldum on the northern coast, occupied from the fifth to the tenth, at Kootwijk in south-eastern Frisia, occupied from the seventh to the tenth, or at Warendorf in southern Saxony, occupied from the mid-seventh to the late eighth, we find the chequerboard of farmsteads that was normal in Denmark, with a long-house in each surrounded by smaller buildings.[149] Danish long-houses were slightly longer than most buildings further south, 20–40 metres being normal at Vorbasse by contrast to 15–30 metres in Frisia or Saxony, and enclosures were often better demarcated in Denmark. Another difference is that more southerly villages, although they could sometimes shift their site, did so less often; even if the shorter periods of occupation of these settlements simply meant that they had moved from and to somewhere close (unlikely for Feddersen Wierde, but possible for several of the others), they still mostly maintained their excavated location for much longer than the peasants of Vorbasse ever managed before 1100. But in other respects these settlements were similar in type. The scale of Frisian and Saxon villages was analogous to Denmark: ten to twenty farmsteads was a common scale, with only Feddersen Wierde slightly larger. The latter also had a substantially larger farmstead for a village leader (called a *Herrenhof*, a 'lord's farmstead', by the excavator), inside an enclosure, unlike the rest of the site, with a concentration of imports and artisanal material inside it. Most recently, the first signs of a settlement hierarchy are beginning to be visible in Frisia, as well.[150]

We can thus propose a similar structure for village society in the whole area from the Rhine mouth to the Swedish border, which existed across our entire period. Peasants organized their lives around concentrated settlements; in these, they maintained a spatial separation between the family units (together with their unfree dependants) living inside each farmstead, each of which could have contained up to twenty-five people.[151] Houses were large, in order to house animals as well as humans, but also very well built. These settlements had their own part-time craftsmen (ironworking and weaving are well documented, pottery less so) and internal hierarchies, although little sign of permanent dominance, either by external or internal lords. They were as effective and coherent foci as any village in Syria or Egypt, even if seldom as large: 200–400 people seems to be the maximum settlement size for villages north of the imperial frontier. They must have

---

[149] Respectively, Haarnagel, *Feddersen Wierde*, II; van Es, *Wijster*; Waterbolk, 'Odoorn'; Besteman, *Wijnaldum*, I; Heidinga, *Medieval settlement*; Winkelmann, 'Warendorf'. Of these Wijnaldum was in many respects the least typical, with its turf houses and an apparent craft specialization. For settlement patterns and their variety see esp. Hamerow, *Early medieval settlements*, pp. 52–77.

[150] Haarnagel, *Feddersen Wierde*, II, pp. 319–21; for settlement hierarchies see the tentative comments in Heidinga, *Frisia*, pp. 26–8.

[151] Donat, *Haus, Hof und Dorf*, p. 123.

been the basic building-blocks of all wider socio-political action, whether at village or sub-regional level, as important as the family as a stage for solidarity, jealousy, and small-scale competitive negotiation.

Further south, by contrast, villages were less coherent. Houses were smaller, seldom including byres, and were often less well built; *Grubenhäuser* were much more numerous; village layouts were less orderly and often more scattered. This was a difference that largely pre-dated the invasion period, with (future) Franks and Alemans making up this southern culture-area, by contrast to the (future) Frisians and Saxons to the north. Although these identities were considerably less clear-cut before 400, there must be an element of cultural difference behind the distinction, with perhaps some ecological justification too, for the climate is warmer, thus making byres for cattle less essential (though this argument should not be pushed too far: climatic difference is not *that* huge). The problem is the Anglo-Saxons, for their settlements in many ways resemble the tradition of the Frankish-Alemannic culture-area—as we shall see, their villages were for long among the simplest and least structured of the southern group; but their origins as a people was, if anywhere, the coastal area of Saxony (and maybe Frisia and Denmark to a lesser extent), as their ceramics make clear, and their own traditions implied as well. They brought Saxon ceramics, that is to say, but not Saxon long-houses. Helena Hamerow argues convincingly that long-houses, whose complexity implies a certain level of social organization, were abandoned in the context of the extreme simplicity of the first century of Anglo-Saxon settlement.[152] The result was, all the same, that Anglo-Saxon England, whatever the origins of its building traditions, came to be closer to the southern group, and we will look at it in that context. Let us look at three southern areas, Alemannia, England, and the Île de France, so as to explore how villages worked there, and how they compare with those of the northern group.

Lauchheim in the rolling hills north of the Danube, in eastern Alemannia, is a good starting-point. The land it occupied had not been in the empire since the end of Roman control of the Black Forest and Neckar valley, in the mid-third century. The village was settled between the sixth and twelfth centuries, without changing markedly. The main houses, post-hole single-aisled buildings, were 10–20 metres long, most of them at the shorter end of this range, although some of the larger ones probably did have animals in them; they were accompanied, as further north, by smaller post-hole buildings and *Grubenhäuser*, in enclosures, which perhaps contained fewer people than in the north—Folke Damminger calculates ten to fifteen each. These building styles and this layout all have roots in pre-medieval, often pre-Roman, settlement beyond the frontier. There were about ten farmsteads

[152] Hamerow, *Early medieval settlement*, pp. 43–9.

at Lauchheim, one of them, as at Vorbasse, rather larger; this *Herrenhof* began in the seventh century and its enclosure had perhaps doubled in size by the eleventh.[153] It is probable that the holder of this farm was more powerful than his analogues in Denmark, for the enclosure had a high number of storage buildings and no *Grubenhäuser*, unlike other farmsteads, perhaps indicating the stockpiling of surplus; and a separate cemetery with rich burials was established in the late seventh century along the edge of the enclosure of the *Herrenhof*. (A cemetery around a newly built church replaced both in the eighth; many such churches are private aristocratic foundations.) It looks as if a local aristocrat was here emerging from village society, even though one could not say from the evidence that he necessarily controlled the village itself.[154] Otherwise, Lauchheim was quite like northern villages in structure, even if its houses were generally smaller. Unlike some villages in the northern group, it did not shift site; although some shifting villages have been identified in Germany (notably Vogelgesang just outside Speyer, in the Middle Rhine), the phenomenon is not well attested in the Frankish–Alemannic culture-area.[155] Villages like Lauchheim, finally, can be seen to fit into a wider settlement hierarchy, at least from the later seventh century, for this was the period of the reoccupation of several Alemannic hill-forts, which had been the political centres of the third to fifth centuries.[156] In the eighth century, documents show an active and rich Alemannic aristocracy, at least in the south of the sub-region, for they are well attested in gifts to St Gallen in north-eastern Switzerland. Such aristocrats could, on the face of it, have lived either in hill-forts or in villages, although exactly what an estate-centre was before 800 in material terms is as yet usually a matter only of assumption—only one is known to me for this area from both documents and excavation, a hill-fort site at Sagogn in the Alps at the top of the Rhine valley, which can be identified with a *sala . . . in castro* in the will of Bishop Tello of Chur in 765. They did not necessarily control the villages they lived in: the St Gallen documents, like other central and southern German collections, mostly indicate the same degree

---

[153] Lauchheim is not fully published; Ingo Stork's interims have appeared regularly in *Archäologische Ausgrabungen in Baden-Württemberg* since 1989. The key ones are 'Zum Fortgang der Untersuchungen' and 'Lauchheim 2000'; see also his short overview, *Fürst und Bauer*, pp. 37–65. Damminger, 'Dwellings, settlements', esp. pp. 60–4, gives summaries and drawings; for people per farmstead, see ibid., pp. 60–1. The latter article is the best current overview for Alemannia; see also Bücher and Hoeper, 'First aspects'. Other important excavations in the German lands include Gladbach in the middle Rhineland (Sage, *Gladbach*) and Kirchheim in Bavaria (Dannheimer, 'Kirchheim').

[154] Stork, 'Zum Fortgang der Untersuchungen', with idem, *Fürst und Bauer*, pp. 52–4, for the *Herrenhof*. For parallels to the separate aristocratic cemetery, see Steuer, *Frühgeschichtliche Sozialstrukturen*, pp 391–2; Böhme, 'Adelsgräber'.

[155] Bernhard, 'Speyer "Vogelgesang" '. A possible parallel is Nomeny south of Metz: see Halsall, *Settlement and society*, p. 180, a cautious account.

[156] Christlein, *Die Alamannen*, pp. 43–9; Koch and Kaschau, 'Ausgrabungen auf dem Runden Berg'.

of fragmented land tenure in villages (*loci* or *villae*) that we have seen for
Dienheim in the middle Rhine (above, pp. 394–7).[157] The emergence
(or better documentation) of aristocratic power here is not in itself
an argument for the tenurial dependence of the villages that have been
excavated, which often seem as prosperous as those of Denmark. But that
prosperity coexisted with stronger aristocratic power than in the North.

Villages in Anglo-Saxon parts of Britain were not, initially, as well structured as Lauchheim. Mucking in Essex, one of the earliest settlements in an
Anglo-Saxon building tradition, occupied from the mid-fifth century to the
early eighth, consisted of post-hole buildings (none of them very large) and
Grubenhäuser, with no enclosures. The fifth-century settlement had only one
visible post-hole building, but excavation conditions were mostly not good
enough in that part of the settlement to detect them; after c. 500 there were
perhaps eight to ten at any one time, with around fourteen *Grubenhäuser.*
The settlement shifted at least twice across the period, but, unlike Vorbasse
and other Continental sites, no clear spatial patternings are visible in it at all.
A second site, West Stow in Suffolk, dating to the same period, was maybe
smaller, with three or four farmstead units at any one time across the same
settlement period; the post-hole buildings were here even smaller, and the
percentage of *Grubenhäuser* higher, maybe four or five of them being
associated with each above-ground building (the excavator of West Stow,
Stanley West, is one of the few archaeologists of our regions who argues that
his sunken-floored huts were sometimes lived in as houses, and some of them
did at least have suspended floors on this site). Here, the settlement did not
shift, even though its house-plots were continually moving in the same area,
but it was as unstructured as was Mucking. In each case, the post-hole
buildings were far smaller than was any major house-type on the Continental North Sea coast; nor was there any sign of any privileged residence in the
village.[158] These features are common to all known early Anglo-Saxon
settlements, and in most cases this is matched by an absence of enclosures
around buildings or obvious planning. The building types in these settlements come from the Continent, probably from the smaller buildings of the
North, but not any element of articulation. The absence of long-houses in
Britain, already discussed, may correlate with the relative absence of small
finds, except ceramics.[159] The early Anglo-Saxon settlement of Britain took

----

[157] St Gallen documents are edited in *Ub. St. Gallen,* I, with some of them re-edited in *ChLA,*
I, II. For Sagogn, see Kaiser, *Churrätien,* pp. 213–15, citing *Bündner Ub.,* n. 17, and Meyer, 'Die
Ausgrabungen der Burgruine Schiedberg'.

[158] Hamerow, *Mucking,* II; West, *West Stow.* West, ibid., pp. 146–50, dates the end of the site
to 650, but the last phases included Ipswich ware, now redated to 720 onwards (Blinkhorn,
'Of cabbages and kings', p. 9).

[159] Some sixth-century enclosures are perhaps visible at Catholme in Staffordshire
(Hamerow, *Early medieval settlement,* p. 92 n.), if the settlement really began as early as
that—see Losco-Bradley and Kinsley, *Catholme;* I am grateful to Helena Hamerow for
letting me see the text in typescript. For other sites, see above, Ch. 6, n. 19. West Heslerton in

place, as argued in Chapter 6 (pp. 306–14), on a small political scale, in a landscape dominated by economic crisis, so great that the British majority (and it will have been a substantial majority, even in Essex and Suffolk) had no effect on the material culture of the next centuries. These settlements, however, show no obvious signs of a stable elite, even among the immigrant population. Cemetery finds, which are rather more differentiated (including at Mucking), show that elites existed, but not necessarily permanent ones, judging from the simplicity of the settlements: even less permanent than in Denmark or Frisia. Eastern Britain in the fifth and early sixth centuries must have had something of a frontier feel to it.

After 600 settlements seem to have become more developed. The earliest excavated royal centre, Yeavering in Northumberland, had already been founded (above, p. 320); others, like Rendlesham in Suffolk, are known from Bede but await excavation. The villages of the seventh century are also more articulated: not the later levels of Mucking and West Stow, it is true, but more recently founded ones, at least. Wicken Bonhunt in Essex (fl. seventh to ninth centuries), Pennyland in Buckinghamshire (fl. sixth to eighth centuries), Yarnton in Oxfordshire (fl. sixth to tenth centuries), Cowdery's Down in Hampshire (fl. sixth to seventh centuries), Catholme in Staffordshire (fl. sixth to tenth centuries), all had at least some enclosures by the seventh century, and their main post-hole buildings were, for the first time, as large as those of sites like Lauchheim, and Gladbach in central Germany.[160] Anglo-Saxon settlements were, that is to say, developing *towards* the modular patterns of the Frankish lands, from the simpler and more inchoate settlements of the fifth and sixth centuries. All the same, only in a few villages (Cowdery's Down after 600 is the clearest example) is there as yet any equivalent to the single larger farmstead which is fairly common on the Continent;[161] and it is not before the eighth century that any English settlement site shows the quality (indeed, as at Cowdery's Down and Catholme, even the quantity) of small finds that is normal in Francia. Settlements remained relatively small, too, with field surveys in midland England showing several in the territories of each modern village up to the mid- to late ninth century; the substantial nucleated

Yorkshire had an apparently planned craft area by the late sixth century: Powlesland, 'Early Anglo-Saxon settlements', pp. 110–13; but this site seems atypical in many ways. For overviews of the early Saxon period see Welch, *Anglo-Saxon England*, pp. 14–53; Arnold, *An archaeology*, pp. 33–66; Hamerow, *Early medieval settlement*, pp. 43–9, 89–95. For the Continental origins of house-types, see above, Ch. 6, n. 10.

[160] Respectively, Wade, 'A settlement site'; Williams, *Pennyland*, pp. 92–5; Dodd and McAdam, 'L'habitat rural', pp. 230–1; Millett and James, 'Cowdery's Down'; see n. 159 for Catholme.

[161] Millett and James, 'Cowdery's Down', pp. 215–17. Powlesland, 'Early Anglo-Saxon settlements', pp. 113, 118–19, hints that West Heslerton may provide a parallel here.

villages of the central middle ages and later only developed in the period 850–1200.[162]

English settlement archaeology reflects what has been argued on other grounds, from cemetery archaeology and written sources (pp. 340–4), about the slow growth of hierarchies in the east of Britain. The absence of any early signs of a stable aristocracy does not seem to be the chance of our evidence. Elites crystallized only late, hardly before 600. But settlements became slowly more stable as they did so. Enclosures for farmsteads began to appear. Eventually, village movement lessened, too; Hamerow dates this to the eighth century for the most part.[163] A clearer nucleation began a century later. From then on, in at least the lowland parts of Britain, villages in their structure resembled those of Francia more and more. Not yet those of Denmark, which, although they had been structured for longer, were still moving around; but Denmark's social hierarchies, too, would not crystallize until the tenth century and later.

The west Frankish heartland presents different problems. Here, I shall focus on the Île de France and Picardy to its north, the best-studied area (together with Normandy) in France, adding parallels from other areas where relevant. Let us begin with one well-excavated (and published) site, Goudelancourt-les-Pierrepont (Aisne), to give an illustration of the sort of pattern we can find there, before generalizing further. At Goudelancourt, not all the site was excavated (this is generally true for Merovingian-period settlements in France), but four post-hole buildings were found, and sixteen _Grubenhäuser_, dating to the sixth and seventh centuries; this may have made up a single house-group. The size of the associated cemeteries might imply that there were around five others, making up a population of some 125 people. It is unclear what the spatial structure of the whole village was; the signs are that it was less coherent than Lauchheim. But the buildings, which were of a Frankish/Alemannic type, were of a good quality, and the central one had a stone foundation. And, although little metalwork was found in the settlement area (there was, as usual, rather more in the cemetery), there was a substantial amount of pottery. This was of medium but at least professional quality; a fifth of it was fine ware (a quarter of it sixth-century Argonne ware, half Merovingian biconic wares), and the rest wheel-turned common wares.[164] There is no indication that the Goudelancourt house

---

[162] For the late development of nucleation, see Foard, 'Systematic field-walking', pp. 364–72; Bowman, 'Contrasting pays', pp. 126–33; Lewis _et al._, _Village, hamlet_, pp. 14–16, 74–95; Dyer, 'Villages and non-villages'.

[163] Hamerow, _Early medieval settlements_, pp. 116–19, modifying her previous later date in 'Settlement mobility', esp. p. 16. Village terminology in Anglo-Saxon charters was vague for a long time, because land units were so large and the concept of the exclusively owned 'estate' not yet available (above, pp. 314–26); 'land at X' is a common formulation. But the concept of the village as a settlement unit did exist by the eighth century, for Bede uses it (he usually calls it a _vicus_): e.g. _HE_, III.10, 28.

[164] See in general Nice, 'Goudelancourt-les-Pierrepont'; Bayard, 'La céramique de... Goudelancourt'.

complex was anything other than a peasant farmstead, but it had access to a wide range of well-made ceramics, much better than those of any site so far referred to in this chapter section. This observation can be generalized to all the Merovingian sites of northern France.

We have already seen that the major cultural shift in northern Gaul occurred in the period 350–450, largely before the century of invasions, which began in 406–7 (above, pp. 475–7). Villas vanished, and were replaced by wooden buildings, often fairly simple ones, small post-hole constructions and *Grubenhäuser*, in a relatively dispersed settlement pattern. The Franks, when they occupied the north from the second third of the fifth century, thus found a housing type which already resembled their own, the result, as proposed earlier, of the cultural militarization of the frontier region. It was not until after 550 or so, however, that more organized village layouts, even ones as loose as Goudelancourt, came in. Frankish cultural influence was not the cause of the move to wooden constructions and farmstead complexes, which were already there; but the assemblage of these complexes into grouped settlements, eventually concentrated villages, may have been influenced by the patterns found in the Frankish origin lands beyond the Rhine. Only relatively few new fifth-century sites have as yet been excavated in the Île de France and Picardy—Herblay (Val d'Oise), Pontavert (Aisne), Pincevent (Seine-et-Marne).[165] After 550 there are many more to match Goudelancourt—Juvincourt-et-Damary (Aisne), Berry-au-Bac (Aisne), Villiers-le-Sec (Val d'Oise), Serris (Seine-et-Marne) are only the best-known.[166] These villages do, as a whole, resemble rather more the settlements of the Rhineland and beyond the old Roman frontier of the Lauchheim type. We can, however, exclude the idea that they were the work of immigrants. It is true that the few such settlements that have been identified in Gaul in the fifth century, such as Neerharem-Rekem in Belgium, are mostly relatively close to the border and have ceramics of types better known beyond the frontier, thus arguably representing Germanic immigrant communities.[167] This cannot, however, be the case for the villages of the late sixth century: it is out of the question that the settlement type that is universal around 600 in a Romance-speaking area should only indicate the presence of Frankish incomers.[168] Anyway, the basic patterns established around 550 extended up to the Carolingian period and beyond.

[165] See n. 95 for Herblay and Pincevent; Bayard, 'Les habitats', pp. 54, 58, for Pontavert.

[166] Respectively, Bayard, 'Juvincourt-et-Damary'; idem, 'Berry-au-Bac'; *Un village aux temps de Charlemagne*; Foucray and Gentili, 'Serris'. See in general the invaluable guide in Peytremann, 'Les structures d'habitat rural'. A new guide to village development in northern Francia is Yante and Bultot-Verleysen, *Autour du 'village'*.

[167] See Van Ossel and Ouzoulias, 'Rural settlement', pp. 149–50, for bibliography. One settlement of this type which is not close to the border is St-Ouen-du-Breuil near Rouen, a mid-fourth-century settlement with close parallels beyond the Rhine: Gonzalez, 'Saint-Ouen-du-Breuil'.

[168] See Farnoux, 'Le fond de cabane mérovingien', for a contrary view.

North French excavation has largely been small-scale, in the context of rescue work; the main archaeological strength of the sub-region for our period is actually in field survey, which we shall come to in a moment. As already noted, whole villages have rarely been excavated, unlike in the northern European countries—although we must recognize that outside the Île de France larger-scale excavations at Sannerville and Mondeville in Normandy, or at Vitry-en-Artois, again show the same sort of patterns that we saw for Lauchheim.[169] The sort of farmstead groups that have been found in the area also have parallels across the whole of northern Europe, with a central building associated with smaller structures, some sunken-floored, presumably the pattern that Latin documents call *casa cum edificiis*, as Guy Halsall has noted,[170] even though how they fit together in northern Gaul, and how many there were in each group, is less clear as yet. There is one clear absence, however, above all from levels pre-dating 650: any buildings that seem to be built on a larger or more complex scale than others. There are after that date a handful of more elaborate buildings: at Serris, four large stone-foundation buildings around a courtyard; at Juvigny (Marne), a 22-metre stone-foundation hall.[171] If this was England, one would be arguing that social hierarchies were beginning to emerge from a village context only around 650. But we know from our extensive documentary sources just how rich the Merovingian-period aristocracy was, by 550 at the latest (pp. 178–95), and much of that aristocracy was based, along with the Neustrian kings, in the Île de France. In material terms, too, the elaboration of ceramic networks (pp. 794–805), which was much greater than that in England, or anywhere outside the former empire, argues for substantial levels of demand; this extended to the peasantry as well, as at Goudelancourt, but had, I would argue, an aristocratic motor. The disjuncture comes only with settlement archaeology, which reflects none of the aristocratic wealth of the written sources, or, still less, of the *palatia*, the royal estates which were common in the Île de France and Picardy too. In this case, we have to conclude that aristocratic residences and royal *palatia* from the Merovingian period have not yet been found. We know this for the *palatia*, for we know where many of them were, and excavations have not yet been carried out

---

[169] See Pilet, 'Le village de Sannerville'; Lorren, 'Le village de Saint-Martin de Mondeville'; for a survey of Vitry, see Louis, 'A de-Romanised landscape', pp. 495–6—I am grateful to Étienne Louis for guidance on the site. The classic village site of Brebières (Nord), close to Vitry, had poor excavation conditions, and no post-hole buildings were found: Demolon, *Brebières*.

[170] Halsall, *Settlement and society*, p. 198. Dolling, *Haus und Hof*, discusses the meanings of the terms found in law-codes, a bit schematically at times; for aristocratic houses see Claude, 'Haus und Hof'.

[171] See n. 166 for Serris; Béague-Tahon and Georges-Leroy, 'Deux habitats ruraux', p. 177, for Juvigny. Outside the Île de France, the substantial stone buildings from the late seventh century at Rigny (Indre-et-Loire) near Tours, which belonged to St-Martin in Tours, may have been for storage, but certainly show architectural ambition: see Zadora-Rio and Galinié, 'La fouille du site de Rigny', pp. 173–9, 197–200, 223–6.

there, except for a sondage at Malay (Yonne), a seventh-century palace, which was probably a two-storeyed stone building. The literary sources show that aristocratic housing (and even the occasional church) could sometimes be in wood, although the solidity of surviving Merovingian stone churches, such as the seventh-century crypt at Jouarre (Seine-et-Marne), closely associated with the aristocratic Faronid family, shows that a stone architectural rhetoric was at least available to Merovingian aristocrats by then.[172] But for further understanding of this issue we shall have to look to the excavations of the future. Even Serris and Juvigny may only have been subsidiary estate-centres, not necessarily places where lords regularly lived. Seen in a village, rather than an aristocratic, context, they may simply be precursors, of a greater move to stone elements in village buildings of all types that is a feature of the Carolingian period. By then, of course, we know from the polyptych of St-Germain that villages could be fairly large (p. 400); the villages of the polyptych are also, mostly, already under modern towns and villages, for this is an area of relatively unshifting settlement. Such a statement also raises the possibility that the later village network was already established by the sixth century; if so, archaeologists in the Île de France have so far largely excavated relatively marginal *habitats intercalaires*, even in the Merovingian period, and we are definitely missing some crucial levels in our evidence.[173]

The field surveys and rescue excavations that have been carried out in recent years, on the other hand, largely in the framework of major stripping work, for *autoroutes*, TGV tracks, airports, or Disneyland Paris, which has in France been done sufficiently recently that the skills necessary for the recognition of early medieval ceramics were by then in place, allow a better sense of the spatial framework of settlement than is common elsewhere in western Europe. In the area along the River Marne known as Marne-la-Vallée, for example, out of twenty Roman sites, 55 per cent were occupied in the seventh century (one of them being Serris); no late Roman ceramics were found, leading surveyors to suppose that there was a settlement break, but the early medieval occupations were all on the same sites, so one could doubt that. Elsewhere, continuity on the same sites into the early middle ages is distinctly rarer, but the figure of around 50 per cent for early medieval occupation recurs—in the Aisne, in Yvelines, and elsewhere too. Overall,

---

[172] Perrugot, 'Le palais mérovingien de Malay'; Barbier, 'Le système palatial franc', for palace lists. Claude, 'Haus und Hof', pp. 333–4, for wood; cf. Samson, 'The Merovingian nobleman's home'. See also above, p. 201. See de Maillé, *Les cryptes de Jouarre*, for Jouarre; a recent argument that the present crypt is much later (de Mecquenem, 'Les cryptes de Jouarre') still dates the capitals to the seventh century (ibid., pp. 19–20); they presumably survive from an earlier church. One of the fifth-century villages which resemble those beyond the Rhine, Gennep in the southern Netherlands, seems to have been a high-status centre (Heidinga, 'Gennep'), presumably for a Frankish aristocrat; this did not survive past 500, however.

[173] See e.g. Halsall, *Settlement and society*, pp. 182–4; Lorren and Périn, 'Images de la Gaule rurale', p. 109.

across the various survey areas, the tendency is for Merovingian-period
settlement to be in river valleys rather than on the low chalky plateaux
that are a general feature of this part of northern France; although some
plateau sites are attested, both in the archaeological record and in documents, there was probably a higher degree of upland abandonment,
which may fit with the figure of 50 per cent fewer sites than in the Roman
period.[174] (Of course, that 50 per cent figure is only significant for global
population if settlements remained the same size, but villas, at least, are
unlikely to have had fewer inhabitants than Merovingian villages.) But the
general density of early medieval sites precludes widespread rural desertion,
particularly if archaeologically identified sites were only intercalatory to the
early medieval—and modern—villages. This conclusion is clearer in the Île
de France and Picardy than in any other part of Continental Europe at
present (though it has close parallels in East Anglia and Essex, where, too,
river valleys show greater settlement continuity than plateaux: above,
p. 312). When these spatial analyses are set against the excavations of
whole settlements, then we shall have a sense of population levels that will
be unusually trustworthy.

This sort of relative settlement continuity, with some possible agricultural
retreat at the margins, showing signs of a population decline since the
Roman period but not a demographic collapse, is beginning to be a common
feature of the evidence for the post-Roman western empire. We can put a
ballpark figure of 50 per cent on it for northern France, thanks to the
precision of some recent field surveys. We can only generalize with caution,
for even in northern France there is a great deal of microregional variability;
but, as just noted, the patterns of settlement retreat from marginal lands
match those of eastern Britain. In southern Europe we would have to be
much more impressionistic, for there is a far greater degree of variability in
the settlement patterns of the post-Roman western Mediterranean than
there is in the North, so even if there were fewer early medieval sites, they
might sometimes be larger than their Roman predecessors; but I would not
be surprised to find a 50 per cent population decline in much of Italy or
Spain, in particular since cities had always been larger in the South, and they
certainly lost some of their population. The causes and contexts of all of this
we shall look at in the next chapter (pp. 547–50). But there is another side to
it, as just implied: this was a decline inside the framework of a continued
occupation of the agrarian landscape. Abandonments were on a small scale,
and were matched by dense continued occupations elsewhere, as, by 800,

---

[174] Daveau, 'Occupation des sols' (for Marne-la-Vallée and elsewhere in the Île de France);
Haslegrove and Scull, 'Romanization and de-Romanization', pp. 12–14; Bourgeois, *Térritoires,
reseaux*, I, pp. 209–13, 240–9. See also, using more extensive methodologies, Périn, 'Le
peuplement', for the Dépt. Ardennes and Halsall, *Settlement and society*, pp. 178–84 for
Lorraine, both arguing for or implying a higher degree of continuity into the early medieval
period than do others.

with the large dependent villages of St-Germain. Only a few larger areas seem to have become substantially depopulated: the Kempen/Campine of northern Belgium and the southern Netherlands, a relatively poor area between Antwerp and the lower Meuse, seems to have lost its (thin) population in the fifth century at the latest, and to have been reoccupied in the late sixth—although the Meuse to its east and the Rhine delta to its north stayed settled. The Ardennes, too, probably lost most of its population—though even there some of the major royal estate-centres which dotted it by the seventh century lay on or by Roman sites and probably had always been occupied. Perhaps other substantial upland areas of the Ardennes type—the Hunsrück, the Vosges—saw similar settlement retreats. But they were surrounded by areas of continuing population.[175]

If there is one area where this sort of picture, of a reduced but consistent settlement continuity, has traditionally been questioned, it is the Rhineland. German scholarship has for long tended to see a sharp separation between Roman-period and Merovingian-period occupation, amounting to a caesura for a century or more in some cases; Frankish settlement in effect would start again.[176] In the context of current views of the patterns of the whole of western Europe (even Britain), I have to say that I find this so anomalous as to be hard to believe. The Rhineland was of course terrain that was in the front line of any invasion of the Roman empire from the east, and was fought over, but this was because of its agricultural wealth as much as because of its border position. It is impossible that the Franks would have wished to see its working population leave, and implausible that such a population movement would have taken place without a more concerted effort than the standard devastations of war-bands would produce. Nor does this image of depopulation fit other elements of the post-Roman Rhenish economy: the wealth of Merovingian Cologne (below, p. 678), or the continued production of the largest-scale industrial product of post-Roman northern Europe, the pottery of Mayen in the lower Eifel (below, p. 796). Some recent work on the lowland zone between Cologne, Aachen, and Krefeld is now showing the same degree of continued occupation that one has come to expect for the Île de France.[177] In future one could expect this further south as well, for the narrower valleys of the Bonn–Trier–Mainz triangle and the wide Middle Rhine valley, and signs of a revised picture are indeed appearing here too.[178] I do not wish to underplay the Roman to

---

[175] For the Kempen, Theuws, 'Landed property', pp. 354–7; for the Ardennes, Müller-Kehlen, *Die Ardennen*, pp. 19–27, 67; for continuities, e.g. ibid., pp. 207–15.

[176] Classic discontinuitist formulations are Janssen, 'Römische und frühmittelalterliche Landerschliessung'; Hinz, *Archäologische Funde*, II, pp. 179–86; Gechter and Kunow, 'Zur ländlichen Besiedlung'. More cautious are Arora, 'Eine frühmittelalterliche Talverfüllung', pp. 273–8, 287–9; Wieczorek, 'Die Ausbreitung', p. 247–53.

[177] Lenz, 'Late Roman rural settlement', pp. 131–7, is the best recent overview. Pirling, *Römer und Franken*, presents Krefeld-Gellep, the cemetery with clearest continuity.

[178] Staab, *Untersuchungen*, pp. 1–175, already presented a strong case; see further, for the crucial fifth century, Staab, *Zur Kontinuität*. Böhner, *Die fränkischen Altertümer*, I,

Merovingian cultural break, and indeed it was stressed in the earlier discussion of the end of villas: Merovingian post-hole buildings and modular farmstead units were profoundly different from the Roman past. But in the Rhine valley, just as in the Seine or Thames valleys, they do not have to represent population replacement and a gap in agricultural exploitation. Local peasantries came to face their landscapes with a partially different material culture (with different building technologies, that is to say, although the same ceramics and tools), and, on the Rhine, language eventually changed as well (if it had not already begun to in the frontier world of the late empire); but one can nonetheless argue that the peasantry and the landscape were the same throughout.

We can see, across the whole of northern Francia (and Alemannia, and Bavaria for that matter), a similar pattern of village structures by the mid-sixth century: groups of modular farmstead units, sometimes arrayed in tight groups (of varying size), sometimes more scattered. Here, unlike anywhere else in the North, we have enough documentation to allow us to get a rough outline of how village identity worked, and we can end this chapter with some discussion of it. We have already seen in Chapter 7 how microregionally variable the word *villa* could be, signifying 'estate' in the Île de France, but 'village' in the middle Rhine; we cannot characterize a single village identity that is valid for the whole of the Frankish lands. But some of its parameters do have some wider applicability, all the same. Let us first look at the meaning of the word *villa* across the texts we have for the post-Roman period. For the most part, it was no longer a word that stably meant 'estate' or 'estate-centre' in Gaul, unlike in the Roman period. Gregory of Tours in the late sixth century uses the word above all to mean 'village', as Martin Heinzelmann has shown, although a secondary meaning is certainly 'rural residence' or 'rural property', thus in effect 'estate'. The formularies are similar: in the *Formulae Andecavenses* from Angers and the *Formulae Arvernenses* from Clermont, some of which are sixth-century, *villa* indicates a geographical territory for the location of parcels of land for the most part, and only occasionally are there references to alienations of a single *villa* (or its synonyms, *locus* and *locellus*) by a landowner.[179] Although the Loire valley and northern Aquitaine were areas of late villas in archaeological terms (above p. 174), it seems that the mental map of writers there was

pp. 285–336, the classic for the Trierer Land, supports the argument too; for Roman continuities in the Moselle valley, established on the basis of placenames and written evidence, see also Ewig, *Trier*, pp. 61–77; Kleiber, 'Mosella romana'. For the Worms–Speyer area of the middle Rhine, see now Bernhard, 'Die Merowingerzeit in der Pfalz', esp. pp. 13–14, 22, 32, 61–7, 84–95, 101–6: material culture changed substantially there in the late fifth century, but without a break in the use of the landscape, much as in England.

[179] Heinzelmann, '*Villa* d'après Grégoire de Tours', gives full lists; see also Lorren and Périn, 'Images de la Gaule rurale', pp. 94–5; Weidemann, *Kulturgeschichte*, II, pp. 105–26. *Form. Andecavenses*, e.g. nn. 28, 33, 46 (estate); *Form. Arvernenses*, 1, 6 (MGH, *Formulae*, pp. 13, 15, 20, 28, 31).

already one of a world of villages, many of which had a variety of land-owners in them. Moving north, we have seen (pp. 400–2) that *villa* in the Île de France in the seventh century usually simply means 'estate', with 'village territory' here only a secondary meaning.[180] This makes the Paris basin distinct from the Loire; but it is worth adding that the two patterns are not necessarily opposed to each other. The Île de France had a higher concentration of large estates than did other parts of France, and the slippage of meaning of the word *villa* from 'village' back to 'estate' would thus have been easier there—the local assumption was that most villages were estates as well, although when they were not, as in a handful of transactions of single fields, and also occasionally in Marculf's *Formulae*, *villa* terminology was still used, implying that the idea that it represented a single geographical territory was stronger than the idea that it simply meant an estate.[181] Moving eastwards past Verdun, landowning was more fragmented again (above, p. 394), and *villa* means 'village' on a normal basis, in the seventh- and eighth-century documents of the Rhineland, from the Netherlands to the Alps. The first village for which this is really clear is Gœrsdorf in Alsace, documented extensively from 693–4 onwards in the Wissembourg cartulary, but it is followed by many others in the next century. By the 820s, even the polyptych of St-Germain, in the Paris basin, uses the word *villa* for settle-ment, rather than estate, units.[182] We can legitimately conclude that the collections of farmsteads visible archaeologically from the Seine to the Danube must have been called *villae* on a regular basis by Latin-speakers, whether they were also estate blocks or not; and, from the Carolingian period onwards, village terminology was normal.[183]

We can say much more about village geography than about the detail of village society. Even Gregory of Tours, who gives us our densest narratives, is seldom concerned with social behaviour inside his *villae*. An exception is the famous Sichar–Chramnesind story, which involved bad behaviour by royal protégés at a drunken party in 585 spiralling out of the control of neighbours and even city authorities; Chramnesind at one point burned down several houses of the *villa* of Manthelan, where Sichar lived, which may mean that the settlement was built of wood, as well as being relatively

---

[180] So also does it in Maine; see Weidemann, *Das Testament*, *passim* (Busson and Ledru, *Actus*, pp. 102–41, with pp. 157–62).

[181] *Marculfi formulae*, II.6 (*MGH, Formulae*, p. 78), is the best example of *villa* probably meaning 'village'; but it means 'estate' in most of the rest of the text. For single fields, see above, Ch. 7, n. 41.

[182] For Gœrsdorf up to 750, see *Trad. Wiz.*, nn. 38, 46, 43, 150, 186, 6, 12, 15, 7, 142, discussed in Wickham, 'L'identité villageoise'. For St-Germain, see *Pol. St-Germain*, most clearly in XII. See in general Schwind, 'Beobachtungen', the best guide.

[183] For the Carolingian period and later see e.g. Bange, 'L'*ager* et la *villa*'; Barthélemy, *La société*, pp. 182–3, as well as the previous note. In eastern Brittany, the *plebs* was the basic settlement term, with *locus* and *villa* (and the vernacular *treb*) denoting hamlets inside it: Davies, *Small worlds*, pp. 36–7, 63–7; here, however, early medieval archaeology is hard to find (Astill and Davies, *A Breton landscape*, pp. 91–115).

concentrated. Elsewhere, *villae* had churches on occasion, and communities of the faithful, and social hierarchies—as with the priest Epachius of Riom in the Auvergne, who was expected to celebrate mass even though he was a drunk, because he was of a senatorial family and the *nobilior* man in the village (*vicus*). Sichar and Epachius were aristocrats who lived in *villae* or *vici*, although not, apparently, owning all the land in them; the villages around Tours and Clermont could evidently be highly stratified. We cannot be more precise about their internal structures, however. Only under the Carolingians, at the end of and after the period discussed in this book, does village society begin to be clearer in our best-documented areas, like the Rhineland (see above, pp. 393–8) and eastern Brittany. The latter has been analysed above all by Wendy Davies; it is atypical of northern Francia less because it was Breton-speaking than because of its unusual peasant autonomy and community identity.[184]

Our other major rural source, the *Pactus legis Salicae* of c.510, in some ways parallels ninth-century eastern Brittany quite closely, but gives us problems of different kinds. First of all, where it relates to is far from clear. It derives from the north-western sub-region later known as Neustria, for clause 47 regards its core area as being between the *silva Carbonaria* (roughly in the centre of modern Belgium) and the Loire, which are the effective bounds of Neustria to the north-east and south; but to regard it as simply reflecting the social practices of that entire sub-region would be naive.[185] It is unlikely that it tells us much about the Paris area, for example, for the *Pactus* is famous for not paying much attention to aristocrats, and the latter were by 600 at the latest very thick on the ground in the Île de France, and arguably always had been (above, pp. 398–406). It is perhaps necessary to add that the *Pactus* is so sketchy a code that its omissions are not significant in themselves; but the attention it pays to the economic activities of free peasants at least shows that the latter were important to its compilers, and around Paris even free peasants were mostly dependent tenants, making them more socially marginal. If the *Pactus* relates to any precise area, it was probably somewhere rather further north than the Seine valley. But it may simply represent a Frankish self-image, in part a (re-)construction of a now-outdated past beyond the Rhine, where its mythical legislators were supposed to have lived.[186] Even then, its imagery is valuable, whether or not its specific enactments are descriptions of real social action. *Villae* in the *Pactus*

---

[184] Gregory of Tours, *LH*, VII.47 with IX.19 (Sichar and Chramnesind); *GM*, n. 86 (Epachius); cf. *VM*, III.33, IV.12, with *GC*, n. 47 (other *villae* with churches). *GC*, n. 80, describing a fire which only touches one farmstead but not its neighbours, also implies a concentrated settlement. For Brittany see Davies, *Small worlds*, *passim*.

[185] *Pactus*, c. 47. Wood, *Merovingian kingdoms*, p. 112, argues for a date not only pre-511 (which is convincing) but pre-507.

[186] For the mythical legislators, see the 'short prologue', pp. 2–3 of the Eckhardt edition of the *Pactus*. For the free peasant focus see e.g. Wickham, *Land and power*, pp. 212–13.

are never estates; they are usually villages; occasionally they seem to be single farmsteads, although we could not deduce from this any reference to dispersed settlement, for the text is not that precise. *Villae* were locations for small-scale landowners, anyway: one law, in a capitulary slightly later than the *Pactus* but attached to it, concerning what to do if a dead man is discovered in the fields (near a *villa*—presumably a concentrated settlement—or between two neighbouring *villae*), with no one admitting his homicide, envisages that the owners of the nearest fields should formally swear with oath-helpers that they were not involved, and that these owners could be socially high or low (*meliores* or *minoflidis*). And in the famous law *De migrantibus*, *villa* inhabitants could veto any incomers to the village, as long as they could gather oath-helpers on four separate occasions—that is to say, as long as a substantial social group backed them up.[187]

These villages were locations for significant social activity, then, and it mattered to their inhabitants who lived there. They were socially divided: between free and unfree, crucially, but also between the richer and poorer free (richer men needed more oath-helpers; they could be rich enough to hire assassins; the richest could be described as *potentes*). But they do not seem to have been formally constituted as communities: or, at least, if they were, such community action was not recorded in the *Pactus*. *De migrantibus* does not envisage any village-wide forum for its veto procedures; the count had to come in to enforce them. A more local court (*mallus*) did exist, run by local legal experts (*rachineburgi*), rather than by wider-ranging authorities such as counts, but there is no sign that each village necessarily had its own *mallus*— the latter were apparently assemblies on a larger scale than that. The *villae* of the *Pactus* were, then, articulated but informal communities: arenas for the action of kin-groups, groups of neighbours, or looser (often violent) groups of associates, *contubernia*.[188] They were defined geographically, as settlements with attached fields, each one distinct from its neighbours. To some extent, this picture resembles the sort of Loire valley communities that Gregory seems to be describing in his anecdotes, and also, for that matter, Dienheim in the eighth-century Rhineland (pp. 394–7), even though there were important landowners in each of these. These two areas were outside the geographical remit of the *Pactus*, but its imagery fits other village communities in the Frankish lands where many landowners lived, no matter how rich they were. And the physical stage of all three probably looked much the same: the loose conglomerations of house-groupings inside enclosures that have been found by archaeologists. These villages may not have

---

[187] *Villa* as a village in *Pactus*, cc. 45 (*De migrantibus*), 102 (the capitulary, an early or mid-sixth-century text); in cc. 3.10, 14.6, 7, it could mean either 'village' or 'farmstead'. In *Lex Ribvaria*, c. 63, it certainly means 'farmstead'. See in general Schmidt-Wiegand, 'Das Dorf'.

[188] Respectively, *Pactus*, cc. 102, 28, 88 (richer and poorer), 45, 56, 57 (*mallus*), 14.6, 42 (*contubernia*). Contrast the visible formality of the local courts of Brittany (Davies, *Small worlds*, pp. 146–60).

been as autonomous as Vorbasse (such a statement is hard to check, given the absence of Danish documents, but it seems likely enough), and they were conceivably less formalized in their internal social relationships (though this second statement is even closer to guesswork than the first is). They were certainly less autonomous than Galatian villages, less stable in their spatial relationships than Syrian villages, less organized in their political structures than Egyptian villages. Nonetheless, they were the bases for local identity, the locations for important social and economic action: inescapable points of reference.

5. Conclusion

With the single major exception of Ireland (above, pp. 354–5), the early middle ages throughout all the regions discussed in this book was a world of villages. This is hardly an unusual statement to make about peasant society, of course, but it needs to be made because the western Roman empire (though not the lands to its east and north) was, by contrast, mostly structured spatially by estates and landowning. The common village identity of early medieval East and West resulted in parallel patterns of development, simply because all village societies have elements in common, collective collaboration set against local tensions, and so on. So Theodoret of Cyrrhus could be linked to the *Life* of Theodore of Sykeōn and the *Nomos geōrgikos*, Gregory of Tours to the *Pactus legis Salicae*; and the two worlds have elements in common too. These elements have sometimes been linked to the common 'sub-Roman' inheritance of both East and West, but it should be said that they are also examples of the common features that all villages have, and one should not be surprised to find equivalents in China or Mexico, too, if one looked for them. Eastern villages were more stable than western ones, however, and materially more solid for that matter. They also had one major difference from most of the West, formal patterns of local organization and government—headmen, community councils and officials, even village-level justice. This was rare in the West in our period; the only area of the West where structured village communities can be talked about really clearly is ninth-century eastern Brittany. But north of our documented areas, it is quite likely that fairly coherent communities existed in regions such as Frisia and Denmark.

This relative informality of western villages is at least in part because, in the former Roman empire, they were new as a way of organizing the landscape—before the end of villas, they were secondary to estate organization, where they existed at all. I have argued that the end of villas was a cultural more than an economic or political change, related to the changing nature of aristocracies, but it had a profound effect on peasant society: it invented the village for them. This happened at both a conceptual and a material level. Peasants began to think territorially rather than in terms of land tenure, and began to construct territorial forms of co-operation. This was partly, perhaps, in some cases, because aristocratic control was in crisis—aristocrats globally became poorer in the crisis of empire, and their hegemony must sometimes have been challenged. In other cases it may be because of Germanic cultural influence, for beyond the border villages had long been normal. But the cultural shift could often simply have resulted from settlement change, as, across most of the former western empire, smaller or greater concentrations of houses began to dominate the landscape. Settlement change could be quite sharp in the end, as villas were abandoned or transformed and villages suddenly appeared. It did not necessarily represent social crisis—it was a catastrophe-flip in mathematical, not social terms (above, p. 13), and often simply marked the moment when old settlement patterns seemed clearly irrelevant, and newer ones more obviously compelling. But villages, even though relatively unstructured in all parts of the post-Roman West (less than both in the East and in the non-Roman North), were the physical carriers of a more organic form of peasant co-operation, which, even if as yet incipient, would clearly be taken up in the future.

I have argued that an important guide to peasant dependence on or autonomy from aristocrats is settlement hierarchy. Aristocrats themselves did not so often live in villages. They were urban-dwelling in most of the Mediterranean, as we shall see in Chapter 10; in the North, they lived in isolated estate-centres in Denmark and probably some of northern Francia. (The most likely archaeological examples of village bases for aristocrats, such as Lauchheim in Alemannia and Cowdery's Down in Hampshire, probably show lords who had been village leaders not long before.) How peasant settlement related spatially to the places where aristocrats did live is thus important if we wish to understand how the two classes related in other ways. But a structured hierarchy of habitat did not necessarily denote domination over a peasantry—both Syria and Denmark disprove that in different ways, with the city landowners of the former not owning much in some of the areas of the most solid village settlement, such as the Limestone Massif, and the magnates of the latter probably not yet having much tenurial power over large structured villages like Vorbasse. Brittany, where local aristocrats lived in an isolated *lis* or *aula* but did not have either a proprietorial or a political dominance over the villages around, is a documentary parallel.[189] But where, as in the eastern Chianti, or parts of the Spanish coast, or in England before 600, all settlement seems relatively fragmented and unstructured, then it is likely that large landowning was relatively weak and the peasantry relatively autonomous. One could also propose that peasantries in this situation had rather less tight social structures than in

---

[189] Davies, *Small worlds*, pp. 36, 140–1.

societies with more organized villages, whether or not these were framed by external powers. In northern Francia, by contrast, where aristocratic power is evident in documents but known settlements are relatively unhierarchized, it is likely that aristocratic estate-centres have not yet been found. One sort of settlement hierarchy that does reflect continuing aristocratic control, although by now in a village environment, may be seen in the partial *perchement* of southern Gaul and Italy. *Perchement*, on the other hand, one must note in passing, is hardly a feature of post-Roman northern Europe at all. The reoccupation of hill-forts in both Alemannia and western Britain (above, p. 327) does parallel it in part; these are, too, rather hillier areas than is the great North European Plain. But the use for settlement of what hills there are there, in more than casual ways, would have to await the development of castles, which only began in the tenth century, well after our period.

One general feature of all our regions, at least in the post-Roman world, is microregional difference. It is hardly appropriate to develop this point in detail again in a conclusion which is trying to stress common themes rather than distinction; but the *fact* of microregional difference is a marker that local constraints, in the form of local ecologies, agricultural strategies, social relationships at the peasant level, or intensities of aristocratic control, had come to be more important for peasantries than any external, overriding, elements such as the effect of senatorial *otium* ideology on local settlement patterns in the Roman period. This really marks out the Roman period, not the early middle ages, as exceptional, given that peasant society is *normally* microregional across time and space; but what the end of that imperial culture did, at least, was to restore to peasantries their ability to control their local environments, and to allow them to choose the way they wanted to organize the detail of their living strategies. Such choices were inevitably going to be microregional, although it is also interesting that several aspects of them were capable of being generalized over rather larger areas, such as the return to wood in Italy or northern Gaul, and the move towards village agglomerations, large or small, which can be found in modified forms in a number of different regions.

Where the early middle ages in the West was different, in both its settlement patterns and in its village identities, is that it was relatively fluid, by comparison with both before and after: the more monumental, but also more static, worlds of the villa on the one hand and the castle on the other. Early medieval western villages were less coherent than either: they sometimes moved about, they were usually relatively disorganized in a spatial sense, and they had, above all, relatively few formal political structures. There are, as a result, historiographical traditions which deny to them the label 'village'. Jean Chapelot and Robert Fossier have argued that 'villages' only appeared in the West around the year 1000, and are associated with settlement concentration or nucleation, a church, organized political structures, maybe a castle, maybe an open field system. In England, too, Christopher Taylor and Christopher Dyer see 'villages' as being created by the settlement nucleation of the ninth to twelfth centuries (above, pp. 503–4), and dispersed settlement patterns, or the more fragmented agglomerations of the early Anglo-Saxon period, as not being those of villages (Dyer has called them 'non-villages'). This is only a question of terminology; nor would I disagree at all with the importance of the tenth and eleventh centuries, in particular, as a moment of political, religious, economic, and spatial aggregation in the West. But the recognition of its importance should not lead us to underestimate the importance of an earlier moment, that in which geographical territories (rather than landowning patterns, as in the western Roman empire) came to be the marker of local collective identity, and the whole landscape became divided up between *villae* (or *vici*, or *loci*), settlements and the agricultural space their inhabitants depended on. This territorialization links the relatively fluid and fragmented settlements of sixth- to eighth-century Francia, England, Spain, Italy, with the much more organized settlements of the eastern Mediterranean and the twelfth-century West. With Fred Schwind and Elizabeth Zadora-Rio, therefore, I would resist the restriction of the word 'village' to the latter, for village territories and identity were clearly in evidence, everywhere, by the end of our period, even if churches were relatively rare before 800 and formal collective practices and institutions rare before 1050.[190] I have argued elsewhere that the latter were the product of the more local, privatized, politics of the world of small-scale lordships that replaced the Carolingian world-order; and, conversely, their absence was made possible in our period, at least in the Romano-Germanic kingdoms, in part because of the overarching presence of public institutions, such as judicial assemblies run by counts, which did not have to exist in every village.[191] But this fluidity was also a marker of relative peasant autonomies. With few exceptions (northern Francia being an important one), aristocracies were weaker in the early middle ages than they were before or after. Individual aristocrats could exercise dominance, over the sections of the peasantry they did still control, as much as ever, but there were fewer of them, and they owned less land; nor were they, in the early middle ages, universally committed to detailed local domination. Globally, there was more chance of any given village being relatively autonomous in the earliest middle ages than in most periods of history. Where there was economic need for it, such villages could organize themselves very coherently, of course, as in Egypt or Anatolia, and maybe in Denmark or eastern Brittany. But, as we see in a number of other places, peasants who did not see

[190] Chapelot and Fossier, *The village and house*, pp. 71, 129; Taylor, *Village and farmstead*, pp. 117–33; Lewis et al., *Village, hamlet*, pp. 191, 198–201; Dyer, 'Villages and non-villages'; Schwind, 'Beobachtungen', pp. 444–5; Zadora-Rio, 'Le village des historiens'.
[191] Wickham, *Community and clientele*, pp. 235–8.

themselves as collectively under threat were often content to construct quite unstructured—fluid—collective environments for themselves. This takes us back to the case studies in Chapter 7, which, as we saw, showed very diverse levels of local collective action. The parameters discussed at the end of that chapter apply to all the local societies discussed in this one, whose internal relationships are only documented, schematically and externally, through settlement archaeology and village identity. They will be developed at a more general level in Chapter 9.

9

Peasant society and its problems

WE HAVE BY NOW looked at some of the empirical issues that concerned the peasantries of our period from several perspectives: how the parameters of the exploitation of peasants by lords changed (Chapter 5); how some well-documented local societies worked (Chapter 7); and how villages operated, spatially and conceptually (Chapter 8)—the latter two seen, as far as possible, from the peasant's point of view. Overall, furthermore, throughout this book, a major sub-theme has been the ways that major landowners dominated over peasantries, whether these were their tenants or their clients or simply their poorer neighbours: by exacting rents, controlling peasant labour, acting as the local agents of the state, establishing local-level political domination, extending coercive patronage relationships, or simply expropriating peasant owners of their land. In other chapters, these issues have been dealt with regionally, and the ways that peasants related to each other and to lords were indeed highly differentiated from place to place. In this chapter, by contrast, I shall focus on generalizing, on the basis of these differences: for, unless we try to look at peasant society as a whole as well, the major vectors of social change risk being made invisible. The chapter will be divided into four parts, each centred on a distinct problem: first, the effect of the end of the Roman empire on the socio-political framework in which peasants lived; second, the basic structures of the economic system in the earliest middle ages in the West, when aristocracies were at their weakest, and peasantries at their most autonomous; third, the main elements of peasant social structure in that period, including status and gender differences; and, fourth, the processes by which western aristocracies took back control over peasantries in both economic and social terms, around the end of our period.

1. Peasants and the end of the Roman empire

It was argued at the start of this book (p. 12) that peasantries saw less change across our period than did aristocracies: essentially, they were subsistence cultivators and continued to be, even if some of the major elements of their external environment changed—their fiscal obligations, at least in the West;

their landlords, sometimes; the intensity of their exploitation, very often; their access to artisanal goods, usually. These external frameworks are discussed elsewhere in some detail (respectively, in Chapters 3, 4, 5, and 11). I argue there that most of these changes were pretty slow processes. Even the breakdown of taxation was not normally immediate, for most of the rulers of the post-Roman successor states wanted to maintain the fiscal system of the empire as long as they could, and in the case of the Arabs managed to do so with conspicuous success; the retreat of aristocratic hegemony, for its part, may occasionally have been faster (though it is hard to be sure), but was seldom at all uniform across a region. (Britain was the only major exception to these statements, as we saw in Chapter 6.) One consequence of this was that the end of the empire, even in the West, was not, for the most part, a process which peasantries would have experienced as immediate, catastrophic, change.[1] It did not result in either liberation or subjugation, at least in the short term. But it was a very substantial change, for all that, when seen structurally: the fifth and sixth centuries, in the West at least, showed a systemic shift for peasant society, which we can associate with the end of the empire.

This can best be seen through an analysis of two debates about the late empire: first, the recently revived debate about the nature of the late Roman colonate; and, second, the arguments about the nature and extent of late Roman patronage. For the tax system of the late empire was sufficiently heavy (above, pp. 62–72) that it seemed important to emperors to underpin its incidence by tying most taxpayers to their professions and locations—a well-known feature of the period, but one which had a particular effect on peasantries; and one of its results was, furthermore, a more overt use of patronage than at other times for the purpose of tax-evasion. Both of these put into relief the importance of the tax system for the construction of rural society as a whole, which has immediate implications for the period after which that system faltered. We shall look at them in turn, followed by a discussion of the evidence for peasant revolts in the late empire (above all those of the Bagaudae); these will enable us to see more clearly the most important changes experienced by peasantries as the empire divided up into successor states.

The debate on the colonate goes back into the nineteenth century and earlier, but for some time it was summed up by A. H. M. Jones, in 1958 and 1964, and his formulations are the most convenient starting-point. Jones argued that early imperial agricultural tenants were often on short-term leases and were free to move about, but that this ended when

---

[1] It must be made explicit that this emphasis on slow change is in direct opposition to one traditional reading of the end of the empire, that is to say as the moment of the breakdown of the slave mode of production. But, as we have seen, the slave mode had long vanished by 400 as a large-scale economic system (above, pp. 262–3).

Diocletian's tax reforms began to register peasants in their villages or estates, and, more generally, tied everyone to their hereditary occupations. In the middle decades of the fourth century we begin to have imperial laws which explicitly tie tenants, *coloni*, to their land, province by province, and generally across the empire by the end of the century. This continued even when the tax laws changed, however, for by now it became increasingly clear, as a law of Theodosius I for Palestine in 386 put it, that tying tenants would 'advantage' (*suffragetur*) landlords. Thus fiscal measures turned into a tool for aristocratic dominance. Tied *coloni* who did not own any of their own land (called by the sixth century *adscripticii*) slowly sank in status, became steadily more subject to lords (*domini*), and even came to resemble slaves, as Justinian commented in 530 (*quae etenim differentia inter servos et adscripticios intellegetur...?*). Not all tied *coloni* were so subject, all the same, for those who also owned land paid their taxes directly (whereas *adscripticii* paid via their landlords), and indeed many tenants continued to have short-term contracts and were not legally subjected to their landlords at all. Jones thought that *adscripticii* were a minority of tenants, but he called them 'serfs', and thus implicitly located them in the metanarrative of the move from (ancient) slavery to (medieval) serfdom—above, pp. 259–64—one aspect of which, the legally subject tenantry, apparently had late Roman roots or at least parallels.[2] The idea that the 'colonate' was 'a new institution, placed between freedom and servitude', has been made explicit by others, supported by laws which state, for example, that a *colonus*, although free, is a *servus terrae*. Here, then, late Roman law had apparently created a close analogue to central medieval legal and social dependence, although one could certainly still argue about whether there were actual continuities between the two.[3]

This picture has recently come under attack from two separate positions. One, more heterogeneous in type, and also related to earlier formulations of the issue (above all by N. D. Fustel de Coulanges in 1885), argued that the colonate of the fourth-century laws was simply a systematization of long-standing relationships of rural subjection based on the power of landlords.[4] The other takes its cue from Jean-Michel Carrié, who argued, in an influential article of 1983, exactly the opposite: that the fourth-century laws on the colonate were *only* intended to specify the taxpaying of the peasantry, not their social position at all, and that the subjection they envisaged was only

---

[2] Jones, *The Roman economy*, pp. 293–307; idem, *LRE*, pp. 795–803. Quotes: *CJ*, XI.51.1 (386), XI.48.21 (530).

[3] e.g. De Martino, 'Il colonato', pp. 791–803 (p. 802 for quote); Marcone, 'Il lavoro nelle campagne', pp. 825–8. De Martino, 'Il lavoro nelle campagne', p. 822, denies any continuity with the middle ages—as also did Marc Bloch, *Mélanges historiques*, I, pp. 373–8, among others—in my view correctly. *Servus terrae*: e.g. *CJ*, XI.52.1, cf. XI.53.1.

[4] e.g. Fustel de Coulanges, 'Le colonat romain'; Mirković, *The later Roman colonate*; Scheidel, 'Slaves of the soil', a review article, is a good starting-point here.

towards the state, not towards landowners. Carrié indeed supposed that tying tenants was not necessarily to the advantage of landlords, for it lessened their flexibility (apart from also weakening the ability of other lords to absorb illegally the peasants of others who were fleeing their tax obligations). He was above all, however, concerned to refute the position that any *coloni* were semi-servile, or indeed even that they had lost status; references to servitude in the laws were only figurative. If they did lose status, it was not because of imperial legislation, but only because of the changing parameters of landlord–peasant relations in the field, which were entirely separate, and which these laws were not designed to cover.[5] This latter argument has attracted both support and vigorous disagreement in the last two decades, with a large variety of variant positions set out.[6]

Whatever one's standpoint, one has to respect the vivacity of this debate; it is more animated than anything analogous concerning the early middle ages, in which discussions of peasant society (outside the framework of debates about labour service, perhaps: above, Chapter 5) have been rather somnolent. There are problems with it, however. The first is the role of imperial legislation itself, the major source of our evidence on *coloni*. Discussions of the colonate very often suppose, both that the two codes which collect late Roman laws are reasonably complete, and that the latter were actually applied, so that it would be sufficient to figure out what the legislator really meant to understand social relations in the countryside. This, as has been argued often in this book, seriously misrepresents how law works. It is true that late Roman rescripts were more specific than early medieval codes, and were often known about very quickly, as with the rapid reception of Anastasius' abolition of the *chrysargyron* tax on commerce in Edessa in 498.[7] In North Africa, however, Augustine wrote to the *iurisconsultus* Eustochius in c.422 to ask for legal opinions on a variety of issues concerning unfreedom and the colonate, including imperial constitutions which he had seen but whose meanings were unclear to him. Augustine, then, who had some judicial authority as a bishop, was legally well informed about some matters, but by no means about everything. Hence, perhaps, the fact that he also

---

[5] Carrié, 'Un roman des origines', developed in a reply to his critics fourteen years later in '"Colonato del Basso Impero"', a sharp-tongued article but more wide-ranging than the former.

[6] In support of Carrié: e.g. Cracco Ruggini, ' "Coloni" e "inquilini" '; Vera, 'Schiavitù rurale'; Grey, *Peasants, patronage*, pp. 7–14, 26–49. Against: e.g. Marcone, 'Il colonato del Tardo impero' (a criticism dating to 1985); Fikhman, 'Du nouveau sur le colonat'; De Martino, 'Il colonato'. See as background two historiographical surveys, Carrié, 'Le "colonat du Bas-Empire" ', and Marcone, *Il colonato tardoantico*, and more recently above all the 1997 article-collection on the entire debate edited by Elio Lo Cascio, *Terre, proprietari e contadini*. Marcone, 'Il colonato tardoantico', in the latter volume, is notably less hostile to Carrié than he was in 1985. Many of the other works cited in nn. 3–6 contain historiographical accounts, with more extensive bibliographies than those cited here; it should be noted that each divides up the historiographical tradition in different, often contradictory, ways.

[7] Joshua the Stylite, *Chronicle*, c. 31; cf. *CJ*, XI.1.1–2.

recorded without comment in the same year the threat made by the *coloni* of an estate that they would leave the land if a tyrannical bishop was appointed over them (above, p. 473), although several laws by now made that entirely illegal.[8] This mixture of knowledge and ignorance could be matched by anyone living today, of course, given the complexity of our own legal systems; but in the late empire it was even harder to know the law, for there were no public legal collections before the Theodosian code itself, issued in 438, which had been very difficult to compile[9]—and that code did not include all the laws on *coloni*, even of the fourth century, for many were not collected until Justinian's code in 529. What 'the law' was may often have been known only to a few people, not necessarily living close by; and this, of course, only exacerbated the fact that it was not necessarily put into practice, given the well-known injustices of the Roman legal system, above all if the people who operated it locally had interests which were affected by the laws—as in the case of any legislation over agrarian matters, given that lawyers and judges were generally landowners.

It must further be added that imperial laws—and, unfortunately, much of the debate on the colonate itself—even when they differentiate between provinces, presume a more homogeneous empire than can ever in reality have been possible. Village registration for 'free' *coloni* must have been a more complex business in those parts of the West where village identity was weak or nonexistent, for example (above, pp. 465–73). Conversely, laws on *coloni*, straightforward in the West where *colonus* (almost always) means a rent-paying peasant, and where their object therefore stably concerned the tenant stratum of rural society, must have had a more problematic resonance in the East, where the only equivalent word, *geōrgos*, meant any peasant or agricultural worker, including wage labourers and both small and medium landowners.[10] Arguments from eastern provinces cannot, therefore, be taken back too readily to Latin-speaking regions. It is, on the other hand, striking that the effects of the laws on the colonate are close to invisible in our best-documented province, Egypt, where leases remained mostly short-term; indeed, *enapographoi geōrgoi* (the exact translation of *coloni adscripticii*) are almost unknown outside the Apion estates and their neighbours in Oxyrhynchos, and, even there, one *enapographos* in 576 was a scribe and a tax-collector, an unusual social role for a 'serf'.[11] This, at the very least,

---

[8] Augustine, *Epp.*, XXIV*, XX*.10, ed. Divjak. For commentary, see (among many) Lepelley, 'Liberté, colonat et esclavage'; Whittaker, 'Agostino e il colonato'.

[9] See *CTh*, I.1.5 for the difficulties the compilers faced, with Matthews, 'The making of the text'. For the purposes of the codes, and of individual rescripts, see Turpin, 'The purpose'; and Harries, *Law and empire* (see pp. 82–8, for rescripts being issued repeatedly to please provincials, rather than always being a sign that the legislation was ignored, as is often argued).

[10] *Geōrgos* as landowner: see e.g. *P. Laur.* III 77 (a. 619), and, in general, Banaji, *Agrarian change*, pp. 192 ff.

[11] Egyptian refs. to *enapographoi*: see Jones, *LRE*, p. 1330, n. 74, not quite a complete list however (see e.g. Banaji, *Agrarian change*, pp. 130, 135); for the citation, *P. Oxy.* LXII 4350 (see Sarris, *Economy and society*, ch. 3).

shows that the totalizing implications of the laws were not generalized across the empire. Not that Egypt allowed its peasants to move around at will; fugitives were pursued by both the late Roman state and by land-owners, and, in the eighth century, with even more vigour, by the Arab state (above, pp. 136–43). This seems simply to have been linked to the general desire of the state to tie people of all kinds to their professions and localities, *curiales* as much as *coloni*, as indeed Carrié argues. But, once again, whether we can use the laws to generalize from these practices, in one of the empire's most tightly governed provinces, to the empire as a whole, is another matter entirely. Overall, it is a good idea to take seriously Domenico Vera's exasperated phrase, 'to continue to do economic and social history starting from the Codes is like crushing water in a mortar'.[12]

This sort of argument thus reinstates the regional realities of the empire, and the local, often microregional, relationships between landowners and dependent peasants (see above, e.g. Chapter 7), as the major parameters which affected rural society, with the exigencies of the fiscal system simply added onto them from the outside. Thus far, I would accept the arguments of Carrié and Vera, and I would agree that the weakening of the social position of peasants, if and when it occurred (and it certainly did sometimes),[13] did not principally derive from the laws on the colonate, partially because the latter had largely fiscal aims, and partially because the specificity of their detail cannot have been applicable to all rural situations. More important were local customs, local parameters for social action, and, above all, local power relations. An unknown African landowner wrote to his neighbour and former teacher Salvius, in the decades around 400, to tell Salvius not to menace his *coloni* in the hill country of Proconsularis, exclaiming: *an aliud aequum Romae sit, aliud Matari?*—'is there one equity for Rome, another for Mateur?'[14] But on one level, there was; Mateur's social relations, like those of Aphroditō (above, pp. 411–19), or those on Libanios' lands behind Antioch (below, p. 527), depended on what one could get away with locally, not on what it said in an imperial rescript.

On the other hand, the laws are not valueless. For a start, they are a guide to changing imperial values and imagery. Justinian did not make *adscripticii* like *servi*, and they never became so, but the fact that he thought they were similar is significant, as is also the fact that fourth-century legislators used the same figurative language, but less forcefully: it seemed a more obvious image by the sixth century than it had in the fourth. Imagery is here a guide both to perceptions of social dependence and to social change. Secondly, laws, although not always obeyed, can be a real transactional element in

---

[12] Vera, 'Schiavitù rurale', p. 320. Cf. Carrié's critique of legal historians in ' "Colonato del Basso Impero" ', pp. 129–34.

[13] See esp., recently, Sarris, *Economy and society*, chs. 7–9.

[14] Lepelley, 'Trois documents méconnus', pp. 240–51.

local social relations, at least if the state is an effective force. As C. R. Whittaker and Peter Garnsey remark, Pliny the Younger, who often complained in the second century about his tenants, would have benefited greatly from a body of legislation tying them to the land. Salvius had formerly, when he was friends with the author of the letter just cited, taught him 'by what law *coloni* are claimed'; the two were both legal experts, and the writer, who uses technical legal vocabulary, was largely aiming to point out to Salvius that he was breaking laws which he, as a lawyer, did know.[15] Furthermore, even if the detail of imperial legislation was known only to a few adepts, there is no doubt that it was generally known that the movement of *coloni* was legally restricted. If legislators had ever tried to invent local social structures from scratch, they would have failed: law is not that powerful, before the twentieth century at any rate. But there is a dialectic between the law and civil society. The words of laws can be used strategically, particularly if they favour the powerful, and the laws on *coloni* in practice did. It would have been that much harder for a tenant to negotiate better terms in a new contract if it was technically illegal to leave the land—not impossible, but harder; even the laws on fugitives, which are sometimes supposed to have been a restraint on larger landowners looking for new manpower, are more likely in practice to have resulted in illegal new tenants having to settle for poor terms in agreements, for they had much more to lose, as illegal immigrants find today. From this standpoint, even though imperial laws were concerned with taxpaying, not labour relations, they objectively favoured landowners: the statement by Theodosius I in his law of 386 that owners were 'advantaged' by the tying of their tenants could be seen from that standpoint as, at the very least, a Freudian slip. Laws of this kind were a serious problem for peasants in their negotiations with landlords, as long as they were accepted as valid, and as long as courts paid attention to them even occasionally: which was until the seventh century and often later in the East, but which did not necessarily outlast the fifth in the West.

Here, then, is one aspect in which the fall of the western empire did indeed directly affect peasants: in the desuetude of laws that tied the legally free to the land and to the remit of specific landowners, in the interests of a (now receding) tax system; and in the weakening of effectively coercive judicial institutions that might enforce such laws, as states slowly lost structural complexity. Not that we can track either in detail in the later fifth and sixth centuries in the West; but at least we can note that most Romano-Germanic legislation did not discuss tied tenure, which had evidently become less of a burning issue for lawmakers. This does not mean that tenants necessarily escaped their landlords in the Romano-Germanic kingdoms; sometimes they did, but sometimes they ended up more legally subject, not less. By now, however, their individual fates in most regions depended entirely on the

---

[15] Ibid.; cf. Whittaker and Garnsey, 'Rural life', p. 291.

nature of their personal autonomy or dependence, and on the local power of their lords, with no automatic legal support for the tied tenure of the free.

We shall look at the implications of these local power relations across much of the rest of this chapter; but it needs to be noted here that these statements are not undermined even by the main apparent counter-example, Visigothic Spain. It is true that the Visigoths promulgated laws in both the late sixth century and the late seventh on fugitives, which present to us a public political effort similar in its all-encompassing activity to late Roman or Arab practice. The Visigothic kings, keen to adopt or adapt late Roman legislative procedures, including the violent rhetoric of imperial laws (above, p. 95), were evidently assiduous in their desire to control rural mobility. In 702 Egica supposed that 'there is hardly a city, castle, village, estate or territory in which *mancipia* are not hiding', and enacted that all the inhabitants of Spain should report all unknown people to a *iudex*, or torture them on the spot to find out their true lords, on pain of between two hundred and three hundred lashes each (except for bishops and counts). If there was ever a law from our period that will never have been properly enforced, it is this one; it well shows the Visigothic commitment to imitate Roman toughness, in the teeth of all real social relationships on the ground. But it is also not the same as the laws on *coloni* at all. It, and its less extreme predecessors, are not laws about free taxpayers, but laws about the unfree, *servi* or *mancipia*; they derive from Roman laws about slavery, not those about the 'colonate'. As such, they do have parallels in other Romano-Germanic codes, in fact.[16] Spain, however, was apparently by the seventh century a region in which rural dependants were mostly unfree; hence the fact that these laws appear to match the Roman laws on *coloni*. Such dependants were beyond doubt tenants, as unfree dependants visibly were in Gaul (above, pp. 281–6); the Diego Álvaro slates, for example, attest to tenancy as the norm in local estate management. There are, conversely, only a handful of references to free tenure in Visigothic Spain, to set against the very many references to *servi*, hence the presumption that it was rare.[17] What remains entirely unclear is whether the tendency of dependent

---

[16] *LV*, IX.1.21 (702); .1–20 for previous laws. Cf. the *Edictum Theoderici*, cc. 84–7, for fleeing *servi* (and once, in 84, a *colonus*) in Ostrogothic Italy; and Rothari 264–76 for fugitive *servi* or *mancipia* in Lombard Italy (in 264 and 268, such fugitives can also be free, but such flight need not be linked to tenure; in 266 the issue is fleeing thieves). Egica's law may not have been all bluff: in *Vita S. Fructuosi*, c. 11, the ill-dressed saint nearly suffered a citizen's arrest by a free *rusticus* as a *fugitivus*, and see below, pp. 560–1, for the general absence of solidarity between free and unfree.

[17] Free tenants: Fita, 'Patrologia visigótica', p. 153, for the donation of Vicentius of Huesca from 551 (*coloni vel servi*); *Form. Wis.*, c. 36 (a lease, *precaria*, for a rent paid *ut colonis est consuetudo*); for Diego Álvaro, see above, p. 224. If we exclude the bald epitome of Roman law which is the *Lex Romana Visigothorum* (e.g. pp. 286–8 for *coloni*), dating to 506, there is only one other reference to *coloni* in Visigothic Spain, II Seville c. 3 (ed. in Vives, *Concilios*, p. 165). We cannot tell from these texts if the word has kept its technical Roman meanings; in contemporary Francia, however, it just meant 'tenant', free or unfree (below, p. 562). The *precaria*

peasants to be unfree was a long-standing characteristic of late Roman Spain—we simply do not know enough about Hispano-Roman land tenure[18]—or whether the accidents of war, or even possibly a Visigothic-period reconceptualization of rural dependence, had reduced the free *coloni* of the past to unfreedom. I would consider the first of these three to be the most likely, without having the proofs to go with it. But the fact that Visigothic kings sought to circumscribe *servi* in the same sort of ways that Roman emperors sought to circumscribe *coloni* shows neither that *colonus* status was in itself 'naturally' tending towards servility nor that Roman legislation on tied free tenure outlasted the specific imperial situations that created it.

The issue of patronage in the late Roman empire to an extent fits together with the 'colonate', at least insofar as it regarded tax. *Patrocinium* in classical Latin meant patronage or protection of any kind, and still did in the late empire; but the laws against it, which mostly date to the years 360–415, but which go on into the sixth century in the East, explicitly link illegal forms of patronage to tax-evasion—to clients seeking patrons who could protect them from paying tax. These laws principally regard Egypt; they are filled out by an oration of Libanios from c.391 on *prostasia*, patronage in Greek, in which it is made clear that Syrian peasants were capable of seeking patrons not only against taxpaying, but against paying rent to their own landlords, including Libanios himself. This imagery has been consistently linked to the weakening of the state at the end of the late empire, although it ought to be recognized by historians who do this that Syria and, especially, Egypt were the very provinces of the empire where taxpaying was least, not most, terminally threatened by private patrons: in Egypt, the Apions were scrupulous taxpayers (above, p. 247), and the Arabs inherited the system with no difficulty.[19] The issue of patronage and tax-evasion can in fact only be linked to the fall of the state in the writings of

---

contract is the best guide to the nature of Spanish free tenure in the period that we have; see further *Form. Wis.*, c. 37; *LV*, X.1.11, 15. The bibliography on this theme tends to assume either that the *servi/mancipia* of the laws are plantation slaves, a position that I see no reason at all to accept (it seems to me a product of the mirror game, criticized earlier, p. 262), or else that these *servi*, unfree tenants, are all former *coloni*, a less implausible position but one based on as little evidence. See, for the former, e.g. King, *Law and society*, pp. 159–72; García Moreno, *Historia de España visigoda*, pp. 243–9; Diesner, 'Sklaven, Untertanen' (all of whom argue for both positions); Castellanos, 'Terminología textual', more cautiously. For the latter, Barbero and Vigil, *La formación*, p. 164.

18 Arce, *El último siglo*, pp. 108–10, 134–5, surveys what little can be said about it.

19 For traditional patronage structures, see e.g. Wallace-Hadrill, *Patronage*; Brown, *Power and persuasion*. For patronage and tax-evasion, the main eastern texts are *CTh*, XI.24.1–6 (360–415), with *CJ*, XI.54.1 (468), 2 (520s), *NJ*, XVII.13 (535); Kaplan, 'Novelle de Tibère II' (578/82); Libanios, *Oration* XLVII. See in general, still, de Zulueta, *De patrociniis vicorum*; good recent accounts, mostly playing down too catastrophist a reading of the texts, include Patlagean, *Pauvreté*, pp. 287–96; Carrié, 'Patronage et propriété militaires'; Krause, *Spätantike Patronatsformen*; Grey, *Peasants, patronage*, pp, 80–8, 114–35; and, for the sixth-century laws, Köpstein, 'Zu den Agrarverhältnissen', pp. 3–39; Kaplan, *Les hommes*, pp. 169–83.

Salvian of Marseille in the 440s (above, pp. 62–3); even setting aside Salvian's many exaggerations and obsessions, he depicts a world in which peasants wished to avoid taxpaying, and, at an extreme, were prepared to surrender their land to patrons and pay rent rather than tax. This has similarities to the eastern evidence just cited, which has thus allowed historians to generalize such forms of tax-evasion across the empire; furthermore, this is in the period of the barbarian invasions, so that the fiscal collapse of the empire in the West was that much nearer.[20]

I would, however, be more cautious than I was two decades ago about the relationship between tax-evasion and the crisis of empire. Actually, the 440s was not a decade of crisis, at least in Gaul; Salvian, like Libanios, was inveighing against a situation of stable corruption, not fiscal breakdown—even for Salvian, the taxes were still being paid, and they continued to be for some time yet (above, pp. 62–115). Nor did this form of rural patronage necessarily turn into stable patterns of local domination, except at least when it resulted in the successful expropriation of peasants, which it presumably sometimes did. Earlier, patronage was briefly discussed as a means through which the pressure of taxation could be negotiated with, and thus (on occasion) defused (above, p. 143). This can be generalized: patronage of this type was a spin-off from taxation, its evil twin; it was a form of rural power that depended for its existence on the continuing structure of the state, and it was illegal because it was against the interests of the state. But this means that if tax-raising ended, which it slowly did in the West, then patronage against it would lose its purpose; such patronage would not of itself *substitute* for the state.[21]

I do not mean by this that rural domination by local aristocrats could not exist without the state, of course. Rather, *this* form of rural domination, a patronage relation that could protect peasants against the negative effects of public power, was pointless without that power. So, in Aphroditō in the sixth century (above, pp. 411–19), we saw that in that, still late Roman, environment there were at least two systems of patronage for peasants, rather than one: one focused on the danger—or protection—of the state, and one focused on the danger—or protection—of private landowners. If peasants were cunning and lucky, they could play one off against the other (although only a minority of peasants were either); anyway, they had to take effective account of both. But if the state ceased to have a local role, what was left was the direct, physical, domination of landowners over their tenants and neighbours, if they could maintain it through armed men and, perhaps sometimes, the memory of the clientelar relationships of the past. So state-orientated

---

[20] Salvian, *De gubernatione dei*, V.28–45; see Krause, *Spätantike Patronatsformen*, pp. 233–83, for the most recent critical analysis. For Salvian linked to the fall of the empire, see recently e.g. Wickham, *Land and power*, pp. 20–3; Whittaker and Garnsey, 'Rural life', pp. 310–11.

[21] Patlagean, *Pauvreté*, p. 294; Krause, *Spätantike Patronatsformen*, p. 336.

systems of patronage would only survive if the successor states had enough of a coercive local impact to generate systems of protection against them. It is not that the Romano-Germanic kingdoms had no coercive role at all; Einhard in the 830s, to take just one example, can be seen acting as a patron to protect a neighbour in central Germany who was evading army service and feared the consequences.[22] But once tax ceased to have an all-embracing structural importance, the major element of the public presence in the countryside ceased as well, and there would henceforth be, above, all, one *kind* of local power, that of lords—although there might well be enough landowners competing in a local area for them to be played off against each other as individuals.

What the two issues of the 'colonate' and the laws on patronage thus had in common was the tax system. As both cases show, the infrastructure of tax-assessment and taxpaying was so complex and all-pervasive that it generated, not just the extraction of large amounts of surplus from peasants, but a whole system of political power, which surrounded and restricted peasants as much as the actual extraction of tax did. The tax structure affected both rural status and the social relations between peasants and landowners, in far-reaching ways. From the peasant standpoint, if the tax-raising role of the state disappeared, what changed above all was twofold: first, they paid less to outsiders; and, second, the frameworks for patronage, for local-level political power, became simpler. Although the fate of taxation was most important for state structures (above, Chapter 3), it had profound effects on the peasantry as well.

This is relevant when we consider peasant resistance in the late empire, too. Peasant revolts are supposed to be against landlords, their primary oppressors; and of course most class conflict at the local level in a society dominated by landowners is over rent and the control of agricultural labour, as, in the late Roman context, in the case of the village of Eukraoi in Galatia (above, p. 408). But when it comes to large-scale revolt, most historic examples occur in the framework of resistance to states: they are struggles against military service, laws on status, and, above all, taxation. It is for this reason that there were few such peasant revolts in the early middle ages (see below, pp. 578–88); they began again in the fourteenth century, when states were more powerful and interfering. It would take us too far from our present theme to discuss the sociology of revolt, although such discussion is rather lacking in accounts of resistance in the late Roman world. Speaking very broadly, however, peasants tend to revolt when they see weaknesses in the structures of domination around them, in the context of lost wars, for example, both because revolt seems actually practicable in such circumstances, and because such weaknesses undermine the ideological hegemony of

[22] Einhard, *Ep.* 42.

their dominators, whether aristocracies or the state (cf. above, p. 440). It may be added that peasant revolts quite often have disaffected aristocratic leaders (usually not from the highest elite strata), but this does not mean that their 'peasantness' is thereby undermined; what marks them out is that, however ill-defined their aims, they threaten the constituted social order, and they are different in that respect from the more standard military or aristocratic rebellions that stud ancient and medieval history. For this reason, they are always misrepresented by our narrative sources, which universally come from the other side: all peasant initiatives are incomprehensible, indeed, to writers for whom current social hierarchies are the only possible ones.[23]

The Bagaudae of the third and fifth centuries are for this reason not easily visible through the distortions of our sources, and as a result have been dealt with in somewhat ideological terms by modern historians too, hailed as an organized rejection of the Roman empire by some, and dismissed as the informal clientèles of local landowners in a situation of political confusion by others.[24] To be brief, in the early 280s and in the 410s–440s in central and/or northern Gaul, and in the 440s–450s in the Ebro valley in Spain, groups of people called Bagaudae or Bacaudae are referred to in our sources, who characterize them as peasants, *rusticani*, *agrestes*, *servitia*, and the like, or *latrones* (brigands), as well as *quasibarbari* (in Salvian's very context-specific terminology). They are universally seen as in some way external to the social order, both in Salvian and in other texts, and as rebellious—armies are routinely sent against them, both Roman and barbarian (the Alan Goar in Armorica, roughly north-western Gaul, in the 440s, on Aetius' instructions; the Visigoth Frederic in Spain in 454, acting *ex auctoritate romana*). Their leaders are sometimes people of some social status, such as the *medicus* Eudoxius in 448. What they stood for is particularly hard to tell, but it is depicted as socially subversive in the rare sources that mention it. If Rutilius Namatianus in 417 was referring to Bagaudae when he described Exuperantius' recent restoration of power in Armorica, which is probable, it is relevant that the latter 'did not allow men to be the slaves of their own servants (*famuli*)'—although we need not be too literal about this as a social programme; that is the sort of thing aristocratic writers always said about peasant revolts. If the comedy *Querolus*, perhaps dedicated to Rutilius Namatianus, was also describing the Bagaudae, which is also probable,

---

[23] See in general e.g. Hilton, *Bondmen made free*; Scott, *Moral economy*, pp. 193–240; Skocpol, 'What makes peasants revolutionary?'. Note that I exclude religious revolts, which were not uncommon in the late empire—the Donatists in the early fifth, or the Samaritans in the early sixth, for example—following Jones, *Roman economy*, pp. 308–29.

[24] For the former, e.g. Thompson, 'Peasant revolts'; Szádeczky-Kardoss, 'Bagaudae'. For the latter, e.g. Van Dam, *Leadership and community*, pp. 25–56; Rubin, 'Mass movements', pp. 137–56; Wood, 'The north-western provinces', pp. 502–4; Neri, *I marginali*, pp. 400–17. Drinkwater, 'Peasants and Bagaudae'; 'Patronage in Roman Gaul'; 'The Bacaudae', is more on the fence. Sánchez León, *Los Bagaudas*, is a sensible overview.

they were associated with a locally based, informal judicial system, a *ius silvestris*, run by *rustici*, on the Loire.[25]

All of these items of evidence are ambiguous and rhetorical. So is all narrative evidence, of course, but, since these apply to peasants, they have been unpicked with unusual suspicion, and have often been discarded. It at least must be said that many of the accusations of 'un-Roman activities' cluster between the Loire and the Seine valleys in the early fifth century; something was going on there that looked neither Roman nor barbarian. Nor could it be absorbed back into the Roman order without violence, as even barbarians could. Gaul was full of competing imperial upstarts in the period around 410, but none of them are accused of subverting the social order; conversely, the leaders of the fifth-century Bagaudae are never put into the category of rival emperors, although the rhetoric of writers of the period had plenty of space for that category, and although even low-ranking soldiers claimed the throne on occasion.[26] We must conclude that, even if such leaders had social status, they did not obey the rules. Take the Ebro Bagaudae, based in an area of Spain that was dominated by prosperous Roman landowners (above, p. 222). Raymond Van Dam has proposed that the Bagaudae were simply these landowners, going it alone in a world of invaders. But they were the object of systematic imperial attack, in 441, 443, and 454, in years when Roman armies in Spain had their hands full with the Suevi; the Ebro Bagaudae, for their part, were not simply autonomist, but attacked cities, killing the bishop of Tarazona and sacking Lleida. It is hard to conceive of ordinary landowners, in a time when (despite barbarian settlements) the Roman political system was still normal, being quite as subversive as that; the conclusion that they opposed the local, as well as the empire-wide, social order, as peasants rather than as landowners, does not seem so hard to draw.[27] For all these reasons, I am happy to see the

---

[25] All refs. are collected in Czuth, *Die Quellen*, not an easy book to find, or, more recently, in Sánchez León, *Les sources*. These cited here are, respectively, Salvian, *De gubernatione dei*, V.22–7; Constantius, *Vita Germani*, cc. 28, 40; Hydatius, *Chronica*, c. 30, ed. Burgess (s.a. 454), *Chronica gallica ad annum 452*, s.a. 448; Rutilius, *De reditu suo*, I.213–16; *Querolus*, c. 30 (the dedication to Rutilius Namatianus, argued for in the introduction, pp. viii–xii, remains unproven, although *a* Rutilius was certainly the dedicatee).

[26] For the third century, one Greek source, Paianios' translation of Eutropius (in *MGH, AA* 2, p. 163), calls the Bagaudic leaders *tyrannoi*, but this is a very vague term, and does not justify the translation by Van Dam (*Leadership and community*, p. 30) as 'native usurpers'. Amandus perhaps claimed the title of *augustus* on coins in the 280s, but these coins have been criticized as forgeries (Sánchez León, *Les sources*, pp. 171–5). Overall, it remains notable how little legitimacy the uprisings are accorded, unlike even the most informal aristocratic usurpers. Neri, *I marginali*, pp. 402 ff., and Sánchez León, *Los Bagaudas*, pp. 48–56, suggest that this may be because the Bagaudae were *culturally* un-Roman; this is hard to show, but anyway does not work well in the highly Romanized Ebro valley.

[27] Hydatius, *Chronica*, cc. 17, 19, 25, 30, ed. Burgess (s.aa. 441, 443, 449, 454); cf. Van Dam, *Leadership and community*, pp. 50–3. Larrea, *La Navarre*, pp. 134–43, the most recent detailed account of the Ebro Bagaudae, is very uncertain who they were.

Bagaudae as rebels who were mostly peasants, and who, whoever their leaders were, had peasant, not aristocratic, aims.

Salvian says flatly that the Bagaudae were the result of oppressive taxation and the injustices of the judicial system. This is the sort of thing that Salvian always says, and we must be very cautious about it, but it does at least fit the profile of peasant revolts elsewhere. The linkage with tax could also be deduced from the *Vita Germani*, at least sequentially, for Germanus of Auxerre both sought tax-exemptions and tried to get pardons for Bagaudic revolt for his local supplicants.[28] The Bagaudae appeared, both in the third and fifth centuries, after local political crises, when the social order had been undermined by civil war and invasion. In that context, taxation and injustice, which had previously been seen by peasants as inescapable burdens, could more easily have come to be regarded as something that resistance could overcome. It is important, as with patronage, not to link them too tightly to the teleology of the fall of the state; they were over by 455, when imperial rule in most of Gaul and in the Ebro valley was still fairly firm. They were revolts against a weakened but still functioning imperial regime. Nor were they a pro-barbarian choice (and barbarians seldom supported them[29]); we have no reliable indication that the end of imperial rule was seen by peasants as liberating, and in fiscal terms, at least initially, it was not. But the Bagaudae do indicate that taxation was something that peasants could reject when the ideological hegemony of the Roman state was weakened. This, it must be added, also exactly fits the other great set of peasant revolts against a state in our period, which are better documented for that matter, the Egyptian tax revolts of the 720s to 830s (above, pp. 140–3). There, the revolts began on a small scale for different reasons, without a background of crisis, but the two main, generalized, uprisings were both set off by civil war among caliphal rivals, in 750 and 812. If there were no weaknesses in the hegemony of tax-raising states over peasantries, then, if tax was perceived as too high, peasants would normally just seek to evade it, by seeking powerful patrons or by flight; but if cracks began to be visible, they could and did resist.[30]

We must finally recognize that, whatever conclusion we come to about the Bagaudae, they remained isolated in the West. In particular, they had no known successors in the periods of disorder that were common in the next

---

[28] Salvian, *De gubernatione dei*, V.24–7; Constantius, *Vita Germani*, cc. 19, 28, 40 (cf. *Chronica gallica ad annum 452*, s.aa. 435, 437).

[29] Only the Suevi once, in 449 (Hydatius, *Chronica*, c. 25, ed. Burgess), as far as we know, although one Bagaudic leader fled to the Huns in 448 (*Chronica gallica ad annum 452*, s.a.).

[30] Only the 779 Mosul tax revolt in northern Iraq seems to have been the result of generalized peasant desperation: above, p. 141. An alternative reaction was brigandage, which is linked to a hostility to taxation in Pisidia by Justinian (*NJ*, XXIV.1). Cf., for the Anatolian mountains in general, Shaw, 'Bandit highlands', pp. 249–70. The socially critical role of Roman brigands as a whole is, however, minimized by the best two surveys, Shaw, 'Bandits in the Roman empire', and Neri, *I marginali*, pp. 367–99.

century. Perhaps when wars were more organized, peasants sometimes made the choice to go with one side or the other, rather than to reject both; we can see them siding with either Goths or Romans in the war in southern Italy in the 540s, for example. The only later tax revolt we know of in the West, in Limoges in 579 against Chilperic's tax changes, was urban, not rural, so does not come into this argument, for urban uprisings are quite different in type; but it might at least allow us to wonder if there were others, outside the purview of city-based chroniclers.[31] But they were presumably highly localized and without wider repercussions, if so. The relative quiescence of peasant political protagonism after the mid-fifth century underpins the basic point that such revolts were the sign of a system that was losing hegemony but had not yet lost its force and coherence. Like patronage to evade taxes, they were a spin-off of a functioning system, not a sign of its imminent demise.

As we saw in Chapter 3, the tax system did indeed slowly break up in the West. By the seventh century it had become marginal (in Gaul and Spain), or had gone altogether (in Lombard Italy). This took a heavy weight off peasantries throughout the West, and, as already argued, lessened the legal constraints and simplified the patronage system they lived inside. The combined result of these changes was radical, even if it was slow, and perhaps often imperceptible to peasants themselves—even in Italy, where the system may have changed fairly quickly, it probably took two generations in the mid- to late sixth century, and in Gaul and Spain it took 150 years or more, across the period c.450–650; only in Britain will its early fifth-century collapse certainly have been consciously felt. By the end, the state had substantially retreated as a mediating force (except for the occasional impact of army muster, or of the judicial ceremonial of the *placitum*), and western peasants were left to face landowners directly. This will be the socio-political context of most of the rest of this chapter.

Some historians, notably Walter Goffart, have concluded that the major beneficiaries of this shift were indeed those landowners, whether Roman or Germanic, secular or ecclesiastical; in particular, aristocrats took over surviving tax obligations and turned them into simple perquisites of landlordship; and, overall, such aristocrats, with their local powers, were well placed to take over from the fading infrastructures of public authority.[32] This did, certainly, sometimes happen. Free peasantries doubtless often became more subject as a result, and may have lost their residual autonomy, perhaps sometimes even their legal freedom. But it is important to note that the clearest examples of the aristocratic 'privatization' of tax burdens are late, deriving from the period after 600 in Francia, when tax levels were already

---

[31] Prokopios, *Wars*, VII.22.2–4, 20–1; Gregory of Tours, *LH*, V.28 (cf. above, p. 107).
[32] Goffart, *Rome's fall*, esp. pp. 198–253.

low and often already fragmentary. And the real problem about supposing that the end of the western empire was simply an aristocratic takeover is the general conclusion that a comparative study of aristocracies (see above, Chapter 4) leads us to: overall, and with the notable exception of Frankish Gaul, post-Roman aristocracies were poorer. Some may have profited as individuals from political and fiscal crisis, as just proposed. But in general we have to conclude that crisis, confusion, and political involution and decentralization did not favour the aristocracy as a class, which instead lost rather than gained wealth and local power. (For an eighth-century example of how this could occur, see above, p. 256.)

The importance of this for peasants in the West can hardly be overstressed. Logically, the less land aristocracies possessed, the more was likely to be in the hands of peasants, and the more there was space for the autonomous actions of peasant proprietors. Such proprietors also did not have to surrender surplus to others in tax. As for dependent tenants, even though their autonomy and often their freedom was much more circumscribed, they too may have lived more easily than under the empire, for the signs are that the intensity of the exploitation of tenants declined considerably in the post-Roman world, even in Gaul (above, pp. 280–7). So, dependants often paid less, and peasant owners paid little or nothing, by the seventh century, in notable contrast to the late Roman world; there were also more such owners; and the involution of the state created more space for a considerable, potential, peasant autonomy. The balance of power had temporarily shifted, favouring peasants rather than lords. I shall argue in Chapter 11 that this also, paradoxically, reduced peasant access to well-made artisanal goods; such autonomy did not improve peasant living conditions in all respects. But it was considerable, and it was new. As a result, the economic parameters of the early medieval West could sometimes be quite distinct from those of previous and successive periods, as we shall see in the next section. It would be a misuse of terms to call this a revolutionary shift: it was only partial; it did not affect the fact that all peasants continued to operate inside circumscribed, subsistence economies; and it was a slow, imperceptible, development for most people. But, for some peasants, for a few centuries the framework in which they lived their lives was transformed.[33]

It must be emphasized that these remarks apply above all to the post-Roman West: to Italy, Spain, and Gaul, and, rather more markedly, to Britain and Mauretania, and probably the Balkans, where even the Roman rules of landownership failed (above, Chapter 6). In the rest of the former empire the state maintained its coherence, and the burdens and constraints of taxpaying continued. All the same, in Egypt and in the Byzantine heartland, and probably also in Africa, aristocracies weakened as well in the

---

[33] I have proposed similar arguments in the past, more schematically: *Land and power*, pp. 33–4, 113–16, 212–25.

Byzantine and Arab period, and to that extent peasants, particularly peasant owners, would have gained accordingly. In several parts of the East—Galatia, the Syrian limestone lands, some Egyptian villages—peasant local autonomy had been considerable even under the late Roman empire (above, pp. 406–28, 443–65); we must assume that it increased further, in the East as in the West. But it did remain framed by the state. Change for peasant societies on the scale that we can propose for the West therefore did not take place. For this reason, the next section, on the parameters of the peasant economy, will deal with the East only in passing; it will return when I discuss peasant society in section 3.

2. The logic of peasant economies in the early middle ages

We have almost no direct evidence about how peasant economies worked from the inside in the early middle ages, and even less evidence about peasant attitudes to them. The more autonomous peasantries were, the further they lived from the world of texts; only Ireland and, later, Iceland give us any guide to peasant economies on the basis of written sources (above, pp. 360–2, 373–4). But, given the statements just made about the particularities of the early medieval West, it is worth trying to reconstruct what their parameters *ought* to have been, on the basis of what we do know, and on the basis of parallels that can be drawn with other economic systems. What would peasants have done when they found that they could keep more of their surplus, and that fewer outsiders sought to intervene in their lives? In order to understand this, we need to engage in some model-building.

Let us first survey, as a point of comparison, the basic structures of the normal economic system of the ancient and medieval periods, the feudal mode of production (see above, pp. 260–1, for the alternatives). In this system, landowners take a surplus, rent, from their tenants, the size of which is ultimately determined by relationships of force.[34] The stronger the landlords, in terms of their access to armed men in the last instance, the more they can extract, and vice versa. The 'struggle for rent' also takes place, however, on a terrain where customary practices have a good deal of weight (above, p. 291), and sometimes public legislation has some influence as well, as with the tying of the late Roman 'colonate' to the land, as we have just seen, or the restrictions of serfdom set out in the legislation of the late middle ages.[35] Landowners in this system have some influence over the local social status of peasants too, as it tends to be related to tenurial condition.

[34] For the feudal mode, see Marx, e.g. *Capital*, III, pp. 917–38 (ch. 47). Kula, *Teoria economica*; Hilton, *Class conflict*, pp. 278–94, remain basic points of reference.

[35] State taxation was another element in feudal surplus extraction, a more systematic and generalized one, where it existed, rather than being a different economic system: see above, pp. 57–61.

They do not, on the other hand, in general control the processes of agrarian production, which tend to remain in the hands of peasants. There are examples of the intensification of landlordly control, as we saw in Chapter 5, over at least some sections of estates, that is to say demesnes, in particular in situations where there is the possibility of large-scale sales of products. Apart from this intensification, however, which was seldom over more than a minority of land, peasants determined how their agriculture was going to work, and sought to ensure that their own subsistence was guaranteed first of all. What aristocrats did dominate in the feudal mode, however, was the main lines of economic exchange, simply because they were the main consumers, using any agricultural product they did not eat in order to buy other agricultural, and especially artisanal, products. The rhythm of the aristocratic economy included the possibility of accumulation, and the development of ever more complex economic structures. Elaborate artisanal production in our period and later could be directed towards many markets, including the peasantry, but it was ultimately dependent on aristocratic—including royal and ecclesiastical—demand (see below, pp. 706–7). The accumulation of surplus, and the creation of a market sufficiently stable to allow artisanal specialization, was thus the work of lords. In the central middle ages, when lords were very powerful, exchange, productive specialization, and semi-industrial artisanal activity would become very complex indeed, and even affected agriculture, as cash-cropping began, although this was as yet never so great as to undermine the subsistence base of peasant communities.

These observations apply to most medieval societies, and do not need to be developed in detail here. How might the economic logic work, however, if peasants did not have to give much surplus to lords, or any other external power? Here, in order to help construct the outlines of what I shall call the 'peasant mode of production', I have mostly read economic anthropology, for this economic system is less discussed by medievalists: Marshall Sahlins, Ester Boserup, and Claude Meillassoux have been particularly useful.[36] The peasant mode had and has many forms, but as an ideal type it can roughly be characterized as follows. First, its basic production unit is the individual

---

[36] Sahlins, *Stone age economics*, pp. 1–148 (esp. pp. 74–99); Boserup, *Conditions*; Meillassoux, *Maidens, meal and money*, pp. 6–7, 33–57, 82–8. Godelier, *Rationality*, pp. 245–319, is also useful. An earlier version of this discussion is in *Land and power*, pp. 224–5. I use the terminology 'peasant' mode of production in the absence of any more satisfactory classification of pre-class economic systems. The main alternatives, 'primitive communal', 'lineage', or 'domestic' (respectively, Marx, *Pre-capitalist economic formations*, e.g. pp. 142–4; Terray, *Marxism and 'primitive' societies*, pp. 95–162; Sahlins, *Stone age economics*, pp. 74 ff.) seem to me either too specific or too generic. The 'peasant' mode would include all autonomous settled peasant cultivators, excluding therefore nomadic pastoralists, and also hunter-gatherers, which have, I would argue, different, even if analogous, economic systems. But we also should not lose ourselves in definitions, as 1970s historiography did; further distinctions will not help a specifically early medieval analysis much.

household; only very seldom do whole villages control agricultural production. The household works the land it controls directly (usually inherited independently, sometimes allocated by the village community or a wider lineage). Households are seldom egalitarian units; gender inequalities may make women work the land as well as inside the home (as in parts of Africa), or, conversely, exclude them from agricultural work altogether (as in parts of Europe); in addition, there may be (often unfree) non-family members in the household, as, in our period, in England or Scandinavia, acting as domestic help and farm labourers. But all able-bodied people in peasant households are expected to work, for at least part of the time.

Household economies are linked together for mutual support. They exchange goods, both to cement social ties (gift-exchange) and to obtain products they do not produce. Peasants exchange goods in all societies, but in the ideal-type peasant mode this exchange is reciprocal, embedded in the network of social relationships, and also based on need. In the peasant mode, surpluses are not easily accumulated; after the acquisition of essential goods like tools and utensils, they are generally given away, as part of the social network, to kin first, to friends next, to other neighbours thereafter; or else they are collectively consumed, in celebrations of different kinds. This also, on one level, discourages any single household from going it alone economically and pushing to improve production, either by increasing its hours of work or improving its technology, for its members will simply end up giving the resultant surplus to the less active and therefore needier people around them; accumulation without such generosity is too risky, as it will cut a household off from its neighbours, and in a bad year it will not receive help from others. The simplicity of this system also discourages any productive specialization that cannot be supported inside relatively small communities, as with the village smith and potter. Occasionally, villages will divide up specialisms (a village of potters, a village of woodworkers, a village of smiths), but there will have to be a stable local network for this to develop. Markets for external, commercial exchange exist, but they are marginal in most versions of the peasant mode.[37]

Another characteristic of many versions of the peasant mode is that, since its members do not have to give surplus to outsiders, they do not work so hard. This largely depends on agrarian technology, it must be stressed. Boserup and Sahlins in the 1960s separately pointed out that the simpler the technology, the smaller the number of hours in the day a peasant household works: lowest for long-fallow systems like slash-and-burn agriculture (less still for hunter-gathering), rather more if plough agriculture has been developed and fallow periods get shorter, most of all if the peasants have developed irrigated agriculture. (Pastoralism is less work-intensive

---

[37] For exchange, Sahlins, *Stone age economics*, e.g. pp. 83, 123–9, 185–230. More generally, Mauss, *The gift*.

than most forms of agriculture too, although it is not self-subsistent, for it usually relies on exchange with agriculturalists.) Of course, the more complex the technology, the more productive the economy; but this does not, for most people, counterbalance the fact that they would have to work longer hours. Why do societies develop agrarian technologies at all, then? Boserup, in explicit opposition to Thomas Malthus, stressed population pressure as the primary cause of agrarian development: only if one has to feed more people is there an incentive to improve technology. This argument seems entirely convincing, at least in the absence of other socio-economic pressures, such as the extraction of surplus by elites in a social hierarchy (that is to say, the introduction of the feudal mode would be a further incentive to intensify agricultural activity). It follows that, for less agriculturally (and work-) intensive systems to survive, then populations have to be restricted in size, by late marriage or by birth control and its equivalents. It must be added that the population-pressure model should mean that agricultural change can also go into reverse, and indeed it does: German and Italian colonists in southern Brazil, for example, faced with unlimited quantities of land, sometimes abandoned crop rotations, or even plough agriculture, which came to seem pointlessly time-consuming. These calculations, however, which privilege leisure time rather than surplus, also mean that households, and communities, can often sail fairly close to the wind when calculating their economic margins. It is not that they normally live badly, for they do not have to give away their surplus, but there can easily be households which do not produce enough, and which become temporarily dependent on their neighbours, or whole communities which run the risk of famine in a run of bad years.[38]

Peasant-mode societies are not necessarily egalitarian. The household generally contains internal inequalities, as already noted, and so can the community. We have seen that household surplus is generally distributed around other households, but this comes at a price. Gifts and the underwriting of collective festivities are acts of power, as Marcel Mauss and Pierre Bourdieu, among others, have stressed; people negotiate socially through reciprocity, aiming to increase their local position. Basically, people who give more than they receive gain status, social rank; they have more ritual importance, or more of a leadership role in decision-making in the community; they can get poorer people to respond to their gifts by doing things for them. People who aim at that local status may indeed choose to work harder, or to develop their productive technology, for the rewards of status are sufficient for them to do so, even if the surplus they produce is eaten or

---

[38] Boserup, *Conditions, passim*; Sahlins, *Stone age economics*, pp. 1–74 (p. 34 for population restrictions, pp. 69–74 for production too close to economic minima). Subsistence calculations do normally take the possibility of bad years into account, all the same, as Horden and Purcell, *The corrupting sea*, pp. 270–4, stress.

otherwise consumed by others almost at once. But, in the ideal-type peasant mode, ranking is not structurally permanent. People have to work for their practical power, by their generosity, by their charisma, or by a capacity to negotiate for others; if they fail at these, or if they overreach themselves and become oppressive, others will withdraw their support. They cannot take power for granted.[39] These societies are, then, at least *relatively* egalitarian. The possibility that social support might be withdrawn keeps both wealth and power from accumulating; it is quite a leap for social differentiation to become permanent, and no longer dependent on the reciprocity, and the choices, of others. When it does, elites will characteristically come to give out less goods, and expect to receive them instead, in return for less tangible forms of service, such as protection: one can then speak of class differentiation rather than ranking, and the feudal rather than the peasant mode.

These, then, are the main elements of the peasant mode, at least as an ideal type. To what extent, however, do they adequately characterize the situation in the early medieval West, or in part of it, at least? The answers to this are inevitably going to be partly speculative, because the early middle ages is ill-documented anyway, and, as already noted, the areas of Europe in that period where peasant choices determined the economic system are likely to be among the areas with the least documentation. In principle, though, if this ideal type was a useful characterization, in material terms one would expect to find a relative lack of economic differentiation, and also a relative lack of artisanal scale and complexity. One would also not be surprised to find relatively restricted population levels, and maybe relatively simple agrarian technologies. These characteristics are, of course, for the most part well-known features of early medieval economies. They have often been interpreted as markers of the failure, the inferiority, of the early middle ages; I would prefer to see them as functional to an economic system in large part dominated by peasants rather than by lords, and as signs of a peasant, as well as or rather than a feudal, economic *logic*. This fits, prima facie, with what we do know to be features of the early medieval West: that it was a period when states and fiscal economic extraction were relatively weak, and that it was a period in which aristocracies were generally, globally, poorer, except in Gaul, both of these developments leaving more space for peasantries. In this sort of environment, therefore, it seems likely that there were substantial parts of Europe where this model, of the way the peasant mode worked, characterized fairly well the way people behaved on the ground.

I would propose, on the basis of the structures of landownership and local society discussed in earlier chapters, that there were two basic patterns for

---

[39] For a major instance of this, Melanesian 'big men', see Sahlins, 'Poor man, rich man, big-man, chief'; for more general theory and other examples, Runciman, *Treatise*, II, pp. 78–80, 150–2, 185–90. For gifts and power, see e.g. Mauss, *The gift*, pp. 33–46; Bourdieu, *Outline*, pp. 5–9. Big-man theory has moved on a lot since Sahlins in 1963, without affecting the elements of the model used here: see Godelier and Strathern, *Big men and great men*.

an autonomous peasant economy in early medieval Europe, although there were intermediate solutions as well. The first was the north European tribal pattern discussed in Chapter 6, in which land tenure was not always organized along Roman lines of exclusive ownership, and thus aristocrats did not have tenants as much as clients. Villages of peasants could owe allegiance, and thus tribute, to an outside lord, or, commonly enough, to a king, but such tributes were small, and did not substantially lessen the economic autonomy of peasantries, with village-level economic decision-making being the crucial element, and surplus accumulation an exceptional process (except for kings). An example of such a village, Malling, was discussed in Chapter 7 (pp. 428–34). Lords did not control any of the economy of such villages, except in the intermediate situation which Anglo-Saxonists call 'inland' (above, p. 323), land on which unfree peasants owed considerably heavier burdens of rents and services—a situation which would eventually lead to a shift to a feudal economy, but had only begun to do so in our period. The peasant mode in its tribal form would have been dominant throughout our period in England, Wales, Ireland, and Denmark (and in other parts of the North as well), in Mauretania, and probably in parts of Spain by the eighth century. Elsewhere, in the 'forest' areas of Francia and Italy (called *forestis* or *gualdus* in our sources), marginal, often wooded, but not uninhabited land, we also find people who were in some way dependent (on kings, until they gave such land away in the eighth and ninth centuries) but were not tenants—they held land independently, even if they paid dues to overlords. There were a fair number of these tracts of land—the Vosges, the *silva Bochonia* of eastern Hesse around Fulda, probably much of the Alps (though the evidence is less good there), parts of the high Appennines in Italy, among others. We could call their inhabitants 'tribal' as well. But they were, precisely, marginal to Frankish and Italian society, islands of the peasant mode in its north European form, and under threat at the end of our period as well, as kings gave such tracts to monasteries, who sought to turn tribal lordship into feudal landlordship (below, pp. 582–3).[40] Elsewhere in these regions, Roman-style landowning continued, and, where the peasant mode predominated, it followed a different pattern.

In most of Francia and Italy, and also doubtless of Spain, there were large landowners, on whose lands the logic of the feudal mode of production generally prevailed, but there were also areas in which there were substantial groups of peasant proprietors, which could, in principle, have favoured the logic of the peasant mode. Here, where peasants were independent

---

[40] Wickham, *Studi sulla società*, pp. 18–44; idem, *Land and power*, pp. 156–68. CDL, II, n. 249 (a. 770) should be added, an example of this sort of tenure from the Emilian Appennines. Innes, *State and society*, pp. 73–7, is the best discussion of the central German examples (including Schwanheim, in *Codex Laureshamensis*, n. 228 (a. 782), cf. 226–7, on the edge of the Odenwald forest but pretty near the Rhine too); the best evidence in that area remains that of marginal land east of the Rhine, i.e. beyond the Roman frontier.

landowners, they owed little or nothing to outsiders—less, indeed, than in tribal societies; but they were much closer to areas of aristocratic power, and were therefore often more at risk. Presumably, full peasant economic autonomy, and the full-scale logic of the peasant mode, would have existed in single villages where there were no outside owners, but there would have been a spectrum from there, running through villages with a small proportion of externally owned land, which, like Anglo-Saxon 'inland', was not yet large enough to affect economic choices, through villages with rather more, and so to villages owned entirely by several outside owners, and villages with a single owner. The latter two, at least, would have been dominated by the feudal mode; but, otherwise, exactly where on this spectrum any village ceased to be economically autonomous and became subject to the logic of the feudal mode is now irrecoverable—and may even then have been locally contingent, as we shall see in a moment. For both this pattern and the tribal pattern, however, the changeover point would have been when larger landowners were influential enough to control the terms by which a village economy worked; once they were, the village would have become part of a feudal economic system.

This second form of the peasant mode, characteristic of areas where Roman-style landowning survived, will thus have existed in a kind of leopard-spot geographical pattern, with areas of dark (the feudal mode, let us say) interspersed with areas of light (the peasant mode), with here the dark predominating—in the Île de France, for example (above, pp. 398–406)—here the light, but with areas of the other colour inside each. Sometimes there must have been a village of independent peasants next door to one of dependent tenants. There will have been friction here, with lords seeking to control the neighbouring economy by force on occasion (if they were sufficiently interested in local domination), with village elites in the autonomous village sometimes seeking to use nearby lords as patrons in their search for a more permanent local authority, or, conversely, with the dependent peasants seeking to emulate the economic autonomy of their neighbours (not an impossible scenario at all, when their lords were weak or distant). It is also likely, however, that in any given microregion one of the two modes of production would have been dominant, would, that is to say, have characterized the basic ground-rules of the economic system at any one time, with, under the peasant mode, even dependent tenants participating in the economy of reciprocity, and, under the feudal mode, even autonomous groupings seeking to accumulate and to participate in the wider exchange economy.

These are, evidently, largely speculative characterizations. Nor do I make any apology for that; one would not expect detailed evidence in this period about such issues, and, conversely, it seems to me that the peasant mode is a logically necessary feature of the early medieval economy, given what else we know about it, and therefore deserves some general description, however hypothetical. But how far can such description be filled out empirically at all? And, not the least important, what criteria could we actually use to identify areas where the peasant mode dominated? The latter, as we have seen, are likely to be areas with exceptionally poor documentation, but we could scarcely hypothesize that every one of such areas was a zone of peasant economy, given the notoriously patchy nature of early medieval evidence as a whole. Let us take these two questions in turn.

Empirically, the peasant mode in the early medieval West does not seem to have often existed in a 'pure' state: there were aristocrats almost everywhere. Independent peasant communities either paid some tribute to them, or were potentially menaced by them, or both. There were, that is to say, rich people in nearly all our societies who could accumulate wealth without giving all of it away; it is just that they did not necessarily have so much wealth or local hegemony that they affected the economic choices of all peasants. In northern Europe in particular, as argued in Chapter 6, and also in the 'Malling' section of Chapter 7, aristocratic lifestyles in this situation were not all so very different from that of peasantries, presumably because aristocrats were still having to give gifts to peasants to gain their support. Status was more sharply defined in Ireland (and, to a lesser extent, in England), in part precisely as a way of distinguishing elites who were much less economically distinct from peasants than they would be in any feudal society. These 'peasant-mode' aristocrats were not elites simply by the consent of their peasant neighbours, and they certainly generally lived off the labour of others, particularly the unfree. But they still had to transact with free peasants, in order to maintain their legitimacy—they were a marker of inequality without as yet representing generalized class subjection.

A second empirical particularity of early medieval Europe was that, inside peasant communities, social ranking seems in some respects to have been more stable than I presented it in my ideal-type characterization of the peasant mode. Members of local elites were, as far as we can tell, distinguished everywhere by having more land and other resources (such as, in Ireland, cattle: above, pp. 356–62), and this created a more permanent imbalance, for the sources of their wealth were heritable, and sometimes— as once again in Ireland—this was buttressed by tightly characterized legal distinctions, also heritable. In central medieval Iceland, too, although this society at least genuinely had no aristocrats for a long time, the position of *goði*, the local politico-religious leader, was heritable and was normally associated with relative wealth. But Iceland is nonetheless a guide as to how such inherited ranks could still fit into a peasant mode, for *goðar*, whatever their legal status, had to be generous, and also effective political dealers, to maintain any practical power in the zones of their theoretical authority. There is little sign of any accumulation of resources or political support here before the thirteenth century, three centuries after the settlement of the island.[41] It was still a considerable step, that is to say, up from local leadership in the style of the peasant mode to even small-scale domination. All the same, given the heritability of a certain level of wealth and ranking in the early medieval West, it was less of a leap than in some societies, and the same process as occurred eventually in Iceland occurred independently in several of our societies, rather earlier.[42] This point may also perhaps be reinforced by a general feature of western European and Mediterranean societies (then and now): seen in a world perspective, they are more violent than many, with an assumption continually made in laws, narratives, sermons, even casually in documents, that men will frequently, driven by anger, attack each other, often with weapons. This accepted male culture of self-assertion, one that seems general across all the societies in this book, legitimized much bad behaviour, including the sort of behaviour that incipient oppressors would have to use in any society, or at least made that behaviour less unexpected.[43]

A further element of stratification concerned the unfree. Peasant households, as we have seen, contained unfree dependants in several parts of Europe, and the regions where the peasant mode was strongest, in Ireland or England or Scandinavia, provide us with the clearest evidence for it (above, pp. 361, 430). As with Irish and Anglo-Saxon aristocracies, it is difficult simply to see this in class terms; unfree workers worked alongside free family members, and their exploitation was for that matter on a continuum with the subjection of free women in peasant households. Where it would become class exploitation would be if the members of the free family which controlled these unfree workers all stopped working, and simply lived off the labour of the unfree, in the same way as rich peasants who leased out some of their land stopped being peasants and started to be low-level feudal landlords once they had so much land that they could lease it all out and live off the rents. It might be supposed that, if a peasant household with unfree dependants really did end up living off unfree labour, then what would emerge would be the slave mode of production, since the unfree had no economic autonomy inside the household, and since the difference between the exploiters and the exploited was defined so clearly along the lines of the free–unfree boundary, just as it had been in early Greece and Rome. It is interesting that this is not what actually happened, however. Although such

---

[41] See in general Byock, *Viking age Iceland*, pp. 99–140, 341–9, and, for this social pattern in Malling described in more detail, above, pp. 428–34.

[42] For ranks becoming classes, see e.g. Friedman and Rowlands, 'Notes', one of the most rigorous of a significant series of processual theories, and Mann, *The sources of social power*, I, pp. 37–40, a good critical survey. Mann sees the process as only occurring under exceptional circumstances; I think he exaggerates its difficulty, although he is right to deny its evolutionary necessity.

[43] See Halsall, *Violence and society*, particularly his introduction, ibid., pp. 1–37; cf., for later periods, Rosenwein, *Anger's past*. For a comparative perspective, see in general Roberts, *Order and dispute*.

peasants did indeed sometimes turn into lords, unfree household labour became steadily less important as time went on in both England and in Scandinavia. Inside the house, at least in England, such dependants tended to become free servants, employed for wages (they were often the as-yet-unmarried children of poorer neighbours). In the fields, too, unfree agricultural dependants turned into tenants, each on their own holding, not into slaves.[44] Tenancy is so much more secure a way of exploiting the labour of others that it has been the default option for nearly every move towards class relationships in human history; the slave mode has been rare, and perhaps dependent on special factors, like the intensity of exchange (above, p. 277). It is, all the same, worth having briefly characterized this road not taken: the slave mode *was* a possible consequence of household inequality, and the fact that it did not develop in the medieval period testifies to the solid force that peasant self-sufficiency had in the framework of all medieval local economies.

These are all elements which made actual early medieval peasant econ-omies slightly different from those of the ideal-type peasant mode that I set out on the basis of anthropological analogies. We shall return to them in the framework of a more social analysis in the next section. But I would argue that none of them undermine the essential elements of that ideal type, in particular the normality of inter-household reciprocity and the absence of economic accumulation, because of the constant need to give in return for political and socio-economic support. And these essential elements are also our best guide if we want to try to recognize the peasant mode on the ground, through its presence rather than its absences from the documentation.

The best guide to the empirical presence of the peasant mode must be archaeology, the only type of source we have that does not privilege the aristocratic or clerical gaze. Above all, if a structure of demand, systematic enough to allow for elaborate artisanal traditions to develop, is a marker of the feudal mode of production, as argued on p. 536, then the weakness of such traditions is at least a marker of a relatively poor aristocracy, and really simple, localized, artisanal practices could be seen as a sign of an econom-ically autonomous peasantry, the peasant mode, that is to say. So, as a rough approximation, areas where utilitarian artisanal goods (i.e. those cheap enough for peasants to buy) are particularly undeveloped in their productive processes are more likely to have been dominated by the peasant mode. A full survey of the productive patterns of our regions will be set out in Chapter 11, based above all on ceramic production, the artisanal process that is easiest to identify and compare across a wide range of sites. Here, I shall anticipate the results of that chapter for a handful of regions and microregions, so as to

---

[44] Karras, *Slavery*, pp. 76–92, 160–3; cf. also Pelteret, *Slavery*, pp. 251–4. For the difference between 'unfree' and 'slave', see above, pp. 261–2.

show the way one could use them to argue for autonomous peasant economic systems.

Ceramic patterns, first of all, single out northern Europe as different. Southern and eastern England, Denmark, north-east Ireland were all regions and sub-regions where pottery was hand-made and very localized in its production from the fifth century at the latest to the eighth century at the earliest, and generally for longer periods still. Wales and the rest of Ireland were aceramic, and relied on wood and metal instead, whose production was equally localized. These are all regions where the peasant mode in its tribal form has been argued to be dominant on other grounds as well, indeed close to universal. Only the very end of our period saw any change in these patterns, with the development of more organized production and exchange (particularly, but not only, of Ipswich-ware pottery) in East Anglia and elsewhere on the coast of eastern England, which may mean that in England the breakdown of peasant autonomy occurred in the east first. (See below, pp. 810–13.) Tribal societies can thus be associated, prima facie, with very simple levels of artisanal specialization, visible over quite wide areas. Early Anglo-Saxon England was also a sub-region with a notably weak settlement hierarchy, an independent indicator of a relative weakness of elites. Although there was slightly more of such a hierarchy in Wales and Ireland, and quite a lot more in Denmark—and also Middle Saxon England—without the tribal nature of society being any the less plausible in the latter regions (above, Chapter 6), this nonetheless gives us a second possible guide to the peasant mode. Broadly, I would propose that either the weakness of artisanal elaboration or the weakness of settlement hierarchy are potential signs of peasant economic autonomy; and where we find both, we can postulate its existence with more confidence.

This is particularly important in the Romano-Germanic kingdoms of the Continent, in Francia, Lombard Italy, and Visigothic Spain, where we know or surmise that there were both landowner-dominated, feudal, microregions and peasant-dominated ones, coexisting in the leopard-spot, variegated, pattern described above. We know that, globally, ceramic distributions were more elaborate in northern Francia and in southern Italy than they were elsewhere in these regions in the early middle ages (below, pp. 794–8, 736–9); we could suppose that the leopard-spots of the peasant mode were smaller there, and this fits what we know about the strength of local aristocracies too (above, pp. 178–95, 206–8)—although this does not mean that autonomous peasantries were entirely absent in either. Inside the other parts of these regions, where ceramics were less elaborate, notably in parts of Spain and north-central Italy, we could similarly suppose that the leopard-spots of the peasant mode were larger, although this, equally, does not simply mean a peasant dominance—for we know that there were some aristocrats in both of the latter regions, and the more localized artisanal traditions in each anyway varied substantially in their elaboration. One would have to look to more specific, locally focused, archaeological analyses to be surer of one's ground here. These are far from numerous, but there are some. One such localized example is the Alicante coast of south-east Spain, where from the late seventh century to the late ninth most pottery was hand-made, demonstrating a degree of productive simplification which is rare in the post-Roman Mediterranean, in this case also linked with a breakdown of rural site hierarchies which was nearly total (above, p. 489; below, pp. 749–51). This must have been a sub-region dominated by the peasant mode. It contrasted notably with the main political and economic foci of Spain such as the Guadalquivir valley; it may have shown a stronger implantation of the peasant mode than Catalonia, too, where ceramics were almost as simple by 700 but site hierarchies seem to have been more elaborated (above, pp. 488–9; below, p. 749). Another example of this kind is the south-eastern Chianti, where local site hierarchies seem to have broken down completely in the sixth to eighth centuries, leaving only isolated houses, scattered across upper hill slopes (above, p. 484). This was not an area of as much ceramic simplification as around Alicante, and small-scale productions of at least medium-quality common wares and wheel-thrown coarse wares persisted. The area was, in fact, both politically and economically associated with a still active urban centre, Siena. All the same, the south-eastern Chianti contrasts so markedly with the Valdelsa, west and north of Siena, where concentrated settlements and estate-centres have been identified at Montarrenti and Poggibonsi, that one could propose a microregion in the south-eastern Chianti, rather smaller than the Alicante area, where the peasant mode dominated, in contrast to other parts of the Senese.[45]

It is in this way, I suggest, that we could begin to be more specific about the dimensions of the leopard-spots of peasant autonomy in the Romano-Germanic kingdoms. At present, such analyses are either very generalized (a whole region with less elaborate ceramics than another), or else so isolated as to be anecdotal, as in the example of Chianti; in future, there will be more. These will give a proper material context to the few peasant economies that we can pin down in the documents, because we can track them losing autonomy to aristocrats in the Carolingian period; these will be discussed in more detail in the last section of this chapter.

It must finally be stressed, in this context, that even in regions of recognized aristocratic power, the dominance of the feudal mode of production was not necessarily complete. The Île de France was at an extreme in the former western empire in its documentation of a powerful aristocracy living

---

[45] Valenti, *Carta archeologica*, I, pp. 360–3, 401–5; cf. Francovich and Valenti, 'La ceramica'; and Cantini, *Le fasi*, for Siena; for the Valdelsa, see above, p. 484, below, pp. 734–5. Note that the eastern Chianti included the area disputed between Siena and Arezzo in 714–15 and onwards, in which dependants even of Senese magnates supported Arezzo (above, pp. 392–3), a sign perhaps of an effective autonomy at other levels too.

on large estates and in the apparent marginality of autonomous peasant communities. In this respect it was unusual even in northern Gaul, for there was less space for peasant autonomies than there was in more tenurially fragmented sections of the region, such as the Rhineland, although there were certainly great aristocrats in the latter area too (see Chapter 7, sections 2 and 3). And, although in general demand for artisanal products was high in the region as a whole (below, pp. 794–805), there must have been space for some substantially autonomous peasant economies, at least somewhere in northern Gaul, or else several sections of the *Pactus legis Salicae* would have made no sense at all, even to its authors. We could not be certain that the autonomy of peasant society visible in parts of the Rhineland always implied a peasant-mode *economy*, dominant even locally (Dienheim, at least, seems to have been an active specialist wine village, presumably for an aristocratic market), but, if any village really resembled those character- ized in the *Pactus*, it would surely have had an autonomous economic structure of some sort.[46] There were, at least, small leopard-spots of auton- omy in northern Gaul/Francia too, then. Unlike the Roman empire, with the powerful unifying force of its tax structure, the feudal mode of the Mero- vingian period was not yet all-encompassing enough to englobe and thus undermine the autonomous economic systems of all villages of peasant owners, even in the heartlands of royal and aristocratic power; there may well have been a few even in the Île de France, although, if so, they will have been very much on the defensive, in an overall economic system structured along feudal lines, and they could not have outlasted the Carolingian period.

These are, in my view, the basic patterns of the various economic systems of the early medieval West. One further implication is more problematic, and that is demography. I shall discuss some of its aspects fairly rapidly here, for they seem to me far from resolved at present. It should first be noted that one element of the early medieval economy that did not visibly simplify was agricultural technology. Plough agriculture was not abandoned; the use of water-mills even extended (including in clearly peasant-mode regions such as Ireland), and were accessible to most peasants in northern Francia by the Carolingian period.[47] Overall, the early medieval peasantry, however au- tonomous, generally maintained relatively intensive agricultural practices, unlike some peasant-mode societies elsewhere (above, pp. 537–8), and the

---

[46] *Pactus*, cc. 2–9, 27, 34, 37, 45, seem to me mostly to reflect peasant-mode economic presuppositions. Cf., Wickham, *Land and power*, p. 213, and above, pp. 512–14.

[47] For mills, see e.g. Lohrmann, 'Le moulin à eau'; Champion, *Moulins et meuniers* (for Carolingian Francia); Rynne, 'The introduction' (for Ireland), over and above Bloch's classic article, republished in *Mélanges historiques*, II, pp. 800–21. The yields of the early middle ages remain unclear; Delatouche's vigorous attack on the excessive pessimism of earlier authors, 'Regards sur l'agriculture', although attractive in many ways, is not conclusive, as Toubert notes (*Dalla terra*, p. 140).

material conditions for class stratification were never absent. But it is also necessary to recognize that populations seem to have declined in this period fairly generally, and there were parts of the West in which intensive agriculture retreated geographically. These phenomena are generally seen, rather vaguely, as part of the package of events that made up the crisis of the Roman empire, or, more precisely, as being caused by external disasters like the bubonic plague. It is worth considering how they fit into the logic of the peasant mode.

The first point is about the incidence of plague. The plague epidemic of the sixth to eighth centuries began in our regions in 541–2 in Constantinople, and is graphically described by Prokopios; John of Ephesus and Evagrios give clear accounts of this and later phases, and it recurs in Arab sources too—eastern narrative sources being in general more explicit than western ones, with the notable exception of Gregory of Tours. Did it kill a lot of people? It must be recognized that it is hard to pin down the impact of the plague in eastern archaeology, and it is also close to invisible in the papyrus documentation of Egypt.[48] It is significant, in fact, that the best evidence for population decline is as yet not eastern at all, but western. Italy and Africa have both been ascribed mid-sixth-century declines, although this could be the result of war as much as of plague (cf. also below, pp. 723, 730). Above all, however, the rough 50 per cent decline for sites, that can be traced in parts of both northern Gaul and eastern England, represents relatively firm data of a kind that cannot easily be matched elsewhere (above, pp. 312, 507). The trouble is that this decline, whatever its cause, cannot be ascribed to plague, for it began in the fifth century, not the sixth, and the later sixth century shows if anything the beginning of the *stabilization* of our archaeological evidence in those sub-regions, the basis for future slow demographic rises from, maybe, the seventh century onwards. Had there been an overall demographic decline visible in the mid- to late sixth century, across all our regions, the plague would have of course been the most plausible cause of it, as the Black Death was in the later fourteenth century. (This is not, one should note, the same as an *economic* 'decline', which cannot so easily be attributed to the Black Death.[49]) But a uniform pattern of demographic decline is, precisely, not what we find. I conclude that the sixth-century plague, however dramatic its local incidences, was a marginal event in the

---

[48] The basic picture is set out in Biraben and Le Goff, 'La peste'; Sarris, 'The Justinianic plague', and the bibliographical survey in Stathakopoulos, 'Plague and pestilence', give guides to recent work. Dauphin, *La Palestine byzantine*, pp. 510–18, gives a very catastrophist account of the impact of the plague there; Liebeschuetz, *The decline*, pp. 390–2, gives plague a major place in his assessment of urban decline. Tate, *Les campagnes*, p. 338, however, cannot find much impact of the plague in the Limestone Massif in northern Syria. The best critique of the impact of the plague in the East remains Durliat, 'La peste du VIᵉ siècle'; evidence brought to light later does not undermine his arguments. For England, Maddicott, 'Plague', stresses the importance of the seventh-century plague, but in my view overstates its incidence and effects.

[49] e.g. Dyer, *Making a living*, pp. 293–362.

demographic history of our period. The population falls that we do see, in a variety of different periods, must have had local causes.[50]

The other significant aspect of the western demographic decline is that it was for the most part internal to areas of continuous agriculture, which only retreated slightly: with the end of the occupation of some poorer lands, particularly in mountain areas, and, in general, the shift of settlement into river valleys, and out of plateaux between them. This does not necessarily mean that the poorer lands were no longer used, but they were probably often used for more extensive forms of agriculture, long-fallow cultivation and rough grazing. In richer lands, there are very few areas of major agricultural abandonment, as pollen analyses are beginning to show. (For all this, see above, Chapter 8.) The same is implied by the regular survival of Roman microtoponyms across wide areas of France or Italy, as well as of the Roman centuriated field patterns of Italy or Tunisia, and the only slightly less regular pre-medieval field patterns of parts of England. These are arguments against systemic agrarian catastrophes of all sorts, and, as noted elsewhere in this book, against all images of generalized depopulation; demographic decline was internal to peasant societies, and probably relatively slow.

If one looks at the different dates for apparent demographic drops in the early middle ages, one discovers that what they correlate most directly with is political crisis: in the fifth century in the North-West, in the sixth in the central Mediterranean, in the seventh in the Byzantine lands, in the eighth or later in Syria. This may indeed make one suspicious, for the dating of archaeological horizons has itself often been twisted by easy assumptions about which periods have prosperity and which periods have war, and so on; and political crisis may affect the availability of archaeologically attested products, independently of demographic change. All the same, political crisis did often produce weaker state structures and weaker aristocracies, and thus more independent peasantries, as we have seen. Could demographic decline be associated with the logic of the peasant mode? Peasants in eastern Britain in the fifth century generally found themselves having to pay out substantially less in rent and tax than they did before; even in northern Gaul, where an aristocracy held on, there were areas of peasant autonomy where much the same would have been the case. How would peasants react? They would doubtless eat more, but there are limits to that. They might spend more on artisanal products, but the crisis in exchange visible at least in Britain would have made that difficult. In the ideal-type peasant-mode model, they would work less, and this seems to me entirely likely; it would immediately explain the phenomenon of the abandonment

---

[50] This argument also works against the latest Great Disaster theory to reach the academic community, the Dust Veil of 536; for a good critical survey plus bibliography, see Arjava, 'The mystery cloud'.

of the cultivation of poorer land, which produces less for the effort taken to work it. The logic of the peasant mode also makes possible the choice to restrict births, as we saw earlier (p. 538), to ward against economic pressure, and, once one begins to operate strategically to keep families small, then long-term population decline is a common next step. Ester Boserup's anti-Malthusian arguments help us, here, to get over what might seem the most counter-intuitive aspect of the model: that a peasant population might restrict its births in order to cope, not with a Malthusian ceiling and resultant famine, as in the early fourteenth century, but with the *relaxation* of economic pressures.[51]

This model fits Britain fairly exactly. It also fits marginal parts of Syria and Palestine, which faced periods of 'abatement', when intensive agriculture was replaced by partially or fully pastoral economies, with often substantially lower populations, in the context of the relaxation of political pressure, although generally not until after our period (above, pp. 457–9). It fits least well the situation in northern Gaul, for the areas where demographic drops have been most clearly pinned down here for the period around 500 are in and around the Île de France, which, *ex hypothesi*, ought to have been the sub-region of the whole of the West that remained most clearly under aristocratic dominance, and therefore not subject to the peasant logic which I have just delineated. Is this because there was a drop in the intensity of tenurial exploitation, at least? Or because there were at least some areas of peasant-mode economy even in the Île de France? These suggestions, however, could too easily be seen as defence mechanisms, to preserve a model's viability against an empirical counter-demonstration. This is a problem for which it is hard to see an easy solution. But it should at least be noted that, even in the Île de France, one can see an *intensification* of aristocratic exploitation in the polyptychs of the early ninth century, with the development of the manorial system, in the context of increased exchange (above, pp. 287–93); and it is precisely in the polyptychs that we have our clearest early medieval evidence of a renewed rise of local population, as shown by Jean-Pierre Devroey for some of the St-Germain-des-Prés estates, and also, in the south, by Monique Zerner for Marseille.[52] Here, population rise and increased exploitation do go together, and they would continue to do so in the West into the thirteenth century. It is thus not inconceivable that we could find the opposite process in the preceding period, even in the Île de France. But its fuller dimensions remain to be explored.

[51] Boserup, *Conditions*, pp. 28–55.

[52] Devroey, 'Les méthodes d'analyse démographique'; Zerner, 'Enfants et jeunes'. Cf. also for Languedoc the pollen-based arguments for ninth-century land-clearance of Aline Durand: below, Ch. 11, n. 105. See in general Toubert, 'The Carolingian moment', pp. 384–8; Verhulst, *Carolingian economy*, pp. 23–8; Devroey, *Économie rurale*, I, pp. 63–75, all duly cautious but in agreement about an upward trend.

3. Peasant social structures in the post-Roman world

I discussed some detailed examples of peasant societies in Chapter 7. Those discussions present most of the main lines of the key structures of peasant society as a whole in our period, in all their regional variety. Here, we shall simply look at some general patterns that can be found across all our regions, East, West and North, in aristocrat- and peasant-dominated societies alike, partly using observations made in Chapters 7 and 8, and partly on the basis of additional material, in particular from Gaul, Italy, and Egypt, globally our best-documented regions. I shall discuss, in turn, kinship and inheritance; the position of women; social status inside the village; and then, more briefly, the village as a social group and aristocratic patronage, two themes already discussed in more detail earlier (pp. 436–41), to frame a characterization of the ways peasants could rise socially.

All the evidence we have indicates that the normal peasant household in our period in all our regions was that of a nuclear family of a married couple and children, with at most an elderly relative or two. It was not universal (39 per cent of the *mansi* in the polyptych of St-Germain were shared between families, even if this does not necessarily show that they shared houses[53]), but it was normal. The nuclear family is a generalized image in narratives, legislation, and documents; other kin are notably less prominent. Peasant families of course did rely on wider kin in times of emergency, or famine, or dispute, as with the *vicini et proximi* who helped a man restore a vineyard, referred to in a sermon of Caesarius of Arles in the 510s, or the *parentes aut amici* whose gifts re-established Paul the Deacon's ancestor in Friuli when he escaped from captivity among the Avars in the seventh century. Conversely, such texts also show that neighbours had a social role alongside kin, and people could for many purposes choose between them.[54] Kin were one's basic resource in feud, but actual participation in violence would presumably have had to be negotiated; in Lombard law, there was provision that oath-helping had to consist of one's closest heirs unless they had good reasons to be absent, which implies that such kin were not always one's automatic first choice even in disputing.[55] Further, the frequency in the eighth-century West of pious gifts to the church by the childless of their whole property, which often only included very small-scale concessions to brothers and cousins, seems to show that one's immediate family loyalty on

---

[53] Figures from Goetz, *Frauen*, p. 253, slightly modified.

[54] Caesarius, *Sermo* LXVII.1; Paul, *HL*, IV.37. Cf. the *vicini* who could in some circumstances inherit in the *Edictum* of Chilperic (*Pactus*, c. 108)—although no one now accepts the organic community of *Gemeinfreie*, the so-called *Markgenossenschaft*, that nineteenth-century historians developed from this and some other clauses of the *Pactus*. See e.g. Dopsch, *Economic and social foundations*, pp. 146–57; Murray, *Germanic kinship structure*, pp. 67–72.

[55] Feud and kin: Liutprand 13 (see, for negotiation, the instructive examples in e.g. *Laxdæla saga*, cc. 48, 50–1, 54, 59). Oath-helping: Rothari 359–60, Liutprand 61—cf. for modern Berber society Gellner, *Saints of the Atlas*, pp. 104–25.

an economic level was above all to one's children.[56] Only Ireland shows more organic attachment to wider kin-groups, the three-generation *gelfine* and the four-generation *derbfine*, and, even there, basic economic activity was carried out by the nuclear family; the potentially parallel *genealogiae* and *genera* on the Continent seem to be above all aristocratic.[57] In most parts of Europe and the Mediterranean, a peasant's basic point of reference was the nuclear family compound, itself usually an articulated social space, often enclosed as well, as excavation and survey show, from the modular units of Denmark and Francia across to the sometimes monumental court-yard units of Syria (above, Chapter 8). Outside that, his or her links to kin and neighbours were usually reliable, but secondary, and subject to choice and negotiation, in the context of exchange.

Inheritance was universally partible; primogeniture cannot be found in any of our societies. Even now, historians often imagine that partible inher-itance undermines family wealth and power, or else is economically irrational in that it divides up properties, which then have to be painstak-ingly pieced together again. These are illusions. They require the improbable hypothesis that societies for millennia continued to reproduce inheritance patterns that were seen to disadvantage family prosperity. The point about division is, of course, to benefit children equally; plenty of societies (includ-ing our own) believe that the stability of family wealth across the generations is not a good thing if it means the reduction of substantial sections of one's descendants to poverty. Furthermore, partition only lessens the family stock of land and movables if there is regularly more than one inheriting child, which cannot be assumed in a fairly static demographic situation like that of the early middle ages; unless population is clearly rising, each family with more than one inheriting child will be matched by a childless family, whose wider kin will inherit their land (unless pious donation to the church inter-venes). To say 'one' inheriting child assumes that sons inherit rather than daughters, which tended to be the case in the West in our period, as we shall see in a moment; but if daughters co-inherit with sons, or else receive a substantial marriage portion from parents (which is much the same in practice), then each marriage will recombine property again. All these procedures certainly fragment landholdings; but there is no evidence at all that peasants (or for that matter large landowners) considered that having

---

[56] See for Lucca, as one instance, *CDL*, I, n. 114, II, nn. 131, 270; *MDL*, V.2, nn. 170 (= *ChLA*, XXXVI, nn. 1065–6), 177, 178, 193, 261, all gifts by the childless, largely or wholly excluding other kin. Kin did matter, though: *CDL*, II, n. 206 (a. 767) involves a father and sons giving their property to the church, 'Quia minime abente filii vel filie aut parente in quem nobis opportet eadem aut causa nostra commendare'.

[57] For Ireland, above, p. 359 n. For *genera*, Rothari, *Prologus*; for *genealogiae*, *Lex Baiuwar-iorum*, III.1. A recent commentary on the latter is Murray, *Germanic kinship structure*, pp. 99–108; cf. ibid., pp. 89–97, a broadly convincing critique of the view that the Lombard *fara* (Rothari 177) was a large-scale kin-group.

ten small fields was more disadvantageous than having one large one.[58] In an age before mechanization, cultivation was generally a slow process; in the enclosed landscapes of the Mediterranean, for example, one could spend a day in one small field and go to the next one the day after. Many scattered fields spread the risk of good land and bad land (or localized crop failure) more evenly; dividing each of three fields between three sons further meant that each son got an equal share of good and bad. Not every society in our period divided single fields between heirs (the Italians and the Palestinians did, the Bretons did not); but it is hardly imaginable that the practice would have continued in Italy and Palestine had it been considered negatively.[59] The peasantries we are dealing with were entirely sanguine about their stock of land constantly changing across time, as inheritance, marriage, and indeed in many places the 'land market', intervened.

The moment of land division itself was, on the other hand, potentially fraught. Doubtless this is one reason why brothers did not always co-operate subsequently: the moment of inheritance exposed potential differences and jealousies, as indeed it does now. Trouble over inheritance seems to have been particularly common in Egypt, in part because Egyptians often lived in what were in effect apartment blocks, which had to be divided room by room (as at Jēme, from where several inheritance disputes over houses survive), in part also perhaps because an irrigated landscape imposed less flexible field partitions—we have some fairly formalized, and therefore perhaps tense, divisions from the irrigated land of Nessana in Palestine, too.[60] Peasants sometimes postponed division, and ran their parents' land as a group. David Herlihy's early statistical work in the 1960s on western European document collections showed that the choice of families not to divide land went in cycles, peaking in the eleventh century in Italy (it was less common in France and Spain)—although neither he nor any successor has managed to explain the cycles satisfactorily. But these *frérèches*, groups of (usually) brothers on undivided land, were normally breakable, and we have plenty of examples of the process by which one person divided his property off from that of a collectively owning group of siblings. Nor did such indivision usually last beyond one generation. Essentially, indivision only postponed division and its potential dangers; it did not abolish it.[61] It was always a matter of choice, the mark of a group of siblings who got on

---

[58] Davis, *Pisticci*, pp. 107–18, is a good anthropological analysis of this.

[59] Wickham, *Community*, pp. 21–2 for Italy; *P. Ness.* 16, 21, 31 for Palestine; Davies, *Small worlds*, pp. 41–7 for Brittany.

[60] Schiller, 'A family archive', for Jēme (cf. above, pp. 419–28); *P. Ness.* 21, 31—and, for an Egyptian-style house division, 22.

[61] Consortial groups of brothers in Italy: Rothari 167, Liutprand 70, 74, and any number of examples in *CDL*. For the partial break-up of continuing peasant consortial groups, see *CDL*, II, nn. 249, 269, and 267 with *MDL*, V.2, n. 155. For Herlihy's figures, see 'Land, family and women', pp. 105, 116–20, and 'Family solidarity', pp. 176–8. For a succinct anthropological example of division and tension, see Cutileiro, *A Portuguese rural society*, pp. 123–6.

particularly well together, rather than a normal marker of lineage co-operation or of the desire to avoid fragmentation.

Inheritance was equal between sons and daughters in Roman law, and this continued into the post-Roman period in Visigothic Spain; Arab rules favoured sons in the division, but did not exclude daughters.[62] In the other Germanic kingdoms, and also in Ireland, female inheritance was more restricted, and generally daughters only inherited land if there were no sons. In Rothari's Lombard law, daughters even then only inherited half the paternal property, with up to a half going to the king, until Liutprand in 714 allowed them the whole estate.[63] Frankish evidence is more ambiguous, and has been much argued over, but I would follow Alexander Murray in his conclusion that Frankish law had always matched the post-714 Italian legal situation, at least as far as land is concerned. In both Italy and Francia, provision also developed to include daughters in the sons' inheritance if the father so chose.[64] All this is from law; more importantly, we can show that in practice the Franks were systematically more generous to daughters than were the Lombards, for, on Herlihy's figures, 17 per cent of land was owned by women in northern Francia in the eighth century, and only 6 per cent in Italy. This is as likely to have come from marriage portions as from inheritance, one must add, above all from husbands, the major contributors at marriage in most Romano-Germanic societies. Frankish custom allowed husbands to give as much as a third of their estates to wives, and in Lombard Italy a 'morning-gift' of a quarter was standard, both in law and documentary practice. (In Spain, where women inherited more, the legal figure was a tenth.) These latter procedures are particularly relevant in that the majority of women recorded in documents as independent owners are likely to have been widows, as we shall see in a moment. Whatever the origins of female-owned land, however, Italy is marked out in its lack of provision for women. The two figures compare instructively with Egypt, the only other region for which one could do such statistics; here, in the fourth century, 15–20 per cent female landowning has been calculated by Roger Bagnall, a similar figure to that for Francia, even though the inheritance system there was theoretically more generous to women. Patriarchal pressures favouring sons probably modified Egyptian legal theory in practice more than in Frankish society.[65]

---

[62] Buckland, *A text-book*, pp. 370–5; *LV*, IV.2.1; Schacht, 'Mīrāth'.

[63] Ireland: Dillon, 'The relationship', pp. 133–4; Germanic societies: see in general Ganshof, 'Le statut de la femme', pp. 33–40, with caution. Lombards: Rothari 158–60; Liutprand 1 (this law, of 714, Liutprand regarded as a major concession: see his *Notitia de actoribus regis*, c. 5).

[64] Murray, *Germanic kinship structure*, pp. 183–215 for discussion and previous opinions; the key texts are *Pactus*, c. 59, the *Edictus* of Chilperic (*Pactus*, c. 108), and *Marculfi formulae*, II.12 (*MGH, Formulae*, p. 83), which shows the voluntary extension of female succession (cf. also Liutprand 102).

[65] Herlihy, 'Land, family and women', pp. 116–17, cf. 105–6. Cf. also examples for Francia in Le Jan, *Famille et pouvoir*, pp. 234–5; Bagnall, *Late Roman Egypt*, p. 130; *LV*, III.1.5. For ninth-century Italy, see further for Frankish and Lombard marriage-portions, Feller,

At least as important as the extent of female landowning (and the possibly parallel extent of female inheritance of peasant dependent tenures[66]) was the degree to which women could really control land in practice, or, beyond that, participate in public life independently of men. Unmarried women were everywhere under the control of their fathers while the latter were alive (so were men, in fact); married women were subjected to their husbands. Only the occasional unmarried heiress, and, above all, widows (if they did not remarry) had any hope of establishing themselves autonomously; and this hope, when achieved, came at the price of the very real dangers to their patrimony from male relatives and other external powers, for the solidarity of kin and neighbours worked less well for women than for men. The Roman tradition, maintained throughout our period in the eastern Mediterranean and in Visigothic Spain, was for widows to have legal responsibility for children. Frankish widows had legal independence too. Lombard law was again by far the most restrictive: women were never to be free of *mundium* (legal guardianship), and even widows with children were technically under the *mundium* of their sons, not vice versa as in Roman law and practice.[67] How far this really happened in practice in Lombard Italy is not clear; we do have examples of widows who seem to be in effective control of their children's estates, whatever the terms of the law, as with Taneldis of Cicilianus (Casale S. Donato) in the Rietino, who disinherited her son's heirs in 768 because her son had done her 'many injuries and bitter trouble and damage', *multas iniurias et amaritudines atque damnietates*, or Alitroda, who seems to have controlled her infant son Atripert's private church just outside Lucca in the years 765–71. Alitroda did this until she made the mistake of sleeping with one of the clerics she had put into the church as legal guardians, her brother-in-law Peter, and was denounced to the bishop for incest by, significantly, her kin and neighbours (*proximi et vicini*); the bishop expelled her for it. It is probably significant, all the same, that both these examples involved trouble for the woman, of one type or another. Lombard women could not do much in public at all; they could not even conduct disputes at court without legal guardians, as women elsewhere did at least sometimes, as documents show. It is indeed possible that women in Lombard Italy were relatively secluded, more than Frankish women,

---

Les Abruzzes, pp. 459–82 (note, pp. 469–71, 487–94, that morning-gifts were the first properties that husbands—and wives—sold off: female land seemed more expendable). For Italy, Hughes, 'Brideprice to dowry', and Skinner, *Women*, esp. pp. 43–7, are significant overviews.

[66] Goetz, *Frauen*, pp. 258–60 shows however how small the figures for female tenant holding are in the polyptychs—up to only 9% for St-Remi-de-Reims, and as little as 0.6% for St-Germain.

[67] Nelson, 'The wary widow', gives a good analysis of the problems on the basis of Frankish evidence. For Italy, Skinner, *Women*, pp. 35–8; for Spain, King, *Law and society*, pp. 242–3, and *LV*, IV.3.1, 3; for Egypt, Beaucamp, *Le statut de la femme*, II, pp. 172–91.

although how much this was really practical at the peasant level is another matter.[68]

These comments are all fairly generic, and are more based on legal theory than is usual in this book. This is above all because the specific cases of female action that survive in our documents so seldom concerned peasants. Taneldis and Alitroda were medium landowners, for example; so were the female litigants over shares of houses at Jēme. Peasant protagonists rarely even have names in this period, but even fewer of these were female. One was Ermansuind, a Bavarian woman whose husband was successfully claimed as unfree by the bishop of Freising in a court in 818, and who thus had herself to negotiate her continued control of her own inheritance in front of the same court, which she did with some skill. Another was Anstruda, who sold her own freedom in 721 in northern Italy but could negotiate over it, as we shall see in a moment (p. 560). These women, however effective, are highly atypical in our sources, all the same. Not even law discusses specifically female peasant acts in much detail: here again the exception is that of the Lombards, apparently precisely because of the peculiar obsession Italian legislators had for excluding and regulating female actions—which included, more generally, laws that specified what constituted the mistreatment of women by men, such as beating them, or not dressing them according to the financial resources of their guardians, or, in another instance, stealing their clothes while they were bathing. Rothari and Liutprand both refer to the inconceivability that women might bear arms; Liutprand in 734 discovered with horror that this meant that the possibility of violent attacks by women on a house or village had been overlooked by legislators, and that, as a result, 'perfidious men, astute in their malice', were setting up women to attack in their place, 'more cruelly than men'. He enacted that they should be shaved and publicly beaten, and that their husbands should pay for their damage. This seems to have been a response to a real event, with female peasant protagonists. Even here, however, the king, at least, assumed that the real perpetrators were men.[69]

Whatever the nature of our evidence, we must conclude, overall, that peasant women were generally subjected in most of our regions, both in

---

[68] Respectively, *CDL*, V, n. 50; *CDL*, II, n. 255. (The bishop tried to expel Atripert too, but the king instructed him that he could not, as the church was private—cf. *CDL*, II, n. 186 for its foundation in 765.) For all this, see La Rocca, '*Multas amaritudines*'. Casale S. Donato has been excavated: see Ch. 8, n. 111, for the excavation and the identification. For seclusion, Paul, *HL*, V.37 (an aristocratic case, however). For courts, Nelson, 'Dispute settlement', p. 58; Beaucamp, *Le statut de la femme*, II, pp. 21–31. Cf. ibid, pp. 344–5, 348–9, with Bagnall, *Late Roman Egypt*, p. 98, for seclusion in Egypt: greater for elites than for peasants.

[69] For Ermansuind, see Brown, 'The use of norms', pp. 29–32, commenting on *Die Traditionen des Hochstifts Freising*, nn. 401c, 402. For Lombard laws, see Liutprand 120, 135 (cf. Rothari 182, Liutprand 125, Aistulf 15), for mistreatment; Rothari 278, 378, Liutprand 141, for arms. See Balzaretti, ' "These are things that men do" '; Skinner, *Women*, pp. 41–2; Wickham, 'Social structures'.

law and in practice, and had little effective autonomy, until widowhood at least, when their autonomy might feel like a threat. They were also boxed in in their daily lives, by moral double standards, and by restrictions on their work to the arena of 'female works', *opera muliebria* (as western sources frequently call it), household management, cooking, gardening, and—above all—weaving; ploughing, by contrast, was an *opus virile*, and a woman ploughing could cause scandal.[70] Overall, they are invisible in many sources, subsumed into discussions about men.

One paradox is that their textual invisibility is matched by a clear archaeological presence, at least at death. Cemeteries, when they contain furnished burials (as is common in the West in the sixth and seventh centuries), show us that women were often dressed much more elaborately than men. In Spanish cemeteries from the Visigothic period, indeed, it is generally the case that only women had furnished burials at all. Guy Halsall has traced the lifecycle of families in the sixth-century cemeteries of the territory of Metz: he showed that the highest quantity of female grave-goods was associated with women in their teens, presumably the marriageable age, whereas the highpoint for men was both later and longer, roughly in their twenties and thirties. One could reasonably conclude that women tended to marry before the age of 20 and men around 30, perhaps after a period of military or other public service. Men had a wider array of grave-goods, and all the weapons; but women had the expensive grave-goods, notably jewellery. These presentations of wealth, publicized in the ritual of burial, need not directly relate to social status; they were competitive claims to ranking rather than simple markers of it (though they did at least provide a minimum guide to what a family could afford). The fact is demonstrated by the relative absence of grave-goods in the tombs of both sexes after their thirties (for women) or their forties (for men); the status of their families would not have been less, but the role of the relatively old in society, and thus the claims made for them at death, were evidently of less social relevance.[71] In this context, however, it is significant that a young woman in the sixth century could be considered to be a shop window for her family, even in death. In public, women were thus physically visible but ideologically invisible at the same moment. Although

---

[70] For overviews of *opera muliebria*, see Herlihy, *Opera muliebria*, pp. 50–5, 75–91; Goetz, *Frauen*, pp. 270–9; Kuchenbuch, 'Opus feminile'. See ibid., pp. 141–2, for the moral scandal of a woman pulling a plough in tenth-century France, in Odo of Cluny's *Vita Geraldi*, I.21.

[71] For Spain, e.g. Hübener, 'Zur Chronologie'; Ripoll, 'La necrópolis', p. 243. For Metz, Halsall, *Settlement*, pp. 75–163, 254–7. In Anglo-Saxon England, there was much less difference between the life-cycles of the two genders in the same period (the twenties were the peak period for both, though there was some regional variation): Stoodley, *The spindle and the spear*, pp. 105–18. A sophisticated survey of gender issues in burial is Hadley and Moore, ' "Death makes the man"?' Cf. Wickham, 'Society', p. 87, for an earlier version of this paragraph. Note that the society of the Metz region did not practise late marriage for women; if it kept its population down, it would have had to have done so by birth control.

paradoxical, however, this need not be surprising to us; it is at least in part true today.

Peasant families lived versions of this life-cycle throughout our period in every region—as indeed in every peasant society in history. Its basic characteristics have been widely discussed on the bases of better-documented periods, and need not be further reprised here. The peasantries of our period also faced the standard dangers of ruin existing in all periods, war, aristocratic bad behaviour, climatic disaster (weather magic is consistently documented across our regions[72]), disease, judicial intervention, and the fortunes of inheritance, whether too many children or too few. If they lived in societies that extracted tax or rent, they were that much closer to disaster. Whether tenants were protected in any way by landlords, in return for paying rent, is undocumented. Peasants were certainly protected by the links of reciprocity they had with kin and neighbours from any disaster that did not affect the whole community, in ways I sketched out earlier, in peasant-mode and feudal-mode societies alike. But it does need to be repeated that gifts need to be returned. Chance imbalances, help given during a temporary illness, grain given to an unlucky neighbour when rain hit the harvest in a single field, can be rectified by return gifts in the following year. But structural imbalances, when one family is permanently in need, and the next family permanently helps them out, turn into structural links of dependence between permanent non-equals. One standard aspect of this from Egypt to Ireland, beside more informal links of reciprocity, was formal credit/debt agreements; in our well-documented regions, loan documents sometimes survive, presumably those that were not cancelled, with land put up as a bond. Uncancelled debt could lead to debtors losing that land, as we saw for Samuel and Phoibammōn in sixth-century Aphroditō (p. 416). (In later periods, churches and monasteries, with their larger resources, would be popular sources of agrarian credit, and would gain from its failure too.)[73] But, overall, all unbalanced reciprocity led to stable links of dependence, and thus to social stratification. None of our regions, whether or not dominated by the peasant mode, are likely to have had anything other than stratified societies at the level of the village, the semi-permanent rankings characterized in the previous section. Let us move on to further aspects of how these stratifications articulated themselves in practice.

In most of our societies, free peasants were described from the outside as a homogeneous group: *geōrgoi*, *rustici*, *ceorlas*, and so on. Their internal differentiations were not, in formulations of this kind, characterized in

---

[72] *Vie de Théodore*, c. 52; Quinisext Council, canon 61 (*Les canons des conciles oecuméniques*, pp. 197–9); *Las pizarras*, n. 104; Agobard of Lyon, *De grandine et tonitriis*.

[73] Creditors are usually churches in our documents, except in Egypt, simply because our collections are ecclesiastical.

law. There were exceptions to this, such as the late Roman laws on the colonate, concerned as they were with fiscal status (pp. 519–26), or the microdifferentiations of Irish law (pp. 359–62)—although even in Ireland the idea of a 'normal' free peasant can be found in the laws. One main reason for this homogeneity was that social stratification among the free, although it always existed, was too variable, too flexible, to be easily codified in any legal system. There was indeed, in most peasant societies, a kaleidoscope of differentiation, founded on the fragmentation of tenure that was normal almost everywhere. It was largely based on economic criteria, with tenants (unfree and free) set against tenants who also owned some land, small owners who also took some land in lease, peasant proprietors, richer peasants who leased fields out, and so on up.[74] These microstratifications were heritable, and could be built on, but they could also vary, as families climbed the ladders and fell down the snakes that existed in each of their societies. There were other status criteria that were more legally clear-cut, like the village leaderships of the East (above, pp. 407–28), or the *goðorð* of Iceland (above, p. 374), or the priests which dominated many village societies (below, p. 568), some of which were heritable too. These may have nuanced the economic criteria of each society, although they usually seem simply to have mapped themselves onto economic differentiation—village headmen, law-finders, or priests who were notably poorer than their neighbours were probably rare. The Lombards regarded formal status, at least among owners, as directly dependent on property or wealth (*qualitas*), and Dopsch argued the same for distinctions such as that between *meliores* and *minoflidis* in Salic law (see further below, pp. 566–9). The de facto importance of wealth was, in practice, the main reason why legal distinctions among the free were vestigial at the peasant level. We do sometimes, it is true, find titles used by peasants in Lombard Italy, particularly *vir devotus* and *vir honestus*. These were somehow inherited from Roman military ranks, and may indicate that position in the Lombard army had some local social resonance. If so, however, it was again vestigial, if only because the army was relatively seldom called out; this, too, was a ranking that probably represented rather than replaced economic wealth.[75] These wealth differentiations were what underpinned the intra-village links of dependence just referred to.

There was one major exception to these flexible economic divisions: the difference between free and unfree, between *liber* or *ingenuus* and *servus/ancilla* or *mancipium*, to use the Latin terminology, although it was as

---

[74] As in the Lucchesia, described above, pp. 387–93.

[75] For the Franks, see e.g. *Pactus*, c. 102 (*Capitulare* III)—cf. Dopsch, *Economic and social foundations*, pp. 214–16, a discussion of all the codes. For the Lombards, Rothari 48 (cf. Liutprand 62, Aistulf 2) for *qualitas* and landholding; cf. Tabacco, 'La connessione'. For military activity, see Gasparri, 'Strutture militari', an article which replaces the substantial previous bibliography. For the parallel link between judicial responsibility and landowning, see above all *MGH, Cap.*, II, n. 193, c. 6 (a. 829), and Manaresi, *I placiti*, n. 66 (a. 864).

important in Greek, Old English, Old Irish, or Old Norse. I have avoided the
word 'slave' when describing most of those of unfree status, for, as argued
earlier (pp. 261–2), this is best reserved for men and women wholly maintained by masters, and liable to unlimited service, with highly restricted
rights to possessions. Such people did exist in our period, but they were
mostly domestic servants, or else the household labourers of the northern
regions. Most *servi/mancipia* in our period, however, as we saw in Chapter 5,
were tenants, who controlled their own holding and could keep its fruits
after rents were paid; it is just that they had no public rights, and, if they
were protected by law from being killed or mistreated by their lords, it was
only a fairly circumscribed protection—late seventh-century Visigothic
kings, for example, disagreed about whether the mutilation of *servi* by
their *domini* should be legal or not.[76]

The free–unfree divide was constantly stressed by legislators, who, for
example, banned intermarriage across the boundary, sometimes fixing extreme penalties such as death by torture. In reality, things were different. As
we have already seen, such intermarriages were very common on the
St-Germain estates (p. 405). In Italy, Rothari stated that intermarriage
would result in death for the servile husband and death or slavery for the
free wife; here too, however, it happened all the same. In 735 at Campione in
the Alpine foothills of Lombardy, Iohannace, a *vir devotus* and evidently a
small landowner at least, sold the *mundium* of his sister Scolastica, who had
married an unfree man (*mancipium*) and had thus become unfree herself, to
her new owners, Sigerad and Arochis. In 721, in an even more anomalous
transaction, Anstruda sold to the same Sigerad and Arochis her own *mundium* (with the consent of her father, a *vir honestus*) and married another of
their *servi*, agreeing with them that her sons would stay unfree but her
daughters could buy their freedom at marriage.[77] These essentially ad hoc
agreements show that, despite the laws, the free–unfree boundary was by no
means impermeable, and that its key elements could be different, not only
from place to place, but even sometimes from *servus* to *servus*, and actually
negotiated over. But they also show that that boundary remained important.
It was the free who policed it: in Italy, where we have several ninth-century

---

[76] *LV*, VI.5.13–14. See Bonnassie, *From slavery*, pp. 19–25, for slave punishments in general.

[77] Bonnassie, *From slavery*, p. 22, for general laws prohibiting intermarriage. For Italy,
Rothari 221, Liutprand 24; the examples cited are *CDL*, I, nn. 53, 29 (note that here and
elsewhere *servus/ancilla* and *mancipium* are generally synonyms). They do show a more serious
situation than at St-Germain, for, unlike around Paris, Italian women who married the unfree
lost status instantly on marriage, and so, normally, did their children. So did the latter in
Bavaria: Hammer, *A large-scale slave society*, pp. 30–2; a little further north, however, the
situation is less clear-cut in Einhard, *Ep.* 46 (cf. also Innes, *State and society*, p. 80). Other Italian
instances are *CDL*, II, n. 204, 274 (children of a free man and his *ancilla* are free—cf. n. 174,
although here marriage is not explicit), III, n. 18 (a royal diploma—cf. Barbero, 'Liberti', p. 20,
though he mysteriously cites *CDL* I, n. 15, a nineteenth-century forgery using *CDL* III, n. 18).
These examples are not exhaustive; intermarriage was evidently common everywhere in
practice.

court-cases about unfree status, the hopeful *servus* or *servi* often lost because of their free neighbours' negative testimony.[78] The parameters of freedom were often hard to be precise about, because free tenants and unfree tenants often looked so similar, and were subject in similar ways. But they existed all the same. Sometimes, obligations were specifically marked as for the unfree (*opus servile*). Nor could the unfree make contracts—in a couple of eighth-century leases from southern Tuscany, the contract is only valid if, as one put it, the tenant 'remained in true freedom', *in vira livertate permanseret*. They could also be moved from tenure to tenure, or sold, in a way that even the most subject free and half-free tenants could not.[79]

As was argued in Chapter 7, the free–unfree division varied in practical importance according to the sort of socio-economic system it was set inside. It was economically fundamental in peasant-mode households where it was the basis for direct, though small-scale, exploitation. It was ideologically important in mixed owner and tenant societies, where poor free peasants were at least protected by their legal position from being at the bottom of the heap, and, if tenants, had at least more negotiating rights than the unfree— although this in practice varied, as we shall see. It was least important in villages where everyone was a dependant—it still mattered as a status marker between tenants, and the unfree may have had less access to the safeguards of village customs, but it could be overcome, as we can see in St-Germain's mixed marriages. These sociological differences did not under-mine the significance of the free–unfree boundary, which continued as long as legal unfreedom did, that is to say, for centuries to come. Indeed, I would see that boundary as one of the main elements which weakened collective peasant co-operation (village cohesion, for example), at least in the West, where unfreedom was more common than in the East. But, as at Campione, exactly how the boundary was experienced was variable, and even negoti-able. For this reason, we need not spend time discussing the details of legal characterizations of unfreedom, of which there were many,[80] or even the full range of variations in practice. I would above all argue that the chief effect of unfreedom was to circumscribe the social position of people who were already tenants, and that most important in any analysis of the character-istics of rural status is to look at how tenure worked, in the changing relationship between freedom and unfreedom.

[78] Manaresi, *I placiti*, nn. 9 (cf. above, p. 388), 58, 117; cf. *CDL*, I, n. 81. Cf. for Spain above, n. 16, and for Francia below, p. 580. Frankish court-cases about status are otherwise not very detailed, however, so it is hard to see what they turned on (for a list, see Nelson, 'Dispute settlement', p. 52 n.).

[79] *CDL*, II, n. 264; cf. I, n. 55, for the free children of a free mother and a half-free father. Italian slave sales include *CDL*, I, n. 36, II, nn. 174, 199. For the half-free (*aldii* in Italy) see most recently Barbero, 'Liberti', pp. 17–20. For *opus servile* see e.g. Goetz, 'Serfdom', p. 42; Hammer, *A large-scale slave society*, pp. 22–3.

[80] Full discussions of legal characterizations can be found in Verlinden, *L'esclavage*, I, pp. 61–122, 637–728, II, pp. 30–96; Nehlsen, *Sklavenrecht*, pp. 153–416. Neither pays any significant attention to practice.

In this context, we must first distinguish between societies whose tenants were largely free and those where they were not. Eastern Mediterranean societies had few unfree tenants. Here, dependency was sometimes individual, sometimes collective, sometimes customary, but overall the relative capacity for protagonism and for village organization, which we have seen among eastern peasantries, does at least fit with a tendency to free status. In the West it was different. In some regions the eastern situation was reversed: in Visigothic Spain, in much of southern Italy, and in the east Frankish/Alemannic/Bavarian lands (modern central-southern Germany), our evidence indicates that tenants were as a whole unfree. In the German lands, the best-documented of these regions (at least after 750), tenure was not absolutely synonymous with unfreedom, but *mancipia* were by far the most common dependants on the royal, lay aristocratic, and ecclesiastical estates we know about. This meant that free tenants too, although doubtless locally privileged, risked being treated as unfree, first informally or terminologically (as when free and unfree tenants were casually referred to together as *servi*), and later in law as well. Judging by other societies, such free tenants might have been best protected if they had at least one plot of land in free ownership; where the legal and the tenurial divide mapped most closely onto one another, this perhaps helped to keep more prosperous tenants on the 'free' side of the line.[81] The origins of the widespread but regionally specific rural unfreedom of Germany are wholly undocumented, and cannot be dealt with here, even speculatively (except to remark that in central Germany it could not have had Roman origins). Its consequence must, however, have been an unusually wide gulf between peasant proprietors and tenants, because the divide was so close to that between being free and unfree. The free peasant protagonists of Dienheim (above, pp. 394–8) were all the more on the defensive because of the dangers of tenure.

In other parts of the West, most of Gaul, north-central Italy, and maybe also North Africa (though the documentation there is fragmentary), free tenure and unfree tenure were characteristically found together in the post-Roman period. Here, the status differentiations found in texts that mention tenants are manifold, but not always either clear or consistent. In Frankish texts from Gaul, such markers can be very vague: the word *colonus*, a free tenant under the empire, sometimes means any peasant, sometimes a free tenant, sometimes someone unfree, for s/he is to be freed as a pious

---

[81] For Spain, see above, n. 17; for Italy, Martin, *La Pouille*, pp. 206–9. There are many good overviews of the German lands; they include Staab, *Untersuchungen*, pp. 331–51; Verhulst, 'Étude comparative'; Rösener, *Strukturen der Grundherrschaft, passim*; Hammer, *A large-scale slave society* (p. 11 for a free beekeeper casually referred to as a *servus* in 768, *Das älteste Traditionsbuch Mondsee*, n. 38)—cf. Goetz, 'Serfdom', p. 35 for dependent *liberi* slipping away from freedom. Renard, 'Les *mancipia*', shows that the term *mancipium* could mean any dependent tenant, free or unfree, in several ninth-century west Frankish polyptychs. For the importance to semi-free tenants of owning plots of land in twelfth-century Tuscany, see Wickham, *Courts and conflict*, e.g. p. 88.

act after his/her owner's death. In Italy, too, the word *massarius* is semantically loose: it denotes an unfree tenant in Rothari's laws, but some *massarii* can make leases in late eighth- and ninth-century Lucca, which means that they, at least, must be free.[82] There may have been chronological changes involved here, both in Italy and in Gaul (where the evidence for free tenure is arguably stronger in the Carolingian period[83]); but what we above all see is differences in emphasis. The point about both *colonus* and *massarius* is that their primary local meaning was 'tenant', and this, in the eyes of early medieval landowners (or notaries), was more important than whether such tenants were free or not. To the tenants, it mattered greatly, and so it did to their free neighbours; the distinction was a relevant one for negotiating purposes even to landlords. But the realities of tenure were winning out over the legal distinctions of the Roman (and also Germanic) world.

The process by which free tenants slowly lost status and unfree ones slowly gained it, both as a result eventually meeting in the category of 'serf', is a cliché of medieval historiography (above, p. 263). It is not entirely a mistaken one; the serfs of the central middle ages genuinely did have this dual origin, and indeed did so above all because the tenurial relationship came to dominate over all other forms of legal dependence, with landowners extending local legal disabilities to tenants as a class, even if not all tenants were ever serfs. The main centuries of this development postdate 800, so we need not consider them—they are anyway extensively discussed by others.[84] But their beginnings do lie in the process just described, in Francia and Italy. (They did not go back to the laws on the late Roman 'colonate': above, pp. 520–6.) The way that landowners were able to impose disabilities on tenants did, conversely, in large part depend on the proportion of them who were originally free or unfree in any given community. The overall capacity of dependent peasants to negotiate their practical status with lords would have been directly affected by the legal position of the majority, with free tenants brought down in practice if the bulk of their neighbours were unfree, and vice versa: German tenants would thus have had a weaker negotiating

---

[82] *Colonus* as any peasant: *Vita Desiderii*, c. 24; *Vita Eligii*, II.61 (certainly a free man); Fredegar, *Continuationes*, c. 50. As largely or almost unfree: *Testamentum Remigii* (a notably imprecise text); cf. Castellanos, 'Propiedad de la tierra'. As free tenants: *Pol. St-Germain*, *passim*. *Massarius* as unfree: e.g. Rothari 132, 234; *CDL*, I, n. 14. As free: e.g. *CDL*, II, n. 176.

[83] This is a difficult statement to make, for it would need to be pursued across many microregions for one to be certain. Compare, however, the references to *mancipia* in detailed texts for Paris-basin estates in the seventh century (e.g. *ChLA*, XIII, n. 569, XIV, n. 594) with the overwhelming dominance of *liberi/coloni* in *Pol. St-Germain*—unless the former term was already as generic in the seventh century as it sometimes was later (Renard, 'Les *mancipia*')? Verhulst, for the ninth century, sees more free tenants west of the Rhine than to the east: 'Étude comparative'.

[84] The classic remains Bloch, *Mélanges historiques*, I, pp. 261–85. Most recently, Barthélemy, *La mutation*, pp. 59–171; Panero, *Servi e rustici*, pp. 15–105; idem, *Schiavi servi*; Davies, 'On servile status'; and the collection of articles in *Mélanges de l'École française de Rome. Moyen âge*, CXII (2000).

situation than Italian ones, and far weaker than Egyptian ones, taken as a whole, even though one would also expect great microregional variation. In this way, legal status continued to matter for a long time for tenants, but as part of the dialectic of lord–tenant relations.

This is equally true when we consider manumission. The pious freed their unfree dependants very frequently, as we can see in countless wills and post-mortem donations, in particular in Gaul/Francia and Italy. Over time, this may have decreased the number of the unfree, although wars, legal penalties, and simple oppression always worked the other way as well. There were restrictions on manumission, in particular on church lands, for clerics held that it undermined church property-holding, which was illegal by canon law, and manumission of ecclesiastical dependants was therefore prohibited in councils in Spain and Gaul, with specific acts of manumission sometimes actually voided (above, p. 221).[85] In general, however, legislators through-out the West, following Roman traditions, were concerned to ensure that freedmen (*liberti, colliberti*) would not easily have the right to leave their former masters, and, sometimes, neither would their heirs. Unfreedom was thus to be replaced by permanent subjection (*tuitio, mundeburdium, defensio*): the freed had, so to speak, gained status but not negotiating rights.[86]

This was the general principle; but there are again signs that it varied in practice. In Francia, we certainly find a presupposition of subjection in many texts, such as some of the best-known wills of our period, of Remigius, Aredius, Bertram, or Abbo. *Liberti* are indeed sometimes casually referred to as *mancipia*, and frequently listed alongside *servi* and *ancillae* in possession clauses. (In the cases of Remigius and Bertram, the freed even included men and women whom the bishops had formerly ransomed from captivity, which sheds a potentially lurid light on the well-known ransoming practices of late Roman and early medieval bishops—such generosity did not always come without strings.)[87] In Lombard Italy, by contrast, there are hesitant signs that not all the freed were quite so subjected. Lombard law has provision for several layers of freedom at manumission, and charters vary in their

---

[85] Spain: I Seville c. 1, IV Toledo cc. 67–9, X Toledo, *Aliud decretum* (ed. in Vives, *Concilios visigóticos*, pp. 151–2, 214–15, 322–4). Gaul: Clichy c. 15 (ed. in *Les canons des conciles*, p. 538)—cf. Bonnassie, *From slavery*, p. 28.

[86] *LV*, V.7.13, 20; Rothari 224–6, Aistulf 11; Wihtred 8. See in general Borgolte, 'Freigelassene'; Panero, *Schiavi servi*, pp. 18–27, 261–6; Grieser, *Sklaverei*, pp. 150–7; Barbero, 'Liberti', pp. 17–22. Finberg, 'Anglo-Saxon England', pp. 440–1, discusses a freedman in Gloucestershire who later buys out his full autonomy. Note that not only did Roman law consider this continued subjection as normal, but so have most other slave-holding societies (Patterson, *Slavery and social death*, pp. 240–7).

[87] *Testamentum Remigii*; *Testamentum S. Aredii*; Weidemann, *Das Testament*, n. 69 (Busson and Ledru, *Actus*, p. 139); for Abbo, Geary, *Aristocracy*, pp. 91–7. Cf. also Busson and Ledru, *Actus*, p. 86 (a. 572) for *comliberti* described as *mancipia*. For bishops ransoming, see Kling-shirn, 'Charity and power'; pp. 201–2 for Remigius and Bertram. For permanent *defensio*, *ChLA*, XIII, n. 569, XIV, n. 592; Pardessus, *Diplomata*, nn. 254, 437; *Cartulary of Flavigny*, n. 1; for the Carolingian period, Epperlein, *Herrschaft und Volk*, pp. 105–52.

provision for them too. In 748, in Pisa, a group of *conliverti* remained under the *defensio* of the bishop, but not all such freeings referred to *defensio* at all. In 778, in Lucca, Bishop Peredeus in his will specified that his freed *aldiones*, half-free dependants, and probably also his freed *servi*, could leave if they wanted. In the 720s–730s, in Campione in northern Lombardy, the freedman Lucius tried to establish his status in court with a charter of King Cunipert (d. 702), which said that he had been freed in church, but this was, as the judge noted, 'prior to the *cartulas* which the lord Liutprand put in his law', that is, Liutprand 23, promulgated in 721, which legalized this particular manumission ritual; the judge therefore determined that he was an *aldius*, not a *liverus*. Lucius had also continued to do labour service for his former masters for thirty years, but he could find no one to witness that this was free service, or that he was personally free, so the judge concluded that he should be held to continue it. Lucius had, therefore, evidently maintained fairly dependent ties with his former owners; all the same, the clear implication is that, if he had had a later charter, and/or friendlier neighbours, he could have escaped these obligations.[88] There thus seems to have been a slightly greater practical space for the activity of freedmen in Italy than in Francia. This I would associate with another Italian particularity, the greater evidence for the existence of individually negotiated, contractual, relationships of peasant tenure than in Frankish Gaul, where free tenure was more collective and customary (not to speak of Germany, where such tenure was much rarer, as we have seen).[89] The manumission process in Italy gave freedmen access to a more complex world of dependence than north of the Alps, which they could sometimes in practice benefit from.

The subjection involved in being a tenant was thus highly variable. Even the unfree, and the freed, were not uniformly dependent; much depended on regional and microregional presuppositions and patterns of power. Free tenants had an even wider range, as just implied, from the customary village-level subjection of St-Germain's *ingenui* to the individual leases of some Italian tenants, leases which are also extensively paralleled in Egypt, where free tenure was normal.[90] These ranges of practical subjection, added to the even wider range of status of peasant owners, meant that every village had its own social structure, usually far removed (for better or worse) from the assumptions found in the laws. In particular, the scope for status negotiation that any peasant had would have been much harder if the bulk of his

[88] For the law, see n. 86. Cited charters, respectively: *CDL*, I, n. 93; *ChLA*, XXXVI, nn. 1065–6 (= *MDL*, V.2, n. 170); *CDL*, I, n. 81. See in general Panero, *Schiavi servi*, pp. 264–5.

[89] Among many Italian leases, see *CDL*, I, nn. 57, 85, 104; II, nn. 166–7, 176, 263–4. *Livellarii*, written leaseholders, were recognized in law: Liutprand 92. See in general Endres, 'Das Kirchengut'; Leicht, 'Livellario nomine'; Andreolli, 'Per una semantica storica'.

[90] Lists for before 650 in Johnson and West, *Byzantine Egypt*, pp. 80–93; and, more completely, Herrmann, *Studien zur Bodenpacht*, pp. 274–88. Some from after 650 are listed above, Ch. 7, n. 106.

or her kin or neighbours were subjected, and much easier if there was more local differentiation: there was a difference, one could say, between an audience for status claims consisting of lords, and one consisting of one's free peasant neighbours. As I have been stressing throughout the last few pages, if one wishes to understand the detail of village social structures, one has to take all these local variabilities into account.

The upper end of peasant society was equally negotiable, at least inside limits. Free peasants were universally defined as free in our period because they had not only legal rights but also—as long as they were male—public obligations. In the East they had to pay taxes; in the West they had to participate in public courts, and, at least in principle, to do army service or its equivalents. In both, they had to do certain labour services, notably the building of roads and defences (in Arab Egypt, quite an array of artisanal and construction work too: above, pp. 136–8).[91] If peasants did not have access to the public sphere in these ways, then their general autonomy would be menaced; this would happen in the West after 800, when the poorer free were decreasingly linked to military activity, and the network of developments began that would lead to structured private lordships run by military elites by the eleventh century. We shall look at the beginning of that process in the next section. Across our period as a whole, however, public services, however occasional they were, were signs of a continuum of free status that stretched right up into the aristocracy. The aristocracy was not formally bounded in any of our regions in the post-Roman period (except Ireland: above, pp. 359–60); the counterpart to this was that peasant, village-level, status was not bounded at the top, either. Peasants at the top of village society could, in principle, continue to 'thrive', until one reached the level of *thegn*, as a later Anglo-Saxon law tract put it (above, p. 319). Such rises cannot have been common, of course. In practice, peasants were as much regarded by elite society as different, inferior, in the early middle ages as before and after. Victor of Vita in the Africa of the 480s (admittedly, still fully Roman in its values) regarded agricultural labour as intrinsically degrading, and so did the Vandals, who punished Catholic aristocrats by forcing them to do it; Cassiodorus in the Italy of the 530s thought that being an urban slave was self-evidently better than being a free peasant in the countryside. Gregory of Tours in the 570s–590s used the word *rusticitas* to indicate a failure to understand the basic assumptions of moral behaviour, and was contemptuous of social upstarts like his rival, Leudast, count of Tours.[92] Peasants were distinguished by their clothes and by their speech, as

---

[91] For a quick survey, Goetz, 'Social and military institutions'.

[92] Victor of Vita, *Historia persecutionis*, I.44, II.10, 16, III.20; Cassiodorus, *Variae*, VIII.33. For Gregory of Tours, see Brown, 'Relics and social status', pp. 230–3, and cf. *LH*, V.48 for Leudast; cf. IV.46, a morality tale about the fate of another upstart, the literary con-man Andarchius.

the Imma story in England shows (above, p. 343). Social ascent thus ran up against the same sort of snobbery as it did in later centuries, for all the relative simplicity of the early medieval period. But it did happen; it is thus worth looking at some of its patterns.

The first element must be the village itself, because local power was a crucial first step for the ambitious. We have seen in Chapter 8 that village coherence, and thus the opportunities for local power, varied very greatly. In the East, villages were structured communities, with official leaderships. The extreme seems to have been Egypt, where the names of annual village headmen (*lashaniou*) were even used to date documents at Jēme (above, p. 422)—notable social status in itself. The *dioikētai* of Palestine and the *prōtopresbyteroi* of Galatia were less locally powerful than that, as it seems. But they were still more stable in their official role than their western equivalents, the *priores loci* of Spain or the priestly families of Brittany or the Pyrenees, which were rather more informal positions;[93] and many western village communities had no visible leaders at all. Village coherence was particularly weak in the western Mediterranean; even its identity could at times be called into question. On the other hand, a de facto village elite group can be identified in most places. In Egypt, they could be called *noc nrōme*, 'big men'; in Galatia, *oikodespotai*, 'house owners'; in the West, very characteristically, *boni homines*, 'good men', an elite whose leaders in 796 in Dienheim on the Middle Rhine (see above, p. 396) were called those who 'have *hereditas*' there.[94] The informality of local status was earlier linked to the complexity of gradations of wealth (p. 559); but the consistency of the link between local landownership and village-level power is made explicit by this network of terms. (The terms *boni homines* and *noc nrōme* were not restricted to villages; such men can be found running legal and other public proceedings in cities, too. See below, p. 600.) These groups of local leaders doubtless established themselves by the usual complex mix of land deals, lucky marriages, successful feasts, well-publicized gifts to churches, patronage networks with their poorer neighbours, and, we can also suppose, mutual support (modified by local rivalries): this is how village leaderships work everywhere. But such leadership was normally an essential starting-point for any upward movement, too.

Village churches were independent power-bases for local elites. If they have not been stressed earlier, it is simply because in many of our regions only a minority of villages had them, as late as 800. They were normal in the East, where almost every archaeological survey, indeed, shows several per settlement. At Jēme, the abbots of the monasteries scattered across the village territory were important patrons and intermediaries, both inside the

---

[93] *Priores loci: LV,* IX.1.8, 9; for priests, see below, n. 96.
[94] *Ub. Fulda,* n. 246. For *boni homines* in general, see Nehlsen-van Stryk, *Die boni homines,* esp. pp. 242–55, 343.

village and outside it (p. 427); at Nessana in Palestine, the village headman and the village priest could be father and son (p. 454). Around Ankara, on the other hand, rural clerics are almost absent from the *Life* of Theodore, perhaps because they were as yet not rich enough to have the transactional influence they had in Egypt.[95] And in the West, village churches were in general only beginning to be founded from the middle of the eighth century onwards in any numbers, and had relatively little socio-economic impact before 800. Such churches would in the future transform peasant political relationships, for they were the foci of pious donations even from the poor, and became rich enough to provide their owners and/or their priests with considerable local prominence. An early example of this is Campori in the mountains north of Lucca, whose church, S. Maria, was founded in the 740s; the family of its holders and priests dominated the village for the next two centuries. The priestly families of some ninth-century Breton villages, and the leaders (frequently priests) of the large collectivities who founded churches in the ninth-century Pyrenees were other examples, from close to the end of our period.[96] Here, to put it schematically, Marc Bloch's politics of land (above, p. 58) could be played out even at the village level, not just among the aristocracy. But the role of churches in the slowly crystallizing structures of village politics in the West, and even in parts of the East, really belongs to the period after ours.

On the basis of these local political positions, ambitious village leaders had two choices, not fully separable: to establish ever firmer local economic and political dominance, or to look for external patronage. The first was possible in the longer term, if one was lucky; it can be seen in the emerging village-level aristocracies of eleventh-century northern Spain, for example, or in the steadily more hierarchical house structures of some excavated north European villages (above, pp. 500–7). Easier was patronage by members of external elites, who were happy to promote individuals from among the *infimes* or *mediocres* as long as they were exceptional: in intelligence (Eligius and Bede, probably), in sanctity (Richer of Centula), in dependability (Leudast, and many humbly born or ex-servile administrators), in physical prowess and sex appeal (Queen Fredegund, the emperor Basil I), or, above all, in military commitment.[97] In the latter category was Ripwin of Bensheim (above, p. 397), and also most of the lower rungs of those famous categories of armed retainers, *boukellarioi/buccellarii* (in the East and in Spain),

---

[95] For village churches in Syria, see Naccache, *Le décor des églises*, I, pp. 23, 300; for Egypt, Wipszycka, *Les ressources*, pp. 50–6. For Galatia, Kaplan, *Les hommes*, pp. 227–8.

[96] Wickham, *Mountains*, pp. 40–51; Davies, *Small worlds*, pp. 100–2; Bonnassie, *From slavery*, pp. 244–7 (with P. Guichard)—see for the latter Baraut, 'Les actes', nn. 1, 4–26. For church-building in general see Wood, *Lords, priests*, chs. 12–14.

[97] *Vita Eligii*, I.1–3; Alcuin, *Vita Richarii*, c. 1 (cf. also *Vita Erminonis*, c. 1; *Vita Pardulfi*, c. 1). For Bede, above, p. 324. For Fredegund, Gregory of Tours, *LH*, IV.27–8; for Basil, *Istorikē diēgēsis Basileiou*, cc. 7–15. A rising administrator from a middling Lombard family is described in Bullough, 'Leo'.

gardingi (in Spain), *gasindi* (in Italy), *trustes* or later *vassi* (in Francia).[98] Armies had always been more open to talent than many other fields of activity, as the low-born emperors of the third century and onwards show. All the same, it must have been easier to catch the eye of aristocratic patrons, whether public or private, if one was already from the social elite of a given village, and perhaps already performing a local public role, like the *boni homines* of the Carolingian world. This was never really easy; but the continuing access of the peasantry to public and military roles at least made it possible. If it became a good deal harder in the West in the eleventh century (never impossible, but harder), it was because that access had ended; the crystallizing, ever more closed, local military aristocracy, often called simply *milites*—and sometimes themselves of rich peasant origin—had in most places pulled up the ladder behind them.[99]

It has, finally, to be stressed that aristocracies did not only, in their patronage networks, pluck village leaders out of their local societies. Aristocrats (including episcopal and major monastic churches) could do many things for peasants, as we saw in Chapter 7 (pp. 438–41): they could offer the possibility of advancement, they could mediate with other powers, they could shore up local authority, they could protect against taxation, military danger, legal defeat, or maybe economic disaster. Important churches got pious donations even from peasants, in part presumably because they mediated with God, but also in part because they were associated with more secular forms of patronage too, as with the private city church of Bishop Peredeus of Lucca, which only got gifts of land while he was bishop (p. 391); in later periods, external religious houses would get peasant gifts in the wake of the piety of secular village-level patrons, too.[100] The tightness of peasant–aristocrat patronage links varied substantially, depending on how dangerous the latter were (as in the Rhineland: pp. 396–8), or on how effective the acceptance of local aristocratic hegemonies were (as in the Lucchesia: pp. 390–2). But they often existed, and presumably they sometimes benefited aristocrats materially (even if not, perhaps, as much as gifts of land benefited churches), for acts of patronage never came entirely free. One crucial question is how much any lord could turn this sort of patronage role, or indeed his local landowning and his direct power over his dependants, into effective local dominance, over village society or (in peasant-mode areas) over the previously autonomous village economy; and how much this would come 'naturally', and how much it depended on deliberate choices to dominate or oppress. For villages did lose their autonomy during the early middle ages, or many of them did at least, especially in the West, including

---

[98] See, among very many, Sánchez-Albornoz, *En torno*, I; Poly, 'Les *vassi*'; Barbero, 'Liberti'; the last two have earlier bibliography.

[99] See e.g., for Italy, Keller, *Adelsherrschaft*, pp. 342–79; Wickham, *Mountains*, pp. 274–92. A good case study for Catalonia is Bonnassie, 'Une famille'.

[100] Wickham, *Mountains*, pp. 190–215; for the lay understanding of piety in Italy, Costambeys, *Piety, property*, ch. 2.

enough of them to mark a trend away from the peasant mode and towards feudalism. This process will be the focus of the last section in this chapter.

4. The return of feudal dominance in the West

As we saw at the end of the second section, in the earliest middle ages in the West, after a retreat of aristocratic landowning in most regions, many areas could be said to have become independent of aristocratic, feudal, economic dominance, either partially or wholly. It is not that we can suppose the existence of whole societies dominated by peasants, as in the *Gemeinfreie* imagery of the early twentieth century; there were aristocrats everywhere, and they were the main protagonists of all political systems. All the same, the earliest middle ages was the low point for their dominance over western peasantries: roughly the sixth and perhaps the seventh centuries in Francia (though aristocrats were always relatively powerful there), the late sixth to early eighth in Italy, the eighth and ninth in Spain, and in Britain, where the process was longer-lasting and more total, the early fifth to the ninth centuries. In the next centuries, however, these processes reversed themselves everywhere. By 1000, and often much earlier, the peasant mode was only vestigial in Francia, Italy, England; by 1100 the same was true of Spain; by 1300 most of non-Roman northern Europe had followed. In its place, aristocratic power, with its feudal economic logic, was supreme, as it had always been in the eastern Mediterranean. The rents peasants paid in the central middle ages could be either heavy or still relatively light, depending on the local situation, but as a whole they structured the economic system, making possible accumulations of surplus, which in their turn underwrote large-scale expenditures: cathedrals, castles, heavy cavalry, universities, and, through aristocratic-fuelled international commerce, the townscapes of Italy and Flanders: the 'medieval world' of first-year survey courses and tourist literature. These patterns long post-date our period; but how the small-scale world of the peasant mode in the early middle ages began to cede ground to aristocratic power is a question whose answer begins before 800, and needs to be considered here. While discussing it, I shall run into the ninth century too, especially when considering peasant resistance to the process, which is better documented then than earlier.

The simple fact that peasants lost ground to aristocrats in the second half of the early middle ages is doubted by almost no one. One would have to believe that there were few independent peasants at all in (say) 700 to think differently, and this has not been the view of many people.[101] By 1000, by

---

[101] The *Königsfreie* school for one, whose views are now generally abandoned (see the bibliographical survey of critiques of it in Wickham, *Land and power*, p. 167 n.); another group is the theorists of the immemorial English manor, such as Chadwick, Aston, and Finberg (see above, p. 319).

contrast, at least in Francia, it has seriously been questioned whether any peasant owners still survived; such arguments are not convincing, but they are at least easier to make than they would be three centuries earlier.[102] All the same, *how* the peasantry lost ground across this period is hardly discussed in any systematic way, outside the Soviet-bloc debates of the 1950s–1970s, which had the disadvantage of basing themselves, as historians did then more often, too heavily on the legal sources.[103] The issue has squarely been faced in the 'feudal revolution' (or 'mutation') debate, focused on the decades around 1000, but that debate hardly used sources from the period before the tenth century. Only rare documentary studies—Robert Fossier for Picardy, Pierre Bonnassie for Catalonia, Rosamond Faith for England, Laurent Feller for central-southern Italy—follow the period after the eighth century as a whole from the peasant standpoint.[104] This book stops too early to add to their number, of course, but it can at least offer models for how the process of peasant weakening began, and what it meant in systemic terms.

I argued earlier that there was a deep structural difference between peasant-mode societies, where status among peasant producers was relatively impermanent, and depended on consent and reciprocal gift-giving, which inhibited accumulation; and feudal-mode societies, where most surplus was taken from peasant producers by lords, and was accumulated and then spent outside the peasant context altogether, leaving village society rather less flexible, its status markers determined largely by tenurial position. It was thus not simply that peasant land was taken by aristocrats in the centuries after 700, but that peasants in many places lost control over the entire economic system and its logic. I say 'in many places', for the peasant mode generally coexisted with areas of aristocratic economic dominance, with leopard-spots of the one interspersed with those of the other, helping to create the microregional differences that characterized the early middle ages as a whole. This was in itself ultimately a strategic weakness for autonomous peasantries, of course, for lords were more powerful than individual peasants. We could posit that the process of change worked, in general, like this. Aristocrats were initially constrained from moving to undermine peasant autonomies in any given village, either by relations of force, when a peasant collectivity could effectively resist them; or by balances of power

[102] Barthélemy, *Vendôme*, pp. 357–61, 441–50, and Duhamel-Amado, 'L'alleu paysan', question the survival of significant peasant landowning; Feller, 'Statut de la terre', effectively defends it. These recent works cite the extensive previous bibliography.

[103] e.g. Njeussychin, *Die Entstehung*; Müller-Mertens, *Karl der Grosse*; Müller-Mertens, *Feudalismus* (reprinting articles largely taken from the *Zeitschrift für Geschichtswissenschaft*, a major venue for debates; it is worth warning the reader that the journal is more widely available than is the book).

[104] Fossier, *La terre*; Bonnassie, *La Catalogne*; Faith, *The English peasantry*; Feller, *Les Abruzzes*. Philippov, *Srednizemnomorskaya Frantsiya*, pp. 358–406, 457–549, achieves the same for southern France, inside the limits of the scarce documentation.

with other aristocrats, who had, for example, isolated holdings in the same village; or by legal and customary restraints, when aristocrats respected them (which was at least sometimes); or by royal opposition to aristocratic oppression; or by links of political patronage between individual aristocrats and individual villagers, which could insulate the village as a whole from a more complete economic dominance; or by a lack of commitment to village-level dominance, because aristocratic interest was situated elsewhere, in royal courts, for example (cf. above, p. 199). If, however, some or all of these constraints were absent, then patronage could turn into coercion, neighbourhood could result in expropriation, the holding of royal office could result in local domination. In tribal economic systems, too, traditional tributes to outside lords could turn into rents, and more and more peasants could find themselves effectively subject to estate relationships. The logic of local economic systems at a given moment would flick over, and feudal-mode processes would become dominant.

An alternative model would be internal to the village, and would focus on village leaders steadily becoming more powerful, turning a relative differ-ence in rank into a local domination that could, in the end, develop into direct control. This was certainly possible in tribal societies: the heirs of the owners of the principal farm in the early medieval versions of Vorbasse in Denmark (pp. 496–7), for example, may have eventually turned into lords of the entire village, and the Malling case described in Chapter 7 (pp. 428–34) had a similar result. In the politically fragmented post-Carolingian world, too, *milites*, that is to say a restricted elite of the militarily active, with their newly crystallizing quasi-public lordship at the village level, the *seigneurie banale* of French historiography, were sometimes the heirs of the richer peasant strata, making good by gaining domination over their neighbours in a period in which military status stretched further down the social ladder than had the more informal aristocratic identity of the past.[105] Our best evidence of this comes from the Iberian peninsula, where *infanzones* in Castile (they had Catalan equivalents as well), who had often started out as militarized peasant elites on the Arab frontier, turned their status into permanent local power, in particular in the eleventh century, a period of rapid social change in Christian Spain.[106] We could suppose that this process occurred in analogous way elsewhere, including in earlier periods, as well.

The problem of how these changes occurred is that we have to rely on models, for we can so seldom see them happening in our sources,

---

[105] Duby, *Hommes et structures*, pp. 400–21; Fossier, *L'enfance*, pp. 964–79; Poly and Bournazel, *La mutation féodale*, pp. 157–83, Le Jan, *Famille et pouvoir*, pp. 147–52 are good guides to the *milites* of Francia around and after 1000 (by no means all of which were former peasants, one must stress). For Italy, see above, n. 99. For a more informal aristocratic identity two centuries earlier, Goetz, ' "Nobilis" '; Airlie, 'The aristocracy'; cf. below, n. 110.

[106] See e.g. Pastor, *Resistencias*, pp. 37–46, 74 ff.; Álvarez, *Poder y relaciones sociales*, pp. 27–51; Larrea, *La Navarre*, pp. 326–36; Bonnassie, *La Catalogne*, pp. 797–808.

ungenerous as they are. We can document examples of such changes anec-
dotally, of course, in, for instance, surviving court-cases in which peasants
tried to preserve their land—these being particularly common in ninth-
century Francia and Italy, where the structure of public power was strong
enough to allow peasants to try to resist such processes. One example which
can stand for many is a case from 845, in which a monastery in Verona took
eight peasants from the diocese of Trento to court, claiming that they did
labour services through their unfree subjection (*per conditionem*). They
argued that they were free men, doing services through a patronage agreement, as the monastery's *commendati*; the monastery conceded their freedom, but, arguing now that these services were rents, successfully claimed
their land. In this case, a patronage agreement seems to have led directly to
the expropriation of the peasants' land, with their legal freedom itself at
risk.[107] But such instances remain anecdotal; moving from an isolated example to the whole economic system remains a speculative process.

There seem to me, in particular, three traps that one can fall into when
speculating in this way. The first is to argue too easily from ad hoc instances
of aristocratic bad behaviour. As noted earlier (p. 177), there is never any
shortage of these. So Querolus at the start of the fifth century wanted to have
the power to treat people badly; Salvian in the 440s depicted the powerful as
forcing their free neighbours into unfree dependence; for Theodahad, an
Ostrogothic aristocrat (later king), in Tuscany around 530, 'to have a
neighbour seemed a kind of misfortune', in Prokopios' words; Gregory of
Tours in the 580s describes graphically the sadism of Duke Rauching, one of
his contemporaries; sixth- and seventh-century laws condemn the aristo-
cratic-led gangs who attacked the houses of others; Rothari in 643 lamented
that *pauperes* suffered from the exactions of those who had 'greater
strength', a lament echoed in Carolingian legislation, and, indeed, that of
tenth-century Byzantium; in the eighth-century *Vita Pardulfi*, nobles could
routinely *usurpare* peasant crops (in this case, mushrooms) as they passed
by; Gerald of Aurillac (d. 909), who made his men pay for their food, was
regarded as so unusual as to be a saint; as the peasants of Cliviano in the
Sabina said in the late eleventh century (far too late for us, but the sentiment
can stand), *seniores tollunt omnia*, 'lords take everything'. Not one of these
well-known texts can be taken at face value as a sign of global aristocratic
encroachment, however, and some of them date from periods of global
aristocratic retreat. What they, and many others, tell us about is how
aristocrats were *considered* by their contemporaries, including themselves—being domineering was simply one of the things that being aristocratic was about. The most they show is that lords were fully capable of
taking advantage of any opportunities that were offered.[108]

---

[107] Manaresi, *I placiti*, n. 49, for the Verona case. Cf. for Italy ibid., n. 36.
[108] *Querolus*, c. 30; Salvian, *De gubernatione dei*, V.38–45; Prokopios, *Wars*, V.3.2; Gregory
of Tours, *LH*, V.3; *LV*, VI.4.2, with *Pactus*, c. 42; Rothari, *Prologus*, with the refs. cit. n. 109,

The second trap is to mix up the economic and the political autonomy of peasants. The free peasantry owed army service, but were too numerous really to be needed for the most part; they performed other burdens instead, road-maintenance or the billeting of troops, but military activity was increasingly seen as the right of aristocrats and their entourages, and the latter increasingly regarded the peasantry as potentially inside their own political domination. Similarly, although attendance at the *placitum* was another duty, in practice peasants were unlikely to participate willingly unless they actually had cases to press, and this crucial arena of public activity was thus in reality a marker of elite participation as well, except insofar as the *placitum* was a locus in which public officials could exact goods and services from the peasantry. The excluded free peasantry were still of interest to kings, however, in particular in the ninth century, when the Carolingians had a wide-ranging sense of public responsibility. Carolingian legislation against the oppression of the free in Francia and Italy is thus detailed, and lists a wide variety of abuses, largely the work of public officials who were themselves turning the public burdens of the *pauperes* into private perquisites. This very fact was the marker of the failure of such legislation, for these were the very officials who should be safeguarding the rights of the peasantry. But we must be careful not to regard these political abuses as proofs of the *economic* weakening of peasantries. In general, of course, the *oppressiones* of the Carolingian aristocracy betray a considerable self-confidence about the latter's practical powers, which extended to economic domination as well: laws against the forced sale of land to lords are a feature of several capitularies. We could probably consider the very existence of texts like these as a prima-facie demonstration that the shift to an aristocratic economic logic had already happened in many or most parts of these two regions by the time of the ninth-century capitularies. But the main aim of the Carolingians was to safeguard their own public power-base; the thrust of these laws depended on that—as did their dating, for that matter.[109]

I stress the problems of these latter laws because the Carolingian period was, in general, indeed a crucial period of aristocratic affirmation, in almost every part of the empire of Charlemagne. Overall, we find more evidence of rich lay aristocracies almost everywhere, and the period 725–850 is also one in which ecclesiastical landowning rapidly advanced, thanks to the gifts of kings and aristocrats very often, but those of peasants as well, as the major

and, for Byzantium, Morris, 'The powerful and the poor', and Kaplan, *Les hommes*, pp. 414–44; *Vita Pardulfi*, c. 9; Odo of Cluny, *Vita Geraldi*, I.33; *RF*, n. 1303, with Toubert, *Les structures*, p. 549.

[109] For all this, Müller-Mertens, *Karl der Grosse*, esp. pp. 97–111, and Tabacco, *I liberi del re*, esp. pp. 37–66, are crucial guides. Laws against the expropriation of peasant land include *MGH*, *Cap.*, I, n. 44, c. 15 and n. 73, cc. 2–3; Müller-Mertens, ibid., pp. 100–1 lists others.

cartularies and document collections make explicit.[110] The generalization of the *régime domanial classique* after 750, at least in northern Francia, and the intensification of the burdens on peasants on such estates, although of course a development in territories already fully under aristocratic control, also attests to a considerable commitment on the part of major landowners to local intervention (above, pp. 283–93). And the archaeologically attested increase in exchange in northern Francia in the same period, although from an already high base, marks a global extension in an economic system associated above all with aristocratic accumulation (below, pp. 801–5). If there was any part of the Carolingian empire where the peasant mode had become vestigial already by around 800, it was northern Francia; these are all signs of it, and the laws on the *pauperes* might be seen only to make that development explicit.

This is an arena, all the same, in which we must proceed very carefully, without overgeneralization. For the third trap is simply put: it is to forget that the real shifts between a peasant and an aristocratic economic logic were not regional at all, but microregional. But if we recognize that, and keep our focus on the (few) local areas for which we can say something securely, then we may be able to move from negative to positive arguments. In northern Francia, we have evidence for some microregions which is occasionally detailed enough to allow us to speculate about such shifts, and they show no such uniformity of dating. In the Île de France, as argued earlier (pp. 398–406), aristocratic economic dominance was probably continuous from the Roman empire into the Carolingian period and beyond, and plenty of Frankish microregions must have been similar. In Lorraine, however, the decline of furnished burials for the ordinary members of society in the seventh century has been seen by Guy Halsall as a marker of the end of status competition among relative equals and of the start of firmer political hierarchies. Although this argument cannot be universally accepted without question (if it was, there could be no established aristocracies where there were furnished burials; cf. above, p. 340), it may well be a valid indicator when associated with other archaeological or documentary signs of a change in the position of elites. Further east, Alemannia may provide us with an example, as with the privileged cemetery and *Herrenhof* in the Aleman village of Lauchheim (p. 501), which are early seventh-century developments, and which are also apparently contemporary with a steady centralization of pottery production and thus a stabilization of demand in areas of the upper Rhine valley; later in the seventh century hill-forts were reoccupied as well, probably as estate-centres. Parts of the Aleman lands thus seem

---

[110] For local studies, see Störmer, *Früher Adel*, pp. 118–56, 357–74; Innes, *State and society*, pp. 13–50; Davies, *Small worlds*, pp. 188 ff.; Feller, *Les Abruzzes*, pp. 187–90. There is no general study of the distribution of aristocratic landowning in the Carolingian period. For church land, see the statistics in Herlihy, 'Church property', pp. 86–8, 103–4.

to see a shift in economic structure in the seventh century, and the return of elites who had not been clear in the archaeology since 500. Similar convergences of shifts will doubtless be identified in the future.[111] A slightly later change can be proposed for the northern fringe of Francia, where, in the Kempen area west of the lower Meuse, Frans Theuws has identified a pattern of hierarchical settlement networks, including estate-centres, beginning in the late seventh century; in this area, the early eighth-century Echternach charters show fully organized landowning structures, but they may well only be a generation old.[112]

These microregions shifted to aristocratic economic dominance well before the Carolingian period (although groups of peasant owners continued to exist in most of them, as we saw for the highly aristocratic middle Rhine area, above, pp. 393–8). Conversely, there were others where such a dominance was considerably later, most visibly in eastern Brittany, where as late as 830 the villages around the monastery of Redon (founded in 832 in the borderlands of effective Frankish control) seem to have been dominated by autonomous peasantries, with local aristocrats who did not control local economic procedures. Here indeed, unusually, we can trace the economic shift in our documentation, for it must have come in the generation after 832, when Redon gained so much in local gifts and wider political patronage that it had attained a generally accepted position of lordship in its hinterland by around 870.[113]

If we want to pin down the shift to aristocratic power in Francia, this sort of pointillistic approach seems to me the only one possible. It must be added, however, that once we have analysed all the microregions we can, we are entitled to generalize, with all due caution. So we can say, for example, that our overall network of documentation, both literary and archaeological, in Francia, even in less well-studied microregions, shows societies which overall resembled the Île de France and Alemannia more than they did Brittany; and this may indeed indicate that the seventh century was a commoner date for the weakening of the peasant mode (where it existed at all) in the Frankish lands than was the ninth. Future work will refine this dating further, and of course add to its microregional complexity. But overall, such a picture supports the proposition that before 800, indeed often before 700, the shift to aristocratic dominance had generally occurred in this region.

In Italy, it is probable that the shift was often slightly later. The eighth-century Lucchesia, discussed as a case study in Chapter 7, must have been an

---

[111] Halsall, *Settlement*, esp. pp. 262–75. For Alemannia, see Christlein, *Die Alamannen*, pp. 39–49, 83 ff.; Châtelet, 'L'évolution de la céramique culinaire tournée'; and Ch. 8, nn. 153–7.

[112] Theuws, 'Landed property', pp. 354–97; cf. Wampach, *Geschichte*, I.2, e.g. nn. 11, 16, 17, 20, 21, 28, 30.

[113] Davies, *Small worlds*, pp. 188–200.

area where the dominant economic logic was aristocratic, but it was none-theless, even though a significant political centre, not one where aristocrats were themselves very wealthy for the most part (above, pp. 387–93). Nor was any part of Italy north of Rome; only between Rome and Naples, and perhaps around Benevento, can we detect richer aristocratic networks before 800 (above, pp. 206–18). It would not be surprising under these circumstan-ces, of relatively restrained aristocratic wealth even in central areas, to find rural peasant-mode microregions, like the south-eastern Chianti (above, p. 546), surviving into the eighth century at least, and indeed even into the ninth in some parts of the peninsula, particularly in marginal economic areas, of which there were many. Only in the ninth century, under Carolin-gian rule, are really rich aristocrats and churches/monasteries documented in north-central Italy (above, p. 218); only by then was the shift to aristocratic dominance probably generalized. These statements are certainly generic ones, but they frame the fact that we can in Italy identify some small peasant-mode areas in marginal lands which fought back, as late as the ninth century, to preserve their rights, or, sometimes, their very survival, as we shall see in a moment: the fact that these last-ditch resistances were relatively late makes them better documented, indeed furnishing us with some of the best documentation we have for peasant resistance in our period.

Other regions saw moves back to aristocratic hegemony that were gener-ally later than our period. In England, the crucial period was the ninth century; this was discussed in Chapter 6, where it was stressed that, although the shift from a peasant to an aristocratic economy was unusually total there, it was probably so slow as to be hard for peasants to perceive, and there was certainly no documented resistance to it (above, pp. 347–51). In Spain, the shift to a peasant mode, where it occurred, was itself later than elsewhere in most places (the seventh century in the south-east, the eighth in parts of the Meseta; only some mountain microregions probably made the change earlier); the eighth and ninth centuries were the period of the widest expansion of peasant economic autonomy, and it was only undermined by Umayyad recentralization in the late ninth and tenth century in the south, and by Asturian-Leonese royal and aristocratic expansion a century later in the north. (For all this, see below, pp. 227–32.) Hence the late date, and also the clarity, of the takeover of autonomous Castilian villages not only by external powers such as monasteries, but also by internally developing aristocracies of *infanzones*; in areas with so much peasant autonomy, in-ternal aristocracies were at least as likely to develop as external ones. Hence also the documentation of peasant resistance to these processes, both in León-Castile and the largely analogous (but Frankish-ruled) areas of Cata-lonia—and, indeed, in the rural areas of the south which fought the wars against the Umayyads known as the first *fitna* (c.880–925); they were more visible to peasants, and so could more easily be fought. Even when feudal hegemony was finally established, some parts of Spain (notably Castile) preserved some elements of local political autonomy for peasants that cannot be seen in many other parts of Europe. But these processes are too late for us to look at them in detail.[114]

The last couple of pages have introduced the issue of peasant resistance to these changes. In England it is invisible, but in every other region there was at least some, in the period before the mid-ninth century: often very localized, often focused on only partial objectives, but at least existing, giving us signs that when the change from a peasant to a feudal mode of production was rapid enough, it could be recognized and opposed. Only in one part of Europe was there a widespread and rapid change from the one to the other: that was Saxony, a tribal sub-region with unusually little political agglomeration, conquered bloodily by Charlemagne between 772 and 804, and rapidly subjected to aristocratic and ecclesiastical domination in the generation that followed. In the half-century c.790–c.840, that is to say, Saxony went through the same economic and political transformations that England experienced in the 300 years between c.600 and c.900. And Saxony also saw the largest peasants' revolt of the early medieval West, the Stellinga rising of 841–2, as a result. We must look at how peasant resistance was structured, for what peasants were opposed to, and how they framed their opposition, is the best evidence we have for understanding how the advent of the feudal mode was actually experienced on the ground. And, although Saxony is not one of the regions focused on in this book, I shall end with the Stellinga, as the best case study of that resistance.

The peasant conflicts of the early medieval West are not more likely to have been recorded faithfully and fairly than were those of the late empire, nor for that matter in any detail. But they were mostly sufficiently small-scale that the single sources which refer to them (often documents, usually of court-cases, rather than chronicles) have little textual association with each other, and their common elements may therefore be significant. Elsewhere, I have offered a typology of such conflicts;[115] here, they will be presented regionally, to draw out their locally common features, before moving to wider generalization. It is fair to say that there are not a huge number of them, but they do share some characteristics, which we can indeed generalize from. Only conflicts involving groups of peasants will be discussed here; isolated examples of individual peasants confronting landlords in court over rents, property, or legal status are less easy to locate in any metanarrative of

---

[114] Pastor, *Resistencias*, pp. 74–112; Bonnassie, *La Catalogne*, pp. 648–50 (here the information is less clear than for Castile); for the *fitna*, e.g. Acién, *'Umar ibn Ḥafṣūn* (not all rebels were peasants, though, by any means); for later political autonomies, see the comparative remarks in Wickham, *Community*, pp. 194–7.

[115] Wickham, 'Space and society'. Much of the material in the next few pages is also discussed there.

aristocratic advance. That the peasants almost always lost in such texts is not significant either, for it was lords—usually churches—who kept the documents. It should be observed, indeed, that the high point for such confrontations was the ninth century, not least because it was then that peasants apparently had most confidence in royal justice, and it is hard to imagine that this would have continued had they never won. But these sorts of conflicts occur in all periods, and do not mark any clear shift.[116]

In Gaul/Francia, Gregory of Tours records no collective rural conflicts for the late sixth-century Loire valley; the closest he gets is his hostile account of the peasant followings of a handful of holy men, whom he regarded as imposters. The violence he recounted in the rural world, with lords and dependants attacking each other, almost casually in some cases, was all individual. There is in fact only one clear Merovingian-period case of group peasant resistance, a *placitum* from near Dijon dating to 664–5. This concerns the invasion of the *villa* of Elariacum (probably Larrey in the hills of the upper Seine valley), given to the monastery of St-Bénigne in Dijon by King Guntram (d. 593), by the men who lived inside its bounds; as the abbot complained, they refused to pay rent, cut down trees, planted vineyards, and cleared land—that is, they acted formally as if they owned the land. These men, called to the court, presented their own *preceptio* from Guntram, which safeguarded their ancestors' land there when he gave the *villa* to St-Bénigne; and also an agreement between their kin and an earlier abbot at the end of an earlier dispute about part of the estate, in which both sides walked the bounds of the *villa* and placed boundary marks. These documents did not, however, persuade the court, which found that St-Bénigne had full rights in the *villa*, 'setting aside and cancelling this confirmation' (that is to say, by Guntram to the peasants). Here, peasant families apparently owned land in a *villa* territory, but were finding their rights of possession increasingly under threat; after a dispute and a compromise, they had lost ground again, and were attempting to recoup their position by force, perhaps as part of a public claim to the land in a case they doubtless regarded as watertight. King Chlotar III and his *proceres*, however, were prepared to override a royal charter in their support of the monastery, and in that context the peasants could not win.[117]

[116] Partial lists for Italy and Gaul are in Wickham, *Early medieval Italy*, p. 215 n. 36; Nelson, 'Dispute settlement', p. 52 n. I know of two cases in which peasants won such disputes, Devic and Vaissete, *HGL*, II, n. 185 (a. 874, for Languedoc), and Manaresi, *I placiti*, nn. 110, 112 (aa. 900–1, for Lombardy).

[117] *MGH, Dip. Merov*, n. 103. This text survives in an eleventh-century cartulary in a poor state, clearly reworked at the beginning and end. Theo Kölzer, its most recent editor, dismisses it as a forgery (ibid., pp. 265–6, and *Merowingerstudien*, II, pp. 87–94). This is largely on the grounds of the apparent implausibility of its content, the peasant protagonists, the overridden royal charter, and so on (see also Bergmann, 'Gerichtsurkunden', pp. 156–9, less suspicious, but equally uneasy about the latter). But the close parallels in Italy to peasants unsuccessfully using royal documentation (below, nn. 123, 125) show that the scenario was one that could indeed

If we move into the Carolingian period, we can find more such examples, although all very localized, and with different objectives. One was described earlier (p. 256), the plea of the monastery of Murbach to Charlemagne in the 780s–790s that its *mancipia* had 'escaped' unfreedom in the context of the Aleman wars of the 740s; these unfree peasants had (if we believe the abbot) established a practical local autonomy without even having to leave their lands. But more common were movements the other way: the monastery of St Gallen establishing its rights over woodcutting and animal pasture in a large *silva*, presumably on the edge of the Alps, perhaps in the 880s, against the opposition of local *pagenses* (though it had to come to terms with them), or Thrudpert of the Breisgau at the end of the eighth century, a saint who was given land in the Black Forest by a local aristocrat and overworked his unfree dependants in order to clear it (they actually killed him, and were of course punished by death).[118] The theme of work reappears in the plea of the peasants of Antoigné near Angers in 828, *coloni* of the monastery of Cormery, who tried to persuade Pippin I of Aquitaine that the abbot's men had increased their rent and services, although they were confounded by the text of an estate survey (*discriptio*) of 801 which listed the obligations of each *mansum*, as sworn to at the time by their forebears. We could suppose that it was around 800, not in the 820s, that rents were raised by Cormery, perhaps in the framework of manorial development (above, pp. 287–91). The theme of freedom recurs in the collective plea by twenty-three peasant families of Mitry, just north-east of Paris, in 861 that they were free *coloni* of St-Denis, not *servi*, although other *coloni* of the same village publicly denied it—this village was evidently seriously divided, with a free tenant elite siding with their lords against their neighbours, whether rightly or wrongly we cannot tell. The peasants of Mitry sought freedom explicitly in order to have their rents recognized as lighter, but it may be noted that as free *coloni* they would also have had access to at least some surviving rights as political protagonists. These, too, were under threat in this period, however, as in the well-known account from the *Annales Bertiniani* for 859 of peasants between the Loire and the Seine (that is to say, in the lands between the last two

exist in the early medieval world; and Kölzer's removal of the imagery to the eleventh century and the *seigneurie banale* raises more problems than it solves. There is no documentary context for such problems in Larrey in the eleventh century, it is worth adding (see *Chartes et documents de Saint-Bénigne*, II); the most one can say is that the eleventh-century monastic chronicle, when summarizing the seventh-century dispute, remarks that *usque hodie successores eorum agere non desinunt* (*Chronique de l'abbaye de Saint-Bénigne*, p. 42, cf. pp. 61–2). I do not see good reason to doubt the core information in the seventh-century text. For Gregory on imposters, *LH*, IX.6; on violence, e.g. V.3, VI.45, VII.47. Note also the will of Abbo of Maurienne in 739 (ed. Geary, *Aristocracy*, p. 66), which envisages penalties if his freedmen ungratefully were to 'wish to rebel'—this fits standard Roman-law concerns of the continued obligations of freedmen to their manumittors (above, p. 564), but may show that tensions in the French Alps in the 730s were higher than elsewhere.

[118] *Form. Morbacenses*, n. 5, *Form. Sangallenses miscellaneae*, n. 9 (MGH, *Formulae*, pp. 331, 383–4); *Passio Thrudperti*, cc. 3–7.

examples) who formed a sworn association (*coniuratio*) against the Vikings, whom indeed they fought, but since their association was made 'incautiously' (*incaute*), the Frankish *potentiores* killed them. Charlemagne had banned *coniurationes* as potentially subversive of royal authority, itself based on oaths; 'incautiously' here may relate to this, but it also must indicate that any autonomous peasant action was by now regarded as illegitimate by aristocrats, and thus dangerous, even if at present aimed at the enemies of the kingdom.[119]

This heterogeneous set does not include any examples of open revolt; even killing one's lord was not strictly that, and the oath-swearers of 859 probably thought they were continuing the royal-sanctioned public obligations of the free, however controversially. The continuing accessibility of the public *placitum* to peasants also helped ensure that their protests kept inside the bounds of legality. But the set does show clear instances of the rearguard resistance of Frankish peasants to aristocratic encroachment (in these cases almost always monastic, although this simply reflects the pattern of the archival preservation of the period). Landowning peasants defended their land, and silvo-pastoral rights. Tenants defended a memory of lower rents, and/or claimed free status. These certainly reflect the picture painted in earlier pages, of a Carolingian period in which aristocrats became steadily richer at the expense of neighbours, more hostile to the residual rights of the free, and more prepared to intensify the exploitation of tenants. Except in 859, however, peasants responded ad hoc, and village by village at most. They accepted the ground-rules of Carolingian society, while contesting their detailed application. But I have also argued that by the Carolingian period aristocratic dominance was *already* close to complete in Frankish Gaul. Under these circumstances, rearguard ad hoc resistance was about all there was space to generate.

Italian resistance was largely along the same lines, but there were some interesting differences. The Antoigné and Mitry cases are both matched by a Piacenza court hearing in 832, in which tenants of the bishop, fighting over levels of labour service, ceded their case in return for a formal recognition of their freedom.[120] The strategic importance of having the lord deny the freedom of his opponents is something we have already seen for Verona in 845 (p. 573). But both of these cases at least saw a lord having to concede something to peasant opponents, a feature less visible in Gaul. Italy also gives us examples of tenants resisting by force, even though not necessarily denying their overall subjection, from quite early on. One example is the *seditio* of the *mancipia* of Clementina, one of the senatorial leaders of

[119] Levillain, *Recueil des actes de Pépin*, n. 12; Tessier, *Recueil des actes de Charles le Chauve*, n. 228; *Annales Bertiniani*, s.a. 859. See Nelson, 'Dispute settlement', pp. 48–52; eadem, *Charles the Bald*, p. 194. For laws against sworn groups, and literary references to peasant tensions, see Epperlein, *Herrschaft und Volk*, pp. 42–50.
[120] Volpini, 'Placiti', pp. 447–51.

Naples, in 592, who had persuaded the dependants of other landlords to attack the papal administrator for the city (Gregory the Great, who described the episode, envisaged punishments for them, but wondered whether they had a *iusta querella* against their lords—as well as whether Clementina herself was implicated); another is the *seditio* condemned by Rothari in 643, which involved peasants uniting into bands (*concilii*) and rebelling, in order to prevent a *dominus* from taking a *mancipium* or movable property from the house of a *servus*. This law, which follows one on such bands attacking a village, aims to reimpose public order on peasants who forcibly resist lordly exercise of prerogatives over their dependants.[121] Both of these examples show tenants in the role of rather more positive (not to say boisterous) protagonists than we have seen for Gaul. Tenants who were slow to give in are also clearly documented in the sequence of cases for Limonta on Lake Como dating from the period 882–957, in which tenants of S. Ambrogio in Milan claimed their freedom (probably rightly), and also contested their obligation to cultivate olives for their landlord. S. Ambrogio was certainly on the offensive here, but it took two generations and more for the peasants to stop resisting.[122]

Italy also has more cases than Gaul in which peasant owners defended land and rights. The Verona case was that too; another is the Flexum case from 824, in which peasants from the Po marshes contested in court the power of the monastery of Nonantola to prevent them from exercising their customary rights of fishing and pasture, presenting a *preceptum* of King Liutprand (d. 744) which confirmed their rights in his *silva*. The monastery had, however, been ceded this land by Aistulf (d. 756), and had won similar cases to this one in the intervening years; the court held that the peasants' rights had been voided by Aistulf's gift. The peasants protested this blatant reversal of standard legal assumptions about prior rights in land, but to no avail; their three leaders were beaten, 'so that they should remember this case'. This case matches the 663 Elariacum case in that a court overthrew a former king's guarantee of the residual rights of peasants; but the Flexum *consortes* were at least only facing the weakening of their extra silvo-pastoral resources, not the loss of their own property. The inhabitants of Flexum are the best candidates so far in this list of resisters for being peasants who were holding out against landlordly encroachment, and so far only conceding little by little.[123]

This sort of resistance has parallels in the marginal lands of central Italy as well. When Farfa was given the *gualdus* of S. Giacinto beside the Tiber in

---

[121] Gregory the Great, *Ep.* III. 1; Rothari 280 (cf. 279, Liutprand 141).

[122] *Codex diplomaticus Langobardiae*, n. 314; Manaresi, *I placiti*, nn. 117, 122. See above all Castagnetti, 'Dominico e massaricio'; Balzaretti, 'The monastery of Sant' Ambrogio'.

[123] Manaresi, *I placiti*, n. 36; see Montanari, 'Conflitto sociale', pp. 22–3—the whole article is the best overview of these Italian texts; see further in general Panero, *Schiavi servi*, pp. 48–57. Not all the men of Flexum were peasants: one was a notary.

745–7, one of those tracts of tribal-style land where Roman rules of land tenure did not fully apply (above, p. 540), its local rights were immediately contested by the inhabitants of the *gualdus*, and it had to agree to a public inquisition in 747 to establish what these rights were, and make concessions to several of the local people.[124] The most dramatic reaction, however, was that of the peasants of the Valle Trita between 779 and 873, known about thanks to eight documents from the cartulary of S. Vincenzo al Volturno, which make reference in all to nine court hearings. Around 758 King Desiderius had given this valley, another *gualdus*, and particularly marginal in this case (it lies under the highest mountains of the Appennines, and is largely silvo-pastoral land), to S. Vincenzo; but its inhabitants also had independent rights, safeguarded by *precepta* of the dukes of Spoleto. S. Vincenzo established an estate there, and regarded the (ex-)public dues owed by the inhabitants as rents; it soon claimed that most of the inhabitants were unfree. In 779 the inhabitants were already refusing dues and services; further refusals occurred in 787, 822–4, 854, and 872–3. In 872 the monastery could only get the openly resisting peasants to court at all because the emperor Louis II and his army were in the vicinity, and the peasants could not take to the hills because of winter, when they were rounded up in January 873. In every case they lost, and S. Vincenzo often managed to coerce them as unfree (as in 854 in particular); but it is easy to see that the situation on the ground was only intermittently under monastic control— Trita is 100 km from the monastery, across two mountain passes. The 873 case may only be the last one because S. Vincenzo was sacked by the Arabs in 881 and did not re-establish control over many of its estates for decades. These texts show how the collective action and the remoteness characteristic of marginal lands could hold off a powerful and determined monastery, even though the latter was backed up by all the state power that was available. Here, the peasant mode was taking on the feudal mode, and, for once, holding out. The next reference to Trita in S. Vincenzo's cartulary is not until 998.[125]

I proposed earlier that the shift to generalized feudal dominance in Italy was in some microregions later than in Gaul, and an eighth- or even a ninth-century phenomenon; these are the main texts that can be used to argue it. Flexum and the *gualdi* were on ecological margins, of marsh, woodland, and mountain pasture, which were both the last places lords would get to and areas of greater than usual collective action; conversely, despite the equal number of such marginal lands north of the Alps, our evidence for such resistance is rather more restricted there (and the closest parallel, Elariacum,

---

[124] *CDL*, IV.1, nn. 4–6; *CDL*, V, nn. 8, 11–13; cf. Wickham, *Land and power*, pp. 162–3, for commentary and bibliography.

[125] Wickham, *Studi sulla società*, pp. 18–28, 104–5; Feller, *Les Abruzzes*, 191–6, 540–6. The texts are *Chronicon Vulturnense*, nn. 23–6, 55, 71–2, 157, 180, and I, pp. 333–7 (the first, sixth and seventh are Manaresi, *I placiti*, nn. 4, 72, 58).

where there was also a silvo-pastoral element, was a century earlier—although the Alps themselves, where we might have expected other similar cases, are particularly ill-documented in our period). Lords were clearly on the offensive in these disputes, and indeed the tide had turned in their favour by the eighth century, in Italy as in Gaul. Other resistances were firmly in the framework of a tenurial domination by landowners that was not in itself contested. But even there, if Italian tenants did resist, they could continue for longer, and sometimes extract cessions from lords. Aristocratic domination was never as complete in Italy; landowners were not so large-scale, peasant owners were more common, there was more of a need for negotiation and mediation. This essential Gaul–Italy difference has been explored in other chapters, but it is relevant here too.

In Spain, finally, the evidence for our period is exiguous, but fits that for central Italy, in that one can link it to ecological margins. Perhaps we should leave aside the Orospeda, subdued by war by King Leovigild in 577, and the Basques, never subdued by anyone, as neither need have been exclusively peasant groups (and exactly where the Orospeda actually lived has never been certain).[126] The only certain account of peasant–lord conflict that we have is of a full-scale revolt in the Asturias, around 770. The two-line record of it in the *Chronicon* of Alfonso III, from perhaps the 880s (the early tenth century at the latest), refers to *servi* (in two of the versions of the text) or *libertini* (in the third version) rising up against their *domini*, until King Aurelius restored them to their 'former servitude'. The Asturias is small and mountainous, and has long been seen as initially tribal, although its earliest documents (for the ninth century) show standard Roman-style land-owning (see above, p. 227); we could see the 770 revolt as one of the moments in which aristocratic landowning imposed itself on neighbouring, autonomous, peasants by force.[127] But it has to be recognized that these laconic records are the only signs we have of such a shift, and we should resist the temptation to make too much of them. Historians of Spain who like to study resistance will be better off in the Duero valley in the eleventh century (above, p. 572). But it may be, all the same, that the Asturian revolt is the best parallel we have to the Valle Trita in the lands of the former western empire, in our period at least.

Put together, most of these examples represent highly localized resistances to increasing aristocratic power. We see free owners resisting expropriation, or the loss of silvo-pastoral rights, or the loss of independence and even freedom as lords turned tribal relationships into estates. We also see tenants

---

[126] For the Orospeda, see John of Biclar, *Chronica*, s.a. 577 (his terminology of a revolt of *rustici* should not be trusted too much; it recurs in the account of Córdoba, an urban centre and thus very different, s.a. 572). For the Basques, see the divergent accounts of Collins, *The Basques*, pp. 78 ff., and Larrea, *La Navarre*, pp. 111–60.

[127] Gil, *Crónicas asturianas*, pp. 136–7, 174, collects all the citations. See Barbero and Vigil, *La formación*, p. 261.

resisting increased rents, or the servile status that would produce increased rents and reduced negotiating rights. Peasants tended to react to detailed changes in their local environments, for this is what they knew, and there was seldom any systematic extra-local pressure on them that could unify them, unlike the tax system that provoked the Bagaudae, or the eighth-century Egyptians (above, pp. 140–3, 529–33). The only positive protagonism that we have seen so far was the 859 Seine–Loire reaction to Viking attack, and this is probably the reason why that reaction was particularly harshly repressed: peasant initiatives were, even if not directed against lords, more dangerous than rearguard reactions. These responses largely failed, whether they were direct/violent or focused on legal proceedings: only the peasants of Trita can be seen to have held off lords for any substantial period of time in the West before 900. But our set of examples does show that peasants were not necessarily resigned to losing against aristocratic oppression. I would see them as the tip of an iceberg: not of *widespread* rural resistance, but of quite *frequent*, small-scale, resistance, and of genuinely widespread opposition of a more muted kind, which might well have been expressed by the 'weapons of the weak' (ineptly carried-out forced labour, for example, or the secret cutting of the lord's vines), but which does not appear in our documentation. One could propose that, even if peasants often assented to aristocratic domination for fear of worse, they did not necessarily accept its legitimacy. The wide range, in time and space, of similar forms of resistance is the best proof of this.

As stated earlier, nowhere in Europe did things change so fast for the worse for peasants as in Saxony. The Saxon political system was highly decentralized before Charlemagne's conquest, with aristocrats (*nobiles, edhilingui*) controlling small territories (*pagi*) politically, all linked together only by an annual assembly (*concilium*), to which the other two free status-groups, *frilingi/liberi* and *lazzi/liti*, also sent representatives according to the *Vita Lebuini*, a suspect source, but partially supported by some of Charlemagne's own legislation. How each *pagus* worked economically is unknown, but it would make most sense to propose a British-style peasant-mode tribal model, with free *frilingi* owing recognitive dues to aristocrats, and with some version of the English 'inland' (cf. above, p. 323) worked by unfree *servi/mancipia*; *lazzi*, who had a version of free status but were clearly more dependent, could have had either economic role. Some Saxon aristocrats were probably richer, and could have been importing Frankish ideas of full landownership from across the permeable border—there are indeed fragmentary signs that some eighth-century landowners owned on both sides of the frontier.[128] Conversely, resistance by the *frilingi* to Christianization,

---

[128] Bede, *HE*, V.10; *Vita Lebuini antiqua*, cc. 4–6, criticized in Wood, *The missionary life*, pp. 115–17; MGH, *Cap.*, I, n. 26, cc. 15, 18–20, 34, n. 27, cc. 4, 8. The latter show Saxony's threefold social division very clearly, and also the importance of assemblies (*conventus,*

potentially the first step to Francicization, is evident in our early mission accounts.

Charlemagne conquered Saxony in the three decades after 772 by war and massacre, *pagus* by *pagus*, and did his best to incorporate the Saxon aristocracy into his new Christian Frankish order, once they had accepted defeat. Broadly, the losers were the other two status-groups, who lost their role in the now-abolished assembly, lost their traditional religion, which had presumably buttressed the legitimacy of their political participation, and who faced steadily increasing aristocratic, and, in particular, ecclesiastical landowning, necessarily at their expense. This rapid feudalization process combined all the ways in which lords could achieve dominance over peasants at once. A new landowning class (particularly of bishops and monasteries—Corvey is the best-documented) was imposed on Saxony from the outside; and Saxon aristocrats must have increased their own control over their free dependants at the same time. Corvey had both *liberi* and *liti* on its estates by the 830s, and used them as an armed following. Although it may be that the *liberi* were not always yet fully economically dependent, for they appear less often in the Corvey charters, *liti* were increasingly put together with *servi* in documentary terminology, and seem to have been regarded simply as tenants on estates, on a standard Romano-Germanic pattern, as soon as we have documents, which is by the 820s (very few texts date from earlier decades). Saxon estates were looser than Frankish ones; demesnes were small, and labour services generally light. But they represented rapidly increasing subjection for both free strata of the peasantry, and their development seems to have been substantially complete by the middle years of the century. The Saxon peasantry, who had been conscious of the threats to their situation even before Charlemagne's invasions, must have felt this change particularly keenly.[129]

This is the background to the Stellinga uprising of 841–2. It began in the framework of the 840–3 civil war between Louis the Pious's sons, Lothar, Louis the German, and Charles the Bald, which also split the Saxon aristocracy, thus fracturing the alliance which had ruled Saxony ever since the 790s; the Stellinga responded to that break in ruling-class hegemony. (Such a quick

---

placita). I am grateful to Stuart Airlie for advice on this. For cross-border landowning, see Wood, 'Before and after mission', pp. 159–61, although his best example, Werden, was in the Frankish lands, not Saxony. Rösener, 'Zur Struktur und Entwicklung', pp. 176–80, the best current survey of Saxon agrarian structures (which also cites previous work), assumes wide preconquest aristocratic landowning, but his evidence, inevitably, all postdates the eighth century.

[129] The ninth-century Corvey documents have had several editions; I have used the most recent, *Die alten Mönchslisten*, pp. 83–131. For *liti* or *lati*, see e.g. nn. 32, 41, 288; *liberi* as dependants appear in n. 107. The monastery of Werden, a later substantial landowner in Saxony, as yet gained little Saxon land in the early ninth-century gifts and sales registered in Crecelius, 'Traditiones Werdinenses', I (not an easy text to find). There is useful commentary on all this in Rösener, 'Zur Struktur und Entwicklung' (p. 202 for few *liberi*); Goldberg, 'Popular revolt', pp. 478 ff.—he cites and discusses the army text at pp. 491–2.

reaction to divisions in the Frankish military machine was not unique; the first Viking raid on Francia, from neighbouring Denmark, was in 834, in the context of Louis's 833–4 conflict with his sons.) The Stellinga were composed of *frilingi* and *lazzi*, as the chronicler Nithard, in particular, makes explicit, and were above all opposed to the Saxon aristocracy; their revolt seems to have included most of Saxony. Their other principal objectives were reportedly the re-establishment of paganism (though this is the sort of thing hostile chroniclers always say) and, most specifically, the re-establishment of 'the custom of the ancient Saxons', the pre-Carolingian socio-political system, in the place of the *lex* of the Carolingians—which indeed Lothar, keen to use the Stellinga against Louis the German, was prepared to grant them. In the winter and spring of 841–2 the Stellinga had the run of Saxony, but in the summer and autumn of 842, once Lothar had been largely defeated, Louis and the reunited Saxon aristocracy put the rising down with great violence.[130] Nor is this surprising; the Stellinga are an unusually good case of a peasants' revolt that was large-scale and (probably) compact, and which had a clear and even practical programme, which essentially involved rolling back the social changes of the last two generations (though perhaps going further, for they were clearly opposed to Saxon aristocrats in general). They were a real danger to feudal power, and had to be crushed if that power was to continue. As soon as the civil war quietened down, they were.

The Saxon revolt of 841–2 is an extreme case, but it makes still clearer what has been proposed here on other grounds: peasants were conscious of increases in aristocratic power, and were opposed to them. Here the main group was free peasants falling into subjection; there were parallels to this elsewhere (in Trita, for example), though other resisters could be tenants of varying social status. (Chroniclers were not likely to get these categories right—one notes the oscillation between freedmen and the unfree in the brief references to the Asturias revolt, and the same oscillation appears in the accounts of the Stellinga; Nithard was quite exceptional in his detail here.) Peasants were, as we have seen, in different measure in different places, resisting pressure on land, on rents, and on status; in Saxony, they were confronting all three. These were genuinely, however, the markers of the advance of the feudal mode; I would argue that peasants knew this, and resisted it where they could. In Saxony, that advance was generalized across an entire region, so the resistance, uniquely in the West in the early middle ages, was also across an entire region. These are indeed the core arguments of the main group of scholars who have discussed such resistance, the

---

[130] The best analyses of the uprising are Epperlein, *Herrschaft und Volk*, pp. 50–68; Müller-Mertens, 'Der Stellingaaufstand'; Eggert, 'Rebelliones servorum'; and Goldberg, 'Popular revolt', the most detailed, and the only one to locate the Stellinga in the political context of the civil wars. The basic texts are Nithard, *Historiarum libri IV*, IV.2, 4, 6; *Annales Bertiniani*, s.aa. 841–2; *Annales Fuldenses*, s.a. 842; *Annales Xantenses*, s.a. 841.

historians of the Soviet bloc; if one sets aside their romanticism about 'die Rolle der Volksmassen', it would be hard to say that they were wrong.[131]

What sort of peasant society was most likely physically to resist aristocratic dominance in the early medieval West? One that witnessed its socio-economic standing weaken very fast, like Saxony or, even more, the Valle Trita. One that was geographically marginal, and thus hard to get to, like Trita—and which also had a more collective, silvo-pastorally orientated economy, like Elariacum and Flexum and the Asturias (and, later, like eleventh-century Castile). One that saw its dominators divided, thus both breaking their hegemony and giving a practical chance at revolt, like Saxony, or perhaps the Seine–Loire peasants facing the Viking crisis, as also in a different context the tax rebels of fifth-century Gaul and eighth- and ninth-century Egypt. One without close patronage links between peasants and the powerful, for sure, a feature of all the resisting groups just listed (cf. above, pp. 438–41). The more of these elements in any given society, the more coherent and large-scale the revolt; this would privilege Saxony and the Valle Trita, as indeed our evidence for them indicates. There cannot have been many other Saxonies, but there could well have been other Tritas. Not so very many—peasants generally lose such conflicts, and many of them are killed as a result; peasants are cautious by nature, and know these risks better than we do—but some, all the same.

The directions and contexts of the peasant resistance we know about give some corporality to the models presented here for the processes by which aristocrats came to dominate over peasants. Overall, the economic shift from the peasant mode to the feudal mode could be seen as a threefold process: first, a steady strengthening of aristocratic status and wealth, inside the constraints of the peasant mode and/or in neighbouring areas; second, a catastrophe-flip from a peasant to a feudal economic logic; third, the steady reduction of areas of continuing peasant autonomy inside the overall dominance of the feudal mode. (The establishment of aristocratic *political* hegemonies, through patronage networks and through the steady exclusion of peasants from public roles, ran parallel to all three phases—the two processes reinforced each other, but must be seen as distinct.) Peasant resistance began in the second phase, and was in particular characteristic of the third. But such resistance would run on, for conflicts over rents, and the legal and political frameworks in which rents could be determined, are characteristic of the feudal mode in all its forms, ancient, medieval, or modern. These were more localized in our period, larger-scale in the fourteenth century, but have continued ever since.

---

[131] Eggert, 'Rebelliones servorum', p. 1148, for the quote.

PART IV

Networks

10

Cities

1. The problem of urbanism

THERE HAS BEEN a great deal of disagreement over the nature of urban continuity into the early middle ages; this has both fruitful and unfruitful aspects. On the positive side, the urban debate has been the focus for much important work in the last couple of decades, and the steadily rising number of urban excavations has tended to be made use of unusually quickly to develop new versions of rival syntheses, with the league table of successful and unsuccessful towns subtly shifting each time; ten or so recent conferences have also contributed to establishing an effective international dimension to the debate.[1] On the negative side, there is a frequent lack of agreement even over the object of debate, not to speak of the criteria that might be used to assess it. One issue, not in itself a negative one, is that historians and archaeologists alike (although they often disagree profoundly over whether documentary or archaeological criteria are more important) have viewed 'the city' with a double vision: through both an economic and a political/institutional framing. Urban centres have an economic function, and if they do not (if, for example, they consist of a handful of administrative or ecclesiastical buildings and nothing else, as with most of the *civitates* of Bede's England), then their urban status is legitimately in doubt. But in nearly all the regions discussed in this book urban centres were also usually defined in politico-administrative terms, as self-governing and tax-raising *municipia* under late Rome, as episcopal centres in every Christian region, as secular administrative centres in the post-Roman world. Indeed, if they were not (as with some of the North Sea *emporia* of the eighth century), then once again there are scholars who doubt their 'real' urban status. Inside any given region this does not have to be a problem, but a comparative analysis has to take the double focus into account, so as to find a common language that can

---

[1] An incomplete list is Rich, *The city*; Christie and Loseby, *Towns in transition*; Francovich and Noyé, *La storia dell'alto medioevo*; Lepelley, *La fin de la cité antique*; Brogiolo and Ward-Perkins, *The idea and the ideal of the town*; Brogiolo, *Early medieval towns*; Brogiolo et al., *Towns and their territories*; Ripoll and Gurt, *Sedes regiae*; Lavan, *Recent research*; Burns and Eadie, *Urban centers and rural contexts*. The best book to start with in this list is the second. Note that Horden and Purcell, *The corrupting sea*, pp. 89–108, argue for the abandonment of urbanism as an analytical category; I disagree entirely.

usefully set Rome, Recópolis, Pella, Dijon, York, and Ribe against each other in the same argument.

The best way to do this, with urbanism as with several other concepts discussed in this book, is to set out the key elements of an ideal type. This, indeed, has been tried by others, and quite successfully as well. Martin Biddle's influential ideal type (he himself uses Edith Ennen's word, *Kriterienbündel*) of a town, developed to analyse Anglo-Saxon England, includes twelve elements: (1) defences, (2) street planning, (3) market(s), (4) a mint, (5) legal autonomy, (6) a role as a central place, (7) a relatively large/dense population, (8) economic diversification, (9) 'urban' house-types, (10) social differentiation, (11) complex religious organization, and (12) judicial functions—he suggests that any three or four of these are needed as a minimum characterization of a town.[2] These elements are not all of equal importance, as Biddle himself warns, and some of them in reality depend on others, but his model still stands, as good a set of guidelines as any that has been proposed for an initial framing of urban characteristics, not least because it is robust enough to be exported to regions as un-English as Syria and Africa. I shall use it as an initial framing as well.

This model has been influential, as already observed; but there are still profound differences of emphasis in debates about urbanism. One major reason is a difference between northern and southern Europeans about where its core characteristics lie. In general, for northern historians and archaeologists, medieval urbanism is regarded as a predominantly economic phenomenon. For them, the 'idea' of the town focuses on active exchange and craft centres, many of which had no formal juridical status for a long time, many of which were wholly unplanned and very casually administered, and all of which were horrifically muddy and unhealthy—all that wood, all that rain. The word 'town' dominates the vocabulary of historians of England, in fact, a word with specifically economic overtones in British English (a 'city', by contrast, was only an episcopal centre for a long time, and the word still denotes institutional privilege in modern Britain). Much the same is true for *ville* in French, or *Stadt* in German. If we move into the Mediterranean, however, the emphasis changes. *Città* in Italian and *ciudad* in Spanish (particularly the former) have a stronger institutional edge, reinforced by the power of central medieval urban political autonomies, as well as by the greater importance of the monumental Roman past. In Italy, indeed, it has needed the coining of a new word, *quasi-città*, by Giorgio Chittolini to force later medievalists to pay more attention to the economic importance of the group of non-episcopal/non-autonomous economic centres ('*borghi*') like Prato or Vigevano or San Gimignano, many of which were huge by north European urban standards, since Italian urban

---

[2] Biddle, 'Towns', p. 100.

historians had hitherto looked so predominantly at the 'real' *città*.[3] When English and French scholars look at the Roman empire, they, too, begin to use 'city' and *cité* for the urban centres they see, and they, too, tend (with different degrees of commitment) to move into a more institutional mode of analysis.

Just to use 'town' or 'city', then, even inside a single language, involves a set of cultural assumptions that need to be made explicit in order to be controlled. Can one sidestep this, and just use the word 'urban', with its spin-offs, 'urbanism' and 'urban centre', which are more neutral words, and are much the same in all western languages? Even then, however, the northern gaze and the southern gaze have largely different cultural assumptions attached to them about what urbanism is. Bryan Ward-Perkins, in an elegant recent article, unpicked some of the assumptions employed, either implicitly or explicitly, by participants in the active Italian debate about early medieval urbanism (including me, and indeed him), drawing clear distinctions between the British and the Italian participants, who argue from, in effect, the opposite ends of the European spectrum of presuppositions about what the core elements of 'townness'/'cityness' should be, the British with (let's say) early medieval Hamwic in the back of their minds, but at least some Italians thinking of imperial Rome.[4]

This is not a framework I can extract myself from, as a British historian with a longstanding commitment to a research debate in Italy. I shall in this chapter be as loose as possible about the details of terminology, with 'city', 'town', and 'urban centre' used as near-synonyms, although I shall use 'city' more in the Mediterranean and 'town' more in the North. (See below, p. 594, for further slight restrictions on the word 'city'.) But my basic definition of urbanism remains dominated by economic criteria, for these seem to me, in the last analysis, the most significant. A relative demographic concentration, a market, and economic activities structurally different from those of the countryside are the core criteria that will be used here (cf. numbers 3, 7, and 8 in Biddle's list), as a minimum characterization of urban activity;[5] if *civitates* (or *poleis*, or *mudun*) ceased to have these characteristics, or never acquired them, then they would no longer be urban, and they will be discussed differently. The evidence for urbanism by this set of criteria is largely archaeological in our period, so these discussions of urban trends will privilege archaeology. The available evidence being as usual also restricted and chance-driven, however, other criteria will sometimes be used, such as the nature of housing and the patterning of streets (cf. numbers 2 and 9 in Biddle's list), to fill these out; 'urban' house-types (leaving aside the potential

[3] Chittolini, 'Quasi-città'.
[4] Ward-Perkins, 'Continuitists, catastrophists'.
[5] An analogous set of definitions is proposed by Scull, 'Urban centres', pp. 271–2, a sharp characterization (it is part of what one could call a 'northern' critique of Biddle's list).

problem of circular argumentation in such a formulation) can be seen as a marker for differentiations in economic activity, while a street plan, although most immediately revealing a political/institutional element, the existence of an authority capable of creating or maintaining regular street alignments, is often a sign of relative population density as well (see below, p. 646).

It must be recognized, nonetheless, that political, institutional, and (more widely) social roles for urban centres were not irrelevant. It mattered enormously for Roman centres that they were *civitates* or *poleis*, with their own *curia* or *boulē* (city council), tax-raising powers, and judicial territories. For a start, the 'kit' of public buildings that every Roman city had to possess, forum, basilicas, theatre, amphitheatre, baths, temples (the latter, from the fourth century, replaced by the cathedral), were a considerable expense and resource, and physically marked 'cities' off from 'non-cities', whatever their economic similarities. Even in the latest Roman and post-Roman period in the West, when the minimum kit had shrunk in monumental terms, becoming restricted for the most part to city walls, cathedral, and royal or comital palace, it still marked difference. For this reason, I shall restrict the word 'city' to urban centres, defined economically, that would have been called *civitates* (or the equivalent in other languages) in our period as well. But we can go further here for more direct economic reasons too. Every Roman *civitas* must count as an urban centre in economic terms, given the amount of public money that passed through it. In the post-Roman period, as well, there was always a dialectic between urban economic activities and administrative centrality. Very rare indeed were economic centres that 'just growed', without any external intervention. The major eighth-century North Sea *emporia*, for example, new towns in nearly every case, seem all to have been royal developments; even when they had older roots, it was kings who elevated them from small maritime landings to substantial exchange centres (below, pp. 681–8). But, apart from this sort of direct royal (or, more generally, princely) intervention, urban centres also depended on another, at least partially political/social, element: aristocratic spending-power. As we will see in more detail in Chapter 11, the scale of private exchange in our period, the late Roman and post-Roman periods alike, depended on aristocratic wealth and taste; the non-agrarian economy was not complex enough to create more broadly based exchange systems. This was indeed true of later centuries too; the exchange growth of the eleventh and twelfth centuries in northern Europe was fuelled by the demand of the new castle-dwelling aristocracies of that period. When aristocracies were rich enough, where they lived was immaterial for urban prosperity; towns could crystallize at the nodes of the communications networks between castles, on those very rare occasions when they were not founded by the aristocrats themselves. But, in our period above all, a strong impulse to urbanism was, simply, the choice that aristocrats could exercise to live in urban centres.

In general, the more aristocrats there were in any settlement, the more other people, including autonomous merchants and artisans, would go there too; that is to say, the more that settlement could operate as a production and exchange centre with an immediate market right on the spot—the key urban characteristics. But why *would* groups of aristocrats want to live in the same urban centre? In the Roman period it was because each city was the locus of tax-raising and political power, which made urban participation virtually inescapable for most aristocrats, at least for parts of the year. In the post-Roman period these imperatives were certainly weaker, and in many areas of the former empire (notably northern Francia and Britain, but also much of Spain and of the Byzantine empire) aristocrats tended to live in the countryside. When, however, they lived in cities, thus underpinning a relative urban survival (as in Italy, Andalucía, Syria-Palestine, or Egypt), they did so in large part because those cities were still important secular administrative centres. In this sense, political/institutional elements could continue to have a directly causal role in the economic criteria that act as my basic definition of urban production; they will therefore be borne in mind as at least secondary indicators of urbanism, supplementing that basic definition.

One final point in this context relates to identity. 'Cityness' has had a strong ideological element in much of history. For the Romans, as is well known, it simply constituted culture, *civilitas*; it would have been a major step for the 'civilized' 'civilian' aristocrat to think that s/he could live without it. Thus, when city-dwelling became less common for the powerful in some parts of the post-Roman world, a major cultural shift took place. The nature of aristocratic identity must have changed already; in particular, the militarization of most post-Roman elites (see above, Chapter 4) made it possible for them, in some regions, to choose non-urban lifestyles for the first time—and also lifestyles that did not depend on monumental building, even in their rural centres (above, Chapter 8). But cities changed too. Their own identities shifted, as they became less the stage for all significant civil aristocratic activity, less the focus for an autonomous, inward-looking, public politics. Public space became more religious, for example, as bishops became more important (the smaller the city, by and large, the more religious its public space became—in the *civitates* of northern Francia and England which kept their bishops but lost their urban economic features, religious ceremonial was all that was left). More generally, in every region of the former empire, the definition of 'cityness' changed considerably from its Roman origins; the ideological pull that cities had for aristocracies shifted accordingly. We cannot always pin this down in our documentary sources, for they are not dense enough, but the new spatial patterns that new ideas of the city generated can be seen in the archaeology. Although this book does not explore cultural change with the same commitment that it explores economic change, the two cannot be fully separated, and in the case of the city, they certainly have to be considered together.

This means that the history of cities, even their strictly economic history, although belonging with the exchange networks that will be the subject of Chapter 11, cannot be entirely cut off from issues discussed earlier on in this book. The fiscal role of cities was discussed in Chapter 3; the wealth and the political locations of aristocrats were discussed throughout Chapter 4; the nature of rural aristocratic housing was discussed in Chapter 8. All these elements are relevant to this chapter, and will recur here as appropriate. This chapter will focus on four main empirical issues, all of them generated by the urban characteristics mentioned above: the changing political structures of cities in the Roman and post-Roman period, and how they fitted into the organization of wider political systems; the location of aristocratic dwelling-places in the post-Roman period, whether inside cities or outside them; the economic activities that can be documented inside towns/cities; and the changing spatial structuration of cities. The first two of these will be discussed separately, but more briefly, for they partially reprise material analysed in previous chapters. Economic and spatial structures will be presented together, divided by region, and at greater length. Finally, we shall look at the situation of urban centres across Europe and the Mediterranean in the eighth century, at the very end of our period, when all the economic changes after the Roman empire (mostly negative ones for urbanism) had been completed, and when, in most of our regions, urban economic activity was either reviving or on the brink of revival.

2. Political changes inside cities

Recent work has made the nature of the basic changes in late Roman city government fairly clear. The *curia* or *boulē*, the formally structured city council with tax-raising powers, ceased to exist nearly everywhere in the fifth and sixth centuries, but this did not in itself mean the failure of city government, as several scholars have shown. Their work allows the process of these changes to be summarized here fairly briefly.[6]

Curiae were the unambiguous foci of local aristocratic political action in the early empire, a period when power was relatively decentralized, and central government positions restricted for the most part to Italians. Councillors (*curiales* or *decuriones* in Latin, *bouleutai* or *politeuomenoi* in Greek) collected taxes and competed for local prestige by constructing public buildings in their cities; that local prestige was usually all that was available to them. The later empire, however, from Diocletian onwards, was characterized by greater central control over tax-raising, thus making curial

---

[6] The main contributions are Claude, *Die byzantinische Stadt*, pp. 107–25, 155–61; Whittow, 'Ruling'; Brandes and Haldon, 'Towns, tax'; Liebeschuetz, *The decline*, pp. 104–202; Laniado, *Recherches*; Rapp, 'Bishops'.

responsibility less remunerative and more risky, and also by a greater openness to a provincial input into the expanding central government. The
senatorial stratum, exempt from city duties, was hugely expanded, thus
making it possible for city aristocrats to rise out of the curial level, just at
the moment when the financial risk involved in curial office was increasing.
Provincial-level senators seldom had much power outside their localities,
and their political activity in practice thus remained restricted to the cities of
their ancestors, but *curiae* suffered, both in prestige (for curial office was not
longer the highest one could aspire to) and in economic security (for the
richer local figures sometimes moved out of the *curiae* altogether, leaving the
underwriting of taxes to lesser players). Essentially, *curiae* were increasingly
out of date in a more centralized political system, where, too, status could be
gained in a greater variety of ways: senatorial, palatine, and provincial
office, and the ecclesiastical hierarchy, were all more prestigious alternatives
to curial status by the fifth century.

Slowly, as we saw earlier (pp. 68–70), *curiae* slipped out of their role as the
authorities that ran cities and raised taxes, and by the end of the sixth
century at the latest tax-raising, in particular, seems to have become entirely
the responsibility of central government officials in both the East and the
West. In the East, city leadership in the later fifth and sixth centuries was in
the hands of a much more informal group, often called *prōteuontes* or
ktētores, 'leading men' or 'landowners' (although other words were used
as well); these consisted of local figures of senatorial rank, the bishop, a
small group of local officials who were central government appointees, and
some *bouleutai/politeuomenoi* (perhaps only the richer and more influential
ones). It was this group—together with the provincial governor—which
chose the city-based officials of the period, such as the *logistēs* (Latin
curator) and the *patēr tēs poleōs*, the 'father of the city', who is best-
documented in provincial capitals.[7] In the West, these new civic offices are
less prominent, and we tend to find bishops exercising a more central role,
beside local senators (sometimes called *honorati*) and surviving *curiae*
(which by the sixth century, however, are ill-documented outside Italy).[8]
It is important for westernists to recognize the stability of this new ruling
group in the cities of the sixth-century East, for the end of the *curia* is even
now often seen in the West as a metonym for the failure of cities and of
urban aristocratic lifestyles themselves, with the urban rich supposedly
driven out of cities by the tax burden falling on the *curia*. This imagery of
urban failure is, of course, given its edge by its rough temporal coincidence

[7] Roueché, 'A new inscription'; Liebeschuetz, *The decline*, pp. 110–24; Laniado, *Recherches*,
pp. 133–223; Alston, *The city*, pp. 309–16.
[8] Liebeschuetz, *The decline*, pp. 124–36, 155–67, is a useful summary, but here the bibliography is extensive. Episcopal takeover of city government was, of course, most complete at
Rome.

with the failure of imperial authority in the West. But, even in the newly Germanic kingdoms, cities could still be run effectively by informal leading groups, as was the Clermont of Sidonius Apollinaris and his brother-in-law Ecdicius in the 470s. Both of these were of senatorial, not curial rank, but Sidonius was committed to the city as its bishop, and Ecdicius as a local warlord, and Sidonius clearly valued what remained of the curial hierarchy, as his letters show. That hierarchy was partly marginalized by the local political role of bishops and lay senators, but was equally, at least in part, strengthened by the latter's urban patriotism, for senators were brought back into local politics by the development of this pattern of political action.[9] It would be for the most part, at least in southern Gaul, senatorial-level families which would lead cities by the sixth century.

The key change was, of course, that a formally constituted body had been replaced by an informal one. Even in the East, no emperor ever institutionalized or defined the *prōteuontes*, and in the West the group never even had a name. Formal positions became determined by status in the hierarchies of central government and the church, not that of the city. The ruling group of city notables did not have the same responsibilities that the *curia* had had: taxes were increasingly collected only by central officials, and city government in a formal sense—the upkeep of streets, public spaces, or poor relief—became the responsibility of the provincial governor or his city-level equivalent in the East, of the bishop in the West. One simple sign of the weakening of the *curia* in many regions was the physical decay of the forum/agora and its associated civic buildings at the centre of cities, which, as we shall see, could happen at the same time as the building or repair of rich private houses and privately founded churches elsewhere in town.[10] The move towards the dominance of informal city notables could thus, as we shall see in more detail later, be represented by the destructuring of the old city centre. And, although provincial governors sometimes can be seen intervening to preserve public spaces (as at Edessa in 497, where the governor cleared the main colonnaded street of illegal shops[11]), overall, as excavation shows in twenty or thirty cities, those spaces were less regularly maintained from the fifth century onwards than they had been when *curiae* were influential. We can interpret the encroachment on public space in two contrasting ways: as a sign of private vitality, even though public buildings and municipal zoning regulations were in decay; and as a sign of a generalized lack of control, a planning crisis, as municipal responsibilities for keeping roads clear, like sewage and street-cleaning, were abandoned, and not taken up by anyone. It is an irony that the proponents of each of these two contrasting

---

[9] Harries, *Sidonius Apollinaris*, pp. 222–38; Sidonius, *Ep.* V.20.

[10] An archaeological overview is Potter, *Towns*, pp. 63–102. For the rarity of references to city councillors in late Roman Palestine in epigraphy, see di Segni, 'The involvement', pp. 322–3.

[11] Joshua the Stylite, *Chronicle*, c. 29; see also below, n. 64.

interpretations have often tended to come from political positions that would lead them to adopt the exact opposite view if they were considering the cities of the late twentieth and early twenty-first century. Leaving that aside, however, it must be recognized that both interpretations are valid to an extent. What would have mattered in any given city in the sixth century would have been the local balance between the two, not the superiority of one principle over the other.

The informality of post-curial government could imply the gradual lessening of local public responsibility, then. It had two other major implications. The first is that cities became more diverse. Every city, large or small, in 250 had a similar range of governing officers. In 550, and still more in 650 and later, this was emphatically no longer true. A small city might only have a bishop and a central government official (a count in Gaul, a pagarch in Egypt, and so on), with no wider penumbra of notables except the family or families these two came from. A larger city, such as Hermopolis or Ravenna or Mérida or Thessaloniki, had a range of local officials, and families of other notables besides. And the terminology of local dominance became different from place to place, as we saw in earlier chapters. In the Ravenna of the 570s, status was still associated with being called a *curialis*; in the Ankara of the early seventh century local notables were called *protiktores*, a title of military origin that seems to have developed a local informal meaning in Galatia; in the Thessaloniki of the seventh century, a range of entirely non-technical titles for notables are used in our major source, the *Miracles* of S. Demetrios; in the Lucca of the eighth, where we can track a dozen significant urban families in our documents, no collective term for them is ever recorded at all. (See above, pp. 209, 233, 238, 212.) We cannot generalize from place to place with any ease when we are faced with this level of difference, and we must remember that we cannot.

We can track this growing lack of homogeneity through late attestations of the word *curialis* (or *bouleutēs*, or *politeuomenos*) itself. In Italy up to 600, it seems to have been used in ways close to its old meaning, but thereafter it fell out of use; when it recurs in Naples in the tenth century it means 'notary'.[12] In Gaul, *curiales* still appear after 600 in occasionally surviving formal registrations of land transfers, particularly in the Loire valley (above, p. 110), but the office seems to have become a ritual one only—one which an inhabitant of Poitiers or Angers might aspire to, but which probably held no more real power or status than the lord-mayorship of a modern British city. In the Ebro valley in the late sixth century, Maximus *curialis* seems simply to have been a local, not even necessarily urban,

---

[12] For Italy, see e.g. *P. Ital.* 7, for Rieti in 557; for Naples in the tenth century, Gallo, 'I curiali napoletani', esp. II, pp. 5–10, 17–25; I am grateful here to Jean-Marie Martin for advice. *Curiales* can also be found in eighth-century Rhaetia, where they were simply local notables: Kaiser, *Churrätien*, pp. 43–4, 199–200.

aristocrat, one of an Ebro-based group who are generally elsewhere called
senatores.[13] In Egypt, the last reference to a functioning *boulē,* in Antinoupolis (Shaykh 'Ibāda), is as late as the 610s, although there are no others
known postdating 450, in a documentation which is very generous in its
references to pagarchs on the one side and to new civic offices such as the
patēr tēs poleōs on the other, in the sixth century in particular. Later
Egyptian references to *politeuomenoi*, of which there are a handful, show
two separate sorts of meaning, at least on the surface. In a Coptic text for
Apollōnopolis Anō (Edfū) of 649, it is a synonym for pagarch. In an Arsinoë
(Madīnat al-Fayyūm) text later in the same century, it denotes a tax-
collector, which ought by now also to mean a pagarch or his dependant. In
two other Edfū papyri, however, the Coptic registration of the arguments of
a dispute held before arbiters in 646, and in 647 the decision of the same
arbiters in Greek, we find that the arbiters are in the latter called *politeuomenoi*, but in the Coptic text they are called *noc nrōme*, 'big men' or 'elders':
that is, simply, 'notables'.[14]

In Egypt, as we shall shortly see, there was no serious weakening of urban
society or economy at any point in our period; these changes in urban
government occurred in a framework of general continuity in most
other aspects of city life. In that region, the pagarch monopolized taxation
by the start of the sixth century, and civic offices became the preserve of the
informal collectivity of notables, such as (only to name the most prominent)
the Apions in Oxyrhynchos (above, p. 248). It is interesting that, in this
active urban environment, a city council could last at least until the 610s; but
its functions must by then have been as vestigial as they were in Poitiers later
in the century. It is in this context that *politeuomenos* could, slowly, become
a term that could apply to any politically active urban notable, pagarchs
included. None of the seventh-century Egyptian references need mean any
more than that, and the 646–7 reference, the most explicit, certainly does
not. What was happening here was the reverse of the process by which
the *boni homines*, 'good men' or, once again, 'notables' of early medieval
Italian cities, the informal elites congregating around bishops and counts,
crystallized into formal consulates when cities became autonomous around

[13] Braulio, *Vita S. Emiliani*, c. 23; cf. Castellanos, *Poder social*, pp. 40–52.
[14] Late references to *boulai* and *politeuomenoi* are collected in Geremek, 'Sur la question des
boulai', and Laniado, *Recherches*, pp. 75–87. I accept, with Laniado and others and against
Geremek, that *bouleutēs* and *politeuomenos* are synonyms. Geremek's wider range of citations
results from the fact that she includes some more metaphorical usages. Those cited here are
Gascou, *Un codex fiscal*, p. 282 (Antinoupolis; a dating to 618–19 seems to me more likely than
633–4); Crum, 'Koptische Zünfte', p. 106 (Edfū in 649); Grohmann, 'Greek papyri of the early
Islamic period', n. 10 (Arsinoë); Schiller, 'The Budge papyrus', p. 88, with Zilliacus, 'Griechische Papyrusurkunden', n. 2017 (Edfū in 646–7). The last citation of all is *CPR* VIII 84, from
c.698, a fragmentary letter from the duke of the Thebaid to the *politeuomenos* Theodore,
probably from Arsinoë. (Laniado, *Recherches*, p. 83, sees the last as *P. Apoll.* 75, but this
should date to 679–80 if we follow the redating of Gascou and Worp, 'Problèmes', not to c.710.)

1100 and counts lost their power or vanished;[15] in Egypt, central authority in the person of the pagarch had become dominant, and *boulai* steadily disintegrated into informal groups of notables. Egypt is the clearest example of this process precisely because cities remained so active, but something similar is regularly apparent elsewhere.

The second point follows on from this: the informality of urban elites coexisted everywhere with two strong and continuous formal hierarchies, those of central government and of the church. Being a 'notable' was flexible and locally diverse; being a bishop or count was rather less so. One could indeed say that the more informal the former was, the more sharply defined the political roles of the latter were, and vice versa. It is also likely that, if urban society hit crisis, it was the informal wider elite that would lose power, status, even coherence, and the small core of the official hierarchies would survive more easily. After all, being an informal but powerful urban notable would only have been attractive if the city itself remained a stable, attractive stage on which to play politics. If that stability weakened at all, simply being a notable would quickly lose its allure. Thessaloniki is a reasonably good example of the process. In the church of Hagios Demetrios, as Leslie Brubaker argues, sixth-century patronage, as represented by donor portraits on the walls, is the work of a wide city elite; after the early seventh century, however, in a period characterized by Slav attack and political isolation, these portraits are restricted to state officials and to the clerical leadership of the city. The notables of the city still existed, as the *Miracles* of the same period show us, but they were becoming eclipsed by the formal hierarchies that still structured the Byzantine empire.[16] We could guess that by now any ambitious citizen in Thessaloniki would be aiming to become either bishop or eparch. Thessaloniki remained important enough for participation in the local informal elite to stay a good second best; but in other cities the ambitious would not have that choice, and instead would probably join the army or the central government in Constantinople and eventually leave the city altogether. Where position in the state became sufficiently more important than informal urban-based status, as in the Byzantine heartland or Francia by 700—but, conversely, not in Italy or Egypt or probably Syria— then urbanism itself might be at risk.

This observation nonetheless needs empirical testing. We can say that, if we have a tax-raising *curia*, we have an urban society, for civic finance would itself under those circumstances have provided a firm economic foundation for urbanism. If we have a clearly characterized informal group of civic notables, then we also normally have an urban society, for a substantial group of the richest owners in a territory were choosing to

---

[15] See e.g. Jones, *Italian city-state*, pp. 120–51.
[16] Brubaker, 'Élites and patronage'; see above, p. 238, for the notables.

identify themselves with, and almost certainly to live inside, the city, thus ensuring the movement of goods from their estates inside the city walls, and the use of their surplus to buy any artisanal goods that urban craftsmen could produce. If all we have in the evidence for any given city is a bishop and a count (or duke, or governor, or pagarch), however, then we will have to look for other indicators if we want to conclude that the *civitas* (or *polis*, or *madīna*) was an urban centre in an economic sense: an identifiable urban archaeology, ideally; otherwise, more hesitantly, numerous churches, or an orthogonal street plan, or at least some form of street plan that indicates a relatively ambitious spatial structuring, and the other major elements of Biddle's ideal type. It is these elements that we shall be looking for later in this chapter.

One could put these points another way. The move from cities dominated by *curiae* to cities dominated by groups of notables to cities dominated by a couple of office-holders is a move from a world in which everyone who is politically important has to live in a city to a world in which, increasingly, they can choose whether to adopt an urban lifestyle or not. Participation in the tax system required city living; simply feeling 'civilized' made city living attractive. But participation in the political retinue of a count could be done from either an urban or a rural base; and counts might not have so much authority that social leaders needed to be in their retinues at all. As our period went on, and as urban government became less organic, urban living became ever more a matter of choice, which tended to have regional regularities, and regional explanations, but no more uniformity than that. Let us look at those regularities from the standpoint of regional aristocracies, first, before investigating the cities themselves.

3. Where did post-Roman aristocrats live?

In the Roman empire, almost every major political figure was urban-based. This bald statement needs immediate qualification, for military leaders did not necessarily have the same identification with a city as did senatorial and curial aristocrats, and indeed frequently came from frontier regions, above all the northern Balkans, where cities were relatively weak; but the higher they rose the more they gravitated to the urban centres of political power, as with Aetius and Aspar, contemporaries of Balkan and Alan origin respectively, whose points of reference were Ravenna and Constantinople, or Belisarios, who was also from the Balkans, but who retired to Constantinople.[17] It must also be stressed that city-based western aristocrats had rural houses as well, the sumptuous villas praised by writers like Sidonius, where they spent the summer months, and occasionally overwintered too (above,

---

[17] *PLRE*, II, s.v. Aetius 7, Aspar; *PLRE*, III, s.v. Belisarius 1, pp. 216–19.

pp. 467–8); where exactly the 'primary' base was for a rich landowner with many such estates, particularly one who was keener on *otium* than on urban or imperial office, may have been no clearer then than it is now. But the exclusive association between city living and the exercise of direct political authority, with all the public money that was attached to it, made it hard for any major figure to turn his back on urban society altogether. Only the antisocial and perhaps the elderly did it, like Asturius, an irascible senator who had retired to the Alpine foothills, probably from Milan, in the early sixth century.[18] It may be that, at the very end of the western empire, city-dwelling was less entirely normal for aristocrats. Apart from Sidonius' letters on the subject, already mentioned, historians tend to cite Cassiodorus' letter of 526/7, requiring the *possessores et curiales* of Bruttii, modern Calabria in the toe of Italy, to return to the 'human society' of the cities, rather than burying themselves in their rural houses. Was this trend restricted to Bruttii, a politically marginal area, or was it more widespread in Italy, and only associated with Bruttii because Cassiodorus was himself from there, and kept more of the letters he wrote about it? We cannot be sure. As long as the Ostrogothic state remained strong in Italy, however, *possessores* who left cities ran the risk of cutting themselves off from political influence and exposing themselves to the power of others—to adopt Sidonius' punning words about the situation in Gaul, 'not so much being praised by the censor (*honorare censor*) as being burdened by the tax-collector (*censetor onerare*)'.[19] So much bad happened in Italy in the next decades, however, that whether this one letter really represents a trend is a bit beside the point; we cannot easily trace the (anyway weak) tradition of rural aristocratic landowning in post-Roman Italy to Bruttii.

In the East, where even summer aristocratic retreats were rare, outside, probably, parts of eastern Anatolia (above, p. 462), the countryside was more marginal still. Rural-based elites under the empire seem never to have been more than medium owners, as at Serjilla and Nessana (above, pp. 447, 454). Moving into the seventh century, the signs are that the Arab conquests did not change much in the conquered lands. As we saw in Chapter 4 (pp. 240–2, 251–2), Roman elites stayed put in their urban environments in Egypt and, as it seems, in Syria and Palestine as well (Edessa is the best-attested case); archaeology certainly supports this for the Levant (below, pp. 613–25). The Arab conquerors, too, were largely urban-based, associated with the garrison cities (*amṣār*) of each province, or, in Syria, with older urban centres, in which they were allotted housing.[20] The ruling Umayyads built substantial rural centres, the *quṣūr* on the desert edge, but Damascus presumably pulled them back for much of the year as well. The only high-status family known to have lived an essentially rural existence

---

[18] Ennodius, *Ep.* I.24, cf. II.12 (*Opera*, nn. 31, 47).
[19] *Variae*, VIII.31; cf. Sidonius, *Ep.* VIII.8.
[20] al-Balādhurī, *Futūḥ al-buldān*, trans. Hitti, pp. 201, 211, 221, etc.

was the 'Abbāsids before they came to power; in the decades around 700 they were a politically marginal family, distantly related to the Umayyads, and relegated to their rural centre at Ḥumayma, inland from 'Aqaba, which has recently been partly excavated. Whether or not there were other such rural families, the marginality of this one is perhaps its most significant aspect.[21]

The Byzantine heartland, on the other hand, was marked by sharp discontinuity; we shall see later in this chapter that most cities here faced crisis in the seventh century. Here, as explored earlier (pp. 233–9), urban aristocracies seem to have faced the choice to go either to Constantinople (or to one of a dozen major provincial cities) or into the army, and away from an urban-based political practice. But it must be said at once that we have no direct evidence at all about where Byzantine aristocrats lived between 650 and the tenth century outside the capital. When, later, we do have such evidence, the middle Byzantine great noble families had largely rural Anatolian bases, and we could legitimately assume that this ruralization had begun by the eighth century at the latest.[22] Our best support for that dating is the urban crisis visible in the archaeology; but the rural basis of tenth-century aristocrats does give us some prima facie independent back-up for such a conclusion. This contrasts with Byzantine and post-Byzantine Africa, where a greater degree of urban continuity into the seventh and even eighth centuries can tentatively be hypothesized on archaeological grounds, as we shall see.

Visigothic Spain gives us slightly more evidence to work with, although it remains on the level of anecdote. Mérida had a clearly defined urban aristocracy, of both Romans and Goths, in the late sixth century. So, probably, did Seville, where two brothers (Leander and Isidore) succeeded each other as bishops. The Ebro valley, by contrast, although very Roman in its politics and aristocratic behaviour, did not necessarily enforce city-dwelling in the same period; Braulio's *Life* of Aemilianus has at least one senator living in the countryside, at Parpalines, and no clear urban focus for any other aristocrat in the text—although Braulio's own family, in the next generation, was clearly orientated towards Zaragoza, where he and his brother were both bishops. Up in the Meseta, the owners of the Diego Álvaro estate and its neighbours in the seventh century (above, p. 224) were almost certainly rural aristocrats, given that no cities are mentioned in their slate archives at all apart from a casual reference to Toledo, the capital. In the Bierzo to the north-west, the *illustris vir* Riccimir was apparently rural-dwelling in the late seventh century.[23] This pointillist picture,

[21] See Foote, 'Frescoes', for aspects of the excavation.

[22] Cheynet, *Pouvoir et contestations*, pp. 213–20.

[23] For Mérida, see above, pp. 221–2. Braulio, *Vita S. Emiliani*, c. 24 (cf. Castellanos, *Hagiografía*, pp. 34–5); *Las pizarras*, n. 75, for Toledo in the slate documents; Valerius, *Ordo querimoniae*, cc. 5, 7.

which has already almost exhausted the direct information we have for the residences of Visigothic aristocrats, seems to show that they could live in both the country and the city in the north, though more often in the city in the south. This would fit the little we know about early al-Andalus, too, for the southern cities are regularly the points of reference of major political leaders, with, by contrast, a greater importance for rural centres such as Gormaz, Catalayud, and Albarracín in the north (though there were certainly exceptions, such as 'Umar ibn Ḥafṣūn's rural base of Bobastro in the far south).[24] Overall, however, both in the Visigothic and Arab periods, political practice was seen as normally urban. The *Historia Wambae*, for example, describing the civil war of 672–3, talks in terms of political centres that are exclusively urban when describing the northern rebel provinces of (what are now) Catalonia and Languedoc.[25] Only the marginal Asturian kingdom of the eighth century adopted rural sites as its political centres.

Francia and Italy provide, as usual, our most detailed document-based guides outside Egypt, and here we are on firmer ground. In Italy, post-sixth-century evidence shows us an aristocracy that was, both in Lombard and Byzantine areas, overwhelmingly urban. We can identify in our documents active urban aristocracies before 800 in Bergamo, Brescia, Rimini, Lucca, Pisa, Rieti, Rome, Benevento, and Naples,[26] and at least individual urban aristocrats from Pavia, Lodi, Senigallia, Pistoia, and Siena.[27] Only documentary absence excludes from these lists Milan, Ravenna, and Spoleto, major centres as we know them to have been. Beyond these cities, we can only speculate how many others were in the same position, but probably at least as many again had urban-based elites, judging by what we know of the immediately succeeding centuries. Lucca (above, pp. 211–12) is the best-documented of these cities, but the evidence for the others is of a similar type: each city had a network of prosperous (although not super-rich) landowning families, often with official titles, who competed for position in the state and episcopal hierarchies associated with each centre.

As important as this is the fact that we so seldom find major aristocrats based in the countryside. There are certainly some, like Rotpert of Agrate, 15 km east of Milan, in 745, or Cunimund of Sirmione on Lake Garda in 765—though Sirmione was itself the centre of an administrative territory. Stavile, *habitante in Sablonaria* (Sabbioneta, prov. Mantua) in 769 was a *civis Brixianus*; was his Brescian identity more important than his quite

---

[24] See Manzano, *La frontera*, pp. 126–8, 139–42, 157–62; Acién, '*Umar ibn Ḥafṣūn*, e.g. p. 74.

[25] Julian of Toledo, *Historia Wambae*, cc. 6, 7, 11–13, 26–8.

[26] Bergamo: *CDL*, II, nn. 226, 293; Brescia: nn. 228, 257 (cf. Paul, *HL*, V.36, 38–9); Rimini: *CB*, nn. 27, 29, 36, 64–75; Lucca: see Ch. 4, n. 154; Pisa: *CDL*, I, n. 116, II, n. 295; Rieti: see Ch. 4, n. 169; Rome: see Coates-Stephens, 'Housing'; Benevento: see Ch. 4, n. 170; Naples: see Ch. 4, n. 144.

[27] Respectively: *CDL*, I, n. 18; II, nn. 137, 155; *CB*, n. 80; *CDL*, II, n. 203; I, n. 50.

distant rural base? Conversely, Walfred, the founder of the remote rural monastery of Monteverdi in 754, came from the city of Pisa (and his brother-in-law and co-donor came from Lucca), and the three founders of the even more remote monastery of S. Vincenzo al Volturno in the 710s came from Benevento.[28] The other firmly rural owners in our eighth-century documents, such as Gunduald of Campori in the Tuscan Appennines, Toto of Campione beside Lake Lugano, and the groups of proprietors around Varsi in the territory of Parma, Monte Amiata in southern Tuscany, and Farfa in the Sabina, were all second-rank figures, prosperous medium owners at best.[29] Of course, such people had to have existed; not all property-owners were ever urban. But they, and the rarer larger rural owners already mentioned, do not undermine the point that urban life was the norm for the political leaders of Italy. This point was already made in Chapter 4, but it must be kept in mind as we assess what we know of the cities themselves; Italy (both its Lombard and Byzantine parts), whatever the limits of its prosperity, is the region of the former empire whose urban aristocracy is best attested in the last century or so of our period, outside Syria-Palestine and Egypt at any rate—but even in these regions, urbanized though they were, we cannot actually name as many eighth-century urban aristocrats as we can for Italy.

In Merovingian Francia we find the opposite, a well-documented aristocracy firmly embedded in the countryside. Again, the basic patterns were set out in Chapter 4, and only need summarizing here. The strongest signs of active urban societies after 550 or so were in the south, centres like Poitiers, Clermont, Limoges, Bordeaux, and Marseille, and in most of these we have some evidence of local urban aristocracies, focusing on episcopal office.[30] All the same, even in the south, not all leading figures had urban origins or a clear urban base. Bishop Aunemund of Lyon (d. after 660) was almost certainly from a local urban family, and Desiderius of Cahors (d. c.650) was probably born in Albi, in which territory he was a major owner. Aredius of Limoges (d. 591) was born in that city, but Eligius of Noyon (d. after 657), another Limousin saint—though, admittedly, from a lesser social background—was born at Chaptelat, 10 km to the north; of bishops of Clermont, Avitus II and Bonitus (d. after 705) were from the city (they were doubtless members of the old Aviti family), but their predecessor Praejectus (d. 676), once again probably of slightly lesser status, seems to have been

[28] Respectively: *CDL*, I, n. 82; II, n. 188 (cf. III, n. 36); n. 228; n. 116 (with Andreas, *Vita Walfredi*, cc. 1, 2); Autpert, *Vita Paldonis, Tatonis et Tasonis*, pp. 104–5.

[29] See for Gunduald, Wickham, *Mountains*, pp. 40–5; for Toto, Rossetti, 'I ceti proprietari', pp. 182–207, and Balzaretti, *Lands of Saint Ambrose*, pp. 205–9; for Varsi, *CDL*, I, nn. 52, 54, 59, 60, 64, 79, 109; II, nn. 129, 159, 291; for Monte Amiata, *Codex diplomaticus Amiatinus*, I (Chiusi, the closest city, is only mentioned three times before 800 in over forty documents, in nn. 14, 19, 24, excluding location clauses); for Farfa, *CDL*, V, *passim*.

[30] For Clermont, see Wood, 'Ecclesiastical politics'; for Marseille, see Gregory of Tours, *LH*, VI.7, 11; see in general Heinzelmann, *Bischofsherrschaft*.

from Issoire, 35 km to the south. Abbo of Maurienne (d. after 739) was probably from Susa, a *civitas* but probably not an urban centre in any economic sense, although his mother's family was apparently from Marseille. Other rural-based figures included Filibert of Jumièges (d. after 678), from the territory of Éauze, and Nizezius, whose huge holdings, listed in a charter of 680, locate him firmly at the Tarn–Garonne confluence some 60 km north of Toulouse. We have here, on the face of it, the same sort of pattern as—more sketchily—in Visigothic Spain, with cities acting, as one might put it, as major points of reference for a rural aristocratic politics as often as actual locations for urban aristocratic living. Braiding of Nîmes, whose will of 813 survives, may be as good a guide to these aristocrats as anyone, for he had three *casae habitationis*, one in the city, one in the mountains to the north, and one on the sea to the south. His focus was urban, but whether he would have been politically marginalized had he switched to his rural estates is much less clear than it would have been four centuries earlier.[31]

North of the Loire, clear evidence of urban aristocrats is very limited indeed. Reims's bishops were nearly all of local origins, but our major source for them, Flodoard, does not at all stress that they actually came from the city, and Bishop Nivard's (d. 673) family monastery, often a good guide in northern Francia to the local base of an aristocratic family, was at Hautvillers, 23 km to the south—although Reims was clearly the focus for the *concives* of the city, including *inlustri viri qui intraurbem commanere videntur*, 'illustrious men who are seen to live in the town', who consent to an episcopal gift in 686.[32] When we have clear reference to the seats of named major aristocrats, they are almost all rural: Ursio (d. 589) in the Woëvre north of Verdun, the Faronids in the Brie close to Meaux (not living in the city, although they did have some land there), the Pippinids on the middle Meuse, Adalgisel-Grimo (fl. 634) probably at Longuyon, north-east of Verdun. Paris was the focus for many important aristocrats (see also pp. 398–406), but we cannot show that they actually lived there; rather, Erminethrudis (fl. c.600) was based at Lagny and Bobigny to the east and north-east, the son of Idda (fl. c.690) at Arthies in the Vexin to the north-west, and Wademir (fl. 690) probably at Précy-sur-Oise, in the royal heartland. All three gave extensively to Paris churches, and thus had an interest in the city, but lived outside it. Only Trier, of the northern cities, was definitely home to important aristocrats, with Germanus of Grandval (d. c.675), of a

---

[31] *Acta Aunemundi*, cc. 2, 3; *Vita Desiderii*, c. 1 (reading *Albige* for *Obrege* in the text—a fairly severe amendment, but one which makes the best overall sense in the context); *Vita Aridii*, c. 3; *Vita Eligii*, I.1; *Vita Boniti*, cc. 1, 4; *Passio Praejecti*, cc. 1–2; Geary, *Aristocracy in Provence*, pp. 38–78, cc. 3, 36; *Vita Filiberti*, c. 1; Devic and Vaissete, *HGL*, II, preuves, pp. 42–4 (Nizezius), 75–9 (Braiding).

[32] Flodoard, *Historia Remensis ecclesiae*, II.7; Pardessus, *Diplomata*, n. 406.

senatorial *prosapia*, born there, and Ermina of Ören, linked to the Pippinids, firmly based there by the time of her will in 697.[33]

There is no need to continue these lists much further. (If I did, I could assign many more Merovingian aristocrats firmly to rural bases, and only a handful, rather uncertainly, to urban ones.[34]) The Frankish evidence used here (for the south as well as the north) is as usual casual, consisting of chance references in narratives, the birthplaces of saints as described in hagiographies, and the centres that emerge from the fullest lists of properties in documents, mostly wills. But, as with our denser eighth-century Italian documentation, it all points in the same direction; so would the explosion of documentary evidence for the eighth-century middle Rhine, which would add Mainz as an aristocratic focus to our list of cities, but dozens of figures to our list of rural aristocrats.[35] It is, of course, not a startling novelty to propose that northern Frankish aristocrats were mostly rural-based—when, at least, they were not following the movements of kings, between the palaces of the Oise and Seine (with stops at Paris) for Neustria, and between the palaces of the Moselle and Rhine (with stops at Metz) for Austrasia. But it is worth noting that there were some cities which seem to have been significant centres for a *rural*-based politics: Paris, certainly; Reims, probably; Trier and Mainz (for the rural owners around them were as important as the few urban owners); also Metz, Verdun, and maybe Meaux. This certainly could have economic implications too, when aristocrats endowed churches inside cities, or if they bought and sold in urban markets. Not all of these centres have significant archaeology to back these observations up, but some do.

On the basis of the location of documented aristocratic bases, we could postulate a rough hierarchy of importance for urbanism in our different regions, as long as we bear in mind that there was a considerable degree of local diversity in each. In 700–50, say, Egypt, Italy, and Syria-Palestine are clearly the regions with the most urbanized aristocrats. Next come southern Spain and southern Gaul, perhaps the Marmara sub-region close to Constantinople (above, p. 234), and maybe Africa, where cities were not the only locations for aristocratic living, but important ones all the same. Greece and Anatolia, northern Spain, and above all northern Gaul, finally, were areas where aristocrats were probably for the most part rural-based. (Britain can be excluded for the moment, for urbanism had effectively vanished as an

---

[33] Respectively, Gregory of Tours, *LH*, IX.9, 12; Jonas, *Vita Columbani*, II.7 (cf. Bergengruen, *Adel und Grundherrschaft*, pp. 65–80); Werner, *Der Lütticher Raum*, pp. 216–27, 341–475; Levison, 'Das Testament'; *ChLA*, XIII–XIV, nn. 592, 569, 571, with 594; Bobolenus, *Vita Germani*, c. 1; Wampach, *Geschichte*, I.2, nn. 3, 4, 6, 9, 10.

[34] Other seventh-century urban aristocrats would include Landibert of Maastricht (*Vita Landiberti*, c. 2), given that that town, a late Roman *castrum*, was certainly economically urban by the late seventh century (below, p. 680), and, probably, Vigilius of Auxerre (Pardessus, *Diplomata*, n. 363, or *Cartulaire général*, n. 8).

[35] For Mainz, see e.g. Falck, *Mainz*, pp. 13–17, 21–2.

economic phenomenon there, until 700 at any rate.) These observations are based, up to here, only on the documents, apart from Africa and, to an extent, Syria-Palestine, where without some reference to archaeology we could say little. We will find, however, that the archaeology does indeed fit this regional urban hierarchy, reasonably well: indeed, it does so sufficiently well for us to be able to use our document-based hierarchy as a predictor even in those sub-regions where the archaeology is weak. There will be some surprises (the urban prosperity of the Rhineland, most notably), but the overall pattern will be maintained. Knowing where to expect post-Roman aristocratic residences will also help us when we are assessing archaeological work, since so few of such residences have actually been found by archaeologists.

4. Urban economies in the eastern Mediterranean

The following sections will largely be based on urban archaeology, which in the last couple of decades has in many regions become rich enough to generate more plausible syntheses than ever before. Documentary references to urban buildings will be used where appropriate as well, however, and also the spatial and topographical analysis of standing buildings (usually churches and city walls, and street plans) when they are available. As usual, we shall look at each region in turn, before coming to wider conclusions.

In Egypt, urban private housing is relatively well understood, thanks to the convergence of detailed sales and leases in the papyri and a handful of significant excavations. To take one example at random, in 535, in the city of Oxyrhynchos, Euphēmia loaned out 2 *nomismata* against a pledge of a room facing east in a house facing north in the Shepherd's Quarter of the city (*amphodos poimenikēs*), together with rights in the rest of the house: the courtyard, the well, the [roof] terraces, and the bread-coolers (*artopsygia*). This image of an apartment building, with rooms opening out into a collective courtyard, probably (to judge from other documents) of several storeys, has plenty of parallels in Egyptian documents from our period; people bought and sold them, leased and pledged them, and went to court over them, that is to say, sets of rooms, or single rooms or, indeed, even subdivided rooms.[36] Excavations in Alexandria, Ṣaqqāra, and Elephantinē

---

[36] *P. Oxy.* XLVII 3355. Probably the same woman, here a large landowner (*geouchousē*), leased a ground-floor room in the Quarter of S. Euphēmia from a baker in 568 (*P. Oxy.* VII 1038). For terminology, the basic guide is Husson, *Oikia*. For the earlier history of quarters, see Alston, *The city*, pp. 130–65. For house transactions, see Johnson and West, *Byzantine Egypt*, pp. 198–203; Husson, 'Houses in Syene'; Saradi, 'Privatisation', pp. 30–43; Schiller, 'A family archive'.

(Aswān) indicate that such courtyards were characteristically long and thin, fitting inside apartment buildings that were roughly the shape of a brick, with (in Alexandria, at the Polish excavation of Kōm el-Dikka) a stairwell at one end. The Kōm el-Dikka buildings from the fifth to seventh centuries had artisans' workshops on the ground floor, specializing in glass-working, and then living quarters on the first floor and probably upper floors as well; the Ṣaqqāra buildings from the seventh to tenth centuries had workshops (for weaving) and kitchens on the ground floor.[37] That sort of division by functions between floors has, once again, parallels in the papyri. The later date of the Ṣaqqāra excavation, unfortunately as yet only published in interim form, shows that this sort of pattern continued without a break up to the end of our period; at the new Arab city of Fusṭāṭ, too, underneath modern Cairo, ground-floor shops on courtyards were found in the French Isṭabl 'Antar site, dating to the early eighth century.[38] Such buildings, in mud brick in the Nile valley, in limestone at Alexandria, must have distantly resembled those of modern cities such as Naples—the best-preserved Kōm el-Dikka building even had external decoration in coloured marble.

An alternative Egyptian pattern was the single house, on its own or part of a terrace, looking onto a street rather than a courtyard. At Syēnē (also part of modern Aswān) the Patermouthis archive from the sixth century refers to several; one, a portion of which was sold by Patermouthis's mother-in-law Tapia to a soldier in 594, had a first-floor dining-room (*symposion*), a second-floor bedroom (*akoubiton*), and a third-floor terrace (*aer* or *dōma*).[39] This house-type has also been found archaeologically, at Tebtynis in the Fayyūm (a seventh- to tenth-century example), in the eighth- and ninth-century levels at Kōm el-Dikka (where, by now, living quarters lay behind a street front of shops), and in an apparently sixth- to tenth-century site at Panopolis (Akhmīm). Buildings like the Syēnē houses must have been impressively articulated, although at Panopolis one has a sense of a lesser degree of monumentality. This was also, as both documents and archaeology show, the dominant house-type in the large village of Jēme in the seventh and eighth centuries.[40]

Egyptian cities are mostly still densely occupied, and large-scale archaeology is difficult there; the relatively few archaeologists who study our period have to take what they can find. One of the happy ironies is that

[37] For Alexandria, see above all Rodziewicz, *Les habitations romaines* (pp. 66–127 for the best-preserved building, House D); for Ṣaqqāra, Ziegler *et al.*, 'La mission archéologique', pp. 270–2; for Elephantinē, Grossmann, *Elephantine II*, pp. 29–34.

[38] Gayraud, 'Isṭabl 'Antar', pp. 66–71; Mathieu, 'Travaux', pp. 524–6 (M.-O. Rousset).

[39] *P. Lond.* V 1733. For a list of all Syēnē house documents, see Husson, 'Houses in Syene'; cf. also Alston, *The city*, pp. 110–12. *Symposion* generally by now just meant 'apartment' (Husson, *Oikia*, pp. 267–71), but here in context it seems to keep a functional meaning.

[40] Rousset, Marchand, and Foy, 'Secteur nord de Tebtynis'; Rodziewicz, *Les habitations romaines*, pp. 335–47; McNally and Schrunk, *Excavations in Akhmīm*, pp. 45–7; Nelson and Hölscher, *Medinet Habu reports*, pp. 51–6, with Schiller, 'A family archive'.

this means that they cannot focus on the monumental centres of cities, as archaeologists only too often tend to do if they have a free hand (and as has been done at the abandoned pilgrimage centre of Abū Mīnā near Alexandria[41]), and the percentage of private housing excavated is unusually high for the East. This of course also coincides with the sort of evidence provided by the papyri, which privileges private transactions, and the social life of private people, whether rich or poor. This focus is exceptionally valuable for us, even if it also means that we have close to no idea what sort of spatial layout Egyptian cities had in our period, and about what elements made up their monumental centres. In Alexandria, Kōm el-Dikka, situated quite near the agora, south of the great ceremonial street, the Canopic Way, maintained the street alignment of the classical city until its abandonment in the tenth century, as Alexandria did in general throughout the medieval period. In Fusṭāṭ, by contrast, orthogonal alignments are hard to find as early as the eighth century. Which of these is more typical of the end of our period in Egypt is as yet unclear.

The crucial point about our Egyptian material is that it stresses urban density. Roger Bagnall and Bruce Frier have calculated, as noted in earlier chapters, that perhaps a third of the population of third- or fourth-century Egypt was urban-dwelling, with Alexandria (the third largest city in the later Roman empire) only the largest of a string of fifty-odd substantial towns.[42] We have seen (p. 600) that urban politics was thriving in Egypt at least up to the end of the eastern Roman empire; in the Arab period, pagarchal administrations were probably more hierarchical, but they were at least coherent and active (pp. 133–8). Did Egyptian urbanism, however, maintain these remarkable Roman demographic levels into the sixth, seventh, or eighth centuries? It is impossible to say as yet. But the papyri and the excavations (even though the latter are as yet small in number) do not easily support an argument for overall population decline.[43] Excavated houses show a meticulous use of all available space, and no substantial changes in material culture across our period (see also below, pp. 759–69). In a pattern we shall see elsewhere in the Mediterranean, the papyri, above all in the sixth century, show a steady tendency to the subdivision of larger houses and the renting of more single rooms on the part of wealthier owners, who were either living in them as well (having fallen on hard times?) or were simply transforming buildings in order to rent them out to more people, presumably

---

[41] Grossmann, *Abū Mīnā I*, covers part of the site.

[42] Bagnall and Frier, *Demography*, pp. 53–6. Alston, *The city*, pp. 331–4, reaches analogous conclusions by different methods.

[43] Hermopolis (Ashmūnayn) may show a settlement retreat, though the Arab levels on the main site are fragmentary: Bailey, *Excavations at el-Ashmunein*, IV, p. 59, V, p. xi. Alexandria certainly did by the ninth century, for clear geopolitical reasons (Haas, *Late Roman Alexandria*, pp. 338–51). The recent Ṣaqqāra and Tebtynis excavations (above, nn. 37, 40) show no retreat until well after our period. Alston's more catastrophist account (*The city*, pp. 361–6) is based on uncertain archaeology, with a wide variation of dating for the end of site occupations.

for profit.[44] It might be argued that this sort of subdivision actually attests to an increased population density in the parts of cities occupied by private housing. Although these might in principle have shrunk (they did, after all, elsewhere in the Mediterranean), we have no clear evidence in Egypt that they did, and the continued importance of street-names and quarter-names in our documents argues against cities becoming particularly small. Fusṭāṭ/Cairo, in particular, grew steadily after its foundation in 653, reaching an estimated population of 250,000 by the eleventh century. This simply parallels Alexandria's roughly estimated population of 200,000 in the sixth, which must have been substantially less by the eleventh, as the city was steadily losing importance after 750 at the latest.[45] But the ability of Egypt to maintain a provincial capital on this sort of demographic scale was probably unaffected throughout; and the same goes, most likely, for its other cities as well.

What made this urban density possible was the Nile, and its associated network of canals, which made transport exceptionally easy, and the sale of Egypt's rich agricultural surplus exceptionally straightforward. Urban produce sales are occasionally documented in sixth-century papyri: two fishmongers in Arsinoë (Madīnat al-Fayyūm), a flower-seller in Antinoupolis (Shaykh 'Ibāda), two vegetable-sellers and charcutiers in the same city. A group of five shops has been excavated along the decumanus in Marea, near Alexandria, with oil jars dating to around 600, which represents the more organized end of urban food sales.[46] In return, cities produced artisanal products of all kinds: cloth above all (wool and linen for the most part), glass, leatherwork, metalwork, stonework, woodwork, and ceramics (though this, the most frequent craft mentioned in documents, was as much rural as urban: see below, p. 764). The Edfū guilds are listed twice in seventh-century documents: in 649 potters, doctors, oil-sellers, butchers, among others; in 679–80 boatmen, embroiderers, fishermen, and potters again, that is to say, a mixture of shopkeepers, artisans, and urban professionals, still as dense as in any previous century.[47] The way the city–country relationship worked is hard to specify in more detail in our period, and after the Arab conquest is still harder to track, for our best evidence is no longer city-focused. If there was any lessening in urban-based exchange, however, it was shortlived; the intensity of such exchange by the eleventh century is very well documented indeed in Egypt, thanks to the Cairo Geniza.[48] We will explore this issue on a wider scale in the next chapter.

---

[44] Saradi, 'Privatisation', pp. 39–43.

[45] See Raymond, *Cairo*, p. 62 for Fusṭāṭ; Haas, *Late Roman Alexandria*, p. 340.

[46] *CPR*, XIV 3 for Arsinoë; *P. Cair. Masp.* 67156, 67164, 67023, for Antinoupolis; el-Fakharani, 'Recent excavations at Marea'.

[47] For craft lists before 640, see Ch. 11, n. 128. For Edfū, Crum, 'Koptische Zünfte'; *P. Apoll.* 75 (following the redatings in Gascou and Worp, 'Problèmes').

[48] Goitein, *A Mediterranean society*, I, *passim*.

Egypt's emphasis on the density of private housing is a necessary counter-weight to the great emphasis on monumental building in the much more numerous excavations from Syria and Palestine. In this latter region, there are many abandoned cities from the late Roman and early Islamic periods, which makes large-scale excavation much easier; as with rural settlements, however (pp. 457–9), the simple fact that the cities are abandoned at once poses the question of when their demographic decline began. Debate has been particularly animated on the subject in the last fifteen years, with 550, 650, 750, and (more tentatively) 850 all supported by someone as the moments for the beginning of urban recession. It can be argued, however, that the answer to the question varies very greatly across the region; with a difference between the north and the south, and also quite a substantial difference between the patterns on the coast and those on the hills and desert fringe of the inland of the region (see above, p. 26).

What is not necessary to do here, however, is to go through the basic findings of the archaeologists in detail, for other recent surveys do this admirably: an article by Clive Foss, two by Alan Walmsley (to name only the most recent), and a book by Wolf Liebeschuetz present detailed and reliable overviews of the situation in the late 1990s, which will remain broadly valid for some time (perhaps a decade, given the speed of research in this area). Even if I would not necessarily agree with all their conclusions, they are the essential initial points of reference at present.[49] Here I shall do something simpler, that is to say, just list the cities with relatively solid archaeological findings, in order to characterize a data-bank, and discuss one, Scythopolis, in more detail, before looking at three general issues: the nature of urban economies in the Levant; the changes in the monumental structure of cities; and the date(s) of urban recession.

The cities with the best evidence, because they have been extensively excavated by people who paid attention to our period, number six: from north to south, Apamea, Bostra (Buṣrā), Scythopolis (Bet She'an), Pella (Tabaqat Faḥl), Gerasa (Jerash), and Caesarea; one should perhaps add the atypical pilgrimage centre of Sergiopolis (Ruṣāfa), and the short-lived Umayyad foundation of 'Anjar. Palmyra and Petra, the other great Roman urban sites, were excavated too early for our period to be studied properly for the most part, but recent work in both has brought to light important material in previously neglected parts of town.[50] Less fully excavated sites, some of which will probably in the next decade figure more prominently in subsequent syntheses, include Gadara (Umm Qays), Abila (Umm al-'Amad),

---

[49] Foss, 'Syria'; Walmsley, 'Byzantine Palestine'; idem, 'Production, exchange'; Liebeschuetz, *The decline*, pp. 54–63, 295–317.

[50] Apamea: Balty, 'Notes sur l'habitat', cf. Foss, 'Syria', pp. 205–26. Bostra: ibid., pp. 237–45. Scythopolis: Tsafrir and Foerster, 'Urbanism'. Pella: McNicoll *et al.*, *Pella*, I and II; Smith and Day, *Pella*, II; Walmsley *et al*, 'The 11th and 12th seasons'. Gerasa: Zayadine, *Jerash*; Gawlikowski, 'Installations omeyyades'. Caesarea: Lentzen, *The Byzantine/Islamic occupation*;

Capitolias (Bayt Rās)—all three close together in the 'Decapolis', an anachronistic but convenient term for the cluster of cities around Lake Galilee
and on the Jordan–Syria border—and Apollonia (Arshaf) on the coast south
of Caesarea.[51] Most of these cities are now abandoned, or else are occupied
only in part. Chalkis (Qinnasrīn) and Elousa (Ḥaluẓa), abandoned sites with
very little recent study, may also soon appear as reference-points. Understandably, however, as elsewhere in the world, still-occupied cities have had
less excavation: most in Antioch, Philadelphia ('Ammān), Madaba, and Ayla
('Aqaba), in all of which substantial urban development only began in the
twentieth century, in post-civil-war Beirut, and also in Jerusalem, where
archaeology has important political implications;[52] considerably less in the
other principal centres of the region, Edessa (Urfa), Callinicum (Raqqa, a
major 'Abbāsid centre), Beroia (Haleb, English Aleppo), Epiphania (Ḥamā,
though there is some work here), Emesa (Ḥimṣ), Damascus, Tyre, Tiberias,
Jericho, and Gaza.[53] This is not a complete list of the cities of the region,
even the main ones, but it is long enough, and is I think representative. One
point must be made at once: almost all the leading cities of the region at
the end of our period, in 800, are in the final category, that of cities which
are still occupied; only Caesarea needs to be added to them. The major
excavations are, that is to say, by definition a misleading guide, if one wants
to consider the question of urban abandonment. But they also do not
in themselves have much homogeneity, and recent work has pointed up
instructive differences, as we shall see.

To get an idea of what one of these cities was like, let us look at Scythopolis, Bet She'an in the Decapolis, just south of Lake Galilee. This is the best-
presented of the major late Roman/early medieval sites, and its late Roman
monumental centre is now almost entirely excavated (although relatively
little private housing has been excavated around it).[54] That centre reached its
height around 500, a little earlier than the typical Syro-Palestinian urban

Raban and Holum, *Caesarea maritima*; Holum *et al.*, *Caesarea papers* 2. Ruṣāfa: see esp.
Mackensen, *Resafa I*; Sack, *Resafa IV*; Brands, *Resafa VI*; Ulbert, 'Beobachtungen'. 'Anjar:
Hillenbrand, ''Anjar'. Palmyra: al-Asʿad and Stępniowski, 'The Umayyad sūq'; Gawlikowski,
'Palmyra, excavations 1995'. Petra: Fiema, 'Byzantine Petra'; idem, 'Late-antique Petra'.

[51] Gadara: Holm-Nielsen *et al.*, 'The excavation of Byzantine baths'; Hirschfeld and Solar,
'The Roman thermae'. Abila: Mare, 'Internal settlement patterns'. Capitolias: Lentzen, 'From
public to private space'; eadem, 'Seeking contextual definitions'. Apollonia: Roll and Ayalon,
'The market street'.

[52] Antioch: Foss, 'Syria', pp. 190–7. 'Ammān: Northedge, *Studies*. Madaba: Piccirillo, *The
mosaics of Jordan*, pp. 49–132, gives a guide. 'Aqaba: Whitcomb, 'The miṣr of Ayla'; Parker,
'The Roman 'Aqaba project'. Beirut: first approaches to rich material are Butcher and Thorpe,
'A note'; Perring *et al.*, 'Bey 006'; see also later issues of *Bulletin d'archéologie et d'architecture
libanaises*. Jerusalem: Magness, *Jerusalem ceramic chronology*, pp. 16–118, gives an account of
major sites.

[53] Ḥamā: Pentz, *Hama*, IV.1. Tiberias: Hirschfeld, 'Tiberias'. For Aleppo, unstudied archaeologically, see Sauvaget, *Alep*, pp. 54–82.

[54] See, for all that follows, Tsafrir and Foerster, 'Urbanism'.

peak under Justinian (perhaps because of the disruption of the Samaritan revolt of 529); a provincial capital for Palaestina II, it may then have had over 30,000 inhabitants. At that time the focus of the city was the agora, an irregular diamond of land between the theatre and the prehistoric tell above it (Scythopolis had straight streets, but they were, atypically in the region, not orthogonal). The agora had colonnades around it, and a group of attached monuments, such as baths and former temples, and an ornate semicircular *sigma* (a commercial centre on top of the former odeon, which had probably been the home of the city council) dated epigraphically to 506–7. In the early sixth century one of the two sets of baths went out of use, and a large hall building was built beside it by the brothers Silvanos and Sallustios, members of an aristocratic Samaritan family of the city, in 515–16, along what the archaeologists call Silvanus Street. (Silvanos was lynched by Christians in 529.[55]) Until then, therefore, older buildings which became obsolescent were replaced by new ones; only later in the sixth century, when the theatre and the (more peripheral) amphitheatre went out of use, did their sites simply decay. An earthquake in the late sixth or seventh centuries is probably responsible for the destruction of porticoes on the northern side of the agora, which were, similarly, not replaced: the street there, and the *sigma* on it, were abandoned, the latter becoming a cemetery. The clear impression that one has from the archaeology is that the old heart of the city had lost its political centrality, although this does not mean that monumental building had ended; four probably sixth-century churches are known from elsewhere inside the city bounds, and the cathedral has not yet been located.[56]

In the seventh and early eighth centuries, however, the city's old centre was still fully occupied, with more utilitarian buildings. The nymphaeum was by now fronted by shops, there were linen workshops in the former eastern baths,[57] and industrial-scale ceramic workshops in the theatre, in the amphitheatre, and on the agora. In the Umayyad period the western baths were abandoned and converted to workshops as well. Private housing expanded into the old public centre. Systematically, colonnades were filled in and shops or workshops created, and buildings in front of them encroached on some streets, notably Valley Street to the east of the agora, at an angle to Silvanus Street. Against this backdrop of an active but more informal urban economy, the caliph Hishām in the 720s rebuilt the area of Silvanos' hall as a monumental line of shops, a *sūq*, with a renewed portico, which was clearly commercially active up to 749.

[55] Cyril of Scythopolis, *Life* of Saba, c. 70; cf. Prokopios, *Secret history*, XXVII.8–9.
[56] Schick, *Christian communities*, pp. 270–1.
[57] Walmsley, 'Production, exchange', p. 307. Scythopolis linen was prized: Jones, *LRE*, p. 848.

The year 749 (or one of the three preceding) is the date of the great earthquake which devastated the Decapolis. Its impact is very striking if one visits Bet She'an now, for white limestone columns lie in regular lines across the black basalt streets and masonry, unmoved since, even by the excavators in some cases. The façade of Hishām's shops fell down onto the street in neat arches, and still lies there. Settlement in the old centre still continued; there are 'Abbāsid houses overlying the infill and the collapsed columns on Valley Street, for example. But no one after Hishām sought to order the area, or to build anything ambitious there.

The excavators of Scythopolis instruct us not to engage in value judgements, but then systematically refer to this steady demonumentalization as 'decay', 'decline', and 'deterioration': the narrowing of streets, the construction of private buildings on public spaces, and the end of street-cleaning and sewage-disposal are clear signs of this to them. We shall see this set of patterns everywhere in the Mediterranean, and they can be read this way if one chooses. If ever there was a site where this demonumentalization might not represent decay, it would, however, be Scythopolis. Here, the quarters containing the post-550 monumental buildings (which, besides churches, included mosques and a governor's palace) have not been excavated, although they certainly existed elsewhere in the city, probably in the latter case on the former tell.[58] Even in the old centre, a thriving commercial and artisanal economy is fully visible in the seventh and early eighth centuries, with some continuities later still. And the area, however politically peripheral it had become, was important enough to be the venue for a substantial monumental intervention, the building of a *sūq*, in the 720s. This, as we shall see, is a common pattern in Syria and Palestine.

The bases of the urban economies of the Levant were the usual mixture of political and fiscal, aristocratic and commercial. The cities of the region were all tax-raising centres until the Umayyad reorganization of the fiscal system, which assigned tax responsibilities to governors, but this region held several Umayyad provinces, and Gaza, Caesarea, Tiberias, Damascus, and Emesa, among others, remained fiscal centres. As for aristocratic city-dwelling, Scythopolis is typical in having at least one major family referred to in the early sixth century; and, although after 650, when inscriptions become fewer, only casual narrative sources tell us about urban families (in Edessa and Damascus: above, p. 241), nonetheless al-Balādhurī makes it clear that the new Arab elites settled in cities like Damascus, Emesa, Laodikeia (Lādhiqīya), and Askalon.[59] Substantial town-houses in use in this period have been discovered by archaeologists in Palmyra, Damascus, Gerasa, and Pella,

[58] For 'decay', 'decline', etc., Tsafrir and Foerster, 'Urbanism', pp. 139, 141. For the governor's palace, Alan Walmsley (pers. comm.).

[59] For inscriptions and their pacing, see di Segni, 'Epigraphic documentation'. For Arab elites, al-Balādhurī, *Futūḥ al-buldān*, trans. Hitti, pp. 189, 201, 211, 221–2.

however. The Palmyra house, just north of the great east–west spinal colonnaded street, seems to have continued in use without a break from the second century to the late eighth, with floors continually kept clean and a steady reshaping of rooms; in the sixth century it was divided into three, apparently more simply; in the eighth it lost an upper storey, but continued to be a focus for economic activity (including an oil-press). The Damascus house, the least well-excavated of this set, seems to have had a sixth-century origin, and Umayyad restorations; it had a mosaic-floored hall and a courtyard, and was located not far from the monumental centre. The Gerasa house was set on the South Decumanus, a major colonnaded sidestreet of that city's north–south spine; it was newly built in the early Umayyad period, and consisted of numerous rooms off a main courtyard. In the 'Abbāsid period it too was divided into three, the courtyard was built over, and the street colonnade was incorporated into one of the houses; around 800 part of it was used as a potter's workshop, and in the ninth century it was abandoned. The Pella house was a large courtyard house, here abandoned after the 749 earthquake. These must have housed urban elite families, and, in all of them except possibly Palmyra, these elites were active in the Umayyad period.[60] These are the most certain examples of rich urban private housing anywhere in the former Roman empire in the century-and-a-half after 650 (though shortly after 800 we find some instances in the West, in Rome and Mérida: below, pp. 649, 661), and they appear to show little change from the Roman period. That they are relatively few even in the Levant can easily be explained by the concentration by excavators on public areas in towns.

It is artisanal activity, continuing into the Arab period, that marks out Syrian and Palestinian urban economies most clearly, however. This is in part precisely because of the demonumentalization of public areas, discussed above for Scythopolis, which in this region did not lead to abandonment, but, most characteristically, to changes in use and the development of inner-city artisan production. At Gerasa, too, ceramic production is extensively documented up to c.800 (it lessened in the ninth century), concentrating in the north of the monumental centre, where the temple of Artemis and the northern theatre became kiln complexes—the area of the southern spinal colonnade remained more monumental and public in that city until after

---

[60] See respectively Gawlikowski, 'Palmyra, excavations 1995'; Saliby, 'Un palais'; Gawlikowski, 'A residential area'; McNicoll *et al.*, *Pella*, I, pp. 135–9. Another example is an immediately extra-urban house in Bostra: Wilson and Saʿd, 'The domestic material culture of Buṣrāʾ', pp. 40–52, 77–8. Alan Walmsley tells me that recent work on the Gerasa house indicates that it had a commercial role from the start; this may not undermine the general argument, given that in Palestine, as in Egypt, it was considered normal for shops to be on the ground floor of a building, residential accommodation on upper floors: see Julian of Askalon, *Urban treatise*, c. 37.1. This latter text, probably from the early sixth century, shows that in Palestine as in Egypt, many-floored apartment buildings were typical; c. 35.2 distinguishes between condominium customs in Caesarea and Askalon.

750, although there is evidence of commercial development here too.[61] Pottery production is also documented in our period in Ayla, Tiberias, Caesarea, Ramla, and the major later centre for fine wares, Raqqa; this is matched by glassmaking in all these cities, except Ramla (where excavation has been only occasional), and also in the 'Abbāsid levels at Pella. Dyeing is attested at Tiberias, Ramla, and Jerusalem, which is of course a sign of other aspects of cloth production. Iron- and copper-work have been located at Caesarea, Pella, and Gerasa. The ovens in the southern baths at Bostra may also have had an industrial purpose, although they may have been for food production, a sign in itself of a substantial urban market.[62] In short, the former monumental areas of these cities were systematically reconverted for a wide range of industrial purposes: a less outwardly impressive sign of civic ambition, but a more significant one at an economic level.

Combining the economic and the monumental are the substantial set, steadily increasing in number, of planned *sūqs* (I use a western plural because this has become an archaeological term) that were set up in the Umayyad period—not all have as firm a date as at Scythopolis, but the archaeological context is fairly clear for most. Rebecca Foote has counted nine known so far, at Ruṣāfa, Palmyra, 'Anjar, Tiberias, Capitolias, Scythopolis, Pella, Gerasa, and Apollonia. The 'Anjar shops were along a colonnaded street, planned as part of the Umayyad foundation of the city, and, like the rest of it, unfinished. Those at Ruṣāfa surround the west and north sides of one of its principal churches, next door to Hishām's large mosque. At Palmyra, the western part of the main colonnaded street was carefully transformed in c.700 into a set of shops, placed on the street itself and facing into the northern portico, which became the new street. Some of these *sūqs* are more architecturally ambitious than others, but all show a systematic concern, probably by public authorities in every case, to take charge of and to structure the steady transformation of the old monumental centres of these cities.[63]

Hugh Kennedy, in an influential article of 1985, defined the terms of the current debate about the transformation from the *polis* to the *madīna* in Syria and Palestine. He developed Jean Sauvaget's proposals about how a lack of public control allowed a steady infill of public spaces, with colonnades converted into shops, buildings encroaching onto streets, open

[61] See in general Julian of Askalon, *Urban treatise*, cc. 4–14, for the density of artisanal activity in sixth-century Palestine. For Gerasa, a quick overview is Gawlikowski, 'Installations omeyyades', pp. 359–61.

[62] All these are listed in Walmsley, 'Production, exchange', pp. 305–9, with references, plus Bahat, 'The physical infrastructure', pp. 54–5, for dyeing in Jerusalem, and al-Balādhurī, *Futūḥ al-buldān*, trans. Hitti, p. 220, for dyeing in eighth-century Ramla.

[63] Foote, 'Commerce, industrial expansion'; I am grateful to her for letting me see relevant sections of her unpublished thesis, which develops this. For 'Anjar, see Hillenbrand, ' 'Anjar', p. 62; for Ruṣāfa, Ulbert, 'Beobachtungen'; for Palmyra, al-As'ad and Stępniowski, 'The Umayyad sūq'.

squares replaced by a maze of semi-permanent then permanent stalls; Kennedy proposed that this marked an urban environment that was often quite as economically active, but which had lost the desire for the monumental framing that had been a feature of the Greco-Roman world. Mosques, the main public areas of a Muslim city, were more enclosed (though mosque precincts contained substantial open spaces); there was no need for squares or wide streets. The lack of the need for open spaces, however, meant that the process of encroachment, always present in cities and resisted in the Roman period (as in the already-cited case of the governor who removed the illegal booths built in the porticoes of Edessa in 496), was no longer resisted—or, perhaps better, less often resisted—under the caliphate. Kennedy argued that the Arabs were less concerned than the Romans had been to keep commerce and artisans out of city centres, for they had more ideological respect for the merchant class. Hence the dominance of commercial streets in the centre of medieval and modern, but not classical, cities.[64]

This basic model has been accepted by nearly everyone in the field; all that has happened since is refinement. Rebecca Foote and Alan Walmsley stress that the Umayyads and 'Abbāsids had their own monumental ambitions, as with the linear *sūqs* just described, or, more generally, with square-planned cities such as Ayla and 'Anjar—something which Kennedy had in fact already noted,[65] and of course with the great mosques of Jerusalem, Damascus, and elsewhere, not to speak of Baghdad and Samarrā' in the 'Abbāsid period. Kennedy may have overstated some subsidiary elements in his argument, such as the financial weakness of the early Arab state (cf. above, p. 133), or the degree to which demonumentalization was already coming to be a feature of Syrian towns before the Arab conquest (cf. above, p. 455). Exactly why the Roman world had needed such elaborate public spaces in the first place has also been too readily taken for granted by scholars in the field. The Roman liking for expressing political affirmation through formal processions in wide streets, for example, which was still strong in the late Roman empire of the fifth and sixth centuries and in Byzantium thereafter, was not the only way of organizing public politics, and it seems not to have been adopted by the Arabs (see also below, p. 634). It must further be observed that that the shift from the classical to the post-classical city did not at all mean that square-planned urban centres were abandoned in favour of the anthill of alleyways of modern cities such as Fès and Marrakesh (neither of them, anyway, former Roman cities): major

---

[64] Kennedy, 'From *polis* to *madina*'. For Edessa, above, n. 11; late Roman laws against encroachment are in *CJ*, VIII, 10.12.3, 6, 10.13. But actually encroachment of public spaces can be found in pre-Arab urban areas in many places in the East: see e.g. McNicoll *et al.*, *Pella*, I, p. 106, and below, p. 634, for the Aegean.

[65] Foote, 'Commerce, industrial expansion'; Walmsley, 'Production, exchange', pp. 274–83; Kennedy, 'From *polis* to *madina*', pp. 16–17.

centres of active urban continuity like Aleppo, Damascus, and Jerusalem have largely kept their classical street plans, better indeed than most western cities outside Italy. But cities in Syria and Palestine did change, slowly and inconsistently, between 650 and 1000, becoming more enclosed, with narrower streets and fewer public monuments, much as Kennedy argued. This change occurred independently of any shift in their economic activities, whether positive or negative. Nor does it link directly with the way urban aristocrats spatially organized their local power and influence, which had been focused on relatively private peristyle courtyards and reception rooms throughout the Roman empire.[66] Nor, finally, is it linked to the weakening of urban political autonomy. This was largely complete by 500, with a resultant abandonment of secular public monuments in old city centres, it is true; but the sixth century in Syria-Palestine is still marked by some bold monumental street planning that was intended to link more widely scattered (often ecclesiastical) buildings with processional ways, as in Justinian's rebuilt Antioch. These overall changes in conceptions of urbanism link most closely to cultural change: above all, changing conceptions of how collective living should be organized. But these issues take us too far from the remit of this book.

The preceding paragraph sidesteps the issue of urban economic 'decline', for, as already noted, this is not what demonumentalization necessarily signifies at all; but it is part of our remit, and must be looked at carefully. The best way to treat the issue is sub-regionally; let us start with the northwest of the Levant.

Antioch and Apamea are particularly clear cases of urban recession. Antioch, the old regional capital, lost its role as the main political focus of the eastern Mediterranean to Constantinople as early as the fourth century, and by 500 was no longer the major point of reference for Palestinian cities, and maybe not inland Syrian ones either, although it was still very large and rich. In the sixth century it faced several earthquakes, and a Persian sack (including the deportation of many people) in 540; these were probably the episodes which marked its retreat to the level of other Syrian cities, a considerable lessening of its importance—although it would remain a substantial centre for many centuries yet. Apamea, further up the Orontes, was still prosperous to the early seventh century (notwithstanding a Persian sack in 573), but the mid-seventh is characterized by the subdivision of larger private houses in the city—the eclipse of the city in the early Arab period is represented by the fact that only one small mosque has been identified there in all the extensive excavations. These two cities lay on the edge of the olive oil-producing Limestone Massif, whose role as one of the richest rural territories of the empire began to dwindle in the early to mid-seventh century (above, pp. 448–9; below, p. 774). Recession in this area seems to

---

[66] Ellis, *Roman housing*, pp. 41–72.

match, as will be argued in the next chapter, the weakening of the eastern Mediterranean exchange network as a whole in that period. The coastal cities of the north have not been excavated, except for parts of Beirut, where similar difficulties seem likely for the seventh century. Overall, however, the fact that, as al-Balādhurī tells it, the Umayyads had to settle new inhabitants in them, may indicate the same economic weakness in the cities most closely linked to the sea. The maritime cities of the north of our region are thus the best candidates for an overall picture of early deurbanization, by 650 at the latest.[67]

The inland north-east shows a different picture. Beroia (Aleppo), Epiphania (Ḥamā), Emesa (Ḥimṣ), and above all Damascus, the Umayyad capital, seem to have been thriving, both politically and economically, in the late seventh and early eighth centuries, and probably expanded in size after the Arab conquest. Three of these cities had large mosques in the eighth century (we cannot be certain about Ḥimṣ); Aleppo and Damascus, as already noted, kept much of their classical street plans.[68] These cities were major political centres until 750, although more marginal thereafter. They were also the main links between the settled lands of Syria, the northern desert, and the middle Euphrates valley, a role which under the caliphate, a political system which linked both halves of the Fertile Crescent, was of long-lasting importance; this importance further increased after 750. They may never have weakened at all, although without excavation we can be less certain of that. Further inland still, Edessa, the great border entrepot of the late Roman empire, kept a commercial role after 650, with, according to its Syriac chroniclers, a class of urban super-rich, one of whom, Athanasios bar Gūmōyē, reputedly owned 300 shops and nine inns in the city around 700—although not all of Athanasios' wealth was commercial, for he was also a great landowner and an enterprising administrator for 'Abd al-Malik (above, p. 241). Ruṣāfa, the pilgrimage city of S. Sergios, whose peak as a cult site was the sixth century (its Christian buildings seem to date from the late fifth to the early seventh), was also patronized by Hishām, who lived there for a while; it may have lost importance thereafter, but, if it did, it probably did so in favour of nearby Raqqa on the Euphrates, which became a major political centre, with large palaces and industrial activity, under Harūn in the period 796–808.[69] These examples further back up the

---

[67] Foss, 'Syria', pp. 190–7, 205–26, with Perring et al., 'Bey 006', pp. 198–9, for Beirut. I doubt this process was caused by Roman landowners fleeing the Arab conquests: above, p. 241. Beirut had revived as a maritime exchange centre by the tenth century: Ibn Ḥawqal (Ibn Hauqal), *Configuration de la terre*, I, p. 173.

[68] Sauvaget, *Alep*, pp. 74–82; Pentz, *Hama*, IV.1, pp. 38, 40, 61–5, 93–6 (for urban continuities rather than intense activity); Sauvaget, 'Le plan antique de Damas'; Sack, *Damaskus*, pp. 16–22.

[69] Edessa: see refs. cit. above, Ch. 4, n. 218, esp. *Chronicle of AD 1234*, pp. 202–4, for Athanasios. For Ruṣāfa, see Brands, *Resafa VI*, pp. 212–35, with Fowden, *The barbarian plain*, pp. 77–94, 175–83. For a brief overview of Raqqa, see Henderson, 'New light'.

argument that the inland Syrian cities did well in the early Arab period, including, in some cases, after 750.

Moving to the south, to the Palestinian coast and hills, we see a much more heterogeneous set of examples. Gaza, full of rich new buildings in the early sixth century according to local authors like Prokopios of Gaza and Chorikios,[70] has hardly been excavated, but may well have run into trouble in the seventh century along with the recession in the wine export on the coast (below, p. 774). Caesarea, however, did not. This city, where excavations have continued for nearly thirty years, is full of large-scale sixth-century building, public structures, private houses, and colonnades with shops. A provincial capital in the sixth century, it was a base of Persian government in the 620s, as we know, because the martyr Anastasios the Persian (d. 628) was imprisoned there; shortly after the end of the Persian war his body was taken back there, and the citizens, 'after common deliberation' (*koinē bouleusamenoi*, a phrase with at least a hint of the city council about it, very late by the 630s), buried him in a new church beside the *tetrapylon* at the city centre, a clear sign of the continued relevance of the old public monumental structure there. In the Arab period some of this building pattern was abandoned; one important example is the governor's palace just south of the port, part of which was carefully replaced with irrigated gardens in the Umayyad period. Much of the rest, however, continued without a break; inland, a colonnaded civic building was converted into an industrial suburb in the late seventh or eighth century; and the inner harbour was bounded by a sea wall in c.750, with a set of private houses built above it, increasing steadily in prosperity into the tenth century.[71] This sort of continuing occupation is matched at Jerusalem, focus of Justinianic redevelopment on a huge scale, including an expanded city wall, and then of the great Umayyad religious buildings on the Temple Mount. Jerusalem was, of course, of interest to emperors and caliphs above all for religious reasons, but it seems that it attracted inhabitants on a long-term basis as well: the City of David hill to the south of the city has prosperous post-Justinianic occupation, abandoned only after 750; and, in the Tyropoeon valley below it, a street and associated houses, built c.600, seems to have continued to be occupied into the central middle ages.[72] Further south and east across the

---

[70] Materials are conveniently collected in Abel, 'Gaza au VIe siècle'.

[71] For Anastasios, see the saint's *Acts*, c. 18 and *Miracles*, c. 7, both edited in Flusin, *Saint Anastase le Perse*, I; the texts date to the 630s. Caesarea is extensively studied but not well presented; Patrich, 'The warehouse complex', presents the irrigated gardens; Raban *et al.*, 'Land excavations', presents the inner harbour; Lentzen, *The Byzantine/Islamic occupation*, pp. 127–9, 403–20, presents the civic building. Holum, 'Archaeological evidence', gives a sensible overview; so does Magness, *The archaeology*, pp. 209–13; Patrich, 'Urban space', while good on the sixth century, overgeneralizes about later ruralization on the basis of the garden excavations, p. 97. Cf. nearby Apollonia's activity: see above, n. 51. These two cities in the middle of the Levantine coast show a continuing prosperity rather greater than on the coast to the north and the south. See further below, p. 774.

[72] See in particular Magness, *Jerusalem ceramic chronology*, pp. 17–27, 51–71.

Red Sea, Petra seems now to have become deurbanized in the seventh century, later than was thought, but well before other cities in this part of the region. The port of Ayla ('Aqaba) at the top of the Red Sea, however, although never a large centre, was clearly in steady expansion, with a prosperous sixth-century settlement, which continued into the Umayyad period even though a new town was added then, just to its south: the latter was constantly rebuilt in the 'Abbāsid and the Fatimid periods.[73]

Finally, in the centre of the region, the cities of the Decapolis, with nearby outliers like Bostra, Philadelphia ('Ammān), and Madaba, can be dealt with together. They are an inland group, located around Lake Galilee and on the uplands between the River Jordan and the desert, on land often good enough to be cultivated without irrigation, although this is less true as one approaches the desert. They are strikingly close together: it is less than 70 km from Tiberias to Gerasa as the crow flies, less than the distance from Marseille to Arles (below, pp. 666–7), and one crosses the lands of Scythopolis, Gadara, Capitolias, Abila, and Pella as one does so. But despite their proximity, they all prospered well into the Umayyad period, and sometimes later; any competition between them does not seem to have led to drastic differences in their success-rates until the early 'Abbāsid period, when their rebuilding after the 749 earthquake was in some cases probably undermined by political marginalization. Gadara shows little as yet after 749; at Scythopolis there is, as we have seen, only unplanned activity after that date. At Bostra, too, an important city under the Umayyads, with a large early eighth-century mosque, 749 marks a break, and rebuilding there was subsequently on a smaller scale. Further south, 'Ammān and Madaba show no substantial monuments after the later eighth century. But the *sūq* at Capitolias was resurfaced in the ninth or tenth centuries; the Gerasa house survived the earthquake and was occupied until the ninth century, when the city did weaken; at Pella, the city centre seems to have shifted up the hill after 749, and the 'Abbāsid houses there again continue until the ninth century. Tiberias, in particular, already a provincial capital under the Umayyads, prospered thereafter as well, with no weakening in the ninth century either, as far as one can see from the sketchy publication of its excavations: substantial building activity both inside and outside the south gate of the city is attested from the late eighth century up to the eleventh. Although some of these sites are at present only partially excavated, it does seem that some cities continued to be active under the 'Abbāsids, even if others did not.[74]

The Decapolis cities are the best-studied urban group in the whole eastern half of the Roman empire in our period, and deserve a little further commentary. If there was any self-sufficient group of cities anywhere in this

---

[73] See above, nn. 50, 52.
[74] For all these sites, see above, nn. 50–2.

region, it would be these, focused on good land, never major political centres (though Scythopolis first, 'Ammān and Tiberias later, had local political importance), and never defined by major commercial routes (though commerce, both with the coast and the desert, at least went through them). Did they remain entirely unchanged up to 749? Not entirely. The steady de-monumentalization described above for Scythopolis is a feature of Gerasa, Pella, and Bostra as well, or at least of their old civic centres, where most excavation has been carried out. Nor can we be sure that this was always just a change in urban culture, with no economic implications. This was argued earlier for Scythopolis; Bostra, Gerasa, and perhaps Gadara would be other candidates for economic continuity; but at Pella, we could see the process differently. Here, the odeon went out of use around 550, the agora a little after 600, the baths in the seventh century, even the cathedral in the early eighth, and were not replaced by other buildings, except in parts of the cathedral precinct. Still-prosperous domestic housing and commercial/in-dustrial reuse of former public buildings did not occupy the same amount of space as these now-abandoned constructions—and the later 'Abbāsid building complexes occupied still less. Pella has been well excavated, al-though by no means completely as yet; on the face of it, it looks as if this city was slowly scaling down already in the seventh century, and possibly since 550.[75]

These changes at Pella may be the sign of an early trend for some of the Decapolis cities to slip behind others. If so, it is perhaps significant that this slippage began in the late sixth century, when, as several historians have argued, Syrian and Palestinian prosperity first began to weaken.[76] It must be stressed, however, that a pre-seventh-century involution of urban prosperity, if it occurred at all, was not generalized—at the present state of research, Antioch is the only really plausible example of it in the whole region. Conversely, Leah di Segni's work on the inscriptions of Palestine argues for continuities in monumental patronage right up to the Persian invasions in the 610s, with the sixth century as a whole far more prominent than the fifth or the fourth (the absolute high point being the first half of Justinian's reign): by now, such monuments were largely ecclesiastical, and after 575 more often rural, but there is no significant decrease in inscriptions in the late sixth century at all.[77] I would myself be agnostic about any late sixth-century urban recession in this region, while conceding that it may be that some specific places could not sustain the intensity of the earlier part of the century; this break in pace also coincided everywhere with the weakening of former civic centres and the move of monumental patronage to more

[75] McNicoll *et al.*, *Pella*, I, pp. 103–9, 126–30; II, pp. 187–8; Smith and Day, *Pella*, II, pp. 7–9. Walmsley, 'Production, exchange', pp. 284–5, is more upbeat about Umayyad Pella.
[76] e.g. Kennedy, 'The last century of Byzantine Syria'; see below, pp. 627–8, for the Aegean.
[77] Di Segni, 'Epigraphic documentation'.

scattered churches. In the seventh century and early eighth, too, cities continued to be important production centres even while their former public buildings fell into ruins, except in the north-west of the region, from Apamea to the coast, and probably also around Gaza. Only after 749–50, after the damaging coincidence of the earthquake that hit so many cities in the centre of the region and the ʿAbbāsid overthrow of the Syria-based Umayyads, did the number of cities with continued prosperity diminish substantially. Even then, several did continue, Ayla, Caesarea, Tiberias, and some of the inland cities of the north-east.

Two elements seem to have underpinned this urban continuity, up to at least 750 and often later. First, regional elites continued to live in cities until the end of our period and beyond, as literary evidence indicates for Edessa and archaeological evidence indicates for cities such as Pella. Second, Syria and Palestine maintained effective city-level economic infrastructures that connected town and country, allowing large-scale artisanal production to be concentrated in towns, which requires that the artisans concerned had access to the food of the countryside. The evidence for both of these elements can in general be deduced from the wealth of the urban archaeology we have just surveyed, which tells us both about the urban rich and about complex artisanal activity in so many cities; I shall explore the best-evidenced example of this, ceramics, in greater detail in the next chapter (pp. 770–80). The wealth of the countryside, which we looked at in Chapter 8 (pp. 443–59), was an essential support to the coherence of these infrastructures; urban and rural prosperity clearly went hand in hand in this region. All these features continued into the Umayyad period, even though most cities lost their fiscal centrality, and even though, as we shall see, wider-scale Mediterranean exchange networks underwent major discontinuities; cities went on, however, without any significant break except to an extent on the coast, in some cases into the ʿAbbāsid period and beyond.

This sort of continuity closely parallels that for Egypt, where our archaeology is much less good, but is comprehensively backed up by Egypt's unique density of written documentation. We cannot know whether Syria-Palestine was ever as intensively urbanized as Egypt, but its cities were certainly numerous and rich, just as in Egypt, and continued to be socio-economic and political centres for their territories, in classical style, right through our period. The continuities in urban landowning, urban artisanal activity, and city–country integration seem to have been much the same for both regions, even though urban elites here were no longer, after the Arab conquest, closely linked to the wider structures of political power. We must conclude that the lasting strength of urban civilization was not, in this corner of the Mediterranean, dependent on the survival of the political and fiscal structures of the Roman empire. But we cannot as yet generalize further, for the simple reason that we will not find, in any other region of the Roman world, a set of urban continuities as pronounced as in Syria-Palestine and Egypt.

Why this was is not at all easy to explain, but let us at least explore its dimensions.

The Byzantine heartland of Greece, the Aegean, and Anatolia shows close parallels to Syrian developments up to the early seventh century, and then abrupt divergencies. Here we have good archaeology from a dozen cities, notably Athens, Corinth, Gortyn, Philippi, Ephesos, Sardis, Miletos, Pergamon, Sagalassos, Aphrodisias, Amorion, Side, and Anemourion (I cite only the ancient names in the case of Turkish sites, as they are not now occupied by more than villages, except for Pergamon and Anemourion, modern Bergama and Anamur),[78] and some more-fragmentary material from as many again, including Constantinople itself.[79] As in Syria-Palestine, however, the cities with the most probable continuity into the eighth century, Thessaloniki, Nicaea (Iznik), Smyrna (Izmir), Attaleia (Antalya), Trapezos (Trabzon), perhaps Nikomedia (Izmit), are still occupied and have had little excavation.

Cities in this region remained prosperous, by and large, until the late sixth or early seventh century. Their monumental centres often became less important, however, just as we have seen in Syria, a process which seems to have begun earlier than in the eastern provinces. In Ephesos, the old civic area of the two agorai and the colonnaded Embolos street that connected them became relatively marginalized in the fifth century, and the buildings that remained there became more residential; new monumental building, the cathedral and the governor's palace, was focused on the area to its north, an area of gymnasia in an earlier period. It is this latter area that was eventually walled, leaving the agorai outside the walls, though the date of that fortification varies from 500 to 700 according to author.[80] In Athens, the 'Greek agora' was clearly becoming demonumentalized by the fifth century, with shops partitioning the colonnade around it by the sixth, and a set of industrial buildings, with evidence of bronze-working, in its southern sector. All the same, good-quality contemporary residential buildings certainly existed to its south, on the Areopagos hill.[81] In contrast to Ephesos and Athens, however, some old central areas, particularly in provincial capitals, retained a monumental vitality into the late sixth century, as at Philippi, Sardis, Aphrodisias, and maybe Side. Building patronage, largely focused on

[78] For recent general surveys, see Haldon, *Byzantium*, pp. 92–124, 459–61; Brandes, *Die Städte Kleinasiens*; idem, 'Byzantine cities'; Sodini, 'L'habitat urbain en Grèce'; Liebeschuetz, *The decline*, pp. 30–54; and see n. 85 for the work of Clive Foss. Individual urban excavations will be cited in the notes that follow.

[79] For Constantinople, see Mango, *Le développement urbain*, pp. 51–62; Magdalino, *Constantinople*, pp. 17–50; the least scrappy excavation in this period is that of Saraçhane (Harrison, *Excavations at Saraçhane*, I; Hayes, *Excavations at Saraçhane*, II).

[80] For overviews, see Foss, *Ephesus*, pp. 46–115 (the wall is post-614: pp. 106–7); Karwiese, *Gross ist die Artemis*, pp. 131–45 (the wall is c.500: p. 140).

[81] Frantz, *The Athenian agora*, XXIV, pp. 79–116. Cf. the situation at Corinth, below, n. 96.

churches, was by now associated with the informal, post-curial, elite, notably the *patēr tēs poleōs*, 'father of the city' (clearly attested, among others, at Aphrodisias and Side).[82] It seems to have been a matter of local choices where to build; it could be in the old agora area, focus of the public buildings of the past, but it did not have to be. Such patronage did in general continue up to 600, or shortly before.

Signs of specifically economic or demographic weakening are more heterogeneous. Some cities were perhaps in trouble already in 500 or before, but for locally specific reasons, like Sagalassos on the Anatolian plateau, a ceramic-production centre probably hit by the success of the Phocaean potteries (below, p. 714), or an array of north Greek cities on the edge of the Balkan military zone, such as Amphipolis.[83] Much more common, however, was an unbroken continuity to 550 at least (with a Justinianic high point), and then more of a divergence, as in Syria, between cities that began to lose momentum around that date and cities that carried on with little perceptible change up to the Persian attacks in the 610s. The church of S. Michael at Miletos was rebuilt on a monumental scale as late as 595–606. Ephesos had little new building after 550, but maintenance, including new ceremonial inscriptions, carried on until the 610s, with some elaborate shops in the Embolos colonnade continuing until then. Much the same is true of Sardis, where a set of shops along the colonnade outside a bath-gymnasion complex, west of the agora, have been particularly well published: these shops were still prosperous right up to their collapse in the 610s, although, elsewhere in the town, the post-550 levels of high-status residential buildings are characterized by subdivisions and a simpler material culture, perhaps indicating a weakening of local elites. Elsewhere, it is harder to be sure about whether the late sixth century is a period of involution, for dating has not always been precise, and, in the absence of inscriptions, the Justinianic decades have sometimes been assumed to be the main moment of building in this period without any real proof. Subdivided private buildings have been found elsewhere in the late sixth century, as at Hierapolis (Pamukkale) and Ephesos, but these do not on their own demonstrate economic weakening. As in Syria, my conclusion is cautiously neutral: there may have been some economic involution after 550, or at least a levelling out of activity after Justinian, but it is far from clear that there were any consistent negative trends. Overall, Aegean and Anatolian

[82] Philippi: Spieser, 'La ville', p. 332. Sardis: Foss, *Byzantine and Turkish Sardis*, pp. 39–52 (and see below, n. 84). Aphrodisias: Roueché, *Aphrodisias*; Cormack, 'Byzantine Aphrodisias'; Whittow, 'Recent research', pp. 142–5. Side: Foss, 'Cities of Pamphylia', pp. 31–47. For the *patēr tēs poleōs* in this region, see Roueché, 'A new inscription'.

[83] Waelkens and Poblome, *Sagalassos*, II, pp. 16–17, 53–5; III, pp. 28–31, 192–3; IV, pp. 101, 170–3, 205–12, 225–52 (the city was not prostrate, all the same, and survived into the seventh century); Dunn, 'The transition from *polis* to *kastron*', and idem, 'From *polis* to *kastron*', for northern Greece.

urbanism was not fundamentally endangered in 600, even if some agorai may have looked rather neglected by then.[84]

The Persian wars, the Arab raids, and (in Greece) the Slav attacks changed this. In Syria and Palestine, cities continued in the Umayyad period with little structural alteration, as we have seen, but this is not true at all of the Byzantine heartland. Twenty-five years of archaeological research, although less dense than in Palestine, has done nothing to undermine the view encapsulated by Clive Foss in the late 1970s that a century-and-a-half of war was crippling for the cities in the region. (Foss then blamed the Persians above all, and it is true that urban crisis in Ephesos and Sardis, his main case studies, already began in the 610s, i.e. the Persian period, but the tendency now is to locate deurbanization within a longer period of disruption.)[85] I have been cautious in this book about ascribing much in the way of major economic change to wars, but this seems a special case, given that the devastations in the Byzantine heartland were prolonged over such a long time, before the Arabs backed off in the later Umayyad period in Anatolia and the Byzantines moved onto the offensive in the Balkans in the 760s. (Cf. above, pp. 125–8.) One test is the Greek islands, which alone of all the sub-regions of the Byzantine heartland were relatively safe from attack: here, also alone in the region, we do find significant seventh-century monumental interventions, in Mytilini on Lesbos and above all Gortyn on Crete. In the latter, probably after an earthquake, Heraclius reconstructed the entire city, extensively rebuilding churches and a judicial/administrative basilica, and also a nymphaeum. A seventh- and perhaps eighth-century artisanal quarter has been found there too, showing continuing economic activity more similar to the Levant than to the Aegean mainland.[86] Gortyn was a key strategic centre, and the capital of Crete, but interventions of this kind were by now entirely unparalleled on the mainlands, even in periods when emperors securely controlled them—all we have by and large for the seventh century is walls. The most we could hypothesize is that surviving major centres like Izmir could have received similar attention to Gortyn, but this is as yet pure guesswork.

[84] Miletos: Müller-Wiener *et al.*, 'Milet 1973–1975', pp. 101–3, 117–25. Ephesos: see above, n. 80, with Roueché, 'Looking for late antique ceremonial'. Sardis: Crawford, *The Byzantine shops*; Rautman, 'A late Roman townhouse'; see in general Russell, 'The Persian invasions', pp. 63–8. A cautiously upbeat picture of the late sixth century in these cities and others is offered by Whittow, 'Recent research'; it seems to me a convincing argument, as against e.g. Liebeschuetz, *The decline*, pp. 43–54, who argues forcibly for 'decline' after c.550.

[85] Foss, *Ephesus*; idem, *Byzantine and Turkish Sardis*; and the articles collected in *History and archaeology* and *Cities, fortresses*. For the disruption as more long-term, see e.g. Haldon, *Byzantium*, pp. 102–12.

[86] For Mytilini, see Martini and Strecker, *Das Gymnasium von Samos*, pp. 38–41. For Gortyn, see di Vita, 'I recenti scavi'; Zanini and Giorgi, 'Indagini archeologiche', and Enrico Zanini (pers. comm.). Note also the urban continuity on the island of Aigina to at least 800, although here without any visible monumentality: Felten, 'Die christliche Siedlung'.

By contrast to Gortyn, the mainland cities show systemic crisis. The way this works in individual locations needs some more detailed characterization, however, to show its dimensions. At Sardis, the shops were abruptly abandoned in the 610s (with no loss of life, but too quickly to remove their contents), and residential buildings collapsed in the same decade; a new street was built over the shops in the mid-seventh century. By then, although street-building implies human activity, only small and scattered areas seem to have been occupied in the lower town, together with the newly fortified *kastron* above it. These dates are established by coin finds, which is problematic. The resultant impression is that activity stopped abruptly around the 610s and then everything ceased except for a flurry in c.660, a pattern paralleled elsewhere (at Ankara, for example), but this is skewed by the fact that Constans II (d. 668) was the last emperor to issue coins on any scale until the ninth century. All the same, a drastic reduction of activity in Sardis by the mid-seventh century can hardly be contested, even if it took as long as a generation.[87] This pattern seems to be matched in less extensive excavations in Ankara, where a gymnasion complex was burnt by the Persians in the sack of 622 (a Sassanian ring-stone was found in the burnt level) and the hilltop *kastron*, made of neatly arrayed spolia, was built by Constans II's reign at the latest (an alternative date being the 630s).[88] In Anatolia, less well-dated excavations seem to show, nearly universally, an absence of any building except fortifications datable to the seventh century, as at Aphrodisias, Ephesos, Miletos, Xanthos, Kyaneai, or Side. At Ephesos, Miletos, Pergamon, and Side, a wall (of unclear date in each case) cut the old city centre in two; the agorai, as already noted, became extramural at Ephesos, and also at Side. At Ephesos, the city remained substantial, for the new wall still included a square kilometre of land and there was also another walled enclosure around the great northern extramural church of S. John.[89] Overall, however, in Anatolia, although there is hardly a single excavation whose chronology for this period is absolutely secure, it would be hard to argue for more than occasional building on most classical urban sites after 650.

What activity did continue in these ancient cities? Hilltop *kastra* are quite frequently attested, at Sardis and Ankara as we have seen, and also Amorion, Prousa (Bursa), Pergamon, and Myra.[90] These are often too small to have sustained urbanism in an economic sense, although they must have

---

[87] Crawford, *The Byzantine shops*; Foss, *Byzantine and Turkish Sardis*, pp. 53–61. For caution about coins, see Hendy, *Studies*, pp. 640–5.

[88] Foss, 'Late Antique and Byzantine Ankara', pp. 68–75; Dunn, 'Heraclius' "reconstruction of cities" ', pp. 798–9, for the 630s.

[89] For an overview see Brandes, *Die Städte Kleinasiens*, pp. 82–111. For the walls, see the list in Liebeschuetz, *The decline*, pp. 51–2 (he plumps for a sixth-century date for each, although Klinkott, *Pergamon*, XVI.1, pp. 22–33, proposes a late seventh-century date in that case), plus Foss, 'Cities of Pamphylia', pp. 43–4 for Side; see n. 80 for Ephesos.

[90] For Amorion, see the interims in *Anatolian studies* since XXXIX (1989). For Pergamon, see Rheidt, *Pergamon*, XV.2, esp. pp. 196–7. For Myra, see Foss, 'The Lycian coast', p. 31.

remained military and perhaps political centres. It could be argued that these fortifications may have acted as foci for more scattered settlement in the unfortified parts of the classical cities, which together might create a complex of occupation with urban dimensions. Frank Trombley has proposed this model on the basis of the *Miracles* of S. Theodore the Recruit, a text of, perhaps, the late eighth century (it certainly postdates the 660s) describing events in Euchaita, a remote town—but also a centre of the Armeniakon theme—on the plateau to the north-east of Ankara. This makes it clear that a fortification acted as a point of reference for wider settlement in the town (*asty*), which included the church of S. Theodore and even a *tetrapylon* and *plateiai*, presumably parts of the classical monumental street network. This specific example has withstood criticism, but it is hard to find archaeological support for its generalization as a model: the most that can be said is that some churches survived in lower areas of cities, as at Amorion.[91] Myra may be the most likely parallel, for here the church of S. Nicholas in the lower town was rebuilt in the eighth century to its full size, with a fortified enclosure; it may not be chance that Myra, like Euchaita, was a pilgrimage centre.[92] The only other towns that seem as yet to have persisted as urban centres, usually on a reduced scale, were Ephesos (where a 'great fair', *panēgyrion*, is referred to by Theophanes for the year 795–6), perhaps Miletos (where houses inside the fortified area seem to be datable to the eighth or ninth century), and the half-a-dozen still-occupied cities already listed, such as Izmir and Antalya.[93] Even allowing for future discoveries, one might guess that centres with genuine urban activity dropped by perhaps four-fifths.

This picture has substantial parallels in mainland Greece. Here, Slav raids began in the 580s, but urban recession seems again to be a seventh-century phenomenon above all, in Athens, Corinth, Delphi, and Butrint.[94] In Athens,

[91] Trombley, 'The decline'; the text is edited in Delehaye, *Les légendes grecques*, pp. 183–201; ibid., pp. 196–200 discusses the town. Zuckerman, 'The reign of Constantine V', proposes a late eighth-century dating. For over-negative criticism, see e.g. Kazhdan, 'Hagiographical notes (17–20)', pp. 197–200; Brandes, 'Byzantine cities', pp. 47–9. Amorion has been used as a model for scattered urban settlement by Haldon, *Byzantium*, pp. 460–1, following Lightfoot's interpretation of the excavation data (e.g. recently, Lightfoot and Ivison, 'The Amorium project', p. 300), but it is not yet clear that there was anything much in the lower town before the tenth century at the earliest apart from a church.

[92] Foss, 'The Lycian coast', p. 31; R. Ousterhout in Brubaker and Haldon, *Iconoclasm. The sources*, pp. 9–10. Myra thus joins Euchaita as the best eastern parallels at present to western *città ad isole*, which will be discussed later in the chapter. Others may appear as pre-tenth-century ceramic dating becomes more refined.

[93] Theophanes, *Chronographia*, pp. 469–70; Müller-Wiener, 'Das Theaterkastell', p. 285, for Miletos; Foss, 'Cities of Pamphylia', pp. 4–13, for Antalya.

[94] Delphi: Pétridis, 'Delphes'; idem, 'Ateliers de potiers', pp. 443–4. Butrint: Hodges and Bowden, 'Butrinto'. For Athens and Corinth, see nn. 95–6. See also Lambropoulou, 'Le Péloponnèse', for the Peloponnesos towns. Area surveys of scrappier data make the same point: Avraméa, *Le Péloponnèse*, pp. 107–15; Karagiorgou, *Urbanism and economy*, pp. 206–19, for Thessaly.

seventh- and eighth-century housing has been found, with in one case continued rebuilding, although using very simple techniques; this city continued as an urban centre through to its ninth-century revival, but was clearly not particularly prosperous.[95] In Corinth, the agora, already undergoing demonumentalization and increasing encroachment by 600, was temporarily abandoned a century later; in the old centre, only the Lechaion Road to its north seems to have continued in use, with shops rebuilt along its former colonnade in the ninth century or so. The city by this time was probably fragmented between several settlement areas, and the agora area had by now become relatively marginal.[96] Corinth's early medieval urbanism has been doubted, perhaps overcritically, but at best it gives us a third Greek site of urban continuity to set beside Athens, and, above all, Thessaloniki. Here, there has been little excavation, but a wealth of surviving churches are known, including one new monumental construction, Hagia Sophia, dating to the seventh century and redecorated in the late eighth, and there are also seals attesting to the city's active political and fiscal centrality.[97] Thessaloniki was exceptional as a major political focus, however, and Corinth, too, was probably the centre of a theme. The rest of Greece, or at least those parts that came under Byzantine control when Constantine V began reconquest in the 760s, was probably run from *kastra*, until urban revival began slowly in the ninth century.

Greece and Anatolia in 550–600 had a similar level of urban prosperity to Syria and Palestine, with, at most, a slightly earlier trend to the demonumentalization of older civic centres, and possibly a slightly higher proportion of cities showing signs of strain in the post-Justinianic period. By 700, however, the two regions were far apart, with a relatively contained pattern of recession in Syria-Palestine (which was far from complete even in 800) but a failure rate of perhaps 80 per cent (a figure which, indeed, some scholars would consider optimistic[98]) for the Byzantine heartland. This contrast is based on similar types of evidence, and it seems to me difficult to contest. I have already stressed that war is one major explanation for this difference. But there have to be others, for war does not necessarily produce deurbanization: it could equally lead to the concentration of a population in fortified urban settlements, for example, rather than to its dispersal across the countryside. Let us finish this section by considering what these contributory factors could be, with the Levantine parallel in our minds as an alternative pattern of development.

---

[95] Frantz, *The Athenian Agora*, XXIV, pp. 117–24.

[96] Scranton, *Corinth XVI*, pp. 27–49; Ivison, 'Burial and urbanism'; Sanders, 'Corinth', the best recent overview.

[97] Spieser, 'La ville', pp. 318–19, gives a brief survey. For Hagia Sophia, see Brubaker and Haldon, *Iconoclasm. The sources*, pp. 6, 10, 23–4. For seals, see Nesbitt and Oikonomides, *Catalogue*, I, pp. 55–64 (XVIII.8, 19, 20, 28–33).

[98] Brandes, 'Byzantine cities', p. 25.

One possibility is that Byzantine cities were less effective as economic foci for their rural territories than those of Syria-Palestine. Until the sixth century, there is no evidence for this. After 600–50 it may be true, but it would be hard to argue that this could operate as an independent cause of urban decline; any rural territory with any degree of economic development has surplus to sell, and if there is a city in the centre of it with any buying power, that city will be able to acquire it. We do not yet know enough about the rural archaeology of either Turkey or Greece to be able easily to assess the prosperity of the countryside, and it is quite possible that there were microregions where demographic or systemic collapse made urban–rural exchange difficult (below, pp. 786–7); but this was not universal, as the land behind Myra may indicate (above, p. 461), and anyway, such collapse itself has other causes.

If cities had any dependence on larger-scale networks of economic exchange, as on parts of the Levantine coast, they would also be exposed if those networks collapsed. It does have to be recognized that, as we shall see in the next chapter, the Byzantine heartland did see considerable macroeconomic breakdown, so that many productions of both amphorae and fine table wares ended in the later seventh century; this, at least, was a systemic collapse. This breakdown was focused on the Aegean, the richest sector of the region, but did not spare the Anatolian plateau or the Adriatic; its underlying context was the political and fiscal crisis of the empire itself, and thus was not geographically restricted. All the same, there were few cities in the region whose prosperity could be assumed to be intimately linked to large-scale exchange.[99] The best example of a collapsing economic network, the end of Phocaean Red Slip production in the decades after 660 (below, p. 785), occurred in the wider hinterland of one of the few cities that survived as an urban centre, Smyrna (Izmir).

The other explanation is the choices of the urban elites of the Byzantine empire. Here, we must be careful to avoid circular arguments: we cannot argue both that urban elites left towns because they were weakening and that towns weakened because the elites left them. It must also be recognized that, as noted earlier (p. 234), we cannot securely locate any Byzantine aristocratic family—apart from those living in Constantinople at any rate—between the sixth and the tenth centuries. But the generally rural bases of middle Byzantine aristocratic families are at least a starting-point. So also are the arguments set out about early medieval Byzantine local aristocracies in Chapter 4 and earlier in this chapter (pp. 236–9, 601): that they probably experienced genealogical continuity in the seventh and eighth centuries, but that they moved into the thematic military hierarchy (or else into the Constantinople-based administrative or ecclesiastical hierarchies), rather than remaining attached to their civilian urban elite origins.

[99] Sagalassos might be one, perhaps: see above, n. 83, and below, p. 784.

We can therefore express that potential circular argument in terms of a dialectic: in a period of political crisis, the attraction to urban elites of the formal hierarchies of the state (and the church) rather than of the informal power of the city patrons of the sixth century, and the economic/demographic weakening of the cities themselves, both acted on each other and made the whole process of deurbanization that much more acute. By the ninth century, even real urban centres were increasingly just called *kastra*, and the idea of there being something special about a *polis* virtually went away.[100]

The enduring pull of Constantinople helps to develop these points, and makes a special feature of this region clearer. An element not to be underestimated when considering the weakening of cities in the Byzantine heartland is, paradoxically, the continued strength and hegemonic force of the state, even in a period of crisis. In Umayyad Syria and Palestine, surviving city elites had no chance of becoming part of the state apparatus unless they converted to Islam, which was as yet a rare choice; the local urban stage was the only plausible alternative, and remained an attractive one. In Byzantium, even at its low point around 700, the state was coherent enough to act as an alternative, and rich enough to offer considerable returns to anyone who abandoned the local urban political network (which itself was henceforth bypassed by the fiscal system: above, pp. 597–601).[101] In this context, indeed, one could almost say that the supersession of the urban stage was planned. Some elite families went, perhaps, to their rural estates; some, in the case of the richest, to Constantinople; but most likely many went to the new political foci, the thematic capitals, which were closer to their rural bases, but were effective centres for tax-raising and military organization. (See above, pp. 125–9.) These thematic capitals were precisely cities like Antalya, Izmir, Trabzon, Nicaea, Thessaloniki: the successful towns of the early middle ages. The 80 per cent deurbanization can thus be seen as the reconfiguration of urban elites around a smaller number of provincial centres, along predetermined state-driven lines.[102] Only a restricted number of urban centres survived on a smaller scale without being the bases for themes: pilgrimage centres like Myra, and a handful of the most important Aegean cities, like Miletos and Ephesos. And, of course, the greatest political centre of all, Constantinople, remained dominant demographically (above, p. 126) and economically (below, pp. 787–90), throughout our period, even allowing for the fact that it declined substantially in size. The catastrophe-flip that caused this shift was certainly war and political crisis, but the

---

[100] A good synthesis is Haldon, 'The idea of the town'.

[101] This economic-political coherence did not extend to Italy, however, where the rules were different: below, pp. 654–5.

[102] These are all cities on or close to the coast; probably the thematic centres of the plateau such as Ankara were as yet too disrupted by war to have a similar social role.

transformation operated in a social context, and it is that social context which is, in the end, more interesting to analyse.

The historiography concerning the demonumentalization of urban centres has focused on Syria and Palestine for good reason: the cities there furnish most of the clearest and best-studied examples of it available. It is probable that the absence of many parallels to this in the Byzantine heartland is only because of the sudden crisis in cities there in the seventh century: the process of demonumentalization in that region was thus arrested early, a fact that underlines the argument that encroachment on the porticoed and colonnaded streets of classical cities is a sign of urban vitality as much as of the weakening of municipal control. Actually, there are a number of sixth-century examples in the region of the beginning of this process, as J. S. Crawford showed in a comparative survey, complementing his study of the Sardis shops (which themselves show encroachment, though only in some shops): we would expect this in a period when *curiae/boulai* were fading fast but building and economic activity continued. Only in a handful of excavated cities did encroachment continue later, indicating a later survival of urban activity.[103] Conversely, however, several surviving towns, such as Thessaloniki and Nicaea, have retained much of their classical street plans. Of course, as explored earlier in the context of cities like Damascus, one can demonumentalize an urban environment without changing street alignments. But it is also probable that, in the smaller number of surviving urban centres in the Byzantine heartland, open-air public activity was differently constructed from that in the Arab world. Although provincial towns give us no usable documentation in this period, the public space of Constantinople, at least, was structured throughout the seventh and eighth century by processions, which marked both formal moments in the ritual year and moments of crisis such as sieges and coups: a Christianization of Roman imperial tradition, but not a structural change in it.[104] It is formal public activity of this kind which gives sense to a city of colonnades; Arab elites, by contrast, put their architects to work on the courtyards of mosques, where their main moments of political affirmation occurred. In Constantinople, therefore, the spatial patterns of the Constantinian and Justinianic city maintained their rationale for much longer. As Paul Magdalino has remarked, the tenth-century city was in this respect not very different from that of the sixth, a statement that could hardly, at our present state of knowledge, be made about many other cities of the former empire at all (outside Italy, at least). Although the Byzantine heartland experienced greater changes across our period than many regions, its capital seems to have stayed remarkably unchanged in this.[105] This public activity may

---

[103] Crawford, *The Byzantine shops*, pp. 107–25 (cf. p. 34 for Sardis).

[104] McCormick, *Eternal victory*, pp. 64–80, 131 ff.; Baldovin, *Urban character*, pp. 174–214; Brubaker, 'Topography and the creation of public space'.

[105] Magdalino, *Constantinople*, pp. 48–50.

have underlain a relative spatial continuity in surviving Byzantine cities elsewhere too.

5. Urban economies in the western Mediterranean

Africa is an instructive counterpoint to the previous two regions, for once again it offers a wealth of abandoned classical cities, whose abandonment generally postdated our period and thus allows an analysis of social change which is not yet necessarily bound up with economic 'decline'. As in Syria-Palestine, its written sources are much scarcer (in this case, after the death of Augustine in 430), which means that the behaviour of urban elites has to be deduced from the archaeology alone, rather than contextualized and/or explained by narrative representations, as (for example) in Gaul. Unfortunately, excavation in Africa began so early, at the beginning of the century in some cases, that the stripping out of post-classical levels was commonplace (these are easy to see on photographs of the Timgad excavations, for example, but one would not know it from the texts of the Timgad publications),[106] and even when they were recorded, the ceramics found in them, which were not then datable, remain unknown. Only a restricted number of urban sites, mostly recently excavated, have good evidence for the fifth century and onwards: apart from Carthage, Thugga (Dougga), Thuburbo Maius, Belalis Maior (Henchir el-Faouar), Bulla Regia and Uchi Maius in Proconsularis (northern Tunisia), Sufetula (Sbeïtla), Ammaedara (Haïdra), and Bararus (Rougga) in Byzacena (southern Tunisia) are the main ones.[107] For this section I shall leave the western provinces, Numidia and the Mauretanias, aside, and also Tripolitania, as more marginal in the period after 439.[108] (The Berber kingdoms of the far west, including their cities, which did persist, are discussed in Chapter 6, pp. 334–7.) These will be the basic points of reference in what follows: a less substantial set of sites than in the Levant or the Aegean (and often rather less well studied than in the Levant, at least), but at least analogous to them.

Africa's urban development in our period has elements of both the eastern and the western Mediterranean. Its economic height, as in the rest of the western Mediterranean, occurred in the fourth century, rather than the early sixth; as we saw in Chapter 8, its urban aristocrats maintained rural

[106] As observed by Gelichi and Milanese, '*Uchi Maius*', p. 91.

[107] For overviews, see Mattingly and Hitchner, 'Roman Africa', pp. 179–87, 209–13; Fentress, 'La Numidia'; Potter, *Towns*; Pentz, *From Roman Proconsularis*, pp. 29–75; Thébert, 'L'evolution urbaine'; idem and Biget, 'L'Afrique'. Thébert's interpretations have been particularly influential for me. For individual cities, see the notes that follow.

[108] The two major Numidian sites are Tebéssa: Lequément, *Fouilles*, pp. 199–241; and Sétif: Mohamedi and Fentress, *Fouilles de Sétif*, pp. 29–92. For Caesarea (Cherchel) in Mauretania, see Benseddik and Potter, *Fouilles du forum de Cherchel*, I, pp. 55–75. Tripolitania is surveyed in Mattingly, *Tripolitania*.

estate-centres and (sometimes) rich country houses, like their Italian or Spanish counterparts but unlike those in Syria. Conversely, it was integrated into the eastern, not the western empire when the (east) Romans reconquered it from the Vandals in 534, and Justinian devoted considerable architectural attention to it; then, from the seventh century onwards, it was occupied by the Arabs, linking it to Syria and Egypt. Africa was thus unique in experiencing both the fifth-century and the seventh-century political crises (although Spain would follow suit for the latter crisis a little later, in the eighth). Of the two, however, the seventh century was arguably more difficult than the fifth in this region, as in the East. It is worth trying to look at Africa through the perspective of the eastern historiography used for the preceding three regions, as a guide for how to compare the East with the West.

In doing so, however, it must be recognized that such an approach runs against the grain of standard accounts of Africa. These focus on the Vandal period (439–534) as one of potential caesura, or else relocate 'decline' to the Byzantine period (534–647/98), seen as the product of a failed reoccupation. Comparatively little attention is paid by either historians or archaeologists to the early Arab period—the eighth century is a particularly serious lacuna, for here, after the end of the great African productive systems of the Roman period (below, pp. 726–8), even the ceramic sequence is not yet known. An imagery of an Arab crisis, either in the post-conquest period, or, more completely, in the eleventh century certainly exists, but it remains all the more strong because it has been so little studied in recent years. I briefly discussed the way this sort of historiography of decline developed in Africa in Chapter 2 (pp. 18–19), and linked it to the other important opposition in the region, that between the desert and the sown, although this latter, at least, can be left out of the present discussion, for none of the Tunisian heartland cities of Africa changed their relationship to an essentially agricultural hinterland in our period, or for a long time later. We shall return to the issue of the Vandal–Byzantine–Arab succession at the end of the section, for the history of state structures in the region is certainly of relevance for understanding the fate of its cities; but let us begin by trying to ignore it, so that we can see how much it forces itself on our attention whether we like it or not.

African cities around 400, like all other aspects of the region's economy, were prosperous according to all known criteria, as both documentary study (as in Claude Lepelley's magisterial survey) and archaeology make clear.[109] From then on, one can track structural changes in cities which have clear eastern analogues. The first is a decrease in use of forum areas and their attached monumental buildings. Of the cities that have been studied in

---

[109] Lepelley, *Les cités*, I, e.g. pp. 15–36, further synthesized in idem, 'Peuplement et richesses'. Earlier pessimistic views of the fourth century are simply wrong, and can be ignored.

Africa, barely any saw any monumental building in the forum area in the century after 450; we find steady neglect (Belalis Maior, Dougga), a transformation of public buildings into housing (Rougga), or their reuse as oil-press installations (Thuburbo Maius, Uchi Maius).[110] Only Sbeïtla, of the well-excavated heartland cities, shows an apparent continuity of use in the forum area; otherwise, we have to go as far west as Cherchel to find an apparent maintenance of the forum as a public space (with a new church) across the fifth century.[111] This apparently systematic development has close parallels in the East a century later, as we have seen in, for example, Scythopolis (pp. 614–16). One can legitimately propose that Africa, earlier than the East, saw the decay of curial institutions and their replacement by more informal structures of urban patronage. *Curiae*, indeed, although strong in the fourth century (as the Timgad album of 361–3 shows), are not documented in any source after 430—Prokopios, for example, refers to 'notables', *dokimoi* and *logimoi*, rather than any more institutionally orientated terms. This argument is contested by several historians, who note that there are references to some curial offices, notably several examples, in inscriptions and the Tablettes Albertini, of men called *flamen perpetuus*, and one of a *procurator* (see above, p. 89) collecting taxes; these references do not, however, have to prove the continued existence of the *curia* itself. The combined weight of the archaeology and the absence of any clear references to city councils (as well as the parallel development in the East) suggests to me that the century after 450 marked their demise, even if some of the titles formerly attached to *curiales* survived longer.[112] The networks of 'notables', who remained rich as church foundations show, probably orientated themselves instead around the local episcopate, as sixth-century eastern *prōteuontes* also would.

The fifth- and sixth-century churches of African cities are often very impressive buildings, with rich mosaic decoration and expert masonry.[113] Indeed, even more than in Palestine, research has often focused on them at the expense of the study of contemporary residential buildings, which means that a key dimension of African urbanism in our period is as yet relatively ill-understood. With that important caveat, it does seem that cities may already

---

[110] Mahjoubi, *Recherches*, pp. 174, 445 (Belalis Maior); Poinssot, *Les ruines de Dougga*, pp. 40–1; Guéry, 'L'occupation de Rougga'; Maurin, 'Thuburbo Maius', pp. 240–1, 249, based on Poinssot and Lantier, 'Rapport' (dating is difficult here, as the excavation is old); Gelichi and Milanese, '*Uchi Maius*', p. 80.

[111] Duval, 'L'urbanisme de Sufetula', pp. 612–13; Benseddik and Potter, *Fouilles du forum de Cherchel*, I, pp. 55–60 (here, the demonumentalization process occurred in the mid-sixth century: pp. 60–6). Segermes, too, has houses on the forum, not exactly dated but subsequent to a late Roman refurbishment: Pentz, *From Roman Proconsularis*, pp. 45–6. For the shift in monumental areas to artisanal production, see in general Leone, 'Topographies of production'.

[112] Prokopios, *Wars*, III.16.10–11; IV.23.18, 23; for the debate about *curiae*, see Ch. 3, n. 88.

[113] See e.g. Duval, *Les églises*, II. One example, the Hildeguns church at Mactar, is discussed in Prévot, *Recherches archéologiques*, pp. 43–5, 190.

have become rather more fragmented in the Africa of c.500 than they would be in the Syria or Anatolia of the next century; the new churches were often on the edge of the old city or outside it altogether, and a move of the 'city centre' to the church areas, as seems to have occurred at all the cities whose fora were demonumentalized, often meant a disaggregation of the concept of 'centre' itself. This may be the reason why in the mid-sixth century the returning Roman ('Byzantine') government in several cities—Dougga and Haïdra most obviously—put a fortress on the site of the former forum itself: to re-establish the centre of the town. Whether or not this was so, however (for fortresses were as often situated on the edges of cities), the foundation of such fortifications represents a shift in concepts of urbanism. Actually, walls around the whole city were commoner in Justinianic Africa, just as they were in the East; but the appearance in even a minority of towns of patterns like that of Haïdra, where a large central fortification acts as a point of reference for networks of continuing settlement around extramural churches, at least indicates a new way of constructing urban monumentality. In parts of the East, in the sixth-century Balkans and seventh-century Anatolia, this spatial structure implies deurbanization. Not in Africa; but the parallel cannot be ignored. The Haïdra fortress may have been intended to recentralize the city, but its very construction in fact closed off one of the main urban areas, and in effect crystallized the tendency of the urban fabric to fragment.[114]

The mid-sixth-century fortifications were the last major secular buildings in most African cities for some time, although some church construction continued later. What little we know of private housing over the next century-and-a-half indicates a steady (if ill-dated) tendency towards subdivided or simpler constructions, as at Thuburbo Maius, Belalis Maior, Dougga, Rougga, and, west of our region, Cherchel. Even so, at Bulla Regia the quality of sixth-century housing seems quite good, and continued wealth, for some, is indicated by the large, early seventh-century gold-coin hoards found at Rougga, Bulla, and Thuburbo Maius. This pattern continues into the seventh and eighth centuries in Rougga and Bulla.[115] In the seventh to ninth centuries, too, at both Belalis Maior and Sbeïtla, excavators have found fortified houses on the edge of town, indicating both renewed expenditure and a further fragmentation of the urban collectivity.[116]

---

[114] Poinssot, *Les ruines de Dougga*, pp. 40–1; Baratte, 'Recherches franco-tunisiennes', with idem *et al.*, *Recherches archéologiques à Haïdra*. For the other Haïdra churches, see the epigraphic account in Duval and Prévot, *Recherches archéologiques à Haïdra*, I: the inscriptions are mostly sixth-century. For a survey of fortresses, see Pringle, *The defence*, esp. pp. 118–19, 171–278; p. 82 for walls around cities.

[115] Poinssot and Lantier, 'Rapport' (Thuburbo Maius); Mahjoubi, *Recherches*, p. 451 (Belalis Maior); Poinssot, *Les ruines de Dougga*, pp. 40–1; Guéry, 'Survivance' (Rougga), with idem *et al.*, *Recherches archéologiques*, for the hoard; Benseddik and Potter, *Fouilles du forum de Cherchel*, I, pp. 62–6; Broise and Thébert, *Recherches archéologiques*, pp. 386–97 (Bulla Regia).

[116] Mahjoubi, *Recherches*, pp. 371–87; Bejaoui, 'Nouvelles données archéologiques', pp. 38–42, for Sbeïtla, with a slightly clearer guide to dating criteria.

Elsewhere, the eighth century is, as observed earlier, difficult to identify as yet on African sites, but at least one can say that in several cities (Rougga, Belalis Maior, Thuburbo Maius, Sbeïtla, Bulla, Haïdra) ninth- or tenth-century glazed wares are widely found in levels above the latest Red Slip types, indicating some continuity of occupation.[117] Although this continuity is, conversely, absent on some other sites (Uchi Maius, for example), one can throw into the equation a number of large and barely excavated cities whose political importance goes back to the early eighth century at least, such as Béja in northern Tunisia, Sousse on the eastern coast, Gafsa on the desert fringe, or the new capital, inland from Sousse, of Kairouan. The government of the Arab province of Ifrīqiya in the eighth century was certainly as much based on the Roman city network as was that of other Arab provinces.[118] The drastic decrease in the number of urban centres that we have seen for the Byzantine heartland seems to have little parallel in this period in Tunisia, and indeed in the ninth and tenth centuries some neglected or abandoned sites seem to have been reoccupied, as at Uchi Maius, and there were new palace-based prestige foundations too, like Raqqada and Sabra al-Mansūriyya.[119] All the same, if one was to identify a low point for urban vitality in Africa, it would have to be the eighth century, as Sauro Gelichi and Marco Milanese point out; even excluding the problem of the absence of fine wares, which is a marker of economic vitality in itself, the ninth and tenth centuries are simply more visible in excavation. In this respect, Africa and Anatolia were moving in parallel once more.

This set of descriptions is aimed at characterizing a whole region (or, at least, the rich Tunisian sub-region at its centre), and risks the collapse of individual urban experiences into that wider whole. Let us, then, look briefly at two specific cities, before I try to explain why African urbanism developed in the way it did: Sbeïtla, summed up by Noël Duval on several occasions, and Carthage itself, the most atypical site of all (and thus ignored up to here), but one whose development has been extensively studied in recent decades.

Sbeïtla was a square-planned town of the first century, and its traditional array of public buildings was rebuilt in the fourth. In the fifth to seventh centuries at least eight churches were constructed, mostly to the north and the east of the former centre; in the north, some late housing has been found too. The forum area was, atypically, a continued focus of activity in Sbeïtla,

[117] See refs. cit. nn. 115–16, with Baratte *et al.*, *Recherches archéologiques à Haïdra*, pp. 83–92 (Arab-period ceramics, but no glaze cited); see further below, pp. 726–8.

[118] Gelichi and Milanese, 'Problems in the transition', pp. 477–80; Thébert and Biget, 'L'Afrique' (pp. 583–4 for Béja). For the prosperity of these cities in the tenth century, see Ibn Hawqal (Ibn Hauqal), *Configuration de la terre*, I, pp. 66–71, 92–5. For Arab government, Djaït, 'La wilāya', I, pp. 117–19; Cambuzat, *L'évolution des cités*, I, pp. 209–13 and *passim* (II, p. 27–32 for Béja).

[119] The palace sites are essentially unpublished, but some of their finds are presented and discussed in an exhibition catalogue, *Couleurs de Tunisie*, pp. 83–96, 118–28.

as already noted; it was given a larger-scale enceinte, probably in this period, and two churches were built beside it (a pattern which has parallels in eastern cities such as Philippi, but fewer in the West), one in the Vandal period (probably), one in the Byzantine period.[120] But it is clear that, otherwise, interest in monumental building had moved away from the forum. Duval has proposed that by the seventh century there were several settlement agglomerations in and around the classical city, which, as we shall see (p. 652), evokes the *città ad isole*, one of the current guiding images of the period for archaeologists in Italy, as well as Euchaita in Anatolia. We should not conclude, however, that this fragmentation calls Sbeïtla's urban status into doubt, for the churches were still rich, and, to the south-east of the city, as already mentioned, several fortified houses begin to appear, with levels beginning in the Byzantine period and continuing to the ninth century (there is Aghlabid glaze on the site). Sbeïtla's wealth must have been largely derived from oil, given its agricultural environment, and late Byzantine oil-presses have been found along the road out of town to the south-east, one of them encroaching substantially on the road. But in the early Arab period there are other signs of continuing urbanism: one of the churches by the forum was converted to artisan workshops, probably in the eighth century, with evidence of metalworking. The city may have fragmented, but it probably had not weakened economically by 800, or indeed 900.[121]

Constructing Sbeïtla's story depends, as usual with urban excavations, on a substantial element of hypothesis, as one proposes, crossing one's fingers, that the best-excavated areas fairly represent the city's development. This is nothing, however, compared to the difficulty presented by Carthage, where dozens of recent scientific excavations have been undertaken, under the aegis of UNESCO in the 1970s and subsequently, by teams from a dozen countries and more, most of which have not been fully published, and the most detailed synthesis for our period, by John Humphrey, dates back as far as 1980. Overall, one plausible reading of them might run as follows.[122]

---

[120] See Duval, 'L'urbanisme de Sufetula', with Duval and Baratte, *Les ruines de Sufetula*, for this and what follows. The forum enceinte is a much simpler wall than the fortresses of towns like Dougga (above, n. 114), but may represent the same closed-off aesthetic, as indeed do the fortified houses (above, n. 116).

[121] Encroaching oil-press: Duval and Baratte, *Les ruines de Sufetula*, pp. 100–2. Church and workshops: Bejaoui, 'Une nouvelle église'. It was supposedly in or near Sbeïtla in 647–8 that the local inhabitants explained to an Arab general that their great wealth came from exporting olives to Byzantium, a famous account recorded in the mid-ninth century by Ibn 'Abd al-Ḥakam (*Conquête de l'Afrique*, pp. 46–9). Precisely because this is unlikely to be a true story, it indicates a continuity in local oil production until well after the end of our period. See below, p. 726.

[122] This account is based on Humphrey, 'Vandal and Byzantine Carthage' (the 1980 survey); Hurst, 'Cartagine'; Ennabli, *Pour sauver Carthage*; Leone, 'Change or no change?'; Ben Abed and Duval, 'Carthage'; and, for specific sites, Lancel, *Byrsa I*; Rakob, *Karthago I*; Hurst and Roskams, *Excavations at Carthage*, I.1; Humphrey, *The circus*, I; Stevens, *Bir el Knissia*, I; Balmelle *et al.*, 'Recherches', and Balmelle *et al.*, 'Vitalité' (for the Odeon); Stevens, 'A late-Roman urban population'; eadem *et al.*, 'Bir Ftouha'.

Carthage was the capital of Africa, a major political and fiscal centre, and channel of much of Africa's wealth overseas in the Roman period. In the period 350–450 its prosperity peaked, as also did its population, which might have reached 100,000 people. Its walls, built in the 420s, blocked some former main access roads, and left some extramural areas to decay. In the Vandal period, too, there are also some signs of a neglect of public buildings, such as those in the forum area and the so-called 'circular monument'; roads often saw encroachment in this period. But the Vandals also built or rebuilt palaces and baths on a lavish scale (one was near the odeon; we also have detailed praise-poems about some of them).[123] Some private housing continued to be rich, such as the House of the Greek Charioteers; and commercial activity remained active, with a continuity of import and export (though this was lessening by 500—see below, p. 723—and the circular harbour, one of Carthage's several harbours, was not fully kept up). After Belisarios' conquest there was a massive rebuilding programme, focusing on public buildings, streets, porticoes, churches, the harbours, and the walls, as befitted a major centre in Justinian's empire; this rebuilding sometimes recognized and systematized former street encroachment. Carthage arguably had a prosperous period up to 600 at least, and maybe even 650, although construction techniques simplified towards the end of this period, and some monuments were converted to private houses. The last known monumental (re-)building dates to c.660, in the southern extramural church of Bir el Knissia;[124] thereafter Carthage underwent a monumental meltdown. Older housing was replaced—and streets even blocked—by numerous poor-quality buildings, the circular harbour and the circus were abandoned (there was seventh-century occupation, probably housing, in the latter, however[125]) and burials intruded on several former occupied areas. Carthage was in the end abandoned, probably in the early eighth century, and replaced by neighbouring Tunis. But the late seventh-century levels of the city, despite their material poverty and their lack of control, do not show terminal population decline; one must conclude that a still-existing population was deliberately moved by the Arabs at some point after their conquest of the city in 698.[126]

Carthage is the only major city in the Umayyad caliphate that the Arabs moved, and why they chose to do so in this case is unclear, but they at least enabled its detailed archaeological reconstruction (and the more nuanced

[123] For the poems, Châlon *et al.*, '*Memorabile factum*'.
[124] Stevens, *Bir el Knissia*, I, pp. 303–8.   [125] Humphrey, *The circus*, I, pp. 99–100.
[126] Post-698 levels may perhaps be visible on one of the Michigan sites and on the Byrsa (Vitelli, *Islamic Carthage*, pp. 15–17, 24–39), and at the church of Bir Ftouha (Stevens, 'Bir Ftouha', pp. 380–1); Caron and Lavoie have recently argued for a late eighth-century mosaic in the Odeon area (Caron and Lavoie, 'Les recherches canadiennes'). But as far as we can yet see, Arab Carthage hardly existed before the tenth century (cf. Vitelli, *Islamic Carthage*, p. 46). On one level, it does not greatly matter if the Arabs moved Carthage to Tunis in 700 or 750.

ones that will follow proper future syntheses), something which cannot be done for Alexandria or Antioch. How widely can we generalize from it, however? Carthage was a capital, and its history tells us above all about political change; its prosperity came from public money more than it did from private (agricultural or commercial) wealth. The crisis that it faced, at all levels except perhaps that of demography, in the later decades of the seventh century may, for example, only mirror the political collapse of the Byzantine administration in Africa in the face of the Arab occupations of Byzacena in the 640s–670s, rather than any wider patterns of urban change. All the same, Carthage's position as Africa's major port (both for the fiscal and the commercial movement of goods) does mean that its overall prosperity could be said to mirror the macroeconomic prosperity of the region; indeed, the downturn around 500, the revival after 550, and the precipitous decline after 650 have exact parallels in the history of African exchange, which is better represented in the history of Carthage than in any so-far excavated urban site. These points will be picked up in the next chapter (pp. 720–8).

It is hardly possible, in the end, to deny the importance of Africa's sequence of invasions when trying to understand how cities changed. Not that this was the result of the different character of the invaders. The Vandals, Byzantines, and Arabs alike valued cities, and used them as the basic elements of their government, which was in each case locally strong. All three polities had major problems with the Berbers, it is true, and seldom exercised much authority outside the Tunisian heartland of Africa; the Vandals had trouble with their Roman subjects too, at least at moments of religious tension. All the same, Africa was tightly governed throughout our period, with the sole exception of the half-century of the Arab conquests, 647–98, which was marked by Arab strategic uncertainty, steady Berber advance, and a near-total absence of any Byzantine military protagonism at all: one cause, beyond doubt, of the fact that the eighth century marked Africa's economic low point in almost all respects. What had changed was, in part, the style of African government; and, in part, the macroeconomic context that these differing political structures had allowed.

The Vandals were, in ideological terms, heavily influenced by the Romans (above, pp. 87–92). Nor do city excavations indicate in any case that their supposed hostility to Catholic hierarchies actually led to an impoverishment of the urban rich, for expensive buildings were still being built. But it is fairly clear that they no longer saw a need for curial tax-raising and local government—thus, ironically, strengthening the local political centrality of their major opponents, the episcopate. *Curiae* vanish from our sources, and secular public areas faced crisis. In urban terms, all the Vandals did was anticipate by a generation the move away from curial government which was already beginning around 500 in the East, and which is also visible elsewhere in the western Mediterranean, in Italy and Spain. But the independence of

Vandal Africa meant that the region was abruptly removed from the fiscally based Mediterranean exchange system (above, pp. 87–8, below, pp. 711–12), which must have disrupted local production, and thus local wealth, at least in the medium term. This may help to explain the fact that the demonumentalization of forum areas seems in many cases to have led to the weakening of the spatial coherence of cities themselves, unlike in the East. The east Roman reconquest did not lead to the recentralization of fragmenting cities, except with the fortifications of places like Haïdra, with the ambiguous consequences already characterized. In effect, the Byzantines found an urban structure that had already moved away from eastern models (although there are parallels in the contemporary Balkans), and they adapted their monumental interventions to this new reality—only in Carthage did a hugely expensive building programme attempt to reverse the process. Africa was by now poorer; even the late sixth-century revival did not return the region to the economic centrality it had enjoyed in 400, for it was now a marginal part of the East, not a focal region of the West.

I shall argue in the next chapter that Africa was worse hit by the breakdown of the Mediterranean world system than any other region. Its natural agrarian wealth meant that urbanism could survive, however, as long as the wealthy continued to live in cities, which, given the continuing expenditure on churches, we can probably assume they did—in, perhaps, the fortified houses of Sbeïtla or Belalis Maior. Even in the remotest cities, there could be leading citizens capable of collective endeavour and expense, as with the fortress underwritten by local *cives* at Aïn Ksar in the high plains of Numidia north of Timgad, in c.580.[127] African cities were never abandoned by their ruling elites, in fact, in all likelihood; there is no sign whatever of the ruralization of the aristocracy, as in (say) Francia, and, conversely, there was never the state-backed reconfiguration of the entire aristocratic hierarchy that we saw in the Byzantine heartland. When that began in the Aegean and Anatolia after 650, the African government was anyway no longer capable of any similar form of systematic intervention; and the Arab conquest will probably have produced the same sort of restriction of Christian elites to their local political stages that we saw in Egypt, Syria, and Palestine. (Early Arab Africa is, unfortunately, so badly documented that this is pure hypothesis.) The city–country relationship was, as a result, never broken in our period, and towns like Béja could even gain in importance under the Arabs. But the wealth of the rich became restricted to the simple ability of landowners to take surplus from tenants, with the extra level of export-led accumulation cut off. After the fifth century there may never again in our period have been enough private wealth to reconfigure the fragmenting urban centres of the region.

[127] Durliat, *Les dédicaces*, pp. 71–7.

Africa's cities changed less than in most western regions (except Italy), and it seems to me that their best parallels remain in Syria-Palestine. But the region's twin political crises created a poorer environment, and thus poorer cities, than in the Levant. Not that the Vandals or the Arabs were themselves devastating forces. But the Vandals removed the region from the fiscal world-system, which was its first major shock; and the half-century of stasis before the Arabs committed themselves to conquering it led to an even more serious productive involution, which took even the Arabs a century to reverse. These themes take us away from our main urban focus, however, and will be explored further in the next chapter.

In Italy, the debate over urbanism has been more intense than in most other regions. This is for three major reasons. First, Italy's particular history, in which political fragmentation around autonomous cities was the stage for the Renaissance, has helped to generate a continuing belief among Italian historians that the fate of cities is of consuming interest (cf. above, p. 36). Indeed, the 'decline of urbanism' in the early middle ages in Italy has often been seen as a simple demonstration of the 'barbarism' of the period, and the cultural superiority of city life, a view assumed by most classical and Renaissance writers, is even now often regarded as normal in historiographic debate; these being views that have much less resonance, for example, beyond the Alps. Second, the debate has been animated by a sharp contrast between the written documentation and the archaeological evidence for urban life. In our Italian narratives and documents, we have numerous references to urban aristocrats, even in the period after 600, a period of economic and political crisis (above, pp. 211–12), and all our evidence for political structures makes it clear that they were routinely based on the city network, in Lombard and Byzantine areas alike, throughout the early middle ages.[128] Archaeological excavations, however, regularly show poor-quality constructions, wooden buildings (a supposedly un-Roman phenomenon), street encroachment, and outright abandonment. The third reason is that scientific post-Roman urban archaeology began to be active in Italy in the early 1980s, five or ten years earlier than in most places in Continental western Europe, and in a period in which processualist archaeological model-builders were particularly active in seeking to replace document-based historical narratives; the discovery that little or nothing could be found by excavators between the sixth and the ninth centuries in some of the urban centres that historians were claiming to be significant political and social foci, as in the early excavations in Brescia, or the Metro excavations in Milan (and, contemporarily, in the French excavations at Tours: below, p. 675), was used with some enthusiasm to fuel that process of replacement.

---

[128] See Harrison, *The early state*, pp. 98–157, for Lombard Italy; Brown, *Gentlemen and officers*, e.g. pp. 55–6, for Byzantine Italy.

The resultant debate had its moment of greatest intensity in the late 1980s. Thereafter, as archaeologists actually began to find evidence in their early medieval levels, and, conversely, historians increasingly recognized the implications of its material simplicity, the debate calmed down, and was replaced in the 1990s by a new trend, the generation of syntheses, where the competitive edge lies in nuance rather than direct confrontation. Italy is thus not only the most debated of our regions, but the most comprehensively synthesized, at least in this field.[129]

I have myself, as noted earlier, contributed to this debate, both in the period of sharper argument and in the period of synthesis, in the last-named context fairly recently. What follows is largely taken from that most recent synthesis, updated to include the latest finds, for we need at least a description of the material changes which took place in Italian cities after the fifth century, in order to allow for useful comparison; after that, however, I shall stand back from the material in order to look at it in a different light, that is to say, from the point of view of the development of cities in the eastern and southern Mediterranean that we have just been following.

Italy is the first region we have looked at where urban continuity is so great that almost all major Roman sites are still occupied, but where archaeologists have managed to target enough areas in contemporary cities to produce significant results. There are high-quality early medieval excavations in Venice (the only non-classical city in this set), Verona, Brescia, Milan, Fidenza, Ravenna, Savona, Luni, Pisa, Florence, Siena, Rome, Ostia, Cagliari, Naples, Pescara, Otranto, and Squillace, and indeed, in more fragmentary form, in numerous other cities. These excavations are not generally large-scale; they are often rescue excavations, and are almost always restricted to small areas, as in the Egyptian sites already mentioned (and as in the Spanish and French/German sites to be discussed below), privileging private houses and churches.[130] One can, nonetheless, fit them into wider contexts rather more easily than in Egypt: in part because there

---

[129] For the 1980s debate, see esp. La Rocca Hudson, '"Dark Ages"' a Verona'; Brogiolo, 'A proposito dell'organizzazione'. For 1990s syntheses, see Zanini, *Le Italie bizantine*, pp. 120–208; Ward-Perkins, 'Continuitists, catastrophists'; Brogiolo and Gelichi, *La città*; Witschel, 'Rom und die Städte Italiens'; Wickham, 'Early medieval archaeology', pp. 11–15, an earlier version of parts of the next few pages.

[130] For Venice, see below, n. 215. For other cities, Hudson, 'Contributi archeologici' (Verona); Brogiolo, *Brescia*; Caporusso, *Scavi MM3* (Milan); Catarsi dall'Aglio, 'Archeologia medievale a Parma e Fidenza'; Ortalli, 'L'edilizia abitativa'; Maioli, 'Strutture economico-commerciali' (Ravenna); Varaldo, 'Lo scavo' (Savona); Ward-Perkins, 'Two Byzantine houses' (Luni); Bruni, *Pisa. Piazza Dante*; Bruni et al., *Ricerche di archeologia medievale a Pisa*; Mirandola, 'Firenze'; Cantini, *Le fasi* (Siena); Paroli and Delogu, *La storia economica di Roma* (including material on Ostia); Santangeli Valenzani, 'Residential building'; Witschel, 'Rom und die Städte Italiens'; Saguì, 'Roma'; Pani Ermini and Spanu, *Aspetti di archeologia urbana* (Cagliari); Arthur, *Il complesso archeologico*; idem, *Naples*; Staffa, 'Scavi nel centro storico di Pescara'; Michaelides and Wilkinson, *Excavations at Otranto*; Donzelli, 'Le strutture tardoantiche'; Raimondo, *Modèles économiques et sociaux* (Squillace). These are only a small proportion of the sites even in these cities, but include the major ones.

are more of them; in part because the spatial structures of Italian cities are better understood.

Briefly put, Italian cities tended to keep their basic classical spatial structures with less disruption than in most regions. More Italian cities still maintain their ancient square plan, in many cases hardly altered at all, than in any other part of the former empire. This is no longer regarded as a flawless argument for urban continuity, as too many sites show such a survival whose economic urbanism was certainly discontinuous, for example Aosta, or those parts of south-east Brescia where Roman *insulae* were turned into early medieval fields, and were only built on again after our period, without, however, disturbing the street plan. As already becomes clear from Paul-Albert Février's survey of the issue in 1973, unchanging street plans do not in themselves prove continuous urbanism: they only show that the temptation to encroach on, or build over, streets is less strong than the power to maintain access and alignment; this could occur both when cities were hardly coherent at all but builders were scarce, and when urban economies were very active, but municipal authorities had the strength to control them.[131] All the same, the particular frequency of surviving street alignments in Italy does seem to be an argument for a tendency to the maintenance of the urban fabric in this region, and most buildings found by excavators for our period respect the ancient grids. These alignments structure a specific early medieval Italian kit of buildings. In Italy, forum areas lost their monumentality, often as early as in Africa, but nonetheless continued to exist at least as open spaces, often with market activity, even after the end of *curiae* in the sixth/seventh centuries (above, p. 69, below, p. 652). Cathedrals were sometimes situated on or near them, although as often in the corners of cities.[132] There was also in most cities a public administrative centre, indeed in some cases two, called the *curtis regia* and the *curtis ducalis* in Lombard cities such as Lucca (above, p. 212), indicating some separation of (still city-based) powers between the king's most immediate agents and the local duke. The cathedral and the centre of public administration acted as rival spatial foci, replacing the forum; but they were sometimes in the same part of town, creating a powerful core of urban activity. The whole was structured not only by streets but also by walls, for the typical Italian city had not only a squared street plan but a square of walls surrounding it as well, although documents show the existence of extramural suburbs in some cities (Lucca, most notably). A dense network of documented churches (thirty-nine from eighth-century texts in Lucca) completes the picture: only a minority have surviving early medieval

[131] For street plans, Ward-Perkins, *From classical antiquity*, pp. 179–82 (partially retracted in 'Continuitists, catastrophists', p. 166 n.); cf. Février, 'Permanence et héritages', pp. 96–104.
[132] Testini *et al.*, 'La cattedrale in Italia', esp. pp. 35–47 (G. Cantino Wataghin), 76–80 (L. Pani Ermini).

elements, but they evidently existed. All of these common elements allow one to locate excavated sites fairly exactly with relationship to the centres of power in any given city.[133]

Conversely, it must at once be recognized that the archaeological record shows that Italian cities collectively underwent several centuries of crisis in our period. The 739 *Versum de Mediolano civitate*, for example, praises Milan in high-flown terms, for its walls, its streets, its churches, and so on; but it was lying when it referred to the 'solid paving', the *firme stratum silice*, of Milan's streets—excavations have only found beaten earth.[134] In general, the urban excavations of early medieval Italy, now fairly numerous as we have seen, tend to show a late fifth- and early sixth-century phase in which Roman town houses begin to be divided up into single rooms, each with their own hearth; a late sixth-century phase when even these are demolished; and a seventh-century and later phase in which they are replaced by rather simpler structures, in reused stone (Verona, Bergamo, Milan, Ravenna, Siena) or wood, the latter constructed either on Roman foundations or simply on wooden beams or post-holes (Brescia, Milan, Luni, Fidenza), or else not by houses at all but by fields, sometimes deliberately created by levelling Roman buildings and putting earth on top (Brescia, Naples). At the same time, paved streets are abandoned, as sewage systems and urban cleaning collapse, and levels of archaeological deposit accumulate as a result—hence the several different levels of beaten earth found in early medieval streets in most urban excavations.[135]

Let us look at some examples of this process. Brescia offers us the most rounded picture of urban change available so far, thanks largely to the work of Gian Pietro Brogiolo. In the early sixth century a palace may have been built near the cathedral, on the western edge of the city, probably by Theoderic, but the eastern edge was getting poorer, with the sort of subdivided houses described above, and in one case a simpler house rebuilt in reused stone. After a fire in the mid-sixth century, these houses were demolished. As already noted, to the south-east, on the Via Alberto Mario, one house was replaced by a field. To the north-east, a dozen wooden huts have been found, respecting the foundations of the preceding Roman buildings, some of them *Grubenhäuser* of a north European type, with evidence of metalworking and ceramic production: demographic and artisanal

---

[133] For Lucca, see Belli Barsali, 'La topografia', pp. 506–15, 525–36. The figure of 39 churches excludes four others listed by Belli Barsali which do not have early documentary references. For later work on Lucca, see below, n. 147.

[134] Cf. the *Versum de Mediolano* with Ceresa Mori, 'Milano', and Caporusso, *Scavi MM3*, I, pp. 165–9, 271. Similarly, the *Versus de Verona* of c.800 praises the paved forum (*foro... sternuto lapidibus*), but it seems to have been largely covered by temporary constructions and house rubble (Hudson, 'Contributi archeologici', p. 338). Both poems are edited in *MGH, Poetae*, I, pp. 24–6, 119–22.

[135] For an overview, see Brogiolo and Gelichi, *La città*, pp. 45–154, with, for Siena, Cantini, *Le fasi*, pp. 60–92; for Naples, Arthur, *Naples*, pp. 53–6.

continuity, therefore (or at least rapid reoccupation), but in radically new, and also far simpler, building styles. In one case, however, on Via Piamarta, much of the Roman street-front was maintained; not every Roman house was in ruins or demolished. In the late seventh century the wooden huts were replaced by stone buildings, probably including a church; in the mid-eighth century this church was rebuilt by King Desiderius as the major urban monastery of S. Salvatore di Brescia, and in the ninth century again as S. Giulia. Brogiolo does not believe that all the seventh-century Bresciani lived in huts; he hypothesizes that the aristocracy lived nearer the cathedral and the palace (by now the *curtis ducalis*), where systematic excavations have not yet taken place. But already at the time of the Lombard conquest, Brescia was a very different city from that which it had been under the Roman empire.[136]

We have more fragmentary information from other cities, but many of the developments found at Brescia are repeated, as single or multiple instances, elsewhere. The best-known parallel to the Via Piamarta in Brescia is the Verona excavation on Via Dante, where a street-front in reused stone, slightly encroaching on the road, was continually rebuilt, as the street-level rose, from the fifth to the eleventh century. The Verona excavations show the abandonment of Roman structures above all in the interior of *insulae*; it would be possible to argue from this that street-fronts were in some places what survived from the Roman past, and that there were courtyards behind them which were most plausibly used as gardens. Such stone street-fronts are less commonly found than are wooden buildings in urban excavations, but there are parallels in both Milan and Bergamo.[137]

Slowly, we are also gaining a sense of the creation of different models for urban building in Italy. One-roomed houses, built in wood, or in a mixture of wood and reused stone and brick, are one new pattern; this is without any parallel in urban housing known from Antiquity, though almost certainly it had been common in the countryside, and maybe in the poorer outer suburbs of Roman towns as well. It may reflect the 'ruralization' of urban building, then, and it certainly has many parallels in early medieval rural excavations. A second, more complex, pattern is the two-storeyed house, with a kitchen and storerooms on the ground floor, external steps, and living quarters on the upper floor: a pattern well known from twelfth- and thirteenth-century houses still inhabited in cities such as Rome and Viterbo, but one very unlike the peristyle houses of Italy during the Roman empire. This two-storey type is known from documents from seventh- and eighth-century Rimini, and, later, from tenth-century Rome and Naples (all Byzantine, not Lombard, cities). A fairly clear archaeological example of it is known from

---

[136] Brogiolo, *Brescia*; Brogiolo, *S. Giulia di Brescia*.
[137] Hudson, 'Contributi archeologici', pp. 336–42; Caporusso, *Scavi MM3*, I, pp. 165–9, 290–3; for Bergamo, see Brogiolo and Gelichi, *La città*, p. 126.

sixth-century Ravenna, and another from the early sixth-century *castrum* of Monte Barro; two particularly well preserved examples have recently been excavated in Rome, on the Forum Nervae, dating to c.800, and the existence of others in Rome has been deduced from older excavation reports. The archaeological examples are thus mostly from Byzantine contexts, which largely match those of the documents; it may be that these new urban building-types had their roots in the final decades of the west Roman empire. They have some analogies to the multistoreyed houses already described for Egypt and Palestine, although the local architecture in Italy was quite different from the East. It is significant, however, that one set of similar structures, only slightly simpler, has also been found in the Lombard kingdom, in the Piazza Dante in Pisa, dating to the eighth century. This is perhaps, then, the type of house that the eighth-century urban aristocracy of our documents lived in, in Lombard Lucca and Brescia as well as in Byzantine Ravenna. By the tenth century, indeed, Roman and Neapolitan documents imply that they were by no means exclusive to aristocrats. It must be recognized, nonetheless, that hitherto they are considerably rarer than one-storeyed and one- or two-roomed wooden houses in our excavations.[138]

It is clear that, universally, after c.550 (the rough date recurs consistently, marking the generalized crisis of the Gothic war) early medieval cities in Italy were poorer than Roman ones. Some indeed vanished altogether, and others lost their urban functions (Luni is the clearest instance among the excavated sites).[139] But even those where urban activities survived, which include every city mentioned in the immediately preceding pages, were very much poorer, with most urban administrative functions (such as street-cleaning) reduced to a minimum, and with often very simple buildings, or Roman buildings fairly crudely reused. Were their populations also reduced? The open fields and internal courtyards might imply so, although one must also note that here, as in the East, one-roomed houses could often imply denser settlement than the generously constructed peristyle houses and extensive temple precincts of the empire. Aristocrats themselves probably occupied fairly simple two-storeyed buildings. Even the houses of the Forum

---

[138] See in general Brogiolo and Gelichi, *La città*, pp. 107–37; Galetti, *Abitare nel medioevo*, pp. 64–92. For two-storey houses found in Ravenna, see Ortalli, 'L'edilizia abitativa', pp. 179–82; Maioli, 'Strutture economico-commerciali', pp. 227–30. For those in Rome, see Santangeli Valenzani, 'Residential building'. For Monte Barro, Brogiolo and Castelletti, *Archeologia a Monte Barro*, I, pp. 30–44. For Pisa, Bruni, *Pisa*, pp. 227–30. Polci, 'Some aspects of the transformation', pp. 89–105, tracks the early history of two-storey houses and links them to palatial reception-rooms (cf. below, n. 140); she argues that the earliest archaeological example is the villa of S. Giovanni di Ruoti, around 460 (Small and Buck, *San Giovanni di Ruoti*, I, pp. 92–5, 412–13). The Rimini documents are *CB*, nn. 64–5, 69, 71–3; cf. Ch. 4, n. 159. For later documents in Rome and Naples, see Hubert, *Espace urbain*, pp. 173–84; Skinner, 'Urban communities', pp. 285–8.

[139] Bandini, 'Luni'; Schmiedt, 'Città scomparse'; La Rocca, '"Castrum vel potius civitas"'.

Nervae, by far the most impressive yet found, do not match the mosaic-floored town houses found regularly in imperial-period levels. If one extends one's sights away from residential building and looks at churches, such as S. Salvatore/S. Giulia in Brescia, or the prestige foundations of Pavia, Cividale, and Spoleto, or any number of eighth- and ninth-century churches in Rome, it is true that one immediately finds good-quality brick- and stone-work, sometimes newly fired or quarried, and also the marble and mosaic traditions of the ancient world. These show a continuity of patronage of skilled artisans, as also do those buildings surviving from the Roman empire up to the present day, for artisans must always have been on hand to make sure their roofs were repaired. The existence of such specialist artisans is further confirmed in documents, such as the eighth-century price-list in the *Memoratorium de mercedibus commacinorum* (above, p. 213). We must conclude, however, that there was not sufficient demand for their services to support *enough* artisans, in any one city, to transform residential housing as well as church architecture. The very richest aristocrats, ducal families for example, may have had houses in new brick, stone, and marble, probably resembling more elaborate versions of the two-storeyed houses of Ravenna and Rome; but they were probably few in number.[140] The rest settled for buildings like those in the Via Dante of Verona or the Piazza Dante of Pisa, and maybe put rich hangings or frescos on the walls to cover the simplicity of the construction. Overall, the aristocracy of early medieval Italy—Byzantine and Lombard alike—although they still lived in cities, were far poorer than their predecessors, or their eleventh-century successors in their tower houses. And their neighbours, artisans or shopkeepers or servants, were poorer still.

It has become common in Italy to argue for a temporal division inside the early middle ages, between roughly the period 550–750 and the period 750–950, the first one of urban crisis, the second one of tentative revival. It is true that the documents for cities would support this, as would the global evidence for greater aristocratic wealth in the Carolingian period (above, p. 218). One could read parts of the archaeology that way too, in particular the greater number of churches, built with good construction techniques, in the second period, and the finding of buildings such as the Forum Nervae houses. Recent excavations in Siena, too, show good-quality stone buildings beginning to be built from the ninth century onwards. I would be cautious, all the same. Rome, at least, is a very atypical city; and church-building follows its own rhythms, independent of any simple

---

[140] See in general Brogiolo and Gelichi, *La città*, pp. 136–64; Ward-Perkins, *From classical antiquity*, pp. 61–3. For S. Salvatore/S. Giulia, Brogiolo, *S. Giulia di Brescia*; for Spoleto, Emerick, *The tempietto*. For episcopal palaces and analogous prestige buildings with first-floor reception rooms, Miller, *The bishop's palace*, pp. 22–76; Polci, 'Some aspects of the transformation', pp. 90–1, 97–8.

correlation with economic prosperity.[141] It could equally well be said that sites like the Via Dante point to much longer continuities of poor construction, and it is also fair to note that the ninth and tenth centuries are as yet less well known archaeologically in most Italian cities than is the seventh. Unhelpfully, the single most unambiguous sign of renewed economic activity after 750 is the huge wealth and artisanal sophistication found in S. Vincenzo al Volturno in the early ninth century; but S. Vincenzo was one of the remotest rural monasteries in Italy.[142] If this is the kind of prosperity that the ninth century could generate, then it needs to be stressed that it has not yet been recognized in most Italian cities. There may very well have been an urban revival in Italy after c.750; but this is a sector of the debate for which we must await more excavation.

With these observations about the changing nature and quality of urban building in mind, let us look again at the issue of the overall structure of Italian cities. An important question that came up in the context of our discussions of Syria and of Africa was the fate of the old forum/agora areas of cities. Italian archaeology does not allow the generation of easy parallels to those debates, for relatively few fora have been subjected to systematic analysis, given the chancy patterning of urban excavations in still-occupied towns. Some have been studied, however, and these tend to situate Italian developments with those of Africa rather than those found in the East, even in the case of major cities. At Verona, there are signs of monumental destructuration (the systematic demolition of the Capitolium) already in the 510s, and sixth-century encroachment on the open square. At Brescia, the ruined Capitolium was reused for ceramic production by 600, indicating an earlier monumental decay. At Milan, sketchier interventions indicate a fifth-century date for the same process. We should also add to this list Luni, whose forum was losing its classical appearance in the fifth century, when it was stripped of marble and underwent a period of formation of silt deposits, before wooden houses were built there in c.550. Luni is different from these other sites, because the city's economy was equally clearly already in trouble (it was the main outlet for Carrara—then Luni—marble, so the stripping of the forum paving is particularly indicative), and it was eventually abandoned; all the same, the early demonumentalization of the forum is significant, for the city's bishops were capable of spending substantial sums on the cathedral up to the ninth century. The forum of Florence, by contrast, seems to have been repaved in the mid-sixth.[143] We should finally add Rome, where

---

[141] Brogiolo and Gelichi, *La città*, e.g. pp. 43, 108, 159–60; Cantini, *Le fasi*, pp. 93–100. Rome's atypicality is discussed in Witschel, 'Rom und die Städte Italiens'; for church-building rhythms see Wickham, *Mountains*, pp. 54–5.

[142] Hodges, *San Vincenzo*, I, II; Hodges and Mitchell, *The basilica of Abbot Joshua*; Marazzi, 'San Vincenzo'.

[143] Hudson, 'Contributi archeologici', pp. 338–9, for Verona; Ch. 11, n. 74 for Brescia; Ceresa Mori, 'Milano'. Contrast, for Luni, Ward-Perkins, 'Two Byzantine houses', with Lusuardi Siena, 'Lo scavo nella cattedrale'. For Florence, see Mirandola, 'Firenze', p. 67.

the forum area was huge and complex; here, the main forum (the Foro Romano as it is now called) was still the focus of monumental building into the seventh century, with the column of Phocas of 608, and the Fora of Nerva and Trajan were still being maintained as late as the ninth century (the start of the century for the former, the end for the latter). As already stressed, Rome was always highly atypical, however. Its *curia* building, on the Foro Romano, was still used by the Senate into the late sixth century (it was converted into a church after 625), and its monuments maintained for a long time an intensity of symbolic meaning and state-supported protection, which those of other cities could never match. All the same, many were in decay by 500—there were simply too many to maintain—and one of the fora, that of Augustus, even though it adjoined those of Nerva and Trajan, was already a quarry in the sixth century.[144]

Fora in Italy maintained a spatial centrality. Many had become markets by the ninth or tenth centuries at the latest, as with Brescia, Milan, Pavia, Florence; others may have done (we do not have the documents elsewhere), and most remained at least open spaces, although these were usually rather smaller than in classical times, that is, substantially encroached on (even if this did not necessarily occur in our period).[145] But it is likely that they began to lose their monumentality by or before the Gothic war, sometimes substantially earlier, much as in Africa. Interestingly, Italian *curiae* seem to have survived longer than in Africa; although they had long since vanished from building inscriptions, they are regarded as normal in the *Variae*, and some (as at Ravenna, Rieti, or Naples) are referred to after 550 in documents and letters.[146] We cannot, that is to say, conclude that a demonumentalized forum automatically means that a *curia* no longer existed. But it is likely, all the same, that the latter were much less important; by 550 practical power in cities was in the hands of bishops, local senators, and other notables, whether or not there was still a *curia*.

Italian archaeologists invented the term *città ad isole* already cited, and there are some cities in the peninsula where some spatial destructuring undoubtedly occurred, following on from the monumental weakening of forum areas. Brescia may be one example, with a cathedral-*curtis ducalis* area in the south-west of the city separated from the public (later monastic) area in the north-east by a decaying and underpopulated forum area. Lucca has been canvassed as another, given the apparently early weakening of the forum area (in the second and third centuries), with a late Roman refocusing

---

[144] Krautheimer, *Rome*, pp. 66–72, for the Foro Romano and a general context; Meneghini, 'L'origine di un quartiere', for the other fora.

[145] Respectively, *Codex diplomaticus Langobardiae*, nn. 571 (a. 942), 290 (a. 879), 393 (a. 901); *S. ecclesiae Florentinae monumenta*, I, p. 84 (prior to 945: cf. Davidsohn, *Storia di Firenze*, I, p. 1248). See in general Ward-Perkins, *From classical antiquity*, pp. 182–6.

[146] See above, p. 69. Brown, *Gentlemen and officers*, pp. 16–17, gives a list of late references; the completest account is now Tabata, *Le città dell'Italia*, pp. 32–55, 241–53.

of the city in the cathedral area in its south-east corner, and, by the eighth century, a wide array of churches in the city's suburbs as alternative settlement foci, with open areas between them. (I have serious doubts about this, all the same, given the even density of the city's numerous intramural churches in the eighth century).[147] A third example of fragmentation is certainly Rome, whose third-century walls included after c.600 only perhaps a twentieth of its late Roman population, grouped, as it would appear from recent work, in a set of what could be called urban villages, maybe as many as a dozen, held together by a common politics and, probably, a continuing ritual of processions across the old classical centre.[148] Brescia and Rome are parallels to the fragmented tendencies of some of the African cities, and indeed Rome is a better example than any of them, although a dangerous one to generalize from, given the huge space inside its walls. How typical they were is, all the same, not clear. Cities fragment because their centres have become less powerful, because new foci, like churches on the edge of town and outside city walls, become more important, and, crucially, because their demography and urban economic activities become too weak to root all these foci in the same urban fabric. My sense of the evidence for Italian cities is that in the case of those which maintained their political importance—as in almost all of the examples cited above—they maintained that essential level of coherence in their urban structure. We have the surviving street plans; we have no cases in Italy of the closed-off urban fortresses documented for some cities in Africa. We have eighth-century evidence of urban artisans (goldsmiths, cauldron-makers, and others) for Lucca, of urban subdivisions for Lucca and Ravenna.[149] And, of course, we have the evidence of the urban aristocrats—the source of demand for the artisans—already cited (pp. 210–13), which fits with what else we know about Italian cities. All of these mark a tendency towards the maintenance of a considerable degree of urban vitality, at least in the successful cities of the peninsula; hence, probably, their continued spatial coherence. The survival of fora as market areas probably reflects that economic vitality, but would have further reinforced the continuing coherence of the urban fabric.

[147] Brescia: Brogiolo, *Brescia*, pp. 85–96 (p. 117 for an instance of the image of the *città ad isole*). Lucca: Ciampoltrini and Notini, 'Lucca', pp. 590–2; Ciampoltrini, 'Città "frammentate" ', pp. 615–20; de Conno, 'L'insediamento longobardo'; Quirós, *Modi di costruire*, pp. 91–3, 101–7; Abela, 'Lucca', a well-balanced account. Siena is possibly a parallel, but the evidence is a bit hypothetical: Cantini, *Le fasi*, pp. 22–4.

[148] Hubert, *Espace urbain*, pp. 70–83; Coates-Stephens, 'Housing'. For processions, see Baldovin, *Urban character*, pp. 158–61; Krautheimer, *Rome*, pp. 278–9. The figure of a twentieth is a pure guess. For an overview of Rome's urban development, see Pani Ermini, 'Forma urbis'.

[149] For artisans in Lucca, *CDL*, I, nn. 69, 113; II, nn. 170, 219, 281; for urban subdivisions, I, n. 69, *MDL*, V.2 , n. 510 (a. 830); with Agnellus, *Liber pontificalis*, cc. 126–9, for Ravenna (a folkloristic account, but presupposing a city divided into quarters in the ninth century at the latest).

Conversely, it must be repeated that the material poverty of Italian cities cannot be denied. Italy's new two-storeyed buildings simply mark changes in the way prosperous town-dwellers wished to live, and represent themselves to others, in the same way that the fortified houses of Sbeïtla and Belalis Maior do; they are signs of vitality, not weakness. But they are a minority. The subdivided houses and the wooden buildings built precariously on Roman foundations show a clear technological involution, which is greater than that visible in Africa. Italian cities, one can propose, maintained a greater density of settlement and structural coherence than did those of Africa, but that density by now consisted of buildings that were very different from those normal in cities elsewhere in the Mediterranean, and indeed much poorer. It has been argued elsewhere in this book that Italy was substantially damaged by the Gothic and Lombard wars, more seriously than any other region was harmed by war in our period apart from, perhaps, the seventh-century Byzantine heartland (e.g. pp. 34–7). After c.600 Italian aristocracies, although still city-dwelling, were also much less rich in their landed property than those of, in particular, Francia (above, Chapter 4). These patterns line up with those described in this chapter. Italy's cities maintained their classical spatial structure, but were unusually poor, in the same way that Italy's political and territorial structures changed rather less than those of elsewhere, and its aristocrats changed their habits less than elsewhere, but were all much poorer.

The seventh-century crisis in the Byzantine heartland produced a process in which the continuing force of the state, and the attraction of its hierarchies, accelerated the abandonment of most of its classical cities, with urban elites concentrating in a smaller number of centres. This process did not occur in Italy, whether Byzantine or Lombard; here, by contrast, cities tended only to fail in economically marginal areas like the southern Appennines, the Alps, or the underpopulated coast of southern Tuscany. In richer areas they persisted in, at times, quite dense networks, as with the southern Exarchate and Pentapolis in the Byzantine lands, or northern Tuscany in the Lombard lands.[150] The reorganization of the Byzantine state in its heartland was much more centralized than in Italy (except in Sicily, above, p. 125; urban archaeology in our period is unfortunately almost absent there); the various sectors of Byzantine power in the peninsula were arguably more conservative than in the Aegean and Anatolian areas, and also steadily drifted away from imperial control. The local state was weaker as well; tax-raising slowly broke down even in Byzantine areas, as it had done in the Lombard kingdom by 600 (pp. 115–17), thus further decreasing the economic hegemony of even local power centres, Rome or Ravenna or Naples. There was thus no obvious reason for a notable from (say) Senigallia to be tempted to relocate to (say) Ravenna, and even less for any such 'rationalization' to

[150] See above, n. 139, for failed cities.

take place in the Lombard lands. City elites, whether rich or poor, stayed in their own cities, and their heirs would eventually act as the core of the autonomous city-based polities of later centuries, urban polities which had no parallel either in the states of the southern and eastern Mediterranean or in the fragmented rural lordships of tenth-century Francia.

Urban Italy was thus both materially poor and culturally conservative in the early middle ages. Signs of this are the praise-poems for Milan (739) and Verona (c.800), which are highly unusual in the centuries after 600 as specific panegyrics of the fabric of cities, with few parallels anywhere in the former empire. (Constantinople and Rome both have them, although in each case they are peculiar texts, with no generic parallels. Alcuin's poem on York spends most of its space on the qualities of local bishops, and very little on the urban fabric. The only other example known to me is the Anglo-Saxon poem *The Ruin*, a nostalgic evolution of barely comprehensible glory.) They praise the walls, the forum, the streets, an aqueduct (in Milan), the amphitheatre (in Verona), and the network of churches in both, in the same way that late Roman panegyrists like Ausonius and Sidonius had—the only novelty was the churches, generally ignored in the late Roman tradition. But, as we have seen, they lied about the state of the fora: the classical image they sought to present evidently did not have to have be directly reflected on the ground. Whether this was simply self-deception, or else, more specifically, the tunnel vision of a rich minority, does not really matter; the fact is that, in cities of mud and poor wooden buildings, it was possible to *talk* as if the buildings of imperial Rome were still standing. Paul the Deacon at the end of the eighth century, too, expressed the devastation of a seventh-century epidemic at Pavia in terms of vegetation being allowed to grow on the *forum* and *plateae* of the city: an image of the country invading the city which has exact parallels in the later Roman empire, but which was still resonant in the very different material world of the early middle ages in Italy. Italian conservatism maintained classical civic ideals, and thus, by extension, the concept of urban living for its elites, through the greatest economic crisis in the history of the peninsula.[151] These ideals were still operative in the period of economic

---

[151] See above, n. 134. Cf. for late Rome Ausonius, *Ordo urbium nobilium* (in *Works*, I, pp. 268–84); Sidonius, *Carmen* XXIII, ll. 37–44. For early medieval Rome, the *Itinerarium Einsiedelnense* can be seen as a simple form of prose evocation of buildings; for Constantinople, see *Parastaseis*, *passim*. For England, see Alcuin, *Versus* (only ll. 19, 196, 220–1, refer to the fabric of the city even in a generic way) and *The Ruin*. Note that the praise-poem for Pamplona, ed. Lacarra, 'Textos navarros', pp. 269–70, probably postdates our period (Larrea, *La Navarre*, p. 140 n.). Paul, *HL*, VI.5, the cited text, is evocative of the horror of the ruralized forum of Vienne in c.473 in Sidonius, *Ep.* VII.1.3. Note finally the characterization of the foundation of Taureana in Calabria in the Greek *Life* of S. Pankratios, ed. Veselovskii, *Iz istorii romana*, pp. 103, 107, a life dating to the decades around 800 (Patlagean, 'Les moines grecs', pp. 581–2, 587–9; Ševčenko, 'Hagiography', p. 113 n.), with a fort, aqueducts, cisterns, a wider

revival, and acute political decentralization, which can be clearly seen in the eleventh century at the latest.

Spain in general fits the western version of the Mediterranean model that is beginning to emerge from in these discussions of Italy and Africa. It shows some of the same elements of secular demonumentalization and a concentration of prestige building activity on churches that is visible in both East and West, but beginning in the fifth century rather than later. In the cities with most prosperity and demographic continuity, a spatial conservatism at least as great as in Italy can sometimes be seen, although, like Africa, no recourse to building in wood has yet been identified in urban excavations, even if the tendency to much simpler construction techniques, on the lines of the western rather than the eastern Mediterranean, seems fairly clear.[152] (Spain and Africa, it should be noted, have less woodland than Italy.) It is harder to offer a clear-cut account of Spanish urbanism in the fifth to eighth centuries than for Italy, however, or even than for Africa. First, because there has simply been less archaeology. Only half-a-dozen classical cities have excavations with substantial results dating from this period—Barcelona, Tarragona, Valencia, Cartagena, Córdoba, Mérida, all of them discussed later, being the main ones. Second, because the extreme geographical and socio-economic heterogeneities of the Iberian peninsula made the fortunes of cities equally diverse, with some sub-regions showing substantial continuities at least in some places (parts of Catalonia and Andalucía, for example, and even, conceivably, Galicia), while others, such as the south-east, show sharp breaks: this, added to the small number of sites and the swift changes in Spanish archaeology at the moment, makes generalization dangerous. Third, because the issue of urban survival has traditionally been (as in Africa) tied up with generalizing assessments of the effects of invasion, in this case by Visigoths and Arabs/Berbers, which were here initially made without any reference to archaeology, and which continue to structure a good deal of the debate even though archaeology can now make a contribution (at least up to the seventh century; the eighth, as in Africa, is little known). But it must also be said that debate on the urban question has been muted, much more so than have arguments about the political and demographic impact of invaders of the peninsula; few syntheses of early medieval

---

fortification, and subsequently luxury houses and baths, i.e. rather more like a classical city in imagery, or the Milan and Verona poems, than anything in contemporary Anatolia. See Noyé, 'Economie et societé', p. 262.

[152] The basic current discussion of the use of wood in Spain, Azcarate and Quirós, 'Arquitectura doméstica', only discusses rural sites for this period. It may only be a matter of time before wooden buildings are discovered in Spanish cities, but stone buildings are still more prominent than in Italy, however basic they are: see Ramallo, 'Arquitectura doméstica en ámbitos urbanos', for a recent survey.

urbanism in Spain have even been attempted.[153] For all these reasons, I shall adopt a sub-regional approach, looking at, in turn, the north-east, the south-east, Andalucía, and the Meseta and the north-west.

As in Italy, one can take an optimistic or a pessimistic view of urban continuity in the north-east, according to taste. Valencia is a good example: here, the forum (the main area excavated) maintained its centrality and even its secular monumentality into the sixth century, with the *curia* rebuilt then and another large building still standing. There was some breakdown of tradition, even so, as when the portico around the forum was filled in with reused material, probably for shops (the date of this is unclear), and one of the other major buildings on the forum, the *macellum*, was abandoned around 450 and replaced by a cemetery; but in the sixth or seventh century a large ecclesiastical complex in turn replaced the cemetery, which may well have been the cathedral. Into the seventh century, then, the forum of Valencia remained a focus for substantial monumental interventions, including ecclesiastical ones, more so indeed than in most cities in the Mediterranean. Conversely, little or nothing has as yet been found in the rest of the town. Is this a sign of a reduction in population solely to that central monumental group? Or is it insignificant as an observation, given the wealth and continuing urban style of the forum area, and the sketchy nature of archaeological intervention elsewhere? And is the absence of eighth-century evidence in the city (the Islamic material begins in the ninth) a sign of terminal decline, or just of our ignorance of the diagnostic signs of the period? These sorts of arguments are reminiscent of the way the debate ran in Italy in about 1985, and I am sure that in Spain it will be resolved one way or the other in the next decade; here, more than elsewhere, we are as yet on the cusp.[154]

Anyway, Valencia is not the only source of evidence in this sub-region of Spain. Certainly, Tarragona offers some parallels. This city, a major provincial capital of the empire, had two secular monumental foci at the start of our period, one for the provincial governor in the upper town, and one for the city in the lower town. By the late empire, the lower town seems to have been in retreat, with the municipal forum in trouble as early as the late fourth century; the rather smaller upper town is the only well-documented settlement area in the city in our period. Even here, however, we have conflicting signals: a public inscription in the provincial forum as late as 470, some repaving in the sixth century, but also a major rubbish dump of

---

[153] Recent partial syntheses include Ramallo, op. cit.; Gurt *et al.*, 'Topografía de la antigüedad tardía hispánica'; Fuentes, 'Aproximación'; Arce, 'La transformación; Gutiérrez, 'De la *civitas* a la *madīna*'; Kennedy, 'From Antiquity to Islam'. The implicit debate between Arce (more optimistic) and Gutiérrez (more pessimistic) has not really been developed.

[154] A recent Valencia synthesis for the monumental centre is Albiach *et al.*, 'Las últimas excavaciones'; an earlier one, Blasco *et al.*, 'Estat actual', discusses the rest of the city as well. For ninth-century material, Pascual *et al.*, 'València', pp. 186-8, 326-8.

around 450. The area seems to have been largely converted to housing by the Visigothic period, with a cathedral complex established a little to its north above a former temple. Elsewhere in the lower town we find several fifth- and sixth-century churches, one in the former amphitheatre still in use in the seventh century, which are evident signs of wealth and patronage (and also of the demonumentalization of the amphitheatre), but with an unclear relationship to areas of settlement. Overall, it would be reasonable to propose post-Roman Tarragona as a relatively fragmented *città ad isole*, especially as a recent excavation also shows occupation into the late seventh century in the port area. As at Valencia, nothing has yet been found for the eighth, or for some time thereafter.[155]

This impression of steady demographic retreat despite some monumental continuity, the former winning out over the latter after 700 or so, can be countered in Barcelona. This is a city which has kept part of its Roman street plan inside its huge fifth-century walls, where the cathedral and the adjoining secular administrative area were foci of monumental building in the sixth century, and again in the tenth, allowing a continuity of use to be proposed; the forum area remained active at least into the seventh, with two churches built beside it, though its monumental identity was probably by now diminished. The rich residential houses of the fourth and fifth centuries in the northern part of the town were subdivided, using simpler construction techniques, in the sixth and seventh, but remained occupied. The southern part of the city, closest to the port, may not have fared so well, and throughout the city the eighth century is no more visible than elsewhere, but the odds are here on a maintenance of the city's urbanism into the ninth century, when it became the political capital of Carolingian Catalonia.[156] On the coast north of Barcelona, Empuries, too, has recently been argued to have stayed prosperous until 700, although nearby Roses seems to have hit trouble (and the end of a substantial fish-processing plant) at the end of the sixth century.[157] Moving inland, finally, we could add to this series Zaragoza, a city with only fragmentary excavation so far but with seventh-century levels found on at least three occasions, and another surviving Roman square-plan; this city remained a significant political centre for both Visigoths and Arabs, a location for Braulio's episcopal dynasty (above, p. 223), and, plausibly, it retained an urban identity in economic terms as well.[158]

---

[155] Keay, 'Tarraco', summarizes work up to 1995. For the repaving of the upper forum and the port excavation, see Vilaseca and Diloli, 'Excavacions', and Adserias *et al.*, 'L'hàbitat suburbà portuari'.

[156] See the surveys of Banks, 'Roman inheritance'; Gurt and Godoy, '*Barcino*'; and Bonnet and Beltrán, 'El primer grupo episcopal', with iidem, 'Nuevas intervenciones'.

[157] Nolla, 'Ampurias'; Nolla, 'Excavaciones recientes en la ciudadela de Roses'.

[158] Paz, 'El bajo imperio', pp. 275–6, gives a guide to 1980s excavations.

It should be clear that in all these cities our evidence is incomplete. Civic buildings do tend to give way to ecclesiastical ones in this sub-region, as elsewhere; a continuing coherence for civic centres that is rather greater than elsewhere is, however, marked by the fact that cathedrals tended to be located on or fairly near to fora. What we cannot be sure about as yet is the demographic back-up to these monuments. It must be observed that all these centres, most of them coastal, imported substantial quantities of African oil and, to a lesser extent, African table wares and eastern Mediterranean products, right up to the end of large-scale Mediterranean sea traffic in the late seventh century: someone had the money to buy them in the north-eastern Spanish cities (below, pp. 748–9). It may be that such people survived in the eighth century, when that traffic—and thus datable ceramics in urban levels—ceased: a continuitist reading of Valencia and Tarragona (both of them, after all, still situated on their Roman sites) certainly cannot be excluded. In regions of the Mediterranean whose scholars are less preoccupied with caesuras, it is likely that there would be no dispute about it.

Whatever we make of the north-east, the south-east is by comparison desolate. Cartagena, another Roman provincial capital and major port, and between 552 and c.628 capital of the thin coastal strip that made up Byzantine Spain, was modestly prosperous up to the Visigothic reconquest, in the same sort of way as Tarragona: much smaller, and with fewer public buildings, than in the first and second centuries, but capable of importing very large amounts of goods from Africa. Its theatre was abandoned in the fifth century, but by the late sixth housed an active quarter of stone houses and shops, each of them small and simple but competently built. This sort of functional activity recalls the southern and eastern Mediterranean, although in this case it may have been created artificially by the needs of the Byzantine public administration. The Visigothic reconquest certainly was harmful: there are no subsequent signs of any urban activity at all until a small-scale reoccupation around 900, even though this is a section of Spain whose eighth-century ceramics are known.[159] Overall, in the wider hinterland of Cartagena, the territory called Tudmīr in the eighth century, cities in that period were mostly by then pretty small, even though some of them were new developments of the sixth and seventh centuries (notably El Tolmo de Minateda, the best-excavated). Nor did this urban network last: the tenth-century territorial structure of the area was based on a largely different urban pattern, focused on Murcia, a new foundation of 825.[160]

A breakdown of the ancient city network seems to be a feature of the whole Spanish coast between Valencia and Málaga (a city which seems, like

---

[159] Recent syntheses are Ramallo, '*Carthago Spartaria*'; Ramallo and Ruiz, 'Cartagena'.

[160] See in general Gutiérrez, *La cora de Tudmīr*, pp. 222–74, 308–11; eadem, 'De la *civitas* a la *madīna*'. The most recent interims for El Tolmo are Abad *et al.*, 'La basílica y el baptisterio'; Gutiérrez, 'El espacio doméstico'; Abad *et al.*, 'La ciudad visigoda'; and Gutiérrez *et al.*, 'Los contextos cerámicos'.

Cartagena, to have enjoyed a period of prosperity in the sixth century, but, unlike Cartagena, seems to have survived, on a much reduced scale). Murcia's development from nothing is matched further south by that of Pechina, established by the 850s, and itself later replaced by Almería. The background to these ruptures has been convincingly argued by Sonia Gutiérrez to be a slow dissolution of urbanism itself between c.600 and c.800.[161] This is matched by a simplification of the material culture of the sub-region from the early seventh century onwards (below, pp. 749–51), and therefore, doubtless, a considerable impoverishment of local elites. We will return to why this was so in the next chapter. The important point to be made here, however, is that it contrasts notably with the sub-region north of Valencia, where the urban network has mostly been preserved, and also arguably with Valencia itself, where, although the eighth century is as yet invisible in the city, a local elite was rich enough to build one of Europe's most impressive rural secular buildings of the seventh/eighth centuries, Pla de Nadal, some 15 km out of town (above, p. 478). It is this sort of contrast that makes generalization so hard in Spain, for why local elites should be so much weaker around Cartagena than around Valencia cannot easily be explained. Conversely, however, the link between the strength or weakness of local elites and the strength or weakness of urbanism, here too, seems a piste that is worth pursuing.

If there was anywhere in which one would expect strong urban continuities in Spain, it would be in the traditional agrarian powerhouse of Baetica (Andalucía), the Guadalquivir valley, to which I shall attach Mérida, just to its north in the Guadiana plain, capital of the whole of Spain in 400. Even here, it has to be recognized, there are uncertainties. The late Roman mining town of Cástulo in the upper Guadalquivir valley failed as an urban centre by the Visigothic period at the latest, and was replaced by Baeza, although there are no signs of urban characteristics in the latter until the ninth or tenth centuries. Granada's ancestry is exceptionally obscure, and it has recently become clearer that its predecessor, the classical city of Elvira, was not in the same location. Conversely, Seville was always a major centre, although it is almost totally unexcavated; Écija, a little to its east, at least keeps its Roman street plan; and the two foci for recent urban archaeology, Córdoba and Mérida, beyond doubt constituted significant urban centres throughout our period.[162] Córdoba is anomalous, for it was the capital of Arab Spain, with

---

[161] For Málaga, Navarro *et al.*, '*Malaca* bizantina'; I have not seen Salado *et al.*, 'Evolución urbana'. For Pechina, Castillo *et al.*, 'Urbanismo e industria'; Castillo and Martínez, 'La vivienda hispanomusulmana'. In general, Gutiérrez, 'De la *civitas* a la *madīna*'.

[162] For Cástulo and Baeza, see the surveys, with bibliography, in Castillo, *La campiña de Jaén*, pp. 290–1, 234–6. Jaén itself developed as an urban centre as late as the tenth century: see the survey in Salvatierra, 'The formation process'. For Granada, see Malpica, *Granada*, with his recent excavations on the cerro del Sombrerete, 'Intervención arqueológica'; but the hinterland of Granada at least maintained a relatively complex economy (below, p. 744). Seville has several generic overviews; Valor, 'La estructura urbana', is useful.

its great mosque taking over a large percentage of the former Roman city, and its urban expansion in the ninth and (especially) the tenth century so precipitous as to overwhelm all previous building (Córdoba has lost its Roman plan, as has Seville). At least we can say that this city had been rich before the Arabs came, as the recent excavation of the huge extramural palace complex of Cercadilla (built c.300, although partially abandoned c.550) shows.[163] But how Córdoba developed in the Visigothic period, between its two major periods of public building, is not as yet sufficiently clear; let us therefore focus our attention on Mérida.

Mérida is the best example in Spain of the sort of standard, low-key urban continuity that is increasingly regarded as characteristic of Italy, and indeed some of the signs of it are materially more complex than have usually been found in Italy. Mérida is another city that has largely kept its street plan. Judging by the *Vitas patrum Emeritensium*, the seventh-century history of its bishops, the cathedral complex and adjoining ducal palace were its focal point in the sixth century, not the forum area, though they were probably only a block away, still in the centre of the city; some solid post-Roman buildings have been found on the forum, however. An alternative ritual centre was the extramural martyrial complex of S. Eulalia, built in the fifth century and recently excavated, by far the most important out of several extramural churches. Even so, the emphasis on S. Eulalia in the *Vitas patrum* gives the clear impression that it was integrated into the community of a coherent and populated city, full among other things of urban aristocrats (above, p. 222), and not in any sense contributing to its destructuration. As in other important but rebellious cities of al-Andalus, the Arab emirs in 835 built an Alcazaba, an intramural fortification, in Mérida; although such constructions could risk, as in Byzantine Africa, the further fragmentation of the spatial structures of cities, this one largely respected the Roman street plan. As for private housing, there are some archaeological signs of fifth-century destructions (Hydatius implies that the city was attacked by Suevi in 429); more important, however, is the recent excavation in the Morería in the south-west corner of the city, which shows a substantial Roman peristyle house divided up into single-room residences, each with its own hearth, in the Visigothic period. This was razed in the late seventh or early eighth century and turned into a dump, before the rebuilding there in the ninth century of a series of notably high-quality houses, which have regular plans, but partially break the Roman street alignment. Mérida was clearly always occupied (even the eighth-century evidence fits that, as the dump shows there was occupation elsewhere); the sixth to eighth centuries may show a

---

[163] For Córdoba syntheses, Acién and Vallejo, 'Urbanismo', is basic, with Marfil, 'Córdoba', for two sixth-century churches. A sharp-edged account of recent archaeology is Scales, 'Córdoba'. Cercadilla is published in Hidalgo, *Espacio público*; idem *et al.*, *El criptopórtico* (pp. 51–9 for the sixth to tenth centuries).

weakening of the city's prosperity, but there was a clear revival in the ninth.[164] Interestingly, in fact, the quality of the local ceramics on the Morería site show an improvement already in the eighth century (below, p. 744); demand for them may have already increased in the earliest Arab period, and it may be that the city's low point was around 700, not any later. This sort of temporary economic weakening, but continued spatial and demographic coherence, must be seen against the framework of the permanent political importance of the city (at least until its sack as a punishment for revolt in 868, and the foundation of Badajoz to replace it). Such a pattern could plausibly be canvassed for other, unexcavated, political centres of Visigothic and Arab Spain, such as Toledo, Seville, or Zaragoza; it may indeed be the model for how successful towns developed in the peninsula.

In this survey, we have proceeded around the eastern and southern edges of Spain, covering at most 40 per cent of the peninsula. About the other 60 per cent, there is much less to be said. Toledo, as just noted, must have been a major centre, above all in the Visigothic period when it was the capital of Spain, with its dozens of intramural and extramural churches (many with fragments of Visigothic-period decoration), its palaces, and its elaborate ceremonial practice; some of this activity probably persisted after 711, given the prominence of the Toledans, the *ahl Ṭulayṭula*, in the ninth century in particular.[165] One hundred kilometres away, Recópolis, a royal foundation dating to 578, matches Iustiniana Prima and 'Anjar as an insight into early medieval ideals of urbanism: smaller than either, it at least shows a planned structure, with palatine buildings and a church around three sides of a square, the whole protected by monumental walls. (This neat planning broke down in the seventh and eighth centuries, as simpler structures infilled around the surviving monuments.)[166] In the central Meseta, however, the site of Complutum, 80 km north-east of Toledo, provides an example of terminal deurbanization. Here, as elsewhere, after fourth-century prosperity, in the fifth century the city was losing its monumental elements, with the baths and the basilica reused for smaller residential structures, although richer housing still existed into the late sixth century, and a small amount of ceramics has been ascribed to the seventh. After that point, however, nothing of a recognizably urban type has been found at all.[167] Nor is there any sign of

[164] Basic surveys are Mateos, '*Augusta Emerita*', and esp. idem and Alba, 'De *Emerita Augusta* a Marida'. For S. Eulalia, Mateos, *La basilica de S. Eulalia*; for the Morería, Alba, 'Ocupación diacrónica', is a useful interim. For documentary sources, Hydatius, *Chronica*, c. 80, ed. Burgess; *Vitas patrum Emeritensium*, IV.7–9 (for supernatural accounts of religious processions, which show, among other things, S. Eulalia's relation to intramural churches—cf. V.11.2); V.10.8 (for the cathedral and ducal palace).

[165] Velázquez and Ripoll, '*Toletum*', is the basic account of the Visigothic city. For before the Visigoths, Carrobles, 'La ciudad de Toledo'; for the ninth century, Manzano, *La frontera*, pp. 261–310.

[166] The most recent account is Olmo, 'Ciudad y procesos de transformación social'.

[167] Recent syntheses are Rascón, 'La ciudad de Complutum'; Sánchez, 'La antigüedad tardía en Complutum'.

urban survival on a larger scale than this in the northern half of the Meseta; Clunia, the classical city to have had most excavation, seems to have been losing its urban characteristics by 500 as well. Only in the far north-west, in Galicia and northern Portugal, are there some signs of settlement continuity in Roman cities, notably in one of the sites excavated at Braga, where occupation apparently continued between the fifth century and the tenth. It is likely that in this area the major episcopal centres kept their ecclesiastical centrality throughout our period, with perhaps some gestures towards a continuing economic urbanism, but even this is uncertain. In the whole expanse of Spain north of Toledo and west of Zaragoza, Braga is anyway the clearest candidate for this as yet.[168] On the basis of what is known so far, northern Spain could be seen as, for the most part, an entirely rural society by the seventh century at the latest, with few if any signs of an involvement by its elites in the former classical city network; a revival of towns here would have to await the eleventh century.

This account of Spanish urbanism is on one level pretty much what one would expect from the evidence discussed in other chapters. We saw or shall see how localized were the patterns of aristocratic dominance in Chapter 4 (pp. 221–5), the patterns of rural settlement in Chapter 8 (pp. 488–93), and the patterns of ceramic production in Chapter 11 (pp. 741–58); city survival follows the same sort of regional differentiation, with a high point in Andalucía, a low point in the south-east and much (but not all) of the north, and with other sub-regions in between. It was argued in Chapter 8 (p. 478) that late villa survival probably represented, at least in part, the continuance of urban taste in the countryside, and the known areas of that survival might therefore be seen as guides to the areas of the survival of urban elites, at least into the seventh century (after which villa-dwelling ended for other reasons): the Catalan–Valencian coast, the Ebro valley around Zaragoza, the area between Mérida and the Atlantic (doubtless including the less well-studied Guadalquivir valley), and the northern Meseta (above, p. 220). Only the northern Meseta fails to fit with the urban excavations discussed here, and this may mean that future archaeological work, in Palencia or León or Salamanca, will nuance my overall picture of an unurbanized Meseta somewhat, up to 700 at any rate.[169] Future work will also have a major effect on our understanding of the boundaries between these very roughly drawn sub-regions. But the available data is at least reasonably homogeneous: we seem to see the same geographical logic

[168] For Clunia, see the surveys in Palol, *Clunia. Historia de la ciudad*, pp. 21–2, and idem, *Clunia O*, pp. 297–300. For Braga, Gaspar, 'Escavações arqueológicas'; for a survey, Martins and Delgado, 'História e arqueologia', pp. 30–3. For a recent sub-regional survey of the far north-west, see Quiroga and Lovelle, 'Ciudades atlánticas en transición'; they argue tentatively for Lugo too.

[169] For the fragmentary archaeology in cities like these, see Fernández, 'La ciudad'; Abásolo, 'La ciudad'.

operative in each sub-region of Spain. The Visigothic kingdom, and the Arab emirate after it, based most government on the city network. The Visigothic tax system was organized by city territories, as the *De fisco Barcinonensi* of 594 shows (above, pp. 96–7), a text which incidentally locates the Catalan fiscal administration in Barcelona rather than the traditional centre of Tarragona, which may help to explain the fact that the former seems to have survived better than the latter. But neither the Visigoths nor the early Arabs had the institutional force to create an urbanized society where one did not previously exist, and the regional differences stressed in this chapter for Spain probably simply represent what would develop in each city territory for local reasons when the homogenizing force of the Roman fiscal system was removed.

The survival or failure of urbanism in any part of the Iberian peninsula must have been, as elsewhere, essentially dependent on the choices and prosperity of local elites. Often in Spain such elites maintained elements of Roman civilian culture surprisingly late, well into the seventh century at least (above, pp. 94–6, 223), which would probably also support their maintenance of urban living and thus the patronage of urban artisans for as long as elites could afford them. But seventh-century cities were generally less impressive than sixth-century ones, which may indicate that elites were once again becoming poorer, even in places like Mérida or the Catalan coast, where urbanism continued best; in the crisis of the eighth century these elites often presumably continued to lose wealth, and the urban stages of their political activity and spending lost wealth with them. This tendency matches the involution in the patterns of exchange, too (below, pp. 742–51). Where, by contrast, cities weakened substantially, as in the south-east and in much of the Meseta, this could either have been because elites changed their culture and lifestyle, and ruralized themselves (as in northern Francia: below, pp. 674–80), or because their wealth collapsed altogether (as in Britain: see Chapter 6). On ceramic grounds, I would argue the former for at least parts of the Meseta, the latter for the south-east, but the demonstration of that will have to await the next chapter.

It is possible, as in Africa, to map urban changes onto the political history of the Iberian peninsula, notably the successive conquests by Suevi, Visigoths, and Arabs, given that city prosperity here seems to have begun to falter in the fifth century, and reached a low point in the eighth. But the fact that Africa, Italy, and Spain, taken as a whole, follow similar trajectories must at least lessen the tendency to see this involution as 'the fault' of any particular political crisis in Spain. The Visigothic state did not, as far as can be seen, cause great disruption when it occupied the peninsula in the 470s. The political confusion of the years 410–70, and, later, 510–60 (cf. above, pp. 93–4) cannot have helped, it is true; conversely, the Visigoths fitted as closely into pre-existing Roman political structures as they could, and cannot be seen in any systemic conflict with pre-existing elites—far less than the Vandals, indeed. Similarly, the Arab conquest was fairly fast, much faster than in Africa (though also accompanied by instability, particularly in the 740s), and only frontier regions are likely to have suffered permanently as a result of it. It is hard to see any specific political reason for the downward trend of urbanism, that is to say, notwithstanding the catastrophism of some accounts of the seventh century, and many accounts of the eighth. At most, the steady weakening of urban prosperity in the seventh century could be one more reason why the legislation of the centralizing kings of the period is so shrill (above, p. 95): it was one more trend that they could not reverse. Overall, we have to conclude that aristocracies were often already getting poorer despite seventh-century political stabilization (and this in richer and poorer sub-regions alike), and continued to do so after 711 in many places, although not necessarily, it seems to me, at a faster rate.

The other point that comes out of this presentation of the Spanish material is that cities in the peninsula, when they give us usable material, seem to show a maintenance of a monumental centrality that is rather greater than in Italy, and much greater than in Africa. Cathedrals are much more frequently situated on fora, or only a block away from them, and ducal/comital palaces often seem to be close by as well. It may be that these institutions identified themselves more tightly with municipal traditions than elsewhere in the West; this may also fit with the tendency of Spanish urban elites to maintain some of their classical culture for longer than in other regions. Above all, however, it means that, although Spanish cities *could* spatially fragment (Tarragona is the most likely example at present), they were at least not encouraged to fragment by the sort of dislocation of central monumental complexes which we have seen in other regions, and probably, for the most part, they maintained their spatial coherence for longer as a result. This is the major particularity of Spanish urbanism in our period that can easily be seen. Otherwise, when cities survived at all in Spain, they tended to fit the parameters of cities in other regions of the western Mediterranean.

This last sentence fits southern Gaul as well as it does Spain, and south French urban archaeology is also relatively scarce, with substantial excavations for the period after 500 restricted to a handful of sites, Marseille, Geneva, Lyon, only the last-named of which gives us much idea of typical urban building. I shall therefore focus on two examples, Lyon and the less well-excavated Arles, and then sketch the urban development of Gaul from the Mediterranean to the Loire with a fairly broad brush, leading into a summing up of western Mediterranean urban patterns. North of the Loire, Gaul's urbanism was somewhat different, and it will be discussed separately.

Lyon has benefited from quite a lot of archaeological attention recently, and more is likely. The signs are that this city, a major political centre throughout our period with a powerful episcopate, developed by the sixth century into the same sort of spatially fragmented *città ad isole* pattern that can be proposed for Tarragona, with several separate areas of occupation inside the bounds of the sprawling classical city, on both sides of the River Saône, each associated with late Roman churches (some of which were large). One of these, the Quartier St-Jean by the cathedral on the west bank of the river, was densely occupied up to c.600, and less densely in the seventh to ninth centuries, before its revival in the tenth, with reused stone buildings, in one case inside a late Roman bath complex. We seem to be looking at an active town, with access to imported goods up to c.600, and documentary references to merchants in later periods too, but with no surviving monumental focus except the scattered network of churches. But the forum was still a public space in 573; Bishop Nicetius' will was read there, *quos lex Romana sanccivit*, 'which Roman law requires', Gregory of Tours says.[170]

Contrast Arles, another significant episcopal centre with a distinguished imperial past (it was capital of Gaul in the fifth century, and sometimes an imperial residence). Arles has archaeological evidence into the sixth century, but almost nothing so far found after 550. This evidence points different ways: simple (although by no means poor) fifth-century constructions built into the outer walls of the circus, which was probably still in use, but also large palatial buildings which survive to the second floor in the modern Hotel d'Arlatan. But no one has argued that Arles ever lost its status and coherence as an urban centre. Its Roman street plan mostly survives; its cathedral was, or soon came to be, situated close to the forum (although the forum itself was being encroached on by the early fifth century, it was still a significant public space in the 460s, and probably the 530s); although there were extramural churches, the classical walled city was still the main settlement focus in the eleventh century (including a private fortification in the amphitheatre), when extramural bourgs along the river developed. If Lyon was Tarragona (or Brescia), Arles was Mérida (or Lucca or Pavia). The general absence (so far) of seventh- or eighth-century levels in Arles indicates a low point for prosperity, doubtless, but there are no signs of the fragmentation found in Lyon.[171] Both cities were foci for city-based elite activity, which will have contributed demographic weight and commercial demand to their surviving political structures; presumably this was sufficiently great in Arles that a critical mass was maintained throughout the early middle ages, preventing the city from flying apart. (Both were also significant nodes on the Rhône–Saône long-distance route, which must have helped their

---

[170] Villedieu, *Lyon St.-Jean*, pp. 40–56, 110–16; Arlaud *et al.*, *Lyon St.-Jean*, pp. 17–19, 42–50; see further the survey in Reynaud, *Lugdunum christianum*, esp. pp. 186–201. For Nicetius, Gregory of Tours, *VP*, VIII.5. A documentary history is Coville, *Recherches*, traditional but full.

[171] Loseby, 'Arles'; Heijmans and Sintès, 'L'évolution', pp. 151–68 (pp. 155–6 for the Hotel d'Arlatan); Heijmans, 'La topographie'. Jean Guyon notes that the buildings infilling the circus had gold coins: 'De la ville', p. 576.

prosperity, even if there is little enough archaeological sign of it as yet after 600.) We cannot tell why this was so in Arles and not Lyon, but we can at least register that both patterns of development were possible in important south Gaulish cities.

The best that one can say of the rest of the cities of the south is that they seem to have lined up with either Arles or Lyon if they were prosperous, or, if they were not, they became much reduced, to a small fortified area (usually around the cathedral), with at most a scatter of settlement elsewhere, but with fewer signs of a generalized breakdown in urban networks than in the materially simpler parts of Spain. Marseille, the main port of Gaul in the sixth and seventh centuries, must have been very successful indeed up to the end of the western Mediterranean exchange network in the late seventh, judging by the excavations in its harbour area. These give little guidance about Marseille's general urban development, but they show intense activity beside the port, both inside and just outside the city's walls, and the availability of a full range of African goods there. What happened in the eighth century cannot yet be said, but Marseille, although much poorer than before, probably maintained an urban coherence parallel to that of Arles. So may Geneva, whose huge cathedral complex, continually rebuilt in every century except the eighth, dominated the (admittedly fairly small) late Roman walled town, and also Toulouse, another city with a partially surviving Roman plan and fragmentary archaeological support for later occupation in several parts of the Roman city.[172] Aix-en-Provence may have been more like Lyon; the most serious excavation has been around the cathedral, which was actually built on part of the forum complex in c.500, but its later history indicates several separate foci for urban activity, which may originate in our period. Further north, so may Poitiers, where a scatter of late Roman and early medieval monuments still persist.[173] Clermont may as well: its late wall was tiny, but the evidence for its urban aristocrats is so extensive (above, pp. 167–8, 171) that one might—at least until serious excavation has taken place—postulate a wider settlement than the wall indicates; its numerous extramural churches support that view. Other reduced enceintes, however, at Rodez or St-Bertrand-de-Comminges, seem to show a real restriction in occupation: at St-Bertrand starting in the fifth century, when the lower town seems to have begun to lose its population; at Rodez not until after the late sixth, the date of a house in the forum portico.[174]

---

[172] Marseille: Loseby, 'Marseille', I and II; Bonifay *et al.*, *Fouilles à Marseille*, esp. pp. 195–6, 355–78; Bouiron, 'La trame urbaine médiévale'. Geneva: Bonnet, *Les fouilles*. Toulouse: Guyon, 'Toulouse'; Pailler, *Tolosa*, pp. 418–21, 445–53.

[173] Aix: Guyon *et al.*, *Atlas*, I, pp. 293–8; cf. Février, *Le développement urbain*, pp. 76, 97–8, 120–2, a topographical classic. Poitiers: Maurin, *Topographie chrétienne*, X, pp. 66–92 (B. Boissavit-Camus).

[174] Clermont: see e.g. Fournier, 'Clermont-Ferrand'; Prévot, *Topographie chrétienne*, VI, pp. 27–40 (building in stone is referred to in the seventh century in the *Passio Praejecti*, c. 11). Rodez: Catalo *et al.*, 'Le forum de Rodez'. St-Bertrand: most recently, Esmonde-Cleary, 'The late Roman defences'; P. Aupert *et al.*, '*Lugdunum* des Convènes'.

The southern half of Gaul was a network of city territories, which in the Merovingian period had rich aristocracies (above, pp. 169–78), powerful bishops, and communities with enough sense of local loyalty that they were capable of fighting each other.[175] The bishops were certainly city-dwelling, and some had considerable ambitions as builders, such as Desiderius of Cahors, who built, his life proudly notes, 'in the style of the ancients, not our Gaulish style', with squared stone; among other things, he repaired the city's aqueduct.[176] These features are not in themselves enough to create urban societies; the bishops, although often rich and by definition city-dwelling, were only one focus for wealth, and might in some cases have been presiding over empty shells of former cities, however much they rebuilt their own living quarters. (This might indeed be true in Geneva; only excavations elsewhere in the city will be able to test it.) We have also seen, however, that at least a percentage of the secular aristocracy still lived in cities in southern Gaul (pp. 606–7), and this percentage will have sometimes provided the economic coherence, the critical mass, to allow for a more wide-ranging urban survival, whether spatially focused or more fragmented into *isole*: Gaulish/Frankish aristocrats could, after all, be very rich and large-scale indeed, with all the entourage and buying-power that this implies. How many cities this actually applied to, however, and what level of wealth we are really talking about, will have to await future work.

The eastern Mediterranean regions offered us a coherent field of study, largely thanks to the clarity of the Syro-Palestinian and probably Egyptian model of demonumentalized economic and spatial continuity in cities; this could be set against the greater discontinuities, but arguably state-influenced ones, in the Byzantine heartland after 600/650. The western Mediterranean is more heterogeneous. The four regions we have looked at had quite divergent histories from as early as the fifth century: quite different state structures, different periods of crisis and war, different economic trajectories. There are considerable variations in the history of western Mediterranean urbanism from region to region as a result, and indeed, as is particularly clear in Spain, inside quite small subsections of regions as well. We need to end this account by asking whether there are any common elements in urban development in the western Mediterranean, or, conversely, any sets of divergences that can be explained regionally or sub-regionally: for it is these patterns that justify the setting out of the empirical material of this section.

---

[175] Local armies: Gregory of Tours, *LH*, VI.31, VII.2, etc. See in general for sixth-century urbanism Gauthier, 'Le paysage urbain'; Loseby, 'Gregory's cities'.
[176] *Vita Desiderii*, cc. 16, 17, 20, 25, 31 (quote); Desiderius, *Ep.* I.13. See Durliat, 'Les attributions civiles'.

One development that western Mediterranean cities had in common with the East was a generalized decrease in importance of the forum area, which often also meant the abandonment or reuse of its monuments. The fact that this development generally coincides with a decrease in the political and economic importance of municipal *curiae* does not seem to be chance; political and monumental interventions normally went with the loci of effective power, and these were moving to cathedral complexes, governors' palaces, and indeed private houses, as informal elites replaced the formal institutions of the past. One cannot be schematic about this; one could in principle have an active *curia* and a demonumentalized forum at the same time, as we saw in the context of sixth-century Italy. All the same, the traditional locus of city government was being bypassed, in terms of both material presence and legal/fiscal role, and the two are unlikely to be unrelated. In the West, there seem to have been two models for what replaced it. One was a set of islands of monumental activity, focused above all on church buildings, often on the edges of the classical town, which as time went on became more and more separate in terms of urban activity as well (the *città ad isole*). The other was a more focused version of the same process, in which the new churches and other monuments were closer together (thus sometimes making a new centre), or else closer to the old forum area (this meant the least topographical change), or else were linked together by a stronger urban fabric. We have seen that the first of these was commoner in Gaul and Africa, the second commoner in Spain and Italy, although both can be found in every region. I have linked this to a greater strength of municipal traditions in the second model, while being aware that there are likely to be other explanations as well, at least in some cases. Each model was, however, stable in itself, and, as in the East, did not represent an 'inferior' form of urbanism to that of the early empire. The weakening of forum areas and urban recession as a whole have frequently been linked by historians and archaeologists, but this is a misreading. There was often little or no gap between the two processes, in the West at least, but they must nonetheless be seen as distinct. The wealth of the spatially decentralized churches of late Roman and Vandal Africa makes the point on its own: ambitious and wealthy patrons were using churches to make major monumental statements, even if (usually) no longer in forum areas.

Urban recession in economic terms did, however, take place in the West too. One common western Mediterranean trend is that cities consistently ran into trouble in the fifth century, and not, as in the East, in the seventh or (at the earliest) the late sixth. From this point onwards, houses began to be rebuilt with poorer masonry or to be subdivided, public spaces of all kinds began to be encroached on, and (in some cases) the urban fabric began to fragment spatially or the population lessened. Such signs of trouble appear at different moments in the fifth century, it is true, and they have different meanings, as we shall see in a moment. Overall, however, in all our western regions the fifth century marks the beginning of a generalized involution in urban prosperity, which continued, at varying speeds, down to a low point in, usually, the eighth century, after which we can often see a revival. This consistent general trend, no matter how diverse its specific versions in our regions, imposes general explanations. I have been stressing aristocratic urban living as a variable, and we shall return to it in a moment, but it must be recognized, before we do, that what the regional differences in aristocratic urbanism and private wealth do is create distinctions in the *way* cities weakened locally; the ultimate background to that generalized weakening must have macroeconomic explanations, which must be, furthermore, specific to the western Mediterranean, for the history of the East was different.

These explanations seem to me to be twofold, and linked: the break-up of the fiscal coherence of the western Roman empire, both as a single unit and inside each of the successor-states; and the slow simplification of the wider patterns of exchange in the western Mediterranean. These are discussed at length elsewhere, in Chapters 3 and 11, but they converge in the history of cities, as much as they do in the history of state-building or of ceramics. Actually, since only a few cities were really closely dependent on interregional exchange for their prosperity (Marseille being the only major example discussed in this section), I would put more weight on the fiscal argument. One could put it, baldly, like this: the fifth century is the period in which the fiscal system of each region of the West began its slow breakdown, as conquering Germanic elites settled on the land, and also the period in which the collection of taxes, one of the most secure forms of the accumulation of wealth in the later Roman empire, began for the first time to bypass cities. The fact that it is also the period in which the material fabric of western cities began to decay simply illustrates the degree to which late Roman urban prosperity was itself tied up in the networks of the state. Meanwhile, although the slow breakdown of exchange structures was more marginal in its effects, it did at least contribute directly to the ways in which cities could maintain themselves. If, for example, the marble trade declined (which it did, from the fifth century in the West, the seventh in the East), then it would hardly be surprising that urban builders began to strip and reuse the marble from older, disused, buildings—which would, of course, also contribute to a further decrease in the cutting of new marble, as spolia began to be seen as normal, and perhaps even desirable, architectural features.[177] The involution in exchange was, also, not just interregional but local; artisans are much less visible in western cities in our period than in

[177] For the marble trade, see e.g. Sodini, 'Le commerce des marbres'. For the aesthetics of spolia in the medieval West, see Greenhalgh, *Survival*, pp. 119–44, and several articles in *Ideologie e pratiche del reimpiego*, II = *Settimane di Studio*, XLVI.2.

eastern ones. But this issue belongs with the next chapter, and will be discussed there.

Against this backdrop of slow macroeconomic simplification, the differences between our regions seem best explained through differences in the behaviour of aristocrats, who, even though they were generally less rich in the early middle ages than in the late empire, remained the only big spenders, the only people capable of paying for entourages, and for artisans to clothe them and to decorate their houses; that is to say, for the basic demographic elements in any successful city, once the fiscal support to the urban economies of the Roman empire was removed. We must add to the basic network of the privately wealthy the dukes/counts, the bishops, and the abbots and abbesses who were based in cities, for their wealth was essentially drawn from the same source as that of the aristocracy, that is to say, landowning. Local secular governors and leading clerics were important in a different way, too: as the dominant monumental builders of the early middle ages, whose choices created the spatial structures of the cities of the end of the period. We thus have two closely related sets of variables: the wealth, taste, and interest in urban living of the rich; and the spatial symbolism of the buildings of local governors and bishops, the 'Christian topography' of cities as it is often called, reflecting the undoubted fact that most monumental buildings were by now churches.

These sets of variables, I believe, are the major elements that help to explain the regional differences we have seen in the western Mediterranean. We have already seen a broad distinction between Spain and Italy on one side and Africa and Gaul on the other in terms of late Roman monumental building; into the post-Roman period, this distinction was maintained (many of the buildings were, of course, the same), and was even accentuated. In parts of Spain, bishops and governors had their prestige buildings in the same places, often quite close to the old monumental centre of the forum; in Italy this could happen as well, but less close to fora—although fora maintained a certain centrality, at least as markets. In Africa, and also in Gaul as Carl-Richard Brühl has argued,[178] cathedrals and secular centres were less often linked; in Frankish Gaul they could even sometimes be seen as in spatial competition, and in Byzantine Africa, on the occasions when the secular power fortified a central area of a city, a clear division was created between a secular focus and the wider scatter of churches (in Gaul, when urban fortresses were built, they were by contrast *around* cathedrals). It would not be surprising, in the light of this contrast, if the fragmented *città ad isole* pattern was more common in Africa and Gaul than in Spain and Italy, even though the Italians actually invented the term.

As for aristocratic choices: in the whole of the West, the clearest documentation for urban aristocrats is in Italy, and this is the region where

---

[178] Brühl, 'The town as a political centre', pp. 424–6.

generalized urban survival is most clearly visible in our archaeology. But Italian aristocrats were not, after the crisis of the sixth century in the peninsula, rich; hence the poverty of these surviving cities. Aristocrats in Gaul remained much richer, but were less fully committed to urban living, even in the south; the unimpressive urbanism that archaeologists have so far found there does not necessarily reflect the most important concentrations of wealth in the region. We have little documentary back-up to tell us about the choices of Spanish aristocrats, which must anyway have been very locally heterogeneous, but I would suppose that they sometimes followed the patterns of Italy (as at Mérida—indeed, Mérida was probably richer than most Italian cities), sometimes those of Gaul. In Africa, too, we only have the archaeology, but using the other regions as analogies we could conclude that African aristocrats remained generally city-dwelling, although not exceptionally wealthy. It must be added that the possibility remains that a rich, urban-dwelling aristocratic elite, closely linked to the church and to secular government, could in principle have replicated in a city of the West the continued material prosperity of eastern cities such as Gerasa or Bostra (even if we exclude those most closely connected with state power, such as Damascus). There were doubtless very few such cities, and none have yet been found, but that does not mean that there were none. Western capitals, Ravenna or Pavia or Toledo, are one possible group (we have seen that Carthage partially fits this up to 650, although it, of course, had the eastern empire behind it). It is not inconceivable that other examples might be located as well: probably not in Italy, where rich aristocrats are close to invisible, but maybe in Aquitaine or Andalucía. If they ever are, however, they will remain exceptional in the West; they would be the possible product of an atypical combination of circumstances, not a model for elsewhere, as in parts of the East.

Two general points conclude this section. The first concerns our understanding of the concept of 'decline', a much-used but unpleasantly value-laden word. We have seen several different versions of the weakening of the material forms of cities, and they do not at all have the same significance: (i) the demonumentalization (or abandonment) of forum areas; (ii) the lessening of monumental building in general; (iii) the fragmentation or destructuration of the spatial coherence of cities, potentially creating *isole* of settlement with unoccupied land between them; (iv) the division of large buildings into smaller houses; (v) the use of simpler construction techniques in building (perhaps including reused material, although this can simply be an aesthetic choice, or else less permanent materials); (vi) the end of the maintenance of public amenities such as roads or sewers; (vii) the beginning of intramural burial; (viii) the straightforward abandonment of urban areas or their conversion to agricultural use. Except for the last named, none of these need indicate urban weakness in itself: (i), as we have seen, does not indicate anything other than a change in city government—although maybe it sometimes involves a new ruling elite who are less interested in 'civic' responsibility, resulting in (vi), as sometimes in the East; (ii) may only indicate changes in the rhetoric of display, with interior decorations replacing external fitments and physical size as rhetorical gestures; (iii) may only indicate a fragmentation in the patterns of urban identity and leadership; (iv) indicates, usually, that the rich are less rich (as (ii) may do as well), but not necessarily that fewer people live in the city; (v) indicates, usually, that there are fewer specialized construction-workers, but this too may only be a marker of the weakening of aristocratic patronage, not of the vitality of urban activity; as for (vii), the least discussed here, it certainly does not mean more than an ideological change, the end of the Roman fear of the dead in settled areas, rather than being a sign of the end of settlement in any given area. There are, it must be remembered, plenty of notably unpublic, unmonumental, indeed chaotic, but highly active cities in the modern Third World, which might not be the preferred residential choices for academics (the heirs in some respects of the senatorial elite of the fourth century), but which nonetheless fit all economic criteria for urbanism.

It seems to me that we must recognize both the polyvalency of changes of this kind, and, at the same time, the implications of their accumulation. We have usually found several of them present in any individual urban case study; put together, they may represent different sorts of cultural change, but they do also mean a steady weakening of the fabric of a city. Indeed, as cities fly apart spatially and lose both their wealthy patrons and their artisanal expertise, they might lose the characteristics that might allow us to call them urban at all (above, p. 593). We shall see that there are examples of Roman cities in northern Gaul that, for a time at least, crossed the boundary between the urbanized and the deurbanized; and the failed cities of Spain or Britain probably broke down in exactly that sort of way, steadily losing their characteristics one by one, until my minima for urbanism, a relative population density and economic activities that were different from those of the countryside, ceased to apply. Even where this did not occur, a city with several of these changes was, in most cases, less prosperous than a city without them: the urban values of the Roman world had not changed so much that people no longer respected impressive public monuments, for example, and patrons still built them when they could, as did Charlemagne at Aachen or the Umayyad emirs at Córdoba. In this framework, it does seem to me legitimate to see the eighth century as clearly urbanistically weaker than the fourth in the western Mediterranean, even in the cities that had survived as urban centres in an economic sense. The indicators were still pointing downwards in the eighth century; how they may have been later reversed we shall see in the next chapter.

The final point concerns my two minimum criteria themselves. Non-agrarian activities, such as markets and artisans, are something we have evidence for; we shall look at them in the next chapter. But how we assess demographic density in the early middle ages is much more difficult. There have been many figures offered for the population of early medieval towns; they have all been fabricated. There are no reliable figures for any population centre between the reasonably well-founded (but all the same widely divergent) calculations for late imperial Rome and Constantinople (see above, p. 73) and those for England in Domesday Book in 1086. Contemporary figures are otherwise entirely rhetorical; modern calculations have been made up out of wholecloth, and can either be ludicrously optimistic or implausibly pessimistic. I shall abstain from offering examples, and will restrict myself to an order of magnitude of my own. If Pisa, after a century and more of rapid growth, had around 25,000 inhabitants in 1228, then it probably had only some 10,000 inhabitants in the eleventh century, and in previous centuries it, and probably every single other western city outside Rome (and, after 900, Córdoba), will have had less.[179] But how much less? We simply cannot say. What we have to recognize at least, however, is the force of *relative* rises, *relative* declines. Overall, the increasingly restricted wealth of urban elites in the early middle ages everywhere meant that their buying-power was less, and that the numbers of their dependants and suppliers will have dropped: this represents a demographic decline relative to the late Roman world, even if we cannot calculate its dimensions. One significant catastrophe-flip in the sequence of that decline will have been when the demographic weight of cities was insufficient to prevent their spatial fragmentation. The next catastrophe-flip would be when the demographic weight was insufficient to support urban crafts, and the minimum criteria for urbanism as a whole no longer held. We can recognize these two moments of change, even if we cannot put figures on them. Until we know much more about our cities, this will have to do as an approximation.

6. Northern Francia and the eighth century

When one reaches the lower Loire from the south, one has come out of the Mediterranean region of Gaul. Although Tours is on the south bank of the Loire, and thus in Aquitaine, its urban structures were already by the sixth century somewhat different from those described in the previous sections. The overall urban development of northern Gaul has a certain homogeneity from the Loire to the Rhine—although, as in southern Gaul, there are sharp divergences in the fates of individual cities—and it will be treated here as a single whole. I do not wish to claim that there are no similarities between the

---

[179] For Pisa in 1228, Salvatori, *La popolazione*, pp. 108–23; for its spatial development up to then, Garzella, *Pisa com'era*.

north and the south in Gaul at all; the north shows a sharper version of some of the trends visible in the south, and anyway the boundary between the two is far from clear (it coincides with some of the zones where there has been less systematic archaeological work in France). It makes most sense, however, to treat the northern cities as structurally separate, for reasons that we shall see. After looking at them, I shall conclude this section with an account of the new urban developments in northern Europe in the eighth century, and a look back at the Mediterranean from this perspective.

The Tours of Gregory of Tours's writings was a bustling place, with numerous churches, including the large extramural burial complex of St-Martin, which was one of Gaul's major pilgrimage sites—Gregory himself recorded the miracles that took place there in his *De virtutibus sancti Martini episcopi*. Inside the city walls there was the cathedral complex, at least one aristocratic residence (that of Eberulf, the *cubicularius* of Chilperic, d. 585), and presumably the administrative buildings associated with the count. Around St-Martin, under a kilometre away, there were large *atria* and a network of churches and monasteries, which were the constant focus for pilgrims and mendicants (who had two houses of poor-relief built for them). Gregory as bishop formally proceeded from the cathedral to St-Martin on feast-days, with, apparently, a substantial congregation; King Clovis on his ceremonial visit to Tours in 508, victorious after the battle of Vouillé, had proceeded in the opposite direction, showering money on the *populus* in Roman style. The city population are less clearly marked in Gregory's writings, it is true; we find that the *cives* of Tours could as easily live in the countryside as in the town. But they could also operate collectively (to oppose bishops, for example), and this sort of aggregation makes most sense if there was a physical concentration of people as well.[180] How interesting, therefore, to read the interims and syntheses of Henri Galinié's extensive Tours excavations, and find that outside the late Roman walled city, itself small enough (about 9 hectares), almost nothing has been found from this period at all except the churches and some cemeteries. It is true that the zone immediately between the cathedral and St-Martin has been less systematically studied, and that a recent excavation in this area, close to the city walls, showed some late occupation. But this was materially very simple, even including hand-made ceramics. Galinié argues that Tours had hardly been an urban centre in archaeological terms since the third century.[181] If one looks carefully at Gregory's words, it is not that he can be proved to tell us

---

[180] See in general Pietri, *La ville de Tours*, pp. 339–430, with pp. 448–59 on processions, and pp. 714–24 on poor relief. For Gregory citations, see *LH*, VII.22 (Eberulf), 23 (a possible comital residence); *VM*, II.25 (Gregory's procession); *LH*, II.38 (Clovis), VII.47 (*cives* in the countryside), V.18 (the possibility of the *populus* opposing bishops).

[181] See, as a recent survey, Galinié, 'Tours de Grégoire' (p. 69 for the extramural excavation). A serious excavation in the area between the city and St-Martin would, however, test this image of the deurbanized city, better than has been done hitherto.

otherwise; his references to *Turonici*, like his *cives*, could largely be to the inhabitants of the city territory; his references to large congregations in churches could include both pilgrims and country-dwellers. Tours is important to him as a religious, rather than economic, centre, and it apparently lacked the political complexity of Clermont, with its rival urban aristocratic families. But it is still striking that a city with such constant activity had so few visible secular inhabitants. This was a *città ad isole* which, on the evidence of the excavations, had gone over the edge into deurbanization; still, to the eyes of its religious leader (and one, we should recall, from the south) it was not structurally different from other *civitates* of Gaul.

Frankish sources talk systematically in terms of *civitates*, which were the building blocks for Merovingian government as much as they were for the Visigoths or the Lombards. But with the example of Tours in mind, one might legitimately wonder whether any of the other towns of the north had more material corporality. Gregory, as has been often noted, only really saw walls and cathedral churches when he sought to describe his cities, wherever they were in Gaul. So Dijon, a mere *castrum*, had imposing walls, and Gregory was thus led to wonder why it was not a *civitas*.[182] Was there anything more?

One thing that one has to say at once is that there were in the Merovingian period many towns in the north, like Tours, that were *città ad isole*—northern archaeologists sometimes use the term polynuclear settlements—at best. Some of them have not had enough excavation for us to be sure how urban they were, but the available evidence stresses groups of agglomerations around churches, largely made up of wooden buildings, both inside and outside the Roman walls. Trier is one such (here the walls delimited a substantial area, unlike at Tours); Bonn, Mainz, and Metz are probably others. Metz, the best-excavated of the four, is an instructive case: an important late Roman military centre (up to 450, perhaps), a royal centre from c.550, with around fifteen known churches in the seventh century and as many as forty-three in the eighth, but also apparently with only scatters of settlement in the early middle ages (up to 800, at least), and very little evidence for occupation at all in the years around 500.[183] The Metz archaeology is interesting in that it offers us a low point in the early sixth century, with a revival already beginning in Gregory's time (although Metz's revival after 550 was also undoubtedly because of royal interest, something that was never the case for Tours, which did not revive until after 900). Overall,

---

[182] *LH*, III.19; see Loseby, 'Gregory's cities', pp. 242–4.

[183] For a brief survey of Trier, see Böhner, 'Urban and rural settlement', pp. 193–6; a brief update is Kuhnen, 'Zwischen Reichs- und Stadtgeschichte'. For Metz, Halsall, *Settlement and society*, pp. 214–41; the occupation gap he postulates for 400–550 must be shorter (or indeed absent) now that Argonne ware can be seen to be continuing into the late sixth century, on the basis of work by Didier Bayard, including a study of the Metz amphitheatre (see Ch. 11, n. 173). For Mainz, Wamers, *Die frühmittelalterlichen Lesefunde*, esp. pp. 11–19, 194–8 (a sudden expansion, on the river-front, around 750). For Bonn, Böhner, 'Bonn'.

in northern Gaul the period 450–600 can probably be seen as a general nadir for urbanism, the seventh century and especially the eighth as a period of revival; this trajectory certainly distinguishes the north of Gaul from the south. It may well also be that other major episcopal centres, with numerous churches, such as Reims (see above, p. 180) or Le Mans, had a similar polynuclear structure to the cities just mentioned.[184] What is much less clear is on which side of the boundary between urban and deurbanized, Lyon as against Tours, any of them lay. Probably Trier and Reims (home of some significant urban aristocrats, above, p. 607), and less certainly Metz (home of kings) were on the Lyon side, Bonn and Le Mans maybe on the Tours side, with Mainz's standing still unclear before its rapid rise after 750, but all this is still largely guesswork. Other episcopal centres in the north were probably rather less successful: Arras, for example, which hit crisis in the fifth century, which shows us at least one *Grubenhaus* in seventh-century levels, and which had a church rebuilt in wood in the Carolingian period, was apparently drifting in the direction of a rural style of economic and material practice. Seen in the context of Arras, Tours is by no means the least impressive one can get; nor did bishops survive in Arras by the eighth century.[185]

Conversely, two northern cities do manage to show something more than these somewhat fragmented patterns: Paris and Cologne. Paris had numerous churches, like the set of towns we have just been looking at, many of which were doubtless foci for settlement. It also had a real centre, however. Its core had shifted from the forum on the Left Bank to the Île de la Cité, where the cathedral and, almost certainly, the royal palace (including a prison) were. This had clear urban characteristics: in the Rue de Lutèce, fourth-century houses are cut by early medieval silos with substantial quantities of pottery, and in front of Notre-Dame there was a shopping street, selling jewellery according to Gregory, which has also left archaeological traces. In 585 there was a serious fire, depicted by Gregory in terms that clearly imply a demographic concentration; in the seventh century we find charter references to houses inside the city walls, including more *taberniae*, shops. This settlement extended southwards to the defended forum area, and probably further south down the Boulevard St-Michel and the Rue St-Jacques (a Roman street) for a kilometre or so, as well as south-east to the amphitheatre, rebuilt in 577; some settlement, artisanal but perhaps more isolated, has been found on the Right Bank too. All this is a secure basis for stating that Paris was an urban centre, which integrated the more scattered network of churches around, throughout the early middle ages—even if we cannot show that any aristocrats lived there (above, p. 607). The St-Denis

---

[184] For Le Mans, L. Pietri and J. Biarne, *Topographie chrétienne*, V, pp. 41–56 (J. Biarne).
[185] Jacques and Hosdez, 'Activité archéologique'; Leman, 'Topographie chrétienne'. I am grateful here to Edward Mills for bibliographical help. For the relatively few failed cities in Gaul, see Loseby, 'Urban failures'.

seasonal market was moved here by 709, giving further weight to the evidence we already have in the sixth century for Parisian merchants (including Syrians and Jews).[186] As for Cologne: it has less documentation, and its archaeology is not fully published, but the eastern part of the city, closest to the Rhine, where the Roman street plan largely survives, was a rich commercial and artisanal centre throughout the early middle ages, as well as having the cathedral and an *aula regia*, where kings often came, and where they might leave their treasure. Roman buildings here were, very unusually for the north of Gaul, reused until the Carolingians rebuilt in both stone and wood; the forum, slightly further away, remained occupied until the tenth century; a synagogue existed here throughout our period too. Imports can be tracked from as far away as Scandinavia, and local metalwork, ceramic, and glass production is visible throughout. This part of the Roman city survived as a clear urban focus, again for (probably) more scattered occupation around peripheral and extramural churches, some of whose cemeteries have been excavated.[187] Paris and Cologne do not at present have significant archaeological parallels in the north, and they may always have been different from their neighbours: Paris was the unrivalled royal centre of north-western Gaul (Neustria) in the centuries after 500, and Cologne one of the two or three major centres of the north-east (Austrasia). But they also stand out in Gaul as a whole: among excavated sites, only Marseille so far matches their prosperity. They may show that Merovingian kings, unreasonably wealthy as we know them to have been (above, pp. 105–13), could on their own create the economic bases for urbanism, even in a relatively ruralized landscape. (This might also encourage us to view Metz, another royal centre, in more buoyant terms.) It should be noticed, however, that even these two towns maintained the polynuclear spatial pattern of the *città ad isole* of the rest of Gaul and of some other parts of the western Mediterranean; it is just that the centre of each was much larger in demographic terms, and much more economically active.

The literary image of Italian cities focused, as we have seen in the cases of the Milan and Verona praise poems, on the traditional monumental imagery of the Roman period. We do not have direct parallels to these texts for this region, but the way Gaulish cities are treated in the narrative literature we

[186] See in general Périn, 'Paris mérovingien'; Picard et al., *Topographie chrétienne*, VIII, pp. 97–129 (N. Duval, P. Périn, and J.-C. Picard); *L'Île de France*, pp. 134–48. For jewellery shops, Gregory of Tours, *LH*, VI.32; for the fire, VIII.33; for the Rue St-Jacques, VI.17; for the amphitheatre (Gregory says *circus*), V.17; for Syrians and Jews, VI.17, X.26. For the St-Denis market, *ChLA*, XIV, n. 586; for houses, XIII, n. 552; Weidemann, *Das Testament*, n. 24 (Busson and Ledru, *Actus*, p. 113).

[187] See Schütte, 'Continuity problems'; Gechter and Schütte, 'Zwischen St. Alban und Juden-viertel'; and now above all Hellenkemper, 'Ausgrabungen'. I am grateful to Sven Schütte for his help. For more scattered occupation outside the centre, see Steuer, *Die Franken in Köln*, esp. pp. 60, 62, 75–86, 97–9; see further Trier, 'Köln'. For the *aula regia*, Gregory of Tours, *VP*, VI.2; for treasure in Cologne, Fredegar, *Chronica*, IV.38.

have is notably different in tone from that surviving from Italy. Here, the south and the north cannot easily be distinguished (Gregory of Tours, for example, saw both in much the same terms), and I shall draw examples from the whole of Gaul to make my points. For a start, secular buildings are rarely referred to, and mostly, it must be said, in the south.[188] Gregory, as we have seen, thought of cities in terms of walls and churches, and our other narratives (largely hagiographical) do so even more, notably stressing churches. Avitus of Vienne in the early sixth century famously stated that churches were a better defence for cities than were walls; Gregory saw the two as at least analogous, as when Clermont was saved from destruction by Theuderic I in c.525 because his duke Hilping stressed the strength of its walls and the churches around it (and the sanctity of its bishop, Quintianus), all recently linked by a procession led by the bishop around the wall circuit, or when Trier was saved from plague in, perhaps, 543 because (as the plague itself said, in a noise like a thunderclap) two saints in their churches guarded the gates, again with the support of the bishop, in his cathedral in the middle of the town.[189] And we find frequent reference, in Gregory and in later texts, to the ritual of procession between the churches of a town. Saintly bishops sometimes did this secretly, presumably on their own, but also—doubtless more often—formally with their clergy, as we have already seen at Tours; aristocrats did so too, as with the formal procession to a church in Soissons of the wife of Duke Rauching and her servants in 587. Processions were used to protect cities, from plague, drought, siege, or other disaster, in a tradition of rogations established by Bishop Mamertus in Vienne in the early 470s; again according to Gregory, plague was held off in Reims by a procession around the city and its *vici* (a reference to the *isole* of settlement around extramural churches?).[190] One could indeed see the city as constituted conceptually by this network of public movement between churches, a humanized parallel to the network of streets of the Roman period.

Such an image is not unique to Gaul. We saw it in Mérida, and in Rome especially (the *città ad isole* par excellence, with particularly powerful churches); the tradition of processions was anyway a classical one, and survived in its imperial version at Constantinople (above, pp. 661–2, 653, 634). But in Gaul it is particularly common; it could be argued that this is because processions were all that most Gaulish cities had to underpin their spatial identity, and that even in the more urban cities, such as Lyon or Trier

[188] Gregory, *LH*, V.45; *Passio prima Leudegarii*, c. 2 (both for Burgundy); *Passio Praejecti*, c. 11; and see n. 176 for Desiderius of Cahors.

[189] See respectively Avitus, *Homilia* XXIV (*Opera*, p. 145); Gregory of Tours, *VP*, IV.2, XVII.4; cf. Loseby, 'Gregory's cities', pp. 252–6.

[190] Secret processions: Gregory, *VP*, XVII.4; *GC*, c. 58. Public processions: *Vita Hugberti*, c. 10; cf. above, n. 180, for Tours. Rauching: Gregory, *LH*, IX.9. Vienne: Sidonius, *Ep.* VII.1. Plague: Gregory, *GC*, c. 78 (cf. the *vici* of Trier in c. 91); cf. also *VP*, VI.6 (Clermont). Drought: *VP*, IV.4; *Vita Nicetii*, c. 6. Siege: Gregory, *GM*, c. 12; *Passio prima Leudegarii*, c. 22. Cf. the general comments in Van Dam, *Saints and their miracles*, pp. 116–35.

or Cologne, they were important to link scattered settlement areas together. Who went on such processions? The clergy, evidently; visiting clerics or aristocrats; also large-scale secular congregations. But these were not necessarily actual urban inhabitants; however large the crowds we find referred to in texts (they tend to be there in hagiographies so as to witness miracles or relic translations, or the burials of saints), they are very seldom explicitly referred to as city-dwellers. As at Tours, they could often be peasants from the city territory, or pilgrims from further off. When in Clermont in the early eighth century a crowd (and aristocrats, and clergy) accompanied the deceased Bishop Bonitus to reburial in the city, the *populus* was so large that it resembled an arrayed army (*exercitus coadunatus*) or the people collected to enjoy a market (*nundinas celebrari*)—the image of the urban crowd was not in the front of this hagiographer's mind, even in a relatively substantial town.[191] We are here a long way from the *Versum de Mediolano*.

Northern Gaul, the Frankish heartland, had many wealthy people, whether kings, bishops, or aristocrats. These mostly did not base themselves in cities, with the notable exception of bishops. Urbanism did not for the most part derive simply from aristocrats being city-dwelling, that is to say, unlike in Italy, although it would certainly be helped along by the sale of goods to the rich, which, as we shall see in the next chapter (pp. 796–805), was a thriving operation in the sixth to eighth centuries and beyond, and which doubtless often, as in Paris, took place in towns. The existence of this internal exchange network might, by the same token, also favour the development of new towns at nodal points for aristocratic (or royal) demand, something that would be all the more feasible as classical cities substantially reduced their populations, making them much less different—indeed, by now probably indistinguishable—from what Roman archaeologists in Gaul call *agglomérations secondaires*, small trading centres, except for the presence of bishops and their substantial entourages and buildings. The political importance of the aristocracy of the middle Meuse (notably the Pippinids) is, for example, one context for the rise of Maastricht: a late Roman *castrum*, but a fast-developing urban centre in the sixth and seventh centuries, with stone houses, some planning, glass and ceramic production (below, p. 797), bronze- and ironwork, antler-working, and substantial cemeteries showing a significant local population, called a *copiosa multitudo virorum* in the *Vita Landiberti* of the 750s–760s. Maastricht was an important mint, and the bishop of Tongeren moved there already in the sixth century; but this did not in itself make it a city—Gregory of Tours might call it an *urbs* and the *Vita Landiberti* an *oppidum* (relatively vague terms), but its coins generally still call it a *vicus*. Einhard, around 830, referring to its numerous merchants, called it a *vicus*, too. It is of course significant that a

---

[191] *Vita Boniti*, c. 40. I am grateful to Leslie Brubaker for ideas about processions. See above, p. 399, for processions in the hinterland of Paris.

new town of the sixth century should so quickly acquire a bishop; Maastricht was absorbed into the patterns of northern political/ecclesiastical administration very fast. This helped to give it a sufficiently secure centrality that it has remained important until the present day. All the same, its administrative status was not secure; in the eighth century it lost its bishop again, to Liège. The point about Maastricht is essentially that it is a marker of the possibilities that exchange relationships could create in the Frankish political heartland, already in the sixth century.[192] There were few new urban centres in the sixth or seventh centuries in any other of our regions; in the most prosperous ones the classical city network was still sufficient, and in the less prosperous ones there was no impetus for such development. The overall lessening in urban size and coherence in northern Gaul, plus the wealth of its elites, together made it possible there. Nor was Maastricht unique in this area; Huy, in particular, also on the Meuse, was not far behind. The Meuse seems, however, to have been particularly favoured in our period; further to the west, the Scheldt saw no significant urban development until the mid-ninth century.[193] This may further underline the importance of aristocratic buying-power and patronage on the Meuse. The other heartland river basins, the Rhine and the Seine, by contrast, had a stronger inheritance of classical urban centres, such as Paris and Cologne, to absorb such exchange, except close to the coast, which was economically slightly different, as we shall see.

The appearance of new towns in sixth- and seventh-century northern Gaul, together with the striking commercial wealth of Cologne, are among the first signs that the old northern frontier of the empire was turning into a political heartland, that of the Merovingian Franks. The rise of Maastricht also points towards the next stage of that development, the definitive concentration of political power in the middle Meuse–lower Rhine area, with the consolidation of Pippinid–Carolingian power, particularly after the civil war of the 710s; in urban terms this would be represented by the prestige development of Aachen by Charlemagne after 792. But the later seventh and especially eighth centuries also saw the appearance of a new type of urban site, the coastal *emporium*, which was designed to focus not only interregional exchange, but also (sometimes almost exclusively) long-distance commerce. The north Frankish coast had several: among others,

---

[192] See for the archaeology Panhuysen and Leupen, 'Maastricht in het eerste millennium', pp. 435–46; Dijkman and Ervynck, *Antler, bone*, pp. 17–23, 80–1. For the political context of the town's development, Theuws, 'Maastricht as a centre of power', which relativizes the episcopal shifts (he argues that bishops in this area largely lived in family estate-centres), and stresses the relation between urban development and political/ecclesiastical patronage. For the quotes, Gregory, *LH*, II.5; *Vita Landiberti*, cc. 2, 4 (note that the *copiosa multitudo* may not all have been town-dwelling); Einhard, *Translatio SS. Marcellini et Petri*, IV.13–14.

[193] Dierkens, 'La ville de Huy'; for the Scheldt, Verhulst, *The rise of cities*, pp. 37–40, 51–6.

Quentovic (Montreuil) on the Canche, Dorestad (Wijk bij Duurstede, the largest by far), and Domburg in the Rhine delta; these were matched in England by York, Ipswich, London, Hamwic (Southampton), and in Denmark by Ribe and Hedeby. (There were also *emporia* further north, outside our research area, in Scandinavia and the Baltic. The largest and best-known is Birka in Sweden.)[194] This new development has been much studied, and only a brief survey is necessary here, to compare it with the changing patterns discussed for other regions in this chapter.

The urban development of these *emporia* (a modern technical term, although it does have contemporary usage: among others, Bede uses it of the international market at London, and the *Miracula Sancti Wandregisili* of Quentovic) tended to follow two main patterns.[195] A minority of towns had seventh-century roots as permanent ports, with a substantial eighth-century expansion: Quentovic, Dorestad, and London are the clearest examples. Quentovic, which has had little study—it was only even located just over a decade ago—may have been the most important in the seventh century, as the main Channel port for England.[196] Dorestad, although known from the 630s for its coins (of the moneyers Rimoald and Madelinus, who had moved there from Maastricht, some 120 km inland), did not begin to expand substantially until c.720, although in its high point, up to the 830s, it became remarkably large, covering over 60 hectares of land. (Its excavators, who have more evidence than usual to work with, estimate its population cautiously at 1,000–2,000; but some idea of the range of demographic hypothesis in this area can be gained by the fact that Hamwic, two-thirds the size of Dorestad, has been ascribed twice this figure, fairly convincingly, by its excavators.) London's mercantile centre (*Lundenwic*), in the modern Strand area of Westminster (i.e. outside the walls of the Roman city), has a few early seventh-century coins, and is documented as active in late seventh-century laws and eighth-century charters; its first quays seem to date from the 670s, and it took off in the 720s.[197] This early eighth-century take-off is matched by the date of the origin of the other group of *emporia*,

[194] The best conceptual introduction remains Hodges, *Dark age economics*; it largely withstands its numerous critiques, some of them shrill (e.g. some of the articles in Anderton, *Anglo-Saxon trading centres*). For more regionally focused updates, Scull, 'Urban centres' (also conceptually sophisticated); Verhulst, 'Roman cities, *emporia*'; Näsman, 'Exchange and politics'; Clarke and Ambrosiani, *Towns*. Blackmore, 'Pottery', an important survey of ceramic distributions in the *emporia* of Francia, England, and Scandinavia, is now a good comparative starting-point.

[195] Bede, *HE*, II.3; *Miracula S. Wandregisili*, c. 15. Other common Latin terms are *portus*, *vicus* (perhaps cf. Old English *-wic*), and *mercimonium*, but there was no standard early medieval terminology.

[196] See in general Lebecq, 'Quentovic'; idem, 'Pour une histoire parallèle'. The town was discovered in the 1980s: Hill *et al.*, 'Quentovic defined'.

[197] Vince, *Saxon London*, pp. 13–25, 99–106; Cowie, 'Mercian London', for a recent survey; Kelly, 'Trading privileges', for charters. Dorestad's population: Verwers, 'Dorestad', p. 55. Hamwic's population: Andrews, *Excavations at Hamwic*, II, p. 253.

which seem to have been deliberately founded, on top of occasional harbours or empty land, in the first decades of the century: Hamwic as a planned site around 700; Ipswich perhaps no earlier than that, although there was apparently a small harbour there in the seventh century; York in the same period, just outside the Roman city but probably on open land; Ribe, again *ex novo*, in 704–10 (we have dendrochronological dating here). We must not exaggerate this convergence of dates; all the same, it would be fair to say that, although in 650 the North Sea and English Channel had a set of harbours, some temporary, others permanent, none of them would have laid much claim to urban status; by 750, however, half-a-dozen of them were large and active economic centres, covering tens of hectares of land apiece, which fulfilled all the main criteria for urbanism outlined above (pp. 591–4).[198]

The sorts of towns *emporia* were needs to be understood here, before we go any further; let us look briefly at Dorestad as an example, drawing parallels from Hamwic and Ribe, the other centres with well-published excavation. Dorestad at its height, around 800, consisted of rows of post-built long-houses of a rural northern European type (above, p. 496), but on much smaller plots than would be normal in a village, separated by streets made out of wooden planks. Closer to the river-harbour on the Kromme Rijn (Dorestad is set well back in the Rhine delta area, some 60 km east of Rotterdam) the houses were slightly smaller and denser, and separated by long causeways running down into the river, which were constantly lengthened (to up to 200 metres) as the river steadily shifted eastwards. Dorestad's inhabitants included peasants, but also a wide range of artisans: woodworkers (including for houses, streets, and ships), boneworkers, weavers, leatherworkers, and smiths. It is unclear whether such artisanal production was primarily intended for fellow residents or was also exported; what is clear, however, is that although this activity was substantial, it was dwarfed by the large quantities of imports on the site. Eighty per cent of the ceramics were imports, mostly from the Rhineland (the other 20 per cent were handmade and probably local). There were also basalt querns from the Eifel, wine in barrels from the middle Rhine (the barrels were reused as wells), glass, metalwork, weapons, and amber (some of which was worked on site). Dorestad was, fairly clearly, the main port for the export of Rhineland products: to other parts of Francia to an extent (though Rhineland ceramics are rather rarer elsewhere in the region), but above all to other parts of the North Sea coastland, England and Denmark in particular. If Dorestad had any form of monumental centre, it has not been found. One probable

---

[198] See in general Scull, 'Urban centres'; for Hamwic and Ribe, see further nn. 200–2. Ipswich has a later dating now that the development of Ipswich ware has been redated to c.720 (Blinkhorn, 'Of cabbages and kings', pp. 8–10). I set aside the temporary liminal markets called by Hodges 'type A *emporia*' (*Dark Age economics*, pp. 50–1), as not being urban centres.

church, again in wood, has been identified, although there must have been others; the town was never a bishopric (it is generally called a *vicus* in our sources), but at least once housed a missionary bishop to the Frisians, Suidberht. The mint may possibly have had a designated building (it would have in southern Europe, although minting technology does not at all require it); so may the *procurator* who controlled the port and its tolls for the king. But the archaeological excavations, which have covered almost half the site, have only really turned up primary economic activity, and little sign of differentiations of wealth.[199]

Other *emporia* have similar structures. At Hamwic, where the port was not excavated, the houses were again of rural type, on an apparently roughly orthogonal plan with metalled roads, and were, in the areas studied, largely devoted to artisanal production, with the same range as found at Dorestad but also including glass, pottery, and copper; here the richest imports were from abroad (mostly the Seine valley, judging by the ceramics, although the Frankish coins imply a wider range), rather than from Wessex, the hinterland of the town, although here over 80 per cent of the pottery was local, and this at least was either made in Hamwic or in its hinterland. Conversely, Hamwic seems not to have had an agrarian element; its food was brought in from outside, arguably in quite a systematic way. Hamwic's macroeconomic role is less clear than that of Dorestad, for it had fewer imports, thus putting more stress on the economic importance of its own crafts, but, conversely, its own crafts and its locally minted coins have rarely been found in its hinterland.[200] Richard Hodges twenty years ago argued strongly that it was founded by King Ine of Wessex (ruling 688–726) as a gateway port, in order to channel goods directly to the royal court, rather than as a standard town providing its hinterland with goods and services. Recent excavators, more struck by Hamwic's own artisanal activities and the relative absence of kingly luxuries, have tried to play down this model, but the absence of its products elsewhere is a limit to any critique of Hodges (see below, p. 809). The town was anyway clearly a planned foundation and closely associated with the kings (it is called a *villa regalis* in 840, and it gave its name to Hampshire by the ninth century at the latest); it must have had a gateway function as well as a local economic role, and was probably more controlled than was Dorestad.[201] In Denmark, Ribe was probably a seasonal market at first, based on planned plots, but had permanent housing in its market and

[199] See for surveys Van Es and Verwers, *Excavations at Dorestad* I, esp. pp. 294–303; Verwers, 'Dorestad'. For Suidberht, see Plummer's commentary on Bede, *HE*, V.11, in vol. II of his edition, p. 291. For the *procurator*, see Lebecq, *Marchands et navigateurs*, I, p. 158; II, pp. 411–12.

[200] Morton, *Excavations at Hamwic*, I, esp. pp. 26–77; Andrews, *Excavations at Hamwic*, II; Andrews, *The coins and pottery*; Hinton, *The gold, silver*, esp. pp. 93–104; Bourdillon, 'The animal provisioning'; for ceramics, see Ch. 11, n. 201.

[201] Hodges, *Dark age economics*; critical are e.g. Hinton, *The gold, silver*, pp. 98–102; Morton, 'Hamwic in its context'. Scull, 'Urban centres', pp. 284–91, is more supportive. *Villa*

port area, and the residential area behind it, by the mid-eighth century. Again, we find textile production and bone- and metalwork on site, with glass bead-making and pottery production (here, an even smaller percentage of ceramics than at Hamwic was imported, only 5–7 per cent, largely from the Rhine); imports included coins, glass, Eifel quernstones, wood from the Elbe, and whetstones from Norway. The patterns resemble Hamwic rather than Dorestad, and Danish archaeologists have no doubt that this was a gateway centre founded by and for kings (cf. above, p. 366). Ribe was rather smaller than some other *emporia*, at 10 hectares, and the intensity of its activity was probably less, fitting the still-restricted levels of Danish royal power.[202]

Emporia were classic examples of new towns. It will be noted that the criteria I have used to discuss them are exclusively commercial and artisanal; they were not centres of political or ecclesiastical power (although they were directly controlled by rulers), and, importantly, they are never described as the residences of the wealthy. London and York were, it is true, episcopal centres (inside the old Roman walls—the *emporia*, as we have seen, were outside), but no contemporary urban activity has yet been found in the vicinity of the cathedrals, which were anyway recent, seventh-century, foundations in England. It is also true that kings kept tight control over the *emporia* and their tolls, as even the poor documentation for England and Denmark makes clear (the same is true for Birka in Sweden, as we can see in the ninth-century *Vita Anskarii*);[203] but only Hamwic and maybe York seem to have been administrative centres for a rural territory. Monumentally, they were far from impressive; Dorestad would have looked very utilitarian to a visitor from Cologne, or even maybe one from Tours, though it was more active an urban centre than the latter by far. *Emporia* were mostly politically marginal centres, and kings were happy that they should remain such. (Dorestad, on the borders with Frisia, actually changed hands politically several times, and was under Frisian control for much of the period 670–720, after which Frisia was conquered by the Franks; London, too, was a border town, with East Saxon, Kentish, and Mercian influence until the Mercians became dominant in the eighth century.) Their raison d'être was as foci for import-export, and this explains why they resemble each other, despite the huge socio-economic differences between Francia on the one side and England and Denmark on the other. It also explains why they flourished so much in the eighth century, and also the ninth, a high point for the North Sea exchange system as that period was; their general lack of

---

regalis: *BCS* 431 (S 288). Hampshire is referred to in *Anglo-Saxon Chronicle*, s.a. 755; the text is late ninth-century, but this entry is generally regarded as being based on a late eighth-century source.

[202] Bencard *et al.*, *Ribe*, IV, esp. pp. 137–48; Feveile and Jensen, 'Ribe'.

[203] Rimbert, *Vita Anskarii*, cc. 19, 26–7.

territorial hinterlands further explains why so many of them failed as economic centres when the trade-routes shifted in the wake of Viking expansion. But they were not simply harbours for that trade; all of them were artisanal production centres too, often of considerable elaboration. The exchange they commanded was sufficiently complex to allow for that.

The urban contexts they were founded in were nevertheless quite different. In Denmark there had never been urban centres before (cf. above, pp. 370–1). Ribe's probably royal founder was thus creating something new, most likely in direct imitation of Frankish *emporia*, but in a much simpler economic environment; and Ribe, like Hamwic, had relatively little impact on its hinterland (below, p. 816). Much the same is true of the English *emporia*. Late Roman Britain had the standard set of *civitates*, but they universally went into crisis at the beginning of the fifth century, together with the state, the aristocracy, and all the infrastructure of large-scale exchange (above, pp. 306–9; below, pp. 806–8). Verulamium and York may have limped on to 450 or so, and some version of non-urban, possibly princely or episcopal, occupation into the sixth century might be proposed for Wroxeter; in Canterbury, we can probably guess at settlement continuity (the currently visible break between the latest Roman levels and the first *Grubenhäuser* around 450 is a generation at most), but, equally probably, no continuity of urbanism, less even than at Arras (above, p. 677); in London, York, Lincoln, seventh-century episcopal centres in former Roman *civitates*, there seems to have been a complete settlement hiatus.[204] The foundation of the coastal *emporia* in the generation around 700 was thus as much of a break with the past here as in Denmark, and is equally likely to have been in conscious imitation of the Frankish ports. As we shall see (pp. 809–10), the English *emporia* did not all develop in the same sort of context. Ipswich is the most likely to have had an exchange relationship with its local hinterland, given the wide distribution across East Anglia of its pottery, Ipswich ware. The local exchange networks of York and London were less developed, although, in the north, a variety of rural sites in the Humber area show rich imports; and Rochester and Canterbury, which had some political links with London, provide us in the 760s with the first clear documentary signs in England of urban housing (unfortunately, this has not yet had any archaeological back-up).[205] Hamwic's lack of an elaborated relationship with its West Saxon hinterland thus shows more similarities

[204] Basic surveys are Esmonde-Cleary, *The ending*, pp. 131–4, 144–54; Brooks, 'A review of the evidence'; Loseby, 'Power and towns'. For York, see Whyman, *Late Roman Britain*, pp. 285–327; for Wroxeter, see Barker *et al.*, *Baths basilica*, and White, 'Wroxeter'; for Canterbury, Blockley, *Marlowe Car Park*, e.g. pp. 18–20 (cf. Brooks, 'The case for continuity', and Loseby, 'Power and towns', p. 338). Clarke and Fulford, 'The excavation of Insula IX', pp. 156–9, 163–4, presents Silchester as another site occupied after c.400, although their terminal date of c.600 is not supported by their evidence.

[205] For Canterbury, *BCS* 192 (S 1182); for Rochester, *BCS* 193, 196, 242 (S 32, 34, 266). For Canterbury see Brooks, *Early history*, pp. 24–30.

with Denmark than with the east coast of England (let alone with Francia). But despite this variety of contexts, early Anglo-Saxon urbanism can generally be argued to be an import from abroad, as much as were the Rhenish and north French pottery, glass, and quernstones which the *emporia* made available in the English kingdoms.

The relationship between Dorestad or Quentovic with the Frankish hinterland was quite different. For a start, they were export, not import, funnels. (It goes without saying that exchange has to be two-way to work, and the Franks must have been importing *something* from England and Denmark, but this was not, probably, manufactured goods. Slaves, fish, and raw materials such as amber and maybe wool and metal are the best bets; the prestige element in this exchange was one-way only.)[206] Secondly, although the coastal ports were unusual in their lack of political centrality and monumentality, they were simply sub-types of the standard urban centre of northern Gaul. They offered the same potential to act as the exchange centre for an immediate hinterland, with major landowners buying and selling there as they needed, as Stéphane Lebecq has shown in his analysis of the use of Quentovic by some of the major Neustrian monasteries, such as St-Wandrille and St-Riquier, both of which owned property there, or St-Germain, which sent goods there to be sold on a regular basis.[207] They were, in a word, more normal as towns; they could simply be seen as the successors of Cologne and Maastricht (and maybe Rouen), products of the increased intensity of Frankish aristocratic-driven exchange in the eighth and early ninth centuries, the age of steady Carolingian expansion, this time across the boundary of the Frankish political system and out into the North Sea. It may be that it was the liminal nature of the *emporia* that made them less attractive as political foci to the Franks; it is interesting that the bishopric of soon-to-be-conquered Frisia was located by Pippin II in the old mission station of Utrecht, not in the far larger settlement of Dorestad, only 20 km away (although it is fair to add that Utrecht, a former Roman *castrum*, may have been a political centre of the Frisians, and Dorestad, a boundary town for the latter as well, certainly was not). The fact that the Frankish *emporia* did not become political foci also meant that they could not easily develop their own territorial hinterlands, and this, added to their boundary position, made them less stable in the long run; all the Frankish *emporia* were abandoned by 900, whereas Cologne, with its continuing local exchange role, and, now, Utrecht as well, continued without a break. But we must guard against seeing the Frankish *emporia* either as atypical, unstable and impermanent ventures, or as brave harbingers of the future, Charlemagne's contribution to the Pirenne thesis. They were, rather, standard north Frankish new towns, as Maastricht had been a century or so earlier, and as

---

[206] Hodges, *Dark age economics*, pp. 117–29.
[207] Lebecq, 'Quentovic', p. 80.

Bruges and Ghent would be a century or so later.[208] This is the sort of recurring urban development that the great wealth of post-Roman aristocratic landowners in northern Gaul would favour in every period, which in this period was also still closely associated with princely interest and patronage. It was this that the English and Danish kings copied in the eighth century, and it is understandable that they did so.

Urban life in general lost momentum nearly everywhere in our period, as states became weaker, exchange less large-scale, and aristocracies less rich. The only important exceptions to this among our regions were Egypt and Syria-Palestine; even Italy, urbanized though it was, saw its cities grow poorer, and the same could be proposed for Tunisia and Andalucía. Different regions had different low points—in the western Mediterranean it was the eighth century, in northern Gaul it was the early sixth—reflecting also the low points for state-building and aristocratic wealth; these relationships will be surveyed and linked together in more detail in the next chapter. It has just been seen, however, that the eighth century shows us quite a lot of urban activity in the regions around the North Sea; let us conclude this chapter by comparing that activity to what can be seen in the same period in the Mediterranean regions discussed earlier.

Dorestad looks like a more active economic centre than most west Mediterranean towns in the eighth century. Its long-distance trade links were certainly wider, and more evidence of artisanal activity has been found there too. The only contemporary archaeological analogues to this degree of exchange intensity in the Mediterranean are as far away as Palestine, cities such as Pella and Gerasa, and their long-distance links were actually, in this century at least, more restricted (below, pp. 774–9). Dorestad was quite spatially extended, too; its 60-plus hectares matches the late Roman walled circuit of Verona, and is not far short of Gerasa.[209] This cannot be a reliable demographic guide, but it does give us an idea of relative scale, at least in the case of the largest of the northern *emporia*. The major structural difference between Dorestad and Verona or Gerasa was that the latter two were political and social centres, with an articulated hierarchy of wealth and power among the urban population, based on landowning; Dorestad, by contrast, was a town dominated by merchants and artisans (and also urban poor, as Rimbert's *Vita Anskarii* remarks[210]), and only existed because of its commercial activities. Using Max Weber's or Henri Pirenne's traditional terminology, this makes it more 'medieval' than the other two—or than the huge majority of eighth-century towns, indeed—although even Dorestad

---

[208] For Utrecht, Alcuin, *Vita Willibrordi*, c. 13 (for Pippin II, see Boniface, *Ep.* 109, by implication); for the succession of urban centres, Verhulst, *The rise of cities*.

[209] Ward-Perkins, 'The cities', p. 374.

[210] Rimbert, *Vita Anskarii*, c. 20 (unlike Birka, which apparently had no poor).

developed largely because of royal patronage and aristocratic buying power, and few if any later medieval cities were really free of the dominance of landowners.[211] Conversely, given the scale of commerce in the early middle ages, Dorestad's reliance on it helps to explain its relative fragility and eventual failure. From this standpoint, Cologne, perhaps as important commercially, but a political/social centre of a more classic type, was better equipped to survive, and has remained important in all these respects ever since.

We shall see in the next chapter that the old impression that there was more commerce in the eighth century in the North Sea than in at least the western part of the Mediterranean is a true one. Are there any equivalents in the Mediterranean to the new urban developments of the North Sea coast, however? In general, no, not in the eighth century, although there are some exceptions. In the Arab-controlled regions of the Mediterranean, there were certainly cities that were doing much better in the eighth century than ever before, such as Damascus, or Raqqa, or Béja; some were very recent foundations, such as Kairouan and Fusṭāṭ; and the biggest of all, to the east of our regions, was entirely new, Baghdad. All these were newly important for entirely political reasons, however; the caliphate's fiscal system was easily strong enough to create new towns from nothing or from very little, and to turn them into major socio-economic centres, as was that of the Romans before. Such moves would continue in the ninth century, too, with the expansion of Córdoba, or the foundation of Murcia and Raqqada. More interesting, perhaps, is that even the Berber tribal kingdoms could do the same, with the foundation of Fès in 790. We cannot even guess at how urban Fès was in that early period, however (Volubilis, which it replaced, was by now not particularly large), and as a city it was seeking to imitate Kairouan, not acting as a structural analogue to Dorestad or Ribe.[212]

Dorestad's role was as a funnel for interregional exchange, at an important nodal point, in this case a meeting-place between the sea lanes and the spinal river traffic of the Rhine, leading directly into a major political heartland region. It must be recognized that the Mediterranean equivalents to this were not doing particularly well in the eighth century. Marseille, near the mouth of the Rhône, was not prospering, and there is no sign at all that its role was being picked up by rivals, such as Arles, or the *cellarium* at Fos, even closer to the Rhône mouth, although there was evident royal interest in the latter.[213] This weakness is significant; the Rhône was still the great route from the Mediterranean to the Frankish north, but it had become marginal to late Merovingian and Carolingian politics. Elsewhere in the Mediterranean, Tarragona, by the mouth of the Ebro, was probably doing even worse

---

[211] Weber, *The city*; Pirenne, *Medieval cities*.
[212] García-Arenal and Manzano, 'Idrīssisme', pp. 15–22.
[213] Ganshof, 'Les bureaux de tonlieu'.

than Marseille. Antioch, too, was in eclipse, although Caesarea was hanging on. Alexandria, at the mouth of the Nile, was still a great city, but had lost its political centrality with the end of the state grain traffic to Constantinople in the early seventh century (much the same is true of Tunis, the heir to Carthage), and there was for the next several centuries no commercial activity that could match that. Constantinople remained more important than all of these, and a major regional economic focus, but this derived above all from its own political role, and there is no sign that it was a real entrepôt in the eighth century. The only real parallel to Dorestad in the Mediterranean, as a coastal nodal point for river traffic to a heartland region, was Venice, the rising centre by the mouth of the Po. Let us end the chapter by looking at it.

In the dissolving, and thus more decentralized, political structure of Byzantine Italy, Venice was ruled by a *dux*, who in the eighth century became more and more separate from the control of either emperor or exarch. It was thus autonomous, unlike the northern *emporia*, from both the Byzantine empire and the kingdom of Italy. All the same, it had close structural links to both; Charlemagne chose not to conquer it in 811, though he used that threat as a means to encourage recognition of his imperial title from the Byzantine emperor Michael I. The city was perfectly situated to become a gateway port, and did indeed do so. It was not for many centuries a major centre for landowners, and the surviving will of the *dux* Justinian in 829 famously involves money more than land, including venture capital (*solidi laboratorii*), the first reference to it in medieval history.[214] The archaeology underlying the rise of Venice is still fragmentary. The lagoon islands were probably first occupied in the late sixth or early seventh century; in the seventh or eighth centuries a glass workshop was active at Torcello, probably for the decoration of the church founded there in 639; on Rialto, piles were laid under S. Pietro di Castello in the late sixth, under S. Lorenzo around 600, in Piazza S. Marco around 700. These are all ninth-century churches, however, as far as we know; literary evidence, too, would tend to date Venice's economic take-off to the late eighth century and early ninth, rather than earlier.[215] Eighth-century commercial uncertainties might, on the other hand, explain the failure of Venice's early rival Comacchio, closer still to the Po mouth, whose boats are referred to on the river in the eighth century and early ninth (see below, p. 733), but which was condemned to sleepy marginality ever after. Venice was not exactly the same as Dorestad. It

---

[214] *Documenti relativi alla storia di Venezia*, I, n. 53. See for Venice's political structure Ortalli, 'Il ducato', pp. 725–58.

[215] For Venice's take-off see most recently Ortalli, 'Il mercante e lo stato', pp. 91–105; Gasparri, 'Venezia'; McCormick, *Origins*, pp. 254–60, 512, 523–31, 546, 632–3, 761–77. For archaeology, Lecziewicz *et al.*, *Torcello*; Tuzzato, 'Venezia'; Ammerman, 'New evidence'; idem, 'More on the origins of Venice'; Ardizzon, 'S. Pietro di Castello'. McCormick, *Origins*, p. 530, argues that church building builds up from the late eighth century.

always had a ruling aristocracy, which restricted the ducal title to members of a small oligarchic group of families; it had, as a result, sharp differences in wealth, and monumental pretension existed from the start. But its prosperity derived from the same basis, commerce. The ninth century in the Adriatic was the earliest moment for the stabilization of long-distance routes, not the eighth, as on the North Sea; they remained unchanged thereafter, however, unlike in the North, and Venice's hegemony over them was never again in question.

Venice was in one way more like Hamwic than like Dorestad. Dorestad's basic role was to export finished goods, often prestige goods, and to import raw materials (and probably slaves) from less economically complex regions; Hamwic and Venice did the opposite, importing prestige goods from more complex regions, Francia and Byzantium/the caliphate respectively. Hamwic's traders were, indeed, probably largely Franks, not Anglo-Saxons; Venice, as Michael McCormick has shown, was heavily involved in the slave trade from Europe to the Byzantine and Arab worlds.[216] But if we set aside the international import-export role of each of these, and look instead at their relationships to a more immediate economic hinterland (relationships which were in general more important than long-distance commerce), then Venice was more like Dorestad: its hinterland in northern Italy, like Dorestad's in northern Francia, was a terrain of regular and integrated exchange, which did not have to be directed in detail by rulers, as Hamwic's probably was. This distinction, too, will be developed in the next chapter. Here, all that needs to be said is that the expanding market relationships that underpinned both Dorestad and, later, Venice are signs of the same process: the stability of the aristocratic hegemony of the Carolingian world, and, as a result, the stability of demand. In Italy, the ninth century was a period of the expansion of aristocratic wealth, rather than the eighth (above, p. 218), hence, probably, the fact that Venice took off then rather than earlier. When other parts of the western Mediterranean developed stable and wealthy aristocracies again, cities elsewhere would follow its lead.

Conversely, however, it must be recognized how atypical these 'commercial barometer' towns were, and remained. The typical city in our period, in 800 as much as 400, and indeed up to the Industrial Revolution, was a focus for the surplus from *local* landowning, *local* aristocratic demand, *local* production, *local* markets for country-dwellers, and *local* political/administrative organization. Its prosperity changed at a far slower pace than that of Marseille or Dorestad or Venice. The ninth-century upturn is much harder to see in Brescia or Milan than in Venice as a result (above, pp. 650–1). I am not alone in predicting that it will be found in the future in major Italian cities, but I would suppose that the signs of ninth-century prosperity will turn out

[216] McCormick, *Origins*, pp. 761–77.

to be less dramatic in Brescia than in Venice, just as they are less dramatic in 800 in Paris than in Dorestad. And it is this, less commercialized and less dramatic, relationship between a city/town and its local hinterland that would mark the solidest economic developments of the future, too.

Systems of exchange

THIS CHAPTER IS in many ways the core of the book. Many of the other chapters refer to the density of exchange as a guide: to the integration of fiscal systems (Chapter 3), to the wealth of the aristocracy (Chapter 4), to the autonomy of the peasantry (Chapter 9), and so on. The arguments in those chapters hang, that is to say, at least in part on the evidence that will be set out here. In this chapter, the presentation of the patterns of and the changes in exchange will largely be based on archaeology, in particular on ceramic distributions; I would argue indeed that ceramics are the firmest support for any account of exchange in our period. If there has been any amount of synthesis of early medieval urban archaeology in recent years, the same cannot be said of exchange; here, the main attempts at archaeologically based reinterpretation have been the stimulating short survey by Richard Hodges and David Whitehouse in 1982 and the important syntheses by Tina Panella of the movement of goods in the late Roman Mediterranean, up to 700, the most recent of which dates to 1993.[1] There is a long-standing and distinguished tradition based on written sources, of course, of which more shortly; but a major part of the argument of this chapter is that written sources are a poor guide to the real patterns of exchange in our period. The importance here of archaeological argument makes it necessary to begin with the development of a set of criteria which will allow us to move from archaeological (in particular, ceramic) evidence towards wider generalizations; these will, in turn, link back to other chapters, and indeed link the whole book together. After an initial methodological section, and then an account of late Roman exchange, the regional analyses that follow will, accordingly, sum up my views of the individual social and economic development of each of the regions of the post-Roman world. This pattern is similar to that of several previous chapters, but the methodological section

---

[1] Hodges and Whitehouse, *Mohammed, Charlemagne*; Panella, 'Merci e scambi'. Reynolds, *Trade*, is a systematic account of the western Mediterranean into the seventh century. An equivalent with a slightly more eastern emphasis is Sodini, 'Productions et échanges'. In the Cambridge histories, Ward-Perkins, 'Specialised production', and Loseby, 'The Mediterranean economy', are also important surveys with a largely archaeological base. McCormick, *Origins*, is the monograph based on written sources that pays most attention to archaeology. For the historiography of early medieval exchange (and economic structures in general), the best account is Petralia, 'A proposito dell'immortalità'.

is particularly important as a justification of what follows, and each of the subsequent sections contains a synthesis of and conclusion to strands developed across the book as a whole. The final chapter will offer a more general conclusion.

1. Methodological issues

'Exchange' is a convenient umbrella as a concept, but it is not a unitary whole. For our purposes, it can be divided up in two separate ways, both of which need discussion here: by its relationship to the profit motive, and by its scale. First, exchange can either be commercial, generated by a desire for profit, or non-commercial. Commercial exchange (or 'commerce') hardly needs much characterization here; it is present whenever people buy and sell commodities. They may do so directly, the producer selling to the consumer, as in a traditional village market or the like; they may do so through middlemen, merchants or pedlars, who live by buying (relatively) cheap and selling (relatively) dear, usually somewhere else. This sort of exchange is simply fuelled by the existence of agrarian surpluses and artisanal production on one side, and demand on the other. Importantly, such exchange does not presuppose personal ties between buyer and seller; both are more concerned with the commodity they are exchanging. Marx famously argued that this preoccupation with the commodity (he called it 'fetishism') hid from all parties the fact that they were part of a wider socio-economic system, which had its own, invisible, logic; the point is a linchpin in his critique of capitalism, and I have always found it entirely compelling, but it holds good for commercial relations in pre-capitalist systems too.[2]

Non-commercial exchange characteristically has two main forms. One is reciprocity or gift-exchange, the exchange of objects or services for the express purpose of establishing social links between two or more parties, as a run of distinguished anthropologists from Marcel Mauss, through Marshall Sahlins, to Marilyn Strathearn have set out; it is distinct from commerce because the maintenance of social relationships is its express intention, rather than being denied.[3] The other is what Karl Polanyi called 'redistribution', that is to say, the transfer of goods from subjects or dependants to the holders of political or tenurial power, and the assignment of those goods by the powerful to others.[4] The tax network of the late Roman empire

---

[2] Marx, *Capital*, I, pp. 163–77 (ch. 1.iv). This section and some of those following are summarized in Wickham, 'The Mediterranean around 800'.

[3] Mauss, *The gift*; Sahlins, *Stone age economics*; Strathearn, *The gender of the gift*. General surveys of exchange types are Davis, *Exchange*; Hodges, *Primitive and peasant markets*; Laiou, 'Economic and noneconomic exchange'; and Moreland, 'Concepts': they take different positions, but are all good guides.

[4] Polanyi, 'The economy as instituted process'.

and its eastern successors is one important example of redistributive exchange; the tribute systems of tribal polities in Ireland or Britain or Scandinavia fit into this category equally well, although their scale was far smaller.
So also do war booty and piracy; so also do the movements of agrarian rents
by a landowner from one estate-centre to another. Rulers and landowners
when they hand out these goods to others can, and do, draw on elements of
the mutual obligations assumed by gift-exchange, as with loyal retainers
who regard themselves as obligated to fight for kings because of royal gifts;[5]
but most redistribution is too large-scale to have a personal element to it—a
city fed, an army paid. Because my interest here is in economic systems,
when non-commercial exchange is discussed in this chapter, it will generally
be redistributive patterns that are meant; gift-exchange, although universal
at all political and social levels, was seldom large-scale enough to characterize whole systems. Some of the archaeologically evidenced patterns of
exchange in Britain and Ireland can, however, best be seen as structured by
reciprocity rather than by either of the other two forms.

There has been much argument inside anthropology and neighbouring
disciplines about whether the economy as a system should be understood
essentially in terms of the rules which characterize exchange for profit,
'market forces' that is to say, or whether the alternative forms of exchange
have to be analysed according to different rules; this latter position, often
called 'substantivist', was set out above all by Karl Polanyi.[6] My acceptance
of the principle that different modes of production have different economic
logics (above, pp. 535–41) leads me naturally to the substantivist side. But
what follows is not dependent on that position. All that is necessary here is a
recognition that there are different sorts of ways in which goods are moved
around and transferred to others; if an object from Egypt is found in
England, then it could have got there by a variety of different means, and
how we interpret it economically depends on which. Conversely, however, it
must be recognized that these subdivisions are ideal types; much actual
exchange will have elements of more than one. One can buy apples from a
shop, or get a gift of apples from a friend; but one can also buy apples from
a friend, perhaps at a special price for friends. This last transaction involves
the contractual obligations of (at least some) commerce—ideally, one ought
to get replacements, or one's money back, if the apples are bad—but,
equally, it also reinforces the personal ties between the parties. Is this 'really'
sale, or gift-exchange? One might perhaps say that this would depend on the
extent to which the price was influenced by 'market forces'; either way,
however, the apples have changed hands and something is expected in
return. Much the same issues arose when the Roman tax system demanded

---

[5] Classic instances are Aneirin, *Y Gododdin*, VIII, XXA, XXI, and *Beowulf*, ll. 2633–8.
[6] For some recent discussions, see Horden and Purcell, *Corrupting sea*, pp. 606–7; Laiou,
'Economic and noneconomic exchange', pp. 681–9.

compulsory sales of agrarian products to the state, usually at a special price (*coemptio* or *synōnē*: above, p. 75). And, at a slightly different level, it must be stressed from the start that all three types of exchange could closely coexist, as in the case of the fiscal grain and oil ships sailing from Africa with extra cargoes of fine pottery for sale on the side—and, doubtless, gifts for port officials as well. These grey areas must discourage us from over-categorization. In practice, I shall distinguish broadly between non-commercial exchange, for the needs of states and rulers above all, and commercial exchange, based on private demand and the willingness to pay to satisfy that demand. Both, as with the apples, involve the same sorts of movement of goods, often on a large scale, and we sometimes cannot easily know which we are dealing with empirically. But, all the same, the implications of each for an understanding of the wider economy were essentially different, and must remain distinct.

The second way in which exchange must be subdivided is related to scale: broadly, one can distinguish between luxury exchange at the top, the exchange of bulk utilitarian goods in the middle, and local small-scale exchange at the bottom. Luxuries exist in any society that is not 100 per cent egalitarian, and are defined as being (relatively) expensive, and/or hard to get hold of, and/or only available to the privileged. They are often traded across very wide geographical ranges, as their expense means that profits can be made on relatively small quantities of them, and carrying-costs are accordingly lower. They are not always the same; gold may possibly be a universal luxury, but spices are not on the Spice Islands, and several early medieval products were utilitarian in one place, luxury in another—African Red Slip pottery, for example, was pretty utilitarian in late Roman Africa or Italy, but a luxury in sixth-century western Britain and Ireland.[7] The crucial point that needs to be made about luxuries is that they are marginal to any economic system, taken as a whole, precisely because they are restricted prestige goods. If they were not economically marginal, it would be because they were more widely available, and they would cease to be luxuries, as happened, for example, to televisions in Britain between 1955 and 1975.

This apparently simple point is so often contested that it deserves a little more elaboration. Of course, there is a grey area, here as elsewhere in economic categorization. Marble, for example, was expensive in the Roman empire, and its use had a prestige element, but it was sufficiently widely available that, for example, churches throughout the late empire could want to have at least some marble fitments, and the marble trade had a certain restricted impact on the imperial economic system as a whole as a result.[8] There were also, in most societies, entrepôts whose prosperity

---

[7] For Britain and Ireland, see e.g. Wooding, *Communication and commerce*, pp. 41–54; see further below, pp. 805–16.

[8] For marble, see Ch. 10, n. 177. Other quasi-luxuries could be said to include silk (very expensive, but sometimes made on a substantial scale) and glass (but this was widely enough

largely derived from luxury trade, particularly specialized frontier trading posts like Edessa or Venice or Ribe, as well as whole social groups (silk merchants, goldsmiths) who lived off that trade. These points do not undermine the basic fact that our understanding of any economic system as a whole does not depend on the availability of luxuries. Anyway, some form of luxuries will always exist, because prestige exists; if the rich cannot get gold they will monopolize silver; if pepper is too freely available they will focus on cumin; and so on. In general, luxuries only *represent* prestige; the real economic system derives from how the wealth underpinning that prestige was built up. Because I am here interested above all in systems, I shall not spend much space analysing luxuries as a category; they are anyway generously discussed elsewhere.

Local small-scale exchange is more important, but will also be discussed relatively briefly in this chapter. In even the most homogeneous agrarian environment, peasants do not have access to exactly the same products (one peasant may have a relatively small apple orchard, though more vineyards; for another, the apple crop may simply have failed this year), thus producing a need for basic agrarian exchange, apples (or cider) for grapes (or wine). Even slight differences in agrarian resources will also tend to produce relative specializations, a hillside village with more vineyards or pasture next door to a valley-bottom village with more grain-fields, which again will tend to encourage the exchange of relative surpluses. This set of patterns exists universally, and therefore historians who seek to distinguish between different sorts of economy will have less to say about it. Not that there are no differences at all here; in fact, there are several types. Societies which allow most of this exchange to operate through the social relationships of reciprocity are economically different from those where sale is more common; societies where sale is carried out directly, often ad hoc, between producer and consumer, are economically different from those which have local markets, or networks of periodic markets (as with the *nundinae* of the Roman period,[9] or the Wednesday-market village beside the Thursday-market village of modern Morocco). In a society where large landowning is elaborate and the level of surplus extraction high, it may be the landlord who demands a wine rent from one village and a grain rent from the next, thus evening out the difference in surplus between the two very substantially—here, the exchange is more redistributive, and the peasants will get to

available that it has been considered here as a bulk good). Slaves were sometimes luxuries, sometimes bulk goods, depending on availability and demand. In our period the slave trade in our regions, although active, was the basis of prosperity only of single entrepôts such as Venice, and for the most part seems to have involved individuals destined for domestic service, rather than for the infrastructure of production. It should be seen as relatively marginal to economic systems as a whole. See most recently McCormick, *Origins*, pp. 244–54, 733–77, who gives it rather more stress than this.

⁹ Shaw, 'Rural markets'.

sell (or give) to each other rather less. These sorts of distinctions are important; by and large, however, in our period they are also ill-documented. We know about their patterns thanks to our knowledge of anthropological and historical parallels, but the late empire and early middle ages tell us relatively little about their operation on the ground.

Two points about different types of local exchange deserve slightly more comment. Peasants in all societies wish to minimize risk, and this is above all true in the case of their own subsistence: they cannot afford to make mistakes. The 'natural' peasant agrarian regime is a mixed one, with a single peasant family producing as many of its food needs as possible; for it is risky to rely on the market, or any other exchange system, for staple foods on a regular basis. If we can find any signs of agrarian specialization in a given area in our sources (whether documents or archaeology) that go beyond the simple hillside versus valley-bottom contrast already referred to, then we can say that the structures of exchange were reliable enough to overcome some of that risk, and that the local economic system of that area was relatively large-scale. Even then, however, as we have seen (p. 271), 100 per cent cash-crop specialization was virtually unknown before the late nineteenth and twentieth centuries; in our period, even specialist wine producers will have had grain-fields as well, as a basic subsistence resource.

The only important ancient and medieval exception to this generalization was full-time pastoralism. This depends in nearly all known cases in the world on a systemic exchange relationship with agriculturalists, with the pastoralists buying staples such as bread, and selling meat, cheese, leather, and (above all, at least in our regions) wool. The Roman empire had a number of specialist pastoral areas, such as much of the southern Appennines, and agrarian exchange there must have been unusually developed. All the same, as is argued elsewhere, it is significant that our documentation for the post-Roman period, above all in the West, shows a substantial lessening in specialist pastoralism, which is hardly documented again before the twelfth century. This is fairly clear in the southern Appennines, and is probable also in the Alps and Pyrenees, although there is less evidence there. Even in northern Spain, where a relative pastoral specialization is clearly documented for some areas when documents begin in the tenth century, we can find references to grain grown in pastoral centres: pastoralists here were securing their basic subsistence in bread. The early middle ages was not a period in which the structures of exchange were reliable enough to overcome much subsistence risk in the West. They were also not a period in which demand was high enough for pastoral products to find large-scale markets, which would limit any temptation to specialize.[10]

This latter point can be generalized, along the lines of arguments made in Chapter 5. There are signs of agrarian specialization in the late Roman

[10] Wickham, *Land and power*, pp. 121–54 (pp. 146–7 for northern Spain).

world: olive-groves in Tunisia or northern Syria, vineyards on the coasts of Palestine or Calabria, and so on. They were not monocultures (see above, p. 445, for Syria), but they certainly existed because of exchange opportunities. These relative specializations must have lessened as market reliability decreased, a process which began slowly in the fifth century in the West and extended to the East in the seventh, as we shall see. In the south-eastern Mediterranean, where exchange held up better, such specializations probably continued later in some places, for example, the papyrus and linen areas of the Nile Delta, the latter of which still existed after 1000, in the period of the Cairo Geniza (see below, p. 765). But elsewhere, by the seventh and eighth centuries, any signs of specialization can be considered surprising, and worth attention: the wine areas of northern France and the Rhineland, for example (see pp. 284-7). In western Europe as a whole, large-scale agrarian exchange between relatively specialized areas did not start until the central middle ages. This point will be returned to in my regional analyses, for it is an important one; it also takes us into the arena of bulk exchange, of which more in a moment.

Peasants do not only need food; they need artisanal products, notably clothing, shoes, ceramic and metal and wooden utensils, wooden and iron agricultural tools. How they obtain these can be expressed in a hierarchy of complexity. They can make some or most of them themselves (this is least likely with metalwork, most likely with clothing); they can buy (or get in gift) from a part-time specialist who is a neighbour; they can buy from a full-time specialist, perhaps 'the' village smith or potter—or from the next village if one village has the smith and the next the potter; they can buy from pedlars; they can go to markets and buy from strangers. These recourses again depend on the scale of exchange in the local economy. But this time they are not simply a set of anthropologically generated possibilities: some sign of them can be picked up archaeologically. Non-local ceramics found in the excavation of a peasant house mean non-local ceramic production and distribution; if there are no loom-weights in a settlement, its inhabitants are probably buying cloth from elsewhere. These issues will be developed as we go; they are the aspect of local exchange that we know most about. They, too, move us into the arena of bulk exchange, which needs now to be introduced.

Luxury exchange and local exchange always exist; not so bulk exchange. I mean by this the movement of goods on a large scale from one region to another (or sub-region, or even microregion), whether foodstuffs or artisanal goods. Food, if it is to be transported more than very short distances before refrigeration, must not be easily perishable: in our period, among goods widely distributed, this means grain, wine, olive oil, living animals, and to a lesser extent fish sauce (in northern lands, above all grain and animals). Almost any artisanal goods can be transported long distances, but bulk exchange tends to be restricted to those items which can be produced in large quantities, cheaply enough for many people to buy but not too cheaply for a profit to be made: ironwork, woodwork (and the raw material for it, timber), clothing, leatherwork, ceramics, papyrus (much later, paper), some types of stone, and, at the top end of the market, copper- and bronzework and glass.[11] These are the main items in all large-scale exchange networks in world history up to the late nineteenth century; cloth, iron, and ceramics (in that order) were, for example, the major elements in the Industrial Revolution in Britain in the decades either side of 1800. They are, quite simply, the principal markers of the scale of any economic system, if they exist at all. (If they do not, then peasant produc- tion, on the local level, must supply all needs for the great majority of people.) The level of productive organization of these goods, the distance they are moved, and the degree to which any given product type dominates local availability in any given area, are all elements that need to be kept in mind when assessing economic scale. The first of these is not always rele- vant; grain production was not much affected by economies of scale before the combine harvester, for instance, and olive harvesting still is not (although olive-oil processing is). In the context of artisanal goods, leatherwork has generally been a small-scale enterprise until recently, too. But clothmaking, pottery production, some metalwork and glasswork can be carried out on a considerable scale even with pre-industrial technologies, and exported else- where in bulk as well, if demand is high enough. The scale of that process is the best guide we have to the complexity of the economy, in our period as before and after, and changes in that scale, as societies move from semi-skilled household production to manufacturing or vice versa, are the best guide to economic change. These issues will be the main theme of the rest of this chapter.

The study of exchange in our period has been dominated by analyses of the written sources; Mikhail Rostovtseff, Moses Finley, A. H. M. Jones for the ancient world, Henri Pirenne, Dietrich Claude, Michael McCormick for the early middle ages, are all scholars whose detailed surveys are classics, and Jones, Claude, and McCormick will be used as points of reference in what follows.[12] But written sources tell us most about luxuries, and far less about the economically crucial level of bulk goods. This is less true of the

---

[11] We should add salt too; but salt is a universal necessity, and always has to be transported if it is not available locally. It is therefore always present, and less useful as a discriminator, except as a sort of evidence in negative: if, in our written sources, salt dominates our evidence for bulk transport in any given area, then it is likely that there was not much else being exchanged on a large scale there. See below, pp. 733, 814.

[12] Rostovtseff, *Social and economic history*; Finley, *The ancient economy*; Jones, *LRE*, pp. 824–72; Pirenne, *Mohammed and Charlemagne*; Claude, *Der Handel*; idem, 'Aspekte des Binnenhandels'; McCormick, *Origins*. These are only the most obvious examples out of a huge bibliography. McCormick focuses above all on routes, an innovative approach to the question, and one that written sources are, overall, a better guide to.

later Roman empire, when the political importance of the provisioning of Rome and Constantinople, the wide scope of Diocletian's Price Edict of 301, and the artisan contracts in Egyptian papyri allow us to say a certain amount about, respectively, oil and grain shipping, relative prices of cloth, and the organization of ceramic production. All the same, the range of disagreement about the exact place of commerce in the late Roman economy is very great, and those who have not used archaeological data have for the most part understated it.[13] In the early middle ages, written evidence for anything except luxuries is scarce and anecdotal. In Dietrich Claude's book on trade in the western Mediterranean after 500, for example, in the thirty-two pages Claude devotes to the types of commodity transported, woollen and linen cloth, together with leather, get a page, iron gets about fifteen lines, and pottery no reference at all; but spices, silk and brocade, gold and jewels, and marble together get thirteen pages. This faithfully represents the balance of evidence in our written sources. At an extreme, Henri Pirenne based his entire theory about the Arab closing of the Mediterranean on only four commodities, gold, silk, papyrus, and spices, three of which were luxuries (papyrus was the only bulk commodity of the set, and arguably an atypical one).[14] These are not reliable guides to the scale of economic activity in our period, simply because they tell us about the wrong things; indeed, historians who focus their attention on luxuries are mostly not writing economic history at all. In the early middle ages in particular, we have to begin again.

If we look at the archaeological record, we find a much more restricted series of indicators. Perishable artefacts rarely survive, except in conditions where air or water are absent, in waterlogged sites and deserts, from where most of our best evidence for cloth and wood comes. Only metal, glass, and ceramics survive abundantly, as they are almost indestructible. But, except for the most expensive metals, these are examples of bulk goods; and they can be analysed in different ways. The technology of production, for example, is directly evidenced if we find kilns or furnaces; and, even if we do not, we can say a great deal about productive scale just from the artefacts themselves—individually made goods can, for example, generally be distinguished from mass-produced goods.[15] Although the range of our sources is

---

[13] For the *annona*, above, pp. 72–9; for cloth, Diocletian, *Edict on Prices*, XIX–XXIX (cloth makes up the largest section of the Edict), and below, n. 19; for Egyptian potters, below, pp. 763–4. For documentary versus archaeological approaches, see e.g. Ch. 8, n. 13. Rare examples of works which talk up late Roman commerce purely on documentary grounds include Ruggini, *Economia e società*, and Banaji, *Agrarian change*; a stimulating critical survey is Carrié, 'Les échanges commerciaux'. For the archaeology, see below, pp. 708–20.

[14] Claude, *Der Handel*, pp. 71–102; non-luxury artisanal work is cited on pp. 87–8, 95, cf. p. 104. (The other pages of this section characterize agrarian products, papyrus, slaves, and salt.) Claude is aware of the problems of his material: see e.g. pp. 117–18. Pirenne, *Mohammed and Charlemagne*, esp. pp. 168–74. Pirenne was extensively criticized, especially in the 1950s; Riising, 'The fate of Henri Pirenne's thesis', sums it up.

[15] A good survey of metalwork in Anglo-Saxon England along these lines is Arnold, *An archaeology*, pp. 77–84; for ceramics, see below, nn. 20, 74, among others.

restricted here, archaeological evidence already makes us better equipped to
answer the range of questions about large-scale exchange that were set out
earlier.

Of all of these, the most useful is ceramics, for two reasons. First, because
pottery is generally the most common human-made find on archaeological
excavations, reaching six-figure sample sizes on the richest Mediterranean
sites, and it can therefore often be quantified with some accuracy. Second,
because it can often be fairly precisely provenanced, on the basis of both
style and fabric analysis (other tests exist too, but are more expensive, and
less often carried out). Few other types of find can have their origins located
at all easily. Metalwork and glass are melted down again, and reused as raw
materials, too often for trace elements to be easy to pin down; wood, even if
it survives, usually has to be from uncommon types of tree for one to be sure
it is not local. Of metal finds, only coins, which generally have a mint mark
stamped on them, can be accurately provenanced.[16] Worked stone is
the other artefact whose origins are often known, and analyses of marble
(a quasi-luxury, as we have seen), or lava querns from the Eifel mountains,
or *pietra ollare* (soapstone) containers from the western Alps are important
additions to our knowledge; but worked stone is much rarer than ceramics
on sites. Otherwise, one has to rely on style, which is a much less certain
indicator, for artisans were sometimes itinerant, and imitations of non-local
products were common across the whole range of artisanal goods; in the
case of pottery, however, one can sometimes distinguish petrologically between imports and identical local imitations. For pottery, therefore, we can
discuss the organization of production, as we can for other artefacts, but
also the distance moved by products; and quantitative analyses of the full
range of dated wares found on any given site can often tell us how much
came from where in any given period. These are precisely the things we most
need to know in order to understand an economic system, and ceramic
analysis is therefore easily our best guide to them.

---

[16] Coinage is, for this reason, the other artisanal product which has been used as an economic
guide, as in Grierson, *Dark age numismatics*; idem and Blackburn, *Early middle ages*; Spufford,
Money, pp. 7–54; Morrisson, *Monnaie et finances*—to name only a few out of many. I have
relied on it less than on ceramics, in part to avoid an over-complex exposition; in part because it
is often unclear how much coin distributions tell us about economics as opposed to the
structures of public administration and of diplomatic gift exchange (see Hendy, *Studies*,
pp. 257–304, 602–13); in part because only copper coins, which were not minted in the post-
Roman West, are much of a guide to non-luxury exchange in our period—the standard silver
denarius of the late eighth-century Carolingian empire, for example, was worth around £12 in
the money of 2004 according to the bread prices in the 794 Synod of Frankfurt (*MGH, Cap.*, I,
n. 28, c. 4). It must be further observed that several moments of considerable economic
prosperity show striking shortages of coin in excavations, such as the fifth century in Palestine,
and the ninth century in both Rome and Iraq: see Magness, *Jerusalem ceramic chronology*,
p. 165; below, n. 87, for Rome; and Ch. 8, n. 20, for Iraq. All the same, coinage is a crucial
indicator, and I would hope that future comparative studies give it proper weight.

It must be clear in the reader's mind exactly what ceramics can be regarded as a guide to. The typical range of pottery on a site can be divided between table wares, cooking wares, storage containers, and transport containers (amphorae). Table wares, such as plates, bowls, and cups, are often 'fine wares': they have good fabrics and finishing, with some pretension to aesthetics, and must have been sold on the basis of the quality of their production, which could often be high, as with the *terra sigillata* (slipped) wares of the Roman empire or some of the glazed wares of the middle ages. Some table wares are less fine: they may have poorer production values and relatively simple decorations, perhaps dabs of paint or fairly rough incisions such as combing or stamping (they are often called 'common wares' by archaeologists; I shall call the most ambitious of them 'semi-fine' on occasion). But they could still be standardized, and exported across substantial distances, and are as important as fine wares for our analyses. Cooking wares and storage containers were more likely to be 'coarse wares': to have rough fabrics and simple shapes, which changed less across the centuries and are thus less easily datable. They were the least likely types to travel long distances, although some did, such as the cooking wares of late Roman Africa and of the neighbouring island of Pantelleria, the latter of which, remarkably, were made on a slow, hand-turned wheel, but were nonetheless widely exported.[17] Amphorae, finally, were regularly exported; their types changed relatively slowly, but they were usually mass-produced.

Table wares and cooking wares were used by almost everyone in our regions. The only (mostly) aceramic regions in this book were Ireland and post-Roman Wales, where wood and metal must have been used exclusively by most inhabitants.[18] Aristocrats, too, nearly everywhere, will have preferred silver or gold plates, and metal or glass cups, where they could get them; but they were less likely to extend this to their entourages and dependants, who would have been the majority of people eating at any aristocratic establishment, and the next social level down would also doubtless have found the best ceramic table wares highly attractive. Indeed, almost every archaeological site mentioned in this book shows ceramics, and they must have been the normal possessions of every social stratum. I would argue that table and cooking wares were in this respect most similar to cloth. These were absolutely standard artisanal products, which could be good/expensive or poor/cheap according to people's resources, what people needed them for, and the range of availability in the area at the time; and they could be made very locally or on a semi-industrial level according to the global scale of people's resources, that is to say, the scale of the local

---

[17] See for these wares Fulford and Peacock, *Excavations at Carthage*, I.2, pp. 8–10, 157–67; Peacock, *Pottery*, pp. 75–80; Reynolds, *Trade*, pp. 86–105; Santoro, 'Pantellerian ware'.

[18] See Edwards, *The archaeology*, pp. 68–78; Arnold and Davies, *Roman and early medieval Wales*, pp. 168–9.

economic system. We can say little about cloth on the basis of archaeology, but ceramics can stand as a guide to this class of bulk artisanal product: not for the exact routes of its distribution, of course, but at least for the scale of its distribution and production. (Iron, the other basic product, tended to have more localized distribution patterns, as far as we can tell, and a more individualized production, although specialist ironworking settlements like Vert-St-Denis in the eighth-century Île de France, and, still more, late Roman arms factories, show that it too could be produced on a considerable scale.)[19]

Amphorae, for their part, are guides to food transport, at least in the Mediterranean (they are rare in the North in our period). They were generally used for transporting wine and oil—more occasionally, *garum* (fish sauce) and other goods. Most wine and oil that was transported by water in the Roman Mediterranean was moved in amphorae, although skins may have been commoner for transport overland to the coast (above, p. 446; below, p. 721). Wine and oil went by different routes, and cannot simply be combined; amphorae must be distinguished as much as possible by content if we are to be properly exact about food transport. Only in recent years has much work been put into distinguishing wine- from oil-amphorae, largely from the pitch used to line the former (more scientific tests for residues are also becoming available), but an approximation to their contents can often be made on the basis of the known products of their places of origin, as we shall see. Globally, the scale of both wine and oil transport may also serve as a very rough guide to the third major food product moved in bulk, grain, although the involvement of the Roman state in grain transport was probably greater than for wine (below, p. 708). When amphorae become less numerous, after 650 or so, we have to be careful; it may be that this is sometimes a sign that wine and oil were more often carried in barrels, as already in the North, rather than because food transport by sea had decreased. But when we have enough evidence of amphora distributions in earlier centuries, their range is significant, and I shall place some weight on it in what follows.

David Peacock has produced an influential and valuable typology of the scale of production of ceramics, based on contemporary ethnographic example: 'household production', inside each household, that is, with very simple technologies, perhaps not even kilns; 'household industry', with part-time local artisans, often in the modern world female, generally not using fast wheels; 'individual workshops', with full-time potters, usually male, and more clearly marked professional skills; 'nucleated workshops', clustered

---

[19] For cloth, see in general Jones, *LRE*, pp. 848–50; Claude, *Der Handel*, pp. 87–8; and below, p. 765, for Egypt. For iron, see Daveau and Goustard, 'Vert-Saint-Denis'; James, 'The fabricae'. A good overview of the range of productive patterns here is Magoula, *Social status*. Iron was not ever uncommon, even in the early medieval West, as Jean-Pierre Devroey stresses (*Économie rurale*, I, pp. 124–9), arguing against the views of Duby (*The early growth*, pp. 14–17) and others.

complexes with greater, often very great, standardization; the 'manufactory', a more controlled and differentiated productive complex; and the 'factory', characteristic of the Industrial Revolution and later.[20] I shall refer to this typology fairly frequently, and it lies at the back of my mind as I write. It is an interpretative typology, however; one does not have direct archaeological evidence of it unless one excavates a kiln complex. If one only has potsherds, one can nonetheless immediately say whether they are hand-made, or made on a slow (hand-moved) wheel, or made on a fast wheel; how elaborate their decoration and production values are (how 'fine' they are); how hard they were fired and in what sort of atmosphere, oxygen-rich ('oxydized') or oxygen-poor ('reduced'), which affects the colour and texture of the pottery. Hand-made pottery generally conforms to Peacock's 'household' production levels, and slow-wheel wares, too, are generally not more than semi-professional (though some, as already noted, could be produced on a large scale). How 'fine' a ware is does not necessarily correlate with the scale of production; we shall see some coarse wares made on a larger scale than contemporary finer wares (e.g. below, pp. 747, 798). The more standardized our ceramic types are, however, the more likely they are to be made at Peacock's 'nucleated workshop' level. This was the most elaborate level normally found in our period; only some of the Egyptian amphora productions may have been 'manufactories' (below, p. 762). Between the simplest hand-coiled pots and African Red Slip ware there was, all the same, a wide spectrum in complexity and scale of production, and I shall try to locate ceramic types as carefully as possible inside that spectrum.

Ceramics are not easy to use. Pottery publications can be brain-numbingly dull lists of types, sometimes with no synthesis at all (in extreme cases, not even typological identifications), or no quantification. Even when we have the latter, the percentages of unknown types or fabrics are on occasion so large that all conclusions would be guesswork (this situation has, however, improved in recent years, as more work has been done, in nearly all our regions). Until recently, dating attributions could on occasion be several centuries apart (the origin of Forum ware in Rome oscillated from the sixth century to the twelfth in the 1960s to 1980s, before settling down securely in the late eighth; both Argonne ware and Ipswich ware have had substantial redatings in the last decade).[21] Many datings are, indeed, still in flux. We must also always wonder how far any single site is typical of a wider area; in Caesarea in Palestine, for example, there are considerable variations in the percentages of ceramic types on different contemporary sites in the

[20] Peacock, *Pottery*, pp. 6–51. His other two types, 'estate' and 'military' production, can be redescribed in terms of the first six.
[21] For Forum ware's changing dates, see Whitehouse, 'Forum ware'; Mazzucato, *Ceramica a vetrina pesante*; Whitehouse, 'Nuovi elementi'; and below, n. 87. For the other wares, see below, nn. 173, 202.

same city.[22] All the same, there are things one can do with ceramics, and they are worth doing. The fact that one can find African Red Slip ware in remote Appennine settlements in 400, or amphorae from Gaza in Marseille in 600, is significant. So is the fact that Mediterranean ceramic types are rare in inland Spain in the late Roman period but common in inland Palestine. So is the fact that, imports aside, Italy's local ceramic productions in 700 were generally more elaborate than those of Spain. So is the fact that wheel-made pottery was normal in northern Francia in the sixth and seventh centuries but all but unknown in neighbouring England. So is the fact that classical fine-ware types were abandoned throughout the former Roman empire by 700 with the exception of Egypt, where they lasted until 1000 and beyond. These observations are archaeologically firm, and they tell us important things about regional economies, as we shall see; they have to be understood in the framework of what else we know, but they are, in my view, surer guides to economic systems than any other form of evidence, taken on its own.

One word of caution needs to be set out about assessing the relationship between the scale of economic systems and the rest of society. We are attuned to seeing economic complexity in teleological, even moral, terms: if an economy gets simpler, it is less 'developed', or 'declines'; if it becomes more complex it 'improves', and society is 'richer'. As was already proposed in Chapter 9, however (p. 536), in any society which does not rely on mass buying-power the people who determined the basic scale and parameters of demand were elites: the privately wealthy and the people who took the benefits from tax systems where these existed, that is to say, landowners and political leaders. If elites were rich, then they were more likely to buy artisanal products on a large enough scale to encourage productive complexity, or from further away (and thus more expensively) if products were seen as better there, thus making long-distance transport more normal, perhaps cheaper. If, furthermore, the state was committed to the movement of goods, then economies of scale were still easier, and transport might be substantially underwritten, as often in the later Roman empire (above, pp. 76–80; below, pp. 708–20). Under these circumstances, peasantries and the urban poor, too, would be able to find good-quality products, sometimes imported from other regions, but still at accessible prices, because the economies of scale had been created already. Often, indeed, goods for the lower end of the market outweighed those for aristocrats and their entourages. But elite consumption structured these large-scale systems, all the same. Peasantries and the poor were not yet a sufficiently consistent, prosperous, market for these economies of scale to exist just for them,

22 Blakely, 'Toward the study', pp. 335–41.

particularly given the absence of sophisticated and responsive structures for the movement of goods.

Conversely, if elites were restricted in wealth, then the scale of their demand would be rather less, and elite identity might be simply marked by a few luxuries; the market for bulk goods would then depend more on the peasantry, and would accordingly be much smaller. This was a common feature of our period. At an extreme, in the tribal systems of the North, where aristocratic lifestyles were least distinct from those of the peasantry, no bulk market can be seen at all, and all production was local, and semi-professional at best (above, Chapter 6; below, pp. 806–9). This creates an important paradox. In these latter societies, elites were less wealthy than under the Roman empire, say, because they were taking less from the peasantry, whose economic activity made up the huge bulk of all pre-industrial production. The peasants, therefore, had to be better off than under the Roman empire, because they were giving less to landowners and rulers. But the infrastructure of large-scale artisanal production under the Roman empire had depended on landowners being wealthier than they now were; peasants were more prosperous, but had less access to goods that were not local, or that required productive complexity. We looked at the implications of this for peasant society and peasant-mode economies earlier (pp. 535–41); here, however, it is the implications for how to understand exchange systems that are more important. In our period, elaborate productive patterns and large-scale bulk exchange are above all signs of exploitation and of the resultant hierarchies of wealth; if one wishes to praise exchange complexity, economic 'development', it is that which one is praising. All the same, the correlation between the complexity of exchange and the accumulation of wealth is a firm one in our period, and it is in this respect above all that the analyses in this chapter underpin the whole of the rest of the book.

A final point needs stressing here. Much traditional medieval economic history has stressed long-distance commerce: partly because documentary sources overstress luxuries, as we have seen, and partly because of what one might call the mercantilist romanticism of Venetian galleys ploughing the seas, and of wharves loaded with bales of cloth. In reality, however, most exchange, and the most important bulk exchange, took place inside rather than between regions. Some of the most important commodities of the later Roman empire had a distribution that covered all or most of the Mediterranean, and that is significant; but it is atypical of our evidence, and even in 400 was only one part of any regional economic reality, which was mostly determined by more local products. The later revival of Mediterranean-wide exchange in the centuries after 1000 was, similarly, a spin-off of regional economies, which slowly ventured back into interregional exchange as they grew more internally complex. Understanding how long-distance routes were organized, where they went, how much traffic they carried (as Michael

McCormick has recently shown in great detail), is undoubtedly important.[23] But the scale of more regionally focused productions will loom rather larger in what follows. Only the next section will give substantial attention to long-distance exchange, and that only as an introduction to the regional surveys which are the main focus of this chapter.

2. The Mediterranean world-system

In Chapter 3 we looked at the spatial patterning of the state's movement of agricultural produce in the later Roman empire. Literary sources make it clear that Rome was fed by grain from Africa and Sicily, pork from southern Italy, and olive oil from Africa, and that Constantinople was fed by grain from Egypt (above, p. 76). This is supported by the (oil-) amphorae from Africa, which are amply attested in Rome and Ostia. If we fill this out with purely archaeological evidence, then we can conclude that Rome largely got its wine from Calabria (in Keay 52 amphorae) and the Aegean (in LRA 3 amphorae);[24] and that Constantinople's wine and oil came from Palestine (LRA 4, 5), Cilicia/north Syria (LRA 1), and the Aegean (LRA 2, 3).[25] These are relatively clear patterns; to them we would have to add the more variegated sources of army supply, such as the oil that went from the Aegean to the Danube, and the grain that may have gone to the Palestinian frontier from Egypt (above, pp. 77–9). How much of this was organized directly by the state, that is, redistributed non-commercially through the fiscal system, has been the subject of some debate; in my view, most of the grain and oil that reached the capitals was supplied by the state, but relatively little of the wine.[26] There is at least no doubt that what was not supplied by the state was encouraged and partly regulated by the state, which could not afford to see its defensive forces and major population centres starve. It should be noted that of the main sources of food supply just mentioned, the products of Egypt and Sicily are not well attested archaeologically in other parts of the Mediterranean, because what they exported did not travel in amphorae; this

[23] McCormick, *Origins*, pp. 501–69.

[24] Panella, 'Merci e scambi', pp. 631–6 (this article, ten years old, remains the basic recent account which underpins this entire section); eadem, 'Rifornimenti urbani'; eadem and Saguì, 'Consumo e produzione a Roma'; Reynolds, *Trade*, pp. 69, 327–30 (the latter being a reclassification of two major fifth-century excavations in Rome); Pacetti, 'La questione delle Keay LII'. I use Keay numbers to characterize west Mediterranean amphorae, and Riley's Late Roman Amphora (LRA) numbers, based on the Michigan Carthage excavations, for the main eastern types; only a few important amphorae types before 700 need be referred to by other classification systems. See respectively Keay, *Late Roman amphorae*; Riley, 'The pottery from the cisterns', pp. 115–22. Red Slip (RS) types are numbered by Hayes types: see Hayes, *Late Roman pottery*.

[25] See Hayes, *Excavations at Saraçhane*, II, pp. 63–6, 94–6 (this being the main Constantinople site for our entire period), on the basis of 'deposit 14', of c.526.

[26] See above, Ch. 3, n. 43.

is an immediate illustration of the limits of archaeology as a guide to the detail of food-transport routes. But it is above all important to recognize the scale of this global picture. From each of these regions, the major exporter regions of the late Roman world, ships sailed with the largest scale of goods that was transported from anywhere to anywhere else in our period. Whether this was commercial or non-commercial exchange, it was dependent on the interests of the state, and, in a real sense, it held the empire together.

The western and the eastern Mediterranean need to be looked at separately, because their exchange systems were largely independent (although there were certainly crossovers—African goods in the East in particular in the early fifth and seventh centuries, Eastern goods in the West in particular in the sixth). The two halves of the Mediterranean also had rather different exchange structures, which have different implications for our regions, and so deserve separate treatment. Each will be tracked here from 400 to 700, after which interregional exchange in the Mediterranean largely dried up; the eighth century will be dealt with in my regional analyses. It should finally be noted that this section will above all discuss Mediterranean sea routes. Land transport was so much more expensive for bulk traffic than routes by water that inland exchange, outside the great river basins at least, was almost always far less important. The state could defy this logic if it wanted to, and in the early empire had, for example, supplied the Rhine frontier from the Mediterranean.[27] It had given up doing so by the late empire, however (above, p. 77); as a result, the other substantial economic network of the empire, that of northern Gaul and the North Sea, was by the start of our period essentially separate, and will be returned to when we look at Gaul itself (pp. 794–805).

In 400 the western Mediterranean was held together by the tax spine from Carthage to Rome. The remarkable dominance of African goods on western sites has by now been described many times, but its basic patterns need at least brief repetition here. African grain and oil supplied Rome, as already stated, and had done so since the first and late second centuries respectively. We cannot be sure that African grain went anywhere else on any scale; at most, perhaps, suppliers might have made windfall profits with it at times of local famines, whether legally or illegally. Oil, however, certainly went elsewhere; African amphorae can be found on every coastal site, and some inland ones, in the western Mediterranean in the fourth century and early fifth. And to this African dominance of food exports, we can add a dominance of artisanal goods. The main *terra sigillata* fine table ware in the

---

[27] See Martin-Kilcher, *Die römischen Amphoren*, pp. 554–65. The best example in the early empire of a land-based distribution pattern was the wide availability in first-century Gaul of *terra sigillata* from La Graufesenque, a remote production site in the Massif Central: see e.g. Woolf, *Becoming Roman*, pp. 195–201.

western Mediterranean was African Red Slip ware (ARS), which can be found even more widely than African amphorae: into the eastern Mediterranean as well, and also further inland than most amphorae reached, including all parts of inland Italy (though rather less of inland Spain and Gaul) by 400.[28] This dominance of interregional exchange was, furthermore, close to complete. African products were a minority with respect to local products on most sites, as imports generally are, but they were far more important than any other imports. No other western fine ware had more than a fragmentary distribution outside its own sub-region—the widest-spread were the so-called *dérivées des sigillées paléochrétiennes* (DSP), a south Gaulish *sigillata* type, whose Provençal and Narbonnais productions could be found in some quantities in Liguria in Italy and in coastal Spain down to Murcia, although ARS was always commoner there too. Similarly, apart from Keay 52, a wine amphora from Calabria and north-east Sicily, which is well documented in Italy and Gaul, no western amphora type except African ones had a significant distribution outside its area of origin—and this even though the Spanish coast had a respectable tradition of *garum* production, lasting into the sixth century, which ought to have had some export value.[29]

The completeness of this African hegemony is one of the most important supports for the argument that the supply network that linked Carthage to Rome was indeed dominated by tax: a commercial supply to the capital would have tended to involve more regions, as indeed the wine-supply seems to have done. But the penetration of oil amphorae and ARS *beyond* Rome must have been commercial, apart, at least, from the supply of the occasional state enterprise, whether an army detachment or a factory. The state had no interest in providing goods for a range of small towns and rural sites, all across the western Mediterranean.[30] One can easily suppose that the *navicularii* of the ships of the grain and oil *annona* had with them more oil than was needed for Rome, and also crates of ARS, cooking-pots, and other products, such as cheap African woollens, on deck.[31] After they had fulfilled their fiscal obligations, they were on the other side of the sea, with their transport costs covered—for they were shipping goods in exchange for tax-exemptions—and they could sell the rest. This has, in fact, some support in

[28] Basic surveys include Hayes, *Late Roman pottery*, pp. 13–299; Tortorella, 'La ceramica fine'; Panella, 'Le anfore tardoantiche'; eadem, 'Merci e scambi'; Reynolds, *Trade*, pp. 6–34; Tortorella, 'La ceramica africana'. For one inland area, upland Molise, see Cann and Lloyd, 'Late Roman and early medieval pottery'.

[29] For DSP in Spain and Italy, see Reynolds, *Trade*, pp. 36–7; ibid., pp. 60–7, for a survey of Spanish amphorae. For Keay 52, see esp. Pacetti, 'La questione delle Keay LII'.

[30] An alternative to state redistribution is that of the movement of rents on great senatorial estates, an argument floated by Whittaker, 'Trade and the aristocracy'. This might help to explain, for example, the presence of African pottery on an important villa site in Italy like S. Giovanni di Ruoti (Small and Buck, *San Giovanni di Ruoti*, I, pp. 82–4, J. Freed), but would not work for most archaeological find-spots, such as those in Molise (above, n. 28).

[31] Cooking wares: see above, n. 17. Woollens: Jones, *LRE*, p. 849.

the sources, as McCormick has shown; the *Codex Theodosianus* has a law of 396 which states that shippers hitherto have had to be back in their port of origin not more than two years after the start of their journey, but that henceforth, although this right is maintained, they have at least to deliver the *annona* in the first year. Even this, however, would have allowed quite enough time for a serious amount of trade on the side, given that the autumn crossing from Carthage to Rome normally only takes around twenty-one days. It is in this way that African commercial goods achieved their spread, riding piggyback on the state grain and oil supply. This scale of commerce must surely have been somewhat greater than the 5 per cent of GNP canvassed by A. H. M. Jones.[32]

The Vandal conquest of Carthage in 439 broke the tax spine. The Vandals used their shipping for military rather than fiscal purposes. It is important to recognize that this did not mean the instant demise of western Mediterranean commercial exchange; the latter was solidly enough implanted to continue, without fiscal support, all through the Vandal century. All the same, the global scale of African exports seems to have dropped at once (this may even have begun before 439, but it anyway continued). So did export penetration, for after c.450 African products are rarer in inland Italy; instead, we find more local imitations of ARS, indicators of a demand that remained greater than supply, and the beginning of imports from the eastern Mediterranean. African merchants under the Vandals seem, however, to have maintained their markets on the coast of Spain and Gaul, even if they cut back more in Italy; they indeed expanded oil exports in Spain.[33] The presence of east Mediterranean amphorae in Carthage itself may indicate that they were selling grain in the eastern empire, and getting wine in return.[34] In theory, grain sales might have underpinned their marketing in the West too, if Africans continued to sell to Rome what they had previously given free; Rome's grain supply had probably at least in part

[32] *CTh*, XIII.5.26; see McCormick, 'Bateaux de vie', pp. 80–93 (p. 89 for crossing times), and cf. Wickham, *Land and power*, pp. 93–7, for a sketchier version of this argument. For Jones's famous calculation, *LRE*, p. 465. A good survey of shippers, focused on the period after 500, is Claude, *Der Handel*, pp. 167–244.

[33] For global scale, see Fentress and Perkins, 'Counting African Red Slip', updated in Fentress *et al.*, 'ARS and its markets'. For inland Italy, see e.g. Cann and Lloyd, 'Late Roman and early medieval pottery', pp. 432–3; Small and Buck, *San Giovanni di Ruoti*, I, pp. 119–21 (J. Freed); Patterson, 'The pottery', pp. 299, 305, for S. Vincenzo al Volturno; and see maps in Tortorella, 'La sigillata africana', pp. 52, 56—overall, ARS becomes rarer inland, but does not entirely disappear from inland sites for another century. For imitations, see above all Fontana, 'Le "imitazioni" ', with Tortorella, 'La ceramica africana', pp. 95–7. For Spain and Italy, see Keay, *Late Roman amphorae*, pp. 423–7; Reynolds, *Trade*, pp. 54–7. Overall, Panella, 'Merci e scambi', pp. 641–54.

[34] Fulford and Peacock, *Excavations at Carthage*, I.2, pp. 119–23, 258–60; Reynolds, *Trade*, pp. 78–9. Cf. Wickham, *Land and power*, pp. 95–6. Most of the eastern amphorae in Carthage were for wine (LRA 2, probably the main exception, is relatively rare), but the commonest, LRA 1, could equally well be for oil (see below, n. 40). It would, of course, be important for arguments here if North Africa did in the end turn out to be importing oil.

switched to Sicily, however, and the size of the capital anyway decreased dramatically during the Vandal period. The overall picture of this period is one of considerable creativity in African exchange patterns, with new ceramic types, new productive structures for oil amphorae (below, p. 722), and some new markets, but a general lessening in quantities. In the early sixth century many central Tunisian ARS workshops ceased to operate, although those of the north stayed prosperous.[35]

The east Roman conquest of Africa in 534 produced some temporary upturns, but did not change this overall downward trend for regional exports. Evidently the re-establishment of the grain and oil *annona*, this time towards Constantinople, and the temporary reunification of most of the Mediterranean coast under Roman rule, did not act to revive the commercial networks that had existed before 439. Some of the possible reasons will be discussed later (p. 725), but the patterns are clear. The sixth century is one in which African amphorae and ARS are still found, in smaller quantities, on the western Mediterranean coasts, but they are more concentrated on Roman political centres, like Rome, Naples, and Cartagena; on military outposts, like S. Antonino di Perti in Liguria and the (non-Byzantine) *castrum* of St-Blaise in Provence; and on the international entrepôt of Marseille. They can be found elsewhere, but they are rarer. At S. Antonino, African imports overwhelmingly dominate over local ceramics, which must be a marker of fiscal distributions to the Byzantine army; a revival of ARS imports in the East also presumably followed the grain *annona*.[36] But the exchange network emanating from Africa was increasingly marginal to local economies. In the seventh century it was ever more restricted to major centres, Naples, Marseille, and, by the end of the century, above all Rome. African links with Rome are shown by the huge pottery dump from the late seventh century found in the Crypta Balbi in Rome: out of some 100,000 sherds, 47 per cent are amphorae, and nearly half of these are African (a fifth are east Mediterranean, a tenth are south Italian, the rest are unidentified and perhaps also Italian), and, although only 3 per cent are fine wares, almost all of these are ARS.[37] But after c.700 African productions can no longer be seen outside the region, and ARS ceased to be made altogether. Without external political intervention—for the Arabs did not take Proconsularis, northern Tunisia, until 698—one of the major artisanal traditions of

[35] For production sites, see below, n. 50. For Rome's decreasing size, see e.g. Durliat, *De la ville antique*, p. 117.

[36] See Panella, 'Merci e scambi', pp. 673–80; Loseby, 'The Mediterranean economy'; Reynolds, *Trade*, pp. 31–4, 57–60; Zanini, 'Ricontando la Terra Sigillata Africana' (for a late sixth-century upturn); idem, 'La ceramica bizantina in Italia'; Tortorella, 'La sigillata africana'. For individual sites, Ramallo *et al.*, 'Contextos cerámicos'; Mannoni and Murialdo, *S. Antonino*, pp. 255–379 (summarized by G. Murialdo on pp. 301–7); Démians d'Archambaud, *L'oppidum de Saint-Blaise*, pp. 86–115 (M.-T. Cavaillès-Llopis and L. Vallauri); Bonifay *et al.*, *Fouilles à Marseille*, pp. 363–5.

[37] Saguì, 'Il deposito della Crypta Balbi'.

the ancient world had ended, after half-a-millennium of history. There must have been a moment, or a set of moments, in which the fall in export volume, rising prices as marginal costs consequently increased, a greater marginality for consumers, and perhaps a greater uncertainty of supply, with further falls in demand as a result, caused a catastrophe-flip (cf. above, p. 13), after which such production seemed abruptly no longer worthwhile, and stopped.

This narrative is well known in its main lines, and has not changed, except in details, in the last fifteen years. The end of African hegemony marks a systemic change of major proportions in the West: the material indicators of the Roman world-system had ended, across the same period as the end of the Roman fiscal system in the post-Roman kingdoms, as described in Chapter 3. The fiscal history of the western Mediterranean did not have exactly the same history as these material indicators, which reflects the fact that the latter represent wider economic relationships than just the state infrastructure. But the fact that by 600 or so both were in close to terminal crisis in the West, as they were not in the still politically united East, shows the ultimate dependence of ARS and food exports from Africa on the fiscal system and the interregional redistribution that went with it. The impact this would have on the different regions and sub-regions of the West would hang on the relation each had to the structures of the world-system itself, and this will have to be looked at case by case. I shall argue that Africa itself was most affected by the process, other regions rather less. But it was not just a problem for Africa. It might be argued that all that happened was that Africa lost its role as the fiscal focus of the western Mediterranean after 439, and, as a result, its commercial hegemony eventually ended as well. But African goods in Gaul, Spain, and Italy were not replaced by goods of the same quality, and regional exchange networks became internally simpler everywhere, sometimes, indeed, very simple. There was here a series of changes internal to regions, which both correlated with the local effects of the end of the world-system, and also acted on it, for the global fall in demand in most of the West was undoubtedly one of the reasons why African productions eventually failed. The causes of these internal changes were not only related to fiscal breakdown, however, as we shall see in later sections.

The eastern Mediterranean exchange network was quite different to the West, and its development took significantly different paths as well. The Alexandria–Constantinople grain *annona* did not, unlike in the African case, result in an Egyptian dominance over any other exchange item in the East that can be identified archaeologically. Here, as already implied, archaeology may mislead: Egyptian papyrus was certainly a bulk commodity, with a monopoly distribution; Egyptian linen was important, too; and the Oxyrhynchos documents attest to a very active textile production there, too, largely in wool, probably also for export. Conversely, Egyptian Red Slip (ERS), and Egyptian wine amphorae (LRA 5/6, 7), although very large-scale productions (see below, pp. 760–2), are relatively rarely attested outside the region. In the case of wine, this is probably because wine was less part of *annona* distributions than was oil, and Egypt had no oil; its wine was also regarded as inferior to Palestinian wine, even in Egypt.[38] ERS may have had too many other eastern competitors, as we shall see in a moment. But it also may be because the Constantinople tax spine was itself less dominant than was the Rome spine in the West. The city was a new foundation, after all, only becoming a true megalopolis shortly before 400, and, although it was certainly larger than the old eastern foci, Alexandria and Antioch, it was perhaps not more than twice their size. These other cities had their own *annona* (above, p. 73), and Antioch, although losing importance and probably population (above, p. 620), remained an exchange focus; more generally, a multiplicity of routes continued to characterize the late empire in the East.

There were two main export-focused wine-production centres in the East, the Aegean and the Palestinian coast, and their amphorae (in particular LRA 3, 4, and 5) crisscrossed the eastern Mediterranean, and indeed sometimes the western, as we have seen. Their hegemony over other wine may have been based on quality as much as on a tradition of export production and the habits of shippers; Gaza wine (LRA 4) was particularly well known and is often praised in our sources, eastern and western; it was, so to speak, the *DOCG* or *premier grand cru* of late Roman wine production.[39] Oil seems to have come from the Aegean (largely in LRA 2 amphorae), and above all from Cilicia, north-east Cyprus, and northern Syria (in LRA 1 amphorae, not all of which were either from this area or for oil, however)—the Limestone Massif behind Antioch has left clear signs of this oil specialization, as we have seen (pp. 443–9).[40] Finally, important eastern Red Slip productions which were exported outside their regions in our period were Phocaean RS from the Smyrna (Izmir) area on the Turkish Aegean coast, and Cypriot RS. Both of these productions originated in the fourth century. Phocaean RS must have expanded so fast because of the new market of Constantinople (although it also succeeded a similar *terra sigillata* production, Candarlı ware, which had been made near Pergamon (Bergama), just to the north);

---

[38] For the relative rarity of Egyptian ceramics elsewhere, see below, n. 120. Palestinian wine is cited as superior in the anonymous *Life* of John the Almsgiver, c. 10.

[39] See Panella, 'Merci e scambi', pp. 663–5; Glucker, *The city of Gaza*, pp. 93–4, is a convenient collection of references to Gaza wine. For the range of Palestinian amphora types see Reynolds, 'Levantine amphorae'; newly prominent are Beirut amphorae and Agora M334, recently located as an 'Akko product in large part.

[40] LRA 1 and 2 could both be used for oil and wine, as was argued, for example, by the excavators of a Samos bath complex, who found a large cache of them: Steckner, 'Les amphores LR1 et LR2'. For a sensible recent survey of LRA 1, see van Alfen, 'New light', pp. 208–10; cf. also Panella, 'Merci e scambi', pp. 665–6; Demesticha, 'Amphora production', for Cypriot kilns. Van Alfen accepts that LRA 1 from Cilicia/Syria/Cyprus are most likely to be for oil, as do I; but this amphora was made along the south Turkish coast too, as far west as Rhodes—it is the commonest, but also the least specific, eastern amphora. For LRA 2 see below, n. 155.

Cypriot RS presumably developed on the back of Cypriot LRA 1 amphorae, and probably also because Cyprus was such a route centre that export from there was easy.[41]

The routes that all these products followed were highly complex, and can only be summarized here. Phocaean and Cypriot RS are found all over the eastern Mediterranean, with an inland penetration throughout Syria and Palestine, though varying across the different microregions of the Levant; Phocaean is not uncommon in the West, too, after 450, although there it had an almost exclusively coastal distribution. (In Egypt, by contrast, ERS dominated except on the coast, where Cypriot RS was most popular; the Anatolian plateau had its own local Sagalassos RS ware, too. See below, pp. 760, 784.) LRA 1 has the widest distribution of all the amphora types, and is the commonest even in parts of the Aegean, as well as being available all through Egypt (in the latter case it must have contained oil, since Egypt had its own wine, and looked to Palestine for wine of quality; it seems mostly to have come to Egypt from Cyprus). LRA 2 and 3 had largely Aegean distributions, and 4 and 5 had largely south-east Mediterranean distributions; these two sets did not greatly overlap, except that they both supplied Constantinople (3 and 4 in particular)—in the West, too, they coexist fairly evenly when they are found.[42]

How these archaeological patterns related to fiscal distribution networks is not fully clear. Although our evidence for *annona* distributions, as we have seen, stresses oil rather than wine, none of the eastern amphora types was exclusively for oil; and Egypt's exports, which would, on analogy with Africa, have been fiscally underpinned, are not attested archaeologically. But, even if LRA 1 amphorae in Constantinople mark non-commercial distribution, their wide Egyptian availability must have been commercially based. Both economic systems must have been complex in the East. Catherine Abadie-Reynal has argued that the relative distribution of ARS and Phocaean RS in the post-fifth-century Aegean, with the former only common in major ports, as well as in Constantinople, suggests that ARS was more part of a long-distance route, such as that of the grain *annona* once Africa had been reconquered (the availability of ARS here rose substantially in the early sixth century); Phocaean RS could be seen by contrast as more of a local commercial good, being moved around on a small scale from harbour to harbour—including, of course, to the capital—from its production sites

---

[41] The basic guides are Hayes, *Late Roman pottery*, pp. 323–86, with his *Supplement*, pp. 525–9. For Phocaean kilns, see n. 154. For the relation between Cypriot RS and LRA 1, see Rautman *et al.*, 'Amphoras and roof-tiles'; the two are certainly closely associated in Egypt: see e.g. Ballet, 'Relations céramiques'.

[42] See Panella, 'Merci e scambi', pp. 657–73, for the basic patterns. For Phocaean RS in the West, see Reynolds, *Trade*, pp. 34–6; Fernández *et al.*, 'Gijón', pp. 117, 120; Martin, 'La sigillata focese'. For the amphorae in the West, see Reynolds, *Trade*, pp. 80–3. For more details, see later sections.

on the Aegean coast.[43] This is a convincing argument as far as the Aegean is concerned. And, although the deep penetration of LRA 1 up the Nile valley probably reflects private commercial demand for oil, the equally deep penetration of all the major RS wares in Syria and Palestine (including ARS), despite the absence of water-courses to help them here, seems most likely to have been helped along by a need to supply the army on the eastern frontier, the largest military concentration in the East (see below, p. 771). Whatever the accuracy of these detailed hypotheses, we can at least say that the complex polycentric pattern shown up in the archaeology matched the polycentricity of state distributions (to the three great cities and to both the eastern and Danube frontiers—for the latter, see below, p. 781), but must have gone beyond them, in an active commercial exchange network which linked Egypt, the Levant, and the Aegean in overlapping ways.

This exchange system had taken form by the early fifth century, and flourished in that century and the one following, which mark a genuine agrarian boom period for the eastern Mediterranean, as we saw in Chapter 8. Until 600/650, its patterns only changed in detail. Phocaean RS seems slowly to have decreased production after c.550, although Cypriot RS continued. Of the amphora types, LRA 2 seems to have developed in the sixth century, possibly at the expense of its Aegean counterpart LRA 3, which is less visible on sites from then on. The other types continued without many changes, in a set of patterns which were by the start of the seventh century very different indeed from those of the West. The fiscal spine continued without a break until then; in the Aegean, Abadie-Reynal argues that it grew in intensity in the sixth century, with an increase in Syro-Palestinian amphorae there as well.[44] The network was thus still in place, hardly touched, when the Persian and Arab invasions started.

Yet this network, so strong for so long, vanished in three generations, much more quickly than did the African system in the West. In 618–29, and then again, finally, after 642, Egypt no longer supplied Constantinople with grain in tax; nor, after 614, would Syria have supplied oil. As with the West in 439, the fiscal spine went at once. Byzantine Africa and Sicily were the only long-distance suppliers to the capital left; after the seventh century only Sicily remained. Nor did the Arabs create their own non-commercial distribution network; their fiscal system was, under the Umayyads, very much localized in the individual provinces of the caliphate (see above, pp. 130–3; below, pp. 778–80). For interregional exchange, commerce was all that was left. It certainly did still exist: the importance of Syro-Palestinian amphorae in the large 'deposit 30' on the Saraçhane site in Constantinople, dating to

---

[43] Abadie-Reynal, 'Céramique et commerce'. Note that African amphorae are relatively rare in the Aegean; if these patterns were indeed *annona*-related it was only the grain supply.

[44] Ibid., pp. 157–9; eadem, 'Les amphores protobyzantines d'Argos'; Hayes, *Excavations at Saraçhane*, II, pp. 63, 66.

655–70 (though with a deposit period spanning a century), shows that Levantine products reached the city in substantial quantities even after the Persian and Arab conquests. The same is true of the Levantine amphorae (around a tenth of the total) in the Crypta Balbi in Rome at the end of the seventh century.[45] But already by 700 nearly every ceramic type mentioned in the last few pages either ceased to be produced, or, if it survived (as with ERS, Egyptian LRA 7, Palestinian LRA 5, or the Aegean successors to LRA 2), ceased to be transported interregionally on any scale. By 700, that is to say, the interregional network was as weak in the East as it was in the West.[46]

The rapidity of this process has caused perplexities among its observers. Some invoke the possibility of a downturn around 550, so as to give it a longer time-span. Some wonder if there was not more interregional exchange after 700 than is generally thought, perhaps with barrels or skins replacing amphorae, or else (since, actually, amphorae remain common on eastern sites) with as-yet-unidentified amphora types.[47] The end of Red Slip products could, conversely, simply be seen as a change in taste, everywhere except in Egypt. This change in taste cannot be denied; all the same, the striking feature of eighth-century collections throughout the East is their localization. Only regional, indeed often microregional, types are found. There is no archaeological support for the maintenance of an interregional network on any scale; this only begins to reappear in the ninth century at the earliest. Conversely, however, in most of the East the productive sophistication of regional-level artefacts in the eighth century remained high (the major exception is the Byzantine heartland). Here, unlike in the West, we cannot see the breakdown of the Roman world-system as either causing or being caused by a breakdown in regional demand.

These points will be discussed in greater detail in the sections that follow. Here, they are set out simply to underline further the paradox that the East presents: a world-system that was in 600 pretty stable, and not tied too much to single routes or commodities, disappeared in a century, even though most of the regions which made it up did not themselves become substantially poorer. This paradox once again throws into relief the importance of the fiscal motor: as in the West, it must have ultimately been the fiscal movement of goods that tied the regions together under the empire. In the West, the tax spine also determined the direction of the main commercial route, but,

---

[45] Hayes, *Excavations at Saraçhane*, II, pp. 100–5; see n. 37 for Rome.

[46] Panella, 'Merci e scambi', pp. 670–2, 678–80; Sodini, 'Le bassin méditerranéen'; and see below, pp. 760, 774, 785. It has recently been argued that Cypriot RS was made for a further century (Pamela Armstrong, pers. comm.), but, if so, it was no longer available in early eighth-century Beirut, an important market for the ware in earlier centuries, and close to Cyprus (Reynolds, 'Pottery and the economy'); again, the interregional network was gone.

[47] See e.g. Walmsley, 'Production, exchange', pp. 326–9, for amphora replacement. Hayes, *Excavations at Saraçhane*, II, pp. 71–3, cf. 111–12, for the range of new types in eighth-century Constantinople.

conversely, commerce outlasted the Africa–Rome fiscal axis by over two centuries. In the East, the opposite was true; trade routes were more independent of the main grain *annona*, although they also broke down much more quickly. The very existence of these contrasts shows that commerce was not, anywhere, *simply* an epiphenomenon of the tax network. It would also, however, on the face of it imply that late Roman exchange across the eastern Mediterranean was more closely linked to taxation than that in the West, which is the opposite of what one might expect. In the East, once political unity was broken by conquest, interregional commerce was not able to hold up independently for long.

Of course, long-distance exchange would be re-established with time. By the twelfth century the Mediterranean was full of ships, many of them carrying bulk goods (including the polychrome glazed pottery which had become the next international ceramic style), and with no help from any overarching state structures.[48] But that system had to be constructed from scratch, using different rules, the first being that merchants could not expect much fiscal support outside their own region. Nor does it seem that the Mediterranean world-system of the central middle ages ever re-created the same sort of bulk-product hegemonies that the state-supported African productions of the Roman empire had at their height; indeed, they have never been created since. It is not inevitable that the Mediterranean, or half the Mediterranean, should be as closely integrated as it was in 400; it is not even 'natural', given the similarity of resources in most Mediterranean regions. It is even less inevitable that interregional products should get substantially inland from coastlines and waterways, given the difficulties of land transport before rail; but this was achieved in at least some areas of the later Roman empire, in Italy and in Syria-Palestine. These processes were largely the products of the political and fiscal underpinning of the Roman world-system, and, when that went away, so in the end did exchange.

At the end of the previous section it was suggested that the basic underpinning of regional economic sophistication was elite demand. Here, we have seen that the basic underpinning of interregional commercial exchange in our period was the fiscal system. These statements are not in contradiction. Elites are seldom so rich that they own outside single regions, at least not regions as large as Italy or Egypt. (The only exceptions in our period were Roman senators who owned on a large scale in both Italy and Africa: see above, pp. 163–4. They undoubtedly helped the integration that the fiscal system provided; but this, too, ended with Vandal confiscations after 439.) Elite demand was the basis for economic complexity at the regional or sub-regional level; but a large-scale infrastructure, such as an institutionally

---

[48] The best guide for the East is Goitein, *A Mediterranean society*, I, esp. pp. 301–52. For some of the scansion of the central medieval world-system, see Abu-Lughod, *Before European hegemony*.

ambitious and complex empire, was needed to link whole regions together at the level of bulk exchange. This is not intended as a generalization which covers the whole of pre-industrial history; the central middle ages after c.1100, and still more the fifteenth century and onwards, operated differently. It was, nonetheless, an abiding feature of the whole of our period. And the putting together of these separate patterns also makes clear a need to recognize a further level of analysis, which is the question of how the two patterns, fiscal and aristocratic, interrelated. It might be best to put it this way. The basic parameters of socio-economic *change* in the post-Roman world could be said to be, not two, but four. First, the changing strength, and geographical scale, of the fiscal system in operation in each region: of the basic machinery of taxation and of other forms of public surplus extraction, and of the geography of the state-backed movement of goods (both internal to the region and between regions). Second, the equivalent strength, scale, and geography of the wealth derived from private landowning, that is, the amount that was channelled in rent from peasants to landowners, where it was taken to, and how this changed across time. Both public and private wealth contributed to the establishment of structures of demand; public powers also, at their most organized, contributed to the wider infrastructure of exchange, as we have seen for interregional exchange in this section. Third, we must recognize the impact of war and generalized destruction, which could occur as different provinces were separated from the Roman state (or, as with the Gothic war in Italy, were violently reattached to it); some regions suffered seriously from this, such as Italy and Anatolia, although others hardly at all. This factor has tended to be referred to here only in passing, but it would be foolish to deny it altogether. Fourth, we can now add the degree to which each region or sub-region had been structurally integrated into the Roman world-system, and would therefore be knocked off course when it ended. The exporter regions discussed in this section would be prime candidates for this. We shall see in the rest of the chapter that these regions were indeed mostly hard hit in the post-Roman world, but there were exceptions, most notably Egypt; conversely, some regions more isolated from the world-system, notably Britain and inland Spain, were hard hit too. It is also interesting that in Italy, the more isolated north faced more serious economic involution than the more Mediterranean-orientated south. Here, the other parameters come into play as well.[49] Only local empirical analysis will, however, allow us to see how all four parameters affected any given society, and how they interrelated. That is the task of the next sections, which will provide, one by one, a final survey of all our regions. They will be

---

[49] These parameters are also briefly characterized in Wickham, 'Studying long-term change'. For the impact of warfare on early medieval long-distance exchange see Horden and Purcell, *Corrupting sea*, pp. 153–72. They minimize it, in fact, convincingly enough, but then conclude—perversely, in my view—that this is an argument against any major retreat of exchange in our period. They do not fully take into consideration the evidence presented here.

divided into three, a western Mediterranean group, an eastern Mediterranean group, and a northern group, since these were the geographical arenas of interregional exchange, when there was any. By 700, in the Mediterranean, this latter was fairly weak, as we have seen; in the North Sea region, however, as we shall see, it was perhaps already a little stronger.

3. The western Mediterranean I: Africa[50]

We have already seen what happened to African exports across our period. How exchange patterns worked inside the region is much harder to discern (until recently it was not much studied), but it is crucial to try to do so, for Africa is the type-example of an exporting region in the later Roman empire, and how this affected the local economy needs to be pinned down as clearly as possible. Our main evidence will be a handful of field surveys, including, however, several kiln-sites; outside Carthage, urban excavations have rarely so far generated detailed ceramic reports.

The ARS kiln-sites that have been best studied, El Mahrine in the Medjerda valley, Oudhna (Roman Uthina) south of Tunis, Sidi Khalifa (Roman Pheradi Maius) on the coast near Hammamet, and, outside this northern set, Sidi Marzouk Tounsi in inland central Tunisia (Byzacena) between Kairouan and Sbeïtla, were all major production centres for clearly identified export ranges, covering most of the post-fourth-century ARS types. Sidi Marzouk Tounsi seems to have ended in the early sixth century; the northern sites, however, continued without a break into the mid-seventh. After that, El Mahrine and Oudhna ended; Sidi Khalifa, whose output was probably already reduced after the early sixth, may have continued on a smaller scale up to 700 and even later. The latest ARS types, from the late seventh century, have not been found at these sites, so there is at least one other major late kiln-site to be found. Each of these were the foci for articulated production systems, which must have employed potters on a considerable scale in 'nucleated workshops' (in Oudhna, an urban site, in several different places in the city).[51] It is therefore significant that the patterns of ceramic availability in Africa itself which are currently known are much more sub-regional, even microregional. Carthage, of course, was a major consumer of

---

[50] This section will only deal with the heartland of the African provinces, that is to say Proconsularis and Byzacena in present-day Tunisia. The western provinces are too little studied to offer more than occasional comparators; see in general above, pp. 335–6.

[51] See respectively Mackensen, *Die spätantiken Sigillata- und Lampentöpfereien*, I, pp. 492–6; Barraud *et al.*, 'L'industrie céramique'; Ben Moussa, 'Production et circulation'—with later dates for Sidi Khalifa than Mackensen and Schneider, 'Production centres', p. 128; ibid., pp. 130–4 (Mackensen and Schneider's whole article is a valuable survey of all kiln-sites). The early sixth-century date for the end of Sidi Marzouk Tounsi fits the end of central Tunisian, 'sigillata C', wares in general: Panella, 'Merci e scambi', p. 649. For the scale of production, see Mackensen, *Die spätantiken Sigillata- und Lampentöpfereien*, I, pp. 471–86.

fine pottery. It is clear, however, that it used above all north Tunisian ARS ('sigillata D') rather than that of central Tunisia ('sigillata C' and 'E'). Indeed, even the main Sidi Khalifa wares, such as Hayes 88, are rare at Carthage, although the two are only 70 km apart.[52] Outside the regional capital, this pattern accentuates. The Segermes field survey, focused on an area close to Sidi Khalifa, shows ARS from that site above all, as one might expect. But the Kasserine survey, which is of an area inland from Sidi Marzouk Tounsi, shows local wares, imitating those from the major kilns, more than the products of those kilns themselves. The Dougga survey, covering an important grain area upstream from El Mahrine, shows no central Tunisian material in our period, although Sidi Marzouk Tounsi would have been accessible by inland routes; El Mahrine wares dominate in the Vandal period, but are matched by apparently local wares in the Byzantine period.[53] The pottery produced from all these kilns can be found across the whole Mediterranean, including in some remote areas, but it is evident that they had a highly incomplete distribution in the African countryside itself. The picture one gains is of a set of productions, substantially for export, focused on separate routes to the coast, and not interconnecting internally. This picture also, less surprisingly, fits work done outside the Tunisian heartland: Jerba had its own local ARS types (as well as importing sigillata D); so did Tripolitania ('Tripolitanian RS'); so did Sétif in east-central Algeria (and its wares were not fully available in its own hinterland, as a survey of the Belezma range to the south-east found).[54] A producer region of a major export commodity whose own access to that commodity is as localized as this is a region whose internal exchange network was much less articulated than its external network. Africa's economic complexity was, that is to say, unusually dependent on Mediterranean-wide exchange.

Oil production is harder to track, for amphorae cannot be pinned down as tightly as fine wares can. Its association with export can be shown, however. Early amphora kiln-sites in Byzacena, the main oil-producing province, are coastal, indicating clearly that oil must have moved from its inland production centres by other means, probably skins (above, p. 446), and that the

[52] For Hayes 88 in Carthage, see Ben Moussa, 'Production et circulation', p. 63; Lund, 'Hellenistic, Roman and late Roman finewares', p. 452.

[53] Segermes: Lund, 'Hellenistic, Roman and late Roman finewares', pp. 466–9, with idem, 'African Red Slip Ware re-evaluated', p. 574. Kasserine: Neuru, 'The pottery', p. 256, with Fentress *et al.*, 'ARS and its markets'. Dougga: De Vos, *Rus africum*, pp. 63–6, cf. 41–6 (A. Ciotola). This pattern is fairly clear now, but has only very recently been confronted by the literature: see also Pentz, *From Roman Proconsularis*, pp. 143–5. As recently as 1991 Jean Peyras could write, concerning his survey of standing buildings in a section of northern Tunisia, 'Nous n'avons pas pu réaliser d'étude systematique des tessons. Ce défaut... ne gêne pas trop l'étude économique' [!] (Peyras, *Le Tell*, p. 444).

[54] Jerba: Fentress *et al.*, 'ARS and its markets'. Tripolitania: Hayes, *Late Roman pottery*, pp. 304–9; Barker *et al.*, *Farming the desert*, II, pp. 321–5. Sétif: Mohamedi and Fentress, *Fouilles de Sétif*, pp. 193–4, cf. Fentress *et al.*, 'Prospectus dans le Belezma', p. 111.

amphorae were for transport by ship. In the Vandal period this changed in part, and kilns for new amphora types begin to be found inland as well, presumably closer to the centres of oil production: one was, again, Sidi Marzouk Tounsi. This does not in itself indicate that the export of oil was less important; the latter site, at least, had well-established links with the coast, and anyway in some parts of the West (notably Spain) there was some increase in export in the Vandal period. Its production was evidently refigured in this period, all the same, maybe because the ownership of olive groves was more localized after the Vandal expropriation of the senatorial aristocracy; the fact that oil was no longer being exported as tax may also have had an effect on production, as Ted Peña has suggested.[55] Its scale seems to have been very large, judging by the number of presses found in the Kasserine survey; it was often a specialized production there.[56] Such production, if repeated widely across Byzacena, as seems likely, would have far surpassed local needs, and would not have helped the integration of local exchange either—for each microregion would have been specializing in the same crop, and would have been separately linked to the coast and the outside world. The oil picture thus matches, and reinforces, the patterns we have seen for ARS.

The early Vandal period does not see much change in these patterns, except for some shifts in amphora production; indeed, the fifth century is generally regarded by rural archaeologists as part of the high point of late Roman economic complexity in Africa. The active exchange of ARS and oil has some counterparts in our sketchier evidence for other products. The scale of grain production cannot be documented archaeologically, but we saw earlier that there is ostrakon evidence in the Vandal period for the demesne production of barley (and also oil) in southern Numidia, and for its careful accounting, which indicates an interest in exchange (see pp. 266, 273). The Tablettes Albertini from the 490s, for their part, show an irrigated agriculture of olives, vines, figs, almonds, and other tree crops, some of which were *nobelli*, newly planted. These texts are all from semi-arid inland areas, on the edge of possible agriculture, but they are economically active in the late fifth century—oil is important in each case, but other types of agriculture are stressed as well. (On the coast, murex production on the island of Jerba seems to have continued throughout the Vandal period too, although that was more of a luxury product.) This may further fit the continuing prosperity of urban elites, as seen in their building programmes (above, p. 637). One might advance an argument that the Vandals had no negative effect on the internal economy of Africa at all; that, if anything, the

---

[55] For the kilns, see Peacock *et al.*, 'Roman amphora production'; iidem, 'Roman pottery production'; Stone *et al.*, 'Suburban land-use', pp. 311–13; Peña, 'The mobilisation', p. 213; Bonifay, 'La céramique africaine', pp. 124–7, who substantially nuances the evidence for the inland move of kilns.

[56] Mattingly, 'Oil presses'; see, in general, idem, 'Oil for export?'.

absence of the external tax burden, and the end of large-scale senatorial landowning there, which had taken so many agrarian rents to Rome and elsewhere in Italy, allowed the commercial economy to bounce forward.[57]

Such a reading would, of course, assume that there were buyers of African products across the western Mediterranean who could afford goods on the same scale as before. We have already seen, however (pp. 711–13), that this is unlikely. Italy was poorer, for a start, simply because it did not receive tax and rent, and the penetration of African goods there seems to have lessened at once. It is not likely that export expansion in Spain made up for this. Something had to give, and in the late Vandal period, after c.500, there begin to be signs of it. The end of ARS production in Byzacena is an important one. The Kasserine survey also seems to show a retreat in agricultural intensity that begins in the early sixth century. This is linked to nomad attacks by some commentators, but it is equally likely that it indicates a fall in export production and thus the beginning of an economic 'abatement' (above, p. 457) of a more inland, drier, export zone.[58] The weakness of African written documentation after the 430s means that how these shifts played out in local socio-economic relationships cannot be observed; we cannot even speculate about whether peasants did worse than aristocrats, for example. We have, however, seen that the late Vandal tax system, while still remaining capable of making political leaders very rich, was also showing signs of structural weakness by the time of the Byzantine reconquest (above, pp. 91–2). This must have had a further impact on the internal movement of goods, which may have become more localized. In many places, on many estates, very little had doubtless changed by 534; but the global economic trends were by now towards simplification.

The later sixth century saw the reintegration of the core African provinces into the empire, a good deal of building in Carthage, which was still doing well in the early decades of the seventh (pp. 640–1), and a substantial investment in the army and the fiscal infrastructure. It did not, however, see a reversal in these trends, which indeed steadily accentuated. All our field surveys, not just Kasserine, show a sharp decrease in sites identified by ARS in the late sixth century and later, which would result in the end of identifiable finds by 700. What this means has to be treated with considerable care, however. It is not uncommon to see it in terms of depopulation, even land abandonment; underpinning interpretations of this kind is the knowledge that much of Africa went pastoral in the end (see above, pp. 18–19),

---

[57] See *Tablettes Albertini*, nn. 3, 11, 24, for *nobelli*; see for comments Mattingly, 'Olive cultivation'. For murex, Elizabeth Fentress (pers. comm.), and Fontana, 'Un "immondezzaio" '. For Vandal-period merchants, see the documentation in Courtois, *Les Vandales*, p. 322, with Ferrandus, *Vita Fulgentii*, c. 8. For the issue of Vandal commercial prosperity, see Fulford and Peacock, *Excavations at Carthage*, I.2, pp. 255–62; cf. Wickham, *Land and power*, pp. 95–6.

[58] For Kasserine and the nomads, see Hitchner, 'Kasserine 1982–1985', p. 180; idem, 'Kasserine 1982–1986', p. 40; cf. Lepelley, 'Progrès dans la connaissance', pp. 279–81.

including all the areas that have been surveyed except for around Segermes and Dougga. But the end-point for the surveys is, of course, simply the final end of ARS as a diagnostic pottery, and in fact Segermes, the best-published Tunisian survey, begins to show a 'society in decline' at just the moment when the largest-scale type from neighbouring Sidi Khalifa, Hayes 88, ceased production. The Dougga survey, the most recent, paid more attention to common wares, and the surveyors found there a seventh century in which sites with only common ware outnumbered sites with ARS three to one—this in addition to the more local ARS types which characterized the Byzantine period.[59] I would argue that most of the changes in these field surveys have to do with ARS availability, which was already relatively localized as we have seen, rather than with settlement. But we must accept that ARS productions and local distributions were indeed steadily retreating across the Byzantine period. The slight increase in exports to the East was from a fairly low level, and was anyway more than matched by the steady decreases in exports in the West (above, pp. 711–13). Oil exports continued, too, but on a similar downward curve, and African amphorae ceased to be exported by 700 as well. Oil production certainly did not cease when ARS production did, as we shall see in a moment, but the intensity of specialization must have decreased here too. The final crisis of the western Mediterranean exchange network was not until the late seventh century, but its scale was greatly reduced as much as a century earlier, and this must have already been felt inside the producer region. There is no archaeological sign of any area doing well in Africa outside Carthage and its hinterland after 550 or so, whether city or countryside, although urban society continued, individuals doubtless maintained their wealth, and at least local production continued almost everywhere.[60]

Byzantine Africa is sometimes regarded as a structural failure, either at once or after around 600: as a demonstration that one of the most long-lasting of Justinian's conquests was useless to the empire, or actively harmful, as fiscal exactions drained its wealth or else were used up in wars against the Berbers. This is unreasonable; rather, after a period of reconstruction, the province seems to have been entirely stable until the Arab attacks began in 647, a century later—stable enough for its army and navy to take Constantinople itself in 610 (above, p. 124).[61] But we must ask what good

---

[59] Segermes: Dietz et al., Africa proconsularis, II, pp. 471–2, 782, 799, cf. pp. 469, 779–80, for Hayes 88, certainly a Sidi Khalifa product (see e.g. Ben Moussa, 'Production et circulation', p. 63). Dougga: De Vos, Rus africum, pp. 65–6, 71, cf. 42–6. For abandonment, see also above, n. 58 for Kasserine. But Islamic pottery has been found on both the Segermes and Kasserine surveys on a small scale: Dietz et al., Africa proconsularis, II, p. 472; Neuru, 'The pottery', p. 259.

[60] For the Carthage hinterland, where little changed until the seventh century, see Greene, 'Une reconnaissance archéologique', a brief taster of a future book.

[61] Diehl, L'Afrique byzantine, esp. pp. 593–5, was fairly negative about the Byzantine state in Africa; more upbeat are Pringle, The defence, pp. 113–15; Cameron, 'Vandal and Byzantine Africa', pp. 561–9; Panella, 'Merci e scambi', pp. 675–7 (until the seventh century, at least).

reintegration into the empire could have done to Africa's economy, even hypothetically. The region's economic high point around 400 was made possible because the imperial world-system made the whole West stable, and a potentially prosperous market for African goods, which was more economically advantageous (for some) than the high taxation on the region was disadvantageous (for others). After 534 this geo-economic situation could have been re-established if Justinian had managed to reintegrate the whole Mediterranean, West as well as East, without economic damage. This he certainly did not manage; Italy was ruined by the Gothic war, and Byzantine Spain, although certainly part of the Mediterranean economy, was only a small section of the Spanish coast. The western markets continued to fragment, and demand for African products continued to drop. Africa was more integrated into the East, it is true, as the rise in ARS exports in the late sixth century shows. Leontios of Neapolis' *Life* of John the Almsgiver, a text of the 620s, refers to the Africa–Egypt route; and the *Teaching of Jacob*, a text of the 640s, shows the apparently normal sale of Constantinople cloth in Carthage.[62] All the same, eastern trade routes could exist perfectly well without Africa, at the other end of the Mediterranean, and did not change greatly as a result of its incorporation into them. Africa was, simply, less essential; and it is probable that these developing eastern links did not compensate for a renewed loss of African tax revenues to the capital. Africa's grain was only vital to imperial survival after Egypt fell to the Persians in 618–19, and this role did not necessarily bring it any economic advantage. What the century 534–647 brought to Africa was a new and reduced role: as a region which, however rich it still was agriculturally, was no longer an export powerhouse because there was nowhere any longer which needed its goods.

How much effect the move to this more limited economic role had on Africa would then depend on how much the region had previously depended on external demand for its artisanal and agricultural specializations to operate. Such demand was not essential for the stability even of exporter regions, as we shall see in the case of Egypt (pp. 759–69). But for Africa to survive the export downturn, it would have to have had its own internal market, an exchange structure sufficiently articulated to absorb local production, and, above all, a rich local aristocracy and/or ecclesiastical and official elite. We cannot say anything directly about aristocratic wealth in the region from our written sources, and urban archaeology, as we have seen (pp. 637–44), is ambiguous about the global wealth of elites after 550 (although some certainly survived).[63] But the ceramic distributions just

---

[62] Leontios, *Life* of John the Almsgiver, cc. 10, 20–1, 25 (cf. cc. 8, 11, 28, for other western links); *Teaching of Jacob*, V.20, ed. in Dagron and Déroche, 'Juifs et Chrétiens', pp. 215–19, commentary at pp. 237–40.

[63] See Ch. 4, n. 141.

discussed strongly support the argument that internal exchange was not very articulated in Africa, and that interregional exchange was its principal motor. It may well have been that elite wealth itself largely derived from export; if that was so, then, far from aristocratic buying-power cushioning the effects of the export downturn, it would have decreased as exports themselves did. All of this means that Africa's economic structures will have had to experience a painful period of adjustment: to a level of production which would fit a vastly reduced level of external demand, and probably a lower level of internal demand as well.

This is what we see in the Byzantine period in Africa: that painful adjustment. Agricultural productive intensities must have dropped; and fine-ware production went into terminal decline. Internal demand alone evidently could not sustain the industrial levels of ARS production; smaller productions, reduced exports, and presumably higher prices eventually generated a catastrophe-flip, and production ceased altogether. We could probably conclude that any other large-scale production—in cloth, for example—would have faced the same problems. These processes must have been well under way before the Arabs arrived in 647. All the same, the final blow to African productions occurred in the second half of the seventh century, when Byzantine rule was restricted, ineffectively, to Proconsularis, northern Tunisia, and any complex economic activity must have become very fragile. El Mahrine went out of production by perhaps 670, and when the Arabs took Carthage in 698 there was probably little left of the old infrastructure. One result is that diagnostic ceramic types are no longer useful guides to rural settlement, which has generated the catastrophist interpretations already alluded to. But, whereas artisanal activity must have simplified considerably, it is less likely that agriculture changed so fast. African oil is written up in at least one ninth-century text (above, p. 640). Already in the tenth century Ibn Ḥawqal refers to oil exports to Egypt from Sfax in former Byzacena, and by the eleventh these can be seen to be extensive in the Geniza documents. It is likely that most of the olive groves survived the intervening period with little change, and that renewed export possibilities simply meant a revival in the intensity of their exploitation. In general, the documentary sources for the tenth century testify to an agrarian wealth that would be hard to explain if agriculture itself had collapsed in the seventh.[64] It is most likely that, after the chaos of the late seventh century, a series of localized economies survived, more or less complex according to local economic conditions, which could be built on when stability returned. Urban archaeology would support this picture, too, with continuities in Sbeïtla or Béja

---

[64] Ibn Ḥawqal (Ibn Hauqal), *Configuration de la terre*, I, p. 67; Goitein, *A Mediterranean society*, I, pp. 272, 302, 344; see for other documentary sources for the eleventh century, ibid., pp. 101–5, 153–5, 224–6 (for cloth); Vanacker, 'Géographie économique'. Some African olive oil was again being exported to Italy as early as the 880s: Citarella, 'Merchants, markets', p. 263.

counterposed to a greater degree of crisis in Uchi Maius (above, pp. 638–40). In general, this archaeology would indicate the eighth century as a low point, with signs of revival appearing in the ninth or tenth. This is the most likely scenario in city and countryside alike.

Documentary references have become more prominent in the previous paragraph; this reflects the poor state of early Arab archaeology in Tunisia, with few sites, and almost no published ceramic reports at all. Oil probably mostly travelled in skins when its export revived, so amphorae do not have to be looked for; but if we are to understand the internal structures of exchange in eighth- and ninth-century Africa, we will need to know much more about table and common wares. We can at least say that they continued to be made, at least locally, with some common-ware types already beginning in the Byzantine period (or earlier), like the often buff-coloured bowls and jugs that have been found in Byzantine Carthage and Sidi Jdidi, and the Red Painted ware of Carthage or Dougga. The dishes in a white fabric imitating the latest Hayes forms, and the stamped and painted common wares, found in Pupput (Hammamet) and Neapolis (Nabeul) in levels from the very late seventh century—indeed, possibly the early eighth—probably show a local kiln shifting away from the ARS tradition. If the Sidi Khalifa kilns did continue past 700, it is presumably these kinds of ware that they produced. Less clearly characterized local wares have been identified at Sbeïtla and Rougga in Byzacena and Belalis Maior in Proconsularis for the eighth and ninth centuries.[65] These wares could be seen as the artisanal counterparts to the localized, less intensive, oil production postulated for the same period. The best ceramic study for North Africa in this period is Nancy Benco's analysis of the Baṣra kilns in northern Morocco, which began in the early ninth century; the first century of production there was dominated by buff common wares, unambitious but of reasonable quality, produced at what Peacock would call the 'individual workshop' level. The Baṣra kilns served the Idrīsid kingdom, a Berber polity rather different to, and probably simpler than, the Arab state in Ifrīqiya; it would be surprising if the local Tunisian wares of the eighth and ninth centuries were at a lower productive level than that, and there is no sign of it. Tunisian ceramics remained skilled enough for potters to be able to adopt polychrome glazed techniques when they came in from the East in the later ninth century, and by the mid-tenth century they were beginning to expand their

[65] See respectively Fulford and Peacock, *Excavations at Carthage*, I.2, pp. 16–17, 198–218, 225–31, with Stevens, *Bir el Knissia*, I, pp. 79–84 (J. Freed), and eadem *et al.*, 'Bir Ftouha', pp. 382–3; Ben Abed *et al.*, 'Note preliminaire', pp. 17–18, 23; De Vos, *Rus africum*, p. 45 (Dougga); Bonifay, 'Les ultimes niveaux' (Pupput and Neapolis: there were also globular amphorae in a post-LRA 2 tradition here, cf. below, n. 167); Ben Moussa, 'Production et circulation', pp. 66–8 (Sidi Khalifa); Bejaoui, 'Nouvelles données archéologiques', pp. 38–42 (Sbeïtla); Guéry, 'Survivance', pp. 401–7 (Rougga); Mahjoubi, *Recherches*, p. 451 (Belalis Maior). I am grateful to Susan Stevens and Elizabeth Fentress for a discussion of these issues. For oil in skins, see Goitein, *A Mediterranean society*, I, p. 344.

production, which became once again in the eleventh one of the region's key exports, north to Italy and, eventually, east to Egypt.[66] Even in the eleventh century Tunisian oil and ceramic exports doubtless did not match those of 400; but the period was nonetheless a prosperous one. The localization of the eighth century had by now, as it seems at present, been substantially reversed.

The African heartland in Tunisia was usually ruled by a single state—the only exception was the crisis period of 647–98—and tax-raising, although perhaps faltering in the early sixth century, survived throughout. We can say less about the private wealth of its elites, but the patterns of urban archaeology seem to imply that a modest level of wealth persisted in many places. Again, except for the late seventh century, it was not dogged by war. These are three of my four parameters for economic change in our period, and the region saw a relative stability in all three. But the complexity of its economy was dramatically reduced between c.500 and c.700, with an eighth century so simple and localized that archaeologists have found it hard to see at all. This emphasizes what I have already argued on other grounds: that Africa was very dependent indeed on the Mediterranean exchange network, far more in fact than any other region taken as a whole, and that its economy was seriously blown off course when that network ended. But this was not the moment when Tunisia abandoned settled agriculture and the traditions of the Mediterranean urban economy. The relatively simple localized economic systems of the eighth century remained stable enough for a renewed complexity to develop, by the tenth century at the latest; artisanal activity never lost a certain minimum of professionalism. This simplicity was a long way from the production and exchange levels of ARS, but it was not, probably, so very far from the productive levels of western regions like northern Italy in 800 or so. African production and exchange changed drastically in our period, but not terminally.

4. The western Mediterranean II: Italy

Italy is much better-documented in its archaeology than is Africa, and there is much more possibility of sub-regional and microregional differentiation

---

[66] Benco, *The early medieval pottery industry*, esp. pp. 66–7, 108–20, 164–71; cf. also the contemporary ceramics of Nakūr, slightly further east but in a different and smaller kingdom, where production was similar but the percentages of hand-made wares were higher: Acién *et al.*, 'Les céramiques tournées', is the most recent survey. For early glaze, see *Les couleurs de Tunisie*, pp. 85–96; Daouatli, 'La céramique médiévale'; and the critical survey of Johns and Kennet, 'An outline of the development of glazed pottery'. Ibn Ḥawqal puts stress on Tunis's polychrome pottery production in the late tenth century (Ibn Hauqal, *Configuration de la terre*, I, p. 70). For export to Italy in the early eleventh century, Berti and Tongiorgi, *I bacini ceramici*, pp. 162–75; to Egypt in the late eleventh, François, *Céramiques médiévales*, pp. 9, 13–19, 157, 181. Glazed wares were never as common on African sites as ARS had been, however.

here, which can, in turn, be related to our written sources in more articulated ways. I shall set out the (mostly ceramic) evidence for exchange first, and then relate this to the wider socio-economic patterns discussed in previous chapters.[67]

Late Roman Italy had its own ceramic productions, to set alongside ARS, which, as we have seen, was available everywhere in the peninsula. These were mostly *acroma depurata*, uncoloured wares with a refined fabric, unpretentious but well made. At the higher end of the market, this ceramic type was decorated with red paint, normally in broad parallel lines or else fairly rough blotches; such semi-fine Red Painted wares were often made on a large enough scale, and in a sufficiently standardized way, that they have been called 'industrial'—in Peacock's terms, the 'nucleated workshop' level—in this respect, at least, paralleling individual ARS productions themselves. Examples of these wares can be found widely in the peninsula, from the Modenese in the north down to Calle di Tricarico in inland Basilicata, in the instep of Italy; some of them imitated ARS forms. In northern Italy, we also find late Roman glazed wares, both in inland parts of the Po plain where ARS was less common, and on the coast. Nearly every part of the peninsula, in fact, had significant local table-ware productions in the fifth century; the only important exception was apparently Rome itself, which could so easily import from elsewhere. Each of these productions had, however, a fairly restricted distribution; the 150 km range of the Calle productions (in a fairly mountainous area, too) and the occasional availability of northern glaze in south-central Italy are unusual.[68] Italy was, in terms of its own table ware, our standard marker for artisan production, a set of largely unrelated sub-regions even at the start of our period, linked together only by the common accessibility of ARS.

Agricultural products had a slightly different distribution. African oil imports into Italy were largely restricted to coastal sites, as amphora patterns imply. Conversely, however, we know from a mixture of sources that internal exchange was more complex, at least in the south. Rome had fiscal links with the south Italian provinces, in that Lucania (Basilicata) and Campania were its sources of pork, a state-supported product. The extensive senatorial and ecclesiastical estates in southern Italy and Sicily will also have channelled rents to Rome, in grain, wine, and oil, to supplement the *annona* (see above, pp. 76, 163). There may also have been an independent grain

[67] These have been discussed in less detail in Wickham, 'Early medieval archaeology', pp. 9–11, and 'Italy at the end of the Mediterranean world system'.

[68] Calle: di Giuseppe, 'La fornace di Calle'. Modena: Gelichi and Giordani, *Il tesoro nel pozzo*, pp. 85–8. Imitations: Fontana, 'Le "imitazioni" '. Glaze: Brogiolo and Gelichi, 'La ceramica invetriata', with Paroli, 'La ceramica invetriata', pp. 35, 38, for late Roman glaze on the Adriatic coast of central Italy, and Sannazaro, 'La ceramica invetriata'. Rome may possibly have had a local RS in the fourth century: Fontana, 'Le "imitazioni" ', pp. 91–5. See, for the whole period up to 700, Saguì, *Ceramica in Italia*.

commerce from Sicily to Rome around 400, as Domenico Vera has argued; and wine from Calabria and north-east Sicily, in Keay 52 amphorae, was common in Rome in the fifth century, as also further afield, as far as Marseille.[69] Thanks to the demand of the capital, internal agrarian exchange covered longer distances than internal artisanal exchange did; this characterized above all the 'senatorial region', stretching down the Tyrrhenian coast from Rome to Sicily. Everywhere in the peninsula, however, local demand for goods seems to have been buoyant at the start of our period.

When ARS began to have distribution problems around 450, these must have been caused by the disruptions of the end of the *annona* in 439, rather than by changes in either production or demand. As we have seen, ARS productions remained stable in the early Vandal period; as for the Italian end, the late fifth century marks the further development of a wide variety of local imitations of ARS forms, whether slipped or Red Painted, often the products of the 'industrial' kiln-sites that already existed, which attest to continuing levels of demand.[70] The fiscal aspects of the distribution of goods in Italy were still in reasonable shape into the Ostrogothic period too; Cassiodorus' *Variae* complain about food supplies, but he takes for granted their normal availability.[71] Nonetheless, the senatorial aristocracy must have been weakened by the loss of their African lands (above, p. 164), and Rome was by now contracting quickly in size, following the end of the *annona*; both of these must have had a considerable effect on agrarian production, at least in southern Italy. Some of the Keay 52 kilns in southern Calabria seem to stop in 500, for example—although Calabrese wine certainly remained available along the south Italian coast and in Rome. Paul Arthur has argued that table ware productions in northern Campania, too, were already in trouble in the early sixth century, which further argues for a general weakening of demand.[72] It is always hard to be certain about the exact date that sites end, but it is plausible, as was already proposed in Chapter 4 (p. 204), to see processes like these as consequences of the breaking of the Africa–Italy fiscal spine, this time at the consumer rather than the producer end. This made the peninsula globally poorer, and necessitated structural adjustments, even before the Gothic war.

The Gothic war of 535–54 nonetheless marked a major break in the Italian economy, and the Lombard invasions and incomplete conquest of

[69] Pork: Barnish, 'Pigs, plebeians'. Sicilian grain: Vera, 'Fra Egitto ed Africa'. Wine: most recently, Pacetti, 'La questione delle Keay LII'; Bonifay *et al.*, *Fouilles à Marseille*, p. 372.

[70] Fontana, 'Le "imitazioni" '. In the Modenese, ARS was hoarded after c.500: above, p. 210.

[71] For a discussion of the evidence of Cassiodorus, and an analysis of the balance between the fiscal and the commercial side of this food distribution, see above all Ruggini, *Economia e società*, pp. 205–359.

[72] For Keay 52, see di Gangi and Lebole, 'Anfore Keay LII', p. 762. They see Keay 52 as stopping in c.550 and being succeeded by another, similar, amphora type ('succedanee' to Keay 52); others have a looser definition, and see the amphora type as continuing to the eighth century. For Campania, Arthur, 'Local pottery'.

the peninsula made permanent its political fragmentation. In exchange terms, the mid-sixth century sees an extension of the trends already seen in previous decades: the Calle kiln-site, for example, probably went out of use at around this time. The Lombards managed to conquer, in the main, those areas with least organic connection to the Mediterranean world-system, and the new political boundaries (which were fought over for some time) made those connections that much more difficult.[73] In the second half of the sixth century it is clearer than ever before that Italy had, in economic terms, become a loose set of unrelated sub-regions, each of which needs to be assessed separately. Here, we shall look at four, each with a relatively clear ceramic history, as they developed across the seventh and eighth centuries.

Northern Italy was never as fully part of the Roman world-system as were the centre and the south, and it had, as we have seen, its own artisanal traditions. These continued into the Lombard period without much of a break. The Lombards themselves imported a ceramic type from Pannonia, usually called *ceramica longobarda* in the modern literature, characterized by a highly burnished exterior and stamped decoration; this had been hand-made in Pannonia, but in Italy was absorbed into the standard pottery-making of the north, professionally made on a wheel by now, and located towards the top end of the market. Kilns from the decades around 590 that were found on the former Capitolium at Brescia (cf. above, p. 651) produced *ceramica longobarda*, glazed wares, standard *acroma* common wares, and cooking-pots: most of the range of the ceramics of the area, at a decent technological level, all together. This is the sort of pattern that one finds elsewhere in the north too, with some interesting cultural/stylistic crossovers (some glazed *ceramica longobarda*, for example, has been found in Pie-monte).[74] They had localized distributions, but, at least initially, there was enough demand in the Lombard north to allow a complex production of fine and semi-fine wares to continue, as with the Red Painted wares found in the 'pozzi-deposito' of the Modenese around 600 (above, p. 209), in some cases alongside simpler, sometimes slow-wheel or hand-made, coarse wares. Imports were by now rare; ARS is only occasional by now, except in Friuli at the top of the Adriatic, which must have had better connections to the sea through Aquileia and Grado (ARS indeed even reached southern Austria, over the Alps, until the early seventh century). There was still a wider level of

---

[73] For the economic fragmentation of Italy, Marazzi, 'The destinies of the late antique Italies'; Zanini, 'La ceramica bizantina in Italia'.

[74] See in general Brogiolo and Gelichi, 'La ceramica comune'; Lusuardi Siena, 'La ceramica longobarda'; and, for details, Olcese, *Ceramiche in Lombardia*. For the Brescia kiln and other Brescia sites, see Guglielmetti, 'La ceramica comune'; Brogiolo *et al.*, 'Associazioni ceramiche'; and the large repertoire of materials in Brogiolo, *S. Giulia di Brescia*, pp. 101–270 (pp. 175–220 being a detailed study of *ceramica longobarda* by M. G. Vitali). For glazed *ceramica long-obarda*, Pantò, 'Produzione e commerci', pp. 267–8.

exchange, nonetheless, marked by *pietra ollare*, soapstone vessels cut in the north-west Alps and generally available in the Po plain (as also, to an extent, the Rhône valley).[75]

The Lombard north went through a further moment of involution, however, in the mid-seventh century. The surviving fine-ware productions ceased; all that was left were highly localized common- and coarse-ware types, usually wheel-thrown still, but much simpler in style: Peacock's 'individual workshop' level at best. It is hard to see why this should have occurred; nothing was going wrong with the Lombard polity around then. We do know, all the same, that the Lombard aristocracy was not, for the most part, enormously wealthy (above, pp. 210–18), and global demand must have decreased; it may well be that c.650 simply marked another catastrophe-flip, when falling demand finally made it impossible to carry on professional ceramic production any longer. Nor did this change back quickly: as far as can at present be seen, there would be no large-scale fine-ware productions in the north again until the late twelfth or thirteenth centuries.[76] Even imports into northern Italy were slow to revive; glazed Forum ware from Rome hardly got beyond the Ravenna area in the ninth century, although by the eleventh, at least, the north had access to some Islamic glaze. The ninth century saw some increased standardization of coarse-ware production, which we will come back to, and *pietra ollare* was by now available down the Adriatic coast, as far as Otranto, indicating some widening of exchange, but the north did not see a major development in ceramic production until well after our period ends.[77]

Northern Italy after 650 is an interesting test case for the proposition that ceramic production and distribution are good guides to economic complexity. (We must from here on focus on table wares and containers; amphorae are rare in the sub-region by now.) On one level, it is paradoxical. Paolo Delogu has seen in the Lombard–Byzantine treaty of 680 the beginnings of a new stabilization in the Italian political structure, which would allow a revival in exchange and general prosperity; we can see trade along the Po in King Liutprand's detailed commercial agreement with Byzantine Comacchio, in the Po delta, in 715 or 730; in Aistulf's reign, *negotiantes* were sufficiently important that his laws of 750 assigned military obligations to them on the basis of movable wealth rather than land; church-building in the eighth century has been seen as one of the markers of an urban revival

[75] Friuli: Villa, 'Alcuni aspetti'. Austria: Ladstätter, *Die materielle Kultur*, pp. 116–17, 203–7, 210. For ARS availability, see in general Tortorella, 'La sigillata africana'. *Pietra ollare*: Bolla, 'La pietra ollare'; Alberti, 'Produzione e commercializzazione'.

[76] Brogiolo and Gelichi, 'La ceramica comune'; iidem, 'Ceramiche, tecnologia'. See for details iidem, *Le ceramiche altomedievali*. I am very grateful to Sauro Gelichi for his advice about this section.

[77] Paroli, 'La ceramica invetriata', p. 45; Gelichi and Sbarra, 'La tavola di S. Gerardo', for Islamic glaze; Alberti, 'Produzione e commercializzazione', p. 338, for *pietra ollare*.

(above, p. 650).[78] After 780–800 Venice developed quickly as an international port, exchanging eastern luxuries for, as it seems, slaves (above, pp. 690–1); the exchange infrastructure of the northern rivers crystallized fast, with new markets mentioned in the sources both in cities and the countryside; the Carolingian aristocracy was markedly wealthier, implying increased demand (above, p. 218); there is some evidence by the end of the century of agrarian production for sale (above, p. 300). Then, in the tenth century, cities expanded in size, and we are into the great centuries of northern Italian urban autonomies—all without ceramics in the north changing much.[79]

These issues take us well out of our period, but they are worth a few comments all the same. Eighth-century exchange undoubtedly existed, but it is far from clear how large-scale it was. As observed in earlier chapters, the inland cities were always relatively substantial, but their inhabitants were still not that rich in the eighth century (see esp. pp. 646–56). Our best two documents for Comacchio, Liutprand's treaty and a court-case from 852 from Cremona (with extensive testimony for the situation in the years before 810), make it clear that the major good the *Comaclenses* brought inland was salt, the only bulk commodity which was transported in every period, and here, then, a sign of the weakness, not the intensity, of large-scale exchange. Excavations at Grado and other coastal sites in the Veneto have shown no imports in eighth-century levels. Even Venice's rise seems to have been less to do with bulk goods than because of its role as a funnel for prestige, long-distance goods from the East to the Carolingian aristocratic elite, in Italy and even over the Alps into Francia. (The Alps were not, of course, easy for bulk goods to cross, and they would not have been the first bulk-good route to be developed in the early middle ages.)[80] There are thus grounds for arguing that non-luxury exchange activity, at least up to 800, was relatively limited, and this fits with the argument that aristocratic demand was also relatively limited. Up to then, the simplicity of ceramic production could be said to fit with the other indicators we have for the economic system of the north.

After 800 aristocratic wealth and generalized exchange activity undoubtedly increased, as we have just seen. As cities increased in size again, their

[78] Delogu, 'La fine del mondo antico', pp. 20–3; for an edition of the Liutprand treaty, Hartmann, *Zur Wirtschaftsgeschichte Italiens*, pp. 123–4 (cf. Balzaretti, 'Cities, emporia', pp. 219–25); Aistulf 3. These are much-cited texts.

[79] For markets, see most recently Settia, ' "Per foros Italiae" ', and Bocchi, 'Città e mercati'; Toubert, *Dalla terra*, pp. 214–45, is basic for agrarian marketing. For urban expansion, the classic is Violante, *La società milanese*, pp. 99–134. For a general context, Jones, 'La storia economica', pp. 1620–64; idem, *The Italian city state*, pp. 92–107.

[80] Manaresi, *I placiti*, n. 56. See above, n. 11, for the issue of salt. The Liutprand text also mentions olive oil, *garum*, and pepper; the Cremona text refers to generic spices; but salt dominates both. For Grado, Brogiolo and Cagnana, 'Nuove ricerche'. More upbeat are Violante, *La società milanese*, pp. 3–70; Wickham, *Early medieval Italy*, pp. 88–91; McCormick, *Origins*, pp. 630–8.

collective demand would also have favoured the revival of artisanal production. But its scale would have been for a long time largely restricted to individual city territories, for that was the range of most aristocratic land-owning (above, p. 216). The rise to international importance of northern Italy's merchants was based on the carrying trade between the East and the Frankish lands for a long time, along the lines pioneered by the Venetians, rather than on Italian bulk productions (of cloth, for example), which cannot easily be attested on an international scale in the north before the twelfth century.[81] This puts the emphasis on evidence for *local* artisanal specializations, and some do exist: soap in Piacenza by 744 and in Pavia around 1000, for example, besides, always, luxury craftsmen such as gold- and silversmiths.[82] In terms of ceramics, what this would lead one to predict would be the revival in the ninth and tenth centuries of standardized types with local distributions: the regularity and the professionalism of their productions would be more significant than their 'fineness' or their wide geographical range. Although Italian pottery is less well studied after 800 or so, this is what we are beginning to find with coarse- and common-ware types; the later ninth century and, still more, the tenth sees a revival of larger-scale and more standardized coarse wares, and by the tenth, in the Romagna in particular, some local glazed pottery in the stylistic tradition of Forum ware and its successors, made in a restricted area in all probability, and available across a circle of a 100 km radius.[83] The only sub-regionally available bulk product in the period remained *pietra ollare*; this shows that there were wider exchange networks in the Po plain, but not that these were as yet more than marginal. It may also mean that some of the more optimistic accounts of the scale of north Italian economic development would need to be played down, at least before 950 or so. More archaeological work is badly needed here.

Other well-documented sub-regions of the Italian peninsula show rather less ceramic breakdown than does the north. Tuscany was under Lombard rule as well, and shared some of the experiences of the north, but not all. Except for on the coast, ARS was only intermittently available after 550 or so, though it did reach some inland centres, notably Siena, into the seventh century. Tuscan semi-fine wares steadily simplified their range of decoration (in red paint and red slip), especially after the seventh century, but never ceased to be produced, with good-quality *depurata* fabrics, at least on a small scale. In Siena, these productions were substantial, and available in some parts of the countryside by the ninth century at the latest; in Siena they largely abandoned paint and slip after 800 or so, but Red Painted wares

[81] Jones, 'La storia economica', pp. 1656–7; for the twelfth century, pp. 1722–8.
[82] *CDL*, III, n. 18; *Die 'Honorantiae'*, pp. 18–22. Still useful as a documentary survey is Monneret de Villard, 'L'organizzazione industriale'.
[83] Brogiolo and Gelichi, 'La ceramica invetriata', pp. 29–30; Gelichi and Sbarra, 'La tavola di San Gerardo'; Sbarra, 'Le ceramiche'.

continued at Pisa. Large-scale productions were reviving, in the Florence area and elsewhere, by c.1000, with a distribution down the Arno valley. Tuscany was also more open to imports from the ninth century. Forum ware has been found in Pisa and elsewhere on the coast, Siena, and at the rural site of Poggibonsi in the Valdelsa; in Pisa, Campanian Red Painted ware was available even in the eighth. All this shows a minimum level of exchange and buying-power which was more elaborate than in the north, and which recovered earlier too. This also fits the continuities in Pisan metallurgy, visible from the seventh century onwards without a break on the Piazza dei Cavalieri site, and the documentary references to artisans in Lucca, which begin in the 730s. But Tuscany, like the north, had a set of small-scale, mostly city-level, economies until the tenth century at the earliest; even Pisa shows no real sign of its commercial future until then.[84]

Lazio had Rome at its centre, which means that it imported ceramics until the end of the seventh century (it may have exported metalwork on a small scale). In Rome's Tiber valley hinterland, imports are less visible after 550, but they still continued to exist, in the wake of the movement of goods to Rome. Some common and coarse wares were made locally, however, some of them by the late seventh century with a combed and white-slipped decoration.[85] Rome was hit hard by the end of African and eastern bulk exchange around 700, and the early eighth-century level in the Crypta Balbi shows a very different ceramic profile to the import-dominated level of the late seventh (above, p. 712): a predominance of local common wares, with a few, apparently local, glazed chafing-dishes. Imported amphorae still existed, however, on a small scale, from Campania and Calabria/Sicily, indicating a continued import of wine from the south. This, the simplest period for Roman ceramics, shows a more elaborate range of productions and imports than anything further north in this period. Amphorae are less common in Rome in the ninth century, by which time the city probably supplied itself from its immediate hinterland (and perhaps in barrels).[86]

[84] See in general Ciampoltrini, 'L'orciolo e l'olla'; Francovich and Valenti, 'La ceramica d'uso comune'; I am grateful to both the latter for advice. For Siena, see above all Cantini, *Le fasi*, pp. 117–431; for Red Painted ware and Campanian imports at Pisa, see Abela, 'Ceramica dipinta in rosso'. For Forum ware imports see e.g. Paroli, 'La ceramica invetriata', p. 45; Valenti, *Poggio Imperiale*, I, pp. 122–3; Bruni, Abela, Berti, *Ricerche di archeologia medievale*, pp. 121–2. For metallurgy, ibid., pp. 72–98. For Lucca, see Ch. 10, n. 149; for Pisan economic expansion in the tenth century, Tangheroni, 'La prima espansione di Pisa', esp. pp. 9–15; Tangheroni, Renzi Rizzo, Berti, 'Pisa e il Mediterraneo'.

[85] See Saguì, 'Il deposito della Crypta Balbi'; eadem, 'Roma, i centri privilegiati'; Reynolds, *Trade*, pp. 69, 327–30; Ricci, 'La ceramica comune'. For the hinterland, and combed and slipped wares, Patterson and Roberts, 'New light' (late Hayes forms have now been found in small quantities in the Tiber valley: Helen Patterson, pers. comm.). For metalwork, Ricci, 'Relazioni culturali'.

[86] Cipriano *et al.*, 'La documentazione ceramica', pp. 99–111; Saguì *et al.*, 'Nuovi dati ceramologici', pp. 42–6; Panella and Saguì, 'Consumo e produzione a Roma', pp. 804–15; for amphorae, Ciarrocchi *et al.*, 'Produzione e circolazione', pp. 239–42. Coinage remained complex until the 730s: Rovelli, 'Monetary circulation', pp. 85–94.

Conversely, Rome's artisanal productions were developing by then. The late eighth century sees the development in the city of Forum ware, a heavy-glazed fine-ware type, often ambitiously (even if, to my eyes, tastelessly) decorated with applied petals: the first new high-status ceramic production in the medieval western Mediterranean. Forum ware probably took its glaze technology from Constantinople, rather than from northern Italy, where glaze production was in abeyance by the eighth century. It became an export product in the ninth century, and has been found across a wide arc from Provence to Sicily at least, at least in small quantities. Rome is the first city in Italy to show clear signs of a locally fuelled growth in demand and economic complexity, which is visible by 800 at the latest; in the early ninth century this would be further shown in the building of a set of large prestige churches, most of which still stand, as well as some elaborate houses. (It managed to do this even though the availability of coinage reached its historic minimum in the city, as indeed in the rest of Carolingian Italy.) But Rome was also by far the largest city in Italy, with, I would guess, 20,000–25,000 people in this period, as well as containing the elaborate and wealthy entourages of the papal court. Its global demand in 800 may not have been matched by other Italian cities until as late as the eleventh century: hence, then, its economic precocity.[87]

The south of Italy is a further set of separate sub-regions and micro-regions, but they largely had parallel developments, and they can be treated here as a single group. The south was, throughout this period, characterized by the survival of Red Painted wares, fine or semi-fine, made in several centres on, as it seems, a substantial scale—although not, or rarely, on the 'industrial' scale of late Roman Calle di Tricarico. Some of these wares were very elaborate, such as the Crecchio ware of the still-Byzantine coast of Abruzzo in the late sixth to mid-seventh centuries, which, remarkably, seems to have imitated Egyptian decorated pottery of the same period. Others were simpler, like the seventh-century types found at Altavilla Silentina, near the coast south of Salerno in the Lombard duchy of Benevento. The political centres of the Lombard duchy are relatively little known archaeologically as yet (although we can say that Benevento itself, well inland, was still getting ARS into the late seventh century), but, taken as a whole, the inland south seems to have been characterized by a set of ceramic traditions, showing a collective inheritance from late Roman styles, but developing largely separately. The eighth- and ninth-century Red Painted ware of S. Vincenzo al

---

[87] For Forum ware, Paroli, 'La ceramica invetriata'; Saguì *et al.*, 'Nuovi dati ceramologici', pp. 44–6. A new article by Paroli *et al.*, 'La ceramica invetriata', pp. 477–80, presents recent finds of seventh-century glazes in the south; if this dating is accepted, it would make the presumption of a borrowing of technology from Constantinople unnecessary. For coinage, Rovelli, 'Monetary circulation', pp. 95–9. For housing, above, Ch. 10, n. 138. For the population guess, Wickham, ' "The Romans according to their malign custom" ', pp. 162–4. See in general for the scale of Rome's economy Paroli and Delogu, *La storia economica di Roma*.

Volturno in the Molise Appennines, for example, is clearly heir to the tradition of kilns like Calle. Benevento, for its part, seems to have matched Naples as a significant production centre. Broadly, good-quality productions are much commoner than simpler ones here.[88]

The Byzantine coastal zones show much greater interconnection, not only up to 700 (when the African link was still strong) but also later. In Naples, there was no break in Red Painted production, and in Miseno and perhaps on Ischia, on the Bay of Naples, eighth-century amphora kilns have been found, presumably for wine, with a distribution that extends from Rome in the north to Sicily in the south. Indeed, in the ninth century there were some amphora connections between the Naples area and as far afield as the Aegean, a much wider range than is by now visible for Rome.[89] Calabrese wine, too, was still available in Rome in the eighth century, as we have seen. In Calabria, agrarian specializations were probably in retreat by 800, but would revive a century or so later; amphorae continued to be made there.[90] Sicilian archaeology is not well developed in this period, but the site of Marettimo on the Egadi islands to the west shows off the Neapolitan links just mentioned particularly well; it should be added that Sicilian oil-lamps were still available in Rome.[91] We have seen that Sicily probably had a close fiscal link with Constantinople, based on grain transport, and an unusually complex local coinage, probably as a result (above, p. 125), but it clearly maintained commercial relations with the major south Italian cities too.

[88] Staffa and Pellegrini, *Dall'Egitto copto*; Staffa, 'Le produzioni ceramiche in Abruzzo', pp. 452–7; Iacoe, 'I corredi tombali' (for Altavilla)—cf. the ceramics of a similar type found at Pratola Serra in the Appennines above Benevento, Saporito, 'Ceramica dipinta', esp. pp. 198–201, and at Mercato S. Severino in the Salernitano, Fiorillo, 'La ceramica'; Lupia, *Testimonianze*, pp. 119–203, esp. 121–2, 134–5, 200–3 (V. Carsana and S. Scarpati, for Benevento); Patterson, 'The pottery', pp. 314–17 (for S. Vincenzo). See in general, and for other examples, Arthur and Patterson, 'A potted history'.

[89] See Arthur, 'Early medieval amphorae'; idem, *Naples*, pp. 122–33; idem, 'Local pottery'. Compare southern Puglia, around Otranto, which shared the Red Painted tradition of the rest of the south, but was also effectively part of the Aegean ceramic network in terms of style and exchange links, as shown in the eighth-century Mitello kiln complex at Otranto, for example. Nonetheless, it was more economically complex after 700 than most of the Aegean, and in this respect, too, conforms to south Italian patterns (cf. below, pp. 785–8). See Arthur *et al.*, 'Fornaci altomedievali ad Otranto'; Arthur and Patterson, 'Local pottery'; Arthur, 'Ceramica in Terra d'Otranto'; Leo Imperiale, 'Otranto cantiere Mitello'.

[90] Pacetti, 'La questione delle Keay LII'; di Gangi and Lebole, 'Anfore Keay LII'; Raimondo, 'La ceramica comune'; di Gangi and Lebole, 'Dal tardo antico al bassomedioevo', pp. 109–14 (for Tropea). Noyé, 'Économie et société', esp. pp. 212–29, provides an overview. Raimondo, *Modèles économiques et sociaux*, esp. pp. 205–26, provides a systematic case study of part of Squillace, which seems after 700 to have been much less linked into interregional exchange than was Tropea, although good-quality ceramics were available in every century there.

[91] Ardizzone *et al.*, 'Il complesso monumentale', pp. 407–11; eadem, 'Rapporti commerciali', an important survey of eighth-century exchange (cf. for the seventh century Saguì, 'Roma, i centri privilegiati', pp. 30–6, another key survey, and Zanini, *Le Italie bizantine*, pp. 320–8). See also Arcifa, 'Per una geografia amministrativa', pp. 237–9, for Naples amphorae on the eastern Sicilian coast in, probably, the eighth century.

The Byzantine parts of the south were, overall, more economically complex than the neighbouring Lombard lands, although the most complex local economies of the interior (like S. Vincenzo, which also developed an elaborate metalwork production in the ninth century) were more similar to those in the Byzantine south than to anywhere north of Rome. What made the Byzantine areas particular was above all the network of eighth-century exchange that linked all the Tyrrhenian coastlands, and extended as far as Rome. There is no reason to hypothesize a fiscal support for this; there is no known fiscal link between the Byzantine heartland and any of the effectively autonomous duchies north of Calabria by the mid-eighth century. As was seen earlier (p. 208), there was also by now no landowning that linked them together, following the disappearance of the papal properties in Calabria and Sicily in the 730s or shortly after. That papal tradition of middle-distance communication might well have left its mark in shipping routes, for rather longer; indeed, McCormick has shown that the only significant East–West route in the eighth century ran down the Tyrrhenian coast. But the crucial point here is that the underpinning of the Tyrrhenian network must have been entirely commercial by now; and, as such, it had no parallel in terms of scale anywhere else in the eighth-century Mediterranean. This sub-regional level of exchange was less articulated than it had been in the sixth century, and more marginal to local economies, but it added to their complexity, and testifies to a buoyancy in demand which joined all the major cities of the coast together. It may well be that some of that connectivity extended inland, to the major Lombard centres; we have a detailed Naples–Benevento treaty, largely covering trade, in 836, and Naples was probably an outlet for S. Vincenzo's production too. Beneventan aristocrats, after all, seem to have been wide-ranging by Lombard standards (above, p. 217). But we should probably conclude that all southern elites, from Rome to Syracuse, were rich by Italian standards, and indeed richer than anyone else in the western Mediterranean by 700. All this must, finally, make it less surprising that the ninth century saw the development of so many trading cities in precisely this area, Gaeta, Amalfi, (Lombard) Salerno, as well as Naples itself—Naples was perhaps temporarily eclipsed by these newer rivals, but was all the same by the tenth century exporting linen, a bulk product. Similarly, when the Arabs conquered Sicily in the ninth century, they could relocate it with ease in their own expanding trading systems, as is shown by its importance in the Cairo Geniza documents from their beginning around 1000. The standard historiography of Italian commerce, focused on Venice and the Po plain as it is, has often found the early role of Amalfi and its neighbours to be an anomaly, to be explained away. Nor should it be overstressed; Amalfi is a pretty small place, and these ports mostly engaged in luxury-level exchange in their interregional activities for a long time. But their location is not anomalous; in 800 the Tyrrhenian sea was the most complex maritime exchange zone in the Mediterranean. The clichéd economic simplicity of southern Italy was by no means a feature of our period.[92]

Early medieval Italy appeared in earlier chapters of this book as a relatively fragmented set of polities, societies, economies. Its fiscal coherence was hit by the Vandal ending of the tax spine from Carthage, and then again by the war and confusion of the sixth century, after which, even in Byzantine areas and still more in Lombard ones, any form of tax-based integration was usually weak (above, pp. 115–20). Its aristocracies were by 600 similarly localized, to single city territories or little more, and were relatively modest in economic terms, in strong contrast to the legendary wealth of the greatest senatorial families around 400: there were only a handful of richer figures, not enough to hold up an exchange system on their own. Identities changed as a result, as these smaller aristocracies adjusted to new militarized political structures (above, pp. 203–19). Villa culture ended in most of Italy in the sixth century (although not in Sicily) as a result of these changing identities (above, p. 477). Conversely, however, city-dwelling as an aristocratic trad-ition did not end. Indeed, cities were unusually coherent in early medieval Italy by western standards, and rather conservative in their ideology, al-though also economically far from prosperous, which fits the material weakness of landowning elites, taken as a whole (above, pp. 644–56). Aristocratic weakness had its counterpart in a relative peasant autonomy. Peasants were often landowners in this period, and had some flexibility of political action, even if they often accepted the patronage of the powerful (above, pp. 387–93). In some areas they could even be autonomous from an aristocratic economic logic, as was hypothesized for the south-eastern Chi-anti on archaeological grounds, and as is likely in the marginal areas of the peninsula which resisted landowners in the ninth century (above, pp. 546, 583). This had ended by 900, but even then landed wealth, though increas-ing, may have stayed modest by the standards of regions such as Francia.

The more detailed survey of exchange in this chapter is intended to underpin that overall picture: it supports it on the basis of different evidence. The weakness of production and exchange in the peninsula as a whole, with the exception of parts of the south, fits the overall weakness of the fiscal systems and the private wealth of Italy after the sixth century. Italy's unusual levels of urbanization, even at its low point for economic complexity—roughly 650–850 on the evidence presented here—helped the coherence of the different polities of the period, despite their lack of fiscal complexity, and must have helped to create the infrastructure for later economic

---

[92] The Naples–Benevento treaty is the *Pactio Sicardi*. For Naples linen, Ibn Ḥawqal (Ibn Hauqal), *Configuration de la terre*, I, p. 197. There is an ample bibliography for the Campanian cities; recent contributions include Skinner, *Family power*; Kreutz, *Before the Normans*, pp. 75–93. For the Tyrrhenian exchange network, see most recently McCormick, *Origins*, pp. 627–30. For Sicily and Egypt, Goitein, *A Mediterranean society*, I, *passim*.

development, which would be very complex by 1100. All the same, in the period 650–850 aristocratic wealth was not great enough, or geographically wide-ranging enough, to sustain developed productive systems or exchange networks on more than a small scale. Of the four parameters for economic change listed earlier in this chapter (p. 719), Italy was affected by all four: fiscal involution, a lessening of aristocratic wealth, particularly disruptive war, and the end of important economic links to other regions. Only the continued elite attachment to city living prevented even sharper changes.

What we can see more clearly now, however, is some of the sub-regional contrasts in the peninsula. Northern Italy had always had a relatively localized aristocracy under the empire, with fewer links to other regions than the landowners of the centre-south, but after the sixth century aristocratic wealth decreased still more; this is very evident in the simplicity of ceramic production there, which may indeed imply that northern wealth has been overestimated in the ninth century or even later. Rome and the south, conversely, seem to have preserved a wealthier aristocratic stratum. The evidence for this is not perfect, it has to be admitted, particularly the documentary evidence, but the material we have for dense landed power-networks in Lazio, plus the fragmentary indicators of a stratum of rich aristocrats in Benevento, do point in the same direction; we might add the presumption of a local fiscal basis for elite wealth in Sicily, although that island is almost undocumented. It is noteworthy that peasant dependence was also more clear cut in the south than the north, with a higher incidence of unfree tenure (above, p. 297); the fact that our best examples of peasant resistance also came from the southern mountains may also show that class struggle was sharper and less mediated there—S. Vincenzo al Volturno, whose artisanal activity was unusually intense, being one of the major protagonists here (above, p. 651). All of these points fit with, and are given more clarity by, the indicators we have just seen for the survival of exchange networks in the south, particularly in the Byzantine lands.

This is interesting, because the south was also the part of Italy whose aristocrats lost much more wealth when the Mediterranean broke up, because they had owned so widely under the empire. It was also the part of Italy most linked to the interregional exchange network of the years around 400. It evidently managed to be blown off course less than one might have predicted: in particular, less than Africa was. This is partly because southern Italy as a consumer region, with its own local productions as well, was less dependent on the world-system than was Africa as a specialized producer region. It is probably also partly because southern Italy's elites, although more reduced in wealth and more localized than ever before, were nonetheless still prosperous by the standards of the western Mediterranean, and aristocratic demand remained the most important basis of any economic complexity. (Unfortunately, we know too little about African elites to push that comparison.) It is also in part because African internal exchange had never been very articulated, so, when external exchange ended, a very localized economy ensued; in southern Italy, however, a network of routes for bulk goods had developed to feed Rome, which allowed for some complementarity of specializations inside the sub-region as well (Sicilian grain, Calabrese and Campanian wine, etc.). These continued to be moved about even in the eighth century, when very little else except luxuries was transported in the Mediterranean at all.

5. The western Mediterranean III: Spain and southern Gaul

As has been observed more than once in earlier chapters, Spanish archaeology is both extremely locally divergent and also at a stage of fast changes in its evidence base. This is as true of ceramics as it is of urban and rural settlement; but its patterns have begun to be clearer in recent years, and there are signs that syntheses are beginning to be possible.[93] I shall add southern Gaul to Spain for convenience, as it had some analogous developments in our period. The south of Gaul was very different from the north, the Seine–Rhine sub-region, which will be discussed separately (pp. 794–805), and there is a wide central region in modern France in which very little ceramic work for our period has been done at all, which further justifies our treating the south and north in different sections. But the choice to add southern Gaul to a chapter section focused on Spain derives above all from a desire to step back from some of the traditional interpretative narratives of Spanish historiography, notably that focused on the break represented by the Arab conquest of 711. The analogous developments in Gaulish exchange existed even though the 711 narrative had very little relevance north of the Pyrenees; we shall see that there are parallels in Italy, too. As in Italy, however, Spain and southern Gaul had highly regionalized ceramic histories, which need to be seen separately before we look for wider interpretations. Accordingly, we will look in turn at the Meseta, inland Andalucía, southern Gaul, and the Spanish Mediterranean coast, in order to try to set out as succinctly as possible their different patterns of development. We will then face the problem of the relationship between archaeological and written sources, which, as was already stressed in Chapter 4 (pp. 219–32), is less straightforward in Spain in particular than it is in many other places.

Unlike Italy, Spain was not at all a homogeneous region in exchange terms in 400. The whole inland plateau of the Meseta, extending down into the Ebro valley in the north-east and into that of the Guadalquivir in the south (Roman Baetica, later the core of al-Andalus), was characterized by an

---

[93] A first synthesis of Spain as a whole is offered by Manzano, 'La cerámica de los siglos oscuros', the conclusion to an important conference, Caballero *et al.*, *Las cerámicas tardorromanas y altomedievales*. For the period before 600, see Reynolds, 'Hispania'.

independent fine-ware production, called by most scholars *terra sigillata hispánica tardía* (TSHT), which had a grey or orange slipped fabric, often decorated with moulds or stamps. TSHT was influenced by ARS forms, and, very often, Gaulish DSP (which it often closely resembles), as well as earlier Spanish *sigillata* traditions. It had its own distinct networks of distribution: a northern network, deriving from kilns on the upper Duero and upper Ebro; a central network (sometimes called TSHT *brillante*) focused on the upper Tajo; and a southern network (TSHT *meridional*) based on the upper Guadalquivir. All are inland networks, however; TSHT is very rare on the coast, except around the Ebro mouth and up to Tarragona. Its distribution is thus almost the exact opposite of ARS, which reached all the coasts of Spain in substantial quantities except for along the northern shoreline, but was seldom available inland at all except a little way up the great rivers, to Zaragoza, Córdoba, and Mérida. Only a small number of locations— apart from these cities, Begastri (Cehegín) and El Tolmo de Minateda, both on the edge of the plateau near the south-eastern coast, are ex- amples—had easy access to both.[94] The distribution of TSHT thus marks with unusual clarity the structural separation of the Spanish interior from the Mediterranean world-system, which was already proposed on the basis of the fiscal movement of goods in Chapter 3 (p. 79).[95]

TSHT was a large-scale commercialized production, reasonably well made with standardized forms in each of its networks, which was widely available in the fourth century even in remote areas. It is indeed a sign of the economic complexity of inland Spain, notwithstanding its lack of connec- tion with the rest of the empire. In the fifth century, however, its availability on rural sites steadily decreased, and it has recently been proposed that TSHT proper ended on the Meseta around 500. It was replaced by a range of local imitations, usually in a brown or grey fabric, filling the gap at the 'semi-fine' level, but made much more simply and on a smaller scale, at Peacock's 'individual workshop' level at most. These local wares, in a late Roman tradition, marked the history of the Meseta for several centuries. They slowly diverged from the *terra sigillata* tradition across time, as their

---

[94] For TSHT, basic are Mayet, *Les céramiques sigillées*, pp. 247–90, and Juan, 'Las industrias cerámicas'; with López, *Terra sigillata hispánica tardía*, and the earlier Mañanes, *La cerámica tardorromana-visigoda*. More recently, see Pérez and García, 'Nuevos datos', for northern kilns; Caballero and Juan, 'Terra sigillata hispánica brillante', for the Tajo network; Orfila, 'Terra sigillata hispánica tardía meridional', for the Guadalquivir (she dates its end to the sixth century, which is too early: see n. 99 for Córdoba, and below for El Tolmo). For ARS and other import distributions, see Járrega, *Cerámicas finas*; Fernández *et al.*, 'Gijon'; Járrega, 'Las cerámicas de importación'. For Begastri, González *et al.*, 'La ciudad hispano-visigoda de Begastri', pp. 1015–17; for El Tolmo de Minateda, Gutiérrez *et al.*, 'Los contextos cerámicos' (where seventh-century ARS and TSHT *meridional* were both found); another example is Braga in northern Portugal, for which see Martins and Delgado, 'História e arqueologia', p. 30.

[95] Arce, *El último siglo*, pp. 111–19, develops this lack of connection; in the fourth century only horses are much mentioned as an export from the interior. Copper and silver may have been others, however: see in general Edmondson, 'Mining', for the problems of the evidence.

fabrics became less fine (this varied from place to place), but their forms stayed Roman until the eighth or ninth centuries, and they were wheel-made. The jars and bottles found in Visigothic-period furnished burials in the Meseta (which have no TSHT) were in this tradition.[96] So were the semi-fine wares found on the settlement sites of Monte Cildá (fifth to ninth centuries) and El Castellar (seventh to tenth centuries) in the northern province of Palencia; so were some of those found at the prestige royal foundation of Recópolis (sixth to ninth centuries). Later ecclesiastical foundations in the southern Meseta, Melque (seventh/eighth to tenth centuries, prov. Toledo) and S. Lucía del Trampal (eighth to ninth centuries, prov. Cáceres), did not have so many Roman forms in their ceramics, but their pattern was similar: good-quality productions and fabrics (less good at El Trampal), made on a microregional scale. It is this ceramic tradition which, particularly in the southern Meseta, gradually picked up forms associated with the future ceramic *koinē* of the Muslim south, which are accordingly termed 'Islamic'; it remained the basic common ware of the plateau when glazed fine wares came in in the tenth century.[97]

This 'post-Roman' Meseta ceramic tradition was localized in the extreme. It can hardly be characterized in more detail here, as it was so locally variable, and new types are being discovered all the time (the northern Meseta is also rather less studied than the area around and south of Madrid). It was, all the same, still at the top of the range for pottery, and its availability was, as a result, locally variable too. At the small rural site of Gózquez (sixth to eighth centuries, prov. Madrid), for example, the percentage of fast-wheel types steadily dropped, and by the eighth century 90 per cent of the ceramics were slow-wheel coarse-ware containers. If there is a moment of greater technological simplicity, it may be the eighth century, although in parts of the far north it may be the ninth, and on some sites no dip in production quality can be seen at all. Overall, however, this tradition does show the survival in most areas of at least geographically localized

---

[96] This account follows Juan and Blanco, 'Cerámica común tardorromana', on imitations of TSHT; see pp. 205–7 for the burial types (developing Izquierdo, 'Cerámica de necrópolis de época visigoda'). Earlier, Luis Caballero had argued, influentially, for a steady deterioration in the quality of TSHT in the fifth and sixth centuries, an internal evolution of a fine ware to the level of a common ware: 'Cerámicas de "época visigoda y post-visigoda" ', pp. 86–9 (cf. the fate of DSP in Marseille: below, n. 103), without pronouncing on the continuity of kiln-sites and of centralized production. The overall loss of fineness in the period is anyway not in dispute. Sixth-century sites with virtually no TSHT include Gózquez (Vigil-Escalera, 'Cabañas de época visigoda', p. 239), and the sites around Zaragoza discussed in Paz, *Cerámica de mesa romana*, pp. 230–5.

[97] Monte Cildá: García Guinea *et al.*, *Excavaciones de Monte Cildá*, pp. 45–9. El Castellar: idem *et al.*, *El Castellar*, pp. 27–9. Recópolis: Lauro Olmo (pers. comm.); cf. idem, 'Ciudad y procesos de transformación social', pp. 387, 390, 393. Melque: Caballero *et al.*, 'Las cerámicas del primer momento'. Trampal: Caballero and Sáez, *La iglesia mozárabe*, pp. 225–47 (with a useful comparative survey). For ceramics in the Meseta after 711 (after 800, really), see the lists in Retuerce, *La cerámica andalusí*; pp. 67–8 for Roman traditions.

productive specialization, and thus demand: on the level of northern Italy after 650, perhaps.[98]

Inland Andalucía's development was analogous. The lower Guadalquivir valley was supplied more by ARS than TSHT, but after 400 the former's distribution was steadily more restricted, to richer sites nearer the river or the Seville–Córdoba road, and after 600/625 ARS ceased to be imported at all. Instead, again, local wares in a late Roman tradition are found, often of good quality, alongside coarse wares for cooking and storage, on the (rather few) sites that have been excavated professionally. In Córdoba, TSHT *meridional* (and perhaps its imitations) continued into the seventh century, losing its fineness slowly, but was replaced by good-quality common wares, some Red Painted, into the ninth century, together with coarse wares on a fast wheel: Córdoba evidently remained a production centre, supplying a demand for professionally made pottery. Further from urban centres, there were often more hand-made coarse types beside the fast-wheel common wares, as just outside Jaén on the Marroquíes Bajos site in the eighth century or at Peñaflor a little to the north, or at Morón de la Frontera in the province of Seville (hand-mades dropped in each to small proportions only after c.850). But even in the countryside there were often places where wheel-thrown types dominated, such as El Castillón de Montefrío (eighth to tenth centuries, prov. Granada) and Ronda (prov. Málaga), becoming slowly influenced by 'Islamic' styles from the ninth; the Loja survey, covering the west of the province of Granada, shows similar patterns. In Mérida, sixth- and seventh-century ceramics were partly hand-made, and both wheel-thrown and hand-made wares survive in a variety of forms, indicating some fragmentation of production; here, after c.700, ceramic production became rapidly more professionalized, with relatively standardized wheel-thrown types. Glazed wares developed in Andalucía in the late ninth century, and mark a clear increase in productive intensity, but were not generalized (and are particularly rare in the countryside) until the late tenth.[99]

---

[98] Vigil-Escalera, 'Cabañas de época visigoda', pp. 237–46, with idem, 'Cerámicas', for Gózquez. For the north, recent updates are Gutiérrez, 'Nuevos desarrollos', esp. pp. 72–4; Larrén *et al.*, 'Ensayo de sistemazición'; Azkarate *et al.*, 'Materiales y contextos cerámicos' (for the very simple productions of the Basque country). See also Fontes and Gaspar, 'Cerâmicas da região de Braga', pp. 208–12, for continuities in Braga.

[99] For the end of ARS, Carr, *Vandals to Visigoths*, pp. 58, 91–4; eadem, 'A changing world', pp. 225–31. Córdoba: Hidalgo *et al.*, *El criptopórtico*, pp. 73–167; Fuertes and Santos, 'Cerámicas tardorromanes y altomedievales'. (The repertory at Córdoba is more similar to that at El Tolmo de Minateda, a town just beyond the mountains at the top of the Guadalquivir, below, n. 110, than it is to the more ruralized area of Jaén in the upper Guadalquivir valley.) Jaén and Peñaflor: Pérez, *Las cerámicas omeyas*, pp. 39–42, 114–18, 125–6; Pérez *et al.*, 'Las primeras cerámicas'; Castillo, *La Campiña de Jaén*, pp. 108–24; see further Ch. 8, n. 134. Morón and Ronda: Acién *et al.*, 'Cerámicas tardorromanas'. El Castillón: Motos, 'La cerámica altomedieval'; eadem, *El poblado medieval*, pp. 94–9. Loja: Jiménez, *El poblamiento*, pp. 32–7. Mérida: Alba, 'Apuntes sobre la cerámica', and Alba and Feijoo, 'Pautas evolutivas'; I am grateful here to help from Santiago Feijoo. For the period after 800, see in general Malpica, *La cerámica altomedieval*.

This array of examples is more variegated than those of the Meseta; urban sites tend to show rather more elaborate ceramic traditions, and so do even some rural ones; Andalucía was, as we saw in Chapter 10 (pp. 660–3), more urbanized than the Meseta, and city–country relationships were accordingly more articulated, covering more of the countryside. The Jaén area was less urbanized, hence the greater simplicity of pottery there (though wheel-thrown techniques remained important); conversely, notwithstanding the weakness of Granada in this period, El Castillón and the Loja field survey show that its hinterland could sustain a demand for well-made ceramics. Distribution patterns were as localized as in the Meseta, however, and were probably restricted to single city territories at best, until glazed pottery was generalized. The only known production in the Guadalquivir valley with a wider range than that between 600 and 850 was not pottery at all, but metalwork: as Gisela Ripoll has shown, the production of bronze belt-buckles, probably in the Seville area, had a wide distribution in the valley and beyond in the seventh century, and was also open to Byzantine cultural influence.[100] Metalworking does not need the productive scale of standard-ized ceramics, and it is quite conceivable that the same restricted level of demand could allow the exchange of good-quality metal products through-out the valley but also be too low to allow large-scale, 'nucleated' ceramic workshops to continue to exist. But it is nonetheless probable that some bulk exchange networks never went away in inland Andalucía, whether or not goods were reaching the region from outside. If so, one comparator sub-region might be the Italian south; but there were rural areas of eighth-century Andalucía where exchange, and thus productive scale, were at a simpler level than anything found in Italy, as the greater frequency of hand-made pottery makes clear.

This account of inland Spain has been deliberately constructed on the basis of the ceramics alone, with as little use of political markers as possible. It must be said, however, that standard political turning-points like Leovi-gild's reunification of the peninsula in the 570s and the Arab conquest in the 710s do not obviously fit the main changes in ceramic production. The breakdown of TSHT in the Meseta in the fifth century must have marked a breakdown of demand; this is the only plausible explanation of it, given that it was made and consumed in the Meseta itself. The fifth century was thus a period of economic simplification, and probably one in which elites became weaker. This was, at least, a time of generalized political uncertainty and occasional confusion, with Vandal, Suevic, and Visigothic attacks and partial settlement, but this confusion would have to be rather greater than

---

[100] Ripoll, *Toréutica*, esp. pp. 166–78, 265–70. Byzantine merchants came up the Spanish rivers, but were probably focused on luxury transport: so *Vitas patrum Emeritensium*, IV.3; *LV*, XI.3.1. See Claude, *Der Handel*, pp. 144–9. For this sort of commerce in the Arab period, see Constable, *Trade and traders*, pp. 185–7.

our scarce sources imply for it to have affected production to such an extent. The stabilization of ceramic production and distribution on a local level predates the *pax Visigothica* of Leovigild and his successors, and there is no sign of any significant bulk exchange facilitated by the Toledo kingdom, except to single high-status sites like Recópolis, which even had access to African oil amphorae—these therefore presumably also came to Toledo itself, as yet unexcavated. But nor do we see any major change resulting from Arab conquest. In some places, a slow technological involution across the Visigothic period is reversed in 700, in others in 850; in others again, no real shift in productive scale occurred at all after the fifth century. The next major change after the end of TSHT is the arrival of glazed pottery, and a more 'Islamic' repertoire of forms, in the late ninth and tenth centuries.[101] The only real difference as yet visible in the intervening period is a tendency for ceramic ranges to be more complex, and for the best types to be technologically more sophisticated, in the more urbanized regions of the south, than in most of the Meseta. (One might also argue for a more variegated socio-economic situation inside the Meseta, as we shall see.) This account of the changes in patterns of exchange substantially flattens out some of the iconic moments in Spanish history. We shall return to its implications shortly.

Southern Gaul is midway between these two Spanish sub-regions in its patterns. It was not cut off from the Mediterranean, even in Aquitaine, but it shared some of the features of the Spanish interior too. Languedoc and Provence imported all the main ARS types, African oil amphorae, and even cooking wares, until the seventh century, as well as eastern products on some sites (notably the major entrepôt of Marseille); in Aquitaine these reached Bordeaux until the seventh, and amphorae reached inland Toulouse until at least the sixth.[102] Conversely, they also made their own fine wares and common wares. DSP, a mostly grey slipped ware, is similar to TSHT, as already noted, and had a wide distribution inside the sub-region and down the Spanish coast. But DSP had several independent networks. It is conventionally divided into Provençal, Languedocian/Narbonnais, and Atlantic (i.e. Aquitainian). The first of these, well known thanks to the Marseille sites, had a great period in the mid-fifth to early sixth centuries, when even ARS took second place in the city; DSP *atlantique*, for its part, is

---

[101] For amphorae at Recópolis, see Gutiérrez, 'Eastern Spain', pp. 182–3. The absence of a sharp material change around 711 also makes it less necessary to be cautious about Luis Caballero's redatings of many 'Visigothic' churches on the Meseta to the eighth century (see Ch. 4, n. 191). The absence of a ceramic tradition brought by the Arabs and Berbers has worried some analysts (see Manzano, 'La cerámica de los siglos oscuros', pp. 553–5, for a discussion), but the issue is surely a non-problem: the Visigoths introduced no ceramic tradition either, and few of the ceramics discussed anywhere in this chapter, except in England (below, pp. 806–7), were brought by immigrant groups.

[102] See CATHMA, 'Importations de céramiques communes'; Bonifay *et al.*, *Fouilles de Marseille*, pp. 361–6, 371–2; Amiel and Berthault, 'Les amphores du Bas-Empire'.

best-attested in the sixth century, and continued in the seventh. This latter sub-type, however, seems itself to be a group of wares with much more local distributions, with Bordeaux the most important, but separate productions at Toulouse and Lezoux (Puy-de-Dôme) and doubtless elsewhere too. These fine-ware types became less easily available, and less fine, across the sixth century, indicating a steady weakening of demand, as already in inland Spain a century earlier.[103] The sixth century thus saw a fragmentation of distribution patterns, again paralleling Spain. But this was countered on the Mediterranean coast by a new ceramic type, a grey common ware called in Languedoc *céramiques à pâte kaolinitique*, found from the fifth and particularly sixth century onwards, kilns for which have been found in the Rhône valley between Uzès and Orange, on both sides of the river. These productions, of a standard quality, can be found on sites from Béziers to Marseille, into the ninth century.[104]

From the seventh century, it is harder to track south Gaulish ceramics. Provence is particularly little known. In Languedoc, all imports had ceased, and fine-ware productions (of, for example, the painted ware of the Lunellois) were microregional in their distribution. In Aquitaine, local productions certainly continued (though sites are few), slowly becoming more influenced by north Frankish elements such as roulette decoration, but not losing their 'fine-ness' completely. The clearest exception to this localization remained the *kaolinitique* tradition, which continued to unify most of Languedoc at the level of the production and exchange of cheap wares. As the CATHMA ceramic group note in their publications, this implies a rather less localized early middle ages than is sometimes assumed. Aquitaine's common and coarse wares are far less studied, but a parallel to the *kaolinitiques* seems to be 'E ware', a seventh-century coarse type made, as it seems, on a substantial scale, probably in Poitou, and exported as far as Britain and Ireland (below, p. 815). Future work may well show equivalents to this in other parts of Aquitaine too.[105] It is interesting that not only DSP but

---

103 For DSP, see Rigoir, 'Les sigillées paléochrétiennes', for the initial survey; for later refs. and the best-dated sequence, see Bonifay *et al.*, *Fouilles de Marseille*, pp. 367–70; for Provence, see also Demians d'Archambaud, *L'oppidum de Saint-Blaise*, pp. 136–60 (Y. and J. Rigoir); Kauffmann *et al.*, 'Les céramiques', for Apt. For Aquitaine, Soulas, 'Presentation et provenance'; Dieulafait *et al.*, 'Céramiques tardives en Midi-Pyrénées'; and Menessier-Jouannet, 'Un four du haut moyen-âge', for the isolated kiln at Lezoux, dated firmly to the seventh century. For Languedoc, see esp. CATHMA, 'Céramiques languedociennes', pp. 112–16, 122–3.

104 Demians d'Archambaud, *L'oppidum de Saint-Blaise*, pp. 161–87 (J.-P. Pelletier and L. Vallauri); CATHMA, 'Céramiques languedociennes', pp. 218–22; CATHMA, 'Céramiques languedociennes: essai de synthèse'; Bonifay, *Fouilles de Marseille*, pp. 370–1. I am grateful to Claude Reynaud for discussion here.

105 For Languedoc, see CATHMA, 'Céramiques languedociennes', *passim* (pp. 213–15 for Lunellois painted pottery), updated in CATHMA, 'Céramiques languedociennes: essai de synthèse' (p. 108 for incomplete localization); see also Garnier *et al.*, 'De la ferme au village', pp. 17–21, for a case study. In the ninth century Languedoc seems to have begun a period of land-clearance, which implies demographic growth, and may mean that the area was beginning to be more economically complex: Durand, *Les paysages médiévaux*, pp. 180, 208–9. For

also the *kaolinitiques* seem to have been exchanged across the Frankish–Visigothic boundary (Languedoc being under Visigothic rule). It is also interesting that the latter apparently carried on without significant change throughout the eighth century, a period of Arab–Frankish wars. The south of Gaul seems to have shown a lessening of demand in the sixth century, then, but after that it stabilized as a network of local production and distribution patterns, with Languedoc's common wares and Poitou's coarse wares unifying rather larger sub-regions. These changes resulted in a general lessening of imports from Africa, too, although these were anyway decreasing for other reasons; only Marseille, a specialist entrepôt, really suffered because the African network ended.[106] How these exchange patterns fit what else we know about southern Gaul we shall see in a moment. It needs to be remembered, though, that the pattern we see here by 700 or so, of largely local exchange networks of a reasonable level of quality, marks substantial sections of the western Mediterranean regions; neither Spain nor Gaul are unusual here.

The Spanish Mediterranean coast has been particularly systematically studied. From the French border down to Málaga, groups of archaeologists offer us a string of sites and field surveys, and have discussed them with an attention that is only recently beginning to be matched elsewhere in the region, particularly up to 700, but in some places (notably the Alicante–Murcia zone) later as well. This coast was, for a long time, dominated by African imports, of ARS, oil amphorae, and even cooking wares. Evidently the coast produced little oil, and indeed oil was probably the core commodity among these imports. What was exported in return can only be guessed at, but fish sauce was one commodity at least—its amphorae have not been pinned down for any area east and north of Málaga, but several production centres have been found. It is striking, however, that the late Roman Spanish coast, unlike any of the other sub-regions discussed in this section, did not have any large-scale ceramic production of its own, only localized semi-fine table-ware and coarse-ware types. The coast was in this respect sharply separated from the Spanish interior, being unusually tied into the Mediterranean exchange system, rather than being unusually separated from it. As we have seen (p. 711), by 500 the Spanish coast absorbed African products (particularly oil) that no longer went to Italy in tax, and indeed the Iberian coastal sites from then on become some of the best indicators of the rise and fall of African (and Levantine) exports, since the latter had so few local competitors, right up to the mid- to late seventh century.[107] After 550

Aquitaine, see Dieulafait *et al.*, 'Céramiques tardives en Midi-Pyrénées'; eadem, 'Existe-t-il une céramique mérovingienne', a text I owe to Simon Esmonde-Cleary. For 'E ware', see Wooding, *Communications and commerce*, pp. 73–83.

[106] Loseby, 'Marseille', II.

[107] See in general Keay, *Late Roman amphorae*, pp. 423–8; Reynolds, *Trade*, pp. 28–34, 54–60; Gutiérrez, 'Eastern Spain'; Reynolds, 'Hispania'; and the Járrega works cit. above, n. 94.

African imports began slowly to lessen, although staying high in the cities, in particular in the parts of the coast the Byzantines occupied between 554 and c.628, which may indicate some state involvement in exchange there; after this, import levels dropped much faster, as did African production, down to its end-point around 700.[108]

The interesting feature of the seventh-century Spanish coast is not so much the particular history of African imports there, but rather the fact that so little replaced them. In the seventh-century Catalan sites discussed in Chapter 8 (p. 488), Puig Rom, on the sea, has some oxydized common wares of reasonable quality; Vilaclara, 40 km inland, has mostly slow-wheel wares, although most of them are oxydized; El Bovalar, slightly further inland, has mostly hand-made and slow-wheel pottery. There is no sign here of the sort of sub-regional common ware that one finds in neighbouring Languedoc, and the eighth century is hardly visible. Nor is it more visible in Valencia, further south.[109] Moving onwards down the coast, Sonia Gutiérrez has established a typology of seventh- to ninth-century wares for the Alicante–Murcia area, but the same patterns are found, for the most part more localized still. She shows that even the local semi-fine table wares of the sixth century ceased to be produced across the seventh, and hand-made productions dominated, at least in the countryside, in the eighth and ninth. Only the urban site of El Tolmo de Minateda (seventh to ninth centuries, prov. Albacete) showed a more complex array of productions, with good-quality common wares all through, some of them semi-fine with slip earlier on, paint later, and glaze by c.850, and very little hand-made pottery in this case. The El Tolmo wares hardly changed in the eighth century, and maintained late Roman forms until after 800. El Tolmo is, however, on the edge of the Meseta, 100 km from the sea, and in some respects fits the interior Spanish patterns that have already been discussed. The coastal cities, by contrast, seem to have failed altogether (above, p. 659), and there were no alternatives to the very simple production patterns of the countryside there; wheel-made ceramics were in a definite minority, and productions were very local indeed. Nothing else existed in this area until the establishment by the

Much recent work is collected in *Arqueo mediterrània*, II (1997). For one case study, see Reynolds, *Settlement and pottery*, esp. pp. 9–27.

[108] For trends, see the previous note, with Cau *et al.*, 'La cerámica del nordeste'. Case studies include Llinàs, 'La excavación de la carretera' (Empúries); Macias and Remolà, 'Tarraco visigoda'; Castanyer and Tremoleda, *La vil.la romana de Vilauba*, pp. 261–76; Pascual *et al.*, 'València'; iidem, 'Cerámicas de la ciudad de Valencia'; Ramallo *et al.*, 'Un contexto cerámico', developing iidem, 'Contextos cerámicos' (Cartagena); Moltó, 'Cerámicas de importación' (Garganes).

[109] See respectively Nolla and Casas, 'Material ceràmic'; Enrich *et al.*, *Vilaclara*, pp. 84–5; Cau *et al.*, 'Algunas consideraciones', pp. 14–15. See in general for Catalonia Cau *et al.*, 'La cerámica del nordeste'; Coll *et al.*, 'Las producciones cerámicas'; Coll *et al.*, 'Contextos ceràmics'; López *et al.*, 'Cerámica tardorromana y altomedieval'. For Valencia, Pascual *et al.*, 'Cerámicas de la ciudad de Valencia', pp. 108–13, for after 700.

Arabs of the first glazed production sites, Murcia here and Pechina (prov. Almería) a little further south, in the late ninth century, and glaze did not become locally common until the tenth.[110]

Gutiérrez argues that this sharp simplification in production and equally sharp localization of distribution is a sign of an equally clear simplification of demand, which was by now largely restricted to peasant needs, and could be supplied by part-time production, Peacock's 'household industry' level, and, in some places, even his individualized 'household production' level. As the direction of argument throughout this chapter shows, I would entirely agree with this. Whereas Gutiérrez can see for the sixth and early seventh centuries several levels of demand, standardized imports for elites, local semi-professional wares for the peasantry, by 700 or so (outside centres like El Tolmo) only local productions were left, and their professionality was lessening too.[111] These, as already argued, are signs of the peasant mode of production (above, pp. 545–6), as also is the weakness of urbanism, and even of rural settlement hierarchies (above, p. 489), in this area. How far this radical destructuring of demand affected the rest of the Spanish coast is not yet clear, given our lack of knowledge of eighth-century typologies elsewhere, but the coastal strip of the province of Granada seems to be substantially similar. By the mid-tenth century the Muslim parts of the coast were economically active, with high-quality ceramic productions and also textile exports through Pechina (later, Almería, the main Mediterranean port of al-Andalus by 1000); but there is no sign of this at all before 850 at the earliest.[112]

However these patterns turn out in detail, it is already clear that the Spanish coast, like the interior, saw a marked fall in the complexity of ceramic production and exchange during our period, which in turn must represent a marked fall in the scale, and geographical range, of demand. This common change is not affected by the fact that on the coast at the start of our period, unlike in the interior, the largest-scale commodities were imports, for local productions on the coast in most places simplified as well; and their continuing simplicity across the whole period 600–850 must indicate that demand remained in most places low. There are two substantial differences between the coast and the interior, however. One is dating: the fall in

[110] Gutiérrez, *La cora de Tudmīr*, esp. pp. 170–203, which replaces earlier surveys (pp. 271–4 for Murcia); eadem *et al.*, 'Los contextos cerámicos', for El Tolmo. For Pechina, see esp. Acién *et al.*, 'Excavación de un barrio artesanal'; Castillo and Martínez, 'Producciones cerámicas'. For glaze, see in general Malpica, *La cerámica altomedieval*. This book tends to link the coast and the interior for al-Andalus, rather than drawing distinctions between them, as here.

[111] Gutiérrez, *La cora de Tudmīr*, pp. 187–98.

[112] Gómez, *El poblamiento*, pp. 423–56 for the Granada coast. At Málaga, too, there is glaze production after 850: Acién *et al.*, 'Cerámicas tardorromanas', pp. 432–3. For textiles and export, see Ibn Ḥawqal (Ibn Hauqal), *Configuration de la terre*, I, pp. 109, 113; Constable, *Trade and traders*, pp. 18–19, 159–60, 173–8.

demand on the coast was almost two centuries later than inland, early seventh-century rather than fifth-century. (The equivalent moment in southern Gaul is the sixth.) The second relates to the degree of simplification of the economy. In 550 the coast would have seemed far more economically complex than the interior, with a diffused level of demand for standardized products that was perhaps only available to royal courts on the Meseta. In 700, however, most of the coastal strip was desolate, with little exchange visible at all beyond the microregional level, and only leopard-spots of more elaborate demand structures. The interior, by contrast, had in many places maintained reasonable levels of productive sophistication, which may have extended across city territories in the Guadalquivir valley; and even on the Meseta, where it was more localized, it did not usually go below the level of productivity associated with wheel-thrown pots—although there were certainly leopard-spots of simpler exchange patterns in both too, more than there were in other regions of the post-Roman world. This contrast in itself makes Spain in the eighth century more locally diverse than Italy, or indeed most of our other regions (see below, pp. 785–9, for some parallels in Greece). One thing that the sudden drop in complexity on the coast in the seventh century, a sub-region which had been so open to exchange for so long, indicates is that it must have been relatively hard hit by the breakdown in the Mediterranean world-system in the same period: it was probably more seriously affected than any other part of the western Mediterranean apart from Africa itself. But its exchange also simplified to levels not even seen in Africa; this must have been caused by other parameters. In order to understand this, we need to look at Spain as a whole.

I argued in Chapter 4 that the documentary evidence and the archaeological evidence for Spain pointed in different directions. This is also true of southern Gaul, to a lesser extent. How this works out in detail needs to be set out here, so that we can see how it can be resolved. Let us first look at the different Spains that have appeared in earlier chapters.

In Chapter 3 (pp. 93–102), we saw that the Visigothic state after the 570s was well organized and ambitious by western standards, and that kings aimed to control and lessen the fragmentation which the geography of the peninsula always supports; they were rich, and the court at Toledo was a magnet, right up to their fall in 711; their often violent rhetoric was essentially a mark of their ambition. The Arab emirs (and, later, caliphs) had the same aims, and taxed more to support their armies, although a coherent and centralized fiscal system only developed fully in the tenth century. The emiral state looks disorganized by the standards of the core lands of the Arab caliphate, but it, and even its Visigothic predecessor, were in fact fairly well structured by the standards of the Romano-Germanic kingdoms of the rest of the West; we should recognize both the objective difficulties rulers faced throughout and their systematic efforts to overcome them. In

Chapter 4 (pp. 219–32), we looked at the documentary evidence for a relatively prosperous and long-lasting aristocracy, which, by the standards of Spanish documentation, is quite consistent; aristocratic groups seem to have been highly localized, city by city, but they were slow to abandon a 'late late Roman' lifestyle—even the militarization of aristocratic culture, normal in the post-Roman world, was maybe incomplete as late as the seventh century. The most likely parallels to this cultural continuity are in Frankish-ruled southern Gaul, although the scale of aristocratic wealth seems to have been rather greater there, particularly in Aquitaine. A dislocation for the aristocracy caused by the Arab conquest can probably be seen in the far north, where microregional societies of different types emerge by 800 or so, but not necessarily elsewhere: there were aristocrats claiming Visigothic descent in al-Andalus up to the civil wars around 900 at least. Taken together, one could argue from the written sources for a Spain which experienced fewer breaks than elsewhere in the West across our period: for a culturally conservative, Romanizing, Visigothic world, which was only different from the later empire (from which Spain had always been fairly cut off) in being less based on taxation and rather more localized—and even this was partly countered by the real political centrality of Toledo. After 711 political culture of course changed, in both al-Andalus and the Christian fringe, but in most of the peninsula the structural relationship between a strong court and a set of inward-looking provinces did not alter until the victory of the caliphs in the tenth century.

The archaeology of rural settlement, cities and exchange shows a different scansion in Spain (see above, pp. 488–91, 656–65). In the fifth century exchange simplified considerably in the interior, and rural villas began to be abandoned, in a process which accelerated in the sixth. Sixth-century cities were still fairly coherent in material terms, but in the seventh they were rather less impressive; the seventh century also saw a collapse of exchange on the coast. The eighth century is difficult to locate almost everywhere; there was some urban continuity of different types, in some places rural settlement hierarchies were maintained, and local exchange networks continued in most places, at least in the interior, but complex economic patterns do not return until the ninth, sometimes the tenth, century. These trends point to a steady weakening of demand, and thus aristocratic wealth, throughout our period. They have parallels everywhere in the West, although the radical breakdown of productive complexity on parts of the Spanish coast marks an extreme. They do not fit very well with the documentary-based continuities that have just been characterized. The Visigothic period, in particular, would appear in this perspective one of continuous economic involution and localization, and the chance that any ruler, even ruthless and determined ones like Leovigild and Chindasuinth, could have reversed it might seem to be limited—it took the Arab emirs two centuries and a civil war to do so.

The archaeology also shows up the acute nature of sub-regional and microregional difference in Spain. This is harder to tell from the written sources, which tend to offer us a central government perspective in both the Visigothic and the emiral periods; local differentiation can be pinned down sometimes, but against the grain of the texts. It is, however, indisputable in the archaeology, and it anyway has to be the most sensible way to view Spain, given its poor communications and the extreme ecological contrasts to be found in the peninsula. The recognition of local difference from a central government perspective appears as a challenge, and appeared as one to rulers in our period too: hence, for example, the importance and wickedness of the Other (whether *servi*, or Jews, or Basques) in Visigothic political rhetoric. But the local was the level at which the huge majority of the population lived, and it must be our starting-point: each sub-region of Spain had a fundamentally different development, and indeed a different time-scale for its development. If we want to resolve the apparent contradictions which have just been set out, this is the level at which we must do it. In terms of the four parameters for social change listed earlier (p. 719), the broad lines of Spain's state structures did not change dramatically in our period, and the continuitist reading of them offered here need not be greatly revised when they are seen from a local perspective—not, at least, until al-Andalus fragmented politically in the eleventh century. The disruptions of war were more localized, and not usually very great, except in frontier areas. Where sub-regional difference above all lay was in the density of aristocratic wealth, and in openness to the Mediterranean. Let us look at how these can be tracked, using the subdivisions already adopted in this chapter, although further dividing the Mediterranean coast into a south-eastern and a north-eastern sector, along lines already proposed in Chapter 10.

Inland Andalucía (including, here as elsewhere, Mérida) shows the greatest continuities. We have documentary evidence for the urban rich in Mérida, at least in the Visigothic period, and our archaeology shows a city which maintained its spatial coherence and some notable concentrations of wealth, with only a minor weakening, in the seventh century in particular. The more fragmentary evidence we have for other parts of the sub-region indicates the survival of prosperous urban elites in many places, although each of them was probably restricted to a single city territory, and although some areas became more ruralized, for example, the upper Guadalquivir valley, the modern province of Jaén. The highly variegated patterns of exchange in our period show that the differences between different urban and rural histories must have been considerable. All the same, notwithstanding this fragmentation, even the Jaén area maintained modest levels of demand for professionally made goods, and also a rural settlement hierarchy (above, p. 490); and some of the cities seem to have remained active centres, with some elements of economic interconnection between them. The economic involution of the seventh and eighth centuries is thus least visible here, and the cultural continuities of our written evidence are not falsified here either. As has often enough been stated, it is understandable that the Arabs should have established their capital at Córdoba, given the natural wealth of the Guadalquivir valley. But it is also worth stressing that the complex patterns of local demand in this sub-region point to some very localized, even if wealthy, aristocracies. Both the Visigoths and the Umayyads had considerable political difficulties with these aristocracies; Leovigild had to confront trouble in both Córdoba and Mérida, for example, and arguably also Seville; Mérida caused difficulties throughout the emirate; and many of the rebellious aristocrats of the first *fitna* at the end of the ninth century came from the south.[113] The late seventh-century kings doubtless dominated the southern cities, and so did the stronger emirs, but their local identities made it harder for rulers to deal with them in all periods.

The south-east shows the greatest discontinuities, moving as it did from being one of the sub-regions with the most complex exchange in the fifth century to that with the simplest patterns, both microregionalized and deprofessionalized, by the eighth, which fits with the radical simplification of its rural settlement structures, and more than one spatial reorientation of its urban hierarchy (El Tolmo de Minateda, atypical in its exchange patterns, was at least typical in this, for it was a new foundation around 600, and failed as a city in the ninth century). This must have been an area where demand mostly collapsed, at any level more elaborate than the needs of the peasantry. The period after the Visigothic reconquest of Byzantine Spain around 628 seems to be the most likely moment for this dramatic shift to have begun. We have already seen that one cause for it is likely to have been the unusual dependence of the sub-region on the Mediterranean-wide exchange network, and the resultant disruption to its economic structures when that network ended at the end of the seventh century. But it must also be that local aristocracies were in serious trouble in the late Visigothic period. We can only speculate as to why, but the process seems clear. This was not an area which would have experienced the seventh century as a period of late Roman continuities. The wealth of its rulers at the time of the Arab conquest, Theudemir (d. 744) and his son Athanagild, was presumably not enough to counteract these tendencies, and Athanagild anyway had no obvious successors; the south-east hardly appears in Arab sources for the next century. This must have been a sub-region where the peasant mode of production was rather more common than elsewhere, as we have seen (p. 546). By the tenth century some of these autonomous peasantries were tribal in their social structure, and Berber in their ethnicity, but the origins of the specificity of the societies of the south-east go back to before the Arab (/Berber) conquest. Berber settlers would not, here, have had as much

---

[113] See above, Ch. 3, n. 98; Ch. 4, nn. 179, 187.

incentive to abandon their tribal social structures as in some other parts of the peninsula.[114]

The north-east, Catalonia, Valencia, and the Ebro valley, had a history of relative urban continuity, at least up to 700, and arguably later too (pp. 657–9), and also some late villa survival, including the new rural prestige foundation of Pla de Nadal near Valencia, from the late seventh or early eighth century: just the sort of building that ought to be rather more common in Spain if our documentary images were taken at face value. This fits with the sorts of aristocratic continuities that are documented at least in the inland parts of the north-east, particularly around Zaragoza (p. 223). It does have to be recognized, on the other hand, that this was also a sub-region that was as open to Mediterranean exchange before the seventh century as was the south-east, and it is quite possible that it was as affected by its end; the difficulty archaeologists have had in tracking the eighth century here may reflect that. Rural settlement at least maintained a village structure, but, as we have just seen, exchange structures in the countryside simplified notably, already before 711. We might conclude that this is a sub-region where elites became substantially less wealthy, but survived, keeping their city orientations; the social structure maintained itself, rather than breaking down as completely as in the south-east, although at a relatively unambitious level. The beginning of this process was probably, as in the south-east, the seventh century. The situation around 700 in the north-east could be regarded as being a simpler version of northern Italy, with relatively poor urban elites surviving in most places. The Carolingian conquest of the northern sector of this sub-region, Catalonia, at the beginning of the ninth century led to an unusually dense documentation in that area a century later, but it is far from clear how far tenth-century Catalan elites had real roots in the Visigothic aristocracy, and it is more likely that they were products of the frontier wars of the Carolingian period—the tenth century is at the other side of a social divide, that is to say.[115] It is more likely that the Carolingians rather than the Arabs are responsible for that divide, but we will need more archaeology in order to be sure.

In a way, the Meseta is the most intriguing problem. It was entirely cut off from the Mediterranean, but it still underwent a considerable simplification in its exchange structures, already in the fifth century, and this must indicate an early weakening of demand and thus global aristocratic wealth. I have already compared it, too, to northern Italy after 650, but here that degree of localization already began two centuries earlier. The Meseta in the

---

[114] *Chronicle of 754*, c. 87, for Theudemir and Athanagild. For tribal communities, see esp. Guichard, *Structures sociales*, pp. 241–90, and Bazzana, Cressier, and Guichard, *Les châteaux ruraux*, for fortified communitarian settlements of the tenth century onwards in the south-east (including the hills behind Valencia); cf. also Ch. 2, n. 47; Ch. 4, n. 195.

[115] See in general Salrach, *El proces de feudalització*, pp. 209–23, slightly more continuitist in this respect than I would be.

Visigothic period did not show any further involution in exchange, and good-quality ceramics remained quite widely available. It was very unevenly urbanized, however, and it is quite likely that the aristocracy of the period were in many places country-dwelling, as well as being at least as local as those of Andalucía; this ruralization makes any Italian parallel less useful. Rich estates (as in the villa areas of the northern Meseta, some of which were owned by kings) probably lay side by side with much more small-scale operations like Diego Álvaro (above, p. 224), and also areas of peasant landowning, more numerous than in Italy. Toledo must have been a major centre, and will have acted as a focus for at least part of the Meseta; it is not clear if it had any parallels, however, on the rest of the plateau. In many ways, this may have been a less difficult terrain for the Visigothic kings to dominate politically than, in particular, Andalucía; it was closer and had better communications, and, above all, its aristocracy would have been less able to resist. The Visigothic Meseta could thus be seen as a *Königslandschaft* like the lands around Paris (above, p. 399), although a poorer and more fragmented one. Diego Álvaro's slates, although showing a very localized economy, also showed an access to a legal culture that probably spread widely across the plateau. This was the basis of the coherence of Visigothic government, the terrain of the ambition of its kings. The harsh rhetoric of their legislation, the sense this gives of a set of rulers grappling with problems that were uncontrollable, had Roman origins, as we have seen (p. 95), but may in part also derive from their awareness of the other regional differences in the peninsula: a rich but potentially autonomous Andalucía, and coastal districts which were slipping fast away from anything that could easily be governed from outside, at least by the seventh century. We could thus recognize both the reality of Visigothic royal power and its geographical limits.

But the Meseta was also surrounded by (and cut in two by) mountains, whose social structures need not be assumed to have been identical. Some of their Visigothic-period inhabitants may have maintained tribal identities from pre-Roman times (like the Basques), or developed them in places where the politics of the fifth century led to particular local confusion (like the *plebs Aunonensis* and the lands of the *senior* Aspidius in southern Galicia).[116] The exchange structures of the Meseta do not show great changes in the eighth century, indicating that the localized economies of the Visigothic period persisted, as the urban elites of Toledo also did. But the northern Meseta was by now, after the 710s, a frontier, and there was close to a no-man's-land in the Duero valley in political terms for two centuries. In this fragmented political environment, some areas of the northern Meseta and the northern mountains probably lost their aristocracies, and some of these developed tribal patterns, perhaps on a Basque model, even if richer

---

[116] Hydatius, *Chronica*, cc. 229, 233, 243, ed. Burgess; John of Biclar, *Chronica*, s.a. 575.

local owners undoubtedly continued in some places. It may well be that some landowners, perhaps of the Diego Álvaro type, turned themselves into tribal leaders, in order to defend their own local power, much as it was earlier proposed that landowners did in fifth-century Britain (above, pp. 330–3). These were consequences of the radical political decentralization of the frontier zone, and therefore, in this area, of the Arab conquest. The way they developed on the ground had everything to do with local realities, rather than external political pressure; but they do not have to invalidate the picture of a stable society on the Meseta in the century before 711.

A sub-regional approach to Spain thus allows us to get over some of the disjuncture between history and archaeology in a fairly simple way: many parts of the post-Roman peninsula showed continuities in social structure from the Roman world, but not all did, and even those which did maintained different elements in different places—here urban living, there complex local exchange structures, and so on. It is also likely that Visigothic political power was by no means undermined by the signs we have that local aristocracies were often poorer than they had been; as in Italy (above, pp. 211, 218), this in itself facilitated the relative dominance of kings who were themselves certainly not poor, and thus the attraction of being part of their clientèles; this argument would extend to the Umayyad emirs as well. Although the history of these sub-regions often hardly links together at all, they can at least be set beside each other in that political framework. Two other conclusions can be drawn from this way of looking at the peninsula. One is that the classic temporal dividing-lines in Spanish history are no easier to see in these syntheses than they were on the basis of the ceramic patterns alone. The fifth-century invasions seem to have had an impact on inland Spain, but 711, in particular, seems nowhere to be a turning-point, with the exception of parts of the northern Meseta. I have argued consistently in this book against overvaluing political explanations of socio-economic change; the Arab conquest of Spain does not seem to be an exception, notwithstanding its importance in the historiography. On the socio-economic level, the geographical contrasts in Spain were more powerful than any political intervention, in our period at least. The second point is that Spain was by no means unique. There are any number of parallels in the West (and indeed the East) to the picture of a set of relatively—sometimes increasingly—localized aristocracies and exchange patterns which characterizes the post-Roman centuries here. Specifically, the north-east of the peninsula had analogies to northern Italy (and also, one can add, Africa), Andalucía to southern Gaul and southern Italy, the Meseta in part to northern Italy. Only the south-east has no parallels in its simplicity in the western Mediterranean. These parallels do not mean that these places were identical; Spain everywhere shows leopard-spots of simpler economies than can be traced in most of Italy, for example. But they seem to me useful, important, to set out. Spain is ill-served if it is regarded as unique in its development.

Let us finally turn to southern Gaul. Here, there is another disjuncture to be faced. In earlier chapters it has become clear that this was, in the sixth to eighth centuries, a sub-region of rich aristocracies, with widely spaced lands, particularly in Aquitaine but (as the will of Abbo of Maurienne shows) in the Rhône valley as well (above, pp. 189–91). These aristocracies were probably less uniformly urbanized than in Italy or much of Spain (pp. 606–7), but they maintained Roman lifestyles as long as did those of Spain, including in some cases villa-living, perhaps into the seventh century (p. 174). Until the Carolingian conquest of the south in the eighth century, they were little affected by political upheaval. The picture of their exchange structures that has here been set out is partially different from this: we have seen ceramic localization and simplification from the sixth century, with only coarse and common wares, the *kaolinitique* exchange system of Languedoc and the Rhône valley, and 'E ware' in Poitou, operating over wide areas. But we should not be misled by the unambitiousness of these ceramic types: they do show demand structures of some complexity. They have parallels in northern Gaul, as we shall see (pp. 796–8), where large-scale exchange systems are in archaeological terms best documented in coarse-ware types, in the seventh century in particular, but surely existed for all that; and, there too, these correlate with a rich and wide-owning aristocracy. The uncertainty here is that Aquitainian coarse wares are not well studied, and it cannot yet be shown that 'E ware' or any equivalent marked exchange systems in the central Garonne valley area in particular. If a localization of Aquitaine's exchange systems were to be confirmed, however, then we might have to conclude that the super-rich elites, people such as Desiderius of Cahors, were more isolated in the sub-region than they at present appear.

In these three sections on the western Mediterranean regions, I have placed strong emphasis on internal social and economic developments, rather than any wider macroeconomic explanatory structure. The common history of these regions does include the end of the Mediterranean exchange network, but the importance of this depended above all on the internal economic structure of each region or sub-region: it was very great in Africa or on the Spanish coast, rather less on the Italian or Gaulish coast, and hardly felt at all in inland Spain or northern Italy. All the same, it does seem generally the case that the eighth century, the first period after the eclipse of the African export system in c.700, is also the low point for the economic complexity of almost every region and sub-region described here. This is in part because the import level was stripped away, leaving only the simpler local production systems for archaeologists to study; in part because local demand was falling anyway, above all because aristocracies in almost all our regions were less wealthy in 700 than they had been in 400, for an array of localized reasons. The eighth century is also emphasized in this way by comparison with the ninth century and later, however, and there is a political context to this. The eighth century was the last period of sharp political change in the western Mediterranean for some time; thereafter, the political map broadly stabilized. By 800 the spheres of influence of the Arab and Frankish worlds were clearly delineated in the western Mediterranean, and, except for the Arab conquest of Sicily, they scarcely altered for over two centuries. Notwithstanding the internal changes inside these two spheres of influence, this overall stability had one important consequence: it allowed aristocracies to root themselves again. Several generations of relatively unchanging political patterns would help the increase of landowning wealth and geographical scale, the re-creation of stable aristocratic hegemonies over peasants (see above, pp. 570–88), and the revival of complex spending patterns as a result. The ninth, and still more the tenth, centuries would see the internal economic complexity of all these regions increase again, sometimes very quickly. This development lies outside our period, but it has parallels elsewhere, as we shall see.

6. The eastern Mediterranean I: Egypt

As we move eastwards, we come to regions where the state never went away, and where we can count on a number of other structural continuities too. But the eastern Mediterranean was no more homogeneous than was the West, and our three major regions had strikingly different ceramic histories in our period, which underpin significant differences in their social structures and socio-economic development.

Egyptian archaeology, as was noted earlier, is undeveloped in our period, but the study of ceramics is one of its most articulated elements, thanks to Pascale Ballet, Donald Bailey, and several other wide-ranging experts, building on the pioneering 1960s–1970s work of Michel Egloff, Mieczysław Rodziewicz, and William Adams.[117] The basic outlines of ceramic production and distribution in Egypt are fairly clear as a result. Egypt in the period up to 700 imported substantial quantities of LRA 1 amphorae, largely from Cyprus, and not much less LRA 4, from Gaza (other amphora types, whether African or eastern, were much less common). These have distributions throughout the region, on most sites; they are common in Hermopolis

---

[117] Egloff, *Kellia*; Rodziewicz, *La céramique romaine tardive*; Adams, *Ceramic industries*. More recently, Ballet and Picon, 'Recherches préliminaires'; Ballet *et al.*, 'Artisanat de la céramique'; Ballet, 'De l'empire romain'; Bailey, *Excavations at El-Ashmunein*, V (and cf. Hayes, *Late Roman pottery*, pp. 387–401, for ERS). Other authors will appear in the next notes. The sophistication of analysis of this material is admirably supported by the niche journal *Cahiers de la céramique égyptienne*. I am grateful to Donald Bailey for advice here.

(Ashmūnayn) in Middle Egypt, for example, together making up nearly all the non-local amphorae (although the figure drops to 12 per cent if local amphorae are included). LRA 1 presumably brought olive oil, which Egypt did not produce, and LRA 4 certainly brought wine, of a higher quality than Egypt's own (p. 714). Egypt did produce plenty of wine by our period, however (wine had replaced the traditional beer by the fourth century), and also its own *lachanon* (vegetable) oil and radish oil for cooking; imports widened the range of Egyptian food, rather than being necessities. All the same, olive oil was widely available, as papyri show, and only up to 50 per cent more expensive than the apparently terrible radish oil in the fifth century—the import of this commodity was evidently very easy.[118] Conversely, fine-ware imports were more restricted. They did exist: ARS can be found throughout the region, even at Elephantinē in the far south, one of the major production centres of Aswān ERS, Egypt's own fine ware. ARS indeed provided many of the models for ERS. But as ERS production expanded, above all in the fifth century, ARS distributions receded. In Hermopolis, another major ERS centre, ARS is rare in the sixth century and absent by the seventh, although it remained common in the Delta. Of the other Mediterranean fine wares, Phocaean RS is relatively rare; Cypriot RS, presumably imported together with LRA 1, is fairly common in Alexandria and the Delta, but it, too, is rare in the Nile valley.[119] ERS and the other Aswān products were evidently seen as of sufficiently good quality that it was not necessary to import competitors, and Egyptian fine wares dominated the market, except for the Mediterranean coast, by 550.

All these imports carried on to the late seventh century and then stopped, with the cessation of Mediterranean trade in general. But it is clear that this had little effect on Egyptian fine wares, which were predominantly local already; at the most, given the quality of Egyptian oil and wine, the regional cuisine would have suffered. The end of the exchange systems would have had more impact on exports: not on fine wares or on wine, for ERS and Egyptian amphorae (LRA 5/6 and 7) are not very often found outside

[118] Overviews for amphorae: Egloff, *Kellia*, pp. 109–19; Ballet and Picon, 'Recherches préliminaires', pp. 21–6, 30–40; Majcherek, 'Late Roman ceramics', pp. 101–11; Bailey, *Excavations at El-Ashmunein*, V, pp. 118–38; Pollard, 'The chronology', pp. 153–8. Gaza (or Askalon) wine appears in papyri in e.g. *P. Oxy.* XVI 1924, LIX 4005. For olive oil (*elaion*) in papyri, see Morelli, *Olio e retribuzioni* (pp. 6–7 for vegetable and radish oil; cf. Bagnall, *Egypt*, pp. 30–1, for the latter's quality and price). Note that *spanelaion* or *elaion spanon* did not come from Spain: Kramer, 'Die Bedeutung von *spanelaion*'.

[119] For ARS and other imports, Bailey, *Excavations at El-Ashmunein*, V, pp. 1–8; Ballet and Picon, 'Recherches préliminaires', pp. 26–9; see n. 41 above for Cyprus. For case studies, see Gempeler, *Elephantine X*, pp. 41–4; Rodziewicz, *La céramique romaine tardive*, pp. 26–46; Majcherek, 'Late Roman ceramics', pp. 84–101, and Bonifay, 'Alexandrie' (for Alexandria); Egloff, *Kellia*, pp. 67–78; Vogt, 'La céramique de Tell el-Fadda' (Pelousion, modern Tell al-Farama, on the coast); Ballet and von der Way, 'Exploration archéologique de Bouto' (also near the coast), pp. 6–8.

the region,[120] but at least on grain, papyrus, and cloth. All the same, the continuities of production inside the region show that, although Mediterranean links always existed in Egypt (unlike in inland Spain or Anatolia), they were always marginal to the internal economy, and their end around 700 was less important than in many places.

Egypt's own ceramic productions were large scale. The Aswān kilns, at Elephantinē and elsewhere, produced several good fine-ware products, with a recognizable kaolinitic fabric: Aswān ERS, the white-slipped Aswān Fine ware, and the painted Aswān Medieval White ware (I use the English classification of Adams and Bailey; the first two are also called Rodziewicz O and W wares). ERS and Aswān Fine ware were produced without a break from the fourth century to the thirteenth; White ware joined them in the eighth. They were available throughout Egypt.[121] In Middle Egypt the Hermopolis kilns (and, doubtless, others nearby) produced another ERS variant, called ERSH by Bailey (Rodziewicz K ware), with a distribution that is most extensive downstream from the site, especially in the Delta; this continued into the ninth century and later. RS productions were not restricted to these two kiln complexes—indeed, as Bailey says, they 'must have been legion' in Egypt—but others were decidedly more local, and imitative of the major productions. In the Fayyūm, for example, an area slightly offset from the main Nile valley, field survey and excavation have found both Aswān and local ERS across our period (and also ARS, up to 600).[122]

Amphorae, too—almost all for wine, as resin deposits show—were produced in enormous numbers. Here, there were also two main production foci, and a myriad of local ateliers, probably in every village that produced wine. LRA 7, a brown (i.e. alluvial clay) carrot-shaped amphora, was largely made at Hermopolis and at Antinoupolis (Shaykh 'Ibāda) just across the river; huge hills of pots survive there, one in Antinoupolis 30 m high. These ceramic mounds are not unparalleled; Rome and Alexandria have them. But those are dumps of throwaway containers in major consumer cities; to have

---

[120] For ERS and amphorae outside Egypt, see Panella, 'Merci e scambi', pp. 658 n., 666; Hayes, *Excavations at Saraçhane*, II, pp. 7, 67; see further below, n. 146. LRA 7 amphorae also went down the Red Sea to Arabia, through 'Aqaba: see below, n. 149, and Ch. 3, n. 192. Note finally Rāġib, 'La plus ancienne lettre arabe de marchand', for a late seventh-century credit note sent from 'Ifriqiya' (Kairouan?) to Egypt: this is more likely to reflect the last years of the Roman world-system than the start of Geniza-type exchange.

[121] See Adams, *Ceramic industries*, II, pp. 525–60; Rodziewicz, *La céramique romaine tardive*, pp. 54–68; Egloff, *Kellia*, pp. 79–89; Gempeler, *Elephantine X*, pp. 22–3, 56–9; Bailey, *Excavations at El-Ashmunein*, V, pp. 8–38; Pierrat, 'Essai de classification', pp. 175–92, 198–203.

[122] Bailey, *Excavations at El-Ashmunein*, V, pp. 38–58 (p. 38 for the quote); Rodziewicz, *La céramique romaine tardive*, pp. 50–3. Note that this classification supersedes that in Hayes, *Late Roman pottery*, pp. 397–401—a rare example of Hayes being superseded. For the Fayyūm, see Rousset and Marchand, 'Secteur nord de Tebtynis', pp. 414–35; Godlewski, 'Coptic pottery', p. 49.

one in a centre of *production* truly indicates the scale that the local kilns must have had. Exactly how the Antinoupolis kilns were organized must await excavation, but this scale implies that Egyptian amphora production may well have been at Peacock's 'manufactory' level; they could indeed have been the only examples of this among ceramic centres in the late empire. This part of Middle Egypt was evidently a serious wine-producing region; this scale is all the more striking when we remember that demand for the wine was nearly all Egyptian.[123] The other main amphora centre as yet known was Abū Mīnā near Alexandria, which was one of the producers of the Egyptian version of the bag-shaped LRA 5/6, as well as common and fine wares (and also ampoules for holy water, souvenirs for the pilgrims to the city). The quality of these amphorae was often fairly low, however, and they may not all have been for wine.[124] Overall, LRA 7 dominated the wine trade, and this amphora type (not all from Hermopolis and Antinoupolis, to be sure) can be found the length of Egypt from Aswān to Alexandria.

These regional production patterns are late Roman ones, but it is important to stress that they did not stop, or change at all, in 700. All that happened after that, apart from the end of imports, was the standard slow evolution of types which any ceramic system generates. Aswān products continued to be dominant in Fusṭāṭ (Cairo) in the eighth century and onwards. The next change was that glazed fine wares were introduced around or shortly after 800 (a date which seems fairly secure, thanks to the Isṭabl 'Antar stratigraphy in Fusṭāṭ), probably following the fashions of Iraq; but they continued to be produced alongside the older fine-ware types and in the same kiln-sites.[125] Egyptian ceramic tastes changed less than those anywhere else in the post-Roman world, without question; and, at least as important, so did the scale of Egyptian productions. In economic terms, this is as close to full continuity across our whole period as we are likely to get.

The clarity of these Egyptian distribution patterns derives from their constancy across wide geographical ranges: Aswān is some 800 km by boat from Fusṭāṭ, and over 1,000 km from Alexandria. If one wants to

---

[123] See Ballet *et al.*, 'Artisanat de la céramique', pp. 134–9 (p. 136 for the pottery dumps); Ballet, 'De l'empire romain'; Bailey, *Excavations at El-Ashmunein*, V, pp. 129–35. For the intensity of wine cash-cropping in late Roman Egypt, see Banaji, *Agrarian change*, pp. 106, 158–9, 167–8, 200–1. Compare the fullest survey of an ARS production site, El Mahrine: Mackensen, *Die spätantiken Sigillata- und Lampentöpfereien*, I, pp. 461–86; Mackensen envisages something on the level of Peacock's 'nucleated workshop' for that site.

[124] See in general Ballet, 'De l'empire romain', pp. 54–5; Empereur and Picon, 'La reconnaissance des productions'; Engemann, 'À propos des amphores d'Abou Mina' (who stresses their poor quality; he doubts that Abū Mīnā amphorae were for wine).

[125] See above all Vogt, 'Les céramiques ommeyyades et abbassides'; see pp. 248–50 and Gayraud, 'Les céramiques égyptiennes', pp. 263–6, for the glaze dating. An earlier dating of the origins of glaze in Egypt to the early eighth century can still be found in recent literature: examples are Engemann, 'Das Ende der Wallfahrten', pp. 163–70; Whitcomb, 'Coptic glazed ceramics', p. 181; Bailey, *Excavations at El-Ashmunein*, V, pp. 112–13. For the evolution of glaze, see further Pierrat, 'Essai de classification', pp. 194–8.

characterize more local productions, especially of common wares and coarse wares, like the Red Painted wares found at Kellia or the flagons of Hermopolis, one runs into the problem that the absolute number of sites in the region is still fairly small. A kiln-site at Gurna in Western Thebes in Upper Egypt, for example, made its own painted wares; these had a fairly restricted distribution, for they hardly reached Tōd, only 20 km to the south. But exactly how wide the range was of the Gurna ceramics, or those of Ṣaqqāra near Cairo (which included local ERS and also imitations of LRA 1), is as yet unknown.[126] What is clear, nonetheless, is that, underneath the fully regional distributions of the major Egyptian productions, there was an elaborate hierarchy of sub-regional and microregional types, with a complex network of local RS, painted and unpainted common wares, amphorae, and cooking wares. Finding out how this hierarchy actually worked, and changed, is a task for the future.[127]

A discussion of Egyptian ceramic production does not, all the same, have to stop here; this is the region of the papyri, and we can say more than usual about the internal structure of artisanal activity. Pottery is, in fact, the best-documented artisanal production in Egypt in our period, particularly in the sixth century, with twenty or more papyri referring to it at least casually (the different groups of clothmaking artisans come next, then brickmaking and metalwork, then stonework). The workshops in our documents are all independent single workshops, mostly in the countryside, but often with urban patrons, in Oxyrhynchos (Bahnasā), or, significantly, Hermopolis. Potters (*kerameioi, kouphokeramoi, keramoplastai*) were sufficiently organized to have guilds, all the same, as seventh-century Apollōnopolis (Edfū) texts show.[128] Exactly what range of pottery they made is partially hidden by unknown technical terms, but their main focus is clear: they made containers for wine, that is to say what we call amphorae. This is often explicit, and even when it is not, the fact that potters also sold pitch, the material for the internal resin coating of wine amphorae, makes the point on its own. We have leases of ceramics workshops; in one, an Aphroditō text from 565, the rent was 2,400 pots (but not the pitch for them). The potters, even if

---

[126] See respectively Egloff, *Kellia*, pp. 47–64; Bailey, *Excavations at El-Ashmunein*, V, pp. 80–90; Myśliwiec, *Keramik und Kleinfunde*, pp. 119–53, 192, with Lecuyot and Pierrat, 'À propos des lieux de production', p. 178, for Tōd (note that Jēme, close to Gurna, was in part supplied by Aswān: see above, p. 421); Ghaly, 'Pottery workshops of Saint-Jeremia'.

[127] The extreme variety of ceramics is best seen in Bailey, *Excavations at El-Ashmunein*, V. Note that Vogt, 'Les céramiques ommeyyades et abbassides', pp. 244–5, proposes that Aswān clay was also itself transported down the Nile to be worked by potters in the north of Egypt, as happens today: a further complexity in ceramic exchange, if it is demonstrated for our period.

[128] For fairly complete lists of artisans, see Johnson and West, *Byzantine Egypt*, pp. 115–25; see also Bagnall, *Egypt*, pp. 84–5. Cockle, 'Pottery manufacture', published some good third-century examples in the *Journal of Roman Studies* in 1981, in an article which surprised the (non-Egyptological) field, because pottery was believed not to be documented—although Johnson and West's lists (not to speak of many of the papyri themselves) had been published for decades. For guilds, see Crum, 'Koptische Zünfte', p. 107; *P. Apoll.* 75.

tenants, were mostly independent operators, who might have their own employees; we have a wage agreement for two employees from Arsinoë (Madīnat al-Fayyūm) in c.600, with a wage in money, bread, and pitched pots. They made contracts with neighbouring landowners to produce containers for the wine-harvest, generally on a sizable scale. An Oxyrhynchos document from 606 is a receipt from the Apions for 3 gold *nomismata* (a low year's salary) to pay for 1,000 'new landlordly pots' (*kainokoupha geouchika*) and a few larger vessels, all pitch-lined, all to be delivered in time for the harvest. Similarly, one of the Apion accounts, from 555, has separate receipts for 1,601 and 764 'new pots'. These were, that is to say, substantial operations, even though scattered across the Nile villages of our documents, which would have produced pretty standardized ceramics. They were a strong organizational foundation for the really big industries of the Aswān and Hermopolis areas.[129]

The papyri, as already noted, also tell us about other artisans. They tend to be operating on a similar scale, that of independent workshops; the major difference is that they were rather more often urban. This was a common difference, for potters often tended to operate closest to where the clays were; in Julian of Askalon's sixth-century urbanism treatise for Palestine, for example, they were the only artisanal group described as working in villages.[130] In Egypt, potters may also have been tied into wine-producing areas (our texts unfortunately tell us little about table wares). But in other respects what we know about other trades fits what we know about ceramics. The textile production of Oxyrhynchos (Bahnasā), for example, has been argued to have been in the third century a quarter of that of medieval Florence at its height. Productions of this kind, even if based on independent workshops, were concentrated enough to fit Peacock's 'nucleated workshop' level. This sort of scale, if it continued into our period, also matches that of most of our ceramic productions except perhaps the very largest; and indeed the larger-scale ceramic productions were urban too. One could expect the big textile productions, for linen and wool, to have various foci in Egypt, just as the major ceramic productions did; and written sources imply that linen, in particular, was exported as well.[131]

---

[129] Respectively, *P. Cair. Masp.* I 67110 (cf. *P. Lond.* III 994); CPR XIV 2; *P. Oxy.* LVIII 3942 (for 3 *nomismata* as a low salary for a manual worker in the period, see e.g. Banaji, *Agrarian change*, pp. 67–8), XVI 1913. For the Apions and pottery production, see Mazza, *L'archivio degli Apioni*, pp. 154–6.

[130] Julian of Askalon, *Urban treatise*, c. 5.1 (cf. cc. 8–13 for other artisans). For Egypt, urban examples include glass in Alexandria (Rodziewicz, *Les habitations*, pp. 141–3, 241–3). For a sample papyrus, see *P. Ross.-Georg.* III 56 (a. 707), a weaver who leases a first-floor veranda in the city of Herakleopolis (Ehnāsiyya) for wool shearing.

[131] For Oxyrhynchos, see van Minnen, 'The volume of the Oxyrhynchite textile trade', based on only one document however; he generalizes the argument in 'Urban craftsmen', not using archaeological evidence. He is followed by Bagnall, *Egypt*, pp. 82–3. See more widely Wipszycka, *L'industrie textile*, esp. pp. 47–102, 157–9, who stresses the small scale and the Egypt-wide distribution of most textile workshops in the period up to 400.

After 700 or so the written evidence we have for artisans lessens, and that for potters largely fades out; but there is more evidence for textiles. We have eighth-century invoices and receipts for cloth, both wool and linen; later, we have a set of documents for a ninth-century Fayyūm merchant which show an extensive trade in cloth, from Qūṣ in Upper Egypt down to Fusṭāṭ. Ninth- and tenth-century narratives and geographers show us the central medieval cloth specializations of Egypt already in operation: the woollens of Bahnasā (by now the major weaving centre in Middle Egypt, along with Madīnat al-Fayyūm), and above all the flax production of the eastern Delta, where centres like Tinnīs and Damietta were virtually one-industry linen-weaving towns. This evidence only begins around 850, and it is not clear whether such an intensity of specialization stretched back to the Roman period without any break (the references we have to linen export in the Roman empire lay stress on the Delta, so production there was old, but not on, for example, Tinnīs as a centre). But it is likely that there was no serious dip in large-scale textile production, given the continuities for ceramics. Egyptian linen was also established on a sufficient scale to provide the raw material for paper, which, first documented in Egypt around 800, almost entirely replaced papyrus (another large-scale Delta product) across the early tenth century. Linen exports probably ended after 700, along with most other interregional exchange, but internal Egyptian demand was sufficient to keep large-scale production going; by 1000 flax and linen were being exported again on a large scale. By then, too, the Cairo Geniza shows a startlingly complex network of urban workshops of all types.[132]

This picture of textile continuity is partially hypothetical, but it is import- ant to repeat that the ceramic archaeology had already prepared us for it. If fine wares from a place as remote as Aswān could remain available through- out the length of the Nile valley, then we can be sure that the scale of exchange in Egypt was always considerable. Egypt formed an integrated market on its own, with sub-regional specializations that were exchanged interdependently: flax/linen and papyrus in the Delta, wine and wool in Middle Egypt, table wares in the south, and, for sure, others again, less known because they lie outside the fields of interest of our written and

---

[132] For invoices, etc., see *APEL* VI 391; *Arabic papyri*, n. 21; *Arabische Briefe*, nn. 49–50. For the Fayyūm merchant, see Rāġib, *Marchands d'étoffes*. For the narratives and geographers, see Lev, 'Tinnīs'; Lombard, *Les textiles*, pp. 36–7, 47–50, 151–74, 222 (and 203–5 for paper); one of the most graphic is, as often, Ibn Ḥawqal (Ibn Hauqal, *Configuration de la terre*, I, esp. pp. 137, 150, 157). There is no papyrus documentation for the Delta, unfortunately. For the organization of papyrus production itself, see Lewis, *Papyrus*, esp. pp. 108–22, for the poor evidence. Linen and woollen cloth were still made in a variety of different places in Egypt on a smaller scale as well, much as ceramics were. For the eleventh century, Goitein, *A Mediterra- nean society*, I, esp. pp. 99–116, 222–8, 362–3, 455–7. The Fusṭāṭ merchants then looked to Bahnasā and the Fayyūm rather than to the Delta even for flax, and they exported flax to the West to be made up into cloth rather than dealing with the Delta weavers: a sign of a further level of economic complexity, but also perhaps of some internal fragmentation of exchange?

archaeological sources. Furthermore, all these integrated, hierarchically, with the more local distribution networks of wine or cloth or ceramics of lesser quality or productive scale, and with the grain trade to Egypt's cities. This system was so substantial, and so solidly implanted, that the end of the Roman world-system in the seventh century had less effect on Egypt than on any other Mediterranean region. But this in itself invites further questions, for one also needs to ask why it was so solidly implanted: the ease of transport along the Nile made the system possible, but it did not create these continuous levels of demand on its own. To answer this we need to step back once more, and look at other aspects of Egyptian society.

Egypt was, as was everywhere in our period, an agrarian society first and foremost. Its economy was based on irrigation, with elaborate dyke and water-control systems, and high fertility. Its villages—almost all concentrated settlements, usually large in size—were coherent units, with active local elites of medium landowners, interspersed with peasant owners in a classic fragmented ownership pattern. Villages were on one level tight societies, with considerable powers for local headmen and a collective loyalty against outsiders, but were also, often, the stages for fluid patterns of social behaviour, with possibilities for movement sideways (peasants becoming artisans, or vice versa) or up and down the social scale. The contrast between tightness and fluidity could produce considerable social tension, which was mediated by patron–client relationships throughout the whole of rural society. Patrons could be village leaders, state officials, landowners, or all three. (See above, pp. 411–28.)

Egyptian aristocrats existed as well, but there were probably fewer of them than in most of our regions, particularly by comparison with the western Roman empire. They were city-dwelling, with land scattered across a single city territory—or two or three in the case of really powerful families, such as the Apions. This family had unusual dominance up to the 620s in and around Oxyrhynchos, controlling a high percentage of its territory and even some whole villages; but there, too, the Apions coexisted with the usual array of medium and smaller owners. Most other cities had less of a concentration of rich landowning. After the Arab conquest few really rich families can be seen in our documentation, and the Arabs themselves rarely bought land on any scale until the ninth century (see above, pp. 242–55). So: concentrations of landed property were relatively scarce in Egypt, and became scarcer in our period. Aristocrats were regularly patrons to peasants and rural elites, but could seldom aim to control them directly, unless they were tenants or employees. This pattern of moderate, city-focused, landed wealth has some parallels to that in Italy after 550, as does its complex articulation with peasant landowning and rural clientèles (cf. above, pp. 387–93).

In Italy, the economic system that resulted from such a pattern was small-scale and materially unprepossessing. Not so in Egypt, where the reverse was the case. Egyptian cities were very large, and full of artisanal activity, throughout our period. They were active societies, with a political protagonism that can still be seen in the local pagarchal politics of the early eighth century. (See above, pp. 133–9, 609–12.) They made up the main buyers for the agricultural surplus of rich and poor alike, and stimulated the articulated and controlled agrarian production of big estates like the Apions, with their wage labour, crop specializations, and complex administration and accounting. (See above, pp. 245–8, 274–6.) There is also good evidence in the documents for an intense Nile traffic, which linked city to city, and allowed for sub-regional productive specializations, as indeed we have just seen; the Apions and others could count on markets hundreds of kilometres up- and downstream, not just on the demand from the nearest city. This exchange activity seems to have existed in every part of the Nile valley and Delta, and was still present in the eighth century, as indeed in the eleventh, as the Geniza documents show. It allows us to regard Egypt as a single region, throughout our period, rather than as a network of microregions with lessening links between them, as in the case of Italy or Spain. Although some places might be less tightly linked to the Nile network than others (as was argued earlier for Jēme as against Aphroditō: above, pp. 421–2), it would be best to see this as a marker of different positions in local economic hierarchies, rather than as a geographical or chronological contrast. It is with this document-based picture of Egypt, urbanized and closely interlinked, that the archaeology of exchange fits best, not with the picture of the region as one of restricted concentrations of private wealth. These indeed became more restricted as time went on without any visible negative impact on the complexity of exchange.

There were two main reasons why Egypt had such a complex economy, despite the weakness of aristocratic demand. The first was its remarkable fertility; simply, more people could live off the land—that is, off the unremitting labour of the peasantry—as a result. It was easier for artisans to exist if there were considerable agrarian surpluses around, some of which could be used to feed them. The ease of communications also meant that artisans could be concentrated in single areas of Egypt if necessary, and so indeed could agricultural specializations. Egypt's rural and urban societies were not in themselves differently structured from those elsewhere (apart from the organization of irrigation, at least), but fertility and cheap transport allowed a rather greater structural complexity, in this period as for centuries (indeed, millennia) before and after.

The second reason was the state. We have seen how elaborate the fiscal system was in Egypt, both in the sixth century and in the eighth, with its concern for exact assessment, collection, and accounting of tax (above, pp. 71–2, 135–6). The quantities of tax taken to Alexandria and Constantinople in the sixth century, to Fusṭāṭ in the eighth, were enormous. The commercial exchange of wine has been stressed in this chapter, because the amphorae attest to it, but it was matched everywhere by the fiscal extraction of grain, and its movement considerable distances in the Nile boats. The land tax, and the fiscal system as a whole, was the main single structure which united Egypt economically. This constant overarching structure—constant even in the century of tax revolts from the 720s to the 830s—made up for the relative localization of the region's privately wealthy; the state created the demand that private owners could not, in 400 and in 800 alike. Egypt was thus united in the same *way* as the Roman Mediterranean was, by the fiscal network; and rather more stably, too.

As with the Roman empire as a whole, however, we must look a little more closely at how that worked, for it is not obvious that simply taking away large amounts of produce from the peasantry creates a complex economic network. It was, of course, in the state's interest to ensure that irrigation continued to work, for fertility (and thus taxation) would be threatened if it did not. Public officials were in charge of making sure that channels and dykes for the Nile flood were repaired;[133] it may also be assumed that fiscal pressure helped to encourage advances in irrigation technology. Beyond this, we can see the state organizing local artisanal production, as when the Arab governors put out boatbuilding and nailmaking to local communities (above, pp. 136–8). Quite a number of Nile transport boats must have been effectively subsidized by state requisitions in all periods, as were those in the Mediterranean (above, p. 710), and artisanal start-up costs could evidently sometimes be covered as well. The form of taxation is relevant here too. It was argued in Chapter 3 (pp. 74–6) that it was in general unlikely that most taxation was moved between regions in the form of money in our period, for the mechanisms by which gold would come back from (say) Constantinople to Egypt on a sufficiently regular basis for the same money to be paid again are impossible to imagine, and anyway it was grain that the capital wanted from Egypt, not gold. Egyptian taxation had a substantial money element in all periods, all the same; some of that money must have been made available through forced sales to the state, as elsewhere, but it is likely, given the unusual levels of buying and selling in Egypt, that peasants could more easily than elsewhere sell their produce in the urban market and get their coin that way. As long as the money did not leave the region, Egypt's exchange structures were elaborate enough to allow the constant circulation of coinage. The fiscal system and the commercial system would in this context help to make each other possible.

Most taxes in money did not, in fact, leave the region; they were designed to pay for civil bureaucrats and military detachments at the provincial level. They could get rich as a result, whether legally or illegally.[134] In the late

133 See Bonneau, *Le régime administratif de l'eau du Nil*, pp. 291–310.
134 See e.g. Macmullen, *Corruption*, pp. 126–32, for a set of references.

empire, many of the landed aristocrats we know about, including the Apions, were indeed the families of state officials who had bought land locally (above, p. 245). Such people, when living in Egypt's cities, were a major source of demand for agrarian and artisanal products, even when local landowners were not. These features did not in themselves make Egypt different from other regions of the empire; but the global scale of taxation here meant that the scale of the buying-power of the official strata was that much greater. And, when in the early Arab period landowning elites grew more modest, this was offset by the fact that almost no tax left Egypt at all; the *muhājirūn* of Fusṭāṭ and the navy at Alexandria absorbed nearly all of it (above, pp. 139–40). Their wealth must have been enormous; and it must also have been almost all spent locally (the eighth century, as we have seen, is a low point for imports, except luxuries at any rate): on servants, retainers, clients, and of course on the artisanal products of the cities and the agricultural products of the countryside. Again, the fiscal system and the commercial system fuelled each other; and here the scale was a regional one, for officials and soldiers got their pay (in money and in kind) from the whole region. It is not clear that this was true of other regions, but we have plenty of evidence, not least the Qurra letters, that it was true for Egypt. The whole of Egypt was thus unified economically, in a self-sustaining structure which did not have to change at all, as long as the fiscal system survived.

If we consider the four parameters for socio-economic change posed earlier in the chapter, Egypt was hardly affected by at least three of them. It experienced little war: there was the occasional civil war, as in the 600s and in the 830s, but none of them lasted long, and the Arab conquest was fairly speedy too. Its fiscal system barely changed at all, except that tax did not leave the region after 640. Its aristocrats became more modest after the early seventh century, but this was balanced by the greater percentage of surpluses that stayed in the region. As for Egypt's exposure to the Mediterranean world-system, it has been argued in this section that this was unusually marginal, given the intensity of the internal regional economy. Egypt and Africa were together the main motors of the Roman state, but Africa's internal exchange system was far less complex, and that region was much more structurally dependent on the Mediterranean network than was its eastern neighbour: it was thus Africa, and not Egypt, that was disrupted when the interregional role of each ceased. Relative population may have had something to do with it too: in the 1950s, before the industrial transformations of the last half-century, Egypt's population was $26\frac{1}{2}$ million, Tunisia's only 4 million. This is a very rough guide indeed, given its late date. But the contrast is considerable all the same. Egypt could shake off the break-up of the Mediterranean more easily than other regions. It remains the type-example for what social and economic continuity in our period looks like.

7. The eastern Mediterranean II: Syria and Palestine

The history of exchange in Syria and Palestine across our period shows up some of the continuities of Egypt, particularly in local productions, while also in other respects resembling the situation in Italy. This region has been more extensively studied by archaeologists than has Egypt, although the density of ceramic work is uneven. There are a scatter of sites in inland northern Syria, from the Limestone Massif east to the middle Euphrates valley; but then in central-southern Syria and Lebanon there is very little usable material. Palestine (in modern terms the states of Israel, Palestine, and Jordan) is much more densely studied, but early ceramic work was based on some very uncertain chronologies, and only in very recent years have there appeared coherent dating criteria for 'Abbāsid-period—indeed, often, Umayyad-period—pottery types, which often still do not have settled, agreed, typologies.[135] I shall do my best to base what follows only on reasonably secure data, even if this will mean that some of the subtleties of microregional difference in this region will be elided. Let us look at fine-ware imports first, then amphora patterns, then local fine- and common-ware productions.

Syria and Palestine were unified in the fifth to seventh centuries by their access to the standard set of Mediterranean *terra sigillata* fine wares. These can be found (although sometimes in small quantities) on virtually every site of the period 400–650 that has been excavated or surveyed in the Levant: not only in cities, but on rural sites, including a long way inland, as on the Kerak plateau in central Jordan, or Andarin on the desert edge in northern Syria, or around Samsat and Deir al-Zōr in the upper and middle Euphrates valley. Syria and Palestine were sufficiently open to the Mediterranean that they are a barometer of maritime trends, with ARS dipping between 450 and 550, Phocaean RS reaching its height in the same period (and continuing in Syria), and Cypriot RS really only becoming available in the late sixth century (especially in northern Palestine)—although this, it must be recognized, is a global image, for individual sites show sharper variations in their import patterns. Overall, Phocaean RS is the commonest type, but few sites do not have at least fragments of all three. (ERS is rare, and restricted to Palestine: see below, p. 774.) These wares coexisted with more local fine wares, as we shall see, but their availability structured the entire region,

---

[135] For illustrations of this point, see the recent arguments about 'Abbāsid pottery in Whitcomb, 'Khirbet al-Mafjar reconsidered'; Falkner, 'Jordan'; de Vries, *Umm el-Jimal*, I, pp. 24–6 (C. J. Lentzen); and the redatings of sites in Magness, 'The dating of the black ceramic bowl'; eadem, 'The chronology of Capernaum'; eadem, *The archaeology*. I generally follow these authors rather than their predecessors, and also the Decapolis-based work of Watson (e.g. 'Change in foreign and regional economic links') and Walmsley (e.g. 'Tradition, innovation'; 'Production, exchange'; 'Turning East'), as the 749 earthquake levels in the Decapolis, especially at Pella, have become an important dating point for northern Palestine. Not all of these authors agree, however, or even use the same terminologies.

including beyond the Arab conquest in 636–8, right up to the end of their productions at the end of the seventh century. It was suggested earlier (p. 716) that their striking inland penetration, further inland than RS reached anywhere else in the late empire away from major rivers, may have been related to the needs of the army, at least before the seventh-century conquest period. Their prominence in the fine-ware repertoire at two military sites on the Dead Sea, En Boqeq and Upper Zohar, in the late sixth and early seventh centuries is an illustration of the point.[136] All the same, the evenness of RS distribution must also testify to its commercial availability, perhaps as a result of diversions from military supply lines. Syria and Palestine exported substantial quantities of goods in the late empire, particularly in the fifth and sixth centuries, and RS was evidently something they bought in return.

Written sources tell us that Syria and Palestine exported cloth, from inland cities such as Damascus and Scythopolis (Bet She'an, an important linen centre) and from coastal dyeing plants, some of which have been excavated.[137] The clearest archaeological evidence we have is for wine and oil, as we saw in Chapter 8 (pp. 444–53; cf. also p. 714). The Palestinian coast specialized above all in wine, exported in LRA 4 (Gaza) and 5 (bag) amphorae, which can be found across most of the eastern Mediterranean. The Gaza amphora was made in a circumscribed zone along the sea between Gaza and Askalon (Ashqelon) and some 10 km inland. LRA 5 was made throughout Palestine, as far inland as the Jordan valley; although it too was exported, it is less frequently found than LRA 4. The export varieties of LRA 5 seem nevertheless largely to be associated with the coast as well, north of Gaza, including the first range of hills inland, as in the case of Sumaqa on Mount Carmel, a wine village of the third to sixth centuries.[138] The LRA 5 amphorae found in inland Palestine, by contrast, do not tend to be of fabrics that were exported. Jerusalem's amphorae are mostly not the same as those on the coast; those of Pella (Tabaqat Faḥl) are for the most part different

---

[136] See in general Hayes, *Late Roman pottery*, pp. 323–86, 460–1; idem, 'Late Roman fine wares'; Sodini and Villeneuve, 'Le passage de la céramique'. For the cited examples, see respectively Miller, *Archaeological survey*, pp. 221–2 (R. M. Brown); Mango, 'Oxford excavations', with eadem, 'Excavations and survey', p. 314; Wilkinson, *Town and country*, p. 242; Römer, 'Die rot engobierte Keramik', p. 354; Gichon, *En Boqeq*, I, pp. 176–97; Harper, *Upper Zohar*, pp. 21–5 (both with the redatings in Magness, 'Redating the forts'). Other good sites for quantities include Riley, 'The pottery from the first session' (Caesarea); Mackensen, *Resafa I*, pp. 40–8; Watson, 'Change in foreign and regional economic links', pp. 242–3 (Pella); Kingsley, 'The Sumaqa pottery assemblage'.

[137] See above, Ch. 10, n. 57. For the dyeing plants, Kingsley, 'Economic impact', p. 45.

[138] LRA 4 kilns: Israel, 'Ashqelon', with the survey at pp. 106–7. Mayerson, 'The Gaza "wine" jar', argues that one can distinguish between Gaza and Askalon jars. See above, n. 39 for literary references. For LRA 5 export, see Kingsley, 'Bag-shaped amphorae'; idem, 'Economic impact', a particularly vigorous defence of a commercial model for export patterns; for Sumaqa, idem, 'The Sumaqa pottery assemblage', pp. 268–70. For LRA 4 and 5 at Caesarea, see among others Riley, 'The pottery from the first session', pp. 26–35; Adan-Bayewitz, 'The pottery from the Late Byzantine Building'. For an overview, see Reynolds, 'Levantine amphorae'.

again. We can conclude that it was above all the maritime strip of Palestine that was focused on export; the inland wine-producers of the sub-region (numerous around Jerusalem, as the distribution of wine-presses shows) were producing for local customers, in the city network of the interior. They still did so on a large scale, but their exchange networks were in that respect more restricted. Indeed, inland Palestine did not buy much Gaza wine either, although its prestige and/or quality at least meant that a little went inland, to Jerusalem, Pella, even Ruṣāfa in northern Syria.[139] Syrian oil production (exported in LRA 1 amphorae) stretched further inland, as far as the Limestone Massif, as we have seen. But here too there was a break in the direction of exchange; to the east, middle Euphrates and desert-edge sites seem to have focused rather more on wine, and are united by the 'North Syrian' carinated amphora. This is not found in a Mediterranean context at all, and may have found a market, apart from in the inland cities, among the troops on the Euphrates frontier.[140]

This separation, between a coast focused on Mediterranean export and an inland with more localized distribution networks, has parallels elsewhere; Spain is one example, Anatolia another. It is less complete than either of those; here, the interior, as we have seen, exported cloth and imported Red Slip table wares. Inland areas of Syria and Palestine were more open to the Mediterranean than inland areas anywhere else. But the separation in wine and oil production would at least make one conclude that the end of the Mediterranean world-system would have different effects in different areas of the region. As we have seen in previous chapters (pp. 457–9, 620–5), this is exactly what happened; the coast suffered badly, the interior hardly at all. We will come back to the point in a moment.

There were also local fine, semi-fine, and common/coarse wares, throughout Syria and Palestine, some of which have good recent studies. Fine Byzantine ware is one, a genuine fine ware, and one of the very few late Roman fine wares anywhere which did not follow or imitate RS traditions (Jodi Magness proposes that it borrowed its aesthetic from metalwork). It was perhaps made in or near Jerusalem from the sixth century onwards, and had a distribution south-west to the Negev, west to the coast at Caesarea (the

---

[139] For Jerusalem, see Magness, *Jerusalem ceramic chronology*, pp. 160–1 (for presses, see Kingsley, 'Economic impact', p. 48, for a map) with, more recently, Rapuano, 'The Hellenistic through early Islamic pottery', pp. 179–81 (some coastal amphorae here). For Pella, Watson, 'Change in foreign and regional economic links', pp. 238–40; for LRA 4 in Ruṣāfa, see Mackensen, *Resafa I*, p. 52. Note that Gaza amphorae are less common than LRA 5 even in some Gaza hinterland sites; LRA 4 was very much an export product. See Tubb, 'The pottery'; Tsafrir, *Rehovot-in-the-Negev I*, pp. 78–96 (R. Rosenthal-Heginbottom).

[140] Harper, 'Athis-Neocaesareia', pp. 337–9; Mackensen, *Resafa I*, pp. 50–2; Lauffray, *Halabiyya*, II, p. 267 (D. Orssaud); Mango, 'Oxford excavations' (N. Pollard), with eadem, 'Excavations and survey', p. 314; Konrad, 'Umayyad pottery', pp. 164–5. This amphora type extended west to Dēhes and other sites in the Limestone Massif: Bavant and Orssaud, 'Stratigraphie et typologie', p. 36; Reynolds, 'Levantine amphorae'.

only coastal site known to me where it has been found) and, above all, north-east into the Decapolis.[141] Jerash bowls, made as the name implies at Gerasa (Jerash)—and also elsewhere—were partially imitative of ARS; their distribution was above all in the Decapolis and Jordan valley, and they too are rare on the coast. In the seventh century RS imitations steadily expanded in number as the import penetration of the parent types slowly decreased; they can be found at, for example, Gerasa, Pella, Madaba, and at Dēḥes in the Limestone Massif.[142] Gerasa saw, indeed, a substantial development of its pottery production after 600 or so and of the density of the distribution of its wares, at least inside the Decapolis; its importance as a ceramic centre continued into the ninth century. None of these types, however, had distributions that were greater than 100–150 km, and it was often rather less.[143] As in Italy, a series of sub-regional and microregional fine-ware exchange networks coexisted across the Levant, unified only by a common access to RS wares. This was true of coarse ware too, although this is less completely studied. One example, Kefar Ḥananya ware, was a kitchen ware which, up to the fifth century, served Galilee only. Brittle ware was another: this was a ceramic type of the Syrian desert fringe, the middle Euphrates valley, and its northern/north-eastern hinterland, what would be called the Jazīra by the Arabs. Brittle ware is interesting for its long duration (into the 'Abbāsid period) and wider than usual availability, for it is found from the coast (where it is uncommon) to the Roman frontier. It is a mixture of partially localized types, but some can be found across the full spread of its distribution; there are Gaulish parallels for coarse wares being available on a wider geographical scale than fine wares (see pp. 747–8, 797–8). Brittle ware also, however, represented a ceramic culture quite distinct from that of the Mediterranean and the Palestinian interior: the middle Euphrates was the focus of a separate exchange network, only superficially overlain by RS availabilities.[144]

---

[141] See for basic surveys Gichon, 'Fine Byzantine wares'; Magness, *Jerusalem ceramic chronology*, pp. 166–71 (the whole of pp. 153–83 stresses how local most Jerusalem pottery was); de Vries, *Umm el-Jimal*, I, p. 213 (S. T. Parker); Harrison, 'Madaba', p. 441; Arnon, 'Islamic and crusader pottery', p. 226 (Caesarea); Walmsley, 'Production, exchange', pp. 322–4.

[142] Basic is Watson, 'Jerash bowls'; see further eadem, 'Production and classification', and, for parallels in a different fabric, Daviau and Beckmann, 'Umayyad painted pottery'. For other RS imitations, Harrison, 'Madaba', p. 442; Sodini *et al.*, 'Déhès', pp. 243–5 (D. Orssaud).

[143] For Gerasa pottery see among many Schaefer and Falkner, 'An Umayyad potters' complex'; Watson, 'Jerash bowls'; Gawlikowski, 'Céramiques byzantines et omayyades'; Walmsley, 'Production, exchange', p. 306 (p. 326 for the figure of 100–150 km).

[144] Adan-Bayewitz, *Common pottery*, for Kefar Ḥananya. For Brittle ware, e.g. Harper, 'Athis-Neocaesareia', pp. 334–7; Northedge *et al.*, *Excavations at 'Ana*, pp. 76–94; Wilkinson and Tucker, *Settlement development*, pp. 69–71; Bartl, *Frühislamische Besiedlung*, pp. 132, 178; Konrad, 'Umayyad pottery', pp. 164–6; Mango, 'Excavations and survey', p. 314. Two important recent syntheses are Orssaud and Sodini, 'Le "Brittle ware"', and Vokaer, 'Syrian Brittle ware'.

When the Mediterranean network disintegrated in the late seventh century, much of the Syro-Palestinian coast hit crisis. LRA 4 amphorae ceased production, and parts of the Negev hinterland of Gaza were abandoned by settled agriculturalists during, as it seems, the eighth century (above, p. 453). In the north, LRA 1 ceased production too, and the Limestone Massif began several centuries of relative stagnation (above, pp. 448–9). This must show the dependence of each area on interregional exchange. Between these two areas, it may be that the coast showed greater resilience. Caesarea and Apollonia (Arshaf) seem to have maintained themselves as cities in the Umayyad period and even later; the former is well documented archaeologically (p. 622). 'Akko, too, is recorded by al-Balādhurī as the first naval centre of the Arabs, being replaced by Tyre, slightly to the north, in the early eighth century.[145] This sector of the coast is, significantly, one of the few in the Levant with an easy low-lying route inland, the Jezreel valley, which connects to the Sea of Galilee and the Decapolis, and from there to Damascus. This must have been the path followed by a handful of late Egyptian imports, particularly ERS from Aswān, visible in the eighth century at Caesarea itself, at Beirut, and at Pella and other Decapolis cities, including (most notably) at Tiberias, the new political centre on the Sea of Galilee. These wares may be signs of a maritime trade that continued on a restricted scale, focused on Caesarea and its neighbours, notwithstanding the crisis of the rest of the coast.[146] If so, Caesarea as an import funnel would have some parallels with Marseille (pp. 667, 746–7, 800).

Inland, by contrast, not much changed at all. Versions of LRA 5 went on into the ninth century in inland Palestine. RS imports ended, but the interior already had in most places local wares of good quality that could replace them. Around Jerusalem, Fine Byzantine ware continued to the eighth or ninth centuries, and indeed became more sophisticated. Jerash bowls did not continue, but Jerash White Painted wares substituted for them. In the Decapolis sub-region (but not, for the most part, extending to Jerusalem) Red Painted wares began in the early eighth century too, generally painted on a good-quality buff fabric (buff and other light fabrics tended to replace

[145] For the prosperity of Apollonia, see Foote, 'Commerce, industrial expansion', pp. 28–9, 36, who stresses glass production and the commercialization of oil and wine. For 'Akko, al-Balādhurī, *Futuḥ al-buldān*, trans. Hitti, p. 181. See in general Walmsley, 'Production, exchange', pp. 290–9, who gives a more upbeat picture of maritime traffic in the eighth century than the one presented here. Beirut, slightly further north, already participated less in this exchange; it had access to Egyptian fine wares in the eighth century and some Byzantine wine amphorae, as well as LRA 5, but its own amphora production had ended: see Reynolds, 'Pottery and the economy'.

[146] See Stacey, 'Umayyad and Egyptian red-slip'; Watson, 'Ceramic evidence for Egyptian links', the basic account, updated in Magness, 'Late Roman and early Islamic pottery', pp. 814–15, and Reynolds, 'Pottery and the economy', p. 726.

red fabrics in this period).[147] The lightest and finest of these fabrics, not usually painted, have recently come to be called Islamic Cream ware, some of which was by the ninth century eggshell thin. One elaborately decorated version of this ware, generally called Mafjar ware, developed after 750; it was also centred on the Jordan valley and the Decapolis, although it can be found further afield, west to Caesarea, south to the Negev and 'Aqaba, and some way north-east, to Ruṣāfa.[148] Mafjar ware had an unusual spread, however; most ceramics remained more localized. North Palestinian types did not generally extend south to 'Aqaba, for example. Here, at the top of the Red Sea, where Egyptian imports had been common in the late Roman period, Umayyad- and 'Abbāsid-period ceramics were more often in an Egyptian tradition, with a variant of the middle Nile LRA 7 amphora made in 'Aqaba kilns in the seventh century. A set of local 'Aqaba fine wares included the late eighth-century type called Mahesh ware. At the other end of the Levant, north Syrian types were distinct again.[149]

Two features thus seem to characterize Syro-Palestinian ceramics between c.650 and c.800. First, they could be of strikingly high quality; in most of the areas we can say anything about there was always at least one fine ware, often several, and then a hierarchy of common and coarse wares, throughout the period. Second, they were mostly highly localized, as much as in the sixth century and indeed more so, for the wider-scale exchange represented by RS wares had gone. We must recognize a few wider exchange links, some of which we have seen already, ERS in Tiberias and Mafjar ware in Ruṣāfa. If there were no Fine Byzantine wares in 'Aqaba, there were at least imitations, marking at least some cultural links between northern and southern Palestine. And black steatite bowls from the Hijāz in Arabia, dating to the eighth century, have been found as far north as Jerusalem, with black ceramic imitations occurring sporadically across the whole of Palestine.[150] But for the most part ceramic traditions were focused on small groups of city territories, with the Jerusalem area, the Decapolis, 'Aqaba and its

[147] See in general for post-650 patterns Sodini and Villeneuve, 'Le passage de la céramique'; Walmsley, 'Tradition, innovation'; idem, 'Production, exchange', pp. 321–31 (important for Red and White Painted wares); Bujard and Joguin, 'La céramique d'Umm el-Rasas'; and above, n. 135.

[148] Walmsley, 'Turning East', is the best survey of Islamic Cream ware; see further 'Production, exchange', pp. 329–30. Walmsley is not fond of the label 'Mafjar ware' (he calls it 'ICW-B'); for that ware (also spelt 'Mefjer', or 'Khirbet al-Mafjar'), not well synthesized given its prominence, see also Whitcomb, 'Khirbet al-Mafjar reconsidered'; Peleg, 'Domestic pottery', pp. 91–104; Grey, 'Tell Jezreel', p. 57; Arnon, 'Islamic and Crusader pottery', pp. 225–6 (Caesarea); Sack, *Resafa IV*, pp. 82–3 (N. Logar); Avner and Magness, 'Early Islamic settlement', p. 50 ('Aqaba).

[149] Melkawi *et al.*, 'The excavation of two seventh-century pottery kilns'; Whitcomb, 'Mahesh ware'; idem, 'Ceramic production at Aqaba'. For north Syria, see in general Sodini and Villeneuve, 'Le passage de la céramique', pp. 211–12.

[150] For Fine Byzantine ware imitations, Avner and Magness, 'Early Islamic settlement', pp. 50–1; Whitcomb, 'Ceramic production at Aqaba'. For steatite bowls, Magness, 'The dating of the black ceramic bowl'; Walmsley, 'Production and exchange', pp. 331–2.

hinterland, the north of Syria, and doubtless many other sub-regions operating with substantially different ceramic histories.

The 'Abbāsid period is often seen as a period of economic simplification for Syria and Palestine. I have already, in the context of both rural and urban archaeology, expressed some caution as to how far this process was general across the region (pp. 467–9, 620–5), and we will return to the point in a moment. But in terms of exchange, as shown in ceramics, the opposite is true: in the ninth century the region was reunified on the level of fine wares, with the appearance and wide dissemination of polychrome glazed pottery. As in Egypt, it cannot any longer be argued that this came in before 800. Polychrome glaze probably began in Iraq first, in imitation of Chinese imports, but in the space of a few decades it spread to Syria and Palestine, Egypt, and soon to North Africa and Spain. This Islamic glazed tradition was the new 'Abbāsid *koinē*, and would come to dominate the taste of the Christian parts of the Mediterranean in the next few centuries too. In the context of Syro-Palestinian ceramics, it is necessary to recognize that much of its production remained local in all likelihood, but the finest types circulated rather more widely, across the whole 'Abbāsid world, and the cultural tradition that underlay its spread was not only regional but interregional. This scale of exchange almost matches that of the Roman empire, except that its focus was, by now, not in the Mediterranean, but in Iraq.[151] Regional demand for high-quality products thus did not lessen in 750 or 800, but on the contrary developed further.

Syria and Palestine were thus similar to Italy—and much less similar to Egypt—in the localization of their ceramic traditions after the end of the Mediterranean world-system. Where they were not at all similar to Italy, however, was in the continuing complexity of each of those local traditions, across the seventh and eighth centuries, which allowed for the introduction of new high-quality wares, with (in some cases) wider distributions, in the ninth. In Italy, by contrast, only Forum ware achieved even a sub-regional distribution in the latter century. (See above, p. 736. Forum ware was another glazed type, of course, but in the Roman tradition of monochrome glazes, and structurally separate from the new Chinese/Islamic glazes of the south-east Mediterranean.) Syria and Palestine maintained complex exchange networks at the local level throughout our period, as no western Mediterranean region did by the eighth century; the only exceptions to this before the 'Abbāsids were the coasts around Antioch and Gaza, which hit crisis in the seventh century. The Levant's local economies, in short, had higher levels of demand than Italy throughout: at a local level, they may

---

[151] The best overview is Northedge, 'Les origines de la céramique à glaçure', reprised in idem, 'Thoughts on the introduction'. Walmsley, 'Turning East', argues for Iraqi influence on Islamic Cream wares too. Gawlikowski, 'Céramiques byzantines et omayyades', p. 85 refers to the period 550–800 as a 'parenthèse vernaculaire' between the RS and glaze systems.

sometimes have remained as high as in Egypt. We need to explain both the localization and the local wealth of the region, bearing in mind the parallels and contrasts elsewhere.

As in Egypt, the impact of war does not seem to have been very extensive in the Levant in our period. Persian raids seem to have damaged the north Syrian cities in the sixth century, but the Persian conquest, Byzantine reconquest, and final Arab takeover in the early seventh seem each to have been quick. Overall, the 610s–630s must have been a difficult and disorientating time, with some episodes of particular violence, such as the sack of Jerusalem in 614, but there was no equivalent to the devastation of the Gothic war in Italy, and Syria and Palestine settled down quickly to be the core Umayyad region.[152] The 'Abbāsid revolution in 750 removed political centrality to Iraq, with some negative impact on the Levant, but, as we have just seen, it is far from clear that the region was globally ruined by that shift, even in the Decapolis, where the earthquake of 749 was so devastating (above, p. 616).

A second area of continuity was that of aristocratic wealth and demand. We have seen that there is not an enormous amount of written evidence for this, but what there is shows a strongly localized urban aristocracy in the late Roman period, which can be seen to have continued under the Umayyads in a few well-documented centres such as Edessa. A continuation of urban wealth is also fully supported by the archaeology, at least up to 750 and sometimes later: there is good evidence for dense artisanal activity in cities and some evidence for rich urban housing as well. Cities appear to have flourished everywhere except around Antioch (Gaza is unstudied), although changing cultural practices led to their steady demonumentalization. (Above, pp. 240–2, 613–25.) It should be clear that this fits the patterns of exchange described in this section very well. Local city–country relationships, whether based on rent-paying or the marketing of goods (or both), were evidently complex and tight. This fits interestingly with the evidence we have for the prosperity of the countryside, well-built villages in particular; in Chapter 8 (pp. 443–59) it was argued that this was in some places a sign of peasant landowning, so urban wealth was not exclusively based on an aristocratic control of all available land. As in Egypt, prosperous villages and prosperous cities went together, and acted as a firm basis for a local exchange network. Although it remains the case that the motor of this must have been aristocratic demand at a level rather higher than that in Italy (outside Rome, at any rate), it may be that part of the wealth that underlay that demand derived from an aristocratic control of elements of the exchange process itself, as we can see for part of the Edessa elite (above, p. 621): that is to say, they could sometimes be active participants in the

---

[152] The briskest account of the material invisibility of the Arab conquest is Pentz, *The invisible conquest*.

production and exchange relationships that underpinned urban prosperity, not simply consumers on the basis of their rents from landowning.

This prosperity continued as long as rich urban elites did, into the early eighth century nearly everywhere, and beyond it in many places, such as Galilee, or the inland north-east. But the economy in each case only extended geographically as far as the elites did, which was usually only across a single city territory or a relatively localized set of territories. The wealthy inhabitants of a city such as Pella had close links to Gerasa, 30 km away, and could buy artisanal or agricultural products there; they looked to Jerusalem, 90 km away (but across difficult country) much more occasionally, and they had no structural links with 'Aqaba, 300 km to the south, at all. In this respect, Syria and Palestine were quite as microregionalized as Italy and Spain, even though each microregion was so much more economically complex. When this complexity became less consistent across the region, from the end of our period onwards, each microregion could have an increasingly divergent history, too, with Pella slipping behind Gerasa already by the seventh century (p. 624), and some wider landscapes facing abandonment or 'abatement' by 800, such as parts of the Negev and the Hawran (pp. 457–9). In both city and countryside, the best-studied landscapes are those of abatement, but in a microregionalized economic environment they need not be generalized, and indeed should not be, for the ecological contrasts in the Levant are so huge. Thus the Hawran may have ceased to practise settled agriculture, but the Balqā' continued to do so, and Galilee was still doing very well, fully participating in the revival of interregional exchange in the ninth century. We need to see that ninth-century revival against a backdrop of a greater microregional differentiation than in the late Roman period. Under Rome, almost every part of the Levant had a complex local economy and was linked into a wider network as well. Under the 'Abbāsids, only some local economies were still complex (around, among others, Jerusalem, Caesarea, Tiberias, Damascus, Ḥimṣ, and Aleppo), and some had become much simpler; the former were better placed to connect with the revived wider network than the latter. But where the local economy was complex, it could remain very articulated indeed, with an exchange density and pockets of wealth matching Egypt, and almost nowhere else in the Mediterranean by 800.

The fiscal system continued throughout our period too, but it experienced sharper changes. Roman taxation was relatively regionally integrated, with poles such as Constantinople and the eastern frontier absorbing revenues from more than one area; the polycentric exchange system of the eastern Mediterranean and, in the Levant, the availability of Mediterranean fine wares throughout the region can both be linked to it, and, as we have seen (pp. 713–18), it is not chance that both of them ended inside two generations of the breaking of the fiscal spine in the East. Umayyad taxation was much more regionalized, with tax staying in the provinces; hence the wealth of the

Arab elites in Egypt, as we have just seen. Syria and Palestine were more decentralized even than Egypt; there were five Umayyad provinces there, excluding the Jazīra, whereas Egypt had only one. It was not until the 'Abbāsid period, from the late eighth century onwards, that effective measures were taken to recentralize fiscal structures on the new capital of Baghdad (p. 133).

Some of the changes in post-Roman exchange in Syria and Palestine fit very clearly into this fiscal narrative. The substantial weakening of exchange links between the Levant coast and Egypt in the late seventh century is one instance. Although these regions were both part of the caliphate, they had no fiscal links, and the basic underpinning of large-scale exchange had gone; only a small number of Egyptian exports continued to go to Caesarea. The end of the fiscally supported world-system, as we have seen, spelt local crisis or stagnation for the sectors of the coast most dependent on it, the Antioch and Gaza areas, which match the Spanish coast and most of Tunisia in the degree of their dislocation. Conversely, the revival of interregional networks in the early ninth century maps onto 'Abbāsid fiscal recentralization. The routes were this time largely by land (at least until Syrian goods reached the Euphrates), but the same basic presupposition as was used for the Roman empire, that transport networks for goods taken in tax could have underpinned commercial exchange as well, applies here too.

Syria and Palestine were thus turned in on themselves in the Umayyad period, just as Egypt was. But Egypt remained an internally integrated region, focused on Fusṭāṭ, while the Levant turned into a set of active, but often quite small, economic microregions. In Egypt, regional-level commercial integration can clearly be linked to the continuing strength of the regional fiscal system, which linked together the local aristocracies, and the local city–country relationships, of the Nile valley. In Syria and Palestine, the situation seems to have been more complicated: we cannot map sub-regional economies onto the five Umayyad provinces (these were Filasṭīn, based by 700 at Ramla, al-Urdunn, based at Tiberias, Dimashq, based at Damascus, Ḥimṣ, and Qinnasrīn). This is for two contrasted reasons. First, the microregional patterns already discussed were substantially smaller than most of the provinces; Jerusalem and Caesarea, whose economies were largely separate, were both in Filasṭīn. (This was a situation that was indeed inherited from the late Roman period, although it had been overlain by RS availability.) Second, because there was a certain degree of fiscal centralization in Syria and Palestine that went well beyond these provinces; the caliphs in Damascus were very wealthy indeed, capable of building an array of rich buildings and indeed whole cities on occasion, and this wealth must have come from more than just the tax of Dimashq. The fiscal system in the Levant must have transcended the autonomy of the provinces there, that is to say. But it was still much less centralized than Egypt. There was a level of ad hoc about the administration of early Islamic Syria and Palestine, which began with the highly decentralized Arab settlement there, and which lasted throughout the Umayyad period, even though tax continued to be paid, and caliphs had a great deal of disposable wealth. Local officials, and Arab settlers on the provincial registers (*dīwān*), were probably paid locally, without tax having to go to Damascus, and probably not even to Ramla or Qinnasrīn. Put simply, Umayyad fiscal structures in this region, unlike in Egypt, or in the Levant under the Roman empire, were not coherent enough to unify the array of local economies into a single system.[153] They were good enough to make a few people very wealthy, but not to underpin the movement of commercial goods long distances on any scale. It is interesting that this was so in the Umayyad political heartland, by contrast not only with Egypt but also with Iraq. We must not be misled by the power of the Umayyad caliphs into concluding that the regional structures of their power were all homogeneous; they were not. In a sense, all the 'Abbāsids did was generalize Iraqi assumptions about fiscal centralization to the whole caliphate; it was they who restored the regional level to the economy of Syria and Palestine. But that economy remained, at base, a collection of, mostly prosperous, sub-regions and microregions.

8. The eastern Mediterranean III: the Byzantine heartland

From the fourth century onwards, the Aegean sea was constantly one of the political and economic foci of the Mediterranean, thanks to Constantinople at its apex. The provisioning of the east Roman, later Byzantine capital was always a key structuring element thereafter, whether or not this was done through taxation (see above, pp. 76, 633, below, pp. 787–90). The 'Byzantine heartland' as defined here included both modern Greece and Turkey, but its core was the Aegean and its immediate coasts, stretching eastwards up the major rivers towards the Anatolian plateau. The plateau itself was largely cut off from that core sub-region, as was the Spanish interior (see above, p. 79; cf. p. 742), and its exchange patterns are furthermore only fragmentarily studied, which means that it will be less discussed here; much the same is true of the mountains of inland Greece. The Aegean will be my principal concern in what follows. Its economic patterns were complex, and remained, even after the seventh-century crisis, more complex than some richer parts of the former empire. An inland sea, dotted with countless islands, has easier internal communications than any of our other regions except Egypt; at least medium-distance exchange is natural there. The Aegean was seriously affected by the breakdown of the Mediterranean system, but its own inward-turned dynamics, plus the pole of Constantinople, allowed a minimum

---

[153] See above, Ch. 3, n. 193. See in general for this discussion Kennedy, *The armies of the caliphs*, pp. 69–72.

of communication to continue there even in the eighth century, the low point for economic complexity in this region as for several others.

The complex overlay of fiscal and more local commercial traffic in the fifth- and sixth-century Aegean has already been discussed in this chapter (p. 715): ARS marked a longer-distance route to the capital with fewer stops (such as Crete and Argos), linked more closely to the fiscal network; Phocaean RS, made in and around Eski Foça north of Smyrna (Izmir), marked a smaller-scale but more complex commercial network, with boats also headed for Constantinople but via many more local ports. Local amphora (i.e. oil and wine) distributions probably had a mixture of fiscal and commercial patterns. LRA 3, probably for wine, which is generally associated with the central part of the Turkish Aegean coast, was most common in Constantinople in the fifth century and less so thereafter, although it continued into the seventh.[154] LRA 2, recently convincingly argued to be largely for oil, was certainly made on Chios, at Porto Cheli near Argos, and probably at several other sites on the Greek coast. It has an interesting distribution, for it dominates the military sites on the Danube (together with LRA 1); some Danube forts, indeed, such as Halmyris (Independenţa) and Nicopolis, were as exclusively supplied from afar in their amphorae and fine wares as were western outposts of imperial power in the sixth century like S. Antonino di Perti in Liguria (above, p. 712). It must have been the choice of the state to send this amphora type through the Bosporos to the frontier, and these distribution patterns must therefore be fiscal. The capillary distribution on a smaller scale of both LRA 2 and 3 in the Aegean, by contrast, is doubtless a sign of a commercial network, linking every type of site on the coast and in the islands, not least the other great cities, such as Smyrna, Ephesos, and Thessaloniki.[155]

This interweaving of ceramic types is incomplete—there were other amphora types, that is, other agrarian distribution patterns, for example—but it

[154] Abadie-Reynal, 'Céramique et commerce' for the general patterns. Phocaea's kilns are identified in Empereur and Picon, 'À propos d'un nouvel atelier'. For LRA 3, not very systematically studied, see Panella, 'Merci e scambi', p. 663 n.; Sodini, 'Productions et échanges', pp. 184–5. For its contraction after the fifth century, see Hayes, *Excavations at Saraçhane*, II, p. 63; Abadie-Reynal, 'Les amphores protobyzantines d'Argos', p. 50. It had a locally made version at Sardis: Rautman, 'Two late Roman wells', pp. 80–1.

[155] The best introduction to LRA 2 and its distribution is Karagiorgou, 'LR2'; see also eadem, *Urbanism and economy*, pp. 188–205; she makes the oil argument as well. See also Poulou-Papadēmētriou, 'Byzantinē keramikē', pp. 242–4. For the problems of the contents of LRA 1 and 2, see above, n. 40. For frontier forts which were dominated by RS imports, see Opaiţ, 'Ceramica', pp. 162–6 for Independenţa; Poulter, 'The Roman to Byzantine transition', p. 351, for Nicopolis; their cooking wares remained local. For the Danube–Aegean fiscal relationship see also above, p. 78. Another fiscal network is represented by the distributions of military metalwork all over the empire: Sodini, 'La contribution de l'archéologie', pp. 165–72. The well-known Yassı Ada wreck of 626 or just after, full of LRA 1 and 2 (or variants) as well as other products, was not necessarily a fiscal transport, although it was certainly a systematic commission. See Bass and Van Doorninck, *Yassı Ada*, I; van Alfen, 'New light'.

is enough to convey the general point that exchange in the Aegean was elaborately articulated. This sub-regional network coexisted, here as elsewhere, with a wide array of more local table wares, mostly not very well analysed, but which seem to have had more restricted distributions. There were, for a start, numerous local RS types, essentially imitations of Phocaean (more occasionally, African) RS; they have been identified all over the Aegean, both on the coast and inland. One of them was at Sardis, which is striking, for that city, 100 km inland, lay on a river which led to Phocaea on the coast; Phocaean distribution networks must have been very sea-orientated. Many of these probably began after about 550, when Phocaean production seems to have started to contract, for unclear reasons; this is certainly the case for the 'local' RS found at Constantinople. (Sardis, however, always had a predominance of local wares.)[156] There were also non-RS fine and semi-fine wares: Central Greek Painted ware, found in Argos, Delphi, and elsewhere in the sixth and seventh centuries; the highly decorated Painted ware of Crete, found at Gortyn and Pseira in the seventh (and later); the half-slipped wares of the Delphi kilns of the late sixth and early seventh; Piecrust Rim ware, found at Anemourion (Anamur) on the south Turkish coast opposite Cyprus, again in the seventh; the slipped Spiral Burnished ware and the painted Monastic ware of the sixth and seventh centuries, found at Alahan in the mountains above Anamur. These types cluster in the seventh century, and, taken together, they show that local taste was beginning to move away from the RS tradition. The range of local wares extends even further, of course, if we include common and coarse wares, although these are almost unstudied.[157]

The most important of these alternatives to *terra sigillata* was Glazed White ware (GWW), made in the capital after about 600. This pottery type—initially, despite its name, brown or green—derived from Roman monochrome glaze traditions. Its seventh-century forms were usually closed

[156] For other Aegean amphorae see e.g. Arthur, 'Eastern Mediterranean amphorae', pp. 165–70, with, for Cretan types, Vogt, 'The early Byzantine pottery', pp. 90–1. For local RS types, see Rautman, 'Two late Roman wells', pp. 41–2, 79–80 for Sardis (where local RS outnumbers Phocaean three to one); Hayes, *Excavations at Saraçhane*, II, p. 8 ('local' RS here was not necessarily made in the capital); Sodini, 'La contribution de l'archéologie', p. 174; Williams, *Anemurium*, pp. 50–3; eadem, 'The pottery', pp. 38–9 (Alahan); Aupert, 'Objets de la vie quotidienne', pp. 417–18 (Argos); di Vita and Martin, *Gortina II*, pp. 201–10; Gelichi and Negrelli, 'La ricognizione', pp. 149–52; Vroom, *After Antiquity*, pp. 137–9 (Askra ware in Boiotia).

[157] For Central Greek Painted ware, Hayes, *Late Roman pottery*, p. 413; Pétridis, 'Delphes', p. 693; for its difference from Delphi productions and for the latter, see ibid., pp. 688–95, and Petridis, 'Ateliers de potiers protobyzantins'. For Cretan Painted wares, Poulou-Papadimitriou, 'Le monastère byzantin à Pseira', pp. 1122, 1126; Poulou-Papadēmētriou, 'Byzantinē keramikē', pp. 236–7; di Vita and Martin, *Gortina II*, pp. 211–17. For Anemourion, Williams, *Anemurium*, pp. 53–7; for Alahan, eadem, 'The pottery', pp. 39–47. It is particularly striking how different these two neighbouring sites are. Monastic ware is found elsewhere in the Göksu river valley around Alahan, but not outside it: Mark Jackson (pers. comm.).

forms like jars and jugs, so not competing with the dishes and bowls of the RS tradition; GWW dishes only appear in the eighth century, when the RS productions had ended, and the GWW ceramic tradition then remained central to Constantinopolitan production right into the thirteenth century. From the start, it was available more widely than the other local fine wares described above; its first dated appearance is in fact on the Yassı Ada wreck, which went down off Bodrum in the southern Aegean, 600 km from the capital, in or just after 626. It arguably spread back down the long-distance fiscal routes to the main cities and islands of the south of the Byzantine empire, which is certainly where GWW has been found in the following century-and-a-half, at Athens, Corinth, Aigina, Melos, on the main sites on Crete and Cyprus, and even at Carthage.[158] Its distribution in no way matched that of Phocaean RS and the other RS types in density, however, and for a long time it is hardly seen outside major sites.

The complexities of this maritime exchange are amply mirrored in our literary sources. One thinks of Nicholas of Sion, picking up ships at Myra on the south-west coast of Turkey in the sixth century that were bound for Askalon and Egypt, and back to Rhodes, almost as if they were regular ferries; further north, Prokopios complained of the overtaxing of ships running through the Bosporos and Dardanelles, evidently on commercial ventures. We have already seen (p. 725) that an anti-Jewish polemic of the 640s represents an entrepreneur sending Constantinople cloth to be sold in Carthage, which is an indicator of other bulk goods apart from GWW that may have gone back down the fiscal routes to be sold commercially—in this case on a small scale, and 'discreetly', probably to avoid customs duties. LRA 2 and 3 perhaps reached seventh-century Rome that way, too. Money from the capital was also widely available in the Aegean, including in villages, in the fifth to early seventh centuries, indicating again a capillarity of exchange.[159] Cities had dense groups of artisans, too. The rich series of several hundred fifth- and sixth-century epitaphs from Korykos on the south-east Turkish coast, between Anemourion and the Cilician plain, show a wealth of trades: to do with the sea, credit, construction, food production and sale, cloth- and leather-working, metal- and glass-working, and ceramics, the largest group with 8 per cent of the total of named trades (did they make LRA 1?). The Sardis shops which were abandoned in the 610s (above, p. 627) included dyers, locksmiths, glass- and copper-workers,

---

[158] Hayes, *Excavations at Saraçhane*, II, pp. 12–18; idem, 'Problèmes de la céramique', p. 379; Poulou-Papadēmētriou, 'Byzantinē keramikē', pp. 238–40; Sanders, 'New relative and absolute chronologies', p. 163 (Corinth); John Hayes (pers. comm.). GWW spread north, too, to Cherson: Paul Arthur (pers. comm.).

[159] For Nicholas, see Ch. 8, n. 53; Prokopios, *Secret History*, XXV. 5–10; see above, n. 62, for Carthage, and n. 37, for Rome. For money in villages, Georganteli, 'Villes et villages'; Callegher, 'Thésaurisation'. Note also the seventh-century wooden price-panel for the Egypt–Constantinople wine trade, discussed in Luzzatto, 'P. Vat. gr. 52'.

and a restaurant.[160] Korykos was presumably on the same sea route as Myra; Sardis was rather more cut off, with its own table wares as we have seen (and even local amphorae), but still had a complex pattern of exchange, presumably with a rural hinterland. This sort of evidence puts a commercial trading network into the foreground; it would be quite wrong to regard exchange in and with the late Roman Aegean as determined only by the needs of the state (although the boats Nicholas of Sion caught could have been carrying fiscal goods too). Here as elsewhere, the late Roman exchange pattern was characterized by an interrelationship between the state and private entrepreneurs. But supplies to the capital, many of them organized directly by the state (oil and grain)—and others at least made possible by the wealth of Constantinople, itself based on taxation—structured the whole Aegean exchange system, and beyond, up to the seventh-century crisis.

This distribution network did not extend into the Anatolian plateau, which seems to have had its own ceramic productions. The best known is Sagalassos RS, an industrially produced *terra sigillata* with a venerable history (it went back to the first century BC, in fact), made in a city in upland Pisidia, which was quite widely available in the eastern Mediterranean before the rise of Phocaean RS. It had a plateau distribution above all, however—in our period, the clearest example is at Amorion, some 150 km to its north—until its terminal decline in the late sixth or early seventh century. Phocaean RS probably spoiled the prosperity of the Sagalassos potters, but not on the plateau itself, where the latter still dominated (Phocaean is hardly visible at Amorion, although it was copied). The dividing-line was probably around the top of the Maiander (Büyük Menderes) valley: both wares seem to be present at Laodikeia, 200 km inland up the river, although at nearby Hierapolis (Pamukkale) only Phocaean has been found. We cannot say much more about the interior, however, for want of sites. At Amorion, apart from RS, a fine grey ware has been found, and a coarse (but wheel-thrown) red gritted ware, both presumably local; the fine wares seem to stop around the seventh century, leaving only the coarse ware to continue on into the central middle ages.[161] This sort of involution of productive complexity in both Sagalassos, a producer centre, and Amorion, a consumer centre, has parallels in other inland sub-regions with few Mediterranean links, such as northern Italy and the Spanish Meseta, and we could

---

[160] For Korykos, see Patlagean, *Pauvrété*, pp. 158–70 (she regards the texts, oddly, as evidence for an underdeveloped economy); Trombley, 'Mediterranean sea culture', pp. 138–46. For Sardis, Crawford, *The Byzantine shops*.

[161] Poblome, *Sagalassos Red Slip ware*, esp. pp. 288, 314–18 (there was a little Mediterranean export even in our period); Lightfoot and Ivison, 'Amorium excavations 1994', pp. 121–2 (C. Wagner); iidem, 'Amorium excavations 1995', pp. 105–6. For local wares in Amorion, Harrison, 'Amorium excavations 1989', pp. 213–15 (L. Bown); idem, 'Amorium excavations 1991', pp. 212–16. For Laodikeia, Gelichi and Negrelli, 'La ricognizione', pp. 149, 152; for Hierapolis, Paul Arthur (pers. comm.)—Hierapolis had its own kilns for amphorae and coarse ware.

assume the same cause as was proposed there, a weakening of local aristocratic demand. In Anatolia, we for once have a clear context for that, too:
wars, for this was indeed a sub-region exposed after the 610s to constant
military attack, by Persians and above all Arabs, for over a century. These
localized patterns also underline the general point that the network of fiscal-
backed exchange never spread very far into Anatolia. Before the seventh-
century crisis the empire was rich but the plateau was marginal; afterwards
the plateau was crucial, as the focus of the whole imperial defence network,
but the empire was globally poorer and also more fiscally decentralized, in
the theme system (above, pp. 79, 125–9). How far we can generalize to the
whole plateau on the basis of Sagalassos and Amorion will obviously need to
be tested in the future, but Amorion was at least a theme capital and an
important strategic centre from the seventh century onwards. If Amorion
did not get either Phocaean RS before 700 or GWW after, it is unlikely that
many other places on the plateau did.

The exchange networks of the Aegean simplified considerably in the
context of the seventh-century crisis, too, and here the evidence for it allows
no doubts. Phocaean RS ceased to be produced in the late seventh century
(later than was thought until fairly recently, thanks to excavations at
Emporio on Chios, Gortyn on Crete, and in the Crimea). It had been
contracting since the sixth century, as we have seen, but the local
RS productions did not replace it, for they ceased as well.[162] LRA 2 and
3 amphorae also stopped being produced, between c.670 and c.700, on
the basis of dating from the Crimea, Saraçhane in Constantinople, and the
Crypta Balbi in Rome. They were replaced by new amphora types; the eighth
century shows a considerable variety on the Saraçhane site, and LRA 2, in
particular, was succeeded by a similar general type of globular amphora
which can be found in a number of places in the Aegean and Black Sea, and
even Italy, as we shall see in a moment. But this replacement of productions
was also a simplification: the new types are less frequently found and
presumably had more local distributions; they are also sometimes more
simply made.[163] Insofar as GWW replaced Phocaean RS as the dominant
fine ware, too, one has to recognize that it had a much more restricted
distribution. As in the Levant, these processes occurred two generations
later than the political divisions which began in the 610s–630s, but were
without doubt linked to them. By 700 exchange was substantially more
localized, and—unlike in the Levant—dealing in technologically simpler
items, than in 600.

---

[162] Ballance *et al.*, *Byzantine Emporio*, pp. 90–6 (J. Boardman); di Vita and Martin, *Gortina
II*, pp. 155–92 (the site ends around 670); Golofast, 'Early Byzantine deposits'. Panella, 'Merci e
scambi', p. 658, had seen the crisis in Phocaean RS production as being early seventh-century.

[163] For the changeover, Sazanov, 'Les amphores', pp. 99–100 (the Crimea); Hayes, *Excavations at Saraçhane*, II, pp. 71–3; Saguì, 'Il deposito della Crypta Balbi'. For post-LRA 2 types,
see n. 167.

This is by now a recognizable story, with extensive parallels in the western Mediterranean in particular. But it is incomplete. Aegean exchange in the eighth century needs, in fact, to be seen at two levels, local productions and distributions, and surviving regional-level patterns: these can be distinguished even though good work in the period is so rare (as Joanita Vroom has recently put it, few site analyses in the sub-region are 'anything more than groping in the dark'). On the local level, Painted wares continued into the eighth century in some places, as at Gortyn and other sites on Crete, and at Hierapolis near the top of the Maiander valley, although their dating on the Greek mainland is less clear. Some local wheel-made common wares, by now resembling later Byzantine types, have been identified in Athens and Corinth, surviving urban centres, that is to say, and also some GWW imitations in eighth-century Athens. Local amphorae were certainly made, as has just been noted. In the areas of central Greece studied in the Boiotia survey, slightly inland from the sea, imports ended entirely, but wheel-made common wares with incised decoration seem to continue; ribbed jugs have also been found at both Aigina and Argos, although the dating here is not tight.[164]

Most striking among these local wares are the hand-made (or, occasionally, slow-wheel) wares which have been found in several parts of mainland Greece, and which can be dated to the seventh and eighth centuries. These were long considered straightforward signs of Slav settlements, for many of them—as far south as a cemetery at Olympia in the Peloponnesos—have parallels in their incised decoration to pottery in the northern Balkans, and indeed north of the Danube. This attribution has recently been questioned by several scholars, who point out that they sometimes have forms that replicate Roman cooking-ware types, and they are indeed found with wheel-made ceramics in a Roman tradition on several sites, such as Sparta and Argos, thus appearing as the lower end of a local market; these are anyway sites the Byzantines never lost control of, unlike Olympia.[165] The ethnic issue seems to me a red herring; as has been argued several times in these pages (e.g. pp. 83, 311), ethnic identities cannot be read off from material culture in any simple way, and 'Romans' could easily use artefacts in a 'Slav'

---

[164] Vroom, *After Antiquity*, pp. 49 (quote), 52 (Argos), 139–41 (no imports in Boiotia). For Painted wares, see above, n. 157; for Aigina, Felten, 'Die christliche Siedlung', pp. 70–3; for Hierapolis, Paul Arthur (pers. comm.). For Corinth and Athens, Sanders, 'An overview', pp. 39–40; Hayes, 'Panorama de la Grèce', pp. 533–4.

[165] The best survey of the hand-made issue is currently Anagnōstakēs and Poulou-Papadēmētriou, 'Ē prōtobyzantinē Messēnē', pp. 252–91; see further Lampropoulou *et al.*, 'Symbolē', pp. 193–5, 215–21. They cite earlier work, which is more ethnicist in style. For Olympia, a recent account is Völling, 'The last Christian Greeks'. Curta, *The making of the Slavs*, pp. 233–4, also argues for later dates for these ceramics, after 650 or so, than did earlier authors. For Sparta, Waywell and Wilkes, 'Excavations', pp. 451–7 (G. D. R. Sanders). For the general issue of hand-mades, and their relationship to more complex products when the two are found together, see Rautman, 'Hand-made pottery'.

tradition if, for example, the latter were culturally hegemonic in any given area. It has to be recognized that the Olympia cemetery, at least, has so many northern parallels (in metalwork and beads, not just ceramics) that, if the dead people were not Slavs, they were at least heavily influenced by Slav culture; in Argos, by contrast, there is no particular reason to believe that Slavs ever settled at all. But more important than either, in a chapter on exchange, is the simple fact that hand-made pottery is so widely attested on the Greek mainland, from (roughly) the seventh century on-wards. Sometimes it coexisted with more complex productions; sometimes, particularly inland from the Aegean coast, hand-mades are all that are found. This latter, regardless of which ethnic groups were involved, testifies to a striking involution in productive expertise, with a return to part-time, semi-professional, 'household industry' production, much like the pattern we saw in south-east Spain (pp. 749–51). Inland and northern Greece, in particular (and northwards from that, into the Balkans), had lost the levels of demand that could sustain any productive complexity. Concentrations of wealth must have been few; fiscal structures must have been sketchy. This was a dramatic shift from the complex exchange patterns of the fifth and sixth centuries, which are well documented in Greece, including the interior.[166]

There were, on the other hand, some wider networks as well, some of them genuinely quite wide. As already noted, GWW is found on several of the southern islands, notably Crete and Cyprus, showing continued ex-change links with the capital some 800 km away (nearly twice as far in the case of Cyprus), in the eighth century. Several of the eighth-century Sara-çhane amphora types have been found in the theatre excavations at Sparta, along with local hand-mades. Of these, the post-LRA 2 globular amphorae are particularly generalized; they have been found in late seventh- or eighth-century levels, apart from Constantinople and Sparta, at Aigina, Gortyn and Pseira on Crete, Cyprus, and even on sites in Africa and Italy. These were not all made in the same place. In Italy, Otranto opposite the Greek coast and Miseno in the Bay of Naples have kilns for this type, for example, and there may have been several centres in the Aegean; the Cypriot and African amphorae were certainly local too. All the same, their homogeneity attests to communications which linked together much of the Aegean coast and went further afield as well. So does the more concrete example of the micaceous brown cooking ware, perhaps (given its petrology) from the Turkish Aegean coast, which has been found in eighth-century levels in

---

[166] Anagnōstakēs and Poulou-Papadēmētriou, 'Ē prōtobyzantinē Messēnē', pp. 288–91, 322. Such technical simplifications help to explain the extreme difficulties surveyors in Greece have had in finding pottery for the eighth and ninth centuries: see above, p. 466. Contrast the Lombards, whose hand-made pottery began to be made on a wheel when they moved into Italy, where productive complexity was greater: above, p. 731.

both Constantinople and Cyprus.[167] These medium-distance patterns privilege the islands, which fits the other evidence we have for their relative prosperity (above, p. 628), but also some of the major maritime centres on the Greek mainland. The ceramic evidence for northern Greece and Turkey is much less well studied for this period, but Thessaloniki, Ephesos, and Smyrna (Izmir), at least, would doubtless have participated in this sub-regional network. Hagiographical works support this latter point. The *Miracles* of S. Demetrios claim that Thessaloniki's city authorities were procuring grain from Thessaly in the 670s, attesting to a bulk traffic in the north-west Aegean which presumably was still needed a century later; Ephesos' fair in 796 has already been mentioned (p. 630); a little later, Ephesos ships were potentially headed for the Sea of Marmara (and thus Constantinople) in large numbers around 830 according to the *Life* of Gregory the Dekapolite, a saint who seems to have travelled fairly easily around the Aegean and across to Sicily and Italy; Lydia (whose major ports were Ephesos and Smyrna) had merchants who organized a consortium, a *koinotēs*, to buy grain from as far away as Sicily, according to the *Life* of Philip of Argyrion, perhaps written in the eighth century or slightly later; a late ninth-century life refers to Smyrna supplying the nearby island of Lesbos with grain during a famine. In major centres, at least, local production and distribution networks, and at least a skeleton sub-regional network, seem to have continued to coexist.[168]

Some of this network was certainly commercial. The hagiographical examples just cited attest to this, except perhaps the first; and a particularly clear sign of it is the *Rhodian sea law*, probably an eighth-century text, which aims largely to regulate deviant behaviour by private persons on ships. Its provisions assume that ships have paying passengers, especially merchants (*emporoi*), who contract with ships' captains (*nauklēroi*) to carry loads of goods: slaves, linen, silk, grain, wine, oil—most of them the sort of bulk goods that characterized the core of Roman-period exchange, and here clearly carrying on into the early middle ages (conceivably, in the case of wine and oil, in globular amphorae). Such trade could extend west as far as Sicily, if we accept the *Life* of Philip of Argyrion. Indeed, it must have extended further, into the surviving Tyrrhenian Sea network described earlier in this chapter (p. 737): this fits, at any rate, the range of post-LRA 2

---

[167] For the amphorae, Hayes, *Excavations at Saraçhane*, II, pp. 71–3, is basic (types 32, 33 and 35–40 are post-LRA 2). See also Poulou-Papadēmētriou, 'Byzantinē keramikē', pp. 242–6; Sodini, 'La bassin méditerranéen'; Arthur and Oren, 'North Sinai survey', p. 207; above, n. 165, for Sparta; Bowden *et al.*, 'Roman and late-antique Butrint', p. 226; above, n. 40 for Cyprus, n. 65 for Africa, and n. 89 for Italy. See also below, n. 169, for recent finds in Beirut. For the cooking ware, Hayes, *Excavations at Saraçhane*, II, pp. 55–7.

[168] *Miracles de St. Démétrius*, II.4 (§ 254); *Vie de St. Grégoire*, c. 9, cf. cc. 10–14; Eusebios, *Life* of Philip of Argyrion, c. 25; *Life* of David, Simeon, and George, c. 13. For these texts, see McCormick, *Origins*, pp. 543–4, 588–9 (a parallel Black Sea route), 880, 915; Laiou, 'Exchange and trade', pp. 707–9 (p. 708 n. for A. Kazhdan's dating of the *Life* of Philip).

amphora types. This link between the Tyrrhenian Sea and the Aegean Sea joined the two areas of the Mediterranean with most maritime activity in the eighth century. Beyond Sicily, it linked the empire and the autonomous polities of Rome and Naples; it must have been commercial. Michael McCormick's documentary study of the routes followed by travellers also specifies this as the only active Mediterranean route in the eighth century. Such a westward link was, all the same, probably fairly tenuous, and this was also true of the eastward one, beyond Cyprus into the Arab world; this did exist, as travellers' accounts again testify, but it may mostly have carried luxuries—although post-LRA 2 amphorae have been found in Beirut in early eighth-century levels.[169] Both these external links were, however, emanations of an Aegean network that was not only fairly active, but was also characterized by a visible presence of private shipping, linking, one could propose, the fairs and markets of the surviving cities of each coast of the Aegean, of which there were still a certain number (above, pp. 630–3). The main one of these was, of course, Constantinople, which still had to be fed. It had lessened substantially in size, but was never small; the grain surpluses of parts of the Aegean and the Black Sea must always have been destined for it, and this alone would have sustained a minimum Aegean traffic. After 618 its grain supply was not free, and this thus potentially underpinned a commercial network. Sicily was part of the grain-supplying hinterland of Constantinople, too, as was argued earlier (pp. 125–6), and it is indeed quite conceivable that the grain in the 'Lydian' ships in the *Life* of Philip was intended for sale in the capital.

There is thus a striking disjuncture in the Aegean sub-region in the eighth century, between, on the one hand, a consistent localization of production and distribution which, away from the coast, could reach extremes of simplicity, and, on the other, a modest but at least consistent maritime traffic, including on occasion in bulk goods, which could extend outside the Aegean, and which was sufficiently consistent to be thought worthy of legal regulation. Even given how uncertain and patchy our archaeological information is, this contrast seems fairly clear; so is its focus on Constantinople, which not only needed food, but also produced the only widespread ceramic type which was definitely the product of a single centre, Glazed White ware. What sort of economic system would produce such a contrast needs some discussion.

Byzantine historians tend to divide between a statist interpretation of exchange in this period and an approach which stresses the development of commerce. The division seems unnecessary to me. The written evidence cited here clearly stresses independent merchants, and some of the ceramic

[169] *Nomos rodiōn nautikos*, esp. III.9–11, 20, 22–5, 27–35, 38–9. I can see no reason to date this text to the late ninth century, as does Schminck, 'Probleme'. For routes east and west, McCormick, *Origins*, pp. 502–8; see Reynolds, 'Pottery and the economy', for Beirut.

evidence fits reasonably well with a commercial model for exchange activity. The focus on the capital, however, even if it is expressed in terms of buying and selling, brings the state more into focus, for Constantinople's size and wealth remained for the most part the product of taxation; the state, furthermore, was very concerned to ensure that the capital never ran out of food, and tenth-century sources show that it both sold grain itself and regulated the market for others.[170] Above all, though, the disjuncture between the local and the sub-regional levels brings the state into focus as a structuring device for all exchange activity, including commerce, in the eighth century (and later) as in the fifth to seventh. In order to characterize this a little more fully, let us look back at how the Byzantine heartland has been seen in earlier chapters.

Running through every account given in this book of the Byzantine empire after c.650 has been the paradox of a crisis-ridden polity which managed to maintain a long-lasting fiscal coherence. The government faced the acute political-military dangers of the mid-seventh century by establishing local fiscal and military structures, each theme with its own army, supported by local taxation in kind; only the lands closest to Constantinople, around the Sea of Marmara, are likely to have maintained taxes in money, one of the clearest signs of a persistence of a local exchange system. (Above, pp. 126–9.) Army supply, in particular, was thus more decentralized than it had been in earlier centuries, much as it was in the early caliphate. But the Byzantine state maintained a centrality, a focus on Constantinople above all, that the Arabs did not match. The thematic hierarchies were not independent, and the capital was the centre of an active, coherent, long-lasting administration. The aristocracies of the empire, which had mostly been focused on individual city territories before 600, shifted to the state and ecclesiastical hierarchies in the face of crisis, whether in the capital or in the thematic armies. Most cities may have ceased to be urban centres in an economic sense, but the main administrative centres continued to be important; aristocrats presumably moved there, except when they adopted a more rural lifestyle on the frontier. The political and fiscal structures of the state thus provided a framework which refigured both aristocratic identity and the fate of urbanism in the empire, in a way that could almost be described as planned. (Above, pp. 233–9, 628–35.) The fact that the system survived in

---

[170] Haldon, 'Production, distribution', updated in Brubaker and Haldon, *Byzantium in the Iconoclast era*, ch. 7; and Laiou, 'Exchange and trade', are the two fundamental recent surveys, with eadem, 'Economic and noneconomic exchange', pp. 690–1. For an earlier version of the state–commerce debate, see Patlagean, 'Byzance et les marchés'; Oikonomides, 'Le marchand byzantin'. Hendy, *Studies*, is another basic contribution to the state model. For tenth-century regulation, see Oikonomides, 'Le marchand byzantin', pp. 656–9; Laiou, 'Exchange and trade', pp. 735–6. Ignatios the Deacon, *Letter* 21, refers to the grain ships of the *dēmosion logon* in Constantinople around 820 (cf. the editor's commentary, pp. 180–1, and McCormick, *Origins*, p. 111); these do not demonstrate the survival of some form of *annona*, but at least show that the state had some involvement in grain supply. Where the grain was from is not specified.

Byzantium meant that the military disasters of the seventh and early eighth centuries, which did indeed bring serious devastation—only sixth-century Italy was as seriously affected by this parameter of social change—did not simply cause chaos, poverty, and the random dissolution of complex social structures. The simplicity of local exchange in the eighth century, as explored in this chapter, would allow one to conclude that in many areas aristocratic demand, that is, resources, weakened considerably, and peasant autonomies doubtless increased. Where this occurred, however, it would have further strengthened the drawing-power of the state, as the securest source of wealth; and even where it did not, the uncertainty of the period would have encouraged even rich aristocrats to accept the ground-rules that the state had laid down.

This picture maps onto the dual-level exchange system described here reasonably well. The Aegean had always been structurally integrated into the Mediterranean world-system, and was undoubtedly greatly disturbed by its demise; hence the collapse of some of its most prominent productive systems, like Phocaean RS. But one pole of that system had always been Constantinople, and that city, although diminished, could still act as a focus for a more modest level of sub-regional exchange in the next century. The dominant role of Constantinople as a fiscally supported centre for commercial exchange matches the dominance of the tax-based state hierarchies for the landed aristocracies of the empire. The fiscal system did not determine all of the social and economic relationships of the Byzantine empire: such power was beyond most states before the twentieth century (although one could make a case for the sixteenth-century Ottomans), and was certainly beyond a state with as many problems as eighth-century Byzantium. Its interests cannot have extended to controlling all exchange relationships, and indeed, with the end of the grain *annona*, more medium- and long-distance exchange was commercial at the end of our period in this region than it had been at the beginning. But the state had more resources than anyone else, by far. This allowed it to set out the basic directions and the ground-rules for exchange, as for many other aspects of society and the economy. The crucial importance of the demand of the capital was enough for that, even without the state regulation of many of the terms of trade, which is documented in later centuries. Given the sharp localization of so much of the productive structure of the empire, with a reduction in demand so great in some places that even full-time artisans found it hard to continue, the survival of medium-distance exchange in the Aegean was ultimately the work of the state. And it may be added that the upturn in exchange in the ninth and, still more, the tenth century, which is attested in both written and archaeological sources (for example, the revival of large-scale wine and wine-amphora production after 900 or so, this time based in the Sea of Marmara), is closely linked to a growing revival and recentralization of state structures, as emperors from Constantine V to Leo VI painstakingly laid the institutional bases for the high point of middle Byzantine political power in the tenth century.[171]

Two final points need to be made here: one microregional, the other comparative. We still know very little indeed about the different micro-regions of the Byzantine heartland. The sketchy information about post-seventh-century local ceramics presented here would lead one to conclude that they were as locally diverse as in Spain. One could propose, on the basis of both written and archaeological evidence, that the Sea of Marmara area, that is to say Thrace and Bithynia, may have maintained a continuous sub-regional complexity, thanks to the fiscal system of the capital and a local concentration of aristocratic landowning (cf. above, p. 234); that there may have been a relatively prosperous local aristocracy in Crete, probably on the Turkish coast around Smyrna (Izmir) and Ephesos, and just possibly, be-tween Corinth and Athens (as also, outside the region, in Byzantine Puglia and, certainly, Sicily); and that there may have been more serious break-downs in fiscal and landowning structures in the western Peloponnesos and probably in much of the Anatolian plateau—not to speak of the rest of inland Greece, which the Byzantines did not stably control in this period. But these characterizations are still no more than the barest hypotheses. Only archaeology will confirm or refute them, and that archaeology is hardly started as yet. One could make predictions: that eighth-century GWW will be found along the Bithynian coast (or indeed, at the end of the longer-distance routes, in Syracuse), or that a decent semi-fine eighth-century ceramic will be found around Izmir; these will certainly be con-firmed or falsified in the future. But the fact of that microregional diversity does seem to be fairly clear. The Byzantine government managed in the end to bind together a region as diverse as Spain, even if it took it another century. So also did the Umayyad emirs and caliphs in Spain, with weaker institutional structures to start with, too (above, pp. 100–2); but the Byzan-tine emperors did it on a rather larger scale, and arguably with a longer-lasting success.

The comparative point also takes us back to the other eastern Mediterra-nean regions. The Byzantine empire was certainly much poorer than the Umayyad caliphate, but it was more focused on its capital. And the clear dominance of Constantinople over the Aegean also means that this sub-region was less internally decentralized than was the region of Syria and Palestine at the end of our period. We saw in the last chapter that the fate of cities was more closely linked to state structures in Byzantium than the Levant (p. 633); this was equally so for exchange. The microregions of

---

[171] See in general Laiou, 'Exchange and trade', pp. 713–14; Haldon, 'Production, distribu-tion'; for the amphorae, Günsenin, 'Le vin de *Ganos*', citing her previous work, with Hayes, *Excavations at Saraçhane*, II, pp. 73–5. The ninth century also saw the development of the Adriatic link to Venice (above, pp. 690–1), and a general expansion in the number of Mediter-ranean routes: McCormick, *Origins*, pp. 508–47.

Syria and Palestine in the eighth century had far more complex economies than the microregions of the Aegean, which in themselves, as we have just seen, more resembled those of Spain; but in the Levant they were hardly linked together at all, whereas in Byzantium some interconnections did exist. Constantinople was more of a regional pole than Damascus was (it was a much larger city, indeed); the movement of goods between the microregions of the Aegean was more complex than that found anywhere between Antioch and 'Aqaba, before the recentralization of the 'Abbāsids and the generalization of polychrome glaze across the Levant. Constantinople was doubtless less of a pole than Fusṭāṭ, and the fiscal system of Egypt created an exchange coherence which could not in any sense be matched in the Aegean; but the circuit of exchange in eighth-century Egypt is the closest parallel to the Byzantine system. For the Byzantines to maintain that despite all their adversities is something of an achievement.

The three regions of the eastern Mediterranean studied in this book were in the fifth and sixth centuries fairly similar, with only minor divergencies in their patterns; it is the seventh that blew them in different directions. In economic terms, the Arab-ruled regions clearly maintained a greater complexity thereafter; they were richer in purely ecological terms than was most of Byzantium, they were not ravaged in the same way that Anatolia was across a century of war, and they would have found it much easier to sustain a high level of military expenditure, one which Byzantium, in order to survive, had to match on a much weaker economic base. Hence the local wealth of both the Levant and Egypt, which has been explored in this chapter. The aristocracies of each for the most part remained more prosperous than those in Byzantium, even bearing in mind their weakening in Egypt. Furthermore, only small sectors of the Arab regions had formerly been structurally linked into the Mediterranean exchange system, perhaps only the Antioch and Gaza areas, whereas a large part of the Aegean sub-region had been before 600. The richest part of the Byzantine heartland would thus have been as hard hit by the breakdown in interregional exchange as the Anatolian plateau was by war. But the Byzantine state managed to hold its provinces together, including the basic patterns of provincial-level taxation, and preserved Constantinople as a focus. As a result, on the regional level its integration has some parallels with that of Egypt, and was rather greater than that of Syria and Palestine. This was the result of the coherence of the fiscal system in both Byzantium and Egypt. Indeed, it had to be, for aristocratic wealth was by now too localized in the eastern Mediterranean, as in the western Mediterranean, to integrate whole regions economically. Only the state could do that—unless, that is, aristocratic wealth operated on a much greater geographical scale than we have seen so far. The test case for that is northern Francia, to which we shall now return.

One final observation. The period of greatest economic localization (and, in Byzantium, economic simplicity) was the eighth century in the eastern Mediterranean, just as it was in the West, but for different reasons. In the western Mediterranean, the eighth century was the culmination of a long period of economic simplification, made only clearer by the end of the last signs of the Roman interregional exchange system, and was essentially a sign of the weakness of aristocracies. In the East, it was the immediate product of seventh-century disruption and of Umayyad fiscal provincialization. There were differences in the way it was reversed, too. In Italy this reversal, from the ninth century onwards, derived from a slow increase in aristocratic wealth, and thus local-level and then regional-level exchange. In the Levant, at the other extreme, it derived above all from the recentralization of the state under the 'Abbāsids. The other regions of the Mediterranean, the Byzantine empire in the East, Africa and Spain in the West, saw a reconstruction of both the state and in some places aristocratic wealth as well: a harder task than the 'Abbāsids faced, and accordingly slower, but moving in the same direction. Slowly, one by one, all these regions came to parallel Egypt more closely in the complexity of their internal economies, and large-scale exchange between regions began again. The tenth and eleventh centuries showed increasing levels of interregional exchange throughout the Mediterranean, even if they would never again reach the uniformity and intensity of those of late Rome. But interregional exchange in every case depended on the prior internal economic complexity of each region, and thus on the different fiscal and aristocratic bases of regional wealth. These different structural bases persisted, and would indeed mark later centuries as well.

9. The North I: northern Gaul/Francia

The Mediterranean world stopped at Lyon, or thereabouts. The north of Gaul, *Germania*, and Britain were not part of it, from the third century at the latest, when Spanish olive oil ceased to be sent to the Rhine army on a large scale, marking, one can assume, a permanent move to animal fats in cooking. Already in the early empire, table wares were Gaulish-made, in the *terra sigillata* traditions of La Graufesenque, Lezoux, Rheinzabern.[172] The Rhône corridor from the Mediterranean continued to matter (below, p. 800), but it was a route between two different exchange systems. The rhythms of development of the North thus did not need to reflect those we have seen in previous sections, and the fact is that they did not. The lands looking down the great rivers to the Atlantic and North Sea saw their crisis early, in the

---

[172] For amphorae, see above, Ch. 3, n. 56. For Gaulish *terra sigillata*, see e.g. Woolf, *Becoming Roman*, pp. 194–203.

fifth century—an incomplete one as far as exchange is concerned—and by the eighth century the standard indicators for wealth accumulation were clearly pointing upwards, when in the Mediterranean economies were unusually localized. I shall focus in this section on the part of the region of Gaul north of a line running from Tours on the Loire, through Dijon in Burgundy, to Basel on the Rhine; there has been less ceramic work for a good distance south of this line, and Aquitaine and the south coast have been discussed in the context of the Mediterranean (pp. 746–8, 758).

In northern Gaul around 400, by far the commonest fine ware, in the *sigillata* tradition, was Argonne ware: an orange or grey ware made in the Argonne forest west of Verdun, often quite elaborately decorated with a roller wheel or roulette (called a *molette* in French), with a 400-km radius of distribution from the Rhine to well south of the Loire, and over into Britain. It was one of a set of late Gaulish fine wares; it was matched to the south by *céramique à l'éponge* in Poitou, Jaulges-Villiers-Vineux ware in northern Burgundy, and the DSP tradition further south again (above, p. 746). Argonne ware was very common in both cities and the Rhine forts, and its distribution, although certainly based on market exchange, must have been buttressed by military demand. This may also explain why its range contracted during the fifth century, the period of the crisis of the political structures of the North. All the same, as Didier Bayard has shown, it continued into the late sixth century; it reached less than 200 km by now, all downstream from its kilns, and rather less densely than before, but survived a century into the Merovingian period as a production on a substantial scale.[173] Argonne ware was matched as a production by an industrial coarse ware, Mayen ware (*céramique rugueuse*, *rauhwandige Drehscheibenware*), made in the Eifel north of Trier. Mayen had almost as wide a distribution as Argonne in the late fourth century, particularly along the Rhine—it is known from Switzerland to Britain; its influence also reached the Paris basin, where it was represented by a local imitation, generally called *céramique granuleuse*.[174] These two types did not exhaust the range of productions in the region, and they always, as everywhere, coexisted with more local ones, of a variety of qualities, but they are as much as we need to

---

[173] See Van Ossel, 'Céramiques', idem, 'La sigillée d'Argonne', and Tuffreau-Libre, 'La céramique de l'antiquité tardive', for late Roman overviews, with, for the strangely named Jaulges-Villiers-Vineux ware, Séguier and Morize, 'Les céramiques tardives'. For Gaulish wares in Britain, see Tyers, *Roman pottery*, pp. 136, 144–5. For the redating of late Argonne ware, see Bayard, 'L'ensemble du grand amphithéâtre de Metz'; idem, 'La céramique dans le Nord de la Gaule'; idem, 'La sigillée d'Argonne'.

[174] The basic account of Mayen ware is Redknap, 'Medieval pottery production'; I am grateful to him for advice about it. For the *céramique granuleuse* of the Paris basin see Petit, 'La céramique de type "Mayen" '; Gentili, 'La céramique des habitats ruraux', pp. 323–4; *L'Île de France*, pp. 248–51 (M. Petit); Bayard, 'La céramique dans le Nord de la Gaule', pp. 121–4; Renel, 'Un ensemble céramique'; Dufour, 'L'occupation', pp. 34–8 (Y.-M. Adrian). There were probably numerous other local imitations or variants of this ceramic type.

give an idea of a northern productive system operating at a considerable scale, paralleling those of the late Roman Mediterranean.

The fifth-century crisis probably undermined the distribution of Argonne ware, as we have just seen. Mayen ware contracted too, and more imitations of it began to be made, in the upper Rhine, the Meuse, the Scheldt. Mayen ware proper only held onto the middle and lower Rhine. Still, this was still an area nearly 300 km in length; and, unlike Argonne ware, Mayen ware did not end in our period—it was still being made in the eleventh century. The Mayen kilns, together with those of Aswān, are the longest-lived workshop complexes known for the whole of the late and post-Roman world. By now they did not restrict themselves to coarse wares: Argonne imitations, carinated wares, Red Painted wares, Tating ware, Carolingian stone ware, the whole basic Frankish ceramic range, all were made at Mayen at some point between 400 and 900. All the same, it was the *rugueuse* tradition which had the widest spread at all times, and which must have been at the core of the production of most kilns.[175]

As these two wares lost their regional-level distributions, local ceramic productions became generally more important. The major development of the fifth century was the introduction of a new ceramic type, called *céramique biconique* by the French, *doppelkonische Keramik* or *Knickwandtöpfen* by the Germans: a carinated, usually black fine ware characterized by often complex roulette decoration. This ware usually had a reasonably high-quality fabric, and it was made at a variety of locations across the whole of northern Gaul. It spread westwards from the Rhineland in the late fifth century and onwards, and has thus often been seen as the Frankish (or Merovingian) ware *par excellence*, but its stylistic and technical antecedents are entirely late Roman, probably derived from the *terra nigra* fine ware that was common in the North up to the fourth century. It was popular as a grave-good when furnished burials returned to Gaul around 500, and, since cemeteries were the main early medieval sites dug in the region until the 1980s, it has long been a fairly well known ceramic type; it is now being found (in smaller quantities) in settlements too, such as Goudelancourt in the Aisne (above, p. 504).[176] By the sixth century and into the seventh, the *biconiques* and the *rugueuses* dominated most ceramic assemblages that have been found in most parts of the North.

This account needs some setting in context. The fifth century was certainly a difficult time in northern Gaul, with a breakdown in fiscal and military

---

[175] Redknap, 'Medieval pottery production'; Gross, 'Die Töpferware', pp. 588–93; for copies, see Van Ossel, 'Céramiques', pp. 64–8; Dijkman, 'La céramique'.

[176] The best quick overview of carinated wares, and of the Merovingian period as a whole, is Gross, 'Die Töpferware'. For cemeteries, see e.g. Young, 'Paganisme, christianisation', pp. 46–7; for settlements, see e.g. Lorren, 'St.-Martin de Trainecourt', pp. 448–9; Bayard and Thouvenot, 'Étude de la céramique', pp. 295–302; Bayard, 'La céramique...de Goudelancourt'; Heege, *Hambach 500*, p. 208.

structures and an often ad hoc takeover by Germanic tribal groups (and local Roman armies), before Clovis's comprehensive conquests in the decades around 500. Recent settlement work, however, rejects earlier apocalyptic arguments for land abandonment and population substitutions (above, pp. 504–10); I have also argued for a continuity of landowning elites in much of the North (pp. 178–97). That argument was partly, but not only, based on the continuities in ceramics just outlined. Notwithstanding a tendency to localization across the fifth century, which is not surprising given the political situation, ceramic production continued on a considerable scale, not least at Mayen, whose continuous history would not have been possible without a continuous, fairly stable, market for its products. Indeed, the period saw the development of a new fine ware in a Roman tradition, which is not easily compatible with any image of chaos—rather, it too indicates a certain level of demand for a decent-quality product, by buyers with sufficient self-confidence to be able to accept innovations, not just imitations of Argonne *sigillata*. This change in taste was generalized in the sixth century, when Merovingian power was hegemonic, but it had begun in the uncertainties of the late fifth. It must be added that there are signs of settlers from beyond the Rhine bringing in their own ceramic traditions, hand-made wares for the most part, but these are restricted to frontier areas: the upper Rhine for the Alemans, the lower Meuse and Rhine for the Franks, the coastal fringe of Flanders and Picardy for, probably, the Anglo-Saxons. In every one of these cases wheel-thrown ceramics came to coexist with them in the sixth century; Germanic immigrants must have picked up Roman pottery habits—and the patterns of market exchange that these entailed—very soon indeed, and they remained the norm south and west of the Rhine, as Gaul turned slowly into Francia, just as they did in Italy and most of Spain.[177] The disruptions of the fifth century in this region thus never led to such a breakdown in demand that professional ceramic production was under threat.

It is not yet easy to be sure how the productions of the sixth and seventh centuries were articulated. We have numerous kilns, at La Saulsotte near Nogent-sur-Seine, Huy, and Maastricht, for example (in most of these both *biconiques* and *rugueuses* were made), which shows the polycentricity of production in this period. But both ceramic types maintained good-quality productive levels, implying trained artisans: they were on the level of Peacock's 'individual workshops' at least, and on that of the 'nucleated workshop' at Mayen. A particularly elaborate set of roulette types in the late sixth-century Paris basin and inland Picardy to its north allowed René Legoux to construct a single (or at most double) ceramic zone stretching

---

[177] See respectively Châtelet, 'La céramique du haut moyen âge', p. 238, with Siegmund, *Alamannen und Franken*, pp. 140–5; De Paepe and Van Impe, 'Historical context', pp. 148–53; Hollevoet, 'Céramiques d'habitats', with Hamerow *et al.*, 'Migration period settlements'.

between them, where the same roulettes were used over an area 180 by 90 km: this was the *Königslandschaft* of the Paris and Oise valley royal palaces, which would doubtless have helped the establishment of a single, sizable, exchange area. Neighbouring areas were clearly distinguishable, and that on the Aisne to the east seems to have had comparable dimensions. This is very tentative work, but it gives us an order of magnitude for an exchange area, which helps us.[178] Interestingly, the coarse *rugueuses* were more centralized in their production patterns than were the *biconique* fine wares, with Mayen ware still dominating 300 km of the Rhineland, as already noted, and the *céramique granuleuse* of the Seine valley also covering a substantial area. This parallels the wide distribution of *céramique kaolinitique* in the lower Rhône, as opposed to the microregional distributions of finer wares in the South (above, pp. 747–8). The important difference is that the *biconiques* were themselves less microregionally distributed in the North, and also culturally homogeneous over nearly all the Loire–Rhine region; only small areas, such as the part-Aleman upper Rhine, developed different traditions of taste (in the northern part of that area, a fairly simple but wheel-thrown Yellow Clay ware replaced both *rugueuses* and *biconiques* in the seventh century). There was thus a hierarchy of exchange areas in northern Gaul/Francia, with a sub-regional distribution of coarse wares, a more localized distribution of fine wares, and also a set of much more local ceramic types, not all well studied (some microregional distribution patterns have, however, been postulated for the Rhineland).[179] The scale of the coarse-ware network is the clearest archaeological guide to a substantial geographical scale for exchange, and fine wares, too, could reach a 100-km radius. Legoux's Paris–Picardy area matches the distribution of fine wares in eighth-century Palestine; fine wares in the latter region were of a higher quality, but their economic scale was similar. But the Mayen distribution network is only paralleled, after the end of the great Roman RS and amphora productions, by those of Egypt, as well as by the rather less dense distribution of GWW in Byzantium.

How internal exchange was actually organized and patterned before the Carolingian period is slightly easier to tell for Francia than for most other

[178] La Saulsotte: see most recently Georges-Leroy and Lenoble, 'La céramique'; Huy: Willems, 'Le quartier artisanal', pp. 18–41, with idem, 'La production de poterie'; Maastricht: Dijkman, 'La céramique'. For the Paris–Picardy area, see Legoux, 'L'art animalier', with Bayard and Thouvenot, 'Étude de la céramique', pp. 305–34, esp. p. 334 for the Aisne.

[179] For the upper Rhine, see Châtelet, 'La céramique du haut moyen âge'; eadem, 'L'évolution de la céramique culinaire tournée'; Gross, 'Beobachtungen'. (The southern and trans-Rhenish Aleman parts of this area maintained much simpler ceramic traditions until the ninth century; see also n. 177, and above, p. 575.) For very localized ceramic areas in the Rhineland, see Verhoeven, 'L'évolution de la céramique', pp. 212–13 (with a map taken, with revisions, from the work of K. Weidemann, *Die frühmittelalterliche Keramik*, which I have not seen), and Roth, 'Zum Handel', pp. 172–80; these areas are rather hypothetical in some cases, and Roth (wrongly in my view) sees them as typical of ceramics in the sub-region, but they are guides to one level in the exchange hierarchy.

regions outside Egypt, for its documentary sources are better. (Italy, our third well-documented region, gives us less information, perhaps reflecting the fact that its exchange was also less elaborate.) There was certainly a network of markets across the Merovingian lands, which are regarded as normal in literary texts, as casual references show. These seem to have been hierarchically arranged, with some major fairs (most notably the annual fair at St-Denis, in existence by the 630s: above, p. 286); a series of urban fairs and markets, presumably present in every city, which sometimes had a range extending into neighbouring city territories; and weekly markets (*nundinae*) in smaller centres.[180] There were in addition professional merchants (*negotiatores, mercatores*), who often dealt locally, but sometimes had a wider range, such as Priscus (d. 582), a Jewish dealer who was a *familiaris* of King Chilperic in the Paris region, and also had links in Marseille. He was not the only merchant with *Königsnähe*, either; John the *negucians*, presumably of Paris, who gave land to St-Denis in the 610s–620s, had his will confirmed by Chlotar II. Some of them were certainly rich, as was Eusebius, *negotiator genere Syrus*, who went so far as to buy the bishopric of Paris in 591. Verdun's traders (*illi negutia exercentes*) were loaned 7,000 *solidi* by Theudebert I, probably in the late 530s, to restore their affairs, and remained affluent in the 580s, when Gregory of Tours (the source for most of this detail) was writing; Verdun must have been a major commercial centre if Gregory was right about the size of the royal loan. Verdun was a nodal point for exchange north down the Meuse, and over the watersheds west down the Marne and south down the Saône, so its merchants may have been more active than in some places; in the tenth century there would be an organized slave trade run from there.[181]

What did these merchants, or the people who went to the markets, buy and sell? Luxuries on occasion, for sure, as with the jewellery shops (*domus negutiantum*) near Notre-Dame in Paris in 583. It is interesting, though, that the casual references in our narratives and other sources are unusually often to bulk products: wine (transported down the Loire from Orléans to Tours in one of Gregory's accounts); the olive oil from the South that was, however, by now most often used for lighting rather than food; salt (transported from Metz to Trier in another of Gregory's stories—the Metz area is a well-documented salt-production area); livestock (as with a letter from the bishop of Reims to the bishop of Metz in the 540s enquiring about pig prices);

---

[180] For markets, see for a full survey Claude, 'Aspekte des Binnenhandels', pp. 45–56 (p. 49 for Cahors people at a market in Rodez; p. 4 for *nundinae*), with Lebecq, 'Les échanges'.

[181] For merchants, see in general Claude, 'Aspekte des Binnenhandels', pp. 62–78; for the examples cited here, Gregory of Tours, *LH*, VI.5, 17 (Priscus), X.26 (Eusebius), III.34 (Verdun); *ChLA*, XIII, n. 550 (John). For Verdun slaves in the tenth century, see Liutprand of Cremona, *Antapodosis*, VI.6. What Verdun merchants were trading in in the 530s cannot be said. Jewish and Syrian merchants are prominent in Gregory and some other sources; Devroey, 'Juifs et Syriens', puts them in context. For the later rise of Frisian merchants, see Lebecq, *Marchands et navigateurs*, I, pp. 23–34.

slaves; and, among artisanal products, cloth. This is, of course, the level of exchange that the ceramic distributions tell us about.[182]

It seems that, at the level of bulk products, there was active exchange at least between neighbouring city territories, throughout the Merovingian period. These relatively localized networks were furthermore linked together, in particular along the main river valleys, the Loire, Seine, Meuse (particularly well attested), Moselle, and Rhine. It was the river network, for example, that transported wine northwards from the specialist viticulture zones of the late Merovingian period stretching from Paris to the Rhine (above, pp. 284–7). This exchange hierarchy fits both the archaeology and our written evidence; it was more elaborated than anything we have seen in the Mediterranean by 700 outside the south-eastern regions. It was also linked into wider markets, above all down the Saône and Rhône, with Marseille regarded as the universal source of Mediterranean goods, as Gregory of Tours's constant references to it, and seventh- and eighth-century trading privileges to St-Denis and Corbie, underline. These texts, so often chewed over in the 'Pirenne thesis' debate, need to be put in perspective by the archaeology, which shows only limited quantities of goods from the Mediterranean in any part of our period. Marseille prospered from its role as a gateway port, as Caesarea in Palestine did (p. 774), but the goods it imported, mostly luxuries, were marginal to the economy as a whole.[183] This exchange was usually commercial, with kings, churches and monasteries, and doubtless aristocrats, acting as important buyers, and with monasteries beginning to be documented as sellers too. Merchants could be either autonomous entrepreneurs or the dependants of these major landowners (or indeed both, as Priscus may show). The goods they moved around will also have run parallel with the large-scale movement of goods taken in rent that must already have characterized the internal economies of royal, ecclesiastical, and aristocratic landowning; there would sometimes indeed have been an interpenetration between them, as when in Carolingian sources inland monasteries are seen sending goods to the sea ports to sell.[184] This

---

[182] Gregory of Tours, *LH*, VI.32 (Paris), VII.46 (wine, cf. idem, *GC*, c. 110); *Vita Filiberti*, c.37 (oil from Bordeaux: see most recently Fouracre, 'Eternal light', pp. 68–78, for lighting); Gregory of Tours, *VM*, IV.29 (salt: cf. *Vita S. Eugendi*, cc. 157–60, for another example, and, for the salt production of the Metz area, Halsall, *Settlement and social organisation*, pp. 208–11); *Epp. Austrasicae*, n. 15 (livestock); Gregory of Tours, *VP*, I.5 (even a hermit buys cloth).

[183] For river routes, see Claude, 'Aspekte des Binnenhandels', pp. 38–45; Devroey, 'Courants et reseaux'. For the most recent discussions of Marseille and the trading privileges, Loseby, 'Marseille', I and II (cf. above, p. 667); the privileges are recently re-edited by Theo Kölzer in *MGH, Dip. Merov.*, nn. 123, 170, 171. The importance of the Meuse as a route fits with the wealth of its aristocracy, particularly the Pippinids (see Ch. 4, n. 97), with the rise of Maastricht (see Ch. 10, n. 192), and with the role also of Huy (above, n. 178).

[184] Claude, 'Aspekte des Binnenhandels', pp. 79–83, argues for a rise of ecclesiastical tied trade at the expense of independent merchants in the seventh century; this argument is nuanced in Devroey, 'Courants et reseaux', and Lebecq, 'The role of the monasteries', pp. 139–48, the best two relatively recent accounts of the late Merovingian period, which stress the role of the

was arguably the Frankish equivalent to the fiscal support for the infrastructure of exchange in the late Roman Mediterranean; indeed, the scale of exchange in seventh-century northern Francia that has been proposed here on both archaeological and documentary grounds fits well with the geographical range of seventh-century aristocratic landowning, as set out in Chapter 4 (pp. 186–92). It constituted a continuous group of interconnected medium-distance networks, in operation without a break across our period, and indeed with roots going back into the empire. If there was a fifth-century dip, it was largely reversed by the early sixth, with only the largest-scale late Roman networks, such as the region-wide distribution of Argonne ware, not re-established.

The eighth century saw further developments, as we can see once again with ceramics. The *biconiques* died out, and were replaced by wares in generally lighter-coloured fabrics, often painted. A major area of their production was the Vorgebirge region near Cologne, particularly Badorf, and Badorf ware in the second quarter of the century spread across the lower Rhine and Meuse valleys, as a more centralized production than the *biconiques*, extending into Frisia and Flanders, and dominating Dorestad's ceramics by 800. Those wares, both fine and less fine, can also be found on several sites in eastern and southern England. Badorf was matched in the Seine valley by other kiln-sites, notably La Londe near Rouen, which supplied Hamwic with much of its imported pottery.[185] It is always necessary to remember when considering these large-scale distribution patterns that much ceramic production remained at a rather more localized level, and there were inland sections of Francia, including economically active ones such as the upper Rhine, which did not see such wares at all. But they are nonetheless signs of the widening of the networks of exchange; Badorf ware was added to Mayen ware, rather than substituting for it. Around 800 there even developed a luxury ceramic type, Tating ware, a fine black ware with tinfoil decoration (made at Mayen at least and probably elsewhere too), which can be found on high-status sites from St-Denis and Mainz up to Scandinavia.[186] These patterns persisted into the late ninth century, and indeed later, although production sites slowly changed.

church as a buyer and seller. It seems to me anyway that the seventh-century shift is largely one of documentation, with Gregory of Tours's anecdotes replaced by ecclesiastical privileges. Gross, 'Beobachtungen', argues that ceramic distributions are above all inside the framework of landlordly economies; the examples he cites for the middle Rhine are telling, but this can only be part of the picture.

[185] For Badorf, Janssen, 'Badorf', is an introduction, with idem, *Die Importkeramik*, pp. 76–130; for Dorestad, Van Es and Verwers, 'Le commerce des céramiques'; for eastern England, Hodges, *The Hamwih pottery*, pp. 37–43, 84–5; for Flanders, Démolon and Verhaeghe, 'La céramique', p. 393; for La Londe, Adrian and Roy, 'Typologie'. See in general Blackmore, 'Pottery'.

[186] For the upper Rhine, Gross, 'Beobachtungen'. Another partially distinct ceramic zone seems to have been the Loire: see Randouin, 'Essai de classification', updated in Zadora-Rio and Galinié, 'La fouille du site de Rigny', pp. 206–17 (P. Husi). For Tating ware, among others, Ring

This ceramic development is matched by many other markers of eighth- and ninth-century economic activity in northern Francia. Paris, Cologne, Maastricht, and Dorestad were discussed in Chapter 10 (pp. 677–90), as prosperous centres in this period, the last of them rather more commercially active at a long distance than anywhere in the Mediterranean by now. The North Sea exchange network, which will be returned to in the next section, is by now well known to both historians and archaeologists; but it also reflected a complex pattern of internal exchange in the Carolingian period. Grain went down the Rhine to the coast; wine went to the lands around the Rhine mouth by ever more complex routes, including, by now, by road; woollens, a speciality of the lowlands of the Rhine delta area, were bought in return. We have also seen that the rapid expansion of the manorial system after 750 or so can best be explained as a development in the intensity of agricultural production and exploitation, aimed at exchange (pp. 287–93). The evidence for merchants, both Frisian and Frankish, steadily increases, and so will, in the ninth century, that for markets; the use of money, notwithstanding its high face value, was quite generalized. Monastic documentation in the ninth century increasingly often cites artisans, above all in iron, leather, and cloth (as with the *gynaecaea*, the female textile workshops, of many monasteries); McCormick has proposed that metalwork and even textiles went north on the back of the wine trade, and it is clear that some artisanal products spread a long way—not only Frankish ceramics, but Frankish glass, and basalt quernstones from the Mayen region, are found in both England and Scandinavia.[187] We do not need to discuss these patterns in greater detail, for the best evidence for them is ninth-century, that is to say, out of our period. But it is at least clear that the hierarchy of exchange already proposed for the sixth and seventh centuries was amply present in northern Francia, and indeed more elaborate, in the eighth and ninth. Local markets, urban markets, sub-regional markets, and regular sub-regional route networks can all be identified, as shown in recent work by Olivier Bruand. The great bulk of this exchange remained relatively local. Bruand analysed the late ninth-century hoards of northern France, and can show that over 80 per cent of the coins in them came from a radius of 100 km, the same scale as the ceramic networks of the Merovingian period; there were microregional differences in his study area (coins from the Seine

and Wieczorek, 'Tatinger Kannen'; Hodges, *The Hamwih pottery*, pp. 64–8; Redknap, 'Medieval pottery production', p. 15; Meyer-Rodrigues, 'Tessons de céramique'. Compare the analogous distributions of Merovingian glass, a bulk ware but above all bought by the relatively wealthy, in Koch, 'Glas', pp. 614–17.

[187] See in general for Carolingian exchange the works cited in Ch. 5, n. 64, with Johanek, 'Der fränkische Handel'; McCormick, *Origins*, pp. 639–68, 698–704 (pp. 651–2 for wine sales underpinning other goods). Bruand, *Voyageurs et marchandises*, gives a particularly articulated account (pp. 203–34, 242–4, for wine and woollens in northern France; pp. 268–70 for road routes). For *gynaecaea*, see refs. cit. in Ch. 9, n. 70. For England and Scandinavia, see e.g. Hodges, *Dark age economics*, pp. 117–26; Näsman, 'Exchange and politics'.

valley, Champagne, and especially the Channel ports spread further, for example), but the tendencies are clear.[188] Exchange at this level was the motor of the economy; finds of coins from very long distances are not uncommon in the period, but they are more marginal. All the same, those local exchange networks were very active, and even more than in the Merovingian period they were linked together, by river and road, in the Seine–Meuse–Rhine sub-region above all, the political core of the Carolingian world as of the Merovingians before. As a secondary development, they extended outwards through *emporia* like Quentovic and Dorestad to the English Channel and North Sea as well, although this exchange was peripheral to the main lines of Frankish local and sub-regional economies.

It is important not to overvalue all these signs of exchange. The late eighth and ninth centuries, the Carolingian period, do show a marked upturn in the intensity of traffic, local, regional, and even interregional; all the same, exchange under the Merovingians had a similar hierarchy, with some products available for hundreds of kilometres. Furthermore, Carolingian exchange, as we have seen in Chapter 5 (pp. 291–2), had limits; exactly who was going to buy all that demesne-produced grain is not fully clear, and the more articulated interregional networks of agrarian specialisms of the twelfth century had not yet appeared. We must not overstate the Carolingian moment, by, for example, ascribing too much conscious protagonism to the royal/imperial court, or too much romantic, future-directed excitement to the trade of the North Sea: these are to introduce presuppositions about how exchange worked that are inappropriate to our period.[189]

All the same, if we look at eighth-century northern Francia with the sort of optic used in the rest of this chapter, which has focused above all on the scale and intensity of local and regional exchange networks, then Frankish exchange still looks pretty active by the standards of most Mediterranean regions. As already noted, Mayen ware, and by now Badorf ware as well, did extend more widely and densely than any ceramic networks in the rest of Europe, and Badorf ware has been widely found on village sites in the areas it reached, showing that the peasantry had access to it too.[190] The articulation and scope of their distribution networks is more important than the quality of their production—for even Badorf ware would have looked simple enough if it had turned up in Egypt or Palestine—and, taken with the increasing documentary evidence for exchange, it shows that, by the standards of the early middle ages, something was going on in the Seine–Rhine sub-region that was second only to the exchange intensity of the Nile valley.

---

[188] Bruand, *Voyageurs et marchandises*, pp. 176–9, 257–72.
[189] See the cautious summary of trends in Verhulst, *Carolingian economy*, pp. 87–113, 132–5.
[190] See e.g. Hollevoet, 'Céramiques d'habitats', p. 200.

In eighth-century Egypt, the regional scale of large-scale exchange was associated with the continuing coherence of the tax system (pp. 766–9). Aristocracies in every part of the Mediterranean were by the end of our period much more localized, in single city territories or sets of neighbouring ones, and even when they were rich (as in Syria and Palestine) they only sustained economic networks at the local level; it took a regional-level fiscal system, as in Egypt or to a lesser extent in Byzantium, to create a wider scale for exchange. This was something that the tax network could not do in northern Francia: it was probably facing crisis already in the mid-fifth century, and was terminally weak by 600 at the latest (except in the Loire valley, where it lasted on a small scale into the eighth: above, pp. 105–15). But here the patterns of private (including royal) landowning were different as well. We have seen that large-scale property-owning continued in Francia, apparently without a break—or, at least, any break was reversed by the early sixth century. By the seventh, our documentation shows a regional-level aristocracy, both secular and ecclesiastical, who had more land in absolute than any other aristocracy of the post-Roman world; and their leaders also had geographical spreads that extended over wide areas, whole sub-regions of the Frankish world, such as Neustria and Austrasia, again in a way that is hardly paralleled elsewhere (above, pp. 178–95). Some parts of northern Francia also had an unusually subject peasantry, notably the Paris region, although this was a more locally varying pattern—peasant landowning is more visible in the Rhineland, for example (above, pp. 393–406). Peasant autonomy was nevertheless on the decrease, as landowners, both lay and ecclesiastical, extended their tenurial power, from the seventh century onwards, and then under the Carolingians both moved against any surviving peasant political protagonism and intensified the exploitation of peasants who were already dependent (above, pp. 289–91, 575–81). The concentration and geographical scale of aristocratic wealth in northern Francia was arguably sufficiently great to compensate for the end of the fiscal system, and the movement of goods between the lands of the great owners, plus the scale of their buying power, were arguably sufficient almost to match the infrastructural importance of the fiscal system for exchange in Egypt. At the end of our period, when infrastructures were weak for a variety of different reasons in most places in the Mediterranean, they were actually getting stronger in Francia, as great landowners became still richer; the contrast with most of the Mediterranean regions simply became more acute.

The documentation for aristocratic wealth in Francia and the documentation for exchange networks thus, as elsewhere, fit together. The rich needed to buy goods in bulk (luxuries too, of course); their demand allowed the maintenance, sometimes the development, of a class of professional artisans, sometimes working on a considerable scale, the level of the 'nucleated workshop', at least in crafts like pottery, glass, or cloth, where that was a practical and useful procedure. The geographical scale of those basic demand networks was regularly around 100 km, as indeed often in the Mediterranean, but the breadth of interest of the richest landowners, and the infrastructure of their internal movement of goods, allowed sub-regional networks of exchange to exist as well, like Badorf ceramics or Parisian and Rhenish wine. Even the most subjected peasants could participate in these networks on occasion, as village pottery distributions show. In the Carolingian period, as under the Merovingians, merchants could engage in entirely autonomous commercial exchange in this environment, but even independent traders were dependent on the buying-power, the commercial patronage, of the rich for any prosperity they could aspire to; they were in practice a structural element in the aristocratic network, even when they sold to peasants as well. Nor would this change in later centuries in most of the north of Francia; the networks of the Carolingian period would remain the bases of the twelfth-century exchange system. There were, of course, interruptions in the intervening period, such as Viking raids, the decline of the *emporia*, the break-up of Carolingian political power, and an increasing geographical localization of the aristocracy in many microregions from the tenth century onwards. These would have their own varying impacts on the local and regional networks of exchange. But the basic feature of northern Francia in our period, the continuing demand of a rich aristocracy, remained a feature of future centuries; and this pattern steadily spread ever further northwards, into England, Saxony, Denmark, as we have also seen (pp. 340–51, 585–8, 364–76).

The Carolingian upturn in aristocratic wealth and political domination on the one hand and in exchange on the other is undeniable; both are products of the stable patterns of political power across the four generations 720–830. The period was one in which very many rich people and ecclesiastical institutions could be found in northern Francia, and therefore one in which substantial quantities of goods were made or distributed to satisfy their needs. This does not, however, make the Frankish economy as a *system* different in type from those of the Mediterranean; it is just that the main buyers were richer, at least by the eighth century. And, notwithstanding that upturn, it must be stressed that they had been rich for a long time. After the upsets of the fifth century in the North, which caused the slow but terminal breakdown of the fiscal system, aristocratic wealth remained great there for ever after. In a sense, then, what marks the early medieval economy of northern Gaul/Francia is less growth, than stability: a stability which, once again, was only surpassed by that of Egypt.

10. The North II: England and its neighbours

This section will concentrate on England, for the simple reason that the evidence for exchange is best there. The models for how exchange worked there can, however, be applied to the other regions and sub-regions of the North, as we shall see at the end.

The breakdown of Roman social and economic structures in Britain in the first half of the fifth century has been discussed in relative detail (above, pp. 306–10), and does not need to be described again here. It is enough to say that it was in that context associated with a meltdown in fiscal and aristocratic demand, and a general tribalization of social structures, which contrasted Britain very sharply with its neighbour, northern Gaul, and puts further into perspective the relatively contained scale of the fifth-century crisis in the latter. The indigenous pottery industries of late Roman Britain all failed, probably across the second quarter of the century, with a speed and a generality which has no parallel anywhere else in the post-Roman world. Surviving sites seem to have become aceramic, at least after their inhabitants stopped using the pottery they had preserved from the past. Only in east Yorkshire has an argument been made for post-Roman pottery production continuing up to the period of the first Anglo-Saxon settlements in the mid-fifth century and onwards.[191] But even there there was no ceramic continuity after that; Anglo-Saxon pottery was utterly different. The settlers brought with them a hand-made tradition with stylistic parallels in northern Germany: Catherine Hills and Martin Weber have argued for such close parallels between the cremation cemetery urns of Spong Hill in Norfolk and those of Issendorf in Lower Saxony that they could have been made by the same potter. Such ceramics could be highly decorated in cemeteries, with probable symbolic content to that decoration, although the equivalents found in settlements are mostly plain. This tradition remained hand-made, and highly localized.[192] It would have lost its ethnic marking very soon, perhaps immediately, as it was by now almost the only ceramic type being made on the island. It dominated in eastern Britain for some four centuries thereafter.

Early Anglo-Saxon hand-made wares are often very simple indeed. Many were probably made at the simplest technological level, family by family, Peacock's 'household production', not using kilns; at most, part-time, village-level potters might have existed on occasion. There are hardly any sites where ceramics might have come from more than short distances away

---

[191] For east Yorkshire, see Whyman, *Late Roman Britain*, pp. 222–4, 343–58; at West Heslerton, one of the earliest Anglo-Saxon sites there, all ceramics are Anglian hand-mades from the start: Haughton and Powlesland, *West Heslerton*, p. 124; Whyman, *Late Roman Britain*, pp. 368–83. For effectively aceramic sites, see e.g. Green, *Poundbury*, I, p. 128; Härke, 'Briten und Angelsachsen', pp. 104–5 (Tatton in Cheshire).

[192] Hills, 'Did the people of Spong Hill'; Weber, 'Das Gräberfeld von Issendorf'. The fullest account of early Anglo-Saxon pottery is Myres, *A corpus*. For decoration and symbolism, see Richards, *The significance of form*. In settlements, 2% of ceramics were decorated at West Stow and 5% at Mucking: West, *West Stow*, I, p. 128; Hamerow, *Excavations at Mucking*, II, p. 51. At Spong Hill, the figure was 24% (Rickett, *Spong Hill, part VII*, pp. 126–7), because the attached cemetery was so important (84% of ceramics were decorated in the cemetery).

before the seventh century, or indeed in many places later. In the late sixth century the 'Illington-Lackford' group, a stamped ceramic type found quite extensively in west Norfolk, west Suffolk, and Cambridgeshire, shows more skilled production values, but even here the movement is more likely to be of the potters than the pottery, for the clays involved are all different; this is even clearer for the 'Sancton-Baston' group, defined by a set of dies found on wares in three cemeteries 160 km apart, stretching from south Lincolnshire to Yorkshire.[193] Such connections do tell us about wider exchange networks, but it is by no means certain that such potters were independent specialists, selling their skills and their wares as they travelled; some form of community gift-exchange is as plausible, perhaps alongside local commercial relationships (cf. above, pp. 694–5). The main point, however, is that levels of demand for basic artisanal goods were at a sufficiently low level in early Anglo-Saxon England that neither full-time professionals nor much of a commercial context needed to exist: the patterns of south-eastern Spain (above, p. 749), but here extended to an entire region. It can be added that household production is even more secure for clothing, for loom-weights are so common on settlement sites that every household could be assumed to have made its own clothes.[194] The contrast between fifth- to eighth-century settlements like West Stow (Suffolk) and Mucking (Essex) and contemporary Gaulish settlements like Goudelancourt (Aisne) is striking: they had similar building technologies, and no obvious high-status inhabitants, but the former had almost exclusively local and hand-made pottery—at Mucking only seventeen sherds of imported wares, mostly from Francia, were identified out of some 32,000—and the latter had a complex repertoire of wheel-made ceramics, some of it of high quality.[195] The relationship of peasant communities to wider exchange systems on each side of the Channel was entirely different.

It is not that peasantries in England had no access at all to wider-scale exchange. The much greater density of archaeological work in England than in some Continental regions allows us to supplement these observations with the evidence for more specialized productions and distributions. Iron or copper-alloy brooches, for example, so common in female graves that they can hardly be regarded as luxuries, can be arranged in localized stylistic groups by the late sixth century, which may indicate some complexity of

---

[193] See Myres, *Anglo-Saxon pottery*, pp. 132–6; Arnold, *An archaeology*, pp. 128–33.

[194] Arnold, *An archaeology*, pp. 92–5. Loom-weights tend to appear in female graves (see e.g. Härke, 'Early Anglo-Saxon social structure', p. 136), supporting the general assumption that weaving is a female occupation—see above, p. 557. John Hines in discussion in Ausenda, *After empire*, p. 70, cites a female grave at Lackford with a pottery die-stamp, which may fit with Peacock's argument, based on modern ethnographic observation, that household-level ceramic production is predominantly female too—see above, p. 704.

[195] West, *West Stow*, pp. 128–38; Hamerow, *Excavations at Mucking*, II, pp. 22–57 (p. 22 for imports); above, Ch. 8, n. 164, for Goudelancourt.

distribution.[196] Gold, silver, jewelled, and enamelled versions of these were, of course, luxuries, both requiring and representing relative wealth for their wearers; so was specialist textile work, like the embroidery Aldhelm mentions in the late seventh century.[197] These could have fairly wide distributions, although again whether this implies independent craftspeople moving from court to court, or dependants attached to single lords, is unclear— probably we can assume there were both. There is relatively little, however, in the Anglo-Saxon world before the late seventh century that implies any developed form of exchange network. The absence of any documentary evidence before that period means that we cannot say much about the origins of markets (even after 700, our evidence for them tends to cluster, significantly, in the coastal ports), although it may be that each kingdom's public assembly had some sort of fair attached to it.[198] But any exchange that did take place there would have been an optional extra; all the signs are that normal exchange was strictly local and small scale, and not necessarily all commercial—gift-exchange is as likely a basis for much of it.

This point is further illustrated by the patterning of imports into England, most of which came from, or through, northern Francia, which have been interestingly analysed by Jeremy Huggett and Chris Arnold. The wide spread of amber and crystal beads (respectively from the Baltic and central Europe) across the sixth- and seventh-century cemeteries of the whole of lowland England show us that there were some light goods being transported very widely in the sub-region, probably by pedlars. The example of Mucking shows that these goods could include pottery in small quantities, at least along the coast. But there is only one part of England where imports are at all common: Kent, the part of the island nearest to the Continent. Kent before 700 or so seems to have had a privileged relationship to Francia, with a substantial number of mostly luxury imports effectively restricted to that kingdom, such as gold, amethyst, and glass. Most Frankish pottery was found in Kent, too. Even when these are found elsewhere in England, they were presumably mostly funnelled through the Kentish ports, such as Sarre, Fordwich, or Dover. There were evidently some relatively rich people in Kent, powerful enough to control this exchange process. They were either rich enough to buy luxuries (although what they exported in return—slaves? wool?—is invisible archaeologically) or they became rich(er) through Frankish political largesse.[199] In principle, they might have been at the core of a

---

[196] See e.g. Hines, *The Scandinavian character*, pp. 117–68; Dickinson, 'Early Saxon saucer brooches', pp. 36–8; Arnold, *An archaeology*, pp. 135–46.

[197] Aldhelm, *Opera*, p. 18, ll. 70–1. For later high-status textiles see Ch. 6, n. 44.

[198] See Sawyer, 'Kings and merchants'; it is significant how generic this article is, for the evidence is so slight.

[199] See Ch. 6, n. 26. Sarre and Fordwich are cited in BCS 189 (S 29). For the patterns of ceramic imports see Evison, *A corpus*, based on cemetery sites up to 1979; for Mucking see above, n. 195.

commercial demand for products, sufficiently consistent that a larger-scale artisan production inside Kent could develop, as would have been normal in Francia or the Mediterranean. But, even in Kent, this did not happen. There was no Kentish wheel-thrown pottery tradition, or, probably, glassmaking either. There may briefly have been a flint-tempered fast-wheel coarse ware in eastern Kent, for a group of such vessels has been found between Canterbury and Thanet, and the geology of their fabric is right; but even this could have come from the chalk of the Calais region. Either way, it is only documented in the middle third of the seventh century, and, if local to Kent, evidently did not take root.[200] This throws into relief the absence of such wares elsewhere. I conclude that even wealthy people in England, even if close to Francia both politically and geographically, did not as yet need production and exchange networks that could be separated from local social hierarchies.

The concentration of imports before the late seventh century on Kent in itself shows that exchange was structured, and probably consciously directed, through political relationships, doubtless above all royal, but also aristocratic, and, increasingly, ecclesiastical. The development of *emporia* in the next century is a further exemplification of this (above, pp. 681–90). The fact that these centres were apparently distributed one per kingdom already makes the point: Hamwic (Southampton) for Wessex, London for Mercia, Ipswich for East Anglia, York for Northumbria (an *emporium* for Kent has not as yet been pinned down, but it had managed for a long while with imports coming through a variety of entry-points, so perhaps still did). Hamwic and Ipswich could well have had structural links to nearby royal centres, Winchester and Rendlesham. Richard Hodges has done the most to characterize the socially embedded exchange that could result from a gateway site like Hamwic, which he calls, following the geographer Carol Smith, a 'dendritic' exchange system: in this model, goods would go from such a gateway directly to political centres, from which they might be exchanged further, either commercially or as prestige gifts from kings. There has been recent debate about this, as already noted (p. 684), for Hamwic pioneered relatively large-scale artisanal production in Britain, and recent scholars have often preferred to see eighth-century Southampton as a standard urban artisanal centre for a surrounding territory. But in fact Hamwic's own pottery, all still hand-made, is hardly attested in its hinterland (the same is true of its coins, Series H sceattas). The distribution of imports, too, both ceramics and metalwork, is highly uneven across mainland Hampshire, privileging, outside Hamwic, Winchester and the subsidiary harbour at Porchester, as Katharina Ulmschneider's work shows. The late eighth-century or (perhaps more certainly) early ninth-century

---

[200] Macpherson-Grant, 'Early–late Saxon continental imports', pp. 173–9; John Cotter (pers. comm.).

iron-smelting site at Ramsbury, not far away in Wiltshire, was also probably in a West Saxon royal centre, and could have been a further part of this restricted political exchange system; the more recently discovered smelting site at Romsey, 15 km from Hamwic, seems to have been similar. The kings who founded (and patronized) Hamwic were evidently capable of operating on a rather larger scale than their predecessors; but these patterns resemble the non-market relationships of Kentish exchange more than they do the networks of the Continent. Even bulk production, which we are now beginning to see for the first time, was still being run in the traditional socially dominated ways. The fact that Hamwic's (and Ramsbury's) own products were fairly utilitarian is not an argument against this, it must be added; kings needed these goods too, as much as they needed imported prestige items, and seem to have remained happy to dominate their distribution.[201]

The only *emporium* to have a visibly different relationship with its political hinterland was Ipswich, and ceramics is a clear guide to that. Ipswich ware, which was made from c.720, was still a partially hand-made ware, but it was finished on a slow wheel; and it was evidently produced on a considerable scale. It is found very widely in East Anglia, effectively on every site, at least in Norfolk, and was, for nearly two centuries, almost the only such production in England. Ipswich ware was in fact the first English ceramic type which we can be certain was even made in a kiln, and a whole area of workshops has been found for the ware, in an organizational leap forward obviously borrowed from Francia—although Frankish fast-wheel technology was evidently considered unnecessary. The availability of the ware across East Anglia again parallels that of local coin types (Series Q and R sceattas), although these two series do not fully overlap, and indicate some microregional differences inside East Anglia. The blanket distribution of Ipswich ware stops abruptly at the political frontier of the kingdom, but it can nonetheless be found fairly widely throughout eastern England, particularly in parts of Yorkshire, Lincolnshire, Cambridgeshire, and Essex, mostly on high-status sites but not only; outside that area, it is somewhat rarer.[202]

This ceramic distribution is a convenient introduction to a distinct subregional development: eastern England, from the Tyne to the Thames, was

[201] Hodges, *Dark age economics*, pp. 16 ff.; idem, *Primitive and peasant markets*, pp. 16–25, 42–9. For the Hamwic debate, see Ch. 10, n. 201. A sensible survey is Yorke, *Wessex*, pp. 299–308. For Hamwic-made pottery types, see Timby, 'The Middle Saxon pottery'; he sees most of them as household types in Peacock's sense (p. 110). For Series H sceattas, see Metcalf, *Thrymsas and sceattas*, III, pp. 321–32. For Hampshire distributions, see Ulmschneider, *Markets, minsters*, pp. 49–52, 64–5, 83–4, 107, with pp. 39, 162, for Romsey; for Ramsbury, Haslam, 'A Middle Saxon iron smelting site' (pp. 56–64 for the royal interest). The basic current survey of pottery distributions in *emporia* as a whole is Blackmore, 'Pottery'.

[202] For Ipswich ware, Blinkhorn, *The Ipswich ware project*, as yet unpublished, will be the basic point of reference; for a summary, see idem, 'Of cabbages and kings'. I am grateful to the author for discussion. For its distribution, see e.g. Hamerow, 'Settlement mobility', pp. 13–14; Williamson, *The origins of Norfolk*, pp. 79–82; Silvester, 'The addition of more-or-less undifferentiated dots', pp. 27–8 (for the boundary of Norfolk as important); Vince, 'The growth of

by the eighth century generating different sorts of exchange patterns to the rest of the island. There are earlier signs of it as well: perhaps already the sixth-century movement of potters, as with the Illington-Lackford group; also, in the seventh century, the beginnings of wider networks of exchange for hand-made wares, like the granite-tempered pottery of Charnwood Forest in Leicestershire, which reached Yorkshire, and the wide distribution across the East Midlands of shell-tempered Maxey ware.[203] Both of these show that more elaborate patterns were developing, perhaps involving market relationships, which Ipswich ware would use in the next century. This was new in England. We cannot be sure about it in the seventh century; but Ipswich ware distributions make it clear in the eighth, for their generality must indicate the existence of commercial networks, no longer channelled exclusively by political relationships, and involving bulk exchange.

There are some parallels to this further north along the coast as well. Some of the monasteries of the north-east, Whitby, Monkwearmouth, Jarrow, are sites on which another eighth-century slow-wheel ceramic type, similar to Ipswich ware but not identical, has been found. These monasteries were also, of course, foci for prestige imports too. As we have seen (p. 341), Flixborough in Lincolnshire is a good example of this, with a wide array of imports (including Ipswich ware, some Continental pottery, and Eifel quernstones) and artisanal production as well. This was coming, by the eighth century, to be increasingly common on the east coast, on high-status sites and more modest sites alike. The network of production and demand on such sites points to an increasingly complex exchange network in eastern England, going in East Anglia some way inland, which, for the first time in the region, faintly resembles those on the Continent. It was not as large-scale as some of those in Francia; even Ipswich ware, the most widely spread product we know of, only had a maximum radius of easy availability of c.180 km, and only sea routes made it as wide as that. Ipswich ware was also not, as far as we can yet see, imitated outside the northern monastic context, even in other *emporia* which imported it, London and York.[204] But we at least find a parallel to Continental patterns emerging in these areas, at the end of our period. This would a century later be taken further by the first

market centres', pp. 188–92 (for its rarity in Mercia and restriction to high-status sites—indeed, one major East Midlands site, Northampton, only had four sherds of Ipswich ware, Williams *et al.*, *Middle Saxon palaces*, pp. 46–53). For the sceattas, see Metcalf, *Thrymsas and sceattas*, III, pp. 483–523, cf. 601–7.

[203] For 'Charnwood ware', Williams and Vince, 'The characterisation'. For Maxey ware, see, still, Addyman, 'A Dark-Age settlement', pp. 47–58, and Hurst, 'The pottery', pp. 307–8.

[204] For north-eastern pottery, Hurst, 'The pottery', pp. 303–7. For Flixborough, see Ch. 6, n. 91. For other Lincolnshire sites, see Ulmschneider, *Markets, minsters*, pp. 31–5, 85 ff. Richards, 'What's so special about "productive" sites?', makes the point that (in eastern England at least) eighth-century sites normally have numerous finds. London: Blackmore, 'La céramique', pp. 136–41, with eadem, 'Pottery', pp. 27, 33 (which wonders if London may have imitated Ipswich ware); York: Mainman, *Pottery*, p. 568.

fast-wheel potteries of England, which developed around the Fens, that is, on the edge of East Anglia, in the late ninth century, at Stamford, Thetford, St Neots, and also at York.[205]

This narrative of a slow and highly patchy development of bulk commercial production and exchange in post-Roman England can be tied reasonably closely to the picture of social development set out in Chapter 6 (pp. 340–51). It was argued there that stable hierarchies of wealth and political power did not crystallize in England before the late sixth century, and only then did polities as large as a single county and upwards begin to appear. From then on, royal power and aristocratic power developed hand in hand. All the same, it was only in the eighth and, above all, the ninth centuries that local tribal hegemonies over partially autonomous peasantries began to sharpen, and develop into more formalized landlord–tenant relationships, that is to say into the patterns of domination and exploitation which had always been normal in Francia. Kings were presumably relatively rich, as Sutton Hoo shows, but it was not until the eighth century and after that the lands of lay aristocrats and churches began to be stable sources of rents and dues on a large scale. The growing articulation of political structures, particularly in eighth-century Mercia, meant that lasting local hierarchies became possible too. From here on, a steady accumulation of power and wealth can be observed, culminating in the unusual centralization of the late Anglo-Saxon state.

If we set this account against the exchange-based narrative just outlined, it can be seen that the very simple productive patterns of the fifth and sixth centuries fit with the relatively undifferentiated socio-political structures of the same period. The seventh century, when kings and aristocrats were crystallizing their power but non-tribal land tenure had not yet developed, can be seen represented in the example of Kent, with no market relationships despite its accumulations of wealth; indeed, it could be proposed that Kent had already developed in this direction earlier than other kingdoms, before the late sixth century. This pattern was still visible, but on a rather larger scale, in eighth-century Wessex. By contrast, East Anglia slowly developed market exchange, which seems to have been generalized by the eighth century. This sub-regional differentiation is only visible in the archaeology; English written documentation gives us a more homogeneous impression (and, for the specific case of East Anglia, is almost entirely lost before the tenth century). But it seems to me clear, all the same; and also not surprising, for there is no reason why such an economically and politically fragmented region as early Anglo-Saxon England should all have developed in the same way. It was East Anglia, and perhaps the east coast of England as a whole (though not Kent), which developed large-scale exchange relationships first, in the eighth century. I would argue that this implies that the elites of East

[205] Hurst, 'The pottery', pp. 314–28; Mainman, *Anglo-Scandinavian pottery*, pp. 400–11.

Anglia were also the first to be properly established as landowners, with a secure control over substantial agricultural rents from peasants, and thus a stable source of wealth and demand, a century earlier than elsewhere in England (above, pp. 347–50).[206] East Anglian kings may have matched Offa's Mercia in their state formation, too, although this is harder to track archaeologically. And it was also in and near East Anglia, as just noted, that good-quality ceramic production finally emerged in the late ninth century, with equivalents found across Wessex and Mercia in the tenth, signs of the final stabilization of aristocratic wealth there too.

This broad-brush characterization obviously covers some sharp micro-regional and sub-regional differences; nor, given the problems of our documentary evidence (p. 348), will we ever have the full picture of exactly how aristocratic power stabilized in each area. Before leaving English developments, however, two more points are worth making, concerning, respectively, East Anglia and Mercia. When East Anglia, and eastern England in general, emerges into our written documentation after 900 or so, it is, certainly, a sub-region with many rich landowners, but it is also one of an unusually widespread independent peasantry by English standards. The early crystallization there of market relations and aristocratic power does not seem to have meant the abolition of peasant landowning, as it would do in much of Midland and southern England. There are various ways this could be explained. These are areas of Danish conquest in the late ninth century, and it may be that Danish lords accepted greater degrees of peasant autonomy, which certainly still existed in Denmark, in the areas they controlled. We also must recognize the generally disruptive effects on aristocratic hegemonies of periods of political confusion. All the same, as Dawn Hadley shows, the fragmented land tenure of the late Anglo-Saxon northern Danelaw is probably pre-Danish in some of its structures.[207] It may be better simply to say that aristocratic tenurial crystallization could happen in different ways in different places, in some areas in large blocks, in others in more fragmented units, and that the east–west contrast in England is an instance of this. But it is also important to remember that it was simply the level and the stability of aristocratic demand that mattered for exchange networks, not the total subjection of all peasant neighbours. East Anglia was in this respect, at least, more similar to the Rhineland and Italy than to Worcestershire or Hampshire.

The second point relates to Mercia. Offa's and Cenwulf's Mercia in the 760s–820s was the first English polity which can be shown to have had sufficiently articulated political structures that one could call it a state,

---

[206] For East Anglian development up to 700, see Scull, 'Before Sutton Hoo'. For the eighth century in eastern England, see above all Moreland, 'The significance of production', pp. 87–98; on pp. 98–104 he argues that these developments took place across wider areas of England than is proposed here.

[207] Hadley, *The northern Danelaw*, esp. pp. 108–31.

rather than a tribal kingdom (above, pp. 344–5). Mercian hegemony was generalized in southern England, with kingdoms like Essex and Kent actually annexed to Mercia (in the case of Kent, with some difficulty). But it is also arguable that the Mercian aristocracy were only then at the beginning of the process by which they established full territorial control over their peasantries. This has parallels in the archaeology. Worcester cathedral, for example, accumulated great quantities of land in the eighth century, thanks to royal and aristocratic grants, as its documents show, but this sort of landed hegemony does not translate into any identifiable concentrations of material wealth on the ground. No known sites in this sub-region remotely match a Flixborough; those that have been excavated, indeed, have hardly any finds at all. Even Droitwich, an important early exchange centre because of its salt, already cited in a royal privilege of 716–17, with productive continuities going back into the Roman period, has only hand-made wares, and few signs of non-local objects of any kind, in the fifth- to eighth-century levels of one of its salt-production sites. Salt distributions, as we have seen (p. 700), do not have to provide a guide to any other form of exchange network, and here evidently did not. Mercia had little coastline, and in particular was cut off from the coasts closest to Francia until it took London in the late seventh century; it would be reasonable to presume that the considerable attention paid to that town by the kings thereafter means that the dendritic route from the port to royal centres in the Midlands (as yet undiscovered) was important. This would, all the same, only make Mercia like Wessex, not like East Anglia. Offa's hegemony included rights in kingdoms that were much more economically developed than the Mercian heartland. He doubtless learnt from them; all the same, it is significant that the most striking material survival yet known from his kingdom is the Dyke, an impressive proof of the aggregation of royal powers over people, but not in any sense a sign of private wealth or commercial exchange. The development of exchange relationships can be seen, broadly, as a sign of the accumulation of wealth, but it need not be a reliable guide to the distribution of political power.[208]

The other regions and sub-regions of the North fit fairly well into this array of patterns. Western Britain, as already noted, went largely aceramic in the early fifth century. Only in the far south-west did local hand-made wares survive, or become established, for they are found on some west Cornish sites, in particular, by the sixth century or perhaps a century later. This does

---

[208] For Worcester's lands, see e.g. Dyer, *Lords and peasants*, pp. 11–16; Bassett, 'Churches in Worcester', p. 238; for Droitwich, see *BCS* 138 (S 97), with Hurst, *A multi-period salt production site*, pp. 69, 75–9. Catholme in Staffordshire has particularly few finds: Losco-Bradley and Kinsley, *Catholme*. For London, Kelly, 'Trading privileges'; for Offa's Dyke, Squatriti, 'Digging ditches'. For Mercia's weak urbanism, see Vince, 'The growth of market centres'.

not in itself have to prove economic simplicity, if glass, wood, and metal filled the gap, but there is little sign of large-scale productions of these either. The high-status sites of the late fifth and sixth centuries in Wales, Cornwall, and Somerset did have imported luxuries, or what were seen as luxuries here at least, African and Phocaean RS, DSP *atlantique*, eastern Mediterranean wine amphorae, and glass (cf. above, pp. 327–8). Political leaders here must have consciously chosen a Mediterranean and Aquitainian connection, clearly distinguishable from the north Frankish connection which came through Kent. On the other hand, the quantities of imports were small, and the Mediterranean link was brief. In the seventh and eighth centuries imports continued (by now they were glass and Aquitainian 'E ware'), but were no more elaborated; and, indeed, there were no further developments in the exchange patterns of Wales and Cornwall across our entire period or for some time later. High-status sites paralleled those of Kent; indigenous productions were highly local and small scale, whether of utilitarian products or of luxuries for rulers (as with the copper-working at Dinas Powys in south Wales, or the gold and silver in early Welsh literature). This fits the fact that in Wales there is no sign of the crystallization of either royal or aristocratic power beyond seventh-century Welsh and English levels, at any time before the eleventh century (above, pp. 351–4).[209]

Ireland was not dissimilar, as we have seen (pp. 354–7). It imported some 'E ware' (in exchange for leather?) in the seventh century, at least to relatively high-status sites; the far north-east also had its own hand-made pottery, Souterrain ware, from then on, which hardly, however, extends outside Counties Antrim and Down. Waterlogged sites show that wood was a widely used alternative, and could be turned with some skill, although it was also unlikely to have been exchanged very far. High-status sites show a fair amount of artisanal activity, copper-working above all, but also iron, bone, and textiles, probably by dependent artisans, but no significant evidence of exchange except for a handful of imports; Lagore in County Meath, the main royal site to have been excavated on the island, was described as being 'almost completely self-contained' by its excavator. Ireland was, of course, further from the Continent, and its closest sea connections were with western Britain, itself materially unprepossessing in this period. But Irish social structures, as we have also seen (pp. 359–63), tended towards the steady redistribution of wealth and the absence of articulated economic hierarchies, and I have already connected this with the simplicity of Irish

---

[209] For local hand-mades, see e.g. Rahtz, *Cadbury Congresbury*, p. 155; for Cornwall, Thomas, 'Grass-marked pottery' and Hutchinson, 'Bar-lug pottery', who disagree about dating. For imports, see Ch. 6, n. 63, summarized by Wooding, *Communication and commerce*, pp. 41–50, 72–84, with the addition of Hill, *Whithorn*, pp. 315–26. For copper-working, see Alcock, *Dinas Powys*, pp. 47–9; cf. e.g. Aneirin, *Y Gododdin*, LXV, XC; *Culhwch ac Olwen*, ll. 60–81, etc., for silver and gold. For the continuing simplicity of Welsh material culture, Arnold and Davies, *Roman and early medieval Wales*, pp. 168–71.

exchange networks. Irish peasants got to keep more of their surplus than their equivalents elsewhere—including in England, after the eighth century—but this in itself militated against the creation of enough demand to generate more than occasional exchange, often directed to and by high-status recipients, or else perhaps focused on the fairs at the annual assemblies, *óenaige*, of each kingdom. For the rest, artisanal activity was the work of households and single dependent craftspeople, and stayed so for an unusually long time.[210]

The Danish situation was a little more complex. It must first be said that this complexity did not lie in its ceramics, which were almost all hand-made, and highly localized, throughout our period and for some centuries to come. Danish pottery is not that well studied (it is not always even published in site reports), although we do have typologies from Stig Jensen and Hans Jørgen Madsen. By 800 or so the region can be roughly divided into four ceramic areas, northern and southern Jutland, Fyn, and the east, with slightly different vessel types in each, but with little sign that even these areas were internally structured by extra-local exchange.[211] Denmark, like other northern regions, had ceramic imports: Norwegian pottery at Stavad in north Jutland in the fourth and fifth centuries, Swedish at Lundeborg on Fyn in the same period, and, on a rather larger scale, Rhineland wares in the eighth century on the high-status site of Sorte Muld on Bornholm or in the *emporia* of Ribe and (after c.780) Hedeby in south Jutland. But Rhineland ceramics did not reach ordinary rural sites until the ninth century at the earliest, even in south Jutland, Denmark's most economically complex area. At Ribe, in the eighth century, there has come to light a local wheel-made ceramic type, using local fabrics but also, evidently, an imported technology, presumably from the Rhine; but, as in Kent, this did not root itself. Clearly, the demand for relatively good-quality pottery was satisfied by imported wares, mostly to high-status sites, and did not need to be supplemented by a local alternative, which did not appear in Denmark until as late as 1200.[212]

One the other hand, the high-status sites of Denmark, its *emporia*, 'central places' and 'magnate farms', are full of more expensive imports too: in

---

[210] See Wooding, *Communication and commerce*, pp. 64–92; Edwards, *The archaeology*, pp. 73–5, and Mallory and McNeill, *The archaeology of Ulster*, pp. 217–19, for Souterrain ware; Hencken, 'Lagore crannog' (p. 12 for the quote). One well-known literary reference to Irish trade with Gaul is *Vita Filiberti*, c. 42, where the Irish are exporting shoes and clothing. For *óenaige*, see Ch. 6, n. 133.

[211] See Jensen, 'Et grubehus fra Darum', with Ethelberg, 'Die eisenzeitliche Besiedlung', pp. 142–50; Madsen, 'Vikingetidens keramik'. I have not managed to see Siemen, *Bebyggelser og keramik*. For the ninth century Hübener, *Die Keramik von Haithabu*, is basic.

[212] See Nissen-Jaubert, *Peuplement*, pp. 222–3 (Stavad); Stilborg, 'Ceramic contacts' (Lundeborg); Madsen, 'Vikingetidens keramik', p. 227 (Sorte Muld); Näsman, 'Exchange and politics', pp. 46–7 (Ribe); Janssen, *Die Importkeramik von Haithabu*. For rural sites in the ninth century onwards Muller-Wille, 'Hedeby und sein Umland'; Madsen, 'Vikingetidens keramik', pp. 227–8. Imports are rare in Vorbasse in the eighth to tenth centuries: Hvass, 'The Viking age settlement', pp. 168–9.

particular, metalwork in gold and silver, and glass (above, pp. 366–8). These have been the focus of attention for recent scholars, and it is easy to see why, with Gudme on Fyn by far the richest early medieval site north of Francia, and a whole host of other interesting sites now available to explore. Denmark was very much richer than any of the sub-regions of Britain, even Kent, in the field of luxury metalwork, and Ireland was very isolated by comparison. All the same, in terms of the patterns of exchange discussed in this chapter, it is with Kent that Denmark can most usefully be compared. It is striking how targeted imports were in Denmark: gold from the Roman empire to the Stevns area of Sjælland in the fourth century or to Gudme (via its port, Lundeborg) in the fifth and sixth, but hardly beyond, even though craftsmen at Gudme itself were certainly active in working that gold; glass to the 'magnate farm' of Dankirke near Ribe, but not to well-excavated villages like Vorbasse. Similarly, the whole array of imports and local crafts in eighth-century Ribe must have largely been destined for a high-status (presumably royal) centre, for they are rather less common elsewhere; the comparator is here Hamwic and Wessex.[213] This fits with the weak local exchange structures implied by Danish ceramics, and it nuances the impression left by all that gold. Danish elites were rich in gold, to be sure, or in silver later, but they were *like* those of Kent or Wessex: they were defined by privileged links to the major source of large-scale production in the North, northern Gaul/Francia. These interregional links were sometimes, perhaps, political exchanges of gifts (or Roman/Frankish gifts in return for deference); sometimes booty from armed attack (in the fifth century, and again in the ninth); sometimes, indeed, even commerce. But once they were on Danish soil they were directed, dendritically, to political centres, and were little exchanged beyond them. The lack of complex internal exchange patterns in our period argues for a generalized aristocratic wealth and dominance that was rather less than Danish luxuries might imply. It fits, however, the tribal hierarchies which I proposed earlier for the region on different grounds (pp. 372–6). Bulk exchange inside Denmark would, once again, have to await the local crystallization of aristocratic power over the peasantry, and this is unlikely to have begun much before the eleventh century.

The North Sea was marginal for the Franks, but the Frankish goods, like the Roman ones before them, which were carried on it were of great importance as the markers of status for all of the regions north of the Rhine mouth and the English Channel. The relationship between the northern regions and Francia was not exactly colonial, for the Franks did not control them politically (although this has been argued for sixth-century Kent, and Frisia and Saxony were indeed conquered in the eighth); but it was not in any sense

---

[213] See Ch. 6, nn. 152, 155, 158, with, in general, Näsman, 'Exchange and politics', an important survey. He is more upbeat about Ribe as a generalized exchange centre (see e.g. p. 42).

a relationship between equals. The Merovingian kingdoms were the super-power of the North, with unusually sharp tenurially based hierarchies, right next door to a set of very small-scale tribal hierarchies with unusually little social differentiation. It is not surprising that all known bulk artisanal production and exchange up to the early eighth century is Frankish, and indeed for that matter the majority of luxury craftworks too. Francia was also the producer of the only foodstuff to have a long-distance distribution in the North, wine. It is very hard to see what Frankish producers got in exchange for the products they sent north, and it is not implausible that many of them were political gifts, sent to increase Frankish prestige; but they were a minor part of Frankish production. Conversely, they made up a high proportion of the locally available luxuries of Britain, Ireland, Denmark alike, and even utilitarian goods like wine and ceramics were in effect luxuries once they crossed the sea. The ways they extended into each of the northern regions operate as a sort of barium meal, which makes clearer the nature of the exchange systems in each, and how they changed over time.

There was a fair amount of North Sea exchange, it is true. By the eighth century there was more of it than could be found on the seaways of at least the western Mediterranean, as is shown by the large size of Dorestad and the lack of any equivalent to that port in our southern regions between the eclipse of Marseille in the late seventh century and the rise of Venice in the late eighth (pp. 689–91). But, as has been stressed repeatedly in this chapter, the important patterns of production and exchange were internal to regions. And here it is clear that northern Francia and the other northern regions were two totally different worlds. In Francia, we find complex production and distribution systems extending up and down all the great rivers and (to a lesser extent) linking river basins too, with high levels of royal, aristocratic, and ecclesiastical demand, and urban centres surviving and developing to satisfy them. In Britain and the rest of the North, by contrast, we find, even after three centuries of slowly increasing political power, above all dendritic exchange, with rulers controlling the distribution of imports and local artisanal production, and probably only East Anglia, after 700, possessing a more commercial exchange system. Aristocracies had not separated themselves enough from their peasant neighbours and depend-ants to become stable sources of large-scale demand. This process was, certainly, beginning by 800, but it would only be developed fully in future centuries. Only then would interregional bulk trade take off in the North, with the Frankish lands by now more evenly matched to those of England or Scandinavia, and regional specializations developing in the eleventh and twelfth centuries—not only wine in the Seine–Rhine region but wool in England and Flanders, fish in Norway, timber in Norway and central Germany (cf. above, p. 292). This exchange was still much less important than the exchange network inside regions, but it was much more active than it had been. It too was, however, ultimately fuelled by aristocratic demand—

as was, by then, the revived commerce of the Mediterranean as well. It is the crucial importance of demand, above all for bulk products distributed internally to regions, which makes macroeconomic models of medieval historical change based on long-distance exchange alone not so much wrong as, largely, irrelevant.

11. Conclusions

My intention throughout this chapter has been to argue for a primacy of causal factors internal to regions when assessing economic change in our period, rather than stressing long-distance relationships as the most important theme to study. The major underpinning of the analysis here has been a study of demand, above all for bulk goods, for the scale of bulk exchange is the main marker of the complexity of regional economic systems. As argued in the first section, the wealth that underpinned large-scale demand was essentially the wealth of the landowning aristocracy; other things being equal, then, a complex economic system meant a rich aristocracy and vice versa. The fiscal system, if it was strong enough on a regional level, could also fund a rich ruling class with its own buying power, as well as creating a movement of goods taken in taxation which itself could act as an infrastructure for commercial distribution. The type-example for a complex regional economy based on aristocratic wealth in our period was northern Francia (with Syria and Palestine a close second, for aristocrats were rich there too, although economic structures were much more localized); the type-example for a complex regional economy based on taxation was Egypt, the most complex of all our regions in fact (with the Byzantine empire offering a greater regional coherence, based on taxation, than could have been expected given the simplicity of some local economies there). Regions like these were the basic building blocks of the economy of the post-Roman world, where indeed we can speak in regional terms at all—for many regions, such as Spain and Italy, were by the end of our period only sets of smaller sub-regional and microregional economies, with relatively few links between them, and our focus must become more local still in order to follow their development.

This stress on the regional level is an empirical, not a methodological, point. It *was* possible in our period to create an interregional economic system based on the large-scale movement of bulk goods, often across long distances. The late Roman empire was one such, with its Mediterranean exchange system (or two systems, western and eastern), in which the density of circulation was facilitated by the needs of the state, but, once established, created its own structures of commercial exchange. These structures outlasted the failure of the fiscal motor (in the western Mediterranean longer than in the East), although they were still ultimately dependent on it, and could not survive indefinitely on their own: a fiscal infrastructure was necessary for regional economies to have more than marginal links with each other.[214] (The central medieval trading system of the Mediterranean was not based on fiscal relationships, it is true, for it was between sovereign states, but it also seems to have been on a smaller scale—foodstuffs, in particular, were generally less important than in the late Roman system, except for some Italian cities.) The Roman world-system lasted long enough for several sectors of the Mediterranean to develop economies dependent on it, which meant that they were seriously disrupted when it ended: the Tunisian heartland of Africa, south-eastern Spain, and the Antioch and Gaza areas, above all, and the Aegean to a lesser extent. Many of their inhabitants would have regarded interregional exchange as of crucial importance. But they were outweighed by those regions for which it was a relatively subordinate factor, for which, that is to say, the end of the Roman world-system was less important than the fate of local aristocracies and fiscal structures. By 800 the post-Roman world was firmly a world of regional and sub-regional economies, and their future histories were dependent on internal parameters, above all the scale of elite demand, except in those regions briefly reunited by 'Abbāsid fiscal recentralization. The way that elite demand was articulated has, accordingly, dominated not only this chapter but several others, notably Chapters 3 and 4 with their focus on fiscal and aristocratic resources respectively, and Chapter 5 with its focus on resource management.

It did prove possible in this chapter to establish at least basic cross-regional groupings, with some features in common. The western Mediterranean showed a common slow involution in demand, a concurrent localization of economic structures and economic simplification even at the sub-regional and microregional level. The extent of this process was different from area to area, and its local causes were different too, but there was a general trend between the fifth and the eighth century for aristocratic elites to become poorer throughout the western Mediterranean, which makes each of the different sub-regions there at least comparable. After our period, the reversal of this process, and the resultant growing internal complexity of sub-regional economies, was also fairly generalized here. In the eastern Mediterranean, one common denominator was the survival of the fiscal structures of the state, even across the seventh-century crisis, when taxation ceased abruptly to unify regions. This had very different consequences in different places, with Egypt maintaining a regional economic integration based on taxation alone, the Levant fragmenting economically until the 'Abbāsid period, and the Byzantine empire, the poorest of the three, keeping a basic fiscal coherence despite everything; here, nonetheless, the dialectic

---

[214] I used this argument in *Land and power*, p. 96, to oppose demand-led models as a whole; my view of how the latter worked was then too simplistic.

between fiscal and landowning structures maintained itself in all three regions, and comparisons between them could be made here too. The North was the most heterogeneous set, in that northern Francia was an unusually coherent economic region, and its northern neighbours, with their tribal aristocracies, were unusually simple and localized in their economies. This generated not so much a comparison as a contrast; the best one can say there is that it is necessary to make clear how much of a contrast it was, given the parallelisms that are regularly drawn between the very different worlds of Charlemagne and Offa. The contrast also generated an interregional exchange system in the North Sea which was, by 800, more articulated than anything in the Mediterranean; but here, too, it remained marginal to regional economies.

These groupings show that, in the matrix of elements which I have outlined as causal factors—fiscal demand, private demand, prior dependence on the Roman world-system—different regions or groups of regions put emphasis on different combinations. How these combinations worked together on the ground is an important framing for understanding the history of each region. But they are guides, above all, to comparison. Each region's economic history did not depend on structural links with its neighbours after the breakdown of the pan-Mediterranean Roman fiscal system, but, rather, on internal developments. Indeed, even the extent of the dependence of exporter regions on the Mediterranean-wide exchange network in the Roman period has to be explained in terms of the internal structures of the economy of each—for Egypt, a major exporter region, was not disrupted when that network ended, whereas Africa was: local economic and social development remained prior. This is true even though, globally, aristocracies became poorer everywhere between 400 and 800 (except in the Levant and Francia), and economies became simpler everywhere as a result (except in Egypt and Francia). The former was, in general terms, a product of instability, a long-term consequence of the break-up of the Roman empire, and the conquest of most of it by new political groupings (above, pp. 80–7); but the way it worked in detail was dependent on factors that were all internal.

It is not a little ironic that the economic history of the early middle ages—a period whose historians are in general transfixed by nuance and qualification—has been so influenced by a single sound-bite, Henri Pirenne's phrase: 'It is thus rigorously true to say that, without Mahomet, Charlemagne is inconceivable.'[215] People still quote it and paraphrase it, seventy years later, indeed perhaps more in recent years than a generation ago. The whole thrust of this chapter opposes its validity. Charlemagne's papal politics (which is what Pirenne was talking about in this passage) would probably not have been significantly different had the eastern Roman empire maintained its Mediterranean compass; and, above all, the wealth and political

[215] Pirenne, *Mahomet et Charlemagne*, pp. 174–5, my translation.

protagonism of the early Carolingians had nothing whatsoever to do with the Mediterranean, either positively or negatively, any more than the trajectories of the Merovingian period had had. To say that 'exchange complexity in the early medieval period was always the product of the accumulation of wealth inside regions' has far less resonance, unfortunately, but it seems to me truer to the past. We have to look at internal demand and its articulation in every case, focusing on how states took resources from their subjects and what they did with them, and on how great landowners did the same thing, that is, how they exploited their peasant dependants; and then how the resultant wealth allowed productive systems of different kinds to operate. These, put together, make up the basic economic history of the early middle ages.

Pirenne's phrase has had so much success in part because it fits in with the longstanding metanarrative of medieval economic history which seeks to explain the secular economic triumph of north-west Europe. In this perspective, there is a moment in time in which a formerly backward region, roughly that delineated by the Seine, Rhine, and Thames, seizes the reins of History (or at least of economic development) from the Mediterranean world. Perhaps this occurred in the reign of Charlemagne, or perhaps with the rural land-clearances and textile specializations of the eleventh and twelfth centuries (Pirenne himself would have said the latter), or indeed later, but at one point or another the *grands échanges* begin again, only in the North Sea this time, not in the Mediterranean (or not only, at least, for the Italian trading cities have to be recognized at least cursorily), and the scene is set for mercantile capitalism, and, eventually, industrialization, with the North-West as a centre and everywhere else a periphery. It must unfortunately be recognized that a metanarrative as simplistic as this is still widely believed, by medievalists and others. It is mistaken because it is teleological, assigning brownie points as it does to developments which produce our own world economy, and marginalizing those which do not; it is mistaken because it is so focused, whether ingenuously or disingenuously, on the countries of origin of most of the influential historians of the last century or so; and it is mistaken because its underlying economic assumptions so profoundly overvalue the determining role of long-distance exchange. We have seen that an interregional exchange network is economically peripheral unless it is in bulk goods, and that bulk exchange over long distances is dependent, in our period at least, on fiscal infrastructures, whether Roman or 'Abbāsid; the bulk commercial exchange between regions that did exist by 1200 (both in the North and in the Mediterranean) was even then a minor part of regional economies, and contributed relatively little to the long-term development of any of them until late in the middle ages. Even local commerce was not yet a causal motor by itself. There were perhaps some local exchange structures in some of our regions, most notably in Egypt, Syria, and Palestine, which were to an extent autonomous from political and tenurial power structures, in that they were based on interdependent specializations, in a hierarchy of market structures; but the ultimate motor of the economy everywhere was landed and fiscal demand. This pattern did not change, in the direction of permanent self-sustaining accumulation, for hundreds of years to come. Local markets, and a wider availability of cheap artisanal products, did gradually spread across nearly all our regions in the central middle ages, to be sure. But it does violence to any proper understanding of our period, or even of the central middle ages, to locate any of it in any teleology towards capitalism. Capitalist development would anyway have seemed more plausible to any future-orientated observer on the Nile, or, further afield, on the Yangtse, than on the Thames or the Rhine, in any century before the thirteenth and probably later still.[216]

Our ceramic evidence is often patchy, and always provisional, but it does allow us to draw broad distinctions between our regions, which fall, around 800, into three rough groups. Egypt was the most internally complex of our regions, followed by northern Francia and then the Levant, and then, probably, the Byzantine empire. A network of more fragmented sub-regions follow, with pockets of complexity and simplicity, southern Italy, southern Gaul, Andalucía, Africa, northern Italy, central Spain, East Anglia, in each of which there was, in most places, enough aristocratic demand to support some professional production and articulated exchange. In some regions and sub-regions concentrations of wealth were not sufficiently great to generate independent exchange systems, as in parts of inland Greece, south-east Spain, Midland and southern England, Wales, Ireland, Denmark. In terms of the scale of artisanal production, as seen in ceramics, Egypt probably had at least one 'manufactory', in Peacock's terms, the Antinoupolis kiln complex (above, p. 762); the first group of regions had a mixture of 'nucleated' and 'individual workshops'; the second group had 'individual workshops' above all; in the third group, the most elaborate ceramics were produced by semi-professional 'household industries', or even, in some parts of the North, inside individual households.

We can assign our different regions and sub-regions to groups of this kind, on the basis of the detailed analyses set out in this chapter. Having done so, however, it must be reiterated that this categorization is not a league-table for economic sophistication, with all the implications for 'development' that such tables have in our own day. Rather, it gives us a rough guide to concentrations of wealth in our regions, and thus to the levels of exploitation in each. The simpler economies had less elaborate artisanal products, but

---

[216] For China shortly after our period, see e.g. Shiba, *Commerce and society*. But the East–West debate about economic transformation currently focuses on a period as late as the eighteenth century: for recent examples, see Pomeranz, *The great divergence*, and his critic, Parthasarathi, 'The great divergence'.

also less dependent peasantries, or at least smaller percentages of dependent peasants. In some places, particularly in the North, peasant communities were—or became in the post-Roman period—economically autonomous to such a degree that we can identify a change in the underlying mode of production, to what I have here called the peasant mode, although in most cases this was fairly short-lived (above, Chapter 9). Elsewhere, aristocracies dominated, but the degree of power and wealth they had varied very greatly. This parameter has constantly been stressed here as, in most cases, the main factor that explains the patterns of local, sub-regional, and regional exchange. Much has been written about early medieval aristocrats, perhaps too much, but one does not have to like them to recognize their importance. The extent to which the peasant majority could organize their lives and their productive activity separately from aristocratic power has been discussed in other parts of this book, in sections of each of Chapters 5–9. But in the context of exchange, it was aristocratic demand that mattered most. Along with the buying power of the representatives of the strongest states, who were, anyway, often the same people, they ultimately determined all the processes described in the last 130 pages.

General conclusions

THIS BOOK STRESSES variability so much that any overall conclusion is bound only to be partial: too many different approaches could be taken. And this is precisely the point. The early middle ages has always resisted synthesis; single generalizations about the motors of its development (Christianization, Roman–Germanic fusion, the breaking of the Mediterranean . . .) have always foundered. Accordingly, I have sought, not to provide 'The Answer', but the *framing* for answers, and generalizations that are consistently qualified by regional variation. Even then, the picture is incomplete. The variables chosen here, fiscal structures, aristocratic wealth, estate management, settlement pattern, peasant collective autonomy, urbanism, exchange, are not the full range that could have been provided. In particular, belief systems, values, gender roles and representations, ritual and cultural practices could in principle have been analysed in the same way, regionally and comparatively.[1] I did not exclude them because they are unimportant; this book absolutely must not be read as a counterblast to the trend towards cultural history as a central element in contemporary historical scholarship, which is a trend I applaud. I chose here to focus on themes I was personally most familiar with, knowing anyway that any framing is only going to be the outer dimensions of the picture—the content, the crucial part, would have to be very much more variegated. But it must at least be said that a set of variables such as those discussed here are intended to be a guide for others, as they seek to fill in the content.

If you analyse any given society (or polity, or culture, or economy), in any aspect of its practices, you have to be aware of how it compares with other societies, and which alternatives are the most useful comparators. Historians who study one society alone, never looking at others, lack an essential control mechanism, and not only risk misunderstanding, of what are real causal elements or turning-points and what are not, but also are in danger of falling into the metanarratives of national identity, the teleologies of what makes Us special, which bedevil the historical enterprise. This book aims at providing for the period 400–800 a framework for understanding which

---

[1] Good cross-cultural examinations of these variables across our period include Herrin, *Formation of Christendom*, and perhaps above all (despite its teleological title) Brown, *The rise of western Christendom*.

societies did have developments similar enough to be compared, and which did not, so that the search for parallels is not entirely unrooted. So Egypt might not very usefully be compared with Britain, at least in the elements discussed in these pages, but it has more structural analogies with Francia than might be expected, and these can be fruitfully developed, as also can those between Britain and Mauretania, and so on. It seems to me at least that the elements chosen here are important enough to be guides to a framing of that kind. It will have been noticed that the regions focused on here often fall into three rough groupings, the eastern and western Mediterranean and the North, with Gaul/Francia sometimes better seen with the western Mediterranean, sometimes with the North, and sometimes divided between the two. These groupings have been useful building blocks for comparison, but, as will also have been seen, they are not the only ones. Each reader may well find others, and I hope, indeed, that that will happen.

Many of the basic comparative points have been made in previous chapters. In Chapter 3, on the state, it was argued that there was a fundamental division between states whose resources were based on taxation and states whose resources were based on landowning, and that the former had much more power to intervene in a wide range of social and economic processes than the latter. This division, after the Roman empire broke up, was essentially one that separated the eastern Mediterranean from the rest; all the same, the way tax broke down in the West and the way this was compensated for by rulers varied considerably, as did the way it persisted in the East. In Chapters 4 and 6, on aristocratic power, the major division ran between regions in which aristocratic landowning was a prominent feature of local societies, maintaining the basic patterns of the Roman world, and those where these patterns broke down, or had never existed, and tribal relationships have to be analysed instead. Here the North was distinct from most of the Mediterranean, with Francia, the region where post-Roman aristocrats remained richest, belonging very firmly with the Mediterranean. Only a few sub-regions further south showed similar social structures to those north of the Rhine and English Channel: Mauretania, parts of southeast and northern Spain, inland Greece (and most of the rest of the Balkans, not analysed here), and, outside these, more isolated leopard-spots of peasant autonomy, as in some of the Appennine valleys, as we saw in Chapter 9. In Chapter 8, on rural settlement, it was the western Mediterranean that was different, with a much more variegated settlement pattern and, often, much weaker village identities than those further north and east, which fitted together with the varying capacities of peasant societies to act collectively against outsiders. In Chapter 11, on exchange, although in general eastern Mediterranean economies remained more active and articulated than those elsewhere, the unfolding of all the other variables showed the northern Frankish heartland as having an economic structure second in its complexity only to Egypt.

Can we discern, in this endless network of variables, any overall trends at all? The answer has to be yes; it is not the aim of this book to lose track of all the distinctiveness of the period, with the interplay of regional differences acting as a sort of camouflage paint, hiding real people and general patterns. There were no single prime movers, and every trend has its exceptions, but one can isolate a set of tendencies, which together mark the distinctiveness of the period 400–800, the period of the end of Roman unity and the earliest middle ages. Let us finish by looking at seven of these, which will also include some comment on tendencies which do not seem to me to be present in the period as well.

First, the early middle ages was a period in which fiscal structures were nearly universally simpler than they had been before. In the Romano-Germanic kingdoms they eventually disappeared altogether, as a result of armies settling on the land; in Byzantium and the Umayyad caliphate they persisted, but became in each case much more regionalized, with Egyptian tax staying in Egypt and tax from the Anatolikon theme essentially used for the army of the Anatolikon. The fiscal structuring that underlay the Mediterranean-wide exchange of the later Roman empire disappeared as soon as Roman control fragmented, but these further simplifications meant that even inside regions one could no longer be sure that there was fiscal support for local economic relationships. Only the continued coherence of tax-raising in Egypt, and the constant need to feed Constantinople and finance its elites from the Aegean sub-region, still supported regional economies by the eighth century; taxation in Arab Spain, and, interestingly, even in the Umayyad heartland of Syria and Palestine, made rulers rich (as it did also for the Merovingians, at least in the sixth century), but had rather less effect on economic complexity as a whole. This regionalization would be reversed after the late eighth century, at least temporarily, in the 'Abbāsid lands, but thereafter we will have to wait until the sixteenth century for any reunification of fiscal structures over large areas in the Mediterranean, under the Ottomans. In the West, effective tax systems did not begin again even at the local level until the eleventh century in England and the late twelfth elsewhere, and were not usually heavy or geographically wide-ranging until the thirteenth and fourteenth. Here, then, post-Roman changes continued to characterize Europe and the Mediterranean for a long time.

Second, the early middle ages marked a period of relative aristocratic weakness: in every post-Roman region except Francia and the Levant, aristocracies were both more localized and poorer than they had been under the empire. This was not the result of war in any simple sense; only Italy in the sixth century and Anatolia in the seventh saw wars that really devastated economies and societies on the regional level for more than short periods. But political uncertainty and regime change led to the displacement of elites in some cases, and to a situation in which aristocracies had less local purchase in nearly all cases (see above, pp. 255–7). This was a retreat in global aristocratic landowning, and also, probably, in local elite dominance over peasantries. Its consequences have been explored at several points in this book. One particularly important one was that a global decrease in aristocratic wealth meant a decrease in buying power, and thus exchange, as was discussed at length in Chapter 11; only in some eastern regions, notably Egypt, could the local state make up for that involution in demand. This trend to aristocratic weakness was generalized above all because political instability was so generalized in the aftermath of the end of imperial unity (and the major exception to this statement, Francia, therefore had to be analysed particularly carefully: pp. 168–203, 331–2). It was for the most part reversed after 800 or so, however, as the major geopolitical blocks of the second half of the early middle ages established themselves: Carolingian Francia, Umayyad Spain, the 'Abbāsid caliphate, the Byzantine empire. These had their own vicissitudes, but the local elites of the early ninth century had time to stabilize and establish greater local hegemonies again—and also more complex exchange systems—in most of our regions. The most dramatic political and structural shift of the late ninth and tenth centuries in our regions, the break-up of the Carolingian empire, was not to the disadvantage of aristocracies as a whole, who on the contrary established fully fledged local dominations in a way that very few of their predecessors and ancestors (not none, but very few) managed in our period. Even here, the aristocracies which survived the Carolingian system were usually different to, and smaller-scale than, their ninth-century predecessors; Carolingian crisis, like Roman crisis, led to a considerable localization. But they maintained greater power over peasantries than in our period, and in this respect the revival of aristocratic wealth after 800 did not end in the Frankish lands. On the contrary, it continued into the central middle ages and later, contributing to the active exchange of the period, as well as to a striking military aggression in all directions.[2]

Two specific consequences of that aristocratic weakening deserve characterization, as our third and fourth trends. Peasantries were, nearly everywhere, more autonomous. Sometimes they were more or less entirely independent of aristocratic domination even in their economic logic, and their economy can be described as being a separate, peasant, mode of production (above, pp. 533–47), particularly in the tribal areas of the North and some of the leopard-spots of peasant autonomy in the Romano-Germanic kingdoms. Even where aristocracies remained economically powerful, peasant landowning increased, and peasant political protagonism is more visible in many of our regions, both at the local level and, more ambiguously, at the level of political systems. The dimensions of peasant economic and political organization are exceptionally difficult to explore, as they left so little trace in written records; several ways of approaching them

---

[2] As explored in Bartlett, *The making of Europe*.

were tried in Chapters 7–9. But at least their outlines are visible, and they mark our period, particularly the sixth to eighth centuries in the West, as different to the ones both before and after.

The aristocracies of our period, weakened and dislocated by political crisis, also changed substantially in their culture and identity. Ancestry became temporarily less important nearly everywhere, as new political regimes came in which respected it less (this is even true in the Byzantine empire, the only regime which survived our period without a political break); and the civilian and secular ideology of the late Roman upper classes (or most of them) vanished nearly everywhere. From now on, aristocracies had a military identity, which lasted into the modern period. One casualty of this change was the literary culture of the Roman aristocratic tradition. This is the major cause of the abrupt changes in source material which mark the early middle ages, and which in the past led to people calling it the 'dark' ages. Actually, it is arguable that the early medieval centuries as a whole, particularly in the West, have a more extensive surviving written documentation than does the Roman empire; the weaknesses in early medieval evidence (especially outside the ecclesiastical sphere), although a problem for us, do not mark a retreat in this respect from the ancient world. But the changes in aristocratic identity and practice which underlie it are real, and must be recognized. (By contrast, the enormous simplification in material culture in our period cannot and should not be argued away; this is a direct consequence of the weakening of fiscal and aristocratic resources, and of peasant economic autonomies as well. But 'dark' age theorists did not, by and large, take it into consideration.) It was also, of course, the case that these aristocracies were in some cases ethnically new, of Germanic or Arab origin in particular. Ethnic difference has, however, been minimized in every case in this book; it seems to me of insignificant importance when the main lines of social and economic structures are considered, and was hardly visible even in cultural terms in many of the post-Roman regions—only in England and the caliphate did immigrant minorities have much effect here. But the *sort* of cultural change that ensued even there has close analogues in regions like Wales, or the Byzantine empire, in which immigration did not take place at all, so the fact of immigration in itself is not so significant as a causal factor.

Fifth, the post-Roman centuries showed much more regional divergence than did the period immediately preceding. This difference is a marker not only of the earliest middle ages, but of all subsequent centuries; but it began here. Of course, the provinces of the empire had not been fully homogeneous either; but our regions did at least have more in common in 400 than in 800. Underlying all this was the end of Roman unity, and the end of a need to maintain a *koinē* of culture from Carlisle to Aswān; it was *possible* for each region to spin off in a different direction, and so they did. The recognition of these differences, and the desire to explore their many parameters, was one of the major impulses behind my choice to study the period. The problem of exactly why each region developed differently from the relative homogeneity of the Roman empire underlies the image of the post-Roman world as an enormous laboratory experiment, in which a more elaborate urban tradition, say, or a more complex tax system, can be measured against each other, to see what patterns of social development each supported. The way the period has been presented in these pages owes much to that image; it is those differences in development which are the raw material for the comparisons that have been attempted at every stage.

Sixth, the regionalization of social development, joined to the weakness of most states and external powers, permitted a notable fluidity in most of our local societies. Of course, even the rigidities of the late empire did not prevent flexibility of practice, as has been true of every society in history, no matter how regulated. But the late Roman state did at least legislate to keep people in their place, and its hierarchies, backed by differential salary rates, were pointillistic in their detail. The early middle ages was in most places rather less structured than that. Titles and social labels were usually vaguer, and often little more than ad hoc status markers, which could be claimed, negotiated over, rather than assigned according to a set of rules. (One example is the word *nobilis*: see above, pp. 155, 182, 211.) Instead, what seems to have marked relative status most profoundly was differences in wealth, which were highly nuanced, and could be expressed in a variety of different ways. This fluidity marked aristocratic and peasant society alike. At the village level, too, peasants had a considerable variety of patronage networks they could connect into (above, pp. 438–41); it was not, in our period, a matter of having to accept the dominance of a single local lord, as in the *seigneurie banale* of much of the central medieval West. Flexibility thus marked the early middle ages by comparison both with preceding and with subsequent periods. It makes our task harder in many ways, but also more interesting: it forces us to look at social practice on every occasion, rather than simply at rules—which tell us little enough in any period, but which are close to meaningless as a guide to real social behaviour in ours.

Underlying all these tendencies—and this is my final point—is the crucial importance of the end of Roman imperial unity. The dissolution of the empire, in the West in the fifth century, in the East in the seventh, set off all these trends. The involution of fiscal systems started from there; and, above all, the weakening of regional aristocracies, and thus of exchange systems and of material culture as a whole, began there. All the continuities that have been tracked across the period by scholars of different persuasions, often (even if not always) rightly, should not counteract the basic fact of this shift. Not that one should engage in facile catastrophism either; life did not stop when the empire ended. The population doubtless dropped (above, pp. 547–50), but the land was not abandoned anywhere in our period, except maybe in some ecologically marginal microregions like the Belgian and

Dutch Campine or the Negev desert (pp. 509, 453). People carried on, using both old and new social strategies, as they generally do across moments of change. One has to recognize both the continuities and the novelties if one wants to study the period. But that there was a major change seems to me a great mistake to deny. How its parameters can be delineated in detail, in each of our very different regions, has been one of the major aims of the book. Some of its effects were beginning to be reversed in the ninth century, as aristocracies became more rooted again and exchange became more complex; a period of relative material simplicity is one of the most consistent markers of the earliest middle ages, of the eighth century above all. But that reversal was differently articulated in every region. Anyone who ever wants to follow that later process of rebuilding of local power structures, cross-culturally and comparatively, as has been attempted here for the period up to 800, will have to recognize the regional differentiation which was the longest-lasting product of the end of the Roman empire. But anyone who does that will, I hope, recognize that only a comparative approach will allow the setting-out of how societies did develop differently, and what those differences tell us about what really caused what in any society. A recognition of the validity and interest of each of these variegated patterns of social development reminds us that social change is overwhelmingly the result of internal factors, not external influences, which has been one of the arguments most often made in this book. Such a recognition is also the best protection against teleological interpretations of history, which are always misleading. If this book contributes to anything in the historical debate at large, I hope it contributes to combating them.

Bibliography

1. PRIMARY SOURCES

Note that primary sources edited in articles, or as parts of books dealing with other matters, will usually be found in the Secondary Sources section. I have often used the most convenient good edition of a text, not necessarily the most recent; *MGH* editions, in particular, have usually been preferred over later ones. In this section, definite articles and 'St' or variants are ignored for alphabetization purposes.

Acta S. Aunemundi, ed. P. Perrier, *Acta Sanctorum*, September, VII (Antwerp, 1760), pp. 744–6.

Actus pontificum cenomannis in urbe degentium, ed. G. Busson and A. Ledru (Le Mans, 1901).

Ägyptische Urkunden aus der königlichen Museen zu Berlin. Koptische Urkunden, I (Berlin, 1902–4).

Das älteste Traditionsbuch des Klosters Mondsee, ed. G. Rath and E. Reiter (Linz, 1989).

AGATHIAS, *History*, ed. R. Keydell, *Agathiae Myrinaei historiarum libri quinque* (Berlin, 1967).

AGNELLUS, *Liber pontificalis ecclesiae Ravennatis*, ed. O. Holder-Egger, *MGH, SRL* (Hannover, 1878), pp. 275–391.

AGOBARD OF LYON, *De grandine et tonitriis*, ed. L. van Acker, *Agobardi Lugdunensis opera omnia* (Turnhout, 1981), pp. 3–15.

ALCUIN, *Versus de patribus regibus et sanctis Euboricensis ecclesiae*, ed. P. Godman, *Alcuin, The bishops, kings and saints of York* (Oxford, 1982).

ALCUIN, *Vita Richarii confessoris Centulensis*, ed. B. Krusch, *MGH, SRM*, IV (Hannover, 1902), pp. 389–401.

ALCUIN, *Vita Willibrordi archiepiscopi Traiectensis*, ed. W. Levison, *MGH, SRM*, VII (Hannover, 1920), pp. 113–41.

ALDHELM, *Opera*, ed. R. Ehwald, *MGH, AA*, XV (Berlin, 1919).

Die alten mönchslisten und die Traditionen von Corvey, ed. K. Honselmann (Paderborn, 1982).

AMMIANUS MARCELLINUS, *Res gestae*, ed. J. C. Rolfe, 3 vols. (Cambridge, Mass., 1935–9).

ANDREAS, *Vita Walfredi*, ed. H. Mierau, in K. Schmid (ed.), *Vita Walfredi und Kloster Monteverdi* (Tübingen, 1991), pp. 38–62.

ANEURIN, *Y Gododdin*, ed. I. Williams, *Canu Aneirin* (Cardiff, 1938).

Anglo-Saxon charters, ed. A. J. Robertson (Cambridge, 1939).

The Anglo-Saxon Chronicle, III: *MS A*, ed. J. M. Bately (Cambridge, 1986).

Annales Bertiniani, ed. F. Grat *et al.*, *Les Annales de Saint Bertin* (Paris, 1964).

Annales Fuldenses, ed. F. Kurze, *MGH, SRG* (Hannover, 1891).

Annales ordinis S. Benedicti occidentalium monachorum patriarchae, ed. J. Mabillon, 6 vols. (Paris, 1703–39).

Annales Regni Francorum inde ab a. 741 usque ad a. 829, ed. F. Kurze, *MGH, SRG* (Hannover, 1895).

Annales Xantenses, ed. B. von Simson, *Annales Xantenses et Annales Vedastini*, *MGH, SRG* (Hannover, 1909), pp. 7–33.

ANTHIMUS, *De observatione ciborum, ad Theodoricum regem Francorum epistola*, ed. E. Liechtenhan (Berlin, 1963).

Anthologia Latina, I, ed. A. Riese (Leipzig, 1869).

The Antinoopolis papyri, ed. C. H. Roberts *et al.*, 3 vols. (London, 1950–67) [*P. Ant.*].

The Aphrodite papyri in the University of Michigan papyrus collection (P. Mich. XIII), ed. P. J. Sijpesteijn (Zutphen, 1977) [*P. Mich.* XIII].

Arabic papyri from Ḥirbet el-Mird, ed. A. Grohmann (Louvain, 1963).

Arabic papyri in the Egyptian library, ed. A. Grohmann, 6 vols. (Cairo, 1934–62) [*APEL*].

Arabic papyri. Selected material from the Khalili collection, ed. G. Khan (Oxford, 1992).

Arabische Briefe des 7. bis 13. Jhts aus den Staatlichen Museen Berlin, ed. W. Diem (Wiesbaden, 1997).

El Archivo condal de Barcelona en los siglos IX–X, ed. F. Udina Martorell (Barcelona, 1951).

ASTRONOMER, *Vita Hludowici imperatoris*, ed. E. Tremp, *MGH, SRG*, LXIV (Hannover, 1995), pp. 280–554.

AUGUSTINE OF HIPPO, *Contra litteras Petiliani*, ed. J.-P. Migne, *PL*, XLIII (Paris, 1845), cols. 245–388.

AUGUSTINE OF HIPPO, *Epistulae*, ed. A. Goldbacher, 4 vols. (Vienna, 1895–1911); ed. J. Divjak, *Lettres 1*–29** (Paris, 1987).

AUGUSTINE OF HIPPO, *Sermones*, ed. J.-P. Migne, *PL*, XXXVIII–XXXIX (Paris, 1841).

AUSONIUS, *Works*, ed. H. G. E. White, 2 vols. (London, 1919–21).

AUTPERT, *Vita Paldonis, Tatonis et Tasonis*, ed. V. Federici, *Chronicon Vulturnense*, I (Rome, 1925), pp. 101–23.

AVITUS OF VIENNE, *Epistulae*, ed. R. Pieper, *Alcimi Ecdicii Aviti Viennensis episcopi, Opera, MGH, AA*, VI.2 (Berlin, 1883), pp. 29–103.

AVITUS OF VIENNE, *Homiliae*, ed. R. Pieper, *Alcimi Ecdicii Aviti Viennensis episcopi, Opera, MGH, AA*, VI.2 (Berlin, 1883), pp. 103–53.

AL-BALĀDHURĪ, *Kitāb futūḥ al-buldān*, trans. P. K. Hitti, *The origins of the Islamic state*, I (New York, 1916).

Bala'izah, ed. P. E. Kahle, 2 vols. (Oxford, 1954).

BARSANOUPHIOS and JOHN, *Correspondance*, ed. F. Neyt, P. de Angelis-Noah, and L. Regnault, 3 vols. (Paris, 1997–2002).

BASIL OF CAESAREA, *The letters*, ed. R. J. Deferrari, 4 vols. (Cambridge, Mass., 1961–70).

BEDE, *Epistola ad Ecgbertum episcopum*, ed. C. Plummer, in Bede, *HE*, I, pp. 405–23.

BEDE, *Historia abbatum*, ed. C. Plummer, in Bede, *HE*, I, pp. 364–87.

BEDE, *Historia ecclesiastica gentis anglorum*, ed. C. Plummer, 2 vols. (Oxford, 1896) [Bede, *HE*].

Beowulf, ed. M. Swanton, 2nd edn. (Manchester, 1997).

BOBOLENUS, *Vita Germani abbatis Grandivallensis*, ed. B. Krusch, *MGH, SRM*, V (Hannover, 1910), pp. 33–40.

BOETHIUS, *De philosophiae consolatione*, ed. E. K. Rand and H. F. Stewart, 2nd edn., rev. S. J. Tester (Cambridge, Mass., 1973).

BONIFACE, *Epistolae*, ed. E. Dümmler, *S. Bonifatii et Lulli epistolae, MGH, Epp.*, III (Berlin, 1892), pp. 215–433.

BRAULIO OF ZARAGOZA, *Epistolae*, ed. L. Riesco Terrero, *Epistolario de San Braulio* (Seville, 1975).

BRAULIO OF ZARAGOZA, *Vita S. Emiliani*, ed. L. Vázquez de Parga (Madrid, 1943).

Breviarium ecclesiae Ravennatis (Codice Bavaro), secoli VII–X, ed. G. Rabotti (Rome, 1985) [*CB*].

Bündner Urkundenbuch, I, ed. E. Meyer-Marthaler and F. Perret (Chur, 1947).

BUSSON and LEDRU, *Actus*, see *Actus*.

CAESARIUS OF ARLES, *Sermones*, ed. M.-J. Delage, *Césaire d'Arles, sermons au peuple*, 3 vols. (Paris, 1971–86).

Canones Wallici, ed. A. W. Haddan and W. Stubbs, *Councils and ecclesiastical documents relating to Great Britain and Ireland*, I (Oxford, 1869), pp. 127–37.

Les canons des conciles mérovingiens (VIe–VIIe siècles), ed. J. Gaudemet and B. Basdevant (Paris, 1989).

Les canons des conciles œcuméniques, ed. P.-P. Joannou (Grottaferrata, 1962).

Carmen de synodo Ticinensi, ed. L. Bethmann, *MGH, SRL* (Hannover, 1878), pp. 190–1.

Le carte private della cattedrale di Piacenza, I, ed. P. Galetti (Parma, 1978).

Cartulaire de l'abbaye de Gorze, ed. A. d'Herbomez (Paris, 1898).

Cartulaire de l'abbaye de Saint-Victor de Marseille, ed. B. Guérard, A. Marion, and L. Delisle, 2 vols. (Paris, 1857).

Cartulaire général de l'Yonne, I, ed. M. Quantin (Auxerre, 1854).

Cartularium saxonicum, ed. W. de G. Birch, 3 vols. (London, 1885–93) [*BCS*].

The cartulary of Flavigny, 717–1113, ed. C. B. Bouchard (Cambridge, Mass., 1991).

CASSIODORUS, *Institutiones*, ed. R. A. B. Mynors (Oxford, 1937).

CASSIODORUS, *Variae*, ed. T. Mommsen, *MGH, AA*, XII (Berlin, 1894).

Catalogue of Arabic papyri in the John Rylands Library, Manchester, ed. D. S. Margoliouth (Manchester, 1933) [*P. Ryl. Ar.*].

Catalogue of the Coptic manuscripts in the collection of the John Rylands Library, Manchester, ed. W. E. Crum (Manchester, 1909) [*P. Ryl. Copt.*].

CATO, *De agricultura*, ed. R. Goujard (Paris, 1975).

Chartae latinae antiquiores, 1st series, 49 vols., general ed. A. Bruckner and R. Marichal (Olten and Zürich, 1954–98) [*ChLA*].

Chartes et documents de Saint-Bénigne de Dijon, ed. G. Chevrier and M. Chaume, 2 vols. (Dijon, 1943–86).

CHORIKIOS OF GAZA, *Orations*, ed. R. Foerster and E. Richtsteig, *Choricii Gazaei opera* (Leipzig, 1929).

Christians and Moors in Spain, III, *Arabic sources*, ed. C. Melville and A. Ubaydli (Warminster, 1992).

Chronica Gallica ad annum 452, ed. R. Burgess, 'The Gallic Chronicle of 452', in R. W. Mathisen and D. Shanzer (eds.), *Society and culture in late Antique Gaul* (Aldershot, 2001), pp. 52–84.

Chronicle of 754, ed. E. López Pereira, *Crónica mozárabe de 754* (Zaragoza, 1980).

Chronicle of AD 1234, trans. in part in A. Palmer, *The seventh century in the West-Syrian chronicles* (Liverpool, 1993), pp. 111–221.

The chronicle of Zuqnīn, parts III and IV, trans. A. Harrak (Toronto, 1999).

Chronicon anonymum pseudo-Dionysianum vulgo dictum, II, trans. R. Hespel (Louvain, 1989).

Chronicon Sanctae Sophiae (cod. Vat. Lat. 4939), ed. J.-M. Martin, 2 vols. (Rome, 2000).

Chronicon Vulturnense, ed. V. Federici, 3 vols. (Rome, 1925–38).

Chronique de l'abbaye de Saint-Bénigne de Dijon, ed. E. Bougard and J. Garnier (Dijon, 1875).

Codex carolinus, ed. W. Gundlach, *MGH, Epp.*, III (Berlin, 1892), pp. 476–657.

Codex diplomaticus Amiatinus, I, ed. W. Kurze (Tübingen, 1974).

Codex diplomaticus Fuldensis, ed. E. F. J. Dronke, 2nd impression (Aalen, 1962).

Codex diplomaticus Langobardiae, ed. G. Porro-Lambertenghi (Turin, 1873).

Codex Euricianus, ed. A. D'Ors, *El Código de Eurico* (Rome, 1960).

Codex Iustinianus, ed. P. Krueger, *Corpus iuris civilis*, II (Berlin, 1929) [*CJ*].

Codex Laureshamensis, ed. K. Glöckner, 3 vols. (Darmstadt, 1929–36).

Codice diplomatico longobardo, I, II, ed. L. Schiaparelli (Rome, 1929–33), III, ed. C. R. Brühl (Rome, 1973), IV.1, ed. C. R. Brühl (Rome, 1981), IV.2, ed. H. Zielinski (Rome, 2003), V, ed. H. Zielinski (Rome, 1986) [*CDL*].

COGITOSUS, *Vita Brigitae*, trans. in S. Connolly, 'Cogitosus's Life of St. Brigit. Content and value', *Journal of the Royal society of Antiquaries of Ireland*, CXVII (1987), pp. 5–27.

COLUMELLA, *Res rustica*, ed. H. B. Ash *et al.*, 3 vols. (Cambridge, Mass., 1941–68).

Concilios visigóticos e hispano-romanos, ed. J. Vives (Barcelona, 1963).

CONSTANTIUS, *Vita Germani*, ed. R. Borius, *Constance de Lyon, Vie de Saint Germain d'Auxerre* (Paris, 1965).

Coptic and Greek texts of the Christian period from ostraka, stelae, etc. in the British Museum, ed. H. R. Hall (London, 1905).

Coptic Ostraca, ed. W. E. Crum (London, 1902) [*CO*].

Coptic ostraka from Medinet Habu, ed. E. Stefanski and M. Lichtheim (Chicago, 1952) [*OMH*].

Corpus inscriptionum latinarum, VIII, ed. G. Wilmanns *et al.* (Berlin, 1881–1916).

Corpus papyrorum Raineri, 22 vols., proceeding (Vienna, 1895–) [*CPR*].

Críth Gablach, ed. D. A. Binchy (Dublin, 1970); trans. E. MacNeill, 'The law of status and franchise', pp. 281–306.

Crónicas asturianas, ed. J. Gil Fernández *et al.* (Oviedo, 1985).

Culhwch ac Olwen, ed. R. Bromwich and D. S. Evans (Cardiff, 1988).

CYRIL OF SCYTHOPOLIS, *Life* of Euthymios, ed. E. Schwartz, *Kyrillos von Skythopolis* (Leipzig, 1939), pp. 5–85.

CYRIL OF SCYTHOPOLIS, *Life* of Saba, ed. E. Schwartz, *Kyrillos von Skythopolis* (Leipzig, 1939), pp. 85–200.

Dai papiri della Biblioteca Medicea Laurenziana, ed. R. Pintaudi, 4 vols. (Florence, 1976–83) [P. Laur.].

Danmarks runeinskrifter, ed. L. Jacobsen and E. Moltke, 4 vols. (Copenhagen, 1941–2).

DESIDERIUS OF CAHORS, *Epistolae*, ed. W. Arndt, *MGH, Epp.*, III (Berlin, 1892), pp. 193–214.

DEVIC and VAISSETE, *HGL*, see *Histoire*.

Digesta, ed. T. Mommsen *et al.*, *Corpus iuris civilis*, I (Berlin, 1928).

DIOCLETIAN, *Edict on prices*, ed. S. Lauffer, *Diokletians Preisedikt* (Berlin, 1971).

Diplomata, chartae, epistolae, leges aliaque instrumenta ad res Gallo-Francicas spectantia, ed. J. M. Pardessus, 2 vols. (Paris, 1843–9) [Pardessus, *Diplomata*].

Diplomata Maiorum domus, ed. K. A. F. Pertz, *MGH, Diplomata imperii*, I (Hannover, 1872), pp. 91–110.

Diplomatarium danicum, I.2, ed. L. Weibull and N. Skyum-Nielsen (Copenhagen, 1963).

Diplomática española del período astur, ed. A. C. Floriano, I (Oviedo, 1949).

Documenti relativi alla storia di Venezia anteriori al Mille, I, ed. R. Cessi (Padua, 1940).

Documentos de época visigoda escritos en pizarra (siglos VI–VIII), ed. I. Velázquez Soriano, 2 vols. (Turnhout, 2000).

Documents comptables de Saint-Martin de Tours à l'époque mérovingienne, ed. P. Gasnault (Paris, 1975).

DRACONTIUS, *Satisfactio*, ed. F. Vollmer, *MGH, AA*, XIV (Berlin, 1905), pp. 114–31.

The early Christian monuments of Wales, ed. V. E. Nash-Williams (Cardiff, 1950).

Early Welsh genealogical tracts, ed. P. C. Bartrum (Cardiff, 1966).

Easter Chronicle, ed. L. Dindorf, *Chronicon Paschale* (Bonn, 1832).

Edictum Theoderici regis, ed. F. Bluhme, *MGH, Leges*, V (Hannover, 1889), pp. 152–68.

Edictus Rothari, ed. F. Beyerle, *Leges Langobardorum 643–866* (Witzenhausen, 1962), pp. 16–94 [Rothari].

EINHARD, *Epistolae*, ed. K. Hampe, *MGH, Epp.*, V (Berlin, 1898–9), pp. 109–45.

EINHARD, *Translatio et miracula SS. Marcellini et Petri*, ed. G. Waitz, *MGH, SS*, XV (Hannover, 1887), pp. 239–64.

Ekloga, ed. L. Burgmann, *Ecloga* (Frankfurt, 1983).

ENNODIUS, *Opera*, ed. F. Vogel, *MGH, AA*, VII (Berlin, 1885).

Epistolae Austrasicae, ed. W. Gundlach, *MGH, Epp.*, III (Berlin, 1892), pp. 111–53.

Epistolae Wisigoticae, ed. W. Gundlach, *MGH, Epp.*, III (Berlin, 1892), pp. 661–90.

EUGENIUS OF TOLEDO, *Carmina*, ed. F. Vollmer, *MGH, AA*, XIV (Berlin, 1905), pp. 231–82.

EUSEBIOS THE MONK, *Life* of Philip of Argyrion, ed. in *Acta Sanctorum*, May, III (Antwerp, 1680), pp. 1*–7*.

Excavations at Nessana, III, *Non-literary papyri*, ed. C. J. Kraemer (Princeton, 1958) [*P. Ness.*].

Expositio totius mundi et gentium, ed. J. Rougé (Paris, 1966).

EUGIPPIUS, *Vita Sancti Severini*, ed. R. Noll and E. Vetter (Berlin, 1963).

FAUSTUS OF RIEZ, *Sermo in natali S. Stephani*, ed. A. Engelbrecht, *Fausti Reiensis opera* (Vienna, 1891), pp. 232–6.

FELIX, *Vita S. Guthlaci*, ed. B. Colgrave (Cambridge, 1956).

FERRANDUS, *Vita beati Fulgentii pontificis*, ed. G.-G. Lapeyre, *Vie de Saint Fulgence de Ruspe de Ferrand, diacre de Carthage* (Paris, 1929).

FIRDAWSĪ, *Shāhnāma*, ed. J. Mohl, *Le livre des rois* (Paris, 1838–78).

Fled Bricrend, ed. E. Windisch, in W. Stokes and E. Windisch, *Irische texte*, 2nd ser., I (Leipzig, 1884), pp. 173–85.

FLODOARD, *Historia Remensis ecclesiae*, ed. M. Stratmann, *MGH, SS*, XXXVI (Hannover, 1998).

FLORIANO, *Diplomática española*, see *Diplomática*.

Formulae Wisigothicae, ed. J. Gil, *Miscellanea wisigothica* (Seville, 1972), pp. 70–112 [*Form. Wis.*].

FREDEGAR, *Chronica*, ed. J. M. Wallace-Hadrill, *The fourth book of the Chronicle of Fredegar with its continuations* (London, 1960), pp. 2–79.

FREDEGAR, *Continuationes*, ed. J. M. Wallace-Hadrill, *The fourth book of the Chronicle of Fredegar with its continuations* (London, 1960), pp. 80–121.

FULGENTIUS OF RUSPE, *Ad Trasamundum*, ed. J. Fraipont, *Sancti Fulgentii Ruspensis opera* (Turnhout, 1968), pp. 97–185.

Gallia christiana novissima, III, ed. J.-H. Albanès and U. Chevalier (Valence, 1901).

Gesta Dagoberti I regis Francorum, ed. B. Krusch, *MGH, SRM*, II (Hannover, 1888), pp. 399–425.

Gesta episcoporum Neapolitanorum, ed. G. Waitz, *MGH, SRL* (Hannover, 1878), pp. 402–36.

Gethyncðo, ed. F. Liebermann, *Die Gesetze der Angelsachsen*, 3 vols. (Halle, 1903–16), I, pp. 456–8.

GILDAS, *De excidio et conquestu Britanniae*, ed. T. Mommsen, *MGH, AA*, XIII (Berlin, 1898), pp. 25–85.

Greek papyri in the British museum, ed. F. G. Kenyon and H. I. Bell, 5 vols. (London, 1893–1917) [*P. Lond.*].

GREGORY THE GREAT, *Dialogi*, ed. U. Moricca (Rome, 1924).

GREGORY THE GREAT, *Registrum epistolarum*, ed. P. Ewald and L. M. Hartmann, *MGH, Epp.*, I, II (Berlin, 1887–99).

GREGORY OF NYSSA, *Letters*, ed. G. Pasquali, *Gregorii Nysseni epistulae* (Leiden, 1959).

GREGORY OF TOURS, *Decem libri historiarum*, ed. B. Krusch and W. Levison, *MGH, SRM*, I.1, 2nd edn. (Hannover, 1951) [Gregory of Tours, *LH*].

GREGORY OF TOURS, *De virtutibus sancti Martini episcopi*, ed. B. Krusch, *MGH, SRM*, I.2 (Hannover, 1885), pp. 584–661 [Gregory of Tours, *VM*].

GREGORY OF TOURS, *Liber in gloria confessorum*, ed. B. Krusch, *MGH, SRM*, I.2 (Hannover, 1885), pp. 744–820 [Gregory of Tours, *GC*].

GREGORY OF TOURS, *Liber in gloria martyrum*, ed. B. Krusch, *MGH, SRM*, I.2 (Hannover, 1885), pp. 484–561 [Gregory of Tours, *GM*].

GREGORY OF TOURS, *Liber vitae patrum*, ed. B. Krusch, *MGH, SRM*, I.2 (Hannover, 1885), pp. 661–744 [Gregory of Tours, *VP*].

Hávamál, ed. S. Bugge, *Norrœn fornkvæði* (Christiania, 1867), pp. 43–64.

Histoire générale de Languedoc, II, ed. C. Devic and J. Vaissete (Toulouse, 1875) [*HGL*].

Die 'Honorantiae civitatis Papie', ed. C. R. Brühl and C. Violante (Cologne, 1983).

HYDATIUS, *Chronica*, ed. R. W. Burgess, *The Chronicle of Hydatius and the Consularia Constantinopolitana* (Oxford, 1993), pp. 70–122.

IBN 'ABD AL-ḤAKAM, *Conquête de l'Afrique du Nord et de l'Espagne (Futûh' Ifrîqiya wa'l-Andalus)*, ed. and trans. A. Gateau, 2nd edn. (Algiers, 1947).

IBN ḤAWQAL (Ibn Hauqal), *Configuration de la terre (Kitab surat al-ard)*, I, trans. J. H. Kramers and G. Wiet (Beirut–Paris, 1964).

IBN KHALDŪN, *Muqaddimah*, trans. F. Rosenthal, 3 vols. (London, 1958).

IBN KHURDĀDHBIH, *Kitāb al-masālik wa'l mamālik*, ed. and trans. M. J. de Goeje, *Bibliotheca geographorum arabicorum*, VI (Leiden, 1889).

IBN AL-QŪṬIYA, *Historia de la conquista de España de Abenalcotía el Cordobés*, trans. J. Ribera, *Colección de obras arábigas de historia y geografía, que publica la Real Academia de Historia*, II (Madrid, 1926), pp. 1–101.

IGNATIOS THE DEACON, *Letters*, ed. C. Mango, *The Correspondance of Ignatios the Deacon* (Washington, DC, 1997).

IGNATIOS THE DEACON, *Life* of Tarasios, ed. S. Efthymiadis (Aldershot, 1998).

ILDEFONSUS OF TOLEDO, *De viris illustribus*, ed. C. Codoñer (Salamanca, 1972).

Inscripciones cristianas de la España romana y visigoda, ed. J. Vives (Barcelona, 1942).

Inscriptiones graecae, XII.2, ed. W. R. Paton (Berlin, 1899).

Inscriptiones latinae christianae veteres, ed. E. Diehl, 3 vols. (Berlin, 1961).

Inscriptiones latinae selectae, ed. H. Dessau, 3 vols. (Berlin, 1892–1916).

Inscriptions antiques du Maroc, II, ed. M. Euzennat *et al.* (Paris, 1982).

Les inscriptions d'Altava, ed. J. Marcillet-Jaubert (Aix, 1968).

Inscriptions de Cilicie, ed. G. Dagron and D. Feissel (Paris, 1987).

Inscriptions grecques et latines de la Syrie, II, ed. L. Jalabert and R. Mouterde (Paris, 1939).

Inscriptions latines de l'Algérie, I, ed. S. Gsell (Paris, 1922).

Inventari altomedievali di terre, coloni e redditi, ed. A. Castagnetti *et al.* (Rome, 1979).

ISIDORE OF SEVILLE, *Etymologiae*, ed. W. M. Lindsay, 2 vols. (Oxford, 1911).

Istorikē diēgēsis tou biou kai tōn praxeōn Basileiou tou doidimou basileōs, ed. J.-P. Migne, *PG*, CIX (Paris, 1863), cols. 225–69.

Itinerarium Antonini Placentini, ed. C. Milani (Milan, 1977).

Itinerarium Einsiedelnense, ed. R. Valentini and G. Zucchetti, *Codice topografico della città di Roma*, II (Rome, 1942), pp. 163–207.

JOHN OF BICLAR, *Chronica*, ed. T. Mommsen, *MGH*, *AA*, XI (Berlin, 1894), pp. 211–20.

JOHN CHRYSOSTOM, *Homilies on Matthew*, ed. J.-P. Migne, *PG*, LVII–LVIII (Paris, 1862).

JOHN CHRYSOSTOM, *Lettres à Olympias*, ed. A.-M. Malingrey, 2nd edn. (Paris, 1968).

JOHN THE DEACON, *Istoria Veneticorum*, ed. L. A. Berto (Bologna, 1999).

JOHN LYDOS, *On powers*, ed. A. C. Bandy (Philadelphia, 1983).

JOHN MALALAS, *Chronographia*, ed. L. Dindorf (Bonn, 1831).

JOHN MOSCHOS, *Spiritual meadow*, ed. J.-P. Migne, *PG*, LXXXVII.3 (Paris, 1863), cols. 2851–3112.

JONAS OF BOBBIO, *Vita Columbani abbatis discipulorumque eius*, ed. B. Krusch, *MGH, SRM*, IV (Hannover, 1902), pp. 61–152.

JORDANES, *Getica*, ed. T. Mommsen, *MGH, AA*, V.1 (Berlin, 1882), pp. 53–138.

JOSHUA THE STYLITE, *Chronicle*, ed. and trans. W. Wright (Cambridge, 1882); trans. F. R. Trombley and J. W. Watt, *The chronicle of pseudo-Joshua the Stylite* (Liverpool, 2000).

JULIAN OF ASKALON, *Urban treatise*, ed. C. Saliou, *Le traité d'urbanisme de Julien d'Ascalon* (Paris, 1996).

JULIAN OF TOLEDO, *Historia Wambae*, ed. W. Levison, *MGH, SRM*, V (Hannover, 1910), pp. 500–35.

Koptische Rechtsurkunden des achten Jahrhunderts aus Djême (Theben), I, ed. W. E. Crum (Leipzig, 1912) [*KRU*].

Koptskie teksty Gosudarstvennogo muzeya isobrazitel'nykh iskusstvimeni A. S. Pushkina, ed. P. V. Jernstedt (Moscow, 1959).

The Ḳurrah papyri from Aphrodito in the Oriental Institute, ed. N. Abbott (Chicago, 1938).

The law of Hywel Dda, trans. D. Jenkins (Llandysul, 1986).

The laws of the earliest English kings, ed. F. L. Attenborough (Cambridge, 1922).

Laxdæla saga, ed. Einar Ólafur Sveinsson, *Íslenzk Fornrit*, V (Reykjavik, 1934).

Leges Aistulfi, ed. F. Beyerle, *Leges Langobardorum 643–866* (Witzenhausen, 1962), pp. 194–204 [Aistulf].

Leges Alamannorum, ed. K. Lehmann, *MGH, Leges*, V.1 (Hannover, 1888).

Leges Baiuwariorum, ed. E. de Schwind, *MGH, Leges*, V.2 (Hannover, 1926).

Leges Burgundionum, ed. L. R. de Salis, *MGH, Leges*, II.1 (Hannover, 1892).

Leges Langobardorum 643–866, ed. F. Beyerle (Witzenhausen, 1962).

Leges Liutprandi, ed. F. Beyerle, *Leges Langobardorum 643–866* (Witzenhausen, 1962), pp. 99–182 [Liutprand].

Leges Ratchis, ed. F. Beyerle, *Leges Langobardorum 643–866* (Witzenhausen, 1962), pp. 183–93 [Ratchis].

Leges Visigothorum, ed. K. Zeumer, *MGH, Leges*, I (Hannover, 1902) [*LV*].

LEONTIOS OF NEAPOLIS, *Life* of John the Almsgiver, ed. A.-J. Festugière, *Léontios de Néapolis, Vie de Syméon le fou et vie de Jean de Chypre* (Paris, 1974), pp. 343–409.

Lex Ribvaria, ed. F. Beyerle and R. Buchner, *MGH, Leges*, III.2 (Hannover, 1954).

Lex Romana Visigothorum, ed. G. Haenel (Leipzig, 1849).

LIBANIOS, *Orations*, ed. R. Foerster, *Libanii opera*, 4 vols. (Leipzig, 1903–8); most of those cited here are also ed. A. F. Norman, *Selected works*, II (Cambridge, Mass., 1977).

Liber historiae Francorum, ed. B. Krusch, *MGH, SRM*, II (Hannover, 1888), pp. 238–328.

Liber Landavensis, ed. J. G. Evans and J. Rhys, *The text of the Book of Llan Dâv* (Oxford, 1893).

Liber largitorius vel notarius monasterii Pharphensis, ed. G. Zucchetti, I (Rome, 1913).

Le Liber Pontificalis, ed. L. Duchesne, 2nd edn. (Paris, 1955).

Life of David, Simeon, and George, ed. in 'Acta graeca SS. Davidis, Symeonis et Georgii', *Analecta bollandiana*, XVIII (1899), pp. 209–59.

Life of John the Almsgiver, ed. H. Deleheye, 'Une vie inédite de Saint Jean l'Aumonier', *Analecta bollandiana*, XLV (1927), pp. 5–74.

Life of Melania, ed. D. Gorce, *Vie de Sainte Mélanie. Texte grec* (Paris, 1962).

The Life of St. Nicholas of Sion, ed. I. and N. P. Ševčenko (Brookline, 1984).

Life of Olympias, ed. A.-M. Malingrey, *Jean Chrysostome, Lettres à Olympias*, 2nd edn. (Paris, 1968), pp. 406–48.

Life of S. Pankratios, partially ed. in A. N. Veselovskii, *Iz istorii romana i povesti*, = *Sbornik otdeleniya russkago yazyka i slovesnosti imperatorskoi Akademii nauk*, XL.2 (1886), pp. 73–110.

Life of Theodore of Studios, B, ed. J.-P. Migne, *PG*, XCIX (Paris, 1860), cols. 233–328.

Liutprand of Cremona, *Antapodosis*, ed. J. Becker, *Liudprandi Opera*, MGH, *SRG*, XLI (Hannover, 1915), pp. 1–158.

Llyfr Iorwerth, ed. A. R. Wiliam (Cardiff, 1960).

Ludovici II Diplomata, ed. K. Wanner, *MGH, Dip. Kar.*, IV (Munich, 1994).

Manaresi, *I placiti*, see *Placiti*.

al-Mas'ūdī, *Murūj al-dhahab*, ed. C. Barbier de Meynard and A. Pavet de Courteille, 9 vols. (Paris, 1861–77).

Memorie e documenti per servire all'istoria di Lucca, IV, ed. F. Bertini, V.2, ed. D. Barsocchini (Lucca, 1818, 1837) [*MDL*].

Methodios, *Life* of Theophanes, ed. V. V. Latyshev, *Zapiski Rossiiskoi Akademii nauk po istoricheskomu-filologicheskomu otdeleniyu*, 8 ser., XIII.4 (1918), pp. 1–40.

Miracles de St Démétrius, see *Plus anciens recueils*.

Miracles of S. Artemios, ed. A. Papadopoulos-Kerameus, *Varia Graeca sacra* (St Petersburg, 1909), pp. 1–75, reprinted with trans. and commentary in V. S. Crisafulli and J. W. Nesbitt, *The miracles of St. Artemios* (Leiden, 1997).

Miracula Austrigisili episcopi Biturigi, ed. B. Krusch, *MGH, SRM*, IV (Hannover, 1902), pp. 200–8.

Miracula S. Wandregisili, partially ed. O. Holder-Egger, *MGH, SS*, XV (Hannover, 1887), pp. 406–9.

MGH, Capitularia, I, II, ed. A. Boretius and V. Krause (Hannover, 1883–97) [*MGH, Cap.*].

MGH, Concilia aevi Karolini, I, ed. A. Werminghoff (Hannover, 1906).

MGH, Diplomata Karolinorum, I, ed. E. Mühlbacher (Berlin, 1906) [*Dip. Kar.*].

MGH, Diplomata regum francorum e stirpe merovingica, 2nd edn., ed. T. Kölzer (Hannover, 2001) [*MGH, Dip. Merov.*].

MGH, Formulae merowingici et karolini aevi, ed. K. Zeumer (Hannover, 1886).

MGH, Poetae latini aevi Carolini, I, ed. E. Dümmler (Berlin, 1880).

Die nichtliterarischen lateinischen Papyri Italiens aus der Zeit 445–700, ed. J. O. Tjäder, 2 vols. (Lund, 1955–82) [*P. Ital.*].

Nikephoros, patriarch of Constantinople, *Short history*, ed. and trans. C. Mango (Washington, DC, 1990).

Nithard, *Historiarum libri IV*, ed. E. Müller, *MGH, SRG* (Hannover, 1907).

Nomos rodiōn nautikos. The Rhodian sea-law, ed. W. Ashburner (Oxford, 1909).

Novellae Iustiniani, ed. R. Schoell and W. Kroll, *Corpus iuris civilis*, III (Berlin, 1928) [*NJ*].

Novellae Maioriani, ed. T. Mommsen and P. M. Meyer, *Theodosiani libri XVI cum constitutionibus Sirmondianis*, II (Berlin, 1905), pp. 156–78 [*Nov. Maj.*].

Novellae Valentiniani, ed. T. Mommsen and P. M. Meyer, *Theodosiani libri XVI cum constitutionibus Sirmondianis*, II (Berlin, 1905), pp. 73–154 [*Nov. Val.*].

ODO OF CLUNY, *Vita S. Geraldi Auriliacensis comitis*, ed. J.-P. Migne, *PL*, CXXXIII (Paris, 1881), cols. 639–704.

OLYMPIODOROS OF THEBES, ed. R. C. Blockley, *The fragmentary classicising historians of the later Roman empire*, II (Liverpool, 1983), pp. 152–208.

The Oxyrhynchus papyri, ed. B. P. Grenfell, A. S. Hunt, *et al.*, 65 vols., proceeding (London, 1898–) [*P. Oxy.*].

Pactio Sicardi, ed. F. Bluhme, *MGH, Leges*, IV (Hannover, 1868), pp. 216–21.

Pactus legis Salicae, ed. K. A. Eckhardt, *MGH, Leges*, IV.1 (Hannover, 1962).

PAIANIOS, *Metaphrasis tēs Eutropiou Rōmaikēs istorias*, ed. H. Droysen, *MGH, AA*, II (Berlin, 1879), pp. 9–179.

PALLADIUS, *Opus agriculturae*, ed. R. H. Rodgers (Leipzig, 1975); partially ed. R. Martin, *Palladius, Traité d'agriculture*, I (Paris, 1976).

Panégyriques latins, ed. E. Galletier, 3 vols. (Paris, 1949–55).

Papiri greco-egizii, III, *Papiri fiorentini*, ed. G. Vitelli (Milan, 1915) [*P. Flor.*].

I papiri vaticani greci di Aphrodito, ed. R. Pintaudi (Rome, 1980) [*P. Vatic. Aphrod.*].

Papyri russischer und georgischer Sammlungen, III, IV, ed. G. Zereteli and P. Jernstedt (Tbilisi, 1927–30) [*P. Ross.-Georg.*].

Papyri Schott-Reinhardt, I, ed. C. H. Becker (Heidelberg, 1906) [*PSR*].

Papyrus Erzherzog Rainer. Führer durch die Ausstellung, ed. J. Karabacek (Vienna, 1894) [*PERF*].

Papyrus grecs d'Apollônos Anô, ed. R. Rémondon (Cairo, 1953) [*P. Apoll.*].

Papyrus grecs d'époque byzantine, ed. J. Maspero, 3 vols. (Cairo, 1911–16) [*P. Cair. Masp.*].

Parastaseis syntomoi chronikai, ed. T. Preger, *Scriptores originum Constantinopolitarum*, I (Leipzig, 1901), pp. 19–73, reprinted with trans. and commentary in A. Cameron and J. Herrin, *Constantinople in the early eighth century* (Leiden, 1984).

PARDESSUS, *Diplomata*, see *Diplomata*.

Passio Praejecti episcopi Arverni, ed. B. Krusch, *MGH, SRM*, V (Hannover, 1910), pp. 225–48.

Passio prima Leudegarii episcopi Augustodunensis, ed. B. Krusch, *MGH, SRM*, V (Hannover, 1910), pp. 282–322.

Passio Thrudperti martyris Brisgoviensis, ed. B. Krusch, *MGH, SRM*, IV (Hannover, 1902), pp. 357–63.

Passio S. Vincentii Aginnensis, ed. B. de Gaiffier, 'La passion de S. Vincent d'Agen', *Analecta bollandiana*, LXX (1952), pp. 160–81.

PATRICK, *Epistola*, ed. A. B. E. Hood, *St. Patrick. His writings and Muirchu's Life* (London, 1978).

PAUL THE DEACON, *Carmina*, ed. E. Dümmler, *MGH, Poetae*, I (Berlin, 1880), pp. 35–73.

PAUL THE DEACON, *Historia Langobardorum*, ed. L. Bethmann and G. Waitz, *MGH, SRL* (Hannover, 1878), pp. 45–187 [Paul, *HL*].

PAULINUS OF PELLA, *Eucharisticos*, ed. C. Moussy, *Paulin de Pella, Poème d'action de grâces et prière* (Paris, 1974).

PELAGIUS I PAPA, *Epistulae quae supersunt*, ed. P. M. Gassó and C. M. Batlle (Montserrat, 1956).

Peri stratēgias, ed. G. T. Dennis, *Three Byzantine military treatises* (Washington, DC, 1985), pp. 10–134.

The Petra papyri, I, ed. J. Frösén, A. Arjava, and M. Lehtinen (Amman, 2002) [*P. Petra*].

Las pizarras visigodas, ed. I. Velázquez Soriano (Murcia, 1988).

I placiti del 'Regnum Italiae', I, ed. C. Manaresi (Rome, 1955).

Les plus anciens recueils des Miracles de Saint Démétrius, ed. P. Lemerle, 2 vols. (Paris, 1979–81).

Das Polyptichon von St.-Germain-des-Prés, ed. D. Hägermann (Cologne, 1993).

Polyptique de l'abbaye de Saint-Germain-des-Prés, ed. A. Longnon, 2 vols. (Paris, 1895) [*Pol. St-Germain*].

POSSIDIUS, *Vita Augustini*, ed. M. Pellegrino (Alba, 1955).

PRISCUS, *Fragments*, ed. R. C. Blockley, *The fragmentary classicising historians of the later Roman empire*, II (Liverpool, 1983), pp. 222–376.

PROKOPIOS, *The anecdota or secret history*, ed. H. B. Dewing (Cambridge, Mass., 1935).

PROKOPIOS, *History of the wars*, ed. H. B. Dewing, 5 vols. (Cambridge, Mass., 1914–28).

Querolus, ed. C. Jacquemard-le Saos (Paris, 1994).

Recueil des actes de Pépin I et Pépin II, rois d'Aquitaine (814–848), ed. L. Levillain (Paris, 1926).

Recueil des actes de Charles II le Chauve, ed. G. Tessier, 2 vols. (Paris, 1943–52).

Recueil des chartes de l'abbaye de St.-Germain-des-Prés des origines au début du XIIIᵉ siècle, I, ed. R. Poupardin (Paris, 1909).

Recueil des chartes de l'abbaye de Stavelot-Malmedy, I, ed. J. Halkin and C.-G. Roland (Brussels, 1909).

Regesto di Farfa, ed. I. Giorgi and U. Balzani, 5 vols. (Rome, 1879–92) [*RF*].

RIMBERT, *Vita Anskarii*, ed. G. Waitz, *MGH, SRG* (Hannover, 1884), pp. 13–79.

The Ruin, ed. G. P. Krapp and E. V. K. Dobbie, *The Exeter book. The Anglo-Saxon poetic records*, III (New York, 1936), pp. 227–9.

RURICIUS OF LIMOGES, *Epistulae*, ed. B. Krusch, *MGH, AA*, VIII (Berlin, 1887), pp. 299–350.

RUTILIUS CLAUDIUS NAMATIANUS, *De reditu suo sive Iter Gallicum*, ed. E. Doblhofer, 2 vols. (Heidelberg, 1972–7).

Sacrorum conciliorum nova et amplissima collectio, XIII, ed. J. D. Mansi (Paris, 1902).

SALVIAN, *De gubernatione dei*, ed. G. Lagarrigue, *Salvien de Marseille, Oeuvres*, II (Paris, 1975).

Sanctae ecclesiae Florentinae Monumenta, I, ed. G. Lami (Florence, 1758).

SĀWĪRUS IBN AL-MUQAFFAʿ, *History of the patriarchs of the Coptic church of Jerusalem*, ed. and trans. B. Evetts, *PO*, I.4, V.1, X.5 (Paris, 1907–10).

Scéla Mucce meic Dathó, ed. R. Thurneysen (Dublin, 1935).

Select English historical documents of the ninth and tenth centuries, ed. F. E. Harmer (Cambridge, 1914).

SEVERUS OF ANTIOCH, *Homélies XVIII à XXV*, ed. and trans. M. Brière and F. Graffin, *PO*, XXXVII.1 (Turnhout, 1975).

Short texts from Coptic ostraca and papyri, ed. W. E. Crum (Oxford, 1921).

SIDONIUS APOLLINARIS, *Carmina* and *Epistolae*, ed. W. B. Anderson, *Poems and letters*, 2 vols. (Cambridge, Mass., 1936–65).

STEPHANUS, *Vita Wilfridi*, ed. B. Colgrave, *The life of Bishop Wilfrid by Eddius Stephanus* (Cambridge, 1927).

SYMMACHUS, *Epistulae*, ed. O. Seeck, *MGH, AA*, VI.1 (Berlin, 1883), pp. 1–317.

SYNESIOS OF CYRENE, *Correspondance*, ed. A. Garzya, 2 vols. (Paris, 2000).

The Syriac life of Saint Simeon Stylites, trans. R. Doran, *The lives of Simeon Stylites* (Kalamazoo, 1992), pp. 103–98.

AL-ṬABARĪ, *Ta'rīkh al-rusul wa'l-mulūk*, ed. M. J. de Goeje *et al.*, 3 vols. in 15 (Leiden, 1879–1901), trans. E. Yar-Shater (ed.), *The history of al-Ṭabarī*, 39 vols. (Albany, NY, 1985–2000).

Tablettes Albertini, ed. C. Courtois *et al.* (Paris, 1952).

Táin Bó Cúailnge, recension I, ed. C. O'Rahilly (Dublin, 1976).

Ten Coptic legal texts, ed. A. A. Schiller (New York, 1932).

Testamentum sancti Aredii, ed. J.-P. Migne, *PL*, LXXI (Paris, 1879), cols. 1143–50.

Testamentum sancti Caesarii, ed. G. Morin, *Sancti Caesarii episcopi Arelatensis opera omnia*, II (Maredsous, 1942), pp. 283–9.

Testamentum Remigii, ed. B. Krusch, *MGH, SRM*, III (Hannover, 1896), pp. 336–40.

Theban ostraca, edited from the originals, now mainly in the Royal Ontario museum of archaeology, Toronto, and the Bodleian library, Oxford, IV, ed. H. Thompson (London, 1913).

THEODORET OF CYRRHUS, *Histoire des moines de Syrie*, ed. P. Canivet and A. Leroy-Molinghen, 2 vols. (Paris, 1977–9).

Theodosiani libri XVI cum constitutionibus Sirmondianis, ed. T. Mommsen and P. M. Meyer, I (Berlin, 1905) [*CTh*].

THEOPHANES, *Chronographia*, ed. C. de Boor, I (Leipzig, 1883).

TÍRECHÁN, *Additamenta*, ed. L. Bieler, *The Patrician texts in the Book of Armagh* (Dublin, 1979), pp. 166–78.

Die Traditionen des Hochstifts Freising, I, ed. T. Bitterauf (Munich, 1905).

Traditiones Wizenburgenses, ed. K. Glöckner and A. Doll (Darmstadt, 1979) [*Trad. Wiz.*].

Urkundenbuch der Abtei Sanct Gallen, I, ed. H. Wartman (Zürich, 1863).

Urkundenbuch des Klosters Fulda, I, ed. E. E. Stengel (Marburg, 1958).

Urkundenbuch zur Geschichte der jetz die Preussischen Regierungsbezirke Coblenz und Trier bilden mittelrheinische Territorien, I, ed. H. Beyer (Koblenz, 1860).

VALERIUS OF BIERZO, *Ordo querimoniae*, ed. C. M. Aherne, *Valerio of Bierzo* (Washington, DC, 1949), pp. 69–109.

Varia Coptica, ed. W. E. Crum (Aberdeen, 1939).

VENANTIUS FORTUNATUS, *Carmina*, ed. F. Leo, *MGH, AA*, IV.1 (Berlin, 1881).

VENANTIUS FORTUNATUS, *Vita Sancti Germani*, ed. F. Leo, *MGH, AA*, IV.2 (Berlin, 1881), pp. 11–27.

Veröffentlichungen aus den badischen Papyrus-Sammlungen, IV, *Griechische Papyri*, ed. F. Bilabel (Heidelberg, 1924) [*P. Bad.*].

VICTOR OF VITA, *Historia persecutionis Africanae provinciae*, ed. C. Halm, *MGH, AA*, III.1 (Berlin, 1879).

La vie de Saint Grégoire le Décapolite et les Slaves macédoniens au IXe siècle, ed. F. Dvornik (Paris, 1926).

Vie de Théodore de Sykéôn, ed. A.-J. Festugière, 2 vols. (Brussels, 1970).

Vita S. Aidi episcopi Killariensis, ed. W. W. Heist, *Vitae sanctorum Hiberniae* (Brussels, 1965), pp. 167–81.

Vita Aridii abbatis Lemovicini, ed. B. Krusch, *MGH, SRM*, III (Hannover, 1896), pp. 581–609.

Vita Audoini episcopi Rotomagensis, ed. W. Levison, *MGH, SRM*, V (Hannover, 1910), pp. 553–67.

Vita sanctae Balthildis, ed. B. Krusch, *MGH, SRM*, II (Hannover, 1888), pp. 482–508.

Vita Bibiani episcopi Santonensis, ed. B. Krusch, *MGH, SRM*, III (Hannover, 1896), pp. 94–100.

Vita Boniti episcopi Arverni, ed. B. Krusch, *MGH, SRM*, VI (Hannover, 1913), pp. 119–39.

Vita S. Cadoci, ed. A. W. Wade-Evans, in *Vitae sanctorum Britanniae et genealogiae* (Cardiff, 1944), pp. 24–140.

Vita Caesarii archiepiscopi Arelatensis, ed. B. Krusch, *MGH, SRM*, III (Hannover, 1896), pp. 457–501.

Vita S. Cainnechi, ed. W. W. Heist, *Vitae sanctorum Hiberniae* (Brussels, 1965), pp. 182–98.

Vita Desiderii Cadurcae urbis episcopi, ed. B. Krusch, *MGH, SRM*, IV (Hannover, 1902), pp. 563–602.

Vita Eligii episcopi Noviomagensis, ed. B. Krusch, *MGH, SRM*, IV (Hannover, 1902), pp. 663–742.

Vita sancti Erminonis episcopi, ed. W. Levison, *MGH, SRM*, VI (Hannover, 1913), pp. 461–70.

Vita Eucherii episcopi Aurelianensis, ed. W. Levison, *MGH, SRM*, VII (Hannover, 1920), pp. 46–53.

Vita S. Eugendi abbatis, ed. F. Martine, *Vie des pères du Jura* (Paris, 1968), pp. 364–434.

Vita Filiberti abbatis Gemeticensis, ed. W. Levison, *MGH, SRM*, V (Hannover, 1910), pp. 583–604.

Vita S. Fructuosi, ed. M. C. Díaz y Díaz, *La vida de San Fructuoso de Braga* (Braga, 1974).

Vita Genovefae virginis Parisiensis, ed. B. Krusch, *MGH, SRM*, III (Hannover, 1896), pp. 215–38.

Vita Hugberti episcopi Traiectensis, ed. W. Levison, *MGH, SRM*, VI (Hannover, 1913), pp. 482–96.

Vita Landiberti episcopi Traiectensis vetustissima, ed. B. Krusch, *MGH, SRM*, VI (Hannover, 1913), pp. 353–84.

Vita Lebuini antiqua, ed. A. Hofmeister, *MGH, SS*, XXX.2 (Leipzig, 1934), pp. 791–5.

Vita S. Lupicini abbatis, ed. F. Martine, *Vie des pères du Jura* (Paris, 1968), pp. 308–62.

Vita Melaniae latina, ed. M. Rampolla del Tindaro, *Santa Melania Giuniore* (Rome, 1905), pp. 3–40.

Vita Nicetii episcopi Lugdunensis, ed. B. Krusch, *MGH, SRM*, III (Hannover, 1896), pp. 521–4.

Vita Pardulfi abbatis Waractensis, ed. W. Levison, *MGH, SRM*, VII (Hannover, 1920), pp. 24–40.

Vita Samsonis, ed. R. Fawtier, *La vie de Saint Samson* (Paris, 1912), pp. 93–177.

Vita Sulpicii episcopi Biturigi, ed. B. Krusch, *MGH, SRM*, IV (Hannover, 1902), pp. 371–80.

Vitas sanctorum patrum Emeretensium, ed. A. Maya Sánchez (Turnhout, 1992).

VIVES, *Concilios*, see *Concilios*.

The Wanderer, ed. G. P. Krapp and E. V. K. Dobbie, *The Exeter Book. The Anglo-Saxon poetic records*, III (New York, 1936), pp. 134–7.

Widsith, ed. G. P. Krapp and E. V. K. Dobbie, *The Exeter Book. The Anglo-Saxon poetic records*, III (New York, 1936), pp. 149–53.

2. SECONDARY SOURCES

Note that authors use different combinations of their initials for different publications; I have tried to regularize these, so as to make it clear that the same author is meant. Authors also, particularly in Spain, use different elements in compound surnames for different publications; these I have left unchanged. I have also left the different transliterations of the same surname in Greek.

ABAD, L. *et al.*, 'La basílica y el baptisterio del Tolmo de Minateda (Hellín, Albacete)', *AEA*, LXXIII (2000), pp. 193–221.

ABAD, L. *et al.*, 'La ciudad visigoda del Tolmo de Minateda (Hellín, Albacete) y la sede episcopal de Eio', in A. Ribera i Lacomba (ed.), *Los orígines del cristianismo en Valencia y su entorno* (Valencia, 2000), pp. 101–12.

ABAD MIR, S., *Pautes de poblament al nordest peninsula*, treball de recerca, Universitat Autònoma de Barcelona (2002).

D'ABADAL, R., *Catalunya carolingia*, III (Barcelona, 1955).

D'ABADAL, R., *Els primers comtes catalans*, 3rd edn. (Barcelona, 1980).

ABADIE-REYNAL, C., 'Céramique et commerce dans le bassin égéen du IVᵉ au VIIᵉ siècle', in *Hommes et richesses dans l'Empire byzantin*, I (Paris, 1989), pp. 143–59.

ABADIE-REYNAL, C., 'Les amphores protobyzantines d'Argos (IVe–VIe siècles)', in V. Déroche and J.-M. Spieser (eds.), *Recherches sur la céramique byzantine* (Paris, 1989), pp. 47–56.

ABÁSOLO, J.-A., 'La ciudad romana en la Meseta norte durante la antigüedad tardía', in García Moreno and Rascón Marqués, *Complutum*, pp. 87–99.

ABEL, F. M., 'Gaza au VIᵉ siècle d'après le rhéteur Chorikios', *Revue biblique*, XL (1931), pp. 5–31.

ABELA, E., 'Ceramica dipinta in rosso', in S. Bruni (ed.), *Pisa, Piazza Dante* (Pisa, 1993), pp. 413–18.

ABELA, E., 'Lucca', in S. Gelichi (ed.), *Archeologia urbana in Toscana* (Mantua, 1999), pp. 23–44.

ABELS, R. P., *Lordship and military obligation in Anglo-Saxon England* (Berkeley, 1988).

ABU-LUGHOD, J. L., *Before European hegemony* (Oxford, 1989).

ACIÉN ALMANSA, M., *Entre el Feudalismo y el Islam. 'Umar ibn Ḥafṣūn en los historiadores, en las fuentes y en la historia*, 2nd edn. (Jaén, 1997).

ACIÉN ALMANSA, M., 'Poblamiento y fortificación en el sur de al-Andalus', *III Congreso de arqueología medieval española, Actas*, I (Oviedo, 1989), pp. 137–50.

ACIÉN ALMANSA, M., and MARTÍNEZ MADRID, R., 'Cerámica islámica arcaica del sureste de al-Andalus', *Boletín de arqueología medieval*, III (1989), pp. 123–35.

ACIÉN ALMANSA, M., and VALLEJO TRIANO, A., 'Urbanismo y estado islámico', in P. Cressier and M. García-Arenal (eds.), *Genèse de la ville islamique en al-Andalus et au Maghreb occidental* (Madrid, 1998), pp. 107–36.

ACIÉN ALMANSA, M. *et al.*, 'Cerámicas tardorromanas y altomedievales en Málaga, Ronda y Morón', in Caballero *et al.*, *Cerámicas tardorromanas y altomedievales*, pp. 411–54.

ACIÉN ALMANSA, M. *et al.*, 'Excavación de un barrio artesanal de Baŷŷāna (Pechina, Almería)', *Archéologie islamique*, I (1990), pp. 147–68.

ACIÉN ALMANSA, M. *et al.*, 'Les céramiques tournées de Nakūr (IXe–Xe siècles)', in Bakirtzis, *VIIe Congrès international*, pp. 621–32.

ADAMS, W. Y., *Ceramic industries of medieval Nubia*, 2 vols. (Lexington, Ky., 1986).

ADAN-BAYEWITZ, D., *Common pottery in Roman Galilee* (Ramat-Gan, 1993).

ADAN-BAYEWITZ, D., 'The pottery from the late Byzantine building (Stratum 4) and its implications', *Qedem*, XXI (1986), pp. 90–121.

ADDYMAN, P. V., 'A Dark-Age settlement at Maxey, Northants', *Medieval archaeology*, VIII (1964), pp. 20–73.

ADRIAN, Y.-M., and ROY, N., 'Typologie et proposition de datation de l'atelier de céramique de la Londe', in Delestre and Périn, *La datation*, pp. 57–68.

ADSERIAS SANS, M. *et al.*, 'L'habitat suburbà portuari de l'antiga Tàrraco', in J. Ruiz de Arbulo (eds.), *Tàrraco 99* (Tarragona, 2000), pp. 137–54.

AIRLIE, S., 'The aristocracy', in R. McKitterick (ed.), *The new Cambridge medieval history*, II (Cambridge, 1995), pp. 431–50.

AKERRAZ, A., 'Les rapports entre la Tingitanie et la Césarienne à l'époque postromaine', *L'Africa romana*, XII (1996), pp. 1435–9.

AKERRAZ, A., 'Recherches sur les niveaux islamiques de Volubilis', in P. Cressier and M. García-Arenal (eds.), *Genèse de la ville islamique en al-Andalus et au Maghreb occidental* (Madrid, 1998), pp. 295–304.

AL-ASʿAD, K., and STĘPNIOWSKI, F. M., 'The Umayyad sūq in Palmyra', *Damaszener Mitteilungen*, IV (1989), pp. 205–23.

ALBA CALZADO, M., 'Apuntes sobre la cerámica de épocas tardoantigua (visigoda) y altomedieval (emiral) en Extremadura a partir del regístro arqueológico emeritense', in P. Mateos Cruz and L. Caballero Zoreda (eds.), *Repertorio de arquitectura cristiana en Extremadura* (Mérida, 2003), pp. 293–332.

ALBA CALZADO, M., 'Ocupación diacrónica del área arqueólogica de Morería (Mérida)', in *Mérida. Excavaciones arqueológicas 1994–1995. Memoria* (Mérida, 1997), pp. 285–301.

ALBA, M., and FEIJOO, S., 'Pautas evolutivas de la cerámica común de Mérida en épocas visigoda y emiral', in Caballero *et al.*, *Cerámicas tardorromanas y alto-medievales*, pp. 483–504.

ALBERTI, A., 'Produzione e commercializzazione della pietra ollare in Italia setten-trionale tra tardoantico e altomedioevo', in S. Gelichi (ed.), *I Congresso nazionale di archeologia medievale* (Florence, 1997), pp. 335–9.

ALBERTINI, E., 'Ostrakon byzantin de Négrine (Numidie)', in *Cinquanténaire de la Faculté des lettres d'Alger (1881–1931)* (Algiers, 1932), pp. 53–62.

ALBIACH, R. *et al.*, 'Las últimas excavaciones (1992–1998) del solar de l'Almoina', in *V Reunió d'arqueologia cristiana hispànica* (Barcelona, 2000), pp. 63–86.

ALCOCK, L. *Cadbury castle, Somerset* (Cardiff, 1995).

ALCOCK, L. *Dinas Powys* (Cardiff, 1963).

ALFÖLDY, G., *Noricum* (London, 1974).

ALGAZE, G. *et al.*, 'The Tigris–Euphrates archaeological reconnaissance project', *Anatolica*, XX (1994), pp. 1–96.

ALSTON, R., *The city in Roman and Byzantine Egypt* (London, 2002).

ÁLVAREZ BORGE, I., *Poder y relaciones sociales en Castilla en la edad media* (Salamanca, 1996).

AMIEL, C., and BERTHAULT, F., 'Les amphores du Bas-Empire et de l'Antiquité tardive dans le Sud-Ouest de la France', *Aquitania*, XIV (1996), pp. 255–63.

AMMERMAN, A. J. *et al.*, 'More on the origins of Venice', *Antiquity*, LXIX (1995), pp. 501–10.

AMMERMAN, A. J. *et al.*, 'New evidence on the origins of Venice', *Antiquity*, LXVI (1992), pp. 913–16.

AMORY, P., *People and identity in Ostrogothic Italy, 489–554* (Cambridge, 1997).

ANAGNŌSTAKĒS, Ē., and POULOU-PAPADĒMĒTRIOU, N., 'Ē protobyzantinē Messēnē (50s–70s aiōnas) kai problēmata tēs cheiropoiētēs keramikēs stēn Pelo-ponnēso', *Symmeikta*, XI (1997), pp. 229–322.

ANČIĆ, M., 'I territori sud-orientali dell'Impero carolingio all'alba della nuova epoca', in C. Bertelli *et al.* (eds.), *Bizantini, Croati, Carolingi* (Milan, 2001), pp. 61–95.

ANDERTON, M. (ed.), *Anglo-Saxon trading centres: beyond the emporia* (Glasgow, 1999).

ANDREOLLI, B., 'Contratti agrari e patti colonici nella Lucchesia dei secoli VIII e IX', *Studi medievali*, XIX (1978), pp. 69–158.

ANDREOLLI, B., 'La corvée precarolingia', in *Le prestazioni d'opera nelle campagne italiane del Medioevo* (Bologna, 1987), pp. 15–33.

ANDREOLLI, B., 'L'evoluzione dei patti colonici nella Toscana dei secoli VIII–X', *Quaderni medievali*, XVI (1983), pp. 29–52.

ANDREOLLI, B., 'Per una semantica storica dello "ius libellarium" nell'alto e nel pieno medioevo', *Bullettino dell'Istituto storico italiano per il medio evo*, LXXXIX (1980–1), pp. 151–91.

ANDREOLLI, B., *Uomini nel medioevo* (Bologna, 1983).

ANDREOLLI, B., and MONTANARI, M., *L'azienda curtense in Italia* (Bologna, 1983).

ANDREWS, P. (ed.), *Excavations at Hamwic*, II, CBA Research Report, 109 (York, 1997).

ANDREWS, P. (ed.), *The coins and pottery from Hamwic* (Southampton, 1988).

ANSELMINO, L. *et al.*, *Il castellum del Nador* (Rome, 1989).

ARCE, J., *El último siglo de la España romana: 284–409* (Madrid, 1982).

ARCE, J., 'La penisola iberica', in A. Carandini *et al.* (eds.), *Storia di Roma*, III (Turin, 1993), pp. 379–404.

ARCE, J., 'La transformación de Hispania en época tardorromana', in *De la Antigüedad al Medievo, ss. IV–VIII* (Madrid, 1993), pp. 227–49.

ARCE, J., 'Un "limes" innecesario', in M. J. Hidalgo *et al.* (eds.), *'Romanización' y 'Reconquista' en la Península Ibérica* (Salamanca, 1998), pp. 185–90.

ARCIFA, L., 'Per una geografia amministrativa dell'altomedioevo in Sicilia', in G. P. Brogiolo (ed.), *II Congresso nazionale di archeologia medievale* (Florence, 2000), pp. 234–41.

ARDIZZON, V., 'Recipienti in ceramica grezza da San Pietro di Castello (Venezia)', in G. P. Brogiolo and S. Gelichi (eds.), *Le ceramiche altomedievali (fine VI–X secolo) in Italia settentrionale* (Mantua, 1996), pp. 36–44.

ARDIZZONE, F., 'Il complesso monumentale in contrada "Case Romane" a Marettimo (Trapani)', in S. Patitucci Uggeri (ed.), *Scavi medievali in Italia 1994–1995* (Rome, 1998), pp. 387–424.

ARDIZZONE, F., 'Rapporti commerciali tra la Sicilia occidentale ed il Tirreno centromeridionale alla luce del rinvenimento di alcuni contenitori di trasporto', in G. P. Brogiolo (ed.), *II Congresso nazionale di archeologia medievale* (Florence, 2000), pp. 402–7.

ARIÑO GIL, E., and DÍAZ, P. C., 'El campo', in R. Teja (ed.), *La Hispania del siglo IV* (Bari, 2002), pp. 59–96.

ARIÑO GIL, E., and DÍAZ, P. C., 'Poblamiento y organización del espacio', *Antiquité tardive*, XI (2003), pp. 223–37.

ARIÑO GIL, E., and RODRÍGUEZ HERNÁNDEZ, J., 'El poblamiento romano y visigodo en el territorio de Salamanca', *Zephyrus*, L (1997), pp. 225–45.

ARJAVA, A., 'The mystery cloud of AD 536 in the Mediterranean sources', *Dumbarton Oaks papers*, LIX (2005).

ARLAUD, C. *et al.*, *Lyon St.-Jean. Les fouilles de l'îlot Tramasse* (Lyon, 1994).

ARNHEIM, M. T. W., *The senatorial aristocracy in the later Roman empire* (Oxford, 1972).

ARNOLD, C. J., *An archaeology of the early Anglo-Saxon kingdoms*, 2nd edn. (London, 1997).

ARNOLD, C. J., 'Territories and leadership', in S. T. Driscoll and M. R. Nieke (eds.), *Power and politics in early medieval Britain and Ireland* (Edinburgh, 1988), pp. 111–27.

ARNOLD, C. J., 'Wealth and social structure', in P. Rahtz *et al.* (eds.), *Anglo-Saxon cemeteries 1979*, BAR, B82 (Oxford, 1980), pp. 81–142.

ARNOLD, C. J., and DAVIES, J. L., *Roman and early medieval Wales* (Stroud, 2000).

ARNON, Y. D., 'Islamic and crusader pottery (area 1, 1993–4)', in K. G. Holum *et al.* (eds.), *Caesarea papers* 2 (Portsmouth, RI, 1999), pp. 225–51.

ARORA, S. K. *et al.*, 'Eine frühmittelalterliche Talverfüllung im Elsbachtal, Rheinland (Frimmersdorf 114)', *Bonner Jahrbucher*, CXCV (1995), pp. 251–97.

ARTHUR, P., 'Ceramica in Terra d'Otranto tra VIII e XI secolo', in S. Patitucci Uggeri (ed.), *La ceramica altomedievale in Italia* (Florence, 2004), pp. 313–26.

ARTHUR, P., 'Early medieval amphorae, the duchy of Naples and the food supply of Rome', *PBSR*, LXI (1993), pp. 231–44.

ARTHUR, P., 'Eastern Mediterranean amphorae between 500 and 700: a view from Italy', in Saguì, *Ceramica in Italia*, pp. 157–83.

ARTHUR, P., 'Local pottery in Naples and northern Campania in the sixth and seventh centuries', in Saguì, *Ceramica in Italia*, pp. 491–510.

ARTHUR, P., *Naples, from Roman town to city-state* (London, 2002).

ARTHUR, P. (ed.), *Il complesso archeologico di Carminiello ai Mannesi* (Lecce, 1994).

ARTHUR, P., and OREN, E. D., 'The North Sinai survey and the evidence of transport amphorae for Roman and Byzantine trading patterns', *JRA*, XI (1998), pp. 193–212.

ARTHUR, P., and PATTERSON, H., 'Ceramics and early medieval central and southern Italy: "a potted history" ', in Francovich and Noyé, *La storia dell'alto medioevo italiano*, pp. 409–41.

ARTHUR, P., and PATTERSON, H., 'Local pottery in southern Puglia in the sixth and seventh centuries', in Saguì, *Ceramica in Italia*, pp. 511–30.

ARTHUR, P. *et al.*, 'Fornaci altomedievali ad Otranto', *AM*, XIX (1992), pp. 91–122.

ASHBURNER, W., 'The farmer's law', *Journal of Hellenic studies*, XXX (1910), pp. 85–108; XXXII (1912), pp. 68–95.

ASTARITA, C., 'La primera de las mutaciones feudales', *Anales de historia antigua, medieval y moderna*, XXXIII (2000), pp. 75–106.

ASTILL, G., and DAVIES, W., *A Breton landscape* (London, 1997).

ASTON, T., 'The origins of the manor in England', *Transactions of the Royal Historical Society*, 5 ser., VIII (1958), pp. 59–83.

AUGENTI, A., 'Dai *castra* tardoantichi ai castelli del secolo X', in Francovich and Ginatempo, *Castelli*, I, pp. 25–66.

AUPERT, P., 'Objets de la vie quotidienne à Argos en 585 ap. J.-C.', in *Études argiennes* (Athens, 1980), pp. 395–457.

AUPERT, P. *et al.*, '*Lugdunum* des Convènes (Saint-Bertrand-de-Comminges/Valcabrère, Haute-Garonne)', *Aquitania*, XVIII (2001–2), pp. 29–77.

AUSENDA, G. (ed.), *After empire* (Woodbridge, 1995).

AUZÉPY, M.-F., 'De la Palestine à Constantinople (VIIIᵉ–IXᵉ siècles)', *Travaux et mémoires*, XII (1994), pp. 183–218.

AUZÉPY, M.-F., 'Les monastères', in B. Geyer and J. Lefort (eds.), *La Bithynie au Moyen Âge* (Paris, 2003), pp. 431–58.

AVNER, U., and MAGNESS, J., 'Early Islamic settlement in the southern Negev', *Bulletin of the American schools of Oriental research*, CCCX (1998), pp. 39–57.

AVRAMEA, A., 'Land and sea communications, fourth–fifteenth centuries', in A. E. Laiou (ed.), *The economic history of Byzantium*, I (Washington, DC, 2002), pp. 57–90.

AVRAMÉA, A., *Le Péloponnèse du IVᵉ au VIIIᵉ siècle* (Paris, 1997).

AXBOE, M., 'Danish kings and dendrochronology', in Ausenda, *After empire*, pp. 217–51.

AXBOE, M., 'Towards the kingdom of Denmark', *Anglo-Saxon studies in archaeology and history*, X (1999), pp. 109–18.

AZKARATE GARAI-OLAUN, A., and QUIRÓS CASTILLO, J. A., 'Arquitectura doméstica altomedieval en la Península Ibérica', *AM*, XXVIII (2001), pp. 25–60.

AZKARATE, A. *et al.*, 'Materiales y contextos cerámicos de los siglos VI al X en el País Vasco', in Caballero *et al.*, *Cerámicas tardorromanas y altomedievales*, pp. 321–70.

BACHRACH, B. S., *Merovingian military organisation, 481–751* (Minneapolis, 1972).

BACHRACH, B. S., 'Was the Marchfield part of the Frankish constitution?', *Mediaeval studies*, XXXVI (1974), pp. 178–85.

BADER, K. S., *Studien zur Rechtsgeschichte des mittelalterlichen Dorfes*, II, *Dorfgenossenschaft und Dorfgemeinde* (Cologne, 1962).

BAGNALL, R. S., 'Agricultural productivity and taxation in later Roman Egypt', *Transactions of the American philological association*, CXV (1985), pp. 285–308.

BAGNALL, R. S., *Egypt in late Antiquity* (Princeton, 1993).

BAGNALL, R. S., 'Landholding in late Roman Egypt', *Journal of Roman studies*, LXXXII (1992), pp. 128–49.

BAGNALL, R. S., and FRIER, B. W., *The demography of Roman Egypt* (Cambridge, 1994).

BAHAT, D., 'The physical infrastructure', in J. Prawer and H. Ben-Shammai (eds.), *The history of Jerusalem. The early Muslim period 638–1099* (Jerusalem, 1996), pp. 38–100.

BAILEY, D. M., *Excavations at el-Ashmunein, IV* (London, 1991); *V* (London, 1998).

BAIRD, D., 'Konya plain survey, central Anatolia', *Anatolian archaeology*, V (1999), pp. 13–14.

BAKER, J. T., *The transition from Romano-British to Anglo-Saxon culture in the Chilterns and Essex region*, Ph.D. thesis, University of Birmingham (2001).

BAKIRTZIS, CH. (ed.), *VIIᵉ Congrès international sur la céramique médiévale en Méditerranée* (Athens, 2003).

BALDINI LIPPOLIS, I., *La domus tardoantica* (Imola, 2001).

BALDOVIN, J. F., *The urban character of Christian worship* (Rome, 1987).

BALLANCE, M. *et al.*, *Excavations in Chios 1952–1955: Byzantine Emporio* (London, 1989).

BALLET, P., 'De l'empire romain à la conquête arabe', in *La céramique médiévale en Méditerranée* (Aix-en-Provence, 1997), pp. 53–61.

BALLET, P., 'Relations céramiques entre l'Égypte et Chypre à l'époque gréco-romaine et byzantine', in H. Meyza and J. Młynarczyk (eds.), *Hellenistic and Roman pottery in the eastern Mediterranean* (Warsaw, 1995), pp. 11–25.

BALLET, P., and PICON, M., 'Recherches préliminaries sur les origines de la céramique des Kellia (Égypte)', *Cahiers de la céramique égyptienne*, I (1987), pp. 17–48.

BALLET, P., and VON DER WAY, T., 'Exploration archéologique de Bouto et de sa région (époques romaine et byzantine)', *Mitteilungen des deutschen archäologischen Instituts. Abteilung Kairo*, XLIX (1993), pp. 1–22.

BALLET, P. *et al.*, 'Artisanat de la céramique dans l'Égypte romaine tardive et byzantine', *Cahiers de la céramique égyptienne*, II (1991), pp. 129–43.

BALMELLE, C., *Les demeures aristocratiques d'Aquitaine* (Bordeaux, 2001).

BALMELLE, C. *et al.*, 'Recherches franco-tunisiennes sur la colline de l'Odéon à Carthage en 1991–1993', in P. Trousset (ed.), *L'Afrique du Nord antique et médiévale* (Paris, 1995), pp. 421–39.

BALMELLE, C. *et al.*, 'Vitalité de l'architecture domestique à Carthage au Ve siècle', *Antiquité tardive*, XI (2003), pp. 151–65.

BALTY, J., *Le mosaïque de Sarrîn (Osrhoène)* (Paris, 1990).

BALTY, J.-C., 'Notes sur l'habitat romain, byzantin et arabe d'Apamée: rapport de synthèse', in J. Balty (ed.), *Actes du colloque Apamée de Syrie* (Brussels, 1984), pp. 471–502.

BALZARETTI, R., 'Cities, emporia and monasteries', in Christie and Loseby, *Towns in transition*, pp. 213–34.

BALZARETTI, R., *The lands of Saint Ambrose*, Ph.D. thesis, University College London (1989).

BALZARETTI, R., 'The monastery of Sant' Ambrogio and dispute settlement in early medieval Milan', *Early medieval Europe*, III (1994), pp. 1–18.

BALZARETTI, R., ' "These are things that men do, not women" ', in Halsall, *Violence and society*, pp. 175–92.

BANAJI, J., *Agrarian change in late Antiquity* (Oxford, 2001).

BANAJI, J., 'Agrarian history and the labour organisation of Byzantine large estates', *Proceedings of the British Academy*, XCVI (1999), pp. 193–216.

BANAJI, J., 'The fictions of free labour', *Historical materialism*, XI.3 (2003), pp. 69–95.

BANDINI, F., 'Luni', in S. Gelichi (eds.), *Archeologia urbana in Toscana* (Mantua, 1999), pp. 11–22.

BANGE, F., 'L'*ager* et la *villa*', *Annales ESC*, XXXIX (1984), pp. 529–69.

BANKS, P., 'The Roman inheritance and topographical transitions in early medieval Barcelona', in T. F. C. Blagg *et al.* (eds.), *Papers in Iberian archaeology*, BAR, I193 (Oxford, 1984), pp. 600–34.

BARATTE, F., 'Recherches franco-tunisiennes sur la citadelle byzantine d'Ammaedara (Haïdra)', *Académie des inscriptions et belles-lettres, comptes rendus* (1996), pp. 125–54.

BARATTE, F. *et al.*, *Recherches archéologiques à Haïdra. Miscellanea 2* (Rome, 1999).

BARAUT, C., 'Els documents, dels segles IX i X, conservats a l'Arxiu capitular de la Seu d'Urgell', *Urgellia*, II (1979), pp. 7–145.

BARAUT, C., 'Les actes de consacracions d'esglésies del bisbat d'Urgell (segles IX–XII)', *Urgellia*, I (1978), pp. 11–182.

BARBERO, A., 'Liberti, raccomandati, vassalli', *Storica*, XIV (1999), pp. 7–60.

BARBERO, A., and VIGIL, M., *La formación del feudalismo en la Península Ibérica* (Barcelona, 1978).

BARBERO, A., and VIGIL, M., *Sobre los orígines sociales de la Reconquista* (Barcelona, 1974).

BARBIER, J., 'Le système palatial franc', *Bibliothèque de l'École de chartes*, CXLVIII (1990), pp. 245–99.

BARCELÓ, M., 'Assentaments berbers i àrabs a les regions del nord-est d'al-Andalus', in P. Sénac (ed.), *La Marche Supérieure d'al-Andalus et l'Occident chrétien* (Madrid, 1991), pp. 89–97.

BARCELÓ, M., *El sol que salió por occidente* (Jaén, 1997).

BARCELÓ, M., 'Els *fulūs* de Ṭanǧa de finals del segle I H./VII d.c., els pactes més antics i el cas de Mallorca i de Menorca', *Gaceta numismática*, CXIV (1994), pp. 5–18.

BARCELÓ, M., 'Vespres de feudals', in *La formació i expansió del feudalisme català* (Girona, 1985–6), pp. 237–49.

BARCELÓ, M. *et al.*, *Les aigües cercades* (Palma de Mallorca, 1986).

BARKER, G. *et al.*, *Farming the desert*, 2 vols. (Tripoli, 1996).

BARKER, P. *et al.*, *The Baths basilica, Wroxeter* (London, 1997).

BARNES, H., and WHITTOW, M., 'The survey of medieval castles of Anatolia (1992–96): the Maeander region', in R. Matthews (ed.), *Ancient Anatolia* (London, n.d., c.1998), pp. 347–58.

BARNISH, S., 'Pigs, plebeians and *potentes*', *PBSR*, LV (1987), pp. 157–85.

BARNISH, S., 'Taxation, land and barbarian settlement in the western Empire', *PBSR*, LIV (1986), pp. 170–95.

BARNISH, S., 'The transformation of classical cities and the Pirenne debate', *JRA*, II (1989), pp. 385–400.

BARNISH, S., 'Transformation and survival in the western senatorial aristocracy, *c.* A.D. 400–700', *PBSR*, LVI (1988), pp. 120–55.

BARNISH, S., LEE, A. D., and WHITBY, M., 'Government and administration', in A. Cameron *et al.* (eds.), *The Cambridge ancient history*, XIV (Cambridge, 2000), pp. 164–206.

BARNWELL, P. S., *Emperor, prefects and kings*, (London, 1992).

BARNWELL, P. S., *Kings, courtiers and imperium* (London, 1997).

BARRAUD, D. *et al.*, 'L'industrie céramique de l'Antiquité tardive', in H. Ben Hassen and L. Maurin (eds.), *Oudhna (Uthina), La redécouverte d'une ville antique de Tunisie* (Bordeaux–Tunis, 1998), pp. 139–67.

BARROW, G. W. S., *The kingdom of the Scots* (London, 1973).

BARTHÉLEMY, D., *La mutation de l'an mil a-t-elle eu lieu?* (Paris, 1997).

BARTHÉLEMY, D., *La société dans le comté de Vendôme de l'an mil au XIVe siècle* (Paris, 1993).

BARTL, K., *Frühislamische Besiedlung im Balīḫ-tal/Nordsyrien* (Berlin, 1994).

BARTLETT, R., *The making of Europe* (London, 1993).

BASILE, B., 'Indagini nell'ambito delle necropoli siracusane', *Kōkalos*, XXXIX–XXXXL (1993–4), pp. 1315–42.

BASS, G. F., and VAN DOORNINCK, F. H., *Yassı Ada*, I (College Station, Tex., 1982).

BASSETT, S. R., 'Beyond the edge of excavation', in H. Mayr-Harting and R. I. Moore (eds.), *Studies in medieval history presented to R. H. C. Davis* (London, 1985), pp. 21–39.

BASSETT, S. R., 'Churches in Worcester before and after the conversion of the Anglo-Saxons', *The Antiquaries journal*, LXIX (1989), pp. 225–56.

BASSETT, S. R., 'How the west was won', *Anglo-Saxon studies in archaeology and history*, XI (2000), pp. 107–18.

BASSETT, S. R., 'In search of the origins of Anglo-Saxon kingdoms', in Bassett, *The origins*, pp. 3–27.

BASSETT, S. R., *The origins of the parishes of the Deerhurst area* (Deerhurst, 1998).

BASSETT, S. R. (ed.), *The origins of Anglo-Saxon kingdoms* (Leicester, 1989).

BATES, M., 'Byzantine coinage and its imitations, Arab coinage and its imitations: Arab-Byzantine coinage', *Aram*, VI (1994), pp. 381–403.

BAUDOUX, J., *Les amphores du nord-est de la Gaule (territoire français)* (Paris, 1996).

BAVANT, B., and ORSSAUD, D., 'Stratigraphie et typologie', in Villeneuve and Watson, *La céramique byzantine*, pp. 33–48.

BAYARD, D., 'Berry-au-Bac (Aisne)', *Archéologie médiévale*, XVIII (1988), pp. 290–1.

BAYARD, D., 'La céramique dans le Nord de la Gaule à la fin de l'Antiquité (de la fin du IVème au VIème siècle)', in Piton, *La céramique*, pp. 107–28.

BAYARD, D., 'La céramique de l'habitat mérovingien de Goudelancourt (Aisne)', *Revue archéologique de Picardie* (1994), 1–2, pp. 65–79.

BAYARD, D., 'La sigillée d'Argonne, un paramètre essentiel pour l'établissement de la chronologie du Ve siècle dans le Nord de la Gaule', in Delestre and Périn, *La datation*, pp. 7–20.

BAYARD, D., 'L'ensemble du grand amphithéâtre de Metz et la sigillée d'Argonne au Ve siècle', *Gallia*, XLVII (1990), pp. 271–319.

BAYARD, D., 'Le village mérovingien du "Gué de Mauchamp" à Juvincourt-et-Damary', in *Archéologie. Grands Travaux. Autoroute A26* (Amiens, 1989), pp. 101–10.

BAYARD, D., 'Les habitats du haut moyen âge en Picardie', in Lorren and Périn, *L'habitat rural*, pp. 53–62.

BAYARD, D., and THOUVENOT, S., 'Étude de la céramique du haut moyen âge (Vème siècle–Xème siècle) dans le département de l'Aisne (France)', in Piton, *La céramique*, pp. 291–340.

BAZZANA, A., CRESSIER, P., and GUICHARD, P., *Les châteaux ruraux d'al-Andalus* (Madrid, 1988).

BÉAGUE-TAHON, N., and GEORGES-LEROY, M., 'Deux habitats ruraux du haut moyen âge en Champagne crayeuse', in Lorren and Périn, *L'habitat rural*, pp. 175–83.

BEAUCAMP, J., *Le statut de la femme à Byzance (4e–7e siècle)*, 2 vols. (Paris, 1990–2).

BECKER, C. H., 'Arabische Papyri des Aphroditofundes', *Zeitschrift für Assyriologie*, XX (1907), pp. 68–104.

BECKMANN, G. A., 'Aus den letzten Jahrzehnten des Vulgärlateins in Frankreich', *Zeitschrift für romanische Philologie*, LXXIX (1963), pp. 305–34.

BEJAOUI, F., 'Nouvelles données archéologiques à Sbeïtla', *Africa*, XIV (1996), pp. 37–63.

BEJAOUI, F., 'Une nouvelle église d'époque byzantine à Sbeïtla', *L'Africa romana*, XII (1998), pp. 1173–83.

BELKE, K., 'Das Byzantinische Dorf in Zentralanatolien', in *XXe congrès international des études byzantines. Pré-actes*, II (Paris, 2001), p. 25.

BELKE, K., and RESTLE, M., *Galatien und Lykaonien, Tabula imperii Byzantini*, IV (Vienna, 1984).

BELL, H. I., 'An Egyptian village in the age of Justinian', *Journal of Hellenic studies*, LXIV (1944), pp. 21–36.

BELL, H. I., 'Two official letters of the Arab period', *Journal of Egyptian archae-ology*, XII (1926), pp. 265–81.

BELL, M., 'Excavations at Bishopstone' = *Sussex archaeological collections*, CXV (1977).

BELLI BARSALI, I., 'La topografia di Lucca nei secoli VIII–XI', in *Atti del V Congresso internazionale di studi sull'alto medioevo* (Spoleto, 1973), pp. 461–554.

BEN ABED, A., and DUVAL, N., 'Carthage, la capitale du royaume et les villes de Tunisie à l'époque vandale', in Ripoll and Gurt, *Sedes regiae*, pp. 163–218.

BEN ABED, A. *et al.*, 'Note préliminaire sur la céramique de la basilique orientale di Sidi Jdidi (Tunisie) (V^e–VIIe s.)', in *La céramique médiévale en Méditerranée* (Aix-en-Provence, 1997), pp. 13–25.

BEN MOUSSA, M., 'Production et circulation des sigillées africaines de la Tunisie septentrionale', *Mésogeios*, VII (2000), pp. 44–78.

BENCARD, M. *et al.*, *Ribe excavations 1970–76*, IV (Esbjerg, 1990).

BENCO, N. L., *The early medieval pottery industry at al-Basra, Morocco*, BAR, I341 (Oxford, 1987).

BENSEDDIK, N., and POTTER, T. W., *Fouilles du forum de Cherchel, 1977–1981*, 2 vols. (Algiers, 1993).

BERESFORD, G., *Goltho* (London, 1987).

BERGENGRUEN, A., *Adel und Grundherrschaft im Merowingerreich* (Wiesbaden, 1958).

BERGMANN, W., 'Untersuchungen zu den Gerichtsurkunden der Merowingerzeit', *Archiv für Diplomatik*, XXII (1976), pp. 1–186.

BERKTAY, H., 'The feudalism debate: the Turkish end', *Journal of peasant studies*, XIV (1987), pp. 291–333.

BERNAL CASASOLA, D., and PÉREZ RIVERA, J. M., 'La ocupación bizantina de *Septem*', *V Reunió d'arqueologia cristiana hispànica* (Barcelona, 2000), pp. 121–33.

BERNARDINI, S. *et al.*, 'Il territorio di Segesta fra l'età arcaica e il Medioevo', in *Atti delle Terze giornate internazionali di studi sull'area elima* (Pisa–Gibellina, 2000), pp. 91–133.

BERNHARD, H., 'Die frühmittelalterliche Siedlung von Speyer "Vogelgesang"', *Offa*, XXXIX (1982), pp. 217–33.

BERNHARD, H., 'Die Merowingerzeit in der Pfalz', *Mitteilungen des Historischen Vereins der Pfalz*, XCV (1997), pp. 7–106.

BERSCHIN, W., *Biographie und Epochenstil im lateinischen Mittelalter*, II (Stuttgart, 1988).

BERTI, G., and TONGIORGI, L., *I bacini ceramici medievali delle chiese di Pisa* (Rome, 1981).

BERTIN, P. *et al.*, 'Une occupation mérovingienne précoce au bord de la Marne', in P. Ouzoulias and P. Van Ossel (eds.), *Document de travail*, VI (Paris, 2003), pp. 121–78.

BERTOLINI, O., 'I vescovi del "regnum langobardorum" al tempo dei Carolingi', in idem, *Scritti scelti di storia medioevale*, I (Livorno, 1968), pp. 71–92.

BESGA MARROQUÍN, A., 'El reino de Asturias y las Vascongadas', in *La época de la monarquía asturiana* (Oviedo, 2002), pp. 391–414.

BESTEMAN, J. C. *et al.*, *The excavations at Wijnaldum*, I (Rotterdam, 1999).

BIDDLE, M., 'Towns', in D. M. Wilson (ed.), *The archaeology of Anglo-Saxon England* (Cambridge, 1976), pp. 99–150.

BIEDENKOPF-ZIEHNER, A., *Untersuchungen zum koptischen Briefformular unter Berücksichtigung ägyptischer und griechischer Parallelen* (Würzburg, 1983).

BIELER, L., 'Towards an interpretation of the so-called "canones Wallici" ', in J. A. Watt *et al.* (eds.), *Medieval studies presented to Aubrey Gwynn, S.J.* (Dublin, 1961), pp. 388–92.

BIERBRAUER, V., 'Frühe langobardische Siedlung in Italien', in *Atti del XVI Congresso internazionale di studi sull'alto medioevo* (Spoleto, 2003), pp. 29–77.

BIERBRAUER, V., *Invillino-Ibligo in Friaul*, I (Munich, 1987).

BIERBRAUER, V., 'Situazione della ricerca sugli insediamenti nell'Italia settentrionale in epoca tardo-antica e nell'alto medio evo (V–VII sec.)', *AM*, XV (1988), pp. 501–15.

BILLY, P.-H., *La 'condamine', institution agro-seigneuriale* (Tübingen, 1997).

BINCHY, D. A., *Celtic and Anglo-Saxon kingship* (Oxford, 1970).

BINTLIFF, J., 'Frankish countryside in central Greece', in P. Lock and G. D. R. Sanders (eds.), *The archaeology of medieval Greece* (Oxford, 1996), pp. 1–18.

BIRABEN, J.-N., and LE GOFF, J., 'La peste dans le haut moyen âge', *Annales ESC*, XXIV (1969), pp. 1484–510.

BITEL, L. M., *Isle of the saints* (Ithaca, NY, 1990).

BITEL, L. M., *Land of women* (Ithaca, NY, 1996).

BLACK-MICHAUD, J., *Cohesive force* (Oxford, 1975).

BLACKMORE, L., 'La céramique du Vème au Xème siècle à Londres et dans la région londonienne', in Piton, *La céramique*, pp. 129–50.

BLACKMORE, L., 'Pottery: trade and tradition', in D. Hill and R. Cowie (eds.), *Wics* (Sheffield, 2001), pp. 22–42.

BLAIR, J., *Anglo-Saxon Oxfordshire* (Stroud, 1994).

BLAIR, J., 'Frithuwold's kingdom and the origins of Surrey', in Bassett, *The origins*, pp. 97–107.

BLAKELEY, J. A., 'Toward the study of economics at Caesarea Maritima', in A. Raban and K. G. Holum (eds.), *Caesarea Maritima* (Leiden, 1996), pp. 327–45.

BLANCHARD-LEMÉE, M., 'La *villa* à mosaïques de Mienne-Marboué (Eure-et-Loir)', *Gallia*, XXXIX (1981), pp. 63–83.

BLANCHARD-LEMÉE, M., *Recueil général des mosaïques de la Gaule*, II.4 (Paris, 1991).

BLANTON, R. E., *Hellenistic, Roman and Byzantine settlement patterns of the coast lands of western Rough Cilicia*, BAR, I879 (Oxford, 2000).

BLASCO, J. *et al.*, 'Estat actual de la investigació arqueològica de l'antiguedat tardana a la ciutat de València', *III Reunió d'arqueologia cristiana hispànica* (Barcelona, 1994), pp. 185–99.

BLEIBER, W., 'Grundherrschaft und Markt zwischen Loire und Rhein während des 9. Jahrhunderts', *Jahrbuch für Wirtschaftsgeschichte* (1982), 3, pp. 105–35.

BLEIBER, W., *Naturwirtschaft und Ware-Geld-Beziehungen zwischen Somme und Loire während des 7. Jahrhunderts* (Berlin, 1981).

BLINKHORN, P., 'Of cabbages and kings', in Anderton, *Anglo-Saxon trading centres*, pp. 4–23.

BLINKHORN, P., *The Ipswich ware project* (in press).

BLOCH, M., *Feudal society* (London, 1961).

BLOCH, M., *Les caractères originaux de l'histoire rurale française* (Oslo, 1931).

BLOCH, M., *Mélanges historiques*, 2 vols. (Paris, 1963).

BLOCKLEY, K. *et al.*, *Excavations in the Marlowe Car Park and surrounding areas*, I (Canterbury, 1995).

BOCCHI, F., 'Città e mercati nell'Italia padana', *Settimane di studio*, XL (1993), pp. 139–85.

BODDINGTON, A., 'Models of burial, settlement and worship', in E. Southworth (ed.), *Anglo-Saxon cemeteries: a reappraisal* (Stroud, 1990), pp. 177–99.

BÖHME, H. W., 'Adelsgräber im Frankenreich', *Jahrbuch des römisch-germanischen Zentralmuseums Mainz*, XL (1993), pp. 397–534.

BÖHME, H. W., 'Das Ende der Römerherrschaft in Britannien und die angelsächsiche Besiedlung Englands im 5. Jahrhundert', *Jahrbuch des römisch-germanischen Zentralmuseums Mainz*, XXXIII (1986), pp. 469–574.

BÖHMER, J. F., *Regesta imperii*, I, re-edited E. Mühlbacher *et al.* (Hildesheim, 1966).

BÖHNER, K., 'Bonn im frühen Mittelalter', *Bonner Jahrbücher*, CLXXVIII (1978), pp. 395–426.

BÖHNER, K., *Die fränkischen Altertümer des Trierer Landes*, 2 vols. (Berlin, 1958).

BÖHNER, K., 'Urban and rural settlement in the Frankish kingdom', in M. W. Barley (ed.), *European towns* (London, 1977), pp. 185–201.

BOIS, G., *La mutation de l'an mil* (Paris, 1989).

BOLLA, M., 'La pietra ollare', in D. Caporusso (ed.), *Scavi MM3*, III. 2 (Milan, 1991), pp. 11–37.

BONIFAY, M., 'Alexandrie. Chantier du théâtre Diana', in J.-Y. Empereur (ed.), *Alexandria I* (Cairo, 1998), pp. 141–8.

BONIFAY, M., 'La céramique africaine, un indice du développement économique?', *Antiquité tardive*, XI (2003), pp. 113–28.

BONIFAY, M. *et al.* (eds.), *Fouilles à Marseille. Les mobiliers (Ier–VIIe siècles ap. J.-C.)* (Paris, 1998).

BONNAL, J.-P., and FÉVRIER, P.-A., 'Ostraka de la région de Bir Trouch', *Bulletin d'archéologie algérienne*, II (1966–7), pp. 239–49.

BONNASSIE, P., *From slavery to feudalism in south-western Europe* (Cambridge, 1991).

BONNASSIE, P., *La Catalogne du milieu du Xe à la fin du XIe siècle* (Toulouse, 1975–6).

BONNASSIE, P., 'Une famille de la campagne barcelonaise et ses activités économiques aux alentours de l'An Mil', *Annales du Midi*, LXXVI (1964), pp. 261–303.

BONNEAU, D., 'Communauté rurale en Égypte byzantine?', *Recueils de la société Jean Bodin*, XLI (1983), pp. 505–22.

BONNEAU, D., *Le régime administratif de l'eau du Nil dans l'Égypte grecque, romaine et byzantine* (Leiden, 1993).

BONNET, C., *Les fouilles de l'ancien groupe épiscopal de Genève (1976–1993)* (Geneva, 1993).

BONNET, C., and BELTRÁN DE HEREDIA, J., 'El primer grupo episcopal de Barcelona', in Ripoll and Gurt, *Sedes regiae*, pp. 467–90.

BONNET, C., and BELTRÁN DE HEREDIA, J., 'Nuevas intervenciones arqueológicas en el Museo de Historia de la Ciudad', *V Reunió d'arqueologia cristiana hispànica* (Barcelona, 2000), pp. 135–44.

BONO, P. *et al.*, 'The water supply of Constantinople', *Environmental geology*, XL (2001), pp. 1325–33.

BORGOLTE, M., 'Freigelassene im Dienst der memoria', *Frühmittelalterliche Studien*, XVII (1983), pp. 234–50.

BOSERUP, E., *The conditions of agricultural growth* (London, 1965).

BOSL, K., 'Der "Adelsheilige" ', in C. Bauer *et al.* (eds.), *Speculum historiale* (Freiburg, 1965), pp. 167–87.

BOSL, K., '*Potens* und *pauper*', in idem, *Frühformen der Gesellschaft im mittelalterlichen Europa* (Munich, 1964), pp. 106–34.

BOUIRON, M., 'La trame urbaine médiévale', in M. Bouiron and H. Tréziny (eds.), *Marseille. Trames et paysages urbains de Gyptis au Roi René* (Aix-en-Provence, 2001), pp. 147–56.

BOURDIEU, P., *Distinction* (London, 1984).

BOURDIEU, P., *Outline of a theory of practice* (Cambridge, 1977).

BOURDILLON, J., 'The animal provisioning of Saxon Southampton', in J. Rackham (ed.), *Environment and economy in Anglo-Saxon England*, CBA Research Report, 89 (York, 1994), pp. 120–5.

BOURGEOIS, L., *Térritoires, reseaux et habitats. L'occupation du sol dans l'Ouest parisien du V au Xe siècle*, Thèse de doctorat, Université de Paris-I (1995).

BOURIN-DERRUAU, M., *Villages médiévaux en Bas-Languedoc*, I (Paris, 1987).

BOURIN, M., and MARTÍNEZ SOPENA, P. (eds.), *Pour une anthropologie du prélèvement seigneurial dans les campagnes médiévales ($XI–XIV^e$ siècles)*, I (Paris, 2004).

BOWDEN, W. *et al.*, 'Roman and late-antique Butrint', *JRA*, XV (2002), pp. 199–229.

BOWDEN, W. *et al.* (eds.), *Recent research on the late antique countryside* (Leiden, 2004).

BOWMAN, A. K., 'Landholding in the Hermopolite Nome in the fourth century A.D.', *Journal of Roman studies*, LXXV (1985), pp. 137–63.

BOWMAN, P., 'Contrasting pays', in J. Bourne (ed.), *Anglo-Saxon landscapes in the East Midlands* (Leicester, 1996), pp. 121–46.

BRANDES, W., 'Byzantine cities in the seventh and eighth centuries', in Brogiolo and Ward-Perkins, *The idea and ideal of the town*, pp. 25–57.

BRANDES, W., *Die Städte Kleinasiens im 7. und 8. Jahrhundert* (Amsterdam, 1989).

BRANDES, W., *Finanzverwaltung in Krisenzeiten* (Frankfurt, 2002).

BRANDES, W., and HALDON, J., 'Towns, tax and transformation', in Brogiolo *et al.*, *Towns and their territories*, pp. 141–72.

BRANDS, G., *Resafa VI* (Mainz, 2002).

BRANIGAN, K., *Latimer* (Bristol, 1971).

BRATHER, S., 'Ethnische Identitäten als Konstrukte der Frühgeschichtlichen Archäologie', *Germania*, LXXVIII (2000), pp. 137–76.

BRAUDEL, F., *The Mediterranean and the Mediterranean world in the age of Philip II* (London, 1972).

BRÉHIER, L., *Les institutions de l'empire byzantin* (Paris, 1949).

BRETT, M., 'The Arab conquest and the rise of Islam in north Africa', in *The Cambridge history of Africa*, II (Cambridge, 1978), pp. 490–555.

BRETT, M., and FENTRESS, E., *The Berbers* (Oxford, 1996).

BRINK, S., 'Political and social structures in early Scandinavia', *Tor*, XXVIII (1996), pp. 235–81.

BROGAN, O., and SMITH, D. J., *Ghirza* (Tripoli, 1984).

BROGIOLO, G. P., 'A proposito dell'organizzazione urbana nell'alto medioevo', *AM*, XIV (1987), pp. 27–45.

BROGIOLO, G. P., *Brescia altomedievale* (Mantua, 1993).

BROGIOLO, G. P., 'Continuità tra tardo antico e altomedioevo attraverso le vicende delle ville', in E. Roffia (ed.), *Ville romane sul lago di Garda* (S. Felice di Benaco, 1997), pp. 299–313.

BROGIOLO, G. P. (ed.), *Early medieval towns in the western Mediterranean* (Mantua, 1996).

BROGIOLO, G. P. (ed.), *Edilizia residenziale tra V e VII secolo* (Mantua, 1994).

BROGIOLO, G. P. (ed.), *La fine delle ville romane* (Mantua, 1996).

BROGIOLO, G. P. (ed.), *Santa Giulia di Brescia, gli scavi dal 1980 al 1992* (Florence, 1999).

BROGIOLO, G. P., and CAGNANA, A., 'Nuove ricerche sull'origine di Grado', in *L'Adriatico dalla tarda antichità all'età carolingia* (in press).

BROGIOLO, G. P., and CASTELLETTI, L. (eds.), *Archeologia a Monte Barro*, 2 vols. (Lecco, 1991–Galbiate, 2001).

BROGIOLO, G. P., and GELICHI, S., 'Ceramiche, tecnologia ed organizzazione della produzione dell'Italia settentrionale tra VI e X secolo', *La céramique médiévale en Méditerranée* (Aix-en-Provence, 1997), pp. 139–45.

BROGIOLO, G. P., and GELICHI, S., 'La ceramica comune in Italia settentrionale tra IV e VII secolo', in Saguì, *Ceramica in Italia*, pp. 209–26.

BROGIOLO, G. P., and GELICHI, S., 'La ceramica invetriata tardo-antica e medioevale nel nord Italia', in L. Paroli (ed.), *La ceramica invetriata tardoantica e altomedievale in Italia* (Florence, 1992), pp. 23–32.

BROGIOLO, G. P., and GELICHI, S., *La città nell'alto medioevo italiano* (Bari, 1998).

BROGIOLO, G. P., and GELICHI, S., *Nuove ricerche sui castelli altomedievali* (Florence, 1996).

BROGIOLO, G. P., and GELICHI S. (eds.), *Le ceramiche altomedievali (fine VI–X secolo) in Italia settentrionale* (Mantua, 1996).

BROGIOLO, G. P., and WARD-PERKINS, B. (eds.), *The idea and ideal of the town between late Antiquity and the early middle ages* (Leiden, 1999).

BROGIOLO, G. P. *et al.*, 'Associazioni ceramiche nei contesti della prima fase longobarda di Brescia-S. Giulia', in idem and Gelichi, *Le ceramiche altomedievali*, pp. 15–32.

BROGIOLO, G. P. *et al.* (eds.), *Towns and their territories between late Antiquity and the early middle ages* (Leiden, 2000).

BROISE, H., and THÉBERT, Y., *Recherches archéologiques franco-tunisiennes à Bulla Regia*, II.1 (Rome, 1993).

BROOKS, D. A., 'A review of the evidence for continuity in British towns in the fifth and sixth centuries', *Oxford journal of archaeology*, V (1986), pp. 77–102.

BROOKS, D. A., 'The case for continuity in fifth-century Canterbury re-examined', *Oxford journal of archaeology*, VII (1988), pp. 99–114.

BROOKS, N. P., 'Alfredian government', in T. Reuter (ed.), *Alfred the Great* (Aldershot, 2003), pp. 153–73.

BROOKS, N. P., 'English identity from Bede to the Millennium', *Haskins Society journal*, XII (2004).

BROOKS, N. P., 'The creation and early structure of the kingdom of Kent', in Bassett, *The origins*, pp. 55–74.

BROOKS, N. P., 'The development of military obligations in eighth- and ninth-century England', in P. Clemoes and K. Hughes (eds.), *England before the Conquest* (Cambridge, 1971), pp. 69–84.

BROOKS, N. P., *The early history of the church of Canterbury* (Leicester, 1984).

BROOKS, N. P., 'The formation of the Mercian kingdom', in Bassett, *The origins*, pp. 159–70.

BROOKS, N. P., review of Hodges, *Anglo-Saxon achievement*, *Speculum*, LXVIII (1993), pp. 169–71.

BROWN, P., *Augustine of Hippo* (London, 1967).

BROWN, P., *Power and persuasion in late Antiquity* (Madison, Wisc., 1992).

BROWN, P., 'Relics and social status in the age of Gregory of Tours', in idem, *Society and the holy in Late Antiquity* (Berkeley, 1982), pp. 222–50.

BROWN, P., 'The rise and function of the holy man in Late Antiquity', *Journal of Roman studies*, LXI (1971), pp. 80–101.

BROWN, P., *The rise of western Christendom* (Oxford, 1996).

BROWN, T. S., *Gentlemen and officers* (Rome, 1984).

BROWN, W., 'The use of norms in disputes in early medieval Bavaria', *Viator*, XXX (1999), pp. 15–39.

BRUAND, O., *Voyageurs et marchandises aux temps carolingiens* (Brussels, 2002).

BRUBAKER, L., 'Élites and patronage in early Byzantium', in J. Haldon (ed.), *The Byzantine and early Islamic Near East*, VI (Princeton, 2004).

BRUBAKER, L., 'Memories of Helena', in L. James (ed.), *Women, men and eunuchs* (London, 1997), pp. 52–75.

BRUBAKER, L., 'Topography and the creation of public space in early medieval Constantinople', in M. de Jong *et al.* (eds.), *Topographies of power in the early middle ages* (Leiden, 2001), pp. 31–43.

BRUBAKER, L., and HALDON, J. F., *Byzantium in the Iconoclast era (ca.680–ca.850)* (Cambridge, in press).

BRUBAKER, L., and HALDON, J. F., *Byzantium in the Iconoclast era (ca.680–850): the sources* (Aldershot, 2001).

BRÜHL, C.-R., *Palatium und civitas*, I (Cologne, 1975).

BRÜHL, C. R., 'The town as a political centre', in M. W. Barley (ed.), *European towns* (London, 1977), pp. 419–29.

BRÜHL, C. R., 'Zentral- und Finanzverwaltung im Franken- und im Langobardenreich', *Settimane di studio*, XX (1972), pp. 61–94.

BRUNI, S. (ed.), *Pisa. Piazza Dante* (Pisa, 1993).

BRUNI, S., ABELA, E., and BERTI, G., *Ricerche di archeologia medievale a Pisa*, I (Florence, 2000).

BUCKLAND, W. W., *A text-book of Roman law from Augustus to Julian*, 3rd edn., ed. P. Stein (Cambridge, 1963).

BUDNY, M., 'The Anglo-Saxon embroideries at Maaseik', *Mededelingen van de Koninklijke academie voor wetenschappen, letteren en schone kunsten van België. Klasse der schone kunsten*, XLV (1984), pp. 57–133.

BÜCKER, C., and HOEPER, M., 'First aspects of social hierarchy of settlements in Merovingian southwest Germany', in C. Fabech and J. Ringtved (eds.), *Settlement and landscape* (Højbjerg, 1999), pp. 441–54.

BUJARD, J., and JOGUIN, M., 'La céramique d'Umm el-Rasas/Kastron Mefaa et d'Umm al-Walid', in Villeneuve and Watson, *La céramique byzantine*, pp. 139–47.

BULLIET, R. W., 'Local politics in eastern Iran under the Ghaznavids and Seljuks', *Iranian studies*, XI (1978), pp. 35–56.

BULLOUGH, D. A., 'Leo, *qui apud Hlotharium magni loci habebatur*, et le gouvernement du *Regnum Italiae* à l'époque carolingienne', *Le moyen âge*, LXVII (1961), pp. 219–45.

BURNS, T. S., and EADIE, J. W. (eds.), *Urban centers and rural contexts in late Antiquity* (East Lansing, Mich., 2001).

BUSCH, J. W., 'Vom Attentat zur Haft', *Historische Zeitschrift*, CCLXIII (1996), pp. 561–88.

BUTCHER, K., and THORPE, R., 'A note on excavations in central Beirut 1994–96', *JRA*, X (1997), pp. 291–306.

BUTLER, H. C., *Publications of an American archaeological expedition to Syria in 1899–1900*, II, *Architecture and other arts* (New York, 1903).

BUTLER, H. C., *Syria*, II B. *Architecture. Northern Syria* (Leiden, 1920).

BYOCK, J., *Viking age Iceland* (Harmondsworth, 2001).

BYRNE, F. J., *Irish kings and high-kings* (London, 1973).

CABALLERO ZOREDA, L., 'Cerámicas de "época visigoda y post-visigoda" de las provincias de Cáceres, Madrid y Segovia', *Boletín de arqueología medieval*, III (1989), pp. 75–107.

CABALLERO ZOREDA, L., 'La arquitectura denominada de época visigoda', in idem and P. Mateos Cruz (eds.), *Visigodos y Omeyas* (Madrid, 2000), pp. 207–47.

CABALLERO ZOREDA, L., and JUAN TOVAR, L. C., 'Terra sigillata hispánica brillante', *Empúries*, XLV–XLVI (1983–4), pp. 154–93.

CABALLERO ZOREDA, L., and SÁEZ LARA, F., *La iglesia mozárabe de S. Lucia del Trampal, Alcuéscar (Cáceres)* (Mérida, 1999).

CABALLERO ZOREDA, L. *et al.*, 'Las cerámicas del primer momento de Santa María de Melque (Toledo), construcción, uso y destrucción', in Caballero *et al.*, *Cerámicas tardorromanas y altomedievales*, pp. 225–71.

CABALLERO ZOREDA, L. *et al.* (eds.), *Cerámicas tardorromanas y altomedievales en la Península Ibérica* (Madrid, 2003).

CADELL, H., 'Nouveaux fragments de la correspondence de Ḳurrah ben Sharik', *Recherches de papyrologie*, IV (1967), pp. 107–60.

CADMAN, G., 'Raunds 1977–1983', *Medieval archaeology*, XXVII (1983), pp. 107–22.

CADMAN, G., and FOARD, G., 'Raunds: manorial and village origins', in M. L. Faull (ed.), *Studies in late Anglo-Saxon settlement* (Oxford, 1984), pp. 81–100.

CAGIANO DE AZEVEDO, M., 'Le case descritte nel *Codex Traditionum Ecclesiae Ravennatis*', *Rendiconti dell'Accademia dei Lincei, classe di scienze morali, storiche e filologiche*, 8 ser., XXVII (1972), pp. 159–81.

CAHEN, C., 'Fiscalité, propriété, antagonismes sociaux en Haute-Mésopotamie au temps des premiers "Abbāsides d'après Denys de Tell-Mahré", *Arabica*, I (1954), pp. 136–52.

CAHEN, C., 'L'évolution de l'iqta' du IXe au XIIIe siècle', *Annales ESC*, VIII (1953), pp. 25–52.

CALLEGHER, B., 'Thésaurisation et circulation monétaire dans le Péloponnèse du Nord entre le Ve et le VIIe siècle', in *XXe Congrès international des études byzantines. Pré-actes*, II (Paris, 2001), p. 49.

CALLEJA PUERTA, M., and BELTRÁN SUÁREZ, S., 'El espacio centro-oriental de Asturias en el siglo VIII', in *La época de la monarquía asturiana* (Oviedo, 2002), pp. 63–109.

CALLOT, O., *Huileries antiques de Syrie du Nord* (Paris, 1984).

CALLOW, C., *Landscape, tradition and power in a region of medieval Iceland*, Ph.D. thesis, University of Birmingham (2001).

CAMBUZAT, P.-L., *L'évolution des cités du Tell en Ifrîkiya du VII au XI siècle*, 2 vols. (Algiers, 1986).

CAMERON, A., 'Vandal and Byzantine Africa', in eadem *et al.* (eds.), *The Cambridge ancient history*, XIV (Cambridge, 2000), pp. 552–69.

CAMERON, F. *et al.*, 'Il castello di Ponte Nepesino e il confine settentrionale del Ducato di Roma', *AM*, XIV (1984), pp. 63–148.

CAMMAROSANO, P., *Italia medievale* (Rome, 1991).

CAMMAROSANO, P., *Nobili e re* (Bari, 1998).

CAMPBELL, E., 'The archaeological evidence for external contacts', in K. R. Dark (ed.), *External contacts and the economy of late Roman and post-Roman Britain* (Woodbridge, 1986), pp. 83–96.

CAMPBELL, E., and LANE, A., 'Longbury bank, Dyfed', *Medieval archaeology*, XXXVII (1993), pp. 15–77.

CAMPBELL, J., *Essays in Anglo-Saxon history* (London, 1986).

CAMPS, G., 'Le Gour, mausolée berbère du VIIe siècle', *Antiquités africaines*, VIII (1974), pp. 191–208.

CAMPS, G., '*Rex gentium Maurorum et Romanorum*', *Antiquités africaines*, XX (1984), pp. 183–218.

CANIVET, P., and REY-COCQUAIS, J.-P. (eds.), *La Syrie de Byzance à l'Islam, VIIe–VIIIe siècles* (Damascus, 1992).

CANN, S. J., and LLOYD, J. A., 'Late Roman and early medieval pottery from the Molise', *AM*, XI (1984), pp. 425–36.

CANTINI, F., *Il castello di Montarrenti* (Florence, 2003).

CANTINI, F., *Le fasi di V–X secolo dello scavo dell'ospedale di S. Maria della Scala*, tesi di dottorato, Università di Siena (2000–2), relatori R. Francovich and A. Molinari.

CANTINO WATAGHIN, G., 'Monasteri in Piemonte dalla tarda antichità al medioevo', in L. Mercando and E. Micheletto (eds.), *Archeologia in Piemonte*, III (Turin, 1998), pp. 101–85.

CAPORUSSO, D. (ed.), *Scavi MM3* (Milan, 1991).

CARANDINI, A., *Anatomia della scimmia* (Turin, 1979).

CARANDINI, A., *Schiavi in Italia* (Rome, 1988).

CARDOT, F., *L'espace et le pouvoir* (Paris, 1987).

CAROCCI, S., 'Signoria rurale e mutazione feudale', *Storica*, VIII (1997), pp. 49–91.

CARON, B., and LAVOIE, C., 'Les recherches canadiennes dans le quartier de la "Rotonde de l'Odéon" en Carthage', *Antiquité tardive*, X (2002), pp. 249–61.

CARR, K. E., 'A changing world—African Red Slip in Roman and Visigothic Baetica', in A. Ferreiro (ed.), *The Visigoths* (Leiden, 1999), pp. 219–61.

CARR, K. E., *Vandals to Visigoths* (Ann Arbor, Mich., 2002).

CARRIÉ, J.-M., ' "Colonato del Basso Impero" ', in Lo Cascio, *Terre, proprietari*, pp. 75–150.

CARRIÉ, J.-M., 'Le "colonat du Bas-Empire": un mythe historiographique?', *Opus*, I (1982), pp. 351–70.

CARRIÉ, J.-M., 'L'economia e le finanze', in *Storia di Roma*, III.1 (Turin, 1993), pp. 751–87.

CARRIÉ, J.-M., 'L'État à la recherche de nouveaux modes de financement des armées (Rome et Byzance, IVᵉ–VIIIᵉ siècles)', in A. Cameron (ed.), *The Byzantine and early Islamic Near East*, III (Princeton, 1995), pp. 27–60.

CARRIÉ, J.-M., 'Les échanges commerciaux et l'État antique tardif', in *Les échanges dans l'Antiquité* (St-Bertrand-de-Comminges, 1994), pp. 175–211.

CARRIÉ, J.-M., 'Observations sur la fiscalité du IVᵉ siècle pour servir à l'histoire monétaire', in *L'"inflazione" del quarto secolo* (Rome, 1993), pp. 115–54.

CARRIÉ, J.-M., 'Patronage et propriété militaires au IVᵉ s.', *Bulletin de correspondance hellénique*, C (1976), pp. 159–76.

CARRIÉ, J.-M., 'Un roman des origines', *Opus*, II (1983), pp. 205–51.

CARROBLES SANTOS, J., 'La ciudad de Toledo en la antigüedad tardía', in García Moreno and Rascón Marqués, *Complutum*, pp. 193–200.

CARRU, D. *et al.*, 'Les *villae* en Provence aux IVᵉ et Vᵉ siècles', in Ouzoulias *et al.*, *Les campagnes*, pp. 475–501.

CARVER, M. O. H., *Arguments in stone* (Oxford, 1993).

CARVER, M. O. H., 'The Anglo-Saxon cemetery at Sutton Hoo: an interim report', in idem (ed.), *The age of Sutton Hoo* (Woodbridge, 1992), pp. 343–71.

CASSANDRO, G., 'Il ducato bizantino', in *Storia di Napoli*, II.1 (Naples, 1969), pp. 3–408.

CASSON, L., 'Tax-collection problems in early Arab Egypt', *Transactions and proceedings of the American philological association*, LXIX (1938), pp. 274–91.

CASTAGNETTI, A., 'Dominico e massaricio a Limonta nei secoli nono e decimo', *Rivista di storia dell'agricoltura*, VII (1968), pp. 3–20.

CASTAGNETTI, A., 'Famiglie e affermazione politica', in L. C. Ruggini *et al.* (eds.), *Storia di Venezia*, I (Rome, 1992), pp. 613–44.

CASTAGNETTI, A., *L'organizzazione del territorio rurale nel medioevo* (Turin, 1979).

CASTANYER I MASOLIVER, P., and TREMOLEDA I TRILLA, J., *La vil.la romana de Vilauba* (Girona, 1999).

CASTELLANA, G., and McCONNELL, B. E., 'A rural settlement of imperial Roman and Byzantine date in Contrada Saraceno near Agrigento, Sicily', *American journal of archaeology*, XCIV (1990), pp. 25–44.

CASTELLANOS, S., *Hagiografía y sociedad en la Hispania visigoda* (Logroño, 1999).

CASTELLANOS, S., *Poder social, aristocracias y hombre santo en la Hispania visigoda* (Logroño, 1998).

CASTELLANOS, S., 'Propiedad de la tierra y relaciones de dependencia en la Galia del siglo VI', *Antiquité tardive*, VIII (2000), pp. 223–7.

CASTELLANOS, S., 'Terminología textual y relaciones de dependencia en la sociedad hispanovisigoda', *Gerion*, XVI (1998), pp. 451–60.

CASTELLANOS, S., 'The political nature of taxation in Visigothic Spain', *Early medieval Europe*, XII (2003), pp. 201–28.

CASTELLANOS, S., and MARTÍN VISO, I., 'The local articulation of central power in the north of the Iberian Peninsula (500–1000)', *Early medieval Europe*, XIII (2005), pp. 1–42.

CASTILLO ARMENTEROS, J. C., *La Campiña de Jaén en época emiral (s. VIII–X)* (Jaén, 1998).

CASTILLO GALDEANO, F., and MARTÍNEZ MADRID, R., 'La vivienda hispanomusulmana en Baŷŷāna-Pechina (Almería)', in *La casa hispano-musulmana* (Granada, 1990), pp. 111–27.

CASTILLO GALDEANO, F., and MARTÍNEZ MADRID, R., 'Producciones cerámicas en Baŷŷāna', in Malpica, *Cerámica altomedieval*, pp. 69–116.

CASTILLO GALDEANO, F. *et al.*, 'Urbanismo e industria en Baŷŷāna. Pechina (Almería)', in *II Congreso de arqueología medieval española*, II (Madrid, 1987), pp. 540–8.

CATALO, J. *et al.*, 'Le forum de Rodez (Aveyron) du IVe au VIIe siècle', in B. Fizellier-Sauget (ed.), *L'Auvergne de Sidoine Apollinaire à Grégoire de Tours* (Clermont, 1999), pp. 113–31.

CATARSI DALL'AGLIO, M., 'Archeologia medievale a Parma e Fidenza', in S. Patitucci Uggeri (ed)., *Scavi medievali in Italia 1994–1995* (Rome, 1998), pp. 33–44.

CATHMA, 'Céramiques languedociennes de haut moyen âge (VII–XIe s.)', *Archéologie du Midi médiéval*, XI (1993), pp. 111–228.

CATHMA, 'Céramiques languedociennes de haut moyen âge (VII–XIe s.): essai de synthèse à partir des acquis récents', in *La céramique médiévale en Méditerranée* (Aix-en-Provence, 1997), pp. 103–10.

CATHMA, 'Importations de céramiques communes méditerranéennes dans le Midi de la Gaule (Ve–VIIe s.)', in *A cerâmica medieval no Mediterrâneo ocidental* (Mértola, 1991), pp. 27–47.

CAU ONTIVEROS, M. A. *et al.*, 'Algunas consideraciones sobre cerámicas de cocina de los siglos IV al VIII', *Quaderns científics i tècnics*, IX (1997), pp. 7–36.

CAU, M. A. *et al.*, 'La cerámica del nordeste peninsular y las Baleares entre los siglos V–X', in *La céramique médiévale en Méditerranée* (Aix-en-Provence, 1997), pp. 173–92.

CECCARELLI LEMUT, M. L., 'Scarlino: le vicende medievali fino al 1399', in R. Francovich (ed.), *Scarlino*, I (Florence, 1985), pp. 19–74.

CECCONI, G. A., *Governo imperiale e élites dirigenti nell'Italia tardoantica* (Como, 1994).

CECCONI, G. A., 'Tradizione e novità nei meccanismi dell'esazione tributaria (Italia, V secolo d. C.)', *Università di Siena. Annali della Facoltà di lettere e filosofia*, XIV (1993), pp. 35–49.

ČEKULOVA, A., 'Fortune des sénateurs de Constantinople du IVe au début du VIIe siècle', in *Eupsychia*, I (Paris, 1998), pp. 119–30.

CÉRATI, A., *Caractère annonaire et assiette de l'impôt foncier au Bas-Empire* (Paris, 1975).

CERESA MORI, A. *et al.*, 'Milano, indagini dell'area del foro', *Notiziario. Soprintendenza archeologica della Lombardia* (1990), pp. 173–85.

CESA, M., '*Hospitalitas* o altre "techniques of accomodation"?', *Archivio storico italiano*, CXL (1982), pp. 539–52.

CHADWICK, H. M., *Studies on Anglo-Saxon institutions* (Cambridge, 1905).

CHALMETA, P., *Invasión e islamización* (Madrid, 1994).

CHALON, M. *et al.*, '*Memorabile factum*. Une célébration de l'évérgetisme des rois vandales dans l'Anthologie latine', *Antiquités africaines*, XXI (1985), pp. 207–62.

CHAMBERS, R. A., 'The late- and sub-Roman cemetery at Queenford Farm, Dorchester-on-Thames, Oxon', *Oxoniensia*, LII (1987), pp. 35–69.

CHAMPION, É., *Moulins et meuniers carolingiens* (Paris, 1996).

CHARMASSON, J., 'L'*oppidum* bas-rhodanien de Lombren (Gard)', *Cahiers rhodaniens*, IX (1962), pp. 64–102.

CHAPELOT, J., 'L'habitat rural', in *L'Île de France de Clovis à Hugues Capet du Ve siècle au Xe siècle* (Paris, 1993), pp. 178–99.

CHAPELOT, J., and FOSSIER, R., *The village and house in the middle ages* (London, 1985).

CHARLES-EDWARDS, T. M., '*Críth Gablach* and the law of status', *Peritia*, V (1986), pp. 53–73.

CHARLES-EDWARDS, T. M., *Early Christian Ireland* (Cambridge, 2000).

CHARLES-EDWARDS, T. M., *Early Irish and Welsh kinship* (Oxford, 1993).

CHARLES-EDWARDS, T. M., 'The distinction between land and moveable wealth in Anglo-Saxon England', in P. H. Sawyer (ed.), *English medieval settlement* (London, 1979), pp. 97–104.

CHARLES-EDWARDS, T. M., 'The social background to Irish *peregrinatio*', *Celtica*, XI (1976), pp. 43–59.

CHARPENTIER, G., 'Les bains de Sergilla', *Syria*, LXXI (1994), pp. 113–42.

CHASTAGNOL, A., and DUVAL, N., 'Les survivances du culte impérial dans l'Afrique du Nord à l'époque vandale', *Mélanges d'histoire ancienne offerts à William Seston* (Paris, 1974), pp. 87–118.

CHÂTELET, M., 'La céramique du haut moyen âge entre les Vosges et la Forêt-Noire (Alsace et Pays de Bade)', in Piton, *La céramique*, pp. 237–44.

CHÂTELET, M., 'L'évolution de la céramique culinaire tournée, du VIe au Xe siècle, dans le Sud du Rhin supérieur (Alsace et Pays de Bade)', in Delestre and Périn, *La datation*, pp. 21–38.

CHAVARRÍA ARNAU, A., 'El món rural al llevant de la Tarraconense durant l'antiguitat tardana', *Butlletí de la Societat catalana d'estudis històrics*, X (1999), pp. 15–32.

CHAVARRÍA I ARNAU, A., 'Els establiments rurals del llevant de la Tarraconesa durant l'antiguitat tardana', *Annals de l'Institut d'estudis gironins*, XXXIX (1998), pp. 9–30.

CHAVARRÍA ARNAU, A., 'Interpreting the transformation of late Roman villas', in Christie, *Landscapes of change*, pp. 67–102.

CHAVARRÍA ARNAU, A., 'Transformaciones arquitectónicas de los establecimientos rurales en el Nordeste de la *Tarraconensis* durante la Antigüedad tardía', *Butlletí de la Reial acadèmia catalana de belles arts de Sant Jordi*, X (1996), pp. 165–202.

CHEYNET, J.-C., 'L'époque byzantine', in B. Geyer and J. Lefort (eds.), *La Bithynie au Moyen Âge* (Paris, 2003), pp. 311–50.

CHEYNET, J.-C., *Pouvoir et contestations à Byzance (963–1210)* (Paris, 1990).

CHITTOLINI, G., ' "Quasi-città". Borghi e terre in area lombarda nel tardo medioevo', *Società e storia*, XIII (1990), pp. 3–26.

CHRISTENSEN, T., 'Lejre beyond legend', *Journal of Danish archaeology*, X (1991), pp. 163–85.

CHRISTIE, N., 'The *limes bizantino* reviewed', *Rivista di studi liguri*, LV (1989), pp. 5–38.

CHRISTIE, N. (ed.), *Landscapes of change* (Aldershot, 2004).

CHRISTIE, N. (ed.), *Three South Etrurian churches* (London, 1991).

CHRISTIE, N., and LOSEBY, S. (eds.), *Towns in transition* (Aldershot, 1996).

CHRISTLEIN, R., *Die Alamannen* (Stuttgart, 1978).

CHRISTYS, A., *Christians in al-Andalus, 711–1000* (Richmond, 2002).

CIAMPOLTRINI, G., 'Città "frammentate" e città fortezza', in Francovich and Noyé, *La storia dell'alto medioevo italiano*, pp. 615–33.

CIAMPOLTRINI, G., 'L'orciolo e l'olla', in Saguì, *Ceramica in Italia*, pp. 289–304.

CIAMPOLTRINI, G., and NOTINI, P., 'Lucca tardoantica e altomedievale', *AM*, XVII (1990), pp. 561–92.

CIAMPOLTRINI, G. *et al.*, 'Materiali tardoantichi e altomedievali dalla valle del Serchio', *AM*, XVIII (1991), pp. 699–715.

CIARROCCHI, B. *et al.*, 'Produzione e circolazione di ceramiche tardoantiche ed altomedievali ad Ostia e Porto', in L. Paroli and P. Delogu (eds.), *La storia economica di Roma nell'alto Medioevo alla luce dei recenti scavi archeologici* (Florence, 1993), pp. 203–46.

CILENTO, N., *Le origini della signoria capuana nella Longobardia minore* (Rome, 1966).

CIPOLLA, C. M., 'Questioni aperte sul sistema economico dell'alto medio evo', *Rivista storica italiana*, LXIII (1951), pp. 95–9.

CIPRIANO, M. T. *et al.*, 'La documentazione ceramica dell'Italia centro-meridionale nell'alto medioevo', in *A cerâmica medieval no Mediterrâneo ocidental* (Mértola, 1991), pp. 99–122.

CITARELLA, A. O., 'Merchants, markets and merchandise in southern Italy in the high middle ages', *Settimane di studio*, XL (1993), pp. 239–84.

CLACKSON, S. J., 'Four Coptic papyri from the Patermouthis archive in the British Library', *Bulletin of the American society of papyrologists*, XXXII (1995), pp. 97–116.

CLAESSEN, H. J. M., 'The early state: a structural approach', in idem and P. Skalník (eds.), *The early state* (The Hague, 1978), pp. 533–96.

CLANCHY, M. T., *From memory to written record* (London, 1979).

CLARK, G. (ed.), *Excavations of Farfa abbey* (London, in press).

CLARKE, A., and FULFORD, M., 'The excavation of Insula IX, Silchester', *Britannia*, XXXIII (2002), pp. 129–66.

CLARKE, H., and AMBROSIANI, B., *Towns in the Viking age*, 2nd edn. (Leicester, 1995).

CLASSEN, P., 'Fortleben und Wandel spätrömischen Urkundenwesens im frühen Mittelalter', in idem (ed.), *Recht und Schrift im Mittelalter* (Sigmaringen, 1977), pp. 13–54.

CLAUDE, D., *Adel, Kirche und Königtum im Westgotenreich* (Sigmaringen, 1971).

CLAUDE, D., 'Aspekte des Binnenhandels im Merowingerreich auf Grund der Schriftquellen', in Düwel *et al.*, *Untersuchungen zu Handel und Verkehr*, III, pp. 9–99.

CLAUDE, D., *Der Handel im westlichen Mittelmeer während des Frühmittelalters* = Düwel *et al.*, *Untersuchungen zu Handel und Verkehr*, II.

CLAUDE, D., *Die byzantinische Stadt im 6. Jahrhundert* (Munich, 1969).

CLAUDE, D., 'Haus und Hof im Merowingerreich nach den erzählenden und urkundlichen Quellen', in H. Beck and H. Steuer (eds.), *Haus und Hof in ur- und frühgeschichtlicher Zeit* (Göttingen, 1997), pp. 321–34.

CLAUDE, D., 'Untersuchungen zum frühfränkischen Comitat', *Zeitschrift der Savigny-Stiftung für Rechtsgeschichte. Germanistische Abteilung*, LXXXI (1964), pp. 1–79.

CLOVER, F. M., 'Emperor worship in Vandal Africa', in idem, *The late Roman West and the Vandals* (Aldershot, 1993), study VII.

COATES-STEPHENS, R., 'Housing in early medieval Rome, 500–1000 AD', *PBSR*, LI (1996), pp. 239–59.

COCKLE, H., 'Pottery manufacture in Roman Egypt: a new papyrus', *Journal of Roman studies*, LXXI (1981), pp. 87–97.

COLL, J.-M. *et al.*, 'Contextos ceràmics de l'antiguitat tardana del Vallès', *Arqueo mediterrània*, II (1997), pp. 37–57.

COLL, J.-M. *et al.*, 'Las producciones cerámicas de época visigoda en la Catalunya central (ss. V–VII)', in *La céramique médiévale en Méditerranée* (Aix-en-Provence, 1997), pp. 193–7.

COLLAVINI, S. M., 'Duchi e società locali nei ducati di Spoleto e Benevento nel secolo VIII', in *Atti del XVI Congresso internazionale di studi sull'alto medioevo* (Spoleto, 2003), pp. 125–66.

COLLAVINI, S. M., *'Honorabilis domus et spetiosissimus comitatus'* (Pisa, 1998).

COLLINS, R., *Early medieval Spain* (London, 1983).

COLLINS, R., 'Mérida and Toledo: 550–585', in E. James (ed.), *Visigothic Spain: new approaches* (Oxford, 1980), pp. 189–219.

COLLINS, R., *The Arab conquest of Spain, 710–797* (Oxford, 1989).

COLLINS, R., *The Basques* (Oxford, 1986).

CONRAD, L. I., 'The conquest of Arwād', in A. Cameron and L. I. Conrad (eds.), *The Byzantine and early Islamic Near East*, I (Princeton, 1992), pp. 317–401.

CONSTABLE, O. R., *Trade and traders in Muslim Spain* (Cambridge, 1994).

CORBIER, M., 'Les familles clarissimes d'Afrique proconsulaire (Ier–IIIe siècle)', in *Epigrafia e ordine senatorio*, II = *Tituli*, V (1982), pp. 685–754.

CORCORAN, S., 'The donation and will of Vincent of Huesca', *Antiquité tardive*, XI (2003), pp. 215–21.

CORMACK, R., 'Byzantine Aphrodisias', *Proceedings of the Cambridge philological society*, XXXVI (1990), pp. 26–41.

CORMACK, R., *Writing in gold* (London, 1985).

COSTAMBEYS, M., *Piety, property and power in eighth-century central Italy*, Ph.D. thesis, University of Cambridge (1998).

Couleurs de Tunisie. 25 siècles de céramique (Paris, 1994).

COULTON, J. J., 'Highland cities in south-west Turkey', in R. Matthews (ed.), *Ancient Anatolia* (London, n.d., c.1998), pp. 225–36.

COUPLAND, S., 'From poachers to gamekeepers', *Early medieval Europe*, VII (1998), pp. 85–114.

COURTOIS, C., *Les Vandales et l'Afrique* (Paris, 1955).

COVILLE, A., *Recherches sur l'histoire de Lyon du Vme siècle au IXme siècle* (450–800) (Paris, 1928).

COWIE, R., 'Mercian London', in M. P. Brown and C. A. Farr (eds.), *Mercia* (Leicester, 2001), pp. 194–209.

CRAWFORD, G. M., 'Excavations at Wasperton, third interim report', *West Midlands archaeology*, XXVI (1983), pp. 15–28.

CRAWFORD, J. S., *The Byzantine shops at Sardis* (Cambridge, Mass., 1990).

CRECELIUS, W., 'Traditiones Werdinenses', I, *Zeitschrift des Bergischen Geschichtvereins*, VI (1869), pp. 1–68.

CRESWELL, K. A. C., *Early Muslim architecture*, II (Oxford, 1940).

CRICK, J., 'Church, land and nobility in early ninth-century Kent', *Historical research*, LXI (1988), pp. 251–69.

CRINITI, N., *La tabula alimentaria di Veleia* (Parma, 1991).

CRONE, P., *Roman, provincial and Islamic law* (Cambridge, 1987).

CRONE, P., *Slaves on horses* (Cambridge, 1980).

CRONE, P., and COOK, M., *Hagarism* (Cambridge, 1977).

CRUM, W., 'Coptic ostraca in the Museo archeologico at Milan and some others', *Aegyptus*, III (1922), pp. 275–83.

CRUM, W., 'Koptische Zünfte und das Pfeffermonopol', *Zeitschrift für ägyptische Sprache und Altertumskunde*, LX (1925), pp. 103–11.

CUBITT, C., *Anglo-Saxon church councils, c.650–c.850* (Leicester, 1995).

CURTA, F., *The making of the Slavs* (Cambridge, 2001).

CUTILEIRO, J., *A Portuguese rural society* (Oxford, 1971).

CZUTH, B., *Die Quellen der Geschichte der Bagauden* (Szeged, 1965).

DAGRON, G., *Constantinople imaginaire* (Paris, 1984).

DAGRON, G., 'Entre village et cité', *Koinônia*, III (1979), pp. 29–52.

DAGRON, G., and DÉROCHE, V., 'Juifs et Chrétiens dans l'Orient du VIIe siècle', *Travaux et mémoires*, XI (1991), pp. 17–273.

DALLAI, L., 'Prospezioni archeologiche sul territorio di Massa e Populonia', in R. Fiorillo and P. Peduto (eds.), *III Congresso di archeologia medievale* (Florence, 2003), pp. 337–43.

DALLAI, L., and FARINELLI, R., 'Castel di Pietra e l'alta valle del Bruna', *AM*, XXV (1998), pp. 49–74.

DAL RI, L., and RIZZI, G., 'L'edilizia residenziale in Alto Adige tra V e VIII secolo', in Brogiolo, *Edilizia residenziale*, pp. 135–48.

DAMMINGER, F., 'Dwellings, settlements and settlement patterns in Merovingian southwest Germany and adjacent areas', in I. N. Wood (ed.), *Franks and Alamanni in the Merovingian period* (Woodbridge, 1998), pp. 33–106.

DANNHEIMER, H., 'Die frühmittelalterliche Siedlung bei Kirchheim (Ldkr. München, Oberbayern)', *Germania*, LI (1973), pp. 152–69.

DAOUATLI, A., 'La céramique médiévale en Tunisie', *Africa*, XIII (1995), pp. 189–204.

DARBY, H. E., and TERRETT, I. B., *Domesday geography of Midland England* (Cambridge, 1954).

DARK, K. R., *Civitas to kingdom* (London, 1994).

DARK, P., 'Palaeoecological evidence for landscape, continuity and change in Britain ca. A.D. 400–800', in K. R. Dark (ed.), *External contacts and the economy of late Roman and post-Roman Britain* (Woodbridge, 1996), pp. 23–51.

DARK, P., *The environment of Britain in the first millennium AD* (London, 2000).

DAUPHIN, C., *La Palestine byzantine*, BAR, I726 (Oxford, 1998).

DAVEAU, I., 'Occupation des sols au Bas-Empire, en Île-de-France', in P. Ouzoulias and P. Van Ossel (eds.), *Document de travail*, III (Paris, 1997), pp. 22–30.

DAVEAU, I., and GOUSTARD, V., 'Vert-Saint-Denis', *Archéologia*, CCCXXX (1997), pp. 42–51.

DAVIAU, P. M. M., and BECKMANN, M., 'Umayyad painted pottery and Abbasid period lamps at Tell Jawa', in Villeneuve and Watson, *La céramique byzantine*, pp. 259–74.

DAVIDSOHN, R., *Storia di Firenze*, I (Florence, 1956).

DAVIES, R. R., *Conquest, coexistence and change. Wales 1063–1415* (Oxford, 1987).

DAVIES, R. R., *The first English empire* (Oxford, 2000).

DAVIES, W., *An early Welsh microcosm* (London, 1978).

DAVIES, W., 'Clerics as rulers', in N. P. Brooks (ed.), *Latin and the vernacular languages in early medieval Britain* (Leicester, 1982), pp. 81–97.

DAVIES, W., 'La comunidad local en las sociedades célticas en la alta edad media', in I. Álvarez Borge (ed.), *Comunidades locales y poderes feudales en la edad media* (Logroño, 2001), pp. 93–114.

DAVIES, W., 'Land and power in early medieval Wales', *Past and present*, LXXXI (1978), pp. 3–23.

DAVIES, W., 'On servile status in the early middle ages', in M. L. Bush (ed.), *Serfdom and slavery* (London, 1996), pp. 225–46.

DAVIES, W., *Patterns of power in early Wales* (Oxford, 1990).

DAVIES, W., 'Sale, price and valuation in Galicia and Castile-León in the tenth century', *Early medieval Europe*, XI (2002), pp. 149–74.

DAVIES, W., *Small worlds* (London, 1988).

DAVIES, W., 'The Latin charter tradition in western Britain, Brittany and Ireland in the early mediaeval period', in D. Whitelock *et al.* (eds.), *Ireland in early Mediaeval Europe* (Cambridge, 1982), pp. 258–80.

DAVIES, W., *The Llandaff charters* (Aberystwyth, 1979).

DAVIES, W., 'Thinking about the Welsh environment a thousand years ago', in G. H. Jenkins (ed.), *Cymru a'r Cymry 2000, Wales and the Welsh 2000* (Aberystwyth, 2001), pp. 1–18.

DAVIES, W., '*Unciae*: land measurement in the *Liber Landavensis*', *Agricultural history review*, XXI (1973), pp. 111–21.

DAVIES, W., *Wales in the early middle ages* (Leicester, 1982).

DAVIES, W., and FOURACRE, P. (eds.), *The settlement of disputes in early medieval Europe* (Cambridge, 1986).

DAVIES, W., and VIERCK, H., 'The contexts of Tribal Hidage', *Frühmittelalterliche Studien*, VIII (1974), pp. 223–93.

DAVIS, J., *Exchange* (Buckingham, 1992).

DAVIS, J., *Land and family in Pisticci* (London, 1973).

DEBUS, K. H., 'Studien zu merovingischen Urkunden und Briefen', *Archiv für Diplomatik*, XIII (1967), pp. 1–109; XIV (1968), pp. 1–192.

DECKER, M., 'Food for an empire', in S. Kingsley and M. Decker (eds.), *Economy and exchange in the east Mediterranean during Late Antiquity* (Oxford, 2001), pp. 69–86.

DE CONNO, A., 'L'insediamento longobardo a Lucca', in *Pisa e la Toscana occidentale nel medioevo*, I (Pisa, 1991), pp. 59–127.

DE JONG, M., 'Adding insult to injury: Julian of Toledo and his *Historia Wambae*', in P. Heather (ed.), *The Visigoths from the migration period to the seventh century* (Woodbridge, 1999), pp. 373–402.

DE JONG, M., *In Samuel's image* (Leiden, 1996).

DELAPLACE, C., 'La Provence sous la domination ostrogothique (508–536)', *Annales du Midi*, CXV (2003), pp. 479–99.

DELATOUCHE, R., 'Regards sur l'agriculture aux temps carolingiens', *Journal des savants* (1977), pp. 73–100.

DÉLÉAGE, A., *La vie économique et sociale de la Bourgogne dans le haut moyen âge* (Mâcon, 1941).

DELEHAYE, H., *Les légendes grecques des saints militaires* (Paris, 1909).

DELESTRE, X., and PÉRIN, P. (eds.), *La datation des structures et des objets du haut moyen âge* (St-Germain-en-Laye, 1998).

DELMAIRE, R., 'Cités et fiscalité au Bas-Empire', in C. Lepelley (ed.), *La fin de la cité antique et le début de la cité médiévale de la fin du IIIe siècle à l'avènement de Charlemagne* (Bari, 1996), pp. 59–70.

DELMAIRE, R., *Largesses sacrées et res privata* (Rome, 1989).

DELOGU, P., 'La fine del mondo antico e l'inizio del medioevo', in Francovich and Noyé, *La storia dell'alto medioevo italiano*, pp. 7–27.

DELOGU, P., 'Lombard and Carolingian Italy', in R. McKitterick (ed.), *The new Cambridge medieval history*, II (Cambridge, 1995), pp. 290–319.

DELOGU, P., 'Longobardi e Romani: altre congetture', in P. Cammarosano and S. Gasparri (eds.), *Langobardia* (Udine, 1990), pp. 111–67.

DELOGU, P., 'Reading Pirenne again', in R. Hodges and W. Bowden (eds.), *The sixth century* (Leiden, 1998), pp. 15–40.

DELUMEAU, J.-P., *Arezzo: espace et sociétés, 715–1230* (Paris, 1996).

DEMANDT, A., *Die Spätantike* (Munich, 1989).

DEMANDT, A., 'The osmosis of late Roman and Germanic aristocracies', in E. K. Chrysos and A. Schwarcz (eds.), *Das Reich und die Barbaren* (Vienna, 1989), pp. 75–86.

DE MARTINO, F., 'Il colonato fra economia e diritto', in *Storia di Roma*, III.1 (Turin, 1993), pp. 789–822.

DE MECQUENEM, C., 'Les cryptes de Jouarre (Seine-et-Marne)', *Archéologie médiévale*, XXXII (2002), pp. 1–29.

DEMESTICHA, S., 'Amphora production on Cyprus during the late Roman period', in Bakirtzis, *VIIe Congrès international*, pp. 469–76.

DEMIANS D'ARCHIMBAUD, G. (ed.), *L'oppidum de Saint-Blaise du Ve au VIIe siècle* (Paris, 1994).

DEMOLON, P., *Le village mérovingien de Brebières (VIe–VIIe siècles)* (Arras, 1972).

DEMOLON, P., and VERHAEGHE, F., 'La céramique du Vème au Xème siècle dans le Nord de la France et la Flandre belge', in Piton, *La céramique*, pp. 385–407.

DE NEEVE, P. W., '*Fundus* as economic unit', *Tijdschrift voor rechtsgeschiedenis*, LII (1984), pp. 3–19.

DE PAEPE, P., and VAN IMPE, L., 'Historical context and provenancing of late Roman hand-made pottery from Belgium, the Netherlands and Germany', *Archeologie in Vlaanderen*, I (1991), pp. 145–80.

DEPREUX, P., 'L'apparition de la précaire à Saint-Gall', *MEFR. Moyen âge*, CXI (1999), pp. 649–73.

DEPREUX, P., *Les sociétés occidentales du milieu du VIe à la fin du IXe siècle* (Rennes, 2002).

DESPLANQUES, H., *Campagnes ombriennes* (Paris, 1969).

DE VOS, M. (ed.), *Rus africum* (Trento, 2000).

DE VRIES, B., 'Continuity and change in the urban character of the southern Hauran from the 5th to the 9th century', *Mediterranean archaeology*, XIII (2000), pp. 39–45.

DE VRIES, B., *Umm el-Jimal*, I (Portsmouth, RI, 1998).

DEVROEY, J.-P., 'Courants et réseaux d'échange dans l'économie franque entre Loire et Rhin', *Settimane di studio*, XL (1993), pp. 327–93.

DEVROEY, J.-P., *Économie rurale et société dans l'Europe franque (VIe–IXe siècles)*, 2 vols. (Paris, 2003–5).

DEVROEY, J.-P., 'Elaboration et usage des polyptyques', in *Akkulturation* (Paris, 2004).

DEVROEY, J.-P., *Études sur le grand domaine carolingien* (Aldershot, 1993).

DEVROEY, J.-P., 'Juifs et Syriens', in J.-M. Duvosquel and E. Thoen (eds.), *Peasants and townsmen in medieval Europe* (Ghent, 1995), pp. 51–72.

DEVROEY, J.-P., 'Les méthodes d'analyse démographique des polyptyques du haut moyen âge', in Devroey, *Études*, study V.

DEVROEY, J.-P., 'Les premiers polyptyques rémois, VIIe–IXe siècles', in A. Verhulst (ed.), *Le grand domaine aux époques mérovingienne et carolingienne* (Ghent, 1985), pp. 78–97 (now in Devroey, *Études*, study II).

DEVROEY, J.-P., 'Problèmes de critique autour du polyptyque de l'abbaye de Saint-Germain-des-Prés', in H. Atsma (ed.), *La Neustrie*, I (Sigmaringen, 1989), pp. 441–65 (now in Devroey, *Études*, study III).

DEVROEY, J.-P., 'Un monastère dans l'économie d'échanges', *Annales ESC*, XXXIX (1984), pp. 570–89 (now in Devroey, *Études*, study XI).

DEVROEY, J.-P., 'Vin, vignes et vignerons en pays rémois au Haut Moyen Âge', in *Vins, vignobles et terroirs de l'Antiquité à nos jours* (Nancy, 1999), pp. 75–92.

DE ZULUETA, F., *De patrociniis vicorum* (Oxford, 1909).

DÍAZ, P. C., 'El testamento de Vicente', in M. J. Hidalgo *et al.* (ed.), *'Romanización' y 'Reconquista' en la Península Ibérica* (Salamanca, 1998), pp. 257–70.

Díaz y Díaz, M. C., 'Un document privé de l'Espagne wisigothique sur ardoise', *Studi medievali*, I (1960), pp. 52–71.

Dickinson, T., 'Early Saxon saucer brooches: a preliminary overview', *Anglo-Saxon studies in archaeology and history*, VI (1993), pp. 11–44.

Dickinson, T., 'The present state of Anglo-Saxon cemetery studies', in P. Rahtz *et al.* (eds.), *Anglo-Saxon cemeteries 1979*, BAR, B82 (Oxford, 1980), pp. 11–33.

Die Franken, Wegbereiter Europas, 2 vols. (Mannheim, 1996).

Diehl, C., *L'Afrique byzantine* (Paris, 1896).

Dietz, S. *et al.*, *Africa proconsularis*, 3 vols. (Århus, 1995–2000).

Dierkens, A., 'La ville de Huy avant l'an mil', in *La genèse et les premiers siècles des villes médiévales dans les Pays-Bas méridionaux* (Brussels, 1990), pp. 391–409.

Dierkens, A., and Périn, P., 'Les *sedes regiae* mérovingiennes entre Seine et Rhin', in Ripoll and Gurt, *Sedes regiae*, pp. 267–304.

Diesner, H.-J., 'König Wamba und der westgotische Frühfeudalismus', *Jahrbuch der österreichischen Byzantinistik*, XVIII (1969), pp. 7–35.

Diesner, H.-J., 'Sklaven, Untertanen und Untertanenverbände im Westgotenreich', *Jahrbuch für Wirtschaftsgeschichte* (1970), 2, pp. 173–94.

Dieulafait, C., 'Existe-t-il une céramique mérovingienne à Saint-Bertrand-de-Comminges?', in press.

Dieulafait, C. *et al.*, 'Céramiques tardives en Midi-Pyrénées', *Aquitania*, XIV (1996), pp. 265–77.

di Gangi, G., and Lebole, C. M., 'Anfore Keay LII ed altri materiali ceramici da contesti di scavo della Calabria centro-meridionale (V–VIII secolo)', in Saguì, *Ceramica in Italia*, pp. 761–8.

di Gangi, G., and Lebole di Gangi, C. M., 'Dal tardo antico al bassomedioevo', in S. Patitucci Uggeri (ed.), *Scavi medievali in Italia 1994–1995* (Rome, 1998), pp. 93–122.

di Giuseppe, H., 'La fornace di Calle di Tricarico', in Saguì, *Ceramica in Italia*, pp. 735–52.

Dijkman, W., 'La céramique du haut moyen âge à Maastricht', in Piton, *La céramique*, pp. 217–25.

Dijkman, W., and Ervynck, A., *Antler, bone, horn, ivory and teeth* (Maastricht, 1998).

Dillon, M., 'The relationship of mother and son, of father and daughter, and the law of inheritance with regard to women', in R. Thurneysen *et al.*, *Studies in early Irish law* (Dublin, 1936), pp. 129–79.

di Segni, L., 'Epigraphic documentation on building in the provinces of Palaestina and Arabia, 4th–7th c.', in J. H. Humphrey (ed.), *The Roman and Byzantine Near East*, II (Portsmouth, RI, 1999), pp. 149–78.

di Segni, L., 'The involvement of local, municipal and provincial authorities in urban building in late antique Palestine and Arabia', in *The Roman and Byzantine Near East* (Ann Arbor, Mich., 1995), pp. 312–32.

di Vita, A., 'I recenti scavi della S.A.I.A. a Gortina', in *XXXVIII Corso di cultura sull'arte ravennate e bizantina* (Ravenna, 1991), pp. 169–83.

di Vita, A., and Martin, A. (eds.), *Gortina II* (Padua, 1997).

Dixon, P., 'How Saxon is the Saxon house?', in P. J. Drury (ed.), *Structural reconstruction*, BAR, B110 (Oxford, 1982), pp. 275–87.

Djaït, H., 'L'Afrique arabe au VIIIe siècle (86–184 H./705–800)', *Annales ESC*, XXVIII (1973), pp. 601–21.

Djaït, H., 'La wilāya d'Ifrīqiya au IIe/VIIIe siècle: étude institutionelle', *Studia islamica*, XXVII (1967), pp. 77–121; XXVIII (1968), pp. 79–107.

Dodd, A., and McAdam, E., 'L'habitat rural en Angleterre durant la période anglo-saxonne', in Lorren and Périn, *L'habitat rural*, pp. 223–34.

Doehaerd, R., 'Au temps de Charlemagne et des Normands. Ce qu'on vendait et comment on le vendait dans le bassin parisien', *Annales ESC*, II (1947), pp. 268–80.

Doehaerd, R., 'La richesse des Mérovingiens', in *Studi in onore di G. Luzzatto*, I(Milan, 1949), pp. 30–46.

Dölling, H., *Haus und Hof in westgermanischen Volksrechten* (Munich, 1958).

Doherty, C., 'Some aspects of hagiography as a source for Irish economic history', *Peritia*, I (1982), pp. 300–28.

Doherty, C., 'The monastic town in early medieval Ireland', in H. B. Clarke and A. Simms (eds.), *The comparative history of urban origins in non-Roman Europe*, BAR, I255 (Oxford, 1985), pp. 45–75.

Dopsch, A., *Die Wirtschaftsentwicklung der Karolingerzeit* (Cologne, 1962).

Dopsch, A., *Economic and social foundations of European civilisation* (London, 1937).

Donat, P., *Haus, Hof und Dorf in Mitteleuropa vom 7. bis 12. Jahrhundert* (Berlin, 1980).

Donner, F. M., *The early Islamic conquests* (Princeton, 1981).

Donzelli, C., 'Le strutture tardoantiche di Scolacium', *MEFR. Moyen âge*, CIII (1991), pp. 485–503.

Drinkwater, J., 'Patronage in Roman Gaul and the problem of Bagaudae', in Wallace-Hadrill, *Patronage*, pp. 189–203.

Drinkwater, J., 'Peasants and Bagaudae in Roman Gaul', *Echos du monde classique/Classical views*, III (1984), pp. 349–71.

Drinkwater, J., 'The Bacaudae of fifth-century Gaul', in idem and Elton, *Fifth-century Gaul*, pp. 208–17.

Drinkwater, J., *The Gallic empire* (Stuttgart, 1987).

Drinkwater, J., and Elton, H. (eds.), *Fifth-century Gaul: a crisis of identity?* (Cambridge, 1992).

Drury, P. J. (ed.), *Excavations at Little Waltham, 1970–71*, CBA Research Report, 26 (London, 1978).

Duby, G., *Hommes et structures du moyen âge* (Paris, 1973).

Duby, G., *La société aux XIe et XIIe siècles dans la région mâconnaise*, 2nd edn. (Paris, 1971).

Duby, G., *The early growth of the European economy* (London, 1974).

Düwel, K. *et al.* (eds.), *Untersuchungen zu Handel und Verkehr der vor- und frühgeschichtlichen Zeit in Mittel- und Nordeuropa*, 4 vols. (Göttingen, 1985).

Dufour, J.-Y., 'L'occupation des Ve et VIe siècles du site de Roissy-en-France/Les Tournelles (Val-d'Oise)', in P. Ouzoulias and P. Van Ossel (eds.), *Document de travail*, V (Paris, 2001), pp. 27–73.

Duhamel-Amado, C., 'L'alleu paysan a-t-il existé en France méridionale autour de l'an Mil?', in R. Delort (ed.), *La France de l'an Mil* (Paris, 1990), pp. 142–61.

Dumville, D., 'Kingship, genealogies and regnal lists', in P. H. Sawyer and I. N. Wood (eds.), *Early medieval kingship* (Leeds, 1977), pp. 72–104.

Dumville, D., 'Sub-Roman Britain: history and legend', *History*, LXII (1977), pp. 173–92.

Dumville, D., 'The idea of government in sub-Roman Britain', in Ausenda, *After empire*, pp. 177–216.

Duncan-Jones, R., *Money and government in the Roman empire* (Cambridge, 1994).

Duncan-Jones, R., *Structure and scale in the Roman economy* (Cambridge, 1990).

Dunn, A., 'From *polis* to *kastron* in southern Macedonia', in A. Bazzana (ed.), *Castrum 5* (Rome, 1999), pp. 399–413.

Dunn, A., 'Heraclius' "reconstruction of cities" and their sixth-century Balkan antecedents', in *Acta XIII Congressus internationalis archaeologiae christianae* (Rome–Split, 1998), pp. 795–806.

Dunn, A., 'The *kommerkiarios*, the *apotheke*, the *dromos*, the *vardarios*, and *the West*', *Byzantine and modern Greek studies*, XVII (1993), pp. 3–24.

Dunn, A., 'The problem of early Byzantine rural settlement in eastern and northern Macedonia', in *XXe Congrès international des études byzantines. Préactes*, I (Paris, 2001), p. 73.

Dunn, A., 'The transition from *polis* to *kastron* in the Balkans (III–VII cc.)', *Byzantine and Modern Greek studies*, XVIII (1994), pp. 60–80.

Durand, A., *Les paysages médiévaux du Languedoc (X^e– XIIe siècles)* (Toulouse, 1998).

Durliat, J., *De la ville antique à la ville byzantine* (Rome, 1990).

Durliat, J., 'La peste du VIe siècle', in *Hommes et richesses dans l'empire byzantin*, I (Paris, 1989), pp. 107–19.

Durliat, J., 'Le salaire de la paix sociale dans les royaumes barbares (V^e–VIe siècles)', in Wolfram and Schwarcz, *Anerkennung und Integration*, pp. 21–72.

Durliat, J., 'Les attributions civiles des évêques mérovingiens', *Annales du Midi*, XCI (1979), pp. 233–54.

Durliat, J., *Les dédicaces d'ouvrages de défense dans l'Afrique byzantine* (Rome, 1981).

Durliat, J., 'Les finances municipales africaines de Constantin aux Aghlabides', in *Bulletin archéologique du Comité des travaux historiques et scientifiques*, XIX B (1985), pp. 377–86.

Durliat, J., *Les finances publiques de Dioclétien aux Carolingiens (284–888)* (Sigmaringen, 1990).

Durliat, J., 'Les grands propriétaires africains et l'état byzantin (533–709)', *Les cahiers de Tunisie*, XXIX (1981), pp. 517–31.

Durliat, J., 'Le vigne et le vin dans la région parisienne au début du IXe siècle d'après le Polyptyque d'Irminon', *Le moyen âge*, LXXIV (1968), pp. 387–419.

Durliat, J., 'Qu'est-ce qu'un polyptyche?', in *Media in Francia. Recueil de mélanges offert à Karl Ferdinand Werner* (Paris, 1989), pp. 129–38.

Duval, N., *Les églises africaines à deux absides*, 2 vols. (Paris, 1971–3).

Duval, N., 'L'urbanisme de Sufetula', in *Aufstieg und Niedergang der römische Welt*, II.10.ii (Berlin, 1982), pp. 596–632.

Duval, N., and Baratte, F., *Les ruines de Sufetula. Sbeïtla* (Tunis, 1973).

DUVAL, N., and PRÉVOT, F., *Recherches archéologiques a Haïdra*, I (Rome, 1975).

DYER, C., *Lords and peasants in a changing society* (Cambridge, 1980).

DYER, C., *Making a living in the middle ages* (New Haven, 2002).

DYER, C., 'Villages and non-villages in the medieval Cotswolds', *Transactions of the Bristol and Gloucestershire archaeological society*, CXX (2002), pp. 11–35.

EBEL-ZEPEZAUER, W., *Studien zur Archäologie der Westgoten vom 5.–7. Jh. n. Chr.* (Mainz, 2000).

EBLING, H., *Prosopographie der Amtsträger des Merowingerreiches von Chlotar II. (613) bis Karl Martell (741)* (Munich, 1974).

EDMONDSON, J. C., 'Mining in the later Roman empire and beyond', *Journal of Roman studies*, LXXIX (1989), pp. 84–102.

EDWARDS, N., *The archaeology of early medieval Ireland* (London, 1999).

EFFROS, B., *Creating community with food and drink in Merovingian Gaul* (Basingstoke, 2002).

EFFROS, B., *Merovingian mortuary archaeology and the making of the early middle ages* (Berkeley, 2003).

EGGERT, W., 'Rebelliones servorum', *Zeitschrift für Geschichtswissenschaft*, XXIII (1975), pp. 1147–64.

EGLOFF, M., *Kellia. La poterie copte*, I (Geneva, 1977).

EL ABBADI, M., 'Historians and the papyri on the finances of Egypt at the Arab conquest', *Proceedings of the sixteenth international congress of papyrology* (Chico, Calif., 1981), pp. 509–16.

EL-FAKHARANI, F., 'Recent excavations at Marea in Egypt', in *Das römisch-byzantinische Ägypten; Aegyptiaca treverensia*, II (Mainz, 1983), pp. 175–86.

EL KHAYERI, A. A., 'Les thermes extra muros à Volubilis', *L'Africa romana*, X (1992), pp. 301–12.

ELLIS, S., 'North African villages in the Byzantine period', *XXe Congrès international des études byzantines. Préactes*, I (Paris, 2001), pp. 74–81.

ELLIS, S., *Roman housing* (London, 2000).

ELMSHÄUSER, K., 'Untersuchungen zum Staffelseer Urbar', in Rösener, *Strukturen*, pp. 335–69.

ELMSHÄUSER, K., and HEDWIG, A., *Studien zum Polyptychon von Saint-Germain-des-Prés* (Cologne, 1993).

EMPEREUR, J.-Y., and PICON, M., 'À propos d'un nouvel atelier de "Late Roman C" ', *Figlina*, VII (1986), pp. 143–6.

EMPEREUR, J.-Y., and PICON, M., 'La reconnaissance des productions des ateliers céramiques', *Cahiers de la céramique égyptienne*, III (1992), pp. 145–52.

ENDRES, R., 'Das Kirchengut im Bistum Lucca vom 8. bis 10. Jht', *Vierteljahrschrift für Sozial- und Wirtschaftsgeschichte*, XIV (1917), pp. 240–92.

ENGELS, F., *Origins of the family, private property and the state* (1884), in K. Marx and F. Engels, *Selected works* (London, 1968), pp. 455–593.

ENGEMANN, J., 'À propos des amphores d'Abou Mina', *Cahiers de la céramique égyptienne*, III (1992), pp. 153–9.

ENGEMANN, P., 'Das Ende der Wallfahrten nach Abu Mina und die Datierung früher islamischer glasierter Keramik in Ägypten', *Jahrbuch für Antike und Christentum*, XXXII (1989), pp. 161–77.

ENNABLI, A. (ed.), *Pour sauver Carthage* (Paris, 1992).

ENRICH I HOJA, J. *et al.*, *Vilaclara de Castellfollit del Boix (el Bages)* (Igualada, 1995).

EPPERLEIN, S., *Herrschaft und Volk im karolingischen Imperium* (Berlin, 1969).

ESCALONA MONGE, J., *Sociedad y territorio en la alta edad media castellana*, BAR, I1079 (Oxford, 2002).

ESHEL, H. *et al.*, 'Khirbet Yattir, 1995–1999', *Israel exploration journal*, L (2000), pp. 153–68.

ESMONDE-CLEARY, S., *The ending of Roman Britain* (London, 1989).

ESMONDE-CLEARY, S. *et al.*, 'The late Roman defences at Saint-Bertrand-de-Comminges (Haute Garonne)', *JRA*, XI (1998), pp. 343–54.

ÉTIENNE, R., 'Ausone, propriétaire terrien et le problème du latifundium au IVe siècle ap. J. C.', in M. Christol *et al.* (eds.), *Institutions, société et vie politique dans l'empire romain au IVe siècle ap. J.-C.* (Rome, 1992), pp. 305–11.

ETHELBERG, P., 'Die eisenzeitliche Besiedlung von Hjemsted Banke, Skaerbaek sogn, Sønderjyllands Amt', *Offa*, XLV (1988), pp. 119–54.

EUZENNAT, M., 'Les edifices de culte chrétiens en Maurétanie tingitane', *Antiquités africaines*, VIII (1974), pp. 175–90.

EVANS, S. S., *The heroic poetry of Dark-age Britain*, (Lanham, Md., 1997).

EVERETT, N., *Literacy in Lombard Italy, c.568–774* (Cambridge, 2003).

EVERETT, N., 'Scribes and charters in Lombard Italy', *Studi medievali*, XLI (2000), pp. 39–83.

EVISON, V. I., *A corpus of wheel-thrown pottery in Anglo-Saxon graves* (London, 1979).

EWIG, E., 'Die fränkischen Teilreiche im 7. Jahrhundert (613–714)', in idem, *Spätantikes und fränkisches Gallien*, I (Munich, 1976), pp. 172–230.

EWIG, E., 'Milo et eiusmodi similes', in idem, *Spätantikes und fränkisches Gallien*, II (Munich, 1979), pp. 189–219.

EWIG, E., *Trier im Merowingerreich* (Trier, 1954).

EYICE, S., 'Ricerche e scoperte nella regione di Silifke nella Turchia meridionale', in C. Barsanti *et al.* (eds.), *Milion*, I (Rome, 1988), pp. 15–58.

FABECH, C., 'Centrality in sites and landscapes', in C. Fabech and J. Ringtved (eds.), *Settlement and landscape* (Højbjerg, 1999), pp. 455–73.

FABECH, C., 'Organising the landscape', *Anglo-Saxon studies in archaeology and history*, X (1999), pp. 37–47.

FABECH, C., 'Reading society from the cultural landscape', in Nielsen *et al.*, *Gudme*, pp. 169–83.

FABECH, C., and RINGTVED, J. (eds.), *Samfundsorganisation og regional variation* (Højbjerg, 1991).

FAITH, R., *The English peasantry and the growth of lordship* (Leicester, 1997).

FAITH, R., 'Tidenham, Gloucestershire, and the history of the manor in England', *Landscape history*, XVI (1994), pp. 39–51.

FALCK, L., *Mainz im frühen und hohen Mittelalter* (Düsseldorf, 1972).

FALKNER, R. K., 'Jordan in the early Islamic period. The use and abuse of pottery', *Berytus*, XLI (1993–4), pp. 39–52.

FANNING, S., 'Emperors and empires in fifth-century Gaul', in Drinkwater and Elton, *Fifth-century Gaul*, pp. 288–97.

FARBER, J. J., 'Family financial disputes in the Patermouthis archive', *Bulletin of the American Society of Papyrologists*, XXVII (1990), pp. 111–22.

FARBER, J. J., and PORTEN, B., 'The Patermouthis archive: a third look', *Bulletin of the American Society of Papyrologists*, XXIII (1986), pp. 81–98.

FARNOUX, C., 'Le fond de cabane mérovingien comme fait culturel', in Lorren and Périn, *L'habitat rural*, pp. 29–44.

FEISSEL, D., 'Magnus, Mégas et les curateurs des "maisons divines" de Justin II à Maurice', *Travaux et mémoires*, IX (1985), pp. 465–76.

FELLER, L., *Les Abruzzes médiévales* (Rome, 1998).

FELLER, L., 'Statut de la terre et statut des personnes', *Études rurales*, CXLV–CXLVI (1997), pp. 147–64.

FELLER, L., GRAMAIN, A., and WEBER, F., 'La marché de la terre dans les Abruzzes au IXe siècle', in L. Feller and C. Wickham (eds.), *Le marché de la terre au moyen âge*, I (Rome, in press).

FELTEN, F., 'Die christliche Siedlung', in H. Walter (ed.), *Alt-Ägina*, I.2 (Mainz, 1975), pp. 55–80.

FENTRESS, E., 'La Numidia', in *Storia di Roma*, III.2 (Turin, 1993), pp. 339–62.

FENTRESS, E., and PERKINS, P., 'Counting African Red Slip ware', *L'Africa romana*, V (1988), pp. 205–14.

FENTRESS, E. *et al.*, 'ARS and its markets', in press.

FENTRESS, E. *et al.*, 'Prospectus dans le Belezma: rapport préliminaire', in *Actes du colloque international sur l'histoire de Sétif* (Algiers, 1993), pp. 107–27.

FERNÁNDEZ MIER, M., *Génesis del territorio en la edad media* (Oviedo, 1999).

FERNÁNDEZ OCHOA, C., 'La ciudad en la antigüedad tardía en la cornisa cantábrica', in García Moreno and Rascón Marqués, *Complutum*, pp. 73–86.

FERNÁNDEZ OCHOA, C. *et al.*, 'Gijón en el período tardoantiguo', *AEA*, LXV (1992), pp. 105–49.

FEVEILE, C., and JENSEN, S., 'Ribe in the 8th and 9th century', *Acta archaeologica*, LXXI (2000), pp. 9–24.

FÉVRIER, P.-A., *Le développement urbain en Provence de l'époque romaine à la fin du XIVe siècle* (Paris, 1964).

FÉVRIER, P.-A., 'Permanence et héritages de l'Antiquité dans la topographie des villes de l'Occident durant le haut moyen âge', *Settimane di studio*, XXI (1974), pp. 41–138.

FIEMA, Z. T., 'Byzantine Petra—a reassessment', in Burns and Eadie, *Urban centers and rural contexts*, pp. 111–31.

FIEMA, Z. T., 'Late-antique Petra and its hinterland', in J. H. Humphrey (ed.), *The Roman and Byzantine Near East*, III (Portsmouth, RI, 2002), pp. 191–252.

FIERRO, M., 'Cuatro preguntas en torno a Ibn Ḥafṣūn', *al-Qanṭara*, XVI (1995), pp. 221–57.

FIKHMAN, I. F., 'De nouveau sur le colonat du bas empire', in M. Capasso *et al.* (eds.), *Miscellanea papyrologica*, I (Florence, 1990), pp. 159–79.

FIKHMAN, I. F., *Oksirinkh—gorod papirusov* (Moscow, 1976).

FINBERG, H. P. R., 'Anglo-Saxon England to 1042', in idem (ed.), *The agrarian history of England and Wales*, I.2 (Cambridge, 1972), pp. 385–525.

FINBERG, H. P. R., *Lucerna* (London, 1964).

FINBERG, H. P. R., *The early charters of the West Midlands* (Leicester, 1961).

FINKELSTEIN, I. *et al.*, *Highlands of many cultures* (Tel Aviv, 1997).

FINLEY, M. I., *The ancient economy* (London, 1973).

FIOCCHI NICCOLAI, V., 'Considerazioni sull'archeologia del territorio laziale nel-l'altomedioevo', in Francovich and Noyé, *La storia dell'alto medioevo italiano*, pp. 403–6.

FIORILLO, R., 'La ceramica della *plebs* di S. Maria di Rota a Mercato S. Severino (SA)', in R. Fiorillo and P. Peduto (eds.), *III Congresso nazionale di archeologia medievale* (Florence, 2003), pp. 127–34.

FISHER, H. L., *Miracle stories and communities*, Ph.D. thesis, University of Birmingham (2001).

FITA, F., 'Patrologia visigótica', *Boletín de la Real Academia de la Historia*, XLIX (1906), pp. 137–69.

FLARAN, X (1988): *La croissance agricole du haut moyen âge*.

FLEMING, R., 'Lords and labour', in W. Davies (ed.), *From the Vikings to the Normans* (Oxford, 2003), pp. 107–37.

FLUSIN, B., *Saint Anastase le Perse et l'histoire de la Palestine au début du VIIe siècle*, 2 vols. (Paris, 1992).

FOARD, G., 'Systematic field-walking and the investigation of Saxon settlement in Northamptonshire', *World archaeology*, IX (1977–8), pp. 357–74.

FONTANA, S., 'Le "imitazioni" della sigillata africana e le ceramiche da mensa italiche tardo-antiche', in Saguì, *Ceramica in Italia*, pp. 83–100.

FONTANA, S., 'Un "immondezzaio" di VI secolo da *Meninx*', *L'Africa romana*, XIII (2000), pp. 95–114.

FONTES, L., and GASPAR, A., 'Cerâmicas da região de Braga na transição da anti-guidade tardia para a idade media', in *La céramique médiévale en Méditerranée* (Aix-en-Provence, 1997), pp. 203–12.

FOOTE, R. M., 'Commerce, industrial expansion and orthogonal planning', *Mediterranean archaeology*, XIII (2000), pp. 25–38.

FOOTE, R. M., 'Frescoes and carved ivory from the Abbasid family homestead at Humeima', *JRA*, XII (1999), pp. 423–8.

FORLIN PATRUCCO, M., and RODA, S., 'Crisi del potere e autodifesa di classe', in A. Giardina (ed.), *Società romana e impero tardoantico*, I (Bari, 1986), pp. 245–72.

FORTACÍN PIEDRAFITA, J., 'La donación del diácono Vicente al monasterio de Asán y su posterior testamento como obispo de Huesca en el siglo VI', *Cuadernos de historia Jerónimo Zurita*, XLVII–XLVIII (1983), pp. 59–64.

FOSS, C., 'Archaeology and the "twenty cities" of Byzantine Asia', *American journal of archaeology*, LXXXI (1977), pp. 469–86 (now in idem, *History and archaeology*, study II).

FOSS, C., *Byzantine and Turkish Sardis* (Cambridge, Mass., 1980).

FOSS, C., 'Cities and villages of Lycia in the Life of St. Nicholas of Holy Zion', *Greek Orthodox theological review*, XXXVI (1991), pp. 303–39.

FOSS, C., *Cities, fortresses and villages of Byzantine Asia Minor* (Aldershot, 1996).

FOSS, C., *Ephesus after Antiquity* (Cambridge, 1979).

FOSS, C., *History and archaeology of Byzantine Asia Minor* (Aldershot, 1990).

FOSS, C., 'Late antique and Byzantine Ankara', *Dumbarton Oaks papers*, XXXI (1977), pp. 29–87 (now in idem, *History and archaeology*, study VI).

Foss, C., 'Syria in transition, A.D. 550–750', *Dumbarton Oaks papers*, LI (1997), pp. 189–269.

Foss, C., 'The cities of Pamphylia in the Byzantine age' (now in idem, *Cities, fortresses*, study IV).

Foss, C., 'The Lycian coast in the Byzantine age', *Dumbarton Oaks papers*, XLVIII (1994), pp. 1–52 (now in idem, *Cities, fortresses*, study II).

Fossier, R., *Enfance de l'Europe* (Paris, 1982).

Fossier, R., *La terre et les hommes en Picardie jusqu'à la fin du XIIIe siècle* (Paris, 1968).

Fossier, R., 'Les tendances de l'économie: stagnation ou croissance?', *Settimane di studio*, XXVII (1981), pp. 261–74.

Fossier, R., *Polyptyques et censiers* (Turnhout, 1978).

Foucray, B., and Gentili, F., 'Le village du haut moyen âge de Serris (Seine-et-Marne), lieudit "Les Ruelles" (VIIe–Xe siècle)', in Lorren and Périn, *L'habitat rural*, pp. 139–43.

Fouet, G., *La villa gallo-romaine de Montmaurin (Hte-Garonne)* (Paris, 1969).

Fouracre, P., 'Attitudes towards violence in seventh- and eighth-century Francia', in Halsall, *Violence and society*, pp. 60–75.

Fouracre, P., 'Cultural conformity and social conservatism in early medieval Europe', *History workshop*, XXXIII (1992), pp. 152–61.

Fouracre, P., 'Eternal light and earthly needs', in W. Davies and P. Fouracre (eds.), *Property and power in the early middle ages* (Cambridge, 1995), pp. 53–81.

Fouracre, P., 'Merovingian history and Merovingian hagiography', *Past and present*, CXXVII (1990), pp. 3–38.

Fouracre, P., 'Merovingians, mayors of the palace and the notion of a "low-born" Ebroin', *Bulletin of the Institute of Historical Research*, LVII (1984), pp. 1–14.

Fouracre, P., 'Observations on the outgrowth of Pippinid influence in the "regnum Francorum" after the battle of Tertry (687–715)', *Medieval prosopography*, V.2 (1984), pp. 1–31.

Fouracre, P., ' "Placita" and the settlement of disputes in later Merovingian Francia', in W. Davies and P. Fouracre (eds.), *The settlement of disputes in early medieval Europe* (Cambridge, 1986), pp. 23–43.

Fouracre, P., 'Space, culture and kingdoms in early medieval Europe', in P. Linehan and J. L. Nelson (eds.), *The medieval world* (London, 2001), pp. 366–80.

Fouracre, P., *The age of Charles Martel* (London, 2000).

Fouracre, P., and Gerberding, R. A., *Late Merovingian France* (Manchester, 1996).

Fourmy, M.-H., and Leroy, M., 'La vie de S. Philarète', *Byzantion*, IX (1934), pp. 113–67.

Fournet, J.-L., *Hellénisme dans l'Égypte du VIe siècle. La bibliothèque et l'oeuvre de Dioscore d'Aphrodité*, 2 vols. (Cairo, 1999).

Fournier, P.-F., 'Clermont-Ferrand au VIe siècle', *Bibliothèque de l'École des Chartes*, CXXVIII (1970), pp. 273–344.

Fournier, G., *Le peuplement rural en Basse Auvergne durant le haut moyen âge* (Paris, 1962).

Fowden, E. K., *The barbarian plain* (Berkeley, 1999).

François, V., *Céramiques médiévales à Alexandrie* (Cairo, 1999).

FRANCOVICH, R., 'Changing structures of settlements', in C. La Rocca (ed.), *Italy in the early middle ages* (Oxford, 2002), pp. 144–67.
FRANCOVICH, R., and HODGES, R., *Villa to village* (London, 2003).
FRANCOVICH, R., and VALENTI, M., 'La ceramica d'uso comune in Toscana tra V–X secolo', in *La céramique médiévale en Méditerranée* (Aix-en-Provence, 1997), pp. 129–37.
FRANCOVICH, R., and GINATEMPO, M. (eds.), *Castelli*, I (Florence, 2000).
FRANCOVICH, R., and NOYÉ, G. (eds.), *La storia dell'alto medioevo italiano (VI–X secolo) alla luce dell'archeologia* (Florence, 1994).
FRANTZ, A., *The Athenian agora*, XXIV (Princeton, 1988).
FRANTZ-MURPHY, G., 'Land tenure in Egypt in the first five centuries of Islamic rule (seventh–twelfth centuries AD)', *Proceedings of the British Academy*, XCVI (1999), pp. 237–66.
FREEDMAN, P., *Images of the medieval peasant* (Stanford, Calif., 1999).
FREISE, E., 'Studien zum Einzugsbereich der Klostergemeinschaft von Fulda', in K. Schmid (ed.), *Die Klostergemeinschaft von Fulda im früheren Mittelalter*, II.3 (Munich, 1978), pp. 1003–269.
FRIED, M. H., *The evolution of political society* (New York, 1967).
FRIED, M. H., *The notion of tribe* (Menlo Park, Calif., 1975).
FRIEDMAN, J., and ROWLANDS, M. J., 'Notes towards an epigenetic model of the evolution of "civilisation" ', in iidem (eds.), *The evolution of social systems* (London, 1977), pp. 201–76.
FUENTES DOMÍNGUEZ, A., 'Aproximación a la ciudad hispana de los siglos IV y V d. C.', in García Moreno and Rascón Marqués, *Complutum*, pp. 25–50.
FUERTES SANTOS, M. DEL C., and HIDALGO PRIETO, R., 'Cerámicas tardorroma-nas y altomedievales de Córdoba', in Caballero *et al.*, *Cerámicas tardorromanas y altomedievales*, pp. 505–40.
FULFORD, M. B., and PEACOCK, D. P. S., *Excavations at Carthage: the British mission*, I.2 (Sheffield, 1984).
FUMAGALLI, V., *Coloni e signori nell'Italia settentrionale. Secoli VI–XI* (Bologna, 1978).
FUMAGALLI, V., *Terra e società nell'Italia padana. I secoli IX e X*, 2nd edn. (Turin, 1976).
FUSTEL DE COULANGES, N. D., 'Le colonat romain', in idem, *Recherches sur quelques problèmes d'histoire* (Paris, 1885), pp. 1–186.
GABBA, E., and PASQUINUCCI, M., *Strutture agrarie e allevamento transumante nell'Italia romana (III–I sec. A.C.)* (Pisa, 1979).
GAGOS, T., and FRÖSÉN, J., 'Petra papyri', *Annual of the Department of Antiquities of Jordan*, XLII (1998), pp. 473–81.
GAGOS, T., and VAN MINNEN, P., *Settling a dispute. Towards a legal anthropology of late antique Egypt* (Ann Arbor, Mich., 1994).
GALETTI, P., *Abitare nel medioevo* (Florence, 1997).
GALETTI, P., 'Un caso particolare: le prestazioni d'opera nei contratti agrari piacen-tini dei secoli VIII–X', in *Le prestazioni d'opera nelle campagne italiane del Medioevo* (Bologna, 1987), pp. 71–103.
GALINIÉ, H., 'Tours de Grégoire, Tours des archives du sol', in N. Gauthier and H. Galinié (eds.), *Grégoire de Tours et l'espace gaulois* (Tours, 1997), pp. 65–80.

GALLO, A., 'I curiali napoletani del medioevo', *Archivio storico per le province napoletane*, N.S., V (1919), pp. 5–47; VI (1920), pp. 5–27; VII (1921), pp. 5–26.

GANSHOF, F. L., 'À propos du tonlieu sous les Mérovingiens', *Studi in onore di Amintore Fanfani*, I (Milan, 1962), pp. 293–315.

GANSHOF, F. L., *Frankish institutions under Charlemagne* (Providence, RI, 1968).

GANSHOF, F. L., 'Le statut de la femme dans la monarchie franque', *Recueils de la société Jean Bodin*, XII (1962), pp. 5–58.

GANSHOF, F. L., 'Les bureaux de tonlieu de Marseille et de Fos', in *Études historiques à la mémoire de Noël Didier* (Paris, 1960), pp. 125–33.

GANSHOF, F. L., 'Quelques aspects principaux de la vie économique dans la monarchie franque au VIIe siècle', *Settimane di studio*, V (1958), pp. 73–101.

GARCÍA ARENAL, M., and MANZANO MORENO, E., 'Idrīssisme et villes idrīssides', *Studia Islamica*, LXXXII (1995), pp. 5–33.

GARCÍA DE CORTÁZAR, J. A., 'La formación de la sociedad feudal en el cuadrante noroccidental de la Península Ibérica en los siglos VIII a XII', *Initium*, IV (1999), pp. 57–121.

GARCÍA GUINEA, M. A. *et al.*, *El Castellar. Villajimena (Palencia)* (Madrid, 1963).

GARCÍA GUINEA, M. A. *et al.*, *Excavaciones de Monte Cildá. Olleros de Pisuerga (PA)* (Madrid, 1973).

GARCÍA LOPEZ, Y., 'La cronología de la "Historia Wambae" ', *Anuario de estudios medievales*, XXIII (1993), pp. 121–39.

GARCÍA MORENO, L. A., 'El estado protofeudal visigodo', in *L'Europe héritière de l'Espagne wisigothique* (Madrid, 1992), pp. 17–43.

GARCÍA MORENO, L. A., 'Imposición y política fiscal en la España visigoda', in *Historia de la hacienda española (épocas antigua y medieval)* (Madrid, 1982), pp. 263–300.

GARCÍA MORENO, L. A., *Historia de España visigoda* (Madrid, 1989).

GARCÍA MORENO, L. A., and RASCÓN MARQUÉS, S. (eds.), *Complutum y las ciudades hispanas en la Antigüedad tardía* (Alcalá de Henares, 1999).

GARNIER, B. *et al.*, 'De la ferme au village', *Archéologie du Midi médiéval*, XIII (1995), pp. 1–78.

GARZELLA, G., *Pisa com'era* (Naples, 1990).

GASCOU, J., 'De Byzance à l'Islam', *Journal of the economic and social history of the Orient*, XXVI (1983), pp. 97–109.

GASCOU, J., 'Documents grecs de Qurnat Mar'y', *Bulletin de l'Institut français de l'ancien Orient*, XCIX (1999), pp. 201–15.

GASCOU, J., 'La table budgétaire d'Antaeopolis (*P. Freer* 08.45 c-d)', in *Hommes et richesses dans l'Empire byzantin*, I (Paris, 1989), pp. 279–313.

GASCOU, J., 'Les grands domaines, la cité et l'état en Égypte byzantine', *Travaux et mémoires*, IX (1985), pp. 1–90.

GASCOU, J., 'Notes critiques sur quelques papyrus des Ve et VIe siècles', *Chronique d'Égypte*, XLVII (1972), pp. 243–53.

GASCOU, J., *Un codex fiscal hermopolite (P. Sorb. II 69)* (Atlanta, Ga., 1994).

GASCOU, J., and MacCOULL, L., 'Le cadastre d'Aphroditô', *Travaux et mémoires*, X (1987), pp. 103–51.

GASCOU, J., and WORP, K. A., 'Problèmes de documentation Apollinopolite', *ZPE*, XLIX (1982), pp. 83–95.

GASPAR, A., 'Escavações arqueológicas na rua de Nossa Senhora do Leite, em Braga', *Cadernos de arqueologia*, 2 ser., II (1985), pp. 51–125.

GASPARRI, S., 'Grandi proprietari e sovrani nell'Italia longobarda dell'VIII secolo', *Atti del VI Congresso internazionale di studi sull'alto medioevo* (Spoleto, 1980), pp. 429–42.

GASPARRI, S., 'Il ducato di Spoleto. Istituzioni, poteri, gruppi dominanti', in *Atti del IX Congresso internazionale di studi sull'alto medioevo* (Spoleto, 1983), pp. 77–122.

GASPARRI, S., 'Il ducato e il principato di Benevento', in G. Galasso and R. Romeo (eds.), *Storia del Mezzogiorno*, II.1 (Naples, 1988), pp. 85–146.

GASPARRI, S., 'Il regno longobardo in Italia', in P. Cammarosano and S. Gasparri (eds.), *Langobardia* (Udine, 1990), pp. 237–305.

GASPARRI, S., 'Il tesoro del re', in S. Gelichi and C. La Rocca (eds.), *I tesori* (Rome, 2004), pp. 49–67.

GASPARRI, S., 'Istituzioni e poteri nel territorio friulano in età longobarda e carolingia', in *Atti del XIV Congresso internazionale di studi sull'alto medioevo* (Spoleto, 2001), pp. 105–28.

GASPARRI, S., 'Strutture militari e legami di dipendenza in Italia in età longobarda e carolingia', *Rivista storica italiana*, XCVIII (1986), pp. 664–726.

GASPARRI, S., 'Venezia fra i secoli VIII e IX', in *Studi veneti offerti a Gaetano Cozzi* (Venice, 1992), pp. 3–18.

GATIER, P.-L., 'Villages du Proche-Orient protobyzantin (4ème–7ème s.)', in G. D. R. King and A. Cameron (eds.), *The Byzantine and early Islamic Near East*, II (Princeton, 1994), pp. 17–48.

GAUTHIER, N., *L'évangélisation des pays de la Moselle* (Paris, 1980).

GAUTHIER, N., 'Le paysage urbain en Gaule au VIe siècle', in eadem and H. Galinié (eds.), *Grégoire de Tours et l'espace gaulois* (Tours, 1997), pp. 49–63.

GAWLIKOWSKI, M., 'A residential area by the South Decumanus', in Zayadine, *Jerash*, pp. 107–36.

GAWLIKOWSKI, M., 'Céramiques byzantines et omayyades de Jerash', in H. Meyza and J. Młynarczyk (eds.), *Hellenistic and Roman pottery in the eastern Mediterranean* (Warsaw, 1995), pp. 83–91.

GAWLIKOWSKI, M., 'Installations omeyyades à Jérash', *Studies in the history and archaeology of Jordan*, IV (Amman, 1992), pp. 357–61.

GAWLIKOWSKI, M., 'Palmyra, excavations 1995', *Polish archaeology in the Mediterranean*, VII (1996), pp. 139–46.

GAYRAUD, R.-P., 'Les céramiques égyptiennes à glaçure, IXe–XIIe siècles', in *La céramique médiévale en Méditerranée* (Aix-en-Provence, 1997), pp. 261–70.

GAYRAUD, R.-P., 'Iṣṭabl 'Antar (Fostat), 1987–1989', *Annales islamologiques*, XXV (1991), pp. 57–87.

GEAKE, H., 'Burial practice in seventh- and eighth-century England', in M. O. H. Carver (ed.), *The age of Sutton Hoo* (Woodbridge, 1992), pp. 83–94.

GEARY, P. J., *Aristocracy in Provence* (Stuttgart, 1985).

GEARY, P. J., 'Ethnic identity as a situational construct in the early middle ages', *Mitteilungen der anthropologischen Gesellschaft in Wien*, CXIII (1983), pp. 15–26.

GEARY, P. J., *The myth of nations* (Princeton, 2002)

GEBÜHR, M., 'Angulus desertus?', *Studien zur Sachsenforschung*, XI (1998), pp. 43–85.

GECHTER, M., and KUNOW, J., 'Zur ländlichen Besiedlung des Rheinlandes in römischer Zeit', *Bonner Jahrbucher*, CLXXXVI (1986), pp. 377–96.

GECHTER, M., and SCHÜTTE, S., 'Zwischen St. Alban und Judenviertel in Köln', *Rheinische Heimatpflege*, XXXV (1998), pp. 37–56.

GELICHI, S., and MILANESE, M., 'Problems in the transition towards the medieval in the *Ifriqya*', *L'Africa romana*, XII (1998), pp. 457–84.

GELICHI, S., and MILANESE, M., '*Uchi maius*', in M. Khanoussi and A. Mastino (eds.), *Uchi Maius*, I (Sassari, 1997), pp. 49–94.

GELICHI, S., and NEGRELLI, C., 'La ricognizione del 1999', in *Laodicea di Frigia*, I (Rome, 2000), pp. 125–64.

GELICHI, S., and SBARRA, F., 'La tavola di San Gerardo', *Rivista di archeologia*, in press.

GELICHI, S., and GIORDANI, N. (eds.), *Il tesoro nel pozzo* (Modena, 1994).

GELLING, M., 'Why aren't we speaking Welsh?', *Anglo-Saxon studies in archaeology and history*, VI (1993), pp. 51–6.

GELLNER, E., *Saints of the Atlas* (London, 1969).

GEMPELER, R. D., *Elephantine X* (Mainz, 1992).

GENTILI, F., 'La céramique des habitats ruraux du Parisis du VIIe siècle à l'An Mil', in *Un village au temps de Charlemagne* (Paris, 1988), pp. 318–31.

GENTILI, F., and HOURLIER, N., 'L'habitat du haut moyen âge de "L'Arpent-Ferret" à Servon (Seine-et-Marne), IVe–XIe siècles', in Lorren and Périn, *L'habitat rural*, pp. 121–33.

GEORGANTELI, E., 'Villes et villages dans la province de Rhodope', in *XXe Congrès international des etudes byzantines. Pré-actes*, II (Paris, 2001), p. 48.

GEORGE, J. W., *Venantius Fortunatus* (Oxford, 1992).

GEORGES-LEROY, M., and LENOBLE, M., 'La céramique du haut moyen âge (7ème–11ème s.) en Champagne méridionale', in Piton, *La céramique*, pp. 245–65.

GEREMEK, H., 'Sur la question des *boulai* dans les villes égyptiennes aux Ve–VIIe siècles', *Journal of juristic papyrology*, XX (1990), pp. 47–54.

GERRETS, D., 'Evidence of political centralisation in Westergo', *Anglo-Saxon studies in archaeology and history*, X (1999), pp. 119–26.

GERSTINGER, H., 'Neue gräko-ägyptische Vertragsurkunden aus byzantinischer Zeit der Sammlung "Papyrus Erzherzog Rainer" ', *Jahrbuch der österreichischen byzantinischen Gesellschaft*, VII (1958), pp. 1–15.

GEUENICH, D. (ed.), *Die Franken und die Alemannen bis zur 'Schlacht bei Zülpich' (496/97)* (Berlin, 1997).

GHALY, H., 'Pottery workshops of Saint-Jeremia (Saqqara)', *Cahiers de la céramique égyptienne*, III (1992), pp. 161–71.

GIANNICHEDDA, E. (ed.), *Filattiera-Soriano* (Florence, 1998).

GIARDINA, A., 'Allevamento ed economia della selva in Italia meridionale', in idem and A. Schiavone (eds.), *Società romana e produzione schiavistica*, I (Bari, 1981), pp. 87–113.

GIARDINA, A., 'Carità eversiva', *Studi storici*, XXIX (1988), pp. 127–42.

GIARDINA, A., 'Le due Italie nella forma tarda dell'impero', in A. Giardina (ed.), *Società romana e impero tardoantico*, I (Bari, 1986), pp. 1–36.

GIARDINA, A., *L'Italia romana* (Bari, 1997).

GIARDINA, A., and GRELLE, F., 'La Tavola di Trinitapoli', *MEFR. Antiquités*, XCV (1983), pp. 249–303.

GICHON, M., *En Boqeq*, I (Mainz, 1993).

GICHON, M., 'Fine Byzantine wares from the south of Israel', *Palestine exploration quarterly*, CVI (1974), pp. 119–39.

GIGLIO, S., *Il tardo impero d'Occidente e il suo senato* (Naples, 1990).

GIL EGEA, M. E., *África en tiempos de los Vándalos* (Alcalá de Henares, 1998).

GLICK, T. F., *From Muslim fortress to Christian castle* (Manchester, 1995).

GLUCKER, C. A. M., *The city of Gaza in the Roman and Byzantine periods*, BAR, I325 (Oxford, 1987).

GOCKEL, M., *Karolingische Königshöfe am Mittelrhein* (Göttingen, 1970).

GODELIER, M., *Rationality and irrationality in economics* (London, 1972).

GODELIER, M., and STRATHEARN, M. (eds.), *Big men and great men* (Cambridge, 1991).

GODLEWSKI, W., 'Coptic pottery from Deir el Naqlun (Fayum)', in idem (ed.), *Coptic and Nubian pottery*, I (Warsaw, 1990), pp. 49–62.

GODLEWSKI, W., *Le monastère de St-Phoibammon* (Warsaw, 1986).

GOETZ, H.-W., 'Bäuerliche Arbeit und regionale Gewohnheit im Pariser Raum im frühen 9. Jahrhundert', in H. Atsma (ed.), *La Neustrie*, I (Sigmaringen, 1989), pp. 505–22.

GOETZ, H.-W., *Frauen im frühen Mittelalter* (Cologne, 1995).

GOETZ, H.-W., 'Herrschaft und Recht in der frühmittelalterlichen Grundherrschaft', *Historisches Jahrbuch*, CIV (1984), pp. 392–410.

GOETZ, H.-W., ' "Nobilis". Der Adel im Selbstverständnis der Karolingerzeit', *Vierteljahrschrift für Sozial- und Wirtschaftsgeschichte*, LX (1983), pp. 153–91.

GOETZ, H.-W., 'Serfdom and the beginnings of a "seigneurial system" in the Carolingian period', *Early medieval Europe*, II (1993), pp. 29–51.

GOETZ, H.-W., 'Social and military institutions', in R. McKitterick (ed.), *The new Cambridge medieval history*, II (Cambridge, 1995), pp. 451–80.

GOFFART, W., *Barbarians and Romans, A.D. 418–584* (Princeton, 1980).

GOFFART, W., 'Old and new in Merovingian taxation', in idem, *Rome's fall*, pp. 213–31.

GOFFART, W., *Rome's fall and after* (London, 1989).

GOFFART, W., *The narrators of barbarian history (A.D. 550–800)* (Princeton, 1988).

GOITEIN, S. D., *A Mediterranean society*, 6 vols. (Berkeley, 1967–93).

GOLDBERG, E. J., 'Popular revolt, dynastic politics and aristocratic factionalism in the early middle ages: the Saxon *Stellinga* reconsidered', *Speculum*, LXX (1995), pp. 467–501.

GOLOFAST, L., 'Early Byzantine deposits from Cherson', *XXᵉ Congrès international des études Byzantines. Pré-actes*, III (Paris, 2001), p. 301.

GÓMEZ BECERRA, A., *El poblamiento altomedieval en la costa de Granada* (Granada, 1998).

GONZÁLEZ, V. *et al.*, 'Saint-Ouen-du-Breuil (Haute-Normandie, Frankreich)', *Germania*, LXXIX (2001), pp. 43–61.

González Blanco, A. *et al.*, 'La ciudad hispano-visigoda de Begastri (Cabezo de Roenas, Cehegín, Murcia)', in *XVI Congreso nacional de arqueología* (Zaragoza, 1983), pp. 1011–22.

González Salas, S., *El castro de Yecla, en Santo Domingo de Silos (Burgos)* (Madrid, 1945).

Goodchild, R. G., *Libyan studies* (London, 1976).

Gorges, J.-G., *Les villas hispano-romaines* (Paris, 1979).

Grabar, O., *City in the desert. Qasr al-Hayr East* (Cambridge, Mass., 1978).

Graham, B. J., 'Early medieval Ireland', in B. J. Graham and L. J. Proudfoot (eds.), *A historical geography of Ireland* (London, 1993), pp. 19–57.

Grahn-Hoek, H., *Die fränkische Oberschicht im 6. Jahrhundert* (Sigmaringen, 1976).

Gramsci, A., *Quaderni del carcere*, ed. V. Gerratana (Turin, 1975).

Green, C. S. (ed.), *Excavations at Poundbury, Dorchester, Dorset 1966–1982*, I (Dorchester, 1987).

Green, D. H., *Language and history in the early Germanic world* (Cambridge, 1998).

Green, J. A., 'The last century of Danegeld', *English historical review*, XCVI (1981), pp. 241–58.

Greene, J. A., 'Une reconnaissance archéologique de l'arrière-pays de la Carthage antique', in A. Ennabli (ed.), *Pour sauver Carthage* (Paris, 1992), pp. 195–7.

Greenhalgh, M., *The survival of Roman antiquities in the middle ages* (London, 1989).

Grey, A. D., 'The pottery of the later periods from Tel Jezreel', *Levant*, XXVI (1994), pp. 51–62.

Grey, C. A., *Peasants, patronage and taxation, c.280–c.480*, Ph.D. thesis, University of Cambridge (2002).

Grierson, P., *Dark age numismatics* (London, 1979).

Grierson, P., and Blackburn, M., *The early middle ages* (Cambridge, 1986).

Grieser, H., *Sklaverei im spätantiken und frühmittelalterlichen Gallien (5.–7. Jh.)* (Stuttgart, 1997).

Grohmann, A., 'Greek papyri of the early Islamic period in the collection of Archduke Rainer', *Études de papyrologie*, VIII (1957), pp. 5–40.

Gross, U., 'Beobachtungen zur Verbreitung frühmittelalterlicher Keramikgruppen in Südwestdeutschland', *Archäologische Informationen*, X (1987), pp. 194–202.

Gross, U., 'Die Töpferware der Franken. Herleitung–Formen–Produktion', in *Die Franken. Wegbereiter Europas* (Mannheim, 1996), pp. 581–93.

Grossmann, P., *Abū Mīnā I* (Mainz, 1989).

Grossmann, P., *Elephantine II* (Mainz, 1980).

Günsenin, N., 'Le vin de Ganos', in *Eupsychia*, I (Paris, 1998), pp. 281–7.

Guérout, J., 'Le testament de Sainte Fare', *Revue d'histoire ecclésiastique*, LX (1965), pp. 761–821.

Guéry, R., 'L'occupation de Rougga (Bararus) d'après la stratigraphie du forum', *Bulletin archéologique du Comité des travaux historiques et scientifiques*, XVII B (1984), pp. 91–100.

GUÉRY, R., 'Survivance de la vie sédentaire pendant les invasions arabes en Tunisie centrale', *Bulletin archéologique du Comité des travaux historiques et scientifiques*, XIX B (1985), pp. 399–410.

GUÉRY, R. *et al.*, *Recherches archéologiques franco-tunisiennes à Rougga*, III (Rome, 1982).

GUGLIELMETTI, A., 'La ceramica comune fra fine VI e X sec. a Brescia, nei siti di casa Pallaveri, palazzo Martinengo Cesaresco e piazza Labus', in Brogiolo and Gelichi, *Le ceramiche altomedievali*, pp. 9–14.

GUICHARD, P., *Structures sociales 'orientales' et 'occidentales' dans l'Espagne musulmane* (Paris, 1977; published in Spanish as *Al-Andalus*, Barcelona, 1976).

GUIDERI, S., 'Il popolamento medievale attraverso un'indagine di superficie', in eadem and R. Parenti (eds.), *Archeologia a Montemassi* (Florence, 2000), pp. 11–37.

GUIDOBALDI, F., 'Le *domus* tardoantiche di Roma come "sensori" delle trasformazioni culturali e sociali', in W. V. Harris (ed.), *The transformations of urbs Roma in late Antiquity* (Portsmouth, RI, 1999), pp. 51–68.

GUNNAR KARLSSON, *Iceland's 1100 years* (London, 2000).

GURT ESPARRAGUERA, J. M., and GODOY FERNÁNDEZ, C., '*Barcino*, de sede imperial a *urbs regia* en época visigoda', in Ripoll and Gurt, *Sedes regiae*, pp. 425–66.

GURT ESPARRAGUERRA, J. M., and PALET MARTÍNEZ, J. M., 'Structuration du territoire dans le nord-est de l'Hispanie pendant l'Antiquité tardive', in Ouzoulias, *Les campagnes*, pp. 303–29.

GURT I ESPARRAGUERA, J. M. *et al.*, 'Topografía de la antigüedad tardía hispánica', *Antiquité tardive*, II (1994), pp. 161–80.

GUTIÉRREZ GONZÁLEZ, J. A., 'Nuevos desarrollos en el estudio de las cerámicas medievales del Norte de España', in C. M. Gerrard *et al.* (eds.), *Spanish medieval ceramics in Spain and the British Isles*, BAR, I610 (Oxford, 1995), pp. 69–87.

GUTIÉRREZ GONZÁLEZ, J. A., 'Sobre los orígines de la sociedad asturleonesa', *Studia histórica. Historia medieval*, XVI (1998), pp. 173–97.

GUTIÉRREZ LLORET, S., 'Algunas consideraciones sobre la cultura material de las épocas visigoda y emiral en el territorio de Tudmīr', in L. Caballero Zoreda and P. Mateos Cruz (eds.), *Visigodos y Omeyas* (Madrid, 2000), pp. 95–116.

GUTIÉRREZ LLORET, S., 'De la *civitas* a la *madīna*', in *IV Congreso de arqueología medieval española*, I (Madrid, 1993), pp. 13–34.

GUTIÉRREZ LLORET, S., 'Eastern Spain in the sixth century in the light of archaeology', in R. Hodges and W. Bowden (eds.), *The sixth century* (Leiden, 1998), pp. 161–84.

GUTIÉRREZ LLORET, S., 'El espacio doméstico altomedieval del Tolmo de Minateda (Hellín, Albacete), entre el ámbito urbano y el rural', in A. Bazzana and É. Hubert (eds.), *Castrum 6* (Rome, 2000), pp. 151–64.

GUTIÉRREZ LLORET, S., *La cora de Tudmīr de la antigüedad tardía al mundo islámico* (Madrid, 1996).

GUTIÉRREZ LLORET, S. *et al.*, 'Los contextos cerámicos altomedievales del Tolmo de Minateda y la cerámica altomedieval en el sudeste de la Península Ibérica', in Caballero *et al.*, *Cerámicas tardorromanas y altomedievales*, pp. 119–68.

886	*Bibliography*

GUYON, J., 'De la ville à la campagne', in Ouzoulias *et al.*, *Les campagnes*, pp. 569–85.

GUYON, J., 'Toulouse, La première capitale du royaume wisigoth', in Ripoll and Gurt, *Sedes regiae*, pp. 219–40.

GUYON J. *et al.*, *Atlas topographique des villes de Gaule méridionale*, I, *Aix-en-Provence* (Montpellier, 1998).

HAARNAGEL, W., *Die Grabung Feddersen Wierde*, II (Wiesbaden, 1979).

HAAS, C., *Alexandria in late Antiquity* (Baltimore, 1997).

HADLEY, D. M., *The northern Danelaw* (Leicester, 2000).

HADLEY, D. M., and MOORE, J. M., ' "Death makes the man"?', in D. M. Hadley (ed.), *Masculinity in medieval Europe* (London, 1999), pp. 21–38.

HÄGERMANN, D., 'Einige Aspekte der Grundherrschaft in den fränkischen formulae und in den leges des Frühmittelalters', in A. Verhulst (ed.), *Le grand domaine aux époques mérovingienne et carolingienne* (Gent, 1985), pp. 51–77.

HÄRKE, H., 'Archaeologists and migrations. A problem of attitude?', *Current anthropology*, XXXIX (1998), pp. 19–45.

HÄRKE, H., 'Briten und Angelsachsen im nachrömischen England', *Studien zur Sachsenforschung*, XI (1998), pp. 87–119.

HÄRKE, H., 'Early Anglo-Saxon social structure', in J. Hines (ed.), *The Anglo-Saxons from the migration period to the eighth century* (Woodbridge, 1997), pp. 125–60.

HÄSSLER, H. J., 'Volkerwanderungs- und Merowingerzeit', in idem (ed.), *Ur- und Frühgeschichte in Niedersachsen* (Stuttgart, 1991), pp. 285–320.

HAIMAN, M., 'Agriculture and nomad-state relations in the Negev desert in the Byzantine and early Islamic periods', *Bulletin of the American Schools of Oriental research*, CCXCVII (1995), pp. 29–53.

HAIMAN, M., 'An early Islamic period farm at Naḥal Mitnan in the Negev highlands', *'Atiqot*, XXVI (1995), pp. 1–13.

HALDIMANN, M.-A., 'Les implantations omeyyades dans la Balqa', *Annual of the Department of Antiquities of Jordan*, XXXVI (1992), pp. 307–23.

HALDON, J. F., *Byzantine praetorians* (Bonn, 1984).

HALDON, J. F., *Byzantium in the seventh century*, 2nd edn. (Cambridge, 1997).

HALDON, J. F., 'Ideology and social change in the seventh century', *Klio*, LXVIII (1986), pp. 139–90 (now in idem, *State, army*, study II).

HALDON, J. F., 'Military service, military lands, and the status of soldiers', *Dumbarton Oaks papers*, XLVII (1993), pp. 1–67 (now in idem, *State, army*, study VII).

HALDON, J. F., 'Production, distribution and demand in the Byzantine world, c.660–840', in I. L. Hansen and C. Wickham (eds.), *The long eighth century* (Leiden, 2000), pp. 225–64.

HALDON, J. F., *State, army and society in Byzantium* (Aldershot, 1995).

HALDON, J. F., 'Synônê', *Byzantine and modern Greek studies*, XVIII (1994), pp. 116–53 (now in idem, *State, army*, study VIII).

HALDON, J. F., 'The fate of the late Roman senatorial élite', in idem (ed.), *The Byzantine and early Islamic Near East*, VI (Princeton, 2004).

HALDON, J. F., 'The feudalism debate once more', *Journal of peasant studies*, XVII (1989), pp. 5–39.

HALDON, J. F., 'The idea of the town in the Byzantine empire', in Brogiolo and Ward-Perkins, *The idea and ideal of the town*, pp. 1–23.

HALDON, J. F., *The state and the tributary mode of production* (London, 1993).

HALDON, J. F., *Warfare, state and society in the Byzantine world, 565–1204* (London, 1999).

HALDON, J. F., review of Brandes, *Finanzverwaltung, Byzantinische Zeitschrift*, XCVI (2003), pp. 715–26.

HALSALL, G., *Early medieval cemeteries* (Glasgow, 1995).

HALSALL, G., *Settlement and social organisation* (Cambridge, 1995).

HALSALL, G., 'The origins of the *Reihengräberzivilisation*: forty years on', in Drinkwater and Elton, *Fifth-century Gaul*, pp. 196–207.

HALSALL, G., 'Violence and society in the early medieval west', in idem, *Violence and society*, pp. 1–45.

HALSALL, G. (ed.), *Violence and society in the early medieval West* (Woodbridge, 1998).

HALSALL, G., *Warfare and society in the barbarian West, 450–900* (London, 2003).

HAMEROW, H., 'Anglo-Saxon timber buildings: the continental connection', in H. Sarfatij *et al.* (eds.), *In discussion with the past* (Zwolle, 1999), pp. 119–28.

HAMEROW, H., *Early medieval settlements* (Oxford, 2002).

HAMEROW, H., *Excavations at Mucking*, II (London, 1993).

HAMEROW, H., 'Migration theory and the migration period', in B. Vyner (ed.), *Building on the past* (London, 1994), pp. 164–77.

HAMEROW, H., 'Settlement mobility and the "Middle Saxon shift" ', *Anglo-Saxon England*, XX (1991), pp. 1–17.

HAMEROW, H., 'The earliest Anglo-Saxon kingdoms', in P. Fouracre (ed.), *The new Cambridge medieval history*, I (Cambridge, in press).

HAMEROW, H. *et al.*, 'Migration period settlements and "Anglo-Saxon" pottery from Flanders', *Medieval archaeology*, XXXVIII (1994), pp. 1–18.

HAMMER, C. I., *A large-scale slave society of the early middle ages* (Aldershot, 2002).

HANDLEY, M. A., 'The origins of Christian commemoration in late antique Britain', *Early medieval Europe*, X (2001), pp. 177–99.

HANSEN, H. J., 'Dankirke', *Kuml* (1998–9), pp. 201–47.

HANSEN, T. E., 'Die eisenzeitliche Siedlung bei Nørre Snede, Mitteljütland', *Acta archaeologica*, LVIII (1987), pp. 171–200.

HANSEN, T. E., 'Et jernalderhus med drikkeglas i Dejbjerg, Vestjylland', *Kuml* (1993–4), pp. 211–36.

HÅRDH, B., and LARSSON, L. (eds.), *Central places in the migration and Merovingian periods* (Lund, 2002).

HARDT, M., 'The Bavarians', in H.-W. Goetz, J. Jarnut, and W. Pohl (eds.), *Regna and gentes* (Leiden, 2003), pp. 429–61.

HARDY, E. R., *The large estates of Byzantine Egypt* (New York, 1931).

HARLOW, M., 'Clothes maketh the man', in L. Brubaker and J. M. H. Smith (eds.), *Gender in the early medieval world* (Cambridge, 2004), pp. 44–69.

HARPER, R. P., 'Athis–Neocaesareia–Qasrin–Dibsi Faraj', in J. C. Margueron (ed.), *Le moyen Euphrate* (Strasbourg, 1977), pp. 327–48.

HARPER, R. P., *Upper Zohar* (Oxford, 1995).

HARRIES, J., *Law and empire in late Antiquity* (Cambridge, 1999).

HARRIES, J., *Sidonius Apollinaris and the fall of Rome* (Oxford, 1994).

HARRISON, D., *The early state and the towns* (Lund, 1993).

HARRISON, R. M., 'Amorium excavations 1989', *Anatolian studies*, XL (1990), pp. 205–18.

HARRISON, R. M., 'Amorium excavations 1991', *Anatolian studies*, XLII (1992), pp. 207–22.

HARRISON, R. M., *Excavations at Saraçhane in Istanbul*, I (Princeton, 1980).

HARRISON, T. P., 'A sixth-seventh century ceramic assemblage from Madaba, Jordan', in *Annual of the Department of Antiquities of Jordan*, XXXVIII (1994), pp. 429–46.

HARTMANN, L. M., *Zur Wirtschaftsgeschichte Italiens im frühen Mittelalter. Analekten* (Gotha, 1904).

HARVEY, P. D. A., '*Rectitudines singularum personarum* and *Gerefa*', *English historical review*, CVIII (1993), pp. 1–22.

HASLAM, J., 'A Middle Saxon iron smelting site at Ramsbury, Wiltshire', *Medieval archaeology*, XXIV (1980), pp. 1–68.

HASLEGROVE, C., and SCULL, C., 'The Romanization and de-Romanization of Belgic Gaul', in M. Wood and F. M. V. R. Queiroga (eds.), *Current research on the Romanization of the western provinces* (Oxford, 1992), pp. 9–24.

HAUGHTON, C., and POWLESLAND, D., *West Heslerton. The Anglian cemetery* (Yedingham, 1999).

HAVET, J., 'Questions mérovingiennes', V, *Bibliothèque de l'École de Chartes*, LI (1890), pp. 5–62.

HAYES, J. W., *Excavations at Saraçhane in Istanbul*, II (Princeton, 1992).

HAYES, J. W., 'Late Roman fine wares and their successors', in Villeneuve and Watson, *La céramique byzantine*, pp. 275–82.

HAYES, J. W., *Late Roman pottery* (London, 1972).

HAYES, J. W., *Late Roman pottery. Supplement* (London, 1980).

HAYES, J. W., 'Panorama de la Grèce (meridionale, sauf Crète, zone centrale, îles)', in Bakirtzis, *VIIe Congrès international*, pp. 529–34.

HAYES, J. W., 'Problèmes de la céramique des VIIème–IXème siècles à Salamine et à Chypre', in *Salamine de Chypre, histoire et archéologie* (Paris, 1980), pp. 375–87.

HEATHER, P., *Goths and Romans, 332–489* (Oxford, 1991).

HEATHER, P., 'New men for new Constantines?', in P. Magdalino (ed.), *New Constantines* (Aldershot, 1994), pp. 11–33.

HEATHER, P., 'Senators and senates', in A. Cameron and P. Garnsey (eds.), *The Cambridge ancient history*, XIII (Cambridge, 1998), pp. 184–210.

HEATHER, P., 'The Huns and the end of the Roman empire in western Europe', *English historical review*, CX (1995), pp. 4–41.

HEATHER, P., 'The western empire, 425–76', in A. Cameron *et al.* (eds.), *The Cambridge ancient history*, XIV (Cambridge, 2000), pp. 1–32.

HEATHER, P., 'Theoderic, king of the Goths', *Early medieval Europe*, IV (1995), pp. 145–73.

HEDEAGER, L., 'Asgard reconstructed?', in M. de Jong *et al.* (eds.), *Topographies of power in the early middle ages* (Leiden, 2001), pp. 467–507.

HEDEAGER, L., *Iron-Age societies* (Oxford, 1992).

HEIDINGA, H. A., 'Frankish settlement at Gennep', in P. O. Nielsen *et al.*, *Gudme*, pp. 202–8.

HEIDINGA, H. A., *Frisia in the first millennium* (Utrecht, 1997).

HEIDINGA, H. A., *Medieval settlement and economy north of the lower Rhine* (Assen, 1987).

HEIDRICH, I., 'Das Breve der Bischofskirche von Mâcon aus der Zeit König Pippins (751–768)', *Francia*, XXIV (1997), pp. 17–37.

HEIJMANS, M., 'La topographie de la ville d'Arles durant l'Antiquité tardive', *JRA*, XII (1999), pp. 142–67.

HEIJMANS, M., and SINTÈS, C., 'L'évolution de la topographie de l'Arles antique', *Gallia*, LI (1994), pp. 135–70.

HEINZELMANN, M., *Bischofsherrschaft in Gallien* (Munich, 1976).

HEINZELMANN, M., *Gregory of Tours* (Cambridge, 2001).

HEINZELMANN, M., 'Villa d'après les oeuvres de Grégoire de Tours', in E. Magnou-Nortier (ed.), *Aux sources de la gestion publique*, I (Lille, 1993), pp. 45–70.

HEINZELMANN, M., and POULIN, J. C., *Les vies anciennes de sainte Geneviève de Paris* (Paris, 1986).

HELLENKEMPER, H., *et al.*, 'Die Ausgrabungen auf dem Kölner Heumarkt III', *Kölner Jahrbuch*, XXXIV (2001), pp. 621–944.

HEN, Y., *Culture and religion in Merovingian Gaul, AD 481–751* (Leiden, 1995).

HENCKEN, H., 'Lagore crannog', *Proceedings of the Royal Irish Academy*, LIII C (1950–1), pp. 1–247.

HENDERSON, J., 'New light on early Islamic industry', in R. J. A. Wilson (ed.), *From River Trent to Raqqa* (Nottingham, 1996), pp. 59–71.

HENDY, M. F., 'From public to private', *Viator*, XIX (1988), pp. 29–78.

HENDY, M. F., *Studies in the Byzantine monetary economy, c.300–1450* (Cambridge, 1985).

HENNING, J., *Südosteuropa zwischen Antike und Mittelalter* (Berlin, 1987).

HERBERT, M., *Iona, Kells and Derry* (Oxford, 1988).

HERLIHY, D., 'Church property on the European continent, 701–1200', *Speculum*, XXXVI (1961), pp. 81–105 (now in idem, *The social history*, study V).

HERLIHY, D., 'Family solidarity in medieval Italian history', in idem, *The social history*, study VII.

HERLIHY, D., 'Land, family and women in continental Europe, 701–1200', *Traditio*, XVIII (1962), pp. 89–120 (now in idem, *The social history*, study VI).

HERLIHY, D., *Opera muliebria* (New York, 1990).

HERLIHY, D., *The social history of Italy and western Europe* (London, 1978).

HERRIN, J., *The formation of Christendom* (Princeton, 1987).

HERRMANN, J., *Studien zur Bodenpacht im Recht der graeco-aegyptischen Papyri* (Munich, 1958).

HERSCHEND, F., *The idea of the good in late Iron Age society* (Uppsala, 1998).

HIDALGO PRIETO, R., *Espacio público y espacio privado en el conjunto palatino de Cercadilla (Córdoba)* (Seville, 1996).

HIDALGO PRIETO, R. *et al.*, *El criptopórtico de Cercadilla* (Seville, 1996).

HIGHAM, N., *Rome, Britain and the Anglo-Saxons* (London, 1992).

HILD, F., and HELLENKEMPER, H., *Kilikien und Isaurien. Tabula imperii Byzantini*, V, 2 vols. (Vienna, 1990).

HILL, D., 'Offa's Dyke: pattern and purpose', *The Antiquaries journal*, LXXX (2000), pp. 195–206.

HILL, D. *et al.*, 'Quentovic defined', *Antiquity*, LXIV (1990), pp. 51–8.

HILL, P., *Whithorn and St Ninian* (Stroud, 1997).

HILLENBRAND, R., 'Anjar and early Islamic urbanism', in Brogiolo and Ward-Perkins, *The idea and the ideal of the town*, pp. 61–98.

HILLS, C., 'Did the people of Spong Hill come from Schleswig-Holstein?', *Studien zur Sachsenforschung*, XI (1998), pp. 145–54.

HILTON, R. H., *Bondmen made free* (London, 1973).

HILTON, R. H., *Class conflict and the crisis of feudalism* (London, 1985).

HILTON, R. H., *The English peasantry in the later middle ages* (Oxford, 1975).

HINES, J., 'Philology, archaeology and the *adventus Saxonum vel Anglorum*', in A. Bammesberger and A. Wollmann (eds.), *Britain 400–600: language and history* (Heidelberg, 1990), pp. 17–36.

HINES, J., 'The Anglo-Saxons reviewed', *Medieval archaeology*, XXXVII (1993), pp. 314–18.

HINES, J., *The Scandinavian character of Anglian England in the pre-Viking period*, BAR, B124 (Oxford, 1984).

HINTON, D. A., *The gold, silver and other non-ferrous alloy objects from Hamwic, and the non-ferrous metalworking evidence* (Stroud, 1996).

HINTZE, F., 'Koptische Steuerquittungsostraka der Berliner Papyrus-Sammlung', in *Festschrift zum 150jährigen Bestehen des Berliner Ägyptischen Museums* (Berlin, 1974), pp. 271–81.

HINZ, H., *Archäologische Funde und Denkmäler des Rheinlandes*, II. *Kreis Bergheim* (Düsseldorf, 1969).

HIRSCHFELD, Y., 'Farms and villages in Byzantine Palestine', *Dumbarton Oaks papers*, LI (1997), pp. 33–71.

HIRSCHFELD, Y., *Ramat Hanadiv excavations* (Jerusalem, 2000).

HIRSCHFELD, Y., 'Tiberias', in E. Stern (ed.), *The new encyclopaedia for archaeological excavations in the Holy Land*, IV (Jerusalem, 1993), pp. 1464–73.

HIRSCHFELD, Y., and SOLAR, G., 'The Roman thermae at Ḥammat Gader', *Israel exploration journal*, XXXI (1981), pp. 197–219.

HITCHNER, R. B., 'Historical text and archaeological context in Roman North Africa', in D. B. Small (ed.), *Methods in the Mediterranean* (Leiden, 1995), pp. 124–42.

HITCHNER, R. B., 'Meridional Gaul, trade and the Mediterranean economy in late Antiquity', in Drinkwater and Elton, *Fifth-century Gaul*, pp. 122–31.

HITCHNER, R. B., 'The Kasserine archaeological survey 1982–1985', *Africa*, XI–XII (1992–3), pp. 158–98.

HITCHNER, R. B., 'The Kasserine archaeological survey 1982–1986', *Antiquités africaines*, XXIV (1988), pp. 7–41.

HITCHNER, R. B., 'The Kasserine archaeological survey 1987', *Antiquités africaines*, XXVI (1990), pp. 231–59.

HLAWITSCHKA, E., *Franken, Alemannen, Bayern und Burgunder in Oberitalien 774–962* (Freiburg, 1960).

HODGES, R., *Dark Age economics* (London, 1982).

HODGES, R., *Primitive and peasant markets* (Oxford, 1988).

HODGES, R., *The Anglo-Saxon achievement* (Ithaca, NY, 1989).

HODGES, R., *The Hamwih pottery*, CBA Research Report, 37 (London, 1981).

HODGES, R., *Towns and trade in the age of Charlemagne* (London, 2000).

HODGES, R. (ed.), *San Vincenzo al Volturno*, 2 vols. (London, 1993–5).

HODGES, R., and BOWDEN, W., 'Butrinto nell'età tardo antica', in G. P. Brogiolo and P. Delogu (eds.), *L'Adriatico dalla tarda antichità all'età carolingia* (Brescia, in press).

HODGES, R., and MITCHELL, J., *The basilica of Abbot Joshua at San Vincenzo al Volturno* (Montecassino, 1996).

HODGES, R., and WHITEHOUSE, D., *Mohammed, Charlemagne and the origins of Europe* (London, 1983).

HÖLSCHER, U., *The excavation of Medinet Habu*, I (Chicago, 1934).

HOLLEVOET, Y., 'Céramiques d'habitats mérovingiens et carolingiens dans la région d'Oudenburg (Flandre Occidentale, Belgique)', in Piton, *La céramique*, pp. 195–207.

HOLM-NIELSEN, S. *et al.*, 'The excavation of Byzantine baths in Umm Qeis', *Annual of the Department of Antiquities of Jordan*, XXX (1986), pp. 219–32.

HOLUM, K. G., 'Archaeological evidence for the fall of Byzantine Caesarea', *Bulletin of the American Schools of Oriental Research*, CCLXXXVI (1992), pp. 73–85.

HOLUM, K. G., *Theodosian empresses* (Berkeley, 1982).

HOLUM, K. G. *et al.*, *Caesarea papers 2* (Portsmouth, RI, 1999).

HOOKE, D., *The Anglo-Saxon landscape* (Manchester, 1985).

HOPE-TAYLOR, B., *Yeavering* (London, 1977).

HOPKINS, K., *Conquerors and slaves* (Cambridge, 1978).

HOPKINS, K., 'Taxes and trade in the Roman empire (200 B.C.–A.D. 400)', *Journal of Roman studies*, LXX (1980), pp. 101–25.

HORDEN, P., and PURCELL, N., *The corrupting sea* (Oxford, 2000).

HOWGEGO, C., 'Coin circulation and the integration of the African economy', *JRA*, VII (1994), pp. 5–21.

HUBERT, É., *Espace urbain et habitat à Rome du Xe siècle à la fin du XIIIe siècle* (Rome, 1990).

HUBERT, É., 'L'incastellamento dans le Latium', *Annales HSS*, LV (2000), pp. 583–99.

HUDSON, P. J., 'Contributi archeologici alla storia dell'insediamento urbano veneto (IV–XI secolo)', in A. Castagnetti and G. M. Varanini (eds.), *Il Veneto nel medioevo*, II (Verona, 1989), pp. 331–48.

HÜBENER, W., *Die Keramik von Haithabu* (Neumünster, 1959).

HÜBENER, W., 'Zur Chronologie der westgotenzeitlichen Grabfunde in Spanien', *Madrider Mitteilungen*, XI (1970), pp. 187–211.

HÜBNER, R., 'Gerichtsurkunden der fränkischen Zeit', in *Zeitschrift der Savigny-Stiftung für Rechtsgeschichte*, XII (1891), appendix, pp. 1–118; XIV (1893), appendix, pp. 1–258.

HUGGETT, J. W., 'Imported grave goods and the early Anglo-Saxon economy', *Medieval archaeology*, XXXII (1988), pp. 63–96.

HUGHES, D. O., 'From brideprice to dowry', *Journal of family history*, III (1978), pp. 262–96.

HUGHES, K., *Early Christian Ireland: an introduction to the sources* (London, 1972).

HUGHES, K., *The church in early Irish society* (London, 1966).

HUMPHREY, J. H., 'Vandal and Byzantine Carthage', in J. G. Pedley (ed.), *New light on ancient Carthage* (Ann Arbor, Mich., 1980), pp. 85–120.

HUMPHREY, J. H. (ed.), *The circus and a Byzantine cemetery at Carthage*, I (Ann Arbor, Mich., 1988).

HURST, H., 'Cartagine, la nuova Alessandria', in A. Carandini *et al.* (eds.), *Storia di Roma*, III.2 (Turin, 1993), pp. 327–37.

HURST, H., and ROSKAMS, S. P., *Excavations at Carthage: the British mission*, I. 1 (Sheffield, 1984).

HURST, J. D. (ed.), *A multi-period salt production site at Droitwich*, CBA Research Report, 107 (London, 1997).

HURST, J. G., 'The pottery', in D. M. Wilson (ed.), *The archaeology of Anglo-Saxon England* (Cambridge, 1976), pp. 283–348.

HUSSON, G., 'Houses in Syene in the Patermouthis archive', *Bulletin of the American society of papyrologists*, XXVII (1990), pp. 123–37.

HUSSON, G., *Oikia* (Paris, 1983).

HUSSON, G., 'Recherches sur les sens du mot "proastion" dans le grec d'Égypte', *Recherches de papyrologie*, IV (1967), pp. 187–200.

HUTCHINSON, G., 'The bar-lug pottery of Cornwall', *Cornish archaeology*, XVIII (1979), pp. 81–103.

HVASS, S., 'Die völkerwanderungszeitliche Siedlung Vorbasse, Mitteljütland', *Acta archaeologica*, XLIX (1979), pp. 61–110.

HVASS, S., 'Jernalderens bebyggelse', in Mortensen and Rasmussen, *Fra stamme til stat*, I, pp. 53–91.

HVASS, S., 'Rural settlements in Denmark in the first millennium A.D.', in K. Randsborg (ed.), *The birth of Europe* (Rome, 1989), pp. 91–9.

HVASS, S., 'The Viking age settlement at Vorbasse, central Jutland', *Acta archaeologica*, L (1980), pp. 137–72.

HVASS, S., 'Wikingerzeitliche Siedlungen in Vorbasse', *Offa*, XLI (1984), pp. 97–112.

IACOE, A., 'I corredi tombali', in P. Peduto (ed.), *Villaggi fluviali nella pianura pestana del secolo VII* (Altavilla Silentina, 1984), pp. 97–102.

Ideologie e pratiche del reimpiego nell'alto medioevo, 2 vols. = *Settimane di studio*, XLVI (1999).

İNALCIK, H., *An economic and social history of the Ottoman empire*, I (Cambridge, 1994).

INNES, M., *State and society in the early middle ages* (Cambridge, 2000).

IRSIGLER, F., *Untersuchungen zur Geschichte des frühfränkischen Adels* (Bonn, 1969).

ISAAC, B., *The limits of empire*, 2nd edn. (Oxford, 1992).

ISLA FREZ, A., 'El "officium palatinum" visigodo', *Hispania*, LXII (2002), pp. 823–48.

ISLA FREZ, A., *La alta edad media. Siglos VIII–XI* (Madrid, 2002).

ISLA FREZ, A., 'Villa, villula, castellum', *Arqueología y territorio medieval*, VIII (2001), pp. 9–19.

ISRAEL, Y., 'Ashqelon', *Excavations and surveys in Israel*, XIII (1993), pp. 100–7.

IVISON, E. A., 'Burial and urbanism at late antique and early Byzantine Corinth (*c.* AD 400–700)', in Christie and Loseby, *Towns in transition*, pp. 99–125.

IZQUIERDO BENITO, R., 'Cerámica de necrópolis de época visigoda del Museo Arqueologico Nacional', *Revista de archivos, bibliotecas y museos*, LXXX (1977), pp. 569–611.

IZQUIERDO BENITO, R., 'Ensayo de una sistematización tipológica de la cerámica de necrópolis de época visigoda', *Revista de archivos, bibliotecas y museos*, LXXX (1977), pp. 837–65.

JACQUES, A., and HOSDEZ, C., 'Activité archéologique: Arras', *Histoire et archéologie du Pas-de-Calais*, XIV (1995–6), pp. 461–3.

JACQUES, F., 'L'ordine senatorio attraverso la crisi del III secolo', in A. Giardina (ed.), *Società romana e impero tardoantico*, I (Bari, 1986), pp. 81–225.

JAMES, E., *Britain in the first millennium* (London, 2001).

JAMES, E., 'Gregory of Tours and the Franks', in A. C. Murray (ed.), *After Rome's fall* (Toronto, 1998), pp. 51–66.

JAMES, E., *The Franks* (Oxford, 1988).

JAMES, S., 'The fabricae', in J. C. Coulston (ed.), *Military equipment and the identity of Roman soldiers*, BAR, I394 (Oxford, 1988), pp. 257–331.

JAMES, S. *et al.*, 'An early medieval building tradition', *Archaeological journal*, CXLI (1984), pp. 182–215.

JAMESON, M. H. *et al.*, *A Greek countryside* (Stanford, Calif., 1994).

JANSSEN, W., 'Badorf', in J. Hoops (ed.), *Reallexikon der germanischen Altertumskunde*, I, 2nd edn. (Berlin, 1973), pp. 594–5.

JANSSEN, W., *Die Importkeramik von Haithabu* (Neumünster, 1987).

JANSSEN, W., 'Römische und frühmittelalterliche Landerschliessung im Vergleich', in W. Janssen and D. Lohrmann (eds.), *Villa–curtis–grangia* (Munich, 1983), pp. 81–122.

JARNUT, J., *Agilolfingerstudien* (Stuttgart, 1986).

JARNUT, J., NONN, U., and RICHTER, M. (eds.), *Karl Martell in seiner Zeit* (Sigmaringen, 1994).

JÁRREGA DOMÍNGUEZ, R., *Cerámicas finas tardorromanas y del Mediterráneo Oriental en España* (Madrid, 1991).

JÁRREGA DOMÍNGUEZ, R., 'Las cerámicas de importación en el Nordeste de la Tarraconense durante los siglos VI y VII d. C.', in *V Reunió d'arqueologia cristiana hispànica* (Barcelona, 2000), pp. 467–83.

JENSEN, S., 'Dankirke-Ribe', in Mortensen and Rasmussen, *Fra stamme til stat*, II, pp. 73–87.

JENSEN, S., 'Et grubehus fra Darum', *Kuml* (1985), pp. 111–21.

JENTGENS, G., *Die Alamannen* (Rahden, 2001).

JIMÉNEZ PUERTAS, M., *El poblamiento del territorio de Loja en la edad media* (Granada, 2002).

JOHANEK, P., 'Der Aussenhandel des Frankenreiches der Merowingerzeit nach Norden und Osten im Spiegel der Schriftquellen', in Düwel *et al.*, *Untersuchungen zu Handel und Verkehr*, III, pp. 214–54.

JOHANEK, P., 'Der fränkische Handel der Karolingerzeit im Spiegel der Schriftquellen', in Düwel *et al.*, *Untersuchungen zu Handel und Verkehr*, IV, pp. 7–68.

JOHN, E., *Land tenure in early England* (Leicester, 1964).

JOHN, E., *Reassessing Anglo-Saxon England* (Manchester, 1996).

JOHNS, J., 'The longue durée', in E. L. Rogan and T. Tell (eds.), *Village, steppe and state* (London, 1994), pp. 1–31.

JOHNS, J., and KENNET, D., 'An outline of the development of glazed pottery in Sicily and the central Mediterranean from late Antiquity to the early 13th century', in J. Johns (ed.), *The Monreale survey* (forthcoming).

JOHNSON, A. C., and WEST, L. C., *Byzantine Egypt: economic studies* (Princeton, 1949).

JOLIVET-LÉVY, C., *La Cappadoce médiévale* (n.p., 2001).

JONES, A. H. M., *The later Roman empire, 284–602* (Oxford, 1964) [Jones, *LRE*].

JONES, A. H. M., *The Roman economy* (Oxford, 1974).

JONES, A. H. M., review of Johnson and West, *Byzantine Egypt, Journal of Hellenic studies*, LXXI (1951), pp. 271–2.

JONES, A. H. M., GRIERSON, P., and CROOK, J. A., 'The authenticity of the "Testamentum S. Remigii" ', *Revue belge de philologie et d'histoire*, XXXV (1957), pp. 356–73.

JONES, G. R. J., 'Post-Roman Wales', in H. P. R. Finberg (ed.), *The agrarian history of England and Wales*, I.2 (Cambridge, 1972), pp. 281–382.

JONES, M. E., *The end of Roman Britain* (Ithaca, NY, 1996).

JONES, P. J., 'La storia economica', in *Storia d'Italia*, II (Turin, 1974), pp. 1469–810.

JONES, P. J., 'L'Italia agraria nell'alto medioevo', *Settimane di studio*, XIII (1966), pp. 57–92.

JONES, P. J., *The Italian city-state* (Oxford, 1997).

JONES, R. F. J. *et al.*, 'The late Roman villa of Vilauba and its context', *The Antiquaries journal*, LXII (1982), pp. 245–82.

JØRGENSEN, L., 'The find material from the settlement of Gudme II', in Nielsen *et al.*, *Gudme*, pp. 53–63.

JØRGENSEN, L., 'The warrior aristocracy of Gudme', in Resi, *Produksjon og samfunn*, pp. 205–20.

JØRGENSEN, L., and PEDERSEN, L., 'Vikinger ved Tissø', *Nationalmuseets arbejdsmark* (1996), pp. 22–36.

JUAN, E., and PASTOR, I., 'Los visigodos en Valencia. Pla de Nadal: ¿una villa aulica?', *Boletín de arqueología medieval*, III (1989), pp. 137–79.

JUAN TOVAR, L. C., 'Las industrias cerámicas hispanas en el Bajo Imperio', in R. Teja and C. Pérez (eds.), *Congreso internacional. La Hispania de Teodosio* (Salamanca, 1997), pp. 543–68.

JUAN TOVAR, L. C., and BLANCO GARCÍA, J. F., 'Cerámica común tardorromana, imitación de sigillata, en la provincia de Segovia', *AEA*, LXX (1997), pp. 171–219.

KAISER, R., *Bischofsherrschaft zwischen Königtum und Fürstenmacht* (Bonn, 1981).

KAISER, R., *Churrätien im frühen Mittelalter* (Basel, 1998).

KAISER, R., 'Royauté et pouvoir episcopal au nord de la Gaule (VIIe–IXe siècles)', in H. Atsma (ed.), *La Neustrie*, I (Sigmaringen, 1989), pp. 143–59.

KAISER, R., 'Steuer und Zoll in der Merowingerzeit', *Francia*, VII (1979), pp. 1–17.

KALDAL MIKKELSEN, D., 'Single farm or village?', in C. Fabech and J. Ringtved (eds.), *Settlement and landscape* (Højbjerg, 1999), pp. 177–93.

KAPLAN, M., *Les hommes et la terre à Byzance du VIe au XIe siècle* (Paris, 1992).

KAPLAN, M., 'Maisons impériales et fondations pieuses', *Byzantion*, LXI (1991), pp. 340–64.

KAPLAN, M., 'Novelle de Tibère II sur les "maisons divines" ', *Travaux et mémoires*, VIII (1981), pp. 237–45.

KARAGIORGOU, O., 'LR2: a container for the military *annona* on the Danubian border?', in S. Kingsley and M. Decker (eds.), *Economy and exchange in the east Mediterranean during late antiquity* (Oxford, 2001), pp. 129–66.

KARAGIORGOU, O., *Urbanism and economy in late antique Thessaly (3rd–7th century A.D.)*, D.Phil. thesis, University of Oxford (2002).

KARRAS, R. M., *Slavery and society in medieval Scandinavia* (New Haven, 1988).

KARWIESE, S., *Gross is die Artemis von Ephesos* (Vienna, 1995).

KAUFFMAN, A. *et al.*, 'Les céramiques de l'Antiquité tardive au XIe siècle dans les fouilles de la Place Jean Jaurès à Apt', *Archéologie du Midi médiéval*, V (1987), pp. 61–84.

KAZHDAN, A. P., 'Hagiographical notes (17–20)', *Erytheia*, IX (1988), pp. 197–209.

KAZHDAN, A. P., 'The formation of Byzantine family names in the ninth and tenth centuries', *Byzantinoslavica*, LVIII (1997), pp. 90–109.

KAZHDAN, A. P., and ŠEVČENKO, N., 'Philaretos the merciful', in A. P. Kazhdan *et al.* (eds.), *The Oxford dictionary of Byzantium*, III (New York, 1991), p. 1650.

KEAY, S., *Late Roman amphorae in the western Mediterranean*, BAR, I196 (Oxford, 1984).

KEAY, S., 'Tarraco in late Antiquity', in Christie and Loseby, *Towns in transition*, pp. 18–44.

KEENAN, J. G., 'A Constantinople loan, A.D. 541', in *Bulletin of the American society of papyrologists*, XXIX (1992), pp. 175–82.

KEENAN, J. G., 'Aurelius Apollos and the Aphrodito village élite', *Atti del XVII Congresso internazionale di papirologia*, III (Naples, 1984), pp. 957–63.

KEENAN, J. G., 'Aurelius Phoibammon, son of Triadelphus', *Bulletin of the American society of papyrologists*, XVII (1980), pp. 145–54.

KEENAN, J. G., 'Egypt', in A. Cameron *et al.* (eds.), *The Cambridge ancient history*, XIV (Cambridge, 2000), pp. 612–37.

KEENAN, J. G., 'Notes on absentee landlordism at Aphrodito', *Bulletin of the American society of papyrologists*, XXII (1985), pp. 137–69.

KEENAN, J. G., 'The Aphrodito murder mystery', *Bulletin of the American society of papyrologists*, XXXI (1995), pp. 57–63.

KEENAN, J. G., 'Village shepherds and social tension in Byzantine Egypt', *Yale classical studies*, XXVIII (1985), pp. 245–59.

KEHOE, D. P., *Management and investment on estates in Roman Egypt during the early empire* (Bonn, 1992).

KEHOE, D. P., *The economics of agriculture on Roman imperial estates in North Africa* (Göttingen, 1988).

KELLER, H., *Adelsherrschaft und städtische Gesellschaft in Oberitalien (9.–12. Jahrhundert)* (Tübingen, 1979).

KELLY, C. M., 'Later Roman bureaucracy: going through the files', in A. K. Bowman and G. Woolf (eds)., *Literacy and power in the ancient world* (Cambridge, 1994), pp. 161–76.

KELLY, F., *A guide to early Irish law* (Dublin, 1988).

KELLY, F., *Early Irish farming* (Dublin, 1998).

KELLY, S., 'Trading privileges from eighth-century England', *Early medieval Europe*, I.1 (1992), pp. 3–28.

KENNEDY, D., and FREEMAN, P., 'Southern Hauran survey 1992', *Levant*, XXVII (1995), pp. 39–73.

KENNEDY, H., 'Central government and provincial élites in the early 'Abbāsid caliphate', *Bulletin of the School of Oriental and African Studies*, XLIV (1981), pp. 26–38.

KENNEDY, H., 'Egypt as a province in the Islamic caliphate, 641–868', in C. F. Petry (ed.), *Cambridge history of Egypt*, I (Cambridge, 1998), pp. 62–85.

KENNEDY, H., 'From Antiquity to Islam in the cities of al-Andalus and al-Mashriq', in P. Cressier and M. García-Arenal (eds.), *Genèse de la ville islamique en al-Andalus et au Maghreb occidental* (Madrid, 1998), pp. 53–64.

KENNEDY, H., 'From *polis* to *madina*', *Past and present*, CVI (1985), pp. 3–27.

KENNEDY, H., *Muslim Spain and Portugal* (London, 1996).

KENNEDY, H., *The armies of the caliphs* (London, 2001).

KENNEDY, H., 'The Barmakid revolution in Islamic government', in C. Melville (ed.), *History and literature in Iran* (London, 1990), pp. 89–98.

KENNEDY, H., 'The financing of the military in the early Islamic state', in A. Cameron (ed.), *The Byzantine and early Islamic Near East*, III (Princeton, 1995), pp. 361–78.

KENNEDY, H., 'The impact of Muslim rule on the pattern of rural settlement in Syria', in Canivet and Rey-Coquais, *La Syrie*, pp. 291–8.

KENNEDY, H., 'The last century of Byzantine Syria', *Byzantinische Forschungen*, X (1985), pp. 141–83.

KEYNES, S., *Anglo-Saxon history. A select bibliography*, 11th edn. (Cambridge, 1996).

KEYNES, S., 'The control of Kent in the ninth century', *Early medieval Europe*, II (1993), pp. 111–31.

KEYNES, S., 'The Fonthill letter', in M. Korhammer (ed.), *Words, texts and manuscripts* (Cambridge, 1992), pp. 53–97.

KIENAST, W., *Die fränkische Vasallität* (Frankfurt, 1990).

KING, G. R. D., 'Settlement patterns in Islamic Jordan', in *Studies in the history and archaeology of Jordan*, IV (Amman, 1992), pp. 369–75.

KING, P. D., *Law and society in the Visigothic kingdom* (Cambridge, 1972).

KINGSLEY, S. A., 'Bag-shaped amphorae and Byzantine trade', *Bulletin of the Anglo-Israel archaeological society*, XIV (1994–5), pp. 39–56.

KINGSLEY, S. A., 'The economic impact of the Palestinian wine trade in late Antiquity', in idem and M. Decker (eds.), *Economy and exchange in the east Mediterranean during late Antiquity* (Oxford, 2001), pp. 44–68.

KINGSLEY, S. A., 'The Sumaqa pottery assemblage', in S. Dar (ed.), *Sumaqa*, BAR, I815 (Oxford, 1999), pp. 263–329.

KLEIBER, W., 'Mosella romana', in Geuenich, *Die Franken*, pp. 130–55.

KLINGSHIRN, W., *Caesarius of Arles* (Cambridge, 1994).

KLINGSHIRN, W., 'Charity and power', *Journal of Roman studies*, LXXV (1985), pp. 183–203.

KLINKOTT, M., *Altertümer von Pergamon*, XVI.1, *Die Stadtmauern* (Berlin, 2001).

KOCH, U., 'Glas—Luxus der Wohlhabenden', in *Die Franken. Wegbereiter Europas* (Mannheim, 1996), pp. 605–17.

KOCH, U., and KASCHAU, B., 'Ausgrabungen auf dem Runden Berg bei Urach, Kreis Reutlingen, 1967–1984', in *Archäologische Ausgrabungen in Baden-Württemberg* (1984), pp. 159–71.

KÖLZER, T., *Merowingerstudien*, 2 vols. (Hannover, 1998–9).

KÖPSTEIN, H., 'Zu den Agrarverhältnissen', in F. Winkelmann *et al.*, *Byzanz im 7. Jahrhundert* (Berlin, 1978), pp. 1–72.

KÖPSTEIN, H., 'Zu einigen Aspekten der Agrarverhältnisse im 7. Jahrhundert (nach den juristischen Quellen)', in eadem and F. Winkelmann (eds.), *Studien zum 7. Jahrhundert in Byzanz* (Berlin, 1976), pp. 23–34.

KOLB, F. *et al.*, 'Spätantike und byzantinische Besiedlung auf dem Gebiet der lykischen Polis Kyaneai', *Klio*, LXXIII (1991), pp. 563–85.

KONRAD, M., 'Umayyad pottery from Tetrapyrgium (Qseir as-Seileh), North Syria', in Villeneuve and Watson, *La céramique byzantine*, pp. 163–91.

KRAMER, J., 'Die Bedeutung von *spanelaion*', *ZPE*, LXXXI (1990), pp. 261–4.

KRAUSE, J.-U., *Spätantike Patronatsformen im Westen des Römischen Reiches* (Munich, 1987).

KRAUTHEIMER, R., *Rome. Profile of a city, 312–1308* (Princeton, 1980).

KREUTZ, B. M., *Before the Normans* (Philadelphia, 1991).

KUCHENBUCH, L., *Bäuerliche Gesellschaft und Klosterherrschaft im 9. Jahrhundert* (Wiesbaden, 1978).

KUCHENBUCH, L., 'Die Klostergrundherrschaft im Frühmittelalter. Eine Zwischenbilanz', in F. Prinz (ed.), *Herrschaft und Kirche* (Stuttgart, 1988), pp. 297–343.

KUCHENBUCH, L., 'Opus feminile', in H.-W. Goetz (ed.), *Weibliche Lebensgestaltung im frühen Mittelalter* (Cologne, 1991), pp. 139–75.

KUCHENBUCH, L., 'Probleme der Rententwicklung in den klösterlichen Grundherrschaften des frühen Mittelalters', in W. Lourdaux and D. Verhelst (eds.), *Benedictine culture, 750–1050* (Louvain, 1983), pp. 132–72.

KUHNEN, H.-P., 'Zwischen Reichs- und Stadtgeschichte—Trier in Spätantike und Frühmittelalter', in *Die Franken. Wegbereiter Europas* (Mannheim, 1996), pp. 138–44.

KULA, W., *Teoria economica del sistema feudale* (Turin, 1970).

Kulturhistorisk leksikon for nordisk middelalder, X, XVIII, XIX (Copenhagen, 1965–75).

LaBIANCA, Ø. S., *Hesban 1, Sedentarisation and nomadisation* (Berrien Springs, Mich., 1990).

LACARRA, J. M., 'Textos navarros del Códice de Roda', in *Estudios de edad media de la Corona de Aragón*, I (Zaragoza, 1945), pp. 193–283.

LADSTÄTTER, S., *Die materielle Kultur der Spätantike in den Ostalpen* (Vienna, 2000).

La época de la monarquía asturiana (Oviedo, 2002).

LAFAURIE, J., 'Eligius monetarius', *Revue numismatique*, 6 ser., XIX (1977), pp. 111–51.

LAING, L., 'The Romanization of Ireland in the fifth century', *Peritia*, IV (1985), pp. 261–78.

LAIOU, A. E., 'Economic and noneconomic exchange', in eadem (ed.), *The economic history of Byzantium*, III (Washington, DC, 2002), pp. 681–96.

LAIOU, A. E., 'Exchange and trade, seventh–twelfth centuries', in eadem (ed.), *The economic history of Byzantium*, III (Washington, DC, 2002), pp. 697–770.

LAMBROPOULOU, A., 'Le Peloponnèse occidental à l'époque protobyzantine (IVᵉ–VIIᵉ siècles)', in K. Belke *et al.* (eds.), *Byzanz als Raum* (Vienna, 2000), pp. 95–113.

LAMPROPOULOU, A. *et al.*, 'Symbolē stēn ermēneia tōn archaiologikōn tekmēriōn tēs Peloponnēsou kata tous "skoteinous aiōnes" ', in E. Kountoura-Galakē (ed.), *Oi skoteinoi aiōnes tou Byzantiou (7os–9os ai.)* (Athens, 2001), pp. 189–229.

LANCEL, S., 'L'affaire d'Antoninus de Fussala', in C. Lepelley (ed.), *Les lettres de saint Augustin découvertes par Johannes Divjak* (Paris, 1983), pp. 267–85.

LANCEL, S. (ed.), *Byrsa I* (Rome, 1979).

LANIADO, A., *Recherches sur les notables municipaux dans l'empire protobyzantin* (Paris, 2002).

LANIADO, A., 'Syntelestēs: notes sur un terme fiscal surinterpreté', *Journal of juristic papyrology*, XXVI (1996), pp. 23–51.

LAPIDGE, M., 'The archetype of *Beowulf*', *Anglo-Saxon England*, XXXIX (2000), pp. 5–41.

LAPORTE, J.-P., 'Pour une nouvelle datation du testament d'Ermenthrude', *Francia*, XIV (1986), pp. 574–7.

LA REGINA, A., 'Ricerche sugli insediamenti vestini', *Memorie dell'Accademia Nazionale dei Lincei, classe Scienze morali, storiche e filologiche*, 6 ser., XIII (1967–8), pp. 359–446.

LA ROCCA, C., ' "Castrum vel potius civitas" ', in Francovich and Noyé, *La storia dell'alto medioevo italiano*, pp. 545–54.

LA ROCCA HUDSON, C., ' "Dark Ages" a Verona', *AM*, XIII (1986), pp. 31–78.

LA ROCCA, C., '*Multas amaritudines filius meus mihi fecit*', *MEFR. Moyen âge*, CXI (1999), pp. 933–50.

LA ROCCA, C., 'Segni di distinzione', in L. Paroli (ed.), *L'Italia centro-settentrionale in età longobarda* (Florence, 1997), pp. 31–54.

LARREA, J. J., *La Navarre du IVᵉ au XIIᵉ siècle* (Brussels, 1998).

LARRÉN, H. *et al.*, 'Ensayo de sistematización de la cerámica tardoantigua en la cuenca del Duero', in Caballero *et al.*, *Cerámicas tardorromanas y altomedievales*, pp. 273–306.

LARSON, L., and HÅRDH, B., 'Uppåkra', *Frühmittelalterliche Studien*, XXXII (1998), pp. 57–71.

LATOUCHE, R., *Les origines de l'économie occidentale (IVᵉ–XIᵉ siècle)* (Paris, 1956).

LAUFFRAY, J., *Ḥalabiyya-Zenobia*, II (Paris, 1991).

LAURANSON-ROSAZ, C., *L'Auvergne et ses marges (Velay, Gévaudan) du VIIIᵉ au XIᵉ siècle* (Le Puy, 1987).

LAVAN, L. (ed.), *Recent research in late-antique urbanism* (Portsmouth, RI, 2001).

LEBECQ, S., 'Les échanges dans la Gaule du Nord au VIᵉ siècle', in R. Hodges and W. Bowden (eds.), *The sixth century* (Leiden, 1998), pp. 185–202.

LEBECQ, S., *Les origines franques, Vᵉ–IXᵉ siècle* (Paris, 1990).

LEBECQ, S., *Marchands et navigateurs frisons du haut moyen âge*, 2 vols. (Lille, 1983).

Lebecq, S., 'Ohthere et Wulfstan', in *Horizons marins, itinéraires spirituels. Mélanges offerts a M. Mollat*, II (Paris, 1987), pp. 167–81.

Lebecq, S., 'Pour une histoire parallèle de Quentovic et Dorestad', in J.-M. Duvosquel and A. Dierkens (eds.), *Villes et campagnes au moyen âge* (Liège, 1991), pp. 415–28.

Lebecq, S., 'Quentovic: un état de la question', *Studien zur Sachsenforschung*, VIII (1993), pp. 73–82.

Lebecq, S., 'The role of the monasteries in the systems of production and exchange of the Frankish world between the seventh and the beginning of the ninth centuries', in I. L. Hansen and C. Wickham (eds.), *The long eighth century* (Leiden, 2000), pp. 121–48.

Lecuyot, G., and Pierrat, G., 'À propos des lieux de production de quelques céramiques trouvées à Tôd et dans la Vallée des Reines', *Cahiers de la céramique égyptienne*, III (1992), pp. 173–80.

Lecziewicz, L. *et al.*, *Torcello. Scavi 1961–62* (Rome, 1977).

Lee, A. D., 'The army', in A. Cameron and P. Garnsey (eds.), *The Cambridge ancient history*, XIII (Cambridge, 1998), pp. 211–37.

Lefort, J., 'The rural economy, seventh–twelfth centuries', in A. E. Laiou (ed.), *The economic history of Byzantium*, I (Washington, DC, 2002), pp. 231–310.

Legoux, R., 'L'art animalier et la symbolique d'origine chrétienne dans les décors de céramiques du VIe siècle après J. C. au nord du Bassin parisien', *Revue archéologique de Picardie* (1992), 1–2, pp. 111–42.

Leicht, P. S., 'Livellario nomine', in idem, *Scritti vari di storia del diritto italiano*, II.2 (Milan, 1949), pp. 89–146.

Leicht, P. S., *Studi sulla proprietà fondiaria nel medioevo*, II (Padua, 1907).

Le Jan, R., *Famille et pouvoir dans le monde franc (VIIe–Xe siècle)* (Paris, 1995).

Le Jan, R., *La société du haut moyen âge* (Paris, 2003).

Le Jan, R. (ed.), *La royauté et les élites dans l'Europe carolingienne (début du IXe siècle aux environs de 920)* (Lille, 1998).

Leman, P., 'Topographie chrétienne d'Arras au VIe siècle', *Revue du Nord. Archéologie*, LXXVII (1995), pp. 169–84.

Lemerle, P., *The agrarian history of Byzantium from the origins to the twelfth century* (Galway, 1979).

Lenoir, E., 'Les fossiles directeurs et l'histoire des sites', in *IIIe Colloque sur l'histoire et l'archéologie d'Afrique du Nord* (Paris, 1986), pp. 239–45.

Lentzen, C. J., 'From public to private space', in *Studies in the history and archaeology of Jordan*, V (Amman, 1995), pp. 235–9.

Lentzen, C. J., 'Seeking contextual definitions for places', *Mediterranean archaeology*, XIII (2000), pp. 11–24.

Lentzen, C. J., *The Byzantine/Islamic occupation at Caesarea Maritima as evidenced through the pottery*, Ph.D. thesis, Drew University (1983) (published Ann Arbor, Mich., 1983).

Lenz, K. H., 'Late Roman rural settlement in the southern part of the province Germania Secunda in comparison with other regions of the Roman Rhineland', in Ouzoulias, *Les campagnes*, pp. 113–46.

Leo Imperiale, M., 'Otranto, cantiere Mitello', in S. Patitucci Uggeri (ed.), *La ceramica altomedievale in Italia* (Florence, 2004), pp. 327–42.

LEONE, A., 'Change or no change?', in P. Baker *et al.*, *TRAC 98* (Oxford, 1999), pp. 121–30.

LEONE, A., 'Topographies of production in North African cities during the Vandal and Byzantine periods', in L. Lavan and W. Bowden (eds.), *Theory and practice in late antique archaeology* (Leiden, 2003), pp. 257–87.

LEPELLEY, C., *Les cités de l'Afrique romaine au Bas-Empire*, 2 vols. (Paris, 1979–81).

LEPELLEY, C., 'Liberté, colonat et esclavage d'après la lettre 24*', in idem (ed.), *Les lettres de saint Augustin découvertes par Johannes Divjak* (Paris, 1983), pp. 329–42.

LEPELLEY, C., 'Peuplement et richesses de l'Afrique romaine tardive', in *Hommes et richesses dans l'Empire byzantin*, I (Paris, 1989), pp. 17–30.

LEPELLEY, C., 'Progrès dans la connaissance des campagnes de l'Afrique proconsulaire', *Antiquité tardive*, III (1995), pp. 277–81.

LEPELLEY, C., '*Quot curiales, tot tyranni*. L'image du décurion oppresseur au Bas-Empire', in E. Frézouls (ed.), *Crise et redressement dans les provinces européennes de l'Empire (milieu du IIIe–milieu du IVe siècle ap. J.-C.)* (Strasbourg, 1983), pp. 143–56.

LEPELLEY, C., 'Trois documents méconnus sur l'histoire sociale et religieuse de l'Afrique romaine tardive, retrouvés parmi les *spuria* de Sulpice Sévère', *Antiquités africaines*, XXV (1989), pp. 235–62.

LEPELLEY, C. (ed.), *La fin de la cité antique et le début de la cité médiévale* (Bari, 1996).

LEQUÉMENT, R., *Fouilles à l'amphithéâtre de Tébessa (1965–1968)* (Algiers, n.d.).

LE ROY LADURIE, E., *Montaillou, village occitan de 1294 à 1324* (Paris, 1975).

LEV, Y., 'Tinnīs: an industrial medieval town', in M. Barrucand (ed.), *L'Égypte fatimide, son art et son histoire* (Paris, 1999), pp. 83–96.

LEVEAU, P., *Caesarea de Maurétanie* (Paris, 1984).

LEVILLAIN, L., 'Les statuts d'Adalhard', *Le moyen âge*, IV (1900), pp. 333–86.

LÉVI-PROVENÇAL, E., *Histoire de l'Espagne musulmane*, 3 vols. (Paris, 1950–3).

LEVISON, W., 'Das Testament des Diakons Adalgisel-Grimo vom Jahre 634', in idem, *Aus rheinischer und fränkischer Frühzeit* (Düsseldorf, 1948), pp. 118–38.

LEWIS, C., MITCHELL-FOX, P., and DYER, C., *Village, hamlet and field* (Macclesfield, 1997).

LEWIS, N., *Papyrus in classical antiquity* (Oxford, 1974).

LEWIT, T., *Agricultural production in the Roman economy, A.D. 200–400*, BAR, I568 (Oxford, 1991).

LEWIT, T., ' "Vanishing villas": what happened to élite rural habitation in the West in the 5th–6th c.?', *JRA*, XVI (2003), pp. 260–74.

LIEBESCHUETZ, J. H. W. G., *Barbarians and bishops* (Oxford, 1990).

LIEBESCHUETZ, J. H. W. G., 'Cities, taxes and the accommodation of the barbarians', in W. Pohl (ed.), *Kingdoms of the empire* (Leiden, 1997), pp. 135–51.

LIEBESCHUETZ, J. H. W. G., 'Civic finance in the Byzantine period: the laws and Egypt', *Byzantinische Zeitschrift*, LXXXIX (1996), pp. 389–408.

LIEBESCHUETZ, J. H. W. G., *The decline and fall of the Roman city* (Oxford, 2001).

LIGHTFOOT, C., and IVISON, E., 'Amorium excavations 1994', *Anatolian studies*, XLV (1995), pp. 105–38.

LIGHTFOOT, C., and IVISON, E., 'Amorium excavations 1995', *Anatolian studies*, XLVI (1996), pp. 91–110.

LIGHTFOOT, C., and IVISON, E., 'The Amorium project: the 1995 excavation season', *Dumbarton Oaks papers*, LI (1997), pp. 291–300.

L'Île-de-France de Clovis à Hugues Capet du Ve siècle au Xe siècle (Paris, 1993).

LIM, R., 'People as power', in W. V. Harris (ed.), *The transformations of urbs Roma in late Antiquity* (Portsmouth, RI, 1999), pp. 265–81.

LINGER, S., 'L'écrit à l'époque mérovingienne d'après la correspondance de Didier, évêque de Cahors (630–655)', *Studi medievali*, XXXIII (1992), pp. 799–823.

LINTZEL, M., *Ausgewählte Schriften*, 2 vols. (Berlin, 1961).

LLINÀS I POL, J., 'La excavación de la carretera de San Martín de Ampurias (Gerona)', *AEA*, LXX (1997), pp. 149–69.

LO CASCIO, E., '*Canon frumentarius, suarius, vinarius*', in W. V. Harris (ed.), *The transformations of urbs Roma in late antiquity* (Portsmouth, RI, 1999), pp. 163–82.

LO CASCIO, E. (ed.), *Terre, proprietari e contadini dell'impero romano* (Rome, 1997).

LOHRMANN, D., 'Le moulin à eau dans le cadre de l'économie rurale de la Neustrie (VIIe–IXe siècles)', in H. Atsma (ed.), *La Neustrie*, I (Sigmaringen, 1989), pp. 367–404.

LOMBARD, M., *Les textiles dans le monde musulman, VIIe–XIIe siècle* (Paris, 1978).

LOOS, M., 'Quelques remarques sur les communautés rurales et la grande propriété terrienne à Byzance (VIIe–XIe siècles)', *Byzantinoslavica*, XXXIX (1978), pp. 3–18.

LÓPEZ MULLOR, A. *et al.*, 'Cerámica tardorromana y altomedieval en la provincia de Barcelona. Siglos VII–X', in Caballero *et al.*, *Cerámicas tardorromanas y altomedievales*, pp. 41–65.

LÓPEZ RODRÍGUEZ, J. R., *Terra sigillata hispánica tardía decorada a molde de la Península Ibérica* (Salamanca, 1985).

LÓPEZ QUIROGA, J., and RODRÍGUEZ LOVELLE, M., 'Ciudades atlánticas en transición', *AM*, XXVI (1999), pp. 257–68.

LORREN, C., 'Le village de St.-Martin de Trainecourt à Mondeville (Calvados) de l'Antiquité au Haut Moyen Âge', in H. Atsma (ed.), *La Neustrie*, II (Sigmaringen, 1989), pp. 439–65.

LORREN, C., and PÉRIN, P., 'Images de la Gaule rurale au VIe siècle', in N. Gauthier and H. Galinié (eds.), *Grégoire de Tours et l'espace gaulois* (Tours, 1997), pp. 93–109.

LORREN, C., and PÉRIN, P. (eds.), *L'habitat rural du haut moyen âge (France, Pays-Bas, Danemark et Grande-Bretagne)* (Rouen, 1995).

LOSCO-BRADLEY, S., and KINSLEY, G., *Catholme* (Nottingham, 2002).

LOSEBY, S. T., 'Arles in late Antiquity', in Christie and Loseby, *Towns in transition*, pp. 45–70.

LOSEBY, S. T., 'Gregory's cities', in I. Wood (ed.), *Franks and Alamanni in the Merovingian period* (Woodbridge, 1998), pp. 239–84.

LOSEBY, S. T., 'Marseille and the Pirenne thesis', I, II, in R. Hodges and W. Bowden (eds.), *The sixth century* (Leiden, 1998), pp. 203–29, and I. L. Hansen and C. Wickham (eds.), *The long eighth century* (Leiden, 2000), pp. 167–93.

LOSEBY, S. T., 'Power and towns in late Roman Britain and early Anglo-Saxon England', in Ripoll and Gurt, *Sedes regiae*, pp. 319–70.

LOSEBY, S. T., 'The Mediterranean economy', in P. Fouracre (ed.), *The new Cambridge medieval history*, I (Cambridge, in press).

LOSEBY, S. T., 'Urban failures in late-antique Gaul' in T. Slater (ed.), *Towns in decline, AD 100–1600* (Aldershot, 2000), pp. 72–95.

LOT, F., *L'impôt foncier et la capitation personnelle sous le bas-empire et à l'époque franque* (Paris, 1928).

LOT, F., 'Un grand domaine à l'époque franque. Ardin en Poitou, contribution à l'étude de l'impôt', in *Cinquanténaire de l'école pratique des hautes études* (Paris, 1921), pp. 109–29.

LOUIS, É., 'A de-Romanised landscape in northern Gaul', in W. Bowden *et al.* (eds.), *Recent research on the late Antique countryside* (Leiden, 2004), pp. 479–504.

LOVELUCK, C. P., 'A high-status Anglo-Saxon settlement at Flixborough, Lincolnshire', *Antiquity*, LXXII (1998), pp. 146–61.

LOYN, H. R., 'Gesiths and thegns in Anglo-Saxon England from the seventh to the tenth century', *English historical review*, LXX (1955), pp. 529–49.

LOYN, H. R., *The governance of Anglo-Saxon England 500–1087* (London, 1984).

LUDWIG, C., *Sonderformen byzantinischer Hagiographie und ihr literarisches Vorbild* (Frankfurt, 1997).

LUND, J., 'African Red Slip Ware re-evaluated', *JRA*, X (1997), pp. 572–4.

LUND, J., 'Hellenistic, Roman and late Roman finewares from the Segermes valley', in Dietz, *Africa proconsularis*, II, pp. 449–629.

LUND, N., 'Scandinavia, c.700–1066', in R. McKitterick (ed.), *The new Cambridge medieval history*, II (Cambridge, 1995), pp. 202–27.

LUND HANSEN, U., 'Himlingøje-undersøgelserne', in Fabech and Ringtved, *Samfundsorganisation*, pp. 85–107.

LUPIA, A., *Testimonianze d'epoca altomedievale a Benevento* (Naples, 1998).

LUSUARDI SIENA, S., 'La ceramica longobarda', in eadem (ed.), *Ad mensam* (Udine, 1994), pp. 55–62.

LUSUARDI SIENA, S., 'Lo scavo nella cattedrale di Luni (SP)', *AM*, XII (1985), pp. 303–11.

LUZZATTO, G., *Dai servi della gleba agli albori del capitalismo* (Bari, 1966).

LUZZATTO, M. J., 'P. Vat. gr. 52', *ZPE*, CXIV (1996), pp. 153–6.

LYNN, C., 'Deer Park Farms, Glenarm, Co. Antrim', in A. Hamlin and C. Lynn (eds.), *Pieces of the past* (Belfast, 1988), pp. 44–7.

MAAS, M., *John Lydus and the Roman past* (London, 1992).

MACIAS I SOLE, J. M., and REMOLÀ VALLVERDÚ, J. A., 'Tarraco visigoda', in *V Reunió d'arqueologia cristiana hispànica* (Barcelona, 2000), pp. 485–97.

MACCORMACK, S. G., *Art and ceremony in late Antiquity* (Berkeley, 1981).

McCORMICK, M., 'Bateaux de vie, bateaux de mort', *Settimane di studio*, XLV (1998), pp. 35–122.

McCORMICK, M., *Eternal victory* (Cambridge, 1986).

McCORMICK, M., *Origins of the European economy* (Cambridge, 2001).

MACCOULL, L. S. B., *Coptic perspectives on late Antiquity* (Aldershot, 1993).

MACCOULL, L. S. B., *Dioscorus of Aphrodito* (Berkeley, 1988).

MacCoull, L. S. B., 'Notes on the social structure of late antique Aphrodito', *Bulletin de la société d'archéologie copte*, XXVI (1984), pp. 65–77 (now in eadem, *Coptic perspectives*, study XX).

MacCoull, L. S. B., 'O. Wilck. 1224: two additions to the Jeme *lashane*-list', *ZPE*, LXII (1986), pp. 55–6.

MacCoull, L. S. B., 'The Aphrodito murder mystery', *Journal of juristic papyrology*, XX (1990), pp. 103–7 (now in eadem, *Coptic perspectives*, study XVIII).

MacCoull, L. S. B., 'The Coptic archive of Dioscorus of Aphrodito', *Chronique d'Égypte*, LVI (1981), pp. 185–93 (now in eadem, *Coptic perspectives*, study II).

MacCoull, L. S. B., 'The Coptic papyri from Apollonos Anô', in eadem, *Coptic perspectives*, study XI.

MacCoull, L. S. B., 'The strange death of Coptic culture', in eadem, *Coptic perspectives*, study XXVI.

McGuire, B. P., 'Patrons, privileges, property', *Kirkehistoriske samlinger* (1974), pp. 5–39.

McGuire, B. P., 'Property and politics at Esrum abbey: 1151–1251', *Medieval Scandinavia*, VI (1973), pp. 122–50.

Mackensen, M., *Die spätantiken Sigillata- und Lampentöpfereien von El Mahrine (Nordtunesien)* (Munich, 1993).

Mackensen, M., *Resafa I* (Mainz, 1984).

Mackensen, M., and Schneider, G., 'Production centres of African red slip ware (3rd–7th c.) in northern and central Tunisia', *JRA*, XV (2002), pp. 121–58.

McKitterick, R., *The Carolingians and the written word* (Cambridge, 1989).

Mackreth, D. F., *Orton Hall Farm*, East Anglian Archaeology, report 76 (Manchester, 1996).

MacMullen, R., *Corruption and the decline of Rome* (New Haven, 1988).

McNally, S., and Schrunk, I. D., *Excavations in Akhmīm, Egypt*, BAR, I590 (Oxford, 1993).

MacNeill, E., 'Ancient Irish law: the law of status and franchise', *Proceedings of the Royal Irish Academy*, XXXVI C (1921–4), pp. 265–316.

McNicoll, A. W. *et al.*, *Pella in Jordan*, 2 vols. (Canberra, 1982–Sydney, 1992).

Macpherson-Grant, N., 'Early–late Saxon continental imports in Kent', in Piton, *La céramique*, pp. 165–87.

McQuitty, A., and Falkner, R., 'The Faris project', *Levant*, XXV (1993), pp. 37–61.

Maddicott, J. R., 'Plague in seventh-century England', *Past and present*, CLVI (1996), pp. 7–54.

Maddicott, J. R., 'Prosperity and power in the age of Bede and Beowulf', *Proceedings of the British Academy*, CXVII (2002), pp. 49–71.

Madsen, H. J., 'Vikingetidens keramik som historisk kilde', in Mortensen and Rasmussen, *Fra stamme til stat*, II, pp. 217–34.

Magdalino, P., *Constantinople médiévale* (Paris, 1996).

Magdalino, P., 'The grain supply of Constantinople, ninth–twelfth centuries', in C. Mango *et al.* (eds.), *Constantinople and its hinterland* (Aldershot, 1995), pp. 35–47.

Magness, J., *Jerusalem ceramic chronology circa 200–800 CE* (Sheffield, 1993).

Magness, J., 'Late Roman and early Islamic pottery from Middle Egypt and some Palestinian connections', *JRA*, XIII (2000), pp. 812–17.

Magness, J., 'Redating the forts at Ein Boqeq, Upper Zohar, and other sites in SE Judaea, and the implications for the nature of the *Limes Palaestinae*', in J. H. Humphrey (ed.), *The Roman and Byzantine Near East*, II (Portsmouth, RI, 1999), pp. 189–206.

Magness, J., *The archaeology of the early Islamic settlement in Palestine* (Winona Lake, Ind., 2003).

Magness, J., 'The chronology of Capernaum in the early Islamic period', *Journal of the American Oriental society*, CXVII (1997), pp. 481–6.

Magness, J., 'The dating of the black ceramic bowl with a depiction of the Torah shrine from Nabratein', *Levant*, XXVI (1994), pp. 199–206.

Magnou-Nortier, E., 'La gestion publique en Neustrie', in H. Atsma (ed.), *La Neustrie*, I (Sigmaringen, 1989), pp. 271–318.

Magoula, O., *The social status of the metalworking artisanate in the early middle ages (500–800 AD)*, M.Phil. thesis, University of Birmingham (2003).

Mahjoubi, A., *Recherches d'histoire et d'archéologie à Henchir el-Faouar (Tunisie)* (Tunis, 1978).

Maillé, Marquise de, *Les cryptes de Jouarre* (Paris, 1971).

Mailloux, A., 'Modalités de constitution du patrimoine épiscopal de Lucques, VIIIᵉ–Xᵉ siècle', *MEFR. Moyen âge*, CXI (1999), pp. 701–23.

Mailloux, A., 'Pour une étude des paysages dans le territoire de Lucques au haut moyen âge (VIIIᵉ siècle)', in M. Clavel-Levêque *et al.* (eds.), *De la terre au ciel*, I (Besançon, 1994), pp. 208–22.

Mainman, A. J., *Anglo-Scandinavian pottery from 16–22 Coppergate*, The archaeology of York, XVI/5 (London, 1990).

Mainman, A. J., *Pottery from 46–54 Fishergate*, The archaeology of York, XVI/6 (London, 1993).

Maioli, M. G., 'Strutture economico-commerciali e impianti produttivi nella Ravenna bizantina', in A. Carile (ed.), *Storia di Ravenna*, II.1 (Venice, 1991), pp. 223–47.

Maitland, F. W., *Domesday Book and beyond* (Cambridge, 1897).

Majcherek, G., 'The Late Roman ceramics from sector "G" (Alexandria 1986–1987)', *Études et travaux*, XVI (1992), pp. 82–117.

Mallory, J. P., and McNeill, T. E., *The archaeology of Ulster from colonisation to plantation* (Belfast, 1991).

Malpica Cuello, A., *Granada, ciudad islámica* (Granada, 2000).

Malpica Cuello, A., 'Intervención arqueológica de urgencia en el cerro de Sombrerete, Madīnat Ilbīra (Atarfe, Granada)', in press.

Malpica Cuello, A. (ed.), *La cerámica altomedieval en el sur de al-Andalus* (Granada, 1993).

Mañanes, T., *La cerámica tardoromana-visigoda, anaranjada y gris, con decoración estampada en la España nor-occidental* (Valladolid, 1980).

Mancassola, N., and Saggioro, F., 'Ricerche sul territorio tra tardoantico e altomedievo: il caso di studio della Garda orientale', in G. P. Brogiolo (ed.), *II Congresso nazionale di archeologia medievale* (Florence, 2000), pp. 127–31.

MANGO, C., *Le développement urbain de Constantinople (IVe–VIIe siècles)* (Paris, 1990).

MANGO, M. M., 'Excavations and survey at Androna, Syria; the Oxford team 1999', *Dumbarton Oaks papers*, LVI (2002), pp. 307–15.

MANGO, M. M., 'Oxford excavations at Andarin (Androna): September 1998', *Annales archéologiques arabes syriennes*, in press.

MANGO, M. M., *Silver from early Byzantium* (Baltimore, 1986).

MANN, M., *The sources of social power*, I (Cambridge, 1986).

MANNONI, T., and MURIALDO, G., *S. Antonino* (Bordighera, 2001).

MANZANO MORENO, E., 'Arabes, bereberes y indígenas', in M. Barceló and P. Toubert (eds.), *'L'incastellamento'* (Rome, 1998), pp. 157–77.

MANZANO MORENO, E., 'El asentamiento y la organización de los ŷund-s sirios en al-Andalus', *al-Qanṭara*, XIV (1993), pp. 327–59.

MANZANO MORENO, E., 'La cerámica de los siglos oscuros', in Caballero *et al.*, *Cerámicas tardorromanas y altomedievales*, pp. 541–57.

MANZANO MORENO, E., 'La conquista del 711: transformaciones y pervivencias', in L. Caballero Zoreda and P. Mateos Cruz (eds.), *Visigodos y Omeyas* (Madrid, 2000), pp. 401–14.

MANZANO MORENO, E., *La frontera de al-Andalus en época de los Omeyas* (Madrid, 1991).

MANZANO MORENO, E., 'Las fuentes árabes sobre la conquista de Al-Andalus: una nueva interpretación', *Hispania*, LIX (1999), pp. 389–432.

MANZANO MORENO, E., 'Señores y emires', *Cuadernos de Madīnat al-Zahrā'*, III (1991), pp. 97–110.

MARAZZI, F., 'Il conflitto fra Leone III Isaurico e il papato e il "definitivo" inizio del medioevo a Roma', *PBSR*, LIX (1991), pp. 231–57.

MARAZZI, F., *I 'patrimonia sanctae Romanae ecclesiae' nel Lazio (secoli IV–X)* (Rome, 1998).

MARAZZI, F., 'The destinies of the late antique Italies', in R. Hodges and W. Bowden (eds.), *The sixth century* (Leiden, 1998), pp. 119–59.

MARAZZI, F. *et al.*, 'San Vincenzo al Volturno. Scavi 2000–2002', *AM*, XXIX (2002), pp. 209–74.

MARCONE, A., 'Il colonato del Tardo impero: un mito storiografico?', *Athenaeum*, LXIII (1985), pp. 513–20.

MARCONE, A., 'Il colonato tardoantico', in Lo Cascio, *Terre, proprietari*, pp. 225–39.

MARCONE, A., *Il colonato tardoantico nella storiografia moderna* (Como, 1988).

MARCONE, A., 'Il lavoro nelle campagne', in *Storia di Roma*, III.1 (Turin, 1993), pp. 823–43.

MARE, W. H., 'Internal settlement patterns in Abila', *Studies in the history and archaeology of Jordan*, IV (Amman, 1992), pp. 309–13.

MARFIL RUIZ, P., 'Córdoba de Teodosio a Abd al-Rahmán III', in L. Caballero Zoreda and P. Mateos Cruz (eds.), *Visigodos y Omeyas* (Madrid, 2000), pp. 117–41.

MARGETIĆ, L., 'La legge agraria', *Rivista di studi bizantini e slavi*, V (1985), pp. 103–35.

MARTIN, A., 'La sigillata focese (Phocaean Red-Slip/Late Roman C Ware)', in Saguì, *Ceramica in Italia*, pp. 109–22.

MARTIN. J.-M., *La Pouille du VIe au XIIe siècle* (Rome, 1993).

MARTIN, J.-M. *et al.* (eds.), *Regesti dei documenti dell'Italia meridionale, 570–899* (Rome, 2002).

MARTIN-KILCHER, S., *Die römischen Amphoren aus Augst und Kaiseraugst*, 3 vols. (Augst, 1987–94).

MARTÍN VISO, I., 'La articulación del poder en la cuenca del Duero', *Anuario de estudios medievales*, XXXI (2001), pp. 75–126.

MARTÍN VISO, I., *Poblamiento y estructuras sociales en el Norte de la Península Ibérica (siglos VI–XIII)* (Salamanca, 2000).

MARTINDALE, J. R. (eds.), *Prosopography of the Byzantine empire*, I, published on CD-Rom (Aldershot, 2001) [*PBE*].

MARTINDALE, J. R. *et al.* (eds.), *Prosopography of the later Roman empire*, 3 vols. (Cambridge, 1971–92) [*PLRE*].

MARTÍNEZ SOPENA, P., *La Tierra de Campos occidental* (Valladolid, 1985).

MARTINI, W., and STECKNER, C., *Das Gymnasium von Samos* (Bonn, 1993).

MARTINS, M., and DELGADO, M., 'História e arqueologia de uma cidade em devir: Bracara Augusta', *Cadernos de arqueologia*, 2 ser., VI–VII (1989–90), pp. 11–39.

MARX, K., *Capital*, trans. B. Fowkes *et al.*, 3 vols. (London, 1976–81).

MARX, K., *Grundrisse*, trans. M. Nicolaus (London, 1973).

MARX, K., *Pre-capitalist economic formations*, ed. E. J. Hobsbawm (London, 1964).

MASLEV, S., 'Die soziale Struktur der byzantinischen Landgemeinde nach dem Nomos Georgikos', in H. Köpstein and F. Winkelmann (eds.), *Studien zum 7. Jahrhundert in Byzanz* (Berlin, 1976), pp. 10–22.

MATEOS CRUZ, P., '*Augusta emerita*, de capital de la diocesis Hispaniarum a sede temporal visigoda', in Ripoll and Gurt, *Sedes regiae*, pp. 491–520.

MATEOS CRUZ, P., *La basílica de S. Eulalia de Mérida* (Madrid, 1999).

MATEOS CRUZ, P., and ALBA CALZADO, M., 'De *Emerita Augusta* a Marida', in L. Caballero Zoreda and P. Mateos Cruz (eds.), *Visigodos y Omeyas* (Madrid, 2000), pp. 143–68.

MATHIEU, B., 'Travaux de l'Institut français d'archéologie orientale en 1999–2000', *Bulletin de l'Institut français d'archéologie orientale*, C (2000), pp. 443–575.

MATHISEN, R. W., 'Fifth-century visitors to Italy', in Drinkwater and Elton, *Fifth-century Gaul*, pp. 228–38.

MATHISEN, R. W., *Roman aristocrats in barbarian Gaul* (Austin, Tex., 1993).

MATHISON, R. W., *Ruricius of Limoges and friends* (Liverpool, 1999).

MATHISEN R. W., and SCHANZER, D. (eds.), *Society and culture in late Antique Gaul* (Aldershot, 2001).

MATTHEWS, J. 'Continuity in a Roman family: the Rufii Festi of Volsinii', *Historia*, XVI (1967), pp. 484–509.

MATTHEWS, J., 'The making of the text', in J. Harries and I. Wood (eds.), *The Theodosian code* (London, 1993), pp. 19–44.

MATTHEWS, J., *Western aristocracies and imperial court, A.D. 364–425* (Oxford, 1975).

MATTHEWS, R. *et al.*, 'Project Paphlagonia', in idem (ed.), *Ancient Anatolia* (London, n.d., c.1998), pp. 195–206.

MATTINGLY, D., 'First Fruit? The olive in the Roman world', in G. Shipley and J. Salmon (eds.), *Human landscapes in classical Antiquity* (London, 1996), pp. 213–53.

MATTINGLY, D., 'Oil for export?', *JRA*, I (1988), pp. 33–56.

MATTINGLY, D., 'Oil presses and olive oil production', *Antiquités africaines*, XXVI (1990), pp. 248–55.

MATTINGLY, D., 'Olive cultivation and the Albertini tablets', *L'Africa romana*, VI (1988), pp. 403–15.

MATTINGLY, D., *Tripolitania* (London, 1995).

MATTINGLY, D., and HITCHNER, R. B., 'Roman Africa: an archaeological review', *Journal of Roman studies*, LXXXV (1995), pp. 165–213.

MAURICI, F., *Medioevo trapanese* (Palermo, 2002).

MAURIN, L., 'Thuburbo Maius et la paix vandale', *Les cahiers de Tunisie*, XV (1967), pp. 225–54.

MAURIN, L. (ed.), *Topographie chrétienne des cités de la Gaule*, X (Paris, 1998).

MAUSS, M., *The gift* (London, 1990).

MAYERSON, P., '*Rouzikón* and *Rogá* in the postconquest papyri', *ZPE*, C (1994), pp. 126–8.

MAYERSON, P., 'Some observations on the Negev archaeological survey', *Israel exploration journal*, XLVI (1996), pp. 100–7.

MAYERSON, P., 'The Gaza "wine" jar (*Gazition*) and the "lost" Ashkelon jar (*Askalônium*)', *Israel exploration journal*, XLII (1992), pp. 76–80.

MAYET, F., *Les céramiques sigillées hispaniques* (Paris, 1984).

MAZOR, G., 'The wine-presses of the Negev' [in Hebrew], *Qadmoniot*, XIV (1981), pp. 51–60.

MAZZA, R., *L'archivio degli Apioni* (Bari, 2001).

MAZZA, R., 'Ricerche sul pagarca nell'Egitto tardoantico e bizantino', *Aegyptus*, LXXV (1995), pp. 169–242.

MAZZOTTI, M., and CURRADI, C., 'La più antica pergamena imolese che si conservi in originale', in *Imola e Val di Santerno* (Imola, 1981), pp. 7–20.

MAZZUCATO, O., *Ceramica a vetrina pesante* (Rome, 1972).

MEE, C., and FORBES, H., *A rough and rocky place* (Liverpool, 1997).

MEILLASSOUX, C., *Maidens, meal and money* (Cambridge, 1981).

MEFR. Moyen âge, CXII (2000).

MELKAWI, A. *et al.*, 'The excavation of two seventh-century pottery kilns at Aqaba', *Annual of the Department of Antiquities of Jordan*, XXXVIII (1994), pp. 447–68.

MENEGHINI, R., 'L'origine di un quartiere altomedievale romano attraverso i recenti scavi del foro di Traiano', in G. P. Brogiolo (ed.), *II Congresso nazionale di archeologia medievale* (Florence, 2000), pp. 55–9.

MENESSIER-JOUANNET, C., 'Un four du haut moyen âge à Lezoux (Puy-de-Dôme)', in B. Fizellier-Sauget (ed.), *L'Auvergne de Sidoine Apollinaire à Grégoire de Tours* (Clermont, 1999), pp. 371–95.

MERCIER, C., and RAYNAUD, C., 'L'habitat rural en Gaule méditerranéenne aux VIᵉ–VIIᵉ s.', in Lorren and Périn, *L'habitat rural*, pp. 193–206.

METCALF, D. M., *Thrymsas and sceattas in the Ashmolean Museum Oxford*, III (London, 1994).

MEYER, W., 'Die Ausgrabungen der Burgruine Schiedberg', in M.-L. Boscardin and W. Meyer, *Burgenforschung in Graubünden* (Olten, 1977), pp. 51–175.

MEYER-RODRIGUES, N., 'Tessons de céramique dite "de Tating" découverts à Saint-Denis', in Piton, *La céramique*, p. 267–74.

MICHAELIDES, D., and WILKINSON, D., *Excavations at Otranto* (Lecce, 1992).

MICHELETTO, E., 'Forme di insediamento tra V e XIII secolo', in L. Mercando and E. Micheletto (eds.), *Archeologia in Piemonte*, III (Turin, 1998), pp. 51–80.

MIGLIARIO, E., *Strutture della proprietà agraria in Sabina dall'età imperiale all'alto medioevo* (Florence, 1988).

MILES, D. (ed.), *Archaeology at Barton Court Farm, Abingdon, Oxon*, CBA Research Report, 50 (London, 1986).

MILLER, J. M. (ed.), *Archaeological survey of the Kerak plateau* (Atlanta, Ga., 1991).

MILLER, M. C., *The bishop's palace* (Ithaca, NY, 2000).

MILLER, W. I., *Bloodtaking and peacemaking* (Chicago, 1990).

MILLETT, M., 'The question of continuity: Rivenhall reviewed', *The archaeological journal*, CXLIV (1987), pp. 434–8.

MILLETT, M., *The Romanisation of Britain* (Cambridge, 1990).

MILLETT, M., and JAMES, S., 'Excavations at Cowdery's Down, Basingstoke, Hampshire, 1978–81', *The archaeological journal*, CXL (1983), pp. 151–279.

MILOŠEVIĆ, A., 'Influenze carolingie nel principato croato alla luce dei reperti archeologici', in C. Bertelli *et al.* (eds.), *Bizantini, Croati, Carolingi* (Milan, 2001), pp. 97–127.

MÍNGUEZ FERNÁNDEZ, J. M., *El dominio del monasterio de Sahagún* (Salamanca, 1980).

MÍNGUEZ FERNÁNDEZ, J. M., 'Ruptura social e implantación del feudalismo en el Noroeste peninsular (siglos VIII–X)', *Studia histórica. Historia medieval*, III (1985), pp. 7–32.

MIRANDOLA, R., 'Firenze', in S. Gelichi (ed.), *Archeologia urbana in Toscana* (Mantua, 1999), pp. 59–72.

MIRKOVIĆ, M., *The later Roman colonate and freedom* (Philadelphia, 1997).

MODÉRAN, Y., 'Gildon, les Maures et l'Afrique', *MEFR. Antiquité*, CI (1989), pp. 821–72.

MODÉRAN, Y., 'La chronologie de la vie de Saint Fulgence de Ruspe et ses incidences sur l'histoire de l'Afrique vandale', *MEFR. Antiquité*, CV (1993), pp. 135–88.

MODÉRAN, Y., *Les Maures et l'Afrique romaine (IVᵉ–VIIᵉ siècle)* (Rome, 2003).

MODÉRAN, Y., 'L'établissement territorial des Vandales en Afrique', *Antiquité tardive*, X (2002), pp. 87–122.

MOHAMEDI, A. *et al.*, ed. E. Fentress, *Fouilles de Sétif 1977–1984* (Algiers, 1991).

MOLINARI, A., 'Il popolamento rurale in Sicilia tra V e XIII secolo', in Francovich and Noyé, *La storia dell'alto medioevo italiano*, pp. 361–77.

MOLINARI, A., 'Insediamento rurale e fortificazioni nella Sicilia occidentale in età bizantina', *Byzantino-Sicula IV* (Palermo, 2002), pp. 323–53.

MOLINARI, A., 'Le campagne siciliane tra il periodo bizantino e quello arabo', in E. Boldrini and R. Francovich (eds.), *Acculturazione e mutamenti* (Florence, 1995), pp. 223–39.

MOLTÓ POVEDA, F. J., 'Cerámicas de importación del yacimiento tardorromano de Garganes', in *V Reunió d'arqueologia cristiana hispànica* (Barcelona, 2000), pp. 529–40.

MONNERET DE VILLARD, U., 'L'organizzazione industriale nell'Italia langobarda durante l'alto medioevo', *Archivio storico lombardo*, 5 ser., XLVI (1919), pp. 1–83.

MONTANARI, M., 'Conflitto sociale e protesta contadina nell'Italia altomedievale', in G. Cherubini (ed.), *Protesta e rivolta contadina nell'Italia medievale* (Bari, 1994), pp. 17–25.

MONTANARI, M., 'La corvée nei contratti agrari altomedievali dell'Italia del Nord', in *Le prestazioni d'opera nelle campagne italiane del Medioevo* (Bologna, 1987), pp. 37–68.

MONTANARI, M., *L'alimentazione contadina nell'alto medioevo* (Naples, 1979).

MOORHEAD, J., *Theoderic in Italy* (Oxford, 1992).

MORELAND, J., 'Concepts of the early medieval economy', in I. L. Hansen and C. Wickham (eds.), *The long eighth century* (Leiden, 2000), pp. 1–34.

MORELAND, J., 'The Farfa survey', *AM*, XIV (1987), pp. 409–18.

MORELAND, J., 'The significance of production in eighth-century England', in I. L. Hansen and C. Wickham (eds.), *The long eighth century* (Leiden, 2000), pp. 69–104.

MORELAND, J., and PLUCIENNIK, M., 'Excavations at Casale San Donato, Castelnuovo di Farfa (RI), 1990', *AM*, XVIII (1991), pp. 477–90.

MORELAND, J. *et al.*, 'Excavations at Casale San Donato, Castelnuovo di Farfa (RI), Lazio, 1992', *AM*, XX (1993), pp. 185–228.

MORELLE, L., 'Les "actes de précaire", instruments de transferts patrimoniaux (France du Nord et de l'Est, VIIIᵉ–XIᵉ siècle)', *MEFR. Moyen âge*, CXI (1999), pp. 609–47.

MORELLI, F., *Olio e retribuzioni nell'Egitto tardo (V–VIII d.c.)* (Florence, 1996).

MORIMOTO, K., 'Land tenure in Egypt during the early Islamic period', *Orient*, XI (1975), pp. 109–53.

MORIMOTO, K., *The fiscal administration of Egypt in the early Islamic period* (Dohosha, 1981).

MORIMOTO, Y., 'État et perspectives de recherches sur les polyptyques carolingiens', *Annales de l'Est*, XL (1988), pp. 99–149.

MORONY, M. G., *Iraq after the Muslim conquest* (Princeton, 1984).

MORRIS, J., *The age of Arthur* (London, 1973).

MORRIS, R., 'The powerful and the poor in tenth-century Byzantium: law and reality', *Past and present*, LXXIII (1976), pp. 3–27.

MORRISSON, C., 'La Sicile byzantine', *Numismatica e antichità classiche*, XXVII (1998), pp. 307–34.

MORRISSON, C., *Monnaie et finances à Byzance: analyses, techniques* (Aldershot, 1994).

MORTENSEN, P., and RASMUSSEN B. (eds.), *Fra stamme til stat i Danmark*, 2 vols. (Højbjerg, 1988–91).

MORTON, A. D., *Excavations at Hamwic*, I, CBA Research Report, 84 (London, 1992).

MORTON, A. D., 'Hamwic in its context', in Anderton, *Anglo-Saxon trading centres*, pp. 48–62.

Moss, J. R., 'The effects of the policies of Aetius on the history of western Europe', *Historia*, XXII (1973), pp. 711–31.

Motos Guirao, E., *El poblado medieval de 'El Castillón' (Montefrío, Granada)* (Granada, 1991).

Motos Guirao, E., 'La cerámica altomedieval de "El Castillón" (Montefrío, Granada)', in Malpica, *La cerámica altomedieval*, pp. 209–37.

Mouterde, R., and Poidebard, A., *Le limes de Chalcis* (Paris, 1945).

Müller, A. E., 'Getreide für Konstantinopel', *Jahrbuch der österreichischen Byzantinistik*, XLIII (1993), pp. 1–20.

Müller-Kehlen, H., *Die Ardennen im Frühmittelalter* (Göttingen, 1973).

Müller-Mertens, E., 'Der Stellingaaufstand', *Zeitschrift für Geschichtswissenschaft*, XX (1972), pp. 818–42.

Müller-Mertens, E., *Karl der Grosse, Ludwig der Fromme, und die Freien* (Berlin, 1963).

Müller-Mertens, E. (ed.), *Feudalismus. Entstehung und Wesen* (Berlin, 1985).

Müller-Wiener, W., 'Das Theaterkastell von Milet', *Istanbuler Mitteilungen*, XVII (1967), pp. 279–90.

Müller-Wiener, W. *et al.*, 'Milet 1973–1975', *Istanbuler Mitteilungen*, XXVII–XXVIII (1977–8), pp. 93–125.

Müller-Wille, M., 'Hedeby und sein Umland', in B. Hårdh *et al.* (eds.), *Trade and exchange in prehistory* (Lund, 1988), pp. 271–8.

Murialdo, G., 'Prima dell'incastellamento', in F. Benente and G. B. Garbarino (eds.), *Incastellamento, popolamento e signoria rurale tra Piemonte meridionale e Liguria* (Bordighera, 2000), pp. 17–35.

Murray, A. C., 'From Roman to Frankish Gaul', *Traditio*, XLIV (1988), pp. 59–100.

Murray, A. C., *Germanic kinship structure* (Toronto, 1983).

Murray, A. C., 'Immunity, nobility, and the *Edict of Paris*', *Speculum*, LXIX (1994), pp. 18–39.

Myhre, B., 'Chieftains' graves and chiefdom territories in South Norway in the Migration Period', *Studien zur Sachsenforschung*, VI (1987), pp. 169–87.

Myres, J. N. L., *A corpus of Anglo-Saxon pottery of the pagan period* (Cambridge, 1977).

Myres, J. N. L., *Anglo-Saxon pottery and the settlement of England* (Oxford, 1969).

Myśliwiecz, K., *Keramik und Kleinfunde aus der Grabung im Tempel Sethos' I. in Gurna* (Mainz, 1987).

Mytum, H., *The origins of early Christian Ireland* (London, 1992).

Naccache, A., *Le décor des églises des villages d'Antiochène du IVe au VIIe siècle* (Paris, 1992).

Naccache, A., 'Le décor des maisons de Syrie du Nord comme produit d'une économie locale: l'exemple de Serdjilla', in C. Castel *et al.* (eds.), *Les maisons dans la Syrie antique du IIIe Millénaire aux débuts de l'Islam* (Beirut, 1997), pp. 305–11.

Näf, B., *Senatorisches Standesbewusstsein in spätrömischer Zeit* (Fribourg, 1995).

Näsman, U., 'Analogislutning i nordisk Jernalderarkæologi', in Mortensen and Rasmussen, *Fra stamme til stat*, I, pp. 125–38.

NÄSMAN, U., 'Det syvende århundrede—et mørkt tidsrum i ny belysning', in Mortensen and Rasmussen, *Fra stamme til stat*, II, pp. 165–76.

NÄSMAN, U., 'Exchange and politics: the eighth–early ninth century in Denmark', in I. L. Hansen and C. Wickham (eds.), *The long eighth century* (Leiden, 2000), pp. 35–68.

NÄSMAN, U., 'The ethnogenesis of the Danes and the making of a Danish kingdom', *Anglo-Saxon studies in archaeology and history*, X (1999), pp. 1–10.

NÄSMAN, U., 'The Justinianic era of south Scandinavia', in R. Hodges and W. Bowden (eds.), *The sixth century* (Leiden, 1998), pp. 255–78.

NARDI COMBESCURE, S., *I paesaggi d'Etruria meridionale* (Florence, 2002).

NAVARRO LUENGO, I. et al., 'Malaca bizantina', in *V Reunió d'arqueologia cristiana hispànica* (Barcelona, 2000), pp. 271–8.

NEGRO PONZI, M. M. (ed.), *S. Michele di Trino (VC)* (Florence, 1999).

NEHLSEN, H., *Sklavenrecht zwischen Antike und Mittelalter*, I (Göttingen, 1972).

NEHLSEN, H., 'Zur Aktualität und Effektivität germanischer Rechtsaufzeichnungen', in P. Classen (eds.), *Recht und Schrift im Mittelalter* (Sigmaringen, 1977), pp. 449–502.

NEHLSEN-VAN STRYK, K., *Die boni homines des frühen Mittelalters* (Berlin, 1981).

NELSON, H. H., and HÖLSCHER, U., *Medinet Habu reports*, I, II (Chicago, 1931).

NELSON, J. L., *Charles the Bald* (London, 1992).

NELSON, J. L., 'Dispute settlement in Carolingian West Francia', in W. Davies and P. Fouracre (eds.), *The settlement of disputes in early medieval Europe* (Cambridge, 1986), pp. 45–64.

NELSON, J. L., 'Queens as jezebels', in eadem, *Politics and ritual in early medieval Europe* (London, 1986), pp. 1–48.

NELSON, J. L., 'The wary widow', in W. Davies and P. Fouracre (eds.), *Property and power in the early middle ages* (Cambridge, 1995), pp. 82–113.

NERI, V., *I marginali nell'Occidente tardoantico* (Bari, 1998).

NESBITT, J., and OIKONOMIDES, N., *Catalogue of Byzantine seals at Dumbarton Oaks and in the Fogg Museum of Art*, 3 vols. (Washington, DC, 1991–6).

NEURU, L., 'The pottery of the Kasserine survey', *Antiquités africaines*, XXVI (1990), pp. 255–9.

NEWMAN, J., 'The late Roman and Anglo-Saxon settlement pattern in the Sandlings of Suffolk', in M. O. H. Carver (ed.), *The age of Sutton Hoo* (Woodbridge, 1992), pp. 25–38.

NICE, A., 'L'habitat mérovingien de Goudelancourt-les-Pierrepont (Aisne)', *Revue archéologique de Picardie* (1994), 1–2, pp. 21–63.

NICHANIAN, M., and PRIGENT, V., 'Les stratèges de Sicile', *Revue des études byzantines*, LXI (2003), pp. 97–141.

NIELSEN, J. N., 'Bejsebakken, a central site near Aalborg in northern Jutland', in Hårdh and Larsson, *Central places*, pp. 197–213.

NIELSEN, L. C., 'Omgård', *Acta archaeologica*, L (1980), pp. 173–208.

NIELSEN, P. O. et al. (eds.), *The archaeology of Gudme and Lundeborg* (Copenhagen, 1994).

NIERMEYER, J. F., *Mediae latinitatis lexicon minus* (Leiden, 1976).

NILSSON, T., 'Stentinget', *Kuml* (1990), pp. 119–31.

NISSEN-JAUBERT, A., *Peuplement et structures d'habitat au Danemark durant les IIIe–XIIe siècles dans leur contexte nord-ouest européen*, Thèse de doctorat, École des hautes études en sciences sociales, Paris (1996).

NJEUSSYCHIN, A. I., *Die Entstehung der abhängigen Bauernschaft* (Berlin, 1961).

NOACK-HALEY, S., and ARBEITER, A., *Asturische Königsbauten des 9. Jahrhunderts* (Mainz, 1994).

NOBLE, T. F. X., *The Republic of St. Peter* (Philadelphia, 1984).

NOËL, R., 'Deux grandes forêts du nord de la Gaule franque', in M. Rouche (ed.), *Clovis, histoire et mémoire*, I (Paris, 1997), pp. 631–69.

NOLLA, J. M., 'Ampurias en la Antigüedad tardía', *AEA*, LXVI (1993), pp. 207–24.

NOLLA BRUFAU, J. M., 'Excavaciones recientes en la ciudadela de Roses', in T. F. C. Blagg *et al.* (eds.), *Papers in Iberian archaeology* (eds.), BAR, I193 (Oxford, 1984), pp. 430–59.

NOLLA, J. M., and CASAS, J., 'Material ceràmic del Puig de les Muralles (Puig Rom, Roses)', *Arqueo mediterrània*, II (1997), pp. 7–19.

NONN, U., 'Eine fränkische Adelssippe um 600', *Frühmittelalterliche Studien*, IX (1975), pp. 186–201.

NORSA, M., 'Un circolare ai *pagarchoi* della Tebaide del secolo VIII', *Annali della Scuola normale superiore di Pisa*, 2 ser., X (1941), pp. 164–70.

NORTHEDGE, A., 'Les origines de la céramique à glaçure polychrome dans le monde islamique', in *La céramique médiévale en Méditerranée* (Aix-en-Provence, 1997), pp. 213–23.

NORTHEDGE, A., *Studies on Roman and Islamic 'Ammān*, I (Oxford, 1992).

NORTHEDGE, A., 'Thoughts on the introduction of polychrome glazed pottery in the Middle East', in Villeneuve and Watson, *La céramique byzantine*, pp. 207–14.

NORTHEDGE, A. *et al.*, *Excavations at 'Āna* (Warminster, 1988).

NOTH, A., *The early Arabic historical tradition*, 2nd edn. (Princeton, 1994).

NOVAK, D. M., 'The early history of the Anician family', in C. Deroux (ed.), *Studies in Latin literature and Roman history*, I (Brussels, 1979), pp. 119–65.

NOYÉ, G., 'Economia e società nella Calabria bizantina (IV–XI secolo)', in A. Placanica (ed.), *Storia della Calabria medievale* (Rome, 1999), pp. 579–655.

NOYÉ, G., 'Économie et société dans la Calabre byzantine (IVe–XIe siècle)', in *Journal des savants* (2000), pp. 209–80.

Ó CORRÁIN, D., 'Nationality and kingship in pre-Norman Ireland', in T. W. Moody (ed.), *Nationality and the pursuit of national independence* (Belfast, 1978), pp. 1–35.

Ó CORRÁIN, D., BREATNACH, L., and BREEN, A., 'The laws of the Irish', *Peritia*, III (1984), pp. 382–438.

Ó CRÓINÍN, D., *Early medieval Ireland 400–1200* (London, 1995).

O'HEA, M., *The conceptual and material transformation of the villa in Aquitanica prima from the third to seventh centuries A.D.*, D.Phil. thesis, University of Oxford (1989).

OIKONOMIDÈS, N., 'Le kommerkion d'Abydos, Thessalonique et le commerce bulgare au IXe siècle', in *Hommes et richesses dans l'empire byzantin*, II (Paris, 1991), pp. 241–8.

OIKONOMIDES, N., 'Le marchand byzantin des provinces (IXe–XIe s.)', *Settimane di studio*, XL (1993), pp. 633–65.

OLAGÜE, I., *Les Arabes n'ont jamais envahi l'Espagne* (Paris, 1969).

OLCESE, G. (ed.), *Ceramiche in Lombardia tra II secolo A.c. e VII secolo D.c.* (Mantua, 1998).

OLDENSTEIN, J., 'Die letzten Jahrzehnte des römischen Limes zwischen Andernach und Selz unter besonderer Berücksichtigung des Kastells Alzey und der *Notitia Dignitatum*', in F. Staab (ed.), *Zur Kontinuität zwischen Antike und Mittelalter am Oberrhein* (Sigmaringen, 1994), pp. 69–112.

OLMO ENCISO, L., 'Ciudad y procesos de transformación social entre los siglos VI y IX', in L. Caballero Zoreda and P. Mateos Cruz (eds.), *Visigodos y Omeyas* (Madrid, 2000), pp. 385–99.

OLSEN, O., 'Royal power in Viking age Denmark', in H. Bekker-Nielsen and H. F. Nielsen (eds.), *Syvende tværfaglige Vikingesymposium* (Odense, 1988), pp. 7–19.

OPAIŢ, A., 'Ceramica din aşezarea şi cetatea de la Independenţa (Murighiol) sec. V î.e.n.-VII e.n.', *Peuce*, X (1991), pp. 133–82.

ORFILA, M., 'Terra sigillata hispánica tardía meridional', *AEA*, LXVI (1993), pp. 125–47.

ORSSAUD, D., 'Le passage de la céramique byzantine à la céramique islamique', in Canivet and Rey-Coquais, *La Syrie*, pp. 219–28.

ORSSAUD, D., and SODINI, J.-P., 'Le "Brittle ware" dans le Massif Calcaire (Syrie du Nord)', in Bakirtzis, *VIIe Congrès international*, pp. 491–504.

ORTALLI, G., 'Il ducato e la "civitas Rivoalti" ', in L. C. Ruggini *et al.* (eds.), *Storia di Venezia*, I (Rome, 1992), pp. 725–90.

ORTALLI, G., 'Il mercante e lo stato', *Settimane di studio*, XL (1993), pp. 85–135.

ORTALLI, J., 'La fine delle ville romane', in Brogiolo, *La fine delle ville*, pp. 9–20.

ORTALLI, J., 'L'edilizia abitativa', in A. Carile (ed.), *Storia di Ravenna*, II.1 (Ravenna, 1991), pp. 167–92.

ØSTERGÅRD SØRENSEN, P., 'Gudmehallerne', *Nationalmuseets arbejdsmark* (1994), pp. 25–39.

OSTROGORSKY, G., *History of the Byzantine state* (Oxford, 1956).

OUZOULIAS, P., 'La déprise agricole du Bas-Empire: un mythe historiographique?', in idem and P. Van Ossel (eds.), *Document de travail*, III (Paris, 1997), pp. 10–20.

OUZOULIAS, P., and VAN OSSEL, P., 'Dynamiques du peuplement et formes de l'habitat tardif', in Ouzoulias, *Les campagnes*, pp. 147–72.

OUZOULIAS, P. *et al.* (eds.), *Les campagnes de la Gaule à la fin de l'Antiquité* (Antibes, 2001).

OVERBECK, M., *Untersuchungen zum afrikanischen Senatsadel in der Spätantike* (Kallmünz, 1973).

PACETTI, F., 'La questione delle Keay LII nell'ambito della produzione anforica in Italia', in Saguì, *Ceramica in Italia*, pp. 185–208.

PÄFFGEN, B., and RISTOW, S., 'Die Römerstadt Köln zur Merowingerzeit', in *Die Franken. Wegbereiter Europas*, (Mannheim, 1996), pp. 145–59.

PAILLER, J.-M. (ed.), *Tolosa* (Rome, 2002).

DE PALOL, P., 'Castro hispanovisigodo de "Puig Rom" (Rosas)', *Informes y memorias de la comisaría general de excavaciones arqueológicas*, XXVII (1952), pp. 163–82.

DE PALOL, P., *Clunia. Historia de la ciudad y guía de las excavaciones* (Burgos, 1994).

DE PALOL, P., *El Bovalar (Seròs; Segrià)* (Barcelona, 1989).

DE PALOL, P. *et al.*, *Clunia O* (Burgos, 1991).

PANELLA, C., 'Le anfore tardoantiche', in A. Giardina (ed.), *Società romana e impero tardoantico*, III (Rome, 1986), pp. 251–72.

PANELLA, C., 'Merci e scambi nel Mediterraneo in età tardoantica', in A. Carandini *et al.* (eds.), *Storia di Roma*, III.2 (Turin, 1993), pp. 613–97.

PANELLA, C., 'Rifornimenti urbani e cultura materiale tra Aureliano e Alarico', in W. V. Harris (ed.), *The transformation of urbs Roma in late Antiquity* (Portsmouth, RI, 1999), pp. 183–215.

PANELLA, C., and SAGUÌ, L., 'Consumo e produzione a Roma tra tardoantico e altomedioevo', *Settimane di studio*, XLVIII (2001), pp. 757–820.

PANERO, F., *Schiavi servi e villani nell'Italia medievale* (Turin, 1999).

PANERO, F., 'Servi, coltivatori dipendenti e giustizia signorile nell'Italia padana dell'età carolingia', *Nuova rivista storica*, LXXII (1988), pp. 551–82.

PANERO, F., *Servi e rustici* (Vercelli, 1990).

PANHUYSEN, T. A. S. M., and LEUPEN, P. H. D., 'Maastricht in het eerste millennium', in *La genèse et les premiers siècles des villes médiévales dans les Pays-Bas méridionaux* (Brussels, 1990), pp. 411–49.

PANI ERMINI, L., '*Forma urbis*', *Settimane di studio*, XLVIII (2001), pp. 255–323.

PANI ERMINI, L., and SPANU, P. G., *Aspetti di archeologia urbana* (Oristano, 1993).

PANTÒ, G., 'Produzione e commerci di vasellame d'uso domestico tra la fine del mondo antico e il medioevo', in L. Mercando and E. Micheletto (eds.), *Archeologia in Piemonte*, III (Turin, 1998), pp. 263–88.

PANTONI, A., *Le vicende della basilica di Montecassino attraverso la documentazione archeologica* (Montecassino, 1973).

PARKER, S. T., 'The Roman 'Aqaba project: the 1996 campaign', *Annual of the Department of Antiquities of Jordan*, XLII (1998), pp. 375–94.

PARODI, A. *et al.*, 'La Vaunage du IIIe siècle au milieu du XIIe siècle', *Archéologie du Midi médiéval*, V (1987), pp. 3–59.

PAROLI, L., 'La ceramica invetriata tardo-antica e medievale nell'Italia centro-meridionale', in eadem (ed.), *La ceramica invetriata tardoantica e altomedievale in Italia* (Florence, 1992), pp. 33–61.

PAROLI, L., and DELOGU, P. (eds.), *La storia economica di Roma nell'alto medioevo alla luce dei recenti scavi archeologici* (Florence, 1993).

PAROLI, L. *et al.*, 'La ceramica invetriata altomedievale in Italia: un aggiornamento', in Bakirtzis, *VIIe Congrès international*, pp. 477–90.

PARTHASARATHI, P., 'The great divergence', *Past and present*, CLXXVI (2002), pp. 275–93.

PASCUAL PACHECO, J. *et al.*, 'Cerámicas de la ciudad de Valencia entre la época visigoda y omeya (siglos VI–X)', in Caballero *et al.*, *Cerámicas tardorromanas y altomedievales*, pp. 67–117.

PASCUAL, J. *et al.*, 'València i el seu territori', *Arqueo mediterrània*, II (1997), pp. 179–202, 326–8.

PASQUALI, G. F., 'I problemi dell'approvvigionamento alimentare nell'ambito del sistema curtense', *AM*, VIII (1981), pp. 93–116.

PASQUALI, G. F., 'La corvée nei polittici italiani dell'alto medioevo', in *Le prestazioni d'opera nelle campagne italiane del Medioevo* (Bologna, 1987), pp. 107–28.

PASQUALI, G. F., 'L'azienda curtense e l'economia rurale degli secoli VI-XI, and 'La condizione degli uomini', in A. Cortonesi, G. F. pasquali and G. Piccinni, *Uomini e campagne* (Bari, 2002), pp. 5–71, 75–122.

PASTOR, R., *Resistencias y luchas campesinas en la época del crecimiento y consolidación de la formación feudal Castilla y León, siglos X–XIII* (Madrid, 1980).

PASTOR DÍAZ DE GARAYO, E., *Castilla en el tránsito de la Antigüedad al feudalismo* (Valladolid, 1996).

PATLAGEAN, É., 'Byzance et les marchés du grand commerce, vers 830–vers 1030', *Settimane di studio*, XL (1993), pp. 587–632.

PATLAGEAN, É., 'Les débuts d'une aristocratie byzantine et le témoignage de l'historiographie', in M. Angold (ed.), *The Byzantine aristocracy IX to XIII centuries*, BAR, I221 (Oxford, 1984), pp. 23–43.

PATLAGEAN, É., 'Les moines grecs d'Italie et l'apologie des thèses pontificales (VIIIème–IXème siècles)', *Studi medievali*, V (1964), pp. 579–602.

PATLAGEAN, É., *Pauvreté économique et pauvreté sociale à Byzance, 4e–7e siècles* (Paris, 1977).

PATRICH, J., 'The warehouse complex and governor's palace', in Holum *et al.*, *Caesarea papers 2*, pp. 71–107.

PATRICH, J., 'Urban space in Caesarea Maritima, Israel', in Burns and Eadie, *Urban centers and rural contexts*, pp. 77–110.

PATTERSON, H., 'The pottery', in J. Mitchell and I. L. Hansen (eds.), *San Vincenzo al Volturno 3* (Spoleto, 2001), pp. 297–322.

PATTERSON, H., and ROBERTS, P., 'New light on dark age Sabina', in Saguì, *Ceramica in Italia*, pp. 421–35.

PATTERSON, N., *Cattle-lords and clansmen* (Notre Dame, Ind., 1994).

PATTERSON, N., 'Patrilineal kinship in early Irish society', *The bulletin of the board of Celtic studies*, XXXVII (1990), pp. 133–65.

PATTERSON, O., *Slavery and social death* (Cambridge, Mass., 1982).

PAZ PERALTA, J. A., *Cerámica de mesa romana de los siglos III al VI d.C. en la provincia de Zaragoza* (Zaragoza, 1991).

PAZ PERALTA, J. A., 'El bajo imperio y el período hispano-visigodo en Aragón', in *Estado actual de la arqueología en Aragón*, I (Zaragoza, 1990), pp. 263–307.

PEACOCK, D. P. S., *Pottery in the Roman world. An ethnoarchaeological approach* (London, 1982).

PEACOCK, D. P. S. *et al.*, 'Roman amphora production in the Sahel region of Tunisia', in *Amphores romaines et histoire économique. Anfore romane e storia economica* (Rome, 1989), pp. 179–222.

PEACOCK, D. P. S. *et al.*, 'Roman pottery production in central Tunisia', *JRA*, III (1990), pp. 59–84.

PEARSON, K. L. R., *Conflicting loyalties in early medieval Bavaria* (Aldershot, 1999).

PELEG, M., 'Domestic pottery', in V. Tzaferis (ed.), *Excavations at Capernaum*, I, *1978–1982* (Winona Lake, Ind., 1989), pp. 31–113.

PELLECUER, C., and POMARÈDES, H., 'Crise, survie ou adaptation de la *villa* romaine en Narbonnaise première?', in Ouzoulias, *Les campagnes*, pp. 503–32.

PELLETIER, J.-P., 'Les céramiques communes grises en Provence de l'Antiquité tardive au XIIIe siècle', in *La céramique médiévale en Méditerranée* (Aix-en-Provence, 1997), pp. 111–24.

PELTERET, D., *Slavery in early medieval England* (Woodbridge, 1995).

PEÑA, I., *The Christian art of Byzantine Syria* (n.p., 1996).

PEÑA, J. T., 'The mobilisation of state olive oil in Roman Africa', in idem *et al.*, *Carthage papers* (Portsmouth, RI, 1998), pp. 117–238.

PENTZ, P., *From Roman Proconsularis to Islamic Ifrīqiyah* (Copenhagen, 2002).

PENTZ, P., *Hama*, IV.1 (Copenhagen, 1997).

PENTZ, P., *The invisible conquest* (Copenhagen, 1992).

PERCIVAL, J., 'P.Ital.3 and Roman estate management', *Latomus*, CII (1969), pp. 607–15.

PERCIVAL, J., 'Seigneurial aspects of late Roman estate management', *English historical review*, LXXXIV (1969), pp. 449–73.

PERCIVAL, J., 'The fifth-century villa', in Drinkwater and Elton, *Fifth-century Gaul*, pp. 156–64.

PERCIVAL, J., *The Roman villa* (London, 1976).

PÉREZ ALVARADO, S., *Las cerámicas omeyas de Marroquíes Bajos* (Jaén, 2003).

PÉREZ ALVARADO, S. *et al.*, 'Las primeras cerámicas de Marroquíes Bajos (Jaén) entre la Tardoantigüedad y el Islam', in Caballero *et al.*, *Cerámicas tardorromanas y altomedievales*, pp. 389–410.

PÉREZ RODRÍGUEZ, F., and GARCÍA ROZAS, M. DEL R., 'Nuevos datos acerca de la producción de terra sigillata hispánica tardía', *Boletín del seminario de estudios de arte y arqueología*, LV (1989), pp. 167–91.

PÉREZ SANCHEZ, D., *El ejército en la sociedad visigoda* (Salamanca, 1989).

PÉRIN, P., 'Paris mérovingien, *sedes regia*', *Klio*, LXXI (1989), pp. 487–502.

PÉRIN, P., 'Le peuplement du diocèse de Reims à l'époque mérovingienne', in W. Janssen and D. Lohrmann (eds.), *Villa–curtis–grangia* (Munich, 1983), pp. 62–80.

PERRIN, E., 'De la condition des terres dites *"ancingae"* ', in *Mélanges d'histoire du moyen âge offerts à M. Ferdinand Lot* (Paris, 1925), pp. 619–40.

PERRING, D. *et al.*, 'Bey 006, 1994–1995, the souks areas', *Bulletin d'archéologie et d'architecture libanaises*, I (1996), pp. 176–206.

PERRUGOT, D., 'Le palais mérovingien de Malay (Yonne)', in A. Renoux (ed.), *Palais royaux et princiers du moyen âge* (Le Mans, 1996), pp. 147–56.

PETIT, J.-P. *et al.* (eds.), *Les agglomérations secondaires* (Paris, 1994).

PETIT, M., 'La céramique de type "Mayen" en région parisienne', *Bulletin du groupement archéologique de Seine-et-Marne*, XVI (1975), pp. 99–110.

PETIT, M., and PARTHUISOT, F., 'L'évolution de la villa de *la Butte à Gravois* à Saint-Germain-lès-Corbeil (Essonne) au Bas-Empire et au début du haut Moyen Âge', in P. Ouzoulias and P. Van Ossel (eds.), *Document de travail*, II (Paris, 1995), pp. 127–33.

PETRALIA, G., 'A proposito dell'immortalità di "Maometto e Carlomagno" ', *Storica* I (1995), pp. 37–87.

PÉTRIDIS, P., 'Ateliers de potiers protobyzantins à Delphes', in Bakirtzis, *VIIe Congrès international*, pp. 443–6.

PETRIDIS, P., 'Delphes dans l'Antiquité tardive', *Bulletin de correspondance hellénique*, CXXI (1997), pp. 681–95.

PEYRAS, J., 'Le *fundus Aufidianus*', *Antiquités africaines*, IX (1975), pp. 181–222.

PEYRAS, J., *Le Tell nord-est tunisien dans l'Antiquité* (Paris, 1991).

PEYTREMANN, E., 'Les structures d'habitat rural du haut moyen âge en France (Vᵉ–Xᵉ siècle)', in Lorren and Périn, *L'habitat rural*, pp. 1–28.

PHILIPPOV, I. S., *Sredizemnomorskaya Frantziya b rannee srednevekov'e* (Moscow, 2000).

PICARD, J.-C. et al., *Topographie chrétienne des cités de la Gaule*, VIII (Paris, 1992).

PICCIRILLO, M., *The mosaics of Jordan* (Amman, 1992).

PICCIRILLO, M., and ALLIATA, E., *Mount Nebo* (Jerusalem, 1998).

PICCIRILLO, M., and ALLIATA, E., *Umm al-Rasas Mayfacah*, I (Jerusalem, 1994).

PIERRAT, G., 'Essai de classification de la céramique de Tôd de la fin du VIIᵉ siècle au début du XIIIᵉ siècle ap. J.-C.', *Cahiers de la céramique égyptienne*, II (1991), pp. 145–204.

PIETRI, C., and PIETRI, L. (eds.), *Prosopographie chrétienne du bas-empire*, II (Rome, 1999).

PIETRI, L., *La ville de Tours du IVᵉ au VIᵉ siècle* (Rome, 1983).

PIETRI, L., and BIARNE, J. (eds.), *Topographie chrétienne des cités de la Gaule*, V (Paris, 1987).

PILET, C. et al., 'Le village de Sannerville, "Lirose" ', *Archéologie médiévale*, XXII (1992), pp. 1–189.

PINTAUDI, R., and SIJPESTEIJN, P. J., 'Testi dell'VIII sec. d.C. provenienti da Aphrodito', *ZPE*, LXXXV (1991), pp. 279–300.

PIRENNE, H., *Mahomet et Charlemagne* (Brussels, 1937), trans. as *Mohammed and Charlemagne* (London, 1939).

PIRENNE, H., *Medieval cities* (Princeton, 1925).

PIRLING, R., *Römer und Franken am Niederrhein* (Mainz, 1986).

PITON, D. (ed.), *La céramique du Vᵉᵐᵉ au Xᵉᵐᵉ siècle dans l'Europe du Nord-Ouest*, Nord-Ouest archéologie, numéro hors-serie (Arras, 1993).

POBLOME, J., *Sagalassos Red Slip ware* (Turnhout, 1999).

POHL, W., *Die Awaren* (Munich, 1988).

POHL, W., *Die Germanen* (Munich, 2000).

POHL, W., *Le origini etniche dell'Europa* (Rome, 2000).

POHL, W., '*Per hospites divisi*. Wirtschaftliche Grundlagen der langobardischen Ansiedlung in Italien', *Römische historische Mitteilungen*, XLIII (2001), pp. 179–226.

POHL, W., 'The empire and the Lombards', in idem (ed.), *Kingdoms of the empire* (Leiden, 1997), pp. 75–133.

POHL, W., *Werkstätte der Erinnerung* (Vienna, 2001).

POINSSOT, L., *Les ruines de Dougga* (Tunis, 1958).

POINSSOT, L., and LANTIER, R., 'Rapport' [an untitled report on the Thuburbo Maius excavations of 1924], *Bulletin archéologique du Comité des travaux historiques et scientifiques* (1925), pp. LXXI–LXXXV.

POLANYI, K., 'The economy as instituted process', in idem et al. (eds.), *Trade and market in the early empires* (Glencoe, Ill., 1957), pp. 243–70.

POLCI, B., 'Some aspects of the transformation of the Roman domus between late Antiquity and the early middle ages', in L. Lavan and W. Bowden (eds.), *Theory and practice in late Antique archaeology* (Leiden, 2003), pp. 79–109.

POLLARD, N. J., 'The chronology and economic condition of late Roman Karanis: an archaeological reassessment', *Journal of the American Research Center in Egypt*, XXXV (1998), pp. 147–62.

POLY, J.-P., 'Les *vassi* du nouvel empire', in E. Bournazel and J.-P. Poly (eds.), *Les féodalités* (Paris, 1998), pp. 83–109.

POLY, J.-P., 'Régime domanial et rapports de production "féodalistes" dans le Midi de la France (VIIIe–Xe siècles)', in *Structures féodales et féodalisme dans l'Occident méditerranéen (X^e–XIIIe siècles)* (Paris, 1980), pp. 57–84.

POLY, J.-P., and BOURNAZEL, E., *La mutation féodale, X^e–XIIe siècles* (Paris, 1980).

POLYAKOVA, S. V., 'Fol'klorniy syuzhet o schastlivom gluptse v nekotorykh pamyatnikakh agiografiy VIII v.', *Vizantiyskiy vremennik*, XXXIV (1973), pp. 130–6.

POMERANZ, K., *The great divergence* (Princeton, 2000).

POPOVIC, A., *La révolte des esclaves en Iraq au IIIe/IXe siècle* (Paris, 1976).

POTTER, T. W., 'Excavations in the medieval centre of Mazzano Romano', *PBSR*, XL (1972), pp. 135–45.

POTTER, T. W., *The changing landscape of South Etruria* (London, 1979).

POTTER, T. W., *Towns in late Antiquity* (Sheffield, 1995).

POTTER, T. W., and KING, A. C., *Excavations at the Mola di Monte Gelato* (London, 1997).

POULOU-PAPADĒMĒTRIOU, N., 'Byzantinē keramikē apo ton ellēniko nēsiōtiko chōro kai apo tēn Peloponnēso (70s–90s ai.)', in E. Kountoura-Galakē (ed.), *Oi skoteinoi aiōnes tou Byzantiou (70s–90s ai.)* (Athens, 2001), pp. 231–66.

POULOU-PAPADIMITRIOU, N., 'Le monastère byzantin de Pseira—Crete: la céramique', in *Akten des XII. internationalen Kongresses für christliche Archäologie* (Münster, 1995), pp. 1119–31.

POULTER, A., 'Cataclysm on the lower Danube', in Christie, *Landscapes of change*, pp. 223–53.

POULTER, A., 'The Roman to Byzantine transition in the Balkans', *JRA*, XIII (2000), pp. 346–58.

POUPARDIN, R., 'Fragments du recueil perdu de formules franques dites "Formulae Pithoei" ', *Bibliothèque de l'École des Chartes*, LXIX (1908), pp. 643–62.

POWER, E., *Medieval people*, 10th edn. (London, 1963).

POWLESLAND, D., 'Early Anglo-Saxon settlements, structures, form and layout', in J. Hines (ed.), *The Anglo-Saxons from the migration period to the eighth century* (Woodbridge, 1997), pp. 101–24.

PRESTWICH, J. O., 'King Æthelhere and the battle of the Winwaed', *English historical review*, LXXXIII (1968), pp. 89–95.

PRÉVOT, F., *Recherches archéologiques franco-tunisiennes à Mactar*, V (Rome, 1984).

PRÉVOT, F., and BARRAL I ALTET, X., *Topographie chrétienne des cités de la Gaule*, VI (Paris, 1989).

PRINGLE, D., *The defence of Byzantine Africa from Justinian to the Arab conquest*, BAR, I99 (Oxford, 1981).

PRINZ, F., *Klerus und Krieg im früheren Mittelalter* (Stuttgart, 1991).

PUIN, G.-R., *Der Dīwān von 'Umar ibn al-Ḫaṭṭāb* (Bonn, 1970).

QUIRÓS CASTILLO, J. A., *Modi di costruire a Lucca nell'altomedioevo* (Florence, 2002).

RABAN, A., and HOLUM, K. G., *Caesarea maritima* (Leiden, 1996).

RABAN, A. *et al.*, 'Land excavations in the Inner Harbor (1993–4)', in Holum *et al.*, *Caesarea papers* 2, pp. 198–224.

RAFTERY, B., *Pagan Celtic Ireland* (London, 1994).

RĀĠIB, Y., 'La plus ancienne lettre arabe de marchand', in idem (ed.), *Documents de l'Islam médiéval* (Cairo, 1991), pp. 1–9.

RĀĠIB, Y., 'Lettres nouvelles de Qurra b. Šarīk', *Journal of Near Eastern studies*, XL (1981), pp. 173–87.

RĀĠIB, Y., *Marchands d'étoffes du Fayyoum au IIIᵉ/IXᵉ siècle*, I (Cairo, 1982).

RĀĠIB, Y., 'Sauf-conduits d'Égypte omeyyade et abbasside', *Annales islamologiques*, XXXI (1997), pp. 143–68.

RAHTZ, P., 'Late Roman cemeteries and beyond', in R. Reece (ed.), *Burial in the Roman world*, CBA Research Report, 2 (London, 1977), pp. 53–64.

RAHTZ, P. *et al.*, *Cadbury Congresbury 1968–73*, BAR, B223 (Oxford, 1992).

RAIMONDO, C., 'La ceramica comune del *Bruttium* nel VI–VII secolo', in Saguì, *Ceramica in Italia*, pp. 531–48.

RAIMONDO, C., *Modèles économiques et sociaux de la Calabre au haut Moyen Âge*, Thèse de doctorat nouveau régime, Université de Paris-X (2001).

RAKOB, F. (ed.), *Karthago I* (Mainz, 1990).

RAMALLO ASENSIO, S. F., 'Arquitectura doméstica en ámbitos urbanos entre los siglos V y VIII', in L. Caballero Zoreda and P. Mateos Cruz (eds.), *Visigodos y Omeyas* (Madrid, 2000), pp. 367–84.

RAMALLO ASENSIO, S. F., '*Carthago Spartaria*, un núcleo bizantino en *Hispania*', in Ripoll and Gurt, *Sedes regiae*, pp. 579–611.

RAMALLO ASENSIO, S. F., and RUIZ VALDERAS, E., 'Cartagena en la arqueología bizantina en *Hispania*', in *V Reunió d'arqueologia cristiana hispànica* (Barcelona, 2000), pp. 305–21.

RAMALLO ASENSIO, S. F. *et al.*, 'Contextos cerámicos de los siglos V–VII en Cartagena', *AEA*, LXIX (1996), pp. 135–90.

RAMALLO, S. F. *et al.*, 'Un contexto cerámico del primer cuarto del siglo VII en Cartagena', *Arqueo mediterrània*, II (1997), pp. 203–28.

RAMSAY, W. M., *The historical geography of Asia Minor* (London, 1890).

RANDOUIN, B., 'Essai de classification de la céramique de Tours du IVᵉ au XIᵉ siècle', in *Recherches sur Tours*, I (Tours, 1981), pp. 103–14.

RANDSBORG, K., 'Gudme-Lundeborg', in Nielsen *et al.*, *Gudme*, pp. 209–13.

RANDSBORG, K., *The first millennium AD in Europe and the Mediterranean* (Cambridge, 1991).

RANDSBORG, K., *The Viking age in Denmark* (London, 1980).

RAPP, C. 'Bishops in late Antiquity', in J. Haldon (eds.), *The Byzantine and early Islamic Near East*, VI (Princeton, 2004).

RAPUANO, Y., 'The Hellenistic through early Islamic pottery from Ras Abu Ma'aruf (Pisgat Ze'ev East A)', *'Atiqot*, XXXVIII (1999), pp. 171–203.

RASCÓN MARQUÉS, S., 'La ciudad de Complutum en la tardoantigüedad', in García Moreno and Rascón Marqués, *Complutum*, pp. 51–70.

RATHBONE, D., *Economic rationalism and rural society in third-century A.D. Egypt* (Cambridge, 1991).

RAUTMAN, M., 'A late Roman townhouse at Sardis', in E. Schwertheim (eds.), *Forschungen in Lydien* (Bonn, 1995), pp. 49–66.

RAUTMAN, M., 'Handmade pottery and social change', *Journal of Mediterranean archaeology*, XI (1998), pp. 81–104.

RAUTMAN, M., 'Two late Roman wells at Sardis', *Annual of the American Schools of Oriental Research*, LIII (1996), pp. 37–84.

RAUTMAN, M. *et al.*, 'Amphoras and roof-tiles from late Roman Cyprus', *JRA*, XII (1999), pp. 377–91.

RAYMOND, A., *Cairo* (Cambridge, Mass., 2000).

RAYNAUD, C. *et al.*, *Le village gallo-romain et médiéval de Lunel Viel (Hérault)* (Paris, 1990).

REBUFFAT, R., 'Recherches sur le bassin du Sebou', *Académie des inscriptions et belles-lettres. Comptes rendus 1986*, pp. 633–52.

REDKNAP, M., 'Medieval pottery production at Mayen', in D. R. M. Gaimster *et al.* (ed.), *Zur Keramik des Mittelalters und der beginnenden Neuzeit im Rheinland*, BAR, I440 (Oxford, 1988), pp. 3–37.

RECCHIA, V., *Gregorio magno e la società agricola* (Rome, 1978).

RÉMONDON, R., '*P. Hamb.* 56 et *P. Lond.* 1419 (notes sur les finances d'Aphrodito du VIᵉ siècle au VIIIᵉ)', *Chronique d'Égypte*, XL (1965), pp. 401–30.

RENARD, É., 'Les *mancipia* carolingiens étaient-ils des esclaves?', in P. Corbet (ed.), *Les moines du Der, 673–1790* (Langres, 2000), pp. 179–209.

RENEL, F., 'Un ensemble céramique du Vᵉ s. découvert à Vanves (Hauts-de-Seine)', in P. Ouzoulias and P. Van Ossel (eds.), *Document de travail*, IV (Paris, 1997), pp. 129–50.

RENFREW, C., and POSTON, T., 'Discontinuities in the endogenous change of settlement patterns', in C. Renfrew and K. L. Cooke (eds.), *Transformations* (New York, 1979), pp. 437–61.

RESI, H. G. (ed.), *Produksjon og samfunn* (Oslo, 1995).

RETUERCE VELASCO, M., *La cerámica andalusí de la Meseta* (Madrid, 1998).

REUTER, T., 'Plunder and tribute in the Carolingian empire', *Transactions of the Royal Historical Society*, 5 ser., XXXV (1985), pp. 75–94.

REUTER, T., 'The end of Carolingian military expansion', in P. Godman and R. Collins (eds.), *Charlemagne's heir* (Oxford, 1990), pp. 391–405.

REYNAUD, J.-F., *Lugdunum christianum* (Paris, 1998).

REYNOLDS, P., 'Hispania in the late Roman Mediterranean: ceramics and trade', in K. Bowes and M. Kulikowski (ed.), *Hispania in late Antiquity* (Leiden, in press).

REYNOLDS, P., 'Levantine amphorae from Cilicia to Gaza', in J. M. Gurt *et al.* (eds.), *Late Roman coarse wares, cooking wares and amphorae in the Mediterranean*, BAR (Oxford, in press).

REYNOLDS, P., 'Pottery and the economy in 8ᵗʰ-century Beirut', in Bakirtzis, *VIIᵉ Congrès international*, pp. 725–34.

REYNOLDS, P., *Settlement and pottery in the Vinalopó valley (Alicante, Spain)* AD 400–700, BAR, I588 (Oxford, 1993).

REYNOLDS, P., *Trade in the western Mediterranean* AD 400–700: *the ceramic evidence*, BAR, I604 (Oxford, 1995).

REYNOLDS, S., *Fiefs and vassals* (Oxford, 1994).

RHEIDT, K., *Altertümer von Pergamon*, XV.2, *Die Stadtgrabung: die byzantinische Wohnstadt* (Berlin, 1991).

RIBERA, J., *Colección de obras arábigas de historia y geografía, que publica la Real Academia de la Historia*, II (Madrid, 1926).

RICCI, M., 'La ceramica comune dal contesto di VII secolo della Crypta Balbi', in Saguì, *Ceramica in Italia*, pp. 351–82.

RICCI, M., 'Relazioni culturali e scambi commerciali nell'Italia centrale romano-longobarda alla luce della Crypta Balbi in Roma', in L. Paroli (ed.), *L'Italia centro-settentrionale in età longobarda* (Florence, 1997), pp. 239–73.

RICH, J. (ed.), *The city in late Antiquity* (London, 1992).

RICHARDS, J., *The significance of form and decoration of Anglo-Saxon cremation urns*, BAR, B166 (Oxford, 1987).

RICHARDS, J., 'What's so special about "productive sites"?', *Anglo-Saxon studies in archaeology and history*, X (1999), pp. 71–80.

RICKETTS, R., *The Anglo-Saxon cemetery at Spong Hill, North Elmham, part VII*, East Anglian Archaeology, report 73 (Dereham, 1995).

RIGOIR, J., 'Les sigillées paléochrétiennes grises et orangées', *Gallia*, XXVI (1968), pp. 177–244.

RIISING, A., 'The fate of Henri Pirenne's thesis on the consequences of the Islamic expansion', *Classica et medievalia*, XIII (1952), pp. 87–130.

RILEY, J. A., 'The pottery from the cisterns 1977.1, 1977.2 and 1977.3', in J. H. Humphrey (ed.), *Excavations at Carthage 1977 conducted by the University of Michigan*, VI (Ann Arbor, Mich., 1981), pp. 85–124.

RILEY, J. A., 'The pottery from the first session of excavation in the Caesarea hippodrome', *Bulletin of the American Schools of Oriental Research*, CCXVIII (1975), pp. 25–63.

RING, E., and WIECZOREK, A., 'Tatinger Kannen aus Mainz', *Archäologisches Korrespondenzblatt*, IX (1979), pp. 355–62.

RINGTVED, J., 'Regionalitet', in Mortensen and Rasmussen, *Fra stamme til stat*, I, pp. 37–52.

RINGTVED, J., 'The geography of power: south Scandinavia before the Danish kingdom', *Anglo-Saxon studies in archaeology and history*, X (1999), pp. 49–63.

RIPOLL, G., 'La necrópolis visigoda de El Carpio de Tajo', *Butlletí de la Reial acadèmia catalana de belles arts de Sant Jordi*, VII–VIII (1993–4), pp. 187–250.

RIPOLL, G., 'Materiales funerarios de la Hispania visigoda', in P. Périn (ed.), *Gallo-Romains, Wisigoths et Francs en Aquitaine, Septimanie et Espagne* (Rouen, 1991), pp. 111–32.

RIPOLL LÓPEZ, G., *Toréutica de la Bética (siglos VI y VII d.c.)* (Barcelona, 1998).

RIPOLL, G., and ARCE, J., 'The transformation and end of Roman *villae* in the West (fourth–seventh centuries)', in Brogiolo *et al.*, *Towns and their territories*, pp. 63–114.

RIPOLL, G., and GURT, J. M. (eds.), *Sedes regiae (ann. 400–800)* (Barcelona, 2000).

RIPOLL, G., and VELÁZQUEZ, I., *La Hispania visigoda. Del rey Ataúlfo a Don Rodrigo* (Madrid, 1995).

RIVERS, T. J., 'Seigneurial obligations and "Lex Baiuvariorum" I, 13', *Traditio*, XXXI (1975), pp. 336–43.

RIZZO, M. S., 'Le dinamiche del popolamento rurale di età tardoantica e medievale nella Sicilia centromeridionale', in G. P. Brogiolo (ed.), *II Congresso nazionale di archeologia medievale* (Florence, 2000), pp. 249–53.

ROBERTS, S., *Order and dispute* (Harmondsworth, 1979).

ROBINSON, C. F., *Empire and elites after the Muslim conquest* (Cambridge, 2000).

ROBLIN, M., *Le terroir de Paris aux époques gallo-romaine et franque*, 2nd edn. (Paris, 1971).

RODA, S., 'Fuga nel privato e nostalgia del potere nel IV secolo d.C.', in idem, *La parte migliore*, pp. 255–69.

RODA, S. (ed.), *La parte migliore del genere umano* (Turin, 1994).

RODRÍGUEZ MARTÍN, F. G., 'La villa romana de Torre Águila (Barbaño, Badajoz) a partir del siglo IV d.C.', in R. Teja and C. Pérez (eds.), *Congreso internacional. La Hispania de Teodosio* (Salamanca, 1997), pp. 697–711.

RODWELL, W. J., 'Relict landscapes in Essex', in H. C. Bowen and P. J. Fowler (eds.), *Early land allotment in the British Isles*, BAR, B48 (Oxford, 1978), pp. 89–98.

RODWELL, W. J., and RODWELL, K. A., *Rivenhall*, CBA Research Report, 55 (London, 1985).

RODZIEWICZ, M., 'Alexandria and district of Mareotis', *Graeco-Arabica*, II (1983), pp. 199–216.

RODZIEWICZ, M., *La céramique romaine tardive d'Alexandrie*, Alexandrie I (Warsaw, 1976).

RODZIEWICZ, M., *Les habitations romaines tardives d'Alexandrie à la lumière des fouilles polonaises à Kôm el-Dikka*, Alexandrie III (Warsaw, 1984).

RÖMER, C., 'Die rot engobierte Keramik im Unteren Habur-Gebiet', in H. Meyza and J. Młynarczyk (eds.), *Hellenistic and Roman pottery in the eastern Mediterranean* (Warsaw, 1995), pp. 351–63.

ROESDAHL, E., *Viking age Denmark* (London, 1982).

RÖSENER, W., 'Strukturformen der adelige Grundherrschaft in der Karolingerzeit', in idem, *Strukturen*, pp. 126–80.

RÖSENER, W., 'Zur Struktur und Entwicklung der Grundherrschaft in Sachsen in karolingischer und ottonischer Zeit', in A. Verhulst (ed.), *Le grand domaine aux époques mérovingienne et carolingienne* (Gent, 1985), pp. 173–207.

RÖSENER, W. (ed.), *Strukturen der Grundherrschaft im frühen Mittelalter* (Göttingen, 1989).

ROFFIA, E., and GHIROLDI, A., 'Sirmione, la villa di via Antiche Mura', in E. Roffia (ed.), *Ville romane sul lago di Garda* (S. Felice di Benaco, 1997), pp. 171–89.

ROLL, I., and AYALON, E., 'The market street at Apollonia–Arsuf', *Bulletin of the American Schools of Oriental Research*, CCLXVII (1987), pp. 61–76.

ROSENWEIN, B. H., *Negotiating space* (Manchester, 1999).

ROSENWEIN, B. H., *To be the neighbor of Saint Peter* (Ithaca, NY, 1989).

ROSENWEIN, B. H. (ed.), *Anger's past* (Ithaca, NY, 1998).

ROSSETTI, G., 'I ceti proprietari e professionali', *Atti del X Congresso internazionale di studi sull'alto medioevo* (Spoleto, 1986), pp. 165–207.

ROSSITER, J. J., 'Roman villas of the Greek east and the villa in Gregory of Nyssa *Ep.* 20', *JRA*, II (1989), pp. 101–10.

ROSTOVTSEFF, M., *The social and economic history of the Roman empire*, 2nd edn. (Oxford, 1957).

ROTH, H., 'Zum Handel der Merowingerzeit auf Grund ausgewählter archäologischer Quellen', in Düwel et al., *Untersuchungen zu Handel und Verkehr*, III, pp. 161–92.

ROUCHE, M., *L'Aquitaine des Wisigoths aux Arabes, 418–781* (Paris, 1979).

ROUCHE, M. (ed.), *Clovis, histoire et mémoire*, 2 vols. (Paris, 1997).

ROUECHÉ, C., 'A new inscription from Aphrodisias and the title *patēr tēs poleōs*', *Greek, Roman and Byzantine studies*, XX (1979), pp. 173–85.

ROUECHÉ, C., *Aphrodisias in late Antiquity* (London, 1989).

ROUECHÉ, C., 'Looking for late antique ceremonial: Ephesos and Aphrodisias', in H. Friesinger and F. Krinzinger (eds.), *100 Jahre österreichische Forschungen in Ephesos* (Vienna, 1999), pp. 161–8.

ROUILLARD, G., *L'administration civile de l'Égypte byzantine*, 2nd edn. (Paris, 1928).

ROUSSET, M.-O., MARCHAND, S., and FOY, D., 'Secteur nord de Tebtynis (Fayyoum). Mission de 2000', *Annales islamologiques*, XXXV (2001), pp. 401–89.

ROVELLI, A., 'Monetary circulation in Byzantine and Carolingian Rome', in J. M. H. Smith (ed.), *Early medieval Rome and the Christian West* (Leiden, 2000), pp. 85–99.

ROVELLI, A., 'Some considerations on the coinage of Lombard and Carolingian Italy', in I. L. Hansen and C. Wickham (eds.), *The long eighth century* (Leiden, 2000), pp. 195–223.

ROWLAND, J., *Early Welsh saga poetry* (Cambridge, 1990).

ROWLANDSON, J., 'Agricultural tenancy and village society in Roman Egypt', *Proceedings of the British Academy*, XCVI (1999), pp. 139–58.

ROWLANDSON, J., *Landowners and tenants in Roman Egypt* (Oxford, 1996).

RUBIN, Z., 'Mass movements in late antiquity—appearances and realities', in I. Malkin and Z. W. Rubinsohn (eds.), *Leaders and masses in the Roman world* (Leiden, 1995), pp. 129–87.

RUGGINI, L. C., *Economia e società nell' 'Italia annonaria'* (Milan, 1961).

RUGGINI, L. C., 'Gli Anicii a Roma e in provincia', *MEFR. Moyen âge*, C (1988), pp. 69–85.

RUGGINI, L. C., 'La Sicilia e la fine del mondo antico (IV–VI secolo)', in E. Gabba and G. Vallet (eds.), *La Sicilia antica*, II.2 (Naples, 1980), pp. 483–524.

RUGGINI, L. C., 'Nobiltà romana e potere nell'età di Boezio', in Roda, *La parte migliore*, pp. 105–40.

RUNCIMAN, W. G., *A treatise on social theory*, II (Cambridge, 1989).

RUNCIMAN, W. G., *Confessions of a reluctant theorist* (Hemel Hempstead, 1989).

RUSSELL, J., 'The Persian invasions of Syria/Palestine and Asia Minor in the reign of Heraclius', in E. Kountoura-Galakē (ed.), *Oi skoteinoi aiōnes tou Byzantiou (70s–90s ai.)* (Athens, 2001), pp. 41–71.

RYNNE, C., 'The introduction of the vertical watermill into Ireland', *Medieval archaeology*, XXXIII (1989), pp. 21–31.

SACK, D., *Damaskus* (Mainz, 1989).

SACK, D., *Resafa IV* (Mainz, 1996).

SAGE, W., *Die fränkische Siedlung bei Gladbach, Kreis Neuwied* (Düsseldorf, 1969).

SAGGIORO, F., *Paesaggi rurali medievali. Il caso della pianura veronese*, 2 vols., tesi di dottorato, Università di Siena (2003).

SAGUÌ, L., 'Il deposito della Crypta Balbi', in Saguì, *Ceramica in Italia*, pp. 305–30.

SAGUÌ, L., 'Roma, i centri privilegiati e la lunga durata della tarda antichità', *AM*, XXIX (2002), pp. 7–42.

SAGUÌ, L. (ed.), *Ceramica in Italia: VI–VII secolo* (Florence, 1998).

SAGUÌ, L. *et al.*, 'Nuovi dati ceramologici per la storia economica di Roma tra VII e VIII secolo', in *La céramique médiévale en Méditerranée* (Aix-en-Provence, 1997), pp. 35–48.

SAHLINS, M., 'Poor man, rich man, big-man, chief', *Comparative studies in society and history*, V (1962–3), pp. 285–303.

SAHLINS, M., *Stone age economics* (London, 1974).

SAID, E. W., *Orientalism* (New York, 1978).

SALADO ESCAÑO, J. B. *et al.*, 'Evolución urbana de la Málaga musulmana, siglos VIII–XV', in I. Cortés Martínez (ed.), *La ciudad en al-Andalus y el Magreb* (Algeciras, 2002).

SALIBY, N., 'Un palais byzantino-omeyyade à Damas', in C. Castel *et al.* (eds.), *Les maisons dans la Syrie antique du IIIe Millénaire aux débuts de l'Islam* (Beirut, 1997), pp. 191–4.

SALRACH, J. M., *El proces de feudalització, segles III–XII* (Barcelona, 1987).

SALVATIERRA CUENCA, V., *La crisis del emirato omeya en el alto Guadalquivir* (Jaén, 2001).

SALVATIERRA, V., 'The formation process of the Islamic town into the Iberian peninsula', in M. Pearce and M. Tosi (eds.), *Papers from the EAA Third annual meeting at Ravenna 1997*, II, BAR, I718 (1998), pp. 197–202.

SALVATIERRA CUENCA, V., and CASTILLO ARMENTEROS, J. C., 'Peñaflor, un établissement rural d'époque émirale dans la Campiña de Jaén', *Archéologie islamique*, V (1995), pp. 11–24.

SALVATORI, E., *La popolazione pisana nel Duecento* (Pisa, 1994).

SAMSON, R., 'The Merovingian nobleman's home: castle or villa?', *Journal of medieval history*, XIII (1987), pp. 287–315.

SÁNCHEZ-ALBORNOZ, C., *Despoblación y repoblación del valle del Duero* (Buenos Aires, 1966).

SÁNCHEZ-ALBORNOZ, C., 'El "stipendium" hispano-godo y los orígines del beneficio prefeudal', in idem, *Estudios visigodos* (Rome, 1971), pp. 255–375.

SÁNCHEZ-ALBORNOZ, C., *En torno a los orígines del feudalismo*, I, 2nd edn. (Buenos Aires, 1974).

SÁNCHEZ-ALBORNOZ, C., 'Ruina y extinción del municipio romano en España y instituciones que le reemplazan', in idem, *Estudios visigodos* (Rome, 1971), pp. 11–147.

SÁNCHEZ LEÓN, J. C., *Les sources de l'histoire des Bagaudes* (Paris, 1996).

SÁNCHEZ LEÓN, J. C., *Los Bagaudas* (Jaén, 1996).

SÁNCHEZ MONTES, A. L., 'La antigüedad tardía en Complutum', in García Moreno and Rascón Marqués, *Complutum*, pp. 249–63.

SANDERS, G. D. R., 'An overview of the new chronology for 9th to 13th century pottery at Corinth', in Bakirtzis, *VIIe Congrès international*, pp. 35–44.

SANDERS, G. D. R., 'Corinth', in A. E. Laiou (ed.), *The economic history of Byzantium*, II (Washington, DC, 2002), pp. 647–54.

SANDERS, G. D. R., 'New relative and absolute chronologies for 9th to 13th century glazed wares at Corinth', in K. Belke *et al.* (eds.), *Byzanz als Raum* (Vienna, 2000), pp. 153–73.

SANNAZARO, M., 'La ceramica invetriata tra età romana e medioevo', in S. Lusuardi Siena (ed.), *Ad mensam* (Udine, 1994), pp. 229–61.

SANTANGELI VALENZANI, R., 'Residential building in early medieval Rome', in J. M. H. Smith (ed.), *Early medieval Rome and the Christian West* (Leiden, 2000), pp. 101–12.

SANTORO, S., 'Pantellerian ware', *L'Africa romana*, XIV (2002), pp. 991–1004.

SAPORITO, P. P., 'Ceramica dipinta e lisciata a stecca', in P. Peduto (ed.), *S. Giovanni di Pratola Serra* (Salerno, 1992), pp. 197–229.

SARADI, H., 'Privatisation and subdivision of urban properties in the early Byzantine centuries', *Bulletin of the American society of papyrologists*, XXXV (1998), pp. 17–43.

SARNOWSKI, T., *Les réprésentations des villas sur les mosaïques africaines tardives* (Wrocław, 1978).

SARRIS, P., *Economy and society in the age of Justianian* (Cambridge, in press).

SARRIS, P., 'The Justinianic plague: origins and effects', *Continuity and change*, XVII (2002), pp. 169–82.

SATO, S., 'L'*agrarium*: la charge paysanne avant le régime domanial, VIe–VIIIe siècles', *Journal of medieval history*, XXIV (1998), pp. 103–25.

SATO, S., 'The Merovingian accounting documents of Tours', *Early medieval Europe*, IX (2000), pp. 143–61.

SAUVAGET, J., *Alep* (Paris, 1941).

SAUVAGET, J., 'Châteaux umayyades de Syrie', *Revue des études islamiques*, XXXV (1967), pp. 1–49.

SAUVAGET, J., 'Le plan antique de Damas', *Syria*, XXVI (1949), pp. 314–58.

SAWYER, B., and SAWYER, P. H., *Medieval Scandinavia* (Minneapolis, 1993).

SAWYER, P. H., *Anglo-Saxon charters. An annotated list and bibliography* (London, 1968; 2nd edn. available at http://www.trin.cam.ac.uk/sdk13/chartwww/eSawyer. 99/eSawyer2.html).

SAWYER, P. H., 'Kings and merchants', in idem and I. N. Wood (eds.), *Early medieval kingship* (Leeds, 1977), pp. 139–58.

SAWYER, P. H., 'Kings and royal power', in Mortensen and Rasmussen, *Fra stamme til stat*, II, pp. 282–8.

SAWYER, P. H. (ed.), *English medieval settlement* (London, 1979).

SBARRA, F., 'Le ceramiche di un villaggio di X secolo nell'area padana', in R. Curina and C. Negrelli (eds.), *1° Incontro di studio sulle ceramiche tardoantiche e alto medievali* (Mantua, 2002), pp. 95–124.

SAZANOV, A., 'Les amphores de l'Antiquité tardive et du Moyen Âge', in *La céramique médiévale en Méditerranée* (Aix-en-Provence, 1997), pp. 87–102.

SCALES, P. C., 'Córdoba under the Umayyads', in G. De Boe and F. Verhaeghe (eds.), *Urbanism in medieval Europe* (Zellik, 1997), pp. 175–82.

SCHAEFER, J., and FALKNER, R. K., 'An Umayyad potters' complex in the North Theatre, Jerash', in F. Zayadine (ed.), *Jerash archaeological project I, 1981–1983* (Amman, 1986), pp. 411–35.

SCHACHT, J., 'Mīrāth, 1', in C. E. Bosworth *et al.* (ed.), *The encyclopaedia of Islam*, 2nd edn., VII (Leiden, 1993), pp. 106–11.

SCHANZER, D., and WOOD, I., *Avitus of Vienne, letters and selected prose* (Liverpool, 2002).

SCHEIDEL, W., 'Slaves of the soil', *JRA*, XIII (2000), pp. 727–32.

SCHICK, R., *The Christian communities of Palestine from Byzantine to Islamic rule* (Princeton, 1995).

SCHILLER, A. A., 'A check list of Coptic documents and letters', *Bulletin of the American society of papyrologists*, XIII (1976), pp. 99–123.

SCHILLER, A. A., 'A family archive from Jeme', in *Studi in onore di V. Arangio-Ruiz*, IV (Naples, 1953), pp. 327–75.

SCHILLER, A. A., 'The Budge papyrus of Columbia University', *Journal of the American Research Centre in Egypt*, VII (1968), pp. 79–118.

SCHLESINGER, W., *Die Entstehung der Landesherrschaft*, 2nd edn. (Darmstadt, 1964).

SCHLINKERT, D., *Ordo senatorius und nobilitas* (Stuttgart, 1996).

SCHMID, K., 'Zur Ablösung der Langobardenherrschaft durch die Franken', *Quellen und Forschungen*, LII (1972), pp. 1–35.

SCHMID, K., 'Zur Problematik von Familie, Sippe und Geschlecht, Haus und Dynastie beim mittelalterlichen Adel', *Zeitschrift für die Geschichte des Oberrheins*, CV (1957), pp. 1–62.

SCHMIDT-WIEGAND, R., 'Das Dorf nach den Stammesrechten des Kontinents', in H. Jankuhn et al. (eds.), *Das Dorf der Eisenzeit und des frühen Mittelalters* (Göttingen, 1977), pp. 408–43.

SCHMIEDT, G., 'Città scomparse e città di nuova formazione in Italia in relazione al sistema di comunicazione', *Settimane di studio*, XXI (1974), pp. 503–607.

SCHMINCK, A., 'Probleme des sog. "*Nomos Rodiōn nautikos*" ', in E. Chrysos et al. (eds.), *Griechenland und das Meer* (Mannheim, 1999), pp. 171–8.

SCHMITT, J., *Untersuchungen zu den liberi homines der Karolingerzeit* (Frankfurt, 1977).

SCHNEIDER. L., 'Entre antiquité et haut moyen âge', in M. Fixot (ed.), *Paul-Albert Février de l 'Antiquité au Moyen Âge* (Aix-en-Provence, 2004), pp. 173–200.

SCHNEIDER, L., 'Nouvelles recherches sur les habitats de hauteur de l'Antiquité tardive et du haut moyen âge en Gaule du Sud-Est', *Les nouvelles de l'archéologie*, XCII (2003), pp. 9–16.

SCHNEIDER, L., '*Oppida* et *castra* tardo-antiques', in Ouzoulias, *Les campagnes*, pp. 433–48.

SCHÜTTE, S., 'Continuity problems and authority structures in Cologne', in Ausenda, *After empire*, pp. 163–75.

SCHULZE, H. K., 'Rodungsfreiheit und Königsfreiheit', *Historische Zeitschrift*, CCXIX (1974), pp. 529–50.

SCHWARZMAIER, H. M., *Lucca und das Reich bis zum Ende des 11. Jahrhunderts* (Tübingen, 1972).

SCHWIND, F., 'Beobachtungen zur inneren Struktur des Dorfes in karolingischer Zeit', in H. Jankuhn et al. (eds.), *Das Dorf der Eisenzeit und des frühen Mittelalters* (Göttingen, 1977), pp. 444–93.

SCOTT, E., *A gazetteer of Roman villas in Britain* (Leicester, 1993).

SCOTT, J. C., *Domination and the arts of resistance* (New Haven, 1990).

SCOTT, J. C., *The moral economy of the peasant* (New Haven, 1976).

SCOTT, J. C., *Weapons of the weak* (New Haven, 1985).

SCRANTON, R. L., *Corinth XVI* (Princeton, 1957).

SCULL, C., 'Approaches to material culture and social dynamics of the migration period of eastern England', in J. Bintliff and H. Hamerow (eds.), *Europe between late Antiquity and the middle ages*, BAR, I617 (Oxford, 1995), pp. 71–83.

SCULL, C., 'Archaeology, early Anglo-Saxon society and the origins of Anglo-Saxon kingdoms', *Anglo-Saxon studies in archaeology and history*, VI (1993), pp. 65–82.

SCULL, C., 'Before Sutton Hoo', in M. O. H. Carver (ed.), *The age of Sutton Hoo* (Woodbridge, 1992), pp. 3–23.

SCULL, C., 'Urban centres in pre-Viking England?', in J. Hines (ed.), *The Anglo-Saxons from the migration period to the eighth century* (Woodbridge, 1997), pp. 269–310.

SEGAL, J. B., *Edessa, 'the blessed city'* (Oxford, 1970).

SÉGUIER, J.-M., and MORIZE, D., 'Les céramiques tardives à revêtement argileux de Jaulges-Villiers-Vineux (Yonne)', in L. Rivet (ed.), *Société française d'étude de la céramique antique en Gaule, Actes du Congrès de Dijon* (Marseille, 1996), pp. 155–78.

Señores, siervos, vasallos en la alta edad media (Pamplona, 2002).

SETTIA, A. A., ' "Per foros Italiae" ', *Settimane di studio*, XL (1993), pp. 188–237.

ŠEVČENKO, I., 'Hagiography of the Iconoclast period', in A. A. M. Bryer and J. Herrin (eds.), *Iconoclasm* (Birmingham, 1977), pp. 113–31.

SHARPE, R., 'Dispute settlement in medieval Ireland', in W. Davies and P. Fouracre (eds.), *The settlement of disputes in early medieval Europe* (Cambridge, 1986), pp. 169–89.

SHARPE, R., *Medieval Irish saints' lives* (Oxford, 1991).

SHAW, B. D., 'Bandit highlands and lowland peace', *Journal of the economic and social history of the Orient*, XXXIII (1990), pp. 199–233, 237–70.

SHAW, B. D., 'Bandits in the Roman empire', *Past and present*, CV (1984), pp. 3–52.

SHAW, B. D., 'Rural markets in North Africa and the political economy of the Roman Empire', *Antiquités africaines*, XVII (1981), pp. 37–86.

SHERESHEVSKI, J., *Byzantine urban settlements in the Negev desert* (Beer-Sheva, 1991).

SHIBA, Y., *Commerce and society in Sung China* (Ann Arbor, Mich., 1970).

SIEGMUND, F., *Alamannen und Franken* (Berlin, 2000).

SIEMEN, P. (ed.), *Bebyggelser og keramik fra 4–9 årh.* (Esbjerg, 1989).

SIJPESTEIJN, P. J., 'A late deed of surety from Oxyrhynchus (P. Princ. inv. AM 11244)', *ZPE*, LXV (1986), pp. 163–7.

SIJPESTEIJN, P. J., 'Der Pagarch Petterios', *Jahrbuch der österreichischen Byzantinistik*, XXX (1981), pp. 57–61.

SILVESTER, R. J., 'The addition of more-or-less undifferentiated dots to a distribution map?', in J. Gardiner (ed.), *Flatlands and wetlands*, East Anglian Archaeology, report 50 (Gressenhall, 1993), pp. 24–39.

SIMONSEN, J. B., *Studies in the genesis and early development of the caliphal taxation system* (Copenhagen, 1988).

SIMS-WILLIAMS, P., *Britain and early Christian Europe* (Aldershot, 1995).

SIMS-WILLIAMS, P., 'Gildas and the Anglo-Saxons', *Cambridge medieval Celtic studies*, VI (1983), pp. 1–30 (now in idem, *Britain*, study I).

SIMS-WILLIAMS, P., *Religion and literature in western England, 600–800* (Cambridge, 1990).

SIRKS, B., *Food for Rome* (Amsterdam, 1991).

SIRKS, B., 'The size of the grain distributions in imperial Rome and Constantinople', *Athenaeum*, LXXIX (1991), pp. 215–37.

SJÖSTRÖM, I., *Tripolitania in transition* (Aldershot, 1993).

SKINNER, A., 'The birth of a "Byzantine" senatorial perspective', *Arethusa*, XXXIII (2000), pp. 363–77.

SKINNER, P., *Family power in southern Italy* (Cambridge, 1995).

SKINNER, P., 'Urban communities in Naples, 900–1050', *PBSR*, LXII (1994), pp. 279–99.

SKINNER, P., *Women in medieval Italian society 500–1200* (Harlow, 2001).

SKOCPOL, T., 'What makes peasants revolutionary?', in R. P. Weller and S. E. Guggenheim (eds.), *Power and protest in the countryside* (Durham, NC, 1982), pp. 157–94.

SKOVGAARD-PETERSEN, I., 'The making of the Danish kingdom', in K. Helle (ed.), *The Cambridge history of Scandinavia*, I (Cambridge, 2003), pp. 163–83.

SMALL, A. M., and BUCK, R. J., *The excavations of S. Giovanni di Ruoti*, I (Toronto, 1994).

SMITH, R. H., and DAY, L. P., *Pella of the Decapolis*, II (Wooster, 1989).

SMYTH, A. P., *Celtic Leinster* (Blackrock, 1982).

SNYDER, C. A., *An age of tyrants* (Stroud, 1998).

SNYDER, C. A., *Sub-Roman Britain (AD 400–600). A gazetteer of sites*, BAR, B247 (Oxford, 1996).

SODINI, J.-P., 'La contribution de l'archéologie à la connaissance du monde byzantin (IVe–VIIe siècles)', *Dumbarton Oaks papers*, XLVII (1993), pp. 139–84.

SODINI, J.-P., 'Le bassin méditerranéen entre le VIIe et le IXe s.', in press.

SODINI, J.-P., 'Le commerce des marbres dans la Méditerranée IV–VIIe s.', in *V Reunió d'arqueologia cristiana hispànica* (Barcelona, 2000), pp. 423–48.

SODINI, J.-P., 'L'habitat urbain en Grèce à la veille des invasions', in *Villes et peuplement dans l'Illyricum protobyzantin* (Rome, 1984), pp. 341–96.

SODINI, J.-P., 'Productions et échanges dans le monde protobyzantin (IVe–VIIe s.): le cas de la céramique', in K. Belke *et al.* (eds.), *Byzanz als Raum* (Vienna, 2000), pp. 181–208.

SODINI, J.-P., and EDDÉ, A.-M., 'Les villages de Syrie du Nord (Massif Calcaire): leur évolution sous l'Islam', in *XXe Congrès international des études byzantines. Pré-actes*, II (Paris, 2001), pp. 26–7.

SODINI, J.-P., and VILLENEUVE, E., 'Le passage de la céramique byzantine à la céramique omeyyade', in Canivet and Rey-Coquais, *La Syrie*, pp. 195–218.

SODINI, J.-P. *et al.*, 'Déhès (Syrie du Nord), campagnes I–III (1976–1978)', *Syria*, LVII (1980), pp. 1–304.

SOT, M., *Un historien et son église au Xe siècle* (Paris, 1993).

SOULAS, S., 'Présentation et provenance de la céramique estampée à Bordeaux', *Aquitania*, XIV (1996), pp. 237–53.

SPECK, P., *Kaiser Konstantin VI.* (Munich, 1978).

SPIESER, J.-M., 'La ville en Grèce du IIIe au VIIe siècle', in *Villes et peuplement dans l'Illyricum protobyzantin* (Rome, 1984), pp. 315–38.

SPRANDEL, R., 'Grundbesitz und Verfassungsverhältnisse in einer merowingischen Landschaft', in J. Fleckenstein and K. Schmid (eds.), *Adel und Kirche* (Freiburg, 1968), pp. 26–51.

SPUFFORD, P., *Money and its use in medieval Europe* (Cambridge, 1988).

SQUATRITI, P., 'Digging ditches in early medieval Europe', *Past and present*, CLXXVI (2002), pp. 11–65.

STAAB, F., 'A reconsideration of the ancestry of modern political liberty', *Viator*, XI (1980), pp. 52–69.

STAAB, F., 'La circulation des biens à l'intérieur de la famille dans la région du Rhin moyen', *MEFR. Moyen âge*, CXI (1999), pp. 911–31.

STAAB, F., *Untersuchungen zur Gesellschaft am Mittelrhein in der Karolingerzeit* (Wiesbaden, 1975).

STAAB, F. (ed.), *Zur Kontinuität zwischen Antike und Mittelalter am Oberrhein* (Sigmaringen, 1994).

STACEY, D., 'Umayyad and Egyptian Red-slip "A" ware from Tiberias', *Bulletin of the Anglo-Israel archaeological society*, VIII (1988–9), pp. 21–33.

STAFFA, A. R., 'Le campagne abruzzesi fra tarda antichità ed altomedioevo (secc. IV–XII)', *AM*, XXVII (2000), pp. 47–99.

STAFFA, A. R., 'Le produzioni ceramiche in Abruzzo tra fine V e VII secolo', in Saguì, *Ceramica in Italia*, pp. 437–80.

STAFFA, A. R., 'Scavi nel centro storico di Pescara, I', *AM*, XVIII (1991), pp. 201–367.

STAFFA, A. R., and PELLEGRINI, W., *Dall'Egitto copto all'Abruzzo bizantino* (Mosciano S. Angelo, 1993).

STATHAKOPOULOS, D., 'Plague and pestilence in late Antiquity and early Byzantium', *Byzantine and Modern Greek studies*, XXIV (2000), pp. 256–76.

STECKNER, C., 'Les amphores LR1 et LR2 en relation avec le pressoir du complexe ecclésiastique des thermes de Samos', in V. Déroche and J.-M. Spieser (eds.), *Recherches sur la céramique byzantine* (Paris, 1989), pp. 57–71.

STEIN, E., *Histoire du Bas-Empire*, 2 vols. (Paris, 1949–59).

STEINHAUSEN, J., 'Die Langmauer bei Trier und ihr Bezirk, eine Kaiserdomäne', *Trierer Zeitschrift*, VI (1931), pp. 41–79.

STEINWENTER, A., *Das Recht der koptischen Urkunden* (Munich, 1955).

STEINWENTER, A., *Studien zu den koptischen Rechtsurkunden aus Oberägypten* (Leipzig, 1920).

STENTON, F. M., *Anglo-Saxon England* (Oxford, 1943).

STENTON, F. M., 'The supremacy of the Mercian kings', *English historical review*, XXXIII (1918), pp. 433–52.

STEPHENSON, P., 'A development in nomenclature on the seals of the Byzantine provincial aristocracy in the late tenth century', *Revue des études byzantines*, LII (1994), pp. 187–211.

STEUER, H., *Die Franken in Köln* (Cologne, 1980).

STEUER, H., *Frühgeschichtliche Sozialstrukturen in Mitteleuropa* (Göttingen, 1982).

STEVENS, S. T., 'A late-Roman urban population in a cemetery of Vandalic date at Carthage', *JRA*, VIII (1995), pp. 263–70.

STEVENS, S. T. (ed.), *Bir el Knissia at Carthage*, I (Ann Arbor, Mich., 1993).

STEVENS, S. T. *et al.*, 'The early Christian pilgrimage complex at Bir Ftouha, Carthage', *JRA*, XI (1998), pp. 371–83.

STILBORG, O., 'Ceramic contacts in the Gudme-Lundeborg area in the Late Roman Iron Age', in Nielsen *et al.*, *Gudme*, pp. 103–5.

STOCKING, R. L., Bishops, councils and consensus in the Visigothic kingdom, 589–633 (Ann Arbor, Mich., 2000).

STÖRMER, W., Früher Adel (Stuttgart, 1973).

STONE, D. L. et al., 'Suburban land use and ceramic production around Leptiminus (Tunisia)', JRA, XI (1998), pp. 304–18.

STOODLEY, N., The spindle and the spear, BAR, B288 (Oxford, 1999).

STORK, I., Fürst und Bauer, Heide und Christ (Stuttgart, 1995).

STORK, I., 'Lauchheim 2000', Archäologische Ausgrabungen in Baden-Württemberg (2000), pp. 154–6.

STORK, I., 'Zum Fortgang der Untersuchungen im frühmittelalterlichen Gräberfeld, Adelshof und Hofgrablege bei Lauchheim, Ostalbkreis', Archäologische Ausgrabungen in Baden-Württemberg (1992), pp. 231–43.

STOUT, M., The Irish ringfort (Blackrock, 1997).

STRATHEARN, M., The gender of the gift (Berkeley, 1988).

STROHEKER, K. F., Der senatorische Adel im spätantiken Gallien (Tübingen, 1948).

STROHEKER, K. F., 'Leowigild', in idem, Germanentum und Spätantike (Zürich, 1965), pp. 134–91.

SZÁDECZKY-KARDOSS, S., 'Bagaudae', in Paulys Realencyclopädie der classischen Altertumswissenschaft, Supplementband, XI (Stuttgart, 1968), cols. 346–54.

TABACCO, G., 'Dai possessori dell'età carolingia agli esercitali dell'età longobarda', Studi medievali, X (1969), pp. 221–68.

TABACCO, G., I liberi del re nell'Italia carolingia e postcarolingia (Spoleto, 1966).

TABACCO, G., 'La connessione fra potere e possesso nel regno franco e nel regno longobardo', Settimane di studio, XX (1972), pp. 133–68.

TABATA, K., Le città dell'Italia nel VI secolo d. C., tesi di dottorato, Università di Pisa (2002).

TAINTER, J. A., The collapse of complex societies (Cambridge, 1988).

TANGHERONI, M., 'La prima espansione di Pisa nel Mediterraneo: secoli X–XII', in G. Rossetti and G. Vitolo, Medioevo Mezzogiorno Mediterraneo, II (Naples, 2001), pp. 3–23.

TANGHERONI, M., RENZI RIZZO, C., and BERTI, G., 'Pisa e il Mediterraneo nei secoli VII–XIII', in Il mare, la terra, il ferro: ricerche su Pisa medievale (secoli VII–XIII) (Pisa, 2004).

TARDIF, J., 'Les chartes mérovingiennes de Noirmoutier', Nouvelle revue historique de droit français et étranger, XXII (1898), pp. 763–90.

TATE, G., Les campagnes de la Syrie du Nord du IIe au VIIe siècle, I (Paris, 1992).

TAYLOR, C., Village and farmstead (London, 1983).

TCHALENKO, G., Villages antiques de la Syrie du Nord, 3 vols. (Paris, 1953–8).

TEALL, J. C., 'The grain supply of the Byzantine empire, 330–1025', Dumbarton Oaks papers, XIII (1959), pp. 87–139.

Teoderico il Grande e i Goti d'Italia, Atti del XIII Congresso internazionale di studi sull'alto medioevo (Spoleto, 1993).

TERRAY, E., Marxism and 'primitive' societies (New York, 1972).

TESTINI, P. et al., 'La cattedrale in Italia', in Actes du XI Congrès international d'archéologie chrétienne, I (Rome, 1989), pp. 5–229.

THÉBERT, Y., 'L'évolution urbaine dans les provinces orientales de l'Afrique romaine tardive', Opus, II.1 (1983), pp. 99–131.

THÉBERT, Y., and BIGET, J.-L., 'L'Afrique après la disparition de la cité classique', in *L'Afrique dans l'Occident romain (1er siècle av. J.-C.–IVe siècle ap. J.-C.)* (Rome, 1990), pp. 575–602.

THEUWS, F., 'Haus, Hof und Siedlung im nördlichen Frankenreich (6.–8. Jahrhundert)', in *Die Franken. Wegbereiter Europas* (Mannheim, 1996), pp. 754–68.

THEUWS, F., 'Landed property and manorial organisation in northern Austrasia', in N. Roymans and F. Theuws (eds.), *Images of the past* (Amsterdam, 1991), pp. 299–407.

THEUWS, F., 'Maastricht as a centre of power in the early middle ages', in M. de Jong et al. (eds.), *Topographies of power in the early middle ages* (Leiden, 2001), pp. 155–216.

THIBAULT, F., 'L'impôt direct dans les royaumes des Ostrogoths, des Wisigoths et des Burgundes', *Nouvelle revue historique de droit français et étranger*, XXV (1901), pp. 698–728; XXVI (1902), pp. 32–48.

THOMAS, C., *English heritage book of Tintagel* (London, 1993).

THOMAS, C., 'Grass-marked pottery in Cornwall', in J. M. Coles and D. D. A. Simpson (eds.), *Studies in ancient Europe* (Leicester, 1968), pp. 311–31.

THOMPSON, E. A., 'Peasant revolts in late Roman Gaul and Spain', *Past and present*, II (1952), pp. 11–23.

THURNEYSEN, R., 'Aus dem irischen Recht', I, II, *Zeitschrift für celtische Philologie*, XIV (1923), pp. 335–94; XV (1924), pp. 238–76.

TILL, W., *Datierung und Prosopographie der koptischen Urkunden aus Theben*, Österreichische Akademie der Wissenschaften, philosophisch-historische Klasse, Sitzungsberichte, CCXL.1 (Vienna, 1962).

TILL, W., *Die koptischen Rechtsurkunden aus Theben*, Österreichische Akademie der Wissenschaften, philosophisch-historische Klasse, Sitzungsberichte, CCXLIV.3 (Vienna, 1964).

TILL, W., *Erbrechtliche Untersuchungen auf Grund der koptischen Urkunden*, Österreichische Akademie der Wissenschaften, philosophisch-historische Klasse, Sitzungsberichte, CCXXIX.2 (Vienna, 1954).

TIMBY, J. R., 'The Middle Saxon pottery', in P. Andrews (ed.), *Southampton finds*, I (Southampton, 1988), pp. 73–124.

TINNISWOOD, A., and HARDING, A., 'Anglo-Saxon occupation and industrial features in the henge monument at Yeavering, Northumberland', *Durham archaeological journal*, VII (1991), pp. 93–108.

TITS-DIEUAIDE, M.-J., 'Grands domaines, grandes et petites exploitations en Gaule mérovingienne', in A. Verhulst (ed.), *Le grand domaine aux époques mérovingienne et carolingienne* (Gent, 1985), pp. 23–50.

TO FIGUERAS, L., 'El marc de les comunitats pageses', in X. Barral (ed.), *Catalunya i França meridional a l'entorn de l'any mil* (Barcelona, 1991), pp. 212–39.

TOMBER, R., 'Quantitative approaches to the investigation of long-distance exchange', *JRA*, VI (1993), pp. 142–66.

TOMLIN, R. S. O., 'A five-acre wood in Roman Kent', in J. Bird et al., *Interpreting Roman London* (Oxford, 1996), pp. 209–15.

TORNBJERG, S. A., 'Bellingegård', *Journal of Danish archaeology*, IV (1985), pp. 147–56.

Torrita di Siena web-page: http://www.archeo.unisi/Web_Torrita

TORTORELLA, S., 'La ceramica africana', in P. Trousset (ed.), *L'Afrique du Nord antique et médiévale* (Paris, 1995), pp. 79–101.

TORTORELLA, S., 'La ceramica fine da mensa africana dal IV al VII secolo d.c.', in A. Giardina (ed.), *Società romana e impero tardoantico*, III (Rome, 1986), pp. 211–25.

TORTORELLA, S., 'La sigillata africana in Italia nel VI e nel VII secolo d.C.', in Saguì, *Ceramica in Italia*, pp. 41–69.

TOUBERT, P., *Dalla terra ai castelli* (Turin, 1995).

TOUBERT, P., *Les structures du Latium médiéval* (Rome, 1973).

TOUBERT, P., 'The Carolingian moment (eighth–tenth century)', in A. Burguière *et al.* (eds.), *A history of the family*, I (Cambridge, 1996), pp. 379–406.

TOUMANOFF, C., *Studies in Christian Caucasian history* (Washington, DC, 1963).

TREADGOLD, W. T., *The Byzantine revival, 780–842* (Stanford, Cal., 1988).

TREADGOLD, W. T., *The Byzantine state finances in the eighth and ninth centuries* (New York, 1982).

TRÉMENT, F., *Archéologie du paysage. Les étangs de Saint-Blaise (Bouches-du-Rhône)* (Paris, 1999).

TRIER, M., 'Köln im frühen Miterlatter', in J. Henning (ed.), *Europa im 10. Jahrhundert* (Mainz, 2002), pp. 301–10.

TROMBLEY, F. R., 'Mediterranean sea culture between Byzantium and Islam, c. 600–850 A.D.', in E. Kountoura-Galakē (ed.), *Oi skoteinoi aiōnes tou Byzantiou (70s–90s ai.)* (Athens, 2001), pp. 133–69.

TROMBLEY, F. R., 'Monastic foundations in sixth-century Anatolia and their role in the social and economic life of the countryside', *Greek Orthodox theological review*, XXX (1985), pp. 45–59.

TROMBLEY, F. R., 'The decline of the seventh-century town: the exception of Euchaita', in S. Vryonis (ed.), *Byzantina kai metabyzantina* (Malibu, Calif., 1985), pp. 65–90.

TROMBLEY, F. R., 'War and society in rural Syria c.502–613 A.D.', *Byzantine and Modern Greek studies*, XXI (1997), pp. 154–209.

TSAFRIR, Y., *Excavations at Rehovot-in-the-Negev*, I = Qedem, XXV (1988).

TSAFRIR, Y., and FOERSTER, G., 'Urbanism at Scythopolis-Bet Shean in the fourth to seventh centuries', *Dumbarton Oaks papers*, LI (1997), pp. 85–146.

TSUJI, S. (ed.), 'The survey of the early Byzantine sites in Ölüdeniz area (Lycia, Turkey)' = *Memoirs of the faculty of letters, Osaka University*, XXXV (1995).

TUBB, J. N., 'The pottery from a Byzantine well near Tell Fara', *Palestine exploration quarterly* (1986), pp. 51–65.

TUFFREAU-LIBRE, M., 'La céramique de l'Antiquité tardive dans le Nord de la France', in Piton, *La céramique*, pp. 91–106.

TURNER, E. G., 'A Roman writing tablet from Somerset', *Journal of Roman studies*, XLVI (1956), pp. 115–18.

TURPIN, W., 'The purpose of the Roman law codes', *Zeitschrift der Savigny-Stiftung für Rechtsgeschichte. Romanistische Abteilung*, CIV (1987), pp. 620–30.

TUZZATO, S., 'Venezia. Gli scavi a San Pietro di Castello (Olivolo)', *Quaderni di archeologia del Veneto*, VII (1991), pp. 92–103.

TYERS, P., *Roman pottery in Britain* (London, 1996).

TZAFERIS, V., *Excavations at Capernaum*, I (Winona Lake, Ind., 1989).

ULBERT, T., 'Beobachtungen im Westhofbereich der grossen Basilika von Resafa', *Damaszener Mitteilungen*, VI (1992), pp. 403–16.

ULMSCHNEIDER, K., *Markets, minsters and metal-detectors*, BAR, B307 (Oxford, 2000).

Un village aux temps de Charlemagne (Paris, 1988).

VALAIS, A., 'La phase Bas-Empire et mérovingienne du site de *Gaillon-le-Bas* à Herblay (Val d'Oise)', in P. Ouzoulias and P. Van Ossel (eds.), *Document de travail*, II, (Paris, 1995), pp. 135–43.

VALENTI, M., *Carta archeologica della provincia di Siena*, I (Siena, 1995).

VALENTI, M., 'La collina di Poggio Imperiale a Poggibonsi', *Miscellanea storica della Valdelsa*, CIV (1998), pp. 9–39.

VALENTI, M., 'La Toscana tra VI–IX secolo', in Brogiolo, *La fine delle ville*, pp. 81–106.

VALENTI, M., *L'insediamento altomedievale nelle campagne toscane* (Florence, 2004).

VALENTI, M., *Poggio Imperiale a Poggibonsi*, I (Florence, 1996).

VALENTI, M., and SALVADORI, F., 'Il periodo altomedievale di Poggio Imperiale (Poggibonsi, SI)', in R. Fiorillo and P. Peduto (eds.), *III Congresso di archeologia medievale* (Florence, 2003), pp. 325–30.

VALLVÉ, J., 'España en el siglo VIII: ejército y sociedad', *Al-Andalus*, XLIII (1978), pp. 51–107.

VALOR PIECHOTTA, M., 'La estructura urbana de la Sevilla islámica prealmohade', in *III Congreso de arqueología medieval española*, II (Oviedo, 1992), pp. 327–40.

VANACKER, C., 'Géographie économique de l'Afrique du Nord selon les auteurs arabes, du IXe siècle au milieu du XIIe siècle', *Annales ESC*, XXVIII (1973), pp. 659–80.

VAN ALFEN, P. G., 'New light on the 7th-c. Yassi Ada shipwreck', *JRA*, IX (1996), pp. 189–213.

VAN DAM, R., *Leadership and community in late antique Gaul* (Berkeley, 1985).

VAN DAM, R., *Saints and their miracles in late Antique Gaul* (Princeton, 1993).

VAN ES, W. A., *Wijster* (Groningen, 1967).

VAN ES, W. A., and VERWERS, W. J. H., *Excavations at Dorestad 1. The harbour: Hoogstraat I* (Amersfoort, 1980).

VAN ES, W. A., and VERWERS, W. J. H., 'Le commerce de céramiques carolingiennes aux Pays-Bas', in Piton, *La céramique*, pp. 227–36.

VANHAVERBEKE, H., MARTENS, F., and WAELKENS, M., 'What survey can tell: late Antique changes in the cityscape of Sagalassos (Pisidia, SW Turkey)', in A. Poulter (ed.), *The transition to late Antiquity* (London, in press).

VAN MINNEN, P., 'The volume of the Oxyrhynchite textile trade', *Münstersche Beiträge zur antiken Handelsgeschichte*, V.2 (1986), pp. 88–94.

VAN MINNEN, P., 'Urban craftsmen in Roman Egypt', *Münstersche Beiträge zur antiken Handelsgeschichte*, VI.1 (1987), pp. 31–86.

VAN OSSEL, P., *Établissements ruraux de l'Antiquité tardive dans le nord de la Gaule* (Paris, 1992).

VAN OSSEL, P., 'Céramiques de la fin du IVe siècle et du Ve siècle en Gaule Belgique', *Bulletin de la société archéologique champenoise*, LXXIX (1986), pp. 63–71.

VAN OSSEL, P., 'La sigillée d'Argonne du Bas-Empire dans le nord de la Gaule', *Alba regia*, XXV (1994), pp. 221–30.

VAN OSSEL, P., 'Structure, évolution et statut des habitats ruraux au Bas-Empire en Île-de-France', in P. Ouzoulias and P. Van Ossel (eds.), *Document de travail*, III (Paris, 1997), pp. 94–119.

VAN OSSEL, P., and OUZOULIAS, P., 'Rural settlement economy in Northern Gaul in the Late Empire', *JRA*, XIII (2000), pp. 133–60.

VARALDO, C. *et al.*, 'Lo scavo della contrada di S. Domenico al Priamàr (Savona)', *AM*, XXIII (1996), pp. 309–99.

VELÁZQUEZ, I., and RIPOLL, G., '*Toletum*, la construcción de una *urbs regia*', in Ripoll and Gurt, *Sedes regiae*, pp. 521–78.

VERA, D., '*Conductores domus nostrae, conductores privatorum*', in M. Christol *et al.* (eds.), *Institutions, société et vie politique dans l'empire romain au IVe siècle ap. J.-C.* (Paris, 1992), pp. 465–90.

VERA, D., 'Dalla "villa perfecta" alla villa di Palladio', *Athenaeum*, LXXXIII (1995), pp. 189–211, 331–56.

VERA, D., 'Enfiteusi, colonato e trasformazioni agrarie nell'Africa Proconsolare del tardo impero', *L'Africa romana*, IV (1986), pp. 267–93.

VERA, D., 'Forme e funzioni della rendita fondiaria nella tarda Antichità', in A. Giardina (ed.), *Società romana e impero tardoantico*, III (Bari, 1986), pp. 367–447.

VERA, D., 'Fra Egitto ed Africa, fra Roma e Costantinopoli, fra annona e commercio', *Kōkalos*, XLIII–XLIV (1997–8), pp. 33–72.

VERA, D., 'Le forme del lavoro rurale', *Settimane di studio*, XLV (1998), pp. 293–342.

VERA, D., '*Massa fundorum*', *MEFR. Antiquité*, CXI (1999), pp. 991–1025.

VERA, D., 'Schiavitù rurale, colonato e trasformazioni agrarie nell'Italia imperiale', *Scienze dell'antichità*, VI–VII (1992–3), pp. 291–339.

VERA, D., 'Strutture agrarie e strutture patrimoniali nella tarda antichità', *Opus*, II (1983), pp. 489–533.

VERA, D., 'Terra e lavoro nell'Africa romana', *Studi storici*, XXIX (1988), pp. 967–92.

VERHOEVEN, A., 'L'évolution de la céramique aux Pays-Bas méridionaux avant l'an Mil', in Piton, *La céramique*, pp. 209–15.

VERHULST, A., 'Étude comparative du régime domanial à l'est et à l'ouest du Rhin à l'époque carolingienne', *Flaran*, X (1988), pp. 87–101 (now in idem, *Rural and urban aspects*, study IV).

VERHULST, A., 'La diversité du régime domanial entre Loire et Rhin à l'époque carolingienne', in W. Janssen and D. Lohrmann (eds.), *Villa–curtis–grangia* (Munich, 1983), pp. 131–48 (now in idem, *Rural and urban aspects*, study III).

VERHULST, A., 'La genèse du régime domanial classique en France au haut moyen âge', *Settimane di studio*, XIII (1966), pp. 135–60 (now in idem, *Rural and urban aspects*, study I).

VERHULST, A., 'Marchés, marchands et commerce au haut moyen âge dans l'historiographie récente', *Settimane di studio*, XL (1993), pp. 23–43.

VERHULST, A., 'Quelques remarques à propos de corvées de colons à l'époque du Bas-Empire et du Haut Moyen Age', in *Revue de l'Université de Bruxelles* (1977), 1, pp. 89–95 (now in idem, *Rural and urban aspects*, study II).

VERHULST, A., 'Roman cities, *emporia* and new towns (sixth–ninth centuries)', in I. L. Hansen and C. Wickham (eds.), *The long eighth century* (Leiden, 2000), pp. 105–20.

VERHULST, A., *Rural and urban aspects of early medieval northwest Europe* (Aldershot, 1992).

VERHULST, A., *The Carolingian economy* (Cambridge, 2002).

VERHULST, A., *The rise of cities in north-west Europe* (Cambridge, 1999).

VERLINDEN, C., *L'esclavage dans l'Europe médiévale*, 2 vols. (Bruges, 1955–Gent, 1977).

VERWERS, W. J. H., 'Dorestad: a Carolingian town?', in R. Hodges and B. Hobley (eds.), *The rebirth of towns in the West, AD 700–1050*, CBA Research Report, 68 (London, 1988), pp. 52–6.

VIGIL-ESCALERA GUIRADO, A., 'Cabañas de época visigoda', *AEA*, LXXIII (2000), pp. 223–52.

VIGIL-ESCALERA GUIRADO, A., 'Cerámicas tardorromanas y altomedievales de Madrid', in Caballero *et al.*, *Cerámicas tardorromanas y altomedievales*, pp. 371–87.

VILASECA I CANALS, A., and DILOLI I FONS, J., 'Excavacions a l'àrea del fòrum provincial', in J. Ruiz de Arbulo (ed.), *Tàrraco 99* (Tarragona, 2000), pp. 47–52.

VILLA, L., 'Alcuni aspetti della circolazione di prodotti di importazione in Friuli tra VI e VII secolo', in Saguì, *Ceramica in Italia*, pp. 275–88.

VILLAVERDE VEGA, N., *Tingitana en la Antigüedad tardía (siglos III–VII)* (Madrid, 2001).

VILLEDIEU, F., *Lyon St.-Jean. Les fouilles de l'avenue Adolphe Max* (Lyon, 1990).

VILLENEUVE, E., and WATSON, P. (eds.), *La céramique byzantine et proto-islamique en Syrie-Jordanie (IVe–VIIIe siècles apr. J.-C.)* (Beirut, 2001).

VILLENEUVE, F., 'L'économie rurale et la vie des campagnes dans le Hauran antique (Ier siècle avant J.-C.–VIe siècle après J.-C.)', in J.-M. Dentzer (eds.), *Hauran*, I (Paris, 1985), pp. 63–136.

VINCE, A., *Saxon London* (London, 1990).

VINCE, A., 'The growth of market centres and towns in the area of the Mercian hegemony', in M. P. Brown and C. A. Farr (eds.), *Mercia* (Leicester, 2001), pp. 183–93.

VIOLANTE, C., 'I traspadani in Tuscia nei secoli VIII e IX', in *Studi di storia economica toscana nel Medioevo e nel Rinascimento in memoria di Federigo Melis* (Pisa, 1987), pp. 403–56.

VIOLANTE, C., *La società milanese nell'età precomunale* (Bari, 1953).

VIOLANTE, C., *Uno storico europeo tra guerra e dopoguerra, Henri Pirenne (1914–1923)* (Bologna, 1997).

VITELLI, G., *Islamic Carthage* (Carthage, 1981).

VÖLLING, T., 'The last Christian Greeks and the first pagan Slavs in Olympia', in E. Kountoura-Galakē (ed.), *Oi skoteinoi aiōnes tou Byzantiou (7os–9os ai.)* (Athens, 2001), pp. 303–23.

VOGT, C., 'La céramique de Tell el-Fadda', *Cahiers de la céramique égyptienne*, V (1997), pp. 1–22.

VOGT, C., 'Les céramiques ommeyyades et abbassides d'Istabl'Antar–Fostat', in *La céramique médiévale en Méditerranée* (Aix-en-Provence, 1997), pp. 243–60.

VOGT, C., 'The early Byzantine pottery', in P. G. Themelēs (ed.), *Protobyzantinē Eleutherna*, I.2 (Rethymno, 2000), pp. 39–199.

VOKAER, A., 'Syrian Brittle ware, 5ᵗʰ–8ᵗʰ centuries', in M. M. Mango (ed.), *Byzantine trade (4ᵗʰ–12ᵗʰ c.): recent archaeological work* (Aldershot, in press).

VOLLRATH, H., 'Herrschaft und Genossenschaft im Kontext frühmittelalterlicher Rechtsbeziehungen', *Historisches Jahrbuch*, CII (1982), pp. 33–71.

VOLPE, G., *Contadini, pastori e mercanti nell'Apulia tardoantica* (Bari, 1996).

VOLPE, G., 'Paesaggi della Puglia tardoantica', in *L'Italia meridionale in età tardo antica* (Naples, 2000), pp. 267–329.

VOLPINI, R., 'Placiti del "Regnum Italiae" (secc. IX–XI)', in P. Zerbi (ed.), *Contributi dell'Istituto di storia medioevale*, III (Milan, 1975), pp. 245–520.

VON RUMMEL, P., 'Habitus Vandalorum?', *Antiquité tardive*, X (2002), pp. 131–41.

VROOM, J., *After Antiquity* (Leiden, 2003).

WADE, K., 'A settlement site at Bonhunt Farm, Wicken Bonhunt, Essex', in D. G. Buckley (ed.), *Archaeology in Essex to AD 1500*, CBA Research Report, 34 (London, 1980), pp. 96–103.

WAELKENS, M., and POBLOME, J. (eds.), *Sagalassos*, II–IV (Leuven, 1993–7).

WALLACE-HADRILL, A. (ed.), *Patronage in ancient society* (London, 1989).

WALLACE-HADRILL, J. M., *Bede's Ecclesiastical history of the English people. A historical commentary* (Oxford, 1988).

WALLACE-HADRILL, J. M., *The long-haired kings* (London, 1962).

WALMSLEY, A., 'Byzantine Palestine and Arabia', in Christie and Loseby, *Towns in transition*, pp. 126–58.

WALMSLEY, A., 'Production, exchange and regional trade in the Islamic east Mediterranean', in I. L. Hansen and C. Wickham (eds.), *The long eighth century* (Leiden, 2000), pp. 265–343.

WALMSLEY, A., 'Tradition, innovation and imitation in the material culture of Islamic Jordan', in *Studies in the history and archaeology of Jordan*, V (Amman, 1995), pp. 657–68.

WALMSLEY, A., 'Turning East', in Villeneuve and Watson, *La céramique byzantine*, pp. 305–13.

WALMSLEY, A. *et al.*, 'The eleventh and twelfth seasons of excavations at Pella (Tabaqat Fahl) 1989–1990', *Annual of the Department of Antiquities of Jordan*, XXXVII (1993), pp. 165–240.

WAMERS, E., *Die frühmittelalterlichen Lesefunde aus der Löhrstrasse (Baustelle Hilton II) in Mainz* (Mainz, 1994).

WAMPACH, C., *Geschichte der Grundherrschaft Echternach im Frühmittelalter*, I.2 (Luxembourg, 1930).

WARD-PERKINS, B., 'Continuitists, catastrophists, and the towns of post-Roman northern Italy', *PBSR*, LXV (1997), pp. 157–76.

WARD-PERKINS, B., *From classical antiquity to the middle ages* (Oxford, 1984).

WARD-PERKINS, B., 'Specialised production and exchange', in A. Cameron *et al.* (eds.), *The Cambridge ancient history*, XIV (Cambridge, 2000), pp. 346–91.

WARD-PERKINS, B., 'The cities', in A. Cameron and P. Garnsey (eds.), *The Cambridge ancient history*, XIII (Cambridge, 1998), pp. 371–410.

WARD-PERKINS, B., 'Two Byzantine houses at Luni', *PBSR*, XLIX (1981), pp. 91–8.

WARD-PERKINS, B., 'Why did the Anglo-Saxons not become more British?', *English historical review*, CXV (2000), pp. 513–33.

WARNER, R. B., 'The date of the start of Lagore', *The journal of Irish archaeology*, III (1985–6), pp. 75–7.

WATERBOLK, H. T., 'Odoorn im frühen Mittelalter', *Neue Ausgrabungen und Forschungen in Niedersachsen*, VIII (1973), pp. 25–89.

WATSON, A. M., *Agricultural innovation in the early Islamic world* (Cambridge, 1983).

WATSON, P. M., 'Ceramic evidence for Egyptian links with northern Jordan in the 6th–8th centuries AD', in S. Bourke and J.-P. Descœudres (eds.), *Trade, contact and the movement of peoples in the eastern Mediterranean* (Sydney, 1995), pp. 303–20.

WATSON, P. M., 'Change in foreign and regional economic links with Pella in the seventh century A.D.', in Canivet and Rey-Coquais, *La Syrie*, pp. 233–47.

WATSON, P. M., 'Jerash bowls', *Syria*, LXVI (1989), pp. 223–61.

WATSON, P. M., 'Pella hinterland survey 1994', *Levant*, XXVIII (1996), pp. 63–76.

WATSON, P. M., 'Production and classification of "Jerash bowls" ', in H. Meyza and J. Młynarczyk (eds.), *Hellenistic and Roman pottery in the eastern Mediterranean* (Warsaw, 1995), pp. 453–62.

WATT, M., 'Sorte Muld', in Mortensen and Rasmussen, *Fra stamme til stat*, II, pp. 89–106.

WAYWELL, G. B., and WILKES, J. J., 'Excavations at the ancient theatre of Sparta 1992–4', *The annual of the British School at Athens*, XC (1995), pp. 435–60.

WEBER, M., 'Das Gräberfeld von Issendorf, Niedersachsen', *Studien zur Sachsenforschung*, XI (1998), pp. 199–212.

WEBER, M., *The city* (London, 1960).

WEIDEMANN, K., *Die frühmittelalterliche Keramik zwischen Somme und Elbe*, Diss. dr. Phil., Göttingen (1964).

WEIDEMANN, M., 'Adel im Merowingerreich', *Jahrbuch des römisch-germanischen Zentralmuseums Mainz*, XL (1993), pp. 535–55.

WEIDEMANN, M., *Das Testament des Bischofs Berthramn von Le Mans vom 27. März 616* (Mainz, 1986).

WEIDEMANN, M., *Kulturgeschichte der Merowingerzeit nach den Werken Gregors von Tours*, 2 vols. (Mainz, 1982).

WELCH, M., *English Heritage book of Anglo-Saxon England* (London, 1992).

WELLHAUSEN, J., *The Arab kingdom and its fall* (Calcutta, 1927).

WENSKUS, R., *Stammesbildung und Verfassung* (Cologne, 1961).

WERNER, K. F., 'Important noble families in the kingdom of Charlemagne', in T. Reuter (ed.), *The medieval nobility* (Amsterdam, 1978), pp. 137–202.

WERNER, K. F., 'Les principautés péripheriques dans le monde franc du VIIIe siècle', *Settimane di studio*, XX (1972), pp. 483–514.

WERNER, K. F., *Naissance de la noblesse* (Paris, 1998).

WERNER, M., *Adelsfamilien im Umkreis der frühen Karolinger* (Sigmaringen, 1982).

WERNER, M., *Der Lütticher Raum in frühkarolingischer Zeit* (Göttingen, 1980).

WEST, S., *West Stow: the Anglo-Saxon village*, 2 vols., East Anglian Archaeology, report 24 (Ipswich, 1986).

WHITBY, M., 'Armies and society in the later Roman world', in A. Cameron *et al.* (eds.), *The Cambridge ancient history*, XIV (Cambridge, 2000), pp. 469–95.

WHITCOMB, D., 'Ceramic production at Aqaba in the early Islamic period', in Villeneuve and Watson, *La céramique byzantine*, pp. 297–303.

WHITCOMB, D., 'Coptic glazed ceramics from the excavations at Aqaba, Jordan', *Journal of the American Research Center in Egypt*, XXVI (1989), pp. 167–82.

WHITCOMB, D., 'Khirbet al-Mafjar reconsidered: the ceramic evidence', *Bulletin of the American Schools of Oriental Research*, CCLXXI (1988), pp. 51–67.

WHITCOMB, D., 'Mahesh ware', *Annual of the Department of Antiquities of Jordan*, XXXIII (1989), pp. 269–85.

WHITCOMB, D., 'The "commercial crescent" ', in L. Conrad (ed.), *The Byzantine and early Islamic Near East*, V (Princeton, in press).

WHITCOMB, D., 'The miṣr of Ayla', in *Studies in the history and archaeology of Jordan*, V (Amman, 1995), pp. 277–88.

WHITE, R., 'Wroxeter and the transformation of late Roman urbanism', in T. R. Slater (ed.), *Towns in decline AD 100–1600* (Aldershot, 2000), pp. 96–119.

WHITE, S. D., 'Clotild's revenge', in S. K. Cohn and S. A. Epstein (eds.), *Portraits of medieval and Renaissance living* (Ann Arbor, Mich., 1996), pp. 107–30.

WHITE, S. D., 'Kinship and lordship in early medieval England', *Viator*, XX (1989), pp. 1–18.

WHITEHOUSE, D. B., 'Forum ware', *Medieval archaeology*, IX (1965), pp. 55–63.

WHITEHOUSE, D. B., 'Nuovi elementi per la datazione della ceramica a vetrina pesante', *AM*, VIII (1981), pp. 583–7.

WHITTAKER, C. R., 'Agostino e il colonato', in Lo Cascio, *Terre, proprietari*, pp. 295–309.

WHITTAKER, C. R., 'Circe's pigs', *Slavery and abolition*, VIII (1987), pp. 88–122.

WHITTAKER, C. R., *Frontiers of the Roman empire* (Baltimore, 1994).

WHITTAKER, C. R., 'Inflation and the economy in the fourth century A.D.', in C. E. King (ed.), *Imperial revenue, expenditure and monetary policy in the fourth century A.D.*, BAR, I76, (Oxford, 1980), pp. 1–22.

WHITTAKER, C. R., 'Trade and the aristocracy in the Roman empire', *Opus*, IV (1985), pp. 49–75.

WHITTAKER, C. R., and GARNSEY, P., 'Rural life in the later Roman empire', in A. Cameron and P. Garnsey (eds.), *The Cambridge ancient history*, XIII (Cambridge, 1998), pp. 277–311.

WHITTOW, M., 'Decline and fall? Studying long-term change in the East', in L. Lavan and W. Bowden (eds.), *Theory and practice in late Antique archaeology* (Leiden, 2002), pp. 404–23.

WHITTOW, M., 'Recent research on the late-Antique city in Asia Minor', in Lavan, *Recent research*, pp. 137–53.

WHITTOW, M., 'Ruling the late Roman and early Byzantine city', *Past and present*, CXXIX (1990), pp. 3–29.

WHITTOW, M., *The making of Orthodox Byzantium, 600–1025* (Basingstoke, 1996).

WHYMAN, M., *Late Roman Britain in transition, AD 300–500*, D.Phil. thesis, University of York (2001).

WICKHAM, C., 'A che serve l'incastellamento?', in M. Barceló and P. Toubert (eds.), *'L'incastellamento'* (Rome, 1998), pp. 31–41.

WICKHAM, C., 'Aristocratic power in eighth-century Lombard Italy', in A. C. Murray (ed.), *After Rome's fall* (Toronto, 1998), pp. 152–70.

WICKHAM, C., 'Asentamientos rurales en el Mediterráneo occidental en la alta edad media', in C. Trillo (ed.), *Asentamientos rurales y territorio en el Mediterráneo medieval* (Granada, 2002), pp. 11–29.

WICKHAM, C., *Community and clientele in twelfth-century Tuscany* (Oxford, 1998).

WICKHAM, C., *Courts and conflict in twelfth-century Tuscany* (Oxford, 2003).

WICKHAM, C., 'Documenti scritti e archeologia per una storia dell'incastellamento', *AM*, XVI (1989), pp. 79–102.

WICKHAM, C., 'Early medieval archaeology in Italy: the last twenty years', *AM*, XXVI (1999), pp. 7–19.

WICKHAM, C., *Early medieval Italy* (London, 1981).

WICKHAM, C., 'Economia e società rurale nel territorio lucchese durante la seconda metà del secolo XI', in C. Violante (ed.), *Sant'Anselmo vescovo di Lucca (1073–1086)* (Rome, 1992), pp. 391–422.

WICKHAM, C., 'Economic and social institutions in northern Tuscany in the 8th century', in idem *et al.*, *Istituzioni ecclesiastiche della Toscana medioevale* (Galatina, 1980), pp. 7–34.

WICKHAM, C., 'Historical and topographical notes on early medieval South Etruria', *PBSR*, XLVI (1978), pp. 132–79; XLVII (1979), pp. 66–95.

WICKHAM, C., *Il problema dell'incastellamento nell'Italia centrale* (Florence, 1985).

WICKHAM, C., 'Italy at the end of the Mediterranean world system', *JRA*, XIII (2000), pp. 818–24.

WICKHAM, C., 'La chute de Rome n'aura pas lieu', *Le moyen âge*, XCIX (1993), pp. 107–26.

WICKHAM, C., 'La signoria rurale in Toscana', in G. Dilcher and C. Violante (eds.), *Strutture e trasformazioni della signoria rurale nei secoli X–XIII* (Bologna, 1996), pp. 343–409.

WICKHAM, C., *Land and power* (London, 1994).

WICKHAM, C., 'Le forme del feudalesimo', *Settimane di studio*, XLVII (2000), pp. 15–51.

WICKHAM, C., 'L'identité villageoise entre Seine et Rhin, 500–800', in Yante and Bultot–Verleysen, *Autour du 'village'*.

WICKHAM, C., 'Lineages of western European taxation, 1000–1200', in M. Sánchez and A. Furió (eds.), *Actes. Col.loqui Corona, municipis i fiscalitat a la baixa Edat Mitjana* (Lleida, 1997), pp. 25–42.

WICKHAM, C., 'Monastic lands and monastic patrons', in R. Hodges (ed.), *San Vincenzo al Volturno*, II (London, 1995), pp. 138–52.

WICKHAM, C., 'Overview: production, distribution and demand, II', in I. L. Hansen and C. Wickham (eds.), *The long eighth century* (Leiden, 2000), pp. 345–77.

WICKHAM, C., 'Paesaggi sepolti', in M. Ascheri and W. Kurze (eds.), *L'Amiata nel medioevo* (Rome, 1989), pp. 101–37.

WICKHAM, C., 'Property ownership and signorial power in twelfth-century Tuscany', in W. Davies and P. Fouracre (eds.), *Property and power in the early middle ages* (Cambridge, 1995), pp. 221–44.

WICKHAM, C., 'Rural society in Carolingian Europe', in R. McKitterick (eds.), *The new Cambridge medieval history*, II (Cambridge, 1995), pp. 510–37.

WICKHAM, C., 'Social structures in Lombard Italy', in P. Delogu and C. Wickham (eds.), *The Langobards from the migration period to the eighth century* (Woodbridge, in press).

WICKHAM, C., 'Society', in R. McKitterick (ed.), *The early middle ages* (Oxford, 2001), pp. 59–94.

WICKHAM, C., 'Space and society in early medieval peasant conflicts', *Settimane di studio*, L (2003), pp. 551–87.

WICKHAM, C., 'Studying long-term change in the West, A.D. 400–800', in L. Lavan and W. Bowden (eds.), *Theory and practice in late antique archaeology* (Leiden, 2003), pp. 385–403.

WICKHAM, C., *Studi sulla società degli Appennini nell'alto medioevo* (Bologna, 1982).

WICKHAM, C., 'The development of villages in the West, 300–900', in C. Morrisson and J.-P. Sodini (eds.), *Les villages dans lempire et le monde fyzantin (V^e-XVe siècle)* (Paris, 2005)

WICKHAM, C., *The mountains and the city* (Oxford, 1988).

WICKHAM, C., ' "The Romans according to their malign custom" ', in J. M. H. Smith (ed.), *Early medieval Rome and the Christian West* (Leiden, 2000), pp. 151–66.

WICKHAM, C., 'Un pas vers le moyen âge?', in Ouzoulias, *Les campagnes*, pp. 555–67.

WIECZOREK, A., 'Die Ausbreitung der fränkischen Herrschaft in den Rheinlanden vor und seit Chlodwig I.', in *Die Franken. Wegbereiter Europas* (Mannheim, 1996), pp. 241–60.

WILBER, D. M., 'The Coptic frescoes of Saint Menas at Medinet Habu', *The art bulletin*, XXII (1940), pp. 86–103.

WILFONG, T., 'The archive of a family of moneylenders from Jême', *Bulletin of the American society of papyrologists*, XXVII (1990), pp. 169–81.

WILFONG, T., 'Western Thebes in the seventh and eighth centuries', *Bulletin of the American society of papyrologists*, XXVI (1989), pp. 89–145.

WILFONG, T., *Women of Jeme: lives in a Coptic town in late antique Egypt* (Ann Arbor, Mich., 2002).

WILKINSON, T. J., *Town and country in southeastern Anatolia*, I (Chicago, 1990).

WILKINSON, T. J., and TUCKER, D. J., *Settlement development in the North Jazira, Iraq* (Warminster and Baghdad, 1995).

WILLEMS, J., 'La production de poterie à l'époque mérovingienne dans la région hutoise', in M. Otte and J. Willems (eds.), *La civilisation mérovingienne dans le bassin mosan* (Liège, 1986), pp. 241–60.

WILLEMS, J., *Le quartier artisanal gallo-romain et mérovingien de 'Batta' à Huy = Archaeologia belgica*, CXLVIII (1973).

WILLIAMS, A., 'Princeps Merciorum gentis', *Anglo-Saxon England*, X (1982), pp. 143–72.

WILLIAMS, B. B., 'Excavations at Ballyutoag, County Antrim', *Ulster journal of archaeology*, XLVII (1984), pp. 37–49.

WILLIAMS, C., *Anemurium* (Toronto, 1989).

WILLIAMS, C., 'The pottery and glass at Alahan', in M. Gough (ed.), *Alahan* (Toronto, 1985), pp. 35–61.

WILLIAMS, D., and VINCE, A., 'The characterisation and interpretation of Early to Middle Saxon granitic tempered pottery in England', *Medieval archaeology*, XLI (1997), pp. 214–20.

WILLIAMS, J. H. *et al.*, *Middle Saxon palaces at Northampton* (Northampton, 1985).

WILLIAMS, R. J., *Pennyland and Hartigans* (Aylesbury, 1993).

WILLIAMSON, T., 'Early co-axial field systems on the East Anglian boulder clays', *Proceedings of the Prehistoric Society*, LIII (1987), pp. 419–31.

WILLIAMSON, T., 'Settlement chronology and regional landscapes', in D. Hooke (ed.), *Anglo-Saxon settlements* (Oxford, 1988), pp. 153–75.

WILLIAMSON, T., *The origins of Norfolk* (Manchester, 1993).

WILSON, J., and SA'D, M., 'The domestic material culture of Buṣrā' from the Nabataean to the Umayyad periods', *Berytus*, XXXII (1984), pp. 35–147.

WILSON, R. J. A., *Sicily under the Roman empire* (Warminster, 1990).

WILSON, S., *Feuding, conflict and banditry in nineteenth-century Corsica* (Cambridge, 1988).

WINKELMANN, F., *Byzantinische Rang- und Ämterstruktur im 8. und 9. Jahrhundert* (Berlin, 1985).

WINKELMANN, F., *Quellenstudien zur herrschenden Klasse von Byzanz im 8. und 9. Jahrhundert* (Berlin, 1987).

WINLOCK, H. E., and CRUM, W. E., *The monastery of Epiphanius at Thebes*, 2 vols. (New York, 1926).

WIPSZYCKA, E., *Les ressources et les activités économiques des églises en Égypte du IVᵉ au VIIIᵉ siècle* (Brussels, 1972).

WIPSZYCKA, E., *L'industrie textile dans l'Égypte romaine* (Wrocław, 1965).

WISE, P. J., 'Wasperton', *Current archaeology*, CXXVI (1991), pp. 256–9.

WITNEY, K. P., *The Jutish forest* (London, 1976).

WITSCHEL, C., *Krise–Rezession–Stagnation?* (Frankfurt, 1999).

WITSCHEL, C., 'Rom und die Städte Italiens in Spätantike und Frühmittelalter', *Bonner Jahrbücher*, CCI (2001), pp. 113–62.

WOLFRAM, H., *History of the Goths*, 2ⁿᵈ edn. (Berkeley, 1988).

WOLFRAM, H., 'Typen der Ethnogenese. Ein Versuch', in Geuenich, *Die Franken*, pp. 608–27.

WOLFRAM, H., and POHL, W., (eds.), *Typen der Ethnogenese*, I (Vienna, 1990).

WOLFRAM, H., and SCHWARCZ, A. (eds.), *Anerkennung und Integration* (Vienna, 1988).

WOOD, I. N., 'Administration, law and culture in Merovingian Gaul', in R. McKitterick (ed.), *The uses of literacy in early medieval Europe* (Cambridge, 1990), pp. 63–81.

WOOD, I. N., 'Before and after mission', in I. L. Hansen and C. Wickham (eds.), *The long eighth century* (Leiden, 2000), pp. 149–66.

WOOD, I. N., 'Ethnicity and the ethnogenesis of the Burgundians', in Wolfram and Pohl, *Typen der Ethnogese*, I, pp. 53–69.

WOOD, I. N., 'Family and friendship in the West', in A. Cameron *et al.* (eds.), *The Cambridge ancient history*, XIV (Cambridge, 2000), pp. 416–36.

WOOD, I. N., 'Forgery in Merovingian hagiography', in *Fälschungen im Mittelalter, MGH, Schriften*, XXXIII.5 (Hannover, 1988), pp. 369–84.

WOOD, I. N., 'The ecclesiastical politics of Merovingian Clermont', in P. Wormald (ed.), *Ideal and reality in Frankish and Anglo-Saxon society* (Oxford, 1983), pp. 34–57.

WOOD, I. N., 'The end of Roman Britain', in M. Lapidge and D. Dumville (eds.), *Gildas: new approaches* (Woodbridge, 1984), pp. 1–25.

WOOD, I. N., *The Merovingian kingdoms, 450–751* (London, 1994).

WOOD, I. N., *The missionary life* (Harlow, 2001).

WOOD, I. N., 'The north-western provinces', in A Cameron *et al.* (eds.), *The Cambridge ancient history*, XIV (Cambridge, 2000), pp. 497–524.

WOOD, S. M., *Lords, priests and churches* (Oxford, 2005).

WOODING, J. M., *Communication and commerce along the western sealanes, AD 400–800*, BAR, I654 (Oxford, 1996).

WOOLF, A., 'Community, identity and kingship in early England', in W. O. Frazer and A. Tyrrell (eds.), *Social identity in early medieval Britain* (London, 2000), pp. 91–109.

WOOLF, G., *Becoming Roman* (Cambridge, 1998).

WORMALD, P., 'A handlist of Anglo-Saxon lawsuits', *Anglo-Saxon England*, XVII (1988), pp. 247–81.

WORMALD, P., *Bede and the conversion of England: the charter evidence* (Jarrow, 1984).

WORMALD, P., 'Bede, "Beowulf" and the conversion of the Anglo-Saxon aristocracy', in R. T. Farrell (ed.), *Bede and Anglo-Saxon England*, BAR, B46 (Oxford, 1978), pp. 32–95.

WORMALD, P., 'Celtic and Anglo-Saxon kingship: some further thoughts', in P. E. Szarmach (ed.), *Sources of Anglo-Saxon culture* (Kalamazoo, Mich., 1986), pp. 151–83.

WORMALD, P., 'Charters, law and the settlement of disputes in Anglo-Saxon England', in W. Davies and P. Fouracre (eds.), *The settlement of disputes in early medieval Europe* (Cambridge, 1986), pp. 149–68.

WORMALD, P., ' "Inter cetera bona . . . genti suae": law-making and peace-keeping in the earliest English kingdoms', *Settimane di studio*, XLII (1995), pp. 963–96.

WORMALD, P., 'Lordship and justice in the early English kingdom', in W. Davies and P. Fouracre (eds.), *Property and power in the early middle ages* (Cambridge, 1995), pp. 114–36.

WORMALD, P., 'The age of Offa and Alcuin', in J. Campbell (ed.), *The Anglo-Saxons* (Oxford, 1982), pp. 101–28.

WORMALD, P., *The making of English law*, I (Oxford, 1999); II (in preparation).

WORMALD, P., 'Viking studies: whence and whither?', in R. T. Farrell (ed.), *The Vikings* (Chichester, 1982), pp. 128–53.

YANTE, J.-M., and BULTOT-VERLEYSEN, A.-M. (eds.), *Autour du 'village'* (Louvain-la-Neuve, 2005).

YEIVIN, Z., 'Chorazin', in E. Stern (ed.), *New encyclopedia of archaeological excavations in the Holy Land*, I (Jerusalem, 1993), pp. 301–4.

YORKE, B., *Kings and kingdoms of early Anglo-Saxon England* (London, 1990).

YORKE, B., *Wessex in the early middle ages* (London, 1995).

YOUNG, B., 'Paganisme, christianisation et rites funéraires mérovingiens', *Archéologie médiévale*, VII (1977), pp. 5–81.

ZACOS, G., and VEGLERY, A., *Byzantine lead seals*, I (Basel, 1972).

ZADORA-RIO, E., 'Le village des historiens et le village des archéologues', in E. Mornet (ed.), *Campagnes médiévales* (Paris, 1995), pp. 145–53.

ZADORA-RIO, E., and GALINIÉ, H., 'La fouille du site de Rigny, 7ᵉ–19ᵉ s. (commune de Rigny-Ussé, Indre-et-Loire)', *Revue archéologique du Centre de la France*, XL (2001), pp. 167–242.

ZANINI, E., 'La ceramica bizantina in Italia tra VI e VIII secolo', in Bakirtzis, *VIIᵉ Congrès international*, pp. 381–94.

ZANINI, E., *Le Italie bizantine* (Bari, 1998).

ZANINI, E., 'Ricontando la Terra Sigillata Africana', *AM*, XXIII (1996), pp. 677–88.

ZANINI, E., and GIORGI, E., 'Indagini archeologiche nell'area del "quartiere bizantino" di Gortina: prima relazione preliminare (campagno 2002)', *Annuario della Scuola archeologica italiana di Atene*, LXXX (2002), pp. 212–32.

ZAYADINE, F. (ed.), *Jerash archaeological project 1, 1981–1983* (Amman, 1986).

ZERNER-CHARDAVOINE, M., 'Enfants et jeunes au IXᵉ siècle', *Provence historique*, XXXI (1981), pp. 355–81.

ZEYADEH, A., 'Settlement patterns, an archaeological perspective', in G. D. R. King and A. Cameron (eds.), *The Byzantine and early Islamic Near East*, II (Princeton, 1994), pp. 117–31.

ZIEGLER, C. *et al.*, 'La mission archéologique du Musée du Louvre à Saqqara', *Bulletin de l'Institut français d'archéologie orientale*, XCVII (1997), pp. 269–92.

ZILLIACUS, H., 'Griechische Papyrusurkunden des VII. Jahrhunderts n. Chr. veröffentlicht und erklärt', *Eranos*, XXXVIII (1940), pp. 79–107.

ZOTZ, T., 'Adel, Oberschicht, Freie', *Zeitschrift für die Geschichte des Oberrheins*, CXXV (1977), pp. 3–20.

ZUCKERMAN, C., 'The reign of Constantine V in the Miracles of St. Theodore the Recruit (*BHG* 1764)', *Revue des études byzantines*, XLVI (1988), pp. 191–210.

General index

This is essentially an index of personal names and placenames, together with some of the more important technical terms used in the book. Definitions of major concepts such as 'state' are also indexed; the main moment where a concept is defined in the text is **bolded**. Also **bolded** are the main discussions of the regions which are the focus of study in this book. Placenames are here linked to countries; these are always the modern countries.

Aachen, Germany 476, 509, 673, 680
Aaron son of Shenoute, Egyptian
    notable 424
d'Abadal, Ramon 230
Abadie-Reynal, Catherine 715, 716
'Abbāsids, 'Abbāsid caliphate 5, 24–5,
    27–9, 58, 60, 68, 81, 84–5, 132–3,
    140–1, 143, 146, 149, 302, 450–1,
    457–8, 604, 614, 616–19, 623–5,
    770, 773, 775–80, 793–4, 820, 822,
    827
Abbo of Maurienne, Frankish
    aristocrat 189, 190, 195, 214, 218,
    283, 564, 580 n.117, 607, 758
'Abd al-'Azīz, governor of Egypt 24
'Abd al-Malik, caliph 24, 241, 621
'Abd al-Rahmān I, amir of
    al-Andalus 40, 101
'Abd al-Rahmān III, caliph of
    al-Andalus 40, 102
Abila (Umm al-'Amad), Jordan 613,
    623
Abraham, bishop of Ermont 421, 423,
    426
Abruzzo, Italy 244, 484 n.115, 736
Abū Mīnā, Egypt 611, 762
Acerisius, Italian aristocrat 217 n.169
Acién, Manuel 493, 494
Acilii, Roman senatorial family 159
Adalgisel-Grimo, deacon of
    Verdun 188–9, 190, 191, 216, 607
Adalhard, abbot of Corbie 300, 301
Adams, William 759, 761
Adelsheiligen 202

Adriatic Sea 217, 244 n.227, 33, 632,
    691, 729 n.68, 731, 792 n.171
adscripticii 523, 524
Áed mac Bricc of Killare, Vita of 355
Aegean Sea 10, 29, 30–2, 76, 78–9,
    125, 129, 239, 277, 327, 446,
    461–2, 626–8, 632–3, 635, 643,
    654, 708, 714–17, 737, 780–93,
    820, 827
Ælfwine, village notable of
    Malling 429, 431, 432
Aemilianus, ascetic in Spain 222–3, 226
Æthelbald, king of Mercia 344–5
Æthelberht, king of Kent 50, 323, 343,
    346
Æthelric, son of Æthelmund, Anglo-
    Saxon aristocrat 316–17
Aetius, Roman general 87 n.82, 158,
    168, 530, 602
Africa 5 n.5, 10, 17–22, 24, 26–7, 29,
    30, 34–5, 37, 40, 65, 69, 75–8,
    80–1, 87–93, 101, 124, 128,
    133 n.195, 149, 163, 166–7, 204,
    207 n.141, 222 n.179, 244, 258,
    263, 266–7, 269–70, 272–4, 276–9,
    286 n.57, 299, 303, 307, 333–5,
    446, 471–3, 474 n.87, 475, 492,
    522, 534, 537, 548, 562, 566, 592,
    604, 608–9, 635–44, 651–4, 656,
    659, 664–5, 669, 671–2, 696, 705,
    708–13, 718, 720–8, 737, 740–1,
    746, 748–9, 751, 757–8, 769, 776,
    787, 794, 815, 820–1, 823, see also
    Arab Africa, ceramics: African Red

Africa (*cont.*)
    Slip, Byzantine Africa, Vandals in
    Africa
Agathias, Roman writer 75
agglomérations secondaires, small
    trading centres 680
Aghlabids, Arab rulers of Africa 22, 640
Agilolfings, Frankish aristocrats 45,
    184, 190, 192, *see also* Faronids
Agilulf, Lombard king 35
agora 611, 615, 624, 626, 627, 629,
    631, *see also* forum
Agrate, Italy 214, 605
agrestes 530
Agrigento, Italy 478
ahl Ṭulayṭula, *see* Toledo
Aigina, Greece 628 n.86, 783, 786–7
Aïn Ksar, Algeria 643
Aisne, River 507, 796, 798
Aistulf, Lombard king 35, 106 n.128,
    214, 582, 732
aithechthúatha, base-client peoples in
    Ireland 358, 360
Aix-en-Provence, France 667
Akhila, Visigothic king 96 n.104
Akhmīm, *see* Panopolis
'Akko, Israel 774
Ala, Danish aristocrat 374–5
Alahan, Turkey 782
Alahis, Lombard king 120
Alahis, 'list' of 216–17
Alans 158, 530, 602
Albacete, Spain 749
Albarracín, Spain 605
Albi, France 190, 606
Albinus, Italian aristocrat 210
Alcuin, Anglo-Saxon writer 655
    Vita Willibrordi 365
Aldhelm, Anglo-Saxon writer 808
aldii, half-freemen 565
Adric, tenant in Francia 404
Alemannia, Germany 46, 198, 256,
    280, 283–4, 287 n.59, 288, 290,
    500–2, 504, 510, 515–16, 562,
    575–6, 580, 797–8
Alemans, Germanic people 45, 102
Aleppo (Beroia, Haleb), Syria 26, 28,
    443, 449, 614, 620–1, 778

Alexander the Great 28
Alexandria, Egypt 22–4, 73 n.47,
    130–1, 135–6, 138–40, 246, 248,
    250–1, 257, 415, 460, 609–12, 642,
    690, 713–14, 760–2, 764 n.130,
    767, 769
Alfonso III, king of the Asturias 39, 584
Alfred, king of Wessex 49, 180,
    318 n.37, 375
Algeria 17, 87, 335, 470, 721, *see also*
    Numidia
Alicante, Spain 230, 481, 489, 490,
    493, 494, 546, 748, 749
Aliperga, Italian notable 217 n.168
Alitroda, Italian notable 555–6
Almanach de Gotha 153
Almería, Spain 40, 660, 750
Alps 30, 33, 34, 190, 219, 297, 501,
    511, 540, 560, 580, 583–4, 603,
    644, 654, 698, 702, 731, 732–3
Alsace, France 77 n.56, 110, 256, 285,
    394 n.23, 511
Altava, Algeria 22, 335–6
Altavilla Silentina, Italy 736
Alteserra, Italy 392
Alto Adige, Italy 486 n.123
Alzey, Germany 103
Amalfi, Italy 738
Amandus, Bagaudic leader 531 n.26
Amay, Belgium 189
amber 682
Ambrose, bishop of Milan 95 n.101
Amiata, *see* Monte Amiata
amicitia 170
Ammaedara (Haïdra), Tunisia 635,
    638–9, 643
'Ammān(Philadelphia), Jordan 26, 241,
    450–1, 614, 623–4
Ammianus Marcellinus, Roman
    writer 66 n.22, 71, 77, 157, 163,
    334
Ammonios, Egyptian landowner 249,
    413, 414, 417
Amorion, Turkey 233, 626, 629–30,
    784–5
Amory, Patrick 83
Amphipolis, Greece 627
amphitheatre 594, 615

amphorae, transport containers 77–9,
132, 327, 445–6, 452, 632, 703–6,
708–10, 712–17, 721–2, 730, 735,
737, 746, 748, 759, 761–3, 768,
770–1, 774–5, 781, 784–9, 791,
798, 815, *see also* ceramics
'Amr, tax-collector in Egypt 142
amṣār, garrison cities 603
'Amudiye, Syria 445
Anamur, *see* Anemourion
Anastasios II, Byzantine emperor 126
Anastasios the Persian, martyr 622
Anastasioupolis, Turkey 233, 407, 462
Anastasius, emperor 30, 69, 75, 162,
522
Anatolia, Turkey 5, 30–2, 36, 37, 75,
77, 79, 125, 127, 129, 164, 232,
237–9, 327, 385–6, 406–7, 440,
443, 463, 460–4, 517, 532 n.30,
603–4, 608, 626–9, 631, 638–40,
643, 654, 656 n.151, 715, 761,
772, 780, 784–5, 792, 793, *see also*
Byzantium
Anatolikon theme 827
Andalucía (Baetica), Spain 37, 39, 40,
44, 79, 220, 226, 229, 595, 656–7,
660, 663, 672, 688, 741, 744–5,
753, 756–7, 823
al-Andalus, Arab Spain 39, 100, 101,
227, 230, 231 n.198, 242, 492,
494, 605, 661, 741, 750, 752,
see also Arabs in Spain
Andarchius, intellectual in
Gaul 566 n.92
Andarin, Syria 449, 455, 770
Andreolli, Bruno 295
Anemourion (Anamur), Turkey 626,
782, 783
angaria, *see* corvées
Angeln, Germany 312
Angers, France 109, 110, 111, 187,
288, 510, 580, 599
Anglo-Saxon Chronicle 346, 685 n.201
Anglo-Saxon England 14, 107, 153,
180, 185, 281, 303, 306, 308, 311,
339–48, 370, 375, 377–9, 351–3,
362, 375–9, 432–3, 435, 475, 496,
500, 502, 515, 517, 543, 545,

557 n.71, 566, 591, 687, 806–8,
812, 816, *see also* England
Anglo-Saxons, Germanic people 47, 49,
691, 797 806
Anicia Juliana, Roman
aristocrat 154 n.4
Anicii, Roman senatorial family 153,
159–65, 171 n.48, 205–6, 244, 270
'Anjar, Lebanon 613, 618, 619, 662
Ankara, Turkey 233, 238, 406–11, 418,
436, 437, 439, 457, 461 n.55, 568,
599, 629, 630, 633 n.102
Annales Bertiniani 580
annona 72–3, 76, 78, 87–8, 91, 98, 103,
110, 125, 163, 271, 710–15, 718,
729–30, 790 n.170, 791
Anstruda, Italian peasant woman 556,
560
Antaiopolis ('Irmāniyya), Egypt 64–6,
134, 245, 249, 412–13, 416–18,
464
Antalya (Attaleia), Turkey 238, 626,
630, 633
Anthemius, emperor 169
Antinoupolis (Shaykh 'Ibāda),
Egypt 252, 422, 600, 612, 761–2
Antioch, Turkey 26, 27, 68, 73 n.47,
76, 164, 240, 443–9, 452–4,
456, 458, 524, 614, 620, 624,
642, 690, 714, 776–7, 779, 793,
820
Antoigné, France 289 n.65, 580, 581
Antonina, Roman aristocrat 154 n.4
Antoninus, bishop of Fussala 473
Antrim, Northern Ireland 52, 815
Antwerp, Belgium 509
Aosta, Italy 646
Apa Apollō (modern Deīr al-Bala'īza),
Egypt 24, 134, 252, 253
Apa Kyros, son of Samuel, village
headman in Egypt 253
Apa Phoibammōn (modern Deir al-
Bahri), Egypt 250, 253, 421, 423
Apa Sourous, Aphroditō, Egypt 414,
419, 424, 425
Apamea, Syria 240, 445, 449, 455, 613,
620, 625
Aphrodisias, Turkey 626, 627, 629

Aphroditō (Coptic Jkōw, modern Arabic
Kōm Ishkāw), Egypt 23–5, 71,
134–40, 142 n.219, 245–6,
249–53, 275 nn.29, 32, 385–6,
411–20, 424 n.104, 426, 435–6,
437, 440, 454, 464, 524, 528, 558,
763, 767
Apion III, Roman aristocrat 165 n.29
Apions, Roman aristocratic family 71,
165–6, 190 n.96, 206, 234, 244–9,
251–3, 266, 269–70, 274–5, 418,
426, 428, 460, 523, 527, 600, 764,
767, 769
Apollinares, Roman aristocratic
family 171, *see also* Sidonius
Apollinaris
Apollinaris, grandfather of Sidonius
Apollinaris 160
Apollonia (Arshaf), Israel 614, 618,
622 n.71, 774
Apollonopolis Anō (Edfū), Egypt 137,
422, 600, 763
Apollōs *boēthos*, son of Dioskoros of
Aphroditō 413 n.74
Apollōs, father of Dioskoros of
Aphroditō 249, 411–14
Appennines, Italy 33, 118, 121,
339 n.86, 387, 469, 471, 484, 540,
583, 606, 654, 698, 706, 737, 826
Appianos, family of, in Roman
Egypt 243, 247
'Aqaba, Jordan 604, 775, 778, 793
Aquileia, Italy 209, 731
Aquitaine, France 38, 41, 42, 43, 44,
45, 46, 77, 82, 102, 103, 107,
110 n.137, 113, 119, 164, 170,
171, 172, 173, 177, 179, 180, 181,
182, 186, 187, 188, 191, 192, 194,
195, 197, 198, 207, 221, 225, 227,
230, 244 n.227, 257, 470, 475,
478, 510, 580, 672, 674, 746, 747,
752, 758, 795, 815
Arabs 4, 11, 18–21, 25–30, 56, 62, 70,
72, 85, 90–2, 114, 130–3, 137–8,
146, 149, 153–4, 158, 167,
207 n.141, 208, 219 n.173, 226–7,
229–31, 234, 237, 240–1, 251,
301–2, 444, 448, 451, 520, 526–7,

535, 548, 554, 583, 603, 605, 616,
628, 634, 636, 689, 691, 701,
716–17, 743, 759, 775–6, 789, 829
in Africa 125, 127, 133 n.195, 305,
636, 639–44, 726–27
in Byzantium (the Byzantine
heartland) 130, 234, 242, 407,
460, 785
in Egypt 101, 125, 126, 130–44,
146–7, 149, 251–5, 257, 302, 422,
441, 566, 610–12, 625, 766, 768–9
in Francia 748
in Italy 661
in Palestine 2, 143–4, 240–1, 444,
448–50, 453, 455, 457, 613, 617,
619–22, 770, 773–7, 779–80
in Persia 130
in Sicily 208, 738
in Spain 2, 39–41, 93, 96, 100–2,
146, 149–50, 219 n.173, 226–7,
229–31, 489–92, 495, 577, 656–58,
660–2, 664, 741, 745–6, 750–2,
754–5, 757, 792, 827–8
in Syria 101, 143, 147, 149, 240–1,
444, 448–50, 455, 457, 613, 617,
619–22, 770, 773–7, 779–80
Arabian desert 18
Arabic, language 24, 28, 130, 134, 140,
168, 241, 421
Aragón, Spain 94
Arbogast of Trier, Roman
general 158 n.13, 169
Ardagh Chalice 356
Ardennes, Belgium 43, 508 n.174, 509
Ardin, Poitou, France 109, 110
Aredius of Limoges 173, 189, 223,
284–7, 564, 606
Arezzo, Italy 118, 212, 392, 393, 485,
546 n.45
Argonne, France 795, 797, *see also*
ceramics: Argonne ware
Argos, Greece 781, 782, 786, 787
Århus, Denmark 366, 428 n.112
Arianism 20, 38, 88, 91
aristocrat, definition of 153–5
Arles, France 77, 160, 161, 168, 170,
623, 665–7, 689
Armant, *see* Ermont

Armenia 5, 24, 237, 238
Armeniakon theme 630
Armorica, France 81, 530
Arno, River 390, 735
Arnold, Chris 808
Arnouville, France 404, 409
Arochis, Italian landowner 560
Arras, France 677, 686
Arsinoë (Madīnat al-Fayyūm),
    Egypt 139 n.213, 165, 243, 248,
    250 n.248, 254 n.254, 274, 422,
    428, 434, 600, 612, 764–5
Artemios, *Miracles* of 129 n.184
Arthies, France 188, 199, 405, 607
Arthur, Paul 730
artisan production 12, 230, 246–8, 259,
    291–2, 310, 320, 353, 355, 371,
    429 n.114, 443 n.1, 456, 472, 476,
    486, 490, 493–4,n 499, 520, 534,
    536–7, 539, 544–7, 549, 566, 612,
    616–19, 625, 628, 637 n.111, 640,
    647, 686, 699, 703, 706, 709, 712,
    725–7, 730, 734, 736, 740, 763,
    764–5, 767–9, 777, 800, 802, 804,
    807, 809, 811, 815–16, 818, 823
artisans 276, 386, 413, 420 n.92, 595,
    602, 610, 650, 653, 664, 670–1,
    673, 683–4, 701–2, 766, 783, 797
Arvandus, praetorian prefect 155 n.5,
    161, 169 n.40
'*aṣabiyya* 358
Astaillac, France 284
Ashmūnayn, *see* Hermopolis
Ashqaw, *see* Aphroditō
Ashqelon, *see* Askalon
Asia 58
Askalon (Ashqelon), Israel 240, 241,
    452, 616, 617 n.60, 771, 783
Aspar, Roman general 158, 165, 602
Aspidius, *senior*, ruler in Spain 94, 756
Aston, Trevor 319
Asturias, Spain 37, 39, 96 n.104,
    227–9, 338–9, 469 n.75,
    489 n.131, 492, 577, 584, 587, 589
Asturius, Roman aristocrat 603, 605
Asulari, Italy 391
Aswān, Egypt 22, 421, 422, 457,
    760–2, 764, 774, 796, 829

Asyūṭ (Lykopolis, Sioout), Egypt 134,
    252
Athanagild, Visigothic king 754
Athanasios bar Gūmōyē, aristocrat of
    Edessa 241, 621
Athanasios, duke of the Thebaid 413
Athens, Greece 12, 235 n.203, 626,
    630–1, 783, 786, 792
Atias, pagarch of Arsinoë, duke of the
    Thebaid 253, 441 n.127
Atlantic Ocean 5 n.5, 18, 38, 40, 43,
    229, 663, 794
Atlas mountains 18
Atripert, Italian landowner 555
Attaleia, *see* Antalya
Attalus, Roman aristocrat 161
Audeliana, Frankish aristocrat 283
Audoin, bishop of Rouen 399
Aufidianus, *fundus*, Tunisia 272
Augsburg, Germany 288, 300
Augustine, bishop of Hippo 20, 87,
    95 n.101, 159, 166, 473, 522–3,
    635
aula regia, in Cologne 678
aula, in Brittany 515
Aunefrid, *clericus* of Guamo 390
Aunemund, bishop of Lyon 606
Aurelios, status marker 414 n.77
Aurelius Tifzalis of Altava 336
Aurelius, king of the Asturias 584
Aurès mountains, Algeria 266
Ausonius of Bordeaux, Roman
    writer 164, 165, 173, 655
Austrasia, France/Germany 46, 104–5,
    112, 171–2, 186, 189–93, 198, 393,
    608, 678, 804, *see also* Francia
Austria 78 n.57, 461, 731
Austrian Academy of Sciences 461
Auteuil, France 402
Auvergne, France 200, 281 n.43,
    284 n.50, 290, 512
Auxerre, France 287, 400 n.39,
    608 n.34
Avars 30, 551
Avitacum, near Clermont, France 467
Aviti of Clermont, Roman senatorial
    family 167, 168, 170, 171, 172,
    173, 606

Avitus I, bishop of Clermont 167
Avitus II, bishop of Clermont 167, 606
Avitus, bishop of Vienne 167, 170, 679
Avitus, *see* Eparchius Avitus
Aydat, France 467
Ayla ('Aqaba), Jordan 132, 450, 614,
    618, 619, 623, 625

Badajoz, Spain 662
Badorf, Germany 801
Baetica, *see* Andalucía
Baeza, Spain 660
Bagaudae (Bacaudae), revolts of 473,
    520, 530–3, 585
Baghdad, Iraq 24, 29, 619, 689
Bagnall, Roger 22, 25, 65, 242, 244,
    414, 427, 554, 611
Bagratuni, Armenian aristocratic
    family 168
Bahnasā, *see* Oxyrhynchos
Bailey, Donald 759, 761
al-Balādhurī, Arab writer 8, 28, 132,
    141 n.219, 241, 301, 616, 621, 774
Bala'īza, *see* Apa Apollō
Balīkh, River 450, 457
Bālis, Syria 241, 301
Balkans 5, 30–1, 81, 126, 165, 338,
    463, 466, 534, 602, 627–8, 638,
    643, 786–7, 826
Ballet, Pascale 759
Balqā', Jordan 241, 450, 451, 456, 459,
    778
Baltic Sea 366, 681, 808
Banaji, Jairus 245, 274
Banū Hīlāl, Arab tribe 19, 305
Banū Qasī, Arab aristocrats in
    Spain 226
Bāra, Syria 443 n.1, 447 n.16, 448–9
Bararus, *see* Rougga
Barbero, Abilio 99, 231
Barceló, Miquel 230, 337
Barcelona, Spain 97, 656–8, 664
Barnwell, Paul 89
barrels, for transportation of
    goods 704, 735, *see also*
    amphorae
Barrow Hills, Oxfordshire,
    England 311

Barton Court Farm, Oxfordshire,
    England 311
Basel, Switzerland 393, 795
Basil I, Byzantine emperor 568
Basil, bishop of Caesarea 68 n.32, 159,
    462
Basilicata, *see* Lucania
Basilika, Byzantine law-code 463 n.60
Basilios, pagarch of Aphroditō 134–7,
    140, 144, 251–3, 454
Basilius, Roman aristocrat 206
Basques 5 n.5, 37, 38, 40, 81, 94, 99,
    227 n.187, 228, 338–9, 584, 753,
    756
Baṣra, Iraq 130
Baṣra, Morocco 727
Bassett, Steven 313, 320, 325, 345
baths 476, 594, 615, 618, 624, 641, 66
Bavaria, Germany 6 n.6, 45, 46, 118,
    122 n.165, 184–5, 191, 197–8,
    281, 283–4, 287, 288, 290, 300,
    339 n.86, 434, 510, 560 n.77, 562
Bayard, Didier 795
beads 808
Beauvais, France 187
Béconcelle, France 402
Bede, Anglo-Saxon writer 49, 50, 314,
    317–18, 323–4, 341–4, 347, 503,
    504 n.163, 568, 591, 681
beer 760
Begastri (Cehegín), Spain 742
Beirut, Lebanon 614, 621, 774, 789
Béja, Tunisia 639, 643, 689, 726
Bejsebakken, Denmark 369
Belalis Maior (Henchir el-Faouar),
    Tunisia 635, 637, 638, 639, 643,
    654, 727
Belezma mountains, Algeria 721
Belfast, Northern Ireland 9
Belgica Secunda 310
Belgium 42, 505, 509, 512, 576, 830–1
Belisarios, Roman general 20, 34, 87,
    89, 165, 602, 641
Bell, H. I. 415
Bellingegård, Denmark 497
Belmonte, Italy 479
belt (*cingulum/balteum*) 175
Benco, Nancy 727

Benedict Biscop 341
Benevento, Italy 35, 118, 120, 121, 203, 204, 217–18, 297, 577, 605, 606, 736, 737, 738, 740
Bensheim, Germany 394, 398
Beowulf 286 n.55, 343, 346, 374, 375
Beqa'a, Lebanon 26
Berbers 19, 21, 26, 39–41, 90, 91 n.93, 96 n.104, 101–2, 165 n.31, 168, 227, 230, 301–2, 305, 333–9, 492, 494, 551 n.55, 635, 642, 656, 689, 724, 727, 754–5
Berclingas 317
Bergama (Pergamon), Turkey 215, 605, 626, 629, 647, 648, 714
Berkeley, England 317
Berkshire, England 48
Berktay, Halil 60
Bernicia, England 48
Beroia, *see* Aleppo
Berry-au-Bac (Aisne), France 505
Bertram, bishop of Le Mans 174, 186–7, 189 n.96, 190, 191 n.100, 199, 214, 216, 218, 281–3, 286, 564
Besançon, France 176
Bet She'an, *see* Scythopolis
Beth Laha, Israel 455
Beule, France 402
Béziers, France 747
Bézu (Eure), France 401 n.41
Bible 159
Biddle, Martin 592
Bierzo, Spain 223, 604
Binchy, Daniel 52
Bingen, Germany 285
Birka, Sweden 681, 685, 688 n.210
birth control, *see* contraception
Bishopstone, Sussex, England 311
Bithynia 29, 31–2, 126, 164–5, 232, 234, 462, 792
Black Death 548, *see also* plagues
Black Forest, Germany 500, 580
Black Sea 31, 785, 788 n.168, 789
Blair, John 318, 320
Bleiber, Waltraut 289
Bloch, Marc 99, 121, 192, 277, 568
boat-building 768

Bobastro, Spain 494, 605
Bobbio, Italy 293, 299, 300
Bobigny, France 401, 403 n.46, 607
Bobo, Frankish *dux* 189
Bochonia, Germany 540
Bodilo, Frankish aristocrat 198
Bodo, Frankish peasant 405
Bodrum, Turkey 783
Boethius, Roman aristocrat 157, 205
Bognetti, Gianpiero 4
Böhme, Horst Wolfgang 309
Boiotia, Greece 466 n.68, 786
boni homines, 'good men' 567, 569, 600
Bonitus, bishop of Clermont 167, 176, 606, 680
Bonn, Germany 393, 509, 676
Bonnassie, Pierre 231, 571
Bonneau, Danielle 427
Book of Llandaff 328
bookland (*bocland*/charter-land) 315–18
Bordeaux, France 43–4, 164, 169, 171, 174, 186, 606, 746–7, 800 n.182
borghi, in Italy 592
Bornholm, Denmark 369, 816
Boserup, Ester 536, 537, 538, 550
Bosporos, Turkey 31, 234, 781, 783
Bostra (Buṣrā), Syria 450, 456, 613, 617 n.60, 618, 623–4, 672
boukellarioi/*buccellarii*, armed retainers 568
boulē, city council 594, 596, 600–1, *see also curia*
bouleutai/*politeuomenoi*, city councillors 69, 596–600, *see also curiales*
Bourdieu, Pierre 538
Bourg, near Bordeaux, France 171, 174
Bourgeois, Luc 401, 402
Bourges, France 106, 108, 109 n.133, 111
Bouzaiai, Turkey 409
Brād, Syria 443 n.1, 448
Braga, Portugal 221, 663
Braiding of Nîmes 195 n.109, 607

Braulio of Zaragoza, Spanish writer 95, 222, 223, 226, 604, 658
Brazil 260, 538
Breatnach, Liam 52
Brebières (Nord), France 506 n.169
brehons (*brithemoin*), Irish lawyers 357, 358
Breisgau, Germany 580
Brescia, Italy 34, 120, 212, 605, 644–9, 651–3, 666, 691–2, 731, *see also* S. Giulia
Breviary of Alaric 69, 526 n. 17
Brevium exempla 290, 299
bricks 763
bridge-making 409
Brie, France 190, 193, 607
brigandage 532 n.30
Bristol Channel 327
Britain 3, 11, 36, 47–50, 77, 79, 81, 113, 148, 155, 163, 169, 179, 182, 244, 258, 303–5, 306–23, 325, 331, 332–3, 337–8, **339–54**, 361, 371, **428–34**, 470, 475, 481, 502–4, 516, 520, 533–4, 549, 570, 595, 608, 695–6, 700, 719, 747, 757, 794–5, 805–15, 817–18, 826, *see also* England, Scotland, Wales
Britain, Roman 11, 47–8, 79, 155, 163, 303, 325–6, 686, 806, 814
Britanni, on the Loire 330
British School at Rome 482, 483
Brittany/Bretons 44–5, 102, 192, 200, 326, 338, 361, 511 n.183, 512, 513 n.188, 514–15, 517, 553, 567–8, 576
Brittonic, language 306
Brogiolo, Gian Pietro 647, 648
bronzework 700, 745
Brooks, Nicholas 315, 342
Brossay, France 282
Brown, Peter 408
Brown, Tom 206
Bruand, Olivier 289, 802
Brubaker, Leslie 601
Bruges, Belgium 688
Brühl, Carl-Richard 671
Brunhild, Merovingian queen 45

Bruttii (Calabria), Italy 165, 204, 206, 603, *see also* Calabria
Brycheiniog, Wales 328
Buckinghamshire, England 307 n.5
Bulgar, Spanish count 122 n.162
Bulgaria 30, 78, 465
bulk goods 696–7, 699–700, 704, 707, 709, 713, 718–19, 733–5, 738, 741, 746, 783, 788, 799, 800, 802 n.186, 804, 810–11, 817–19, 822
Bulla Regia, Tunisia 635, 638–9
Burgundofara, Frankish aristocrat 189 n.96
Burgundy 44–5, 46, 81, 84–5, 103, 107, 110, 169–72, 285, 400 n.39, 679 n.188, 795
burials 179, 225–6, 340–1, 367, 431, 557, 641, 743, 796, 807–8, *see also* cemeteries, graves
Bürstadt, Germany 394
Burunitanus, saltus (Souk el-Khmis), Tunisia 274
Butila, Gothic priest in Italy 85
Butler, H.C. 444
Butrint, Albania 630
Byrne, Francis John 52
Byzacena, *see* Tunisia
Byzantine empire/Byzantium 3, 11, 19, **29–32**, 35, 56–7, 70, 85, 89, 90, 94–6, **124–30**, 131, 144–6, 149–50, 154, 168, 184, 203–4, 207–8, 209, 211, 213, 225, 231, **232–40**, 241–2, 257–8, 268, **406–11**, 460, 463–4, 534, 535, 549, 573, 595, 601, 604, 619, 625, **626–35**, 636, 639, 640 n.121, 643, 654, 668, 691, 712, 717, 732, 736, 772, 774, **780–94**, 798, 804, 819, 823, 827–9
in Africa 207 n.141, 334–5, 604, 636, 638, 640, 642–3, 661, 671, 716, 721, 723–4, 726–7
in Egypt 427
in Greece 631, 786
in Italy 116, 204, 207–9, 211, 213, 225, 231, 234, 237, 239–40, 257, 480, 487–8, 605–6, 644, 648–50, 654, 690, 737–40

Byzantine empire/Byzantium (*cont.*)
in Sicily 208
in Spain 38, 659, 725, 745, 749, 754
in Syria-Palestine 777

Cáceres, Spain 743
Cadbury, Somerset, England 328 n.63
Cadog, Welsh saint 329
Caedwalla, king of Wessex 318
Caeionii, Roman senatorial family 159, 163
Caserta, Italy 205
Caesarea (Cherchel), Algeria 335, 637–8
Caesarea, Israel 26, 130, 240, 613–14, 616, 617 n.60, 618, 622, 625, 690, 705, 771 n.138, 772, 774–5, 778–9, 800
Caesarea (Kayseri), Turkey 451, 462 n.56
Caesariensis, *see* Mauretania Caesariensis
Caesarius, bishop of Arles 170, 240, 471, 551
Cagliari, Italy 645
Cahors, France 124, 186, 187, 190, 606
Cáin Aicillne 359
Cáin Sóerraith 359, 360
Cairo, *see* Fusṭāṭ
Cairo Geniza 612, 699, 726, 738, 765, 767
Calabria, Italy 33, 76, 208, 272, 486 n.123, 603, 655 n.151, 699, 708, 710, 730, 735, 737, 738, 741, *see also* Bruttii
Calahorra, Spain 226
Calais, France 809
Calama, Algeria 166
Calle di Tricarico, Italy 205
Callinicum, *see* Raqqa
Cambridgeshire, England 807, 810
Cammarosano, Paolo 211
Campania, Italy 33, 163, 164, 205–6, 208, 729–30, 735, 741
Campine, Belgium 509, 576, 830–1
Campione, Italy 297, 560–1, 565
Campori, Italy 568
Camps, Gabriel 337

Canada 340
Canche, River 682
Cantabria, Spain 94, 229
Canterbury, England 307, 318 n.38, 319 n.40, 321, 336, 346, 348, 686, 809
Capernaum, Israel 452
Capetians 393
capitalism 260, 694, 823
Capitolias (Bayt Rās), Jordan 614, 618, 623
Capitulare de villis, Frankish capitulary 267–8, 278, 289–90
Cappadocia, Turkey 31, 164, 232, 411, 461, 462
Capracorum, domusculta of 483
Silva Carbonaria, Belgium 512
Caria, Turkey 78, 239
Caribbean 260
Cariliacum, *see* Les Carriès
Carlisle, England 829
Carolingians 3, 5, 35, 45–6, 55, 81, 103–4, 106–7, 113, 117, 120, 122, 129 n.187, 145, 176, 181, 192–5, 199, 204, 237, 257, 267–8, 280, 288, 292, 294, 346, 364, 379, 393, 397, 399, 505, 507, 511–12, 517, 546–7, 563, 564 n.87, 569, 573, 574–7, 580, 581, 587, 650, 677–8, 680, 687, 689, 691, 702 n.16, 733, 736, 798, 800, 802–5, 822, 828, *see also* Francia
in Italy 11, 117, 120, 204, 209, 212, 294, 391
in southern Gaul 758
in Spain 391, 658, 755
Carrara, Italy 651
Carrié, Jean-Michel 25, 521–2, 524
Cartagena, Spain 94, 656, 659, 660, 712
Carthage, Tunisia 17, 21, 22, 24, 63, 76, 87–90, 115, 124, 204, 255, 272, 635, 639–43, 672, 690, 708 n.24, 709–11, 720–1, 723–7, 739, 783
Casale S. Donato, Italy 483, 555, 556 n.68
Casauria, Italy 296 n.79
Cashel, Ireland 52

Cassiodorii of Squillace, Roman
    aristocratic family 165
Cassiodorus 159, 160 n.17, 165, 172,
    206, 477, 566, 603
    Variae 36, 80, 92, 96, 115, 652,
    730
Castagnetti, Andrea 488
Casteldebole, near Bologna, Italy 480
Castelldwyran, Pembrokeshire,
    Wales 327
castellum, see castrum
Castelnuovo di Berardenga, Italy 484
Castile, Spain 572, 577, 578, 589
Castillo, Juan Carlos 490
castles 486, 493, 494, 516, 517, 594,
    see also castrum
castrum, castellum 473, 479–80, 486,
    488–9, 495, 649, 676, 680, 687,
    712
Cástulo, Spain 660
Catalayud, Spain 605
Catalonia, Spain 5 n.5, 37, 39, 44,
    94, 220, 227, 229, 474, 479, 488,
    489, 492, 493, 546, 569 n.99,
    571, 572, 577, 605, 656, 658, 663,
    664, 749, 755
cathedrals 594, 624, 626, 646, 647,
    652, 653, 657, 658, 661, 665, 667,
    675, 678, 685, 814
CATHMA 747
Catholicism 3–4, 20, 88
Catholme, Staffordshire,
    England 502 n.159, 503,
    814 n.208
Cato, *De agricultura* 289
cattle, in Ireland 356, 360–3, 542
Catuvellauni 332
célsine, Irish clientage 360
Celtic, culture 44, 352
Celtic, languages 311, 332
cemeteries 313, 474–5, 480, 501,
    503–4, 557, 575, 615, 680, 657,
    786–7, 806
Cenél nEógain, Irish people 52,
    305, 360
census, see tributum
censuses, in the Roman empire 70
centinarii 390 n.14

Centro Italiano di Studi sull'Alto
    Medioevo 1
Cenwulf, king of Mercia 303, 318 n.38,
    344–5, 350, 378, 813
ceorlas, peasants 319, 322, 323, 324,
    343, 349, 558
ceramics 9–10, 13, 79, 181–2, 184, 195,
    204–5, 209, 214, 219, 225–6,
    229 n.192, 230, 248, 254, 307,
    327, 328, 341, 355, 420 n.92, 421,
    449–51, 461 n.53, 472, 486,
    488–90, 493–4, 500, 502, 504–7,
    509–10, 544–6, 575, 617–18, 625,
    627, 635–6, 647, 659, 662, 664,
    670, 677, 680, 683, 685, 693,
    699–705, 728, 729, 731, 734–6,
    741, 745–6, 764–6, 770, 783, 787,
    795–6, 798, 810, 823
    acroma depurata 729
    amphorae, *see* amphorae
    Argonne ware 181, 504, 676 n.183,
        705, 795–7, 801
    Badorf ware 801, 803, 805
    brittle ware 773
    Candarlı ware 714
    carinated wares (*biconiques*) 181,
        796, 797, 798, 801
    central Greek Painted ware 782
    céramique granuleuse 798
    coarse wares 703, 732, 734–5, 744,
        747–8, 758, 763, 772–3, 775, 782,
        784, 795, 798, 809
    common wares 703, 727, 731, 735,
        743–4, 746–7, 749, 758, 762–3,
        770, 775, 782, 785
    dérivées des sigillées paléochrétiennes
        (DSP) 710, 742, 746–7, 795, 815
    fine wares 703, 705–6, 709, 712, 721,
        731, 736, 743, 746–7, 760–2,
        770–6, 778, 781–5, 795, 796–8,
        801
    Forum ware 482, 705, 734–6, 776
    glazed wares 703, 729, 731, 734–6,
        743–4, 746, 750, 762, 776, 793
    Glazed White Ware (GWW) 782–83,
        785–6, 787, 789, 792, 798
    hand-made 786–7, 806, 809–11,
        814–16

ceramics (*cont.*)
  'Illington-Lackford' group 807, 811
  Ipswich ware 545, 682 n.198, 686,
    705, 810–11
  Islamic wares 743, 746, 750, 775
  Jerash ware 774
  kaolinitique 747, 748, 758, 798
  LRA (1) 708, 714–16, 759, 760, 763,
    772, 774, 781, 783
  LRA (2) 708, 714–15, 717, 781, 783,
    785, 787–9
  LRA (3) 708, 714–15, 781, 783, 785
  LRA (4) 708, 714–15, 759–60,
    772 n.139, 774
  LRA (5) 708, 714–15, 717, 771,
    772 n.139, 774
  LRA (5/6) 713, 760, 762
  LRA (7) 713, 717, 760–1, 775
  Mafjar ware 775
  Mahesh ware 775
  Maxey ware 811
  Mayen ware (*rugueuse*) 181, 795–8,
    801, 803
  Painted wares 782, 786
  Piecrust Rim ware 782
  Red Painted ware 210, 727, 729–31,
    734, 735–7, 744, 763, 774–5, 796
  Red Slip ware 13, 453, 632, 639, 696,
    714–17, 729 n.68, 734, 760, 763,
    770–5, 776 n.151, 779, 781–4,
    791, 815, *see also* terra sigillata
  Red Slip, African (ARS) 210, 334,
    336–7, 480, 482, 706, 710–13,
    715–16, 720–31, 734, 736, 742,
    744, 746, 748, 758, 760–1, 770,
    772–4, 759, 761, 763, 772, 781,
    805
  Red Slip, Egyptian (ERS) 713–15,
    717, 760–1, 763, 770, 774–5;
    ERSH 761
  Red Slip, Phocaean 446, 632, *see also*
    Phocaea
  'Sancton-Baston' group 807
  semi-fine ware 734, 736, 742–3, 772,
    782, 792, 801
  Souterrain ware 355, 815, 816 n.210
  Spiral Burnished ware 782
  Tating ware 796, 801 n.186
terra nigra 796
terra sigillata hispánica tardía
    (TSHT) 13, 220, 230, 742–6
terra sigillata 13, 703, 709–10, 714,
    720 n.51, 721, 730, 770, 782, 784,
    794, *see also* Red Slip ware
  Yellow Clay ware 798
Cercadilla, Córdoba, Spain 661
Cethegus, consul 205–6
Cethegus, son of consul Cethegus 206
Chaalis, France 401
Chabrignac, France 284
Chadwick, H.M. 319, 321
Chael, son of Psmo, Egyptian
    headman 422
chalk 809
Chalkis (Qinnasrīn), Syria 449, 614
Chalon-sur-Saône, France 170
Champagne, France 103, 181, 184,
    191 n.100, 210, 286 n.56, 803
Chapelot, Jean 516
Chaptelat, France 606
Charibert, Merovingian king 80, 171
Charlemagne, Carolingian emperor 35,
    46–8, 57, 145, 120, 215, 256, 290,
    346, 365–7, 372, 395, 574, 578,
    580–1, 585–6, 673, 680, 687, 690,
    821–2
Charles Martel, Frankish mayor of the
    palace 46, 104–5, 124, 195–6,
    197 n.115
Charles the Bald, Carolingian
    emperor 150 n.228, 586–7
Charles II, king of England 153
Charnwood Forest, England 811
Chaussy, France 188
Cherchel, *see* Caesarea
Chertsey, England 318, 322, 325,
    337
Chianti, Italy 392, 484–5, 494, 515,
    546, 577, 739
Chicago, University of 419, 420
Childebert II, Merovingian king 108,
    122 n.163, 183, 198
Childebert III, Merovingian king 105,
    109
Childeric II, Merovingian king 46,
    105

Chilperic, Merovingian king 80, 107, 111, 533, 551 n.54, 554 n.64, 675, 799

China 133, 158, 514, 776, 823 n.216

Chindasuinth, Visigothic king 39, 94–5, 221, 223, 752

Chios, Greece 781, 785

Chiragan, near Toulouse, France 466, 469

Chittolini, Giorgio 592

Chlochilaich, Danish King 54 n.53

Chlotar I, Merovingian king 108

Chlotar II, Merovingian king 45, 106, 112, 113, 176, 187, 188 n.93, 196, 197, 346, 799

Chlotar III, Merovingian king 579

Chorazin, Israel 452

Chorikios of Gaza, Roman writer 240, 622

chōrion, village, 463, 488

Chramnelen, *dux* in Francia 176

Chramnesind, Frankish aristocrat 178, 511

Christianity 4, 11, 38, 40–1, 46, 48, 50, 53–4, 180, 202–3, 257, 306, 346, 752, 776, 825

Christopher, pagarch of Herakleopolis 251

Chronicle of 754 100, 101

Chronicon of Alfonso III 584

chrysargyron, tax 522

Chulberta, Frankish peasant 401

Chur, Switzerland 200, 501

Churchill, Winston 153

Cicilianus, Italy 483 n.111

Cilicia, Turkey 26, 76, 445, 449, 460, 708, 714, 783

circumcelliones, in Africa 473

città ad isole 640, 652, 658, 665, 668, 671, 676–8

city councils, *see boulē, curia, sigma*

city walls 594, 622, 626, 638, 641, 646–7, 653, 662, 666–7, 675–6, 679

city, definition of 591–6

Cividale, Italy 650

Civil War, English 3, 12

Claessen, Henri 57

Claude, Dietrich 3, 201, 700, 701

Claudius, *dux* of Mérida 222

Clementina of Naples, Roman aristocrat 581, 582

Cleopatra, Egyptian pharaoh 24

Clermont, France 105 n.123, 107–8, 110, 168, 170–2, 174, 192 n.103, 197, 213, 276, 467, 510, 512, 598, 606, 667, 676, 679–80

Clichy, France 193, 399
  Council of (626–7) 112

Cliviano, Sabina, Italy 573

clothmaking 700–4, 725–6, 734, 761, 763, 766, 771–2, 783, 800, 802, 804, 807–8, 816 n.210, *see also* textiles

Clovis, Merovingian king 44–5, 48, 94, 103–4, 179, 180, 182, 184, 187, 194–5, 310, 358, 370, 403, 675, 797

Clovis II, Merovingian king 176

Clunia, Spain 663

Codex Theodosianus 30, 66, 711

Codice Bavaro 279 n.42

coemptio 75, 271

Cogitosus, *Vita S. Brigitae* 358

coinage 125, 446, 449, 488, 629, 638, 666 n.171, 680–1, 684, 702, 735 n.86, 736–7, 768, 802, 809–10

Cologne, Germany 44, 46, 102–3, 285, 307, 393, 509, 677, 678, 680–1, 685, 687, 689, 801–2

coloni adscripticii, see adscripticii

coloni, tenants 269, 273, 274, 279, 521–7, 529, 535, 559, 562–3, 580

Columella, Roman writer 263–4, 268, 466

Comacchio, Italy 690, 732, 733

comites, see counts

commendati 573

Como, Lake, Italy 582

comparatio 271

Compiègne, France 104, 193, 399

Compludo, monastery, Spain 99

Complutum, Spain 662

concilium, assembly in Saxony 585–6

Conda, Frankish aristocrat 194

conductores 270–1

coniurationes 581

Connaught, Ireland 52
Constans, son of Constantine III 220
Constans II, Byzantine emperor 125, 407, 629
Constantine I, emperor 29
Constantine III, emperor 220
Constantine V, Byzantine emperor 31, 127, 631, 634, 791
Constantinople, Turkey 20–1, 29–31, 33, 35, 72–3, 75–6, 78–9, 124–6, 129, 131, 149, 154 n.4, 155, 157, 161, 163–6, 193, 206, 208, 232, 234–6, 238, 240 n.215, 248, 257, 406, 408, 412, 447, 461 n.53, 462, 548, 602, 604, 608, 620, 626, 632–4, 655, 674, 679, 690, 701, 708, 712–16, 724–5, 736–7, 767–8, 778, 780–5, 787–8, 789–93, 827
Constantius, *Vita Germani* 334 n.76
contraception 538, 550, 557 n.71
Contrada Saraceno, near Agrigento, Italy 478
contubernia 513
conviva regis 196
Copenhagen, Denmark 367
copperwork 355, 618, 700, 742 n.95, 783, 815
Coptic, culture 24, 415
Coptic, language 134, 168, 420, 422, 600
Corbie, France 300, 800
Corbon, France 402 n.42, 404 n.50
Cordillera Cantábrica, Spain 491
Córdoba, Spain 37–9, 94, 99, 101–2, 126, 226–27, 229, 490–1, 494, 584 n.126, 656, 660–1, 673–4, 689, 742, 744, 754
Corinth, Greece 626, 630–1, 783, 786, 792
Corippus, Roman writer 21
Cormery, France 289 n.65, 580
Cornino, Italy 215, 216
Cornwall, England 814–15
Coroticus, British ruler 331 n.71
Corsica, France 216
corvées 273–4, 278–80, 294–9, 300 n.86
Corvey, Germany 586

Council of the Seven Provinces 161 n.19
Courtois, Christian 87, 337
Cowdery's Down, Hampshire, England 341, 370, 429 n.113, 503, 515
crannógs 354
Crawford, J.S. 634
Crecchio, Italy 736
Cremona, Italy 733
Crete, Greece 31, 628, 781–3, 785, 786–7, 792
Crimea, Ukraine 785
Crispinus, bishop of Calama 166
Críth Gablach 359
Croatia 338 n.84
Crone, Patricia 143
crop rotations 538
Cruithni, Irish people 305
Crum, Walter 420
Cunedda, Welsh king 168 n.37
Cunimund of Sirmione, Italian aristocrat 605
Cunipert, Lombard king 120, 565
curator 597
curia, city council 594, 596–9, 600–2, 615, 622, 637, 642, 646, 652, 657, 669, *see also boulē*
curiales, councillors 62–3, 68, 69, 84, 156, 167–8, 524, 596, 598 n. 10, 599, *see also bouleutai*
curtis ducalis 646, 648, 652
curtis regia 646
Cyprus 76, 78, 445, 714–16, 717 n.46, 759, 760, 770, 782–3, 787–9
Cyrenaica, Libya 6 n.6, 333, 465
Cyril of Scythopolis, Roman writer 276
Cyrrhus, Syria 240, 447

Dagobert I, Merovingian king 45–6, 104, 106, 109, 113, 124, 176, 188 n.93, 198, 399
Dagobert II, Merovingian king 112 n.144
Dál Ríata, Irish-Scottish kingdom 52
Damascus, Syria 26, 28, 130–2, 136, 140, 241, 450, 465–6, 511, 603,

Damascus, Syria (*cont.*)
614, 616–17, 619, 620–1, 634, 672, 689, 771, 774, 778–80, 793
Damietta, Egypt 765
Danegeld 150
Danelaw, England 813
Danevirke, Danish defensive dyke 54, 366
Dankirke, near Ribe, Denmark 370, 373, 817
Dannenbauer, Heinrich 185
Danube, River 30, 34, 45, 74, 77–9, 81, 115, 191, 290, 333, 708, 716, 781, 786
Daphnē, near Antioch, Turkey 454
dar al-Islām 21
Dardanelles, Turkey 31, 129 n.186, 783
Davies, Wendy 50, 313, 328, 353, 512
De fisco Barcinonensi 96–7, 664
Dead Sea 451 n.25, 771
Decapolis 26, 614, 616, 623–4, 770 n.135, 773–5, 777
Decii, Roman senatorial family 159, 206
decuriones, see curiales
Deerhurst, Gloucestershire, England 317
Dēhes, Syria 444–6, 448–50, 772 n.140, 773
Deir al-Zōr, Syria 770
Deir Sim'an, Syria 444
Deira, England 48, 313
Dejbjerg, Denmark 373 n.163
Delogu, Paolo 116, 732
Delphi, Greece 630, 782
Delta, of the River Nile, Egypt 22, 23, 131, 138, 140, 141, 250, 251, 254, 421, 460, 760, 765, 767
demesne (*pars dominica*) 263, 272–3, 273–80, 288–91, 536, 586, 722, 803, *see also* feudal mode of production
Demetae, *see* Dyfed
Demetrios of Thessaloniki, S., *Miracles* of 129, 238, 599, 788
demography 538–9, 547–50, 830
demons 408–9
Denmark 2, 5, 14, 17, 44, 53–5, 56, 303, 304, 312, 339–40, 342, 355,

364–76, 376–9, 428 n.112, 496–9, 500–1, 503–4, 514–15, 517, 540, 545, 552, 572, 587, 682, 684–8, 805, 813, 816–17, 818, 823
Dennett, Daniel 132
Deodatus, bishop of Siena 392
derbfine, kin-group in Ireland 552
Desenzano, Italy 466
Desiderius, bishop of Cahors 124, 176, 188 n.93, 189 n.96, 190, 196 n. 112, 606, 668, 679 n.188, 758
Desiderius, *dux* of Albi 176, 196 n.112
Desiderius, Lombard king 118, 214 n. 160, 583, 648
Devroey, Jean-Pierre 286, 289, 550
Díarmait mac Cerbaill, Irish king 52
Dido, bishop of Poitiers 197 n.114
Didymus, Roman aristocrat 220
Diego Álvaro, Spain 39, 223–5, 228, 231, 247, 252, 267, 526, 604, 756–7
Dienheim, Germany 394–8, 437, 502, 513, 547, 562, 567
Dijon, France 190, 579, 592, 676, 795
Dimashq, Arab province 779
Dinas Powys, Wales 815
Diocletian, emperor 62, 448 n.18, 521, 596, 701
Dioskoros of Aphroditō, Egyptian notable 139 n.212, 249, 250, 253, 411, 413, 415, 421, 427, 440
Dodo, Frankish aristocrat 178
Doherty, Charles 52
dokimoi 637
Domburg, Netherlands 682
Domesday Book 349, 350, 353, 674
dominicus/-atus 273, 283
Domminger, Folke 500
Domna, *see* Julian and Domna
Domnolus, bishop of Le Mans 282
domuscultae 297, 483, 486
Donatism 20, 88, 166, 530 n.23
Donegal, Ireland 52
Donnchad mac Domnaill, Irish king 358 n.134
Dopsch, Alfons 1, 2, 4, 559
Dordogne, France 286

Dorestad (Wijk bij Duurstede), Netherlands 682–5, 687, 688–92, 801–3, 818
Dougga (Thugga), Tunisia 637–8, 640 n.120, 721, 724, 727
Doukai, Byzantine aristocratic family 237
Dover, England 808
Down, Ireland 815
Droitwich, Worcestershire, England 348, 814
dryhten, Anglo-Saxon lord 375
Dublin, Ireland 9
Duby, Georges 1, 293
Duero, River 37, 220, 227, 230, 584, 742, 756
Dumio, near Braga, Portugal 221
Dumville, David 342
Dunbarton, Scotland 331 n.71
Durliat, Jean 81–2, 116, 286, 446
Dust Veil (of 536) 549 n.50
Duval, Noël 639–40
Duyūk, Israel 455
dyeing 618, 771, 783, 807
Dyer, Christopher 517
Dyfed, Wales 48, 305, 326–7, 332, 337

Ealhmund, *gesith*, village notable of Malling 429–32
Eanswith, English tenant 348
earthquakes 13, 27, 443, 615, 616, 617, 620, 623, 625, 770 n.135, 777
East Anglia, England 48, 50, 310, 312–14, 343, 377, 495, 508, 545, 686, 809–14, 818, 823
Éauze, France 174, 607
Eberulf, *cubicularius* in Francia 183, 675
Ebro, River 37, 39, 94, 220, 222–3, 225–27, 229–30, 530–2, 599, 600, 604, 663, 689, 741–2, 755
Ebroin, Frankish mayor of the palace 46, 104, 193, 401 n.40
Ecdicius, Roman general 167–8, 174, 193 n.103, 220, 598
Ecgbert, bishop of York 317, 347
Ecgfrith, king of Mercia 324, 346

Echternach, Luxembourg 186, 285, 286, 576
Écija, Spain 660
Edessa (Urfa), Turkey 240–2, 276 n.35, 522, 598, 603, 614, 616, 619, 621, 625, 697, 777
Edfū *see* Apollonopolis
Edinburgh, Scotland 285
Edward the Elder, king of England 318 n.37
Egadi islands, Italy 737
Egica, Visigothic king 95, 97 n.106, 142, 526
Egloff, Michel 759
Egypt 5, 11, 12, 14, 21, 22–5, 28– 30, 32–3, 36, 41, 61, 64–6, 69–78, 92, 101, 124–6, 130–2, 133–44, 146–7, 149, 165–6, 168, 206, 232, 238, 241, 242–55, 256–9, 264, 266–9, 272–8, 293, 302, 324, 384 n. 3, 413, 427, 441, 443, 457, 459–60, 462, 499, 514, 517, 523–4, 527, 532, 534–5, 548, 551, 553–4, 558, 564–8, 585, 589, 595, 599–601, 603, 606, 608, 609–12, 617 n.60, 625, 636, 643, 645, 649, 668, 688, 695, 701, 705–6, 708–9, 713–17, 719, 725–6, 728, 736, 759–69, 770, 776–7, 779–80, 783, 793–4, 798, 799, 803–5, 819, 821–3, 826–8, *see also* Arabs in Egypt, ceramics: Egyptian Red Slip, Roman empire in Egypt
Eifel mountains, Germany 509, 682, 702, 795, *see also* quernstones
Einhard, Frankish writer 529, 680
Ekloga, Byzantine law-code 127, 463
El Bovalar, Spain 488–9, 749
El Castellar, Spain 743
El Castillón de Montefrío, Spain 490, 744–5
El Mahrine, Tunisia 720–1, 726
El Tolmo de Minateda, Spain 659, 742, 744 n.99, 749–50, 754
Elariacum (Larrey), France 579, 582–4, 589
Elbe, River 685

Elephantinē (Aswān), Egypt 609–10, 760–1, *see also* Aswān
Eligius of Limoges, bishop of Noyon 8, 103, 108–9, 176, 568, 606
Elizabeth, daughter of Epiphanios, Egyptian notable 424
Elousa (Ḥaluẓa), Israel 452, 455, 614
Elvira, Spain 660, *see also* Granada
embolē 244–5, *see also annona*
embroidery 808
Emesa (Ḥimṣ), Syria 26, 130, 240, 614, 616, 621, 778–9
Emilia, Italy 118 n.154, 204 n.132, 293, 471, 480, 540 n.40
emporia 292, 342, 366, 375, 591, 594, 680–8, 690, 803, 805, 809–11, 816
Emporio, Chios, Greece 785
Empuries, Spain 658
En Boqeq, Israel 771
enapographoi geōrgoi 523, *see also adscripticii*
enclosures 341, 354, 429, 496, 499–502, 504, 513, 552–3
Engels, Friedrich 259
England 2, 5–7, 44, 47–50, 53–6, 150, 265, 290, 302, 306–26, 339–51, 428–34, 502–4, 537, 540, 543–5, 548–9, 567, 570–1, 578, 593, 674, 682, 685, 687–8, 695, 706, 801–2, 805–14, 823, *see also* Anglo-Saxon England, Britain
English Channel 683, 803, 807, 817, 826
English, language 48
Ennen, Edith 592
Ennodii, Roman aristocratic family 165
Ennodius, bishop of Pavia 80, 159 n.15, 170, 477
Eodimia, Frankish tenant 404 n.51
Eóganacht Chaisil, Irish people 360
Eóganachta, Irish royal family 52, 357
eorlas 323
Epachius of Riom, Roman notable 512
eparch 601
Eparchius Avitus, emperor 160–1, 167–8, 174
Ephesos, Turkey 626–30, 633, 781, 788, 792

Epimachos, pagarch of Aphroditō 135 n.200, 251
Épinay, France 400
Epiphania (Ḥamā), Syria 26, 240, 614, 621
Epiphanios, Egyptian abbot 421, 423, 427 n.107
Epiphanios, Egyptian notable 424
Epiros, Greece 164
Ercamberta, *see* Wademir
Erchinoald, Frankish aristocrat 193
Erfo, duke of Friuli 214 n.160
Ergyng (Ariconium), Welsh kingdom 328–9
Ermansuind, Bavarian peasant 556
Ermenold, Frankish tenant 404
Ermentrudis, wife of Bodo, Frankish tenant 405
Ermina, abbess of Ören in Trier 190 n.96, 608
Erminethrudis of Paris, Frankish landowner 189 n.96, 285, 287, 401, 403, 607
Ermont (Greek Hermōnthis, Arabic Armant), Egypt 254 n. 254, 419, 422, 426, 441
Ervig, Visigothic king 39, 95, 97, 98, 99, 100
Eski Foça, Turkey 781, *see also* Phocaea
Esmonde-Cleary, Simon 308, 309
Espaly, France 174
Essex, England 310, 313, 314, 503, 508, 685, 810, 814
estate, definition of, 319
Étampes, France 188
Euchaita, Turkey 630, 640
Eucherius, bishop of Orléans 120, 197
Eudoxius, doctor in Gaul 530
Eugenius, landowner in Gaul 282
Eugippius, *Vita Severini* 339 n.86
Eukraoi, Turkey 408, 409, 529
Euphēmia, Egyptian landowner 609
Euphrates, River 26, 28, 78, 131, 240–1, 301, 446, 449, 450, 621, 770, 772–3, 779
Euphronius, bishop of Tours 172
Euric, Visigothic king 44, 85, 176
European Science Foundation 1, 82

Eusebius, merchant in Gaul 799
Eustochius, Roman lawyer 522
Eutolmios, notable in Anatolia
   408–10
Eutropius, Roman writer 531 n.26
Evagrios, Roman writer 548
Everett, Nick 116
Évreux, France 188
Ewig, Eugen 4, 114
exchange, definition of **694–700**
Exeter, England 47
exiles 347 n.104
Expositio totius mundi 78
Exuperantius, Roman general 530
Eynsham, England 318 n.38

Fabech, Charlotte 368
fairs 799
Faith, Rosamond 320, 329, 347, 349,
   571
family, nuclear 551–2
fara, Lombard kin-group 552 n.57
Faremoutiers, France 193
Farfa, Italy 217, 296–7, 582–3, 482–3,
   606
Farmer's law (*Nomos geōrgikos*) 457,
   462–4, 514
Faronids, Frankish aristocratic
   family 190, 191 n.98, 193, 507,
   607, *see also* Agilolfings
Fatimids, Arab ruling family 623
Faustus, bishop of Riez 177–8, 206
Fayyūm, Egypt 142 n.222, 245,
   255 n.256, 459, 610, 761, 765
feasting 195–6, 201, 333, 357 n.130,
   362
Feddersen Wierde, Germany 498–9
Feidlimid mac Crimthainn, Irish
   king 358 n.134, 378
Felix III, pope 160
Feller, Laurent 571
Fens, England 812
Fertile Crescent 28, 29, 621
Fès, Morocco 18, 22, 336, 619, 689
Festugière, André-Jean 407
feudal mode of production 391,
   535–6, 539–47, 558, 571–2, 578,
   583, 587, 589

feudalism, feudal society 6, 7, 9, 60–1,
   304–6, 379, 570–1, 577–8, 586
feud 551
Février, Paul-Albert 646
Fidelis, bishop of Mérida 222
Fidenza, Italy 645, 647
field systems 308–9, 311, 332, 497,
   517, 549
Filasṭīn, Arab province 779
Filattiera, Italy 484
Filibert of Jumièges 607, 816 n.210
Finberg, H.P.R. 319
Finley, Moses 700
Firdawsī, *Shāhnāma* 242
Firmus, Roman aristocrat 334
fishing rights 582
fitna, in Spain 494, 577, 754
flamen perpetuus 637
Flanders, Belgium 570, 797, 801, 818
Flaochad, aristocrat in Burgundy 120
Flavigny, France 110, 285 n.54
Flavios, status marker 414
flax 765
Fleury (St-Benoit-sur-Loire),
   France 400 n.39
Flexum, Italy 582–3, 589
Flivenasa, near Auxerre, France 287
Flixborough, England 320, 341, 370,
   811, 814
Flodoard of Reims, *Historia Remensis
   ecclesiae* 181, 607
Florence, Italy 126, 215, 645, 651, 652,
   735, 764
Florentinus, Roman writer 80
Fontenay, France 282
Foote, Rebecca 618, 619
Fordwich, England 808
forestis 540
Forêt de Sénart, France 402
Formulae Andecavenses 174 n.53, 510
Formulae Arvernenses 174 n.53, 510
Formulae Marculfi 111, 112, 123, 287,
   399 n.36, 439, 511
Formulae Wisigothicae 225
forum 594, 598, 636–40, 643, 646,
   651–3, 657, 665–6, 669, 671–2,
   677–8, *see also* agora
Fos, France 689

Foss, Clive 461, 613, 628
Fossier, Robert 293, 516, 571
Fouracre, Paul 194, 197
France 2, 4, 42, 479, 496, 549, 553,
    592, 593, 645
Francia 5, 6, 11, 34–6, 38, 41–7, 49,
    53–4, 81–2, 84, 86, 95, 99, 100,
    102–15, 117–24, 145, 148–50,
    168–203, 206, 209, 212, 225,
    255–6, 264–5, 267, 280–93, 296,
    298–302, 316, 324, 346, 353,
    364–7, 369–70, 372, 375–9, 387,
    393–406, 500, 503–4, 505–14, 515,
    517, 533–4, 540, 545, 547, 552,
    554, 561 n.78, 562, 564–5, 570–1,
    573–6, 579, 581, 586–7, 595, 601,
    605, 643, 654–5, 665–8, 671,
    674–81, 682, 685, 687, 691, 706,
    733–4, 739, 747–8, 752, 759, 793,
    794–805, 807–12, 814, 815,
    817–18, 821, 823, 826–8, *see also*
    Austrasia, Carolingians, Franks,
    Gaul, Germany, Merovingians,
    Neustria
Frankfurt, Germany 393, 394,
    702 n.16
Frankish annals 365, 366
Franks, Germanic people 39, 44, 45, 46,
    797, *see also* Francia
Fredegar, Frankish writer 104,
    106 n.128
Fredegund, Merovingian
    queen 154 n.4, 108, 568
Frederic, Visigothic aristocrat 530
Freise, Eckhard 396, 397
Freising, Germany 556
French Revolution 3, 12
French, language 18, 48
frérèches, groups of brothers 553
Frier, Bruce 23, 611
frilingi/liberi, free men in
    Saxony 585–6, 587
Frisia, Netherlands 5, 53, 312, 365,
    370, 376, 377, 498–9, 500, 503,
    514, 684, 685, 687, 799 n.181,
    801, 802, 817
Frithuwold, sub-king of Surrey 318
Friuli, Italy 214 n.160, 551, 731

Fructuosus of Braga, abbot 99, 100,
    526 n.16
Fulda, Germany 186, 394, 395, 397,
    540
Fulgentius, bishop of Ruspe 89, 91
fundi, Roman units of
    ownership 470–3, 487, 488
Fussala, Algeria 473
Fusṭāṭ (Cairo), Egypt 24, 25, 130,
    134–6, 138–9, 140 *and* n.215, 144,
    250 n.248, 251, 253, 422, 459,
    610–12, 689, 762, 765, 767, 769,
    779, 793
Fustel de Coulanges, N.D. 521
Fyn, Denmark 53, 54, 365, 368, 369,
    372, 374, 816–17

Gadara (Umm Qays), Jordan 613,
    623–4
Gaeta, Italy 738
Gafsa, Tunisia 639
Gaidoald of Pistoia, Italian
    aristocrat 214 n.160, 215
Galatia, Turkey 164, 232, 406–7,
    410–11, 418, 439, 440, 461, 514,
    535, 567, 599
Galicia, Spain 37–8, 40, 81, 94, 227,
    656, 663, 756
Galilee, Israel 26, 452, 455, 614, 623,
    773, 778
Galilee, Sea of 774
Galinduste, Spain 224
Galinié, Henri 675
Galla Placidia, empress 154 n.4
García Moreno, Luís A. 99
Garda, Lake, Italy 466, 486 n.123,
    605
gardingi, armed retainers, in Spain 569
Garfagnana, Italy 484
Garnsey, Peter 525
Garonne, River 43, 171, 173, 607,
    758
garum, fish sauce 37, 704, 710,
    733 n.80, 748
Gascou, Jean 64, 65
gasindi, armed retainers, in Italy 569
Gasparri, Stefano 117
Gaudiosus, Italian peasant 392–3

Gaul 5, 10, 11, 34, 41–7, 49, 61,
  66 n.22, 69–70, 77, 79, 80, 86,
  94–5, 102–15, 148, 159–66,
  168–203, 216–17, 234, 244, 257,
  268, 277, 280–93, 309–10, 331,
  346, 378, 393–406, 469–70, 473,
  475–7, 479, 485–6, 488, 492,
  505–14, 516, 526, 528, 530–1,
  533–4, 539, 547–8, 550–1, 562–4,
  579, 582–4, 589, 598–9, 603, 608,
  635, 665–8, 669, 671–2, 674–81,
  709–11, 713, 741, 746–51, 757–8,
  773, 794–805, 806–7, 823, 826, *see
  also* Francia, Merovingians,
  Carolingians
Gausprand, son of Peredeus 389
Gaza, Palestine 26–7, 69, 144,
  240–1, 266, 276, 452–3, 458, 614,
  616, 622, 625, 706, 714, 759,
  771–2, 774, 776–7, 779, 793, 820
Geiseric, Vandal king 20, 87–88, 91–2,
  131
gelfine, kin-group in Ireland 552
Gelichi, Sauro 639
Gelimer, Vandal king 9
Gello, Italy 294
Gemeinfreie 551 n.54, 570
gemot, Anglo-Saxon assembly 431
genera, kin-groups 552
Geneva, Switzerland 44, 172, 665, 667,
  668
Geniza, *see* Cairo Geniza
Gennep, Netherlands 507 n.172
Genoa, Italy 203
Genovefa, Roman ascetic 103, 184
George, author of *Life* of Theodore of
  Sykeōn 324, 406, *see also*
  Theodore of Sykeōn
George, headman of Nessana 454
George, senior official of Apion estates
  in Egypt 246, *see also* Victor
geōrgoi, peasants 523, 558
Gerald of Aurillac 200, 557 n.70, 573
Gerasa (Jerash), Jordan 133 n. 193,
  613, 616–18, 623–4, 672, 688, 773,
  778
German, language 168, 420
Germania 794

Germanic society, politics, kingdoms 2,
  60, 80–4, 176, 311, 326, 333, 352,
  515, 829, *see also* Romano-
  Germanic kingdoms
Germanos, Egyptian notable 424, 425
Germanus, abbot of Grandval 607–8
Germanus, bishop of Auxerre 532
Germany 2, 20, 42, 44–5, 49, 53–4,
  496, 498, 501, 503, 538, 562, 592,
  645, 806, 818, *see also* Alemannia,
  Bavaria, Francia, Saxony
Gernsheim, Germany 393
Gerticos, Spain 223
gesith, gesithcundman, Anglo-Saxon
  aristocrat 153, 429–32
gesta municipalia (gesta publica) 70, 97,
  110
Gewissae 305, *see also* Wessex
Ghent, Belgium 688
Ghirza, Libya 333, 334
Ghittia, Italian nun 217
Giardina, Andrea 269
Gibraltar 37, 335
gift-exchange 175, 196, 374, 389 n.11,
  391, 429, 537–9, 541–2, 544, 551,
  558, 571, **694–6**, 702 n.16, 807–8,
  818
Giglio, Stefano 156
Gildas, British writer 50, 309, 327, 331
Gildo, governor of Africa 124, 165, 334
Girona 489 n.131
Gisulf of Lodi, Italian
  landowner 214 n.160
Gladbach, Germany 503
Glamorgan, Wales 328, 351
glasswork 373, 696 n.8, 700–3,
  764 n.130, 774 n.145, 783, 802,
  804, 808, 809, 815, 817
Glavendrup, Denmark 374
Gloucestershire, England 564 n.86
Glywysing (Glamorgan and Gwent),
  Wales 48, 326, 351
Goar, Alan king 530
goðar, Icelandic political leaders 373,
  432 n.118, 542, 559
Godin, Frankish aristocrat 198 n.119
Godofrid, king of Denmark 55, 365–7,
  369, 375, 378–9

goðorð, *see goðar*
Gœrsdorf, France 511
Goetz, Hans-Werner 405
Goffart, Walter 84–6, 101, 106, 112, 116, 533
Göksu, River, Turkey 782 n.157
goldwork 126, 696–7, 701, 734, 764, 768, 808, 815 n.209, 817
Goltho, England 348
Gómez, Antonio 490
Gorges, Jean-Gérard 220
Gorm, Danish king 54, 366
Gormaz, Spain 605
Gortyn, Crete, Greece 31, 626, 628, 629, 782, 785, 786, 787
Gorze, France 285, 286
Gothic war in Italy 35–6, 45, 115, 160, 203, 205, 209, 278, 474, 477, 478 n.96, 533, 649, 652, 654, 719, 725, 730, 777
Goths 34, 206, 225, 533, 604, *see also* Ostrogoths, Visigoths
Goudelancourt-les-Pierrepont (Aisne), France 504–6, 796, 807
Gózquez (Madrid), Spain 743
Grado, Italy 203, 731, 733
Grahn-Hoek, Heike 184, 185
grain production 10, 43, 64–5, 76, 79, 291–2, 295, 696–7, 699–701, 704, 708–9, 711–12, 721, 725, 729–30, 737, 741, 761, 766, 768, 784, 788–91, 802–3
Gramsci, Antonio 440
Granada, Spain 230, 481, 490, 493, 494, 660, 744, 745, 750
graves 179, 181–2, 557, *see also* burials, cemeteries
Greece 3, 30–3, 230, 262, 277, 415, 465–6, 482, 543, 608, 626–8, 630–2, 751, 780–1, 786–8, 792, 823, 826, *see also* Aegean, Byzantium
Greek, language 24, 134, 168, 241, 258, 275, 276, 421–2, 560, 600
Gregorius, exarch of Africa 21
Gregory of Nyssa, Roman writer 462
Gregory, bishop of Tours 8, 41, 104, 107–8, 111–13, 116, 171–2, 174,
177, 179, 182, 184, 194, 198, 202, 276, 510–11, 513–14, 548, 566, 573, 579, 666, 675–76, 679–80, 799, 800, 801 n.184
Gregory the Dekapolite, *Life* of 788
Gregory the Great, pope 36, 70, 159, 160, 164, 166, 204–6, 208, 247, 266, 270–1, 276, 278, 280, 297, 582
Grimoald, Frankish mayor of the palace 46, 400–1
Grubenhäuser, sunken-floored dwellings 179, 307, 310, 476, 496, 500–2, 504–5, 647, 677, 686
gsur (Classical Arabic *quṣūr*) 333
Guadalquivir, River 37, 40, 220, 226, 230–1, 490, 546, 660, 663, 741–2, 744, 745, 751, 753–4
Guadiana, River 37, 660
gualdus 339 n.86, 540, 582, 583
Guamo, Italy 294, 390
Gudme, Fyn, Denmark 53, 54, 55, 368, 369, 371, 817
Guichard, Pierre 230
Guidonids, Frankish family 192
Guipúzcoa, Spain 227 n.190
Gulf of Syrtis 17, 465
Gundoin, Frankish aristocrat 193 n.104
Gunduald of Campori, Italian notable 212 n.154, 606
Gundulf, *dux* of Austrasia 172, 176
Gunthar, Frankish tenant 404
Gunthram Boso, Frankish duke 183
Guntram, Merovingian king 579
Gurna, Egypt 421, 763
Gutiérrez, Sonia 489, 660, 749–50
Gwent (Venta), Wales 327–9, 337, 351
Gwynedd, Wales 48, 326–7, 330
gynaecaea, female textile workshops 802

Hadley, Dawn 320, 813
Hadrian I, pope 297
Hadrian's Wall, England 5 n.5, 47, 306, 309, 332 n.72
Haïdra, *see* Ammaedara
al-Ḥakam II, caliph of al-Andalus 102

Haldon, John 60, 127–8
Halmyris (Independenţa), Romania
    781
Halsall, Guy 506, 557, 575
Hamerow, Helena 500, 504
Hammamet (Pupput), Tunisia 720, 727
Hampshire, England 48, 515, 684, 813
Hamwic (Southampton), England 320,
    342, 593, 681–6, 691, 801, 809–10,
    817
Harald Blåtand (Bluetooth), Danish
    king 54, 366
Hardy, E.R. 243, 245
Harodos, Lombard aristocratic
    family 211
Harūn al-Rashīd, caliph 621
Harvington, England 348
Hatshepsut, Egyptian pharaoh 421
Haute-Garonne, France 469
Hautvillers, France 607
Hávamál 374
Hawran, Syria/Jordan 443, 450–1,
    456–9, 778
Hayes, John 727
Heather, Peter 83
Hedeager, Lotte 367, 368
Hedeby, Germany 54, 366–7, 371, 378,
    681, 816
Heinzelmann, Martin 510
Henchir Mettich, *see* Mappalia Siga
Hendy, Michael 73, 125, 127
Henry I, king of England 153
Henry II, king of England 107
Heraclius, Byzantine emperor 21, 24,
    30, 124, 126, 241, 406–7, 628
Heraclius, exarch of Africa 21, 124
Hērakleios, Egyptian peasant 417
Herakleopolis (Ehnāsiyya),
    Egypt 139 n.213, 245, 248, 251,
    254 n.254, 764 n.130
Herāt, Afghanistan 12
Herblay (Val d'Oise), France 505
Heremod, Danish king 347
Herlihy, David 553, 554
Hermenegild, son of Visigothic king
    Leovigild 94 n.98
Hermopolis (Ashmūnayn), Egypt 138,
    141, 243, 245, 249, 275 n.32, 428,

434, 599, 611 n.43, 759–50,
    760, 761, 762, 763, 764
Herrenhof 499, 501, 575
Hesban, Jordan 451 n.25, 457
Hesse, Germany 540
hides, of land 318–19, 321,
    323, 342
Hierapolis (Pamukkale), Turkey 627,
    784, 786
Hierios, Roman senator 164
Highland Zone, Britain 47, 48, 51
Hijāz, Saudi Arabia 132, 775
Hilderic, gastald of Rieti 217 n.169
Hills, Catherine 806
Hilping, Frankish general 679
Himnechild, Merovingian
    queen 192 n.103
Ḥimṣ, *see* Emesa
Hines, John 311
Hippo (Annaba), Algeria 87
Hishām, caliph 29, 615, 616,
    618, 621
Hjemsted, Denmark 497
Hlothhere, king of Kent 429 n.114
Hodges, Richard 1, 289, 378, 684, 693,
    809
Homer, Greek poet 159
honorati, local senators 597
Honorius, emperor 88, 310 n.18
Honorius, Spanish aristocrat 223
Hopkins, Keith 74
Horden, Peregrine 447
Horic I, king of Denmark 365, 375
Horic II, king of Denmark 365
horses 742 n.95
horta, of Valencia 37, 492
Ḥorvat Din'ila, Israel 452
hospitalitas, and Germanic
    settlement 84, 86, 90
hospitality rights 344, 374
House of Lords 153, 154
Hraban Maur, abbot of Fulda,
    archbishop of Mainz 394–6
Hrothingas, Anglo-Saxon people 305
Huesca, Spain 222, 229
Huggett, Jeremy 808
Ḥumayma, Jordan 604
Humber, River 341, 686

Humphrey, John 640
hundred court 431
Huneric, Vandal king 88–9, 90 n.90
Hungary 78
Huns 180, 532 n.29
Hunsrück, Germany 509
Huntbert, Frankish landowner 283
hunter-gatherers 536 n.36
Hurstborne Priors, Hampshire,
    England 349
ḥuṣūn, fortifications in Spain 489–90,
    493, 495
Huwariya, Egypt 460
Huy, Belgium 189, 681, 797, 800 n.183
Hwicce, kingdom of, England 313, 314,
    315, 344
Hydatius, Roman writer 661

Ianuarius, Italian merchant 300
Iberian peninsula, *see* Spain
Ibn 'Abd al-Ḥakam, Arab
    writer 640 n.121
Ibn al-Qūṭiya, Arab writer 100, 226
Ibn Ḥawqal, Arab writer 726, 728 n.66
Ibn Ḥazm, Arab writer 226
Ibn Khaldūn, Arab writer 18, 337, 358
Ibn Khurdādhbih, Arab writer 128
Iceland 332, 361, 374, 377, 433, 535,
    542–3, 559
iconoclasm 31, 242
Idda, son of, Frankish aristocrat 188,
    189, 199, 607, 403, 405
Idrīs b. 'Abd Allāh, 'Alid king in
    Morocco 22
Idrīsids, ruling family in Morocco 22,
    727
Ifrīqiya, *see* Africa
Ignatios the Deacon, *Life* of the
    patriarch Tarasios 234
Île de France 42, 46, 193, 393, 385–6,
    398–406, 418, 430, 435, 439–40,
    476–7, 495, 500, 504–11, 541,
    546–7, 550, 575–6, 704
Illington, England 807
Illyricum 164, 279 n.42, 465
Imma, Northumbrian aristocrat 343,
    567
Imola, Italy 297

incastellamento 483–5, 487, 495
India 52
Indo-European, language 52
Industrial Revolution 691, 700, 705,
    822
Ine, king of Wessex 320–2, 324, 330,
    343, 347, 362, 375, 378,
    429 n.114, 684
infanzones, aristocrats in Spain 572,
    577
inferenda, Merovingian tax 109, 110
infimes, poor 568
ingenui, free 565
Innes, Matthew 397
Invillino, Italy 479
Iocos, harpist in Gaul 283
Iohannace, Lombard landowner 560
Ipswich, England 320, 342, 545, 682–3,
    686, 809, 810
Ipswich ware, *see* ceramics
Iran 6, 85, 131, 242
Iraq 24, 28, 29, 92, 130, 131, 132, 133,
    141, 277, 449, 457, 532 n.30,
    702 n.16, 776, 777, 780
Ireland 2, 5, 9, 49, 50–3, 54, 56, 237,
    303, 304–5, 327, 339–40, 351,
    354–64, 370–2, 374–9, 433–4, 514,
    535, 540, 542–3, 545, 547, 552,
    554, 558–9, 566, 695–6, 703, 747,
    815–16, 817–18, 823
Irene, Byzantine empress 127, 145,
    235 n.203
Irmitrudis, landowner in Gaul 283
Iron Age 52, 54, 308, 367
ironwork 618, 699–701, 704, 802, 810
irrigation 133, 246–7, 266, 273–4,
    301–2, 333, 390, 419, 426, 449,
    450, 452, 454, 457, 459, 464, 471,
    490, 492, 495, 516–17, 537, 553,
    622–3, 722, 766–8
Irsigler, Franz 184, 185
Ischia, Italy 737
Isidore of Seville 95, 221, 223, 604
Iskenderun, Turkey 241
Islam 25, 28, 657, *see also* Arab empire
Isle of Wight, England 318, 321
Israel 5 n.5, 26–7, 443, 451, 770
Issendorf, Germany 806

Issoire, France 607
Istria, Slovenia/Croatia 129 n.187
Italy 2, 5, 9–11, 29, 30, 33–7, 40, 44–5,
    49, 69, 75 n.52, 70, 74, 78–9, 81,
    85–6, 88, 92, 110, 113, 115–20,
    121, 147, 159–70, 193, 201,
    203–19, 212, 214, 218, 243–4, 262,
    264–5, 269, 272, 277, 279–80, 291,
    293–9, 316, 324, 379, 387–93,
    470–2, 474–5, 477, 478 n.96,
    479–81, 482–8, 491–92, 508,
    533–4, 538, 540, 545, 548–9, 551,
    553–54, 556, 562–6, 570–1, 573–4,
    576–7, 581–4, 592, 595, 599, 601,
    603, 605–6, 608, 620, 633 n.101,
    634, 636, 640, 642, 644–56, 661,
    664–5, 669, 671–2, 679–80, 688,
    696, 706, 708, 710, 713, 718–19,
    723, 725, 726 n.64, 728–41, 751,
    755, 757–8, 767, 770, 773, 776–8,
    784–5, 787–8, 791, 797, 799, 813,
    819, 822–3, 827, *see also* Arabs in
    Italy, Byzantine empire in Italy,
    Carolingians in Italy, Lombard
    Italy, Ostrogoths in Italy
Iulius Leontius 336
ius ecclesiasticum 315
ius haereditarium 317–18
Izmir, *see* Smyrna

Jaén, Spain 230, 490, 493–4, 744–5,
    753
Japan 133
Jarrow, England 811
Jaulges-Villiers-Vineux, France 795
Jazīra, Syria Iraq 28, 131, 133 n.195,
    141, 241–2, 773, 779
Jelling, Denmark 366
Jēme (Memnonia), Egypt 24–5, 134,
    250, 253, 269, 385–6, 411, 419–27,
    435–41, 459, 490–1, 553, 556–7,
    610, 763 n.126, 767
Jensen, Stig 816
Jerash, *see* Gerasa
Jerba, Tunisia 721, 722
Jericho, Palestine 26, 133 n.193, 614,
    775
Jerome, Roman writer 95 n.101

Jerusalem, Israel/Palestine 26, 132, 240,
    614, 618–20, 622, 771–2,
    773 n.141, 774–5, 777–9
Jezreel valley, Israel 774
Jiménez, Miguel 491
Jkōw, *see* Aphroditō
John Chrysostom, patriarch of
    Constantinople 164, 276 n.34
John Lydos, Roman writer 161–2, 233,
    235
John Moschos, Roman writer 456
John of Damascus, writer 242
John of Ephesos, Roman writer 548
John the Almsgiver, patriarch of
    Alexandria 250, 725
John Troglita, Roman general 334
John, bishop of Zaragoza 223
John, duke of Persiceta 214 n.160
John, Egyptian headman 423 n.100
John, Eric 317–19
John, merchant in Francia 799
John, Palestinian ascetic 69
Jones, A.H.M. 7, 63–4, 74–5, 156, 444,
    446, 520–1, 700, 711
Jordan, River 5 n.5, 19, 26–7, 36,
    443, 450–1, 614, 623, 770, 773,
    775
Joseph, Egyptian tenant 416
Joshua the Stylite, Roman
    writer 276 n.35
Jouarre (Seine-et-Marne), France 193,
    507
Jouy, France 400
Jovinus, Roman aristocrat 161
Judaism/Jews 39, 678, 753, 783, 799
Judea, Israel/Palestine 451 n.26
Julian of Askalon, Roman writer 764
Julian of Toledo, *Historia
    Wambae* 95 n.102, 96, 120, 605
Julian, and Domna, Syrian village
    notables 447, 455–6
Julian, emperor 66 n. 22
Julian, pagarch of Antaiopolis 413
Julius Nepos, emperor 169 n.40
Justinian I, emperor 27, 29, 30, 34, 65,
    69, 70, 73, 78, 90, 92, 115, 124,
    128, 141 n.219, 161, 206, 412,
    462, 521, 523–4, 532 n.30, 615,

Justinian I, emperor (*cont.*)
  620, 622, 624, 627, 631, 634, 636,
  638, 641, 724–5
  Novels 69, 164, 232, 411
Justinian II, Byzantine emperor 462
Justinian, *dux* of Venice 690
Jutland (Jylland), Denmark 53–5,
  365–7, 369, 371–2, 496–8, 816
Juvenal, Roman writer 157
Juvigny (Marne), France 506–7
Juvincourt-et-Damary (Aisne), France 505

Kabylie, Algeria 165 n.31, 334–5, 339
Kairouan, Tunisia 21, 639, 689, 720
Kaisarios of Antioch, Roman
  aristocrat 240
Kaiser, Reinhold 114
Kaiseraugst, near Basel, Switzerland 77
Kanhave, Denmark 366
Kaper Koraon, Syria 240 n.216, 447–8
Kaplan, Michel 408, 410, 446
Karakabaklı, Turkey 449 n.21
Karanis, Egypt 459
Karkabo (Alakilise), Turkey 460–1
Kasserine, Tunisia 469, 471, 721–3,
  724 n.59
kastra 451, 453, 629, 631, 633
Keenan, James 413, 415–16
Kefar Hananya, Israel 773
Kellia, Egypt 763
Kempen, *see* Campine
Kennedy, Hugh 133, 618–19, 620
Kent, England 48, 305, 313–14,
  319 n.40, 325, 330, 332, 342,
  344–6, 348, 352, 428 n.112, 685,
  808–10, 812, 814–17
Kerak, Jordan 451 n.25, 770
Kerry, Ireland 357
Khirbet Faris, Jordan 451
kilns 181, 205, 220, 452, 490, 617, 705,
  715 n.41, 720–2, 727, 730–31,
  737, 742, 747, 761–3, 775, 782,
  784 n.161, 787, 795–7, 801,
  806–7, 810
al-Kindī, Arab writer 140
kinship 40, 41, 551–2
Khirbet al-Mafjar, Jericho, Palestine 775
Klysma (Suez), Egypt 132, 135

koinotēs, village community 463, 465,
  788
Kolb, Frank 461
Kollouthos, son of Konstantinos,
  Egyptian headman 424
Kolōje, Egyptian moneylender 419
Kōm Ishqāw, *see* Aphroditō
komē, village 412
Komes, son of Chael, Egyptian
  headman 422, 424
Königslandschaft, royal landscape 46,
  393, 399, 756, 798
Königsnähe 154–5, 160, 183, 196,
  197–8, 200, 210–11, 219, 799
Konya, Turkey 461
Kootwijk, Netherlands 499
Koptos (Qift), Egypt 422
Korykos, Turkey 783–4
Kosmas, Apion official in Egypt 246
Kosmas, *technitēs* 445
kouratores 462
Köwerich, Germany 285
Krefeld, Krefeld-Gellep,
  Germany 182–3, 509
Kromme Rijn, River 683
ktētores, landowners 413, 597
Kuchenbuch, Ludolf 291
Kūfa, Iraq 130
Kyaneai, Turkey 460–1, 629
Kynopolis, Egypt 245
Kyros, pagarch of Herakleopolis 251

La-Celle-St-Cloud, France 405
La Chartre, France 281
La Cocosa, near Mérida, Spain 466,
  478 n.99
La Graufesenque, France 709 n.27, 794
La Londe, near Rouen, France 801
La Saulsotte, France 797
La Yecla, Spain 479
LaBianca, Øystein 19, 457
Lackford, England 807
læn, lease in England 432
Lagny-le-Sec, France 400–3
Lagny-sur-Marne, France 401, 607
Lagore, Ireland 355, 815
Laguatan, Berber federation 22, 305,
  333–4

Laifin, *maior* at Secqueval 404
Lancashire, England 327
land-clearance 280, 288, 292–3, 402,
    747 n.105, 822
Landibert of Maastricht 178, 608 n.34,
    680
Langres, France 172
Languedoc (Septimania), France 44–5,
    94, 96, 94, 170, 469 n.75, 485,
    489, 579 n.116, 605, 746–9, 758
Laodikeia (Lādhiqīya), Syria 616, 784
Laon, France 124, 181, 283, 285
Larrey *see* Elariacum
lashane, Egyptian headman 137, 139,
    422–5, 438
Latin, language 48, 168, 306, 311, 430,
    448
Latopolis (Esnā), Egypt 138, 422
Latouche, Robert 4
Lauchheim, Germany 500–6, 515, 575
Lauricius, Roman landowner 270
law-codes 383–4, 426, 506 n.170
    Alamannic 287 n. 59
    Anglo-Saxon 319, 320, 323, 343,
        347, 566
    canon 564
    Carolingian 587
    Frankish 179, 182, 510, 513, 559, *see
        also Pactus legis Salicae*
    Irish 50, 357–62, 559
    Lombard 551, 554–6, 559, 560,
        563–5, *see also* Rothari
    Roman 325–6, 521–3, 526 n. 17,
        527, 554–5, 559, 580 n.117, 583
    Visigothic 39, 93–5, 97, 225, 526–7,
        560
Laxdæla saga 551 n.55
Lazio, Italy 33, 167, 208–9, 217, 482,
    485, 487–8, 491, 735, 740
lazzi/liti, free men in Saxony 585, 586,
    587
Le Jan, Régine 43, 191
Le Mans, France 109–11, 186, 195,
    197, 281–2, 285–6, 290, 400, 677
Leander, bishop of Seville 604
leatherwork 700–1, 783, 802, 815
Lebanon 26, 770
Lebecq, Stéphane 289, 687

Lebissos, Turkey 460
Legoux, René 797–8
Leibulf, Frankish aristocrat 195 n.109
Leicestershire, England 811
Leinster, Ireland 52
Lejre, Sjælland, Denmark 370
Lenin 96
Leo I, emperor 412
Leo III, Byzantine emperor 30
Leo III, pope 297
Leo VI, Byzantine emperor 791
Leodegar, bishop of Autun 96 n.103,
    120, 176, 197
León, Spain 39, 577, 663
Leontii of Bordeaux, Roman aristocratic
    family 171, 174
Leontios of Neapolis, *Life* of John the
    Almsgiver 250, 725
Leontius I, bishop of Bordeaux 171
Leontius II, bishop of Bordeaux 171
Leovigild, Visigothic king 38, 94, 98–9,
    220, 222, 584, 745–6, 752, 754
Lepcis Magna, Libya 466
Lepelley, Claude 68, 636
Les Carriès, near La Chartre,
    France 281
Lesbos, Greece 277, 278, 628, 788
Leudast, count of Tours 566, 568
Levant 26–9, 276, 443, 450, 453–60,
    603, 613, 616–17, 620, 628, 632,
    635, 644, 715–17, 748, 770,
    773–80, 785, 792–4, 820–1, 823,
    827, *see also* Palestine, Syria
Lezoux (Puy-de-Dôme), France 747,
    794
Libanios of Antioch, Roman
    writer 68, 199, 440, 447–8, 456,
    524, 527–8
Liber pontificalis 297
Liberios, pagarch of Apollōnopolis
    251
liberti, freedmen 564, 565, 584
Libya 5 n.5, 18, 22
Libyan Valleys Survey 22
Liceria, Italian aristocrat 210–11
Liebeschuetz, Wolf 25, 85, 613
Liège, Belgium 43, 190, 193, 681
Liguria, Italy 710, 712, 781

Limestone Massif, Syria 27, 33, 443–9, 450, 452–3, 455–7, 515, 535, 548 n.48, 620, 714, 770, 772–4

Limoges, France 103, 107, 109 n.133, 172, 533, 606

Limonta, Italy 582

Limousin, France 108, 284, 285

Lincoln, England 686

Lincolnshire, England 807, 810–11

linen 699, 713, 739 n.92, 764–5, 771, 788

lis, in Brittany, *see aula*

Liutprand, Lombard king 35, 117–19, 122 n.163, 216–17, 389 n.11, 551 n.55, 554, 556, 565, 582, 732–3

Llancarfan, Wales 329

Lleida, Spain 222, 229, 488, 531

Lloyd George, David 153

loci, villages 491, 502, 517

locksmiths 783

Lodi, Italy 605

logimoi 637

logistēs 597

Loire, River 43–4, 82, 84, 106–13, 123, 169, 170–4, 178–9, 188, 286, 330, 510–13, 530–1, 579, 580, 585, 589, 599, 607, 665, 674, 795, 798–800, 804

Loja, Spain 490–1, 493, 745

Lombard Italy 34–7, 45, 81, 84, 86, 93, 95, 106 n.128, 115–23, 129, 145, 149, 185, 191, 203–4, 206–19, 225, 257, 278, 293–302, 324, 338, 391, 480–1, 487–8, 526 n.16, 533, 545, 551, 554–6, 559–60, 563–5, 568 n.97, 579 n.116, 605–6, 644, 646, 648–50, 654–5, 676, 730–2, 734, 736, 738–9, 787 n.166, *see also* Italy

Lombren, France 479

London, England 9, 292, 342, 344, 681–2, 685–6, 809, 811, 814

Longuyon, France 188–9, 607

looms 807

Lorraine, France 508 n.174

Lorsch, Germany 186, 393–5, 397

Lot, Ferdinand 108

Lothar, Carolingian emperor 586, 587

Louhac, France 284

Louis II, Carolingian emperor in Italy 300, 583

Louis the German, Carolingian king 586–7

Louis the Pious, Carolingian emperor 586–7

Loveluck, Chris 341

Lowland Zone, Britain 47–50

Lucania (Basilicata), Italy 33, 729

Lucca, Italy 36, 118–19, 206, 212–13, 215, 217, 294, 298, 385–93, 400, 418, 435, 440, 436, 485, 495, 555, 563, 565, 568, 599, 605–6, 646, 649, 652–3, 666, 735

Lucchesia, Italy 204–5, 215–16, 387, 388–94, 430, 434, 437, 438, 440–1, 485, 487, 556, 569, 576–7

Lucius of Campione, Italian peasant 565

Lugano, Lake, Italy/Switzerland 606

Lundeborg, Fyn, Denmark 368, 816, 817

Lunel, France 469, 486

Luni, Italy 645, 647, 649, 651

Lunigiana, Italy 484

Lupus, abbot of Ferrières, Frankish writer 176

Lupus, duke of Champagne 174, 181, 184, 210

Lusitania, Spain/Portugal 220, 229

luxury goods 696–7, 699–701, 707, 722, 733, 741, 745 n.100, 769, 799, 804, 807–8, 811, 815, 817–18

Lycia, Turkey 32, 460–2, 464

Lydia, Turkey 788–9

Lyon, France 43, 112, 168, 172, 180, 400, 606, 665–7, 677, 679, 794

Maastricht, Netherlands 178, 189, 476, 608 n.34, 680–1, 687, 797, 800 n.183, 802

MacCoull, Leslie 415, 419

Macedonia 465

Macerias, near Laon, France 283

Mâcon, France 283

Mactar, Tunisia 163

Madaba, Jordan 240 n.216, 241,
450–1, 456, 614, 623, 773
Madelinus, Dorestad moneyer 681
Madīna, Saudi Arabia 132
madīna, city 593, 602, 618
Madīnat al-Fayyūm, *see* Arsinoë
Madīnat Habū, *see* Jēme
Madrid, Spain 491, 743
Madsen, Hans Jørgen 816
Mafia 330–1
Magdalino, Paul 126, 634
Maghreb 21–2
magic 558
magnate farms, Denmark 498 n.148,
816–17
Magnentius, emperor 474
Magness, Jodi 772
Magnou-Nortier, Elisabeth 82
Magulf, aristocrat in Gaul 176
Maiander (Büyük Menderes),
River 238, 784, 786
Main, River 190–1
Maine, France 285 n.54, 511 n.180
Mainz, Germany 197, 281 n.43,
393, 435, 437, 509, 608, 676,
677, 801
maior domus/maior palatii, mayor of the
palace 45, 104, 198
Maitland, Frederic 320–2
Makedonia, Greece 164
Málaga, Spain 37, 473, 482, 494,
659–60, 748
Malay (Yonne), France 507
Malaysia 440
Malling 428–36, 439, 497, 540, 542,
572
mallus, Frankish court 513
Malthus, Thomas 538, 550
Mamertus, bishop of Vienne 679
Mamikonean, Armenian aristocratic
family 168
Mampsis (Mamshit), Israel 453
al-Ma'mūn, caliph 141
Mancian tenures 269, 273
mancipia 282, 291, 301 n.90, 559–60,
562, 563 n.83, 564, 580–1, 582
Mango, Cyril 126
Manicheism 88

Mann, Michael 9
manorial system 273, 550, 802, *see also*
régime domanial classique, sistema
curtense
Mansour, *see* John of Damascus
al-Manṣūr, caliph 102
Manṣūr b. Sarjūn (Sergios),
administrator in Damascus 241
Manthelan, France 511
Mantua, Italy 605
manumission 388, 564–5, 580 n.117
Manzano, Eduardo 231
Mappalia Siga (Henchir Mettich),
Tunisia 274, 278
Marazzi, Federico 209
marble 651, 670, 696, 701–2
Marboué (Eure-et-Loir), France 478
Marculf, formulary of, *see Formulae*
Marculfi
Marcus, Merovingian tax collector
(*referendarius*) 107
Marea, near Alexandria, Egypt 612
Marettimo, Italy 737
Maria, mother of Theodore of
Sykeōn 406, 410
Marius Maximus, Roman writer 157
Majorian, emperor 160
market activity 593, 595, 608, 612, 616,
619, 653, 673, 677–8, 684, 691,
695, 697, 699, 706–7, 725, 799,
813, 823
Marmara, Sea 31, 79, 125–6, 193, 232,
234, 239, 461–2, 608, 788, 790–2
Marne, River 507, 799
Marne-la-Vallée, France 507
Maroveus, bishop of Poitiers 107–8
Marrakesh, Morocco 619
marriage 538, 552, 554, 557, 560–1,
567
Marseille, France 267 n.12, 286 n.57,
469, 550, 606–7, 623, 665, 667,
670, 678, 689–91, 706, 712, 730,
743 n.96, 746–8, 774, 799, 800, 818
Marwnad Cynddylan 326 n.60
Marx, Karl 60, 145, 259, 261, 694
Maslāma b. 'Abd al-Malik, Umayyad
prince 301
Masona, bishop of Mérida 222

massae, Roman estate complexes 470
massarius 563
Massiesa, African landowner 266
Massif Central, France 43, 173,
    709 n.27
al-Mas'ūdī, *Meadows of gold* 242
Masuna, Berber king 335
Mateur, Tunisia 524
Matthews, John 169
Maule, France 401–2, 404
Mauretania 21, 30, 81, 199 n.122, 163,
    466, 534, 540, 635, 826, *see also*
    Tingitana
Mauretania Caesariensis, Algeria 18,
    165, 334–7, 339, 373
Mauretania Sitifensis, Algeria 18
Mauri, see Berbers
Maurice, emperor 30, 406
Mauricius, duke of Rimini 209 n.146
Maurontus, patrician of Provence 176
Maurusius, Roman landowner 467–8
Mauss, Marcel 340, 538, 694
Maximus, Roman senator 162
Maximus, Spanish aristocrat 223, 599
Mayen, Germany 509, 795, 797, 802,
    see also ceramics: Mayen ware
Mayer, Theodor 185
Mazzano Romano, Italy 484
McCormick, Michael 1–2, 3, 691, 700,
    707–8, 711, 738, 789, 802
Meath, Ireland 52, 357, 815
Meaux, France 190, 191 n.98, 607–8
mediocres 568
Mediterranean Sea 5, 10, 13, 17, 18,
    26–31, 33, 36, 37, 41–3, 55, 77, 79,
    131, 163, 169, 203, 206, 209, 220,
    265–80, 286, 298, 301, 327, 465,
    475, 482, 485, 490, 495, 515, 555,
    562, 689, 693, 701–2, 704, 706–7,
    709–10, 718–20, 723–5, 728,
    737–8, 741–2, 746–8, 750, 753,
    755, 757, 759, 761, 766, 768–70,
    772–4, 776, 778, 780, 784, 789,
    791–2, 794, 795, 800, 802, 804–5,
    809, 815, 818–22, 825–6
Medjerda, River 720
Megas, *komēs*, Roman
    aristocrat 240 n.216, 447

Megethios, tax collector in Galatia 408
Meillassoux, Claude 536
Melanesia 374, 539 n.39
Melania the younger, Roman
    aristocrat 162–3, 277
Melissēnoi, Byzantine aristocratic
    family 237
Melissēnos, Michael, *strategos* of the
    Anatolikon theme 237
Melminii, Italian aristocratic
    family 209
Melos, Greece 12, 783
Melque (Toledo), Spain 743
*Memoratorium de mercedibus
    comacinorum* 213, 650
Memphis, Egypt 140
Mēnas, Egyptian soldier 417
Mēnas, pagarch of
    Antaiopolis 139 n.212, 412, 427
Menzingen, Germany 394
Mercato S. Severino, Italy 737 n.88
Mercia, England 48, 303, 313–14, 342,
    344–5, 347, 350, 358, 367, 372–3,
    375, 377–8, 685, 599, 604, 617,
    656, 660–4, 666, 672, 679, 809,
    811 n.202, 813–14
Mérida, Spain 37, 94, 220–2, 226, 466,
    478 n.99, 661, 662 n. 164, 742,
    744, 753–4
Merovingians 44–6, 102–14, 118–19,
    121–4, 145, 148–50, 153, 257,
    281–4, 306–7, 318, 338, 399, 469,
    504, 506, 508–10, 547, 579, 606–8,
    668, 678, 680, 689, 795–7, 799,
    800, 802–3, 805, 818, 827, *see also*
    Gaul, Francia
Meseta, Spain 37–40, 77, 79, 220, 223,
    225–7, 229, 230, 234, 267, 338–9,
    491, 577, 657, 662–4, 741–6, 749,
    751, 755–7, 784
Mesopotamia, Iraq 26
metalwork 310, 320, 327, 353–4,
    504, 545, 640, 647, 682, 685,
    699–703, 735, 745, 763,
    781 n.155, 783, 787, 802, 809,
    815, 817
Methodios, *Life* of the chronicler
    Theophanes 234

Metz, France 46, 75, 77 n.56, 103, 112,
189, 193, 288 n.62, 400 n.39,
501 n.155, 557, 608, 676–8, 799,
800 n.182
Meurig ap Tewdrig, Welsh king 351
Meuse, River 103, 171, 189, 476, 509,
576, 607, 680–1, 796–7, 799, 800,
803
Mexico 514
mezzadria, Italian land
contract 269 n.16
Michael I, Byzantine emperor 690
Micheldever, England 431 n.116
Midlands, England 48, 313, 811,
813–14, 823
Milan, Italy 34, 126, 165, 214, 582,
603, 605, 644–5, 647–8, 651–2,
655, 656 n.151, 678, 691
Milanese, Marco 639
Miletos, Turkey 626–7, 629, 630, 633
military aristocrats/*milites* 153, 566,
568–9, 572, 574, 602, 632, 732
Millán, *see* Aemilianus
Millett, Martin 312
mills 356 n.127, 401, 404, 547
millstone-cutter 246
mining 228
Mínguez, José María 231
Miseno, Italy 737, 787
Mitello, Lecce, Italy 737 n.89
Mitry, France 580–1
Modena, Italy 209–10
Modenese, Italy 480, 729, 730 n.69,
731
Moesia II, Bulgaria 78
Mola di Monte Gelato, Italy 205, 482,
483, 484, 485
molette, roulette 795
Molise, Italy 710 nn.28, 30, 737
Mondeville, France 505
Mongols 12, 180
Monkwearmouth, England 324, 341,
811
Montarrenti, Italy 484, 546
Monte Amiata, Italy 294, 297, 484,
487, 606
Monte Barro, Italy 479, 649
Monte Benichi, *see* Alteserra

Monte Cildá, Spain 479, 743
Montecassino, Italy 218, 483
Monteverdi, Italy 606
Montmaurin, near Toulouse,
France 468–9
Moreland, John 482
Morimoto, Kosei 140
'morning-gift', in Lombard Italy 554,
555 n.65
Morocco 18, 21, 22, 335–6, 697, 727
Morón de la Frontera (Seville),
Spain 744
Mørup, Jutland, Denmark 498 n.148
Moselle, River 43, 46, 103, 189, 285–6,
510 n.178, 608, 800
Mosul, Iraq 141, 144, 241, 532 n.30
Muʿāwiya, caliph 132
Mucking, England 311, 807, 502–3,
808
Mugnano, Italy 390
muhājirūn, Arabs in Egypt 140, 769
Muḥammad, prophet 28
Mummolus of Auxerre, general in
Gaul 176, 183
Munderic, Frankish aristocrat 182
mundium 555
municipium 591
Munster, Ireland 52, 357, 359, 361
Murbach, France 110–11, 186, 256,
580
Murcia, Spain 230, 489–90, 660, 689,
710, 748–50
Murray, Alexander 554
Musciano, Italy 390
Muslims 11, 22, 24, 30, 130, 138, 241,
492, 619, *see also* Arabs
Mynyddog, king of Gododdin 285
Myra, Turkey 461–2, 629–30, 633,
783–4
Mytilini, Lesbos, Greece 628

Nador, Morocco 466
nailmaking 136, 768
Nakūr, Morocco 728 n.66
Nanctus, Spanish ascetic 567
Naples, Italy 35, 203–4, 207–8, 473,
577, 581–2, 599, 605, 610, 645,
647–9, 652, 654, 712, 737–8, 789

Naples, Bay of, Italy 737, 787
Narbonne, France 168, 222 n.179, 710, 746
Näsman, Ulf 368
Natalis, Italian master builder 389
Navarre, Spain 229
Neapolis (Nabeul), Tunisia 727
Neauphlette, France 404–5
Neble, Sjælland, Denmark 369
Neckar, River 500
Neerharem-Rekem, Belgium 505
Negev, Israel 26, 27, 132, 443, 452–4, 457–8, 772, 774–5, 778, 831
Négrine, oasis of, Algeria 266
Nepotianus, Roman aristocrat 223
Nessana (Niẓẓana), Israel 27, 65 n.20, 132, 134, 143–4, 247, 266, 452–5, 457, 553, 568, 603
Netherlands 42, 53, 495–6, 507 n.172, 509, 511
Neustria 41–2, 46, 49, 104–5, 112–13, 171, 186–8, 191–4, 399–400, 506, 512, 608, 678, 687, 804, *see also* Francia
Níall Noígíallach, Irish king 52
Nicaea (Iznik), Turkey 626, 633–4
Nicaea, Second Council of 235
Nicetius, bishop of Lyon 666
Nicholas, abbot of Sion 461, 783–4
Nicopolis, Bulgaria 781
Nikephoros I, Byzantine emperor 127
Nikomedia (Izmit), Turkey 233, 626
Nile, River 23, 33, 65, 136, 140, 247–8, 251, 269, 412, 415, 419, 421, 426, 459, 610, 612, 690, 699, 716, 760, 763 n.127, 764–8, 775, 779, 803, 823
Nîmes, France 469
Nithard, Frankish writer 587
Nivard, bishop of Reims 188, 607
Nizezius, aristocrat in Gaul 283, 607
nobilis 155, 179, 182, 211, 214, 220–1, 323, 388, 585, 830
nobilitas 185, 194, 202, 331
noc nrōme, 'big men', of Egypt 424, 426, 436, 567, 600
Nogent-sur-Seine, France 797
nomads 18, 19, 457, 536 n.36, 723

Nomeny, France 501 n.155
nomes, Egyptian city territories 244–5, 249, 251, 274
Nomos geōrgikos, see Farmer's law
Nonantola, Italy 582
Norfolk, England 806–7, 810
Noricum, Austria 74, 78 n.57
Normandy, France 42, 180, 187, 399, 504
Nørre Snede, Denmark 497
North Africa, *see* Africa
North European Plain 43, 47, 292
North Sea 378, 502, 591, 594, 683, 685, 687–9, 691, 709, 720, 794, 802–3, 817–18, 821–2
Northampton, England 811 n.202
Northumberland, England 48
Northumbria, England 48, 314, 317, 345, 377, 809
Norway 53, 365, 374, 377, 685, 816, 818
notitiae, from Diego Álvaro 224, *see also* Diego Álvaro
Novalesa, Italy 483
Noyon, France 103, 176, 606
Nozo, son of Raduald of Vicopelago, Italian landowner 389
Nubel, Roman-Berber *regulus* 199 n.122, 334, 335
numerarius, tax-collector 98
Numidia, Algeria 18, 19, 65, 66 n. 21, 74, 87, 162–3, 266, 273, 334 n.76, 434, 635, 643, 722
nundinae, weekly markets 697, 799

Ó Corráin, Donnchadh 52
Obodrites, Slavic tribe 365
Odenwald, Germany 540 n.40
Odo of Cluny, *Vita Geraldi* 200 n.126, 557 n.70
Odoorn, Netherlands 499
óenaige, Irish assemblies 816
Offa, king of Mercia 48-50, 180, 303, 322, 344–5, 348, 350, 358, 367, 372–3, 375, 378, 379, 813–14, 821
Offa's Dyke 48–9, 342, 344, 366, 814
Ohthere, *see* Wulfstan and Ohthere

oikodespotai, 'house owners', in
    Galatia 567
Oise, River 103, 188, 398, 403, 403,
    608, 798
Olagüe, Ignacio 40, 83
Old English, language
Old Irish, language 50, 560
olive oil production 37, 43, 76–7, 79,
    286 n.57, 444–6, 448–9, 452, 488,
    582, 620, 637, 640, 659, 696–7,
    699, 701, 704, 708–9, 711, 714–16,
    721–2, 724, 726–9, 733 n.80, 746,
    748, 760, 771–2, 774 n.145, 781,
    784, 788, 799, 800 n.182
Olympia, Greece 786–7
Olympias, Roman aristocrat 164
Olympiodorus, Roman writer 162, 271
Omgård, Denmark 497
Ongendus, king of Denmark 54n.73,
    365
opera muliebria 557
Opilonicus, dependant in Provence 284
Oppenheim, Germany 394
oppidum 680
Oppila, Spanish aristocrat 99
opus virile 557
Orange, France 747
Orientalism 3
Orléans, France 110, 186, 197, 799
Orly, airport, France· 400
Orontes, River 240, 443, 620
Orospeda, Spain 94, 584
Orton Hall Farm, near Peterborough,
    England 307–8, 311
Oslo, Norway 365
Osred, ruler of the Hwicce 344
Ostia, Italy 645, 708
Ostrogoths 34, 35, 37, 45, 80, 81, 84,
    85, 86, 477, 573, *see also* Goths
    in Gaul 170
    in Italy 69, 75 n.52, 92–3, 115, 164,
        170, 176, 205, 207, 216, 526 n.16,
        603, 730
    in Spain 38, 96
otium 80, 157, 158 n.12, 174, 201–2,
    206, 270, 467, 472, 479, 516, 550,
    603
Otranto, Italy 203, 645, 737 n.89, 787

Ottoman empire 85, 131, 304, 791, 827
Oudhna (Uthina), Tunisia 720
Ouzoulias, Pierre 476
Ovid, Roman writer 11
Oviedo, Spain 39, 227
Oxfordshire, England 313
Oxyrhynchos (Bahnasā), Egypt 23, 71,
    165, 243–5, 247–51, 269 n.15,
    274–5, 287, 418, 426–8, 434, 460,
    523, 600, 609, 763–6

Pactio Sicardi 739 n.92
Pactus legis salicae, Frankish law-
    code 179, 182, 184–5, 196, 283,
    320, 462, 512–14, 547, 551 n.54,
    554 n.64
Padua, Italy 273, 278–9
Paeonius, praetorian prefect 161
paganism 587
pagi, territories in Saxony 585–6
Paianios, Roman writer 531 n.26
palaces 46, 594, 608, 621–2, 626, 639,
    641, 647, 650 n.140, 661–2, 666,
    669, 798
Palaestina II 615
Palaiseau, France 299, 400, 402–3, 405
Palencia, Spain 663, 743
Palermo, Italy 330
Palestine 2, 5, 11, 12, 14, 19, 26–9, 30,
    32, 65, 69, 76, 78–9, 92, 125, 130–3,
    143–4, 149, 168, 232, 240–2, 254,
    257–8, 266, 272, 301, 411–12,
    443–59, 460, 550, 553, 567–8, 595,
    598 n.10, 603, 606, 608–9, 613–26,
    628, 631–5, 637, 643–4, 649, 668,
    688, 699, 702 n.16, 705–6, 708,
    714–16, 718, 764, 770–80, 792–3,
    798, 800, 803–4, 819, 822, 827, *see
    also* Arabs, Syria
Palladius, *Opus agriculturae* 268–9,
    271, 468
Pallars, Spain 229
Palmyra (Tadmor), Syria 26, 613, 616–18
Pamphylia, Turkey 32, 239, 462
Pamplona, Spain 228 n.190, 655 n.151
Pando, Italian aristocrat 217 n.169
panegyrics, of cities 655, 676
panēgyrion, great fair 630

Panella, Clementina 693
Pankratios, *Life* of 655 n.151
Pannonia, Hungary 35, 78, 731
Panopolis (Shmin, Akhmīm),
 Egypt 142, 250, 422, 428, 610
Pantelleria, Italy 703
papacy 166, 208, 218, 257
Papas, pagarch of Apollonopolis Anō
 (Edfū) 137–8, 251
paper, production of 700, 765
Papostolos, Constantine, Egyptian
 passport-holder 143
papyrus, production of 699, 700–1,
 713, 761, 765
Parastaseis 129 n.184, 235
Pardulf, ascetic in Aquitaine 177, 573
Paris, France 43–4, 46, 75, 102–4,
 112–13, 176, 183–4, 186, 188,
 193, 196, 204, 280, 282, 285–8,
 292, 299, 307, 398–9, 401, 403,
 409, 439, 478, 511–12, 560 n.77,
 580, 607–8, 677–8, 680–1, 692,
 756, 795, 797–800, 802, 804–5, *see
 also* St-Germain-des-Prés
Parma, Italy 212, 487, 606
Parpalines, Spain 604
pars dominica, see demesne
Parthenius of Clermont, Roman
 aristocrat 167–8, 170
pastoralism 537–8, 582, 698, 723–4
patēr tēs poleōs, father of the city 597,
 600, 627
Patermouthis of Syene (Aswān),
 Egyptian notable 250, 610
Patiens, bishop of Lyon 103
Patlagean, Évelyne 446
Patrick, Roman writer 331
Patrikia, pagarch of
 Antaiopolis 249–50
patrocinium, see patronage
patronage 71, 98–9, 391–2, 398–9,
 412, 416–18, 426–7, 430–4,
 438–41, 454–5, 461, 464,
 519–20, 527–9, 532–3, 551,
 567–9, 572–3, 576, 589, 601,
 624–7, 637, 650, 658, 664,
 669, 681, 689, 739, 763,
 766, 830

Patterson, Orlando 260
Patti Marina, Italy 204
Paul the Deacon, *Historia
 Langobardorum* 115–17, 120,
 211–12, 551, 655
Paul, bishop of Mérida 222, 407
Paul, Roman senator 162
Paul, Visigothic king 96, 98
Paulinus, bishop of Nola 164–5, 169,
 171, 194
Paulinus of Pella, Roman
 aristocrat 161, 164
pauperes 574, 575
Pavia, Italy 34, 106 n.128, 118, 120,
 122, 165, 203, 210, 215–17, 487,
 605, 650, 652, 655, 666, 672, 734
Peacock, David 704, 727, 729, 732,
 742, 750, 762, 764, 797, 806, 823
peasant, definition of **386–7**
peasant mode of production 304–5,
 536–40, 541–50, 558, 561, 571,
 575–8, 583, 585, 589, 700, 750,
 824
peasant revolts 140–2, 147, 532,
 578–88, 768, *see also* Bagaudae,
 Stellinga
Pechina (Almería), Spain 490, 660, 750
Pektēs, Egypt 252
Pekysios, Egyptian headman 423 n.100
Pelagia, aristocrat in Gaul 284, 285–6,
 see also Aredius
Pella (Tabaqat Faḥl), Jordan 29, 451,
 592, 613, 616–18, 623–5, 688,
 770 n.135, 771–4, 778
Peloponnesos, Greece 630 n.94, 786,
 792
Pelousion (Tell al-Farama), Egypt 22,
 460, 760 n.119
Peña, Ted 722
Peñaflor, Spain 490, 493, 744
Pennyland, Buckinghamshire,
 England 503
Pentapolis, Italy 654
Pente Pediades, near Aphroditō,
 Egypt 139 n.213
pepper 733 n.80
Perche, France 402 n.42
perchement 485–6, 493, 516

Peredeus, bishop of Lucca 214 n.160,
   295, 299, 387, 391, 395,
   565, 569
Pergamon, *see* Bergama
Permetaia, Galatia, Turkey 409
Persians 23–4, 26–8, 30, 62,
   78, 130–1, 240–1, 444,
   448, 620, 622, 624,
   627–9, 716–17, 725, 777
   in Byzantium 234, 406, 785
   in Egypt 249, 251
   in Syria-Palestine 444, 448–9
Pescara, Italy 203, 645
Pesynthios, Egyptian headman 423
Peter, cleric from the Lucchesia 555
Peter, Frankish tenant 404 n.51
Peter, priest in Langres 172 n.49
Peter, son of Komes, *lashane* in
   Egypt 423
Peterborough, England 308
Petra, Jordan 26–7, 240, 455, 456,
   613, 623
Petronia, wife of Felix III 160
Petronii, Roman senatorial
   family 159–60, 162 n.21
Petronius Maximus, emperor 157, 162
Petronius Probus, Roman
   senator 157–8, 160, 163
Petterios, pagarch of Arsinoë 251
Pğōl, deacon in Egypt 252
Philadelphia, *see* 'Ammān
Philaretos, *Life* of 234
Philip of Argyrion, *Life* of 788–9
Philippi, Greece 626, 640
Phocaea, Turkey 627, 632,
   714–16, 760, 770, 781–5, 791, 815
Phocas, emperor 124, 652
Phoibammōn of Aphroditō, Egyptian
   peasant 416, 426, 558
Phokades, Byzantine aristocratic
   family 237
Phrygia, Turkey 164
Piacenza, Italy 117, 212, 240 n.213,
   297, 581, 734
Picardy, France 42, 504–5, 508, 571,
   797–8
Picts 52
Piemonte, Italy 731

pietra ollare, soapstone containers 702,
   732, 734
Pietri, Luce 173
pilgrimages, pilgrims 630, 633, 675,
   680
Pinhas, notable in Palestine 455
Pincerais, France 401
Pincevent (Seine-et-Marne), France 505
Pinianus, Roman aristocrat 162–3, 277,
   see also Melania
Pippin I, Carolingian king of
   Aquitaine 580
Pippin II, Frankish mayor of the
   palace 46, 104, 105 n.123, 190,
   687
Pippin III, Carolingian king 46, 402
Pippinids, Frankish aristocratic
   family 104, 105 n.123, 190–3,
   198, 607–8, 680, 800 n.183
Pirenne, Henri 1, 4, 687–8, 700–1, 800,
   821–2
Pirling, Renate 182
Pisa, Italy 9, 217, 295, 387, 565, 605–6,
   645, 649–50, 674, 735
Pisidia, Turkey 232, 411, 532 n.30, 784
Pisões, Portugal 478 n.99
Pistoia, Italy 215, 605
Pithou, France 288
Pîtres, Edict of 301
Pla de Nadal, near Valencia, Spain 478,
   660, 755
Placidina, Roman aristocrat 171, *see*
   Leontius II
placitum, assembly 574, 579, 581,
   585 n.128
plagues 457, 461, 548–9, 558, 679
Plassac, France 174
Platōn, pagarch of Latopolis 138
plebs Aunonensis, Spain 756
Plectrudis, Frankish aristocrat 46, 190
Pliny the Younger, Roman writer 525
Po, River 33–5, 78, 115, 118, 204, 209,
   215, 218, 278, 293, 297,
   480 n.105, 582, 690, 732, 734, 738
Poggibonsi, Italy 484, 546, 735
Pohl, Walter 116
Poitiers, France 107, 110–12, 599, 600,
   606, 667

Poitou, France 109, 174, 181, 188, 289 n.65, 747, 748, 758, 795
Poland 292
Polanyi, Karl 694, 695
polis 593–4, 602, 618, 633
politeuomenoi, see bouleutai
polyptychs, estate surveys 115 n.148, 288 n.62, 290–3, 295, 299, 399, 401, 550, 562 n.81, *see also* Bobbio, St-Germain-des-Prés, S. Giulia di Brescia
Pomaria (Tlemcen), Algeria 336
Pontavert (Aisne), France 505
Ponte Nepesino, Italy 484
Pontius Leontius, Roman aristocrat 171
Pontoise, France 399
Pontos, Turkey 462
population density, in urban centres 309, 458, 508, 593, 595, 611–12, 627, 633, 641–2, 649–50, 652–53, 657–9, 661, 666, 674, 680–1, 688, 713, 723, 769, 797, *see also* demography
Porchester, England 809
Porto Cheli, Greece 781
ports 667, 681, 684, 686–7, 711, 733, 738, 750, 788, 800, 803, 808–9, 817–18
Portugal 5 n.5, 37, 220, 663
post-hole buildings 476, 496, 500, 502–5, 506 n.169, 510, 683
potentes, in Francia 182
potlatch 340, 368
Poto, Italian aristocrat 218 n.170
potters and pottery, *see* amphorae, ceramics
Poukhis, Egypt 72
Poundbury, Dorset, England 308, 328 n.63
Pousire (Busiris, Abū Ṣīr Banā), Egypt 138
Power, Eileen 405
Powys, Wales, 326
pozzi di deposito, in Emilia 480
Praeiectus, bishop of Clermont 197, 606–7
praetor 157–8
Prato, Italy 592

Pratola Serra, Italy 737 n.88
prebendarii 300–1
precariae, Frankish leases 395, 401, 526–7 n.17
preceptum 582
Précy-sur-Oise, France 607
priores loci, of Spain 567
Priscus, Jewish merchant in Gaul 799, 800
Prittlewell, Essex 341
private housing, in urban centres 609–11, 613–15, 617, 622, 638, 647–50, 654, 658, 661, 669
proasteia, estate-centres 460
Probus, son of Olympius, Roman senator 162
proceres, aristocrats 153
processions 431, 619, 653, 662, 675, 679–80
proconsul, of Africa 158
Proconsularis, Tunisia 17–21, 76, 87, 90, 125, 163, 338, 524, 635, 712, 720 n.50, 726–7
procurator 89, 637, 684
Prokopios of Caesarea, Roman writer 20, 41, 80, 87, 90, 92, 99, 165, 240, 335, 456, 548, 573, 783
Prokopios of Gaza, Roman writer 622, 637
pronoia 85
prostasia, patronage 527
prōteuontes, leading men 597–8, 637
protiktores, of Anatolia 411, 599
prōtopresbyteroi, of Galatia 567
Prousa (Bursa), Turkey 629
Provence, France 103, 165, 169, 170–1, 173 n.51, 186, 190, 195, 209, 485, 489, 710, 712, 736, 746–7
Pseira, Crete, Greece 782, 787
Psimanobet of Aphroditō, Egyptian notable 253 n.253, 412–15, 417, 419, 423
Psmo, son of Komes, Egyptian headman 422
Puglia, Italy 33, 67–8, 76, 204, 470, 482, 737 n.89, 792
Puig Rom, Spain 479, 488, 749
Pulcheria, Roman empress 154 n.4

Pupput, *see* Hammamet
Purcell, Nicholas 447
Pyrenees 5 n.5, 37, 38, 43, 223, 227, 229, 489, 494, 567–8, 698, 741
Pyrrus, *tribunus* 270

Qa'lat Sim'ān, Syria 444
Qinnasrīn (Chalkis), Syria 449, 779–80
quaestor 157
quaestura exercitus 78
quasi-città, in Italy 592
Quentovic (Montreuil), France 681–2, 687, 803
querns/quernstones 682, 685, 687, 702, 802, 811
Querolus, Roman comic figure 177, 530–1, 573
Quierzy, France 399
Quintianus, bishop of Clermont 679
qurā (Spanish *alquerías*), villages in Arab Spain 491–2
Qu'rān 357
Qurra ibn Sharīk, governor of Egypt 134–7, 139–40, 142–4, 246, 769
Qūṣ, Egypt 765
quṣūr, fortifications 451, 603

Rabat, Morocco 18
Ramesses III, Egyptian pharaoh 419, 420
Ramla, Israel 618, 779–80
Ramsbury, England 810
Randsborg, Klavs 368
Randuic, Frankish tenant 404
Raqqa, Syria 450, 618, 621, 689
Raqqada, Tunisia 639, 689
Ratchis, Lombard king 214 n.160
Rathbone, Dominic 243, 274
Rauching, Frankish duke 573, 679
Raunds, Northamptonshire, England 348
Ravenna, Italy 34–6, 64, 66, 86, 110, 115–16, 129, 165, 203–4, 206–9, 270, 278, 470, 599, 602, 605, 645, 647, 649–50, 652–4, 672, 732
al-Rāzī, Arab writer 100, 101
Rebais, France 193

Reccared, Visigothic king 38, 94
Reccesuinth, Visigothic king 39, 95, 223
reciprocity, *see* gift-exchange
Recópolis, Spain 592, 662, 743, 746
Red Sea 26, 132, 450, 623, 775
Redon, France 199, 576
referendarius 107
Reggio Emilia, Italy 203, *see also* S. Tommaso
régime domanial classique 280, 284, 288–90, 292–3, 296, 575, *see also* manorial system, *sistema curtense*
Rehovot, Israel 453
Reihengräberfelder 182
Reims, France 43, 75, 112, 124, 180–1, 187–8, 193, 195, 285, 555 n. 66, 607–8, 677, 679, 799
Remigius, bishop of Reims 180–1, 184, 210, 223, 285, 310, 564
Rémondon, Roger 138
Renaissance 36, 644
Rendakioi, Byzantine aristocratic family 236
Rendlesham, Suffolk, England 503, 809
Rentenlandschaften 291
Reynolds, Paul 489
Rhaetia, Switzerland 200, 599 n.12
Rheinzabern, France 794
Rhine, River, Rhineland 5 n.5, 41–6, 74–5, 77, 79, 102–3, 113, 124, 171, 179, 182, 185–6, 192–3, 200, 243–4, 256, 280–1, 285, 286 n.56, 288, 290, 308, 324, 331, 332 n.72, 333, 385–6, 391, 393–9, 400–1, 418, 434–7, 440, 476, 496, 499, 501, 505, 509–12, 540 n.40, 547, 567, 569, 575, 608–9, 674, 678, 681–3, 685, 689, 709, 741, 794–8, 800–5, 813, 816–18, 822–3, 826
Rhodes, Greece 246, 714 n.40, 783
Rhodian sea law 463, 788
Rhône, River 41, 43–4, 46, 77, 103, 111, 119, 169–71, 173, 182, 186, 195 n.109, 469, 471, 666, 689, 732, 747, 758, 794, 798, 800
Rhuulfr, Danish aristocrat 374

Ribe, Denmark 54, 366, 367, 370–2,
    592, 682–4, 686, 689, 697, 816–17
Riccimir, bishop of Dumio 221, 223
Riccimir, *illustris vir* of Bierzo 604
Richer, abbot of Centula 568
Rieti, Italy 120 n.161, 217, 605, 652
Rietino, Italy 296, 555
Rift Valley 26
Rigny (Indre-et-Loire),
    France 506 n.171
Rihbald, Rhineland landowner 288,
    289 n.62
Rimbert, *Vita Anskarii* 366–7, 688
Rimini, Italy 209, 213, 605, 648
Rimoald, Dorestad moneyer 681
ringforts 354, 355 n.122, 361, 363,
    379
Ringtved, Jytte 368, 370
Riothamus, Roman general 169, 330
Ripoll, Gisela 745
Ripwin of Bensheim, Rhineland
    landowner 397–8, 436, 568
Risorgimento 36
Rivenhall, Essex, England 307 n.5,
    311 n.19
road-building 430, 566, 574, 598, 802
Roblin, Maurice 402
Roc de Pampelune, France 479
Rochester, England 686
Roderic, Visigothic king 39
Rodez, France 667
Rodziewicz, Mieczysław 759, 761
rogations 679
Romagna, Italy 297 n.81, 734
Roman empire 2–5, 10–14, 26–33,
    55–9, 62–80, 82, 84, 86–8, 90–3,
    138, 146–7, 149, 153–4, 155–68,
    175, 203, 220, 255, 286, 288, 318,
    324, 326, 332, 364, 369, 434,
    464–70, 470, 500, 507–10, 514,
    517, 519–20, 525–6, 528, 531,
    547–8, 584, 603–4, 619–20, 625,
    634, 636, 648–50, 698, 701, 703,
    706–9, 719–20, 752, 754, 758,
    768, 776, 779–80, 784, 794, 801,
    817, 820–2, 826–31
  in Africa 86–7, 90, 334–5, 641–2,
    696, 703, 712

  in Britain 11, 47–8, 79, 155, 163,
    303, 325–6, 686, 806, 814
  in Egypt 138, 459, 611, 765–6, 769
  in Gaul 43, 45, 509–10, 575, 758,
    797
  in Italy 92–3, 204, 696, 729
  in Spain 38, 40, 489, 663, 748, 752
  in Syria/Palestine 452, 777, 613, 619
Roman law 521–5, 559, 580 n.117,
    583
Romance, language 37
romanitas 83
Romano-Germanic kingdoms 12–13,
    85–6, 120–2, 140, 146, 148, 164,
    174, 178, 231, 256, 306, 517, 525,
    529, 545–6, 554, 586, 751, 827–8,
    see also Germanic kingdoms
Rōmanos, landowner in Palestine 276
Rome, Italy 10, 20, 33–5, 37, 50, 53,
    72, 76, 78, 84, 86–8, 92, 102, 115,
    124–6, 149, 155–67, 174–5, 203–8,
    255, 296, 305, 482–3, 543, 577,
    592–4, 605, 617, 645, 648–55,
    674, 679, 701, 702 n.16, 708–12,
    714, 717–18, 723, 729–32, 735–6,
    737–8, 741, 761, 772, 777, 783,
    785, 789, 794
Romsey, England 810
Romulf, bishop of Reims 176, 181, 188
Rösener, Werner 289
Roses, Spain 658
Rosignano, Italy 295, 299
Rossiter, John 462
Rostovtseff, Mikhail 700
Rothari, Lombard king, 35, 117, 119,
    211, 487, 526 n.16, 551 n.55,
    552 n.57, 553 n.61, 554, 556, 560,
    563, 573, 582
Rotpert, *vir magnificus* of Agrate 214,
    605
Rotterdam, Netherlands 683
Rouche, Michel 43, 177, 188
Rouen, France 399, 687, 801
Rougga (Bararus), Tunisia 637–9, 727
Rufii Festi, Roman senatorial
    family 159, 205
Ruhalt, Danish aristocrat 374
Ruin, The 655

Runciman, W. G. 57
runes 53, 374
Rupert, Frankish count 396
Rupertiner/Robertines, Frankish
    aristocratic family 192, 393–5, 397
rural-based aristocrats 602–8, 633,
    635–6, 643, 648, 655, 668, 680
Ruricii, Roman aristocratic family 171
Ruricius, bishop of Limoges 170–1
Ruṣāfa (Sergiopolis), Syria 613, 618,
    621, 772, 775
Russia 147
Russian Revolution 12
rustici/rusticani, peasants 530–1, 558,
    566, *see also* peasants
Rusticiana, mother-in-law to Apion
    III 165 n.29, 206
Rutilius Namatianus, Roman
    senator 530, 531 n.25

Sabaria, Spain 94
Sabbioneta (Mantua), Italy 605
Sabina, Italy 204 n.132, 293, 296, 298,
    434, 487 n.126, 573, 606
Sabra al-Mansūriyya, Tunisia 639
Sagalassos, Turkey 626–7, 715, 784–5
Sagogn, Switzerland 501
Sahal, pagarch of Armant 253 n.254
Sahara 5 n.5, 17, 18, 26
Sahlins, Marshall 536, 537, 694
St-Benoit-sur-Loire, *see* Fleury
St-Bénigne, Dijon, France 579
St-Bertin (St-Omer), France 186, 400
St-Bertrand-de-Comminges, France 667
St-Blaise, France 469, 471, 479, 712
St-Denis, France 109–10, 112, 186–7,
    193, 286, 399, 400–1, 403, 580,
    677–8, 799, 800–1
St-Gallen, Switzerland 186, 287 n.59,
    501, 580
St-Germain-des-Prés, Paris,
    France 115 n.148, 244, 278, 286,
    288, 295, 299, 399, 401–2, 404–6,
    507, 509, 511, 550–1, 555 n.66,
    560–61, 563 n.83, 565, 687
St-Martin, Tours, France 108 n.131,
    109, 110, 114, 191 n.100,
    506 n.171, 675

St Neots, England 812
St-Ouen-du-Breuil, near Rouen,
    France 505 n.167
St-Rémy-la-Varenne, France 174
St-Riquier (Centula), France 687
St-Wandrille, France 687
Saintes, France 186
Salamanca, Spain 223, 224, 491, 493,
    663
Salernitano, Italy 737 n.88
Salerno, Italy 736, 738
Sallust, Roman writer 159
Sallustios, notable in Scythopolis 615
Salobreña, Spain 481, 490
salt 348, 700 n.11, 701 n.14, 733, 799,
    800 n.182, 814
Salvian of Marseille 8, 9, 62–4, 86, 199,
    528, 530, 532, 573
Salvius, African landowner 524–5
Samaria, Palestine 27, 451 n.26, 452,
    530 n.23
Samarrā', Iraq 619
Sammac, Roman aristocrat 334–5
Samosata (Samsat), Turkey 450, 770
Samsø, Denmark 366
Samson, Welsh/Breton monastic
    founder 326
Samuel, Egyptian landowning
    soldier 416, 558
Samuel, *kyrios* of Gaza 241
S. Antonino di Perti, Liguria, Italy 712,
    781
S. Cornelia, Italy 483
S. Giacinto, Sabina, Italy 582
S. Giovanni di Ruoti, Italy 204–5,
    649 n.138, 710 n.30
S. Gimignano, Italy 592
S. Giulia/Salvatore di Brescia,
    Italy 293–4, 298–300,
    648, 650
S. Lucía del Trampal (Cáceres),
    Spain 743
S. Maria Alteserra, Italy 392
S. Tommaso di Reggio, Italy 267 n.12,
    300
S. Vincenzo al Volturno, Italy 217–18,
    296, 392, 483, 583, 606, 651,
    711 n.33, 736–8, 740

Sánchez-Albornoz, Claudio 4, 40, 99, 230, 491
Sandos, Turkey 408–9
Sannerville, France 506
Saône, River 44, 46, 111, 171–2, 290, 666, 799, 800
Ṣaqqāra, Egypt 609, 610, 611 n.43, 763
Sarapammōn, Egyptian notable 417
Sardinia, Italy 33, 69, 76, 87, 89 n.88, 166, 276
Sardis, Turkey 626–9, 634, 782–4
Sarre, England 808
Sarris, Peter 247, 274
Sassanians, *see* Persia
Saulieu, France 285
Sauvaget, Jean 618
Savona, Italy 645
Sawīrus ibn al-Muqaffaʿ 140, 142, 143
Saxony, Germany 5, 53, 290, 376, 377, 498–500, 578, 585–9, 805–6, 817
Sbeïtla (Sufetula), Tunisia 635, 637–40, 643, 654, 720, 726–7
Scandinavia 5, 53, 54, 277, 439, 537, 543, 544, 678, 681, 695, 801–2, 818, *see also* Denmark
Scarborough, England 47
Scarlino, Italy 485
Scauriniacum, France 284
Scéla Mucce meic Dathó 357 n.130
Scheldt, River 681, 796
Schiller, Arthur 420, 424
Schlesinger, Walter 185
Schleswig, Germany 53
Schwind, Fred 517
Scolastica, Italian peasant 560
Scotland 6 n.6, 47, 51, 52
Scott, James 440
Scythia, Romania 78
Scythopolis (Bet She'an), Israel 613–18, 623–4, 637, 771
seals, Byzantine 127
Secqueval, France 404
Secundus of Non, Italian writer 116
Segermes, Tunisia 721, 724
di Segni, Leah 624
seigneurie banale 572, 830
Seine, River 43, 103, 171, 181, 185, 187–8, 191, 215, 256, 280–2,

286, 290, 398, 401–2, 404, 476, 510–12, 531, 579–80, 585, 589, 608, 681, 684, 741, 798, 800–3, 818, 822
Selsey, England 323
Senator, Italian aristocrat 210, 211
Senigallia, Italy 209, 240, 605, 654
Sens, France 111, 288
Septem (Ceuta), Spain/Morocco 335
Septimania, *see* Languedoc
Sergiopolis, *see* Ruṣāfa
Sergios, priest of Nessana 454
Sergios/Sarjūn b. Manṣūr, administrator in Damascus 241
Serjilla, Syria 447, 455–6, 603
Serris (Seine-et-Marne), France 505–7
Servon (Seine-et-Marne), France 476, 483
Seti I, Egyptian pharaoh 421
Sétif, Algeria 721
Severn, River 47, 327
Séviac, France 174
Seville, Spain 37, 94, 226, 490, 604, 660–2, 744–5, 754
Sfax, Tunisia 726
Shenoute, Egyptian headman 423–4, 427 n.107
shipping 701, 709–11, 718, 722, 734, 768, 774 n.145, 783–4, 788–9
Shmin, *see* Panopolis
Shmoun, *see* Hermopolis
shoes 816 n.210
Sichar, Frankish aristocrat 178, 511–12
Sichild, Merovingian queen 187
Sicily, Italy 30, 33–5, 76, 78, 81, 87, 124–7, 163–4, 166, 204–6, 208, 244, 262, 266, 270–2, 278, 279 n.42, 297, 470, 475, 478, 654, 708–10, 712, 716, 729–30, 736–41, 759, 788–9, 792
Sicorius, Spanish aristocrat 223
Side, Turkey 626–7, 629
Sidi Jdidi, Tunisia 727
Sidi Khalifa (Pheradi Maius), Tunisia 720–1, 724, 727
Sidi Marzouk Tounsi, Tunisia 720–2

Sidonius Apollinaris, Roman writer 80,
86, 95, 155 n.5, 160–1, 169 n.40,
170, 174, 193 n.103, 194, 199,
201, 268, 270, 467–8, 472, 598,
602, 655
Siena, Italy 118, 212, 392–3, 484, 546,
605, 645, 647, 650, 734–5
Sigerad, Italian landowner 560
Sigfrid, Danish king 54n.73, 365
Siggo, Rhineland landowner
397 n.33
Sigibert I, Merovingian king 173
sigma, home of the city council of
Scythopolis 615
Sijpesteijn, Peter 251
Síl nÁedo Sláne, Irish people 52
Silchester, England 686 n.204
silk 696 n.8, 697, 701, 788
Silly-le-Long, France 400–1
Silo, king of the Asturias 219 n.173
Silvanos, notable in Scythopolis, 615
silver 734, 742 n.95, 808, 815 n.209,
817
silvo-pastoral economy 584, 698
Simeon the Stylite, Syrian ascetic 444,
455
Sims-Williams, Patrick 328
Sioout, *see* Asyūṭ
Sioussac, France 284
Sipha (Çemkale), Turkey 410 n.67
Sirks, Boudewijn 87
Sirmione, Italy 215, 605
sistema curtense 293–301, *see also*
manorial system, *régime domanial
classique*
Sjælland, Denmark 53–4, 367, 369–70,
372, 374, 497, 817
Skåne, Sweden 53, 365, 369
Sklēroi, Byzantine aristocratic
family 237
slaves 141, 259–63, 263–5, 272, 276–8,
279, 281–3, 285, 296, 300–1, 323,
356, 435, 543–4, 560, 687, 691,
697 n.8, 701 n.14, 788, 799 n.181,
800, 808
Slavs 5, 30, 129, 377, 463, 601, 628,
630, 786–7
Smith, Carol 809

Smyrna (Izmir), Turkey 238, 626, 628,
630, 632–3, 714, 781, 788, 792
soap 734
Sobata (Shivta), Israel 453, 455
Soissons, France 102, 169, 186, 679
Somerset, England 327, 815
Sorte Muld, Bornholm, Denmark 369,
816
sortes (land-shares) 90
Sousanna, mother of Germanos,
Egyptian notable 425
Sousse, Tunisia 639
South Etruria Survey 482, 495
Southampton, *see* Hamwic
Soviet Union 10, 571, 588
Spain 2, 5, 7, 10, 11, 17, 20–21, 30, 34,
37–41, 43–5, 47, 49, 51, 64–5, 69,
70, 74, 77, 79, 81, 87, 93–102, 110,
113, 117, 120–1, 128, 146, 149–50,
159, 163–4, 168, 193, 201, 219–32,
244, 254, 258, 352, 470, 473, 475,
478–9, 481, 486, 488–95, 508, 515,
517, 526, 530, 533–4, 540, 546,
553–4, 561 n.78, 564, 567–8, 570,
572, 577–8, 584, 592, 595, 608,
636, 642, 645, 656–65, 667–9,
671–2, 706, 710–11, 713, 719,
722–3, 725, 741–58, 761, 772, 776,
778–80, 784, 787, 792–4, 797,
819–20, 823, 826–8, *see also* Arab
Spain, Byzantine empire,
Carolingians, Iberian peninsula,
Ostrogoths, Roman empire,
Visigoths, Vandals
Sparta, Greece 786–7
Speyer, Germany 393, 395, 501,
510 n.178
Spice Islands 696
spices 696, 701
Spoleto, Italy 1, 35, 118, 120–1, 192,
203–4, 217, 296, 487 n.126, 583,
605, 650
Spong Hill, Norfolk, England 311, 806
Squillace, Italy 206, 645, 737 n.89
Staffelsee, Germany 288, 300–1
Staffordshire, England 814 n.208
Stalin 302
Stamford, England 812

Stanhamstead, England 321
state, definitions of 57–9, 303–4
Stavad, Jutland, Denmark 497, 816
Stavelot-Malmedy, Belgium 186
Stavile of Sabbioneta, Italian
	landowner 605
steatite bowls 775
Stein, Ernst 156
Steleco, Roman aristocrat 478 n.97
Stellinga, revolt of 578, 586–8
Stentinget, Jutland, Denmark 369
Stenton, Frank 4, 49, 320, 322
Stephanus, *Life* of Wilfrid 323
Stephen III, pope 208 n.143
Stevns, Sjælland, Denmark 54, 367,
	369, 817
Stoke Prior, England 315, 318
stonework 700, 763
stormandsgårder, Danish magnate
	farms 370, 498
Strategios II, Roman aristocrat from the
	Apion family 248
Strathearn, Marilyn 694
Suavegotha, Merovingian
	queen 181 n.77
Suevi, Germanic people 38, 94,
	184 n.85, 531, 532 n.29, 661, 664,
	745
Suffolk, England 503, 807
sugar production 302
Suidberht, missionary bishop 684
Sullecthum (Salakta) 89
Sulpicius Severus, Roman writer 108
Sumaqa, Israel 771 n.138
Sunderad, Italian aristocrat 387
sūqs, monumental markets in Syria-
	Palestine 616, 618–19, 623
Surrey, England 325, 332
Susa, Italy 607
Sussex, England 313, 323, 332, 344,
	428 n.112
Suti, Danish carver 375
Sutton Hoo, Suffolk, England 320, 341,
	812
Sweden 53, 365–6, 367, 373, 377, 499,
	681, 685, 816
Switzerland 42, 393, 501, 795
Syagrius, Roman general 169

Syēnē (modern Aswān), Egypt 610, *see
	also* Aswān
Sykeōn, Turkey 233, 406–7
Symmachi, Roman senatorial
	family 159
Symmachus, Roman senator 68, 158,
	162–63, 205
synagogues 452, 678
Synesios, bishop of Cyrene 333
Synod of Frankfurt 702 n.16
syntelestai, Roman taxpayers 417 n.85
Syracuse, Italy 208 n.143, 738, 792
Syria 5, 12, 14, 18, 19, 26–9, 30, 32–3,
	272, 276 n.35, 76, 78–9, 92, 101,
	125, 130–3, 143, 147, 149, 168,
	240–2, 244, 254–5, 301, 406–7,
	411, 417 n.85, **443–59**, 460, 462,
	472, 514–15, 527, 535, 548 n.48,
	549–50, 552, 592, 595, 601,
	603, 606, 608–9, **613–26**, 627–8,
	631–6, 638, 643–4, 651, 668, 678,
	688, 699, 714–16, 718, 770–80,
	792–3, 799 n.181, 804, 819, 822,
	827, *see also* Arabs, Palestine,
	Roman empire
Syriac, language 28

Tabacco, Giovanni 211
al-Ṭabarī, Arab historian 28
taberniae, shops in Paris 677
Tablettes Albertini 20, 266 n.10, 270,
	471, 637, 722
tagmata, part of Byzantine army 31
Taido of Bergamo, Italian
	aristocrat 214 n.160, 215
Taín Bó Cúailnge 356
Tajo, River 220, 742
Taneldis of Cicilianus, Italian
	notable 555–6
Tanger, Morocco 17, 18
Tapia, Egyptian landowner 610
Tara, Ireland 52
Tara Brooch 356
Tarasios, patriarch of
	Constantinople 234
Tarazona, Spain 531
Tarn, River 607
Tarraconensis, Spain 94, 96

Tarragona, Spain 94, 656–9, 664–6, 689, 742
Taso, *centinarius* 294
Tassilo, Italian landowner 216
Tate, Georges 443–9, 455
Taureana, Italy 655 n.151
Taurus mountains 26, 30
Taut, Egypt 423
taxation, definition of 57–8, 60, 70
Taylor, Christopher 517
Tchalenko, Georges 444–7
Teaching of Jacob 725, 783
Tebéssa, Algeria 266
Tebtynis, Egypt 610, 611 n.43
Teilreich, Frankish kingdom 45, 118
Tel Jezreel, Israel 452
Tell al-Fadda, Egypt 460
Tello, bishop of Chur 501
Telmissos (Fethiye), Turkey 460
Tertry, battle of, France 46
Teuspert, Italian notable 217 n.168
textiles 765, 822, *see also* cloth
Thagaste (Souk Ahras), Algeria 163
Thames, River 345, 510, 810, 822–3
Thanet, Kent, England 809
Thebaid, Egypt 74, 137–8, 248, 250, 413, 415–17, 422, 600 n.14
Thebes (al-Uqsur/Luxor), Egypt 24, 134, 140, 419, 421, 763
thegnas, Anglo-Saxon aristocrats 374, 432, 566
Thekla of Apollōnopolis, Egyptian notable 250, 251
themes 236, 631, 633, 827
Theodahad, Ostrogothic king 573
Theoderic II, Visigothic king 80, 166
Theoderic Strabo, Roman general 30
Theoderic the Amal, Ostrogothic king 30, 34, 36, 45, 80, 92, 166, 205, 647
Theodora, empress 154 n.4, 412, 413
Theodorakios, pagarch of Herakleopolis 251
Theodore of Stoudios, Byzantine writer 234
Theodore of Sykeōn, ascetic in Anatolia 8, 233, 276 n.34, 324,

386, 406–11, 439, 461, 464, 514, 568
Theodore of Tarsus, archbishop of Canterbury 315
Theodore the Recruit, *Miracles* of 630
Theodore, *politeuomenos* of Arsinoë 600 n.14
Theodoret, bishop of Cyrrhus 27, 240, 447, 455–6, 461, 514
Theodoros, Apion official 246
Theodosioupolis, Egypt 248
Theodosius I, emperor 220, 521, 523, 525
Theodosius *megaloprepestatos*, Egyptian aristocrat 72
Theodota of Pavia, Italian aristocrat 210
Theodotos, Byzantine state treasurer 236
Theophanes, Byzantine writer, 127, 128 n.180, 234, 236, 241, 630
Thessaloniki, Greece 31, 129, 238, 599, 601, 626, 631, 633–4, 781, 788
Thessaly, Greece 788
Thetford, England 812
Theudebert I, Merovingian king 167, 799
Theudemir, Spanish aristocrat 96 n.104, 219 n.173, 754
Theuderic I, Merovingian king 679
Theuderic III, Merovingian king 105 n.123
Theudis, Visigothic king 99, 221 n.176
Theuws, Frans 576
Thiais, France 400
thing, Scandinavian assembly 367, 431
thingmenn, in Scandinavia 373
Thogonoetum, Algeria 473
Thomas, Syrian landowner 455
Thrace, Greece/Turkey 29, 31, 126, 164, 232, 792
Thrasamund, Vandal king 80, 166
Thrudpert of the Breisgau, ascetic 580
Thuburbo Maius, Tunisia 635, 637–9
Thucydides, Greek writer 159
Thugga, *see* Dougga
Thurgau, Switzerland 287 n.59

Thuringia, Germany 45–6, 198
Tiber, River 582, 735
Tiberias, Israel 130, 614, 616, 618, 623–5, 774–5, 778–9
Tidenham, England 330 n.69
Tigris, River 28, 131
Till, Walter 420
timar, Ottoman tax unit 85
timber 818
Timgad, Algeria 635, 637, 643
Timothy of Eukraoi, landowner in Galatia 409–10
Tingitana, Morocco 18, 335–7
Tinnīs, Egypt 765
Tipperary, Ireland 360
Tissø, Denmark 371 n.158
Tits-Dieuaide, Marie-Jeanne 281, 282, 283
Tōd, Egypt 763
Toledo, Spain 38–9, 94–6, 98, 104, 118, 122, 221–3, 225, 491, 604, 662, 663, 672, 743, 746, 751–2, 756
  councils of 38, 221
tolls 344
Tongeren, Belgium 680
Torcello, Italy 690
Torre Águila, Spain 478 n.99
Totila, Ostrogothic king 206
Toto of Campione, Italian landowner 606
Toto, *dux* of Nepi 209 n.147
Toubert, Pierre 289, 296
Toulouse, France 44, 283, 469, 607, 667, 746–7
Touraine, France 109
Tours, France 106–10, 116, 171–4, 178, 268, 506 n.171, 512, 644, 674–5, 677, 679–80, 685, 795, 799, *see also* St-Martin
town, *see* city
Trabzon (Trapezus), Turkey 238, 626, 633
Trajan, emperor 132, 135
Trebur, Germany 393
Treis Pediades, near Aphroditō, Egypt 253
Trent, battle of, England 343

Trento, Italy 85, 573
Tresson, France 282
Treviso, Italy 120
Tribal Hidage 313, 325
tribal societies 40, 41, 305–6, 313, 322, 540–1, 545, 572, 578, 583–5, 695, 707, 756–7, 797, 814, 817–18, 821
tribute system 70, 321–3, 695
tributum/census 7, 107–8, 112, 115–116
Trier, Germany 44–5, 75, 77, 102–3, 160, 168–70, 184, 189–90, 197, 285, 403, 466, 476, 509, 607–8, 676–7, 679, 795, 799
Trinitapoli, Italy 67–8, 70
Tripoli (Tarābulus), Lebanon 241
Tripolitania, Libya 5 n.5, 18, 21, 333, 334 n.76, 334, 336–7, 465, 466 n.67, 635, 721
Trombley, Frank 630
Troyes, France 103
trustes/vassi, armed retainers in Francia 569
Tshenoute, daughter of Epiphanios, Egyptian notable 424
túath, Irish people 51–2, 357–62
Tudela, Spain 226
Tudmīr, Spain 96 n.104
Tuletianos, *fundus*, Tunisia 270, 273–4, 471
Tullianus, Roman aristocrat 206, 220
Ṭūlūnids, ruling family in Egypt 25
Tunis, Tunisia 21, 641, 690, 720
Tunisia 17–21, 76, 87, 90, 125, 207 n.141, 266, 270, 338, 469, 470, 471, 549, 635–6, 639, 642, 688, 699, 712, 720–4, 726–8, 769, 820
turf houses 499 n.149
Ṭurīn, Syria 448
Turkey 3, 26, 31–2, 78, 239, 407, 626, 632, 714, 780–3, 787–8, 792
Tuscany, Italy 9, 33, 35, 118, 204, 212, 215–16, 243, 281, 293–4, 296, 300 n.86, 387, 441, 482, 484, 486–7, 491, 561, 562 n.81, 573, 606, 654, 734–5
Tyne, River 810
Tyre, Lebanon 614

Tyrone, Ireland 52, 360
Tyrrhenian Sea 730, 738, 788–9

'Ubayd Allāh, tax official in Egypt 140,
    142 n.219
Uchi Maius, Tunisia 635, 637, 639, 727
Uí Chennselaig, Irish people 305
Uí Néill, Irish royal family 52, 357
Ulmschneider, Katharina 809
Ulster, Ireland 52, 354
'Umar I, caliph 91–2, 130
'Umar II, caliph 254 n.154
'Umar ibn Ḥafṣūn, Spanish
    aristocrat 226, 494, 605
Umayyads, Ummayad caliphate 24, 26,
    28–9, 60, 100–1, 128, 131–3,
    137–8, 140–4, 146–7, 149, 241–2,
    301–2, 451, 453–5, 458, 491, 495,
    577, 603–4, 613, 615–19, 621–3,
    625, 628, 633, 641, 673, 716, 754,
    757, 770, 774–5, 777–80, 792,
    794, 827–8
Umm al-Jimal, Jordan 450
Umm al-Rasas, Jordan 451
UNESCO 640
United States 147, 260
Uppåkra, Sweden 369
Upper Zohar, Israel 771
Uracius, Frankish tenant 284
Uraicecht Becc 359–60
urbanism, *see* city
al-Urdunn, Arab province 779
Urgell, Spain 229
Ursio of the Woëvre, Frankish
    aristocrat 183, 607
Utrecht, Netherlands 687
Uzappa, Tunisia 163
Uzès, France 747

Vaccoli, Italy 390
Val d'Ambra, Italy 392, 393 n.20
Val d'Oise, France 193
Valdelsa, Italy 484, 546, 735
Valencia, Spain 30, 37, 229, 478, 492,
    656–60, 663, 749, 755
Valens, emperor 126
Valenti, Marco 484
Valentinian I, emperor 67

Valentinian III, emperor 63, 88
Valerii, Roman senatorial family 162
Valerius of Bierzo, Spanish ascetic 223
Valle Trita, Italy 296, 583, 584–5, 587,
    589
Van Dam, Raymond 531
Van Ossel, Paul 476
Vandals, Germanic people 19, 20, 23,
    30, 37, 69, 76, 80–1, 87–92, 97,
    106, 121, 124, 131, 566, 636,
    718, 730
  in Africa 84, 86–8, 121, 124, 163,
    204, 207 n.141, 335, 636, 640–4,
    711–12, 721–3, 739
  in Spain 38, 665, 745
Varsi, Italy 487, 606
vassi, see trustes
Vaunage, France 469
vega, irrigated land in Spain 490
veizla, in Scandinavia 376 n.167
Velay, France 174
Veleia, Italy 471, 487 n.126, 488
Venantius Fortunatus, Roman
    writer 80, 159, 171, 175, 182, 194
Venice, Italy 35, 203, 237, 645, 690–2,
    697, 707, 733, 738, 792 n.171,
    818
Vera, Domenico 269, 279, 524, 730
Verdun, France 124, 188–90, 400, 511,
    607–8, 795, 799
Verenianus, Roman aristocrat 220
Verhulst, Adriaan 280–1, 283, 288–9
Verina, empress 154 n.4
Verona, Italy 34, 215, 480 n.105,
    486 n.123, 573, 581–2, 645, 647–8,
    650–1, 655, 656 n.151, 678, 688
Verrières, France 400
Versum de Mediolano civitate 647, 680
Ver-sur-Launette, France 401
Vert-St-Denis, France 704
Verulamium, England 307, 686
Vestfold, Norway 365
Vexin, France 188, 399, 405, 607
Vicentius, bishop of Huesca 219 n.173,
    222–3, 526 n.17
Vicenza, Italy 120
vicini 487, 551
Vicopelago, Italy 389

Victor of Vita, Roman writer 89 n.87, 90 n.90, 91 n.93, 566
Victor, chief administrator of Apion estates in Egypt 246, 252, 269, 270
Victor, nephew of Apollōs of Aphroditō 412
Victor, villager in Aphroditō 417
Victorids, ruling family of Rhaetia 200
Victorius, duke in Clermont 176
vicus 468, 487–8, 504 n.163, 517, 679–80, 684
Vienne, France 167–8, 655 n.151, 679
Vierck, Hayo 313
Vigevano, Italy 592
Vigil, Marcelo 99, 231
Vigilius of Auxerre 608 n.34
Vikings 48–9, 51–2, 54, 150, 355, 358, 363, 365, 367, 496–7, 581, 585, 587, 589, 686, 805
Vilaclara, Sapin 488, 749
villa, estate-centre, xv, 175, 281–2, 307, 466–81, 602, 663, 739, 752, 755–6, 758
villa xv, 400, 488–9, 492, 502, 510–18, 579
Villandro, Italy 486 n.123
village, definition of 516–18
Villiers-le-Sec (Val d'Oise), France 505
Vincentius, *dux Hispaniarum* 176
vindices, Roman tax officials 69
vineyards 43, 284–7, 290, 295, 299, 401, 551, 699, *see also* wine
Virgil, Roman writer 80, 95 n.101, 157, 159, 472
Visigoths, Germanic people 20, 44–5, 49, 176, 184 n.85, *see also* Goths
  in Aquitaine 103
  in Gaul 86, 94, 169–70, 748
  in Italy 85–6, 658
  in Spain 14, 38–40, 45–6, 64–5, 80–1, 83–6, 91, 93–100, 103, 105–6, 117, 119, 121–3, 128, 145, 149, 219–21, 225–32, 234, 257, 267–8, 301–2, 337–8, 489–92, 494, 526–7, 545, 554–5, 557, 562, 604–5, 607, 656, 658–60, 662, 664, 676, 743, 745–6, 748, 751–8
Vita Aemiliani 222–3, 226, 604, 658

Vita Anskarii 366–7, 688
Vita Brigitae 358
Vita Cadoci (of Llancarfan) 328
Vita Cainnechi 356 n.125
Vita Eligii 8, 103, 108–9, *see also* Eligius of Limoges
Vita Eucherii 197
Vita Filiberti 816 n.210
Vita Fructuosi 526 n.16
Vita Genovefae 103, 184
Vita Geraldi 200 n.126, 557 n.70
Vita Germani 532
Vita Landiberti 680
Vita Lebuini 585
Vita Melaniae latina 162–3, 469 n.74
Vita Pardulfi 177, 573
Vita Severini 74
Vita Wilfridi 343
Vitas patrum Emeritensium 221, 661
Viterbo, Italy 648
Vitry-en-Artois, France 506
Vogelgesang, Speyer, Germany 501
Völkerwänderung 496, 498
Volubilis, Morocco 18, 22, 336, 689
Vorbasse, Denmark 429 n.1, 496–9, 501–2, 514–15, 572, 816 n.212, 817
Vorgebirge, Germany 801
Vortigern, ruler in Britain 337
Vortipor, Welsh king 327, 334 n.76, 378
Vosges, France 43, 189, 509, 540
Vouillé, France 94, 675
Vroom, Joanita 786

Wademir, Frankish landowner 187, 189 n.96, 190, 403, 607
Wadulf, Italian aristocrat 218 n.170
Walaram, Rhineland aristocrat 394–6
Wales 5, 47–51, 56, 303, 306, 308, 326–30, 335, 337, 339–40, 344, 351, 352–4, 356, 371–2, 377–9, 540, 545, 703, 814–15, 823, 829
Walfred of Pisa, Italian aristocrat 214 n.160, 606
Walmsley, Alan 613, 619
Walpert, duke of Lucca 212

Walprand, bishop of Lucca 212, 215 n.162
Wamba, Visigothic king 95–6, 98
Warattonids, Frankish aristocratic family 104, 193
Ward-Perkins, Bryan 593
Warendorf, Germany 499
Warnefrit, gastald of Siena 393
Weald, England 332
weapon sacrifices 367
weather 558
Weber, Martin 806
Weber, Max 688
Welschbillig, near Trier, Germany 403, 466
Welsh, language 48, 168
Wenskus, Reinhard 82
Werden, Germany 586 nn.128, 129
Werner, Karl Ferdinand 183
Werner, Matthias 43
Wessex, England 48, 313–14, 318, 320, 342–5, 347, 350, 377, 684, 686, 809–10, 812–14, 817
West Heslerton, England 503 nn.159, 161
West Stow, England 311, 502, 503, 806 n.192, 807
West, Stanley 502
Westbury on Trym, England 322
Westminster, London, England 681
Whitby, England 811
Whitehouse, David 1, 693
Whittaker, C.R. 331, 476–7, 525
Wicken Bonhunt, England 503
Widerad of Flavigny, Frankish aristocrat 189 n.96, 190
Widsith 317 n.35
Wihtred, king of Kent 343, 429 n.114
Wijnaldum, Netherlands 499
Wijster, Netherlands 498–9
Wilfong, Terry 419–20, 424
Wilfrid, bishop of Ripon 318, 323, 346 n.101
Willebad of Burgundy, Frankish aristocrat 120
William I, king of England 49
Wiltshire, England 810
Winchester, Engand 809

wine production 77, 79, 292, 393, 398, 450, 452–3, 547, 622, 682, 699, 704, 708, 713–15, 729–30, 737, 741, 760–7, 771–2, 774 n.145, 781, 783 n.159, 788, 791, 799, 800, 802, 805, 815, 818, *see also* vineyards
Winkelmann, Friedhelm 236, 238
Wissembourg, France 123, 186, 288 n.62, 394 n.23, 395, 511
Witiza, Visigothic king 96 n.104, 227 n.187
Woëvre, France 607
Wolfram, Herwig 82
women 45, 249, 537, 543, 551–2, 554–7, 802, 807
wood 430–1, 486, 491, 496, 505, 507, 511, 516, 540, 545, 580, 644, 647–8, 656 n.152, 676–7, 685, 699, 700, 815
Wood, Ian 213
wool 713, 764–5, 808, 818
Worcester, England 314, 317, 322, 348, 814
Worcestershire, England 50, 319, 813
Worms, Germany 393, 510 n.178
Wroxeter, England 307, 327, 328 n.63, 336, 686
Wulfred, archbishop of Canterbury 348
Wulfstan, and Ohthere, ninth-century travellers 366 n.146

Xanthos, Turkey 629

Yangtse, River 823
Yarnton, England 503
Yassı Ada, shipwreck, Turkey 781 n.155, 783
Yazīd, pagarch of Akhmīm 142
Yeavering, England 320, 341, 371, 503
Yemen 130
York, England 306–7, 342, 467, 592, 655, 682–3, 685–6, 809, 811–12
Yorke, Barbara 342
Yorkshire, England 48, 332 n.72, 806, 807, 810–11
Yrieix, *see* Aredius
Yucatán, Mexico 133

Yugoslavia 30
Yvelines, France 507

Zacharias, pope 297
Zadora-Rio, Elisabeth 517
Zanj, slave revolt 141

Zaragoza, Spain 222–3, 226, 604, 658, 662–3, 742, 755
Zeno, emperor 30, 34
Zerner, Monique 550
Zeugma, Turkey 450
Zotto, Italian landowner 392, 393